Complete Tenth Edition

Pearson Education International

Digital Planet: Tomorrow's Technology and You

George Beekman
Ben Beekman

Prentice Hall

Boston Columbus Indianapolis New York San Francisco Upper Saddle River
Amsterdam Cape Town Dubai London Madrid Milan Munich Paris Montréal Toronto
Delhi Mexico City São Paulo Sydney Hong Kong Seoul Singapore Taipei Tokyo

To students all over the world—

The promise of the future

lies not in technology

but in you.

—G.B.

—B.B.

If you purchased this book within the United States or Canada you should be aware that it has been imported without the approval of the Publisher or the Author.

Editor in Chief: Michael Payne
Associate VP/Executive Acquisitions Editor: Stephanie Wall
Executive Editor: Jenifer Niles
Product Development Manager: Eileen Bien Calabro
Development Editor: Nancy Lamm
Editorial Project Managers: Virginia Guariglia and Meghan Bisi
Editorial Assistant: Nicole Sam
Director of Digital Development: Zara Wanlass
Editor, Digital Learning & Assessment: Paul Gentile
Product Development Manager, Media: Cathi Profitko
Editorial Media Project Manager: Alana Coles
Production Media Project Manager: John Cassar
Director of Marketing: Kate Valentine
Senior Marketing Manager: Tori Olson Alves
Marketing Coordinator: Susan Osterlitz
Marketing Assistant: Darshika Vyas
Senior Managing Editor: Cynthia Zonneveld
Associate Managing Editor: Camille Trentacoste
Production Project Manager: Ruth Ferrera-Kargov
Manager of Rights and Permissions: Hessa Albader
Senior Operations Specialist: Natacha Moore
Art Director: Anthony Gemmellaro
Text and Cover Designer: Anthony Gemmellaro
Manager, Visual Research: Karen Sanatar
Photo Researcher: Heather Kemp AV
Cover Art: Matthew Hurst/Science Photo Library
Full-Service Project Management: GEX Publishing Services
Composition: GEX Publishing Services
Printer/Binder: Webcrafters Inc.
Cover Printer: Lehigh-Phoenix Color/Hagerstown
Text Font: Times Roman 10/12

Pearson Education Ltd., London
Pearson Education Singapore Pte, Ltd.
Pearson Education, Canada, Ltd.
Pearson Education-Japan
Pearson Education Australia PTY, Limited
Pearson Education North Asia Ltd., Hong Kong
Pearson Educación de Mexico S.A. de C.V.
Pearson Education Malaysia, Pte, Ltd.
Pearson Education, Upper Saddle River, New Jersey

10 9 8 7 6 5 4 3 2 1

Prentice Hall
is an imprint of

ISBN 13: 978-0-13-273751-7
ISBN 10: 0-13-273751-5

Contents

Chapter 1 Exploring Our Digital Planet 2

Chapter 2 Hardware Basics: Inside the Box 36

Chapter 3 Hardware Basics: Peripherals 64

Chapter 4 Software Basics: The Ghost in the Machine 104

Chapter 5 Productivity Applications 144

Chapter 6 Graphics, Digital Media, and Multimedia 188

Chapter 7 Database Applications and Privacy Implications 234

Chapter 8 Networking and Digital Communication 270

Chapter 9 The Evolving Internet 314

Chapter 10 Computer Security and Risks 358

Chapter 15 Is Artificial Intelligence Real? 550

Appendix A Basics 583

Appendix B ACM 607

Glossary 615

Credits 635

Index 639

About this Book

Even if you're **on the right track**, you'll get run over if you **just sit on it**.

—Pat Koppman

In the world of information technology, it seems like change is the only constant. In less than a human lifetime, this technological torrent has transformed virtually every facet of our society—and the transformation is just beginning. As old technologies merge and new technologies emerge, far-fetched predictions routinely come true and even the most forward-thinking pundits are caught off guard by unpredictable developments. This headlong rush into the high-tech future poses a challenge for all of us: How can we extract the knowledge we need from the deluge of information? What must we understand about information technology to survive and thrive in an increasingly technological future? *Digital Planet: Tomorrow's Technology and You* is designed to aid travelers on their journey into that future.

Meeting this challenge means going far beyond knowing how to read a budget spreadsheet, create a Web page, or find facts on the Internet. A deeper understanding of digital technology will help you answer much more meaningful questions. What kinds of new media will emerge from the next generation of Internet technology, and how will our lives change as a result? What should you do to protect yourself from spam, spyware, identity theft, and Internet fraud? How can you build a home network that's ready for the future? How can you use mobile technology and social networks to your advantage without sacrificing your personal privacy? How will technological breakthroughs change the global political landscape? What is the impact of digital technology on artificial intelligence—and human intelligence? How will technology affect your future career prospects, and what can you do to maximize your chances of getting the job you want?

Digital Planet is designed to help you explore these and many other questions. It goes beyond simply describing the latest gadgets and explains many of the benefits we derive (and risks we tolerate) when we incorporate new technology into our lives.

What Is *Digital Planet*?

Digital Planet explores information technology on three levels:

- Explanations: *Digital Planet* clearly explains what a computer is and what it can (and can't) do; it describes the basics of digital technology, from smart phones and multimedia PCs to the Internet and beyond.
- Applications: *Digital Planet* illustrates how computers and networks are—and will be—used as practical, versatile tools to solve problems and extend human capabilities.
- Implications: *Digital Planet* puts technology in a human context, illustrating how our ever-growing network of digital devices affects our lives, our world, and our future.

Here's a quick rundown of the book's chapters:

Chapter 1 offers a solid foundation by presenting a big-picture view of our digital planet. This chapter provides a perspective for understanding the future by emphasizing trends and storylines rather than historical details and technical trivia. It opens with profiles and perspectives on a particularly powerful digital trend—the Web 2.0 phenomenon. The *Inventing the Future* box near the end of the chapter provides an overview of strategies for predicting the future—strategies that are applied in later chapters.

Chapters 2 through 4 provide clear explanations of the basic concepts of computer hardware and software. Many of these concepts are often misunderstood by students—even those who have considerable computer experience. These chapters, like later chapters in the book, include optional *How It Works* boxes that provide more technical detail for those who want or need to know more.

Chapters 5 through 7 survey a variety of PC, smart phone, and Internet applications, from familiar office tools to cutting-edge multimedia and database applications.

Chapters 8 and 9 go into greater depth on network technology in general and the Internet in particular. These chapters cover emerging technologies that are rapidly changing the way we use the Internet—technologies that many casual Internet users don't understand. The face of the Internet tomorrow will be vastly different than it is today, and we will feel its impact everywhere. Material in these chapters should make it easier for students to predict their networked futures.

Chapter 10 provides a focal point for a variety of ethical and social issues related to information technology. Many of these issues—privacy, security, reliability, and more—are discussed throughout the book. This chapter, though, pulls all of these concepts together. The chapter closes with a discussion of big questions about our relationship to technology—important questions for all citizens of the future to think about.

Chapter 11 surveys the applications and implications of digital technology in our three most important social institutions: our homes, our schools, and our workplaces.

Chapters 12 and 13 are targeted at students who need or want to know more about the application of information technology in business. Chapter 12 focuses on digital tools for managing all kinds of businesses. Chapter 13 covers electronic commerce, from traditional e-business models to future trends in e-commerce.

Chapter 14 goes beyond the introduction in Chapter 4 to software technology, exploring programming, systems design, and computer science concepts in more depth.

Chapter 15 covers one of the most intriguing fields of computer science: artificial intelligence. The chapter demystifies and clearly explains the basics of AI, robotics, and artificial life. It ends with speculation about a future in which machine intelligence may radically alter our world.

The appendix provides a friendly introduction for students who have little or no experience with PCs and the Internet. This unique feature addresses the most commonly reported problem of introductory computer concepts classes—the diverse backgrounds of students in those classes. Most instructors report that the majority of their new students have PC and Internet experience. These students don't need to be told about keyboarding or navigating a Web site. But if these topics aren't covered, the inexperienced students are at a distinct disadvantage. The appendix is designed for those beginners, so they can fill in gaps in their knowledge before launching into the rest of the book.

In general, the book's focus flows from the concrete to the controversial and from the present to the future. Individual chapters have a similarly expanding focus. After a brief introduction, each chapter flows from basic concepts toward abstract, future-oriented questions and ideas. Most chapters raise ethical issues related to the use and misuse of digital technology. Every chapter asks readers to think about trade-offs associated with technological innovations. The book provides a framework to help readers think about ways to use present and future technology to help them achieve their goals.

About the Authors

George Beekman is an Honorary Instructor in the School of Electrical Engineering and Computer Science at Oregon State University (OSU). For more than two decades he designed and taught courses in computer literacy, interactive multimedia, computer ethics, and computer programming at OSU. His innovative computer literacy course served as the inspiration for *Computer Currents*, the first edition of the book that evolved into *Digital Planet*. George Beekman has taught workshops in computer literacy and multimedia for students, educators, and economically disadvantaged families from the Atlantic to Alaska. He has written many books on computers, information technology, and multimedia, as well as more than 100 articles and reviews for *Macworld* and other popular publications. George also bikes, hikes, and runs on Oregon trails and roads, produces and plays acoustic and electronic music, shoots and edits photos and videos, and cultivates community connections on and off line.

Ben Beekman is a multimedia designer, writer, and technical consultant based in Portland, Oregon. Ben has developed multimedia Web sites for businesses, nonprofits, artists, and musicians. He has done extensive desktop publishing, page layout, and design for periodicals and one-shot publications. He has written blogs for the Web and technology reviews for print media. He has worked behind the scenes on several books, and co-authored the last two editions of this one. Ben also composes, mixes, and remixes music and video, tracks the evolving Internet, consumes comedy, plays disc golf, and enjoys the outdoors with friends and his dog Gizmo.

Acknowledgments

We are deeply grateful to all of the people who have come together to make *Digital Planet* a success. Their names may not be on the cover, but their high-quality work shows in every detail of this project.

We're grateful to Stephanie Wall, the savvy Executive Editor who worked with us to ensure that we had the resources and help we needed to produce a first-rate text. Stephanie put together a terrific team to work on this book. Special thanks to project manager extraordinaire Virginia Guariglia, who skillfully, cheerfully, and tirelessly kept this project on course and on schedule. When Virginia's skills were required on other projects, Meghan Bisi ably guided the project through to completion. This edition is also far better thanks to the careful, thoughtful, and timely work of development editor Nancy Lamm, copyeditor Mark Goodin, and technical editors Ann Taft and Mary Carole Hollingsworth.

Many others brought their considerable talents to *Digital Planet*. Designer Anthony Gemmellaro turned our cover idea into a beautiful work of art and created the striking design that graces every page. Ruth Ferrera-Kargov worked on all aspects of production, helping ensure that the project could make all those nearly impossible deadlines. Heather Kemp uncovered many of the new photos for this edition. Joanna Green secured permissions for hundreds of images and other resources in the book and on the Web site. Marisa Taylor and the team at GEX Publishing Services, compiled the final book from all of the raw materials supplied by the others listed here.

All of this effort would be wasted if *Digital Planet* didn't reach its intended audience. Thankfully, Prentice Hall's amazing marketing and sales team, including Tori Olson Alves, does a phenomenal job of making sure that professors and their students have access to our books, and we can't thank them enough for their efforts.

We both owe special thanks to our family and community, here in Oregon and all around our digital planet, who provided unbelievable support throughout this project. We're especially grateful to Susan Grace Beekman, who somehow managed be there whenever we needed her in spite of the fact that she was immersed in an extremely challenging project of her own.

There are others who contributed to *Digital Planet* in all kinds of ways, including critiquing chapters, answering technical questions, tracking down obscure references, guiding us through difficult decisions, and being there when we needed support. There's no room here to detail their contributions, but we want to thank the people who gave time, energy, talent, and support during the years that this book was under development, including: Mike Quinn, Liz-e Patton, Evan Scheessele, Jeremy Smith, Mina Carson, Michael Hulse, Randy Primeaux, Brad Upchurch, Arthur Kaneen, Stephanie Sireix, Robert Rose, Gabe Guzman, Skyler Corbett, Johanna Beekman, Maureen Spada, Dave Trenkel, Mark Dinsmore, Natalie Anderson, Naftali Anderson, Martin Erwig, Otto Gygax, Francisco Martin, Jim Folts, Jan Dymond, Johanna Beekman, Mike Johnson, Margaret Burnett, Sherry Clark, Walter Rudd, Cherie Pancake, Bruce D'Ambrosio, Bernie Feyerherm, Rajeev Pandey, Dave Stuve, Clay Cowgill, Keith Vertanen, Gary Brent, Marion Rose, Megan Slothover, Claudette Hastie Baehrs, Melissa Hartley, Breitenbush, Gracewinds Music, Shjoobedebop, Oregon Public Broadcasting, Mary Pape, Darrel Karbginsky, Keith J. Conners, Anita Ross, Fani Zlatarova, Ilga Higbee, Karl Smart, Harold Smith, Wayne Morris, Adeleye Bamkole, Marie Taylor Harper, Alan L. Matthews, Kathy Harvey, Phil Zwieg, and all of the editors and others who helped with previous editions. Thanks also to all the hardware and software companies whose cooperation made our work easier.

Visual Walk-Through

Digital Planet is designed to help you provide students with the background they need to survive and prosper in a world transformed by information technology. The tenth edition comes in two forms, the Introductory Edition and the Complete Edition, and both books include a variety of supplements and ancillary materials designed to help you enhance your students' learning experience.

About this Edition

From its earliest days, this book has been about the future. The first edition, *Computer Currents: Navigating Tomorrow's Technology*, was unique among introductory computing books because it devoted a *whole page* to that experimental network of networks called the Internet. Today, of course, the Internet is everywhere, both in our lives and in this book. To stay ahead of the ever-rising technological curve, the book has gone through several major revisions. Two constants have anchored it through the changes: an engaging writing and presentation style that clarifies complex ideas, and an uncompromising eye on the technological horizon that will define our future.

Changes in the technology and its impact on our lives have been particularly profound since the last edition of this book, *Tomorrow's Technology and You*, was published. Consequently, this latest edition is one of the most thorough revisions we've ever done. The new title reflects the planetary scope of the digital revolution and its impact on readers. The entire book has been rewritten to reflect the growing importance of mobile devices, alternative platforms, cloud computing, collaborative technologies, and the global information economy. We've expanded our future focus to encompass the latest technological trends. At the same time, we've looked in more depth at the impact of these new technologies on our brains, our thoughts, our productivity, our communities, and our planet.

Here is a chapter-by-chapter summary of improvements and additions to this edition.

Chapter 1, "Exploring Our Digital Planet." This chapter provides a broad overview of the information technology trends that are transforming our society, while providing a solid foundation for the chapters that follow. The opening profile sets a personal tone by telling the human stories behind Facebook, Flickr, YouTube, Twitter, and other popular Web 2.0 applications. The chapter includes expanded coverage of smart phones, tablets, firmware, and cloud computing. The four phases of the Information Age illustrated in the Digital Technology Time Line are covered in more detail in the chapter. Placing Web 2.0 in the context of our ever-more-digital time line provides a perspective that makes it easier to understand what kind of changes are ahead—and how those changes are likely to transform our lives.

Chapter 2, "Hardware Basics: Inside the Box," and Chapter 3, "Hardware Basics: Peripherals." Both of these chapters have been updated to clearly describe the latest hardware technology, from processors to peripherals. The chapters include expanded and updated coverage of multicore technology, clusters, digital cameras, sensors, monitors (including discussions of aspect ratio and the relationship between computer screens and HDTV), and audio output. A new visual index of computer ports makes it easy to make sense of the web of wires connected to a typical PC or Mac. The "Green Computing" and "Ergonomics and Health" *Working Wisdom* boxes provide more tips for minimizing the negative impact of our digital tools on personal and planetary health. The *Inventing the Future* boxes for both chapters have been rewritten to cover cutting-edge hardware emerging from research facilities around the world.

Chapter 4, "Software Basics: The Ghost in the Machine." This chapter includes expanded and updated coverage of Web applications, operating systems, documentation, plug-ins, and mashups.

Chapter 5, "Productivity Applications." This chapter has been updated to include current productivity and simulation software. A newly titled and expanded section covers e-books, e-readers, and e-paper. A new *Screen Test* box, "Productivity on a Student Budget," showcases shareware and freeware alternatives to Microsoft Office and other productivity software. The all-new *Inventing the Future* box at the end of the chapter builds on the *Tomorrow's User Interface* box in Chapter 4, focusing on multisensory interfaces.

Chapter 6, "Graphics, Digital Media, and Multimedia." This chapter has been revised to include new material on graphics, digital audio, digital video, and multimedia, covering both amateur and professional applications. The discussion of image bit-depth has been moved here from Chapter 3. The "Multimedia on a Student Budget" *Screen Test* has been revised to cover the latest free software that can deliver high-end results for Windows and Mac users. The *Inventing the Future* box has been revised to reflect the latest developments in virtual reality, augmented reality, and other types of shared virtual spaces.

Chapter 7, "Database Applications and Privacy Implications." This chapter includes updated coverage of special-purpose databases. A completely rewritten *Screen Test*, "The Big Sync," clarifies the options for sharing address books, calendars, and email on smart phones, PCs, and the cloud. The section on privacy implications includes timely new material, including tips on protecting personal privacy.

Chapter 8, "Networking and Digital Communication." This chapter contains expanded and updated coverage of network technologies, including in-depth coverage of 3G/4G technology and its impact on mobile Internet access. The section on social networks has been rewritten to cover current technology, applications, and implications. The "Netiquette and Messaging Etiquette" *Working Wisdom* box includes new tips for using social networks effectively. The all-new *Inventing the Future* box covers science fiction-like mind-machine interfaces, their applications, and their implications.

Chapter 9, "The Evolving Internet." This chapter has also been rewritten to reflect changes in Internet technology, applications, and implications. The section on domain names has been updated to include new domains and clarify the global naming system. The section on Web programming tools now includes more material on content-management systems, Web site personalization, and HTML 5. A new *Screen Test* box, "Building A Dynamic Site," shows the set up of a content management system that can be easily maintained by a nontechnical user. The chapter also has updated coverage of ethical and political issues, including net neutrality, access, and censorship.

Chapter 10, "Computer Security and Risks." The sections on computer crime, malware, backups, and security have all been updated to reflect current trends and issues. *Working Wisdom* tips on protecting yourself from identity theft and safe computing have been revised. The section on backups has been expanded and rewritten to describe the four different types of backups every serious PC owner should know about—and employ. The section on smart weapons has been revised to cover these important new tools of warfare. There's new material on the growing threat of cyberwar and its relationship to hacking. The new *Inventing the Future* box covers layered security, human security issues, and the emerging threat of biohacking.

Chapter 11, "Computers at Work, School, and Home." This chapter contains updated material on office automation, including a discussion of desktop virtualization. The section on high-tech schools has been thoroughly rewritten to reflect current trends and research in educational technology, from smart phones and e-Learning 2.0 systems in K–12 schools to comprehensive educational Web systems in higher education. A new *Working Wisdom*, "Maximizing Brain Power in the Digital Age," is packed with practical tips based on solid research relating digital technology to brain function. The section on the digital home includes coverage of social television and other trends. The *Inventing the Future* box has been revised to cover the XO-3 and its relationship to the iPad and other current technologies.

Chapter 12, "Information Systems in Business," and Chapter 13, "E-Commerce and E-Business: The Evolving Internet Economy." These two chapters have been updated with the latest business-related software and hardware examples. They include new material on international information systems and global markets. The Chapter 13 *Inventing the Future* box describes emerging marketing and sales techniques and technologies that have the potential to turn every waking moment into a commerce-driven game.

Chapter 14, "Systems Design and Development." This chapter has been updated to reflect changes in technology and techniques of software design and development. A new section on aspect-oriented programming and a revised section on programming for the Web cover emerging programming technologies.

Chapter 15, "Is Artificial Intelligence Real?" This chapter includes updated examples of applied AI in a variety of fields, including robotics. An all-new section covers question-answering systems, including Wolfram Alfa and IBM's Jeopardy-playing Watson. There's more in-depth and cutting-edge coverage of artificial life in the rewritten *Inventing the Future* box, "Artificial Life."

Appendix A, "Basics." The appendix contains introductory material updated to cover the latest software and hardware.

All of these changes are packaged in a clean, inviting new design that better reflects the future-friendly spirit of the book.

Special Focus Boxes

Digital Planet includes several unique feature boxes that add value for students, instructors, and casual readers. Many of these boxes are new or updated for this edition.

How It Works

How It Works boxes provide additional technical material on more complex topics. For classes where this kind of technical detail isn't necessary, students can skip these boxes.

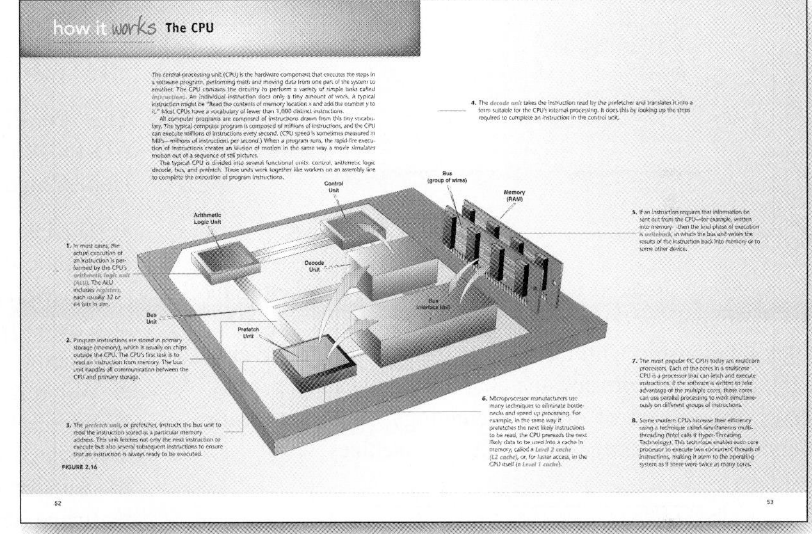

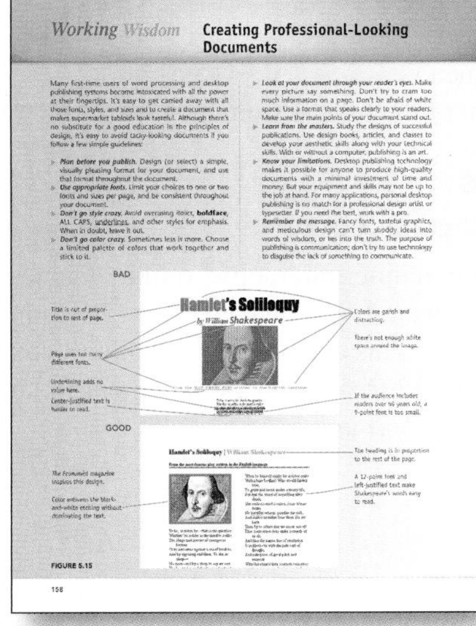

Working Wisdom

Working Wisdom boxes contain relevant and intriguing tips that can help readers produce better results and steer clear of trouble.

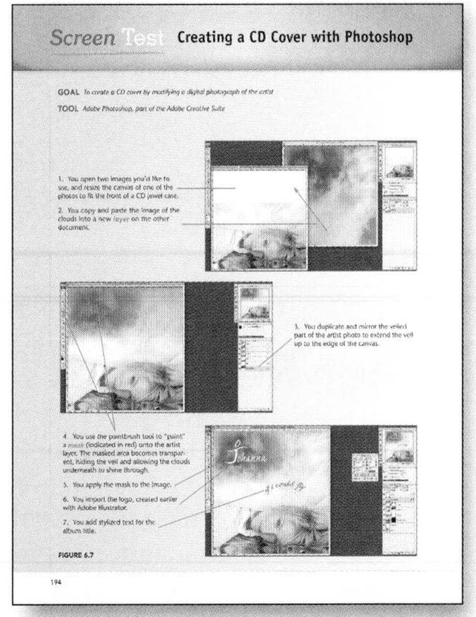

Screen Test

Screen Tests show what it's like to use a software application to achieve specific goals. They provide students with a glimpse of programs they might not otherwise experience.

Inventing the Future

Inventing the Future boxes provide futuristic perspectives at the end of every chapter.

Inventing the Future ▸ Multisensory Interfaces

FIGURE 5.34

180

Crosscurrents

Completely updated **Crosscurrents** articles are some of the best contemporary, short essays focusing on our complex relationship with technology. Topics include the erosion of personal privacy, the abuse of intellectual property laws, the impact of digital technology on human brain function, and the ethics of intelligent machines.

Crosscurrents Your Brain Online

by Sharon Begley

Discussion Questions

307

Other Resources

Companion Web Site

This text is accompanied by a Companion Web site at **www.pearsonhighered.com/beekman**. This Web site brings you and your students a richer, more interactive Web experience than ever before. Features of this site include an interactive study guide, end-of-chapter materials, additional Internet exercises, and crossword puzzles to enhance your understanding of key concepts and terms from each chapter.

CourseSmart

CourseSmart is an exciting new choice for students looking to save money. As an alternative to purchasing the printed textbook, students can purchase an electronic version of the same content. With a CourseSmart eTextbook, students can search the text, make notes online, print out reading assignments that incorporate lecture notes, and bookmark important passages for later review. For more information, or to purchase access to the CourseSmart eTextbook, visit **www.coursesmart.com**.

Instructor Resources

The Prentice Hall Instructor's Resource Center on CD-ROM includes the tools you expect from a Prentice Hall Computer Concepts text, like:

- The instructor's material in Word format
- Solutions to all questions and exercises from the book and Web site
- Customizable PowerPoint slide presentations for each chapter
- Web resources
- Internet exercises
- Discussion questions
- Additional assignments
- Image library of all of the figures from the text

CourseCompass
www.coursecompass.com

CourseCompass is a dynamic, interactive online course-management tool powered exclusively for Pearson Education by Blackboard. This exciting product allows you to teach market-leading Pearson Education content in an easy-to-use, customizable format.

Blackboard
www.pearsonhighered.com/blackboard

Prentice Hall's abundant online content, combined with Blackboard's popular tools and interface, results in robust Web-based courses that are easy to implement, manage, and use—taking your courses to new heights in student interaction and learning.

WebCT
www.pearsonhighered.com/webct

Course-management tools within WebCT include page tracking, progress tracking, class and student management, a grade book, communication tools, a calendar, reporting tools, and more.

Digital Planet: Tomorrow's Technology and You

1

Exploring Our Digital Planet

OBJECTIVES

After you read this chapter you should be able to:

- Describe digital technology's critical role in our lives
- Discuss several key trends in the evolution of computers and digital technology
- Describe the major types of computers and their principal uses
- Explain how the growth and evolution of the Internet is changing our lives
- Explain how our information age differs from any time that came before
- Discuss the social and ethical impact of information technology on our society

The culture of generosity is the very backbone of the Internet.

Caterina Fake, co-founder of Flickr

Creating Communities on the Living Web

You may not realize it, but you're probably helping build one of the most important and complex structures ever created: the World Wide Web. The Web isn't new; it's been around since the 1990s. But until recently, most people treated it like a television set or a library. They surfed and searched for information, images, and experiences, but they didn't add anything new. That's changing, thanks to Web pioneers who are designing sites that depend on our creative contributions. Today some of the most vital parts of the Web are being built by everyday people working (and playing) together in virtual communities that span the globe.

One of the best known examples of the living Web is MySpace, founded in 2003 by Tom Anderson and Chris DeWolfe. Inspired by Match.com and Friendster, these two Los Angeles entrepreneurs set out to create an online community experience for young people. But unlike other popular social networking sites, MySpace enabled—and encouraged—members to create personal Web sites to share words and pictures with other members. They also designed MySpace so that it was easy for musicians to connect with fans, bypassing corporate PR portals. According to Anderson, "The idea was that if it was a cool thing to do online, you should be able to do it on MySpace." MySpace's success was immediate and overwhelming. Within three years it became one of the most popular Web destinations. In 2005, MySpace was purchased by Rupert Murdoch's News Corp. for U.S. $580 million.

But by 2008 MySpace had lost its "cool" to Facebook. Facebook was founded just four years earlier by Harvard student Mark Zuckerberg. Facebook was originally designed for Harvard students. Today it's open to just about anyone, anywhere—except in a handful of countries where it's banned by dictators who fear the free exchange of ideas. Facebook now generates more than a billion dollars in annual revenue by providing online space for hundreds of millions of members to create and share comments, content, and connections.

The online worlds of Facebook and MySpace aren't trouble-free. Unsuspecting users reveal personal information and photographs, naively assuming that all of their "friends" can be trusted, and that only their friends will see their postings. Online stalking, harassment, and bullying incidents have forced both companies to deal with

FIGURE 1.1a MySpace founders Tom Anderson and Chris DeWolfe.

FIGURE 1.1b Facebook founder Mark Zuckerberg.

difficult questions about the balance between personal security and privacy—the same kinds of questions that plague communities in the nondigital world.

Flickr is an online community with a different purpose and a different story. Caterina Fake and Stewart Butterfield, a married couple in Vancouver, B.C., Canada, founded their company to create a massive multiplayer Web game. When one of their engineers developed a clever way for players to share pictures, they decided to build a photo-sharing site around that technology. "It turned out the fun was in the photo sharing," Fake says. Their game didn't survive, but Flickr became an instant hit after its 2004 launch. Within two years it was snapped up by Yahoo! for an estimated U.S. $35 million. Flickr members generously share their photographs—from personal portraits to late-breaking news images—with millions of other members. They decide collectively how Flickr's online galleries should be organized and categorized. They develop a sense of community based on shared interests and trust.

There are many variations on these stories, including some unlikely successes. In 2005 Chad Hurley, Steve Chen, and Jawed Karim launched a Web site for sharing videos. Few people at the time thought the Internet was ready to handle the demands of a massive video-based site. But their creation, YouTube, became a global cultural phenomenon before being purchased by Google for $1.65 billion less than two years later. In 2006, Jack Dorsey, Biz Stone, and a few other young creative Web workers started Twitter so that individuals could send short messages to groups of people. They went against conventional wisdom by requiring that every message be limited to 140 characters or less. This made it possible for people to use their phones to send and receive "tweets." Today millions of people around the world tweet about everything from the personal to the political. And then there's Wikipedia, the written-by-volunteers, funded-by-donations encyclopedia that has become the Web's most popular general reference work since it was launched in 2001 by Larry Sanger and Jimmy Wales.

The creators of these Web sites didn't just build pages—they created communities. And we're all invited to be part of that creative process. These sites and other similar sites are referred to as Web 2.0 because they're transforming the Web into a different kind of experience. As Steven Levy and Brad Stone wrote in *Newsweek,* these Web 2.0 sites "aren't places to go, but things to do, ways to express yourself, means to connect with others and extend your own horizons." ■

Computers and the Internet are so much a part of modern life that we tend to take them for granted. We hardly notice when some technical marvel—Facebook, Twitter, iTunes, Google, or whatever's next—changes the way we live. And we're even less conscious of the computer-controlled devices humming away in the background, maintaining the infrastructure of our civilization. But we'd certainly notice if they suddenly stopped working. Imagine...

Living in a Nondigital World

I've suffered a great many catastrophes in my life. **Most of them never happened.**
—*Mark Twain*

You wake up with the sun well above the horizon and realize your alarm clock hasn't gone off. You wonder if you've overslept. You have a big research project due today. The TV and radio don't work. The lights don't work either, so that clinches it: there is no power. But that's not all. The face of your phone stares back at you blankly. Your laptop isn't just sleeping; it's dead. The morning newspaper is missing from your doorstep. You'll have to guess the weather forecast by looking out the window.

Your microwave isn't working, so you decide to go out for breakfast, but your car won't start. In fact, the only cars moving are antiques from the 1970s or earlier. Dejected, you pull out the camping stove, carry it out to the deck behind your apartment, and heat some water for coffee. Leaning against the rail of the deck, you notice how quiet the city is.

By noon the water faucets and toilets no longer work: there is no more fresh water. You've spent a good part of the morning talking to your neighbors about the apparent failure of all things digital. Under normal circumstances you rarely see most of these people, but the techno-crisis seems to have sparked a sense of community.

As you discuss plans with your neighbors, you hear popping sounds from the direction of the nearby mall. Could that be gunfire? Where are the police?

Our story could go on, but the message should be clear enough by now. Computers are everywhere, and our lives are directly affected in all kinds of ways by their operation—and nonoperation. It's truly amazing that computers have infiltrated our lives so thoroughly in such a short time.

FIGURE 1.2 This utility company control room depends on digital technology (left). Complex computer technology works behind the scenes to support creative artists and dazzle audiences in Cirque du Soleil performances (right).

Computers in Perspective

> It's almost impossible to know **which grain of sand is going to start an avalanche.**
> *—Brian Eno, musician and digital artist*

Although computers have been with us for less than an average human lifetime, these extraordinary machines are built on centuries of insight and effort.

Computers grew out of a human need to quantify. Early humans were content to count with fingers, rocks, or other everyday objects. As cultures became more complex, so did their counting tools. The abacus (a type of counting tool and calculator used by the Babylonians, the Chinese, and others for thousands of years) and the Hindu-Arabic number system are examples of early calculating tools that had an immediate and profound effect on the human race. (Imagine trying to conduct business without a number system that allows for easy addition and subtraction.)

By the early nineteenth century, the capitalist culture's appetite for mathematics had outgrown its tools. A "computer" was a person who performed calculations to produce mathematical tables. Unfortunately, to err is human, and the tables they produced were riddled with mistakes. A pair of British visionaries, Charles Babbage and Augusta Ada King, the Countess of Lovelace (commonly called Ada Lovelace today), imagined the construction of an Analytical Engine—a mechanical computer that would automatically and reliably perform these tasks. They never completed their dream machine, and it took about 125 years for engineers to transform their vision of a computing machine into a reality. The journey from Analytical Engine to working computer produced some amazing stories:

- In 1939 a young German engineer named Konrad Zuse completed the Z1, the first programmable, general-purpose digital computer. "I was too lazy to calculate and so I invented the computer," Zuse recalled. In 1941, Zuse and a friend asked the German government for funds to build a faster electronic computer to help crack enemy codes during World War II. The Nazi military establishment turned him down, confident that their aircraft would quickly win the war without Zuse's devices.
- At about the same time, the British government was assembling a top-secret team of mathematicians and engineers to crack Nazi military codes. In 1943 the team, led by mathematician Alan Turing and others, completed Colossus. This special-purpose computer allowed British military intelligence to eavesdrop on even the most secret German messages throughout the remainder of the war.
- In 1939, Iowa State University professor John Atanasoff and graduate student Clifford Berry created the Atanasoff-Berry Computer (ABC), which was capable of solving systems of linear equations. When Atanasoff approached International Business Machines for funding, he was told "IBM will never be interested in an electronic computing machine."
- Harvard professor Howard Aiken was more successful in financing the automatic, general-purpose calculator he was developing. Thanks to a $1 million grant from IBM, he completed the Mark I in 1944. This 51-foot-long, 8-foot-tall monster used noisy, slow, electromechanical relays, but it proved its worth by computing ballistics tables for the U.S. Navy.
- After consulting with Atanasoff and studying the ABC, John Mauchly teamed up with J. Presper Eckert to help the U.S. war effort by constructing a machine that could calculate ballistics tables for the army. The machine was the Electronic Numerical Integrator and Computer (ENIAC), a 30-ton behemoth that broke down about once every seven minutes. When it was running, it could calculate 500 times faster than the existing electromechanical calculators—about as fast as a modern pocket calculator. The ENIAC wasn't completed until two months after the end of World War II in 1945, but it convinced its creators that large-scale computers were commercially feasible. After the war Mauchly and Eckert started a private company and designed the UNIVAC I, the first

FIGURE 1.3 J. Presper Eckert (left) describes the UNIVAC I computer to CBS correspondent Walter Cronkite before the 1952 presidential election. When 5 percent of the votes had been reported, UNIVAC correctly predicted that Eisenhower would win the election, but CBS cautiously chose to withhold the prediction until most of the votes were reported.

general-purpose commercial computer built in the United States. Calculator maker Remington Rand bought them out in 1950, completed the UNIVAC I, and delivered it to the U.S. Census Bureau in 1951.

FIGURE 1.4 A vacuum tube, a transistor, and an integrated circuit.

Computer hardware evolved rapidly from those early days, with new technologies replacing old every few years. The first computers were big, expensive, and finicky. Only a large institution such as a major bank or the U.S. government could afford a computer, not to mention the climate-controlled computing center needed to house it and the staff of technicians needed to program it and keep it running. But with all their faults, computers quickly became indispensable tools for scientists, engineers, and other professionals.

The **transistor** was invented in 1948 as a substitute for the vacuum tube, and transistors first appeared in computers eight years later. Computers that used transistors were radically smaller, more reliable, and less expensive than computers that used vacuum tubes to store and manipulate data. Because of improvements in software at about the same time, these machines were also much easier to program and use. As a result, computers became more widely used in business, science, and engineering.

After the Soviet Union's successful launch of the Sputnik satellite in 1957, the United States was desperate to catch up with its Cold War rival. America's fledgling space program needed computers that were even smaller and more powerful than the transistor-based machines, so researchers developed the **integrated circuit**: a small **silicon chip** containing hundreds of transistors and other electronics. By the mid-1960s, transistor-based computers were replaced by smaller, more powerful machines built around these new integrated circuits.

Integrated circuits rapidly replaced transistors for the same reasons that transistors superseded vacuum tubes:

- *Reliability.* Machines built with integrated circuits were less prone to failure than their predecessors because the chips could be rigorously tested before installation.
- *Size.* Single chips could replace entire boards filled with hundreds of transistors and other electronics, making it possible to build much smaller machines.
- *Speed.* Because electricity had shorter distances to travel, the smaller machines were faster than their predecessors.
- *Efficiency.* Because chips were so small, they used less electrical power. As a result, they created less heat.
- *Cost.* Mass production techniques made it easy to manufacture inexpensive chips.

Just about every breakthrough in computer technology since the dawn of the computer age has presented similar advantages over the technology it replaced.

The inventions of the vacuum tube, the transistor, and the silicon chip had tremendous impact on our society. But the impact was even bigger when, in 1971, Intel engineers developed the first **microprocessor**—a single silicon chip containing *all* of a computer's computational components. The research and development costs for the first microprocessor were enormous. But once the assembly lines were in place, silicon computer chips could be mass-produced cheaply. The raw materials were certainly cheap enough; silicon, the main ingredient in beach sand, is the second most common element (after oxygen) in the Earth's crust.

U.S. companies soon flooded the marketplace with watches and calculators built around inexpensive microprocessors. The economic effect was immediate: mechanical calculators and slide rules became obsolete overnight, electronic hobbyists became wealthy entrepreneurs, and California's San Jose area gained the nickname **Silicon Valley** when dozens of *semiconductor* manufacturing companies sprouted and grew there.

The personal computer revolution began in the late 1970s, when Apple, Commodore, Tandy, and other companies introduced low-cost, microprocessor-based microcomputers as powerful as many of the room-sized computers that had come before. **Personal computers**, or **PCs**, are now common in offices, factories, homes, schools, and just about everywhere else. Microprocessors have found their way into countless other devices, from phones and game machines to robots and space stations. Every year brings more silicon surprises.

All of these digital innovations are possible because of **Moore's law**. In 1965 Gordon Moore, the chairman of chipmaker Intel, predicted that the number of transistors that can be packed into a silicon chip of the same price would roughly double every two years. Moore's law has been widely misquoted. The most common misstatement of Moore's law is that computer power doubles every 18 months; Moore insists he never said that. Still, Moore's law has been remarkably accurate through the years. This type of exponential growth has powerful implications over an extended period of time: a quantity that doubles every two years grows by a thousand in two decades—and by a million in four decades.

A microprocessor's performance doesn't necessarily double with its transistor count. Still, the phenomenal growth of computing power over the last few decades is largely due to the effects of Moore's law. In fact, all of the five factors listed earlier in this section—reliability, size, speed, efficiency, and cost—have continually improved as engineers find ways to pack more transistors into those tiny slabs of silicon. (According to Intel, similar progress in the airline industry would have resulted in one-second transatlantic flights that cost about a penny!) Moore's law has also resulted in a steady increase in computer memory capacity. At

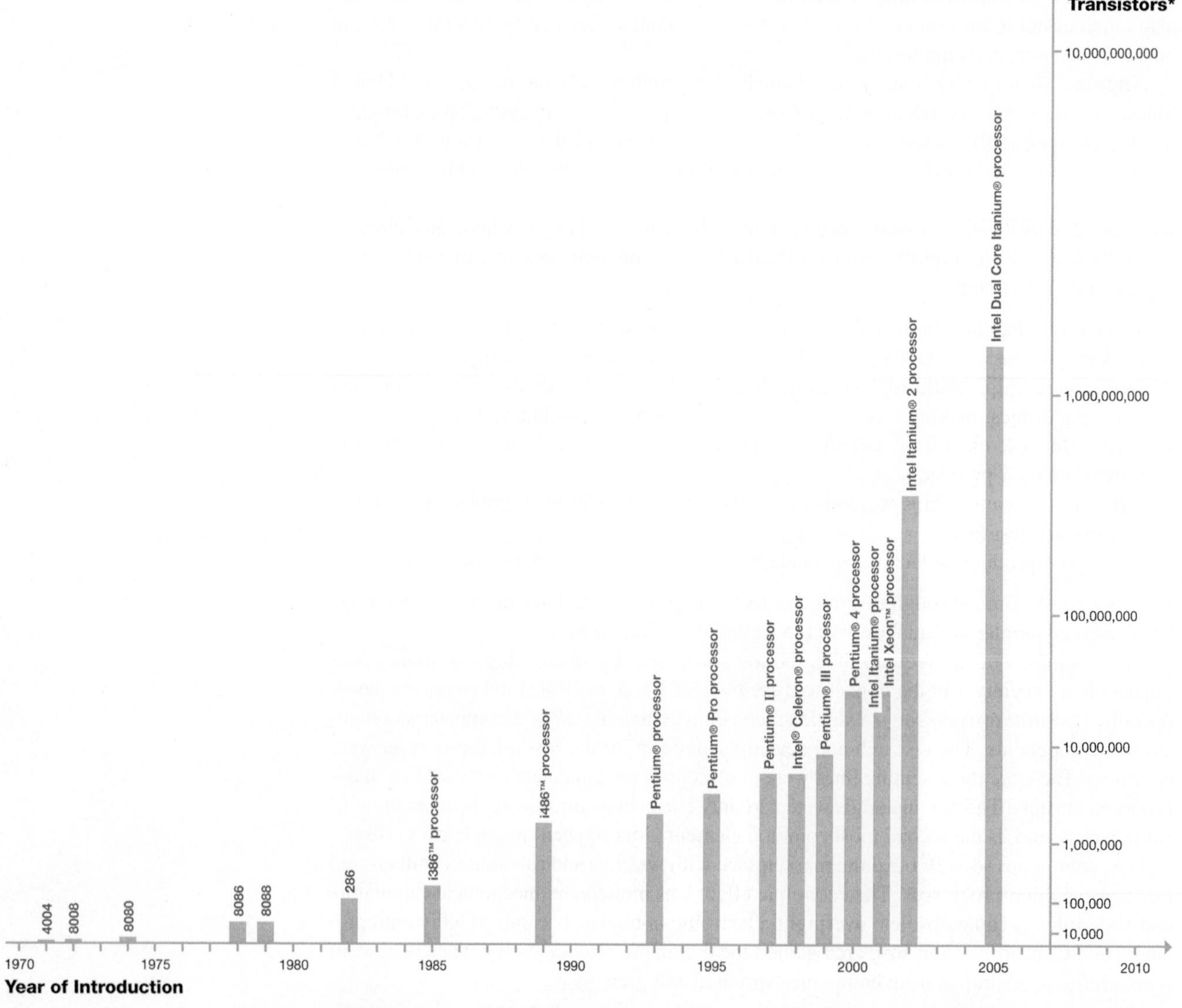

FIGURE 1.5 This chart was created by Intel to commemorate the 40th anniversary of Moore's Law. According to Moore's law, the number of transistors per chip doubles every two years. Computer power continues to increase as a result.

the same time, technological improvements have resulted in exponential growth in hard disk capacity and network capacity. Software engineers have been in a continual race to keep up with the relentless progress on so many hardware fronts. And there's no reason to believe this exponential progress won't continue for a decade or more.

Computers Today: A Brief Taxonomy

I've come up with a set of **rules that describe our reactions to technologies.**

1. Anything that is in the world when you're born is **normal and ordinary** and is just a natural part of the way the world works.
2. Anything that's invented between when you're fifteen and thirty-five is **new and exciting and revolutionary** and you can probably get a career in it.
3. Anything invented after you're thirty-five is **against the natural order of things**.

—*Douglas Adams, author of* The Hitchhiker's Guide to the Galaxy

Thanks to an abundance of low-cost microprocessors, today's world is populated with an incredible variety of computers, each particularly well suited to specific tasks. We'll take a quick look at the major computer classes here, starting with the devices that most people don't think of as computers.

Embedded Systems

More than 90 percent of the world's microprocessors are hidden inside common household and electronic devices. A microprocessor used as a component of a larger system is called an **embedded system**. You can find embedded systems inside thermostats, traffic lights, wristwatches, toys, game machines, TVs, camcorders, cars, and ovens. Just about anything that's powered by electricity—battery or house current—has become a candidate for a microprocessor implant.

The microprocessors inside embedded systems are, at their core, similar to those in general-purpose personal computers. But unlike their desktop cousins, these special-purpose machines typically have their programs etched in silicon so they can't be

FIGURE 1.6 Embedded computers are so common in today's world that they are all but invisible. This home energy management system uses embedded computer chips for indoor climate control and energy efficiency (left). Computers control and coordinate traffic lights to reduce traffic delays and make intersections safer (middle). The IntelliCap is an "intelligent pill" that uses built-in sensors to navigate to the diseased area in the digestive tract before releasing medicine (right).

altered. When a program is immortalized on a silicon chip, it becomes known as **firmware**—a hybrid of hardware and software. Technically speaking, there's no clear line between firmware and software. Firmware usually refers to programs that run when a device is starting up or taking care of routine, behind-the-scenes business. Some devices, including many music players, home entertainment systems, phones, and cars, store firmware in a type of memory that can be updated.

Personal Computers and Workstations

A personal computer (PC) is, generally speaking, designed to be used by one person at a time as a tool for enhancing productivity, creativity, or communication. PCs can be classified as desktop computers, workstations, and laptop computers.

As the name implies, a **desktop computer** is a personal computer designed to sit on a desk or table for extended periods of time. The most common type of desktop computer has several separate components, including a tower (containing the microprocessor and several other critical components), monitor, keyboard, mouse, and speakers. The tower, or system unit, doesn't really need to sit on the desktop, so it's often stashed under or beside the desk. Another type of desktop computer eliminates the tower by hiding all of its components inside the monitor casing. A desktop computer has one or more power cables connecting it to an electrical outlet.

A **workstation**—a high-end desktop computer with massive computing power—is used for computationally intensive interactive applications, such as large-scale scientific data analysis. As workstations become less expensive and desktop computers become more powerful, the line that separates them is becoming as much a marketing distinction as a technical one.

A **laptop computer** (sometimes called a **notebook computer**) is a personal computer designed with portability in mind. A typical laptop computer weighs less than seven

FIGURE 1.7 PCs today come in a variety of shapes and sizes.

pounds and relies on an internal battery to power its electronics. To keep size and weight down, manufacturers often leave out some components that would be standard equipment on desktop machines. For example, some laptops don't have built-in optical drives for playing or recording CDs or DVDs. Most have ports that enable external drives, keyboards, mice, and monitor screens, referred to as **peripherals**, to be attached with cables. Extra-small, extra-light, no-frills notebooks are sometimes called **netbooks** because they're designed mainly as portable Internet connection devices.

Many laptop computers are built around microprocessors similar to those that drive desktop models. But portability comes at a price: Notebooks (and especially netbooks) aren't as powerful or fast as their desktop counterparts, and if they are, they generally cost more than comparable desktop machines. They're also more difficult to upgrade than tower systems when newer hardware components become available.

Handheld Devices

Many computing devices are small enough to tuck into pockets and serve the needs of users who value mobility over a full-sized keyboard and screen. ***Personal digital assistants (PDAs)*** were originally designed to serve as pocket-sized digital address books and day planners that could share data with PCs, but they quickly evolved into multipurpose handheld computers.

Today's digital **smart phones** have made PDAs all but obsolete. A smart phone typically combines the functions of a phone, a camera, a PDA, a game machine, and a music/video player with Internet connectivity and the ability to run **apps**—small software applications. The iPhone, Droid, Blackberry, and other smart phones are powerful, pocket-sized computers that use apps to perform all kinds of functions that previously required a full-sized PC—and some that can't be done with a PC.

Another type of device, the **tablet computer**, bridges the shrinking gap between the smart phone and the notebook/netbook PC. Keyboardless tablet PCs have existed for many years, but for most people these bulky devices offered no advantage over laptops. Newer, smaller, simpler, lighter tablets like Apple's 1.5 pound iPad, on the other hand, serve as attractive compromises between portability and power.

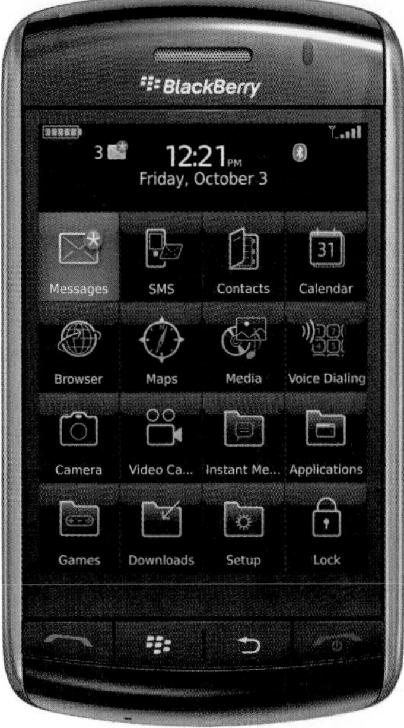

FIGURE 1.8 The Droid and Blackberry are pocket-sized computers marketed as smart phones. The iPad's large touch screen makes it an ideal media/communication/entertainment device for people who need more than a smart phone but don't want to lug a laptop.

FIGURE 1.9 Rack-mounted servers don't need built-in displays because they can be remotely controlled through other computers.

Servers

A **server** is a computer that provides other computers connected to the network with access to data, programs, or other resources. For example, Web servers respond to requests for Web pages, database servers handle database queries, and print servers provide other computers access to a printer. Although just about any desktop computer can be used as a server, some computers are specifically designed with this purpose in mind. Servers may have faster processors, more memory, or faster network connections than typical desktop systems. Servers are often clustered together in groups to increase their processing power.

Mainframes and Supercomputers

Before the microcomputer revolution, most information processing was done on **mainframe computers**—room-sized machines with price tags to match. Today large organizations, such as banks and airlines, still use mainframes for big computing jobs. But their use of microprocessors means that today's mainframes are smaller and cheaper than their ancestors; a typical mainframe today might be the size of a refrigerator and cost around US$50,000. These industrial-strength computers are largely invisible to the general public because they're hidden away in climate-controlled rooms.

But the fact that you can't see them doesn't mean you don't use them. When you make an online airline reservation or deposit money in your bank account, a mainframe computer is probably involved in the transaction behind the scenes. Your travel agent and your bank teller might communicate with a mainframe using a computer **terminal** or **thin client**. A terminal is a combination keyboard and screen with little local processing power that transfers information to and from a mainframe computer or server; a smart client is similar, but typically has more on-board processing power than a bare-bones terminal. The mainframe or server might be in another room or even in another country halfway around the globe.

A mainframe computer can communicate with several users simultaneously through a technique called **timesharing**. For example, a timesharing system allows travel agents

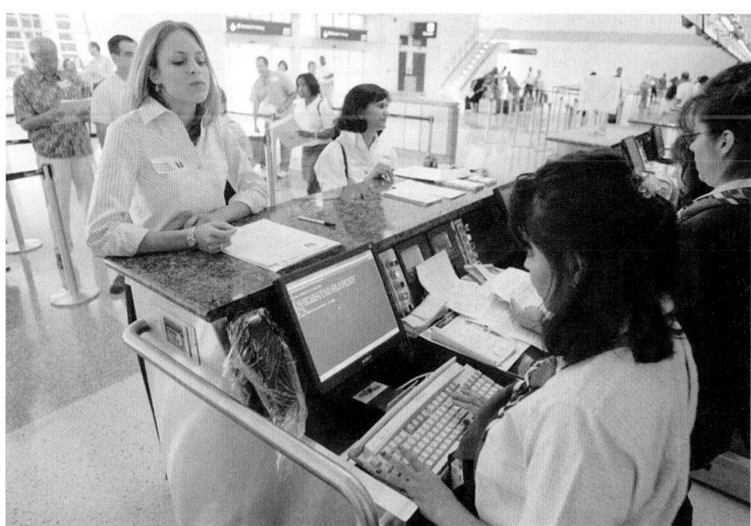

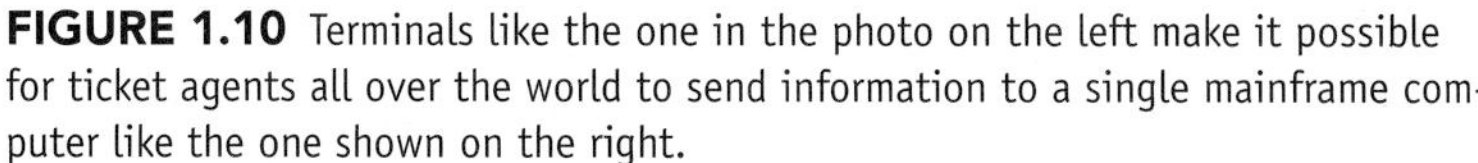

FIGURE 1.10 Terminals like the one in the photo on the left make it possible for ticket agents all over the world to send information to a single mainframe computer like the one shown on the right.

all over the country to make reservations using the same computer and the same flight information at the same time.

Timesharing also makes it possible for users with diverse computing needs to share expensive computing equipment. Many research scientists and engineers, for example, need more mathematical computing power than they can get from PCs. Their computing needs might require a powerful mainframe computer. A timesharing machine can simultaneously serve the needs of scientists and engineers in different departments working on a variety of projects.

Many researchers can't get the computing power they need from a mainframe computer. Traditional "big iron" may not be enough for some calculation-intensive work, including weather forecasting, telephone network design, simulated car crash testing, oil

FIGURE 1.11 IBM BlueGene/L supercomputer.

exploration, computer animation, and medical imaging. Power users with these special requirements need access to the fastest, most powerful computers made. These superfast, superpowerful computers are called **supercomputers**. A typical supercomputer is constructed out of thousands of microprocessors.

Computer Connections: The Internet Revolution

> The grand design keeps getting grander. **A global computer is taking shape,** and we're all connected to it.
>
> —*Stewart Brand, in* The Media Lab

Microprocessors have worked their way into everything from music players to supercomputers. The microprocessor's impact has been magnified by the development of **networks** to connect many of those devices together.

In the late 1960s, a group of visionary computer scientists and engineers, with financial backing from the U.S. government, began work on an experimental network for connecting computers. As the network evolved, it became known as the **Internet**. As late as the 1980s, the Internet was still the domain of researchers, academics, and government officials, who used it to transfer files and exchange **electronic mail (email)** messages. The Internet wasn't designed for casual visitors; users had to know cryptic commands and codes that only a programmer could love.

But in the 1990s, Internet software took giant leaps forward in usability. The most significant breakthrough was the development of the **World Wide Web** (or just **Web**), a vast tract of the Internet accessible to just about anyone who could point to buttons on a computer screen. This led to the Internet's transformation from a text-only environment into a multimedia landscape incorporating pictures, animation, sounds, and video. Millions of people now connect to the Internet each day through **browsers**—programs like Internet Explorer and Firefox that serve as navigable windows into the Web. **Hypertext links** on Web pages loosely tie together millions of pages created by diverse authors, making the Web into a massive, ever-changing global information space.

Widespread email and Web use have led to astounding Internet growth, from a few million users in the mid-1990s to about two billion today—more than one out of four people on the planet! In the late 1990s, Internet users tended to be young, educated, male, white, and middle-class. But as the Internet's population has grown, it has come to look more like

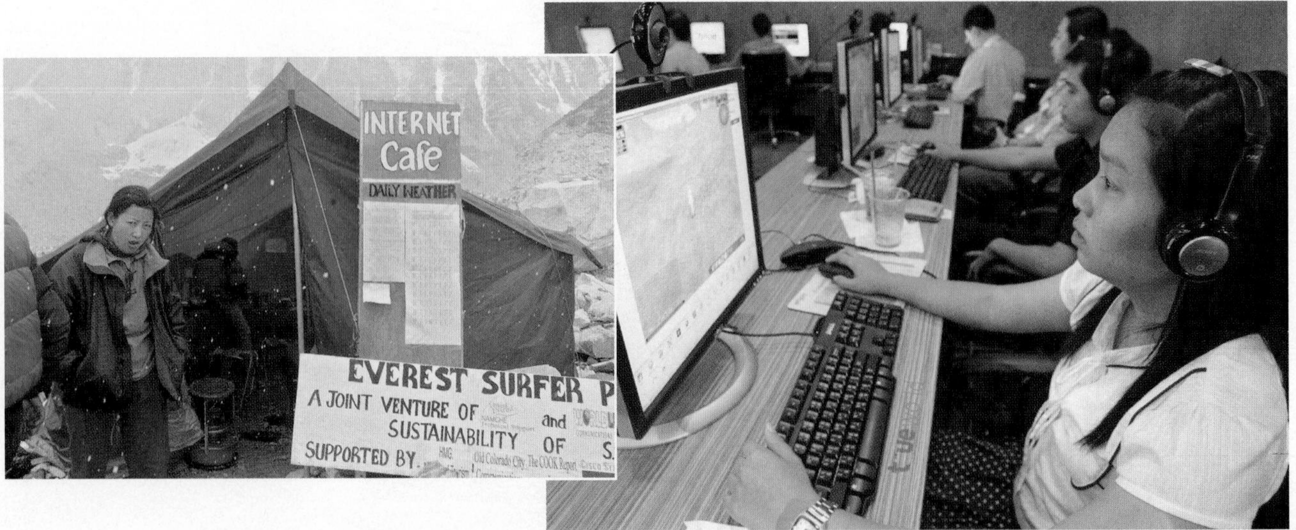

FIGURE 1.12 People throughout the world use Internet cafés to access the Web and socialize.

the population at large. More than half of all active Internet users are now female. And while there are still some areas with no Internet access, those areas are becoming harder to find. In just about any city on Earth, you can rent time on a PC to check your email or explore the Web. The Internet is growing faster than television, radio, or any other communication technology that came before it.

Internet-based computing goes beyond traditional PCs. Video game consoles, including Microsoft's Xbox 360, Sony's PlayStation 3, and Nintendo's Wii, provide Internet access through TVs sets. Smart phones and other handheld devices provide easy access to email and other Internet services. Many home entertainment systems, security systems, and other devices can connect to the Internet, monitoring all kinds of data that can have an impact on our lives and our livelihoods.

The explosive growth of the Internet is largely fueled by the rapid expansion of commerce on the Web. The Internet economy generates hundreds of billions of dollars in revenues and millions of jobs each year. Online stores, auctions, and service bureaus have transformed the way people do business worldwide. Multiplayer games and virtual communities connect people all over the planet. Internet advertising supports a myriad of free services, from email and search engines to radio stations and social networks.

But a surprising amount of Internet traffic is still noncommercial. Academics and researchers collect data and collaborate through global networks. Governments, nonprofits, political candidates, and activists communicate through the Web. Ad-hoc communities form to create not-for-profit encyclopedias, art galleries, and software.

At the beginning of this chapter we met the creators of some of the Web's most important sites—sites that are built largely by the people who visit them. Facebook, Twitter, Wikipedia, YouTube, and countless other Web 2.0 sites exist only because global communities of people share their ideas, words, images, sounds, and artwork to them. For many people who visit these sites daily, it's hard to remember what life was like without them. And for many people who use phones, tables, game machines, and TVs to connect to data and applications stored in the Internet "cloud," the desktop PC seems clunky and old-fashioned.

Like the digital technology it's built upon, the Internet is a work in progress—a work that seems to transform itself into something new every few years. And with each transformation it plays a more central role in our lives.

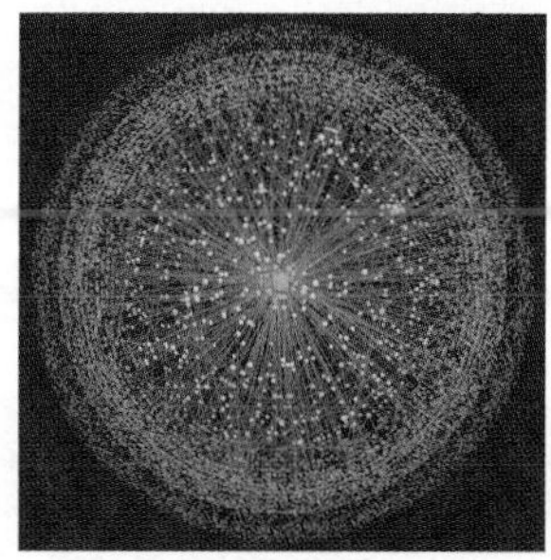

FIGURE 1.13 This graph is a computer-generated "map" of the Internet—a visualization showing the complex network of interconnecting nodes, with the most highly-connected nodes in the center. The image on the cover of this book is another computer-generated visualization of the Internet.

FIGURE 1.14 This family is playing a game with other Internet-connected gamers who might be anywhere in the world.

Screen Test Windows into the World of Web 2.0

Web 2.0 sites are built around contributions from Web users. Here are several popular examples.

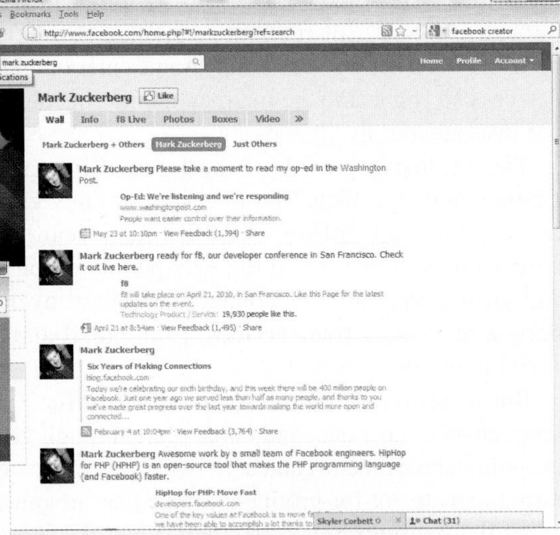

FIGURE 1.15a Facebook is the most popular social networking site on the Web. Facebook members can join groups, keep track of friends, play games with other members, and even write programs to enhance the Facebook experience.

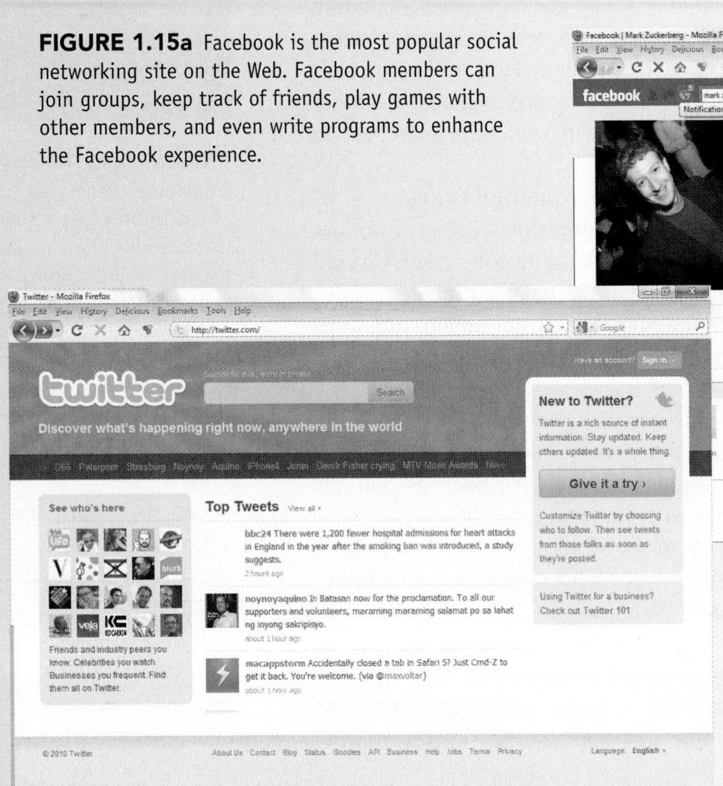

FIGURE 1.15b Millions of Twitter users send and receive tweets—very short text messages—using PCs and smart phones.

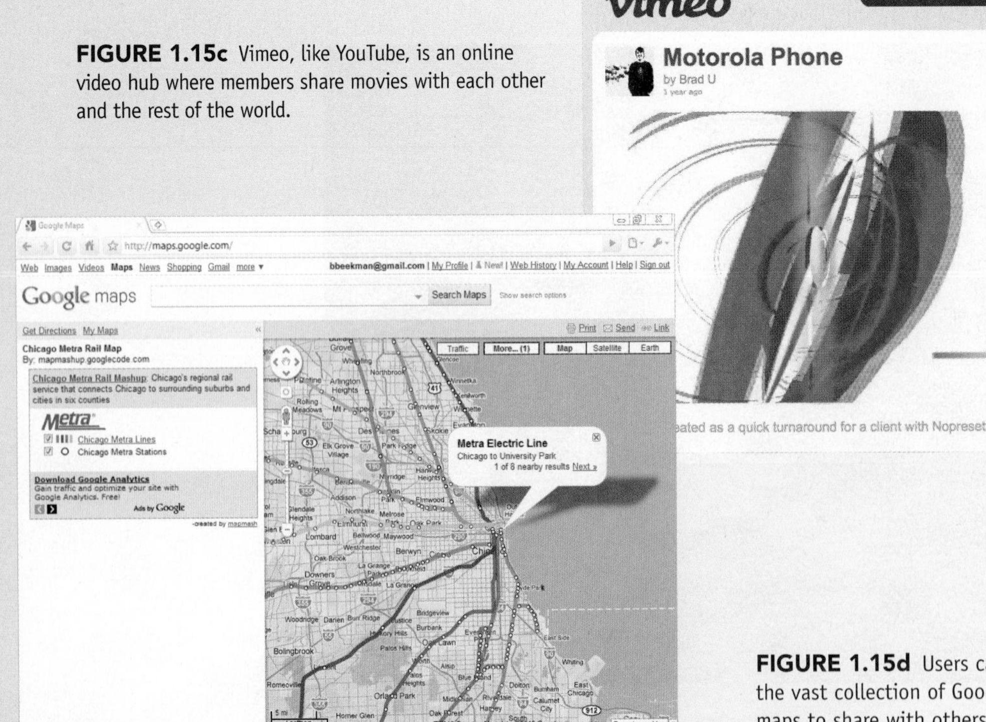

FIGURE 1.15c Vimeo, like YouTube, is an online video hub where members share movies with each other and the rest of the world.

FIGURE 1.15d Users can easily add information to the vast collection of Google Maps, creating custom maps to share with others.

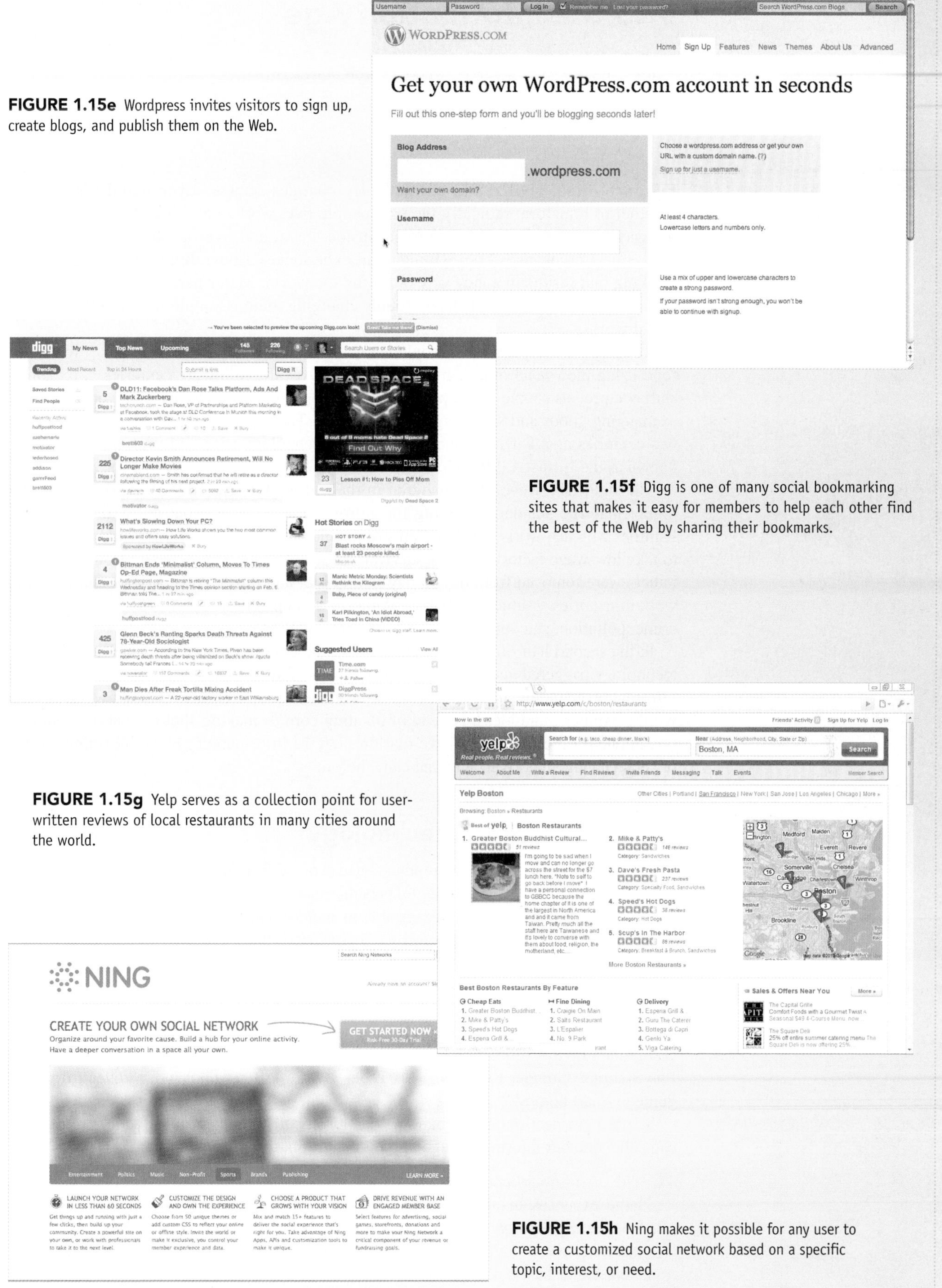

FIGURE 1.15e Wordpress invites visitors to sign up, create blogs, and publish them on the Web.

FIGURE 1.15f Digg is one of many social bookmarking sites that makes it easy for members to help each other find the best of the Web by sharing their bookmarks.

FIGURE 1.15g Yelp serves as a collection point for user-written reviews of local restaurants in many cities around the world.

FIGURE 1.15h Ning makes it possible for any user to create a customized social network based on a specific topic, interest, or need.

Into the Information Age

In the short term, the impact of new technologies like the Internet will be less than the hype would suggest. **But in the long term, it will be vastly larger than we can imagine today**.

—*Paul Saffo, technology forecaster*

Every so often, civilization dramatically changes course. Events and ideas come together to transform radically the way people live, work, and think. Traditions fall by the wayside, common sense is turned upside down, and lives are thrown into turmoil until a new order takes hold. Humankind experiences a **paradigm shift**—a change in thinking that results in a new way of seeing the world. Major paradigm shifts take generations because individuals have trouble changing their assumptions about the way the world works.

Roughly 10,000 years ago, people learned to domesticate animals and grow their own food using plows and other agricultural tools. Over the following centuries, a paradigm shift occurred as people gave up nomadic hunter–gatherer lives to live and work on farms, exchanging goods and services in nearby towns. The **agricultural age** lasted until about two centuries ago, when advances in machine technology triggered what has come to be known as the **Industrial Revolution**.

The Industrial Revolution ushered in the **industrial age**. Factory work promised a higher material standard of living for a growing population—but not without a price. Families who had worked the land on sustainable farms for generations found it necessary to take low-wage factory jobs for survival. As work life became separate from home life, fathers were removed from day-to-day family life, and those mothers who didn't have to work in factories assumed the bulk of domestic responsibilities. As towns grew into cities, crime, pollution, and other urban problems grew with them.

In the second half of the twentieth century, the convergence of computer and network technology triggered another paradigm shift—the shift from an industrial economy to an information economy. In the **information age**, most people earn their living working with words, numbers, and ideas. Instead of planting corn or making shoes, most of us shuffle bits in one form or another. As we roar through the information age, we're riding a wave of social change that rivals any that came before.

Living with Digital Technology

In less than a human lifetime, computers have evolved from massive, expensive, unreliable calculators into (mostly) dependable, versatile machines that have worked their way into just about every nook and cranny of modern society. The pioneers who created and marketed the first computers did not foresee these spectacular advances in computer technology. Thomas Watson, Sr., the founding father of IBM, declared in 1943 that the world would not need more than five computers! And the early pioneers certainly couldn't have predicted the extraordinary social changes that resulted from the computer's rapid evolution, not to mention the interconnections among those computers as networks encompass the globe. In the time of UNIVAC, who could have imagined netbooks, iPhones, PlayStations, Google, Facebook, YouTube, Twitter, eBay, robot moon rovers, or laser-guided "smart bombs"?

To get a perspective on our changing relationship to computers and all things digital, we can subdivide our information age into four short phases:

1. The *institutional computing phase*, starting about 1950. Computer specialists used large, expensive mainframes for corporate and government data storage and calculation.
2. The *personal computing phase*, starting about 1975. Millions of PCs joined mainframes in business and government, but they also found their way into schools and homes. Nontechnical users could now create, store, and distribute digital documents.

3. The *interpersonal computing phase*, starting about 1995. Networks connected the PCs and mainframes, the Internet went public, and digital communication changed the world.
4. The *collaborative computing phase*, starting about 2005. Smart phones, tablets, and other digital devices join PCs on the Internet. Web 2.0 sites encourage visitors to create, contribute, and connect with each other. Applications and documents begin migrating from PCs to the Internet "cloud."

Technological breakthroughs encourage further technological change, so we can expect the rate of change to continue to increase in coming decades. It's just a matter of time, and not very much time, before today's state-of-the-art PCs look as primitive as ENIAC looks to us—and before the Web we know seems as quaint as a Model T Ford. Similarly, today's high-tech society just hints at a future world that we haven't yet begun to imagine.

What do you really need to know about digital technology today? The remaining chapters of this book provide answers to that question by looking at the technology on three levels: explanations, applications, and implications.

Explanations: Clarifying Technology

You don't need to be a computer scientist to coexist with computers and networks. But your encounters with digital technology will make more sense if you understand a few basic concepts. Computer hardware and software details change every few years. And the Internet is evolving even faster; some suggest that one normal year is equal to several "Internet years," a phrase coined by Intel co-founder Andy Grove. But most of the underlying concepts remain constant as computers and networks evolve. If you understand the basics, you'll find that it's a lot easier to keep up with the changes.

Applications: Digital Technology in Action

Application programs, also known simply as **applications**, are the software tools that transform general-purpose computers, from smart phones to supercomputers, into special-purpose tools useful for meeting particular needs. Most applications are designed to be stored and run on particular computers. ***Web applications*** are stored on the Web so they can be accessed and used by multiple computers with Internet access. Many computer applications in science, government, business, and the arts are far too specialized and technical to be of use or interest to people outside the field. And many operate almost invisibly, taking care of business without demanding our attention. On the other hand, some applications are general-purpose tools with mass consumer appeal.

Regardless of your background or aspirations, you can almost certainly benefit from knowing a little about these applications:

- *Network applications.* A network application is a door into a world of online communication, communities, and commerce. Email, instant messaging, Web browsing, Web publishing, and social networks just scratch the surface of the possibilities that a networked computer offers. For many people, a computer is of no value when it's disconnected from the Internet.
- *Word processing and desktop publishing.* Word processing is a critical skill for anyone who communicates in writing—on paper, via digital documents, or on the Web. Desktop-publishing software can transform written words into polished, visually exciting publications.
- *Spreadsheets and other number-crunching applications.* In many businesses, the spreadsheet is the PC application that pays the rent—or at least calculates it. If you work with numbers, spreadsheets and statistical software can help you turn those numbers into insights.
- *Databases.* Electronic record-keeping databases reign supreme in the world of mainframes and servers. Of course, databases are widely used on PCs, too. Even if you don't have database software on a PC, database-searching skills are important for finding what you're looking for on the Internet.

These Time covers represent our changing relationship to computers and digital technology. Notice that the beginning of each new "phase" doesn't mean the end of the old ways of computing. Today we live in a world of institutional, personal, interpersonal, and collaborative computing.

TIME
MACHINE OF THE YEAR
The Computer Moves In

1950

1975

Institutional Computing Phase

A few large, expensive, mainframe computers in climate-controlled room

Controlled by experts and specialists

Used mainly for data storage and calculation

Personal Computing Phase

Millions of small, inexpensive PCs in offices, schools, homes, and elsewhere

Controlled mostly by users

Used mostly for document creation, data storage, and calculation

FIGURE 1.16 Digital time line: Four phases of the information age.

1995

2005

Interpersonal Computing Phase

Networks of interconnected computers in offices, homes, schools, and elsewhere

Controlled by users (clients) and network administrators

Used mostly for communication, document creation, data storage, and calculation

Collaborative Computing Phase

Global network of PCs, handhelds, embedded computers, and other clients connected to a "cloud" of servers providing online applications, storage, and other services

Controlled by users, groups, and network administrators

Used mostly for collaborative creation, self-expression, information sharing, communication, document creation, data storage, and calculation

FIGURE 1.17 Smart bombs, such as those employed in both Gulf wars, helped the U.S. armed forces target enemy installations with greater accuracy than was possible in earlier wars.

- *Graphics and image processing.* Computers make it possible to produce and manipulate all kinds of graphics, including charts, drawings, digital photographs—even realistic 3-D animation. As graphics tools become more accessible, visual communication skills become more important for all of us.
- *Audio, video, and multimedia.* Most PCs and many handheld devices and set-top boxes can play music, videos, and games. But audio and video applications can also open up creative possibilities for all kinds of people, from amateur podcasters to professional filmmakers. Multimedia documents and Web sites, by combining graphics, video, audio, and interactivity, open up all kinds of opportunities for entertainment and information exploration.
- *Programming and customized problem solving.* People often use computers to solve problems. Most people use applications written by professional programmers, but you may want to use computers to solve problems for which off-the-shelf applications or Web applications don't exist. Programming languages allow you to build custom application programs or customize existing applications. Many computer users find that their machines become more versatile and valuable when they learn a little about programming.
- *Artificial intelligence.* Artificial intelligence is the branch of computer science that explores the use of computers in tasks that require intelligence, imagination, and insight—tasks that have traditionally been performed by people rather than machines. Until recently, artificial intelligence was mostly an academic discipline—a field of study reserved for researchers and philosophers. But that research is paying off today with commercial applications that exhibit intelligence, from basic speech recognition to sophisticated expert systems that can solve problems formerly requiring the knowledge of a human expert.

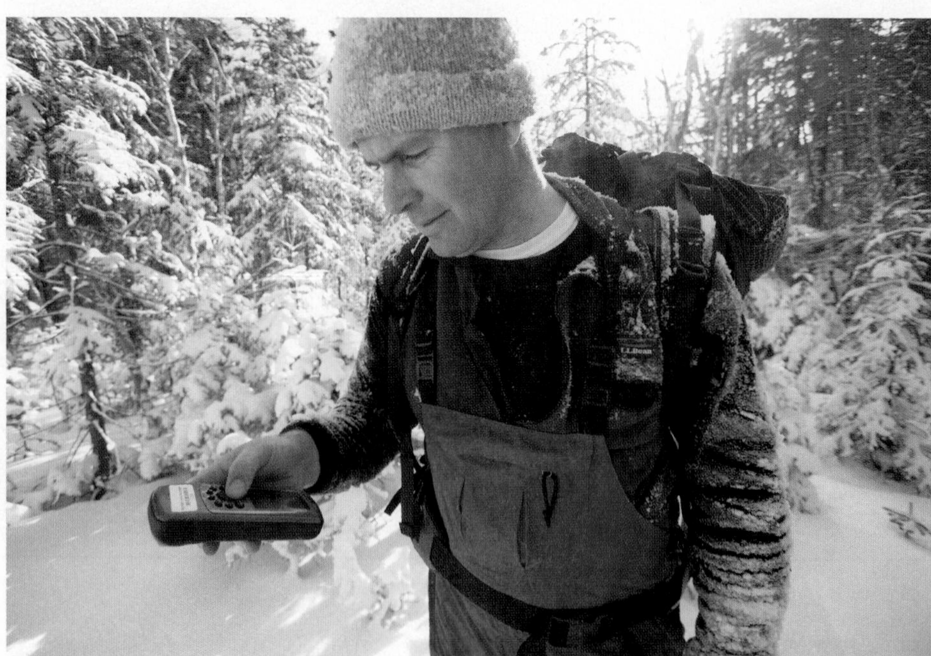

FIGURE 1.18 This search-and-rescue team member's handheld GPS device uses computer and network technology to provide critical location information.

Implications: Social and Ethical Issues

Digital technology is transforming the world rapidly and irreversibly. Jobs that existed for hundreds of years are being eliminated by automation, while new careers are built on emerging technology. Start-up businesses create new markets overnight, while older companies struggle to keep pace with "Internet time." Instant worldwide communication changes the way businesses work and challenges the role of governments. Computers routinely save lives in hospitals, keep space flights on course, and predict the weekend weather.

More than any other recent technology, computers and networks are responsible for profound changes in our society. To recognize their impact, all we need to do is imagine a world without them, as we did at the beginning of the chapter. Of course, computer scientists and computer engineers are not responsible for all the technological turbulence. Developments in fields as diverse as genetic engineering, medicine, and atomic physics among others contribute to the ever-increasing rate of social change. But researchers in all these fields depend on computers and the Internet to produce and communicate their results.

Although it's exciting to consider the opportunities arising from advances in digital technology, it's just as important to pay attention to the potential risks. Here's a sampling of the kinds of social and ethical issues we'll confront in this book:

- *The threat to personal privacy posed by large databases and computer networks.* When you use a credit card, buy an airline ticket, place a phone call, visit your doctor, send a text message, or explore the Web, you're leaving a trail of personal information in one or more computers. Who owns that information? Is it OK for the business or organization that collected the information to share it with others or make it public? Do you have the right to check its accuracy and change it if it's wrong? Do laws protecting individual privacy rights place undue burdens on businesses and governments?

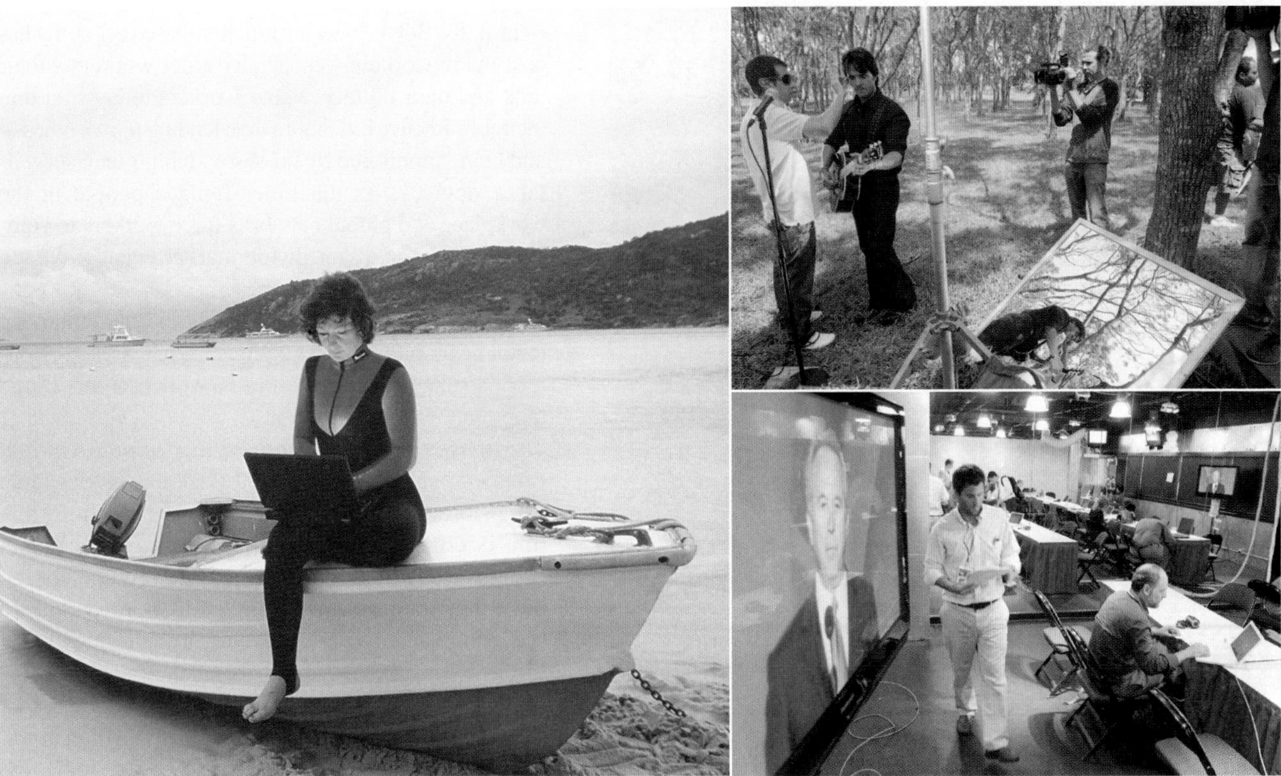

FIGURE 1.19 PC applications make it possible for people to work in ways that aren't possible otherwise. A marine biologist (left) uses a laptop computer to record research notes and analyze data in the field. A videographer (top right) can capture and edit footage for a music video using portable gear. A blogger (bottom right) can provide timely news and commentary to a worldwide audience.

FIGURE 1.20 This robot security guard helps protect a convention center from vandals and thieves. But does it threaten the jobs of human security guards?

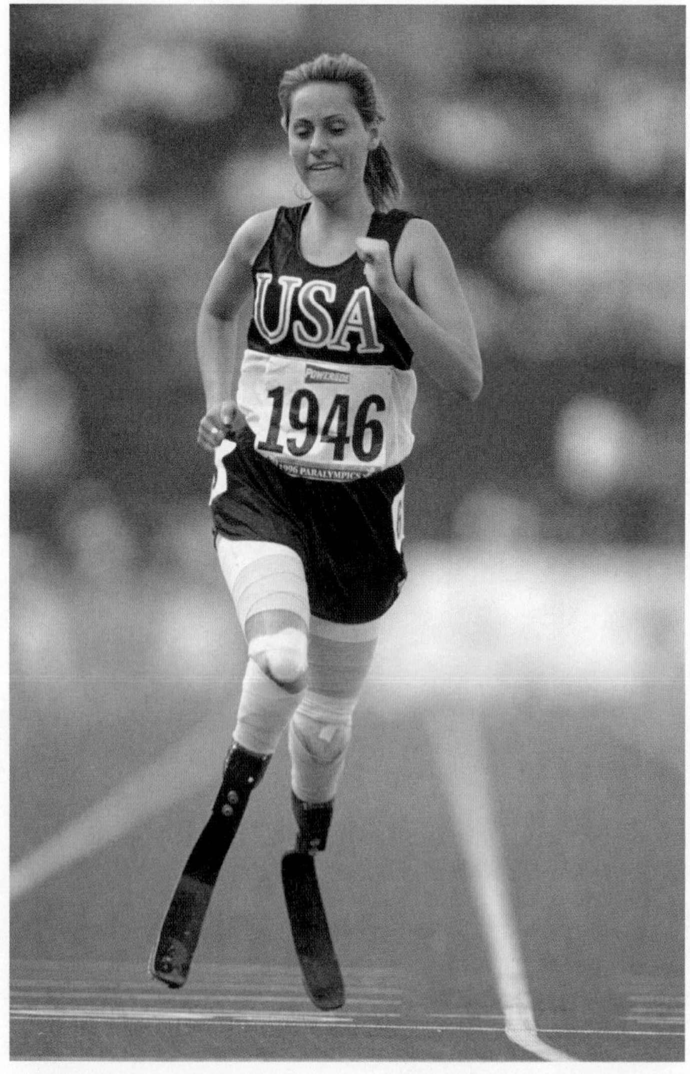

FIGURE 1.21 Athlete, model, and activist Aimee Mullins uses a variety of experimental prosthetic legs, including these special "cheetah" legs that, she says, give her "super powers."

- *The hazards of high-tech crime and the difficulty of keeping data secure.* Even if you trust the institutions and businesses that collect data about you, you can't be sure that data will remain secure in their computer systems. Computer crime is at an all-time high, and law enforcement officials are having a difficult time keeping it under control. How can society protect itself from information thieves and high-tech vandals? How can lawmakers write laws about technology that they are just beginning to understand? What kinds of personal risk do you face as a result of computer crime?
- *The difficulty of defining and protecting intellectual property in an all-digital age.* Software programs, musical recordings, videos, and books can be difficult and expensive to create. But in our digital age, all of these can easily be copied. What rights do the creators of intellectual property have? Is a teenager who copies music files from the Web a computer criminal? What about a shopkeeper who sells pirated copies of Photoshop for $10? Or a student who posts a clip from *The Daily Show* on his Web site? Or a musician who uses a two-second sample from a Beatles song in an electronic composition?
- *The threat of automation and the dehumanization of work.* Computers and the Internet fueled unprecedented economic growth in the last decade of the twentieth century, producing plenty of new jobs for workers with the right skills. But the new information-based economy has cost many workers—especially older workers—their jobs and their dignity. Many workers today find that their jobs involve little more than tending to machines—and being monitored by bosses with high-tech surveillance devices. As machines replace people in the workplace and global networks force workers to compete for jobs in a worldwide market, what rights do displaced workers have? Does a worker's right to privacy outweigh an employer's right to read employee email or monitor worker actions? What is the government's role in the protection of worker rights in the high-tech workplace?
- *The abuse of information as a tool of political and economic power.* The computer age has produced an explosion of information, and most of that information is concentrated in corporate and government computers. The emergence of low-cost computers and the Internet makes it possible for more people to access information and the power that comes with that information. But the majority of the people on the planet have never made a phone call, let alone used a computer. Will the **digital divide** between information technology "haves" and "have nots" leave the "have nots" behind? Do information-rich people and countries have a responsibility to share technology and information with the information-poor?
- *The dangers of dependence on complex technology.* Every once in a while, a massive power blackout,

Working Wisdom Computer Ethics

Ethics is moral philosophy—philosophical thinking about right and wrong. Many people base their ethical beliefs on religious rules, such as the Ten Commandments or the Buddhist Eightfold Path. Others use professional codes such as the doctor's Hippocratic oath, which includes the often quoted "First do no harm." Still others use personal philosophies with principles like "It's OK if a jury of observers would approve." But in today's changing world, deciding how to apply the rules isn't always easy. Sometimes the rules don't seem to apply directly, and sometimes they contradict each other. (How should you "Honor thy father" if you learn that he's using his computer to embezzle money from his employer? Is it okay to allow a friend who's broke to borrow your Microsoft Office CD for a required class project?) These kinds of ***moral dilemmas*** are central questions in discussions of ethics. Information technology poses moral dilemmas related to everything from sampling music to reporting a coworker's sexist screen saver or racist email.

Computer ethics can't be reduced to a handful of rules; the gray areas are always going to require thought and judgment. But principles and guidelines can help to focus thinking and refine judgments when dealing with technology-related moral dilemmas. The Association for Computing Machinery (ACM) Code of Ethics, reprinted in the appendix of this book, is the most widely known code of conduct specifically for computer professionals. The ACM Code is worth understanding and applying even if you don't plan to be a "computer professional." Who shouldn't "Contribute to society and human well-being" or "Honor confidentiality"? But these principles take on new meaning in an age of Facebook and eBay.

Here are some other guidelines that might help you to decide how to "do the right thing" when faced with ethical dilemmas at school, at work, or at home:

- ***Know the rules and the law.*** Many laws, and many organizational rules, are reflections of moral principles. For example, almost everyone agrees that plagiarism—presenting somebody else's work as your own—is wrong. It's also a serious violation of rules in most schools. And if the work is copied without permission, plagiarism can become copyright infringement, a serious legal offense even if the work is not explicitly copyrighted.
- ***Don't assume that it's okay if it's legal.*** Our legal system doesn't define what's right and wrong. How can it when we don't all agree on morality? The law is especially lax in areas related to information technology because the technology changes too fast for lawmakers to keep up. It's ultimately up to each individual to act with conscience.
- ***Think scenarios.*** If you're choosing between different actions, think about what might happen as a result of your actions. If you suspect your employer is falsifying spreadsheets to get around environmental regulations, what's likely to happen if you snoop around on his computer and blow the whistle on him? What's likely to happen if you don't? What are your other alternatives?
- ***When in doubt, talk it out.*** Discuss your concerns with people you trust—ideally, people with wisdom and experience dealing with similar situations. For example, if you're unsure about the line between getting computer help from a friend and cheating on homework, ask an instructor.
- ***Make yourself proud.*** How would you feel if you—or your family and friends—saw your actions on YouTube, cable news, the *New York Times*, or your family's hometown newspaper? If you'd be embarrassed or ashamed, you probably should choose another course of action.
- ***Remember the golden rule:*** *Do unto others as you would have them do unto you.* This universal principle is central to every major spiritual tradition, and it is amazingly versatile. One example: Before you download that bootleg MP3 file of that up-and-coming singer, think about how you'd feel about bootleggers if you were the singer.
- ***Take the long view.*** It's all too easy to be blinded by the rapid-fire rewards of the Internet and computer technology. Consider this guiding principle from a Native American tradition: In every deliberation, consider the impact of your decision on the next seven generations. Musician and digital artist Brian Eno coined the phrase "the long now" to represent this kind of future-oriented decision making. (Visit longnow.org for more on the Long Now Foundation that Eno co-founded.)
- ***Do your part.*** In a democratic society, we're responsible for our own actions. But as citizens and voters, we're also responsible for making sure our representative government is acting ethically. Are your local, state, and national governments using technology in ways that we can be proud of? Is your country following the golden rule in its relationships with other countries? Is it taking the long view when dealing with information technology, natural resources, national debt, and education policies? If not, it's up to you to do something about it. And thanks to the Internet, it's never been easier to take an active role in our democratic process.

FIGURE 1.22 What impact will computer technology have on traditional cultures that evolved for thousands of years without computers?

Internet virus, or database crash reminds us how much we have come to depend on this far-from-foolproof digital technology. Are we, as a society, addicted to computer technology? Should we question new technological innovations before we embrace them? Can we build a future in which technology never takes precedence over humanity?

- *The emergence of biodigital technology.* Today thousands of people walk around with computer chips embedded in their bodies, helping them overcome disabilities and lead normal lives. At the same time, researchers are attempting to develop computers that use biology, rather than electronics, as their underlying technology. As the line between organism and machine blurs, what happens to our vision of ourselves? What are the limits of our creative powers, and what are our responsibilities in using those powers?

History of the Future

> First we shape our tools, thereafter **they shape us.**
>
> —*Marshall McLuhan*

Today's technology raises fascinating and difficult questions. But these questions pale in comparison to the ones we'll have to deal with as the technology evolves in the coming years. Imagine...

You wake up to the sound of your radio playing songs and news stories that match your personal interest profile. The newscaster is talking about the hacker uprising that has crippled China's infrastructure, but you have other things on your mind.

Today's the day of your big trip. You're looking forward to spending time in the same room with Tony, your Italian lab partner. Over the past few months you've become close friends, working and chatting by videophone, conquering virtual reality games together, and creating truly terrible music in those late-night long-distance jam sessions. Still, there's no substitute for being in the same space, especially after Tony's accident. Tony says that the chip implant and the prosthetic hand will make him almost as good as new, but you know he can use some moral support while he recovers.

On the way to the airport, your electric car's computer pipes up, "Ben's Bagels ahead on the right is running a special on cinnamon bagels. Nobody is at the drive-up window, so you can pick up a bagel and still make your flight."

"I thought I told you already: I don't like cinnamon bagels," you grumble.

Noting your annoyance, the car responds, "Sorry. I knew you didn't like cinnamon buns. No more cinnamon bagel ads or notifications, either." You wonder if the computer's spam and ad filter needs fixing, or you just forgot to tell it about your bagel preferences. Before you can ask, the computer announces that the next freeway entrance is blocked because of an accident. It suggests another entrance and talks you through the traffic to that entrance.

Once you get on the freeway, you join the "auto train" in the fast lane. Your car, now controlled by a network computer, races along at exactly the same speed as the car that's a few feet in front of it. You take this opportunity to ask your phone, "Which bus do I take to get from the Rome airport to Tony's place?" The phone responds, "Bus 64. Watch out for pickpockets." You shiver when you remember what

FIGURE 1.23 The "Meteor" subway line of the Paris Metro is completely automated. The trains have no drivers.

happened the last time you lost your wallet; it took months to undo the damage from that identity thief.

At the airport, you step out of the car near the shuttle station, remove your suitcase, and tell the car to park itself in the long-term lot. It says "Goodbye" and glides away.

On the shuttle you use your phone to try to learn a few Italian phrases. You say "Translate Italian" then, "I would like to convert dollars into Euros." The phone responds, "Vorrei convertire i dollari in Euro," into your tiny wireless earpiece. You know the phone can translate for you on the fly, but you'd like to be able to say a few things without its help.

At the security station, you insert your passport into the slot, put your hand on the scanner, and put your face into a shielded enclosure. After the system confirms your identity by taking your handprint and scanning your retinas, it issues a boarding pass, baggage claim slip, and routing tag. Under the watchful eye of the security guard, you attach the routing tag to your bag and place it on the conveyer belt leading to the baggage handling area. You notice that a nearby passenger is being vigorously questioned, and you hope that she's not the victim of yet another security system error.

You realize you forgot to pack your jet lag medication. You enter the airport gift shop and insert your medical ID card under the pharmacy scanner. A dispenser issues a vial of pills that should work well with your genetic structure. You also download a best-selling book into your phone for the trip. As you leave the store, a sensor detects your two purchases. Your phone tells you that $33.97 has just been deducted from your account and asks if you want to know the remaining balance. You don't answer; you're trying to remember the last time you bought something from a human cashier.

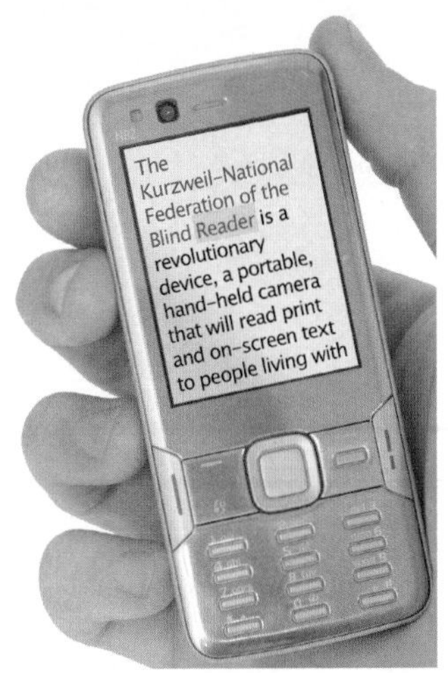

FIGURE 1.24 The Kurzweil KNFB Mobile Reader makes it possible for a blind person to read signs, menus, and money.

This isn't far-fetched fantasy. Early versions of most of the devices in this story already exist. And exponential growth in computing power (remember Moore's law?) makes it likely that you'll see similar technology in your everyday life in just a few years.

For better and for worse, we will be coexisting with information technology until death do us part. As with any relationship, a little understanding can go a long way. The remaining chapters of this book will help you gain the understanding you need to survive and prosper on our digital planet.

Tomorrow Never Knows

There is no denying the importance of the future, but the future isn't always easy to see. In 1877, when Thomas Edison invented the phonograph, he thought of it as an office dictating machine and lost interest in it; recorded music did not become popular until 21 years later. A 1900 Mercedes-Benz study estimated that worldwide demand for cars would not exceed 1 million, primarily because of the limited number of available chauffeurs. When the Wright brothers offered their invention to the U.S. government and the British Royal Navy, they were told airplanes had no future in the military. In 1977 Ken Olson, the founder of Digital Equipment Company, said, "There is no reason anyone would want a computer in their home."

History is full of stories of people who couldn't imagine the impact of new technology. Technological advances are hard to foresee, and it is even harder to predict the impact that technology will have on society. Who could have predicted in 1950 the profound effects, both positive and negative, television would have on our world?

Computer scientist Alan Kay has said, "The best way to predict the future is to invent it." Kay's visionary research at XEROX more than four decades ago defined many of the essential qualities of today's PCs. Of course, we can't all invent world-changing tools. But Kay says there are other ways to predict the future. For example, we can look in the research labs today to see the commercial products of the next few years. Of course, many researchers work behind carefully guarded doors, and research often takes surprising turns.

A third way is to look at products from the past and see what made them succeed. According to Kay, "There are certain things about human beings that if you remove, they wouldn't be human any more. For instance, we have to communicate with others or we're not humans. So every time someone has come up with a communications amplifier, it has succeeded the previous technology." The pen, the printing press, the telephone, the television, the PC, the smart phone, and the Internet are all successful communication amplifiers. What's next?

Kay says we can also predict the future by recognizing the four phases of any technology or media business: hardware, software, service, and way of life.

- ***Hardware.*** Inventors and engineers start the process by developing new hardware. But whether it's a television set, a PC, or a global communication network, the hardware is of little use without software.
- ***Software.*** The next step is software development. Television programs, sound recordings, video games, databases, and Web pages are examples of software that give value to hardware products.
- ***Service.*** Innovative hardware and clever software aren't likely to take hold unless they serve human needs. Computer and Internet companies that focus on serving their customers are generally the most successful.
- ***Way of life.*** The final phase happens when the technology becomes so entrenched that people don't think about it anymore; they notice only if it isn't there. We seldom think of pencils as technological tools. They're part of our way of life, so much so that we'd have trouble getting along without them. Similarly, the electric motor, which was once a major technological breakthrough, is now all but invisible; we use dozens of motors every day without thinking about them. For most of us, computers and the Internet have become a way of life, too.

Kay's four phases of predicting the future don't provide a foolproof crystal ball, but they can serve as a framework for thinking about tomorrow's technology. In the remaining chapters of this book, we'll examine trends and innovations that will shape future digital hardware and software. Then we will look at how this technology will serve users as it eventually disappears into our way of life.

FIGURE 1.25 The 1930 movie *Just Imagine* presented a bold, if not quite accurate, vision of the future; here Maureen O'Sullivan sits in her personal flying machine.

Crosscurrents

That Whole Internet Thing's Not Going To Work Out

by Farhad Manjoo

Predicting the future is anything but easy. In this article, first posted on Slate.com *in March, 2010 (edited here for length), technology columnist Farhad Manjoo shows how we can learn from one very wrong prediction.*

In 1995, Clifford Stoll published a column in *Newsweek* with a doozy of a headline: "The Internet? Bah!" Stoll wrote. "The truth is no online database will replace your daily newspaper, no CD-ROM can take the place of a competent teacher and no computer network will change the way government works."

Stoll wasn't a Luddite; indeed, he'd been working on the Internet for decades. The Internet that Stoll knew was "a wasteland of unfiltered data" where it was impossible to find anything useful. "Logged onto the World Wide Web, I hunt for the date of the Battle of Trafalgar," he wrote. "Hundreds of files show up, and it takes 15 minutes to unravel them..."

Stoll also dismissed the notion that anyone would ever shop online. For one thing, engineers hadn't invented a secure way to send money through computers. The Internet was [also] "missing a most essential ingredient of capitalism: salespeople." For Stoll, this was the Internet's biggest failing—it lacked any capacity for "human contact." The Internet would never take off because "computers and networks isolate us from one another."

Stoll [recently] called his piece a "howler" and said he thinks back to it often as a reminder that he can be very, very wrong. But Stoll's article is good for more than just a laugh. Terrible predictions can be instructive—in their wrongness, we can see the flaws of our own visions for the future.

The future is unknowable—especially in the digital age, when we're constantly barraged with new technologies. Still, it would be nice to have some idea of which predictions to trust and which to dismiss. Here are a few rules for separating the good from the bad.

Good predictions are based on current trends. In his *Newsweek* piece, Stoll argued that e-books would never take off because reading on a screen was a chore, and you couldn't take your computer to the beach. He was right, based on the computers of 1995. Stoll's mistake was to believe that computers would stay the same.

Don't underestimate people's capacity for change. Stoll's belief that we needed salespeople to help us shop was firmly rooted in his time. But wasn't it possible that we'd learn new ways to shop? After all, we'd done that before—general stores had given way to supermarkets and malls, which had themselves been usurped by strip malls and big-box stores. Nothing in commerce had ever remained fixed, so why couldn't we abandon salespeople, too?

New stuff sometimes comes out of the blue. You can't fault Stoll for thinking that the Internet would always remain a chore to navigate. It also wasn't obvious that we'd find a way to create good content online. And then a few magical things came and changed everything. The date of the Battle of Trafalgar? It took me a second and a half to find out that it took place on Oct. 21, 1805. Thank you, Google and Wikipedia.

What Stoll missed here was the potential for collective intelligence to arise out of the online cacophony. Google's founders saw that they could suss out good content from bad by looking at linking patterns; Wikipedia's founders saw that by letting people edit each other's content, they could create a reference that was both comprehensive and uncannily accurate.

But Google and Wikipedia weren't predictable. Before they were invented, no one would've believed such technologies could work so fantastically well. And that's the thing about the prediction business. Some of the most important developments of our lifetimes couldn't have been anticipated. Rather, they came about because a few innovators had brilliant ideas that no one else had foreseen.

These days it's best to err on the side of optimism. Stoll's forecast is unusual for being too conservative; he thought the future would most likely resemble his present. Perhaps there's a lesson in that. In the digital age, the future is approaching faster than we think. As a result, the tech that comes tomorrow will probably be far more awesome than you can imagine today. Recent history supports this theory. Many of the technologies that we now take for granted—online social networks, Web video, and photo libraries—weren't invented a decade ago.

In the realm of outlandish predictions, I feel more comfortable with the extreme optimists. Ray Kurzweil—the acclaimed technologist who in 1990 correctly predicted that a computer would beat the best human chess player by the end of the decade—believes that humans will soon "transcend biology." He says we're on the cusp of "the singularity"—a point when technology will have advanced so far that human beings will essentially become immortal. It's hard to believe. But Kurzweil's predictions are based on current trends, and nothing about them seems really impossible. I doubt the singularity is just around the corner. But, hey, maybe he's right.

Discussion Questions

1. Do you agree with the author's four rules for evaluating predictions? Why or why not?
2. Can you think of other examples of predictions that have proven to be wrong?

Summary

Mechanical computing devices date back hundreds of years, but the first real computers were developed during the 1940s. Computers have evolved at an incredible pace since those early years, becoming consistently smaller, faster, more efficient, more reliable, and less expensive. At the same time, people have devised all kinds of interesting and useful ways to put computers to use in work and play.

Computers today come in all shapes and sizes, with specific types being well suited for particular jobs. Mainframe computers and supercomputers provide more power and speed than smaller desktop machines, but they are expensive to buy and operate. Timesharing makes it possible for many users to work simultaneously at terminals connected to these large computers. At the other end of the spectrum, PCs and handheld devices provide computing power for those of us who don't need a mainframe's capabilities. Microprocessors aren't just used in general-purpose computers; they're embedded in appliances, automobiles, and a rapidly growing list of other products.

Connecting to a network enhances the value and power of a computer; it can share resources with other computers and facilitate electronic communication with other computer users. The Internet is a collection of networks connecting the computers and other devices around the globe. Email provides hundreds of millions of people with near-instant worldwide communication capabilities. With browsing software, those same Internet users have access to billions of pages on the World Wide Web—a distributed network of interlinked multimedia documents. Although it started as a tool for scientists, researchers, and scholars, the Internet has quickly become a vital center for entertainment and commerce. In the last few years there's been a trend toward Web 2.0 sites—sites created by their users—social networks, media sharing sites, blogs, and more.

Computers and information technology have changed the world rapidly and irreversibly. Our civilization is in a transition from an industrial economy to an information economy, and this paradigm shift is having an impact on the way we live and work. Computers and digital technology are central to our information age, and we can easily list dozens of ways in which computers now make our lives easier and more productive. PC and Web applications, from word processing and email to multimedia and database applications, have become essential tools for people everywhere. Emerging technologies, such as artificial intelligence, offer promise for future applications. At the same time, computers threaten our privacy, our security, and perhaps our way of life. As we rush into the information age, our future depends on computers and on our ability to understand and use them in productive, positive ways.

Key Terms

agricultural age....................(p. 18)
apps....................(p. 11)
application program (application)....................(p. 19)
browsers....................(p. 14)
desktop computer....................(p. 10)
digital divide....................(p. 24)
electronic mail (email)....................(p. 14)
embedded system....................(p. 9)
firmware....................(p. 10)
hypertext link....................(p. 14)
industrial age....................(p. 18)
Industrial Revolution....................(p. 18)
information age....................(p. 18)
integrated circuit....................(p. 7)
Internet....................(p. 14)
laptop computer....................(p. 10)
mainframe computer....................(p. 12)
microprocessor....................(p. 7)
Moore's law....................(p. 8)
netbook....................(p. 11)
network....................(p. 14)
notebook computer....................(p. 10)
paradigm shift....................(p. 18)
peripherals....................(p. 11)
personal computer (PC)....................(p. 7)
server....................(p. 12)
silicon chip....................(p. 7)
Silicon Valley....................(p. 7)
smart phones....................(p. 11)
supercomputer....................(p. 14)
tablet computer....................(p. 11)
terminal....................(p. 12)
thin client....................(p. 12)
timesharing....................(p. 12)
transistor....................(p. 7)
workstation....................(p. 10)
World Wide Web (Web)....................(p. 14)

Companion Website Projects

1. The *Digital Planet* Web site, **www.pearsonhighered.com/beekman**, contains self-test exercises related to this chapter. Follow the instructions for taking a quiz. After you've completed your quiz, you can email the results to your instructor.
2. The Web site also contains open-ended discussion questions called Internet Exercises. Discuss one or more of the Internet Exercises questions at the section for this chapter.

True or False

1. If all computers stopped working, people would use their phones much more to get necessary information.
2. Because it can be programmed to perform various tasks, the PC is a general-purpose tool, not a specialized device with one use.
3. One of the first computers helped the Allies crack Nazi codes during World War II.
4. According to Moore's law, the power of a silicon chip of the same price would double about every 8 years for at least 100 years.
5. A smart phone is a pocket-sized digital computer that can also be used as a phone.
6. A microcomputer is a smart phone or PDA—any computer small enough to fit in your pocket.
7. A netbook is a small notebook computer designed mostly for Internet access.
8. About 30 percent of the world's microprocessors are hidden inside common household and electronic devices.
9. Only about half of the world's countries have Internet connectivity.
10. There's been a steady trend away from individual uses of computers and toward institutionalized computing.

Multiple Choice

1. When did personal computers become available?
   a. Before 1950
   b. Between 1950 and 1965
   c. Between 1966 and 1990
   d. Between 1991 and 2005
   e. After 2005
2. When did the World Wide Web become available?
   a. 1960s
   b. 1970s
   c. 1980s
   d. 1990s
   e. 2000s
3. When did Web 2.0 sites like Facebook and YouTube become popular?
   a. 1960s
   b. 1970s
   c. 1980s
   d. 1990s
   e. 2000s
4. For which of the following do we depend on computer technology?
   a. Controlling our money and banking systems
   b. Keeping our transportation systems running smoothly
   c. Making many of our household appliances and gadgets work properly
   d. All of the above
   e. None of the above

5. PCs are extremely versatile tools because they can accept instructions from a wide variety of
   a. hardware.
   b. software.
   c. network connections.
   d. PDAs.
   e. semiconductors.

6. Many of the most important developments in the earliest days of the computer were motivated by what event?
   a. World War I
   b. The Great Depression
   c. World War II
   d. The prohibition of alcohol in the United States
   e. The launch of Sputnik by the USSR

7. Which of these technologies was developed first?
   a. The smart phone
   b. The laptop computer
   c. The netbook
   d. The embedded computer
   e. The desktop computer

8. Which of these technologies was developed most recently?
   a. The smart phone
   b. The laptop computer
   c. The netbook
   d. The embedded computer
   e. The desktop computer

9. Which represents the order in which computer circuitry evolved through three generations of technology?
   a. Vacuum tube, silicon chip, transistor
   b. Transistor, vacuum tube, silicon chip
   c. Vacuum tube, transistor, silicon chip
   d. Transistor, silicon chip, vacuum tube
   e. Silicon chip, vacuum tube, transistor

10. As computers evolved, they
    a. grew in size.
    b. became faster.
    c. consumed more electricity.
    d. became less reliable.
    e. cost more.

11. When a bank clerk transfers money into your account, where is the actual transaction probably being processed and stored?
    a. A PC
    b. A netbook
    c. A terminal
    d. A mainframe
    e. A Web page

12. Some computers are able to maintain simultaneous connections to many users through a technique called
    a. nanolinking.
    b. hot syncing.
    c. spider syncing.
    d. parallel processing.
    e. timesharing.

13. Silicon Valley is a nickname for
    a. the region in California that contains most of the world's silicon mines.
    b. the part of the Internet where most of the traffic is channeled through silicon cables.
    c. the part of a computer that's used to transport data from the hard drive to the processor.
    d. the dip in productivity on a timeline that inevitably happens when new computer technology is introduced.
    e. the area in Northern California where many of the most important digital technology companies are based.

14. Which of these principles is *not* a useful guideline for making ethical decisions related to technology?
    a. The Golden Rule.
    b. Take the long view.
    c. Think about how you would feel if your actions were widely viewed as a YouTube video.
    d. If it's legal, it's ethical.
    e. If you have any doubts, discuss them with knowledgeable people before taking action.

15. An application program is
    a. a program that lets users create new applications.
    b. a program that lets users apply for jobs.
    c. a program that lets someone use a computer for a particular purpose.
    d. a program that updates the operating system of a computer.
    e. None of the above

Review Questions

1. List several ways you interact with hidden computers in your daily life.
2. What is the most important difference between a computer and a calculator?
3. How are computers today similar to the first computers? How are they different?
4. The way people use the Internet has changed since the early days. How?
5. What is the difference between a supercomputer and a microcomputer? What are the advantages and disadvantages of each?
6. What kinds of computer applications require the speed and power of a supercomputer? Give some examples.
7. Is a smart phone a computer? Explain your answer.
8. What types of applications are particularly well suited for handheld devices? What common applications are particularly well suited for PCs?
9. Why is it important for people to know about and understand computers?
10. Describe some of the benefits and drawbacks of the information age.

Discussion Questions

1. What do people mean when they talk about the information age? Why is it a societal paradigm shift?
2. Do you expect another "age" to follow the information age? What do you think it might be?
3. The Digital Time Line in this chapter divided the information age into four computer-related phases: the institutional computing phase, the personal computing phase, the interpersonal computing phase, and the collaborative computing phase. Talk about each of these phases, and speculate about what the next phase might be.
4. How would the world be different today if a wrinkle in time transported a state-of-the-art notebook computer, complete with software, peripherals, and manuals, onto the desk of Woodrow Wilson? Adolf Hitler? Albert Einstein?
5. The automobile and the television set are two examples of technological inventions that changed our society drastically in ways that were not anticipated by their inventors. Outline several positive and negative effects of each of these two inventions. Do you think, on balance, that we are better off as a result of these machines? Why or why not? Now repeat this exercise for the computer and the Internet.
6. Should all students be required to take at least one computer course? Why or why not? If so, what should that course cover?
7. Computerphobia—fear or anxiety related to computers—is a common malady among people today—especially people who grew up before computers were everywhere. What do you think causes it? What, if anything, should be done about it?
8. Suppose a company were marketing a tiny microprocessor designed to be implanted in your brain behind your right ear. The device is designed to help you remember people's names. It is particularly popular among people who work with the public. You plan to have a career in sales. Would you consider getting such an implant? Why or why not? What questions would you want to have answered before you agreed to have the device implanted in your brain?

Projects

1. Take an inventory of all the computers you encounter in a single day. Be sure to include embedded computers, such as those in cars, appliances, entertainment equipment, and other machines. *Hint*: If a device has an LCD screen or LED numbers (digital numbers made out of light segments), it contains a microprocessor.
2. The title "Inventor of the Computer" has been given to Charles Babbage (for the Analytical Engine), Konrad Zuse (for the Z1, Z2, and Z3), John Atanasoff and Clifford Berry (for the Atanasoff-Berry Computer), John Mauchly and J. Presper Eckert (for the ENIAC), and F. C. Williams, Tom Kilburn, and Geoff Tootill (for the Small-Scale Experimental Machine). Research these inventors and their machines. Draw a table comparing the features of these computing devices. Decide for yourself who deserves the title "Inventor of the Computer."
3. Make a graph that charts how the price of an entry-level personal computer system changed over the last 20 years. Use the Consumer Price Index inflation calculator, found at **http://www.bls.gov/cpi/home.htm**, to adjust all the prices to the same real dollar value. Of course, a price graph won't tell the whole story. Attach a short description of how the features and power of the entry-level system changed over time.
4. Develop a questionnaire to try to determine people's awareness of the computers around them. You can ask them about how often they use a computer, the uses to which they put a computer, the most valuable thing a computer does for them, and so on. Once you have collected the answers, analyze them. What percentage of the people assumed you were talking about "personal computers" when you asked them about their computer use? How many of them mentioned embedded computers, such as the computers in phones, microwaves, music players, ATM machines, and cars?

Sources and Resources

Books

Everyware: The Dawning Age of Ubiquitous Computing, by Adam Greenfield (New Riders). We tend to think of computers as PCs and mainframes—general-purpose devices running programs to do our bidding. But computers are in all kinds of other devices, from clothing to furniture. We're entering an age of ubiquitous computers—computers everywhere. Designer and writer Adam Greenfield refers to this phenomenon as *everyware*. In this book he explores the implications of everyware in a series of short, thought-provoking essays. Welcome to the future.

The Difference Engine, by William Gibson and Bruce Sterling (Bantam). How would the world of the nineteenth century be different if Charles and Ada had succeeded in constructing the Analytical Engine 150 years ago? This imaginative mystery novel takes place in a world where the computer revolution arrived a century early. Like other books by these two pioneers of the "cyberpunk" school of science fiction, *The Difference Engine* is dark, dense, detailed, and thought-provoking.

A History of Modern Computing, by Paul E. Ceruzzi (MIT Press). This book traces the first 50 years of computer history, from ENIAC to Internetworked PCs. The social context of the technology is clear throughout the book.

Crystal Fire: The Invention of the Transistor and the Birth of the Information Age, by Michael Riordan and Lillian Hoddeson (Norton). One of the defining moments of the information age occurred in 1947, when William Shockley and his colleagues invented the transistor. *Crystal Fire* tells the story of that earthshaking invention, clearly describing the technical and human dimensions of the story.

Accidental Empires: How the Boys of Silicon Valley Make Their Millions, Battle Foreign Competition, and Still Can't Get a Date, by Robert X. Cringely (Collins). Robert X. Cringely is the pen name for *InfoWorld's* computer-industry gossip columnist. In this opinionated, irreverent, and entertaining book, Cringely discusses the past, present, and future of the volatile personal computer industry. When you read the humorous, colorful characterizations of the people who run this industry, you'll understand why Cringely didn't use his real name. *Triumph of the Nerds,* a 1996 PBS TV show and video based loosely on this book, lacks much of the humor and insight of the book but includes some fascinating footage of the pioneers reminiscing about the early days.

The Black Swan: The Impact of the Highly Improbable, by Nassim Nicholas Taleb (Random House). One of the hazards of predicting the future is that we need to base our predictions on what's most likely to happen, and that's not always what happens. Taleb's book deals with the phenomenon of the "black swan"—the highly improbable event that can't easily be predicted.

The World is Flat 3.0: A Brief History of the Twenty-first Century, by Thomas Friedman (Picador). Thomas Friedman's *The World is Flat* described in clear prose the new globalized, interconnected world. The world has changed since he wrote the first edition, and this new edition reflects those changes.

Periodicals

Wired **(wired.com)**. This highly stylized monthly started out as "the first consumer magazine for the digital generation to track technology's impact on all facets of the human condition." Today *Wired* devotes more pages to hawking the latest gear for the techno-chic lifestyle, but it's still one of the most important and influential sources for thought-provoking, future-oriented articles about technology and its impact on our future.

Technology Review **(technologyreview.com).** This periodical from MIT provides excellent coverage of technology in the labs today that will change our lives tomorrow.

Scientific American **(scientificamerican.com).** This old standby still provides some of the best writing on science and technology, including emerging information technologies.

PC World **(pcworld.com).** This periodical is one of the most popular sources for keeping up with developments in the PC world. The companion Web site offers up-to-the-minute information along with archives from past issues.

PC Magazine **(pcmag.com).** *PC Magazine* is a popular PC periodical, containing news, reviews, and feature articles for a variety of interests.

Macworld **(macworld.com).** This is the premier periodical for Apple users, covering hardware, software, and Internet issues with clear, easy-to-read articles and reviews.

InfoWorld **(infoworld.com).** This magazine covers business computing, including applications for mainframes, servers, and other behind-the-scenes machines that aren't typically covered in PC-centric publications.

ComputerWorld **(computerworld.com).** InfoWorld's older sibling covers the broad spectrum of computers and information technology from the perspective of the computer professional.

Hardware Basics
Inside the Box

OBJECTIVES

After you read this chapter you should be able to:

- Explain in general terms how computers store and manipulate information
- Describe the basic structure and organization of a computer
- Discuss the computer system's main internal components and the ways they interact
- Explain why a computer typically has different types of memory and storage devices

Every once in a while a **revolutionary product** comes along that **changes everything.** It's very fortunate if you can work on just one of these in your career....Apple's been very fortunate in that it's introduced a few of these.

—*Steve Jobs*

Steve Wozniak, Steve Jobs, and the Garage that Grew Apples

The seeds of Apple were planted in the early 1970s by Steve Wozniak and Steve Jobs, two young guys with uncommon talent and vision. Wozniak, a brilliant engineer called Woz by his friends, worked days as a calculator technician at Hewlett-Packard (HP); he was refused an engineer's job because he lacked a college degree. At night he designed and constructed a scaled-down computer system that would fit the home hobbyist's budget. When he completed it in 1975, he offered it to HP, but the company turned it down.

FIGURE 2.1 Steve Wozniak.

Wozniak took his invention to the Homebrew Computer Club in Palo Alto, where it caught the imagination of another college dropout, Steve Jobs. A freethinking visionary, Jobs persuaded Wozniak to quit his job in 1976 to form a company born in Jobs's garage. They marketed the machine as the Apple I.

With the help and financial backing of businessman A. C. Markkula, the two Steves turned Apple into a thriving business. Wozniak created the Apple II, a more refined machine, and in the process invented the first personal computer disk operating system. Because it put computing power within the reach of individuals, the Apple II became popular in businesses, homes, and especially schools. Apple became the first company in American history to join the Fortune 500 in less than five years. Still in his mid-twenties, Jobs was running a corporate giant.

When IBM introduced its PC in 1982, it overshadowed Apple's presence in the business world. Other companies developed PC clones, treating the IBM PC as a standard—a standard that Apple refused to accept. Inspired by a visit to Xerox's Palo Alto Research Center (PARC), Jobs worked with a team of Apple engineers to

FIGURE 2.2 Steve Jobs.

develop the Macintosh (Mac), a futuristic computer Jobs hoped would leapfrog IBM's advantage. When Jobs insisted on focusing most of Apple's resources on the Mac, Wozniak resigned to pursue other interests.

Businesses failed to embrace the Mac, and Apple stockholders grew uneasy with Jobs's controversial management style. In 1985, a year and a half after the Mac was introduced, Jobs was ousted. He went on to form NeXT, a company that produced expensive workstations and software. He also bought Pixar, the computer animation spin-off of Lucasfilms, Inc. After Apple's fortunes declined under a string of CEOs, the company bought NeXT in 1997 and invited an older and wiser Jobs to retake the helm. He agreed to share his time between Pixar and Apple. Under his leadership, Apple has regained its innovative edge. Though its share of the global PC market is relatively small, Apple continues to maintain and expand a fanatically loyal customer base, especially in the consumer, creative, and education markets.

For Jobs, Apple is *not* just a computer company. Since his return, Apple has introduced a string of elegant and trendsetting products that position it at what Jobs calls "the intersection of technology and liberal arts." The iPod revolutionized the way millions of people listened to music; its companion iTunes Store legitimized the online music industry, rapidly becoming the biggest music store on the planet. The iPhone was the first smart phone to truly capture the imagination of consumers and software developers; its App Store did for software what iTunes did for music. The iPad has the potential to take book, magazine, and multimedia publishing into uncharted territory.

While Apple was changing the consumer electronics landscape, Pixar was redefining the art of animation in cinema. Beginning in 1995 with *Toy Story*, the first computer-generated full-length motion picture, Pixar released an unbroken string of critically acclaimed blockbusters, including *Finding Nemo*, *WALL-E*, and *Up*. In 2006 the Disney Corporation bought Pixar, making Steve Jobs the single largest stockholder in the entertainment giant.

His phenomenal success at running Pixar and Apple makes Jobs something of a legend in the business world. He has been criticized for being authoritarian and secretive, but few can deny his accomplishments. In 2009, *Fortune Magazine* named him CEO of the decade and *Forbes* listed him as one of the world's most powerful people.

Woz, on the other hand, leads a more low-key life, developing technology companies out of the public spotlight. ■

Computers schedule airline flights, predict the weather, play and even create music, control space stations, and (usually) keep the world's economic wheels spinning smoothly. How can one kind of machine do so many things?

To understand what really makes computers tick, you would need to devote considerable time and effort to studying computer science and computer engineering. Most of us don't need to understand every detail of a computer's inner workings any more than a parent needs to explain wave and particle physics when a child asks why the sky is blue. We can be satisfied with simpler answers, even if those answers are only approximations of the technical truth. We'll spend the next three chapters exploring answers to the question, "How do computers do what they do?"

The main text of each of these chapters provides simple, nontechnical answers and basic information. "How It Works" boxes use text and graphics to dig deeper into the inner workings of the computer. Depending on your course, learning style, and level of curiosity, you may read these boxes as they appear in the text, read them after you've

FIGURE 2.3 PCs are assembled in highly automated factories such as this one owned by Dell Computer. In this chapter and the next, we'll examine the hardware components that make up a modern computer.

completed the basic material in the chapter, or (if you don't need the technical details) bypass some or all of them. Use the "Sources and Resources" section at each chapter's end for further explorations.

What Computers Do

> Stripped of its interfaces, a bare computer boils down to little more than a pocket calculator that can **push its own buttons and remember what it has done**.
>
> —*Arnold Penzias, in* Ideas and Information

The simple truth is that computers perform only four basic functions:

- *Receive input.* Computers accept information from the outside world.
- *Process information.* Computers perform arithmetic or logical (decision-making) operations on information.
- *Produce output.* Computers communicate information to the outside world.
- *Store information.* Computers store and retrieve information from memory and storage devices.

Every computer system contains hardware components—physical parts—that specialize in each of these four functions:

- **Input devices** accept input from the outside world. The most common input devices today are keyboards and pointing devices such as mice and touch pads.
- **Output devices** send information to the outside world. A typical computer uses a video monitor as its main output device, a printer to produce paper printouts, and speakers to output sounds.
- A **microprocessor**, also called the **processor** or **central processing unit (CPU)**, is, in effect, the computer's "brain." The CPU processes information, performs arithmetic calculations, and makes basic decisions by comparing information values.

- **Memory** and **storage devices** both store information, but they serve different purposes. The computer's memory (sometimes called *primary storage* or **random access memory (RAM)** is used to store programs and **data** (information) that need to be instantly accessible to the CPU. Storage devices (sometimes called *secondary storage*), including hard disk drives and a variety of removable media devices, serve as long-term repositories for data.

These four types of components, when combined, make up the hardware part of a computer system. Of course, the system isn't complete without software—the instructions that tell the hardware what to do. But for now, we'll concentrate on hardware. In this chapter, we take a look at the central processing unit and the computer's memory; these components are at the center of all computing operations. In the next chapter, we look at the input, output, and storage devices—the **peripherals** of the computer system. Because every computer hardware component is designed to transport or to transform information, we start with some facts about information.

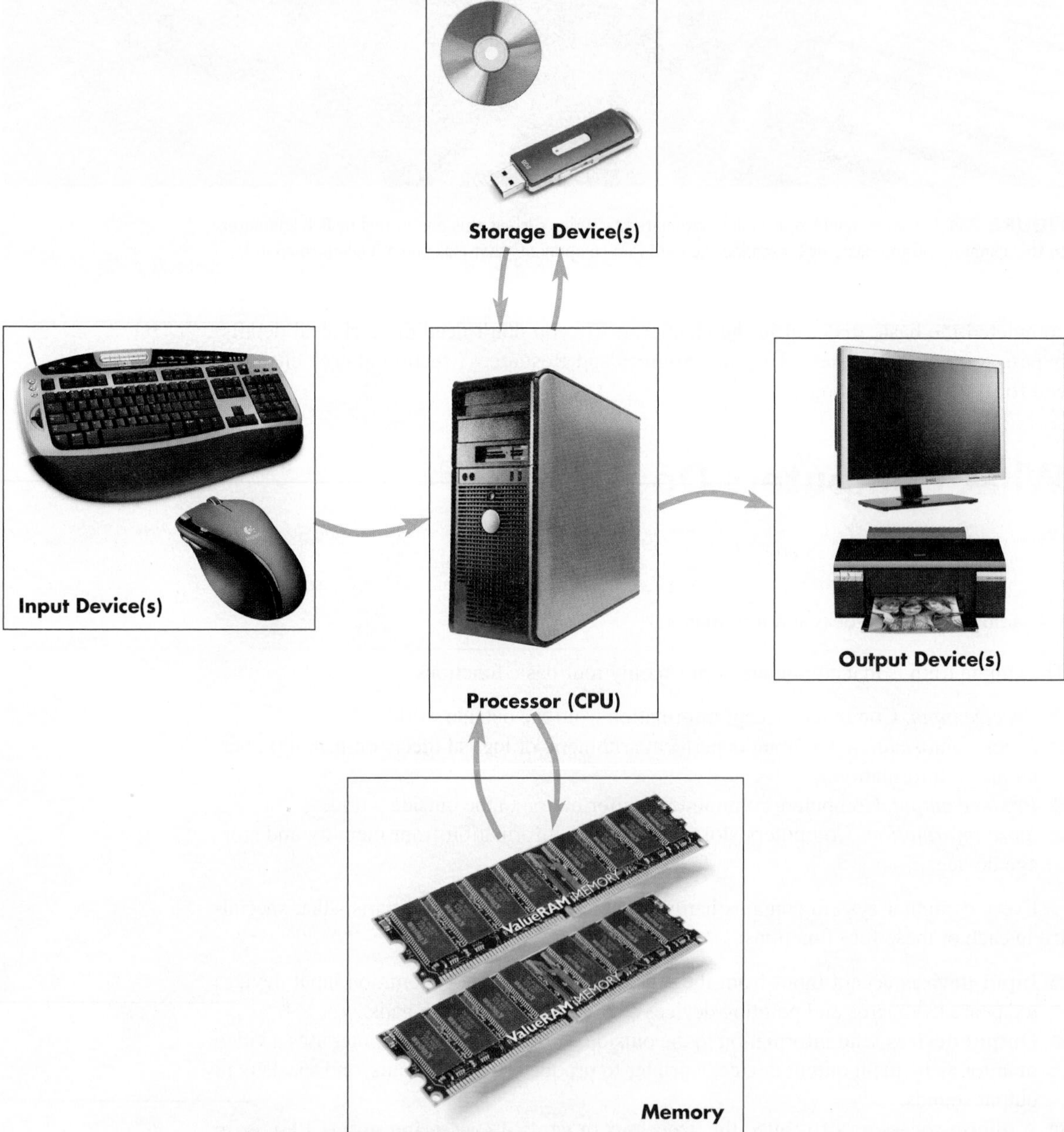

FIGURE 2.4 The basic components of every computer system include the central components (the CPU and memory) and various peripherals.

A Bit About Bits

Everybody gets **so much information** *all day long that they lose their common sense.*

—Gertrude Stein, American Writer

The term **information** is difficult to define because it has many meanings. According to one popular definition, *information* is communication that has value because it *informs*. This distinction can be helpful for dealing with data from television, magazines, computers, and other sources: information has value, data doesn't. But it's not always clear, and it's not absolute. As educator and author Richard Saul Wurman points out, "Everyone needs a personal measure with which to define information. What constitutes information to one person may be data to another. If it doesn't make sense to you, it doesn't qualify."

At the opposite extreme, one communication theory defines information as anything that can be communicated, whether it has value or not. By this definition, information comes in many forms. The words, numbers, and pictures on these pages are symbols representing information. If you underline or highlight this sentence, you're adding new information to the page. Even the sounds and pictures that emanate from a television commercial are packed with information, though it's debatable whether most of that information is useful.

Some people attempt to apply strictly the first definition to computers, claiming that computers turn raw data, which has no value in its current form, into information, which is valuable. This approach emphasizes the computer's role as a business data processing machine. But in our modern interconnected world, one computer's output is often another's input. If a computer receives a message from another computer, is the message worthless data or valuable information? And whose personal measure of value applies?

For our purposes, describing the mechanics of computers in these chapters, we lean toward the second, more objective, approach and use the terms *data* and *information* more or less interchangeably. In later chapters, we present plenty of evidence to suggest that not all computer output has value. In the end, it is up to you to decide what the real information is.

Bit Basics

Whatever you call it, in the world of computers, information is **digital**: This means it's made up of discrete, countable units—**digits**—so it can be subdivided. In many situations people subdivide chunks of information into simpler units to use them effectively. For example, a child trying to pronounce an unfamiliar word might sound out each letter or syllable individually before tackling the whole word.

A computer doesn't understand words, numbers, pictures, musical notes, or even letters of the alphabet. Like a young reader, a computer can't process information without dividing it into smaller units. In fact, computers can digest information only if it has been broken into bits. A **bit**, or binary digit, is the smallest unit of information a computer can process. A bit can have one of two values: 0 or 1. You can also think of these two values as yes and no, on and off, black and white, or high and low.

If you think of the inner components of a computer as collections of microscopic on/off switches, it's easy to understand why computers process information bit by bit. Each switch stores a tiny amount of information: a signal to turn on a light, for example, or the answer to a yes/no question. (In modern integrated circuits, high and low electrical charges represent bits, but these circuits work as if they were really made up of tiny switches.)

Remember Paul Revere's famous midnight ride to warn the American colonists of the British invasion? His co-conspirators used a pair of lanterns to convey a choice between two messages, "One if by land, two if by sea"—a **binary** choice. It's theoretically possible to send a message like this with just one lantern. But "One if by land, zero if by sea" wouldn't have worked very well unless there had been some way to know exactly when the message was being sent. With two lanterns, the first lantern could say, "Here is the message," when it was turned on. The second lantern communicated the critical bit's worth of information: land or sea. If the revolutionaries had wanted to send a more complex message, they could have used more lanterns ("Three if by subway!").

In much the same way, a computer can process larger chunks of information by treating groups of bits as logical units. For example, a collection of 8 bits, called a **byte**, can represent 256 different messages ($256 = 2^8$). If you think of each bit as a light that can be either on or off, you can make different combinations of lights represent different messages. (Computer scientists usually speak in terms of *0* and *1* instead of on and off, but the concept is the same either way.) The computer has an advantage over Paul Revere in that it sees not just the number of lights turned on, but also their order, so 01 (off–on) is different from 10 (on–off).

FIGURE 2.5 The MITS Altair, the first popular personal computer, came with no keyboard or monitor. It could be programmed only by manipulating a bank of binary switches on the front panel for input. Binary patterns of lights provided the output. (Source: Courtesy of The Computer History Museum.)

Building with Bits

What does a bit combination such as 01100110 mean to the computer? There's no single answer to that question; it depends on the context and convention. A string of bits can be interpreted as a number, a letter of the alphabet, or almost anything else.

Bits as Numbers

Because computers are built from switching devices that reduce all information to *0*s and *1*s, they represent numbers using the ***binary number system***, a system that denotes all numbers with combinations of two digits. Like the 10-digit decimal system you use every day, the binary number system has clear, consistent rules for every arithmetic operation.

The people who worked with early computers had to use binary arithmetic. But today's computers include software that converts decimal numbers into binary numbers automatically, and vice versa. As a result, the computer's binary number processing is completely hidden from the user.

Decimal representation	Binary representation
0	0000
1	0001
2	0010
3	0011
4	0100
5	0101
6	0110
7	0111
8	1000
9	1001
10	1010
11	1011
12	1100
13	1101
14	1110
15	1111

FIGURE 2.6 In the binary number system, every number is represented by a unique pattern of *0*s and *1*s.

Bits as Codes

Of course, computers don't just compute. They work with all types of information—especially text. To make words, sentences, and paragraphs fit into the computer's binary-only circuitry, programmers have devised codes that represent each letter, digit, and special character as a unique string of bits.

The most widely used code, **ASCII** (an abbreviation of American Standard Code for Information Interchange, pronounced "as-kee"), represents each character as a unique 8-bit code. Out of a string of 8 bits, 256 unique ordered patterns can be made—enough to make unique codes for 26 letters (upper- and lowercase), 10 digits, and a variety of special characters.

As the world shrinks and our information needs grow, ASCII's 256 unique characters simply can't meet the challenge. ASCII is too limited to accommodate Chinese, Greek, Hebrew, Japanese, Arabic, and other languages. To facilitate multilingual computing, the computer industry is embracing **Unicode**, a coding scheme that supports more than 100,000 unique characters—more than enough for all major world languages.

Of course, today's computers aren't just manipulating numbers and text. A group of bits can also represent colors, sounds, quantitative measurements from the environment, or just about any other kind of information that we need to process. You've probably heard of MP3 music files and JPEG photographs; these are just two examples of binary encoding schemes. We explore these and other types of information in later chapters.

Bits as Instructions in Programs

So far we've dealt with the ways bits represent data. But another kind of information is just as important to the computer: the programs that tell the computer what to do with the data you give it. The computer stores programs as collections of bits, just as it stores data.

how it works Binary Arithmetic

A computer's memory is made up of millions of microscopic switches that can be either "on" or "off." A single switch can represent only two symbols: 0 and 1. Two symbols are all a computer needs to represent numbers and do arithmetic. Let's look at the inner workings of a calculator to see how this is done.

1. When you use a calculator, you use the keys 0 through 9 to type decimal (base 10) numbers. The calculator's microprocessor stores the numbers as binary (base 2) digits—think of them as strings of *0*s and *1*s.
2. Just as we use more than one decimal digit to represent numbers larger than 9, the processor uses more than one binary digit (bit) to represent numbers larger than 1. A collection of 8 bits is called a byte.

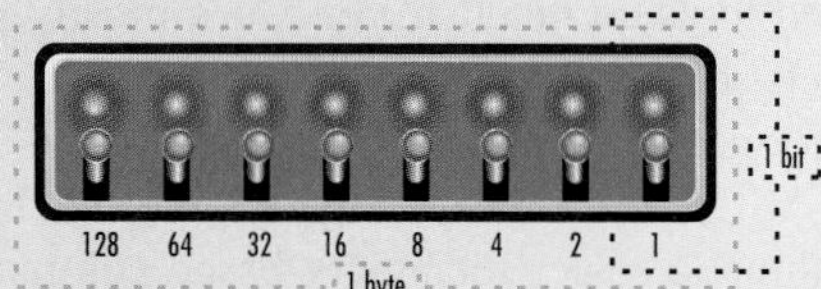

3. A byte can represent all the numbers between 0 and 255. The positional values are powers of 2, not 10. They start at 1 (the units' place) and double in value for each additional place. If all 8 bits are 0, the value is 0; if all 8 bits are 1, the value is 255 (1 + 2 + 4 + 8 + 16 + 32 + 64 + 128).
4. To represent values larger than 255, processor designers combine bytes. Two bytes, with 16 bits, can represent all the numbers from 0 to 65,535.

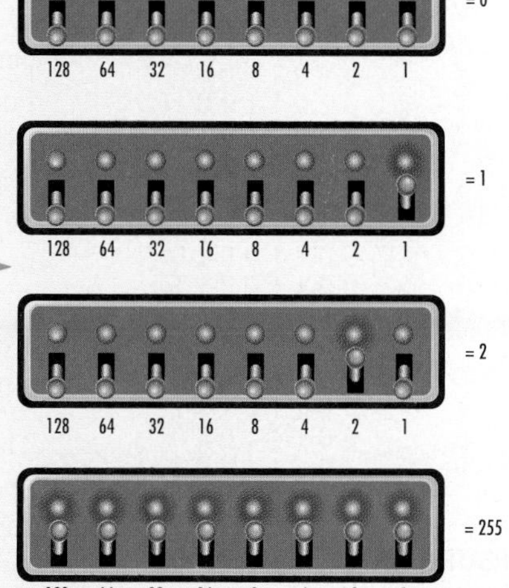

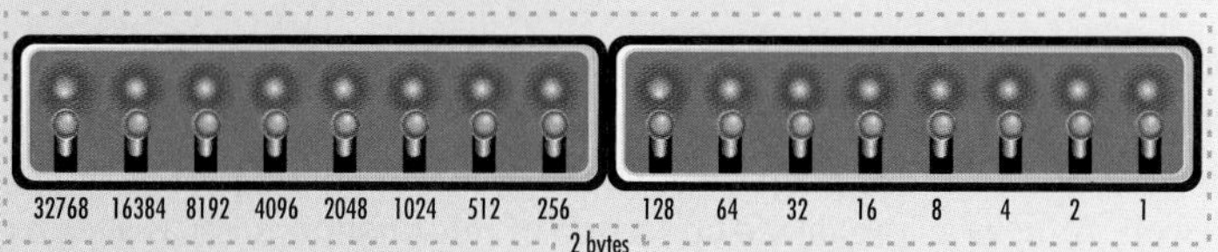

5. For computers, adding binary numbers is simpler than adding decimal numbers because there are fewer rules to remember.

0	0	1	1
+0	+1	+0	+1
0	1	1	10

6. Using these rules, we can compute the binary sum of 12 and 10:

```
 1100
+1010
10110
```

7. The calculator transforms the sum from binary back into a decimal number displayed on the calculator's screen.

FIGURE 2.7

Character	ASCII binary code
A	01000001
B	01000010
C	01000011
D	01000100
E	01000101
F	01000110
G	01000111
H	01001000
I	01001001
J	01001010
K	01001011
L	01001100
M	01001101
N	01001110
O	01001111
P	01010000
Q	01010001
R	01010010
S	01010011
T	01010100
U	01010101
V	01010110
W	01010111
X	01011000
Y	01011001
Z	01011010
0	00110000
1	00110001
2	00110010
3	00110011
4	00110100
5	00110101
6	00110110
7	00110111
8	00111000
9	00111001

FIGURE 2.8 The capital letters and numeric digits are represented in the ASCII character set by 36 unique patterns of 8 bits each. (The remaining 92 ASCII bit patterns represent lowercase letters, punctuation characters, and special characters.)

Program instructions, like characters, are represented in binary notation through the use of codes. For example, the code 01101010 might tell the computer to add two numbers. Other groups of bits—instructions in the program—contain codes that tell the computer where to find those numbers and where to store the result. You'll learn more about how these computer instructions work in later chapters.

Bits, Bytes, and Buzzwords

Trying to learn about computers by examining their operation at the bit level is a little like trying to learn about how people look or act by studying individual human cells; there's plenty of information there, but it's not the most efficient way to find out what you need to know. Fortunately, people can use computers without thinking about bits. Some bit-related terminology does come up in day-to-day computer work, though. Most computer users need to have at least a basic understanding of the following terms for quantifying data:

- *Byte:* A logical group of 8 bits also referred to as an octet. If you work mostly with words, you can think of a byte as one character of ASCII-encoded text.
- **Kilobyte (KB, K)**: About 1,000 bytes of information. For example, about 5 KB of storage is necessary to hold 5,000 characters of ASCII text. (Technically, 1 K is 1,024 bytes because 1,024 is 2^{10}, which makes the arithmetic easier for binary-based computers. For those of us who don't think in binary, 1,000 is often close enough.)
- **Megabyte (meg, MB)**: Approximately 1,000 KB, or 1 million bytes.
- **Gigabyte (gig, GB)**: Approximately 1,000 MB, or 1 billion bytes.
- **Terabyte (TB)**: Approximately 1 million MB or 1 trillion bytes. This massive unit of measurement applies to the largest storage devices commonly available today.
- **Petabyte (PB)**: This astronomical value is the equivalent of 1,024 terabytes, or 1 quadrillion bytes. While it's unlikely that anyone will be able to store 1 PB of data on a home PC anytime soon, we're definitely heading in that direction.

The abbreviations *KB*, *MB*, *GB*, *TB*, and *PB* describe the capacity of memory and storage components. You could, for example, describe a computer as having 4 GB of memory (RAM) and a hard disk as having a 2 TB storage capacity. The same terms are used to quantify sizes of computer files as well. A **file** is an organized collection of information, such as a term paper or a set of names and addresses, stored in a computer-readable form. For example, the text for this chapter is stored in a file that occupies about 400 KB of space on a hard disk drive.

To add to the confusion, people often measure data transfer speed or memory size in ***megabits (Mb, Mbits)*** rather than megabytes (MB). A megabit, as you might expect, is approximately 1,000,000 bits—one-eighth the size of a megabyte. When you're talking in bits and bytes, a little detail such as capitalization can make a significant difference.

Most of us have a hard time grappling with these gigantic numbers. It's hard to get an intuitive grasp on gigabits and terabytes. And even if we could, those numbers don't necessarily translate into meaningful values. As astronomer Carl Sagan once said, "All of the books in the world contain no more information than is broadcast as video in a single large American city in a single year. Not all bits have equal value."

The Computer's Core: CPU and Memory

> The microprocessor that makes up your personal computer's central processing unit, or CPU, is the **ultimate computer brain, messenger, ringmaster, and boss**. All the other components—RAM, disk drives, the monitor—exist only to bridge the gap between you and the processor.
>
> —*Ron White, in* How Computers Work

It may seem strange to think of ATMs, smart phones, and supercomputers as bit processors, but whatever it looks like to the user, a digital computer is, at its core, a collection of on/off switches designed to transform information from one form to another. The

how it works Representing the World's Languages

The United States has long been at the center of the computer revolution—that's why the ASCII character set was originally designed to include only English-language characters. ASCII code numbers range from 0 to 127, but this isn't enough to handle all the characters used in the languages of Western Europe, including accents and other diacritical marks.

The Latin I character set appends 128 additional codes onto the original ASCII 128 to accommodate additional characters.

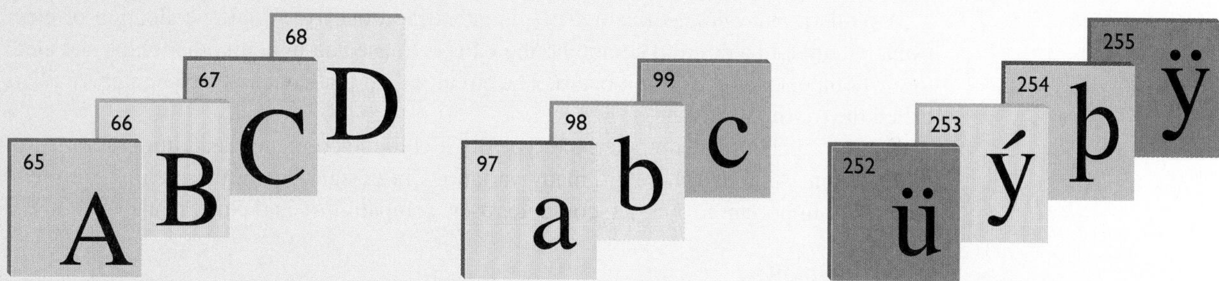

Both the ASCII and the Latin I character sets can use 8 bits—1 byte—to represent each character, but there's no room left for the characters used in languages such as Arabic, Greek, Hebrew, and Hindi, each of which has its own 50- to 150-character alphabet or syllabary. Asian languages, such as Chinese, Korean, and Japanese, present bigger challenges for computer users. Chinese alone has nearly 50,000 distinct characters, of which about 13,000 are in current use.

Unicode's international standard character set is designed to facilitate multilingual computing by allowing for more than 100,000 distinct codes. In Unicode, the first 256 codes (0 through 255) are identical to the codes of the Latin I character set. The remaining codes are distributed among the writing systems of the world's other languages.

Most major new software applications and operating systems are designed to be transported to different languages. Making a software application work in different languages involves much more than translating the words. For example, some languages write from right to left or top to bottom. Pronunciation, currency symbols, dialects, and other variations often make it necessary to produce customized software for different regions even where the same language is spoken.

Computer keyboards for East Asian languages don't have one key for each character. Using phonetic input, a user types a pronunciation for a character using a Western-style keyboard then chooses the character needed from a menu of characters that appears on the screen. The software can make some menu choices automatically based on common language-usage patterns.

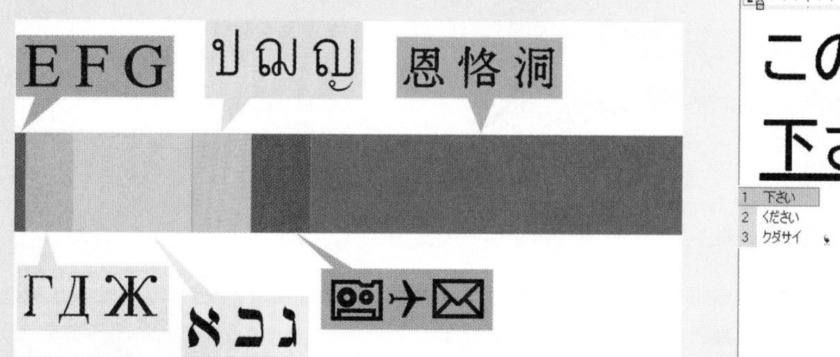

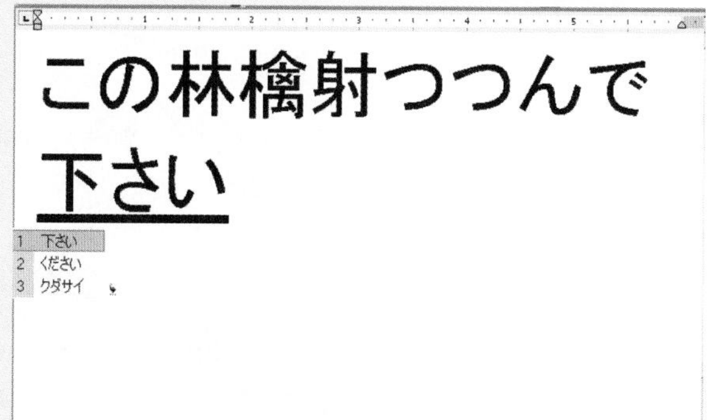

FIGURE 2.9 After entering a phonetic pronunciation of a Japanese character, a user can choose the correct character from a pop-up menu.

user provides the computer with patterns of bits—input—and the computer follows instructions to transform that input into a different pattern of bits—output—to return to the user.

The CPU: The Real Computer

The CPU, often just called the *processor*, performs the transformations of input into output. Every computer has at least one CPU to interpret and execute the instructions in each program, to perform arithmetic and logical data manipulations, and to communicate with all the other parts of the computer system indirectly through memory.

A modern *microprocessor*, or CPU, is an extraordinarily complex collection of electronic circuits. In a desktop computer, the CPU is housed along with other chips and electronic components on a circuit board. The circuit board that contains a computer's CPU is called the **motherboard**.

When you choose a computer, the type of CPU in the computer is an important part of the decision. Although there are many variations in design among these chips, only two factors are important to a casual computer user: compatibility and performance.

Compatibility

Not all software is **compatible** with every CPU; that is, software written for one processor may not work with another. Every processor has a built-in instruction set—a vocabulary of instructions the processor can execute. CPUs in the same product family are generally designed so newer processors can process all instructions handled by earlier models. For example, chips in Intel's Core i7 processor family are **backward compatible** with the Core i5, Core i3, Core 2 duo, Celeron, Pentium, 486, 386, and 286 chips that preceded it, so they can run most software written for those older CPUs. (Likewise, many of the processors designed by Advanced Micro Devices—AMD—are purposefully made to be compatible with those made by Intel.) In contrast, the ARM processors used in many smart phones and netbook PCs have a different instruction set from Intel CPUs. An ARM

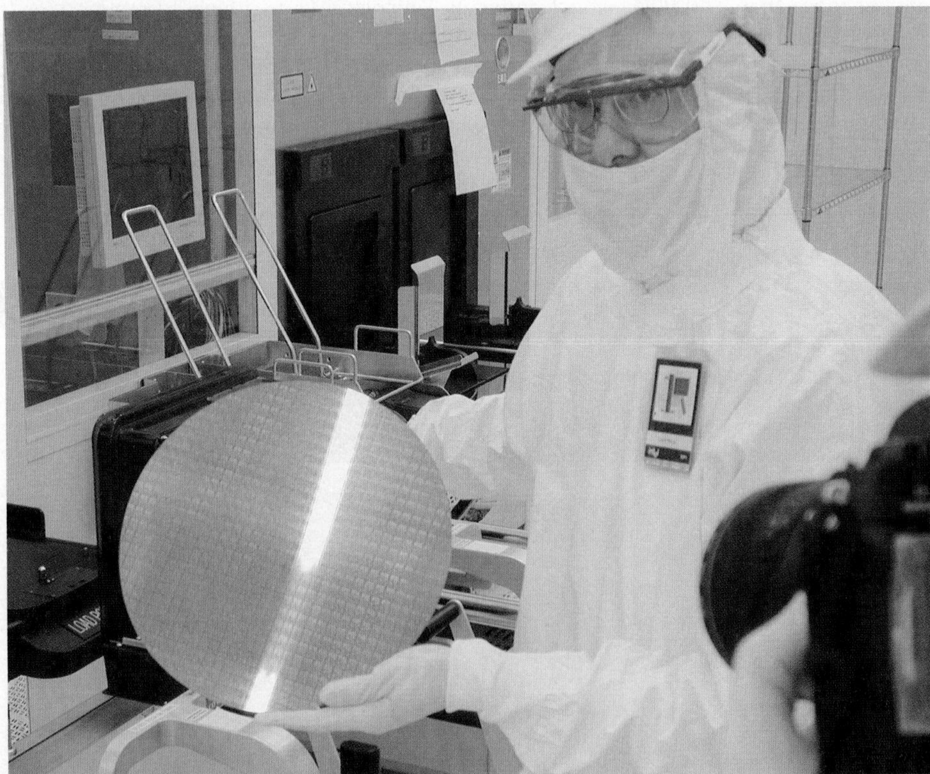

FIGURE 2.10 This chip specialist is examining a silicon wafer before it is sliced into many silicon chips.

FIGURE 2.11 The motherboard of a typical PC has places for the CPU, memory, and several other important chips and components.

CPU can't (without additional translation software) decipher Intel Pentium instructions and vice versa.

A related issue involves the software systems that run on these hardware processors. Programs written for Linux, a popular operating system, can't run on Windows, even though both operating systems can be installed on PCs powered by an Intel microprocessor. In Chapter 4, you will learn more about these issues and see how virtual machine software can often overcome incompatibility problems by translating instructions written for one CPU or software system into instructions that another can execute.

Performance

When it comes to handling information, some processors are much faster than others. Most computer applications, such as Web browsing, are more convenient to use on a faster machine. Some computationally intensive applications, such as statistical programs, graphic design programs, and many computer games, *require* faster machines to produce acceptable results.

A computer's overall performance is determined in part by the speed of its microprocessor's internal *clock*—the timing device that produces electrical pulses to synchronize the computer's operations. A modern computer's clock speed is measured in units called *gigahertz (GHz)*, for billions of clock cycles per second. (One hertz equals one clock cycle per second.) Ads for computer systems sometimes emphasize gigahertz ratings as a measure of speed. But these numbers can be misleading; judging a computer's speed by its gigahertz rating alone is like measuring a car's speed by the engine's RPM (revolutions per minute). For example, two processors may have the same clock speed, but one processor may outperform the other if it can access its memory faster.

PC performance can also be affected by the **architecture** of the processor—the design that determines how individual components of the CPU are put together and work together on the chip. For example, newer chips can manipulate more bits simultaneously than older chips can, which makes them more efficient, and therefore faster, at performing

Working Wisdom Green Computing

When compared with heavy industries, such as automobiles and energy, the computer industry is relatively easy on the environment. But the manufacturing and use of computer hardware and software does have a significant environmental impact, especially now that so many of us are using the technology. Fortunately, you have some control over the environmental impact of your computing activities. Here are a few tips to help minimize your impact:

- ***Buy green equipment.*** Today's computer equipment uses relatively little energy, but as world energy resources dwindle, less is always better. Many modern computers and peripherals are specifically designed to consume less energy. Look for the Environmental Protection Agency's Energy Star certification on the package.
- ***Use a laptop.*** Portable computers use far less energy than desktop computers. They're engineered to preserve precious battery power. But if you use a laptop, keep it plugged in when you have easy access to an electrical outlet. Batteries wear out from repeated usage, and their disposal can cause environmental problems of a different sort. Some batteries last longer if you occasionally drain and recharge them; check online to see what's best for your particular battery. (If you're the kind of person who always needs to have the latest and greatest technology, a notebook isn't the best choice because notebooks are difficult or impossible to upgrade.)
- ***Take advantage of energy-saving features.*** Most systems can be set up to go to sleep (a sort of suspended animation state that uses just enough power to preserve RAM) and turn off the monitor or printer when idle for more than an hour or so. If your equipment has automatic energy-saving features, use them. You'll save energy and money.
- ***Turn it off when you're away.*** If you're just leaving your computer for an hour or two, you won't save much energy by turning the computer off. But if you're leaving it for more than a few hours and it's not on duty receiving faxes, email, or other messages, you'll do the environment a favor by turning it off or putting it to sleep.
- ***Save energy, not screens.*** Your monitor may be the biggest power guzzler in your system, especially if it's not a flat-panel display. (If you don't have a flat-panel monitor, consider upgrading to one. Old-style CRTs aren't ecofriendly.) A screen saver can be fun to watch, but it doesn't save your screen, and it doesn't save energy, either. As long as your monitor is displaying an image, it's consuming power. Use sleep as your screen saver, and you'll save energy, too.
- ***Turn it all the way off.*** Many electronic devices consume power even when they're turned off. Some stay in a "ready" state so there's no delay when they're turned on; others just continue to consume power because it was easier or cheaper to design them that way. If you plug your system components (CPU, monitor, printer, external drives, audio/video gear) into a power strip with a switch, you can use that switch to cut off power completely to all of them, saving yourself time, energy, and money. Similarly, you'll save energy by unplugging your mobile phone charger from the wall when it's not charging your phone.
- ***Avoid moving parts.*** In general, things that move consume more energy than things that don't. Disk drives are the movers and shakers of the PC world. If you can store your information on a flash drive instead of a hard disk or optical disk, you'll save energy.

FIGURE 2.12 Laptop computers consume less energy than desktop PCs. This makes it possible to use solar panels to power them in remote locations.

- ***Print only once.*** Don't print out a rough draft just to proofread; try to get it clean on-screen. (Most people find this one hard to follow 100 percent of the time; some errors just don't seem to show up until you proofread a hard copy.)
- ***Use a green font.*** Some fonts use less ink than others. The Internet offers many options for environmentally-friendly fonts that can save ink, save the environment, and save money. The University of Wisconsin, Green Bay, found that it could save thousands of dollars per year when it switched its default font in its email system to Century Gothic, a font with a thin print line.
- ***E-cycle your waste products.*** When you reprint that 20-page report because of a missing paragraph on page 1, recycle the flawed printout. When your printer's inkjet or toner cartridge runs dry, ship or deliver it to a company that can refill or recycle it. The company may even pay you a few dollars for the empty cartridge. When a battery in one of your portable electronics dies, follow the manufacturer's instructions for recycling it. If your computer or printer dies, don't bury it in the landfill. Take advantage of the gear-recycling programs offered by many companies and communities. While you're in recycling mode, don't forget all those computer magazines and catalogs.
- ***Pass it on.*** When you outgrow a piece of hardware or software, don't throw it away. Donate it to a school, civic organization, family member, or friend who can put it to good use. Make sure to delete your data first, though, or you might end up the victim of identity theft.
- ***Send bits, not atoms.*** It takes far more resources to send a letter by truck, train, or plane than to send an electronic message through the Internet. Whenever possible, use your Internet connection instead of your printer.
- ***Consider hidden environmental costs of your decisions.*** The amount you pay for something doesn't always reflect its true cost. Somebody, somewhere, at sometime will pay for the environmental damage done by companies that refuse to be good citizens of the planet. You may pay a few dollars less for a gadget produced by such a company, but is it worth it? If you want to do comparative ecoshopping, you can find environmental scorecards for most big companies on the Web.

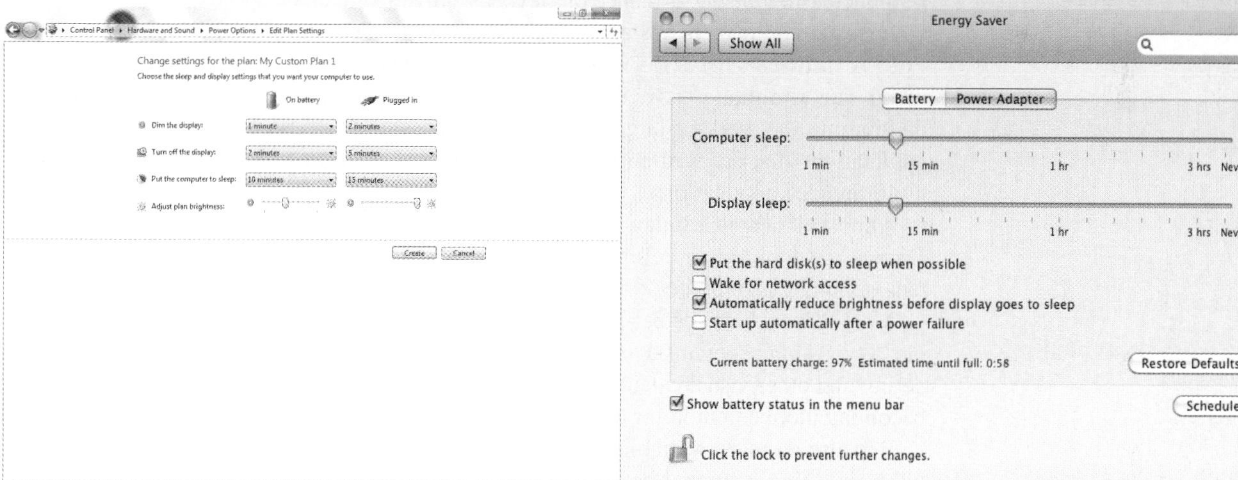

FIGURE 2.13 Windows and Mac OS X systems have advanced energy-saver control panels that can be used to switch the monitor, hard drive, and CPU to lower-power sleep modes automatically after specified periods of inactivity.

FIGURE 2.14 The Intel Core i7 (left) and AMD SixCore Opteron chips contain circuitry that looks like geometric patterns when magnified.

most operations. The number of bits a CPU can process at one time—typically 32 or 64—is sometimes called the CPU's *word size*. More often, though, people use the number without a label, as in "AMD produced the first 64-bit processor for consumer PCs." Some embedded and special-purpose computers still use 8- and 16-bit processors because their performance needs are smaller and these chips cost less.

The amount of heat generated by a CPU increases as the clock speed increases. CPUs with high clock speeds need large heat sinks and fans to keep them from overheating. The heat dissipation problem is one reason chip manufacturers have realized it is impractical to keep increasing the performance of CPUs by only raising clock speeds.

Instead, chip makers design and manufacture multicore processors for almost all new PCs. A **multicore processor** is a single chip that contains multiple CPUs, or **cores**, which run simultaneously. Each core handles threads of instructions independently, dividing up the work of larger processes so that the work can be done faster. Software applications that are written to take advantage of multiple cores are sometimes called multithreaded applications.

Almost all new PCs today have at least two cores, and quad-core CPUs such as the Intel Core i7 are common in PCs. More powerful experimental *manycore* machines may have tens or hundreds of processors per chip.

Most PCs include special-purpose processors to supplement the basic CPU. For example, a typical PC contains a **graphics-processing unit (GPU)** to handle 3-D graphics rendering and other visual calculations. This frees the main CPU to work on other tasks. It's becoming more common for a PC CPU to include an integrated GPU on the same chip.

Because so many variables affect the performance of a computer, it's impossible to tell from a single number how well it performs in day-to-day work or play situations. To aid comparison shoppers, computer magazines, consumer Web sites, and other organizations report on *benchmark tests* that provide solid data in side-by-side comparisons of various machines.

From Multicore to Cluster

Before we move on to talk about memory, it's worth mentioning that some of the performance-enhancing techniques we've seen aren't confined to the insides of CPU chips. The divide-and-conquer parallel processing techniques used in multicore PCs are applied on a much larger scale in high-end server systems. Instead of adding more cores to a CPU, a large system might simply add more machines to a network. This way, the processing resources of

FIGURE 2.15 A single-core CPU can handle multiple applications by rapidly switching between applications. A multicore CPU can (with the right software) divide the work load between processors, assigning multiple cores to labor-intensive tasks such as photo or video editing.

multiple servers can be grouped together in a **cluster** to improve rendering speeds in lifelike computer graphics or calculate the sums of complex financial trading computations more quickly. Google uses a cluster of thousands of PCs to handle hundreds of millions of search queries a day. Server clusters are also used for reliability reasons: If one machine in a cluster shuts down because of errors, or to be serviced, the other servers can pick up the slack.

Parallel processing (sometimes called **symmetric multiprocessing** or just **multiprocessing** in the PC world) has been used in high-end servers and workstations for some time. The threaded processing in multicore CPUs is like a microscopic version of parallel processing used in some of the world's biggest computing networks.

The Computer's Memory

> "What's one and one and one and one and one and one and one and one and one and one?" "I don't know," said Alice. "I lost count." "**She can't do addition,**" said the Red Queen.
>
> —*Lewis Carroll, in* Through the Looking Glass

The CPU's main job is to follow the instructions encoded in programs. But like Alice in *Through the Looking Glass*, the CPU can handle only one instruction and a few pieces of data at a time. The computer needs a place to store the rest of the program and data until the processor is ready for them. That's what RAM is for.

Random access memory (RAM) is the most common type of primary storage, or computer memory. RAM chips contain circuits that store program instructions and data temporarily. The computer divides each RAM chip into many equal-sized memory locations. Memory locations, like houses, have unique addresses so the computer can tell them apart when it is instructed to save or retrieve information. You can store a piece of information in any RAM location—you can pick one at random—and the computer can, if so instructed, quickly retrieve it. Hence, the name is random access memory.

how it works The CPU

The central processing unit (CPU) is the hardware component that executes the steps in a software program, performing math and moving data from one part of the system to another. The CPU contains the circuitry to perform a variety of simple tasks called ***instructions***. An individual instruction does only a tiny amount of work. A typical instruction might be "Read the contents of memory location *x* and add the number *y* to it." Most CPUs have a vocabulary of fewer than 1,000 distinct instructions.

All computer programs are composed of instructions drawn from this tiny vocabulary. The typical computer program is composed of millions of instructions, and the CPU can execute millions of instructions every second. (CPU speed is sometimes measured in MIPs—millions of instructions per second.) When a program runs, the rapid-fire execution of instructions creates an illusion of motion in the same way a movie simulates motion out of a sequence of still pictures.

The typical CPU is divided into several functional units: control, arithmetic logic decode, bus, and prefetch. These units work together like workers on an assembly line to complete the execution of program instructions.

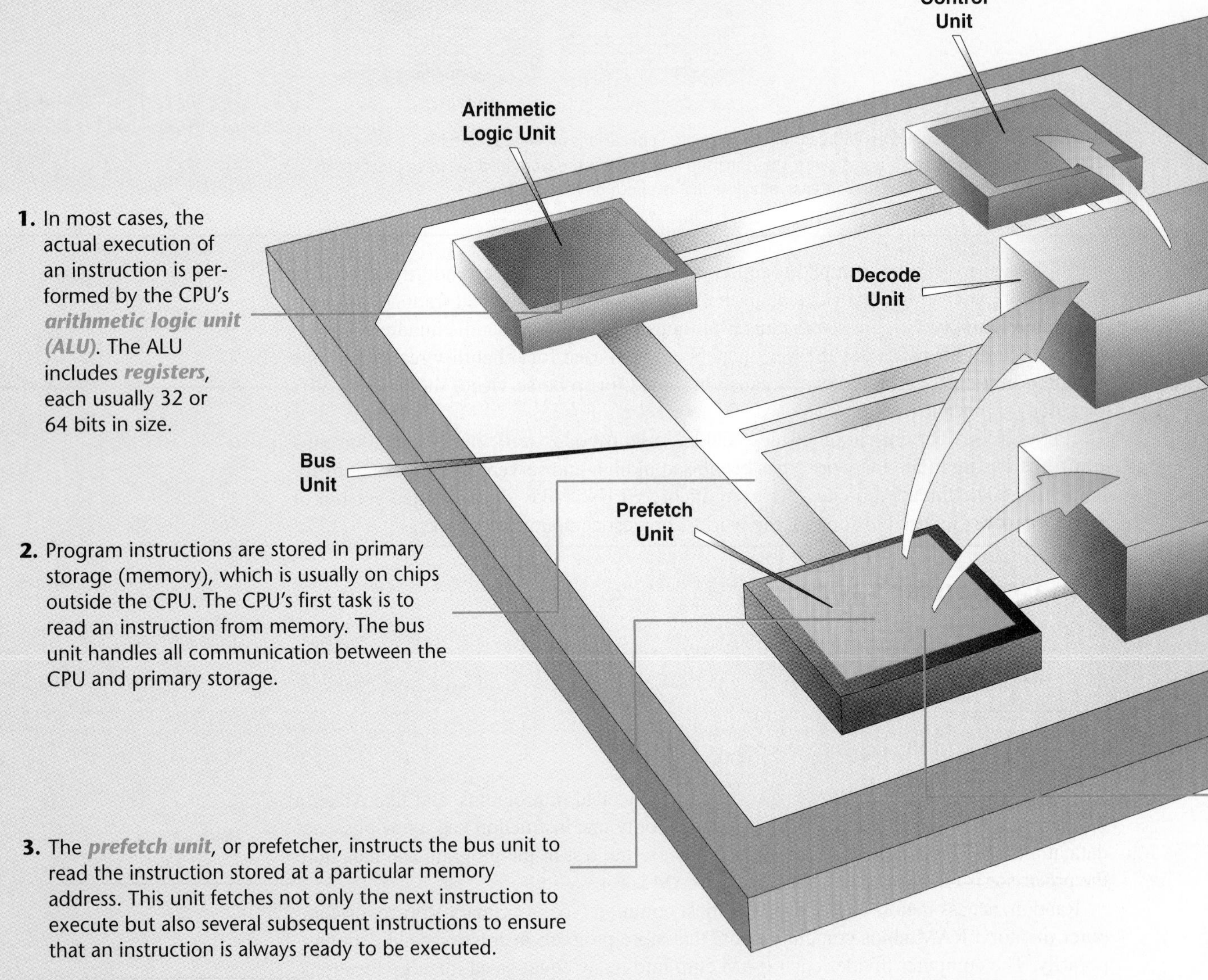

1. In most cases, the actual execution of an instruction is performed by the CPU's ***arithmetic logic unit (ALU)***. The ALU includes ***registers***, each usually 32 or 64 bits in size.

2. Program instructions are stored in primary storage (memory), which is usually on chips outside the CPU. The CPU's first task is to read an instruction from memory. The bus unit handles all communication between the CPU and primary storage.

3. The ***prefetch unit***, or prefetcher, instructs the bus unit to read the instruction stored at a particular memory address. This unit fetches not only the next instruction to execute but also several subsequent instructions to ensure that an instruction is always ready to be executed.

FIGURE 2.16

4. The ***decode unit*** takes the instruction read by the prefetcher and translates it into a form suitable for the CPU's internal processing. It does this by looking up the steps required to complete an instruction in the control unit.

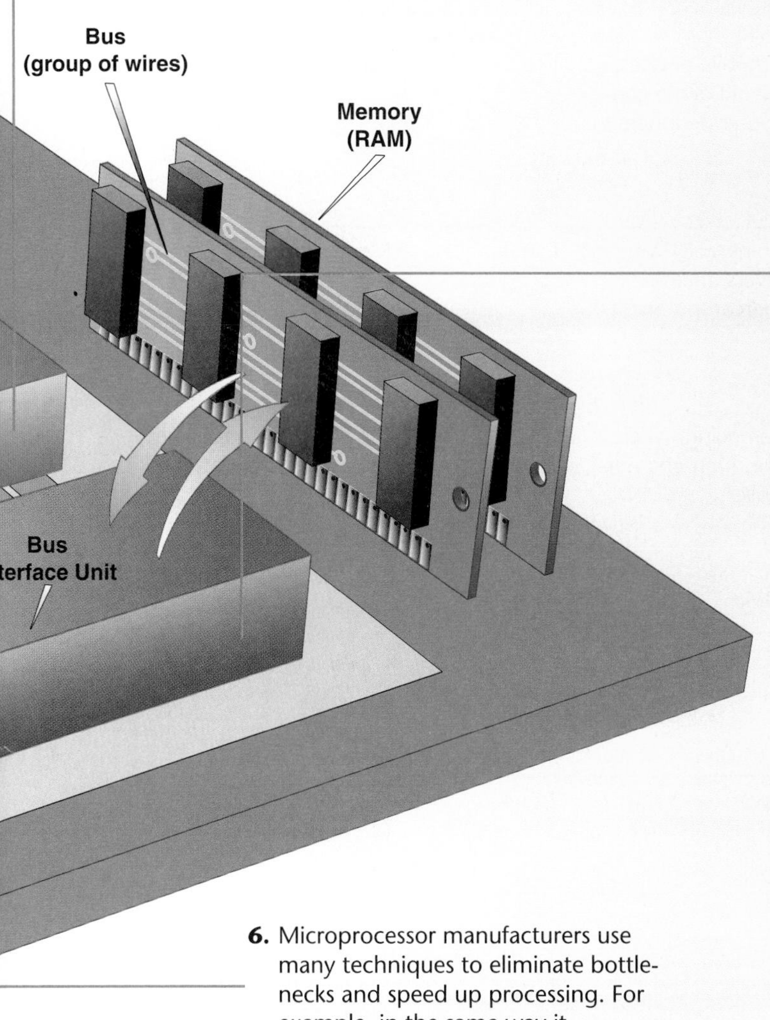

5. If an instruction requires that information be sent out from the CPU—for example, written into memory—then the final phase of execution is ***writeback***, in which the bus unit writes the results of the instruction back into memory or to some other device.

6. Microprocessor manufacturers use many techniques to eliminate bottlenecks and speed up processing. For example, in the same way it prefetches the next likely instructions to be read, the CPU prereads the next likely data to be used into a cache in memory, called a ***Level 2 cache (L2 cache)***, or, for faster access, in the CPU itself (a ***Level 1 cache***).

7. The most popular PC CPUs today are multicore processors. Each of the cores in a multicore CPU is a processor that can fetch and execute instructions. If the software is written to take advantage of the multiple cores, those cores can use parallel processing to work simultaneously on different groups of instructions.

8. Some modern CPUs increase their efficiency using a technique called simultaneous multithreading (Intel calls it Hyper-Threading Technology). This technique enables each core processor to execute two concurrent threads of instructions, making it seem to the operating system as if there were twice as many cores.

Popular CPUs and Where to Find Them

CPUs are designed for a wide variety of computers and applications. In general, more powerful processors tend to consume more energy and produce more heat.

Photo	Name	Used In	# of Cores	Energy Requirements
	Intel Xscale	Mobile and embedded devices	1	Minute (half a watt)
	ARM (variations are manufactured by many companies; for example, Apple's A4)	Embedded devices, MP3 players, many smart phones and mobile handheld devices, gaming devices	1	Very low (2–10 watts)
	Intel Atom	Netbooks, mobile phones, PDAs, handheld game consoles, computer peripherals	1 to 2	Very low (2–10 watts)
	Cell processor (IBM, Sony, and Toshiba)	Game machines, HDTVs, gaming servers, mainframes, supercomputers	1 to 8	Medium low (30 watts)
	Tilera TILEGX line	Video conferencing, wireless base stations, high-end network controllers.	16 to 100	Medium low to medium high (10 to 55 watts)
	Intel Core 2	PCs and servers	2 to 4	Medium low to medium high (17 to 45 watts)
	Intel i3/5/7	PCs and servers	2 to 4	Medium to high (25 to 65 watts)
	AMD Athlon I & II, Phenom 1 & II	PCs and servers	2 to 6	Medium to very high (40 to 110 watts)
	Cray XT5-HE Opteron Six Core 2.6 GHz (the world's fastest supercomputer)	Supercomputers	224162	Extremely high (roughly 1500 watts)

FIGURE 2.17

how it works Memory

Memory is the work area for the CPU. For the CPU to execute instructions or manipulate data, these instructions or data must be loaded into memory. Think of memory as millions of tiny storage cells, each of which can contain a single byte of information. Like mailboxes in a row, bytes of memory have unique addresses that identify them and help the CPU keep track of where things are stored. PCs contain a large amount of random access memory (RAM) and a small amount of read-only memory (ROM).

The CPU can store (write) information into RAM and retrieve (read) information from RAM. The information in RAM may include program instructions, numbers for arithmetic, codes representing text characters, digital codes representing pictures, and other kinds of data. RAM chips are usually grouped on small circuit boards called ***dual in-line memory modules (DIMMs)*** and are plugged into the motherboard. RAM is volatile memory, meaning that all the information is lost when power to the computer is turned off.

On the other hand, information is permanently recorded on the ROM, meaning the CPU can read information from the ROM but cannot change its contents. On most computer systems, part of the operating system is stored in ROM. Programs stored in ROM are called firmware.

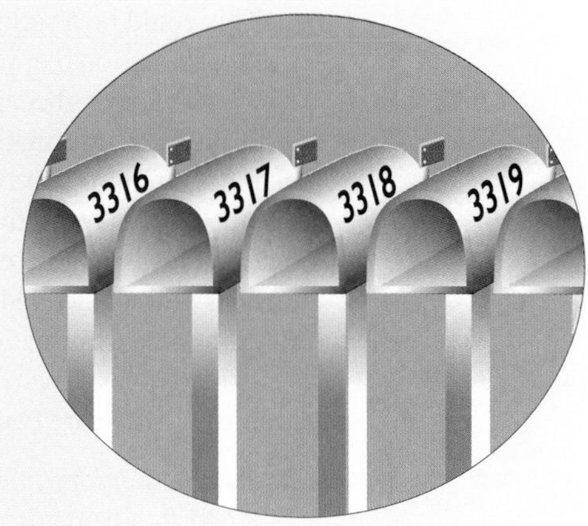
3316
3317
3318
3319

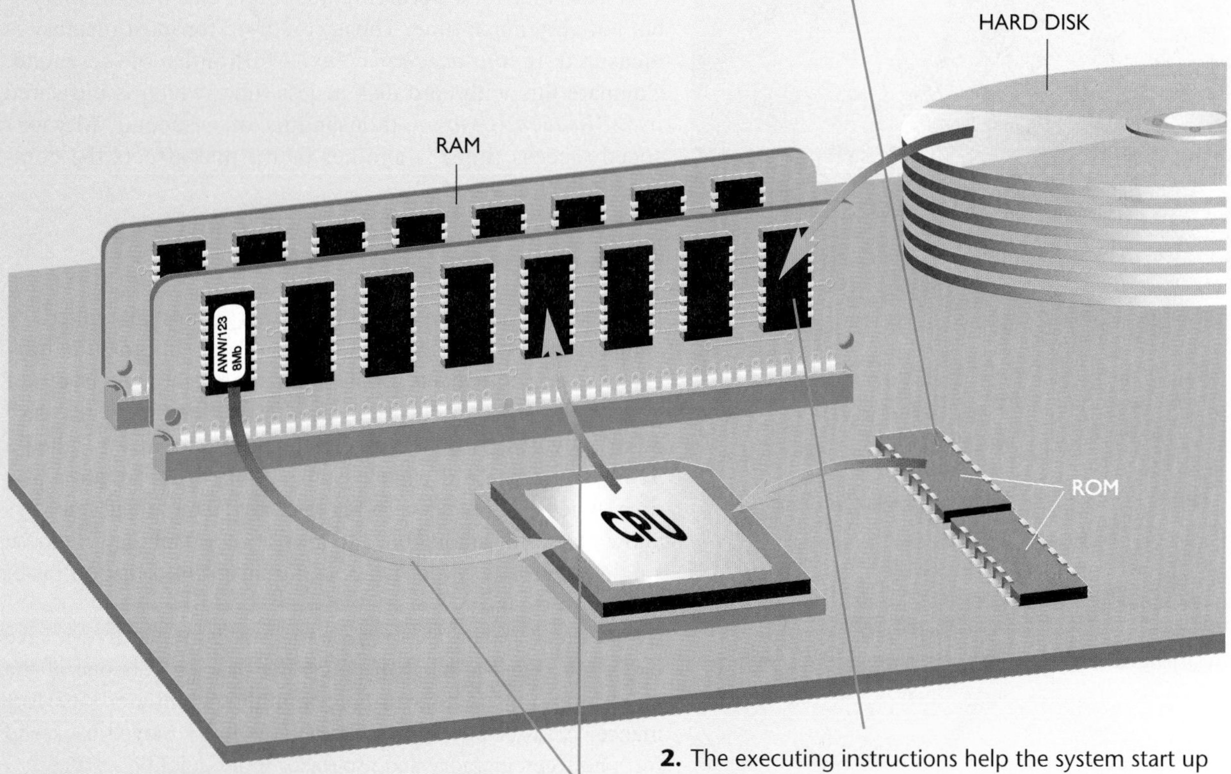
1. When you turn on the computer, the CPU automatically begins executing operating system instructions stored in ROM.
HARD DISK
RAM
AWW/123
8Mb
CPU
ROM
2. The executing instructions help the system start up and tell it how to load the operating system—copy it from disk into RAM.
3. Once instructions for the operating system are loaded into RAM, the CPU is able to execute them.

FIGURE 2.18

The information stored in RAM is nothing more than a pattern of electrical current flowing through microscopic circuits in silicon chips. This means that when the power goes off, the computer instantly forgets everything it was remembering in RAM. RAM is sometimes referred to as volatile memory because information stored there is not held permanently.

This could be a serious problem if the computer didn't have another type of memory to store information that you don't want to lose. This nonvolatile memory is called **read-only memory (ROM)** because the computer can only read information from it; it can never write any new information on it. The information in ROM was etched in when the chip was manufactured, so it is available whenever the computer is operating, but it can't be changed except by replacing the ROM chip. All modern computers use ROM to store start-up instructions and other critical information. You can also find ROM inside preprogrammed devices with embedded processors, such as calculators and microwave ovens. Printers use ROM to hold information about character sets.

Other types of memory are available; most are seldom used outside of engineering laboratories. There are two notable exceptions:

- *Complementary metal-oxide semiconductor (CMOS)* is a special low-energy kind of RAM that can store small amounts of data for long periods of time on battery power. CMOS RAM stores the date, time, and calendar in a PC along with other system settings. (CMOS RAM is called *parameter RAM* or PRAM in Macs.)
- *Flash memory* chips, like RAM chips, can be written and erased rapidly and repeatedly. But unlike RAM, flash memory is nonvolatile; it can keep its contents without a flow of electricity. Digital cameras, cell phones, pagers, portable computers, handheld computers, PDAs, and other digital devices use flash memory to store data that needs to be changed from time to time. Data flight recorders also use it. In spite of its relatively high cost, flash memory is sometimes used for storage instead of (or in addition to) the hard drive. Unlike a spinning disk-based hard drive, a flash-based solid-state drive (SSD) has no moving parts.

It takes time for the processor to retrieve data from memory—but not very much time. The *access time* for most memory is measured in *nanoseconds (ns)*—billionths of a second. Compare this with hard disk access time, which is measured in *milliseconds (ms)*—thousandths of a second. Memory speed (access time) is another factor that affects the computer's overall speed.

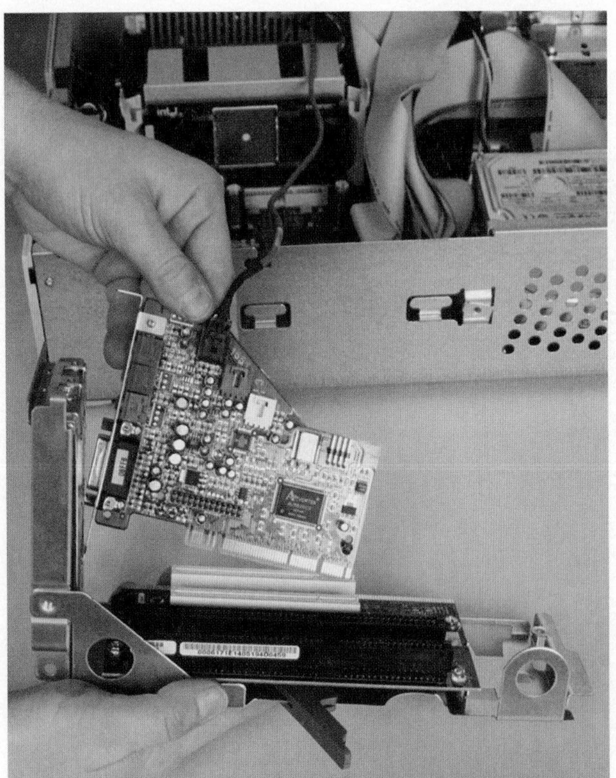

FIGURE 2.19 Slots and ports enable the CPU to communicate with the outside world via peripheral devices. Here an add-on card is being inserted into an internal slot in the PC. (The circuit board containing the slot has been removed for easier viewing.)

Buses, Ports, and Peripherals

In a desktop computer, the CPU, memory chips, and other key components are attached to the motherboard. Information travels between components on the motherboard through groups of wires called **internal buses**, or just **buses**. Buses typically have 32 or 64 wires, or data paths; a bus with 32 wires is called a *32-bit bus* because it can transmit 32 bits of information at a time, twice as many as a 16-bit bus. Just as multilane freeways allow masses of automobiles to move faster than they could on single-lane roads, wider buses can transmit information faster than narrower buses.

The bus is the bridge between the processor and RAM. Like clock speed and number of cores, the bus speed is one of the most important factors in determining a computer's performance. A faster bus allows instructions to be moved back and forth between memory and processor more quickly.

Buses connect to storage devices in **bays**—open areas in the system box for disk drives and other devices. Buses also connect to **expansion slots** (sometimes just called *slots*) inside the computer's housing. Users can customize their computers by inserting special-purpose circuit boards (called **expansion cards**, or just *cards*) into these slots. Buses also connect to **ports**—sockets on the outside of the computer chassis. These ports are generally used to attach peripherals—external devices that enable the CPU to communicate with the outside world and store information for later use. The peripherals are connected to the ports through ***external buses***—cables designed to transmit data back and forth between computers and peripherals.

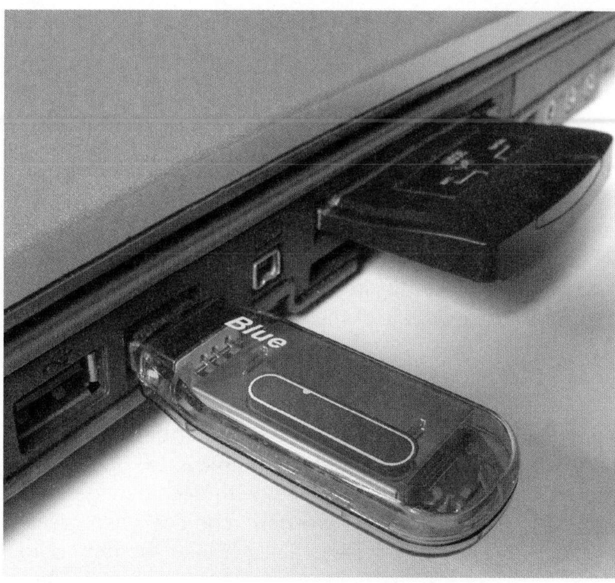

FIGURE 2.20 Most laptop computers have ports and slots for attaching external storage devices and other peripherals.

A computer typically has a variety of ports to meet diverse needs: one or more video ports for connecting monitors; audio jacks for connecting speakers and/or headphones; and ***USB ports*** for connecting keyboards, pointing devices (such as a mouse), printers, cameras, disk drives, portable storage devices, and more. Some ports are connected directly to the system board. Others, such as the video port, may be attached to an expansion card. In fact, many expansion cards do little more than provide convenient ports for attaching particular types of peripherals. In many computers—especially portable computers, where size is critical—most ports go directly to the system board. Because portable computers don't have room for full-sized cards, many have slots for **ExpressCards** or **PC cards**—small removable cards that contain memory, miniature peripherals, or additional ports. PC cards are the size of credit cards; newer such cards are considerably smaller. These cards and ExpressCards are *hot-swappable*—they can be inserted or removed from a computer's slot while the system is running.

Slots and ports make it easy to add peripherals to the computer system. Without peripherals, CPU and memory together are like a brain without a body. Some peripherals, such as keyboards and printers, serve as communication links between people and computers. Other peripherals link the computer to other machines. Still others provide long-term storage media. In the next chapter, we explore a variety of input, output, and storage peripherals and then revisit the buses, slots, and ports that connect those peripherals to the CPU and memory.

Inventing the Future ▸ Energy, Atoms, and Light: Tomorrow's Computer Processors

Researchers are working on a variety of fronts to produce future generations of computers that are smaller, faster, more powerful, and more energy efficient than today's state of the art. Some labs are concentrating their efforts on shrinking computer components. Others are experimenting with alternatives to circuits etched in silicon. In this section we'll explore a few of these paths into the future.

SHRINKING CPUS: SPEED, ENERGY, AND SIZE

We've seen how silicon chips have relentlessly, obediently followed the dictates of Moore's Law, packing more circuitry into smaller spaces with each new generation. CPU designers have two basic choices when creating a chip that's physically smaller: Make the new chip faster, or make it more energy efficient. In the early days of the PC, chip designers emphasized speed because of the growing appetite for computing power. But in today's wireless world, battery life is a bigger issue than processor speed for most computer users. So as the circuitry continues to shrink, many researchers are focusing on creating ultralow-power CPUs for portable computing devices.

Today's cutting edge chips employ **nanotechnology** (or nanotech)—technology that approaches the molecular or atomic level. (A nanometer is a billionth of a meter—the unit of measure that can be applied to molecule-sized structures.) Researchers are working on molecular-scale electronics (moletronics) that might eventually produce computers that perform *billions* of times faster than today's fastest machines. Scientists at IBM, HP, and elsewhere have experimented with silicon nanowire technology that may help extend Moore's Law for a couple of decades. But silicon circuits can't shrink forever; sooner or later Moore's Law will run up against more fundamental laws of physics and chemistry.

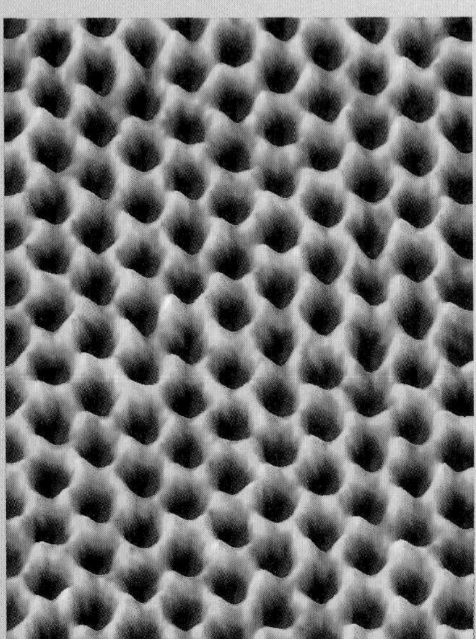

FIGURE 2.21 Graphene is a honeycomb lattice made of carbon atoms.

Many researchers believe carbon-based nanoscale processors could be much smaller and consume far less electricity than conventional silicon-based microprocessors. A one-atom-thick sheet of carbon known as ***graphene*** shows promise as a material for making future processors. Researchers have produced a graphene transistor one atom thick and 10 atoms wide, as well as fully functional graphene integrated circuits. According to one MIT report, commercial graphene processors might soon run more than 100 times faster than today's silicon CPUs.

Nanotechnology breakthroughs may be steppingstones on the road to **quantum computers**—computers based on the properties of atoms and their nuclei and the laws of quantum mechanics. According to Christian Joachim of the French National Scientific Research Centre, "Atomic-scale computing researchers today are in much the same position as transistor inventors were before 1947. No one knows where this will lead."

SUPERCONDUCTORS AND OPTICAL COMPUTERS

Researchers are pursuing other radical research technologies, too. Superconductors that transmit electricity without heat loss could increase computer speed a hundredfold. Unfortunately, superconductor technology generally requires a supercooled environment, which isn't practical for most applications. The search goes on for superconductors that can function at room temperature.

Another possibility for future CPUs is the **optical computer**, which transmits information in light waves rather than in electrical pulses. Optical computing is sometimes called photonic computing because it uses photons (light particles) instead of electrons to transmit bits. Optical computers outside research labs are currently limited to a few narrow applications, such as robot vision. But when the technology is refined, general-purpose optical computers may process information hundreds of times faster than silicon computers do.

It's not clear which of these technologies will survive the relentless race into the future. But whatever future CPUs are made of, people will find ways to push them to their limits. In the words of Bjarne Stoustrup, designer of the C++ programming language, "The only thing that has consistently grown faster than hardware in the last 40 years is human expectation."

Crosscurrents

The Clock of the Long Now

by Stewart Brand

According to one Native American tradition, it's important to think about each decision in terms of its impact seven generations into the future. In today's fast-paced, technology-driven society, few people take the time to think more than a few years—or even days—ahead. The Long Now Foundation is a visionary group dedicated to encouraging long-term thinking. Its pioneering members include writer and consultant Stewart Brand, musician and artist Brian Eno, and computer scientist and inventor Danny Hillis. (The organization's name was coined by Eno, who noticed when he moved to New York City that "here" and "now" meant "this room" and "this five minutes," as opposed to the bigger here and longer now of his native England.) In this short essay from The Long Now Foundation's Web site, Brand describes the rationale behind the group's most well-known artifact: The Clock of the Long Now. This clock is sometimes referred to as "the world's slowest computer."

FIGURE 2.22 A prototype for the Clock of the Long Now.

Civilization is revving itself into a pathologically short attention span. The trend might be coming from the acceleration of technology, the short-horizon perspective of market-driven economics, the next-election perspective of democracies, or the distractions of personal multi-tasking. All are on the increase. Some sort of balancing corrective to the short-sightedness is needed-some mechanism or myth which encourages the long view and the taking of long-term responsibility, where 'long-term' is measured at least in centuries. Long Now proposes both a mechanism and a myth. It began with an observation and idea by computer scientist Daniel Hillis:

> *"When I was a child, people used to talk about what would happen by the year 2000. For the next thirty 30 years they kept talking about what would happen by the year 2000, and now no one mentions a future date at all. The future has been shrinking by one year per year for my entire life. I think it is time for us to start a long-term project that gets people thinking past the mental barrier of an ever-shortening future. I would like to propose a large (think Stonehenge) mechanical clock, powered by seasonal temperature changes. It ticks once a year, bongs once a century, and the cuckoo comes out every millennium."*

Such a clock, if sufficiently impressive and well engineered, would embody deep time for people. It should be charismatic to visit, interesting to think about, and famous enough to become iconic in the public discourse. Ideally, it would do for thinking about time what the photographs of Earth from space have done for thinking about the environment. Such icons reframe the way people think.

Hillis, who developed the 'massive parallel' architecture of the current generation of supercomputers, devised the mechanical design of the Clock and is now building the second prototype (the first prototype is on display in London at the Science Museum). The Clock's works consist of a binary digital-mechanical system which is so accurate and revolutionary that we have patented several of its elements. (With 32 bits of accuracy it has precision equal to one day in 20,000 years, and it self-corrects by 'phase-locking' to the noon Sun.) For the way the eventual Clock is experienced (its size, structure, etc.), we expect to keep proliferating design ideas for a while. In 01999 Long Now purchased part of a mountain in eastern Nevada whose high white limestone cliffs may make an ideal site for the ultimate 10,000-year Clock. [The Long Now Foundation uses five- digit dates; the extra zero is to solve the deca-millennium bug which will come into effect in about 8,000 years.] In the meantime Danny Hillis and Alexander Rose continue to experiment with ever-larger prototype Clocks.

Long Now added a "Library" dimension with the realization of the need for content to go along with the long-term context provided by the Clock—a library of the deep future, for the deep future. In a sense every library is part of the 10,000-year Library, so Long Now is developing tools (such as the Rosetta Disk, The Long Viewer the Long Server) that may provide inspiration and utility to the whole community of librarians and archivists. The Long Bets project—whose purpose is improving the quality of long-term thinking by making predictions accountable—is also Library-related.

The point is to explore whatever may be helpful for thinking, understanding, and acting responsibly over long periods of time.

Discussion Questions

1. Do you think the Long Now Clock is a good idea? Why or why not?
2. Can you think of other ways to encourage long-term thinking?

Summary

Whether it's working with words, numbers, pictures, or sounds, a computer manipulates patterns of bits—binary digits of information that it can store in switching circuitry and that are represented by two symbols. Groups of bits can be treated as numbers for calculations using the binary number system. Bits can be grouped into coded messages that represent alphabetic characters, pictures, colors, sounds, or just about any other kind of information. Even the instructions that computers follow—the software programs that tell the computer what to do—must be reduced to strings of bits before the computer accepts them. Byte, kilobyte, megabyte, terabyte, and other common units for measuring bit quantities are used in descriptions of memory, storage, and file size.

The microprocessor, or central processing unit (CPU), follows software instructions to perform the calculations and logical manipulations that transform input data into output. Not all CPUs are compatible with each other; each is capable of processing a particular set of instructions, so a software program written for one family of processors can't necessarily be understood by a processor from another family. Engineers are constantly improving the clock speed and architecture of CPUs, making computers capable of processing information faster. Most modern CPUs employ multicore or manycore processing systems that speed calculations using parallel processing.

The CPU uses RAM (random access memory) as a temporary storage area—a scratch pad—for instructions and data. Another type of memory, ROM (read-only memory), contains unchangeable information that serves as reference material for the CPU as it executes program instructions.

The CPU and main memory are housed in silicon chips on the motherboard and other circuit boards inside the computer. Buses connect to slots and ports that enable the computer to communicate with internal devices and external peripherals.

Key Terms

Companion Website Projects

1. The *Digital Planet* Web site, **www.pearsonhighered.com/beekman**, contains self-test exercises related to this chapter. Follow the instructions for taking a quiz. After you've completed your quiz, you can email the results to your instructor.
2. The Web site also contains open-ended discussion questions called Internet Explorations. Discuss one or more of the Internet Exploration questions for this chapter.

True or False

1. For a computer to add two numbers, the numbers first must be converted to Unicode.
2. A simple on/off switch can store exactly two bits of information.
3. The data processed by digital computers is made up of discrete units, or digits.
4. The contents of RAM cannot be changed.
5. If a processor is backward compatible with another, older processor, it can run older programs written for that processor.
6. A gigabyte (GB) is ten times as big as a megabyte (MB).
7. The information stored in RAM is nothing more than a pattern of electrical current flowing through microscopic circuits in silicon chips.
8. Benchmark tests are used to determine CPU clock speed, which is the most accurate measure of a CPU's performance.
9. Slots and ports make it possible for the CPU to communicate with the outside world through peripherals.
10. The access time for most memory is faster than the access time for a typical hard disk.

Multiple Choice

1. Why will software written for the Core 2 Duo CPU generally run on the Core i7 CPU?
   a. Microsoft uses special encoding techniques when they build Core CPUs.
   b. The Core 2 Duo has special compatibility registers in RAM.
   c. The Core i7 is designed to be backward compatible with earlier Core chips.
   d. Every CPU is, by definition, compatible with the Core processor.
   e. It doesn't; software written for one processor won't run on another CPU.
2. ExpressCards are
   a. cards that are designed to be inserted into expansion slots on desktop PCs.
   b. high-speed cards that are designed to work with multicore CPUs.
   c. compact cards that are designed to work with portable computers.
   d. cards that are necessary for parallel processing to work.
   e. None of the above
3. One terabyte equals approximately
   a. 1,000 bits.
   b. 1,000 bytes.
   c. 1,000 megabytes.
   d. 1,000 gigabytes.
   e. 1,000 terabits.
4. How many values can be represented by a single byte?
   a. 2
   b. 8
   c. 16
   d. 64
   e. 256
5. Transformation of input into output is performed by
   a. peripherals.
   b. memory.
   c. storage.
   d. the CPU.
   e. the ALU.
6. A coding scheme that supports 100,000 unique characters has the name
   a. parallel processing.
   b. binary.
   c. Unicode.
   d. ASCII.
   e. HTML.
7. What does the speed of a processor depend on?
   a. The architecture of the processor
   b. The clock speed of the processor
   c. The word size of the processor
   d. The number of cores in the processor
   e. All of the above
8. Why are program instructions represented in binary notation within the computer?
   a. Binary notation is more compact than other representations.
   b. Computer memory is made out of binary digits (bits).
   c. There are only two different directions for electricity to move along a wire.
   d. Computer programmers prefer to think in binary.
   e. A CPU can execute no more than two instructions at one time.

9. A computer's internal bus can be connected to an external bus through
   a. a depot.
   b. a CPU.
   c. a port.
   d. a flash.
   e. a megabit.
10. When you first turn on a computer, the CPU is preset to execute instructions stored in
   a. RAM.
   b. ROM.
   c. flash memory.
   d. the CD-ROM.
   e. the ALU.
11. When you are working on an unsaved document on a PC, where is the document temporarily stored?
   a. RAM
   b. ROM
   c. The CPU
   d. The Internet
   e. The CD-ROM
12. Information travels between components on the motherboard through
   a. flash memory.
   b. CMOS.
   c. bays.
   d. buses.
   e. peripherals.
13. Which of these is the best indicator of real-world performance of a computer?
   a. Benchmark tests published in computer magazines
   b. The CPU's clock speed
   c. The number of cores in the CPU
   d. The amount of memory
   e. The bus speed
14. A collection of bits in the computer's memory might be treated as
   a. binary numbers that can be added and subtracted.
   b. ASCII codes representing letters and other characters.
   c. program instructions that tell the computer what to do.
   d. Any of the above
   e. None of the above
15. Storage devices can be connected to the CPU and memory via
   a. expansion slots.
   b. ports.
   c. bays.
   d. All of the above
   e. None of the above

Review Questions

1. Provide a working definition of each of the keywords listed in the "Key Terms" section. Check your answers in the glossary.
2. What is the main hardware obstacle to running xBox software on a PC?
3. Draw a block diagram showing the major components of a computer and their relationships. Briefly describe the function of each component.
4. Why is the international computer industry shifting from ASCII to Unicode for representing text?
5. Why do many PC manufacturers include graphics-processing units (GPUs) in their machines?
6. The number of cores in a CPU is one factor in determining a CPU's processing speed. What is another?
7. Explain how symmetrical multiprocessing can increase a computer's performance. Use an example or a comparison with the way people work, if you like.
8. Why do computer manufacturers typically make their new processors backward compatible with earlier processors?
9. How is a cluster of servers similar to a multicore CPU?
10. Describe several ways you can minimize your negative impact on the environment when you purchase and use a computer.

Discussion Questions

1. How is human memory similar to computer memory? How is it different?
2. Why are computer manufacturers constantly releasing faster computers? How do computer users benefit from the increased speed?
3. Does information always have value? Explain your answer.
4. Do you think the computer industry has more of a positive or negative effect on preserving global ecosystems?

Projects

1. Collect computer advertisements from newspapers, magazines, and other sources. Compare how the ads handle discussions of speed and performance. Evaluate the usefulness of the information in the ads from a consumer's point of view.
2. Use the Web to window shop for a computer. Try to determine how the choice of CPU and memory affect price and performance.
3. Interview a salesperson in a computer store. Find out what kinds of questions people ask when buying a computer. Develop profiles for the most common types of computer buyers. What kinds of computers do these customers buy, and why?
4. Systems supporting the keyboard input of Chinese can be put into three types, depending on whether they rely on encoding, pronunciation, or the structure of the characters. Research these systems, and report on the relative strengths and weaknesses of each system type.

Sources and Resources

Books

iCon Steve Jobs: The Greatest Second Act in the History of Business, by Jeffrey S. Young and William L. Simon (Wiley). Business pundits will be writing about Steve Jobs long after he has moved on from Apple and Pixar. This book tells the amazing story of his reemergence as one of the most influential visionaries of our time.

Apple Confidential 2.0: The Definitive History of the World's Most Colorful Company, by Owen Linzmayer (No Starch Press). This may be the most comprehensive history of Apple you'll find. The author has covered Apple from the early days through the dark years to its spectacular reemergence under Steve Jobs.

Inside Steve's Brain, by Leander Kahney (Portfolio). Steve Jobs is a contentious, complex, and private person who has achieved fame that rivals rock stars. *Inside Steve's Brain* is one of the better biographies of this enigmatic visionary.

iWoz: Computer Greek to Cult Icon: How I Invented the Personal Computer, Co-founded Apple, and Had Fun Doing It, by Steve Wozniak with Gina Smith (W. W. Norton). This is the story of Apple's slightly less famous Steve in (mostly) his own words.

How Computers Work, by Ron White (Que). The first edition of *How Computers Work* launched a successful series that inspired many imitators. After nine editions, this book is still a great tool for people who want to know more about what's going on inside their PCs. By combining beautiful illustrations with clear prose, *How Computers Work* takes much of the mystery out of the machine.

How Computers Work: Processor and Main Memory, by Roger Young (1st Book Library). This book is much more technical than *How Computers Work* by Ron White. If you're interested in decoding the circuit diagrams that serve as blueprints for silicon chips, this book may be a good place to start.

Inside the Machine: An Illustrated Introduction to Microprocessors and Computer Architecture, by John Stokes (No Starch Press). Computer architecture is a complex and highly technical field. Most books on the subject are written in a language only engineers can understand. This book uses color illustrations and clear prose to make the material accessible to a larger audience.

The Soul of a New Machine, by Tracy Kidder (Back Bay Books). This Pulitzer Prize–winning book provides a journalist's inside look at the making of a new computer in the late 1970s, including lots of insights into what makes computers (and computer people) tick. It's still a good read—and highly relevant.

High Tech Trash: Digital Devices, Hidden Toxics, and Human Health, by Elizabeth Grossman (Island Press). We don't like to talk about it, but we're leaving a toxic trail of digital discards behind us as we rush into the future. In this book, the author makes the case that the environmental impacts of our high-tech tools and toys "are now being felt by communities from the Arctic to Australia, with poorer countries and communities receiving a disproportionate share of the burden." Parts of the book are fairly technical, but there's also a practical appendix: "How to Recycle a Computer, Cell Phone, TV, or Other Digital Device."

The Clock of the Long Now: Time and Responsibility: The Ideas Behind the World's Slowest Computer, by Stewart Brand (Basic Books). Brand is one of the prime movers of the Long Now Foundation, an organization dedicated to promoting the long view and overcoming civilization's "pathologically short attention span." Brand's books are always thought provoking, and the foundation attracts some of the most forward-thinking people on the planet. This book presents many of the basic concepts of the Long Now.

Web Sites

www.apple.com. This site showcases Apple's hardware, software, services, and online store.

www.pixar.com. This is the site of Steve Jobs' other success story, the wildly successful computer animation company that's now part of Disney, Inc.

Check the Digital Planet Web Site, **www.pearsonhighered.com/beekman**, for links to Web sites related to this chapter's material.

3

Hardware Basics
Peripherals

OBJECTIVES

After you read this chapter you should be able to:

- List several examples of input devices and explain how they can make it easier to get different types of information into the computer
- List several examples of output devices and explain how they make computers more useful
- Explain why a typical computer has different types of storage devices
- Diagram how the components of a computer system fit together

No one gets to vote on whether technology is going to **change our lives.**

—*Bill Gates*

Bill Gates Rides the Digital Wave

In the early days of the PC revolution, Bill Gates and Paul Allen formed a company called Microsoft to produce and market a version of the BASIC programming language for personal computers, then commonly referred to as microcomputers. Microsoft BASIC quickly became the standard language installed in virtually every microcomputer.

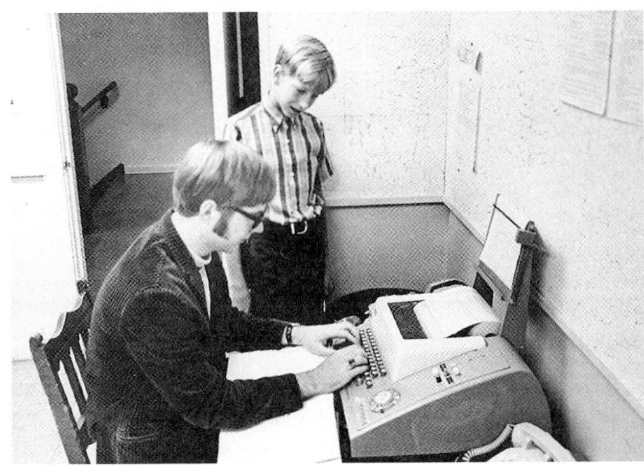

FIGURE 3.1 Bill Gates and Paul Allen as students.

When IBM went shopping for an operating system for its PC, Microsoft moved aggressively to get IBM's business. Microsoft purchased an operating system from a small company, reworked it to meet IBM's specifications, renamed it MS-DOS (for Microsoft Disk Operating System), and charged IBM only $80,000 for a nonexclusive, royalty-free license to use MS-DOS forever. Gates's goal was to make money by licensing MS-DOS to other manufacturers making PC-compatible computers. His gamble paid off. MS-DOS became the dominant operating system for the IBM PC, and Microsoft made billions of dollars providing it to other PC makers and users. In the years that followed, Microsoft's Windows replaced MS-DOS, PC shipments soared, and Microsoft became a giant corporation.

Today Microsoft dominates the PC software industry, selling operating systems, application programs, server software, and software development tools. Microsoft Windows and Microsoft Office are the two products that generate the bulk of Microsoft products. They've made Gates one of the richest men on Earth.

Microsoft's desktop dominance was threatened in the mid-1990s by the Internet explosion. For many people, computers became little more than portals into the Internet. Gates wisely responded by making the Internet a critical part of Microsoft's software strategy. Today Microsoft's desktop applications have links to the Internet, other MS applications are designed specifically for Internet use, and the company has partnerships with dozens of Web-related businesses worldwide.

Microsoft also markets keyboards, mice, game machines, music players, and other hardware devices. To prepare for an all-digital future, the company has extended its reach into all kinds of information-related business ventures, from online banking and shopping to the MSNBC cable TV network.

Many competitors and customers insist that Microsoft has used unethical business practices to ruthlessly—and sometimes illegally—stomp out competition and choice. In 1998, 20 states joined the U.S. government in a widely publicized lawsuit against Microsoft's anticompetitive practices. That same year the European Union filed two antitrust lawsuits against the company. Microsoft responded with arrogant denials and a massive PR campaign; one state official received pro-Microsoft form letters from hundreds of people, including some who had died years before. The company was found guilty of antitrust violations in the United States and the EU, but the resulting penalties had little effect on the company's dominance.

Ironically, Microsoft's digital domain is more threatened by the rise of another near-monopoly: Google. Microsoft has so far had little success in controlling the online world, where operating systems and PC applications are less important than emerging Web applications. In general, Microsoft runs a distant second to Google in search engines, Web mail, and other markets where it competes directly with Google.

FIGURE 3.2 Bill Gates.

In early 2000, Gates stepped aside as CEO of Microsoft to become the company's chairman and chief software architect. That same year he formed the Bill and Melinda Gates Foundation to channel his unprecedented wealth into global causes such as public health, education, libraries, at-risk families, and global climate change. In 2008, he left behind most of his duties at Microsoft so that he could focus full time on philanthropy work. However, he still continues to serve as Microsoft's chairman and an advisor on key development projects. When Bill Gates applies his relentless, results-driven approach to solving problems that plague the poor, he gives hope to people all over the world. ■

In this chapter, we'll complete the tour of hardware we started in the previous chapter. We've seen the CPU and memory at the heart of the system unit; now we'll explore the peripherals that radiate out from those central components. We'll start with input devices, then move on to output devices, and finish with a look at external storage devices. As usual, the main text provides the basic overview; if you want or need to know more about the inner workings, consult the How It Works boxes scattered throughout the chapter.

Input: From Person to Processor

> A computer... is an **interface** where the **mind and body can connect with the universe and move bits of it about.**
>
> —*Douglas Adams, author of* The Hitchhiker's Guide to the Galaxy

The nuts and bolts of information processing are usually hidden from the computer user, who sees only the input and output, or as the pros say, *I/O*. This wasn't always the case. Users of the first computers communicated one bit at a time by flipping switches on massive consoles or plugging wires into switchboards; they had to be intimately familiar with the inner workings of the machines before they could successfully communicate with them. In contrast, today's users have a choice of hundreds of input devices that make it easy to enter data and commands into their machines. Of these input devices, the most familiar is the computer **keyboard**.

The Keyboard

In spite of nearly universal acceptance as an input device, the QWERTY keyboard (named for the top row of letter keys) seems strangely out of place in a modern computer system. The weird arrangement of letters dates back to the earliest manual typewriters. The letter layout was chosen to reduce typing speed, making it less likely that a typist would hit two keys at the same time and cause the machine to jam. Technological traditions die hard, and the QWERTY keyboard became standard equipment on typewriters and later on virtually all PCs.

Some computer keyboards stray from the traditional typewriter design to save wear and tear on our bodies. Typing on a standard keyboard, with keys lined up in straight rows, forces you to hold your arms and wrists at unnatural angles. Evidence suggests that long hours of typing this way may lead to medical problems, including **repetitive-stress injuries**, such as tendonitis and carpal tunnel syndrome. **Ergonomic keyboards** place the keys at angles that are easier on your arms and hands without changing the ordering of the keys.

Whether it's straight or ergonomic, a typical keyboard sends signals to the computer through a cable of some sort—most commonly a USB cable. A battery-powered ***wireless keyboard*** doesn't need a cable connecting it to the rest of the system. Many wireless keyboards use a radio technology called Bluetooth (described in Chapter 8).

Other variations on keyboard design include miniature keyboards built into pocket-sized devices, screens on phones or laser projections that display keys that react to touch or movement, one-handed keyboards for people who need to (or prefer to) keep one hand free for other work, and keyboards printed on membranes that can be rolled or folded like paper. Innovative ideas are still emerging from that ancient typewriter technology.

Regardless of its design, a keyboard has keys for typing letters, numbers, and special characters, and

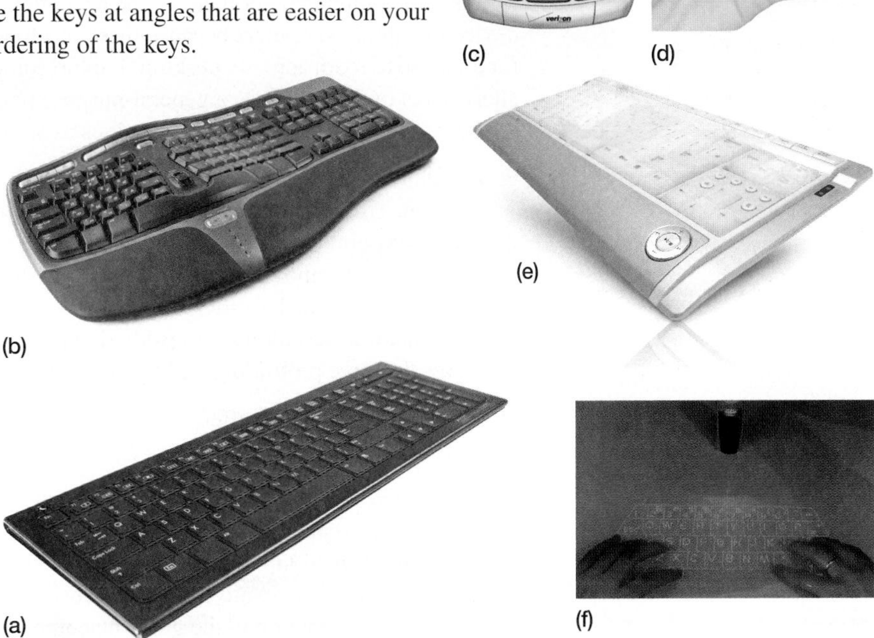

FIGURE 3.3 (clockwise from lower left) a. A standard wireless computer keyboard has a straight row of keys. b. An ergonomic keyboard puts the keys at an angle to allow your wrists to assume a more natural position while you type. c. Many pocket computers and phones, such as the BlackBerry, have QWERTY keyboards, even though they are too small for touch typing. d. The iPhone, like many smart phones, displays a keyboard on a touch-sensitive screen when needed to input text. e. The keys on the Luxeed Dynamic Pixel LED keyboard can be individually set to glow or be animated in different colors depending on the software being used. f. The Virtual Laser Keyboard (VKB) can turn just about any flat surface into a QWERTY keyboard.

Command	Windows Shortcut	Mac Shortcut
Open	Ctrl-O	Cmd-O
Print	Ctrl-P	Cmd-P
Select All	Ctrl-A	Cmd-A
New (window, document)	Ctrl-N	Cmd-N
Save	Ctrl-S	Cmd-S
Copy	Ctrl-C	Cmd-C
Cut	Ctrl-X	Cmd-X
Paste	Ctrl-V	Cmd-V
Close Window	Ctrl-W	Cmd-W
Bold (selected text)	Ctrl-B	Cmd-B
Italic (selected text)	Ctrl-I	Cmd-I

FIGURE 3.4 Common Keyboard Shortcuts.

other keys that can modify meanings of keystrokes. For example, holding the Shift key while pressing the *s* key types a capital *S*, while Ctrl+S tells a Windows application to save the current document. A keystroke just causes a digital signal to be sent to the computer; it's up to the software to assign a meaning to that signal.

Pointing Devices

Computer users today use keyboards mostly to enter text and numeric data. For other functions, such as sending commands and positioning the cursor, they typically use a mouse or an alternative pointing device. The **mouse** is designed to move a pointer around the screen and point to specific characters or objects. The typical mouse uses reflected light and an optical sensing device to detect movement.

Most mice have two or more buttons. In a standard configuration, the left button sends standard "click" and "drag" messages, while the right button is used to issue additional commands. A mouse may contain a scroll wheel between the two buttons to streamline the process of scrolling through documents. Apple's Magic Mouse has no visible buttons, but its touch-sensitive shell can detect left-clicks, right-clicks, and multi-touch gestures (see next section). For most mice, software can be used to customize the functions of various buttons. ***Wireless mice*** use Bluetooth or other wireless frequencies (see Chapter 8) to send their signals; they require batteries to power tiny radio transmitters.

It's virtually impossible to find a new computer today that doesn't come with a mouse as standard equipment, but there is one exception: The mouse is impractical as a pointing device on laptop computers because these machines are often used where there's no room for a mouse to roam across a desktop. Laptop computer manufacturers provide a variety of alternatives to the mouse as a general-purpose pointing device, and some of these devices are becoming popular as desktop solutions as well:

- The **touchpad** (sometimes called ***trackpad***) is a small flat panel that's sensitive to light pressure. The user moves the pointer by dragging a finger across the pad.
- The **trackpoint** is a tiny handle that sits in the center of the keyboard, responding to finger pressure by moving the pointer in the direction in which you push it. It's like a miniature embedded joystick.
- The **trackball** resembles an upside-down mouse. It remains stationary while the user moves the large protruding ball to control the pointer on the screen.

Other pointing devices offer advantages for specific types of computer work (and play). Here are some examples:

- ***Game controllers*** come in a variety of forms. A ***joystick*** is a gearshift-like device used to control movement in arcade games and flight simulators. A ***gamepad*** is a multibutton device that is held in both hands and typically includes a small joystick. The Nintendo Wii remote is an innovative three-dimensional pointing device that sends position and movement information to the game machine.
- The **graphics tablet** is popular with artists and designers. Most touch tablets are pressure sensitive, so they can send different signals depending on how hard the user presses on the tablet with a stylus. The ***stylus*** also performs the same point-and-click functions as a mouse.
- The **touch screen** responds when the user points to or touches different screen regions. Computers with touch screens are frequently used in public libraries, airports, and shopping malls, where many users are unfamiliar with computers. Touch screens are also used in many handheld computers and smart phones.

FIGURE 3.5 Popular pointing devices. a. The Microsoft mouse, like most mice, has multiple buttons and a scroll wheel to streamline the process of scrolling through documents or graphical windows. b. Apple's Magic Mouse has no visible buttons, but the pressure-sensitive surface responds like a multibutton mouse and recognizes multi-touch gestures. c. Many laptops, including this HP Pavilion, have a built-in touchpad as a pointing device. d. The Lenovo ThinkPad has a tiny pointing stick called a trackpoint, embedded in the center of its keyboard. e. A trackball is an alternative pointing device for a PC. f. A joystick can be used to control movements in arcade games and flight simulators. g. A game controller typically includes several buttons and joystick-like controls. h. A graphics tablet uses a stylus as a pointing, writing, and drawing tool. i. Touch screen displays are often used in kiosks, ATM machines, self-service retail devices, smart phones, and tablet devices.

Multi-Touch Input Devices

Sometimes pointing isn't enough. With a **multi-touch** input device, it's possible to use multi-finger or multi-hand gestures to accomplish complex tasks quickly. A multi-touch device might be a touch-sensitive screen, a touch tablet, or a trackpad that can recognize the position, pressure, and movement of more than one finger or hand at a time.

Probably the best known example of a multi-touch device is the screen of Apple's iPhone. Multi-touch technology enables the iPhone's tiny screen to recognize two-fingered movements and gestures. The phone's software can interpret those movements and gestures as complex commands. For example, zooming in for a close-up view of part of a map is as simple as spreading two fingers apart on the map. The iPhone was the first popular consumer device with multi-touch capability, but many other smart phones have similar technology built in today.

Many manufacturers use multi-touch technology in laptop trackpads and tablet computer touchscreens. A multi-touch trackpad is more than a simple pointing device. Multi-touch gestures and movements can trigger a variety of complex operations, depending on how the computer's software interprets them. For example, you might be able to rotate a photo by simply "touching" opposite corners of the picture and rotating your fingers, just as you would with a physical photograph on a smooth table.

Multi-touch input is also useful in many professional applications. For example, the Lemur Jazzmutant gives a musician or multimedia artist the freedom to control multiple devices, sounds, or images simultaneously. An audio or video technician can replace a myriad of knobs, switches, and sliders with a well-designed multi-touch device.

One of the most ambitious products based on multi-touch technology is Microsoft's Surface. Surface is, in essence, a computer embedded in a table with a large touch-sensitive tabletop that serves as the monitor. Surface is initially designed for use by restaurants,

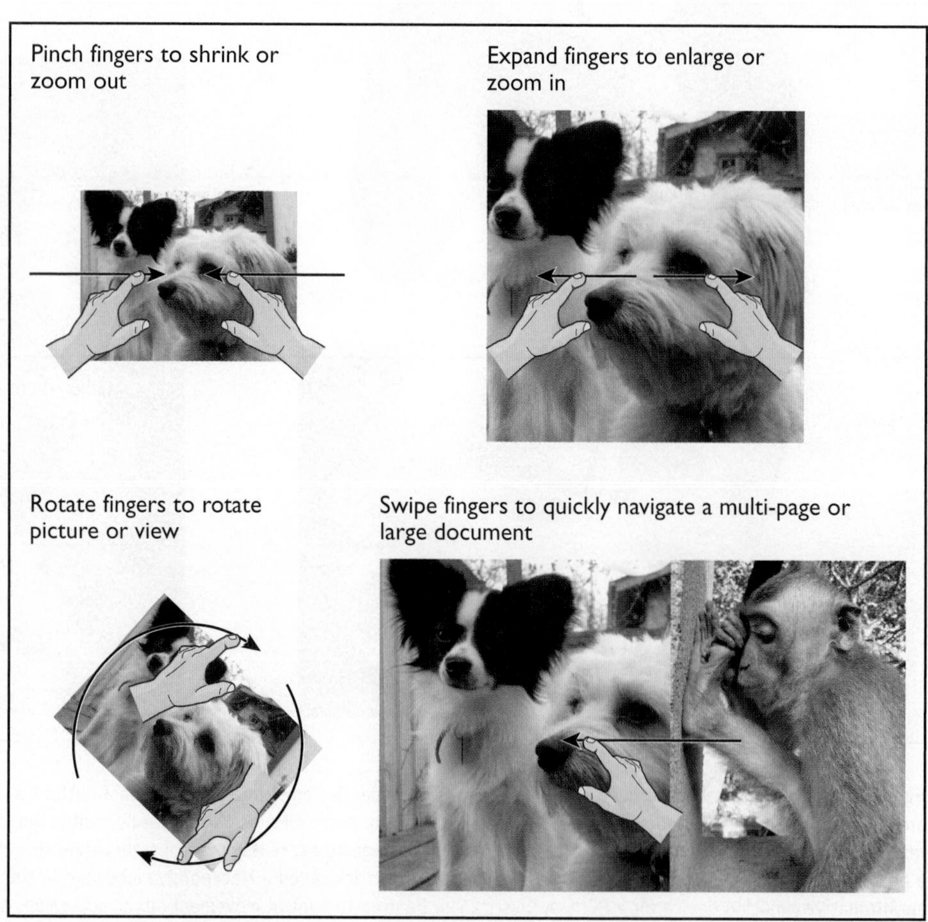

FIGURE 3.6 Common multi-touch gestures.

hotels, retail stores, and military applications. Surface can recognize 50 or more touches at a time, and can be programmed to recognize many physical objects. For example, it might display a wine menu when a diner sets a wine glass on its surface.

Futuristic multi-touch technology has appeared in science fiction films such as *Minority Report* and *Avatar*. As the technology develops and prices drop, it will undoubtedly become common in business machines, home entertainment systems, appliances, and other electronic devices.

Reading Tools

In spite of their versatility, pointing devices are woefully inefficient for the input of large quantities of text into computers, which is why the mouse hasn't replaced the keyboard on the standard PC. Still, there are alternatives to typing

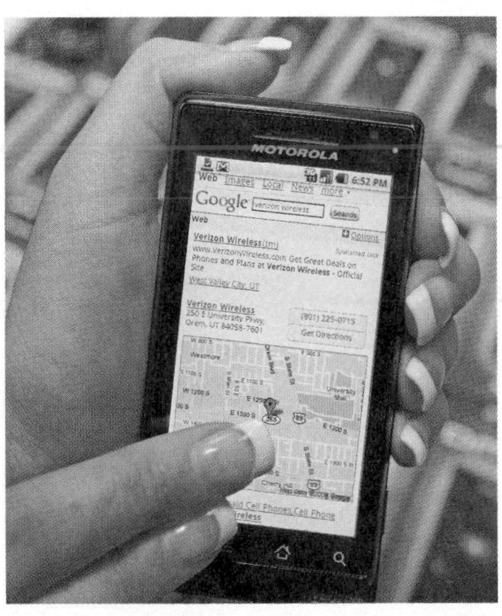

(a)

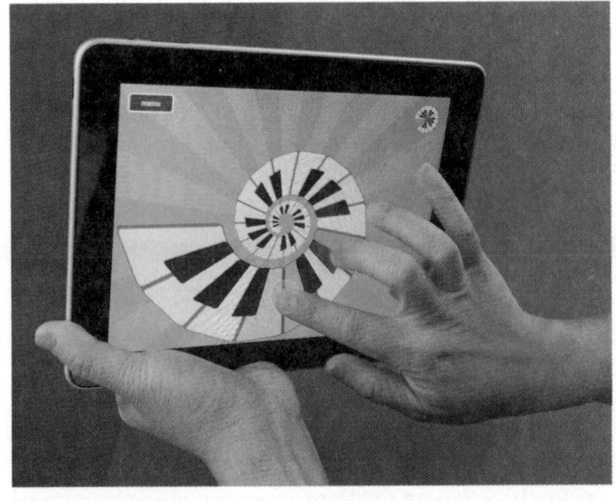

(b)

(c)

(d)

(e)

FIGURE 3.7 Multitouch input devices. a. The Motorola Droid is one of many smart phones that uses multi-touch technology. b. The glass screen on Apple's iPad recognizes a variety of one- and two-fingered movements. c. Many laptops and netbooks include multitouch trackpads or multitouch displays that can interpret a variety of multidigit gestures as commands. d. Lemur's Jazzmutant is a popular multi-touch control surface for musicians, multimedia artists, and technicians. e. In this mockup of a future application, pictures pour out of a camera phone placed on Microsoft Surface, where they can be sorted, rearranged, and resized using simple hand gestures.

FIGURE 3.8 Computers use specialized input devices to read information stored as optical marks, bar codes, and specially designed characters.

for entering numbers and words into computers. Some types of devices, specifically designed for computer input, allow computers to read marks rapidly that represent codes:

- **Optical mark readers** use reflected light to determine the location of pencil marks on standardized test answer sheets and similar forms.
- **Magnetic ink character readers** read those odd-shaped numbers printed with magnetic ink on checks.
- **Bar code readers** use light to read *universal product codes (UPCs)*, inventory codes, and other codes created from patterns of variable-width bars. In many stores, bar code readers are attached to **point-of-sale (POS) terminals**. These terminals send scanned information to a mainframe computer. The computer determines the item's price, calculates taxes and totals, and records the transaction for future use in inventory, accounting, and other areas.
- **Radio frequency identification (RFID) readers** use radio waves to communicate with **radio frequency identification (RFID) tags**. When energized by a nearby RFID reader, an RFID tag broadcasts its unique identification number to the reader, which digitizes the information for input into a computer. An RFID tag can be as large as a deck of cards or as small as a grain of rice. Larger tags can be read from a greater distance. The hard plastic antitheft cards attached to clothes at department stores contain RFID tags. RFID tags are also used to identify railroad cars, automobiles at toll booths, library books at checkout counters, and pallets of goods being shipped to stores.

Because test forms, magnetic ink characters, bar codes, and RFID tags were designed to be read by computers, the devices that read them are extremely accurate. Reading text from books, magazines, and other printed documents is more challenging because of the great variety of printed text. **Optical character recognition (OCR)** is the technology of recognizing individual characters on a printed page, so they can be stored and edited as text.

Before a computer can recognize handwriting or printed text, it must first create a digital image of the page that it can store in memory. This is usually done with an input device known as a *scanner*. There are many types of scanners, as you'll see in the next section. A scanner doesn't actually read or recognize letters and numbers on a page—it just makes a digital "picture" of the page available to the computer. The computer can then use OCR software to interpret the black-and-white scanned patterns as letters and numbers.

Actually, a few special-purpose scanners take care of the OCR work themselves. *Pen scanners* look like highlighters, but they're actually wireless scanners that can perform character recognition on the fly. When you drag a pen scanner across a line of printed text, it creates a text file in its built-in memory, where it's stored until you transfer it into your computer's memory through a cable or wireless connection. A wireless pen scanner actually contains a small computer programmed to recognize printed text. This kind of optical character recognition isn't 100 percent accurate, but it's getting better all the time.

FIGURE 3.9 This self-service POS terminal uses three input devices for gathering information about a purchase: A touch screen for entering commands and answering questions, a bar code reader for scanning product information, and a scale for security and accuracy. Before the transaction is completed, another input device reads information encoded in the magnetic strip on the customer's credit card.

FIGURE 3.10 A pen scanner can capture text from a printed document and transfer it to a PC.

Handwriting recognition is far more difficult and error prone than printed character recognition is. But handwriting recognition has many practical applications today, especially in tablet PCs. A tablet PC can work without a keyboard and can accept input from a stylus applied directly to a flat-panel screen. The computer electronically simulates the effect of using a pen and pad of paper. **Handwriting recognition software** translates the user's handwritten forms into computer-readable characters. In the past, such systems required users to modify their handwriting so that it was consistent and unambiguous enough for the software to decipher reliably. Today's handwriting-recognition devices are much more forgiving and accurate.

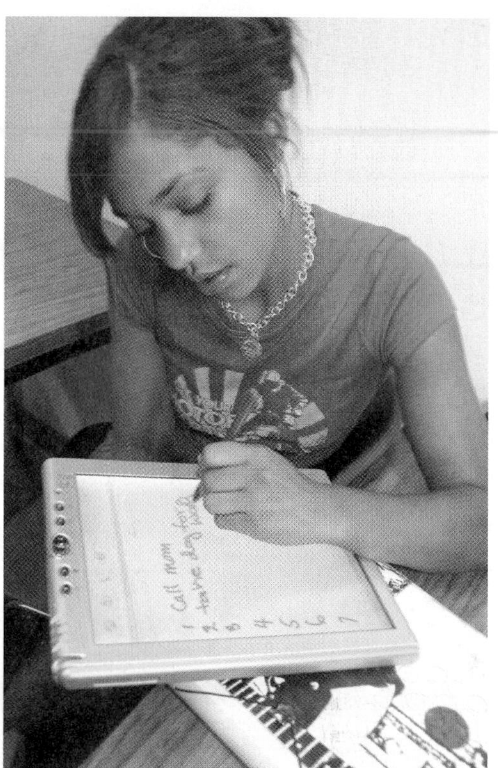

FIGURE 3.11 A Tablet PC is a computer with stylus or finger touch input capabilities.

Digitizing Devices and Sensors

Because real-world information comes in so many forms, a variety of input devices have been designed for capturing and **digitizing** information—converting it into a digital form. In this section we'll examine several of these devices, from common scanners to exotic sensors.

A **scanner** is an input device that can create a digital representation of typed text, handwritten text, graphics, and objects. The most common models today are *flatbed scanners*, which look and work like photocopy machines, except that they create computer files instead of paper copies. (In the section on printers later in the chapter, we'll discuss printer/scanner/copier/fax all-in-one devices.) Inexpensive flatbed scanners are designed for home and small-business use. More expensive professional models are capable of producing higher-quality reproductions of paper documents and, with attachments, photographic negatives and slides.

Some scanners, called *film scanners* can scan only slides and negatives; they're used in professional settings where batches of slides or negatives need to be converted into collections of high-quality digital images. *Drum scanners* are larger and more expensive than flatbeds are; they're used for museum archival and high-end publishing, where image quality is critical. Regardless of its type or capabilities, a scanner converts photographs, drawings, charts, and other printed information into bit patterns that can be stored and manipulated in a computer's memory.

In the same way, a **digital camera** can capture snapshots of the real world as digital images. A digital camera stores bit patterns on flash memory cards or other digital storage media. Similarly, a *digital video camera* (or camcorder) can digitize and store video (and audio) signals on a memory

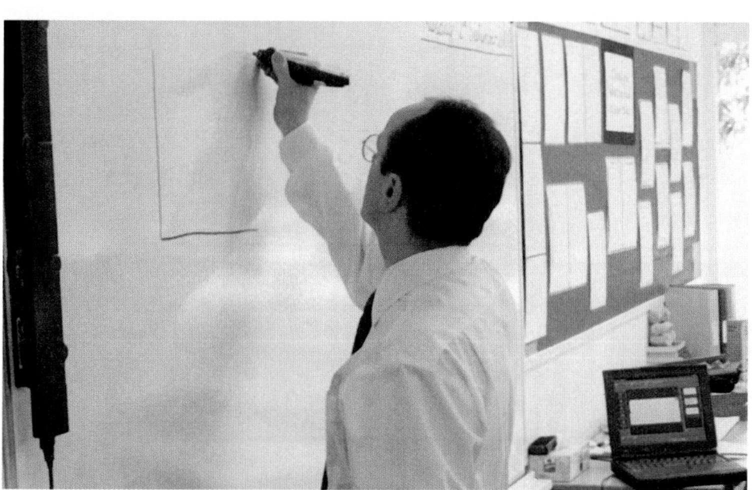

FIGURE 3.12 A smart whiteboard can send its contents to a PC, simplifying and streamlining the note-taking process for meetings and classes.

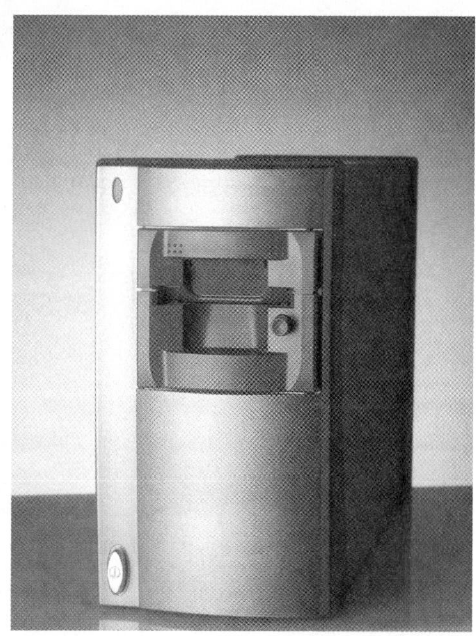

FIGURE 3.13 A slide scanner can capture and digitize images from photographic negatives and slides.

card, disc, or tape. Most digital cameras today can take digital videos, and most digital camcorders can take still pictures, so the line between these two types of devices is blurring. Many phones can capture digital images and videos, although they generally can't compete with stand-alone cameras for image quality.

However they are created, digital photos and videos can be transferred from camera to computer, where they can be stored, edited, and viewed using software described in later chapters. It's possible to transfer video from older analog camcorders and VHS players into a computer, but not without a separate *video digitizer* to convert the analog signals into digital data.

One type of digital video camera, commonly called a *webcam*, is either attached to or built into a computer monitor; it can't function as a stand-alone camera. Webcams are typically used for capturing and posting images or videos to the Web and for desktop *videoconferencing*. With videoconferencing software and hardware, people in diverse locations can see and hear each other while they conduct long-distance meetings; their video images are transmitted through networks.

Sounds, like images, can be captured into memory and processed by computers, provided they first are digitized—converted into digital data. Virtually all modern PCs contain circuitry to convert audio signals from microphones or other sound sources into digital signals.

FIGURE 3.14 Digital cameras. a. Consumer cameras sell for a few hundred dollars or less; professional models can cost much more. b. Many mobile phones include picture- and movie-taking capabilities and can send these images to other phone users. c. A webcam can continuously feed still pictures or video directly to a PC or Mac. d. Digital video cameras can deliver video directly to a PC or Mac. e. This laptop includes a built-in webcam above the screen.

Many PCs include built-in microphones. Some sound sources—USB microphones, digital recorders, professional sound mixers, and smart phones—provide digital signals that don't need to be digitized by the computer's internal circuitry.

Of course, audio digitizers can capture spoken words as well as music and sound effects. But digitizing spoken input isn't the same thing as converting speech into text. Like scanned text input, digitized *voice input* is just data to the computer. *Speech recognition* software, a type of artificial intelligence software, can convert voice data into words that can be edited and printed. Speech recognition software has been available for years, but until recently it wasn't reliable enough to be of much practical use. The latest products are too limited to replace keyboards for most people. They generally work best when the speaker articulates clearly in a quiet environment, the program has been trained to recognize an individual's speech patterns, or input is limited to preset vocabulary (such as in a telephone menu system). However, they are invaluable for people with disabilities and others who can't use their hands while they work. The promise and problems of automated speech recognition will be explored in later chapters.

One way to think about input devices is to compare them to our sensory organs. A webcam or digital camera capturing visual information is like an eye to the computer, while a microphone allows the computer to "hear." Engineers have developed a variety of devices that provide computers with other "senses." These **sensors** measure or detect real-world conditions—temperature, humidity, motion, pressure, radioactivity, or even odor—and provide computers with digital representations of those conditions.

Sometimes sensors are used simply to help a computer or electronic device function better. Many computers use heat sensors to determine when to turn on internal cooling fans. Many laptops contain *accelerometers* that can detect rapid motion changes so hard drives can be protected from hard falls. Pressure sensors tell the Roomba robotic vacuum cleaner when it's close to stairs and other hazards.

Sensors also unlock entirely new applications for computers and digital devices. The sensors in Guitar Hero's game controller detect a player's finger positioning and gestures. The Nintendo Wii game controller includes a motion detector that enables it to recognize gestures and other movements, so it can behave like a virtual golf club, bowling ball, or light saber. The iPhone's accelerometer makes it possible to shuffle an audio playlist with a shake, switch to a wider landscape view of an image with a twist, scroll through a document with a twist, or use the phone as a carpenter's level. Similar technology makes it possible for antishake technology in a digital camera to prevent many blurry photos.

FIGURE 3.15 Audio input devices. a. This microphone plugs into the computer's USB port. b. This digital recorder stores digital audio signals on flash memory cards so they can be transferred to a PC for processing and playback.

FIGURE 3.16 Because of a brain injury, Logan Olson has difficulty using a keyboard. Speech recognition software makes it easier for her to publish her magazine for disabled women.

how it works Digitizing the Real World

We live in an analog world, where we can perceive smooth, continuous changes in color and sound. Digital computers store all information as discrete binary numbers. To store analog information in a computer, we must digitize it—convert it from analog to digital form.

Digitizing involves using an input device, such as a digital camera or recorder, to take millions of tiny samples of the original image or sound. A sample of an image might be one pinpoint-sized area of the image; each sample from an audio source is like a brief recording of the sound at a particular instant. The digitizing device might be inside the computer (a sound chip or sound card) or outside the computer (a digital camera). Either way, the digitization process must be completed before the computer can work with the data.

The value of a sample can be represented numerically and, therefore, stored on a computer. A representation of the original image or sound can be reconstructed by assembling all the samples in sequence.

In the example below, you can see how a digital camera, a microphone, and a computer can capture photographs and sound recordings of a wolf.

ANALOG INPUT

A digital camera captures the wolf's image.

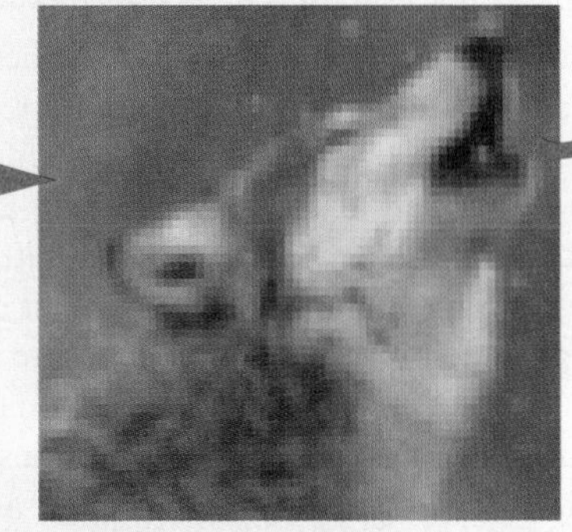

Inside the camera, the image is mapped onto a grid of tiny cells called pixels. Filters separate light into the three primary colors: red, blue, and green. A *CCD (charge-coupled device)* or *CMOS (complimentary metal oxide semiconductor)* converts light into electrons. An *analog-to-digital converter (ADC)* converts the electrical charges into discrete values. A single byte (eight bits) represents the intensity of each primary color; a three-byte code represents the color of each pixel. After compression, the byte codes are stored as a JPEG file.

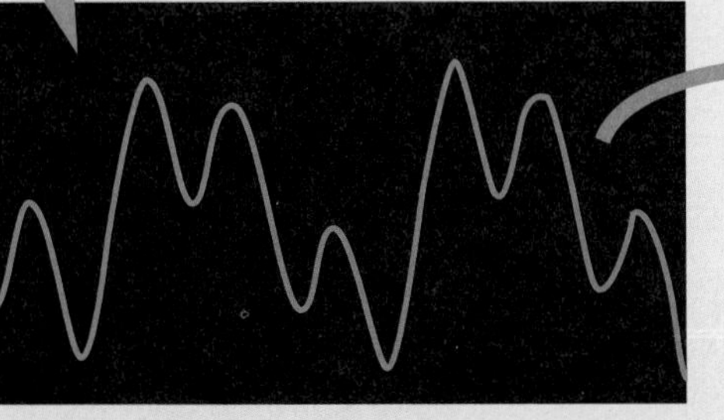

A microphone transmits the wolf's howl to an analog-to-digital converter (ADC). The ADC might be built into the microphone (common for USB mics) or on a circuit board inside the computer.

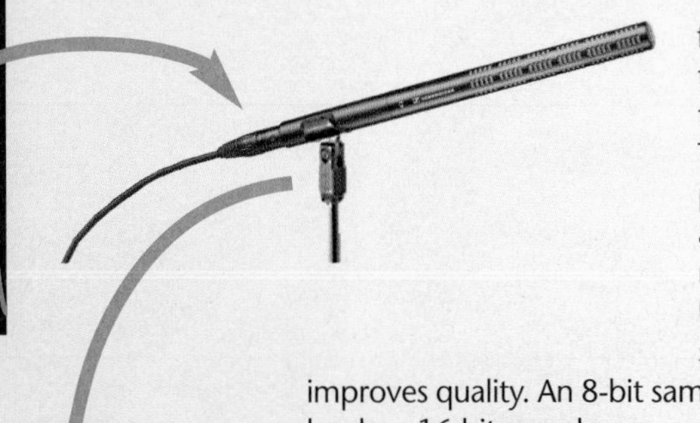

The ADC samples the wave frequently—44,000 or more times per second—and stores the sound level as a number. The higher (faster) the sampling frequency is, the more accurately the digital recording represents the original sound. Using more storage to represent the sound level also improves quality. An 8-bit sample can represent 256 different levels; a 16-bit sample can represent 65,536 different levels.

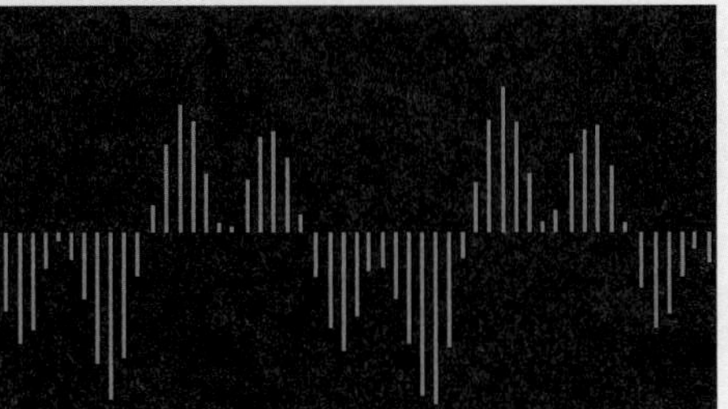

A *DSP (digital signal processor)* compresses the stream of bits before it is transmitted to the CPU.

FIGURE 3.17

DIGITAL REPRESENTATION

ANALOG OUTPUT

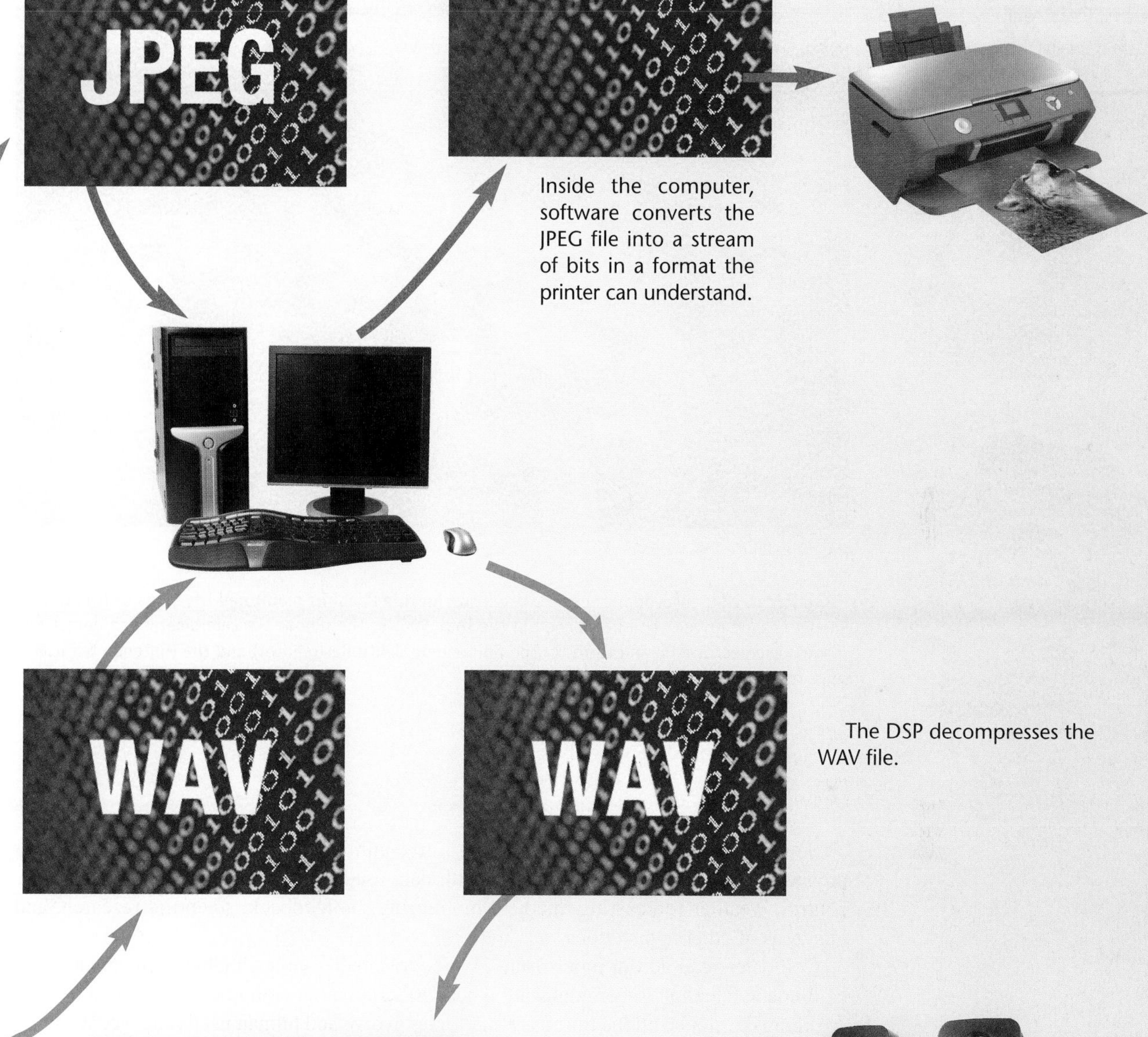

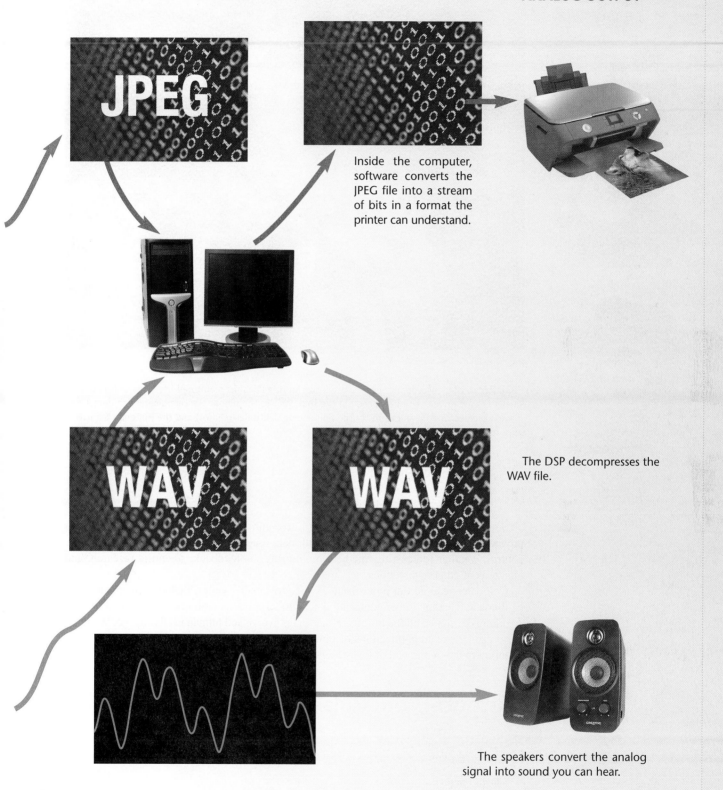

Inside the computer, software converts the JPEG file into a stream of bits in a format the printer can understand.

The DSP decompresses the WAV file.

The speakers convert the analog signal into sound you can hear.

A *DAC (digital-to-analog converter)* converts the digitized wave form into an analog signal. The DAC might be part of the computer's internal circuitry or (for USB speakers) built into the speakers.

(a)

(c)

(b)

FIGURE 3.18 Sensor input devices. a. Sensors in this LifeShirt monitored life signs of this Indy Racing League driver when he crashed in the Indy 500. b. The iPhone's accelerometer can detect shakes, wiggles, twists, and turns. c. The Guitar Hero controller (shown) and the Nintendo Wii use sensors to track each player's movements.

Sensors designed to monitor temperature, humidity, pressure, motion, and other physical quantities provide computers with data used in robotics, environmental climate control, weather forecasting, medical monitoring, biofeedback, scientific research, and hundreds of other applications.

Computers can accept input from a variety of other sources, including manufacturing equipment, telephones, communication networks, and other computers. New input devices are being developed all the time as technologies evolve and human needs change. We'll see more examples and applications of input devices in later chapters; for now we turn our attention to the output end of the process.

Output: From Pulses to People

As a rule, men **worry more about what they can't see** than about what they can.

—*Julius Caesar*

A computer can do all kinds of things, but none of them is worth anything to us unless we have a way to get the results out of the box. Output devices convert the computer's internal bit patterns into a form that humans can understand. The first computers were limited to flashing lights, teletypes, and other primitive communication devices. Most computers today produce output through two main types of devices: display screens for immediate visual output and printers for permanent paper output.

Screen Output

The **display**, also called a **monitor**, serves as a one-way window between the computer user and the machine. Early computer displays were designed to display characters—text, numbers, and tiny graphic symbols. Today's displays are as likely to present graphics, photographic images, animation, and video as they are to display text and numbers.

Display size, like television size, is measured as the length of a diagonal line across the screen; a typical desktop display today measures from 17 to 30 or more inches diagonally, but the actual viewable area is often smaller. Images on a display are composed of tiny dots, called *pixels* (for picture elements). A square inch of an image on a display is typically a grid of about 96 pixels on each side. Such a monitor has a **resolution** of 96 dots per inch (dpi). Higher-resolution screens display clearer images because the pixels are closer together.

Another way to describe resolution is to refer to the total number of pixels displayed on the screen. Assuming that two displays are the same size, the one that places the dots closer together displays more pixels and creates a sharper, clearer image. When describing resolution in this way, people usually indicate the number of columns and rows of pixels rather than the total number of pixels. For example, a 1,024 × 768 image is composed of 1,024 columns by 768 rows of pixels, for a total of 786,432 pixels.

Over the years, display resolutions have risen with improvements in technology. A decade ago a standard PC monitor was 640 × 480. Today a 640 × 480 image wouldn't cover half of a typical PC's screen. Larger, higher-resolution screens make it easier to work with large documents; they also make it possible to view more documents at the same time. The end result, according to research, is a general increase in productivity.

Today's monitor is also likely to have a different aspect ratio than the one it replaced. The *aspect ratio* is the fractional relationship between the width and height of a display. Older monitors, like older TVs, typically had aspect ratios of 4 × 3 (or 4:3), so the image was only 1/3 wider than it was tall. Today's widescreen monitors are more likely to have something closer to a 16 × 9 aspect ratio—the standard for most high-definition TV (HDTV) programming. Besides improving the viewing experience for movies and TV programs, widescreen monitors make it easier to work with two or more documents at the same time.

Many older computers use **cathode-ray tube (CRT) monitors** that resemble twentieth-century televisions. But today virtually all new monitors use flat-screen **liquid crystal display (LCD)** technology. **Video projectors** also use LCDs to project computer screen images for meetings and classes. (Not all projectors use LCD displays; some pocket projectors use laser technology to beam images onto screens.)

Many PCs are capable of driving multiple monitors. For example, a laptop might have a display port (and additional graphics circuitry) so a monitor or projector can be used alongside the built-in display. The second display might *mirror* the contents of the main monitor (so, for example, it could be viewed by an audience). Or the second monitor might *extend* the main display so that more documents are visible at a time. System software allows the user to switch between these two options.

Most PCs today have all of the necessary video circuitry built into the motherboard. But in some tower systems the video ports and video controllers are on removable *video cards*. Plug-in video cards are most popular with gamers, 3-D designers, and video professionals who need high-end video capabilities.

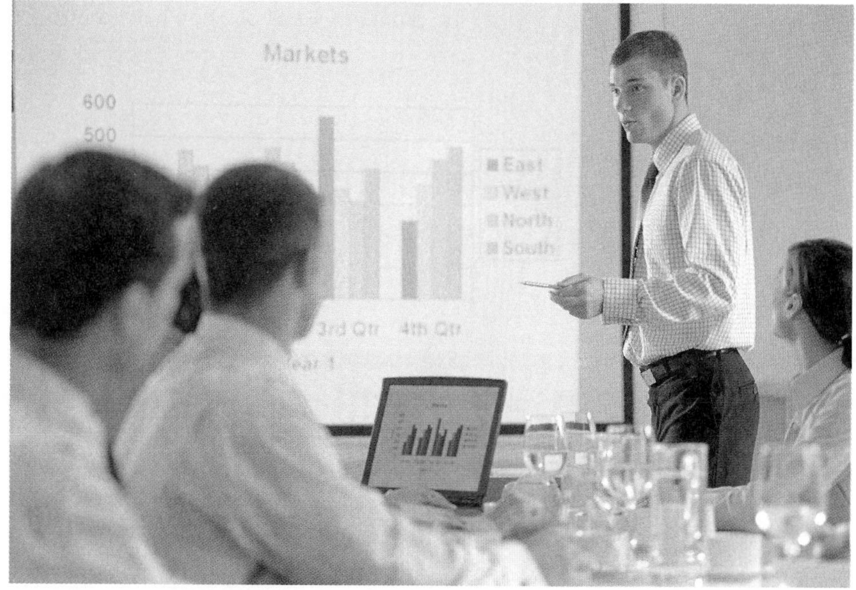

FIGURE 3.19 This laptop has circuitry to support a second monitor or projector. The projector in this case mirrors what we see on the laptop screen.

how it works Color Display

An image on a computer display is made up of rows of tiny colored pixels. LCD pixels are square and CRT pixels are round, but they're so small that they don't appear as individual squares or circles to us. A monitor's image is refreshed many times per second; with each refresh, the color displayed by each pixel might change.

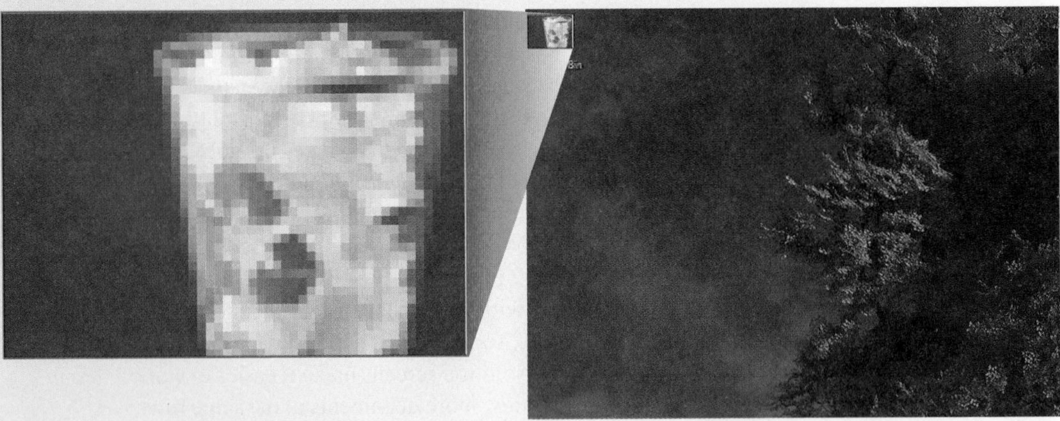

Each pixel is made up of a mixture of red, green, and blue light. A pixel with maximum values of red, green, and blue appears white; a pixel with maximum red and blue but no green appears magenta; and so on. By varying the luminosity (brightness) of the three colored lights that make up each pixel, a monitor can display millions of unique colors. This process of creating colors by combining colored lights is called additive color synthesis.

Additive color synthesis is really a kind of optical illusion. Pixels that combine red and green light appear to the human eye to be yellow, even though the light they produce is not truly yellow.

Red, green, and blue are the three additive primary colors. Additive color synthesis that is based on red, green, and blue uses the *RGB color model*.

The RGB color model is device dependent—an image might look different on two different monitors because of the way the primary colors are generated. Graphic designers and photographers depend on color management hardware and software to fine-tune displays so they're consistent with each other and with other output devices. Image editing programs like Photoshop have controls for adjusting RGB values in individual images.

FIGURE 3.20

Paper Output

Output displayed on a monitor is immediate but temporary. A **printer** can produce a hard copy on paper of any static information that can be displayed on the computer's screen. Printers come in several varieties, but they all fit into two basic groups: impact printers and nonimpact printers.

Impact printers form images by physically striking paper, ribbon, and print hammer together, the way a typewriter does. Mainframes use **line printers** to print bills, forms, and reports; these speedy, noisy beasts hammer out thousands of lines of text per minute, but can't print graphic images. Instead of printing each character as a solid object, a **dot matrix printer** uses pinpoint-sized hammers to transfer ink to the page, so it can print low-resolution graphics as well as text.

Except for those applications, such as billing, where multipart forms need to be printed, **nonimpact printers** have replaced impact printers in most offices, schools, and homes. The two main types of nonimpact printers are laser printers and inkjet printers. **Laser printers** can quickly print numerous pages per minute of high-quality text and graphical output. Because of their speed, durability, and reliability, they're often shared among PCs in office environments. Laser printers use the same technology as photocopy machines: A laser beam creates patterns of electrical charges on a rotating drum; those charged patterns attract black toner and transfer it to paper as the drum rotates. Color laser printers can print multicolor images by mixing different toner shades.

Inkjet printers spray ink directly onto paper to produce printed text and graphic images. Inkjet printers are smaller and lighter than laser printers. Portable inkjet printers designed to travel with laptops weigh only a couple of pounds each. Specialized inkjets called **photo printers** are designed to print high-quality photos captured with digital cameras and scanners; these printouts are often indistinguishable from the photos you might order from a professional photo-printing service.

Inkjet printers are popular with home users and others whose printing needs are light to medium. High-quality color inkjet printers cost far less than color laser printers. But for businesses and others with heavy print loads, lasers tend to be more cost-effective because of the lower *cost per page* for consumables. The ink used in an inkjet printout costs, on average, more than the toner used to print the same image with a laser printer. Inkjets also generally print fewer pages per minute than laser printers do.

Both laser and inkjet printers produce high-resolution output—usually 600 or more dots per inch. At these resolutions, it's hard to tell that characters and pictures are, in fact, composed of dots.

Multifunction printers (MFP), also called *all-in-one devices*, take advantage of the fact that different tools can use similar technologies. A multifunction printer usually combines a scanner, a laser or inkjet printer, and a fax modem (described in the next section). Such a device can serve as a printer, a scanner, a color photocopy machine, and a fax machine.

One other type of nonimpact printer, the *thermal printer*, can't compete with inkjet and laser printers for image quality. Thermal printers print images by selectively heating coated thermal paper. They're relatively fast and quiet. Thermal printers are common in gas station pumps, ATM machines, and point-of-sale terminals.

For certain scientific, engineering, and design applications, a **plotter** is more appropriate than a printer for producing hard copy. A plotter is an automated drawing tool that can produce large, finely scaled drawings, engineering blueprints, and maps by moving the pen and/or the paper in response to computer commands.

Fax Machines and Fax Modems

A **facsimile (fax) machine** is a tool for long-distance copying of paper documents. When you send a fax of a paper document, the sending fax machine scans each page, converting the scanned image into a series of electronic pulses and sending those signals over phone lines to another fax machine. The receiving fax machine uses the signals to construct and print black-and-white facsimiles of the original pages. In a sense, a pair of connected fax machines serves as a long-distance photocopy machine.

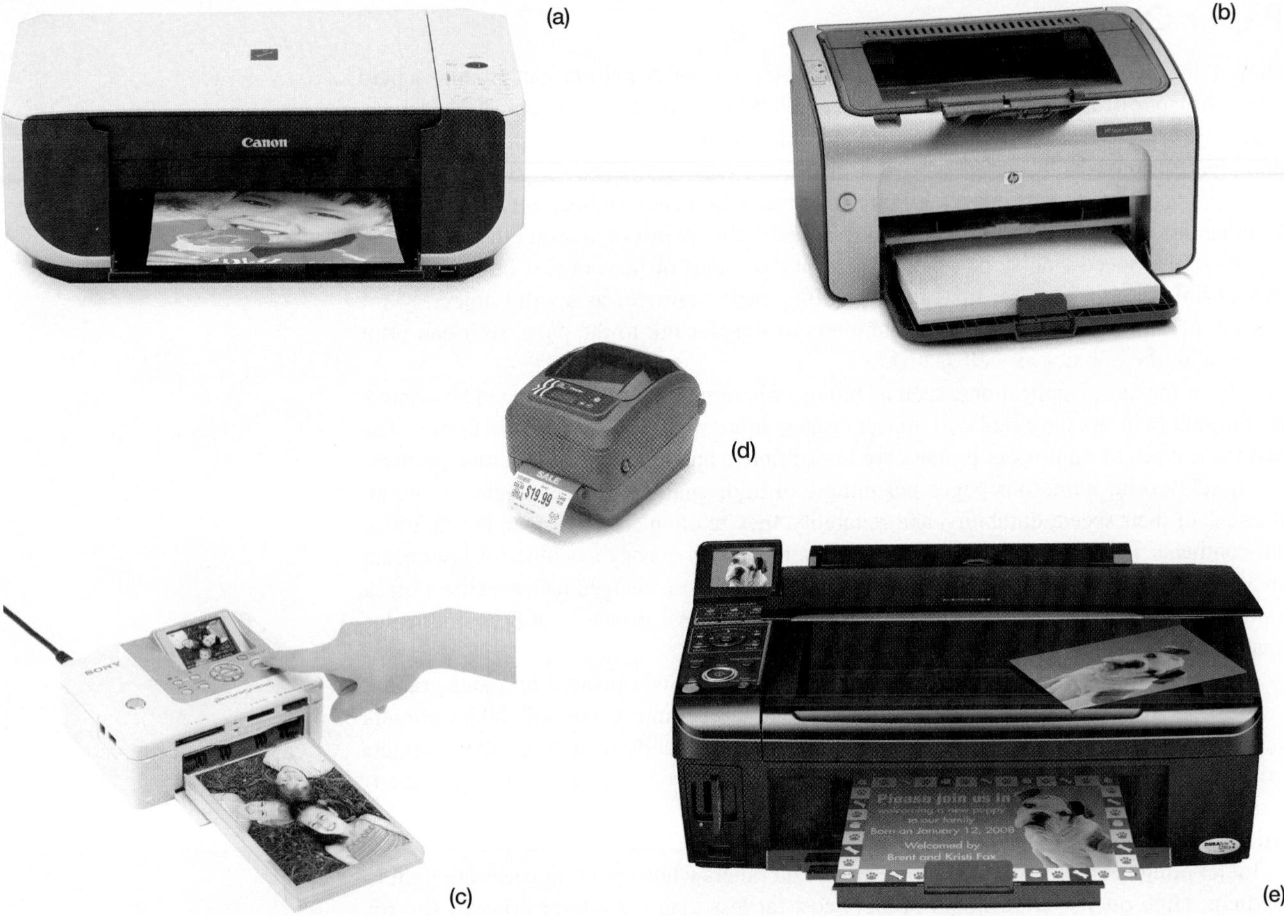

FIGURE 3.21 Printers. a and b. Inkjet printers and laser printers are both widely used for printing black-and-white and color documents in offices and homes. c. Some inkjets are specifically designed for printing photographs. d. Thermal printers are typically used to print receipts at point-of-sale terminals and gas pumps. e. Multifunction printers combine the functions of printers, copiers, scanners, and fax machines.

A computer can send on-screen documents through a fax modem or an Internet connection to a receiving fax machine. The **fax modem** translates the document into signals that can be sent over phone wires and decoded by the receiving fax machine. In effect, the receiving fax machine acts like a remote printer for the document. A computer can also use a fax modem or an Internet connection to receive transmissions from fax machines, treating the sending fax machine as a kind of remote scanner. A faxed letter can be displayed on-screen or printed to paper, but it can't immediately be edited the way an email message can. Like a scanned document, a digital facsimile is nothing more than a collection of black-and-white dots to the computer. Before a faxed document can be edited, it must be processed by optical character recognition (OCR) software.

Output You Can Hear

Most PCs have internal speakers. The small speakers built into computers—especially portable computers—are designed mostly for playing system sounds and spoken recordings, not for high-fidelity music playback. Fortunately, virtually all PCs today have sound output jacks for headphones, powered speakers, and other audio output devices. Some audio jacks, especially on laptops and smart phones, can transmit audio signals in both directions, so they can be used with headsets that combine microphones and earphones. Headsets are particularly useful for telephone and teleconferencing applications. PCs can also transmit sound data to peripherals through USB interfaces to speaker systems, monitors with built-in speakers, professional sound boards, and other USB-compatible devices.

how it works Color Printing

Printed colors can't be as vivid as video colors because printed images don't produce light the way monitors do; they only reflect light. Most color printers use subtractive synthesis to produce colors: they mix various amounts of cyan (light blue), magenta (reddish purple), yellow, and black pigments to create a color. Colors mixed this way follow the CYMK color model (for Cyan, Yellow, Magenta, and blacK).

Most printers, like monitors, form images from tiny dots. Each dot is made up of a mixture of the primary subtractive colors.

You can demonstrate subtractive synthesis by painting overlapping areas of cyan, magenta, and yellow ink. The combination of all three is black; combinations of pairs produce red, green, and blue, which are secondary colors of the subtractive system.

Matching on-screen color with printed color is difficult because monitors use additive color synthesis to obtain the color, whereas printers use subtractive synthesis. Monitors are able to display more colors than printers can, although printers can display a few colors that monitors can't. The range of colors that humans can perceive extends beyond either technology.

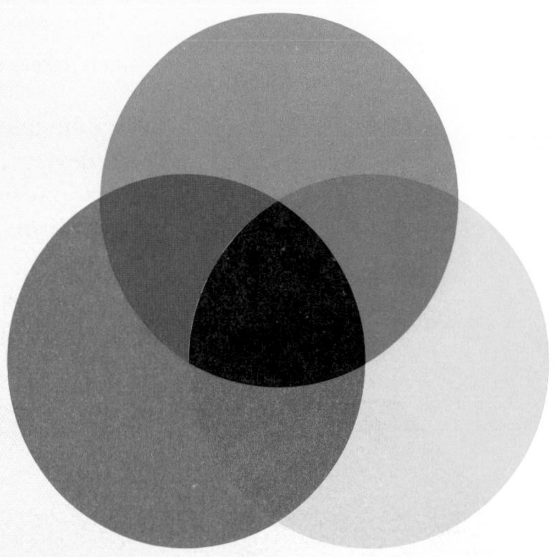

FIGURE 3.22

Most modern PCs include all the necessary sound circuitry on the main system board. People with older tower systems or needs that go beyond the built-in components can buy and install removable **sound cards**. A sound card typically contains audio jacks, chips for digitizing and processing sounds, and a synthesizer for creating sounds.

Controlling Other Machines

In the same way that sensors convert real-world conditions into digital pulses, many output devices work in the other direction, taking bit patterns and turning them into nondigital movements or measurements. Robot arms, telephone switchboards, transportation devices, automated factory equipment, spacecraft, and a host of other machines and systems accept their orders from computers.

In one example familiar to computer gamers, an enhanced input device delivers output. Controllers with ***force feedback***, also known as ***haptic feedback***, can receive signals from a computer and give tactile feedback—jolts, scrapes, and bumps—that matches the visual output of the game or simulation. Many video arcades take the concept further by having the computer shake, rattle, and roll the gamer's chair while displaying on-screen movements that match the action.

Of course, computers can send information directly to other computers, bypassing human interaction altogether. The possibilities for computer output are limited only by the technology and the human imagination, both of which are stretching further all the time.

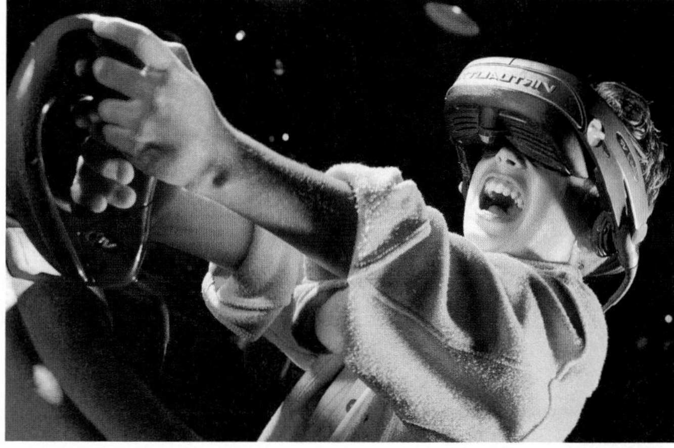

FIGURE 3.23 Using output devices that operate on similar principles, computers control the movements of spacecraft and virtual reality arcade games.

Storage Devices: Input Meets Output

> You can count how many **seeds are in the apple**, but not how many **apples are in the seed**.
>
> —*Ken Kesey, author of* One Flew over the Cuckoo's Nest

Some computer peripherals are capable of performing both input and output functions. These devices, which include tape and disk drives, are the computer's **storage devices**. They're sometimes referred to as *secondary storage* devices because the computer's memory is its *primary storage*. Unlike RAM, which forgets everything when the computer is turned off, and ROM, which can't learn anything new, storage devices enable the computer to record information semipermanently so it can be read later by the same computer or by another computer.

FIGURE 3.24 This back-up device stores large quantities of data on magnetic tape cartridges.

Magnetic Tape

Tape drives are common storage devices on most mainframe computers and some PCs. A tape drive can write data onto, and read data off of, a magnetically coated ribbon of tape. **Magnetic tape** can store massive amounts of information in a small space at a relatively low cost. The spinning tape reels that symbolized computers in old science fiction movies are history, but today's tape cartridges are based on similar technology.

Tape is a **sequential-access** medium; the computer must read through information in the order in which it was recorded. Retrieving information from the middle of a tape is too time consuming for most modern applications because people expect immediate response to their commands. As a result, magnetic tape is used today primarily for backing up data and a few other operations that aren't time sensitive.

Magnetic Disks

Like magnetic tape, a *magnetic disk* has a magnetically coated surface that can store encoded information; a *disk drive* writes data onto the disk's surface and reads data from the surface. But unlike a tape drive, a disk drive can rapidly retrieve information from any part of a magnetic disk in any order. Because of their **random access** capability, disks are popular media for everyday storage needs.

Virtually all PCs include hard disks as their main storage devices. A **hard disk** is a rigid, magnetically sensitive disk that spins rapidly and continuously inside the computer chassis or in a separate box connected to the computer through a USB, FireWire, or Ethernet cable. A hard disk might hold hundreds of gigabytes (thousands of megabytes) of information—more than enough room for every word and picture in this book, an entire music collection, several movie-length video clips, and years of photographs.

FIGURE 3.25 Internal hard drives and smaller microdrives are based on very similar technologies, despite the differences in size.

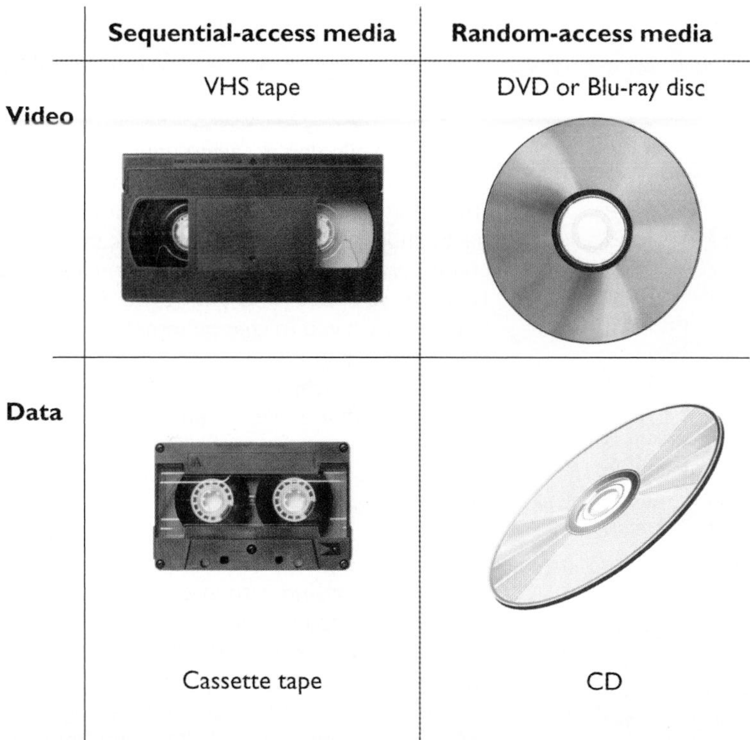

Sequential-access media
Random-access media
Video
VHS tape
DVD or Blu-ray disc
Data
Cassette tape
CD

FIGURE 3.26 In the typical home entertainment system, sequential-access devices—cassette and VHS tape decks—have been replaced by random-access devices—CD, DVD, Blu-ray, and MP3 players (not shown). The advantages of random access are the same for video and audio players as for computers.

Long-time computer users are familiar with the diskette (floppy disk)—a magnetically sensitive plastic wafer in a plastic case. Because of the diskette's limited capacity and slow speed, it is rarely used today. The same is true of Zip disks and other higher-capacity removable magnetic disk cartridges. Magnetic cartridge drives have all but disappeared as a result of advances in portable hard disk, optical disc, and flash memory storage technology.

Optical Discs

An **optical disc drive** uses laser beams rather than magnets to read and write bits of data on a reflective aluminum layer of the disc. ("Disc" is generally spelled with a "k" when it refers to magnetic media and with a "c" when it refers to optical media.) A transparent plastic disc surface protects the aluminum layer from routine physical damage while letting laser light through. Access speeds are slower for optical discs than for magnetic hard disks. While optical discs are generally reliable for long-term storage, they can deteriorate. A severe scratch in the plastic coating can allow air to reach the aluminum layer, leading to oxidation and a loss of information. Surprisingly, the upper surface of the disc (with the label) is more sensitive to scratching than the lower surface because the protective plastic layer is thinner on that side.

From CD-ROM to BD-RW, there's an alphabet soup of choices in optical discs and drives for PCs today. The names can be especially confusing because they aren't consistent. Does *R* stand for Read, Recordable, Rewritable, or Random? It depends on the context.

The oldest type of optical drive in computers is the CD-ROM drive. A CD-ROM drive can read data from **CD-ROM** (compact disc—read-only memory) discs—data discs that are physically identical to music compact discs. The similarity of audio and data CDs is no accident; it makes it possible for CD-ROM drives to play music CDs. A CD-ROM can hold up to about 800 MB of data—more raw text than you could type in your lifetime. But because CD-ROM drives are read-only devices, they can't be used as storage devices. That's why they're seldom found in PCs today; they've been replaced by drives that can write as well as read optical discs.

Working Wisdom Ergonomics and Health

Along with the benefits of computer technology comes the potential for unwelcome side effects. For people who work long hours with computers, the side effects include risks to health and safety. Many heavy computer users suffer from *repetitive-stress injuries*, such as *carpal tunnel syndrome*, a painful affliction of the wrist and hand that results from repeating the same movements over long periods. Prolonged computer use also increases the likelihood of headaches, eyestrain, fatigue, and other symptoms of "techno-stress."

Ergonomics (sometimes called *human engineering*) is the science of designing work environments that enable people and things to interact efficiently and safely. Ergonomic studies suggest preventative measures you can take to protect your health as you work with computers:

- ***Choose equipment that's ergonomically designed.*** When you're buying computer equipment, look beyond functionality. Use Web site and magazine reviews, manufacturer's information, and personal research to check on health-related factors, such as monitor glare, fan noise levels, and keyboard layout. Avoid temptation to use older equipment that doesn't meet today's health and safety standards. A growing number of computer products, such as split, angled ergonomic keyboards, are specifically designed to reduce the risk of equipment-related injuries.
- ***Create a healthful workspace.*** Keep the paper copy of your work at close to the same height as your screen. Position your monitor and lights to minimize glare. Sit at arm's length from your monitor to minimize eyestrain.
- ***Build flexibility into your work environment.*** Whenever possible work with an adjustable chair, an adjustable table, an adjustable monitor, and a removable keyboard. Change your work position frequently.
- ***Protect your ears.*** Loud sounds—especially when they're prolonged—can do permanent damage to your hearing. Choose equipment that's quiet so you don't need to turn up music or talk loudly to drown it out. If you're forced to work in a noisy environment, use ear plugs, earbuds, or headphones to protect your ears. But don't be tempted to crank up the volume on your headset to drown out the noise. No technology available today can replace lost hearing.
- ***Let the technology work for you.*** If your work involves frequent repetitive typing, consider using a software utility to automate the repetition. If you do lots of typing, consider voice recognition software.
- ***Rest your eyes.*** Look up from the screen periodically and focus on a faraway object or scene. Blink frequently. Take a 15-minute break every couple of hours.
- ***Stretch.*** While you're taking your rest break, do some simple stretches to loosen tight muscles. Occasional stretching of the muscles in your arms, hands, wrists, back, shoulders, and lower body can make hours of computer work more comfortable and less harmful.
- ***Listen to your body.*** If you feel uncomfortable, your body is telling you to change something or take a break. Don't ignore it.
- ***Don't leave healthy habits at home.*** If you're not careful, your mobile devices can do as much damage as desktop machines—or more. Texting excessively on tiny keyboards and keypads can lead to repetitive stress injuries. A heavy laptop can pull your spine out of alignment if you always carry it on one side of your body. And of course, any kind of mobile tech work, from texting to choosing a song on an MP3 player, can be fatal when combined with driving.
- ***Seek help when you need it.*** If your wrists start hurting when you work, you have persistent headaches, or you are feeling some other problem that may be related to excessive computer work, talk to a professional. A medical doctor, chiropractor, physical therapist, or naturopath may be able to help you to head off the problem before it becomes chronic.

FIGURE 3.27 A healthful workspace can reduce the chances of developing computer-related injuries.

A *CD-RW drive* can read data from CD-ROMs, play music from audio CD, and *burn*, or record, data onto CD-R and CD-RW disks. **CD-R** (compact disc-recordable) disks are *WORM* (write-once, read-many) media. That is, a drive can write onto a blank (or partially filled) CD-R disk, but it can't erase the data after it's burned in. **CD-RW** (compact disc-rewritable) discs have the advantage of being erasable. A drive can write, erase, and rewrite a CD-RW disk repeatedly.

Today, CD-R and CD-RW media are commonly used to make back-up copies of data files and personal music CDs and for transporting data between machines. But CD-ROM and CD-RW *drives* have been replaced by drives that can work with DVDs as well as CDs. **DVD** originally stood for *digital video disc*, because the discs were designed to replace VHS tapes in video stores. Today, many people say DVD stands for *digital versatile disc* because these high-capacity discs are used to store and distribute all kinds of data.

A DVD can hold between 4.7 and 17 GB of information, depending on how the information is stored. A single-layer DVD can hold up to 4.7 GB of information. A second layer approximately doubles the data capacity of the disc. Most commercial DVD movies are encoded on dual-layer DVDs. It's possible to double the capacity again by recording on both sides of the disc. *DVD-ROM drives* can play DVD movies, read DVD data discs, read standard CD-ROMs, and play audio CDs. They're seldom found in PCs today; they're mostly used in home DVD players.

Rewritable DVD drives, or *DVD burners*, are commonplace in PCs today. These versatile drives can read and write on CD and DVD media. They may be called *DVD-RW*, *DVD+RW*, *DVD+/-RW*, or *DVD/RW* drives. Discs for DVD/RW drives come in write-once (*DVD-R* or *DVD+R*) or rewritable (DVD-RW or DVD+RW) forms. Within each of these categories, it's possible to choose single-layer or more expensive dual-layer media, although not all DVD burners can burn dual-layer discs. In the early days of rewritable DVD drives (just a few years ago), two competing formats, DVD-RW and DVD+RW, were incompatible. Fortunately, newer drives can read and write data on both DVD-RW and DVD+RW disks.

With the right software, most of these recordable DVD drives can be used to create DVD videos that you can play on DVD movie players. Unfortunately, some older DVD players have trouble reading DVDs burned on computer drives. Single-layer, write-once discs are the least likely to cause compatibility problems on other machines, including DVD players.

Early DVD burners were rated with speeds of 1X—it might take as long to record a movie as it does to watch it. Today's drive speeds are measured in multiples of 1X. For example, a 16X drive might record data 16 times faster than a 1X drive. Speed can also be affected by the type of media, the type of connection to the computer, and the computer's software.

DVD drives are gradually being supplanted by **Blu-ray** drives (BD) that can read and write on media that hold up to 50 GB on two layers—enough for full-length high-definition (HD) movies with plenty of room to spare. *BD-R* drives can read data from Blu-ray discs, DVDs, and CDs; *BD-RW* drives can read and record on all of those types of media.

Internal and External Drives

Hard disk drives and optical disc drives come in two basic forms: internal drives and external drives. An **internal drive** resides inside the casing of a computer. In a tower computer, each internal drive resides in a *bay*—a standardized space designed to hold one drive. A tower PC often includes a hard disk in one bay and some kind of optical drive in a second bay. Some PCs have extra bays for additional internal hard drives or removable media. Non-tower desktop systems and laptops generally lack expansion bays for adding additional drives.

But even if there's no room in the system unit for additional internal drives, **external drives** can be connected to the system through USB or FireWire ports, discussed later in this chapter. Because they're contained in their own cases, external drives are relatively easy to transport between locations and share between computers. For example, a

Disk Storage

MAGNETIC DISKS

Both hard disks and floppy disks are coated with a magnetic oxide similar to the material used to coat cassette tapes and videotapes. The read/write head of a disk drive is similar to the record/play head on a tape recorder; it magnetizes parts of the surface to record information. The difference is that a disk is a digital medium—binary numbers are read and written. The typical hard disk consists of several *platters*, each accessed via a read/write head on a movable *armature*. The magnetic signals on the disk are organized into concentric tracks; the tracks in turn are divided into sectors. This is the traditional scheme used to construct addresses for data on the disk.

Hard disks spin much faster than floppy disks do and have a higher storage density (number of bytes per square inch). The *read/write head* of a hard disk glides on a thin cushion of air above the disk and never actually touches the disk.

CD-ROM

A CD-ROM drive contains a small laser that shines on the surface of the disk, "reading" the reflections. Audio CDs and computer CD-ROMs have similar formats; that's why you can play an audio CD with a CD-ROM drive. Information is represented optically—the bottom surface of the CD, under a protective layer of plastic, is coated with a reflective metal film. A laser burns unreflective pits into the film to record data bits. After a pit is burned, it can't be smoothed over and made shiny again; that's why CD-ROMs are read-only.

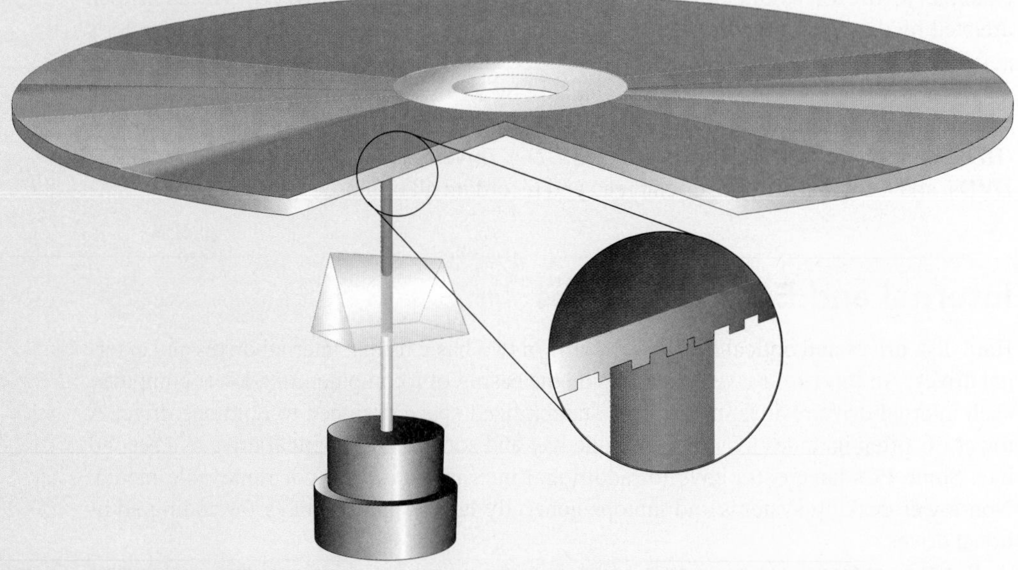

FIGURE 3.28

DVD AND BLU-RAY DRIVES

The main difference between DVD and CD technology is that the pits are packed much closer together on a DVD, so about seven times as many can fit on the DVD's surface. (To read these tightly packed bits, the DVD-ROM uses a narrower laser beam.) A DVD can hold even more data—up to 8.5 GB—if it has a second layer of data. On a layered DVD, the top layer is semireflective, allowing a second readback laser to penetrate to the layer below. The laser can "see through" the top layer, just as you can see through a picket fence when you look at it from exactly the right angle. For massive storage jobs, a DVD can have data on both sides—up to 17 GB. Two-sided usually have to be turned over for the reader to read both sides; future drives may allow additional readback lasers to read the second side without flipping the disk. A Blu-ray disc can pack almost six times as many bits on a disc as a DVD by using a blue-violet laser, which has a shorter wavelength than the lasers used in DVD drives.

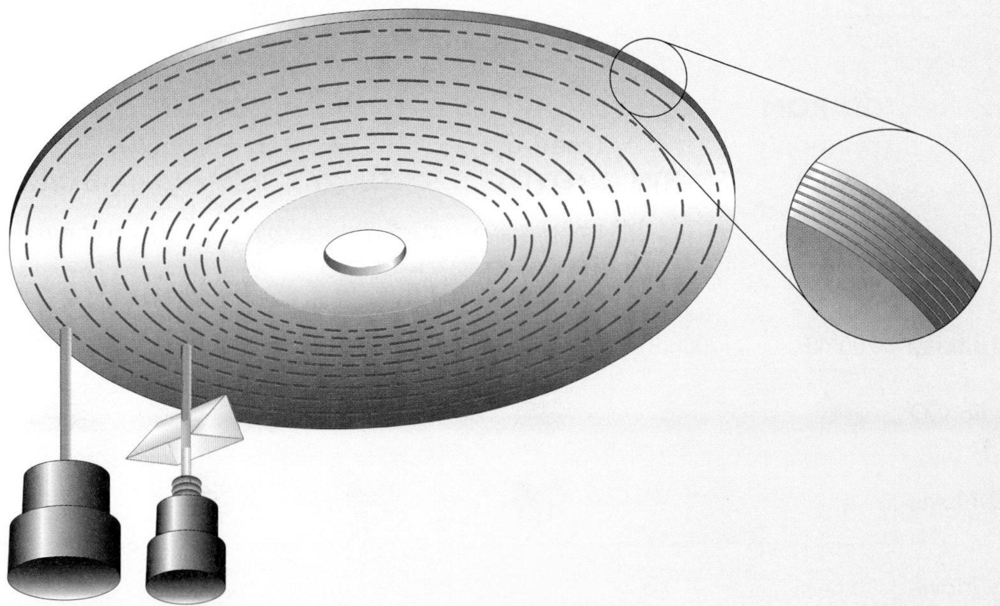

RECORDABLE DRIVES

Recordable CD, DVD, and Blu-ray drives use laser beams to write data on recordable disks. But recordable optical media have layers with chemical structures that react to different temperatures created by different types of lasers. To write data, a high-intensity laser beam produces high temperatures that break down the crystalline structure of the original surface. The resulting pits dissipate, rather than reflect, low-level lasers during the process of reading recorded data. To erase data, a laser heats the pits to about 400 degrees, causing them to revert to their original reflective crystalline state.

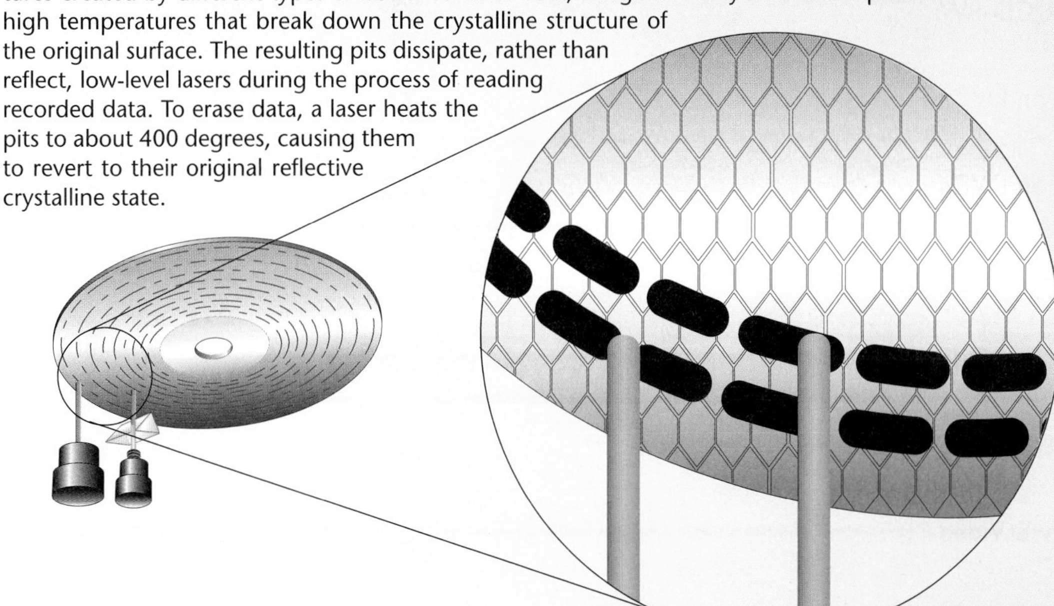

FIGURE 3.29 This drive can read from and write to CDs, DVDs, and Blu-ray discs.

photographer might copy a large photo library from an office PC's internal hard drive onto an external hard drive, take the drive home, attach it to a Mac, and copy the photo library onto the Mac's internal hard drive. (This kind of *cross-platform* data transfer is generally simple, provided that the disk format is recognizable by both Macs and PCs. Disk formatting and operating systems are discussed in the next chapter.)

Most external drives include their own power supplies that must be plugged into separate AC outlets. Some portable hard drives are designed to draw their power from their host computers through their USB or FireWire connections.

	CD-ROM (read-only CD)	**CD-RW**	**DVD-ROM (read-only DVD)**	**DVD/RW**	**BD/ROM (read-only Blu-ray)**	**BD/RW**
Capacity	700MB	700MB	4.7GB (single-layer disc), 9.4GB (dual-layer disc)	4.7GB (single-layer disc), 9.4GB (dual-layer disc)	27GB (single-layer disc), 50GB (dual-layer disc)	27GB (single-layer disc), 50GB (dual-layer disc)
Play Audio CD	●	●	●	●	●	●
Play DVD Movie			●	●	●	●
Play HD Blu-ray Movie					●	●
Read CD-R, CD-RW	●	●	●	●	●	●
Write CD-R, CD-RW		●		●		●
Read Data on DVDs			●	●	●	●
Write Data on DVDs				●		●
Read Data on Blu-ray Disc					●	●
Write Data on Blu-ray Disc						●
Record DVD Video				●		●
Record HD Video						●

FIGURE 3.30 This table summarizes the capabilities of different types of optical drives. (Older drives may require specific + or – media formats for compatibility.)

Flash Memory Storage Devices

In spite of their popularity, disk drives aren't without problems. Their moving parts are more likely to fail than other computer components. Experienced computer users know that it's not a question of *if* their hard drives will fail, but *when* they'll fail. For airline travelers and others who must depend on battery power for long periods of time, spinning drives consume too much energy. Disk drives can be noisy—a problem for musicians and others who use computers for audio applications. And disk drives are bulky when compared with computer memory; they're often not practical for smart phones and other applications where space is tight and battery life is at a premium.

Until recently, disk drives were the only realistic random-access storage devices for most computer applications. **Solid-state storage** devices—rewritable memory devices with no moving parts—were far too expensive to be practical for most uses. But that's changing rapidly with the declining cost of **flash memory**—a type of erasable memory chip that can serve as a reliable, low-energy, quiet, compact storage alternative for many applications. ***Flash memory cards***, including SD (Secure Digital) cards, Compact Flash cards, Memory Sticks, and other cards, are used to store images in digital cameras and sounds in digital recorders. A flash memory card can also be read and written to by a PC, provided it's connected to the PC through a camera, recorder, or ***flash media card reader***. (Some PCs, monitors, and keyboards have built-in flash media card readers. And a few memory cards include wireless transmitters for communicating with PCs.) Flash memory is also used in MP3 players, smart phones, and many other electronic devices.

USB flash drives (also called ***thumb drives*** and ***jump drives***) are popular for storing and transporting data files. A key-sized flash drive can plug directly into a USB port; from the computer's point of view, it looks and acts like a small removable hard drive. It can be loaded with data, removed, and plugged into another computer's USB port—regardless of the make and model of each computer. Many people carry flash drives on keychains so they can easily transport documents, pictures, songs, and even movies between computers. Today's devices hold gigabytes of data.

Flash memory is still too expensive to replace spinning drives in all computers. But as prices drop and production rises, solid-state memory is almost certain to become the storage standard.

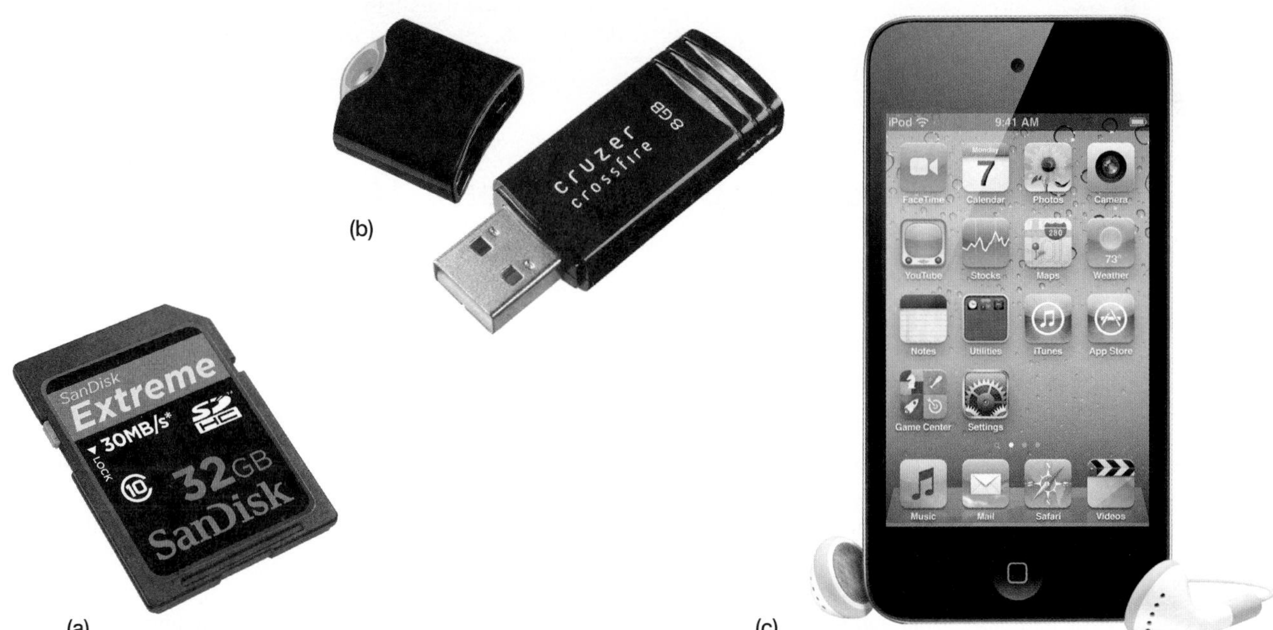

FIGURE 3.31 Flash memory devices. a. An SD flash memory card is one of the most popular kinds of solid-state storage used in digital cameras and other digital media devices. b. A USB flash (thumb) drive can store gigabytes of data and plug into a computer's USB port. c. An Apple iPod Touch stores music and other data using flash memory.

Storage Medium	Capacity	Advantages	Disadvantages
Hard disk	100 GB–3 TB or more	Relatively high capacity, fast, and inexpensive per GB.	Not easily portable. Moving parts make data more vulnerable to drive failure.
CD (CD-R and CD-RW)	700 MB	Can contain audio data compatible with audio CD players. Data CDs can be read by nearly any optical drive.	Smallest capacity of all optical discs. CD-R discs can't be erased and rewritten. CD-RW discs must be reformatted before being rewritten.
DVD (DVD-R, DVD+R, DVD-RAM, DVD-RW, and DVD+RW)	4.7 GB–9.4 GB	Can contain DVD video compatible with most consumer DVD players.	Smaller capacity than Blu-ray discs. Discs can't be used in CD drives. DVD-R and DVD+R discs can't be erased and rewritten. DVD discs that can be rewritten must be reformatted first.
Blu-ray (BD-ROM, BD-R, and BD-RE/BD-RW)	27 GB–50 GB	Highest-capacity optical media option. Can contain HD video playable in many home theater systems.	Relatively expensive. Discs can't be used in CD or DVD drives. BD-ROM and BD-R discs can't be erased and rewritten. BD-RE discs must be reformatted before being rewritten.
Flash drive	1 GB–64 GB or more	No card reader required; works with any computer with a USB port. Extremely portable.	Relatively expensive per GB of storage. Requires a spare USB port.
Flash memory card	1 GB–64 GB or more	Can be used in most digital cameras, recorders, and other portable devices. Slightly cheaper than flash drive per GB.	Relatively expensive per GB of storage. May require a card reader to connect to computer.

FIGURE 3.32 Popular storage media compared.

The Computer System: The Sum of Its Parts

Invention breeds **invention**.

—*Ralph Waldo Emerson*

Most personal computers fall into one of four basic design classes:

- *Tower systems*—tall, narrow boxes that generally have more expansion slots and bays than other designs
- Flat *desktop systems* (sometimes called "pizza box" systems) designed to sit under the monitor like a platform
- *All-in-one systems* that combine monitor and system unit into a single housing
- *Laptop computers*, which include all the essential components, including keyboard and pointing device, in one compact box

Whatever the design, a PC must allow for the attachment of input, output, and storage peripherals. That's where slots, ports, and bays figure in. Now that we've explored the peripherals landscape, we can look again at the ways of hooking those peripherals into the system.

Working Wisdom Computer Consumer Concepts

Any brand-specific advice on choosing computer equipment quickly becomes outdated, but some general principles remain constant while the technology races forward. Here are some consumer criteria worth considering if you plan to buy your own computer:

- ***Cost.*** Don't make the mistake of spending your entire budget on the computer itself. Save some funds for peripherals. Depending on how you're going to use the system, you may need one or more of these peripherals: printer, scanner, microphone, webcam, digital camera, video camera, or external storage devices—not to mention wireless network hardware. If you're buying a laptop, you may want to buy an external monitor, keyboard, and/or mouse so it can function like a full-fledged desktop machine at home. You'll almost certainly need some additional software, too. Don't be tempted to copy copyrighted software from your friends or public labs; software piracy is against the law. When comparing computers, think about the software included in the purchase price. Some systems come with truly useful software that will save you money later; others are bundled with "bloatware" that's little more than hard-drive clutter.
- ***Capability.*** Is it the right tool for the job? Buy a computer that's powerful enough to meet your needs; don't expect a $300 netbook to be a multimedia powerhouse. On the other hand, don't think that you have to have the fastest processor available. The difference in performance between one system with a 4-core CPU and an otherwise identical system with a 8-core CPU may not be worth paying an extra several hundred dollars. What's more likely to be a barrier to high performance is having inadequate RAM. Many applications today don't run well on computers with less than 2 GB RAM, and some of these applications exhibit much better performance on computers with 4 GB or more of RAM.
- ***Capacity.*** If you plan to do graphic design, publishing, or multimedia authoring, you'll be surprised how quickly you can fill up a 250 GB disk. Make sure your machine has enough disk storage to support the resource-intensive applications you'll need. Consider adding removable media drives for saving, backing up, and transporting large files.
- ***Creativity.*** If you want to burn your own DVDs or Blu-ray discs, make sure the system has the appropriate drive—or plan on buying an external drive that can do the job. If you're going to be editing video using a FireWire-equipped camcorder, make sure your computer has a FireWire port. If you'll be recording music or live audio, check the noise level of the computer's fan before you buy.
- ***Customizability.*** Most people don't care if they can swap out PC components; they just want their computer to do what they need it to do. But some users want or need to customize their machines for specialized work or play. If you need specialized graphics cards for video work or gaming, or if your scientific research requires an instrument-monitoring sensing device, make sure the system you buy will accept your add-ons.
- ***Compatibility.*** Will the software you plan to use run on the computer you're considering? Most popular computers have a good selection of compatible software, but if you have specific needs, such as being able to take your software home to run on Mom's computer, study the compatibility issue carefully. Total compatibility isn't always possible or necessary. Many people don't care if all their programs will run on another kind of computer; they just need data compatibility—the ability to move documents back and forth between systems on disk or through a network connection. It's common, for example, for Windows users and Mac users to share documents over a network, even though they can't run identical versions of a software application.
- ***Connectivity.*** A computer today isn't fully functional unless it can connect to the Internet. Sometimes a wireless connection is all you need; sometimes an Ethernet connection is necessary. Make sure you buy the system that will make connecting as easy as possible.
- ***Convenience.*** Just about any computer can do most common jobs, but which is the most convenient for you? Do you value portability over having all the peripherals permanently connected? Is it important to you to have a machine that's easy to install and maintain so you can take care of it yourself? Or do you want to choose the same kind of machine as the people around you so you can get help easily when you need it?
- ***Company.*** If you try to save money by buying an off-brand computer, you may find yourself the owner of an orphan system. Even well-constructed computers may need parts and service at some point. Some small companies have provided superior sales and service for many years, but others vanish overnight. Buy from companies that you judge will be around for a while.
- ***Conservation.*** Ivan Illich warned, "In a consumer society there are inevitably two kinds of slaves: the prisoners of addiction and the prisoners of envy." Avoid becoming a prisoner to consumerism. Will the latest model computer really make a difference in how productively you use your time, or are you making the purchase to satisfy an impulse or keep up with others? Conservationists do the planet a favor (and save a lot of money) by using things until they are no longer useful then disposing of them properly. If your computer is obsolete, you'll know it.

Ports and Slots Revisited

From the earliest days of the PC's history, designers recognized the need to have standard ports for connecting peripherals. In general, these ports followed **interface standards** agreed on by the hardware industry so that devices made by one manufacturer could be attached to systems made by other companies. For many years industry standard PCs had *serial ports* that could send and receive data one bit at a time and *parallel ports* for attaching printers and other devices that send and receive bits in groups. Additional ports were typically included for keyboard, video displays, and audio equipment. The downside of industry standards is that they can sometimes hold back progress. By today's standards those serial, parallel, and keyboard ports—often referred to as *legacy ports*—are far too slow for today's needs. It's rare to find a new PC containing those pokey ports today.

From the beginning, most standard PCs had an **open architecture**—a design that enabled users and technicians to add expansion cards and peripherals as needed. For example, a computer owner might install a network card into an older machine so that the computer could communicate with other computers through an Ethernet port. Many hobbyists, taking advantage of open architecture and interface standards, have used the same computers for years; they just swap in new cards, drives, and even CPUs and motherboards to keep their systems up to current standards. But most computer users today don't want to take their computers apart. And many of today's desktop and laptop machines are closed systems, not intended to have their internal hardware modified by consumers. Fortunately, new interface standards enable casual computer users to add the latest and greatest devices to their systems without cracking the box.

Today, most external peripherals (except for monitors and speakers) are connected to desktop and laptop computers using two newer industry standard interfaces: USB and FireWire.

The original **USB (universal serial bus)** standard allowed for data to be transmitted at approximately 11 megabits per second (Mbps)—roughly 100 times faster than the legacy PC serial port. USB 1.0 is fast enough for transmitting signals from keyboards and mice, but not for transferring large amounts of data (such as media files) to and from hard drives. Fortunately, USB 1.0 has been all but replaced by **USB 2.0**, which has data transfer rates of up to 480 Mbps, and later by USB 3.0, with a data transfer rate of more than 3 Gbps. Theoretically, up to 126 devices, including keyboards, mice, digital cameras, scanners, and storage devices, can be chained together from a single USB port. USB devices can be **hot swapped**—removed and replaced without powering down—so the system instantly recognizes the presence of a new device when it is plugged in. And USB is *platform independent*, so USB devices can often work on both PCs and Macs.

FIGURE 3.33 This tower system has its side panel removed so you can see the storage bays containing disk drives (top left) and the expansion boards inserted into slots (lower right).

Virtually all new PCs and Macs include one or more USB ports. Although it is common for some of these ports to be on the back of the box so cables that are seldom removed can be kept out of sight, many PCs have USB ports on the front or side so flash drives, cameras, MP3 players, and other temporary peripherals can be plugged in quickly and easily.

It's easy to expand the number of available USB ports by attaching a *USB hub* so several USB peripherals can share the same port. Many monitors and keyboards include USB hubs. USB can supply small amounts of power to peripherals, so many low-power USB devices don't need AC connections or batteries. There's a practical limit to the number of USB devices that can draw power from a single port, so many USB hubs are powered. When plugged into AC outlets, they can overcome the power limitations of their host computer's USB ports.

Another important interface standard is **FireWire**, a high-speed connection standard developed by Apple. Some PC makers refer to FireWire by the less friendly designation, *IEEE 1394*, assigned by the Institute of Electrical and Electronic Engineers when they

Symbol	Port	Cable	Used For
USB 	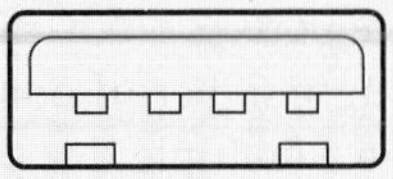	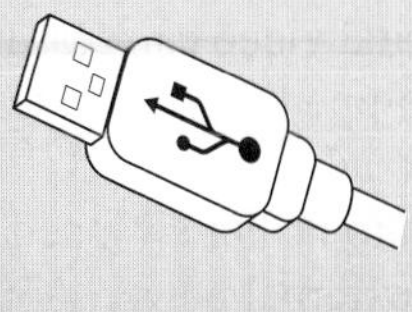	Input devices such as keyboards and mice, Output devices such as printers, scanners, external storage devices, MP3/PDA/smart phone syncing
FireWire 400/ FireWire 800/ IEEE 1394 	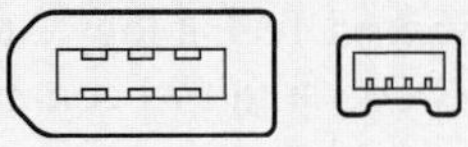	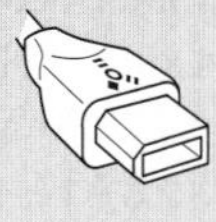	External storage devices, digital video transfer
eSATA (SERIAL ATA 3 Gb/s)	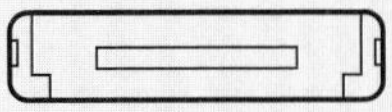	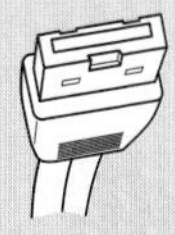	External hard drives and other jobs that require high transfer rates
Audio Line In 		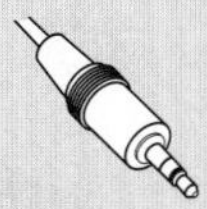	External microphone or other audio source
Audio Line Out 		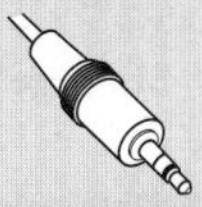	Headphones, speakers, or other external audio devices
VGA 	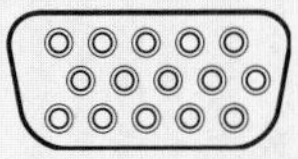	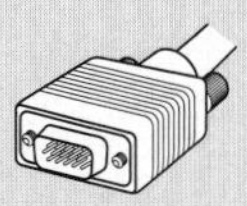	LCD displays, CRT monitors
DVI 	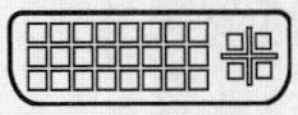		LCD displays
HDMI (HDMI™)	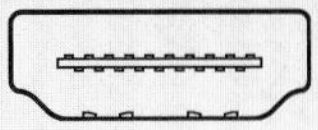	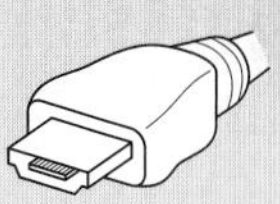	High-definition TV and other video gear
S-Video  (S→)	 4 3 2 1	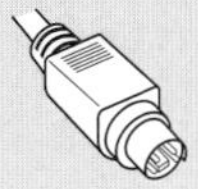	Video output
RJ-11/Modem 	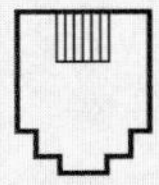	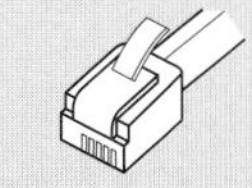	Internal dial-up modem connection, phone dialing software
Ethernet 	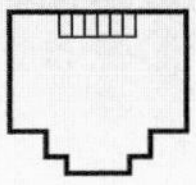	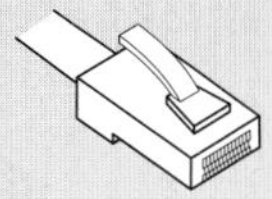	Local network and/or the internet

FIGURE 3.34 The most common PC ports can usually be recognized by shape and symbol.

approved it as a standard. (Sony calls its version iLink.) FireWire can move data between devices at 400 Mbps (the original version) or 800 Mbps (the newer FireWire 800)—faster than most peripheral devices can handle. Most professional and many consumer digital video cameras have FireWire ports, so they can be connected directly to FireWire-equipped PCs or Macs. (A growing number of consumer camcorders have USB ports instead.) Like USB, FireWire allows multiple devices to be connected to the same port and to be hot swapped. FireWire can also supply power to peripherals so they don't need an external power supply.

Another interface standard for connecting computers to hard drives and optical drives is *Serial-ATA* or *SATA* (Serial Advanced Technology Attachment). Serial ATA can transfer data at up to 1200 Mbps. SATA ports aren't as common as USB and FireWire ports on PCs, but the SATA protocol is becoming increasingly common for connecting internal storage devices in PCs.

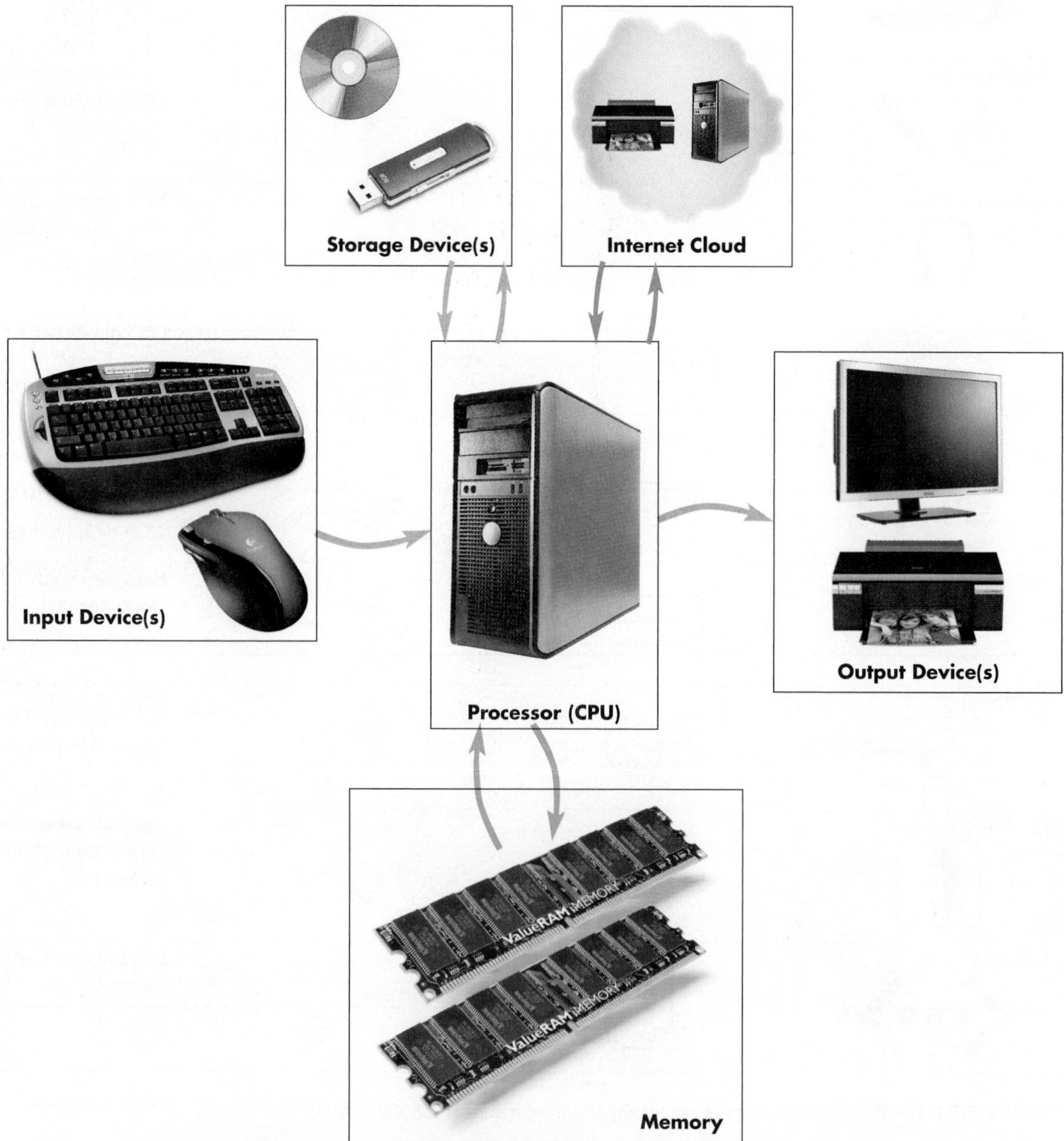

FIGURE 3.35 A basic computer system includes peripherals for input, output, and storage. But in today's networked world, many of those peripherals can exist in the Internet cloud.

USB, FireWire, and SATA are likely to go through speed-enhancing improvements in coming years. Eventually, though, they'll probably be replaced by other technologies that make these standards seem as quaint as the legacy ports on early PCs seem today.

Wireless Peripherals, Network Peripherals, and the Cloud

Three technological trends are already changing the way people think about and use computer peripherals: wireless technology, computer networks, and the Internet "cloud." Wireless keyboards, mice, cameras, and printers are common today. Even tiny flash memory chips can have built-in wireless transmitters. From a practical standpoint, just about any peripheral could be designed to communicate wirelessly.

With or without wires, a growing number of peripherals communicate with multiple PCs through networks. The days of one-printer-per-computer are long gone in most offices, because printers can serve multiple PCs through wired or wireless network connections. Those same PCs can easily be set up to share storage on networked hard disks.

Since most computer networks are connected to the Internet, it's becoming more and more common for computers to use peripherals—especially storage devices—that are located somewhere in the cloud. It's possible and practical for many mobile computer users to save their files without having any idea where they're being stored. In Chapters 8 and 9, we'll take an in-depth look at the technology that enable computers to treat far-away digital devices as if they were directly connected peripherals. The next few chapters will focus on the software that drives all of this hardware.

Inventing the Future ▸ Tomorrow's Peripherals

Here's an overview of some of the ways computer storage, output, and input are likely to change as a result of today's research. We'll explore many of these technologies and their applications in more detail in upcoming chapters.

TOMORROW'S STORAGE

Last chapter you saw how a computer's memory (DRAM) serves as the temporary repository for work in progress. This chapter we discussed several forms of longer-term storage, including hard disks and flash memory drives. For many years researchers have been searching for a **universal memory**—a fast, low-energy, nonvolatile form of memory that can replace hard disks, flash memory, and DRAM.

One possibility is racetrack memory, under development in IBM research labs. Racetrack memory records information in magnetic patterns on nanoscopic wires. Another possible universal memory technology is MRAM—magnetoresistive random access memory. MRAM stores data not as electrical charges but as magnetic patterns in ferromagnetic plates. Both racetrack memory and MRAM promise huge improvements in capacity, size, performance, reliability, and cost of future storage devices on PCs and handheld devices.

HP researchers are exploring a technology called the memristor. A memristor, or memory resistor, is a nano-scale switch that can remember an electrical charge after the power is turned off. Storage devices made of memristors could be faster, smaller, and cheaper than today's flash memory devices. They also have the potential to replace DRAM and hard disks. Further down the road, they may even be able to handle processing tasks without the aid of a CPU. If this line of research pans out, future computers could merge processing and storage, much as our brains do.

FIGURE 3.36 This circuit with 17 memristors was photographed using an atomic force microscope.

TOMORROW'S OUTPUT

Today's research will almost certainly result in steady improvements in the output devices we use with our computers. OLED (organic light-emitting diode) technology will continue to improve, and flexible, roll-up displays may soon be commonplace. Researchers are exploring other technologies, from lasers to nanocrystals, as possible future alternatives to LCD screens. There's also a growing interest in incorporating 3-D into computer displays. Several technologies, including stereoscopic display, computer-generated holographs, and lasers, have potential for creating computer-generated 3-D experiences.

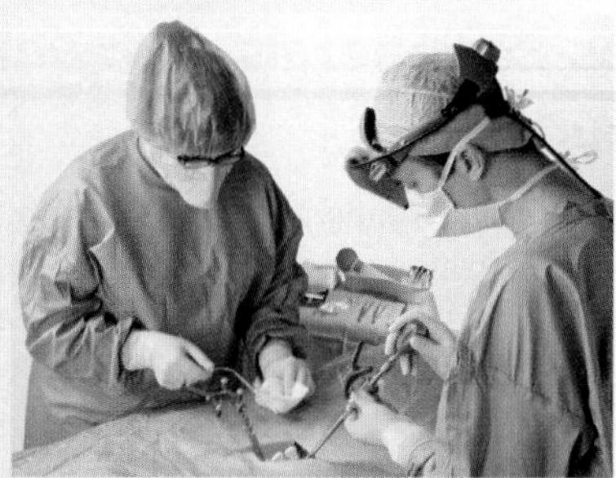

FIGURE 3.37 This surgeon's retinal scanner display makes video images and the patient's vital signs continually visible throughout the surgical procedure.

You've probably seen or tried a **head-up display**—a semitransparent display that allows you to view a computer image or data without looking away from a real-world scene. Head-up displays are used in aircraft, cars, swim goggles a **retinal display** that works without a screen; it shines a focused beam of light through the wearer's pupil, moving across the field of vision to draw pixels directly on the retina. Fighter pilots, neurosurgeons, and people with limited vision use these displays to see critical computer data without taking their eyes off of their work.

TOMORROW'S INPUT

Researchers in industry and academia are developing input devices with all kinds of potential applications. Some of these are simply refinements of existing technology—larger, more accurate multitouch surfaces, for example. Others are unusual devices that open up new possibilities for computer applications. Many of the most revolutionary applications are likely to be associated with sensors that enable digital devices to monitor the analog world. Temperature sensors, optical sensors, motion sensors, and other types of sensors enable computers to track a variety of real-world activities and conditions. But as these technologies mature, more sophisticated devices will serve as eyes, ears, and other types of sense organs for computer networks. Technology forecaster Paul Saffo wrote in a special anniversary issue of the *Communications of the ACM*:

> ***Two parallel universes currently exist—an everyday analog universe that we inhabit, and a newer digital universe created by humans, but inhabited by digital machines. We visit this digital world by peering through the portholes of our computer screens, and we manipulate with keyboard and mouse much as a nuclear technician works with radioactive material via glovebox and manipulator arms.... Now we are handing sensory organs and manipulators to the machines and inviting them to enter into analog reality. The scale of possible surprise this may generate over the next several decades as sensors, lasers, and microprocessors coevolve is breathtakingly uncertain.***

Crosscurrents

3D Printers Are Adding a Whole New Dimension to Design

by Grant Buckler

We tend to think of printers as devices for producing two-dimensional paper output. In this March 8, 2010 Globe and Mail *article, Grant Buckler surveys Canadian research in 3-D printers and their global applications.*

Joint replacements, like artificial knees and hips, are increasingly common. They're a boon for people with failing joints, but the replacement parts aren't as durable as the originals. Usually made of metal and plastic and often cemented to the bone, they can deteriorate and come loose, and usually need replacing after 20 to 25 years.

But what if implants were made from materials that would actually allow bone and cartilage to grow into them and eventually replace them? A University of Waterloo research lab, with Toronto's Mount Sinai hospital and University of Toronto, is working on it.

It's one example of the innovative things Canadian researchers are doing with rapid prototyping, also sometimes referred to as three-dimensional printing.

Printers work by depositing toner or ink on the surface of paper. Three-dimensional printing doesn't stop at one layer. These machines lay down layer after layer of material — it may be in liquid or solid form — to build up an object.

As the name rapid prototyping implies, 3D printing has mostly been thought of as a relatively quick way to make models of products in the design stage. But 3D printing is good for more than prototyping, says Dr. Ehsan Toyserkani, a Waterloo associate professor of mechanical and mechatronics engineering, director of Waterloo's Rapid Prototyping Laboratory and one of the researchers in the artificial implant project.

For an artificial implant to really become part of the body, it must be made of material that the body can absorb without harm and be porous enough that tissue can grow slowly into tiny cavities in the artificial part.

It's one thing to machine the outer shape of a part out of suitable material, says Mr. Toyserkani, but "we cannot actually control internal structures." That's where 3D printing comes in. Because it builds up the part in layers rather than carving it out of a block of material, this process can easily leave openings, or pores, throughout the part.

Implants produced this way have been tested in animals, Mr. Toyserkani says, and the researchers hope to move on to human trials soon, with clinical use possible in three to five years.

Researchers in Montreal have put 3D printing to an entirely different use.

Philippe Lalande and Martin Racine are associated with Hexagram, the Institute for Research/Creation in Media Arts and Technologies, which is supported by Concordia, Université du Quebec à Montreal, Université de Montreal, McGill and commercial sponsors. Mr. Lalande says he was interested in rapid prototyping, while Mr. Racine was exploring sustainable design.

So they embarked together on a series of projects linking rapid prototyping and sustainable design.

The first was PRéco, which explored the idea of making consumer products last longer by using 3D printers to make replacement parts on demand. Too many household gadgets are thrown away because replacement parts are hard to find, Mr. Lalande explains. If there were 3D printing machines in hardware stores and parts carried code numbers allowing a store employee to download the design for a part, people could get replacement parts at local stores much as they get keys copied today.

"We found that basically it was a practical scenario," Mr. Lalande says, "but to be really effective, products would have to be designed from the outset with the idea of their being replaced with rapid prototyping."

So in their Metamorphose project the researchers moved on to designing products that could easily be repaired and adapted to other purposes. Using rapid prototyping, they created a series of light fixtures able to be altered to fit different locations and lighting needs, or even turned into other objects — a lamp shade becoming a fruit bowl, for example.

After seeing how difficult these adaptable designs were, Mr. Lalande and Mr. Racine decided to launch an adaptable design contest. Their year-old Metacycle contest has brought more than 130 entries, some produced using rapid prototyping.

Rapid prototyping plays a role in other research work. At University of Calgary, Dr. Simon Park of the Mechanical and Manufacturing Engineering department uses it to create larger-scale models of nano-scale designs such as tiny pumps. Carleton University set up a rapid prototyping lab several years ago with machines available for student and researcher use.

The Waterloo lab is also exploring the use of 3D printing to manufacture tools with embedded sensors that can measure factors like heat and impact. Today such sensors are usually placed on the surface of the tool, Dr. Toyserkani says. Readings would be more accurate with the sensor built in, but that's hard to do with traditional manufacturing methods. Three-dimensional printing could be the answer.

Discussion Questions

1. Can you think of other uses for 3-D printers?
2. Do you expect 3-D printers to eventually be included in home computer systems?

Summary

A computer with just a CPU and internal memory is of limited value; peripherals allow that computer to communicate with the outside world and store information for later use. Some peripherals are strictly input devices. Others are output devices. Some are external storage devices that accept information from and send information to the CPU.

The most common input devices today are the keyboard and the mouse, but a variety of other input devices can be connected to the computer. Trackballs, touch-sensitive pads, touch screens, and joysticks provide alternatives to the mouse as a pointing device. A growing number of devices, from trackpads to touch screens, support multi-touch technology that can recognize gestures made with multiple fingers or hands. Bar code readers, optical mark readers, and magnetic ink readers are designed to recognize and translate specially printed patterns and characters. Scanners and digital cameras convert photographs, drawings, and other analog images into digital files that the computer can process. Sound digitizers do the same thing to audio information from microphones, other external audio devices, and synthesized sounds. Sensors can detect motion, temperature, pressure, and other characterisics of their environment. All input devices are designed to do one thing: convert information signals from an outside source into a pattern of bits that the computer can process. This conversion process can happen inside the system unit (as it does when a microphone is plugged into an audio-in port) or inside the peripheral (as it does when a digital camera is connected to a computer's USB port).

Output devices perform the opposite function: They accept strings of bits from the computer and transform them into a form that is useful or meaningful outside the computer. Again, the conversion process might happen outside or inside the peripheral. Video monitors are almost universally used to display information continually as the computer functions. A variety of printers are used for producing paper output. Fax modems let you share printed information with fax machines using standard phone lines; it's also possible to communicate with fax machines via the Internet. Sound output from the computer, including music and synthesized speech, is delivered through audio speakers and headphones. Output devices also allow computers to control other machines.

Unlike most input and output peripherals, storage devices such as disk drives and flash (thumb) drives are designed to send and receive large quantities of data. Because of their high-speed random-access capability and large capacity, magnetic hard disks are the most common forms of storage on computers. Sequential-access tape devices are generally used to archive only information that doesn't need to be accessed often. Optical discs (CD, DVD, and Blu-ray) are the most common removable storage media. Most optical drives can read and write data. Solid-state flash memory is rapidly replacing disks and tapes for many applications. USB thumb drives, SD memory cards, and solid-state internal memory have many advantages over the spinning media that have dominated computer storage for decades.

The hardware for a complete computer system generally includes at least one processor, memory, storage devices, and several I/O peripherals for communicating with the outside world. With the hardware components in place, a computer system is ready to receive and follow instructions encoded in software.

Key Terms

Companion Website Projects

1. The *Digital Planet* Web site, **www.pearsonhighered.com/beekman**, contains self-test exercises related to this chapter. Follow the instructions for taking a quiz. After you've completed your quiz, you can email the results to your instructor.
2. The Web site also contains open-ended discussion questions called Internet Exercises. Discuss one or more of the Internet Exercises at the section for this chapter.

True or False

1. Blu-ray drives can read data on CDs, DVDs and Blu-ray discs.
2. USB thumb drives use flash memory technology to store data.
3. A monitor with an aspect ratio of 16 × 9 is better suited for displaying two pages side-by-side than a monitor with a 4 × 3 aspect ratio.
4. Because bar codes were designed to be read by computers, the devices that read them are extremely accurate.
5. A scanner creates an analog representation of a printed digital image.
6. An image on a standard LCD monitor is made up of thousands of tiny squares of colors called pixels.
7. Thermal printers are commonly used to print receipts at point-of-sale terminals.
8. Laser printers are generally more expensive than comparable inkjet printers, but they may be cheaper in the long run because of the lower cost per page of laser printouts.
9. A DVD-R drive can be used to store and back up data files.
10. Multi-touch technology was developed so that a PC could be connected to several pointing devices at the same time.

Multiple Choice

1. The mouse is standard equipment on virtually all modern PCs *except*
   a. PCs without USB or FireWire ports.
   b. tower PCs.
   c. all-in-one PCs.
   d. laptop and tablet PCs.
   e. The mouse is standard equipment on all PCs.
2. Which of these is both an input and an output device?
   a. A bar-code reader
   b. A flatbed scanner
   c. A touch screen
   d. A sensor
   e. A plotter
3. Which of these peripherals is generally connected to a standard desktop PC through a port that's not a USB port?
   a. Mouse
   b. Monitor
   c. Keyboard
   d. External drive
   e. Digital camera
4. Why was the arrangement of keys on the QWERTY keyboard chosen?
   a. Because it corresponds to alphabetical order in the Esperanto language
   b. Because it corresponds to alphabetical order in Latin
   c. To reduce typing speed
   d. To minimize finger motion to reach the most commonly typed characters
   e. To honor Harold Qwerty, the inventor of the keyboard
5. Optical character recognition can be used to extract text from writing on
   a. smart whiteboards.
   b. tablet PCs.
   c. photographs of typewritten documents.
   d. scanned letters.
   e. All of the above
6. Which of these input devices is least likely to use multi-touch technology?
   a. A touch-sensitive display
   b. A touch tablet
   c. A keyboard
   d. A trackpad
   e. A smart phone

7. LCD technology is used in
   a. notebook computer displays.
   b. desktop computer displays.
   c. video projectors.
   d. smart phone displays.
   e. All of the above
8. The size of a display is measured
   a. across the top of the display.
   b. down the left side of the display.
   c. across the middle of the display.
   d. down the center of the display.
   e. from the upper-left corner to the lower-right corner of the display.
9. Which of these is most like the open architecture of the modern PC?
   a. A modern car with a computer-controlled emissions system that can be adjusted by factory-authorized mechanics
   b. A "smart" microwave with an embedded computer that allows for complex recipes and scheduling
   c. A stereo system that allows speakers, disc players, and other components to be replaced by the owner
   d. A handheld computer with built-in firmware for all of the most common PDA tasks
   e. A music keyboard that includes a built-in synthesizer and an LCD display
10. External drives are typically connected to the computer by
    a. USB.
    b. FireWire.
    c. VGA.
    d. Both A and B
    e. None of these
11. A multifunction printer generally includes all of these except
    a. a scanner.
    b. an inkjet or laser printer.
    c. a port for connecting to a phone line.
    d. a port for connecting to a PC or a network.
    e. a hard disk drive.
12. USB flash drives have all of the following advantages over other storage options *except*
    a. they are small and portable.
    b. they are cheaper per MB than other storage options.
    c. they can be used to access and store your data on virtually any computer with a USB port.
    d. they can plug into almost any modern digital camera.
    e. they are less prone to being damaged if dropped or scratched.
13. Hard disk drives have the disadvantage that
    a. they hold less information than CDs do.
    b. they are more likely to fail than other computer components.
    c. they cannot be backed up.
    d. their contents are lost when they lose power.
    e. All of the above
14. Most digital cameras today store images using
    a. DVD-RAM.
    b. hard disks.
    c. flash memory.
    d. digital ink.
    e. None of the above
15. Which of these technologies is considered a "legacy" port today because it has been replaced by other technologies in modern PCs?
    a. The USB port
    b. The Ethernet port
    c. The serial port
    d. The express slot
    e. The Wi-Fi connection

Review Questions

1. Provide a working definition for each of the key terms listed in the "Key Terms" section. Check your answers in the glossary.
2. List five input devices and three output devices that might be attached to a PC. Describe a typical use for each.
3. Describe the advantages of storing your data on Blu-ray discs instead of DVD discs. Are there any disadvantages?
4. Name and describe three special-purpose input devices and one output device people commonly use in public places, such as stores, banks, and libraries.
5. Many people find that the mouse is impractical for use as a pointing device on a laptop computer. Describe at least three alternatives.
6. What are the advantages and disadvantages of flash memory devices over hard disks as storage media?
7. Describe at least three common audio output devices for PCs, and explain how each of them might be used.
8. Describe how multi-touch technology can make common input tasks more efficient.
9. Some commonly used peripherals can be described as both input and output devices. Explain.
10. List several devices that might be connected to a PC through USB and FireWire ports.

Discussion Questions

1. What kinds of new input and output devices do you think future computers might have? Why?
2. If we think of the human brain as a computer, what are the input devices? What are the output devices? What are the storage devices?
3. What do you think are the major health risks associated with excessive computer use? How do you think you can minimize those risks?
4. Many computer users have become addicted to multiplayer online role-playing games. Some of them spend eight hours or more a day playing these games. Do you think computer addiction will become a bigger problem when more sophisticated peripherals such as LCD goggle displays become commonplace?

Projects

1. The keyboard is the main input device for computers today. If you don't know how to touch-type, you're effectively handicapped in a world of computers. Fortunately, many personal computer software programs are designed to teach keyboarding. If you need to learn to type, try to find one of these programs and use it regularly until you are a fluent typist.
2. Using a Web browser to research prices, try to break down the cost of a desktop computer to determine, on the average, what percentage of the cost is for the system unit (including CPU, memory, and disk drives), what percentage is for input and output devices, and what percentage is for software. How do the percentages change as the price of the system goes up?
3. Visit several local businesses. Find and write about unusual input and output devices that you wouldn't find on a typical home PC.
4. Visit a bank, store, office, or laboratory. List all the computer peripherals you see, categorizing them as input, output, or storage devices.

Sources and Resources

Books

Hard Drive: Bill Gates and the Making of the Microsoft Empire, by James Wallace and Jim Erickson (Collins). This book covers the early years of the Bill Gates story. It doesn't pull punches, often painting Gates as ruthless and difficult. This is a good read on an important era in the Gates legacy. Still, the world is due for a serious biography of the older, wiser, and more generous Bill Gates—the one whose charitable work is changing lives the world over.

Gates: How Microsoft's Mogul Reinvented an Industry—and Made Himself the Richest Man in America, by Stephen Manes and Paul Andres (Touchstone). This well-written book by two prominent technology journalists illustrates how the Bill Gates story is intertwined with the story of the birth of the PC.

How Digital Photography Works, by Ron White and Timothy Edward Downs (Que). Ron White's phenomenally popular *How Computers Work* (see Chapter 2 Sources and Resources) has helped countless people figure out what's going on inside their PCs. This book takes a similar approach to digital cameras. White's clear explanations combine with Timothy Edward Downs's illustrations to produce a visually appealing way to understand digital camera technology. As with most technology, an understanding of the inner workings can produce a more satisfying user experience—and better results.

Disclosure, by Michael Crichton (Ballantine Books). This book-turned-movie provides an inside look at a fictional Seattle corporation that manufactures computer peripherals. Even though the author has clearly tampered with credibility for the sake of a suspenseful plot, the story provides insights into the roles money and power play in today's high-stakes computer industry.

Real World Scanning and Halftones, by David Blanner, Conrad Chavez, Glenn Fleishman, and Steve Roth (Peachpit Press). It's easy to use a scanner, but it isn't always easy to get high-quality scans. This illustrated book covers scanner use from the basics to advanced tips and techniques.

The Digital Photography Book, Volumes 1, 2, and 3, by Scott Kelby (Peachpit Press). In these three books (also available as a boxed set), master photographer and writer Kelby shares his expertise without getting bogged down in the theory of photography. In his words, these books are about "you and I shooting, and I answer the questions, give you advice, and share the secrets I've learned just like I would with a friend, without all the technical explanations and without all the techno-photo-speak." Each page covers a single trick or tip for taking pictures like the pros.

Photopedia: The Ultimate Digital Photography Resource, by Michael Miller (Que). Tools, techniques, and tips, from camera to computer. This easy-to-read book contains a wealth of information for anyone interested in digital photography.

Yoga for Computer Users: Healthy Necks, Shoulders, Wrists, and Hands in the Postmodern Age, by Sandy Blaine (Rodmell Press). Like any activity, computer work can be hazardous to your health if you don't exercise care and common sense. This book describes stretching and relaxation exercises for deskbound workers and students. If you spend hours a day in front of a computer screen, these activities can help you to take care of your body and mind.

Software Basics
The Ghost in the Machine

OBJECTIVES

After you read this chapter you should be able to:

- Describe three fundamental categories of software and their relationships
- Explain the relationship of algorithms to software
- Compare and contrast PC applications and Web applications
- Describe the role of the operating system in a modern computer system
- Explain how file systems are organized
- Outline the evolution of user interfaces from machine-language programming to futuristic interfaces
- Describe some challenges of applying intellectual property laws to software

> **Any program is only as good as it is useful.**
>
> —*Linus Torvalds*

Linus Torvalds and the Software Nobody Owns

When Linus Torvalds bought his first PC in 1991, he never dreamed it would become a critical weapon in a software liberation war. He just wanted to stop waiting in line to get a terminal to connect to his university's mainframe. Torvalds, a 21-year-old student at the University of Helsinki in Finland, had avoided buying a PC because he didn't like the standard PC's "crummy architecture with this crummy MS-DOS operating system." But Torvalds had been studying operating systems, and he decided to try to build something on his own. "I had no idea what I was doing," he recalls. "I knew I was the best programmer in the world. Every 21-year-old programmer knows that. How hard can it be? It's just an operating system?"

He based his work on Minix, a scaled-down textbook version of the powerful UNIX operating system designed to run on PC hardware. Little by little, he cobbled together pieces of a kernel, the part of the system where the real processing and control work is done.

When he mentioned his project on an Internet discussion group, a member offered him space to post it on a university server. Others copied it, tinkered with it, and sent the changes back to Torvalds. The communal work-in-progress eventually became known as Linux (pronounced "Linn-uks" by its creator). Within a couple of years, it was good enough to release as a product.

Instead of copyrighting and selling Linux, Torvalds made it freely available under the GNU General Public License (GPL) developed by the Free Software Foundation. According to the GPL, anyone can give away, modify, or even sell Linux, as long as the source

FIGURE 4.1 Linus Torvalds talking to Linux fans.

code—the program instructions—remain freely available for others to improve. Linux is the best known example of open-source software, and now it spearheads the popular open-source software movement.

Thousands of programmers around the world have worked on Linux, with Torvalds still at the center of the activity. Some do it because they believe there should be alternatives to expensive corporate products; some do it because they can customize the software; others do it to be part of a global community of programmers; still others do it just for fun. As a result of all their efforts, Linux has matured into a powerful, versatile product with millions of users.

Today Linux powers Web servers, film and animation workstations, scientific supercomputers, handheld computers, some general-use PCs, and even Internet-savvy appliances such as refrigerators. Linux is especially popular among people who do computing on a tight budget—particularly in debt-ridden Third World countries.

The success of Linux has inspired Apple, Sun, Hewlett-Packard, and other software companies to release products with open-source code. Even the mighty Microsoft is paying attention as this upstart operating system grows in popularity, and the company has responded with a pseudo–open-source strategy covering its embedded products that compete directly with Linux.

Today Torvalds is an Internet folk hero. Web pages pay homage to him, his creation, and Tux, his stuffed penguin that has become the Linux mascot. In 1996 he completed his master's degree in computer science and went to work for Transmeta Corp., a chip design company in Silicon Valley. In 2003 he moved to the Open Source Development Labs, which merged with the Free Standards Group to become the Linux Foundation. He has become wealthy thanks to stock options donated by grateful companies that built their products on Linux. He maintains a relatively low profile, but still champions the open-source cause.

FIGURE 4.2 A novel use of the Linux operating system is in the NASA personal satellite assistant, currently under development. The six-inch sphere will float around the International Space Station and act as an environmental monitor and communications device. Its design was inspired by the light saber training droid used by Luke Skywalker in the movie Star Wars.

Chapters 2 and 3 told only part of the story about how computers do what they do. Here's a synopsis of our story so far:

On one side we have a person—you, me, or somebody else—it hardly matters. We all have problems to solve—problems involving work, communication, transportation, finances, and more. Many of these problems cry out for computer solutions.

On the other side, we have a computer—an incredibly sophisticated bundle of hardware capable of performing all kinds of technological wizardry. Unfortunately, the computer hardware *recognizes only zeros and ones.*

A great chasm separates the person who has a collection of vague problems from the stark, rigidly bound world of the computer. How can humans bridge the gap to communicate with the computer?

That's where software comes in. Software enables people to communicate certain kinds of problems to computers and makes it possible for computers to communicate solutions back to those people.

Modern computer software didn't materialize out of the atmosphere; it evolved from the plug boards and patch cords and other hardware devices that were used to program early computers such as the ENIAC. Mathematician John von Neumann, working with ENIAC's creators, J. Presper Eckert and John Mauchly, wrote a 1945 paper suggesting that program instructions could be stored with the data in memory. Every computer created since has

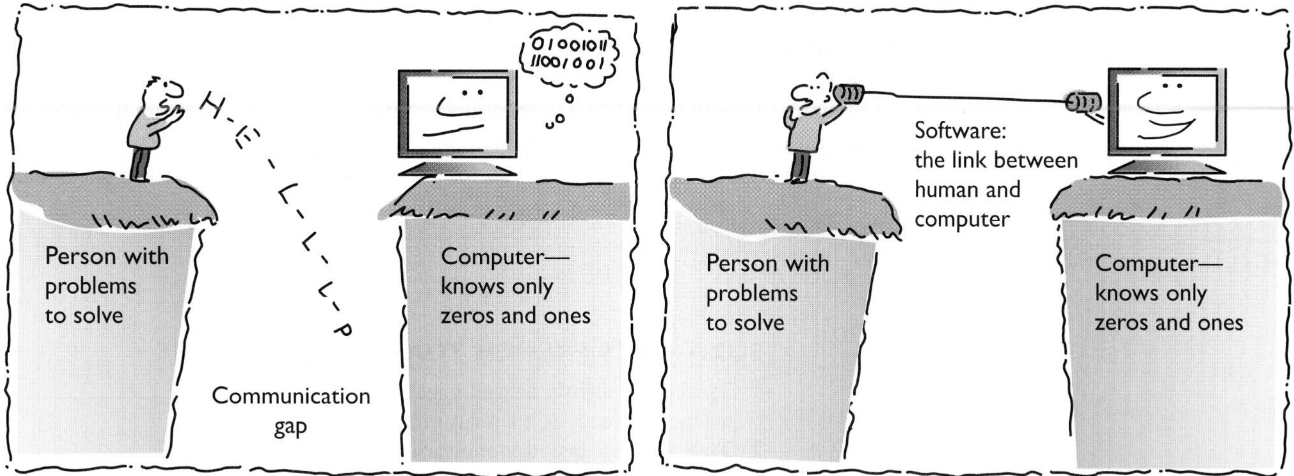

FIGURE 4.3a The communication gap. . .

FIGURE 4.3b . . . and the software solution.

been based on the *stored-program concept* described in that paper. That idea established the software industry.

Instead of flipping switches and patching wires, today's programmers write *programs*—sets of computer instructions designed to solve problems—and feed them into the computer's memory through keyboards and other input devices. These programs are the computer's software. Because software is stored in memory, a computer can switch from one task to another and back to the first without a single hardware modification. For instance, the computer that serves as a word processor for writing this book can, at the click of a mouse, become a window into the World Wide Web, a reference library, a math machine, a drawing table, a video-editing workstation, a musical instrument, or a game machine.

What is software, and how can it transform a mass of circuits into an electronic chameleon? This chapter provides some general answers to that question along with details about each of the three major categories of software:

- Compilers and other translator programs, which enable programmers to create other software
- Software applications, which serve as productivity tools to help computer users solve problems
- System software, which coordinates hardware operations and does behind-the-scenes work the computer user seldom sees

Processing with Programs

> Leonardo da Vinci called music **"the shaping of the invisible"** and his phrase is even more apt as a description of software.
>
> *—Alan Kay, conceiver of the notebook computer and user-interface architect*

Software is invisible and complex. To make the basic concepts clear, we start our exploration of software with a down-to-earth analogy.

Food for Thought

Think of the hardware in a computer system as the kitchen in a short-order restaurant: It's equipped to produce whatever output a customer (user) requests, but it sits idle until an order (command) is placed. Robert, the computerized chef in our imaginary kitchen, serves as the central processing unit (CPU), waiting for requests from the users/customers. When somebody provides an input command—say, an order for a plate of French toast—Robert responds by following the instructions in the appropriate recipe.

As you may have guessed, the recipe is the software. It provides instructions telling the hardware what to do to produce the output the user desires. If the recipe is correct, clear, and precise, the chef turns the input data—eggs, bread, and other ingredients—into the desired output—French toast. If the instructions are unclear, or if the software has **bugs**, or errors, the output may not be what the user wanted.

For example, suppose Robert has this recipe for "Suzanne's French Toast Fantastique."

SUZANNE'S FRENCH TOAST FANTASTIQUE

1. Combine 2 slightly beaten eggs with 1 teaspoon vanilla extract, 1/2 teaspoon cinnamon, and 2/3 cup milk.
2. Dip 6 slices of bread in mixture.
3. Fry in small amount of butter until golden brown.
4. Serve bread with maple syrup, sugar, or tart jelly.

FIGURE 4.4 Suzanne's French Toast Fantastique.

This seemingly foolproof recipe has several trouble spots. Because step 1 doesn't say otherwise, Robert might include the shells in the "slightly beaten eggs." Step 2 says nothing about separating the six slices of bread before dipping them in the batter; Robert would be within the letter of the instruction if he dipped all six at once. Step 3 has at least two potential bugs. Because it doesn't specify what to fry in butter, Robert might conclude that the mixture, not the bread, should be fried. Even if Robert decides to fry the bread, he may let it overcook while waiting for the butter to turn golden brown, or he may wait patiently for the top of the toast to brown while the bottom quietly blackens. Robert, like any good computer, just follows instructions.

A Fast, Stupid Machine

> The most useful word in any computer language is **"oops."**
>
> —*David Lubar, in* It's Not a Bug, It's a Feature

Our imaginary automated chef may not seem very bright, but he's considerably more intelligent than a typical computer's CPU. Computers are commonly called "smart machines" or "intelligent machines." In truth, a typical computer is incredibly limited, capable of performing only the most basic arithmetic operations (such as 7 + 3 and 15 – 8) and a few simple logical comparisons ("Is this number less than that number?" "Are these two values identical?").

Computers *seem* smart because they can perform these arithmetic operations and comparisons quickly and accurately. A typical PC can perform millions of calculations in the time it takes you to pull your pen out of your pocket. A well-crafted program can tell the computer to perform a sequence of simple operations that, when taken as a whole, print a term paper, organize the student records for your school, or simulate a space flight. Amazingly, everything you've ever seen a computer do is the result of a sequence of extremely simple arithmetic and logical operations done very quickly. The challenge for software developers is to devise instructions that put those simple operations together in ways that are useful and appropriate.

Suzanne's recipe for French toast isn't a computer program; it's not written in a language that a computer can understand. But it could be considered an algorithm—a set of step-by-step procedures for accomplishing a task. A computer program generally starts as an **algorithm** written in English or some other human language. Like Suzanne's recipe, the initial algorithm is likely to contain generalities, ambiguities, and errors.

The programmer's job is to turn the algorithm into a program by adding details, hammering out rough spots, testing procedures, and debugging—correcting errors. For example, if we were turning Suzanne's recipe into a program for our electronic-brained short-order cook, we might start by rewriting it like the recipe shown here:

SUZANNE'S FRENCH TOAST FANTASTIQUE: THE ALGORITHM

1. Prepare the batter by following these instructions.
   1a. Crack 2 eggs so whites and yolks drop in bowl; discard shells.
   1b. Beat eggs 30 seconds with wire whisk, fork, or mixer.
   1c. Mix in 1 teaspoon vanilla extract, 1/2 teaspoon cinnamon, and 2/3 cup milk.
2. Place 1 tablespoon butter in frying pan and place on 350° heat.
3. For each of six pieces of bread, follow these steps:
   3a. Dip slice of bread in mixture.
   3b. For each of the two sides of the bread do the following steps:
      3b1. Place the slice of bread in the frying pan with this (uncooked) side down.
      3b2. Wait 1 minute then peek at underside of bread; if lighter than golden brown, repeat this step.
   3c. Remove bread from frying pan and place on plate.
4. Serve bread with maple syrup, sugar, or tart jelly.

FIGURE 4.5 Suzanne's French Toast Fantastique: The algorithm.

We've eliminated much of the ambiguity from the original recipe. Ambiguity, while tolerable (and sometimes useful) in conversations between humans, is a source of errors for computers. In its current form, the recipe contains far more detail than any human chef would want but not nearly enough for a computer. If we were programming a computer (assuming we had one with input hardware capable of recognizing golden brown French toast and output devices capable of flipping the bread), we'd need to go into excruciating detail, translating every step of the process into a series of absolutely unambiguous instructions that could be interpreted and executed by a machine with a vocabulary smaller than that of a two-year-old child!

The Language of Computers

> The programmer, like the poet, works only slightly removed from pure thought-stuff. He builds **castles in the air, created by exertion of the imagination**. Yet the program construct, unlike the poet's words, is real in the sense that **it moves and works**, producing visible outputs separate from the construct itself.
>
> —*Frederick P. Brooks, Jr., in* The Mythical Man-Month

Every computer processes instructions in a native machine language. Machine language uses numeric codes to represent the most basic computer operations—adding numbers, subtracting numbers, comparing numbers, moving numbers, repeating instructions, and so on. Early programmers were forced to write every program in a machine language, tediously translating each instruction into binary code. This process was an invitation to insanity; imagine trying to find a single mistyped character in a page full of zeros and ones!

how it works Executing a Program

Most programs are composed of millions of simple machine-language instructions. Here we'll observe the execution of a tiny part of a running program: a series of instructions that computes the 5 percent sales tax on a $99.00 purchase. The machine instructions are similar to those in actual programs, but the details have been omitted. The computer has already loaded (copied) the program from disk into RAM so that the CPU can see it.

The program counter inside the CPU keeps track of the address of the next instruction to be executed. The instruction execution cycle has a three-step rhythm: fetch the instruction, increment the program counter, and perform the specified task. In this example, four instructions tell the CPU to read two numbers from memory (locations 2000 and 2004), multiply them, and store the result in memory (location 2008). The CPU goes through 12 steps to execute these four instructions.

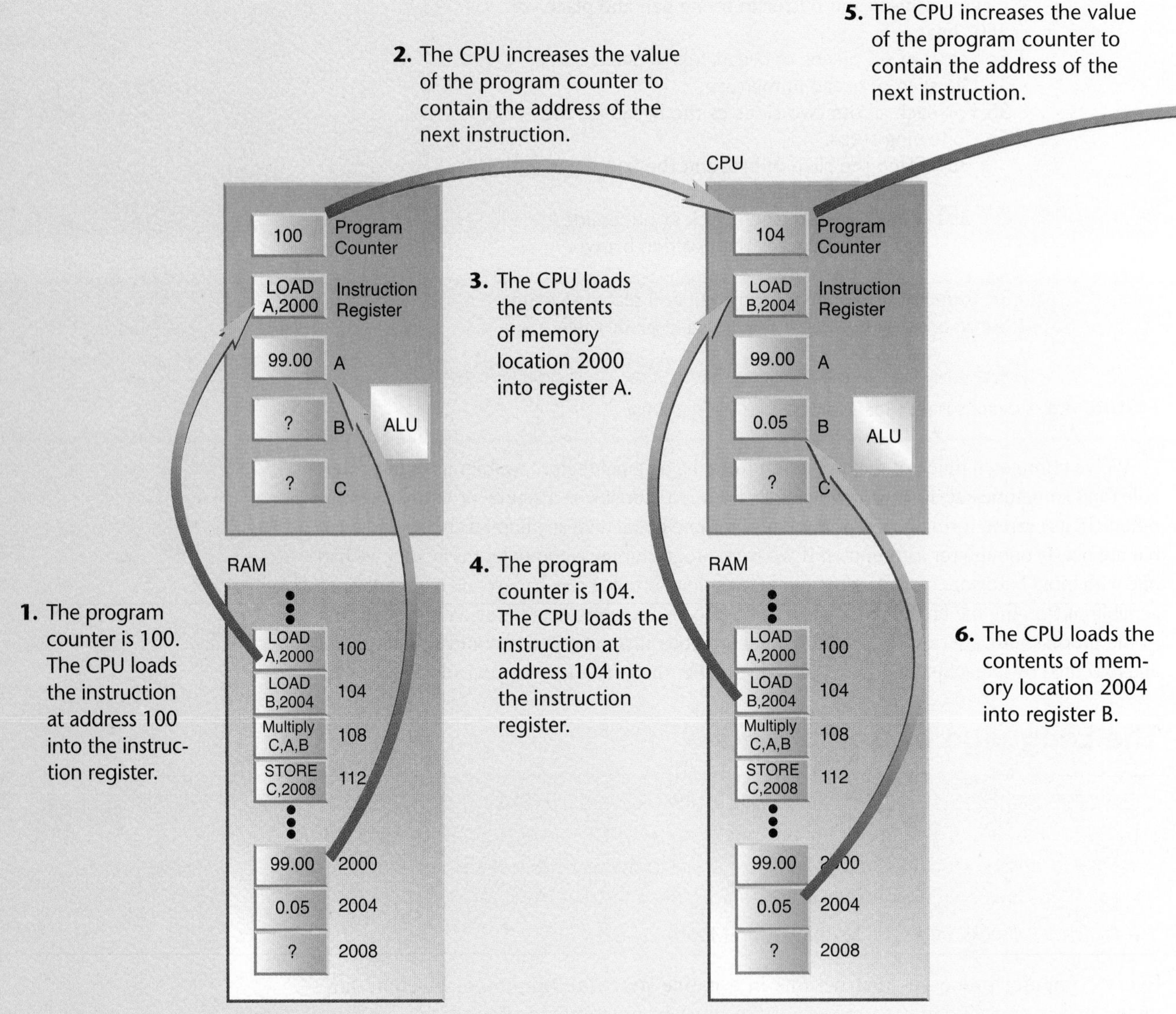

1. The program counter is 100. The CPU loads the instruction at address 100 into the instruction register.
2. The CPU increases the value of the program counter to contain the address of the next instruction.
3. The CPU loads the contents of memory location 2000 into register A.
4. The program counter is 104. The CPU loads the instruction at address 104 into the instruction register.
5. The CPU increases the value of the program counter to contain the address of the next instruction.
6. The CPU loads the contents of memory location 2004 into register B.
CPU
100
Program Counter
LOAD A,2000
Instruction Register
99.00
A
?
B
ALU
?
C
RAM
LOAD A,2000
100
LOAD B,2004
104
Multiply C,A,B
108
STORE C,2008
112
99.00
2000
0.05
2004
?
2008
104
Program Counter
LOAD B,2004
Instruction Register
99.00
A
0.05
B
ALU
?
C

FIGURE 4.6

Translated into English, the instructions at memory addresses 100–112 look like this:

- (100) Copy the number stored in memory location 2000 into register A inside the CPU.
- (104) Copy the number stored in memory location 2004 into register B inside the CPU.
- (108) Multiply the contents of registers A and B, putting the result in register C.
- (112) Copy the contents of register C into memory location 2008.

In this example, memory location 2000 contains the purchase price (99.00), and memory location 2004 contains the sales tax rate (0.05).

The computer actually stores all instructions and data values as binary numbers, but we have represented them as letters or decimal numbers to make the example easier to follow.

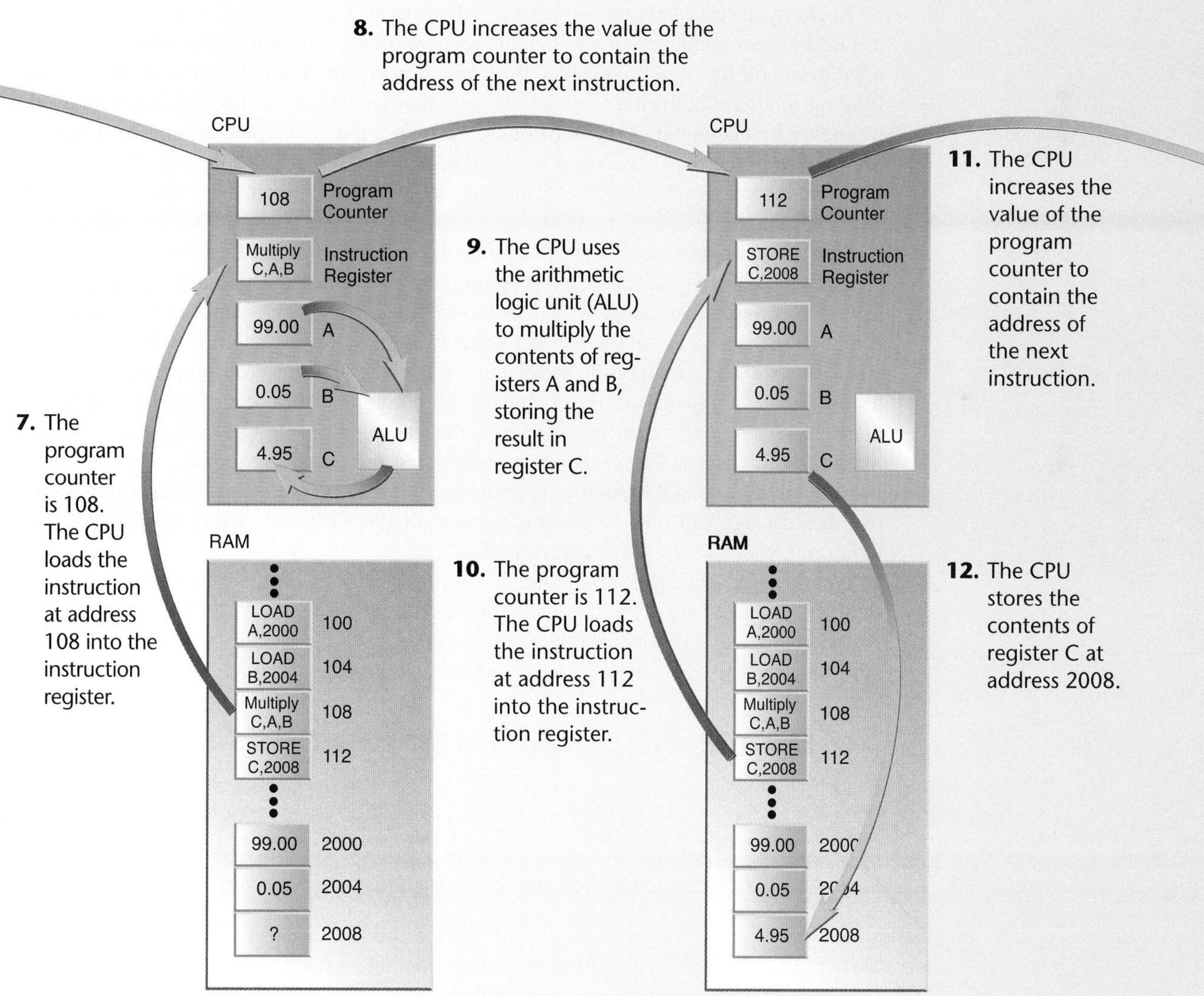

8. The CPU increases the value of the program counter to contain the address of the next instruction.
CPU
108
Program Counter
Multiply C,A,B
Instruction Register
99.00
A
0.05
B
4.95
C
ALU
RAM
LOAD A,2000
100
LOAD B,2004
104
Multiply C,A,B
108
STORE C,2008
112
99.00
2000
0.05
2004
?
2008
7. The program counter is 108. The CPU loads the instruction at address 108 into the instruction register.
9. The CPU uses the arithmetic logic unit (ALU) to multiply the contents of registers A and B, storing the result in register C.
10. The program counter is 112. The CPU loads the instruction at address 112 into the instruction register.
CPU
112
Program Counter
STORE C,2008
Instruction Register
99.00
A
0.05
B
4.95
C
ALU
RAM
LOAD A,2000
100
LOAD B,2004
104
Multiply C,A,B
108
STORE C,2008
112
99.00
0.05
4.95
2008
11. The CPU increases the value of the program counter to contain the address of the next instruction.
12. The CPU stores the contents of register C at address 2008.

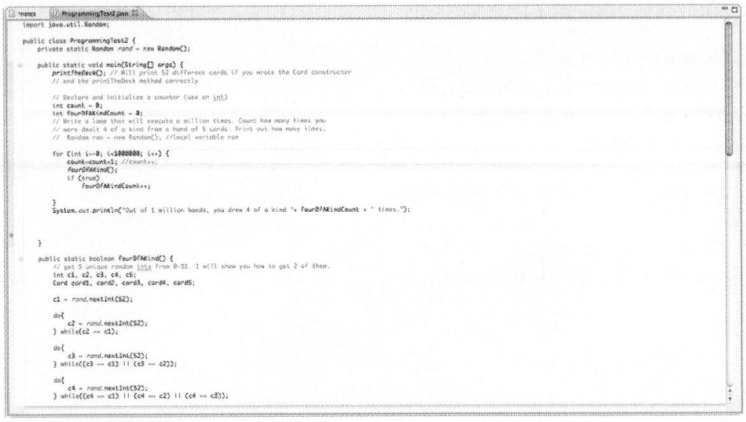

FIGURE 4.7 Compilers enable programmers to write in high-level languages, such as Java (shown), C#, or C++.

Today most programmers use programming languages, such as C++, Java, and Visual Basic, that fall somewhere between natural human languages and precise machine languages. These languages, referred to as **high-level languages**, make it possible for scientists, engineers, and businesspeople to solve problems using familiar terminology and notation rather than cryptic machine instructions. For a computer to understand a program written in one of these languages, it must use a translator program to convert the English-like instructions to the zeros and ones of machine language. The most common type of translator program is called a **compiler** because it compiles a complete translation of the program from a high-level computer language (such as C#) into machine language before the program runs for the first time. The compiled program can run again and again; it doesn't need to be recompiled unless instructions need to be changed.

To clarify the translation process, let's go back to the kitchen. Imagine a recipe translator that enables our computer chef to look up phrases such as "fry until golden brown." Like a reference book for beginning cooks, this translator fills in all the details about testing and flipping foods in the frying pan, so our computer cook, Robert, understands what to do whenever he encounters "fry until golden brown" in any recipe. As long as Robert is equipped with the translator, we don't need to include so many details in each recipe. We can communicate at a higher level. The more sophisticated the translator, the easier the job of the programmer.

Programming languages have steadily evolved during the past few decades. Each new generation of languages makes the programming process easier by taking on, and hiding from the programmer, more of the detail-oriented work. The computer's unrelenting demands for technical details haven't gone away; they're just handled automatically by translation software. As a result, programming is easier and less error prone. As translators become more sophisticated, programmers can communicate in computer languages that more closely resemble **natural languages**—the languages people speak and write every day.

Even with state-of-the-art computer languages, programming requires a considerable investment of time and brainpower. Fortunately, many tasks that required programming two decades ago can now be accomplished with spreadsheets, graphics programs, Web tools, and other easy-to-use software applications.

Programming languages are still used to solve problems that can't be handled with off-the-shelf software, but virtually all computer users manage to do their work without programming. Programming today is done mainly by professional software developers, who use programming languages to create and refine the applications and other programs the rest of us use.

Software Applications: Tools for Users

> The computer is **only a fast idiot**; it has no imagination; it cannot originate action. It is, and will remain, **only a tool to man**.
>
> *—American Library Association reaction to the UNIVAC computer exhibit at the 1964 New York World's Fair*

Software applications enable users to control computers without having to think like programmers do. We now turn our attention to applications.

Consumer Applications

Computer stores, consumer electronics stores, mail-order houses, and Internet stores sell thousands of software titles: publishing programs, accounting software, personal-information managers, graphics programs, multimedia tools, educational titles, games, and more. The process of buying computer software is similar to the process of buying music or movies, but there are some important differences.

Documentation

A computer software package, whether downloaded (copied) from a Web site or purchased on a disc, generally includes **documentation**—instructions for installing and using the software. The documentation might be provided in the form of printed manuals, digital files for on-screen reading, or some combination of the two. Software packages generally include *Read Me* files with installation instructions and last-minute release notes. They also might include paper or digital user's guides, tutorials, and reference manuals. But many software companies have replaced traditional manuals with *help files* that appear on-screen at the user's request. Help files are supplemented and updated with *online help* that can be accessed through the local help files or at the company's Web site. Online help sometimes includes video tutorials and other multimedia experiences that aren't possible in paper manuals. Many programs are so easy to use that it's possible to put them to work without reading the documentation. But they often include advanced features that aren't obvious through trial-and-error experimentation.

FIGURE 4.8 Adobe's Web site includes video tutorials designed to introduce features of Photoshop and other Adobe programs.

Updating and Upgrading

Most software companies continually improve their programs by removing bugs and adding new features. A typical company might release minor free **updates** (containing bug fixes and minor enhancements) several times a year and major **upgrades** (with significant new features and/or improvements) every year or two. Microsoft and other companies occasionally release free *service packs* containing bundled updates. An upgrade to the next major version of a program typically costs an upgrade fee. To distinguish between versions, program names often include version numbers, as in FileMaker Pro 11. Most companies use decimals to indicate minor revisions and whole numbers to indicate major revisions. For example, iTunes 9.0.1 is only slightly different than iTunes 9.0.0, but it's a major improvement over iTunes 8. Many product names, such as Quicken 2011, use years to indicate versions. Still others use name changes. For example, the last few versions of Microsoft's consumer operating system have been marketed as Windows 98, Windows Millennium Edition (Windows Me), Windows XP Home Edition, Windows Vista Home (Basic or Premium), and Windows 7 Home Edition (Basic or Premium).

Some applications are designed so they can be customized with add-ons called plug-ins. A *plug-in* (or plugin) is a program that interacts with the host application, extending its functionality in some way. A plug-in might be created and distributed by the same company that produced the host application, or it might be developed by another company. For example, the Adobe Reader plug-in allows you to view PDF documents (discussed in Chapter 5) in a Web browser.

Compatibility

A computer software buyer must be concerned with **compatibility**. When you buy an audio CD, you don't need to specify the brand of your CD player because all manufacturers adhere to common industry standards. But no complete, universal software standards exist in the computer world, so a program written for one type of computer system or smart phone may not work on another. Software packages contain labels with statements such as "Requires Windows 7 with 2 GB of RAM." These demands should not be taken lightly; without compatible hardware and software, most software programs are worthless.

Disclaimers

According to the little-read warranties included with many software packages, some applications might technically be worthless even if you have compatible hardware and software. Here's the first paragraph from a typical software warranty, which is part of a longer **end-user license agreement (EULA)**, pronounced "yoo-la":

> *This program is provided "as is" without warranty of any kind. The entire risk as to the result and performance of the program is assumed by you. Should the program prove defective, you—and not the manufacturer or its dealers—assume the entire cost of all necessary servicing, repair, or correction. Further, the manufacturer does not warranty, guarantee, or make any representations regarding the use of, or the result of the use of, the program in terms of correctness, accuracy, reliability, for being current, or otherwise, and you rely on the program and its results solely at your own risk.*

Software companies hide behind disclaimers because nobody's figured out how to write error-free software. Remember our problems providing our cook, Robert, with a foolproof set of instructions for producing French toast? Programmers who write applications such as word processing programs must try to anticipate and respond to all combinations of commands and actions users might perform under any conditions. Given the difficulty of this task, most programs work amazingly well—but not perfectly.

Licensing

When you buy a typical computer software package, you're not actually buying the software. Instead, you're buying a **software license** to use the program. (This is also true for most movies and songs, whether purchased online or on disc.) While end-user licensing agreements vary, most include limitations on your right to install and use the software on multiple computers, copy discs, install software on hard drives, and transfer information to other users. Many companies offer ***volume licenses***—special licenses for families, companies, schools, or government institutions. Some companies even rent software to corporate and government clients.

Virtually all commercial software is copyrighted. **Copyrighted software** can't be legally duplicated for distribution to others. Some software CDs and DVDs (mostly entertainment products) are ***copy protected*** with **digital rights management (DRM)** technology to ensure that they can't be duplicated with conventional copying techniques. A milder, more common form of copy protection is to require the user to type his or her name and a product serial number before a newly installed program will work. Between these two extremes, many software companies require new owners to complete an online authorization process.

Because programming is so difficult, software development is expensive. Software developers use copyrights and copy protection to ensure that they sell enough copies of their products to recover their investments and stay in business to write programs.

Software piracy is the unauthorized copying and selling of software. By some estimates, global software piracy costs U.S. companies tens of billions of dollars in lost revenues every year. At the end of this chapter and in later chapters, we'll discuss laws protecting the rights of software developers.

Distribution

Software is distributed through direct sales forces to corporations and other institutions. Software is sold to consumers through retail stores and online outlets. Web distribution makes it possible for companies to offer software without packaging or disks. It also makes it easy for companies to offer trial versions of programs. For example, you might download (copy) a demo version of a commercial program from a company's Web site or some other source; the demo program is identical to the commercial version, but with some features disabled or a time limit placed on its usage. After you try the program and decide you want to buy it, you can purchase a code to unlock the disabled features of the program.

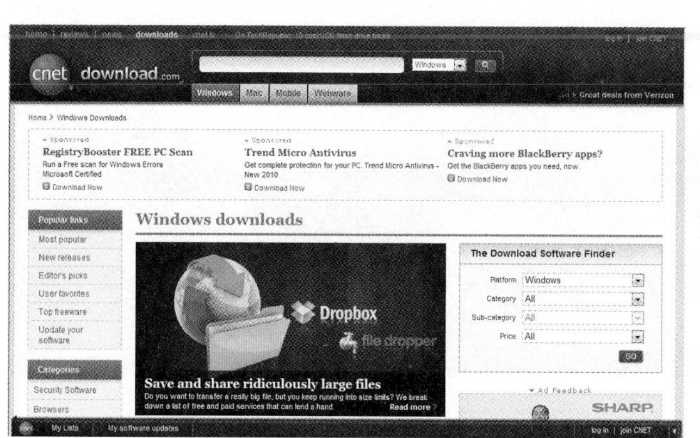

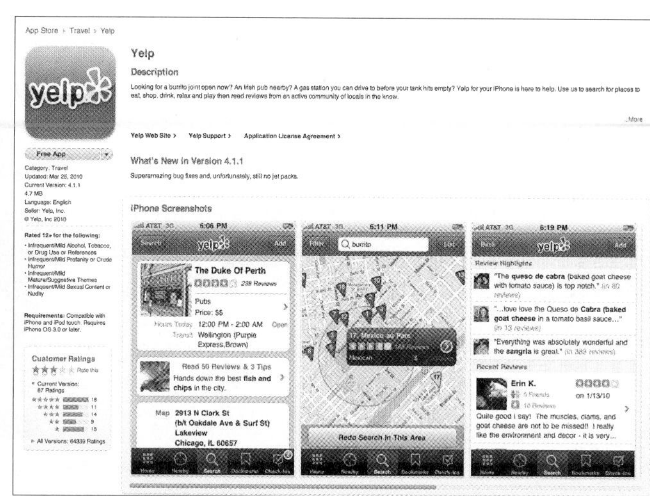

FIGURE 4.9 Download.com (left) is one of many Web sites where you can download freeware, shareware, and commercial software for PCs, Macs, and smart phones. The iTunes App store (right) provides a similar service for users of Apple's iPhones, iPads, and iPod Touches.

Not all software is copyrighted. Web sites, user groups, and other sources commonly offer **public-domain software** (free for the taking) and **shareware** (free for the trying, with a send-payment-if-you-keep-it honor system) along with demo versions of commercial programs. The term *open source* refers to freely accessible software in which the program's source code is part of the distribution. (Linux, discussed at the beginning of this chapter, is open-source software.) Public-domain software, shareware, demo software, and open-source software can be legally copied and shared freely.

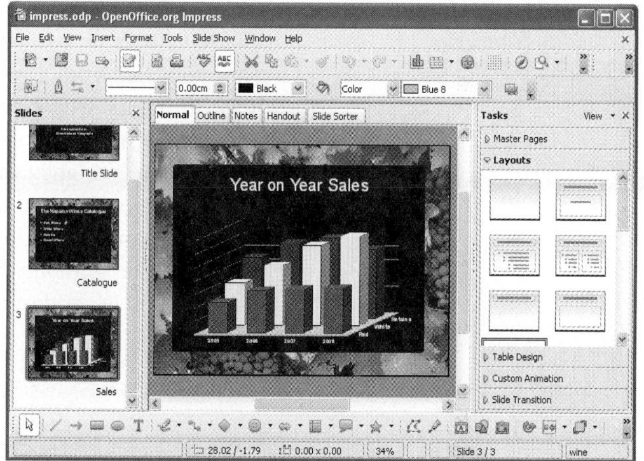

FIGURE 4.10 The open-source application suite OpenOffice.org provides compatibility with Microsoft Office documents but runs on a variety of platforms, including Windows, Linux, and the Mac OS.

Web Applications

There's a growing trend toward using **Web applications**—applications that run on remote Internet servers rather than on local PCs. A Web application typically (but not always) requires a Web browser to work. It might be designed for use by the general public via the Internet, or by a smaller group of individuals on a corporate or institutional network.

Some Web applications look and perform like PC applications. Google Docs includes full-featured word processor, spreadsheet, and presentation graphics software. These programs enable users to edit documents and save them on remote servers or local disks using standard Web browsers. Similarly, Photoshop.com is a simplified Web version of Adobe's popular photo editing and organization program. Webmail programs, including Gmail, Hotmail, and Yahoo! Mail, perform the same functions as the mail programs that come with Microsoft Office or Mac OS X.

Other Web applications take care of business that can't be handled by standard desktop applications. A multiplayer online game turns the Internet into a playing field, enabling global competition and cooperation. A wiki—a collection of Web pages that can be edited by anyone who accesses it—is a type of interactive, collaborative document that can't exist on an isolated PC; the encyclopedia Wikipedia is the best-known example. Retail sites such as Amazon.com and Gap.com use complex Web applications to make shopping simple for their customers. Online auctions such as eBay connect buyers and sellers all around the world. Online communities such as Facebook are built on ever-growing clusters of Web applications that link members to each other. Other Web applications provide instant access to maps, driving directions, weather reports, newsfeeds, Internet radio stations, on-demand video, and much more.

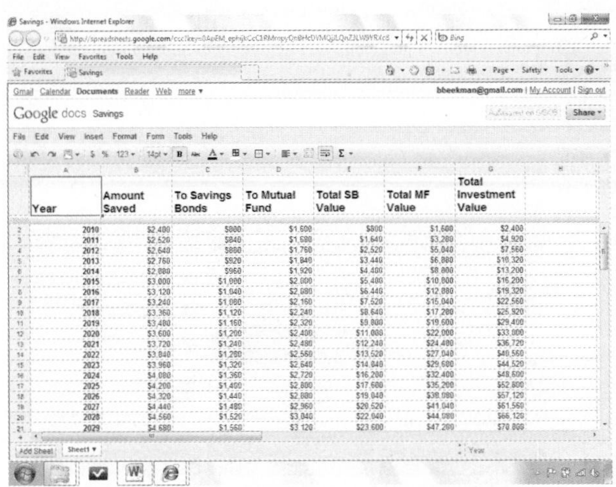

Year	Amount Saved	To Savings Bonds	To Mutual Fund	Total SB Value	Total MF Value	Total Investment Value
2010	$2,400	$800	$1,600	$800	$1,600	$2,400
2011	$2,520	$840	$1,680	$1,640	$3,280	$4,920
2012	$2,640	$880	$1,760	$2,520	$5,040	$7,560
2013	$2,760	$920	$1,840	$3,440	$6,880	$10,320
2014	$2,880	$960	$1,920	$4,400	$8,800	$13,200
2015	$3,000	$1,000	$2,000	$5,400	$10,800	$16,200
2016	$3,120	$1,040	$2,080	$6,440	$12,880	$19,320
2017	$3,240	$1,080	$2,160	$7,520	$15,040	$22,560
2018	$3,360	$1,120	$2,240	$8,640	$17,280	$25,920
2019	$3,480	$1,160	$2,320	$9,800	$19,600	$29,400
2020	$3,600	$1,200	$2,400	$11,000	$22,000	$33,000
2021	$3,720	$1,240	$2,480	$12,240	$24,480	$36,720
2022	$3,840	$1,280	$2,560	$13,520	$27,040	$40,560
2023	$3,960	$1,320	$2,640	$14,840	$29,680	$44,520
2024	$4,080	$1,360	$2,720	$16,200	$32,400	$48,600
2025	$4,200	$1,400	$2,800	$17,600	$35,200	$52,800
2026	$4,320	$1,440	$2,880	$19,040	$38,080	$57,120
2027	$4,440	$1,480	$2,960	$20,520	$41,040	$61,560
2028	$4,560	$1,520	$3,040	$22,040	$44,080	$66,120
2029	$4,680	$1,560	$3,120	$23,600	$47,200	$70,800

FIGURE 4.11 Google Spreadsheets is a Web application similar to Microsoft Excel and other PC spreadsheet programs. Another Web application, Photoshop.com, allows you to upload, organize, and edit your photos using a Web browser.

Some Web applications, called ***mashups***, provide new services by combining data or functionality from two or more external sources. For example, a Web site might combine crime statistics from a police Web site with maps from Google to create visual representations of exactly where crimes are occurring in a city. Another might combine language translation with Web search to allow a user to search for terms in another language. Some Web sites are designed to encourage mashups; their programmers think of them as modules that can be plugged into other Web applications. A small but growing number of programmers work in worldwide communities creating modules that can be combined into mashups. (The term *mashup* is also used to describe video and audio works created from multiple sources, as described in Chapter 6.)

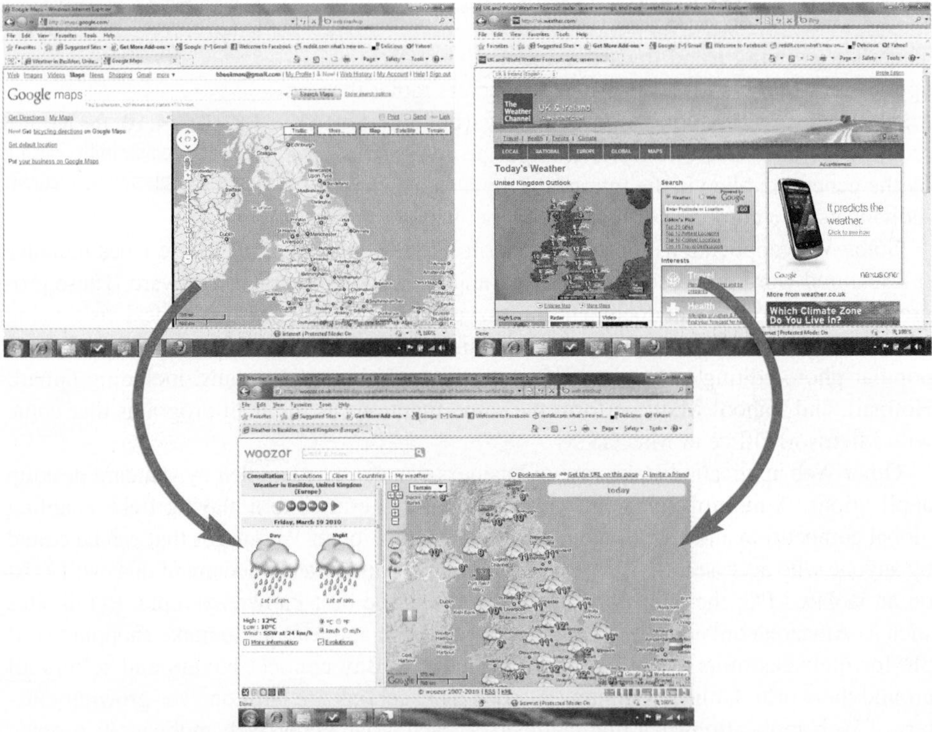

FIGURE 4.12 Woozor.com is a Web mashup that combines data from Google maps and the Weather Channel to produce dynamic custom weather maps.

For most Web applications users, software compatibility is not an issue. Most Web applications are designed to work without modification on computers running Windows, Mac OS, Linux, or other operating systems. Using a Web application, a person can start and save a job on a Windows PC at work, continue it on a Mac at home, complete it on a Linux machine in an Internet café, and recheck it on an iPhone while waiting for a ride home.

Web applications offer other advantages. Users of Web applications don't have to worry about application upgrades and updates, as long as they keep their Web browsers up to date. And most Web applications are free (although some sites pay their bills by barraging users with advertisements).

FIGURE 4.13 Vertical-market software helps this researcher track geographic information.

Vertical-Market and Custom Software

Because of their flexibility, basic office applications are used in homes, schools, government offices, and all kinds of businesses. But many computer applications are so job specific that they're of little interest or use to anybody outside a given profession. Medical billing software, library cataloging software, legal reference software, restaurant management software, and other applications designed specifically for a particular business or industry are called **vertical-market applications** or **custom applications**. A custom application might run on a single computer, or it might be a mashup that combines data and applications from several different business systems across the Web.

Vertical-market applications tend to cost far more than mass-market applications because companies that develop the software have fewer potential customers to recover their development costs from. In fact, some custom applications are programmed specifically for single clients. For example, the software used to control the space shuttle was developed with a single customer—NASA—in mind.

System Software: The Hardware-Software Connection

> Originally, operating systems were envisioned as a way to handle one of the most complex input/output operations: communicating with a variety of disk drives. But, **the operating system quickly evolved into an all-encompassing bridge** between your PC and the software you run on it.
>
> —*Ron White, in* How Computers Work

When you're typing a paper or writing a program, you don't need to concern yourself with low-level details, such as which parts of the computer's memory hold your document, the segments of the word processing software currently in the computer's memory, or the output instructions sent by the computer to the printer. **System software**, a class of software that includes the operating system and utility programs, handles these details and hundreds of other tasks behind the scenes.

What the Operating System Does

Every general-purpose computer today, whether it's a timesharing supercomputer or a laptop PC, depends on an **operating system (OS)** to keep hardware running efficiently and to make the process of communication with that hardware easier. Operating system software

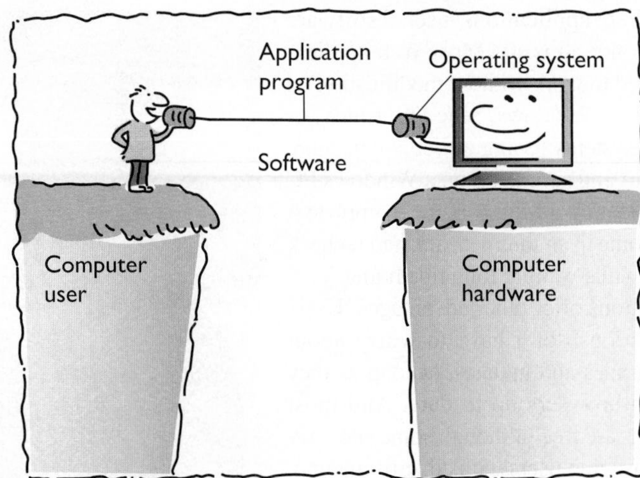

FIGURE 4.14 The user's view: When a person uses an application, whether a game or an accounting program, the person doesn't communicate directly with the computer hardware. Instead, the user interacts with the application, which depends on the operating system to manage and control hardware.

runs continuously whenever your computer is on, providing an additional layer of insulation between you and the bits-and-bytes world of computer hardware. Because the operating system stands between the software application and the hardware, application compatibility is usually defined by the operating system as well as by the hardware.

The operating system, as the name implies, is a system of programs that performs a variety of technical operations, from basic communication with peripherals to complex networking and security tasks.

- The operating system maintains the file system that keeps track of the location on the hard drive of all programs and data files. (There's more on how the operating system stores files on disks later in this chapter.)
- To support **multitasking**—the concurrent execution of multiple applications—the operating system creates dozens of processes (also called tasks). For example, there is usually at least one process associated with every window on the computer's screen. Because the CPU can execute only one process at a time, the operating system must do task scheduling, allocating blocks of CPU time to the processes to enable them to make progress.
- Operating systems manage **virtual memory**—space on a hard disk (or other storage device)—that simulates random access memory. Virtual memory is useful when there isn't enough RAM to store all of the necessary data and instructions for currently running applications. From the software's point of view, virtual memory is just like RAM (except that it has slower access time). Virtual memory is divided into same-sized blocks called pages. When a process is not running on the CPU, its pages can be held temporarily on a hard disk. When a process is running, the pages containing the instructions and data needed by the CPU are brought into RAM, displacing pages used by an idle process.
- On multiuser systems, the operating system is responsible for ***authentication*** (determining that users are who they claim to be) and ***authorization*** (ensuring that users have permission to perform a particular action). An example of an authentication mechanism is requiring a user to enter a login name and password before using the computer. An example of an authorization mechanism is allowing only those with administrative privileges to install or uninstall application programs.

Utility Programs and Device Drivers

Even the best operating systems leave some housekeeping tasks to other programs and to the user. **Utility programs** serve as tools for doing system maintenance and repairs that aren't automatically handled by the operating system. Utilities make it easier for users to copy files between storage devices, repair damaged data files, translate files so that different programs can read them, guard against viruses and other potentially harmful programs (as described in Chapter 10), compress files so they take up less disk space, and perform other important, if unexciting, tasks.

The operating system can directly invoke many utility programs, so they appear to the user to be part of the operating system. For example, **device drivers** are small programs that enable I/O devices—keyboard, mouse, printer, and others—to communicate with the computer. Once a device driver—say, for a new printer—is installed, the printer driver functions as a behind-the-scenes intermediary whenever the user requests that a document be printed on that printer. Some utility programs are included with the operating system. Others, including many device drivers, are bundled with peripherals. Still others are sold or given away as separate products.

Where the Operating System Lives

Some computers—mostly game machines, handheld computers, smart phones, and special-purpose computers—store their operating systems permanently in ROM (read-only memory) so they can begin working immediately when the user turns them on. But because ROM is unchangeable, operating systems on these machines can't be modified or upgraded without hardware transplants. Some computers, including many handheld devices, store their operating system in flash memory so it can be upgraded. But most computers, including all modern PCs, hold only a small portion of the operating system in ROM. The remainder of the operating system is loaded into memory in a process called **booting**, which occurs when you turn on the computer. (The term *booting* is used because the computer seems to pull itself up by its own bootstraps.)

Most of the time the operating system works behind the scenes, taking care of business without the knowledge or intervention of the user. But occasionally it's necessary for a user to communicate directly with the operating system. For example, when you boot a PC, the operating system takes over the screen, waiting until you tell it—with the mouse, the keyboard, or some other input device—what to do. If you tell it to open a graphics application, the operating system locates the program, copies it from disk into memory, turns the screen over to the application, and accepts commands from the application while you draw pictures on the screen.

Interacting with the operating system, like interacting with an application, can be anywhere from intuitive to challenging. It depends on something called the user interface. Because of its profound impact on the computing experience, the user interface is a critically important component of almost every piece of software.

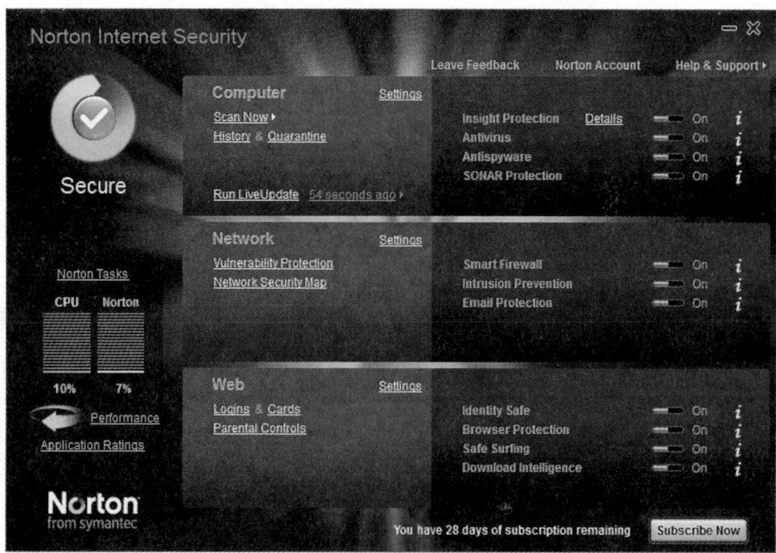

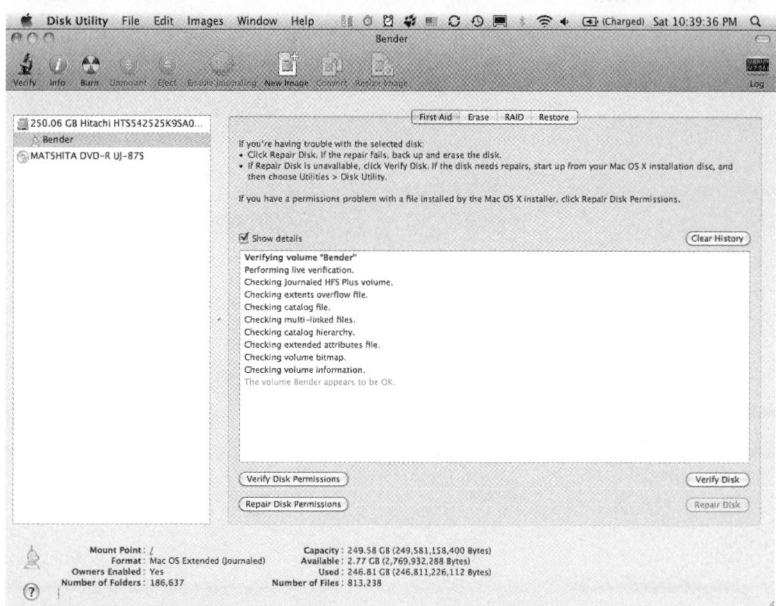

FIGURE 4.15 Norton Internet Security is a utility that provides protection from viruses, spyware, and other Internet risks. Disk Utility is a Mac utility that includes diagnostic and repair tools for hard disks.

how it works The Operating System

Most of what you see on screen when you use an application program and most of the common tasks you have the program perform, such as saving and opening files, are being performed by the operating system at the application's request.

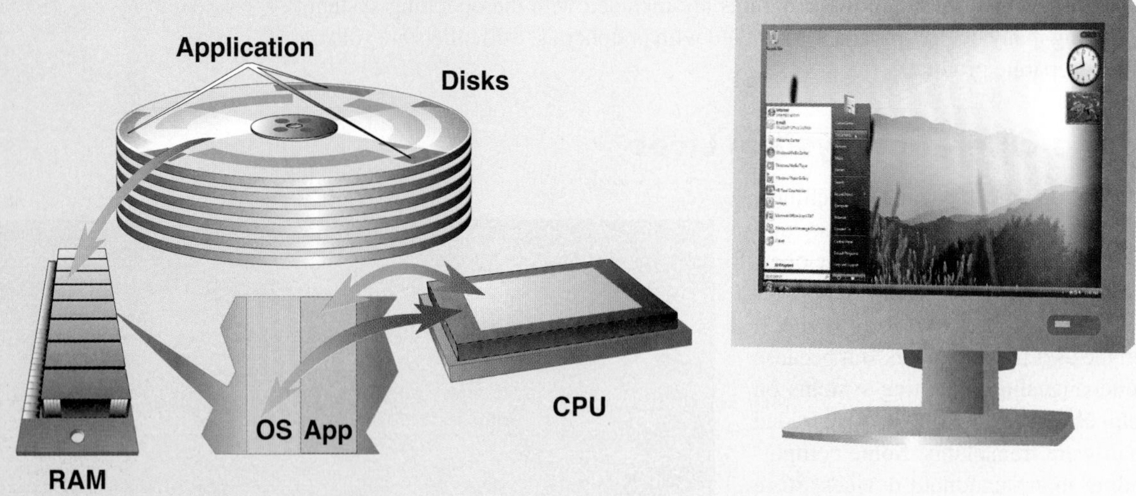

When a computer is turned off, there's nothing in RAM (random access memory), and the CPU isn't doing anything. The operating system (OS) programs must be in memory and running on the CPU before the system can function. When you turn on the computer, the CPU automatically begins executing instructions stored in ROM (read-only memory). These instructions help the system boot, and the operating system is loaded from the disk into part of the system's memory.

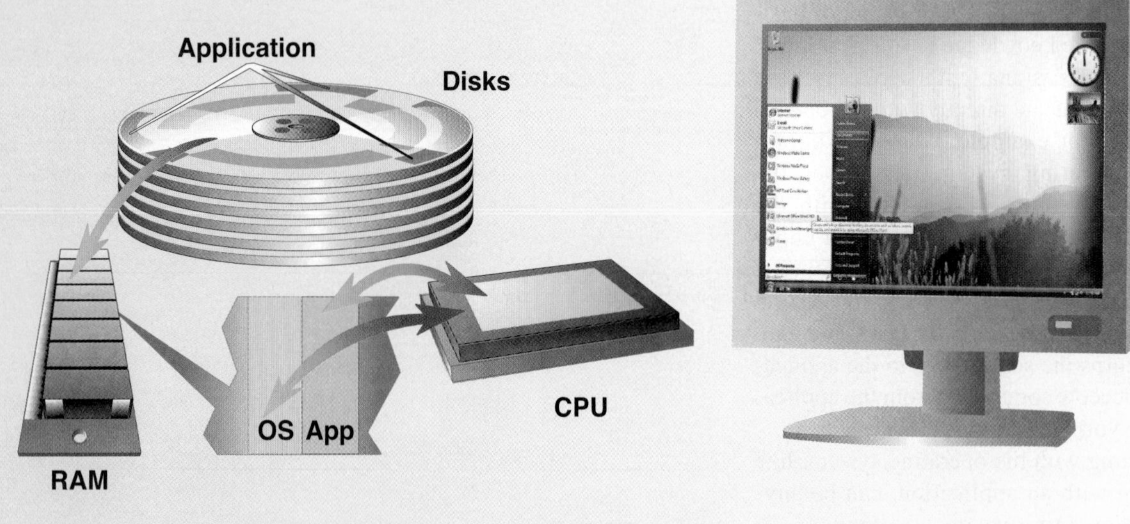

FIGURE 4.16

Using the mouse, you "ask" the operating system to load a word processing application program into memory so it can run.

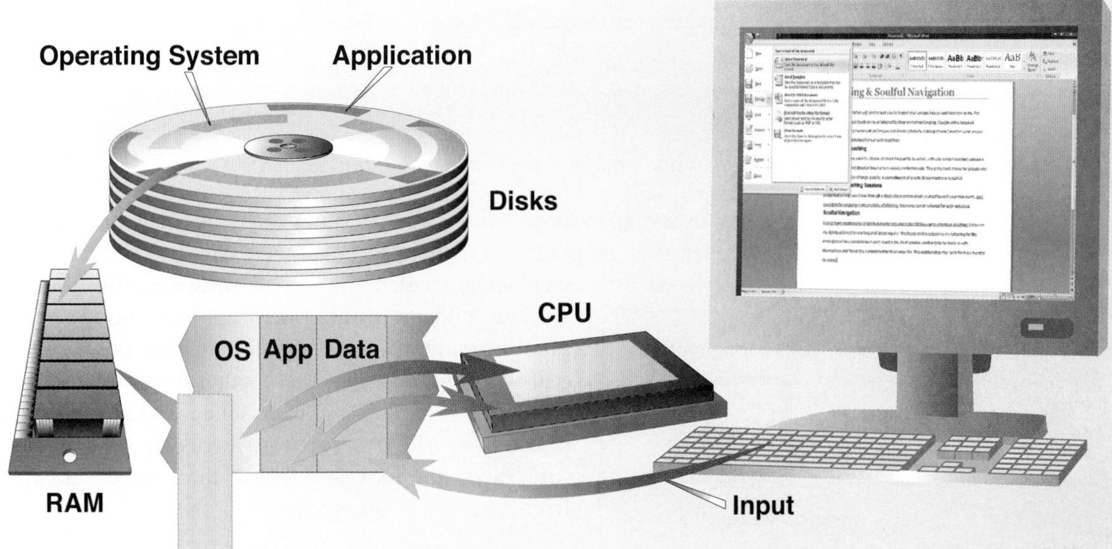

The loaded application occupies a portion of memory, leaving that much less for other programs and data. The OS remains in memory, so it can provide services to the application program, helping it to display on-screen menus, communicate with the printer, and perform other common actions. Because the OS and application are in constant communication, control—the location in memory where the CPU is reading program instructions—jumps around. If the application calls the OS to help display a menu, the application tells the CPU, "Go follow the menu display instructions at address *X* in the operating system area; when you're done, return here and pick up where you left off."

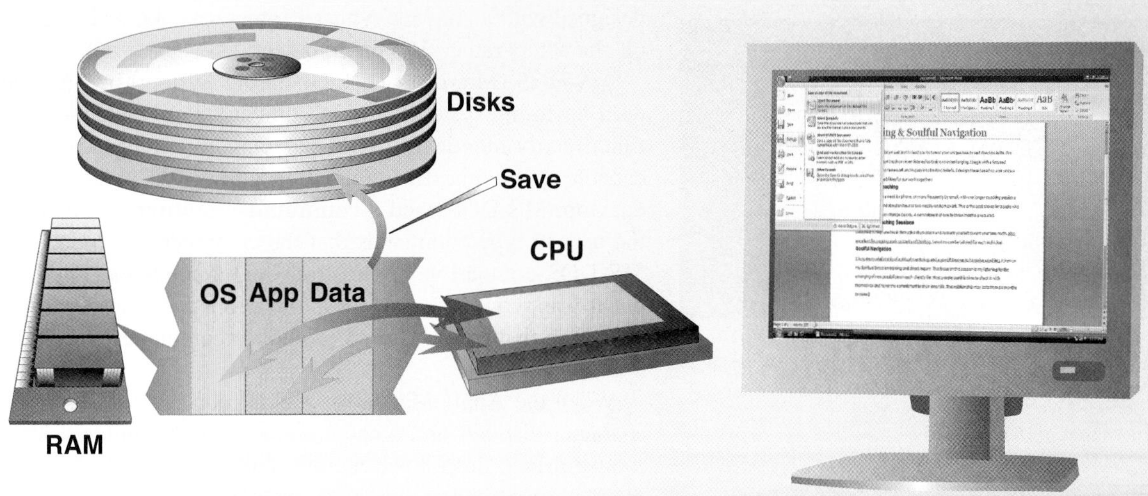

To avoid losing your data file when the system is turned off, you save it to the disk, meaning you have the OS write it into a file on the disk for later use. The OS handles communication between the CPU and the disk drive, ensuring that your file doesn't overwrite other information. (Later, when you reopen the file, the OS locates it on the disk and copies it into memory so the CPU—and, therefore, any program—can see it and work with it.)

The User Interface: The Human–Machine Connection

> The anthropologist Claude Levi-Strauss has called human beings **tool makers and symbol makers**. The user interface is potentially the most sophisticated of these constructions, one in which **the distinction between tool and symbol is blurred**.
>
> *—Aaron Marcus and Andries van Dam, user interface experts*

Early computer users had to spend tedious hours writing and debugging machine-language instructions. Later users programmed in languages that were easier to understand but still technically challenging. As PC software evolved, most users worked with preprogrammed applications, such as word processors, that simulated and amplified the capabilities of real-world tools. Today's computer users supplement those tools with programs and experiences unlike anything in the physical world. As software evolves, so does the **user interface**—the look and feel of the computing experience from a human point of view.

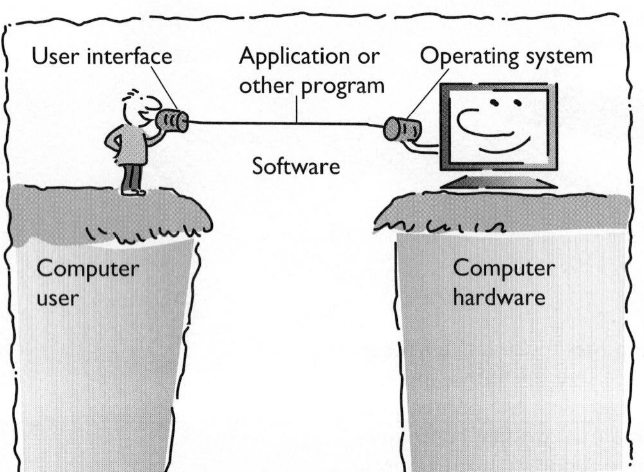

FIGURE 4.17 The user's view revisited: The user interface is the part of the computer system that the user sees. A well-designed user interface hides the bothersome details of computing from the user.

```
    cd \winnt\profiles\username\programs\start menu
is the same as:
    cd "\winnt\profiles\username\programs\start menu"
which is what you would have to type if extensions were di
D:\Documents and Settings\Stephanie>dir
 Volume in drive D has no label.
 Volume Serial Number is D4FD-D98A

 Directory of D:\Documents and Settings\Stephanie

01/13/2004  02:14 AM    <DIR>          .
01/13/2004  02:14 AM    <DIR>          ..
01/27/2004  07:58 PM    <DIR>          Desktop
01/13/2004  02:26 AM    <DIR>          Favorites
01/14/2004  06:13 AM    <DIR>          My Documents
09/16/2003  08:47 PM               906 reglog.txt
```

FIGURE 4.18 MS-DOS users work with a character-based interface.

FIGURE 4.19 Many consumer devices today, including some phones, label printers, and equipment controllers, have character-based user interfaces.

Desktop Operating Systems

The earliest PC operating systems, created for the Apple II, the original IBM PC, and other machines, looked nothing like today's Mac and Windows operating systems. When IBM introduced its first personal computer in 1981, a typical computer monitor displayed 24 80-column lines of text, numbers, and/or symbols. The computer sent messages to the monitor telling it which character to display in each location on the screen. To comply with this hardware arrangement, the PC's dominant operating system, MS-DOS, was designed with a **character-based interface**—a user interface based on characters rather than on graphics.

MS-DOS (Microsoft Disk Operating System) became the standard operating system on IBM-compatible computers—computers functionally identical to IBM personal computers and, therefore, capable of running IBM-compatible software. Unlike the Windows desktop, MS-DOS used a **command-line interface** that required the user to type commands that the computer responded to. Some MS-DOS-compatible applications had a command-line interface, but it was more common for applications to have a **menu-driven interface** that enabled users to choose commands from on-screen lists called **menus**.

When the Apple Macintosh was introduced in 1984, it replaced character displays and typed commands with windows, icons, and mouse-driven drop-down menus. The Mac was the first low-cost computer that had an operating system designed with a **graphical user interface (GUI)**, pronounced "gooey." But the **Mac OS**, was eclipsed by **Microsoft Windows**, which quickly became the most popular operating system for PCs. (For an introduction to Windows and Mac OS, see Appendix A).

Windows and the Mac OS have evolved over the years, adding new features to their GUIs to make them easier to use. The Windows **taskbar** provides one-click access to open applications, making it easy to switch back and forth among different tasks. **Hierarchical menus**

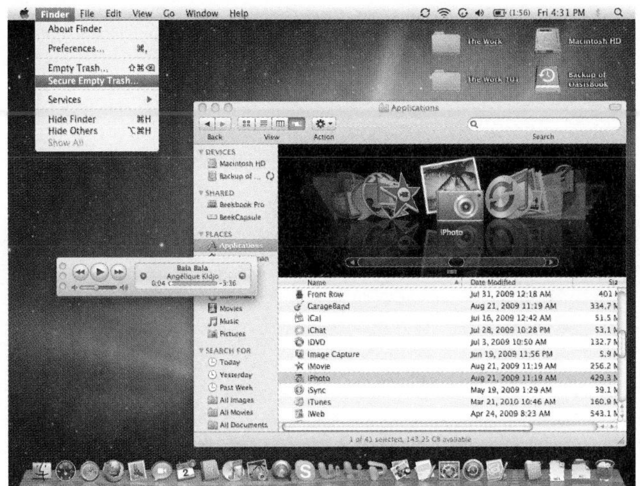

FIGURE 4.20 Mac OS X refines the traditional graphical user interface with a modern take on windows, icons, and directories.

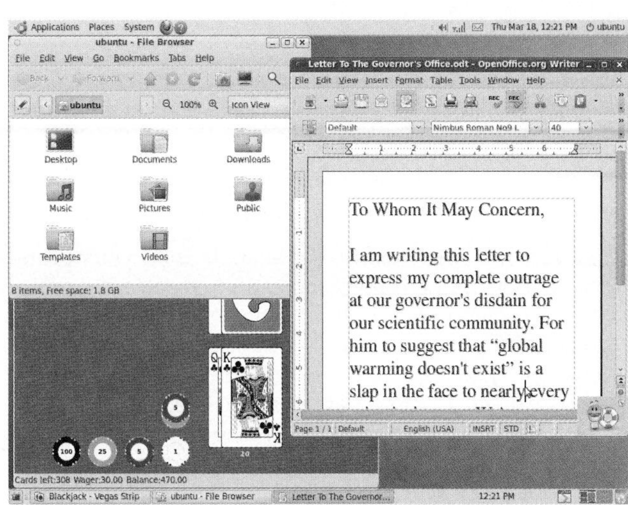

FIGURE 4.21 Many versions of Linux, including Ubuntu Linux, use menus and icons in ways that would be familiar to Windows and Macintosh users.

in Windows and Mac OS organize frequently needed commands into compact, efficient submenus, and pop-up menus can appear anywhere on the screen. Context-sensitive menus offer choices that depend on which on-screen object the user has currently selected.

While there are many differences between Windows and Mac OS, the two now have user interfaces that are more alike than different. Many applications, including Adobe Photoshop and Microsoft Office, are almost identical on Windows and the Mac OS.

Both Windows and the Mac OS started as single-user operating systems. But today both support multiple users. Both are available in server versions that can be used as alternatives to UNIX, the OS that has ruled the server market for decades.

UNIX and Linux

Because of its historical ties to academic and government research sites, the Internet is still heavily populated with computers running the UNIX operating system. UNIX, developed at Bell Labs more than a decade before the first PCs, enables a timesharing computer to communicate with several other computers or terminals at one time. UNIX has long been the operating system of choice for workstations and mainframes in research and academic settings. In recent years it has taken root in many business environments. In spite of competition from Microsoft, UNIX is still favored by many who require an industrial-strength, multiuser operating system. Some form of UNIX is available for personal computers, workstations, servers, mainframes, and supercomputers.

Commercial brands of UNIX are available from Sun (Solaris), Hewlett-Packard (HP-UX), and IBM (AIX). Most Mac users don't know it, but Mac OS X is built on top of a version of UNIX. Linux, a UNIX clone described at the beginning of this chapter, is widely distributed for free and supported without cost by a devoted, technically savvy group of users.

At its heart, in all its versions, UNIX is a command-line, character-based operating system. The command-line interface (or shell) is similar to that of MS-DOS, although the commands aren't the same. For most tasks the UNIX command-line interface feels like a single-user system,

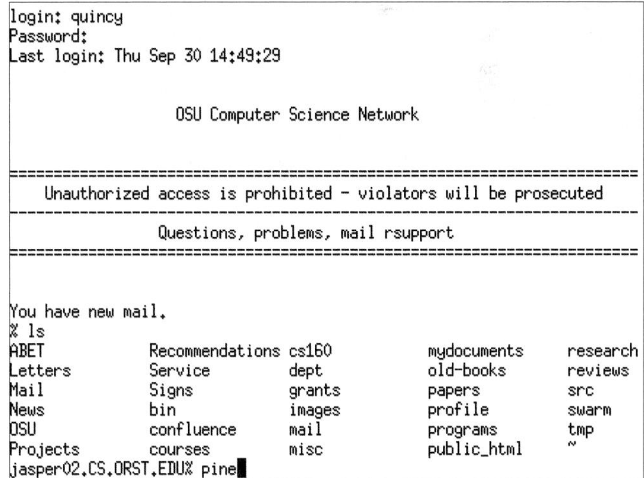

FIGURE 4.22 In its basic form, UNIX is a character-based operating system. This screen shows the beginning of a session on a school's multiuser UNIX mainframe. After the user (quincy) types his login name and password, the system responds with some introductory messages and a prompt (in this case, %). Quincy types the "ls" command to view the names of files in his home directory. The system lists the files and displays a new prompt. Quincy types "pine" to run the pine email program. The session continues this way until Quincy responds to a prompt with a command to log off the system. In practice, many UNIX users never see this type of command-line interface because of software shells with GUIs similar to Windows or Mac OS.

Working Wisdom When Good Software Goes Bad

Even the best software can fail when you need it most. These tips should help you deal with program freezes, system crashes, and other bugs that plague computer users.

- ***Restart the application.*** If the application you're running starts misbehaving, you can often solve the problem by saving your work, closing the application, and relaunching it. If you can't close it because it's frozen, use the system's force quit option. In Windows, press the Ctrl + Alt + Del keys at the same time, and then click Task Manager; then select the frozen program and click End Task. On a Mac, press Command-Option-Esc or choose Force Quit from the Apple menu; then select the frozen application from the list and click Force Quit. You may lose the last of your work with that application, but that's better than losing all of your work in every open application.
- ***Recover your work.*** If the application is frozen, you may not be able to save your work before closing. Fortunately, many applications can autosave your work every few minutes, so you don't lose more than a few minutes of work in a freeze or crash. Plan ahead: Save each document the minute you start working on it, and make sure you have your applications configured to autosave.
- ***Reboot the system.*** A surprising number of problems can be solved with a simple restart of the computer. A reboot can clear memory of bad data and reset parameters that might have been messed up by "buggy" software. If the computer is completely locked up, you can force a shutdown by holding down the power button on your computer for a few seconds.
- ***Recheck for updates.*** Sometimes the problem is out-of-date software. Check the Web to make sure you're using the current version of the misbehaving program and the OS. If you're not, download and install the latest patches.
- ***Reboot in safe mode.*** Some problems can be traced to hidden utilities, widgets, drivers, and other programs that run in the background while you're working with your computer. One of these hidden programs may have become corrupted, or may be clashing with some other program. You can start your machine in safe mode to disable most of these extra programs temporarily. On a Windows machine, press and hold the F8 key on the keyboard as the machine is booting, then use the arrow keys to select Safe Mode in the Windows Advanced Options Menu that

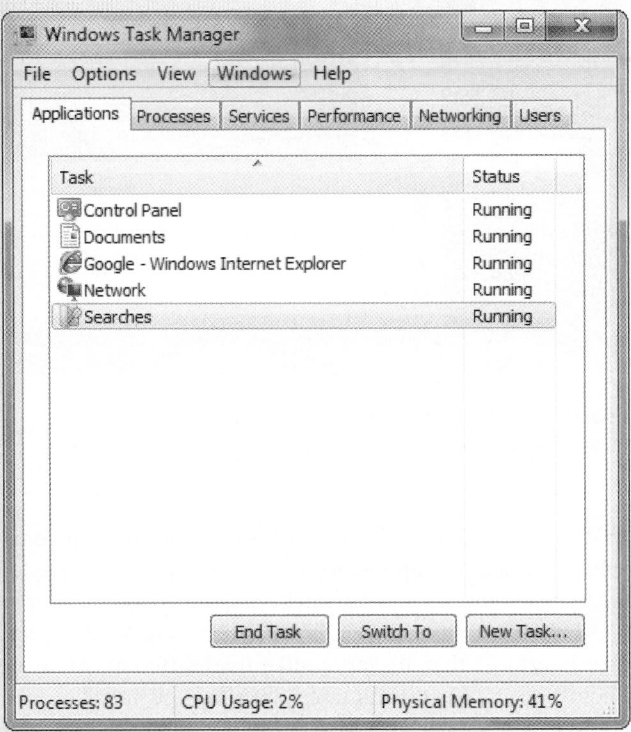

FIGURE 4.23a When an application freezes, you can use the Windows Task Manager to select the errant application and press End Task to terminate it.

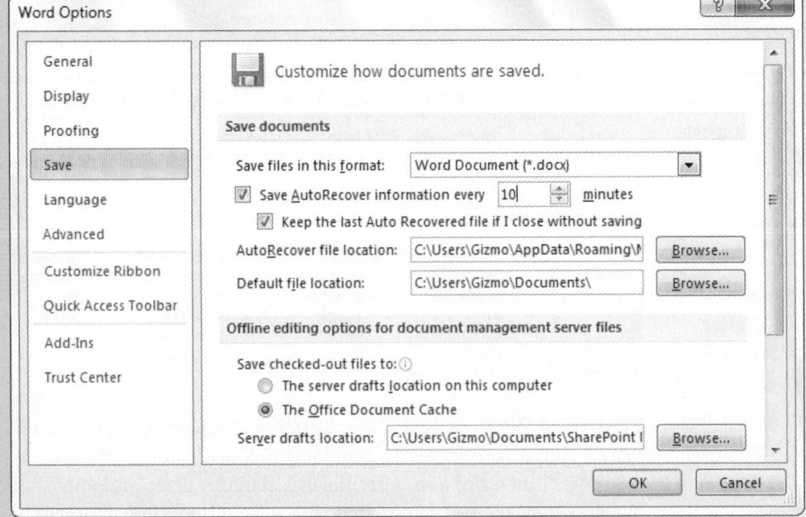

FIGURE 4.23b Microsoft Word, like many applications, includes an autosave option in its Preferences. Here the program is set to automatically save each open document every 10 minutes.

appears. On a Mac, hold down the Shift key while restarting until the Apple logo appears. If everything works fine in safe mode, but not otherwise, you'll probably need to do some detective work to identify the suspect software. (On a PC, you may also want to try loading the last known good configuration from the Windows Advanced Options Menu.)

- ***Research your problem.*** Check the Web for similar problems. Try using a few keywords in a search engine. If the program displayed an error message, you might try typing that into the search engine in quotes. You might also want to check forums and FAQs on the software company's Web site, or check popular sites that specialize in troubleshooting.
- ***Request help.*** Software technical support varies in quality and price from company to company. Sometimes it's free and very good; sometimes it's neither. But in some situations, it's your best shot at solving the problem.
- ***Reinstall the program.*** If the easy fixes fail, try uninstalling and reinstalling the software. Many programs can be downloaded from the Web, but you may need to type in your original serial number or perform some kind of initialization.
- ***Restore the operating system.*** The most serious problems may require you to back up your data onto another drive, wipe your hard disk clean, and perform a clean install of the OS and applications to start fresh.
- ***Repair the hardware.*** If all your software fixes fail, you may be dealing with hardware problems—a faulty circuit board, a failing hard drive, a short in a connector, or something else. You may need to ask a technician whether it's cost effective to troubleshoot and fix the problem. If it's an older computer or the problem is severe, you may need to look at the final solution—replace the system.
- ***Replace the system.*** If nothing else works, you'll have to start over with fresh hardware, and take consolation in the fact that your new system is faster and more powerful than your old one. But before you move on, don't forget to recycle your old computer.
- ***Recycle your old computer.*** Return it to the company through their recycling program or pass it on to someone who can recover any usable or recyclable parts.

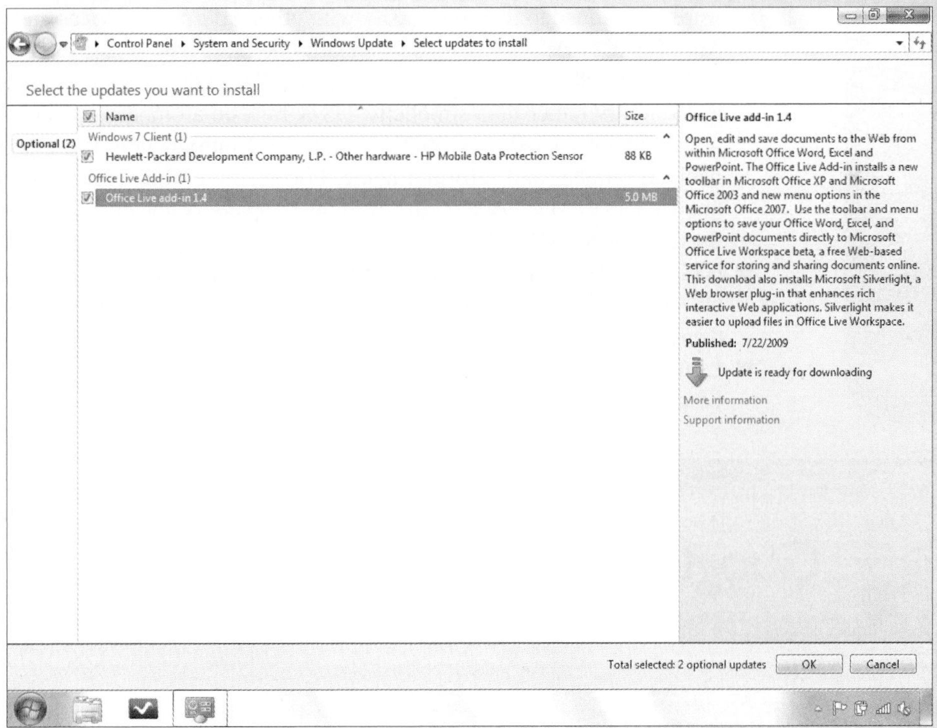

FIGURE 4.23c Windows Update (in Control Panels) checks the Web to see if there are any updates or patches for the currently running Windows OS. It's generally wise to install any updates soon after they're available.

even when many users are *logged in*—connected to and using the system. But today's UNIX systems work with more than just typed commands. Several companies, including Apple, Sun, and IBM, market UNIX variations and shells with graphical interfaces.

Hardware and Software Platforms

In most electronic devices, the operating system operates invisibly and anonymously. But some operating systems, especially those in PCs, are recognized by name and reputation. The most well-known operating systems include:

- **Microsoft Windows 7.** This is Microsoft's flagship product, introduced in 2009 to replace Windows Vista. Microsoft sells several different versions of Windows 7, including Windows 7 Starter, for simple home computing needs; Windows 7 Home Premium, which includes Windows Media Center software; Windows 7 Business, for business users; Windows 7 Enterprise, for global organizations with complex IT infrastructures; and Windows 7 Ultimate, the most feature-rich version of the operating system, with capabilities for home computing, mobile computing, and entertainment. All versions share the same code base. Even though Windows 7 has been around for a while, there are still many PCs around the world running Windows Vista, Windows XP, and other earlier Windows incarnations.
- **Microsoft Windows Server.** The server-based version of Windows runs on everything from small Web servers to the mightiest hardware on the planet. This product competes with UNIX and Linux.
- **Windows Embedded CE.** This stripped-down Windows variant is designed for embedded, connected devices, such as robots, voting machines, music players, and medical equipment.
- **Windows Phone 7.** A relatively new operating system for mobile phones. The software is designed to integrate easily with other Microsoft devices and programs.
- **Mac OS X (10).** OS X is the standard operating system for the Mac. Underneath its stylish, friendly exterior, OS X is built on UNIX, the powerful OS known for security and stability rather than simplicity. OS X runs on all modern Macs. Apple has released several major upgrades to OS X since its 2001 introduction. Each upgrade has a unique decimal number and informal name. For example, the version introduced in 2009 is known both as Mac OS 10.6 and as Snow Leopard. A few older Macs still run Mac OS 9, the original non-UNIX Mac OS.
- **iOS.** Apple's iPhone, iPad, and iPod Touch devices run on this efficient, easy-to-use OS. Although it's a variation of Mac OS X, programs that run on Macs can't run on iOS devices, or vice versa.
- **Linux, Sun Solaris, and other UNIX variations.** Some forms of UNIX or Linux can be found on PCs, Macs, workstations, supercomputers, mainframes, and a variety of other devices. Linux is especially popular because it is free—and freely supported by its partisans. Because Linux doesn't offer as many application programs as Windows does, some people use *dual-boot PCs* that can switch back and forth between Windows and Linux by simply rebooting.
- **Google Chrome OS.** This is a Linux-based OS designed for low-cost PCs, netbooks, and tablet devices. Chrome is designed with the Internet in mind—data is stored in the cloud rather than on local machines.
- **Google Android.** Like Google Chrome OS, this is Linux-based, but it's designed for smart phones. Google made headlines by making the entire OS available as open source, and promoting an open standard for mobile devices. (Most smart phone

FIGURE 4.24 Google has developed the Chrome OS for PCs and the Android OS for smartphones.

competitors control their source code and restrict the software that can be installed on it.)

- **BlackBerry OS.** The BlackBerry is a smart phone manufactured by Canadian company Research in Motion (RIM). The BlackBerry has a proprietary multitasking operating system that supports wireless communication with PCs.
- **Palm WebOS.** The Palm WebOS is another smart phone OS with a touch-screen interface. It runs on the Linux kernel, supports multitasking, and uses many proprietary components.

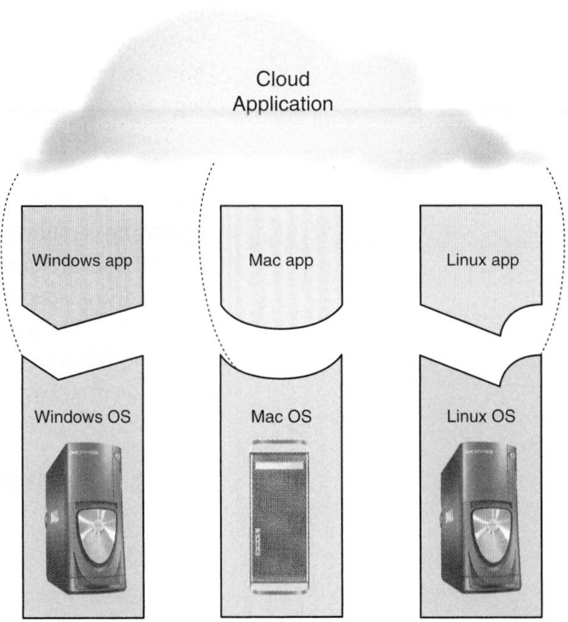

FIGURE 4.25 Compatibility issues: Operating systems are designed to run on particular hardware platforms. Applications are designed to run on particular operating systems. Most cloud applications are designed to run on multiple platforms.

Operating systems by themselves aren't very helpful. They need applications so they can do useful work. But application software can't exist by itself; it needs to be built on some kind of platform. People often use the term platform to describe the combination of hardware and operating system software that application software is built on. But some applications aren't built on a hardware/OS platform—they're built on a Web platform. *Cross-platform applications*, such as Microsoft Office and Adobe Photoshop, are programs that are available in similar versions for multiple platforms.

The trends are unmistakable. In the early days of the personal computer, there were dozens of different platforms—machines from Apple, Atari, Coleco, Commodore, Tandy, Texas Instruments, and other companies. All of these products have vanished from the marketplace, sometimes taking their parent companies with them. Today's market for new PC hardware and software is dominated by three general platforms: Windows in all its variations, the Mac OS, and various versions of UNIX/Linux. UNIX is mostly used in servers and high-end workstations, ultra-low-cost systems, and specialized applications. While the Mac OS commands a decent share of specialized markets such as education, graphic design, publishing, music, video, and multimedia, it runs far behind Windows in the massive corporate and government markets.

Even though Windows software isn't designed to run on the Mac platform, software solutions make it possible for Mac users to run most Windows programs. A software emulation program can create a simulated Windows computer within the Mac environment. An *emulation* program translates all Windows-related instructions into instructions the Mac's operating system and CPU can understand. Translation takes time, however, so emulation isn't adequate when speed is critical. Because modern Macs use the same type of CPU used in Windows machines, it's possible to install the Windows OS alongside the Mac OS and choose at system boot-up time which operating system to use. Many CPUs support *virtualization*—the creation of a virtual computer within a computer, enabling multiple operating systems to run simultaneously. Because software doesn't need to translate instructions to a different CPU's native language, there's no loss of speed when running Windows software on Intel Macs. With virtualization, it's possible to have Windows, Mac OS, and Linux all running simultaneously on one Mac. (Because the Mac OS is designed to work with specific hardware configurations, this trick doesn't work in the other direction: a standard Windows PC can't run the Mac OS.)

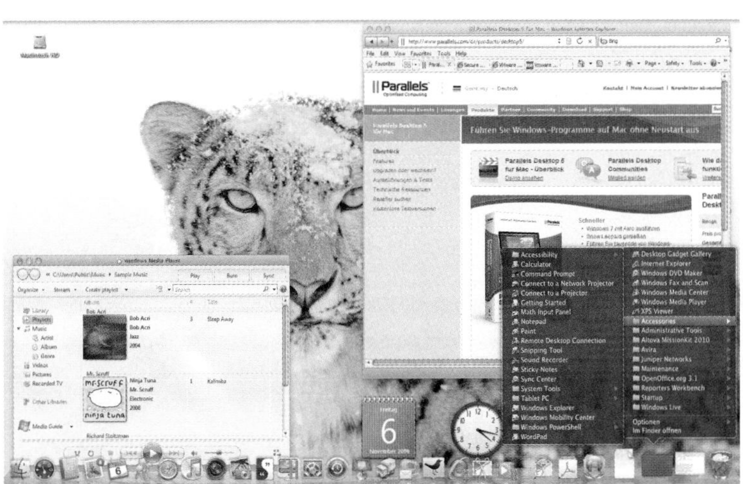

FIGURE 4.26 Virtualization software, such as Parallels, lets users run Windows and Linux environments inside of a window on the host OS (in this case, Mac OS X) and move data between the virtual machine and the host OS.

With the growing importance of networks, future applications may be more tied to networks than to desktop computer platforms. Computer users are spending less time dealing with information stored locally on their desktop computers and more time on the Web. Microsoft has responded to that trend with .NET, a strategy that enables programmers to ignore many processor-specific considerations. .NET blurs the line between the Web and Microsoft's operating systems and applications. As .NET evolves, more and more software components are being delivered by the network rather than residing on the desktop.

Microsoft's .NET strategy is a response to the popularity of **Java**, a platform-neutral computer language developed by Sun Microsystems for use on multiplatform networks. Programs written in Java can run on computers running Windows, Mac, UNIX, and other operating systems, provided those computers have ***Java virtual machine*** software installed. Like emulation software, Java applications run more slowly than applications targeted to a specific OS platform do. In 2007 Sun made Java available for free to other companies. Similar technologies are emerging from the open-source community. It's now possible for computer users to do their work without knowing—or caring—where in the world their software is.

File Management: Where's My Stuff?

> The first principle of human interface design, whether for a doorknob or a computer, is to keep in mind the human being who wants to use it. **The technology is subservient to that goal**.
>
> —*Donald Norman, in* The Art of Human–Computer Interface Design

You've seen how the operating system provides an interface layer between the computer user and the user's data. In this section we'll look behind the Windows and Mac GUIs to see how information is stored and organized on a computer's hard disk.

Organizing Files and Folders

As we've seen, Windows and the Mac OS employ a user interface that makes an analogy between a computer system and a business office. The monitor becomes a virtual desktop, and the reports, photographs, and other objects manipulated by the computer become files appearing on the desktop. To prevent the desktop from becoming too cluttered, files may be placed inside folders. The number of visible folders can quickly

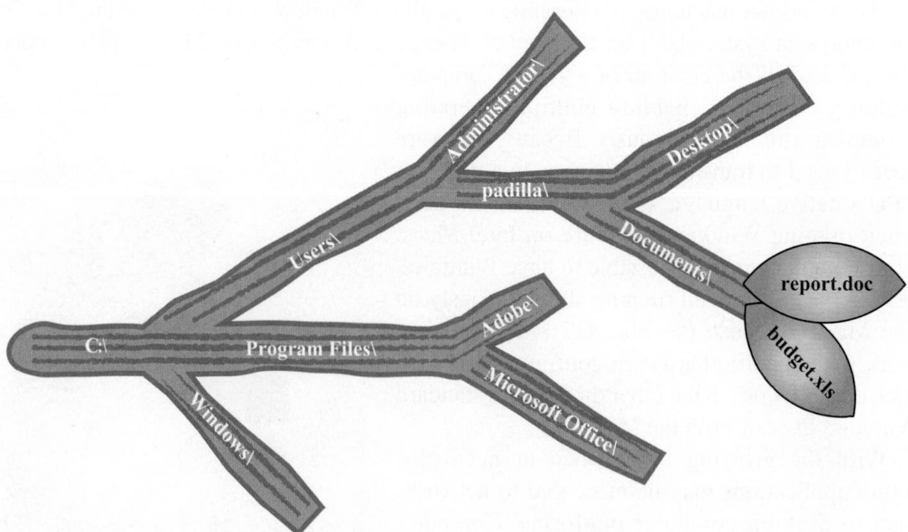

FIGURE 4.27 Because many folders and files may be put into the same folder, you can think of the file directory structure as a kind of tree, where the root directory is the trunk, the folders are the branches, and the files are the leaves. In this particular file directory structure the pathname C:\Users\padilla\Documents\budget.xls refers to an Excel spreadsheet.

become overwhelming, so operating system designers stretch the analogy and allow users to place folders inside folders.

A computer's files and folders are stored on a nonvolatile storage device, such as a hard disk flash drive, or optical disc. The Windows operating system uses letters to refer to particular storage devices. A Windows PC's primary hard disk is usually given the letter *C*. Every file and folder has a unique **pathname**, which describes the nesting of folders containing it. Within the pathname, the backslash character "\" separates the names of the folders.

For example, on a Windows 7 system, the files and folders appearing on the desktop of user "padilla" are most likely kept in the directory

C:\Users\padilla\Desktop

Let's interpret this pathname. The main folder on the C drive, called the **root directory**, contains all the other files and folders kept on the disk. The beginning of the pathname, "C:\", refers to the root directory. The root directory contains a folder named "Users." Within folder "Users" is another folder named "padilla." Within folder "padilla" is another folder named "Desktop." Within folder "Desktop" is a list of the files and folders appearing on the Windows desktop of user "padilla." (Pathnames on Macs are similar to Windows pathnames, except that there's no requirement that drives be given one-letter names. As a result, most drives have names such as "Macintosh HD" and "Backup drive" rather than C and D.)

Windows Explorer and the Finder: File Managers

A **file-management utility** (sometimes called a ***file manager***) makes it easy to view, rename, copy, move, and delete files and folders. In the Mac OS, the built-in file manager is called the Finder; in Windows it is called Windows Explorer. In both cases the file manager is included with the operating system. Few computer users know they're using a separate program when they use these utilities.

You can use a file-management utility to see the location of a file or folder in a storage device's hierarchy and view its pathname. You can also configure it to display information about a particular file, such as its size, its type, and the last time it was modified.

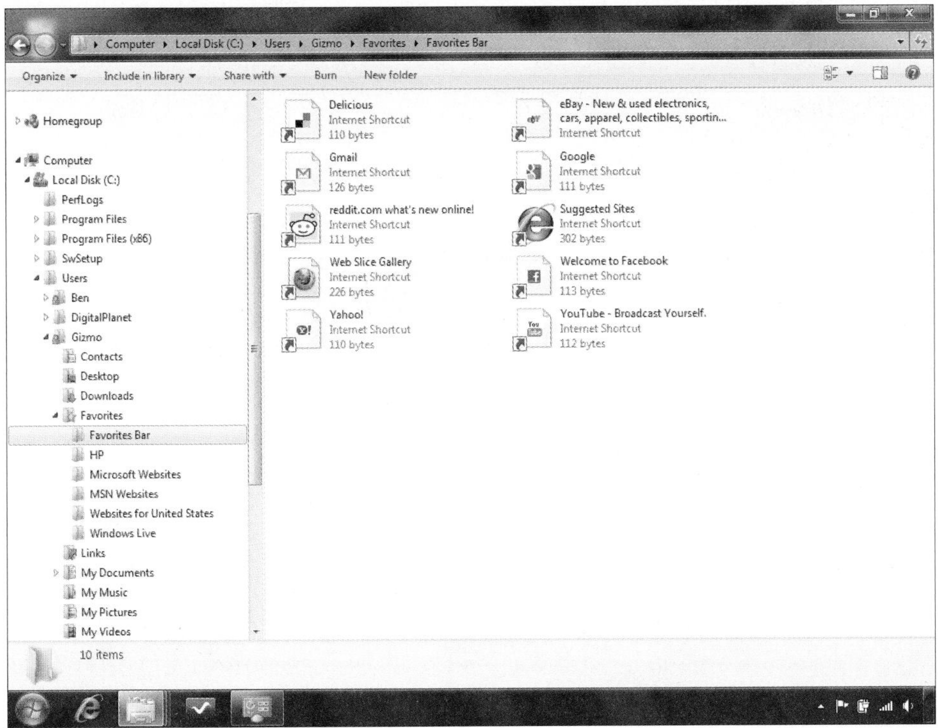

FIGURE 4.28 Windows Explorer allows you to see both the contents of a folder and the location of the folder in the storage device's hierarchy.

Managing Files from Applications

Most applications manipulate objects that can be stored in files. For example, a word processor allows you to type a new document or start with a previously saved document. In either case, you have the ability to save a copy of the new or revised document. An email program allows you to save some or all of the emails you have sent or received. An entertainment application may give you the opportunity to save the state of a game and restart the game from that point. Most applications support four basic file-management operations: Open, Save, Save As, and Close.

The *Open* operation allows you to select the file containing the project you would like to work on. After you select the file, the application reads its contents into memory. The state of the application changes to reflect the contents of the file. For example, when you open a file containing a spreadsheet, the contents of the spreadsheet file are displayed for you to view and manipulate.

The *Save* operation writes the current state of the application as a disk file. Suppose you are enhancing a spreadsheet that has been in existence for a while. You used the Open operation to retrieve the previous version of the spreadsheet. After adding some new formulas to the spreadsheet, you replace the previous version with the new, improved version. The Save operation overwrites the prior version of the spreadsheet with the enhanced version.

The *Save As* operation allows you to choose the location and name of the file you want to contain the current state of the application. When you're working with a new file, Save As is the same as Save. For example, suppose you are running a word processor to create a report from scratch. Because you began with a blank document, there is no filename associated with it. The first time you save the report, the application must be given the name and location of the file. Save As is also useful when you don't want to overwrite the previously saved version. Suppose you open a file containing a photograph and use a photo editor to touch it up. You would like to save your work, but you don't want to lose the original. You can keep the original copy and save the new copy by using the Save As operation to give the new copy a different name than the original.

The *Close* operation allows you to stop working on a project without quitting the application. A Close operation is often followed by an Open or New operation to read in or start a new project. When you Close a document, changes made since the last Save or

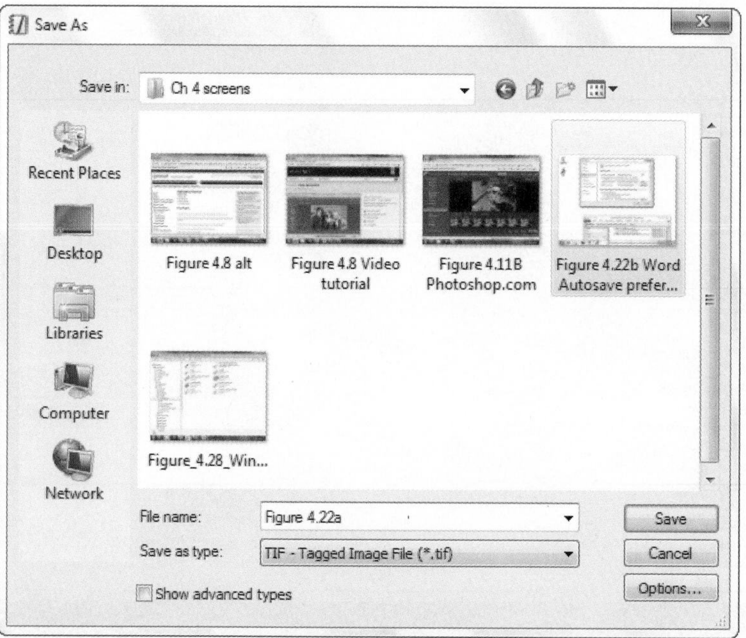

FIGURE 4.29 The Save As operation lets you choose the location and the name of the file that will store the current state of the application.

Save As operation are lost. If you attempt to close a modified document without saving it, the application probably will display a pop-up window that asks if you would like to save the project before closing it.

Locating Files

Even if you start with a brand-new computer, it doesn't take long to create a huge number of files scattered all over the file system. It's hard to manage data that you can't find. Of course, it's easier to find files if they're organized logically. To this end, both Windows and the Mac OS support common system folders with self-explanatory names. For example, your documents might be stored in a folder called Documents, photos in Pictures, and music in Music. These folders are specific to each user, so multiple users on a single PC have their own Documents, Pictures, and Music folders.

Modern operating systems include search tools that can help you find files wherever they're stored. The Search and Find commands are designed to help answer the common computer user's question, "Where's my stuff?" You can search for filenames or for words or phrases inside a file. So if you don't know the name of a file but do know some text that might be contained in that file, you can use the search tool to find your data.

Today's Windows and Mac operating systems go beyond the limitations of the folders-and-windows GUI for cataloging, organizing, and finding files. They enable you to create virtual folders ("smart folders" in Mac OS X) that can display collections of files that match specific criteria, and automatically update those collections. For example, a virtual folder might "contain" all of the Word documents on your hard drive that include your school name and were created in the last three months. If you create a new Word document with your school's name in it, it automatically shows up in that folder, regardless of where on the disk you actually saved the file.

Search tools and virtual folders are based on database interface technology discussed in Chapter 7. They make it easier for computer users to find their stuff while shielding them from the intricacies of the hardware and software. Google and other search engines

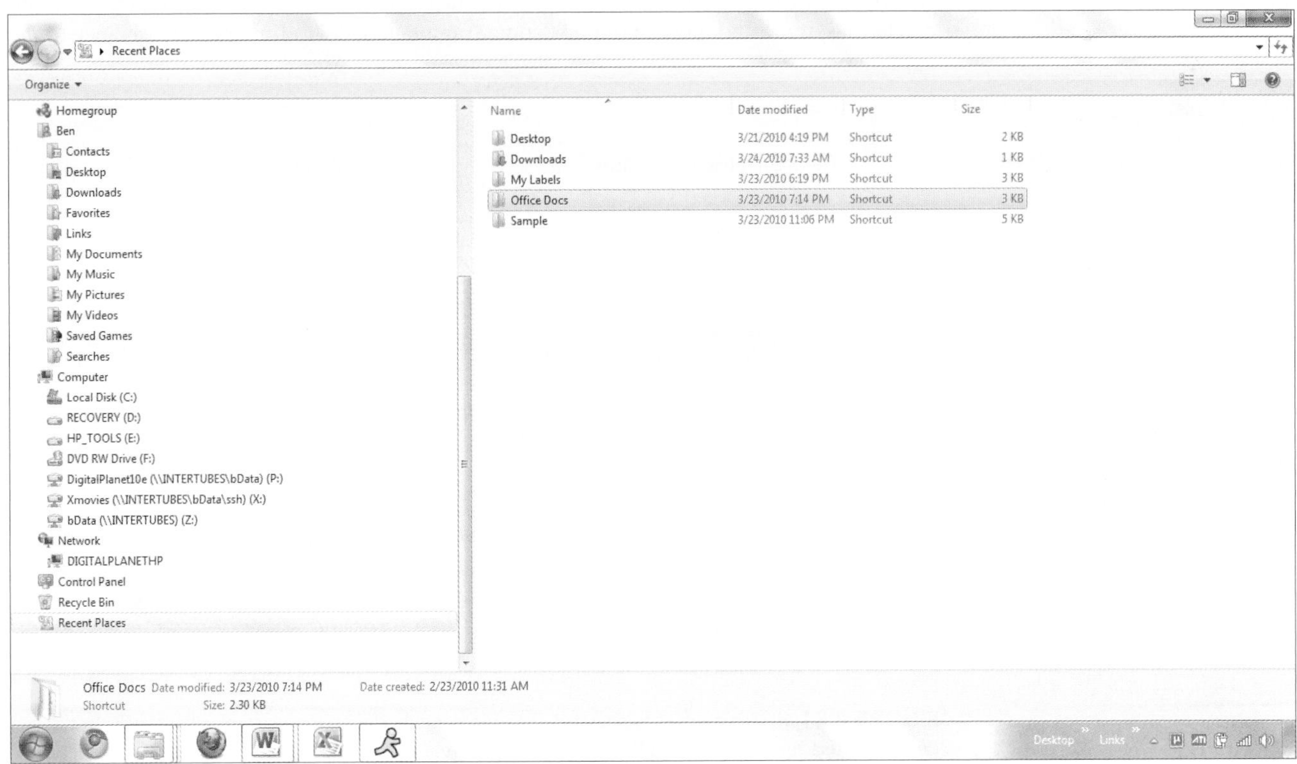

FIGURE 4.30 This Windows 7 virtual folder shows all of the user's most recently used folders, regardless of where they're stored.

provide similar capabilities across the Internet. The trend toward cloud computing is likely to blur the lines that separate local and global search tools.

Disk Formatting and Defragmentation

Before the operating system can store files on a hard disk, the disk must be formatted. **Formatting** a disk means putting electronic marks on the disk, dividing the disk into a series of concentric *tracks* and dividing each track into a collection of *sectors*. (You may never have had to format a hard disk yourself because computer manufacturers format the hard disks of new computers before installing the operating system and application programs.) Formatting removes any information that was previously stored on the disk, so you should make sure you never reformat a disk that contains important information.

Sectors are small compared to the size of the files most frequently stored on a disk, so disk drives usually bundle sectors into *clusters* or *blocks*. Because many files are larger than a single cluster, the file system must provide a way to link multiple clusters to store large files. To keep track of the files kept on a disk, the file system maintains a table (also stored on the disk) that indicates which clusters are assigned to each file. The file system also maintains a list of empty clusters. It dips into the pool of empty clusters when you want to create a new file or add to an existing file.

Accessing the information in a file is faster if the file is assigned to contiguous clusters. That way, the disk head reading the information does not have to move from track to track as often. Moving the disk head takes several milliseconds, a long time on PCs that can perform more than a million instructions every millisecond.

As you work with a file, its contents may become scattered over distant clusters. Suppose you have been editing a Word document, and you ask the file system to save a newer, longer version of the document. If the document no longer fits in the cluster(s) to which it was assigned, the file system looks to see whether the next cluster is empty. If so, it can allocate that cluster to the document, keeping it stored in contiguous clusters. If the next cluster is already allocated to another file, the OS must find another empty cluster. A **fragmented file** is a file allocated to noncontiguous clusters. As you create, edit, and delete files, more and more of them become fragmented, degrading the performance of the hard disk.

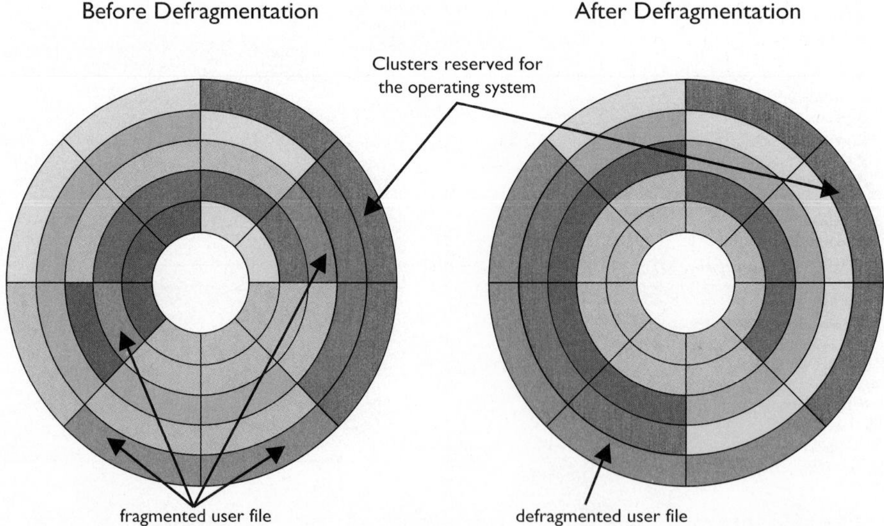

FIGURE 4.31 Having a lot of fragmented files can degrade the performance of a hard disk. In this figure, clusters reserved for operating system files are red. Each additional color represents an application or a document file. After defragmentation, files are assigned to contiguous clusters whenever possible. For example, before defragmentation, the four sectors holding the light blue file are scattered over three tracks. After defragmentation, all four sectors occupy a single track.

A **defragmentation utility** eliminates (as much as possible) fragmented files by changing the assignment of clusters to files. Depending on how fragmented a disk is, the defragmentation process may take hours. Mac OS X and Windows 7 both handle routine defragmentation automatically, so if your computer uses either of those it's unlikely you'll need to manually defragment your drive.

Software Piracy and Intellectual Property Laws

> **Information wants to be free. Information also wants to be expensive.** Information wants to be free because it has become so cheap to distribute, copy, and recombine—too cheap to meter. It wants to be expensive because it can be immeasurably valuable to the recipient. **That tension will not go away.**
>
> —*Stewart Brand, in* The Media Lab

Software piracy—the illegal duplication of copyrighted software—is rampant. Millions of computer users have made copies of programs they don't legally own and distributed them to family members, friends, and total strangers. Because so few software companies use physical copy protection methods to protect their products, copying software is as easy as duplicating an audio CD or photocopying a chapter of a book. Unfortunately, many people aren't aware that copying software, recorded music, and books can violate federal laws protecting intellectual property. Many others simply look the other way, convinced that software companies, music companies, and publishers already make enough money.

The Piracy Problem

The software industry, with a world market of more than $88 billion a year, loses billions of dollars every year to software pirates. The Business Software Alliance (BSA) estimates that more than one-third of all software in use is illegally copied, costing the software industry tens of thousands of jobs. Piracy can be particularly hard on small software companies. Developing software is just as difficult for them as it is for big companies such as Microsoft and Oracle, but they often lack the financial and legal resources to cover the losses they suffer through piracy.

Software industry organizations, including the BSA and SPA Anti-Piracy (a division of the Software & Information Industry Association), work with law enforcement agencies to crack down on piracy. At the same time, they sponsor educational programs to make computer users aware that piracy is theft because laws can't work without citizen understanding and support. Software piracy is a worldwide problem, with piracy rates highest in developing nations. In China approximately 82 percent of all new software installations are pirated; in Armenia the piracy rate is 93 percent. A few developing nations refuse to abide by international copyright laws. They argue that the laws protect rich countries at the expense of underdeveloped nations. In 1998 the Argentine Supreme Court ruled that the country's copyright laws don't apply to computer software.

FIGURE 4.32 In 1999 Moscow police attempted to make a dent in the illegal software market by destroying mountains of pirated software. Their efforts were largely unsuccessful. Today about three out of every four software programs in Russia are pirated.

Intellectual Property and the Law

Legally, the definition of **intellectual property** includes the results of intellectual activities in the arts, science, and industry. **Copyright** laws have traditionally protected forms of literary expression, including books, plays, songs, paintings, photographs, and movies. **Trademark** law has protected symbols, pictures, sounds, colors, and smells used by a business to identify goods. **Patent** law has protected mechanical inventions, and **contract** law has covered trade secrets. Software doesn't fit neatly into any of these categories under the law. Copyright laws protect most commercial software programs, but a few companies have successfully used patent laws to protect software products.

The purpose of intellectual property laws is to ensure that mental labor is justly rewarded and to encourage innovation. Programmers, inventors, scientists, writers, editors, filmmakers, and musicians depend on ideas and the expression of those ideas for their incomes. Ideas are information, and information is easy to copy—especially in this electronic age. Intellectual property laws are designed to protect these professionals and encourage them to continue their creative efforts so society can benefit from their future work.

Most of the time, these laws help them to achieve their goals. A novelist can devote two or three years of her life to writing a masterpiece, confident that she won't find bootleg copies for sale on street corners when she finishes it. A movie studio can invest hundreds of millions of dollars in a film, knowing that the investment will be returned, a little at a time, through ticket sales and video rentals. An inventor can work long hours to create a better mousetrap and know that MegaMousetrap City won't steal her idea.

But sometimes intellectual property laws are applied in such a way that they may stifle the innovation and creativity they're designed to protect. In 1999 Amazon.com was awarded a controversial patent for "one-click shopping," preventing other e-commerce sites from giving their customers a similar, simple shopping experience. Similarly, SightSound patented all paid downloads of "desired digital video or digital audio signals." RealNetworks patented streaming audio and video, and British Telecom claims to hold a 1976 patent that covers every Web hyperlink! Most experts agree that these ideas are too simple and broad to be owned by one company. And in many cases, the patent owner isn't the inventor of the concept; Douglas Engelbart demonstrated hyperlinking as early as 1967 at Stanford Research Institute. Such broad patents generally end up in court, where legal experts and technology experts debate the merits and scope of the ideas and the laws designed to protect them. Meanwhile, legislators attempt to update the laws to address ever-changing technological advances.

Most existing copyright and patent laws, which evolved during the age of print and mechanical inventions, are outdated, contradictory, and inadequate for today's information technology. Many U.S. laws, including the Computer Fraud and Abuse Act of 1984, clearly treat software piracy as a crime. The NET (No Electronic Theft) Act of 1997 closed a narrow loophole in the law that allowed people to give away software on the Internet.

The Digital Millennium Copyright Act (DMCA) of 1998 represents the most comprehensive reform of U.S. copyright law in a generation. The DCMA implements two 1996 treaties of the World Intellectual Property Organization. According to the law, it is illegal to produce, distribute, or use technology that circumvents digital rights management (DRM) schemes, regardless of whether copyrights are violated. The law as written applies to DVDs, electronic books, computer software, or any other form of intellectual property protected by DRM technology. The DMCA also makes it a crime to share information about how to crack copy protection. It increased the penalties for copyright infringement on the Internet, while limiting the liability of Internet service providers whose sites contain copyrighted material posted by their customers. In 2001 the European Union passed the Copyright Directive (EUCD), a law similar in many ways to the DMCA. Critics argue that these laws suppress freedom of speech, academic freedom, and the principle of fair use—the time-honored right to make copies of copyrighted material for personal and academic use and for other noncompetitive purposes. Controversial provisions of the DMCA have been challenged in court, and challenges are likely to continue for years to come.

In 2001 the Recording Industry Association of America (RIAA) used the DMCA to shut down the Napster music-sharing service; by 2003 the RIAA was invoking the DMCA to force Internet service providers to reveal the identities of individual song pirates. While the courts eventually ruled that Internet service providers did not have to give this information to the RIAA, questions about the scope and reach of the DMCA remain. Meanwhile, millions of people continue to exchange music, movies, and other copyrighted works over Kazaa, Bit Torrent, and other file-sharing networks. Some organizations, such as the Electronic Frontier Foundation, are advocating reforms of the copyright system that would

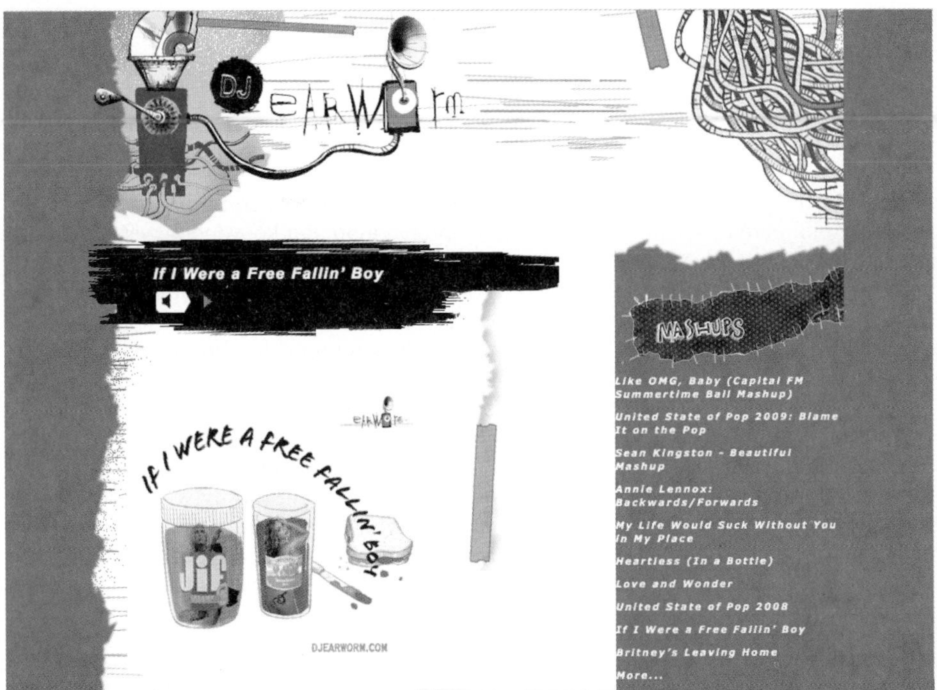

FIGURE 4.33 DJ Earworm is one of many mashup artists whose creations test the limits of fair use of intellectual property.

legalize file sharing while still providing a way for musicians and other content creators to receive a fair financial return for their creative efforts.

The growing popularity of *mashups*—in software, music, and video media—raise even more questions about current intellectual property laws and customs. When a Web site is built from plug-in modules created by several programmers using data from other Web sites, who, if anyone, owns the intellectual property rights for that site? When a DJ uses a drumbeat from a classic rock track in a remix, are the property rights of the original record's drummer or publisher violated? And when a college student uploads to YouTube a video mashup that combines scenes from 1950s cartoons with a homemade soundtrack, can the cartoon owners sue the student or YouTube?

Strict proponents of intellectual property laws say that these examples constitute theft, and they should be prosecuted as such. Others argue that the world's creative works have always been built on the works of others. Shakespeare, Beethoven, and Picasso might not have produced their masterpieces if they'd been threatened with lawsuits for borrowing ideas from their predecessors. (We'll revisit intellectual property issues related to music and art in Chapter 7.)

In matters of software, the legal system is sailing in uncharted waters. Experts debate online and off about whether current intellectual property laws encourage or stifle innovation. Whether dealing with issues of piracy or monopoly, lawmakers and judges must struggle with difficult questions about innovation, property, freedom, and progress. The questions are likely to be with us for quite a while.

Inventing the Future ▸ Tomorrow's User Interfaces 1: From WIMP to SILK

Thirty years ago, the typical computer could be operated only by a highly trained data-processing professional or programmer. Today preschoolers can make computers do their bidding. The graphical user interface pioneered by Xerox and popularized by Apple and Microsoft is an industry standard, making it possible for users to move between machines almost—but not quite—as easily as drivers adjust to different brands of cars. But today's WIMP (windows, icons, menus, and pointing devices) interface isn't the end of user interface evolution.

Several years ago researcher Raj Reddy coined an acronym to describe some of the most important emerging user interface technologies: SILK, for speech, image, language, and knowledge capabilities. We'll explore each of these technologies in later chapters. Here are some snapshots of where they're headed:

- ***Speech.*** Although we still don't have a reliable language-translating telephone or a foolproof dictation-taking "talkwriter," speech technology is rapidly maturing into a practical alternative to keyboard and mouse input. Voice-recognition technology is used for security systems, automated voicemail systems, hands-free Web navigation, medical report transcription, and countless other applications. New applications are being developed every day.
- ***Image.*** Today's two-dimensional desktop metaphors will give way to animated 3-D interfaces—virtual workspaces unlike anything we use today. Virtual reality (VR) user interfaces will create the illusion that the user is immersed in a world inside the computer—an environment that contains both scenes and the controls to change those scenes. Augmented reality user interfaces combine virtual information with real-world scenes, supporting rather than replacing standard visual information. (Virtual reality and augmented reality are discussed in more detail in the "Inventing the Future" features in upcoming chapters.)
- ***Language.*** With or without speech, natural-language processing will be part of future user interfaces. We'll routinely communicate with computers in English, Spanish, Japanese, or some other natural language. Today computers can reliably read subsets of these languages or can be trained to understand spoken commands and text. Tomorrow's machines should be able to handle much day-to-day work through a natural-language interface, written or spoken. Researchers expect that we'll soon use programs that read documents as we create them, edit them according to our instructions, and file them based on their content.
- ***Knowledge.*** Advances in the technology of knowledge will enable engineers to design self-maintaining systems that can diagnose and correct common problems without human intervention. But knowledge will also enable software agents to really be of service to users. Agents are programs designed to be managed rather than manipulated. An intelligent software agent can ask questions as well as respond to commands, pay attention to its user's work patterns, serve as a guide and a coach, take on its owner's goals, and use reasoning to fabricate goals of its own. Computer industry analyst Esther Dyson explained agents this way: "I don't want to sit and move stuff around on my screen all day and look at figures and have it recognize my gestures and listen to my voice. I want to tell it what to do and then go away; I don't want to babysit this computer. I want it to act for me, not with me."

Many PC applications include *wizards* to guide users through complex tasks and answer questions. Computer opponents in games are also intelligent agents. The Internet is home to countless bots—software robots that crawl around the Web collecting information, helping consumers make decisions, playing games, and even posing as humans in online chats and messaging sessions. Software agents can keep you posted on articles on subjects that interest you, manage appointments, track communications, and defend systems and homes from security breaches and privacy threats. But today's wizards, bots, and agents aren't smart enough to consistently manage the many details that a human assistant might juggle.

Agents are often portrayed with human characteristics; *2001*'s Hal and the computers on *Star Trek* are famous examples. Of course, agents don't need to look or sound human—they just need to possess considerable knowledge and intelligence.

Future agents may possess a degree of sensitivity, too. Researchers are developing *affective computing* technology that factors emotional states into the human/computer communication. A machine might analyze speech patterns, facial expressions, and/or body gestures to determine the user's emotional state—and respond accordingly. Affective computers might also be programmed to exhibit or simulate emotions when communicating with users. Affective computing is still in its infancy, but it's already found practical applications: customer support phone systems that can detect when callers are angry or impatient, virtual pets that can provide comfort and companionship to medical shut-ins, and more. Still, it will take much more research to produce an emotional robotic butler along the lines of *Star Wars*' C3PO.

Crosscurrents

Copyrights—and Wrongs

by Sascha Segan

Do our copyright laws encourage or discourage creativity? That's the question at the center of this PC Magazine *column from July 2008.*

Did you break the law today? If you've created something on the Internet, probably. Artists, librarians, tech geeks, and software engineers are now fighting over a miserably shrinking public domain. This isn't what copyright was supposed to be about, and only a popular uprising will stop the current trend.

Copyright law was designed to "promote the Progress of Science and useful Arts, by securing for limited Times to Authors and Inventors the exclusive Right to their respective Writings and Discoveries." That's from the U.S. Constitution, thus the weird capitalization.

The way "the exclusive Right" promotes progress is by giving creators a monopoly over selling their works, or letting them sell the rights to someone else, so they can make a living and thus keep creating.

There's an amusing utopian argument against all copyright, but it assumes too many random acts of generosity. Before copyright, only the wealthy, or those with wealthy patrons, could afford to spend time making art. In our market-oriented world, people will buy things if they consider them affordable and valuable—and if there's a punishment for stealing them. When the price and restrictions are too high, people will steal. The record labels still claim to be shocked—shocked!—that their unacceptable terms lead to thievery. But if there's no punishment at all for stealing, nobody will pay, and fewer things will be created because artists will spend time finding ways to feed their families instead.

One of the great tech stories of the past decade has been how technology has enabled a tremendous explosion of creativity. This is why the Electronic Frontier Foundation (EFF), the Consumer Electronics Association, and the Center for Democracy and Technology are involved in the debate over a new Orphan Works Act, which is supposed to expand the public domain. Your camera-phone photos, YouTube mashups, blog posts, home-burned DVDs, iMovies of your kids—even your Facebook status updates—are creative works.

Right now, more Americans are creating lasting works than ever before, and if you borrow content, you're likely violating copyright law. That's nothing new—do you think Shakespeare had an original plot? If you're concerned about legality, the pool of stuff in the public domain that you can legally use to create new brilliance has gotten proportionally smaller with time.

At some point in the 20th century, most works went from being created by people (who die) to being created by corporations (which are immortal). The immortal corporations wanted their rights to extend to their immortal life spans. The Constitution prohibits an unlimited copyright term, so they just keep extending the term. They're immortal and you aren't, so they'll keep doing this until people make them stop.

As a creator, I don't see why I should keep profiting from something I wrote even 50 years down the line. There needs to be some term of exclusivity to give the work value, but beyond a certain point, that exclusivity discourages creativity. If I can live off one book for 90 years, I have no incentive ever to write another book, and nobody else can use my creativity as a springboard to build the next masterpiece.

So now we get to fighting over scraps. Because copyrights now extend until the fall of Western civilization, the Orphan Works Act is supposed to let people reuse stuff whose provenance they can't identify. An example: If you find an old studio photograph of your grandmother as a young girl, Walmart won't copy it for you, because the estate of the photographer (presumably dead) still holds the copyright. The new law would let you rescue Grandma from the depths of time. If you could tell who created the photo, you'd have to pay for the privilege, but if not, you could still use the image.

This sounds good, but the law's opponents, mostly visual artists and photographers, say that all someone needs to do is pretend not to be able to find the creator. You could submit your work to a registry to protect yourself, but that basically amounts to paying protection money.

Yes, a well-written Orphan Works Act that would accommodate everyone is not impossible. The EFF suggests mandating that the copyright registry be free, and that people have to look very, very hard for the original creator. The artists, of course, fear smooth-talking lawyered folks who can convince a judge that they're looking very, very hard when they aren't. The Orphan Works Act isn't the answer. Returning to a sensible copyright regime is.

The power to create that technology gives us is a heady drink, and a vibrant public domain is the best chaser for it. Endless copyright terms don't encourage creativity or protect individual creators. Tell Congress to cut through all this nonsense and enhance the public domain by shortening the length of copyright terms, not by throwing a few scraps and bones to the public.

Discussion Questions

1. What do you think is a "sensible copyright regime?" Why?
2. How have you broken copyright laws?

Summary

Software provides the communication link between humans and their computers. Because software is soft—stored in memory rather than hardwired into the circuitry—it can easily be modified to meet the needs of the computer user. By changing software, you can change a computer from one kind of tool into another.

Most software falls into one of three categories: compilers and other translator programs, software applications, and system software. A compiler is a software tool that enables programs written in English-like languages such as Visual Basic and C++ to be translated into the zeros and ones of the machine language the computer understands. A compiler frees the programmer from the tedium of machine language programming, making it easier to write quality programs with fewer bugs. But even with the best translators, programming is a little like communicating with an alien species. It's a demanding process that requires more time and mental energy than most people are willing or able to invest.

Fortunately, software applications make it easy for most computer users today to communicate their needs to the computer without learning programming. Applications simulate and extend the properties of familiar real-world tools such as typewriters, paintbrushes, and file cabinets, making it possible for people to do things with computers that would be difficult or impossible otherwise. Applications and accompanying documentation can be delivered on physical media or downloaded from the Web. Either way, the software purchaser generally buys a license with some restrictions about how the software can be used and shared. Web applications are tools that users typically access through Web browsers. Programmers for businesses and public institutions develop vertical-market and custom packages for situations in which a general commercial program won't do the job.

Whether you're writing programs or simply using them, the computer's operating system is functioning behind the scenes, translating your software's instructions into messages that the hardware can understand. Popular desktop and laptop operating systems today include several versions of Microsoft Windows, Mac OS X, and Linux. An operating system serves as the computer's business manager, taking care of the hundreds of details that need to be handled to keep the computer functioning. A timesharing operating system has the particularly challenging job of serving multiple users concurrently, monitoring the machine's resources, keeping track of each user's account, and protecting the security of the system and each user's data. One of the most important jobs of the operating system is managing the program and data files stored on hard disks and other storage media. Utility programs can handle many of those system-related problems that the operating system can't solve directly.

Applications, utilities, programming languages, and operating systems all must, to varying degrees, communicate with the user. A program's user interface is a critical factor in that communication. User interfaces have evolved over the years to the point where sophisticated software packages can be operated by people who know little about the inner workings of the computer. A well-designed user interface shields the user from the bits and bytes, creating an on-screen façade, or shell, that makes sense to the user. Today the computer industry has moved away from command-line interfaces toward a friendlier graphical user interface that uses windows, icons, menus, and pointing devices in an intuitive, consistent environment. Tomorrow's user interfaces are likely to depend more on voice, three-dimensional graphics, and animation to create an artificial reality.

One of the challenges of working with a computer is keeping track of the masses of information that can be collected, edited, and stored on discs. Most computers use some kind of hierarchical file system involving directories, or folders, to organize files. But modern operating systems have built-in search functions that make it easy to locate files without knowing their exact locations.

Commercial software programs enjoy legal copyright protection in most countries. To encourage creativity, most countries grant copyrights to the creators and publishers of software, music, movies, books, and other intellectual property. But copyright law can stifle creativity if it prevents people from building on the work of others. A tension exists between the needs and desires of producers and the needs and desires of consumers. Despite copyright protections for computer programs, software piracy has flourished in many countries around the world.

Key Terms

agents .... (p. 136)
algorithm .... (p. 108)
autosave .... (p. 124)
booting .... (p. 119)
bug .... (p. 108)
character-based interface .... (p. 122)
command-line interface .... (p. 122)
compatibility .... (p. 113)
compiler .... (p. 112)
context-sensitive menus .... (p. 123)
contract .... (p. 133)
copyright .... (p. 133)
copyrighted software .... (p. 114)
custom application .... (p. 117)
debugging .... (p. 109)
defragmentation utility .... (p. 133)
device drivers .... (p. 119)
digital rights management (DRM) .... (p. 114)
documentation .... (p. 113)
end-user license agreement (EULA) .... (p. 114)
file-management utility .... (p. 129)
force quit .... (p. 124)
formatting .... (p. 132)
fragmented file .... (p. 132)
graphical user interface (GUI) .... (p. 122)
hierarchical menus .... (p. 122)
high-level language .... (p. 112)
intellectual property .... (p. 133)
Java .... (p. 128)
Linux .... (p. 105)
Mac OS .... (p. 122)
machine language .... (p. 109)
menu .... (p. 122)
menu-driven interface .... (p. 122)
Microsoft Windows .... (p. 122)
multitasking .... (p. 118)
natural language .... (p. 112)
open-source software .... (p. 106)
operating system (OS) .... (p. 117)
patent .... (p. 133)
pathname .... (p. 129)
platform .... (p. 127)
pop-up menus .... (p. 123)
public-domain software .... (p. 115)
root directory .... (p. 129)
safe mode .... (p. 124)
shareware .... (p. 115)
shell .... (p. 123)
software license .... (p. 114)
software piracy .... (p. 114)
system software .... (p. 117)
taskbar .... (p. 122)
trademark .... (p. 133)
UNIX .... (p. 123)
update .... (p. 113)
upgrade .... (p. 113)
user interface .... (p. 122)
utility program .... (p. 118)
vertical-market application .... (p. 117)
virtual memory .... (p. 118)
Web applications .... (p. 115)

Companion Website Projects

1. The *Digital Planet* Web site, www.pearsonhighered.com/beekman, contains self-test exercises related to this chapter. Follow the instructions for taking a quiz. After you've completed your quiz, you can email the results to your instructor.
2. The Web site also contains open-ended discussion questions called Internet Exercises. Discuss one or more of the Internet Exercises questions at the section for this chapter.

True or False

1. Microsoft Windows was the first operating system with a user interface based on windows and icons.
2. An algorithm is a computer program written in an algorithmic programming language.
3. When you buy a software program, you're really buying a license to use the program according to rules specified by the software company.
4. Shareware is a type of software application used for sharing files over a network or the Internet.
5. An operating system is necessary in a PC, but not in a smart phone.
6. Your computer can't print documents on a connected printer unless it has a device driver for that printer.
7. Digital rights management (DRM) technology protects the rights of computer users to copy software.
8. It is impossible to run Windows applications on a Mac computer.
9. A PC can have more than one operating system installed on its hard disk so that it can run software written for different platforms.
10. Cross-platform Web applications can be run using Web browsers on computers with different operating systems.

Multiple Choice

1. Which of the following is the most famous example of open-source software?
   a. Microsoft Windows
   b. Mac OS X
   c. UNIX
   d. Linux
   e. Google
2. What is correcting errors in a program called?
   a. Compiling
   b. Debugging
   c. Undoing
   d. Interpreting
   e. Oopsing
3. A compiler translates a program written in a high-level language into
   a. machine language.
   b. an algorithm.
   c. Java.
   d. C#.
   e. natural language.
4. What does a program's end-user license agreement (EULA) typically include?
   a. Rules specifying how the software may be used
   b. Warranty disclaimers
   c. Rules concerning the copying of the software
   d. All of the above
   e. None of the above
5. When you buy a typical computer software package, you are purchasing
   a. a guarantee that the software has no bugs in it.
   b. a share of stock in the company making the software.
   c. the software.
   d. a license to use the software.
   e. free upgrades to the software.
6. The original rationale for copyright and patent laws was to
   a. place software development under a legal umbrella.
   b. discourage the spread of bad technology.
   c. encourage innovation by ensuring rewards for creative work.
   d. prevent international piracy.
   e. provide a legal platform for mashups.
7. When a PC crashes or freezes while you're using it, the problem might be caused by
   a. a bug in the application program that you were using.
   b. a bug in the operating system.
   c. a clash between two pieces of software that were running at the same time.
   d. a hardware failure.
   e. Any of the above
8. Which of the following can handle most system functions that aren't handled directly by the operating system?
   a. Vertical-market applications
   b. Utilities
   c. Algorithms
   d. Web applications
   e. Compilers
9. The operating system is stored in ROM or flash memory in most
   a. Windows and Mac computers.
   b. mainframes and supercomputers.
   c. smart phones.
   d. open-source and public-domain computers.
   e. computers, regardless of size or function.
10. What happens when you boot up a PC?
    a. Portions of the operating system are copied from disk into memory.
    b. Portions of the operating system are copied from memory onto disk.
    c. Portions of the operating system are compiled.
    d. Portions of the operating system are emulated.
    e. None of the above
11. Which of the following is a necessary part of a software agent?
    a. Natural language processing technology
    b. Synthetic speech technology
    c. Knowledge technology
    d. 3-D graphics technology
    e. All of the above
12. What is the main folder on your PC's hard drive called?
    a. A drive
    b. Start menu
    c. Home page
    d. Root directory
    e. Device driver
13. A mashup
    a. happens when two programs occupy the same memory locations at the same time.
    b. is the result of data compression utility software being applied to a large database.
    c. is the combining of data or functionality from two or more external services in a single Web application.
    d. is a necessary part of the process of compiling a computer program.
    e. is none of the above.

14. Future PC user interfaces will almost certainly involve more use of
    a. machine language.
    b. natural language.
    c. high-level language.
    d. assembly language.
    e. algorithmic language.

15. Most commercial software programs enjoy a form of intellectual property protection called
    a. digital rights management (DRM) technology.
    b. copy protection.
    c. copyright.
    d. trademark.
    e. patent.

Review Questions

1. What is the relationship between higher level languages and machine language?
2. Most computer software falls into one of three categories: compilers and other translator programs, software applications, and system software. Describe and give examples of each.
3. Why is a Web browser different than another type of software platform?
4. Write an algorithm for washing the dishes. Check your algorithm carefully for errors and ambiguities. Then have a classmate or your instructor check it. How did your results compare?
5. What are some of the ways that operating systems and user interfaces have evolved since the earliest PCs were introduced?
6. What is the purpose of DRM technology? Give some examples.
7. What is the relationship between a utility and an operating system?
8. Is the character-based interface completely obsolete? Explain your answer.
9. Describe several steps you might take to solve the problem if your word processing program locks up while you're writing a paper.
10. What is the difference between the Save and Save As commands? When is each useful?

Discussion Questions

1. In what way is writing instructions for a computer more difficult than writing instructions for a person? In what way is it easier?
2. Speculate about the user interface of a typical computer in the year 2015. How would this user interface differ from those used in today's computers?
3. Some people believe Web applications will soon replace PC applications for most purposes. What do you think? What would it take to make this practical?
4. How do you feel about the open-software movement? Would you be willing to volunteer your time to write software or help users for free?
5. The second-to-last paragraph in the section on intellectual property (p. 135) raises several questions about mashups. Give your opinion about how these questions should be answered.
6. Suppose you've spent all your spare time for the past eight months programming a new PC game. Your friends have tried it and say it is great. They have started bugging you for copies of the game. Would you give the game away or try to sell it?
7. Suppose Whizzo Software Company produces a program that looks, from the user's point of view, exactly like the immensely popular BozoWorks from Bozo, Inc. Whizzo insists that it didn't copy any of the code in BozoWorks; it just tried to design a program that would appeal to BozoWorks users. Bozo cries foul and sues Whizzo for violation of intellectual property laws. Do you think the laws should favor Bozo's arguments or Whizzo's? Why?

Projects

1. Take an inventory of PC and Web applications available on the Web related to your field of study. Describe the major uses for several of these applications.
2. Interview five people who own a PC running a version of the Windows operating system, and interview five people who own a Mac. Ask each person to explain what he or she likes best about the computer's operating system, as well as what he or she dislikes the most about the computer's operating system. After you are done with your interviews, look for similarities and differences between the likes and dislikes of Windows and Mac users.

Sources and Resources

Books

Just for Fun: The Story of an Accidental Revolutionary, by Linus Torvalds and David Diamond (HarperBusiness). The executive editor of *Red Herring* magazine convinced Linus Torvalds to tell his story. The result is this book, a quirky collection of tidbits from the life of the creator of Linux.

Rebel Code: Linux and the Open Source Revolution, by Glyn Moody (Perseus). This book tells the Linux story in a style that's more conventional, and for many readers, more readable, than the Torvalds/Diamond book.

The Cathedral and the Bazaar: Musings on Linux and Open Source by an Accidental Revolutionary, by Eric S. Raymond (O'Reilly). This widely praised book is an expanded version of the original manifesto for the open-source software movement—the movement that threatens to revolutionize the software industry. Tom Peters calls it "wonderful, witty, and, ultimately, wise."

Windows 7 for Dummies Book + DVD Bundle, by Andy Rathbone (John Wiley & Sons). The Dummies series that started with *DOS for Dummies* has expanded to cover everything from antiquing to yoga. The quality varies from book to book, but the best titles in the Dummies family have served as easy-to-read tutorials for millions of people, dummies or not. This popular package combines a dummies introduction to Windows with a DVD that walks viewers through many of the basic processes. Of course, the Dummies series doesn't have a Windows monopoly. There are hundreds of books on Windows for dummies and nondummies alike.

Microsoft Windows 7 Visual Quickstart Guide, by Chris Fehily (Peachpit Press). This book covers the basics of Windows, from setup to security, using the popular VQS formula: short, step-by-step tutorials explaining how to do each task, liberal use of screen shots, and plenty of bonus tips.

The Little Mac Book, Snow Leopard Edition, by Robin Williams (Peachpit Press). Robin Williams has written many great books about computers, desktop publishing, graphic design, Web design, and (especially) the Mac. She's known for her clear, approachable writing style. In this book she explains the ins and outs of the Mac and its operating system. It's one of the best gentle introductions to the Mac you'll find anywhere.

Switching to the Mac: The Missing Manual, Snow Leopard Edition, by David Pogue (Pogue Press). If you're already Windows-savvy but you feel a little lost on a Mac, this book should help. David Pogue's book combines an intimate knowledge of both Mac and Windows with a clear, humorous writing style.

UNIX and Linux: Visual QuickStart Guide, by Deborah S. Ray and Eric J. Ray (Peachpit Press). Many UNIX and Linux books assume that you speak fluent technojargon and that you want to know all about the operating system and how it works. This book is designed for people who want to (or need to) use UNIX or Linux but don't particularly want to read a massive volume of OS lore. No book can make mastering UNIX or Linux simple, but this one at least makes getting started simpler.

Linux in a Nutshell, by Ellen Siever, Aaron Weber, Stephen Figgins, Robert Love, and Arnold Robbins (O'Reilly Media). O'Reilly has a large list of quality computer books, including the excellent Missing Manual series. O'Reilly is especially strong in its coverage of open-source software, including Linux. This massive multiauthor book is one of their most popular titles. It's a useful reference manual, rather than an introductory tutorial.

Google Apps for Dummies, by Ryan Keeter and Karl Barksdale (For Dummies). Google has transformed itself from a search engine into an online platform for Web applications of all types. This book provides a practical overview of the growing Google toolbox. But Google's online tools are always changing, so you'll need to supplement this (or any) book on the subject with online documentation and help.

Things That Make Us Smart: Defending Human Attributes in the Age of the Machine, by Donald A. Norman (Perseus). Norman left his position as the founding chairman of the Department of Cognitive Science at the University of California, San Diego, to work in the computer industry. His research on the relationship between technology and the human cognitive system is especially relevant in an industry where user interface decisions affect millions of users every day. This book, like Norman's others, is informative and thought provoking.

Ethics for the Information Age, by Michael J. Quinn (Pearson Addison-Wesley). This book contains in-depth discussions of many ethical issues raised by the introduction of information technology. One of its chapters focuses on intellectual property and debates issues related to the rights of producers and consumers, including whether creators of computer programs and music have a right to own their creations and whether consumers have an obligation to respect copyright laws.

The Pirate's Dilemma: How Youth Culture Is Reinventing Capitalism, by Matt Mason (Free Press). Are pirates terrorists or freedom fighters? That's the question at the heart of Matt Mason's book. He argues that many of the most important advancements in culture have occurred as a result of what we now call piracy. Everybody from Thomas Edison to Andy Warhol has been accused of piracy. Today's intellectual property laws are, on the surface, designed to encourage innovation. But according to Mason, they may have just the opposite effect. Today's youth culture, steeped in hip hop and open-source ideas, may transform our capitalistic system into one that encourages collaboration and openness. It should come as no surprise that the author's Web site includes viral video mashups extolling the ideas in the book.

The Myths of Innovation, by Scott Berkum (O'Reilly Media, Inc.). O'Reilly has a well-established catalog of books on software design, development, and use. Many of its most popular titles deal with open-source technology. In this highly praised book, Scott Berkum explores the nature of innovation, including software innovation. Dozens of examples from technology, business, and the arts show how ideas can become successful, world-changing innovations.

Legal Guide to Web and Software Development (book with CD-ROM), by Stephen Fishman (NOLO Press). NOLO Press specializes in books about law for non-lawyers. This book, like many NOLO books, can demystify legal contracts and concepts, making it easier for creators of intellectual property to protect that property.

Getting Permission: How to License and Clear Copyrighted Materials Online and Off, (book with CD-ROM), by Stephen Fishman (NOLO Press). This NOLO book looks at the other side of the coin: How to get permission to use intellectual property of others. It doesn't have to be hard, as long as you understand the law. That's where this book comes in.

The Public Domain: How to Find and Use Copyright Free Writings, Music, Art, and More, by Stephen Fishman (NOLO Press). If you don't want to—or can't—get permission to use copyrighted materials in your work, you might want to go the tried and true route of exploring the public domain. If you do, this book should tell you what you need to know about the law as it applies to public domain works.

5

Productivity Applications

OBJECTIVES

After you read this chapter you should be able to:

- Describe how PC and Web applications have revolutionized writing and publishing
- Discuss the potential impact of desktop publishing and Web publishing on freedom of the press
- Speculate about future developments in digital publishing
- Explain how computers can be used to answer what-if questions
- Describe the functions and applications of spreadsheets and other types of statistical and simulation programs
- Explain how computers are used as tools for simulating mechanical, biological, and social systems

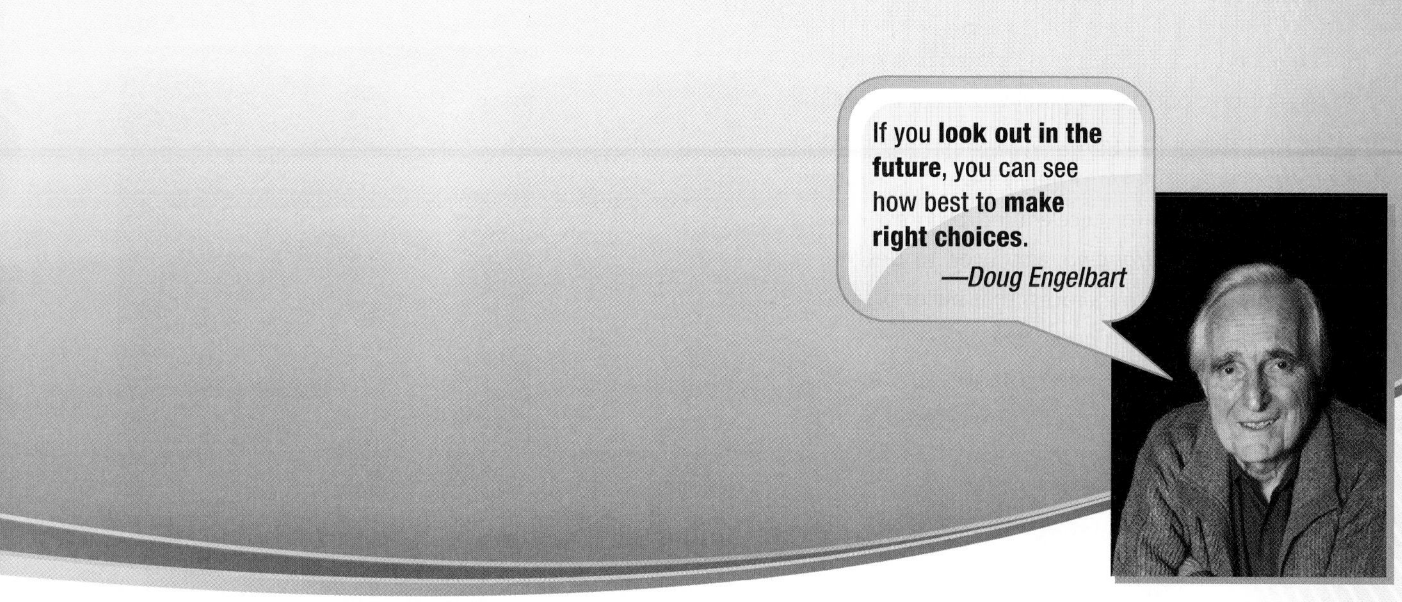

If you **look out in the future**, you can see how best to **make right choices.**
—*Doug Engelbart*

Doug Engelbart Explores Hyperspace

On a December day in 1950, Doug Engelbart looked into the future and saw what no one had seen before. Engelbart had been thinking about the growing complexity and urgency of the world's problems and wondering how he could help solve those problems. In his vision of the future, Engelbart saw computer technology augmenting and magnifying human mental abilities, providing people with new powers to cope with the urgency and complexity of life.

Engelbart decided to dedicate his life to turning his vision into reality. Unfortunately, the rest of the world wasn't ready for Engelbart's vision. His farsighted approach didn't match the prevailing ideas of the time, and most of the research community denounced or ignored Engelbart's work. In 1951 there were only about a dozen computers in the world, and those spent most of their time doing military calculations. It was hard to imagine ordinary people using computers to boost their personal productivity. So Engelbart put together the Augmentation Research Center at the Stanford Research Institute to create working models of his visionary tools.

In 1968 he demonstrated his Augment system to an auditorium full of astonished computer professionals and changed forever the way people think about computers. A large screen showed a cascade of computer graphics, text, and video images, controlled by Engelbart and a coworker several miles away. "It was like magic," recalls Alan Kay, one of the young computer scientists in the audience. Augment introduced the mouse, video-display editing (the forerunner to word processing), mixed text and graphics, windowing, outlining, shared-screen video conferencing, computer conferencing, groupware, and hypertext. Although Engelbart used a large computer, he was really demonstrating a futuristic "personal" computer—an interactive multimedia workstation for enhancing individual abilities.

Even though Engelbart's lab was responsible for many of the most important innovations in the history of computing, those innovations weren't fully appreciated until decades later. Engelbart is widely recognized for one small part of his vision—the mouse—but he never received any royalties for it. When the PC revolution started in the 1970s, many members of the Augment research team lost interest in Engelbart's vision of a networked, collaborative computing environment.

But Engelbart stayed true to his vision of using shared technology to solve our shared problems. He founded the Bootstrap Institute, a nonprofit think tank dedicated to helping organizations solve problems using a strategic *bootstrapping* approach for accelerating progress toward goals. (The term *bootstrapping,* also used to describe a computer startup, refers to a process that builds on itself—that pulls itself up by its own bootstraps.)

Today Engelbart is Founder Emeritus of the Doug Engelbart Institute, an organization he created with his daughter, Christina Engelbart. In a world where automation can dehumanize and eliminate jobs, he and his institute are still committed to replacing automation with augmentation. But they focus more on the human side of the equation, helping people chart a course into the future guided by intelligent, positive vision. He talks about turning organizations into "networked improvement communities" and explores ways of raising our collective IQ. If anyone understands how to build the future from a vision, Doug Engelbart does. ■

FIGURE 5.1 Doug Engelbart.

FIGURE 5.2 Doug Engelbart's visionary 1968 presentation showed the world how computers could be used as collaborative tools.

Doug Engelbart was one of the first people to recognize that computer technology could be used to augment human capabilities. Thanks in large part to his visionary work, people all over the world use computer applications to enhance their abilities to write papers and articles, publish periodicals and books, perform complex calculations, conduct scientific research, and even predict the future.

In this chapter we survey a variety of applications that people use to manipulate words and numbers. We consider software tools for working with words, from outliners to sophisticated reference tools, and numbers, from spreadsheets to statistical packages and money managers. We look at how digital technology has transformed the publishing process and provided more people with the power to communicate through written words. We examine how scientific visualization software can help us understand relationships that are invisible to the naked eye and how computers simulate reality for productivity and pleasure.

The Wordsmith's Toolbox

> I ... **cannot imagine now** that I ever wrote with a typewriter.
>
> —*Arthur C. Clarke, author and scientist*

In a single human generation the writing process has been transformed by word processing software. Instead of suffering through the painful process of writing and rewriting (or typing and retyping) in pursuit of a "clean" draft, a writer can focus on developing ideas and let the machine take care of laying out words on the page.

Word Processing Tools and Techniques

Working with a word processor involves several steps:

- Entering text
- Editing text
- Formatting the document
- Proofreading the document
- Saving the document
- Printing the document

Early word processing systems generally forced users to follow these steps in a strict order. Today's word processors allow writers to switch freely between editing and formatting—or do both at the same time. Words appear on the screen almost exactly as they will appear on a printed page. This feature is often referred to as ***WYSIWYG***, short for "what you see is what you get" and pronounced "wizzy-wig." (If you're new to word processing, you'll find more on the subject in Appendix A.)

Text formatting commands enable you to control the format of the text—the way the words will look on the page. Word processors include commands for controlling the formats of individual characters and paragraphs as well as complete documents.

With character formatting commands, you can select the font and the font size of the document's characters. Other character formatting commands let you change the color of a character, put it in boldface and/or italics, underline it, and more.

Other formatting commands apply to paragraphs rather than characters; they control space between lines, indentation, tab stops, and justification. **Justification** refers to the alignment of text on a line. Four justification choices are commonly available: align text left (with a smooth left margin and ragged right margin), align text right, justify (both margins are smooth), and center justification.

Some formatting commands apply to entire documents. For example, Microsoft Word's Page Setup command enables you to control the margins that apply throughout the document. Other commands enable you to specify the content, size, and style of **headers** and **footers**—text that appears at the top and bottom of every page, displaying repetitive information, such as chapter titles, author names, and automatically calculated page numbers.

Advanced editing and formatting features enable you to perform the following tasks:

- Define **styles** for each of the common elements in a document. (For example, you can define a style called "subhead" as a paragraph that's left-justified in a boldface, 12-point Helvetica font with standard margins and apply that style to every subhead in the document without reselecting all three of these commands for each new subhead. If you decide later to change the subheads to 14-point Futura, your changes in the subhead style are automatically reflected throughout the document.)
- Define alternate headers, footers, and margins so left- and right-facing pages can have different margins, headers, and footers.
- Create documents with multiple variable-width columns.
- Create, edit, and format multicolumn tables.
- Incorporate (and even edit) graphics created with other applications.
- Generate tables of contents and indexes for books and other long works (with human help for making judgments calls).
- Attach hidden comments that aren't visible in the final printed document.
- Record and reuse ***macros***—multistep sequences of instructions that can save time and effort by automating repetitive task. (More on macros in the spreadsheet section of this chapter.)
- Store presets of any or all of the above in ***templates*** so they can be used as starting points for similar future documents.

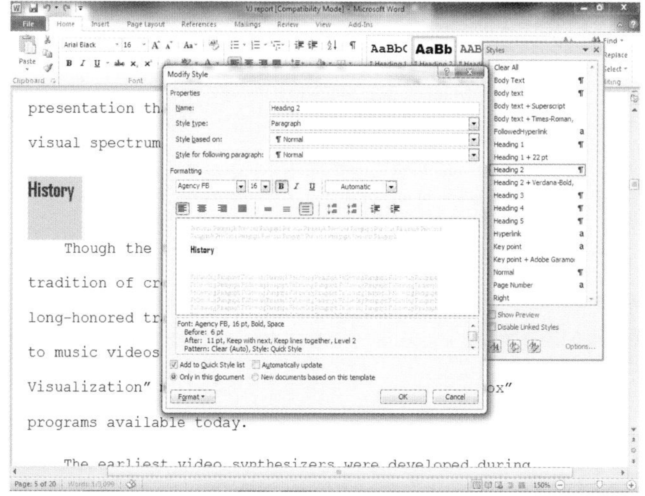

FIGURE 5.3 Microsoft Word's styles allow for quick formatting modifications throughout the document. For example, when the style "Heading 2" is redefined, every Heading 2 paragraph with that Heading 2 style attached automatically changes to reflect changes in the style definition.

how it works Font Technology

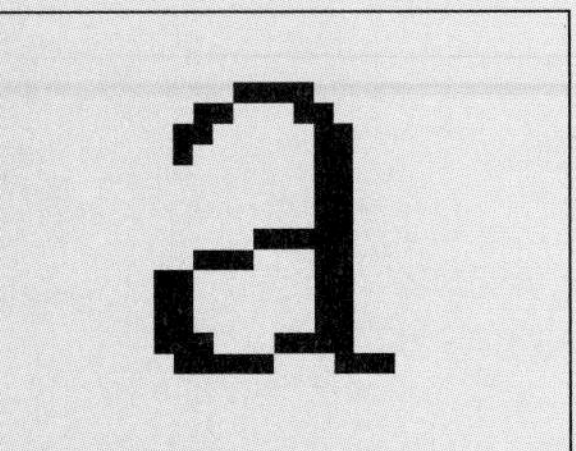

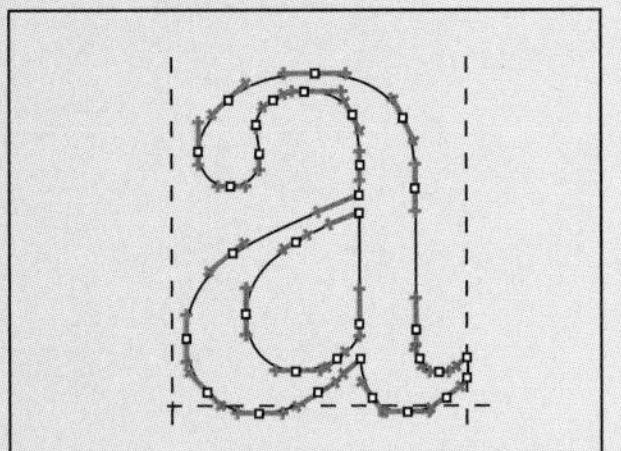

When a computer displays a character on a monitor or prints it on paper, the character is nothing more than a collection of tiny dots or squares in an invisible grid. Bitmapped fonts store characters in this way, with each pixel represented as a black or white bit in a matrix. A bitmapped font usually looks fine on screen in the intended point size but doesn't look smooth when printed on a high-resolution printer or enlarged on screen.

Most computer systems now use scalable outline fonts to represent type in memory until it is displayed or printed. A scalable font represents each character as an outline that can be scaled—increased or decreased in size without distortion. Curves and lines are smooth and don't have stair-stepped, jagged edges when they're resized. The outline is stored inside the computer or printer as a series of mathematical statements about the position of points and the shape of the lines connecting those points.

Downloadable fonts (soft fonts) are stored in the computer system (not the printer) and downloaded to the printer only when needed. These fonts usually have matching screen fonts and are easily moved to different computer systems. Most important, you can use the same downloadable font on many printer models.

A laser printer is really a dedicated computer system that contains its own CPU, RAM, ROM, and specialized operating system. Printer fonts are stored in the printer's ROM and are always available for use with that printer, but you may not be able to achieve WYSIWYG if your computer doesn't have a screen font to match your printer font. And if you move your document to a different computer and printer, the same printer font may not be available on the new system.

Until recently, fonts were most commonly available in two scalable outline forms: Adobe PostScript and Apple's TrueType. Because Apple and Microsoft have included TrueType downloadable fonts with their operating systems for many years, TrueType fonts are more popular among general computer users. PostScript fonts usually require additional software but are the long-time standard among many graphics professionals. PostScript is actually a complete page description language particularly well suited to the demands of professional publishers.

In recent years thousands of fonts have been released in a format that combines TrueType and PostScript technology: OpenType, co-developed by Adobe and Microsoft. According to Adobe, "The two main benefits of the OpenType format are its cross-platform compatibility (the same font file works on Macintosh and Windows computers), and its ability to support widely expanded character sets and layout features, which provide richer linguistic support and advanced typographic control." OpenType enables character shapes to travel with documents in compressed forms so a document transmitted electronically or displayed on the Web will look like the original even if the viewer's system doesn't include the original document's fonts.

1st, 2nd, 3rd	1st, 2nd, 3rd
Rectangle	Rectangle
Quick Brown Fox	*Quick Brown Fox*

FIGURE 5.4 Many OpenType fonts (right) contain expanded character sets and layout features that make them more flexible than their TrueType equivalents (left).

- Use **automatic footnoting** to save you from having to place footnotes and endnotes; the program automatically places them where they belong on the page.
- Use **automatic hyphenation** to divide long words that fall at the ends of lines.
- Use **automatic formatting (autoformat)** to apply formatting automatically to your text; for example, to number lists automatically (such as the exercises at the end of this chapter) and apply proper indentation to those lists.
- Use **automatic correction (autocorrect)** to correct common typing errors. For example, if you type *THe* or *Teh*, the software will automatically change it to *The*.
- Convert formatted documents to **HTML (hypertext markup language)** so they can be easily published on the Web.
- Use coaching or help features (sometimes called **wizards**) to walk you through complex document formatting procedures.

In addition to basic editing and formatting functions, a typical word processor includes a built-in outliner, spelling checker, and thesaurus.

Outliners and Idea Processors

> If any man wishes to write in a clear style, let him **first be clear in his thoughts**.
>
> —*Johann W. von Goethe*

For many of us, the hardest part of the writing process is collecting and organizing our thoughts. Traditional English-class techniques, including outlines and 3-by-5 note cards, involve additional work. But technology transforms these time-honored techniques into high-powered tools for extending our minds and streamlining the process of turning vague thoughts into solid prose.

Outliners, such as the ***Outline View*** option built into Microsoft Word, are, in effect, idea processors. Outliners are particularly effective at performing three functions:

1. Arranging information into hierarchies, or levels, so each heading can be fleshed out with more detailed subheads, which can then be broken into smaller pieces
2. Rearranging ideas and levels so subideas are automatically moved with their parent ideas
3. Hiding and revealing levels of detail as needed so you can examine the forest, the trees, or an individual leaf of your project

For a project that requires research, you can use an outliner as a replacement for note cards. Ideas can be collected, composed, refined, rearranged, and reorganized much more efficiently when they're stored in an outline. When the time comes to turn research into a research paper,

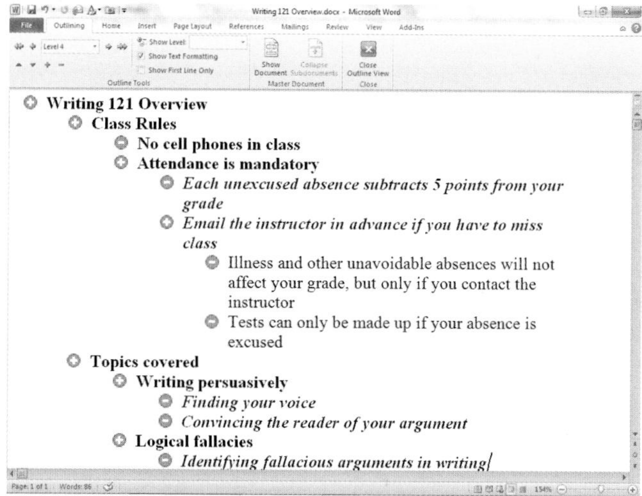

FIGURE 5.5 Microsoft Word's Outline View enables you to examine and restructure the overall organization of a document, while showing each topic in as much detail as you need. When you move headlines, the attached subheads and paragraphs follow automatically.

FIGURE 5.6 Microsoft Word's Thesaurus feature puts synonyms at your fingertips. In this case, the computer is providing synonyms for the word *retire*.

you don't need to retype the notes; you can polish them with standard text-editing techniques. If the outliner is built into the word processor, the line between notes and finished product blurs to the point where it almost disappears.

Digital References

> The difference between the right word and the almost-right word is **the difference between the lightning and the lightning bug**.
>
> —*Mark Twain*

Writers rely on dictionaries, quotation books, encyclopedias, atlases, almanacs, and other references. Just about all of these resources are now available on the Web and on disk. Mac OS includes a built-in spell checker and dictionary that works automatically in many applications. Microsoft Office and many other applications include dictionary and thesaurus tools.

The classic synonym finder, or *thesaurus*, is an invaluable tool for finding the right word, but it's not particularly user-friendly. With a computerized thesaurus, it's a simple matter to select a word and issue a command for a synonym search. The program provides almost instant gratification, displaying all kinds of possible replacements for the word in question. If you find a suitable substitute in the list, you can indicate your preference with a click or a keystroke; the software even makes the switch for you.

Reference materials abound on the Web. Unfortunately, not all of those sources are useful or reliable. Still, the Web offers a combination of speediness, timeliness, and cross-referencing that can't be found in any other reference source. Because pictures, maps, and drawings consume bandwidth and storage, they're sometimes removed or modified on the Web and disc. On the other hand, many digital references include sound, animation, video, and other forms of information that aren't possible to include in books.

Copying quotes electronically is faster and more accurate than retyping information from a book. Of course, this kind of quick copying makes plagiarism—using someone else's words without giving credit—easier than ever and may tempt more writers to violate copyright laws and ethical standards. If you're tempted to plagiarize someone else's writing, remember that electronic references make detecting plagiarism easier than ever, too!

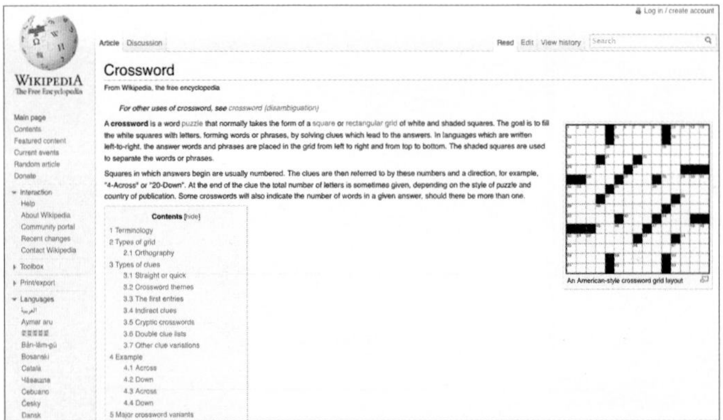

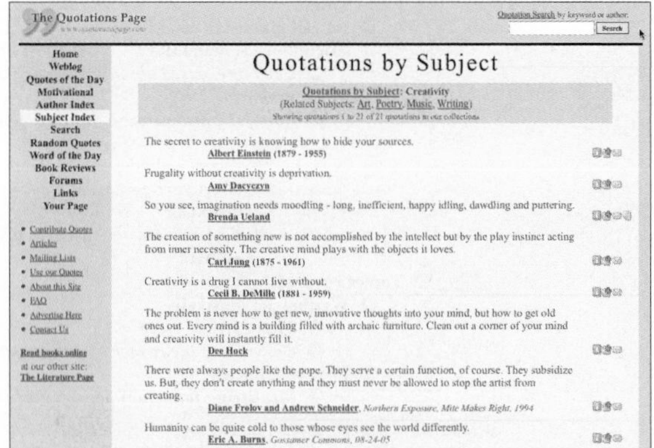

FIGURE 5.7 Students and other researchers can save time when searching for facts, quotes, ideas, or inspiration by using specially designed reference sites on the Web.

Spelling Checkers

> It is a damn poor mind indeed which can't think of **at least two ways to spell any word.**
>
> —*Andrew Jackson*

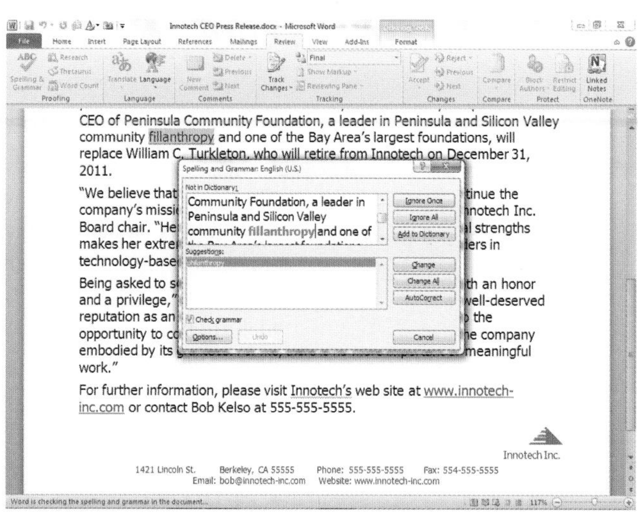

FIGURE 5.8 Most spelling checkers, including the one in Microsoft Word, offer the user several choices for handling words that aren't in the dictionary.

Although many of us sympathize with Jackson's point of view, the fact remains that correct spelling is an important part of most written communication. That's why a word processor typically includes a built-in **spelling checker**. (The Mac OS includes a spelling checker that works in most applications.) A spelling checker compares the words in your document with words in a disk-based dictionary. Every word that's not in the dictionary is flagged as a suspect word—a potential misspelling. In many cases the spelling checker suggests the corrected spelling and offers to replace the suspect word. Ultimately, though, it's up to you to decide whether the flagged word is, in fact, spelled incorrectly.

Spelling checkers are wonderful aids, but they can't replace careful proofreading by alert human eyes. When you're using a spelling checker, it's important to keep two potential problems in mind:

1. *Dictionary limitations and errors.* No dictionary includes every word, so you have to know what to do with unlisted words—proper names, obscure words, technical terms, foreign terms, colloquialisms, and other oddities. If you add words to your spelling checker's dictionary, you run the risk of adding an incorrectly spelled word, making future occurrences of that misspelling invisible to the spelling checker and to you.
2. *Errors of context.* The fact that a word appears in a dictionary does not guarantee that it is correctly spelled in the context of the sentence. The following passage, for example, contains eight spelling errors, none of which would be detected by a spelling checker:

> *I wood never have guest that my spelling checker would super seed my editor as my mane source of feed back. I no longer prophet from the presents of an editor while I right.*

Grammar and Style Checkers

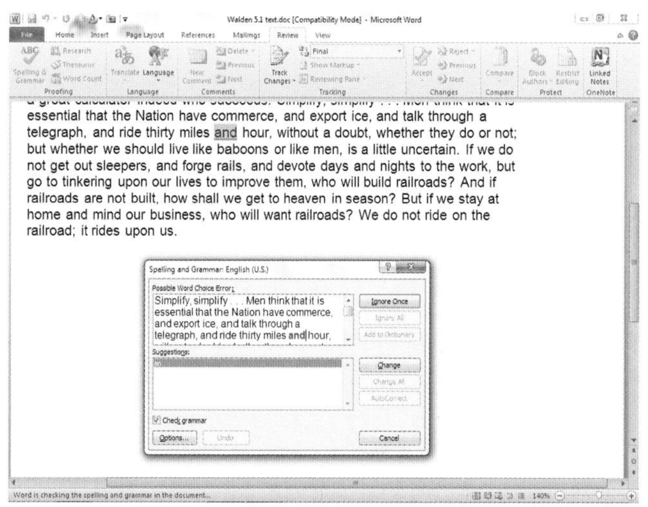

FIGURE 5.9 Grammar-and-style-checking software flags possible errors and makes suggestions about how they might be fixed. Here, Microsoft Word points out that "and" doesn't make sense in this sentence, and guesses that you mistyped "an."

The errors in the preceding quote would have slipped by a spelling checker, but many of them would have been detected by a **grammar and style checker**. In addition to checking spelling, grammar-and-style-checking software analyzes each word in context, checking for errors of context (I wood never have guest), common grammatical errors (Ben and me went to Boston), and stylistic foibles (Suddenly the door was opened by Bethany). In addition to pointing out possible errors and suggesting improvements, it can analyze prose complexity using measurements such as sentence length and paragraph length. This kind of analysis is useful for determining whether your writing style is appropriate for your target audience.

Grammar-and-style-checking software is, at best, imperfect. A typical program misses many true errors, while flagging correct passages. Still, it can be a valuable writing aid, especially for students who are mastering the complexities of a language for the first time. But software is no substitute for practice, revision, editing, and a good English teacher.

Form-Letter Generators

> **Congratulations, Mr. <last name>**. You may already have won!
>
> —*Junk mail greeting*

Most word processors today have **mail merge** capabilities for producing personalized form letters. When used with a database containing a list of names and addresses, a word processor can quickly generate individually addressed letters and mailing labels. Many programs can incorporate custom paragraphs based on the recipient's personal data, making each letter look as if it were individually written. Direct-mail marketing companies exploited this kind of technology for years before it became available in inexpensive PC software.

Collaborative Writing Tools

Most large writing projects, including the one that produced this book, involve groups of people working together. Computer networks make it easy for writers and editors to share documents, but it's not always easy for one person to know how a document has been changed by others. **Groupware**—software designed to be used by a workgroup—can keep track of a document's history as it's passed among group members and make sure that all changes are incorporated into a single master document. Using groupware, each writer can monitor and make suggestions concerning the work of any other writer on the team. Editors can "blue pencil" corrections and attach notes directly to the electronic manuscript. The notes can be read by any or all of the writers—even those who are on another continent. This kind of collaborative writing and editing doesn't require specialized software anymore; it can be done with many word processing and publishing programs. For example, Microsoft Word's Track Changes option can record and display contributions from several writers and editors; it can also compare document versions and highlight differences between versions.

Word's Track Changes feature does not allow multiple users to make changes *simultaneously*. Instead, team members pass the document back and forth, making sequential changes. But Word and many other programs, including Google Documents, Gobby, and Writeboard, allow many writers to work on a document at the same time through a network.

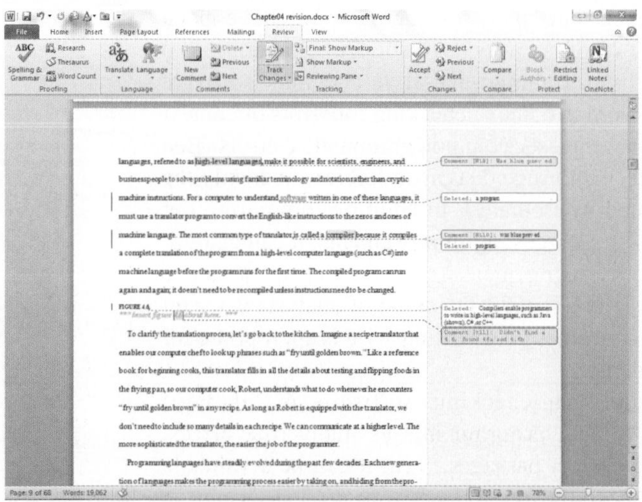

FIGURE 5.10 The Track Changes feature in Microsoft Word enables writers, editors, and other collaborative document creators to contribute to the same document and see each other's changes.

Emerging Word Tools

The real technology—behind all of our other technologies—is language. It actually **creates the world our consciousness lives in**.

—*Norman Fischer, Abbot, Green Gulch Farm Zen Center*

Word processing software has evolved rapidly in the past few years. The evolution isn't over; current trends suggest big changes are coming in word processing technology.

Processing Handwriting and Speech

For a small but growing population, pen-based systems provide an alternative tool for entering text. Handwriting recognition doesn't come easy to computers; it requires sophisticated software that can interpret pen movements as characters and words. The diversity in handwriting makes it difficult for today's software to translate all of our scribbles into text. Powerful pen-based systems such as the Tablet PC work reliably because they use all the processing punch of modern notebook PCs and advanced handwriting-recognition algorithms.

Ultimately, most writers long for a computer that can accept and reliably process *speech* input—a *talkwriter*. With such a system, a user can tell the computer what to type—and how to type it—by simply talking into a microphone. The user's speech enters the computer as a digital audio signal. **Speech recognition software** looks for patterns in the sound waves and interprets sounds by locating familiar patterns, segmenting input sound patterns into words, separating commands from the text, and passing those commands to the word processing software.

Speech recognition software systems have been around for years, but until recently, most were severely limited. It takes a great deal of knowledge to understand the complexities of human speech. A computer, lacking a child's experience with English, might interpret, say, "recognize speech" as "wreck a nice beach." Research in speech recognition today focuses on producing systems that can:

- Recognize words reliably without being trained to an individual speaker, an ability known as *speaker independence*
- Handle speech without limiting vocabulary
- Handle continuous speech—natural speech in which words run together at normal speed

Researchers are making great strides toward these goals, making speech recognition practical for applications in health care, the military, telephony, and elsewhere. Most of us have navigated through automated customer-service menus by speaking commands rather than punching phone buttons. Many cars and cell phones have speech recognition systems designed to recognize basic commands and names. Speech-recognition systems are especially important for people who can't use their hands because of physical limitations, injuries, or job restrictions.

Dictation software—software designed to turn continuous speech into written text—can achieve accuracy approaching 100 percent under ideal conditions. Accuracy generally improves as the program "trains" to the speaker's voice and mannerisms. The best dictation software integrates seamlessly with word processors, email programs, and other applications. Some Web sites offer dictation and messaging services via cell phone, translating spoken passages into email messages. For many writers, speech recognition software increases productivity while reducing the risk of repetitive strain injuries.

FIGURE 5.11 This student is able to dictate to his computer using Dragon Naturally Speaking speech recognition software.

Intelligent Word Processors

Speech recognition is just one aspect of artificial intelligence research that's finding its way into the writing process. Many experts foresee word processing software that is able to anticipate the writer's needs, acting as an electronic editor or coauthor. Today's grammar and style checkers are primitive forerunners of the kinds of electronic writing consultants that might appear in a few years.

Here are some possibilities:

- As you're typing a story, your word processing software reminds you that you've used the word *delicious* three times in the past two paragraphs and suggests that you choose an alternative from the list shown on the screen.
- Your word processing software continuously analyzes your style as you type, determines your writing habits and patterns, and learns from its analysis. If your writing tends to be technical and formal, the software modifies its thesaurus, dictionary, and other tools so they're more appropriate for that style.
- You're writing a manual for a large organization that uses specific style guidelines of documentation. Your word processing software modifies your writing as you type so it conforms to the organizational style.
- You need some current figures to support your argument on the depletion of the ozone layer. You issue a command, and the computer does a quick search of the literature on the Web and reports to you with several relevant facts.

All these examples are technically possible now. The trend toward intelligent word processors is clear. Nevertheless, you're in for a long wait if you're eager to buy a system with commands such as Clever Quote, Humorous Anecdote, and Term Paper.

The Desktop Publishing Story

> Freedom of the press belongs to **the person who owns one**.
>
> —*A. J. Liebling, the late media critic for the* New Yorker

Just as word processing changed the writer's craft in the 1970s, the world of publishing was radically transformed in the 1980s when Apple introduced its first LaserWriter printer and a new company named Aldus introduced PageMaker, a Mac program that could take advantage of that printer's high-resolution output capabilities. Publishing—traditionally an expensive, time-consuming, error-prone process—instantly became an enterprise that just about anyone with a computer and a little cash could undertake.

What Is Desktop Publishing?

The process of producing a book, magazine, or other publication includes several steps:

- Writing text
- Editing text
- Producing drawings, photographs, and other graphics to accompany the text
- Designing a basic format for the publication
- Typesetting text
- Arranging text and graphics on pages
- Typesetting and printing pages
- Binding pages into a finished publication

In traditional publishing, many of these steps required expensive equipment, highly trained specialists to operate the equipment, and lots of time. With **desktop publishing (DTP)** technology, the bulk of the production process can be accomplished with tools that are small, affordable, and easy to use. A desktop publishing system generally includes one or more Macs or PCs, a scanner, a digital camera, a high-resolution printer, and software. It's now possible for a single person with a modest equipment investment to do all the writing, editing, graphic production, design, page layout, and typesetting for a desktop publication. Of course, few individuals have the skills to handle all of these tasks, so most publications are still the work of teams that include writers, editors, designers, artists, and supervisors. But even if the titles remain the same, each of these jobs is changing because of desktop publishing technology.

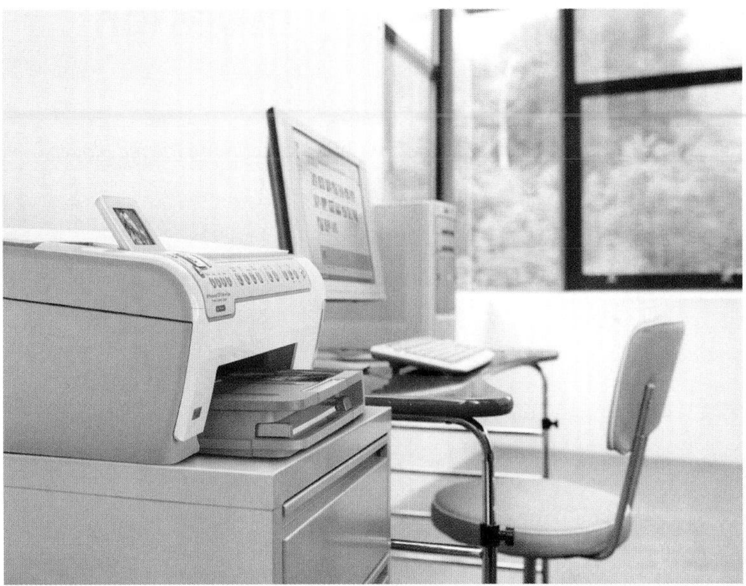

FIGURE 5.12 A typical desktop publishing system includes a personal computer, a high-resolution printer, a scanner and other imaging hardware, and a variety of graphical software programs.

The first steps in the publishing process involve producing **source documents**—articles, chapters, drawings, maps, charts, and photographs that are to appear in the publication. Desktop publishers generally use standard word processing and graphics programs to produce most source documents. Scanners with image-editing software are used to transform photographs and hand-drawn images into computer-readable documents. **Page-layout software**, such as Adobe InDesign, QuarkXPress, Microsoft Publisher, or Apple's Pages, is used to combine the various source documents into a coherent, visually appealing publication. Pages are generally laid out one at a time on-screen, although most programs have options for automating multiple-page document layout.

Page-layout software provides graphic designers with control over virtually every element of the design, right down to the spacing between each pair of letters (***kerning***)

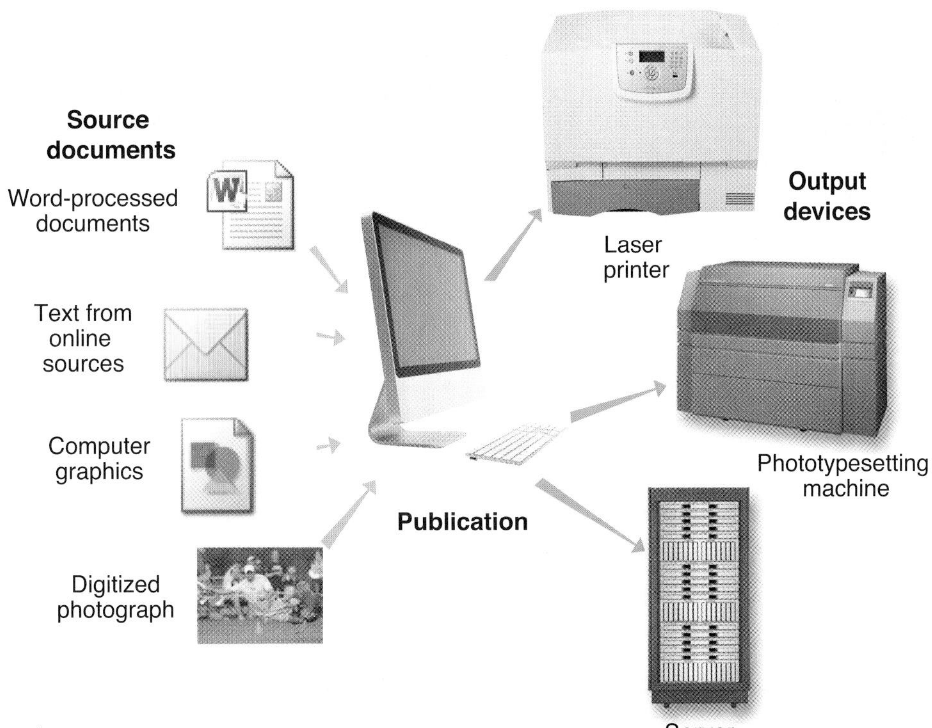

FIGURE 5.13 Source documents are merged in a publication document, which can be printed on a laser or inkjet printer, printed on a high-resolution phototypesetter, or published on the Web.

Screen Test Desktop Publishing with Adobe InDesign

GOAL *To create a four-page newsletter for ultimate frisbee players*

TOOLS *Adobe Photoshop, Adobe InDesign*

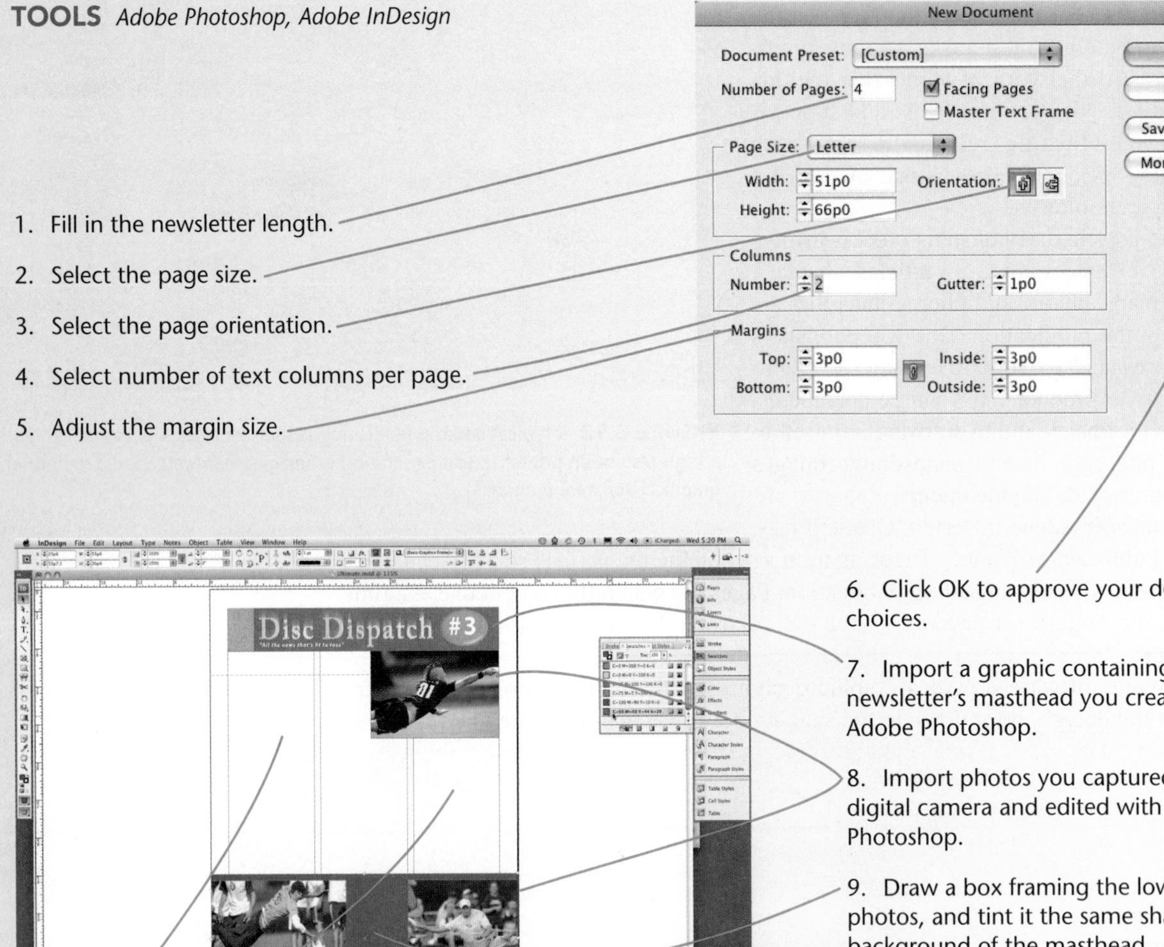

1. Fill in the newsletter length.
2. Select the page size.
3. Select the page orientation.
4. Select number of text columns per page.
5. Adjust the margin size.
6. Click OK to approve your design choices.
7. Import a graphic containing the newsletter's masthead you created with Adobe Photoshop.
8. Import photos you captured with a digital camera and edited with Adobe Photoshop.
9. Draw a box framing the lower two photos, and tint it the same shade as the background of the masthead.
10. Create text boxes to hold the cover story.
11. Use the Get Text command to import text from a Word document.
12. Modify the size of the article's title.
13. Add another text box between the photos at the bottom and type a quote into it. Color the text white.
14. Continue the layout process on the remaining pages, and print the finished document.

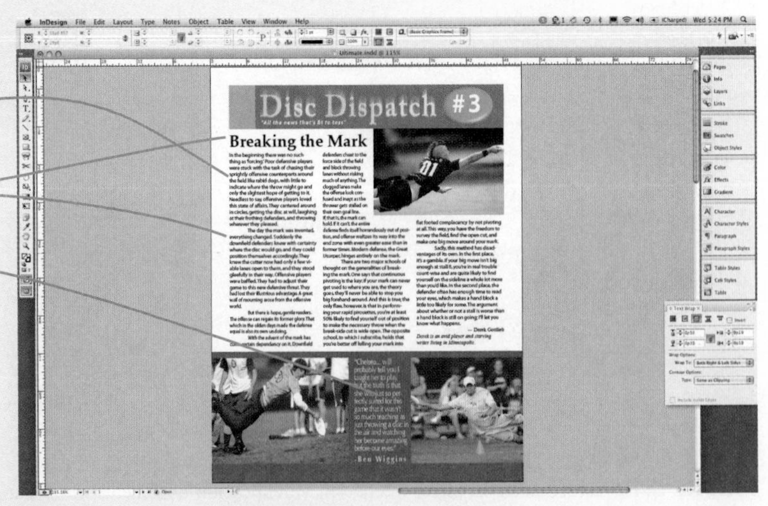

FIGURE 5.14

and the spacing between lines of text (*leading*). Today's word processing programs include basic page-layout capabilities, too; they're sufficient for creating many types of publications. But to produce more complex layouts for newspapers, newsletters, magazines, and flyers, publishers need the kind of advanced formatting capabilities found only in dedicated desktop publishing applications. (Word processing and desktop publishing software often works hand in hand: For example, writers usually use word processing software to create the text that is poured into a desktop publishing layout.)

For users without backgrounds in layout and design, most page-layout and word processing programs include professionally designed **templates**—"empty" documents that can be easily adapted to specific user needs. Most programs have options for saving documents as templates, so future documents can be created using the same layout and styles. Even without templates, it's possible for beginners to create professional-quality publications with a modest investment of money and time.

Desktop publishing becomes more complicated when color is introduced. *Spot color*—the use of a single ink color (or sometimes two) to add interest—is relatively easy. But *full-color* desktop publishing, including color photos, drawings, and paintings, must deal with the inconsistencies of different color output devices. Because printers and monitors use different types of color-mixing technologies, as described in the How It Works boxes in Chapter 3, what you see on the screen isn't always what you get when you print it. It's even difficult to get two monitors (or two printers) to produce images with exactly the same color balance. Still, color desktop publishing is big business, and advances in *color-matching* technology are making it easier all the time.

Most desktop publications are printed on color laser printers capable of producing output with a resolution of at least 600 dots per inch (dpi). The number of dots per inch influences the resolution and clarity of the image. Output of 600 dpi is sufficiently sharp for most applications, but it's less than the 1200 dpi that is the traditional minimum for professional typesetting. High-priced devices, called phototypesetting machines or imagesetters, enable desktop publications to be printed at 1200 dpi or higher. Many desktop publishers rely on outside service bureaus with phototypesetting machines to print their final camera-ready pages—pages that are ready to be photographed and printed.

Why Desktop Publishing?

Desktop publishing offers several advantages for businesses. Desktop publishing saves money. Publications that used to cost hundreds or thousands of dollars to produce through outside publishing services can now be produced in-house for a fraction of their former cost. Desktop publishing also saves time. The turnaround time for a publication done on the desktop can be a few days instead of the weeks or months it might take to publish the same thing using traditional channels. Quality control is easier to maintain when documents are produced in-house. And desktop publishing makes it easy to repurpose content for use on the Web.

The real winners in the desktop publishing revolution might turn out to be not big businesses, but everyday people with something to say. With commercial TV networks, newspapers, magazines, and book publishers increasingly controlled by a few giant corporations, many media experts worry that the free press (guaranteed by the U.S. First Amendment and similar proclamations in other countries) is seriously threatened by de facto media monopolies. Desktop publishing technology offers hope for every individual's right to publish. Writers, artists, and editors whose work is shunned or ignored by large publishers and mainstream media have affordable publishing alternatives. If, as media critic A. J. Liebling suggested, freedom of the press belongs to the person who owns one, that precious freedom is now accessible to more people than ever before.

Working Wisdom Creating Professional-Looking Documents

Many first-time users of word processing and desktop publishing systems become intoxicated with all the power at their fingertips. It's easy to get carried away with all those fonts, styles, and sizes and to create a document that makes supermarket tabloids look tasteful. Although there's no substitute for a good education in the principles of design, it's easy to avoid tacky-looking documents if you follow a few simple guidelines:

- ***Plan before you publish.*** Design (or select) a simple, visually pleasing format for your document, and use that format throughout the document.
- ***Use appropriate fonts.*** Limit your choices to one or two fonts and sizes per page, and be consistent throughout your document.
- ***Don't go style crazy.*** Avoid overusing *italics*, **boldface**, ALL CAPS, underlines, and other styles for emphasis. When in doubt, leave it out.
- ***Don't go color crazy.*** Sometimes less is more. Choose a limited palette of colors that work together and stick to it.
- ***Look at your document through your reader's eyes.*** Make every picture say something. Don't try to cram too much information on a page. Don't be afraid of white space. Use a format that speaks clearly to your readers. Make sure the main points of your document stand out.
- ***Learn from the masters.*** Study the designs of successful publications. Use design books, articles, and classes to develop your aesthetic skills along with your technical skills. With or without a computer, publishing is an art.
- ***Know your limitations.*** Desktop publishing technology makes it possible for anyone to produce high-quality documents with a minimal investment of time and money. But your equipment and skills may not be up to the job at hand. For many applications, personal desktop publishing is no match for a professional design artist or typesetter. If you need the best, work with a pro.
- ***Remember the message.*** Fancy fonts, tasteful graphics, and meticulous design can't turn shoddy ideas into words of wisdom, or lies into the truth. The purpose of publishing is communication; don't try to use technology to disguise the lack of something to communicate.

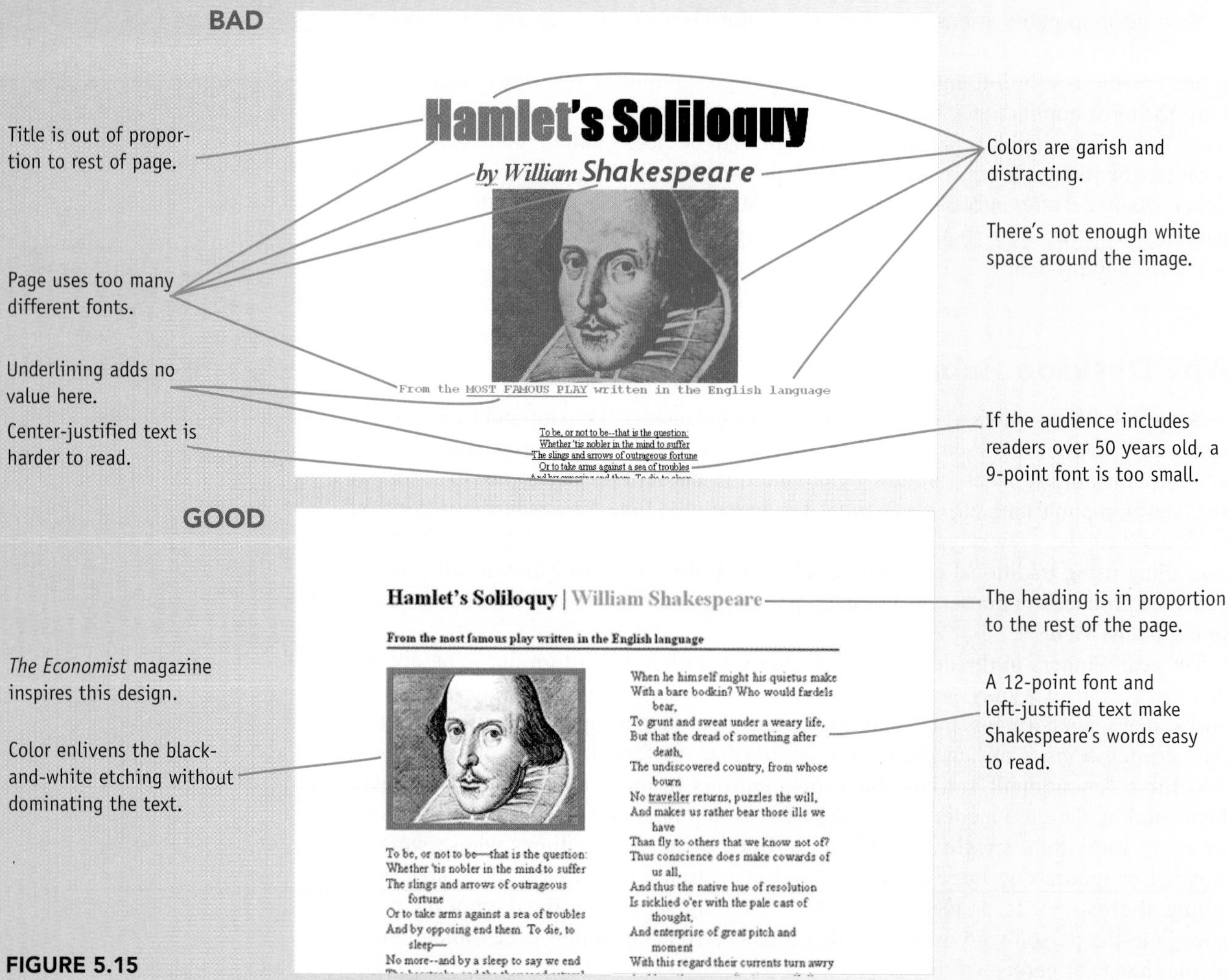

FIGURE 5.15

Beyond the Printed Page

> **Paper, often underrated as a communication medium, will not be eliminated** by the growth of electronic media. It remains inexpensive, extremely portable, and capable of carrying very high-resolution images.
>
> *—Mark Duchesne, Vice President, AM Multigraphics*

The first books were so difficult to produce that they were considered priceless. They were kept in cabinets with multiple locks so they couldn't be removed without the knowledge and permission of at least two monks. Today we can print professional-quality publications in short order using equipment that costs less than a used car. But the publishing revolution isn't over yet.

Paperless Publishing and the Web

A common prediction is that paper publishing will be replaced by paperless electronic media. Paper still offers advantages for countless communication tasks. Reading printed words on pages is easier on the eyes than reading from a screen. Paper documents can be read and scribbled on almost anywhere, with or without electricity. And there's no electronic equivalent for the aesthetics of a beautifully designed, finely crafted book. Predictions aside, the printed word isn't likely to go away anytime soon.

Still, digital media forms are likely to eclipse paper for many applications. Email messages now outnumber post office letter deliveries. Online encyclopedias have all but replaced their overweight paper counterparts. Adobe's ***PDF (Portable Document Format)*** enables documents of all types to be stored, viewed, or modified on virtually any PC making it possible for organizations to reduce paper flow.

The Web offers unprecedented mass publishing possibilities to millions of Internet users. Programs as diverse as Microsoft Word, Adobe InDesign, and Apple Pages can save documents in HTML format, so they can be published on the Web. Other programs, specifically designed for Web publishing, offer advanced capabilities for Web layout, graphics, animation, and multimedia publishing. (We'll explore some of these tools in later chapters when we discuss multimedia and the Web in greater depth.)

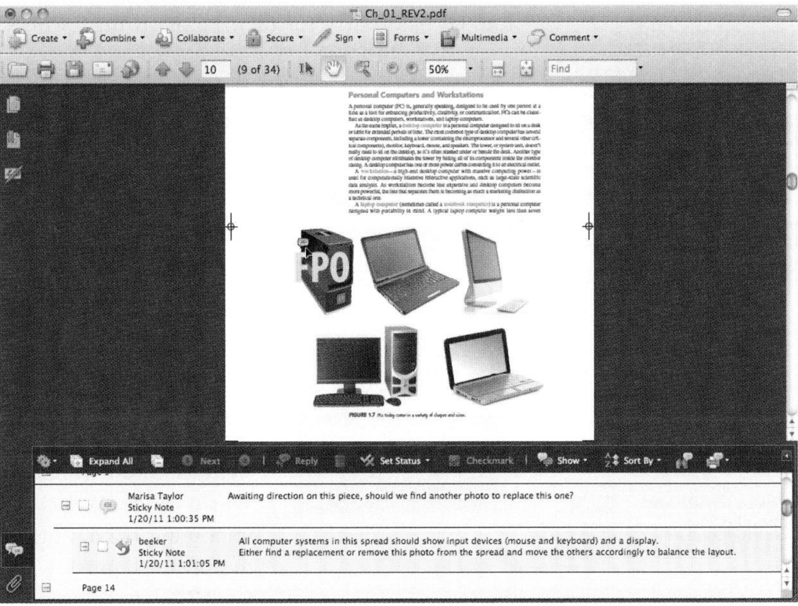

FIGURE 5.16 Adobe Acrobat Pro is a cross-platform software program that enables the electronic sharing of PDF documents, eliminating the need for paper in many publishing projects. People who worked on *Digital Planet* attached their comments to PDF pages and shared them electronically using Acrobat Pro. (Adobe's free Acrobat Reader can display, but not edit, PDF documents.)

FIGURE 5.17 Mountains of waste paper such as this one should become less common as paperless publishing grows in popularity. That's the theory, anyway.

Never before has a communication medium made it so easy or inexpensive for an individual to reach such a wide audience. For a few dollars a month, an Internet service provider can supply you with space to publish blogs, essays, stories, reviews, photos, and art. It doesn't matter whether you're a student, a poet, an artist, a government official, a labor organizer, or a corporate president; on the Web all URLs are created equal.

Of course, the most popular commercial Web sites cost their owners more than a few dollars a month. A typical Web storefront costs a million dollars just to build. And one of the biggest challenges in Web publishing is attracting people to your site once it's online. Copyright protection is another problem for Web publishers; anything that's published on the Web for the world to see is also available for the world to copy. How can writers and editors be paid fairly for their labors if their works are so easy to duplicate?

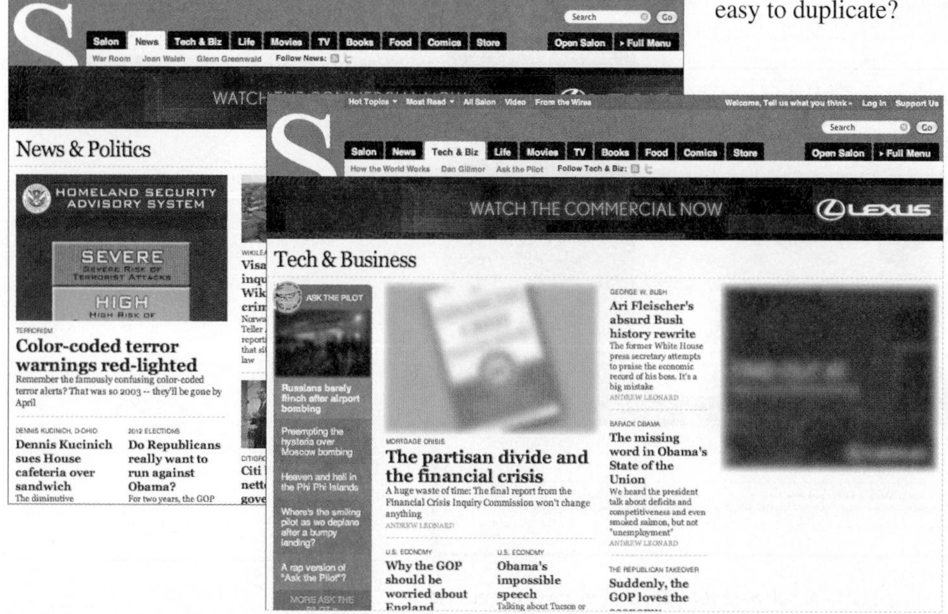

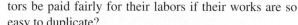

FIGURE 5.18 Many popular periodicals, from *Wired* to *Rolling Stone*, are published electronically on the Web. *Salon* is an example of a high-quality, popular magazine that is available only on the Web.

Still, the Web is far more accessible to small-budget writers and publishers than any other mass medium. And many experts predict that Web technology will eventually include mechanisms for automatic payment to content creators whose works are downloaded. In any case, the free flow of ideas may be more significant than the flow of money. In the words of writer Howard Rheingold, the World Wide Web "might be important in the same way that the printing press was important. By expanding the number of people who have the power to transmit knowledge, the Web might trigger a power shift that changes everything."

E-Books, E-Readers, and E-Paper

Paper publications also have growing competition from **e-books (electronic books)** and other digital publications. An e-book is a digital version of a book. An e-book might be readable on a computer, a PDA, a smart phone, and/or an **e-reader (e-book reader)**—a handheld device designed primarily for reading digital publications. E-book readers have been produced and marketed by Amazon, Sony, Barnes and Noble, and other companies. Apple's iPad isn't a *single-purpose* e-reader, but it was the first major multifunction device designed to compete with e-readers as a delivery platform for digital publications. Depending on how it's designed, an e-reader (or similar device) might download digital publications from a connected computer, from an online bookstore via a wireless connection, or both.

The iPad and most other tablet computers use the same LCD display technology found in most computers and smart phones. There are many advantages to LCD: They can produce vivid color images, they can display and respond to rapid movements, and they can provide bright backlit images even in the dark. But LCD displays lose their images when they run out of power, and they can be hard to read in bright sunlight. Most e-readers use another display technology called **e-paper (electronic paper)**. E-paper is designed to look more like ordinary paper. An e-paper display can't refresh (change) as quickly as an LCD display. An e-paper display isn't backlit—it reflects light like a paper page does—so it can't be seen in the dark, but it doesn't lose visibility in bright sunlight. An e-paper display can stay on even when the device is powered down. Some types of e-paper are flexible, so foldable digital newspapers might make their way into our daily lives as the technology improves.

One advantage of an e-book, e-magazine, or e-newspaper, is that it can be downloaded into, and read on, a variety of devices. You might start reading a book on the beach using the Amazon Kindle's e-paper display. After the sun goes down you might switch to an iPad (or even an iPhone) because of its bright backlit display. And you might refer back to the book later on your desktop PC.

E-books also offer advantages in convenience and portability. A student might be able to download a year's worth of textbooks into an e-reader the size of a small notebook, and receive automatic updates from the publisher when books are revised. Assuming, of course, that all of those books are available in a digital format that's compatible with the student's e-reader.

Unfortunately, there is no universal standard for e-books. E-books, like digital music files, come in many different formats. An e-book might be a simple text file or a PDF document. More often, it's encoded in a format developed specifically for e-books. Many are encoded using an open standard called EPUB, a format supported by many companies and compatible with many e-readers and other devices. Some e-book files include

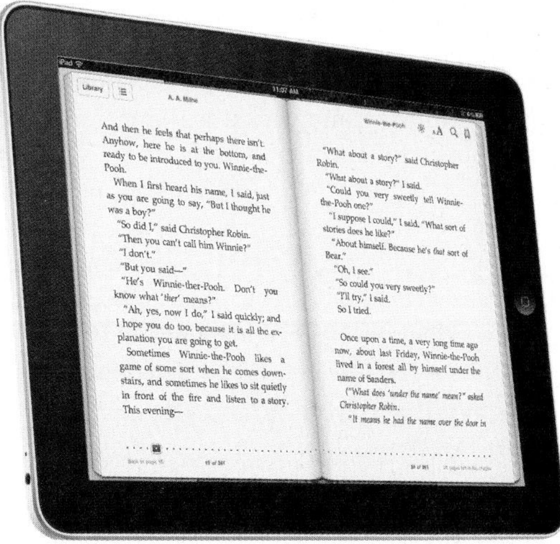

FIGURE 5.19 Amazon's Kindle is a popular electronic book reader. Apple's iPad includes an app that turns it into an e-book reader. Both products are designed to work seamlessly with online bookstores, making it easy to browse, buy, and download books wirelessly.

FIGURE 5.20 Compared to an LCD display, electronic paper looks more like real paper, making for a reading environment that is easier on the eyes. Electronic paper is beginning to appear in consumer products. Sony's Reader (left) uses electronic paper to present book pages. This Lexar flash drive (right) uses electronic paper as a storage capacity indicator. The display can be read even when the drive is not plugged in.

DRM (digital rights management) technology (see Chapter 4) to prevent rampant piracy. (The EPUB format includes DRM options.)

The electronic publication industry is young, so it's likely to go through lots of changes over the next few years. E-publications won't completely replace paper books, magazines, and newspapers. But the future of e-publishing looks very bright.

The Spreadsheet: Software for Simulation and Speculation

> Compare the expansion of business today to the conquering of the continent in the nineteenth century. The spreadsheet in that comparison is like the transcontinental railroad. **It accelerated the movement, made it possible, and changed the course of the nation.**
>
> —*Mitch Kapor, creator of the Lotus 1-2-3 spreadsheet software*

From the earliest days of the PC revolution, the spreadsheet has changed the way people do business. In the same way word processing software gives people control over words, **spreadsheet software** enables computer users to take control of numbers, manipulating them in ways that would be difficult or impossible otherwise. A spreadsheet program can make short work of tasks that involve repetitive calculations: budgeting, investment management, business projections, grade books, scientific simulations, checkbooks, and so on. A spreadsheet can also reveal hidden relationships between numbers, taking much of the guesswork out of financial planning and speculation.

The Malleable Matrix

> The goal was that it had to be **better than the back of an envelope**.
>
> —*Dan Bricklin, inventor of the first spreadsheet program*

Almost all spreadsheet programs are based on a simple concept: the malleable matrix. A spreadsheet document, called a **worksheet**, typically appears on the screen as a grid of numbered rows and lettered **columns**. The box representing the intersection of a row and

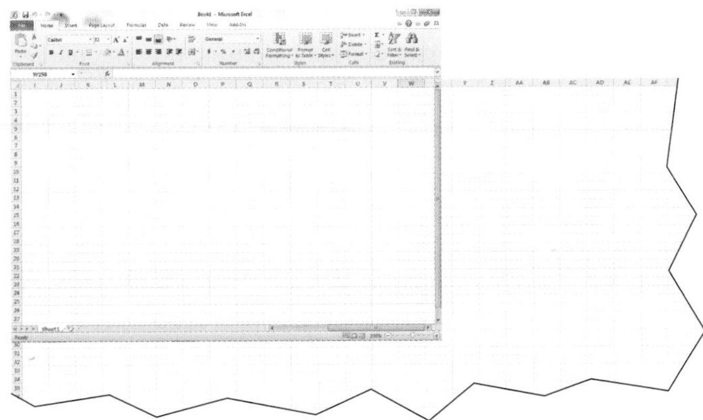

FIGURE 5.21 The worksheet may be bigger than what appears on your screen. The program enables you to scroll horizontally and vertically to view the larger matrix. (After column Z, columns are labeled with double letters: AA, BB, and so on.)

a column is called a **cell**. Every cell in this grid has a unique **address** made up of a column letter and row number. For example, the cell in the upper-left corner of the grid is called cell A1 (column A, row 1) in most spreadsheet applications. All the cells are empty in a new worksheet; it's up to the user to fill them. Each cell can contain a numeric value, an alphabetic label, or a formula representing a relationship with numbers in other cells.

Values (numbers) are the raw material the spreadsheet software uses to perform calculations. Numbers in worksheet cells can represent wages, test scores, weather data, polling results, or just about anything that can be quantified.

To make it easier for people to understand the numbers, most worksheets include **labels** at the tops of columns and at the edges of rows, such as "Monthly Wages," "Midterm Exam 1," "Average Wind Speed," or "Final Approval Rating." To the computer, these labels are meaningless strings of characters. The label "Total Points" doesn't tell the computer to calculate the total and display it in an adjacent cell; it's just a road sign for human readers.

To calculate the total points (or the average wind speed or the final approval rating), the worksheet must include a **formula**—a step-by-step procedure for calculating the desired number. The simplest spreadsheet formulas are arithmetic expressions using symbols, such as + (addition), – (subtraction), * (multiplication), and / (division). For example, cell B5 might contain the formula =(B2+B3)/2. This formula tells the computer to add the numbers in cells B2 and B3, divide the result by 2, and display the final result in the cell containing the formula, cell B5.

You don't see the formula in cell B5; you see only its effect. It doesn't matter whether the numbers represent test scores, dollars, or nothing at all; the computer obediently calculates their average and displays the results. If the number in cell B2 or B3 changes, the number displayed in B5 automatically changes, too. In many ways, this is the most powerful feature of a spreadsheet.

Different brands of spreadsheets, such as those included in Microsoft Office, Google Docs, StarOffice, OpenOffice.org, and iWork, are distinguished by their features, their user interfaces, and which operating system platforms they use. In spite of their differences, all popular spreadsheet programs work in much the same way and share most of these features:

- *Lists.* Despite the availability of powerful and advanced features in virtually all spreadsheets, most people still use these applications for fairly mundane tasks, such as making and managing lists of grocery items, to-do tasks, phone numbers, and other related information.

	A	B	C	D	E
1	Comparison of Car Loans				
2	Selling Price	$ 14,400.00			
3	Down Payment	$ 2,200.00			
4	Principal	$ 12,200.00			
5		Option 1	Option 2		
6	Term (in years)	5	4		
7	Annual Interest Rate	7%	6%		
8	Monthly Payment	$ 241.57	$ 286.52		
9	Total Payout	$ 14,494.48	$ 13,752.83		
10	Interest Expense	$ 2,294.48	$ 1,552.83		

FIGURE 5.22 This simple spreadsheet calculates the true cost of car loans.

- *Automatic replication of values, labels, and formulas.* Most worksheets contain repetition: budgetary amounts remain constant from month to month; exam scores are calculated the same way for every student in the class; a scheduling program refers to the same seven days each week. Many spreadsheet commands streamline the entry of repetitive data, labels, and formulas. **Replication** commands are, in essence, flexible extensions of the basic copy-and-paste functions found in other software. The most commonly used replication commands are the Fill Down and Fill Right commands. Formulas can be constructed with *relative references* to other cells, as in the example on the previous page, so they refer to different cells when replicated in other locations, or as *absolute references* that don't change when copied elsewhere.
- *Automatic recalculation.* **Automatic recalculation** is one of the spreadsheet's most important capabilities. It not only makes possible the easy correction of errors, but also makes it easy to try different values while searching for solutions.
- *Predefined functions.* The first calculators made computing a square root a tedious and error-prone series of steps. On today's calculators a single press of the square-root button tells the calculator to do all the necessary calculations to produce the square root. Spreadsheet programs contain built-in **functions** that work like the calculator's square-root button. A function in a formula instructs the computer to perform some predefined set of calculations. For example, the formula =SQRT(C5) calculates the square root of the number in cell C5. Spreadsheet applications include libraries of predefined functions. Many, such as SUM, AVERAGE (or AVG), MIN, and MAX, represent simple calculations that are performed often in all kinds of worksheets. Others automate complex financial, mathematical, and statistical calculations that would be extremely difficult to calculate manually. The IF function enables the worksheet to decide what to do based on the contents of other cells, giving the worksheet logical decision-making capability. (For example, if the number of hours worked is greater than 40, calculate pay using the overtime schedule.) Like the calculator's square-root button, these functions can save time and reduce the likelihood of errors.
- *Macros.* A spreadsheet's menu of functions, like the menu in a fast-food restaurant, is limited to the most popular selections. For situations in which the built-in functions don't fill the bill, most spreadsheets enable you to capture sequences of steps as reusable **macros**—custom-designed procedures that you can add to the existing menu of options. Some programs require you to type macros using a special macro language; others enable you to turn on a macro recorder that captures every move you make with the keyboard and mouse and records those actions in a macro transcript. Later, you can ask the computer to carry out the instructions in that macro. Suppose, for example, you use the same set of calculations every month when preparing a statistical analysis of environmental data. Without macros, you'd have to repeat the same sequence of keystrokes, mouse clicks, and commands each time you created the monthly report. But by creating a macro called, for instance, Monthstats, you can effectively say, "Do it again" by issuing the Monthstats command.
- *Formatting.* Most spreadsheets enable you to control typefaces, text styles, cell dimensions, and cell borders. They also enable you to include pictures and other graphic embellishments in documents.
- *Templates and wizards.* Even with functions and macros, the process of creating a complex worksheet from scratch can be intimidating. Many users take advantage of worksheet templates that contain labels and formulas but no data values. These reusable templates produce instant answers when you fill in the blanks. Some common templates are packaged with spreadsheet software; others are marketed separately. A similar feature, called a wizard, automates the process of creating complex worksheets that meet particular needs. Well-designed templates and wizards can save considerable time, effort, and anguish.
- *Validation.* To help users check complex worksheets for consistency of entries and formula logic, spreadsheet programs now include *validators*—the equivalent of spelling and grammar checkers for calculations. For example, suppose you enter six numbers into consecutive cells of a Microsoft Excel spreadsheet; then you create a formula that finds the sum of only the first five of these values. Excel produces a warning message suggesting that you may have left out a value from the sum.

Screen Test Creating a Worksheet with Microsoft Excel

GOAL *To create a computerized version of a worksheet showing projected expenses for one college student's fall term*

TOOLS *Microsoft Excel*

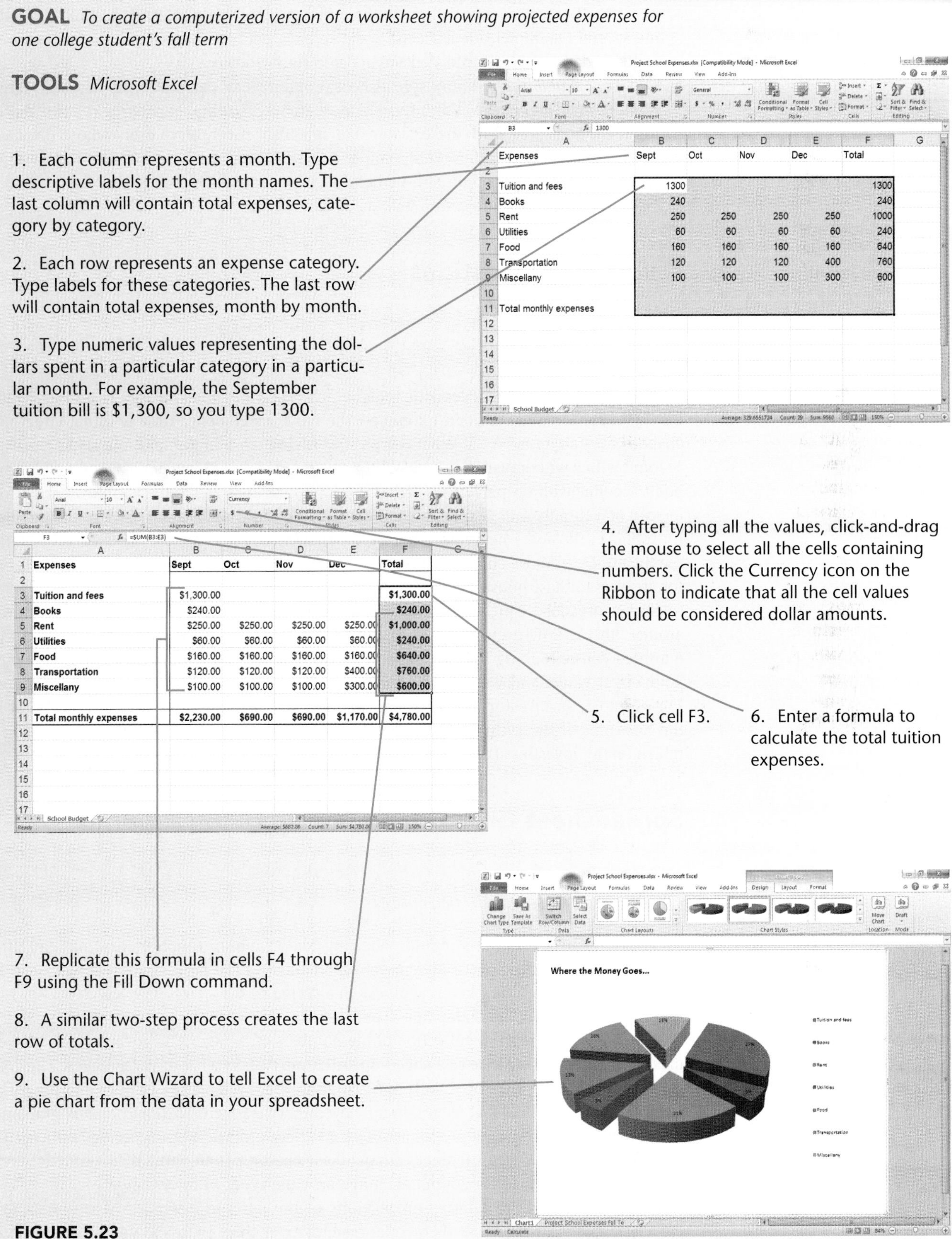

1. Each column represents a month. Type descriptive labels for the month names. The last column will contain total expenses, category by category.

2. Each row represents an expense category. Type labels for these categories. The last row will contain total expenses, month by month.

3. Type numeric values representing the dollars spent in a particular category in a particular month. For example, the September tuition bill is $1,300, so you type 1300.

4. After typing all the values, click-and-drag the mouse to select all the cells containing numbers. Click the Currency icon on the Ribbon to indicate that all the cell values should be considered dollar amounts.

5. Click cell F3.

6. Enter a formula to calculate the total tuition expenses.

7. Replicate this formula in cells F4 through F9 using the Fill Down command.

8. A similar two-step process creates the last row of totals.

9. Use the Chart Wizard to tell Excel to create a pie chart from the data in your spreadsheet.

FIGURE 5.23

- *Linking.* Sometimes a change in one worksheet produces changes in another. For example, a master sales summary worksheet for a business should reflect changes in each department's sales summary worksheet. Most spreadsheet programs can create **automatic links** among worksheets so when values change in one, all linked worksheets are updated automatically. Some programs can create three-dimensional worksheets by stacking and linking several two-dimensional sheets. Some spreadsheet programs can create links to Web pages so data can be downloaded and updated automatically.
- *Database capabilities.* Many spreadsheet programs can perform basic database functions: storage and retrieval of information, searching, sorting, generating reports, merging mail, and such. With these features, a spreadsheet can serve users whose database needs are modest. For those who require a full-featured database management system, spreadsheet software might still be helpful; many spreadsheet programs support automatic two-way communication with database software.

"What If?" Questions

> The purpose of computation is **not numbers but insight**.
>
> —*R. W. Hamming*

A spreadsheet program is a versatile tool, but it's especially valuable for answering **"what if?" questions**: "What if I don't complete the third assignment? How will that affect my chances for getting an A?" "What if I put my savings in a high-yield, tax-sheltered IRA account with a withdrawal penalty? Will I be better off than if I leave it in a low-yield passbook account with no penalty?" "What if I buy a car that gets only 15 miles per gallon instead of a slightly more expensive car that gets 40? How much more will I pay altogether for fuel over the next four years?" Because it enables you to change numbers and instantly see the effects of those changes, spreadsheet software streamlines the process of searching for answers to these questions.

Some spreadsheet programs include **equation solvers** that turn "what if?" questions around. Instead of forcing you to manipulate data values until formulas give you the numbers you're looking for, an equation solver enables you to define an equation, enter your target value, and watch while the computer determines the necessary data values. For example, an investor might use an equation solver to answer the question "What is the best mix of these three stocks for minimizing risk while producing a six percent return on my investment?"

Spreadsheet Graphics: From Digits to Drawings

> **Our work** ... is to present things that are **as they are**.
>
> —*Frederick II (1194–1250), King of Sicily*

Most spreadsheet programs include charting and graphing functionality that can turn worksheet numbers into charts and graphs automatically. The process of creating a chart is usually as simple as filling in a few blanks in a dialog box.

The growth in election campaign spending seems more real as a line shooting toward the top of a graph than as a collection of big numbers on a page. The government's budget makes more (or less?) sense as a sliced-up dollar pie than as a list of percentages. The correct chart can make a set of stale figures come to life, awakening our eyes and brains to trends and relationships that we might not have otherwise seen. The charting and graphing functionality in spreadsheet programs offers a variety of basic chart types and options for embellishing charts. The differences among these chart types are more than aesthetic; each chart type is well-suited for communicating particular types of information.

Pie charts show the relative proportions of the parts to a whole. **Line charts** are most often used to show trends or relationships over time or to show relative distribution of one variable through another. (The classic bell-shaped normal curve is a line chart.) **Bar charts** are similar to line charts, but they're more appropriate when data falls into a few categories. Bars can be stacked in a **stack chart** that shows how proportions of a whole change over time; the effect is similar to a series of pie charts. **Scatter charts** are used to discover, rather than display, a relationship between two variables. A well-designed chart can convey a wealth of information, just as a poorly designed chart can confuse or mislead.

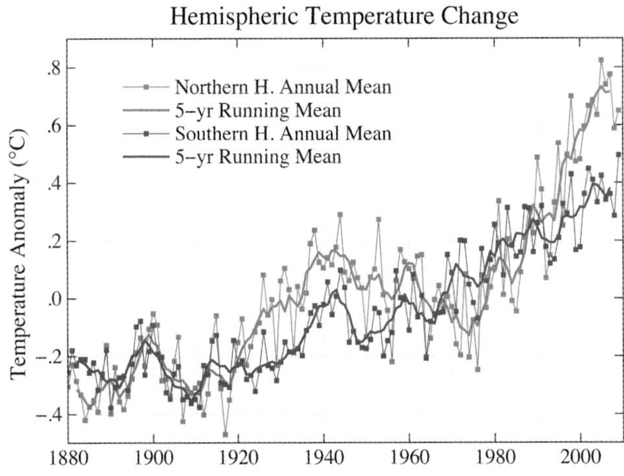

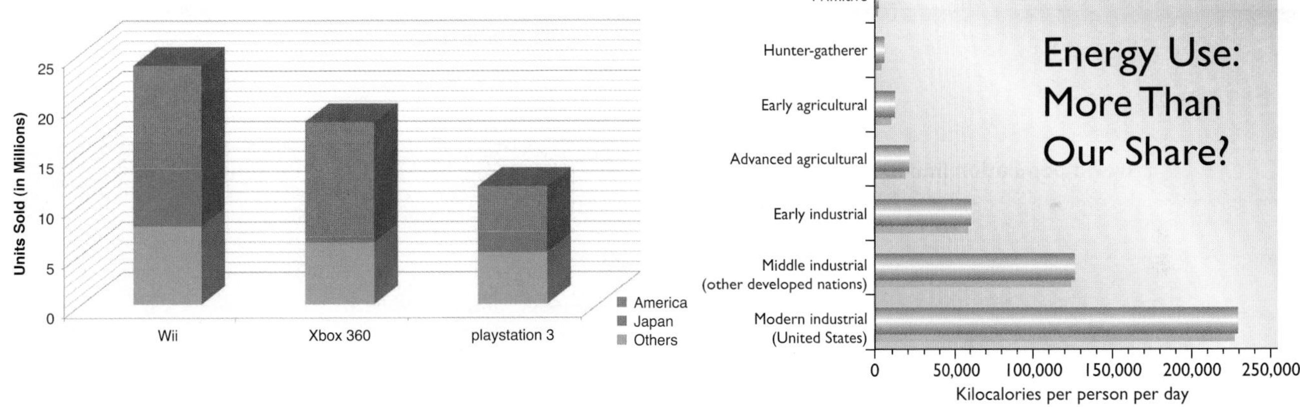

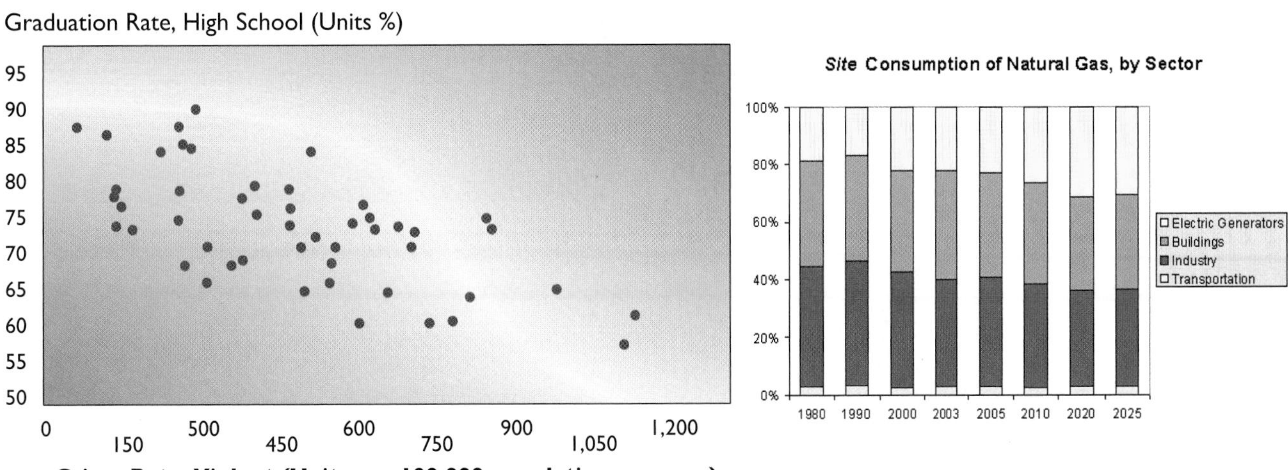

FIGURE 5.24 Line and bar charts show trends over time and/or distribution over categories. Scatter charts show relationships between variables.

Working Wisdom Avoiding Spreadsheet and Charting Errors

Spreadsheet errors are easy to make and easy to overlook. And even if the calculations are correct, a spreadsheet might create charts and graphs that are confusing or misleading. When creating a worksheet and/or a chart, you can minimize problems by following a few basic guidelines.

- ***Plan the worksheet before you start entering values and formulas.*** Think about your goals, and design the worksheet to meet those goals.
- ***Make your assumptions as accurate as possible.*** Answers produced by a worksheet are only as good as the assumptions built into the data values and formulas. A worksheet that compares the operating costs of a gas guzzler and a gas miser must make assumptions about future trips, repair costs, and, above all, gasoline prices. The accuracy of the worksheet is tied to all kinds of unknowns, including the future of Middle East politics. The more accurate the assumptions, the more accurate the predictions.
- ***Double-check every formula and value.*** Values and formulas are input for worksheets, and input determines output. Computer professionals often describe the dark side of this important relationship with the letters **GIGO—garbage in, garbage out**. One highly publicized spreadsheet transcription error for Fidelity Investments resulted in a $2.6 billion miscalculation because of a single missing minus sign! You may not be working with values this big, but it's still important to proofread your work carefully.
- ***Make formulas readable.*** If your software can attach names to cell ranges, use meaningful names in formulas. It's easier to create and debug formulas when you use readily understandable language, such as payrate*40+1.5*payrate*overtime, instead of a string of characters, like C2*40+1.5*C2*MAX(D2-40,0).
- ***Check your output against other systems.*** Use another program, a calculator, or pencil and paper to verify the accuracy of a sampling of your calculations.

A chart can clarify, confuse, mislead, or confound...

CLEAR

world population (millions)

The data values come first, and the trend is clear: Human population has grown exponentially since 1750.

CLUTTERED

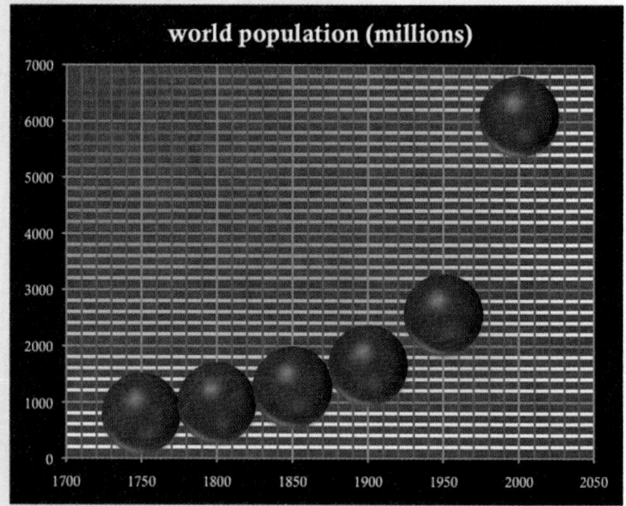

This chart confuses the viewer by applying glitz and gimmicks liberally.

FIGURE 5.25

- ***Build in cross-checks.*** Compare the sum of row totals with the sum of column totals. Does everything add up?
- ***Change the input data values and study the results.*** If small input adjustments produce massive output changes, or if major input adjustments result in few or no output changes, something may be wrong.
- ***Take advantage of preprogrammed functions, templates, and macros.*** Why reinvent the wheel when you can buy a professionally designed vehicle?
- ***Use a spreadsheet as a decision-making aid, not as a decision maker.*** Don't put too much faith in an answer just because it was produced by a computer. Stay alert and skeptical. Some errors aren't obvious, and others don't show up immediately.
- ***Take advantage of built-in error-checking tools.*** Spreadsheet programs have a variety of built-in tools to help you identify errors and track down faulty formulas.
- ***Choose the right chart for the job.*** Think about the message you're trying to convey. Line charts, bar charts, and scatter charts are not interchangeable. Pie charts are rarely appropriate.
- ***Put the data first in your charts.*** Avoid adding elements to your charts that obscure the data values. Too many grid lines make the data values hard to see. If your purpose is tabulating values, a table might be better than a chart.
- ***Avoid graphic distractions.*** The chart should encourage the reader to think about the meaning of the data values, not which program was used to create the chart or its interesting color scheme. Avoid filling in blank spaces with clip art or other design elements that have nothing to do with the data.
- ***Make it easy to compare data in your charts.*** If the chart illustrates a single trend, make sure the trend is clear. If the chart shows multiple trends, make sure the reader can distinguish among trends and compare them.
- ***Don't distort data.*** By hiding the baseline, you can deceive a reader into thinking that the actual change in a data value is larger or smaller than it really is. Your goal should be to reveal the truth, not hide it.
- ***Relate your chart to the rest of the document.*** If your chart is part of a written report, make sure that the information you provide in your chart is consistent with the descriptions and analyses in your report.
- ***Learn from the experts.*** Use high-quality charts in magazines, books, and newspapers as models.

MISLEADING

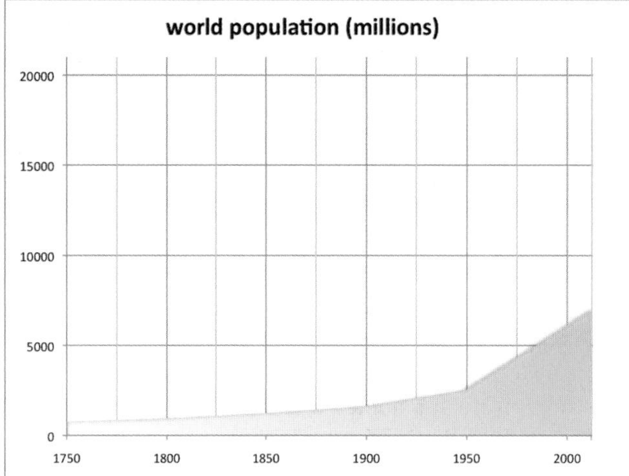

This chart shows one way data can be distorted to lead viewers to a different conclusion. The data is the same, but the horizontal axis has changed—and with it, the apparent rate of population growth.

CONFUSING

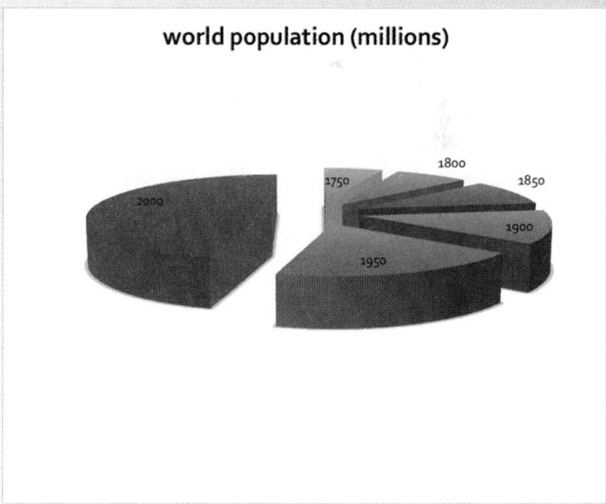

This pie chart displays the same data, but confuses rather than clarifies the trend. A pie chart is not an appropriate way to show a trend over time. The only use for a pie chart is to show how various parts add up to a whole. Even then, pie charts reveal little information for the amount of space they occupy.

Statistical Software: Beyond Spreadsheets

> Yet to calculate is **not in itself to analyze.**
>
> —*Edgar Allan Poe*

Spreadsheet software is versatile, but no program is perfect for every task. Other types of number-manipulation software are available for situations in which spreadsheets don't quite fit the job.

Money Managers

Spreadsheet software has its roots in the accountant's ledger sheets, but spreadsheets are seldom used for business accounting and bookkeeping. Accounting is a complex concoction of rules, formulas, laws, and traditions, and creating a worksheet to handle the details of the process is difficult and time consuming. Instead of relying on general-purpose spreadsheets for accounting, most businesses (and many households) use professionally designed **accounting and financial-management software**.

Whether practiced at home or at the office, accounting involves setting up accounts—monetary categories to represent various types of income, expenses, assets, and liabilities—and keeping track of the flow of money among those accounts. An accountant routinely records transactions—checks, cash payments, charges, and other activities—that move money from one account to another. Accounting software automatically adjusts the balance in every account after each transaction, whether the transaction is typed in to the program or downloaded from a financial institution's Web site. What's more, it records every transaction so you can retrace the history of each account step by step. This audit trail is a necessary part of business financial records, and it is one reason accountants use special-purpose accounting packages rather than spreadsheet programs.

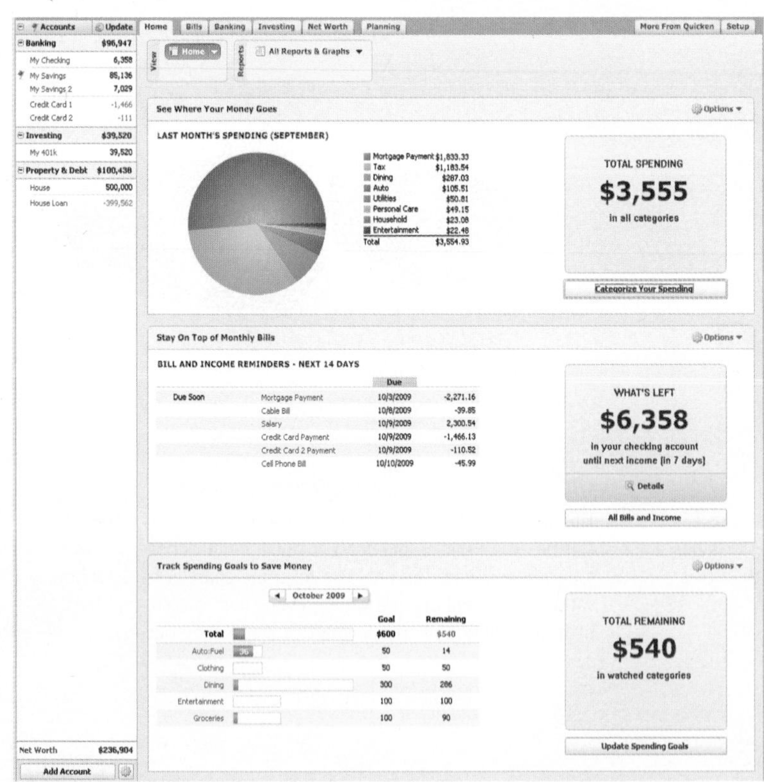

FIGURE 5.26 Quicken is one of the most popular programs for managing personal and small business finances.

In addition to keeping records, financial-management software can automate check writing, bill paying, budgeting, and other routine money matters. Periodic reports and charts can provide detailed answers to questions such as "Where does the money go?" and "How are we doing compared to last year?"

Financial management programs can use Internet links to recommend investments based on up-to-the-hour performance statistics, as well as track investment portfolios, comparison shop for insurance and mortgages, and link to specialized online calculators and advisors.

The most popular financial management software for homes and very small businesses is Intuit's Quicken, which comes in various versions for Windows, Mac OS, and the cloud (Quicken.com). Quickbooks, from the same company, includes many additional features for businesses, including payroll tracking and invoice generation. These programs, and similar programs from other companies, have all but eliminated paper ledgers—and the tedium of creating those ledgers—for millions of individuals, families, businesses, and nonprofit organizations.

Most accounting and financial-management programs don't calculate income taxes, but they can export records to programs that do. **Tax-preparation software** works like a prefabricated worksheet. As you enter numbers into the blanks in on-screen forms, the program automatically fills in other blanks. Every time you enter or change a number, the bottom line is recalculated automatically. When the forms are completed, they're ready to print, sign, and mail to the Internal Revenue Service. Many taxpayers now bypass paper forms altogether by submitting the completed forms electronically.

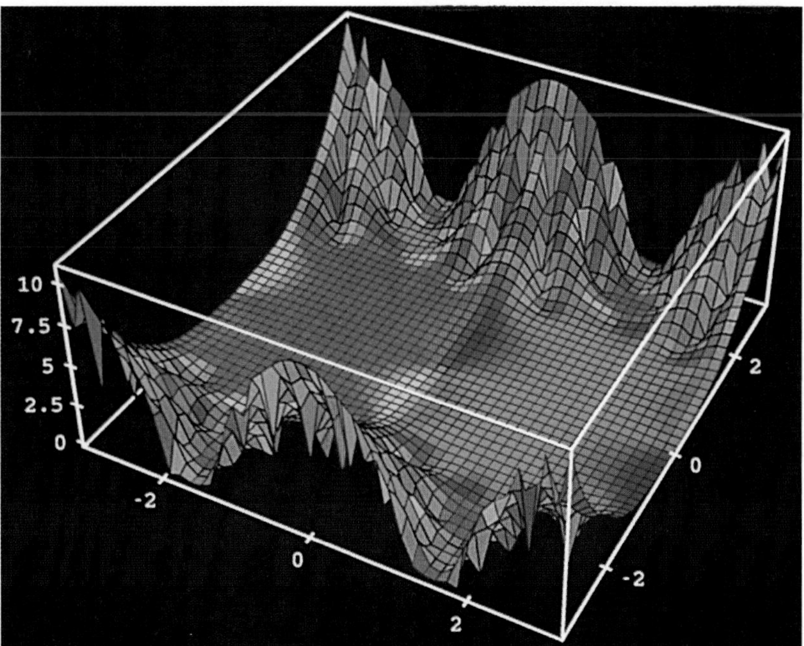

FIGURE 5.27 An abstract mathematical relationship is easier to understand when it is turned into a visible object with software, such as Mathematica.

Automatic Mathematics

Most of us seldom do math more complicated than filling out our tax forms. But higher mathematics is an essential part of the work of many scientists, researchers, engineers, architects, economists, financial analysts, teachers, and other professionals. Mathematics is a universal language for defining and understanding natural phenomena as well as a tool for creating all kinds of products and structures. Whether or not we work with it directly, our lives are constantly being shaped by mathematics.

Many professionals and students whose mathematical needs go beyond the capabilities of spreadsheets depend on symbolic **math-processing software** to grapple with complex equations and calculations. Math processors make it easier for mathematicians to create, manipulate, and solve equations in much the same way word processing software helps writers. Features vary from program to program, but a typical math processor can do polynomial factoring, symbolic and numeric calculus, real and complex trigonometry, matrix and linear algebra, and three-dimensional graphics.

A math processor generally includes an interactive, wizard-like question-and-answer mode, a programming language, and tools for creating interactive documents that combine text, numerical expressions, and graphics. Since math processors were introduced in the late 1980s, they've changed the way professionals use mathematics and the way students learn it. By handling the mechanics of mathematics, these programs enable people to concentrate on the content and implications of their work.

Statistics and Data Analysis

One branch of applied mathematics that has become more important in the computer age is **statistics**—the science of collecting and analyzing data. Modern computer technology provides us with mountains of data—census, political, consumer, economic, sports, weather, scientific, and more. We often refer to the data as statistics. ("The government released unemployment statistics today.") But the numbers by themselves tell only part of the story. The analysis of those numbers—the search for patterns and relationships among them—can provide meaning for the data. ("Analysts note that the rise in unemployment is confined to cities most heavily impacted by the freeze on government contracts.") Statisticians in government, business, and science depend on computers to make sense of raw data.

Do people who live near nuclear power plants run a higher cancer risk? Does the current weather pattern suggest the formation of a tropical storm? Are rural voters more likely to support small-town candidates? These questions can't be answered with absolute certainty; the element of chance is at the heart of statistical analysis. But **statistical-analysis software** can suggest answers to questions such as these by testing the strength of data relationships. Statistical software can also produce graphs showing how two or more variables might relate to each other. Statisticians can often uncover trends by browsing through

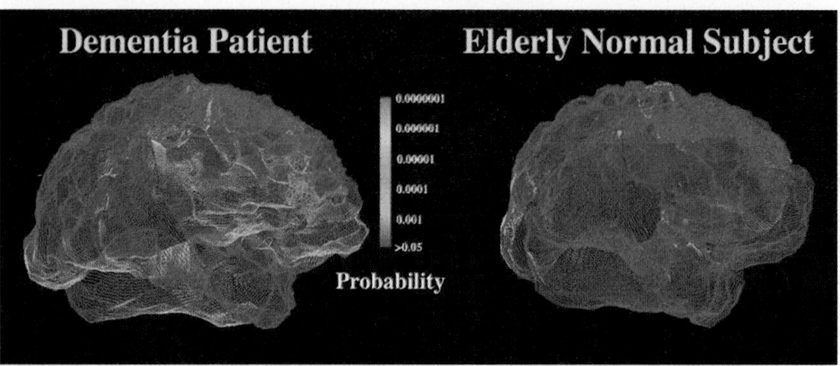

FIGURE 5.28 These two visualizations, created at the Laboratory of Neuro Imaging (LONI), map physical differences between a normal human brain and one with a form of dementia.

two- and three-dimensional graphs of data, looking for unusual patterns in the dots and lines that appear on the screen. This kind of visual exploration of data is an example of a type of application known as scientific visualization.

Scientific Visualization

> The wind blows over the lake and stirs the surface of the water. Thus, **visible effects of the invisible** are manifested.
>
> —*The I Ching*

Scientific-visualization software uses shape, location in space, color, brightness, and motion to help us understand relationships that are invisible to us. Like mathematical and statistical software, scientific-visualization software is no longer confined to mainframes and supercomputers; some of the most innovative programs have been developed for use on PCs, working alone or in conjunction with other computers.

Scientific visualization takes many forms, all of which involve the graphical representation of numerical data. The numbers can be the result of abstract equations, or they can be data gleaned from the real world. Either way, turning the numbers into pictures enables researchers and students to see the intangible and sometimes, as a result, to know what was previously unknowable. Here are two examples:

- Margaret Geller of Harvard University created a 3-D map of the cosmos from data on the locations of known galaxies. While using her computer to "fly through" this three-dimensional model, she saw something that no one had seen before: the mysterious clustering of galaxies along the edges of invisible bubbles.
- Dr. Mark Ellisman of the University of California, San Diego, School of Medicine used a 30-foot electron microscope to collect data from cells of the brain and enter it into a supercomputer, which rendered a 3-D representation of the brain cell. When Ellisman's team displayed the data on a graphic workstation, they saw several previously undiscovered aberrations in brains of patients who had Alzheimer's disease—aberrations that may turn out to be clues for discovering the cause and cure for this disease.

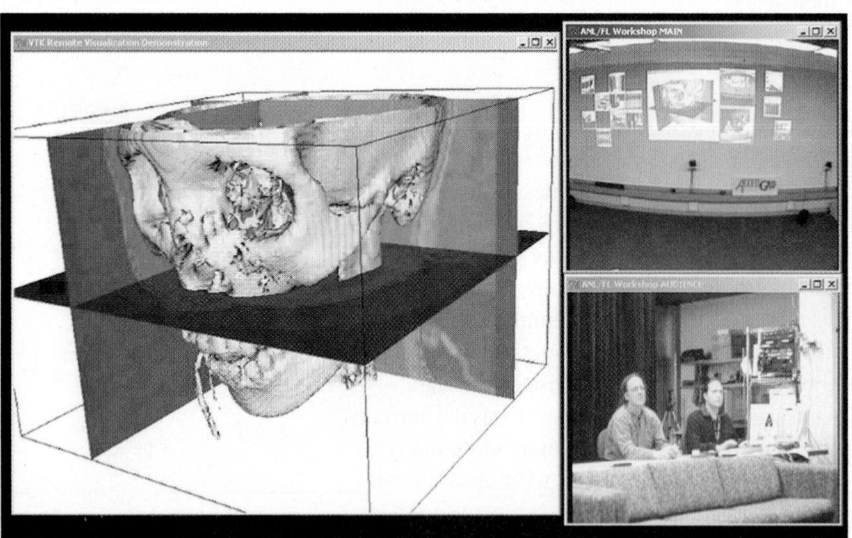

FIGURE 5.29 Using a tool called Access Grid, researchers (shown in the lower-right window) work with a shared visualization called the Visible Human (visible in the other two windows).

how it works Fractal Geometry and Simulation

Computers have long been used to analyze and visualize scientific data collected through experiments and observation. A computer can also serve as a virtual laboratory that simulates a physical process without real-world experiments. Of course, an inaccurate simulation can give incorrect results. The problems of creating an accurate simulation helped initiate the study of chaos and fractals. Chaos is now a vast field of study with applications in many disciplines.

The "Chaos Game" illustrates how computers can quickly complete repetitive tasks in experiments that would otherwise be impractical or impossible. You could perform the first few steps of such an experiment with pencil, paper, and ruler, like this:

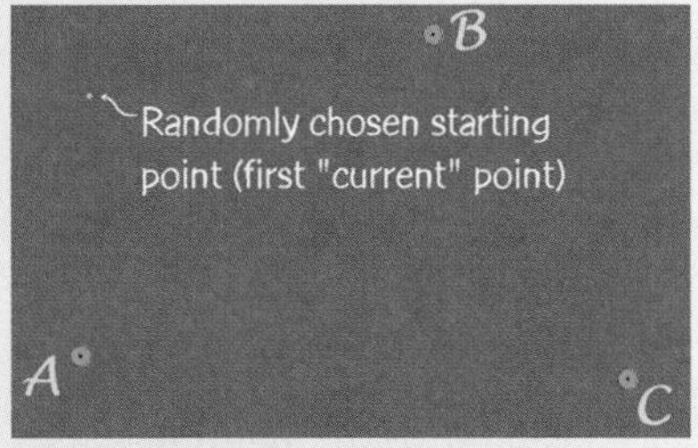

1. Draw three widely separated points on the paper to form a triangle; label the points A, B, and C. Draw a random starting point anywhere on the paper. This will be the first "current" point.

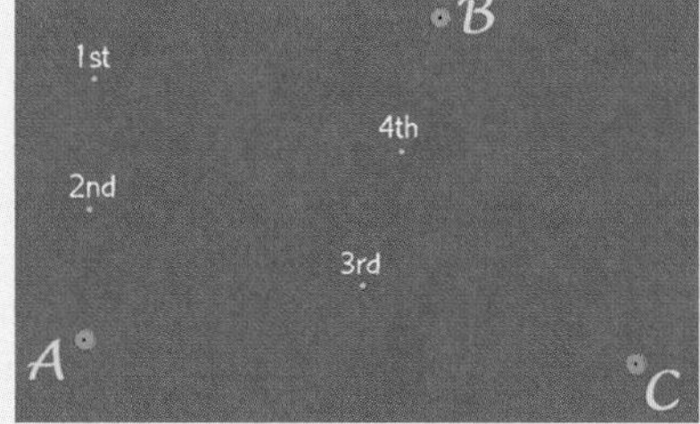

2. Repeat the following process four times: Randomly choose from among points A, B, and C, and draw a new point halfway (on an imaginary straight line) between the current point and the chosen point. The newly drawn point then becomes the new current point.

3. If you use a simple computer program to plot 100,000 repeats of step 2 (excluding the first few points from the drawing), you'll see a pattern emerge rather than a solid mass of dots. This pattern, called a Sierpinski gasket, is a fractal—an object in which pieces are miniatures of the whole figure. You will see a pattern like this.

FIGURE 5.30 Because some fractal formulas mimic the patterns of natural objects, such as coastlines and mountains, chaos has found applications in computer-generated scenery and special effects for movies and television shows.

The Mandelbrot set, discovered by the mathematician Benoit Mandelbrot (who coined the term *fractal*) while he was working at IBM's Thomas J. Watson Research Facility, is one of the most famous fractals to emerge from chaos theory.

In these examples and hundreds of others like them, visualization helps researchers see relationships that might have been obscure or even impossible to grasp without computer-aided visualization tools.

Calculated Risks: Computer Modeling and Simulation

> We are reaching the stage where problems that we must solve are going to become insolvable without computers. **I do not fear computers; I fear the lack of them.**
>
> *—Isaac Asimov, scientist and science fiction writer*

Whether part of a simple worksheet or a complex set of equations, numbers often symbolize real-world phenomena. Computer **modeling**—the use of computers to create abstract models of objects, organisms, organizations, and processes—can be done with spreadsheets, mathematical applications, or standard programming languages. A business executive who creates a worksheet to project quarterly profits and losses is trying to model the economic world that affects the company. An engineer who uses a math processor to test the stress capacity of a bridge is modeling the bridge mathematically. Even a statistician who starts by examining data collected in the real world creates statistical models to describe the data.

Computer models aren't always serious; most computer games are models. Chessboards, pinball games, battlefields, sports arenas, ant colonies, cities, medieval dungeons, rock concerts, interplanetary cultures, and mythological societies have all been modeled in computer games. Students use computer models to travel to distant lands, explore the subatomic world, invest in the stock market, and dissect digital frogs.

Whether it's created for work, education, or play, a computer model is an *abstraction*—a set of concepts and ideas designed to mimic some kind of system. But a computer model

FIGURE 5.31 These two popular strategic life-simulation games put sophisticated simulation technology in the hands of gamers. The Sims and its sequels simulate the daily activities of virtual people, called Sims. Civilization 5 is drawn on a much bigger canvas—it simulates the evolution of an entire civilization.

isn't static; you can put it to work in a computer simulation to see how the model operates under certain conditions. A well-designed model should behave like the system it imitates.

Suppose, for example, an engineer constructs a computer model of a new type of airplane to test how the plane will respond to human commands. In a typical flight simulation, the "pilot" controls the plane's thrust and elevator angle by feeding input data to the model plane. The model responds by adjusting air speed and angle of ascent or descent, just as a real plane would. The pilot responds to the new state of the aircraft by adjusting one or more of the controls, which causes the system to respond by revising the aircraft's state again. This **feedback loop**, where plane and pilot react to data from each other, continues throughout the simulation.

FIGURE 5.32 Flight simulators for home computers and video game consoles (top photo) are based on the same simulation technology that's used in professional flight trainers (bottom photo).

A flight simulator might have a graphical user interface that makes the computer screen look and act like the instrument panel of a real plane so human pilots can run it intuitively. Or it might display nothing more than numbers representing input and output values, and the input values might be generated by a simulated pilot—another computer model! Either way, it can deliver a wealth of information about the behavior of the plane, provided the model is accurate.

Computer Simulations: The Rewards

Computer simulations are widely used for research in the physical, biological, and social sciences and in engineering. Schools, businesses, and the military also use simulations for training. There are many reasons:

- *Safety.* Although it's safer to learn piloting skills while sitting in front of a computer rather than actually flying in the air, it's still possible to learn to fly without a computer simulation. Some activities, however, are so dangerous that they aren't ethically possible without computer simulations. How, for example, can scientists study the effects of a nuclear power plant meltdown on the surrounding environment? Unless a meltdown occurs, there's only one practical answer: computer simulation.
- *Economy.* It's far less expensive for an automobile manufacturer to produce a digital model of a nonexistent car than to build a prototype out of steel. The company can test the computer model for strength, handling, and efficiency in a series of simulations before it builds and tests a physical prototype. The cost of the computer model is small when compared with the expense of producing a possibly defective car.
- *Projection.* Without computers, it could take decades for biologists to determine whether the introduction of a nonnative plant on an island threatens other species, and by the time they discover the answer, it would be too late to do anything about it. A computer model of the island's ecosystem could speed up natural biological processes so scientists could measure their effects over several generations in a matter of minutes. A computer simulation can, in effect, serve as a time machine for exploring one or more possible futures.
- *Visualization.* Computer models make visualization possible, and visualization enables researchers and students to see and understand relationships that might otherwise go unnoticed. Computer models can speed time up or slow it down; they can make subatomic particles big and the universe small.
- *Replication.* In the real world, it can be difficult or impossible to repeat a research project with slightly different conditions. But this kind of repetition is an important part of serious research. An engineer needs to fine-tune dimensions and angles to achieve peak performance. A scientist studies the results of one experiment and develops a new hypothesis that calls for further testing. An executive needs to test a business plan under a variety of economic scenarios. If the research is conducted on a computer model, replication is just a matter of changing input values and running a new simulation.

Computer Simulations: The Risks

The downside of computer simulation can be summed up in three words: Simulation isn't reality. The real world is a subtle and complex place, and capturing even a fraction of that subtlety and complexity in a computer simulation is a tremendous challenge.

GIGO Revisited

The accuracy of a simulation depends on how closely its mathematical model corresponds to the system being simulated. Mathematical models are built on assumptions, many of which are difficult or impossible to verify. Some models suffer from faulty assumptions; others contain hidden assumptions that may not even be obvious to their creators; still others go astray simply because of clerical or human errors.

The daily weather report is the result of a complex computer model. Our atmosphere is far too complex to capture exactly in a computer model; that's why the weather forecast is sometimes wrong. Occasionally simulation errors produce disastrous results. Faulty computer models have been responsible for the deadly flooding of the Colorado River, the collapse of the roof of a Salt Lake City shopping mall, and the crash of a test plane on its first flight. These kinds of disasters are rare. It's much more common for computer models to help avert tragedies by pointing out design flaws. In fact, sometimes things go wrong because people *ignore* the results of accurate simulations. Still, *garbage in, garbage out* is a basic rule of simulation.

Making Reality Fit the Machine

Simulations are computation intensive. Some simulations are so complex that researchers need to simplify models and streamline calculations to get them to run on the best hardware available. Even when there's plenty of computing power available, researchers face a constant temptation to reshape reality for the convenience of the simulation. In one classic example, a U.S. Forest Service computer model reduced complex old-growth forests to "accumulated capital." Aesthetics, ecological diversity, and other hard-to-quantify factors didn't exist in this model.

Sometimes this simplification of reality is deliberate; more often it's unconscious. Either way, information can be lost, and the loss may compromise the integrity of the simulation and call the results into question.

The Illusion of Infallibility

Risks can be magnified because people take computers seriously. People tend to emphasize computer-generated reports, often at the expense of other sources of knowledge. Executives use worksheets to make decisions involving thousands of jobs and millions of dollars. Politicians decide the fate of military weapons and endangered species based on summaries of computer simulations. Doctors use computer models to make life-and-death decisions involving new drugs and treatments. All of these people, in some sense, are placing their trust in computer simulations. Many of them trust the data precisely because a computer produced it.

A computer simulation, whether generated by a PC spreadsheet or churned out by a supercomputer, can be an invaluable decision-making aid. The risk is that the people who make decisions with computers will turn over too much of their decision-making power to the computers.

Screen Test Productivity on a Student Budget

A computer is worthless without software, and the right software can make that same computer priceless. But productivity software isn't without a price; it can easily cost more than the hardware that runs it. Fortunately, there are many low-cost or free alternatives for students and others on tight budgets. Some are Web applications that require an Internet connection to work; others can be installed on Windows, Mac, or Linux computers so they'll work on or off the grid.

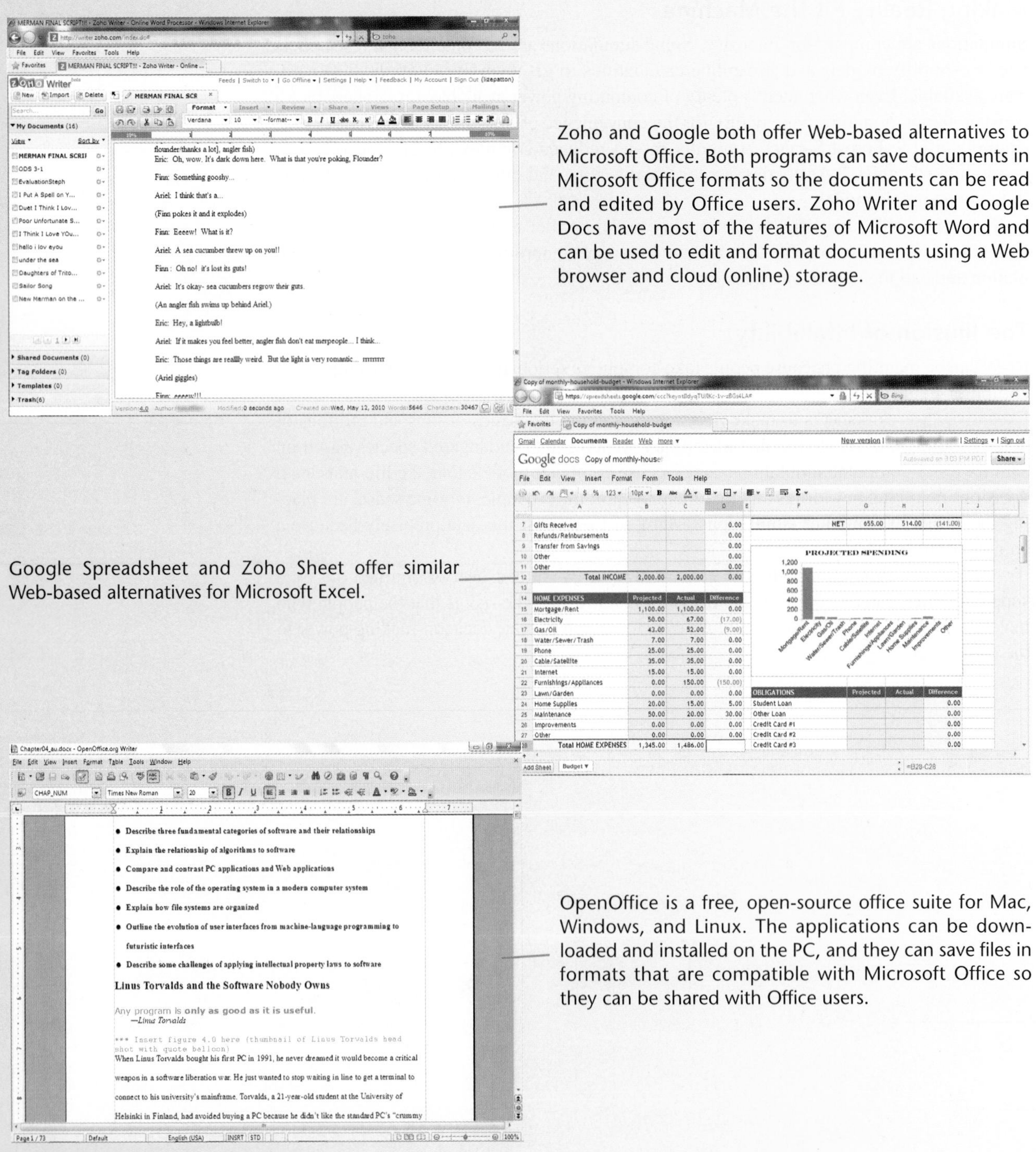

Zoho and Google both offer Web-based alternatives to Microsoft Office. Both programs can save documents in Microsoft Office formats so the documents can be read and edited by Office users. Zoho Writer and Google Docs have most of the features of Microsoft Word and can be used to edit and format documents using a Web browser and cloud (online) storage.

Google Spreadsheet and Zoho Sheet offer similar Web-based alternatives for Microsoft Excel.

OpenOffice is a free, open-source office suite for Mac, Windows, and Linux. The applications can be downloaded and installed on the PC, and they can save files in formats that are compatible with Microsoft Office so they can be shared with Office users.

FIGURE 5.33

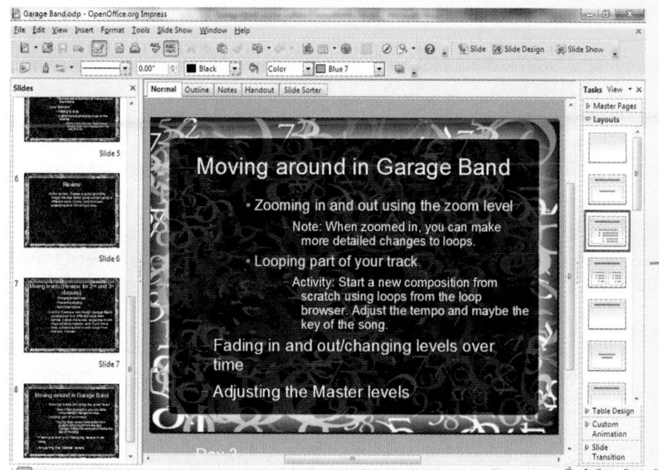

Zoho Show and OpenOffice Impress are excellent free alternatives to PowerPoint for slideshow presentations.

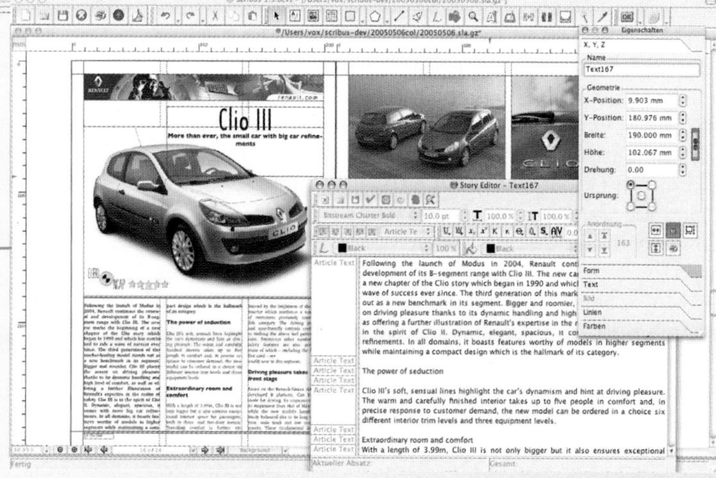

Scribus is a free open-source desktop publishing application that offers many professional page layout features.

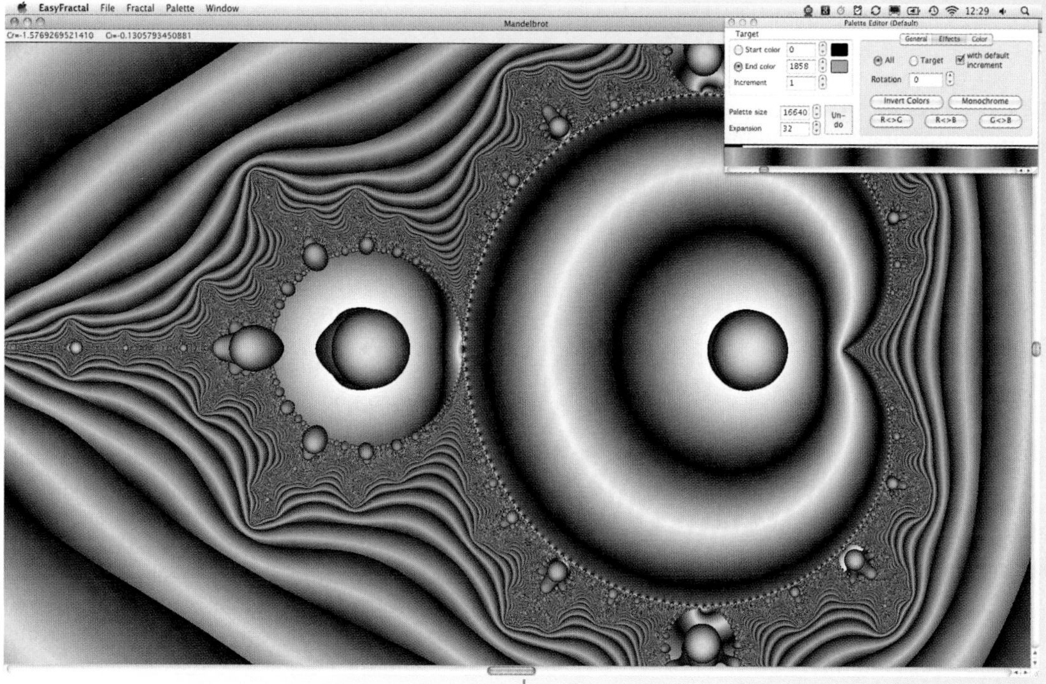

Fractal eXtreme for Windows and EasyFractal for Mac are inexpensive shareware visualization programs for exploring fractals.

Inventing the Future ▸ Multisensory Interfaces

Early human/computer communication involved two of our senses: touch and sight. People flipped switches, pressed buttons, and typed on keyboards to get information into computers; the machines responded by turning on lights, displaying characters on screens, and printing text on paper. Today's multimedia machines communicate with us through multiple senses, and the possibilities expand as research progresses.

Touch. After a half-century of computing, we still depend on keyboards for delivering data to our computers. We use a variety of other touchy-feely devices, including mice, trackpads, and touch screens. Multitouch devices, from smart phones to wall-sized displays, are becoming more sophisticated all the time. The current limitations of multi-touch technology—for example, the number of touches that can be recognized at a time—will recede as the technology develops. It's not hard to imagine a multiplayer game in which several players simultaneously move their hands around on a "live" table to control the action. And haptic feedback—when the device responds to touch by moving or vibrating—can make for an even more compelling experience. Touch input won't be limited to screens and pads. Devices with pico-projectors, infrared sensors, and acoustic sensors should make it possible to turn just about any surface, including your skin, into a multitouch device.

Sight. It's rare to find a computer today that doesn't use graphical elements to organize information on a screen. Recent research is making it possible for 3-D to migrate from the big screen to the PC, the game machine, and the smart phone. A variety of 3-D technologies are working their way into our digital devices—3-D screens with or without glasses, 3-D glasses that don't require screens, wraparound displays, holograms, and more.

FIGURE 5.34 The g-speak "spatial operating environment" responds to gestures rather than keystrokes and mouse movements.

But visual communication can go both directions. While we're looking at our computers, they can look back at us. Microsoft's Kinect is a popular gaming device that accepts input from multiple players without game controllers. The system uses a visual sensor to detect body movements and gestures. G-speak is a gesture-controlled UI system that lets users shuffle through information by waving their hands. For people with amyotrophic lateral sclerosis (ALS) and others who can't use their hands, eye-tracking technology turns eye movements into computer input.

Sound. We've discussed the importance of speech and language in future user interfaces. But audio is more than spoken words. State-of-the-art sound, including surround (3-D) sound, can have a profound impact on computer user experiences. Future computers will most likely include technology that is being developed by and for professional sound designers, musicians, and engineers today.

Smell and taste. For the most part, these two related senses haven't been used for either input or output in today's digital technology. Some environmental hazard detectors use a primitive sense of "smell" for input, but those devices are typically limited to recognizing a few chemical traces in the air. Aromatic computer *output* is another matter. Smells can instantly evoke deep memories and subconscious feelings. There are many possible applications for an aromatic output device: A Web site that includes scenes and aromas from restaurants along with reviews; an exploration game that evokes jungle or desert smells; a surf-scented music video. But smells are hard to model mathematically, so they aren't as easy to simulate as sights and sounds. Primitive smell devices may show up in our technological devices within a few years, but a fully functional chemical "printer" for smells—or, for that matter, tastes—won't happen anytime soon.

Brain waves. With the right sensors, a computer can even read human brain waves. Wearing a cap covered with electrodes, a person can play a video game, choose letters from an on-screen keyboard, or manipulate a robot. The technology is still primitive, but it's likely that this kind of brain-to-machine communication will eventually find all kinds of practical applications, from helping disabled people take care of their daily business to waking drivers when they start to nod off.

Each of these technologies has a potential place in our digital world. For example, Kinect's hand-waving technology is great for gaming, but inappropriate on a crowded airplane. Three-dimensional graphics are terrific for immersive simulations, but possibly too distracting for car computers. As these multisensory technologies evolve, they put more "reality" into virtual reality and augmented reality environments. We'll focus on VR and AR in next chapter's "Inventing the Future."

Crosscurrents

The New Literacy

by Clive Thompson

You've probably heard it many times: the younger generation is spending too much time playing online games or exploring social networks and not enough time reading and writing. But recent research suggests that this widely stated truth may not be true after all. Clive Thompson's Wired *columns provide monthly insights into the ways our lives are changing as a result of digital technology. In this column, first posted August 24, 2009, Thomson argues that all of that time online may, in fact, be responsible for the most literate generation ever.*

As the school year begins, be ready to hear pundits fretting once again about how kids today can't write—and technology is to blame. Facebook encourages narcissistic blabbering, video and PowerPoint have replaced carefully crafted essays, and texting has dehydrated language into "bleak, bald, sad shorthand" (as University College of London English professor John Sutherland has moaned). An age of illiteracy is at hand, right?

Andrea Lunsford isn't so sure. Lunsford is a professor of writing and rhetoric at Stanford University, where she has organized a mammoth project called the Stanford Study of Writing to scrutinize college students' prose. From 2001 to 2006, she collected 14,672 student writing samples—everything from in-class assignments, formal essays, and journal entries to emails, blog posts, and chat sessions. Her conclusions are stirring.

"I think we're in the midst of a literacy revolution the likes of which we haven't seen since Greek civilization," she says. For Lunsford, technology isn't killing our ability to write. It's reviving it—and pushing our literacy in bold new directions.

The first thing she found is that young people today write far more than any generation before them. That's because so much socializing takes place online, and it almost always involves text. Of all the writing that the Stanford students did, a stunning 38 percent of it took place out of the classroom—life writing, as Lunsford calls it. Those Twitter updates and lists of 25 things about yourself add up.

It's almost hard to remember how big a paradigm shift this is. Before the Internet came along, most Americans never wrote anything, ever, that wasn't a school assignment. Unless they got a job that required producing text (like in law, advertising, or media), they'd leave school and virtualy never construct a paragraph again.

But is this explosion of prose good, on a technical level? Yes. Lunsford's team found that the students were remarkably adept at what rhetoricians call *kairos*—assessing their audience and adapting their tone and technique to best get their point across. The modern world of online writing, particularly in chat and on discussion threads, is conversational and public, which makes it closer to the Greek tradition of argument than the asynchronous letter and essay writing of 50 years ago.

The fact that students today almost always write for an audience (something virtually no one in my generation did) gives them a different sense of what constitutes good writing. In interviews, they defined good prose as something that had an effect on the world. For them, writing is about persuading and organizing and debating, even if it's over something as quotidian as what movie to go see. The Stanford students were almost always less enthusiastic about their in-class writing because it had no audience but the professor: It didn't serve any purpose other than to get them a grade. As for those texting short-forms and smileys defiling *serious* academic writing? Another myth. When Lunsford examined the work of first-year students, she didn't find a single example of texting speak in an academic paper.

Of course, good teaching is always going to be crucial, as is the mastering of formal academic prose. But it's also becoming clear that online media are pushing literacy into cool directions. The brevity of texting and status updating teaches young people to deploy haiku-like concision. At the same time, the proliferation of new forms of online pop-cultural exegesis—from sprawling TV-show recaps to 15,000-word videogame walkthroughs—has given them a chance to write enormously long and complex pieces of prose, often while working collaboratively with others.

We think of writing as either good or bad. What today's young people know is that knowing who you're writing for and why you're writing might be the most crucial factor of all.

Discussion Questions

1. Do you think you write more than your parents did at your age? If so, do you think your writing is better as a result? Explain your answer.
2. Do you think the results of Andrea Lunsford's research would have been different if she had studied people who didn't go to college instead of Stanford students? Why or why not?

Summary

Even though the computer was originally designed to work with numbers, it quickly became an important tool for processing text as well. Word processing software enables the writer to use commands to edit and format text on the screen before printing a finished document. Word processing software can be used to control the typefaces, spacing, justification, margins, columns, headers, footers, footnotes, hyphenation, and graphics in a document. Outlining tools turn the familiar outline into a powerful, dynamic organizational tool. Spelling checkers and grammar and style checkers partially automate the proofreading process, although they leave the more difficult parts of the job to literate humans. Thesauruses, dictionaries, and other computer-based references, both online and off, simplify basic writing research.

As word processing programs becomes more powerful, they take on many of the features previously found only in desktop publishing software. Still, many publishers use word processing and graphics programs to create source documents for page-layout programs. Desktop publishing enables publishers and would-be publishers to produce professional-quality text-and-graphics documents at a reasonable cost.

The Web makes it possible for potential publishers to reach mass audiences without the problems associated with printing and distributing paper documents. Electronic books, magazines, and newspapers, whether viewed on e-readers, smart phones, tablets, or PCs, will continue to grow in importance. Typing may no longer be a necessary part of the writing process as handwriting and speech recognition technologies improve, and word processing software that incorporates other artificial intelligence technologies may coach and teach future writers.

Spreadsheet programs, first developed to simulate and automate the accountant's ledger, can be used for tracking financial transactions, calculating grades, forecasting economic conditions, recording scientific data, and just about any other task that involves repetitive numeric calculations. Spreadsheet documents, called worksheets, are grids with individual cells containing alphabetic labels, numbers, and formulas. Changes in numeric values can cause the spreadsheet to update any related formulas automatically. The responsiveness and flexibility of spreadsheet software make it particularly well suited for providing answers to "what if" questions. Most spreadsheet programs include charting commands to turn worksheet numbers into a variety of graphs and charts. The software can do most of the work of creating a professional-looking chart, but it's up to the user to ensure that the chart clearly illustrates, rather than distorts, the trends in the data.

Number crunching often goes beyond spreadsheets. Specialized accounting and tax preparation software packages perform specific home and business financial functions without the aid of spreadsheets. Symbolic mathematics processors can handle a variety of higher mathematics functions involving numbers, symbols, equations, and graphics. Statistical-analysis software is used for data collection and analysis. Scientific visualization can be done with math processors, statistical packages, graphics programs, or specialized programs designed for visualization.

Modeling and simulation are at the heart of most applications involving numbers. When people create computer models, they use numbers to represent real-world objects and phenomena. Simulations built on these models can provide insights that might be difficult or impossible to obtain otherwise, provided that the models reflect reality accurately. If used wisely, computer simulation can be a powerful tool for helping people understand their world and make better decisions.

Key Terms

Companion Website Projects

1. The *Digital Planet's* Web site, **www.pearsonhighered.com/beekman**, contains self-test exercises related to this chapter. Follow the instructions for taking a quiz. After you've completed your quiz, you can email the results to your instructor.
2. The Web site also contains open-ended discussion questions called Internet Exercises. Discuss one or more of the Internet Exercises questions at the section for this chapter.

True or False

1. OpenType fonts are identical to TrueType fonts, but are open source.
2. WYSIWYG stands for "what you simulate is what yields garbage."
3. Text editing and text formatting are two different terms for the same process.
4. Almost all e-book readers use the same LCD technology that's used in laptop computers.
5. Desktop publishing refers to the use of a computer to publish Web pages.
6. Charting software, such as the chart tools built into spreadsheet software, generally contains safeguards that prevent the misrepresentation of information.
7. The most difficult part of using accounting and financial-management software is the tedious, but necessary, process of typing in a transaction for each check or credit card transaction.
8. Statistical-analysis software can suggest answers to scientific questions by testing the strength of data relationships.
9. Electronic publishing is replacing some forms of print publishing, but paper documents aren't likely to go away anytime soon.
10. People tend to be more skeptical of computer-generated reports than they are of other types of reports.

Multiple Choice

1. Video display editing (a forerunner to word processing) and on-screen outlining were introduced by
   a. Douglas Engelbart before PCs became popular.
   b. Bill Gates shortly after the first PCs went on the market.
   c. Steve Jobs when he introduced the Apple 1.
   d. IBM when they introduced the DisplayWriter.
   e. the U.S. government during World War II.
2. If you change the definition of the style called BodyText that you've assigned to body paragraphs, but not headings, in a document,
   a. every paragraph that's assigned to that style automatically changes to reflect the changes.
   b. the change only applies to new paragraphs assigned to that style.
   c. every paragraph in the document, regardless of assigned style, changes in appearance.
   d. the contents of each BodyText paragraph changes, but the formatting remains unchanged.
   e. It's not possible to change the definition of a style once the style has been applied.
3. To which of the following does justification generally apply?
   a. Individual characters
   b. Words
   c. Paragraphs
   d. Fonts
   e. All of the above

4. Left justification is particularly useful when formatting
   a. a column of numbers representing your daily expenses.
   b. the paragraphs of an informal document.
   c. text in font sizes larger than 72 point.
   d. the title of a document.
   e. All of the above

5. When is centered justification generally the best choice?
   a. For paragraphs of text in a narrow column
   b. For a column of numbers with a total at the bottom
   c. For the body text of a two-column document
   d. For the title of a document
   e. For any of the above

6. A serif font is generally better than a sans serif font when formatting
   a. titles and subtitles.
   b. the body of a long document (pages of text).
   c. figure captions.
   d. numbers in a spreadsheet.
   e. All of the above

7. A document created with a desktop publishing system can be
   a. printed on a color printer.
   b. converted into a PDF document for electronic distribution.
   c. displayed on the Web.
   d. printed on a phototypesetting machine at a service bureau.
   e. All of the above

8. Which of the following is a fundamentally important feature of spreadsheets?
   a. They can easily convert bar charts and pie charts into numerical data.
   b. They never change the values of cells unless explicitly instructed to by the user.
   c. They're designed to accept input in PDF format.
   d. Formulas automatically recalculate results when any of their inputs change.
   e. All of the above

9. To represent full-color images accurately, what must desktop publishing systems use?
   a. Inkjet printers
   b. Service bureaus
   c. Color-matching technology
   d. Spot color
   e. E-paper displays

10. If you change the value of numbers in a spreadsheet,
    a. nothing else changes unless the spreadsheet is linked to other spreadsheets.
    b. the spreadsheet macros will check for data-entry errors.
    c. the labels at the column heads should automatically change to reflect the new values.
    d. cells containing formulas may change to reflect the new numeric values.
    e. the WYSIWYG checker will apply a template to your changes.

11. Which type of chart is most appropriate for showing the changes in the average annual temperature of a mountain lake over a 100-year period?
    a. Circle chart
    b. Line chart
    c. Scatter chart
    d. Pie chart
    e. Bullet chart

12. Which of these types of software is used for creating models?
    a. Spreadsheet software
    b. Accounting software
    c. Math-processing software
    d. All of the above
    e. None of the above

13. Scientific-visualization software
    a. requires visual input devices to work properly.
    b. is the scientific equivalent of desktop publishing software.
    c. creates pictures from numbers.
    d. requires supercomputer power to run.
    e. doesn't exist yet, but it will be a reality before the end of the decade.

14. Simulation software offers many advantages, including all of these *except*:
    a. It can save money.
    b. It can be much safer than real-world experience.
    c. It is generally more accurate than standard experimental research.
    d. It can save time.
    e. It makes experimental replication easier.

15. A wizard inside a PC application is a primitive example of
    a. an intelligent agent.
    b. a spreadsheet program.
    c. a scientific simulation.
    d. a computer virus.
    e. a fractal.

Review Questions

1. Provide a working definition for each of the key terms listed in the "Key Terms" section.
2. How is working with outline view in a word processor different than working with the WYSIWYG page layout view?
3. Describe three different ways a spelling checker might give incorrect feedback.
4. How is word processing different from desktop publishing?
5. Describe several different types of "paperless" publishing, and discuss their impact on traditional print media.
6. How many different ways can a paragraph or line of text be justified? When might each be appropriate?
7. What kinds of basic reference tools are included in popular word processing programs?
8. An automated speech-recognition dictation system might have trouble telling the difference between a "common denominator" and a "comedy nominator." People who use these programs heavily tend to have fewer of these types of errors over time. Why?
9. In what ways are word processing and spreadsheet programs similar?
10. What are some advantages of using a spreadsheet over using a calculator to maintain a record of sports scores or workout summaries? Are there any disadvantages?
11. If you enter "=A1*B1" in cell C1 of a worksheet, the formula is replaced by the number 125 when you press the Enter key. What happened?
12. List several advantages and disadvantages of using computer simulations for decision making.
13. Explain the difference between a numeric value and a formula in a worksheet.
14. Describe or draw examples of several different types of charts, and explain how they're typically used—and misused.
15. Describe several software tools used for numeric applications too complex to be handled by spreadsheets. Give an example of an application of each.

Discussion Questions

1. Like Gutenberg's development of the movable-type printing press more than 500 years ago, the development of desktop publishing puts powerful communication tools in the hands of more people. What impact will desktop-publishing technology have on the free press and the free exchange of ideas guaranteed in the United States Constitution? What impact will the same technology have on free expression in other countries? Answer the same questions about publishing on the Web.
2. What do you think of the arguments that word processing reduces the quality of writing because it makes it easy to write in a hurried and careless manner and it puts the emphasis on the way a document looks rather than on what it says?
3. The statement "Computers don't make mistakes, people do" is often used to support the reliability of computer output. Is the statement true? Is it relevant?
4. Spreadsheets are sometimes credited with legitimizing the personal computer as a business tool. Why do you think they had such an impact?
5. Word processing and spreadsheet software were invented before the Internet explosion; both these types of applications were conceived as tools for producing paper documents. Do you think that the Web will eventually make these software categories irrelevant? Explain your answer.
6. Computer models and simulations have been blamed for some of the most serious financial disasters of the last decade. What do you think?

Projects

1. Analyze the stylistic elements of one or more magazines of your choice. Create a table that documents the fonts and styles of titles, subtitles, figure captions, text boxes, article bodies, and color palettes. How are these elements varied within each magazine? If these magazines have companion Web sites, repeat the process for each Web site. Then note what design elements are common between each magazine and its companion Web site.
2. Use a word processing or desktop publishing system to produce a newsletter, brochure, or flyer in support of an organization or cause that is important to you. Base your design on good design principles as they're applied in other publications.
3. Use a spreadsheet to track your grades in each of your classes. If appropriate, apply weightings from the course syllabus to your individual scores, calculating a point total based on those weightings. Create line charts to track your grades and pie charts to show how each class's grades are made from multiple pieces (for example: 40 percent from tests, 30 percent from class assignments, 20 percent from projects, 10 percent from quizzes).
4. Use a spreadsheet or a financial-management program to develop a personal budget. Try to keep track of your income and expenses for the next month or two, and record the transactions with your program. At the end of that time, evaluate the accuracy of your budget.
5. Scan print and Web publications for poorly designed or misleading charts and graphs. Find a graphic that distorts the data values by hiding the baseline. Find a graphic containing superfluous elements that distract from the data values. Find a graphic that makes it difficult to compare data values (for example, a pie chart used inappropriately).
6. Use a spreadsheet to search for answers to a "What if" question that's important to you. Possible questions: If I lease a car instead of buying it, am I better off? If I borrow money for school, how much does it cost me in the long run?

Sources and Resources

Books

Bootstrapping: Douglas Engelbart, Coevolution, and the Origins of Personal Computing, by Thierry Bardini (Stanford University Press). This long-overdue book shines a spotlight on the visionary, revolutionary work of Douglas Engelbart at SRI.

Office 2010: The Missing Manual, by Nancy Conner and Matthew MacDonald (Pogue Press). There are hundreds of books on Microsoft Office. This one is part of David Pogue's highly successful Missing Manual series. It follows a tried-and-true formula that should help you learn the ins and outs of this complex software suite. Similar titles exist for a wide variety of software and hardware tools.

Microsoft Office 2008 for Macintosh: Visual QuickStart Guide, by Steve Schwartz (Peachpit Press). Peachpit's Visual Quickstart series covers a variety of applications for multiple platforms, but they're particularly strong on Mac programs because of Peachpit's emphasis on design and creativity titles. This book covers the Mac version of Office.

The Non-Designer's Design and Type Book, Deluxe Edition, by Robin Williams (Peachpit Press). In this perennially popular book, Robin Williams provides a friendly introduction to the basics of design and page layout in her down-to-earth style. The first section of the book illustrates the four basic design principles (proximity, alignment, repetition, and contrast). The second section focuses on using type as a design element. This edition combines two previously separate books and adds full-color illustrations. This book is highly recommended for anyone new to graphic design.

The Elements of Style, Fourth Edition, by William Strunk, Jr., and E. B. White (Allyn & Bacon,). Through a half century and four editions, this book has been helping writers to communicate more clearly.

The Chicago Manual of Style, Fifteenth Edition (University of Chicago Press). This is considered by many to be the definitive writing style guide. The latest edition includes much new material on electronic publishing and online publication.

Adobe Acrobat 9 Classroom in a Book, by Adobe Creative Team (Adobe Press). Adobe's PDF is the industry standard for paperless publishing, and Acrobat is the standard tool for creating and editing PDF documents. This tutorial, like others in Adobe's excellent *Classroom in a Book* series, explains the ins and outs of the software in an easy-to-follow format.

Print is Dead: Books in Our Digital Age, by Jeff Gomez (Macmillan). The title raises the question; the book attempts to answer that question. What is the future of the book in the age of electronics? You may not agree with Gomez, but this book should at least start some interesting conversations about our future.

Quicken 2010: The Official Guide, by Maria Langer (McGraw-Hill). Quicken is far-and-away the most widely used personal accounting and money management program. This "official" book covers the basics of the Windows version of the program, with tips for setting up accounts, creating a budget, recording transactions, banking online, investing, and more.

Super Crunchers: Why Thinking-by-Numbers is the New Way to Be Smart, by Ian Ayres (Bantam). There's a wealth of numeric data out stored in computers today. Ian Ayers argues that intelligent analysis on this data is the right way to make smart decisions today. He uses a variety of real-world examples to illustrate the power of thinking statistically and analytically.

The Visual Display of Quantitative Information, by Edward R. Tufte (Graphics Press). Tufte is widely recognized as a master of statistical graphics. In this book he presents his rules for good design and illustrates them with dozens of wonderful (and terrible) graphics that have actually appeared in print.

How to Lie with Statistics, by Darrell Huff (W. W. Norton). This classic book, first published in 1954, has more relevance in today's computer age than it did when it was written.

Stat-Spotting: A Field Guide to Identifying Dubious Data, by Joel Best (University of California Press). Best is a sociology professor and the author of several books about the ways that numbers can hide the real truth.

6

Graphics, Digital Media, and Multimedia

OBJECTIVES

After you read this chapter you should be able to:

- Explain the difference between painting software, image-processing software, drawing software, and 3-D modeling software
- Explain effective techniques for improving the quality of slides prepared with presentation-graphics software
- Describe how digital technology is used in video and audio production today
- Describe how data compression works
- Describe several present and future applications for multimedia technology

The whole idea you can have some idea and make it happen means that **dreamers all over the world should take heart and not stop.**

—Tim Berners-Lee, *creator of the World Wide Web*

Tim Berners-Lee Weaves the Web for Everybody

The Internet has long been a powerful communication medium and a storehouse of valuable information. But until recently, few people mastered the cryptic codes and challenging languages that were required to unlock the Internet's treasures. The Net was effectively off-limits to most of the world's people. Tim Berners-Lee changed all that when he single-handedly invented the World Wide Web and gave it to all of us.

Tim Berners-Lee was born in London in 1955. His parents met while programming the Ferranti Mark I, the first commercial computer. They encouraged their son to think unconventionally. He developed a love for electronics and even built a computer out of spare parts and a TV set when he was a physics student at Oxford.

Berners-Lee took a software engineering job at CERN, the European Particle Physics Laboratory in Geneva, Switzerland. While he was there, he developed a program to help him track all his random notes. He tried to make the program, called Enquire, deal with information in a "brainlike way." Enquire was a primitive hypertext system that allowed related documents on his computer to be linked with numbers rather than mouse clicks. (Back in 1980, PCs didn't have mice.)

Berners-Lee wanted to expand the concept of Enquire so he could link documents on other computers to his own. His idea was to create an open-ended, distributed hypertext system without boundaries, so scientists everywhere could link their work.

Over the next few years, he single-handedly built a complete system to realize his dream. He designed the URL scheme for giving every Internet document a unique address. He developed HTML, the language for encoding and displaying hypertext documents on the Web. He created HTTP, the set of rules that allows hypertext documents to be linked across the Internet. And he built the first software browser for viewing those documents from remote locations.

When he submitted the first paper describing the Web to a conference in 1991, the conference organizers rejected it because the Web seemed too simple to them. They thought that Berners-Lee's ideas would be a step backward when compared to hypertext systems that had been developed by Ted Nelson, Doug Engelbart, and others over the previous 25 years. It's easy to see now that the simplicity of the Web was a strength, not a weakness.

Rather than try to own his suite of inventions, Berners-Lee made them freely available to the public. Suddenly, vast tracts of the Internet were open to just about anyone who could point and click a mouse. Other programmers added multimedia capabilities to the Web, and its popularity spread like a virus. In a few short years, the Internet was transformed from a forbidding fortress of cryptic codes into an inviting multimedia milieu for the masses.

When he created the Web, Tim Berners-Lee created a new medium of communication. Few people in history have had so great an impact on the way we communicate. In the words of writer Joshua Quittner, Tim Berners-Lee's accomplishments are "almost Gutenbergian."

FIGURE 6.1 Tim Berners-Lee, the inventor of the World Wide Web. *(Source: © Sam Ogden.)*

In 1994, Tim Berners-Lee founded the World Wide Web Consortium (W3C). The W3C is a standards-setting organization dedicated to helping the Web evolve in positive directions rather than disintegrate into incompatible factions. He has since become a champion of net neutrality, advocating that Internet service providers should not discriminate based on content, sites, or platforms. In 2009, he launched the World Wide Web Foundation to "Advance the Web to empower humanity by launching transformative programs that build local capacity to leverage the Web as a medium for positive change." Tim Berners-Lee continues to work to ensure that his greatest creation, the World Wide Web, belongs to everyone. ■

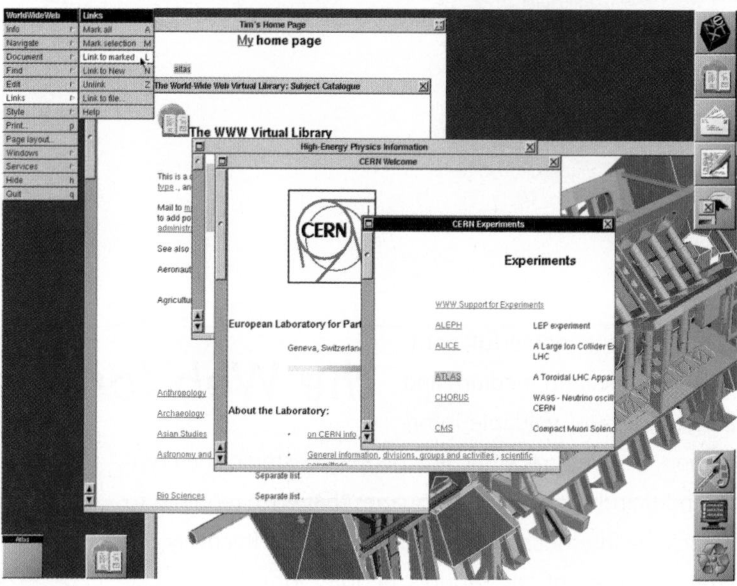

FIGURE 6.2 Berners-Lee implemented the first Web browser on a NeXT workstation in 1990.

The work of Tim Berners-Lee brought multimedia to millions of people around the world. Today, the Web is a source of images, sounds, animations, video clips, and rich interactive documents that merge multiple media types. Even without the Web, though, today's PC can serve as a digital hub for a network of creative media tools, from digital cameras and graphics tablets to musical instruments and video systems. In this chapter we look into these technologies and see how they're changing the ways we create and communicate.

Focus on Computer Graphics

> Expression has been the one constant among artists from the Stone Age until now. **The only thing that has changed is the technology**.
>
> —*Steven Holtzman, author of* Digital Mantras

The previous chapter explored a variety of computer applications, from basic word-processing and desktop publishing software to mathematical programs that can analyze data and generate charts and graphs from numbers. But computer graphics today go far beyond page layouts and pie charts. In this section we explore a variety of graphical applications, from simple drawing and painting tools to complex programs used by professional artists and designers.

Painting: Bitmapped Graphics

> **Everything you imagine** is real.
>
> —*Pablo Picasso*

An image on a computer screen is made up of a matrix of **pixels**—tiny dots of white, black, or color arranged in rows. The words, numbers, and pictures we see on the computer display are nothing more than patterns of pixels created by software. Most of the time, the user doesn't directly control those pixel patterns; software creates the patterns automatically in response to commands. For example, when you press the *e* key while word processing, the software constructs a pattern that appears on the screen as an *e*. Similarly, when you issue a command to create a bar chart from a spreadsheet, software automatically constructs a pixel pattern that looks like a bar chart. Automatic graphics are convenient, but they can also be restrictive. When you need more control over the details of the screen display, another type of graphics software might be more appropriate.

Painting software enables you to "paint" pixels on the screen with a pointing device. A typical painting program accepts input from a mouse, joystick, trackball, touch pad, or stylus, translating the pointer movements into lines and patterns on-screen. A professional artist might prefer to work with a stylus on a pressure-sensitive tablet because it can, with the right software, simulate a traditional pen or paintbrush more accurately than other pointing devices can. A painting program typically offers a **palette** of tools on-screen. Some tools mimic real-world painting tools, while others can do things that are difficult, even impossible, on paper or canvas.

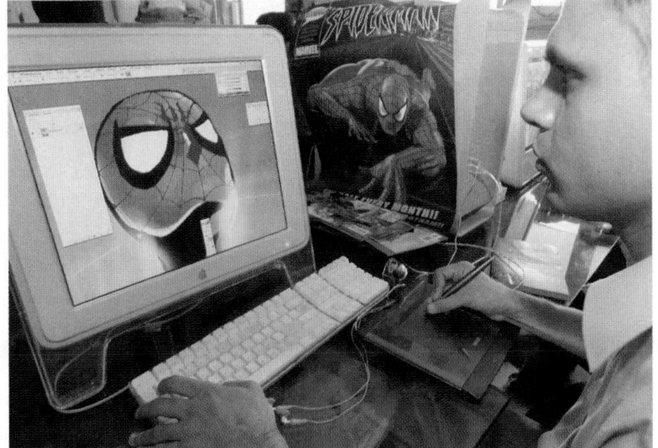

FIGURE 6.3 When it's used with compatible software, a stylus on a pressuresensitive tablet can simulate the feel of a paintbrush on paper. As the artist presses harder on the stylus, the line becomes thicker and denser on the screen.

FIGURE 6.4 Natural painting programs such as Corel Painter allow artists and nonartists to create paintings with digital tools that simulate real-world tools such as watercolors, oil paints, and charcoal.

FIGURE 6.5 These four images show the same photograph displayed in four different bit depths: 1, 4, 8, and 24 bits.

Painting and photo-editing programs create **bitmapped graphics**, or, as they're sometimes called, ***raster graphics***. To the computer, these pictures are simple maps showing how the pixels on the screen should be represented. For the simplest bitmapped graphics, a single bit of computer memory represents each pixel. Because a bit can contain one of two possible values, *0* or *1*, each pixel can display one of two possible colors, usually black or white. Allocating more memory per pixel, so each pixel can display more possible colors or shades, produces even higher-quality graphics. **Gray-scale graphics** allow each pixel to appear as black, white, or one of several shades of gray. A program that assigns 8 bits per pixel allows up to 256 different shades of gray to appear on the screen—more than the human eye can distinguish.

Realistic color graphics require more memory. Many older computers have hardware to support 8-bit color, allowing 256 possible colors to be displayed on the screen at a time—enough to display rich images, but not enough to reproduce photographs exactly. Modern PCs use 24 or 32 bits of memory to display millions of colors at a time—photorealistic color.

The number of bits devoted to each pixel—called **color depth** or **bit depth**—is one of two technological factors limiting an artist's ability to create realistic on-screen images with a bitmapped graphics program. The other factor is **resolution**—the density of the pixels, described in ***pixels per inch*, or *PPI*** (in print, this density is measured in ***dots per inch*, or *DPI***). Not surprisingly, these factors are important in determining image quality in monitors, as described in Chapter 3. But some graphics images are destined for the printer after being displayed on-screen, so the printer's resolution comes into play, too. When displayed on a 96-dpi computer screen—on a Web page, for example—a 96-dpi picture looks fine. But when printed on paper, that same image lacks the fine-grained clarity of a photograph. Diagonal lines, curves, and text characters have tiny *jaggies*—jagged, stair-step-like bumps that advertise the image's identity as a collection of pixels.

Painting programs get around the jaggies by allowing you to store an image at 300 dots per inch or higher, even though the computer screen can't display every pixel at that resolution and normal magnification, and by using a technique called **anti-aliasing** to smooth the artifacts created by less-than-ideal resolutions. Of course, these high-resolution pictures demand more memory and disk space. But for printed images, the results are worth the added cost. The higher the resolution, the harder it is for the human eye to detect individual pixels on the printed page.

Practically speaking, resolution and bit-depth limitations are easy to overcome with today's hardware and software. Artists can use paint programs to produce works that convincingly simulate watercolors, oils, and other natural media, and transcend the limits of those media. Similarly, bitmapped image-editing software can be used to edit photographic images.

Image Processing: Photographic Editing by Computer

> **The aim of every artist is to arrest motion, which is life,** by artificial means and hold it fixed so that a hundred years later, when a stranger looks at it, **it moves again since it is life**.
>
> —*William Faulkner*

Like a picture created with a high-resolution paint program, a digitized photograph or a photograph captured with a digital camera—often simply referred to as a *digital photo*—is

FIGURE 6.6 This painting served as the cover art for a Herbie Hancock CD called *Dis is de Drum*. Photographer Sanjay Kothari created the image through the process of digital photographic manipulation. Several of the photos used in the final collage are shown along the side of the main image. At the bottom of the collage, three small images show how the photos were merged to create the final image.

a bitmapped image. **Image-processing software** enables the photographer to manipulate digital photos and other high-resolution images with tools similar to those found in paint programs. Image-processing software, such as Adobe Photoshop, is in many ways similar to paint software; both are tools for editing high-resolution bitmapped images.

Digital image-processing software makes it easier for photographers to remove unwanted reflections, eliminate "red eye," and brush away facial blemishes. These kinds of editing tasks were routinely done with magnifying glasses and tiny brushes before photographs were digitized. But digital photographic editing is far more powerful than traditional photo-retouching techniques. With image-processing software, it's possible to distort photos, apply special effects, and fabricate images that range from artistic to otherworldly.

Screen Test Creating a CD Cover with Photoshop

GOAL *To create a CD cover by modifying a digital photograph of the artist*

TOOL *Adobe Photoshop, part of the Adobe Creative Suite*

1. You open two images you'd like to use, and resize the canvas of one of the photos to fit the front of a CD jewel case.

2. You copy and paste the image of the clouds into a new ***layer*** on the other document.

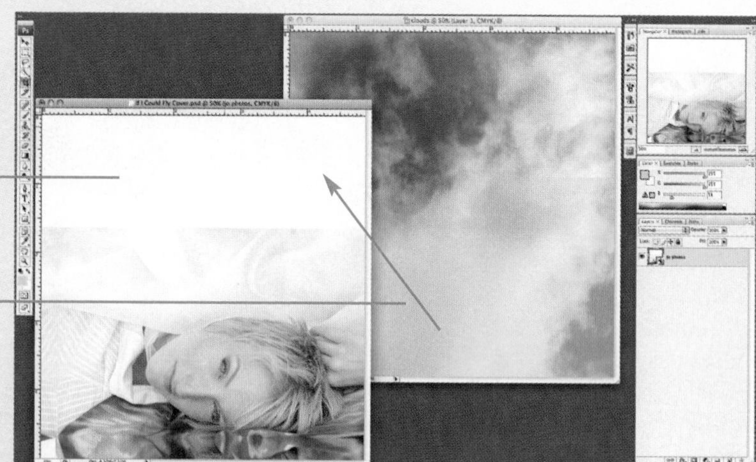

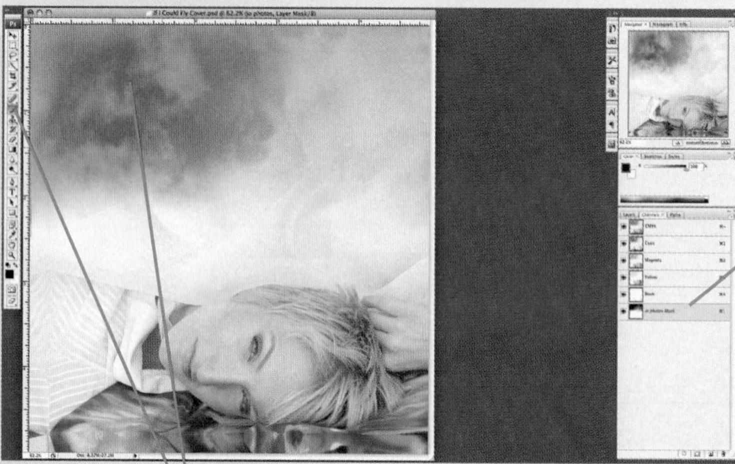

3. You duplicate and mirror the veiled part of the artist photo to extend the veil up to the edge of the canvas.

4. You use the paintbrush tool to "paint" a ***mask*** (indicated in red) onto the artist layer. The masked area becomes transparent, hiding the veil and allowing the clouds underneath to shine through.

5. You apply the mask to the image.

6. You import the logo, created earlier with Adobe Illustrator.

7. You add stylized text for the album title.

FIGURE 6.7

It's also possible to combine photographs into composite scenes that show no obvious evidence of tampering. Supermarket gossip tabloids routinely use these tools to create sensationalistic cover photos. Many experts question whether photographs should be allowed as evidence in the courtroom now that they can be doctored so convincingly.

A digital camera typically stores images on a flash memory card. Images are usually downloaded from camera to computer via a USB connection or memory card reader. Digital *photo management software* programs such as Apple iPhoto, Google Picasa, and Adobe Lightroom simplify and automate common tasks associated with capturing, organizing, editing, and sharing digital images. Most consumer-oriented digital photo managers make it easy to import photos from digital cameras, remove red eye, adjust color and contrast, fix small errors, print photos on a color printer, upload images to a Web site, email copies to friends and family, store photo libraries on CD or DVD, and order paper prints or hardbound photo albums online.

FIGURE 6.8 Apple's iPhoto, like many PC photo applications, makes it easy to import, edit, and organize photos. iPhoto also automates the creation of custom photo albums that can be turned into professionally bound books via an online store.

Drawing: Object-Oriented Graphics

Actually, **a root word of technology, *techne,* originally meant "art."** The ancient Greeks never separated art from manufacture in their minds, and so never developed separate words for them.

—*Robert Pirsig, in* Zen and the Art of Motorcycle Maintenance

Because high-resolution paint images and photographs are stored as bitmaps, they can make heavy storage and memory demands. Another type of graphics program can economically store pictures with virtually *infinite* resolution, limited only by the capabilities of the output device. **Drawing software** stores a picture not as a collection of dots, but as a collection of lines and shapes. When you draw a line with a drawing program, the software doesn't record changes in the underlying pixels. Instead, it calculates and remembers a mathematical formula for the line. A drawing program stores shapes as shape formulas and text as text. Because pictures are collections of lines, shapes, and other objects, this approach is often called **object-oriented graphics** or **vector graphics**. In effect, the computer is remembering "a blue line segment goes here and a red circle goes here and a chunk of text goes here" instead of "this pixel is blue and this one is red and this one is white."

Many drawing tools—line, shape, and text tools—are similar to painting tools in bitmapped programs. But the user can manipulate objects and edit text without affecting neighboring objects, even if the neighboring objects overlap. On the screen, an object-oriented drawing looks similar to a bitmapped painting. But when it's printed, a drawing appears as smooth as the printer's resolution allows. (Of course, not all drawings are designed to be printed. You may, for example, use a drawing program to create images for publication on a Web page. Because many Web browsers recognize only bitmapped images, you'll probably convert the drawings to bitmaps before displaying them.)

Most professional drawing programs, including Adobe Illustrator, can store images as **PDF (portable document format)** documents. PDF is a file format developed by Adobe that enables digital documents to be exchanged between programs independent of application software, hardware, or operating system. A PDF file is, in effect, a complete description of a two-dimensional document, including text, fonts, images, and vector graphics. PDF has become an open standard, and is widely used in illustration programs,

Creating Smart Art

Graphics software isn't just for professional artists. Almost anybody can create pictures and presentations. Here are some guidelines to help you make the most of the computer as a graphic tool:

- ***Reprogram yourself...relax.*** For many of us, the hardest part is getting started. We are programmed by messages we received in our childhood, which for many of us included "You aren't creative" and "You can't draw."

Format	Used in	Advantages	Disadvantages
GIF	***Simple Web graphics and animations***	Lossless compression ideal for simple illustrations, logos, and simple animated sequences. Supports transparency, allowing you to define areas where the background shows through the image.	Inadequate for photos or illustrations with thousands of colors and complex textures. Text can't be searched or copied.
JPG	***Photographs, especially on the Web***	JPG compression can produce excellent photo images with relatively small file sizes. Options range from slightly compressed (best quality) to highly compressed (smallest file size). Most popular and supported image format on the Web.	Lossy compression. Line and shape drawings and illustrations may look blurry or pixellated. Over-compression can do the same to photos. Text can't be searched or copied.
PNG	***Web photographs and illustrations***	Photographs and gradients may look better than comparable JPG images. Supports transparency, allowing background to show through some areas. Color depth can range up to 24-bit, higher than JPG or GIF.	File size can be larger than JPG. Text can't be searched or copied when compressed for Web.
PDF	***All kinds of documents on the Web (with plugin), on a PC, or printed***	Text can be searched and copied. Excellent for articles and books containing both graphics and text. Supports transparency, layers, vector graphics and (in some cases) advanced Adobe Illustrator features. Optimized for print, but widely used as a paperless alternative to print documents.	Requires a plugin and/or separate program for Web viewing (although most browsers have the plugin installed by default).
PSD	***Photoshop's native format for editing photos and other images for print or screen***	Widely used and supported format for manipulating print-quality images. Supports advanced Photoshop features such as Smart Layers and Layer Effects.	Relatively large file size. Not supported by most applications that can display or edit photos.
TIF	***Photographs, especially for print***	Popular format for desktop publishing and print design. Supports layers, transparency, and lossless compression.	Large file size. Not as easy to edit as PSDs.
EPS	***Complex printed documents***	Supports both print and vector graphics as well as transparency; optimized for printer output.	Large file size, difficult to edit.
RAW	***Photographs, especially for print***	Native format for many professional cameras; allows for more accurate corrections to the image because the file contains all of the information captured with the photo.	File sizes are extremely large (much larger than PSD and TIF). Not supported by all applications. Image processing can be very slow.
AI	***Adobe Illustrator's native format; used for vector graphics***	Shapes, colors, text, and gradients are easy to change, output looks smooth and crisp at any size. Supports layers, transparency, and advanced Illustrator features like Gradient Meshes.	Not supported by many non-vector graphics applications, can't open newer AI files in older versions.

FIGURE 6.9 Comparison of the most common graphic formats.

Fortunately, a computer can help us overcome this early programming and find the artist locked within us. Most drawing and painting programs are flexible, forgiving, and fun. Allow yourself to experiment; you'll be surprised at what you can create if you're patient and playful.

- ***Choose the right tool for the job.*** Will your artwork be displayed on the computer screen or printed? Would color enhance the finished work? Will the finished project be viewed from a distance or at close range? Your answers to these questions will help you determine which software and hardware tools are most appropriate. As you're thinking about options, don't rule out low-tech tools. The best approach may not involve a computer, or it may involve some combination of computer and nonelectronic tools. For example, you might create sketches, paintings, or collages, scan them, and incorporate them into digital drawings or paintings.
- ***Always keep a native copy.*** By default, a typical graphic application saves files in a native format—one that's specifically designed for that application. Always save your work in that native file format—it's the only way you can be sure that everything is saved in a way that it can be modified later. Even when you think you're done editing, keep a native file in a safe place, just in case. You may be surprised how often you want or need to change a "finished" document.
- ***Know your graphics file formats.*** A native file for one application might not be readable by another application or tool. For example, a digital picture frame may not be able to display images manipulated in Photoshop unless they're saved in an industry standard format. The most common graphics file types are JPEG (or JPG), TIFF (or TIF), and RAW, generally used for photographs; GIF, generally used for Web art; PNG, generally used for Web art and photographs; and PDF, a general-purpose format especially well-suited for documents that combine graphics and text. (There's more on these file types later in this chapter.)
- ***Borrow from the best.*** Art supply stores sell *clip art*—predrawn images that artists can legally cut out and paste into their own pictures or posters. Computer artists can choose from countless digital clip art collections. Computer clip art images can be cut, pasted, and edited electronically. Some computer clip art collections are in the public domain (that is, they are free); others can be licensed for a small fee. Computer clip art comes in a variety of formats, and it ranges from simple line drawings to scanned color photographs. If you have access to a scanner, you can create your own digitized clip art from your photos and drawings.
- ***Don't borrow without permission.*** Computers, scanners, and digital cameras make it all too easy to create unauthorized copies of copyrighted photographs, drawings, and other images. There's a legal and ethical line between using public domain or licensed clip art and pirating copyrighted material. If you use somebody else's creative work, make sure you have written permission from the owner.
- ***Understand your rights.*** Copyright laws aren't just to protect other people's work. Your creative work is copyrighted, too—the papers you write, the photographs you take, even the doodles you put down on napkins. As soon as your creative work takes on a fixed form, it is your property and enjoys copyright protection. (If an employer is paying you to create the work, the employer is considered to be the author for copyright purposes.) If one of your creations is particularly valuable, you may want to register it with the U.S. Copyright Office. For more information, go to the U.S. Copyright Office Web site: (**www.copyright.gov**).
- ***Consider letting others build on your work.*** Under current copyright law, you can't use someone else's work without asking their permission. That means others can't use your work either without asking your permission. If you want to allow certain uses of your creative work, or if you want it to become public domain (freely usable by anyone), you can give your permission, up front, by associating a Creative Commons license with your work. See the Creative Commons Web site for more details (**www.creativecommons.org**).

FIGURE 6.10 The Web offers a multitude of sources for photos and other digital images. Images on Fotolia.com are contributed by users; contributors receive royalties when other users buy those images.

Pixels versus Objects How do you edit a picture? It depends on what you're doing and how the picture is stored.		
The task . . .	**Using bitmapped graphics**	**Using object-oriented graphics**
Moving and removing parts of pictures 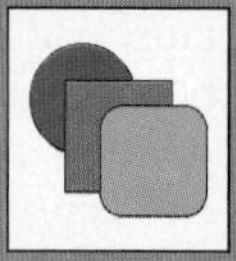	Easier to work with regions rather than objects, especially if those objects overlap 	Easier to work with individual objects or groups of objects, even if they overlap 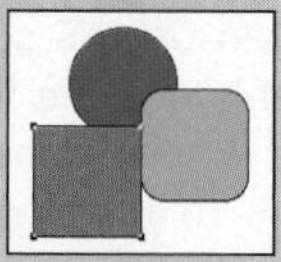
Working with shapes 	Shapes stored as pixel patterns can be edited with eraser and drawing tools 	Shapes stored as math formulas can be transformed mathematically 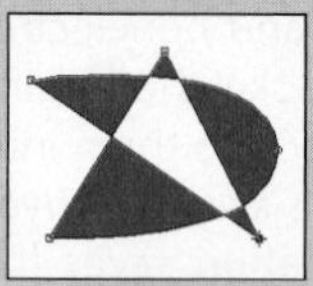
Magnification 	Magnifies pixels for fine detail editing 	Magnifies objects, not pixels 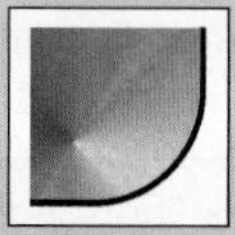
Text handling Text	Text "dries" and can't be edited, but can be moved as a block of pixels When paint text "dries" it can't be edited like other text	Text can always be edited Draw text always can be changed
Printing	Resolution of printout can't exceed the pixel resolution of the stored picture	Resolution is limited only by the output device
Working within the limits of the hardware	Photographic quality is possible but requires considerable memory and disk storage	Complex drawings require considerable computational power for reasonable speed

FIGURE 6.11 Pixels versus objects.

desktop publishing programs, and other applications. Web browsers can display PDF documents using Adobe's Acrobat Reader plug-in. A PDF document might be created in Microsoft Word on a Windows PC, embellished with Adobe Illustrator on a Mac, and posted on the Web using a Linux server.

Object-oriented drawing and bitmapped painting each offer advantages for certain applications. Bitmapped image editing programs give artists and photo editors unsurpassed control over textures, shading, and fine detail; they're widely used for creating screen displays (for example, in video games, multimedia presentations, and Web pages), for simulating natural paint media, and for embellishing photographic images. Object-oriented drawing and illustration programs are better choices for creating printed graphs, charts, and illustrations with clean lines and smooth shapes.

Some programs merge features of both in a single application, blurring the distinction and offering new possibilities for amateur and professional illustrators. For example, a Photoshop document can contain multiple layers with different properties. Two layers might be photographic images, a third layer might contain some drawn shapes, and a fourth layer might contain text. Each layer can be edited separately before they're merged into a single image that can be printed, posted to the Web, or imported into other applications.

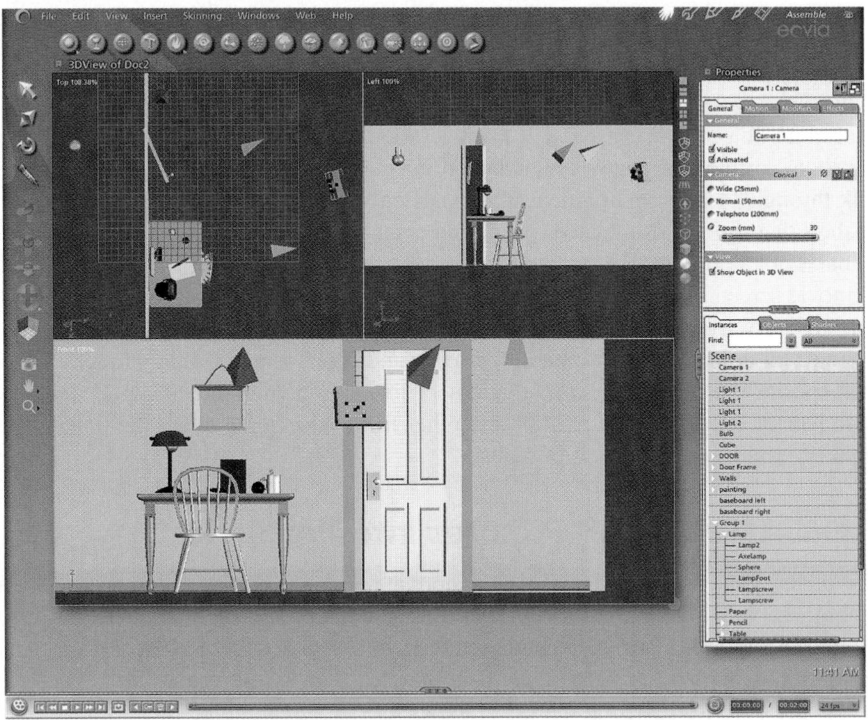

FIGURE 6.12 This scene was created using 3-D modeling software. The upper screen shows three different views of the scene being modeled. The lower screen shows the completed scene, including lighting and surface textures.

3-D Modeling Software

Working with a pencil, an artist can draw a representation of a three-dimensional scene on a two-dimensional page. Similarly, an artist can use a drawing or painting program to create a scene that appears to have depth on a two-dimensional computer screen. But in either case, the drawing lacks true depth; it's just a flat representation of a scene. With **3-D modeling software** graphic designers can create 3-D objects with tools similar to those found in conventional drawing software. You can't touch a 3-D computer model; it's no more real than a square, a circle, or a letter created with a drawing program. But a 3-D computer model can be rotated, stretched, and combined with other model objects to create complex 3-D scenes.

Illustrators who use 3-D software appreciate its flexibility. A designer can create a 3-D model of an object, rotate it, view it from a variety of angles, and take two-dimensional "snapshots" of the best views for inclusion in final printouts. Similarly, it's possible to "walk through" a 3-D environment that exists only in the computer's memory, printing snapshots that show the simulated space from many points of view. For many applications, the goal is not a printout, but an animated presentation on a computer screen, a TV screen, or a movie screen. Animation software, presentation-graphics software, and multimedia-authoring software (all described later in this chapter) can display sequences of screens showing 3-D objects being rotated, explored, and transformed. Many modern TV and movie special effects involve combinations of live action and simulated 3-D animation. Techniques pioneered in *Up, Avatar,* and other films and video games continually push computer graphics to new levels of realism.

CAD/CAM: Turning Pictures into Products

Three-dimensional graphics also play an important role in the branch of engineering known as **computer-aided design (CAD)**—the use of computers to design products. CAD software allows engineers, designers, and architects to create designs on-screen for products ranging from computer chips to public buildings. Today's software goes far beyond basic drafting and object-oriented graphics. It allows users to create three-dimensional "solid" models with physical characteristics such as weight, volume, and center of gravity. These

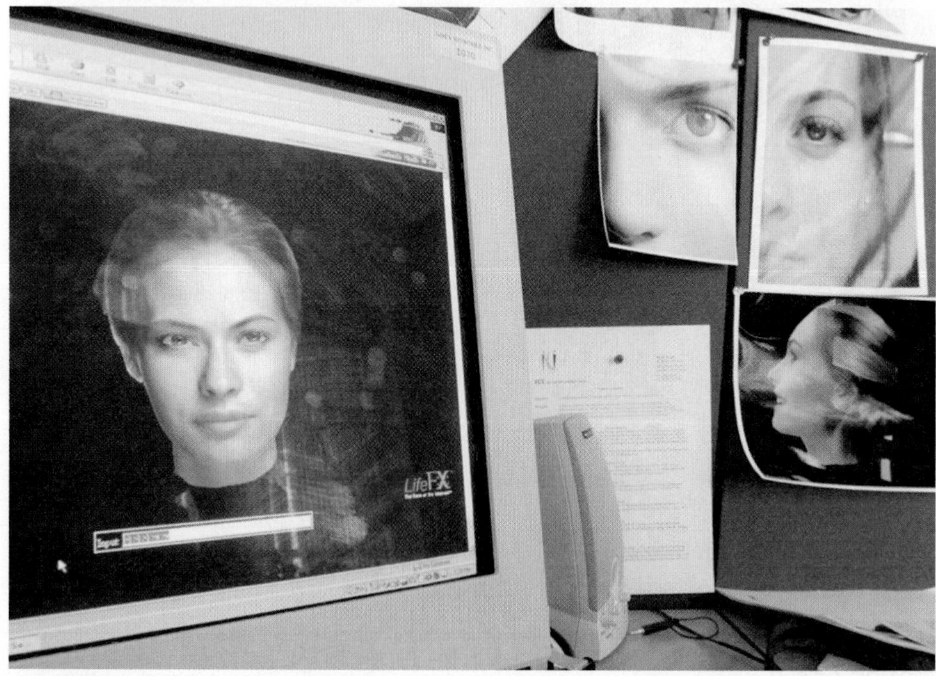

FIGURE 6.13 Animated 3-D figures using technology from LifeFX can simulate human expressions for use in Internet-based video communications.

FIGURE 6.14 Engineers use CAD software to design everything from microscopic electronic circuits to massive structures.

models can be visually rotated and viewed from any angle. The computer can evaluate the structural performance of any part of the model by applying imaginary force to the object. Using CAD, an engineer can crash-test a new model of an automobile before it ever leaves the computer screen. CAD tends to be cheaper, faster, and more accurate than traditional design-by-hand techniques. What's more, the forgiving nature of the computer makes it easy to alter a design to meet project goals.

Computer-aided design is often linked to **computer-aided manufacturing (CAM)**. When the design of a product is completed, the numbers are fed to a program that controls the manufacturing or prototyping of products. For electronic parts, the design translates directly into a template for etching circuits onto chips. The emergence of CAD/CAM has streamlined many design and manufacturing processes. The combination of CAD and CAM is often called **computer-integrated manufacturing (CIM)**; it's a major step toward a fully automated factory.

Dynamic Media: Beyond the Printed Page

A picture is worth a thousand words. **An interface is worth a thousand pictures.**

—*Ben Shneiderman*

Most PC applications—painting and drawing programs, word processors, desktop publishers, and so on—are designed to produce paper documents. But many types of modern media can't be reduced to pixels on printouts because they contain dynamic information—

Working Wisdom Making Powerful Presentations

You've probably had to suffer through at least one terrible computer-assisted presentation—a speech or lecture that used ugly, hard-to-understand computer-generated slides to distract from, rather than drive home, the basic messages of the talk. Presentation-graphics software makes it easy to create presentations, but it doesn't guarantee that those presentations will be good. These guidelines will help you produce first-rate presentations.

Before you create any slides...

- ***Remember your goal.*** Know what you're trying to communicate. Keep your goal in mind throughout the process of creating the presentation.
- ***Remember your audience.*** How much do they know about your topic? How much do they *need* to know? Do key terms need to be defined?
- ***Plan a story.*** Determine the best way to take your listeners from where they are to where you want them to be. A powerful presentation smoothly guides the audience from one point to the next, as if it were telling a story.
- ***Determine your slide count.*** Depending on topic and speaking style, you'll probably spend between 30 seconds and 2 minutes per slide. Figure out how many slides you need to match the total presentation time. Then estimate how many slides to devote to each point you want to make.
- ***Tell them what you're going to tell them, then tell them what you told them.*** It's the speechmaker's fundamental rule, and it applies to presentations, too.

As you create the slides...

- ***Outline your ideas.*** If you can't express your plan in a clear, concise outline, you probably won't be able to create a clear, concise presentation. After your outline is done, you can import it into your presentation-graphics software and massage it into a presentation.
- ***Don't expect too much from one slide.*** A visual presentation is not a replacement for a detailed written report with data-rich diagrams.
- ***Keep each slide focused.*** Each screen should convey one idea clearly, possibly with a few concrete supporting points.
- ***Be stingy with words.*** Limit yourself to seven lines per list and no more than seven words per line. Whenever possible, eliminate low-information-content words such as *a, an, and,* and *the.*
- ***Use signposts.*** Help listeners keep track of where you are in the presentation. An occasional signpost slide lists the major topics and indicates which one is going to be covered next.
- ***Use a consistent design.*** Make sure all your slides look like they belong together. Use the same backgrounds and colors throughout your presentation. Consider using predesigned templates.
- ***Don't go font crazy.*** It's generally wise to choose one or two fonts and use them throughout your presentation.

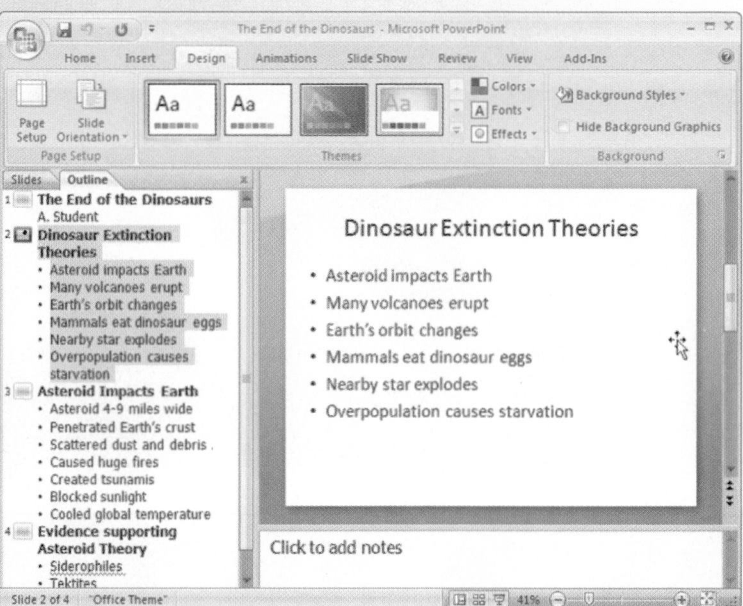

The presentation software converts an outline into slides.

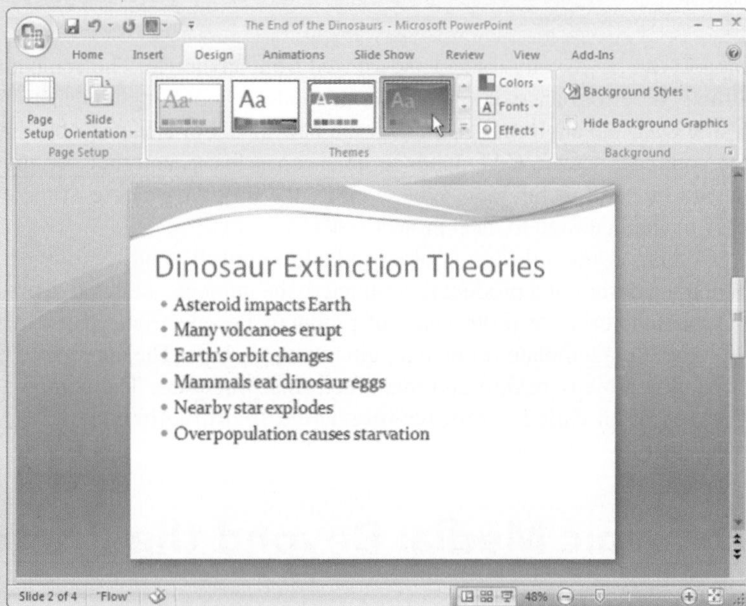

You can choose a professionally designed template from a collection provided with the software.

FIGURE 6.15

- ***Cool colors make better backgrounds.*** Blues and greens are better than yellows, oranges, and reds. It's hard to go wrong with a dark blue background.
- ***Use large letters.*** The smallest letters on the slide should be at least 24 point to ensure readability for audience members in the back of the room.
- ***Avoid use of all capital letters.*** TEXT PRINTED IN ALL CAPITAL LETTERS IS HARDER TO READ.
- ***Be smart with art.*** Don't clutter your presentation with random clip art. Make sure each illustration contributes to your message. Use simple graphs that support your main points. Make sure you coordinate illustrations with the colors and design of the rest of the presentation.
- ***Keep it simple.*** Avoid useless decorations and distractions. Avoid fancy borders and backgrounds. Don't use a different transition on each slide.

When you make your presentation...

- ***Do a test run before the audience arrives.*** You may lose your communication edge—and your audience—if you spend your opening minutes figuring out how to make the computer and projector work together.
- ***Stand to the left of the screen.*** The eyes of the audience members won't have to cross the screen when they shift their gaze from you to a new slide or list item.
- ***Don't read your slides.*** Talk in complete sentences but only put short phrases on the slides.
- ***Reveal no line before its time.*** If you unveil the entire contents of a slide all at once, expect audience members to read the slide rather than listen to you.
- ***Use wipe right to reveal lines.*** The wipe right animation allows audience members to begin reading the text before it is completely written.
- ***Pause when you reveal a new slide or bullet.*** Give your listeners a chance to read the slide title or list item before you elaborate on it.
- ***Vary pace or volume to make a point.*** To emphasize a particular point, you can repeat yourself, pause for a moment after saying it, or noticeably change the volume of your voice.

BAD

Blue on red and red on blue are among the worst color combinations.

Each bullet contains a complete sentence. The audience will be tempted to read the sentences, not listen to you speak.

The excessive number of words causes text to be too small.

Background is a hot color.

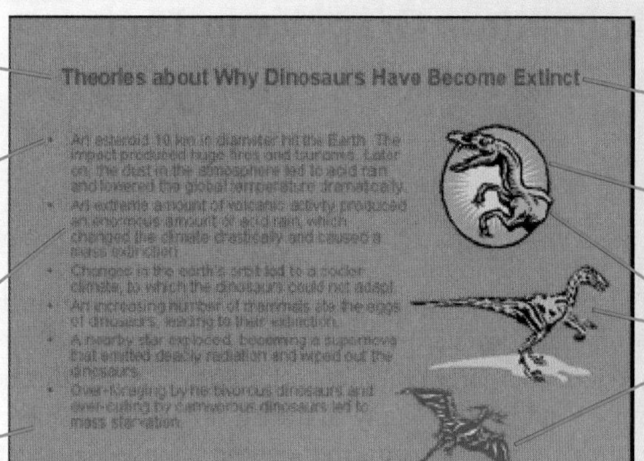

Title is too long, forcing letter size to be too small.

Graphic images do not add information. Images distract from text.

Images are taken from different libraries and do not match each other.

GOOD

High contrast between letters and background improves readability.

Because there are only six lines and only three or four words per line, text is large and easy to read.

Dinosaur Extinction Theories

- Asteroid impacts Earth
- Many volcanoes erupt
- Earth's orbit changes
- Mammals eat dinosaur eggs
- Nearby star explodes
- Overpopulation causes starvation

65 million years ago

Background is a cool color.

Short title allows large text size.

The graphic contributes information. An animation in which the "No" symbol stamps out the dinosaur would be a nice touch.

information that changes over time or in response to user input. Today's multimedia computers enable us to create and edit dynamic presentations, animated sequences, video clips, sound, and music along with text and graphics. Just as words and pictures serve as the raw materials for desktop publishing, dynamic media such as animation, video, audio, and hypertext are important components of interactive multimedia projects.

Presentation Graphics: Bringing Lectures to Life

Presentation-graphics software helps automate the creation of visual aids for lectures, training sessions, sales demonstrations, and other presentations. Presentation-graphics programs are most commonly used for creating and displaying a series of on-screen "slides" to serve as visual aids for presentations. Slides might include photographs, drawings, spreadsheet-style charts, or tables. These different graphical elements are usually integrated into a series of **bullet charts** that list the main points of a presentation. Slides can be output as transparencies or handouts. More commonly, though, they're presented as "slide shows" directly on computer monitors or LCD projectors, including animation, audio, and video clips along with still images. Some presentation applications can convert presentations into Web pages automatically or convert slide shows into video files that can be published on the Web or incorporated into other video products.

Because they can be used to create and display on-screen presentations with animated visual effects and video clips, presentation-graphics programs, such as Microsoft's PowerPoint, Apple's Keynote, and Google Docs Presentations, are sometimes called multimedia presentation tools. These programs make it easy for nonartists to combine text, graphics, and other media in simple multimedia presentations or incorporate them into other video products.

Animation: Graphics in Time

> We're on the threshold of a moment in cinematic history that is unparalleled. **Anything you can imagine can be done.** If you can draw it, if you can describe it, we can do it. It's just a matter of cost.
>
> *—James Cameron, director of* Avatar *and* Titanic, *two of the top-grossing films of all time*

Creating motion from still pictures—this illusion is at the heart of all **animation**. Before computers, artists drew animated films by hand, one still picture, or **frame**, at a time. Modern computer-graphics technology has transformed amateur and professional animation by automating many of the most tedious aspects of the animation process.

In its simplest form, the techniques used in creating computer-based animation are similar to traditional frame-by-frame animation techniques; each frame is a computer-drawn picture, and the computer displays those frames in rapid succession. With an animation program, an animator can create key frames and objects and use software to help fill in the movement of the objects in the in-between frames—a process known as ***tweening***. The most powerful animation programs include tools for working with animated objects in three dimensions, adding depth to the scene on the screen.

Animation on the Web ranges from simple GIF animations to complex cartoon animations created with programs such as Adobe Flash. An animated GIF is simply a bundle of bitmapped GIF images that appear in a sequence similar to the pages of a children's flip book. A more sophisticated way to represent an animation is through the use of vector graphics. A vector graphics animation describes a collection of objects and how they change over time. The two most popular vector graphics formats are ***Shockwave Flash Format (SWF)***, associated with the Adobe Flash player, and ***Scalable Vector Graphics (SVG)***, an open standard promoted by the W3C.

As a way of representing Web animations, vector graphics animations have several advantages over animated GIFs. Vector graphics animations occupy less space, which means they can be downloaded faster. Because vector graphics animations describe images in terms of objects and locations, rather than colored pixels, it is possible to write software

FIGURE 6.16 Pixar has created a string of blockbuster feature films, including Wall-E, that use digital animation to create compelling characters and engaging stories.

that makes the images look good on a wide variety of displays, from smart phones to HDTVs. Finally, SVG files represent the words inside images as plain text characters. Future versions of Web search engines may include the contents of animations in their indexes, making it easier for them to return animations in response to queries.

Computer animation has become commonplace in everything from television commercials to feature films. Sometimes computer animation is combined with live-action film; Harry Potter, Spider-Man, and a host of other characters depend on computer animation to make their larger-than-life actions seem real. Other films, including *Toy Story, Shrek,* and *Up* use computer animation to create every character, scene, and event, leaving only the soundtrack for live actors and musicians to create.

Desktop Video: Computers, Film, and TV

> **Digital technology is the same revolution** as adding sound to pictures and the same revolution as adding color to pictures. **Nothing more and nothing less.**
>
> *—George Lucas, filmmaker*

There's more to the **digital video** revolution than computer animation. Computers can be used to edit video, splice scenes, add transitions, create titles, and do other tasks in a fraction of the time—and at a fraction of the cost—of precomputer techniques. The only requirement is that the video be in a digital form so the computer can treat it as data.

Analog and Digital Video

In the twentieth century and the first part of the twenty-first century, almost all television programs, videos, and movies were stored and broadcast as analog (smooth) electronic waves. But analog video technology is rapidly being replaced by digital video technology. In the United States, all new televisions (as of 2009) are digital. They receive signals that are broadcast as digital data. Many of these digital TVs are **HDTVs**—high-definition

Screen Test Creating a Flash Animation

GOAL *To create an animated spaceship for a science fiction fan Web site*

TOOLS *Adobe Flash*

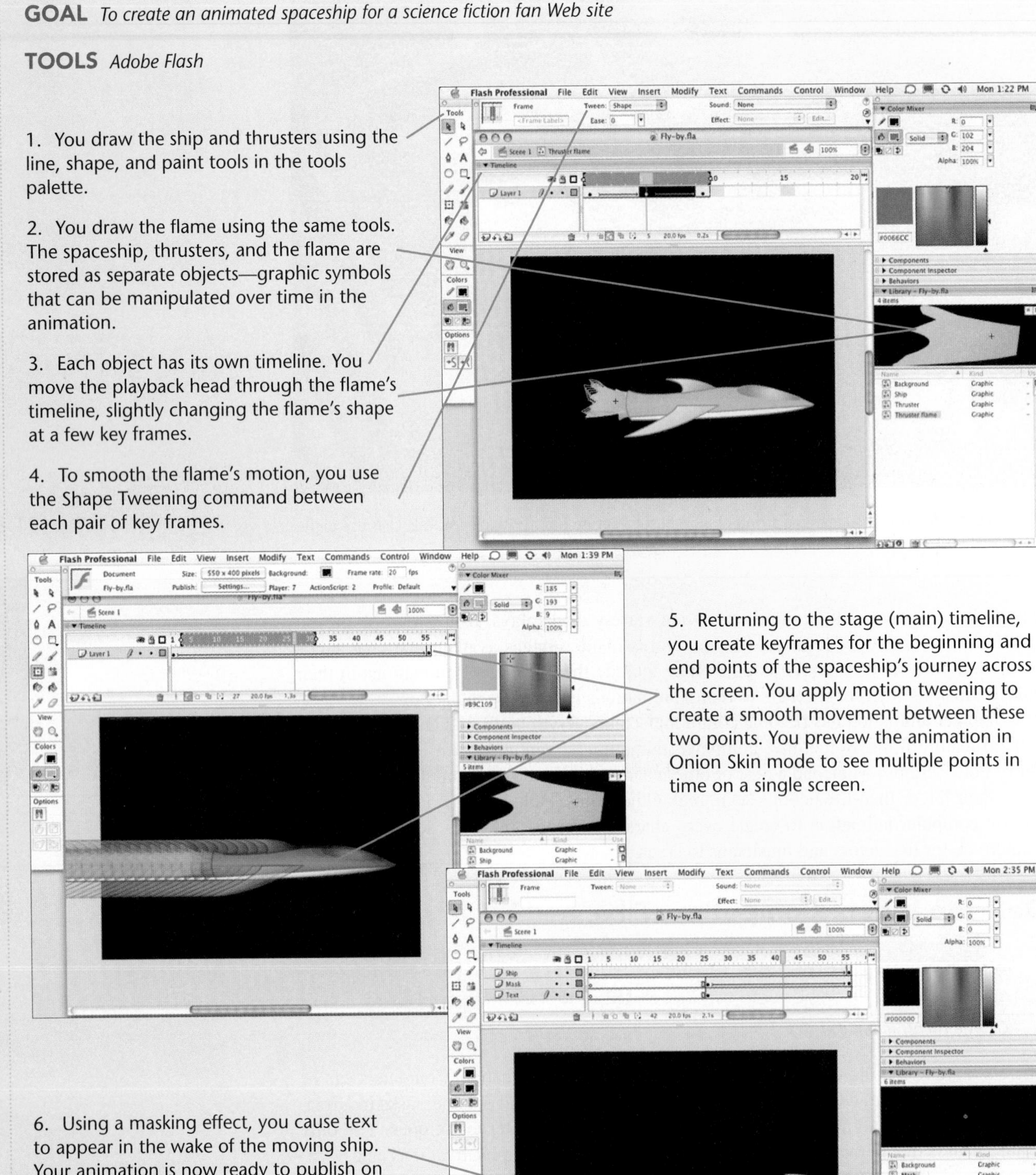

1. You draw the ship and thrusters using the line, shape, and paint tools in the tools palette.

2. You draw the flame using the same tools. The spaceship, thrusters, and the flame are stored as separate objects—graphic symbols that can be manipulated over time in the animation.

3. Each object has its own timeline. You move the playback head through the flame's timeline, slightly changing the flame's shape at a few key frames.

4. To smooth the flame's motion, you use the Shape Tweening command between each pair of key frames.

5. Returning to the stage (main) timeline, you create keyframes for the beginning and end points of the spaceship's journey across the screen. You apply motion tweening to create a smooth movement between these two points. You preview the animation in Onion Skin mode to see multiple points in time on a single screen.

6. Using a masking effect, you cause text to appear in the wake of the moving ship. Your animation is now ready to publish on a Web page.

FIGURE 6.17

televisions capable of receiving and displaying high-resolution images, videos, and broadcasts. New camcorders, from consumer grade to professional, are mostly all digital. Many big-screen films are captured using digital camcorders. And analog VHS videotapes have little relevance in a world of DVDs, Blu-ray discs, and digital movie downloads. (Analog videos and broadcasts can be digitized—converted to a newer digital format—with a *video digitizer*. A video digitizer can be part of a consumer home entertainment system or part of a computer system.)

A digital camcorder might store data on mini-DV tapes, digital-8 tapes, rewritable optical discs, flash memory cards, or a hard disk—different models have different storage capabilities. Most digital video cameras have FireWire (IEEE 1394) or USB ports that can be used to copy raw video footage from camera to computer and later copy the edited video back from computer to camera. A camera connected to a computer can also bypass its own tape or disc storage and transfer images directly to a computer in *real time*—at the same time they're being captured by the camera's lens. Because digital video can be reduced to a series of numbers, it can be copied, edited, stored, and played back without any loss of quality.

FIGURE 6.18 *The Lord of the Rings* trilogy combined live action with computer-generated animation to bring J.R.R. Tolkien's fantasy world to life. In *Avatar,* the visually rich 3-D world of Pandora is populated with alien creatures and plants that seem more real than many live action movie characters.

Video Production Goes Digital

A typical video project starts with an outline and a simple *storyboard* describing the action, dialogue, and music in each scene. The storyboard serves as a guide for shooting and editing scenes.

Today, most video editing is done using *nonlinear editing (NLE)* technology. Because the video and audio clips are stored on the computer's hard disk(s), the editing can happen in any sequence—it isn't limited to the linear sequence of the video footage. Nonlinear editing is faster and easier than older editing techniques, and it allows filmmakers to do things that aren't possible without computers. Video editing makes massive storage and memory demands on a computer. But thanks to falling hardware prices and technological advances, even an off-the-shelf laptop PC or Mac can serve as a digital video studio.

Video-editing software, such as Adobe Premiere, Apple iMovie, and Microsoft Windows Movie Maker, makes it easy to eliminate extraneous footage, combine clips from multiple takes into coherent scenes, splice together scenes, insert visual transitions, superimpose titles, synchronize a soundtrack, and create special effects. High-end programs such as Final Cut Studio and Avid Media Composer go beyond the basics, providing professionals and serious amateurs with state-of-the-art video production tools. Just about anything is possible with these tools: color correction to compensate for a setting sun in a long shoot, chroma keying an ancient Roman background into a scene shot in front of a green screen, morphing a man into a werewolf, painting one or two frames with a surrealistic effect and applying that effect to an entire scene, and much more.

After it's edited, a video can be turned into a DVD or Blu-ray movie using software such as Apple's iDVD or Sonic's MyDVD. Video clips can also be imported into multimedia presentations using PowerPoint and other presentation programs. But many videos reach their widest audiences through the Web. TV networks, movie studios, and other businesses are distributing countless videos online—often for free. Many amateur videographers and performers distribute their works as video podcasts—programs delivered on demand or by subscription through iTunes or other Web outlets. And countless others post their work—and play—on YouTube.com and other video-friendly Web sites. YouTube has democratized video distribution like nothing that has come before it, creating instant celebrities, capturing politicians making compromising statements, and spreading ideas like viruses.

Data Compression

Digital movies can make heavy hardware demands; even a short full-screen video clip can quickly fill a hard disk or slow a digital download to a crawl. To save storage space and allow the processor to keep up with the quickly changing frames, digital movies designed for the Web are often displayed in small windows with fewer frames per second than the standard 30. In addition, data **compression** software and hardware squeeze data out of movies so they can be stored in smaller spaces, often with a

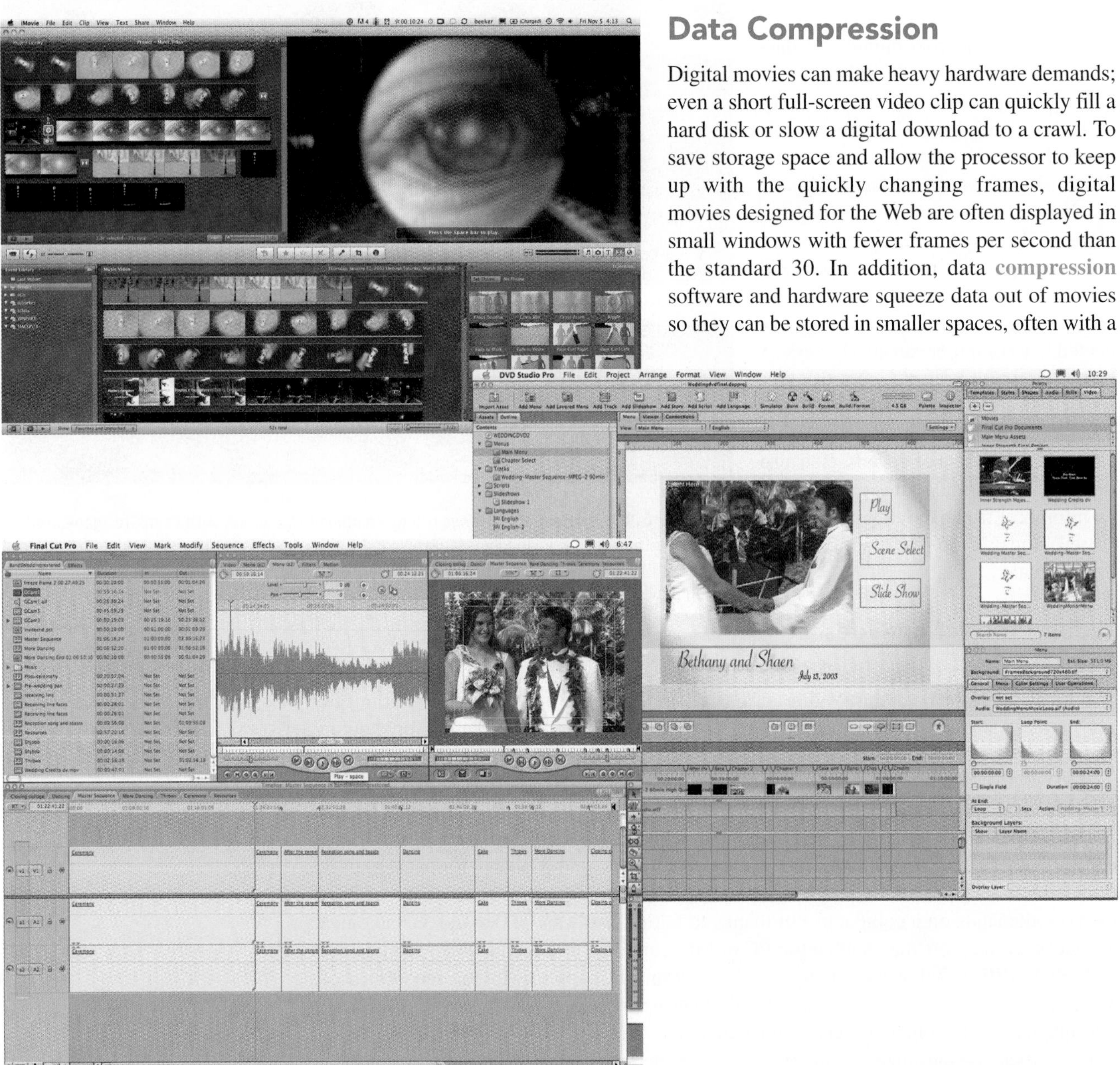

FIGURE 6.19 Software can turn a desktop or laptop computer into a video-editing and production station. Programs for non-professionals, such as those included in Apple's iLife Suite (top), make it easy to capture and edit video footage, add special effects and audio, and share final products on the Web or on DVDs. Professional tools, such Apple's Final Cut Studio, are more difficult to master, but they offer maximum power and flexibility.

FIGURE 6.20 Many Web sites deliver streaming video content to viewers with fast broadband Internet connections (left). Compressed video can also be displayed on a variety of pocket-sized devices, from iPods to cell phones (right).

slight loss of image quality, though formats such as MPEG-4 and Windows Media Video 9 reduce the problem. General data compression software can be used to reduce the size of almost any kind of data file; specialized *image-compression software* is generally used to compress graphics and video files. Modern media players, such as QuickTime and Windows Media Player, include several common software compression schemes. Some compression schemes involve specialized hardware as well as software.

Even highly compressed video clips gobble up storage space quickly. As compression and storage technologies continue to improve, digital movies are becoming larger, longer, smoother, and more common in everyday computing applications.

Low-cost desktop video systems are transforming the film and video industry in the same way that desktop publishing has revolutionized the world of the printed word. They're also making it possible for individuals, schools, and small businesses to create near-professional-quality videos.

The Synthetic Musician: Computers and Audio

> It's easy to play any musical instrument: all you have to do is **touch the right key at the right time and the instrument will play itself.**
>
> —*J. S. Bach*

Sound and music can turn a visual presentation into an activity that involves the ears, the eyes, and the whole brain. For many applications, sound puts the *multi* in *multimedia.* Computer sounds can be sampled—digitally recorded—or **synthesized**—synthetically generated. Today's computers can produce sounds that go far beyond the basic beeps of early computers.

Digital Audio Basics

An **audio digitizer** can record just about any sound as a **sample**—a digital sound file. Digitized sound data, like other computer data, can be loaded into the computer's memory and manipulated by software. Sound-editing software can change a sound's volume and pitch, add special effects such as echoes, remove extraneous noises, and even rearrange musical passages. Sound data is sometimes called *waveform audio* because this kind of editing often involves manipulating a visual image of the sound's waveform. To play a digitized sound, the computer must load the data file into memory, convert it to an analog sound, and play it through a speaker.

how it works Data Compression

Graphic images, digital video, and sound files can consume massive amounts of storage space on disk and in memory; they can also be slow to transmit over computer networks. Data-compression technology allows large files to be temporarily squeezed to reduce the amount of storage space and network transmission time they require. Before you can use them, you must decompress compressed files. (In the physical world, many companies "compress" goods to save storage and transportation costs: When you "just add water" to a can of concentrated orange juice, you're "decompressing" the juice.)

All forms of compression involve removing bits; the trick is to remove bits that can be replaced when the file can be restored. Different compression techniques work best for different types of data.

Suppose you want to store or transmit a large text file. Your text compression software might follow steps similar to those shown here:

1. Each character in the uncompressed ASCII file occupies eight bits; a seven-character word—*invoice,* for example—requires 56 bits of storage.

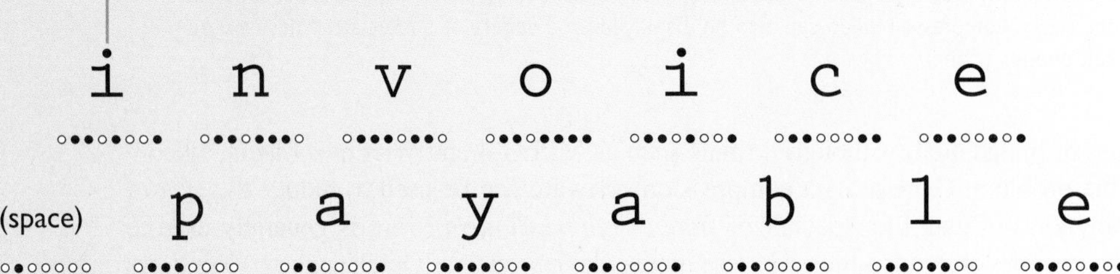

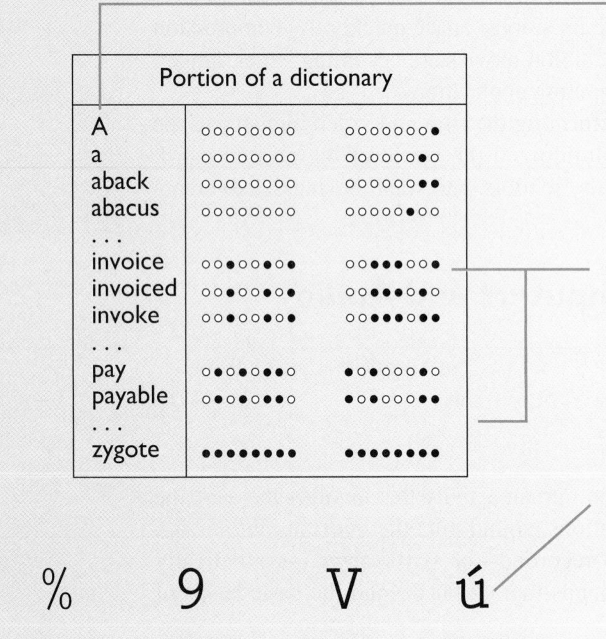

2. A two-byte binary number can contain code values ranging from 0 to 65,535—enough codes to stand for every commonly used word in English. This partial code dictionary shows the code values for a few words, including *invoice* and *payable*.
3. To compress a file using a code dictionary, the computer looks up every word in the original file; in this example, *invoice* and *payable*. It replaces each word with its two-byte code value. In this example, they are % 9 and V ú. The seven-character word now takes up only 16 bits—less than one-third of its original size.
4. In a compressed file, these two-byte code values would be used to store or transmit the information for *invoice* and *payable,* using fewer bits of information either to increase storage capacity or to decrease transmission time.
5. To reverse the process of compression, the same dictionary (or an identical one on another computer) is used to decompress the file, creating an exact copy of the original. A computer program quickly performs all the tedious dictionary lookup.

FIGURE 6.21

Compression programs work on patterns of bits rather than on English words. One type of video compression stores values for pixels that change from one frame to the next; there's no need to store values repeatedly for pixels that are the same in every frame. For example, the only pixels that change in these two pictures are the ones that represent the unicycle and the shadows. In general, compression works because most raw data files contain redundancy that can be "squeezed out."

Lossless compression systems allow a file to be compressed and later decompressed without any loss of data; the decompressed file will be an identical copy of the original file. Popular lossless compression systems include ZIP, TAR, and DMG. GIF is a specialized lossless compression system for graphical images. A *lossy compression* system can usually achieve better compression than a lossless one, but it may lose some information in the process; the decompressed file isn't always identical to the original. This is tolerable in many types of sound, graphics, and video files but not for most program and data files. JPEG is a popular lossy compression system for graphics files.

MPEG is a popular compression system for audio and video. (MP3 and AAC are forms of MPEG compression that are widely used for digital audio.) An MPEG file takes just a fraction of the space of an uncompressed audio or video file. Because decompression programs demand time and processing power, the playback of compressed video files can sometimes be jerky or slow. Many professional video workstations get around the problem with MPEG hardware boards that specialize in compression and decompression, leaving the CPU free for other tasks.

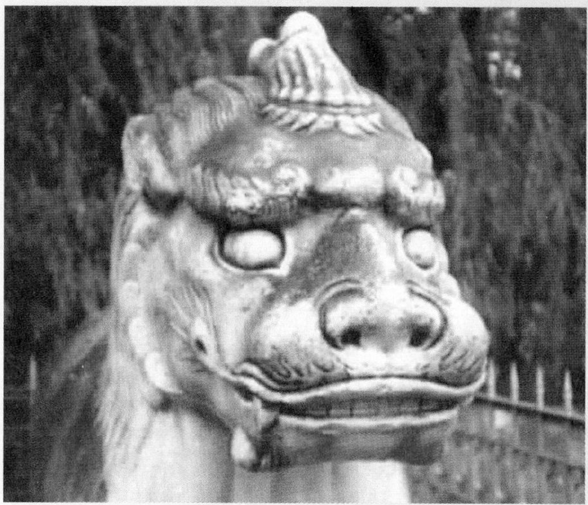

The original photographic image (above) has an uncompressed size of 725 KB. With aggressive JPEG compression, the image on the right occupies only 1/38 as much disk space (19 KB), but looks almost as good.

Recorded sound can consume massive amounts of space on disk and in memory. As you might expect, higher-quality sound reproduction generally requires more memory. The difference is due in part to differences in *sampling rate*—the number of sound "snapshots" the recording equipment takes each second. A higher sampling rate produces more realistic digital sounds in the same way that higher resolution produces more realistic digital photographs; it allows for more accurate modeling of the analog source. The number of bits per sample—usually 8, 16, or 24—also affects the quality of the sound; this is similar to a digital photograph's bit depth.

Music is digitized on audio CDs at a high sampling rate and bit depth—high enough that it's hard to tell the difference between the original analog sound and the final digital recording. Because computers can read standard audio CDs, it's easy to *rip*, or copy, songs from a CD to the computer's hard drive, and *burn*, or create, audio CDs containing ripped songs.

But CD audio is memory intensive; a three-minute song takes about 30 megabytes of space on a compact disc. Files that large can be expensive to store and slow to transmit through networks. That's why many sound files are compressed during or after the recording process. Sound data compression, like image compression, can significantly shrink a file's size with little loss of quality from the listener's point of view. Several popular compression technologies, including MP3 (MPEG-1 Audio Layer 3), *AAC* (Advanced Audio Codec), and *WMA* (Windows Media Audio), can squeeze audio files to a fraction of their original CD file sizes with only a slight loss of fidelity. Compression makes it practical to transmit recordings through the Internet, store them on hard disks, and play them on phones and other pocket-sized devices.

Free music files are available on hundreds of Web sites. Many are contributed by undiscovered musicians who want exposure. Others are ripped from CDs and distributed through illicit *peer-to-peer (P2P) file sharing* networks (giving a new meaning to the old phrase *ripped off*). Internet music piracy has taken a serious toll on the industry, robbing musicians and record companies and forcing the closure of countless record stores. But the net has also provided new legal channels for distributing music. Apple's iTunes Music Store, the giant of this emerging industry, has sold billions of songs, becoming one of the world's biggest music retailers in the process. Customers play their purchases on their computers, burn them to CDs, and download them into iPods and other portable music players. Many competitors follow Apple's pay-by-the-song model; others rent access to music libraries on a month-by-month basis. Audio files are also distributed as podcasts—radio-style programs that can be downloaded on demand or automatically by subscription. (Ethical and legal issues raised by digital audio files will be discussed in more detail in Chapters 9 and 10.)

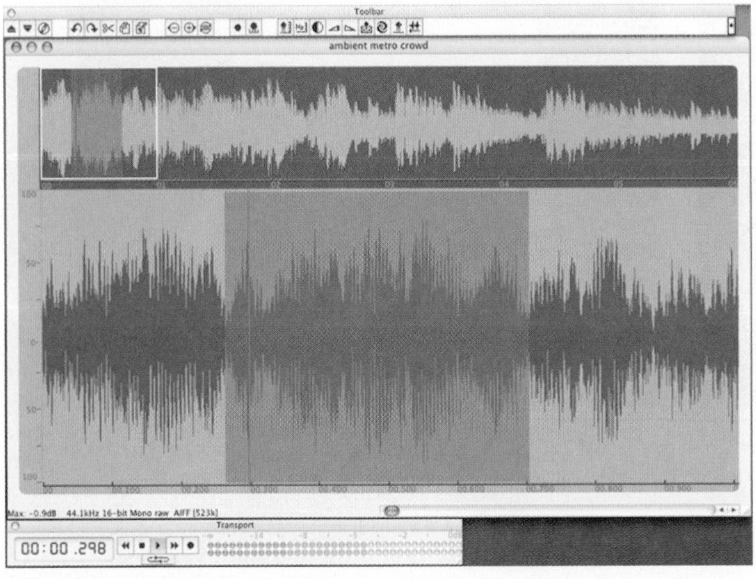

FIGURE 6.22 You can edit waveform audio files in a variety of ways using software tools such as Peak, from Bias, Inc.

Samplers, Synthesizers, and Sequencers: Digital Audio and MIDI

Multimedia computers can control a variety of electronic musical instruments and sound sources using Musical Instrument Digital Interface (MIDI)—a standard interface used to send commands between computers and musical instruments. MIDI commands can be interpreted by a variety of music *synthesizers* (electronic instruments that synthesize sounds using mathematical formulas), *samplers* (instruments that can digitize, or sample, audio sounds, turn them into notes, and play them back at any pitch), and hybrid instruments that play sounds that are part sampled and part synthesized. But most PCs can also interpret and execute MIDI commands using

Working Wisdom Digital Audio Do's and Don'ts

Whether you are digitizing your audio CD collection or are subscribing to an online music service, your digital audio experiences will go more smoothly if you understand a few simple rules.

- ***Don't steal.*** It's OK to copy audio CDs to your PC, use those songs on portable audio devices, and mix CDs you create, but only if you own the originals. If you believe that people should be fairly compensated for their work, don't "borrow" music from a friend or steal music online.
- ***Understand downloading and streaming.*** Music is typically delivered from the Web to your computer in one of three ways: downloadable audio, streaming audio, and pseudo-streaming audio. When you download an audio file (for example, from the iTunes Music Store or a band's Web site), your computer stores the entire file on its hard disk. Once the file is transferred from the server to your computer, it can be played by an application (such as iTunes), copied to another device (such as an iPod or a smart phone), backed up, used in a video project, burned to a CD, or edited, depending on the rights granted by the DRM (discussed next). Streaming audio—the type typically used by Internet radio stations—isn't downloaded to your computer's hard disk. Instead, it's played as it is being delivered to your computer. Once a segment of the audio file is played, it disappears from your computer's memory. Pseudo-streaming audio is downloaded to your hard disk, but it begins playing shortly after the first part of the file is transmitted.
- ***Know your file formats.*** Uncompressed audio CD files can gobble up hard disk space at an alarming rate. The MP3 compression format is popular because it produces files that sound almost identical to uncompressed audio files. But MP3 isn't the only popular audio compression format. Many audio files are stored in AAC format used by iTunes or Microsoft's WMA format. A music file compressed with AAC or WMA technology can have better sound quality than a comparable MP3 file. AAC and WMA also offer options for including *digital rights management (DRM)* technology in compressed files. A file compressed with DRM is protected against casual copying to protect the artists' intellectual property. Today most legally purchased audio files are DRM-free, so they can be freely moved between devices.
- ***Don't overcompress.*** Audio compression is lossy, so there's always a loss of quality when you compress a sound file. There's no way to put back the bits that you squeeze out in the compression process. Most people can't distinguish between a 160 Kbps MP3 file or a 128 Mbps AAC or WMA file and an original audio CD recording. But if you choose too low a bit rate when compressing a file, you may squeeze the life out of the music.
- ***Protect your ears.*** The most important tool in your audio toolkit is your ears, and they can't be replaced or upgraded. Loud music or noise—especially if it's prolonged—can do permanent damage to your eardrums. Do what you need to do to protect them. Keep the volume low in your studio and on your MP3 player. Use earplugs with tight seals if you're in a loud environment where you can't control the volume.

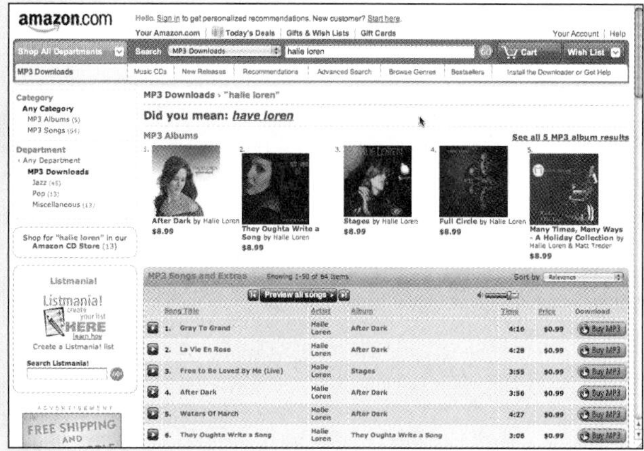

FIGURE 6.23b The Amazon store sells MP3 music files that are compatible with a wide variety of computers, music players, and smart phones.

Format	Description
WAV, AIFF	Standard formats for uncompressed audio for Windows and the Mac OS, respectively. Both formats are supported on Windows, Mac OS, and Linux. Both create large files. Both are lossless—a CD track encoded with WAV or AIFF sounds identical to the original.
MP3	A popular format for transmitting audio on the Internet. A CD track converted to MP3 format can be 1/10 the size of the original—or smaller—but still sound very similar.
WMA	An alternative to MP3 developed by Microsoft for Windows. WMA compression can result in smaller files of higher fidelity. WMA files may be protected by DRM.
AAC	Apple's alternative to MP3 and WMA is used primarily by iTunes and the iTunes Music Store. AAC compression is sonically superior to MP3 compression. AAC files may be protected with DRM.
OGG	Similar to WMA and AAC in sound quality and compression, Ogg Vorbis is open source and freely available—not controlled by any company.

FIGURE 6.23a Popular digital audio formats.

sampled sounds built into their hardware or stored in software form. Whether the sounds are played back on external instruments or internal devices, the computer doesn't need to store the entire recording in memory or on disk; it just has to store commands to play the notes in the proper sequence. A MIDI file containing the MIDI messages for a song or soundtrack requires only a few kilobytes of memory.

Anyone with even marginal piano-playing skills can create MIDI music files. A piano-style keyboard sends MIDI signals to the computer, which interprets the sequence of MIDI commands using **sequencing software**. (While the keyboard is the most common MIDI controller for sequencing, MIDI communication capabilities are built into other types of instruments, including drums, guitars, and wind instruments.) Sequencing software turns a computer into a musical composing, recording, and editing machine. The computer records MIDI signals as a musician plays each part on a MIDI controller. The musician can use the computer to layer instrumental tracks, substitute instrument sounds, edit notes, cut and paste passages, transpose keys, and change tempos, listening to each change as it's made. The finished composition can be played by the sequencing software or exported to any other MIDI-compatible software, including a variety of multimedia applications.

Music recording and composition software isn't limited to sequencing MIDI commands; most programs can record digital audio tracks as well as MIDI tracks, making it possible to include voices and nonelectronic instruments in the mix. The audio and MIDI data is recorded directly onto the computer's hard disk, making tape unnecessary.

A typical electronic music studio includes a variety of synthesizers, samplers, and other instruments. But the trend today is to replace many bulky, expensive hardware devices with ***virtual instruments***—instruments that exist only in software. With today's powerful CPUs and massive storage devices, it's possible to have a professional-level multitrack recording and editing studio that fits in a suitcase.

Most musicians today use ***DAW (digital audio workstation)*** software that incorporates sequencing, recording, and mixing capabilities in a single program. **Mixing** involves combining multiple tracks, adding audio effects, and balancing volumes and audio placement for the best possible recording. The final mix might take the form of a mono recording for a podcast, a stereo recording for a CD, a multichannel surround sound mix for a movie soundtrack, or something else. Some audio artists specialize in creating ***remixes***—complete reworking of songs using fresh instrumentation, rhythms, and audio samples.

Professional musicians use computers for composing, performing, recording, mixing, and publishing music, and for educating would-be musicians. Digital audio technology cuts across genres; it's used for everything from Bach to rock. The technology has spawned whole new branches of music that fit loosely into a category called ***electronica***—music designed from the ground up with digital technology. Just as computer graphics technology has changed the way many artists work, electronic music technology has transformed the world of the musician. What's more, computer music technology has the power to unleash the musician in the rest of us.

FIGURE 6.24 Digital audio technology has revolutionized the music recording process for hobbyists and professionals alike.

FIGURE 6.25 Music software allows musicians to put Mac and Windows PCs to work in a variety of ways. Serato Scratch Live (top) is a software/hardware package that enables DJs to mix music from hard drives using turntables as control devices. Pro Tools (middle) is widely used for recording, sequencing, and editing music. Sibelius (bottom) is a music notation program that can create sheet music from MIDI files and other sources.

how it works Computer-Based Music Production

Music-processing software comes in a variety of forms, but most programs are built on the same fundamental concepts. A musical composition is typically made up of several tracks that represent individual instrumental and vocal parts. For example, a song might have a lead vocal track, a guitar track, a bass track, a drum track, and three backup vocal tracks. You can record and edit each of these tracks separately; you can play them back in any combination.

A software mixer can adjust the relative volumes to achieve the desired balance before you mix the piece down to a final digital stereo recording. The same principles apply for acoustic, electric, or electronic music; the differences between these types of music are reflected mainly in the way the individual tracks are created and stored. Most software can work with two kinds of tracks: digital audio samples, represented as waveforms, and MIDI sequences, depicted as a series of bars representing notes.

1. Real-world instruments and sounds can be sampled by plugging an instrument or microphone into the sound in port on the computer. You can also buy professionally recorded samples and legally use them in your music productions.

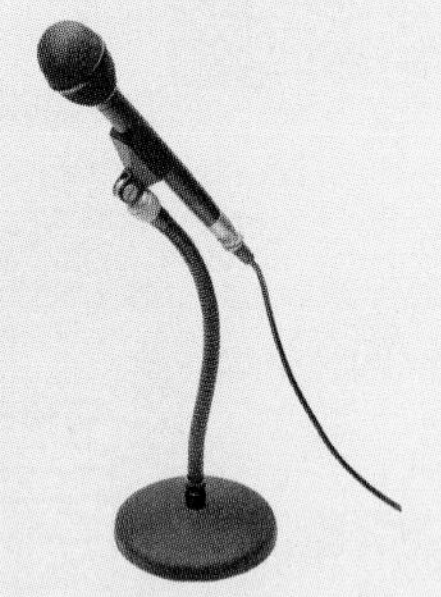

2. Any sample, such as this recording of a percussionist playing a drum kit, can be looped, so that the sample repeats as many times as necessary to reach the desired length.

3. Because waveforms are stored as a series of numbers, many music production tools use math to manipulate those numbers and alter qualities, such as the tempo, pitch, and volume of the recording.

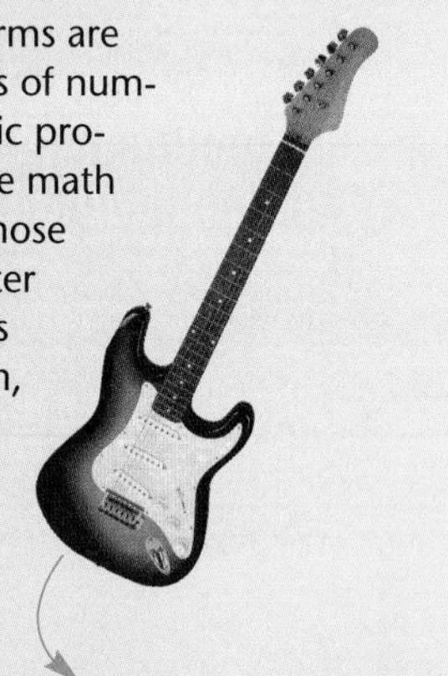

4. Software-based filters can be used to manipulate the sonic qualities of your samples and loops; this particular effect lends an acoustic, echo-filled, ethereal quality to the guitar part.

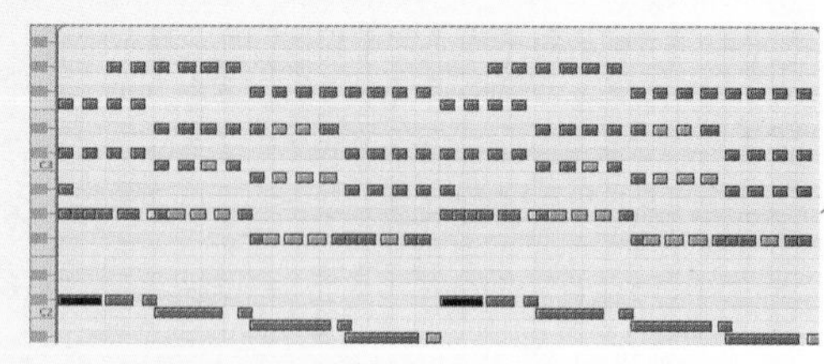

5. MIDI instruments send performance information, such as when and where each note is played in a sequence and how hard each note is struck. Because MIDI stores your performance as a series of notes rather than an audio sample, you are able to later correct notes, transpose to a different key, alter the tempo, and even change the instrument used to play back your performance. You can easily correct for human error using a feature known as quantizing, which cleans up the timing of a passage by "rounding off" performance data to the nearest points on the rhythmic grid.

FIGURE 6.26

6. Software allows you to control characteristics of sound over time. For example, the master volume controller fades the song out as it nears the song's end.

7. A finished composition can be output in a variety of forms.

8. The final mix can be exported as a stereo waveform.

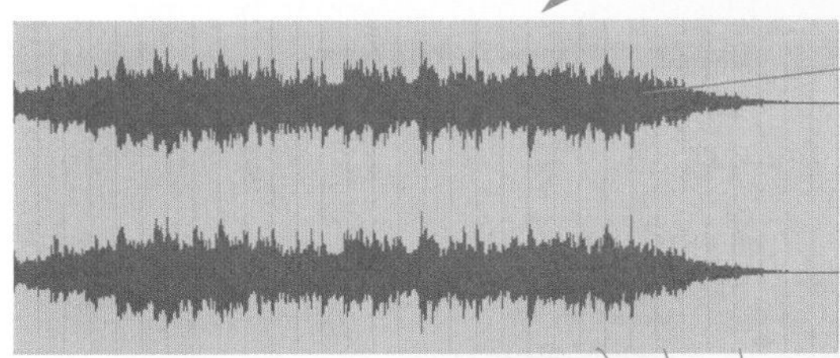

11. Compression software can produce a much smaller sound file.

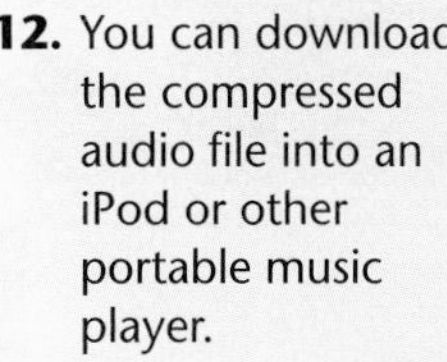

12. You can download the compressed audio file into an iPod or other portable music player.

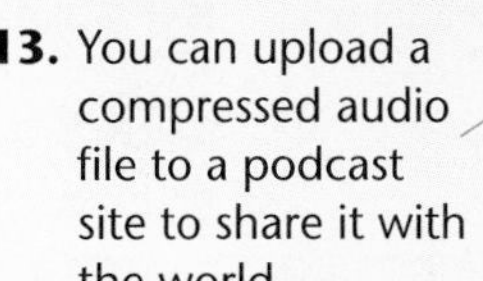

9. Speakers or headphones attached to the computer provide the most direct output, giving the composer and performers immediate sonic feedback.

10. You can burn the stereo file onto an audio CD.

13. You can upload a compressed audio file to a podcast site to share it with the world.

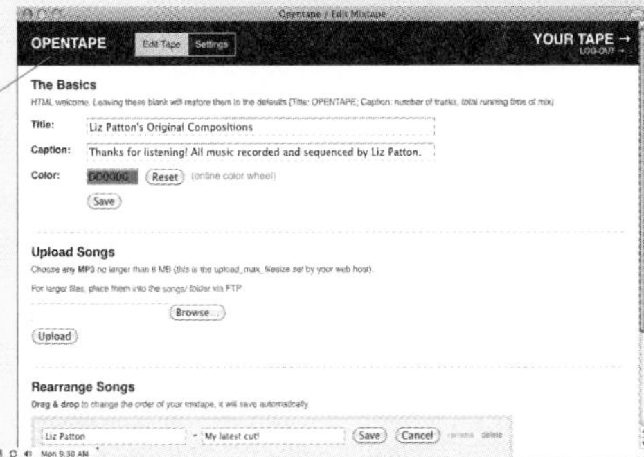

14. You can import the audio file into a video-editing program for use in a movie soundtrack.

Screen Test — Multimedia on a Student Budget

Professional multimedia software can be very expensive. It's not unusual to pay hundreds—or even thousands—of dollars for state-of-the-art software tools for creating and manipulating graphic images, animation, video, or audio files. If you're creative but cash-poor, you can take advantage of many free alternatives to the big-ticket packages. Here's a sampler:

For photo library organization and basic image editing, it's hard to beat iPhoto (left), part of the iLife suite that ships with every Mac. Google Picasa (above) is a free program with similar capabilities for Windows and Mac. Picasa also allows you to organize, edit, and post videos to YouTube.

For cloud-based photo retouching, Splashup.com offers a sophisticated palette-based interface patterned after Photoshop.

Blender 3-D is a cross-platform 3-D modeling and rendering tool.

FIGURE 6.27

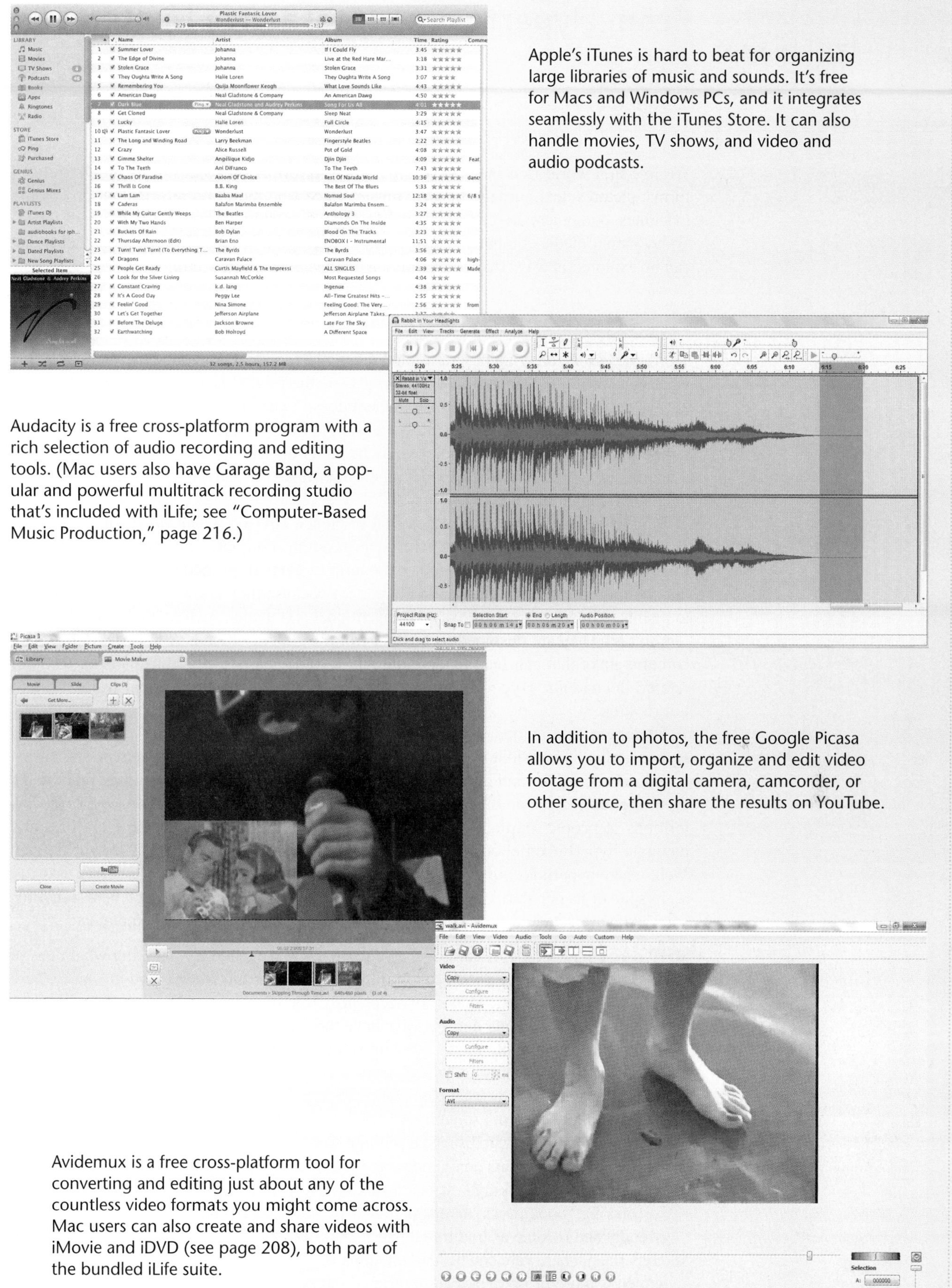

Apple's iTunes is hard to beat for organizing large libraries of music and sounds. It's free for Macs and Windows PCs, and it integrates seamlessly with the iTunes Store. It can also handle movies, TV shows, and video and audio podcasts.

Audacity is a free cross-platform program with a rich selection of audio recording and editing tools. (Mac users also have Garage Band, a popular and powerful multitrack recording studio that's included with iLife; see "Computer-Based Music Production," page 216.)

In addition to photos, the free Google Picasa allows you to import, organize and edit video footage from a digital camera, camcorder, or other source, then share the results on YouTube.

Avidemux is a free cross-platform tool for converting and editing just about any of the countless video formats you might come across. Mac users can also create and share videos with iMovie and iDVD (see page 208), both part of the bundled iLife suite.

From Hypertext to Interactive Multimedia

The hybrid or the meeting of two media is **a moment of truth and revelation from which a new form is born.**

—*Marshall McLuhan, in* Understanding Media: The Extensions of Man

We live in a world rich in sensory experience. Information comes to us in a variety of forms: pictures, text, moving images, music, voice, and more. As information-processing machines, computers are capable of delivering information to our senses in many forms. Today's multimedia computers allow users to work with information-rich documents that can be explored in ways that could only be imaged a generation ago.

Hypertext and Hypermedia

Word processors, drawing programs, and most other applications today are WYSIWYG—what you see (on the screen) is what you get (on the printed page). But WYSIWYG isn't always necessary or desirable. If a document doesn't need to be printed, it doesn't need to be structured like a paper document. If we want to focus on the relationship between ideas rather than the layout of the page, we may be better off with another kind of document—a dynamic, cross-referenced super document that takes full advantage of the computer's interactive capabilities.

Since 1945 when President Roosevelt's science advisor, Vannevar Bush, first wrote about such an interactive cross-referenced system, computer pioneers such as Doug Engelbart and Ted Nelson, who coined the term **hypertext**, pushed the technology toward that vision. Early efforts were called hypertext because they allowed textual information to be linked in ***nonsequential*** ways. Conventional text media, such as books, are linear, or ***sequential***: They are designed to be read from beginning to end. A hypertext document contains links that can lead readers quickly to other parts of the document or to other related documents. Hypertext invites readers to cut their own personal trails through information.

Hypertext first gained widespread public attention in 1987 when Apple introduced HyperCard, a hypermedia system that could combine text, numbers, graphics, animation, sound effects, music, and other media in hyperlinked documents. (Depending on how it's used, the term **hypermedia** might be synonymous with interactive multimedia.) Today, millions of people routinely use hypertext whenever they consult online Help files and navigate hyperlinked ebooks. But the biggest hypermedia platform is the World Wide Web, where hyperlinks connect documents all over the Internet.

In spite of its popularity, hypertext won't completely replace paper documents any time soon. Web users and others who use hypertext have several legitimate complaints:

- Hypermedia documents can be disorienting and leave readers wondering what they've missed. When you're reading a book, you always know where you are and where you've been in the text. That's not necessarily true in hypermedia.
- Hypermedia documents don't always have the links readers want. Hypermedia authors can't build every possible connection into their documents, so some readers are frustrated because they can't easily get "there" from "here." How can writers develop effective plot lines if they don't know what path their readers will choose through their stories?
- Hypermedia documents sometimes contain "lost" links, especially on the Web, where even a popular page can disappear without a trace.
- Hypermedia documents don't encourage scribbled margin notes, highlighting, or turned page corners for marking key passages. Some hypermedia documents provide controls for making "bookmarks" and text fields for adding personal notes, but they aren't as friendly and flexible as traditional paper mark-up tools.
- Hypermedia hardware can be hard on humans. Most people find that reading a computer screen is more tiring than reading printed pages, although modern font-rendering software seeks to reduce this problem. Many people complain that extended periods of screen

gazing cause eyestrain, headache, backache, and other ailments. Research suggests that hypermedia links in a document can distract readers and reduce their ability to remember what they've read.

The art of hypermedia is still in its infancy. Every new art form takes time to develop. It will only get better as writers and artists learn more about how to create interactive works, from basic hypertext documents to interactive multimedia masterpieces thoroughly interwoven into our lives, as technologies and techniques improve.

Interactive Multimedia: Eye, Ear, Hand, and Mind

The term **multimedia** generally means using some combination of text, graphics, animation, video, music, voice, and sound effects to communicate. By this definition an episode of *Sesame Street* or the evening news might be considered multimedia. In fact, computer-based multimedia tools are used heavily in the production of *Sesame Street,* the evening news, and hundreds of other television programs. Entertainment-industry professionals use computers to create animated sequences, display titles, construct special video effects, synthesize music, edit soundtracks, coordinate communication, and perform dozens of other tasks crucial to the production of modern television programs and motion pictures.

So when you watch a typical TV program, you're experiencing a multimedia product. With each second that passes, you are bombarded with millions of bits of information. But television and video are passive media; they pour information into our eyes and ears while we sit and take it all in. We have no control over the information flow. Modern computer technology allows information to move in both directions, turning multimedia into interactive multimedia. Unlike TV, radio, and video, **interactive multimedia** allows the viewer/listener to take an active part in the experience. The best interactive multimedia software puts the user in charge, allowing that person to control the information flow.

Interactive multimedia software is delivered to consumers on a variety of platforms. Today, multimedia computers equipped with fast processors, large memories, optical drives, speakers, and wireless Internet connections are everywhere. Thousands of education and entertainment multimedia programs are available on CD-ROM and DVD-ROM for these machines. Many more multimedia software titles are designed to be used with TVs and controlled by game machines and other *set-top boxes* from Sony, Microsoft, Nintendo, and other companies. Many multimedia documents are created for use in kiosks in stores, museums, and other public places. A typical multimedia kiosk is a PC-in-a-box with a touch screen instead of a keyboard and mouse for collecting input.

Interactive multimedia materials are all over the Web, too. Multimedia on the Web today is full

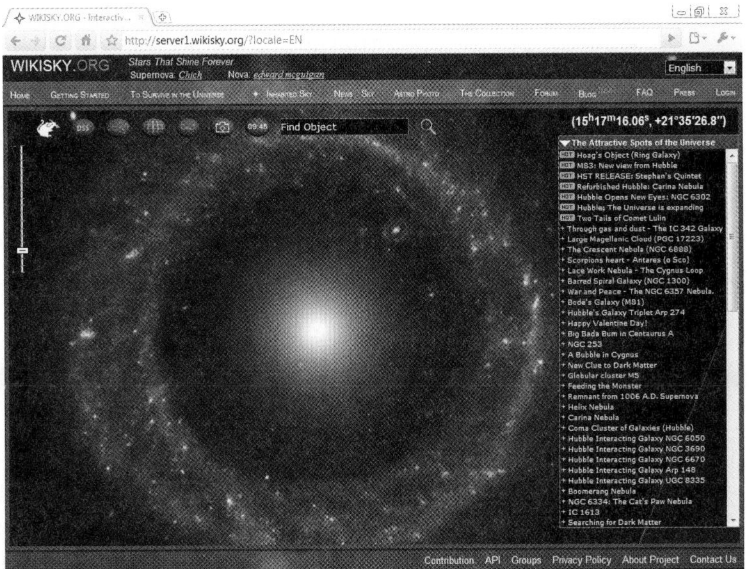

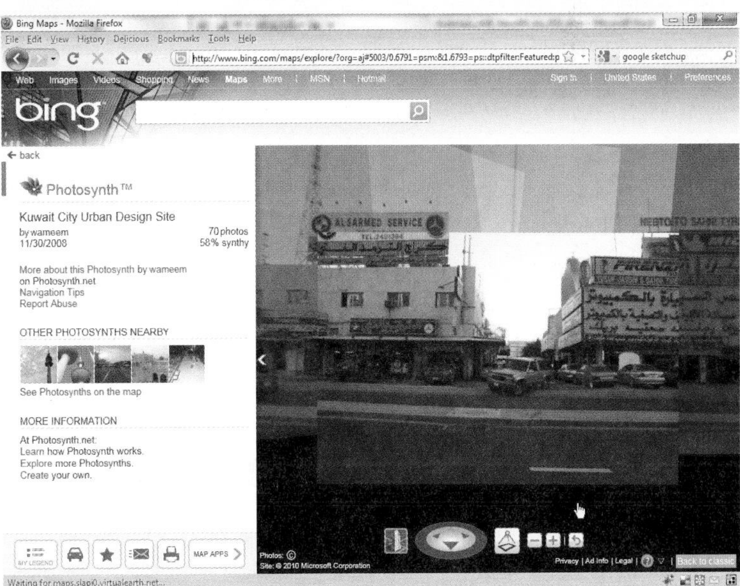

FIGURE 6.28 Interactive multimedia experiences often combine education with entertainment. Wikisky is an online map of the heavens that's updated and enhanced by other users. Bing's Photosynths automatically stitch together user-uploaded images from the same location into interactive 3-D panoramas combining information from all of the perspectives.

of compromises because many of today's Web pipelines can't deliver large media files quickly enough. Still, Web technology is improving rapidly, and more people are connecting to the Net with faster broadband technology, making many experts wonder whether disk-based multimedia will soon be unnecessary. In the meantime, cable, telephone, and other companies are rushing to provide multimedia services, including video on demand.

Multimedia Authoring: Making Mixed Media

> Style used to be an interaction between the human soul and tools that were limiting. **In the digital era, it will have to come from the soul alone.**
>
> —*Jaron Lanier, virtual reality pioneer*

Multimedia-authoring software is used to create and edit multimedia documents. Similar to desktop publishing, interactive multimedia authoring involves combining source documents—including graphics, text files, video clips, and sounds—in an aesthetically pleasing format that communicates with the user. Multimedia-authoring software, like page-layout software, serves as glue that binds documents created and captured with other applications. But since a multimedia document can change in response to user input, authoring involves specifying not just *what* and *where* but also *when* and *why*. Some authoring programs are designed for professionals. Others are designed for children. Many are used by both.

The presentation-graphics program PowerPoint uses a slideshow metaphor, with each screen being represented by one slide. PowerPoint was designed as a tool for creating linear presentations, but it includes capabilities for adding hyperlinks. The World Wide Web uses metaphorical pages to represent screens of information; many authoring tools are designed specifically to create Web pages. Adobe Flash, a popular tool for creating multimedia Web applications, has a different kind of user interface with a timeline similar to those seen in video-editing software. A Flash document is like an interactive movie. A link can transport a user to another frame of a movie rather than to another card or page.

The authoring tool's interface metaphor is important to the person creating the multimedia document, but not to the person viewing the finished document, who sees only the user interface that was built into the document by the author.

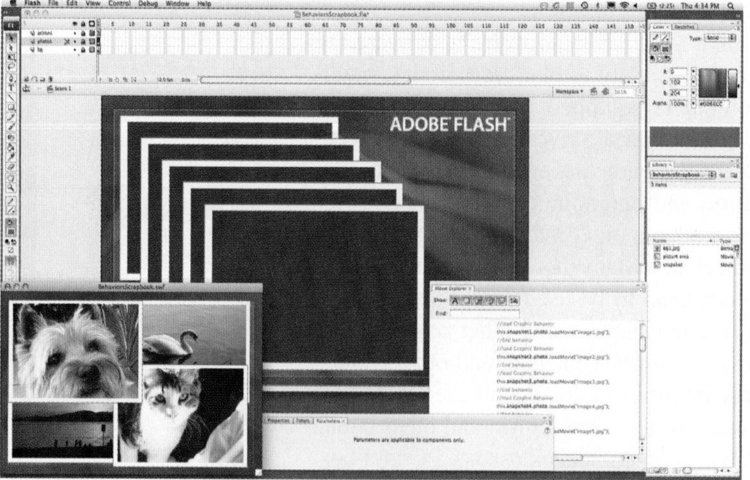

FIGURE 6.29 Multimedia authoring involves programming objects on the screen to react, or behave, in particular ways under particular circumstances. Adobe Flash allows you to create advanced interactivity using scripts and prewritten behaviors that can be attached to on-screen buttons, images, and other objects.

Working Wisdom Creating an Effective Interactive Experience

Whether you're creating a simple presentation or a full-blown multimedia extravaganza, your finished product will communicate more effectively if you follow a few simple guidelines:

- ***Be consistent.*** Group similar controls together, and maintain a consistent visual appearance throughout the presentation.
- ***Make it intuitive.*** Use graphical metaphors to guide viewers, and make your controls do what they look like they should do.
- ***Strive for simplicity.*** A clean, uncluttered screen is more inviting than a crowded one—and easier to understand, too.
- ***Keep it lively.*** If your presentation doesn't include motion, sound, or user interaction, it probably should be printed and distributed as a paper document.
- ***The message is more important than the media.*** Your goal is to communicate information, not saturate the senses. Don't let the bells and whistles get in the way of your message.
- ***Put the user in the driver's seat.*** Include controls for turning down sound, bypassing repetitive animation, and turning off annoying features. Provide navigation aids, search tools, bookmarks, online help, and "Where am I?" feedback. Never tell the user, "You can't get there from here."
- ***Let real people test your designs.*** The best way to find out whether your multimedia works is to test it on people who aren't familiar with the subject. If they get lost or bored, find out why, fix the problem, and test it again.

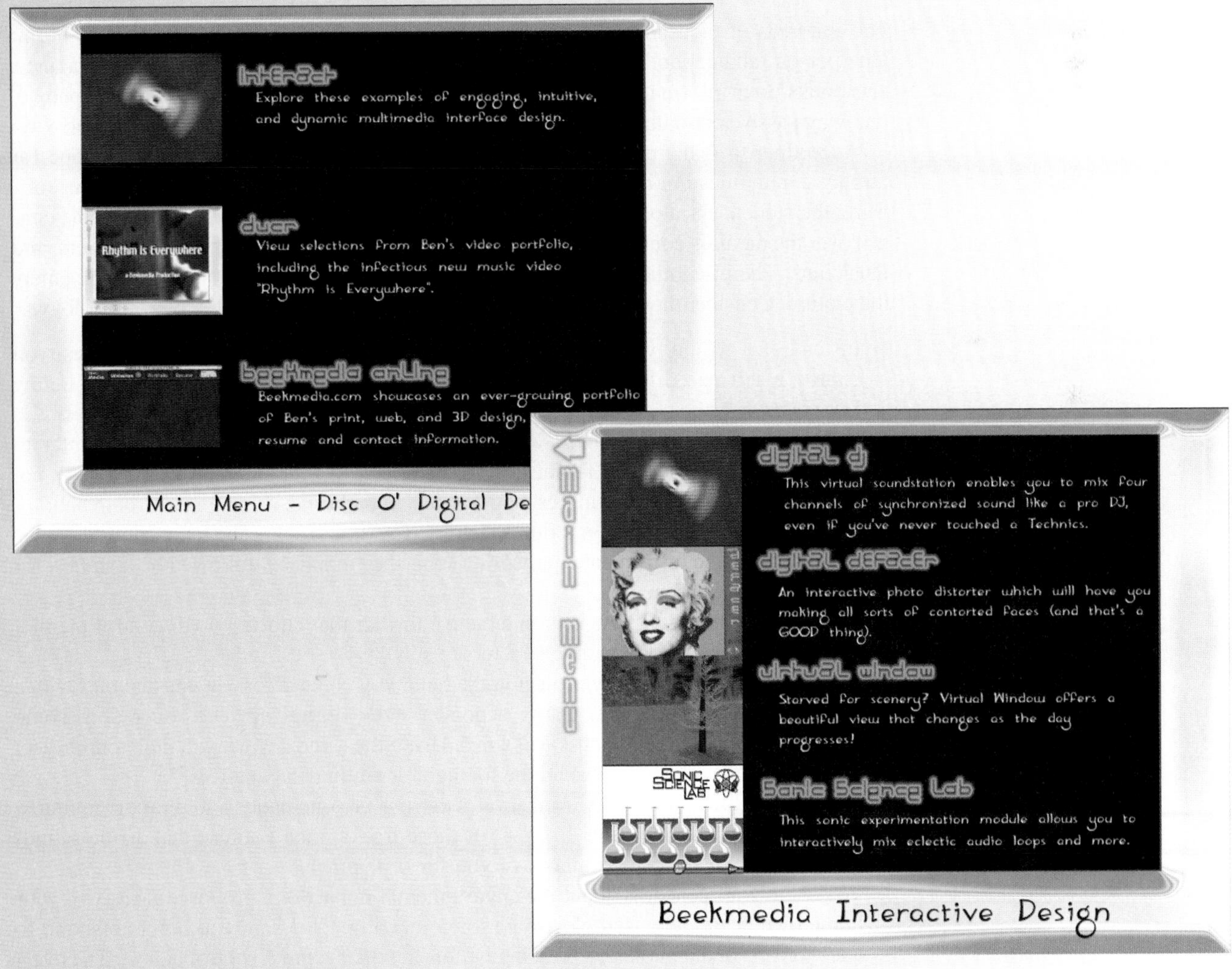

FIGURE 6.30 These two screens from a multimedia CD-ROM portfolio use interactive motion menus and a consistent, intuitive user interface to guide the user through the disk's contents.

In the twenty-first century the Web has replaced CD-ROMs as the most popular multimedia platform. But even with compression, the Internet isn't fast enough to deliver the high-quality audio and video that's possible with a local disc. On the other hand, the contents of a disc are static; they can't be continually updated like a Web site. And CD-ROMs don't offer opportunities for communication with other people the way a Web site can. Many multimedia manufacturers today produce hybrid discs—media-rich CD-ROMs and DVD-ROMs that automatically draw content and communication from the Web.

Many of the problems with hypertext and hypermedia outlined earlier are even more serious when multiple media are involved. Still, the best multimedia productions transcend these problems and show the promise of this emerging technology.

Interactive Media: Visions of the Future

> For most of recorded history, the interactions of humans with their media have been primarily passive in the sense that marks on paper, paint on walls, even motion pictures and television, do not change in response to the viewer's wishes. [But computers can] respond to queries and experiments—so that **the message may involve the learner in a two-way conversation.**
>
> —*Alan Kay*

For hundreds of thousands of years, two-way interactive communication was the norm: One person talked, another responded. Today television, radio, newspapers, magazines, and books pour information into billions of passive people every day. For many people, one-way passive communication has become more common than interactive discourse.

According to many experts, interactive multimedia technology offers new hope for turning communication back into a participatory sport. With interactive multimedia software, the audience is a part of the show. Interactive multimedia tools can give people control over the media—control traditionally reserved for professional artists, filmmakers, and musicians. The possibilities are far reaching, especially when telecommunication enters the picture. Consider these snapshots, all of which are possible with today's technology.

- Instead of watching your history professor flip through overhead transparencies, you control a self-paced interactive presentation complete with video footage illustrating key concepts.
- Using an electronic whiteboard, a professor's writings are automatically transmitted to your wireless notebook or Tablet PC, allowing you to take notes on what he says, not what he writes. Students can present questions in real time, using an electronic ballot.
- In your electronic mailbox you find a "letter" from your sister. The letter shows her performing all of the instrumental parts for a song she composed, followed by a request for you to add a vocal line.
- Your favorite Internet show is an interactive thriller that allows you to control the plot twists and work with the main characters to solve mysteries.
- While working on a biology project in the field, you come across an unusual bird with a song you don't recognize. Using a pocket-sized digital device, you record some audio/video footage of the bird as it sings. Using the same device, you dial your project partner's phone number and send the footage for editing and analysis.
- You legally download tracks from several of your favorite bands and remix them into a mashup combining elements from all of those tracks; then you use that as the soundtrack for a reedited scene from one of your favorite movies.
- You share your concerns about the environmental impact of a proposed factory in your hometown at the televised electronic town meeting. Thousands of others respond to questions from the mayor by pressing buttons on their remote control panels. The overwhelming citizen response forces the city council to reconsider the proposal.

Of course, the future of interactive multimedia may not be all sunshine and roses. Many experts fear that these exciting new media possibilities will further remove us from books, other people, and the natural world around us. If television today can mesmerize so many people, will tomorrow's interactive multimedia TVs cause even more serious addiction problems? Or will interactive communication breathe new life into the media and the people who use them? Will interactive electronic media make it easier for abusers of power to influence and control unwary citizens, or will the power of the push button create a new kind of digital democracy? Will interactive digital technology just turn "sound bites" into "sound bytes," or will it unleash the creative potential in the people who use it? For answers, stay tuned.

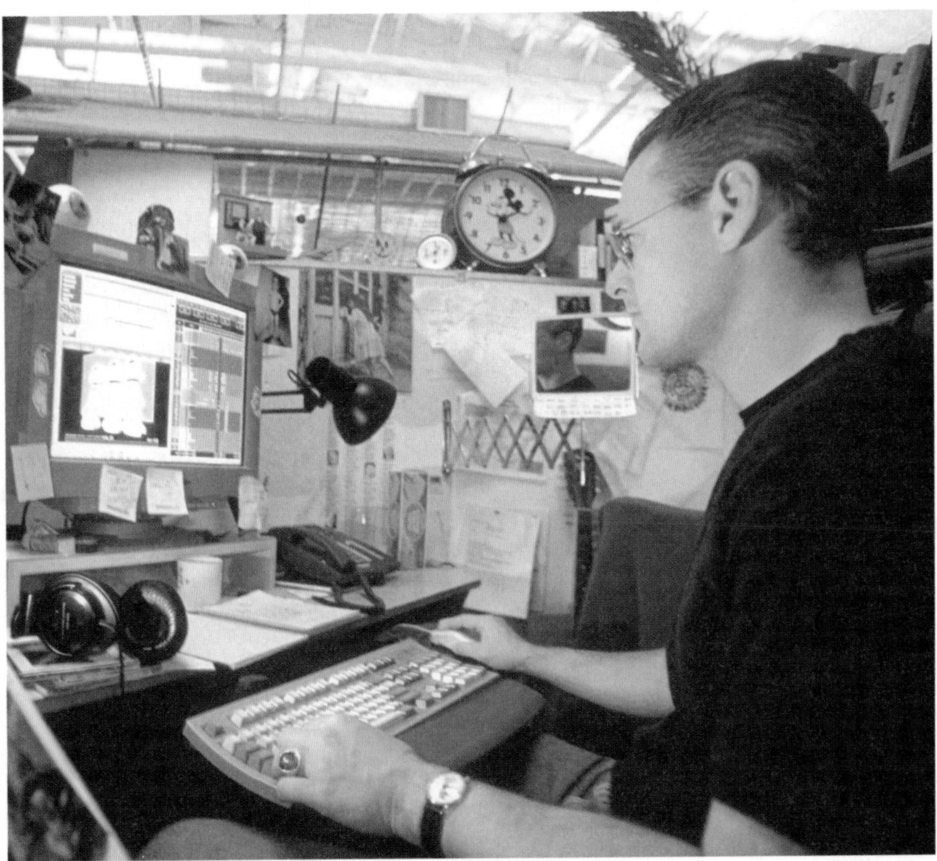

FIGURE 6.31 Animators at Pixar Studios work on film projects, including the popular *Toy Story* trilogy. Many of these projects spawn games, educational software programs, and other interactive multimedia products.

Inventing the Future ▸ Shared Virtual Spaces

Tomorrow's multimedia is likely to extend beyond the flat screen, creating immersive experiences that challenge our notion of reality.

Since the 1960s researchers have experimented with *virtual worlds*—computer-generated worlds that create the illusion of immersion. Virtual worlds typically involve special hardware, including sensors, but the exact form of those sensors varies from application to application. Virtual reality and augmented reality hardware commonly includes:

- Accelerometers, gyroscopes, compasses, and GPS devices to detect orientation, motion, and position
- Webcams with image recognition to translate the camera's view into data about position
- Body sensors and/or gloves equipped with motion sensors that detect body position and movement
- A display—either head-mounted or built into a handheld device—that changes what it displays as its position and environment change.

This equipment, when coupled with appropriate software, enables the user to explore an artificial world of data as if it were three-dimensional physical space. Tomorrow's systems may not require the use of special headgear.

AUGMENTED REALITY

One approach to creating more immersive experiences is called augmented reality (AR)—the use of computer displays that add virtual information to a person's sensory perceptions. AR supplements rather than replaces the world the user sees. There are hundreds of AR phone apps that superimpose data—about travel, shopping, real estate, and more—on the camera's view of the real world. On a PC, AR software combined with a webcam can enhance toys, books, maps, and other objects by revealing hidden data, displaying 3-D images, and launching interactive games. But the most interesting and practical applications for AR involve emerging hardware and software technology that eliminate the need to be tethered to a PC or phone screen.

With AR, a repair person might see instructions superimposed on machine parts; a surgeon might see inside a patient with live ultrasound scans of internal organs overlaid on the patient's body; a firefighter might see the layout of a burning building displayed on protective goggles.

AR researcher Steven K. Feiner predicts

> *The overlaid information of AR systems will become part of what we expect to see at work and at play: labels and directions when we don't want to get lost, reminders when we don't want to forget and, perhaps, a favorite cartoon character popping out from the bushes to tell a joke when we want to be amused. When computer user interfaces are potentially everywhere we look, this pervasive mixture of reality and virtuality may become the primary medium for a new generation of artists, designers, and storytellers who will craft the future.*

TELE-IMMERSION

The next step beyond basic AR is tele-immersion—the use of multiple cameras and high-speed networks to create an environment in which multiple remote users can interact with each other and with computer-generated objects. Participants move around in shared virtual spaces, while maintaining their unique points of view. Today's systems require participants to wear special glasses; future versions may not.

Jaron Lanier, who coined the term virtual reality, is a multimedia artist and computer scientist known for his research in tele-immersion. Lanier was a consultant for Spielberg's *Minority Report*, a movie that shows the direction that this research might lead.

IBM and other businesses employ tele-immersion technology to hold virtual long-distance meetings instead of financing expensive business trips for face-to-face meetings. Tele-immersion systems will allow engineers, archaeologists, and artists, among others, to collaborate long-distance in shared virtual workspaces. It may allow musicians and actors to give personal interactive performances.

VIRTUAL REALITY

Virtual reality eliminates the real world altogether, creating virtual spaces that can be experienced by one or more "visitors." In the typical VR setup, participants see representations of each other, sometimes called *avatars*. Most VR setups involve sensors that detect the position of each participant's head, arms, and (maybe) bodies.

VR setups aren't just for games and escapism. Ford uses VR headsets and tracking sensors to examine new vehicle lines firsthand for any problems that might arise in manufacturing, years before they hit the production line. "In the absence of this technology, years ago we would stand in our pilot plant with physical parts and then we'd identify a problem in production," Harrington said. "Now we're identifying inadequacies to the build of the vehicle two to three years before the vehicle ever launches."

Today's AR and VR experiences can be exciting and disorienting, but few people would confuse them with "real" reality. Labs around the world are developing technologies that are making those alternative realities more real.

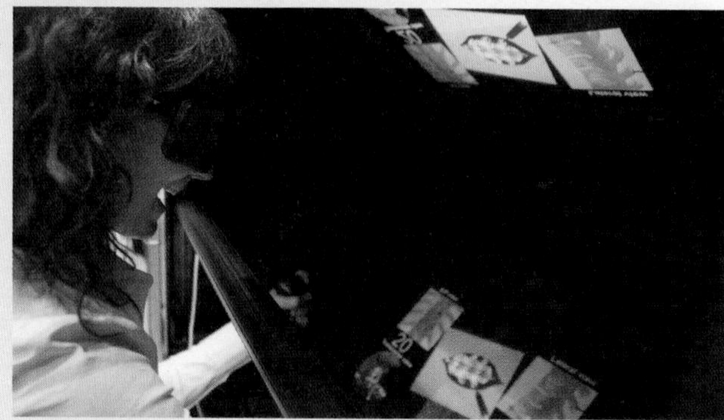

FIGURE 6.32 This medical researcher is exploring a 3-D virtual reality and haptic simulation of a musculoskeletal system.

Crosscurrents

The Age of Music Piracy Is Officially Over

by Paul Boutin

The music industry hasn't adjusted easily to the digital revolution. Steadily declining revenues have devastated publishing companies, record companies, record stores, and musicians. Most observers place the blame on music piracy—illegal duplication and downloading of "free" music. This article, first published in the December 2010 issue of Wired, *addresses the most common reasons for music piracy and argues that most of those reasons are no longer valid. (Ironically, the Beatles' music library was released on iTunes between the time the column was written and the time the magazine was released.)*

Mark down the date: The age of stealing music via the Internet is officially over. It's time for everybody to go legit. The reason: We won. And all you audiophiles and copyfighters, you know who fixed our problems? The record labels and online stores we loved to hate.

Granted, when Apple launched the iTunes Music Store in 2003 there was a lot to complain about. Tracks you bought on computer A often refused to play on gadget B, thanks to that old netizen bogeyman, digital rights management. (It's crippleware!) My local Apple store was actually picketed by nerds in hazmat suits attempting to educate passersby on the evils of DRM.

Well played, protesters: In January 2009, Apple announced that it would remove the copyright protection wrapper from every song in its store. Today, Amazon and Walmart both sell music encoded as MP3s, which don't even have hooks for copyright-protection locks. The battle is over, comrades.

A few years ago, audiophiles dismissed iTunes' 128-Kbps resolution as anemic, even though it supposedly passed rigid blind testing against full-bandwidth CD tracks of the same song. The sound is compressed, connoisseurs said. The high end is mangled. Good work, audiophiles: Online stores have cranked up the audio quality to a fat 256 Kbps. To most ears, it's indistinguishable from a CD. (Actually, most ears are listening through crummy earbuds anyway, but whatever.) It's certainly better than most of the stuff out on BitTorrent. If you still hate the sound of digital music, you probably need to go back to vinyl. You can get a pretty good turntable for around $500. Which, I'll just point out, is not free. And when you steal vinyl records, it's called shoplifting.

Haters might get a bit more traction with the gripe that official stores still don't carry every track ever recorded. You won't find, say, AC/DC or the Beatles* in iTunes. For other artists, contract restrictions mean some songs can't be downloaded in every country, which indeed seems dumb for a store on the border-free Internet. Americans, for example, can't buy Daniel Zueras' 2007 Spanish hit "No Quiero Enamorarme" from the iTunes store for Spain. Still, the available inventory keeps growing, including artists' back catalogs. I recently discovered that Salt City Orchestra's limited-edition, vinyl-only 1997 nightclub fave "The Book" has been kicking around iTunes since 2008. Way back in the day, I had to trade favors with a pro DJ to get that record. It's getting harder and harder to find the few holdouts to hang a reasonable complaint on.

That leaves one last war cry: Music should be free! It's art! Friends, a song costs a *dollar*. Walmart has pushed some of its MP3s down to 64 cents. At Grooveshark, you can sample any song you want before you buy. Rdio charges $5 a month for all the music you can eat, served up via the cloud.

So there's really no reason not to buy—and surely you understand by now that there are reasons why you should. When you buy instead of bootlegging, you're paying the band. Most download retailers send about 70 percent of each sale to the record companies that own the music. Artists with 15 percent royalty deals get 15 percent of that 70 percent, or about 10.5 cents per dollar of sales. Those who write their own music and own their own music publishing companies—an increasingly common arrangement—get another 9.1 cents in "mechanical royalties." Every download sends almost 20 cents straight to the band.

A recent court ruling against Universal Records—and in favor of the rapper Eminem—might even lead to downloads of older music being treated not as sales but as licensed music. (Newly written contracts tend to address digital music sales directly.) That would bump the artist's split with the label from around 15 percent to an average of 50 percent. If that happens and you can still rationalize not throwing four dimes Eminem's way, then maybe there's another reason you're still pirating music: You're cheap.

*Yes, we know: Since we published this article, Apple brought the Beatles to iTunes.

Discussion Questions

1. Do you agree with the author's point that the main reasons for music piracy are no longer valid? Why or why not?
2. Do you think it's possible for musicians and music companies to reverse the downward trend of the industry? How?

Summary

Computer graphics today encompass more than quantitative charts and graphs generated by spreadsheets. Bitmapped painting programs enable users to "paint" the screen with a mouse, pen, or other pointing device. The software stores the results in a pixel map, with each pixel having an assigned color. The more possible colors there are and the higher the resolution (pixel density) is, the more the images can approach photorealism. Object-oriented (vector) graphics programs also allow users to draw on the screen with a pointing device, with the results stored as collections of geometric objects rather than as maps of computer bits.

Bitmapped graphics and object-oriented graphics each offer advantages in particular situations; trade-offs involve editing and ease of use. Both types of graphics have applications outside the art world. Bitmapped graphics are used in high-resolution image-processing software for on-screen photo editing. Object-oriented graphics are at the heart of 3-D modeling software and computer-aided design (CAD) software used by architects, designers, and engineers.

With today's computers, you aren't limited to working with static images; they're widely used to create and edit documents in media that change over time or in response to user interaction. Presentation-graphics software automates the process of creating computer-based presentations and accompanying handouts. For animation and digital video work, PCs mimic many of the features of expensive professional workstations at a fraction of the cost. Similarly, today's PCs can perform a variety of sound- and music-editing tasks that used to require expensive equipment and numerous musicians.

The interactive nature of the computer makes it possible to create nonlinear documents that enable users to take individual paths through information. Early nonlinear documents were called hypertext because they could contain only text. Today, we can create or explore hypermedia documents—interactive documents that mix text, graphics, sounds, and moving images with on-screen navigation buttons—on disk and on the World Wide Web.

Multimedia computer systems make a new kind of software possible—software that uses text, graphics, animation, video, music, voice, and sound effects to communicate. Interactive multimedia documents are available for desktop computers, video game machines, set-top boxes connected to televisions, and (especially) the Web. Regardless of the hardware, interactive multimedia software enables the user to control the presentation rather than watch or listen passively. Only time will tell whether these new media will live up to their potential for enhancing education, training, entertainment, and cultural enrichment.

Key Terms

3-D modeling software..........(p. 200)
animation..............................(p. 204)
anti-aliasing..........................(p. 192)
audio digitizer.......................(p. 209)
augmented reality (AR).........(p. 226)
bit depth................................(p. 192)
bitmapped graphics ....(p. 192)
bullet charts ....(p. 204)
color depth............................(p. 192)
compression..........................(p. 208)
computer-aided design (CAD)..............................(p. 200)
computer-aided manufacturing (CAM) ....(p. 201)
computer-integrated manufacturing (CIM)...............................(p. 201)
digital video..........................(p. 205)
drawing software..................(p. 195)
frame....................................(p. 204)
gray-scale graphics................(p. 192)
HDTV...................................(p. 205)
hypermedia...........................(p. 220)
hypertext..............................(p. 220)
image-processing software....(p. 193)
interactive multimedia...........(p. 221)
MIDI.....................................(p. 212)
mixing..................................(p. 214)
MP3......................................(p. 212)
multimedia............................(p. 221)
multimedia-authoring software ....(p. 222)
object-oriented graphics........(p. 195)
painting software..................(p. 191)
palette ....(p. 191)
PDF (portable document format).............................(p. 195)
pixel.....................................(p. 191)
podcast.................................(p. 212)
presentation-graphics software ....(p. 204)
public domain.......................(p. 197)
resolution..............................(p. 192)
sample..................................(p. 209)
sequencing software ....(p. 214)
synthesized ....(p. 209)
tele-immersion......................(p. 226)
vector graphics ....(p. 195)
video-editing software...........(p. 207)
virtual reality ....(p. 226)

Companion Website Projects

1. The *Digital Planet* Web site, www.pearsonhighered.com/beekman, contains self-test exercises related to this chapter. Follow the instructions for taking a quiz. After you've completed your quiz, you can email the results to your instructor. The Web site also contains open-ended discussion questions called Internet Exercises. Discuss one or more of the Internet Exercises questions at the section for this chapter.
2. The Web site also contains open-ended discussion questions called Internet Exercises. Discuss one or more of the Internet Exercises questions at the section for this chapter.

True or False

1. PDF is the native document format of Photoshop; it's specifically designed for storing photographic images with maximum resolution.
2. Photographic image-editing software can't approach traditional darkroom techniques for producing fabricated images that look like a real courtroom.
3. Based on trends in animation technology today, it's likely that the first fully computer-animated feature-length film will be released in the second decade of the twenty-first century.
4. Sequencing software allows musicians to record audio and MIDI tracks, edit them, and play them back.
5. Because uncompressed video requires massive amounts of storage, virtually all digital video files are compressed.
6. Through the use of mathematical formulas, vector graphics represent lines, shapes, and characters as objects.
7. The idea of hypertext was first conceived by Tim Berners-Lee, the creator of the World Wide Webstyle.
8. Photographic image-editing software is based on vector graphics technology.
9. Presentation-graphics programs, such as Microsoft PowerPoint, can automatically generate pie charts and bar charts but not bullet charts.
10. Multimedia on the Web isn't true interactive multimedia because the user is geographically separated from the media.

Multiple Choice

1. Computer animation today
   a. typically involves automatically adding movements to hand-drawn 2-D images.
   b. can't be combined with live action video without expensive sequencers and synthesizers.
   c. requires high-end workstations because PCs don't have adequate storage capacity.
   d. is routinely used in television and movies to create effects that would be difficult or impossible to achieve without computers.
   e. All of the above
2. Which kind of technology are photographic image-editing programs largely based on?
   a. Object-oriented graphics
   b. Presentation graphics
   c. Bitmapped graphics
   d. PDF graphics
   e. GIF graphics
3. If a photographic image looks fine when displayed on a computer screen but appears jagged and rough when printed, the problem has to do with the image's
   a. bit depth.
   b. dimensions.
   c. vector.
   d. TIFF.
   e. resolution.
4. Which of the following might professional artists, seeking an input device that can more accurately simulate a pen or paintbrush, choose to draw with?
   a. A mouse
   b. A joystick
   c. A trackball
   d. A stylus on a pressure-sensitive pad
   e. An infrared system that tracks eye movements

5. Which technology is 3-D graphics software based largely on?
   a. Video graphics
   b. Object-oriented graphics
   c. Bitmapped graphics
   d. Photo graphics
   e. Hyper graphics

6. A well-designed slide for a presentation typically
   a. contains at least ten bullet points.
   b. uses at least three different fonts.
   c. has a bright red or yellow background.
   d. has a focal point for drawing in the viewer's eyes.
   e. has at least two different animated objects to keep viewer interest.

7. Data compression is commonly used for reducing the file size of
   a. digital photographs.
   b. digital video clips.
   c. digital music files.
   d. digital text files.
   e. All of the above

8. The process of tweening in animation is similar to which of these video concepts?
   a. Mixing
   b. Morphing
   c. Sequencing
   d. Synthesizing
   e. Sampling

9. What must you do to use a computer to edit footage captured with a digital video camera?
   a. Store the video clips on a DVD or Blu-ray disc.
   b. Digitize the video footage.
   c. Import the video footage from the camera.
   d. All of the above
   e. None of the above

10. During the nonlinear video-editing process, the edited video and audio clips are typically stored on
    a. tape.
    b. optical disks.
    c. CD-ROM.
    d. thumb drives.
    e. hard disk(s).

11. When a musician plays an electronic keyboard in a music studio, the sounds that it plays might be
    a. synthesized sounds generated by the keyboard.
    b. sampled sounds stored in the instrument's memory.
    c. generated by another electronic instrument connected to the keyboard via MIDI.
    d. created using virtual instruments in a PC.
    e. Any or all of the above

12. Why is MP3 a popular format for music file sharing?
    a. MP3 files contain DRM technology.
    b. MP3 files work equally well for text, graphics, and music.
    c. MP3 files contain VRM technology.
    d. MP3 compression is lossless.
    e. None of the above

13. Why is a MIDI file of a Beethoven piano concerto much smaller than a CD audio file of the same piece?
    a. MIDI uses efficient MP3 technology.
    b. MIDI uses MPEG-4 compression.
    c. MIDI uses software rather than hardware for compression.
    d. The MIDI file contains only instructions for playing notes; the note sounds are stored in the computer or musical instrument.
    e. Actually, MIDI files are larger than MP3 files.

14. What does hypermedia software give computer users?
    a. Nonsequential access to text, numbers, graphics, music, and other media
    b. Incredibly fast access to documents stored anywhere on the Web
    c. Instantaneous downloading of full-length feature movies
    d. Immersive virtual-reality interaction with other computer users
    e. None of the above

15. What is the most important difference between an interactive multimedia version of *Sesame Street* and a *Sesame Street* television program?
    a. The interactive multimedia version allows the viewer to have more control over the experience.
    b. The interactive multimedia version offers a richer mix of media types.
    c. The interactive multimedia version requires a joystick or game controller.
    d. The interactive multimedia version can't be displayed on a standard TV screen.
    e. The interactive multimedia version exists only in theory; it's not technically possible yet.

Review Questions

1. Define or describe each of the key terms listed in the "Key Terms" section. Check your answers using the glossary.
2. Presentation-graphics software can produce good presentations and bad presentations. Describe several factors that distinguish the two.
3. Why is compression an important part of digital audio and video technology?
4. Remixing songs has become popular as a result of the emergence of digital audio technology. Explain why these two trends are related.
5. Why is it important to save a creative work in the graphic application's native format? What are the disadvantages of *only* saving a file in the application's native format?
6. Which two technological factors limit the realism of a bitmapped image? How are these related to the storage of that image in the computer?
7. What are the main disadvantages of hypermedia when compared with conventional media such as books and videos?
8. Is it possible to have hypermedia without multimedia? Is it possible to have multimedia without hypermedia? Explain your answers.
9. What is the main advantage of storing a copy of a graphic image as a PDF file?
10. Explain how virtual instruments make it possible to create and edit music tracks without using physical musical instruments.

Discussion Questions

1. How does modern digital image-processing technology affect the reliability of photographic evidence? How does digital audio technology affect the reliability of sound recordings as evidence? How should our legal system respond to this technology?
2. Many people enjoy creating mashups—hybrid songs or videos combining pieces of many other songs or videos. Because many of the original songs and videos are copyrighted, this kind of activity can violate copyright laws. Do you think the law should allow this kind of creative expression?
3. Thanks to modern electronic music technology, one person working in a garage can make a recording that would have required dozens of musicians and an expensive studio 20 years ago. What impact will electronic music technology ultimately have on the music profession?
4. Digital technology makes it easier than ever for people to violate copyright laws. What, if anything, should be done to protect the intellectual property rights of the people who create pictures, videos, and music? Under what circumstances do you think it's acceptable to copy sounds or images for use in your own work?
5. Try to answer each of the questions posed at the end of the "Interactive Media: Visions of the Future" section.

Projects

1. Draw a familiar object or scene using a bitmapped painting program. Draw the same object or scene with an object-oriented drawing program. Describe how the process changed using different software.
2. Produce a short video on a subject related to one of your classes. Begin by creating a storyboard outlining the action, dialogue, and music in each scene. Record the scenes. Download the video and music files into a computer. Edit the movie using a video-editing software. Save the finished movie on DVD or upload it to the Web. Reflect on the movie production process. Describe possible improvements to the software that would have made your job easier.
3. Compose some original music using a synthesizer, a computer, and a sequencer. Reflect on the process of producing the piece of music. Describe possible improvements to the software that would have made your job easier.
4. Modify a photograph using an image-processing software package such as Adobe Photoshop. If the photograph is not already in digital form, use a scanner to

create a digitized image. Add some special effects that demonstrate the power of the software to create images that can't be seen in the "real world." Which features of the software tools were easiest to use? Which features were hardest to use?

5. Create visual aids for a speech or lecture using presentation-graphics software. In what ways did the software make the job easier? What limitations did you find?

Sources and Resources

Books

Most of the best graphics, video, music, and multimedia applications books are software specific. When you decide on a software application, choose books based on your chosen software and on the type of information you need. If you want quick answers with a minimum of verbiage, you'll probably be delighted with a book from Peachpit's *Visual Quickstart* series. Most of the titles in the following list aren't keyed to specific applications.

Weaving the Web: The Original Design and Ultimate Destiny of the World Wide Web, by Tim Berners-Lee. (Harper San Francisco). This is the story of the creation of the Web straight from the word processor of the man who did it. Few people in history have had more impact on the way we communicate than this unassuming man.

The New Drawing on the Right Side of the Brain, by Betty Edwards (HarperCollins). If you're convinced you have no artistic ability, give this book a try; you might surprise yourself.

Digital Photography Top 100 Simplified Tips & Tricks, by Rob Sheppard (Visual). If you want to take pictures that are more than snapshots, this highly graphical book can help. It's packed with useful tips accompanied by clear illustrations.

Photoshop CS4, Volume 1: Visual Quickstart Guide, by Elaine Weinmann and Peter Lourekas (Peachpit Press). Peachpit's *Visual Quickstart Guides* are popular because they provide maximum instruction for a minimal investment of time. This Photoshop guide is one of the best. Using lots of pictures and few words, it unlocks the secrets of the program that is the industry standard for professional photo- and bitmap-editing software.

Adobe Creative Suite Bible, by Ted Padova and Kelly L. Murdock (Wiley). The Adobe Creative Suite includes Photoshop, InDesign, Acrobat, Illustrator, Flash, and other industrial-strength digital media applications. Many books cover individual applications; this one provides an overview of the entire package.

The Art of 3-D Computer Animation and Effects, by Isaac V. Kerlow (Wiley). Films like *Toy Story* and *Shrek* have turned 3-D graphics into a big business and a popular art form. This book provides in-depth descriptions of the technology and the industry that make it all possible.

Presentation Zen: Simple Ideas on Presentation Design and Delivery, by Garr Reynolds (New Riders). There's more to a successful presentation than bullet charts. This book deals with the entire presentation experience. Audiences everywhere will be better served if presenters read this book before turning on the projector.

Becoming a Digital Designer: A Guide to Careers in Web, Video, Broadcast, Game and Animation Design, by Steven Heller and David Womack (Wiley). The title says it all: This is the book to read if you want to break into the field of digital design.

Developing Digital Short Films, by Sherri Sheridan (New Riders). This illustrated guide is a great companion for budding digital filmmakers. The focus is on the art of storytelling through video, rather than technical trivia. An accompanying CD-ROM includes a music video project, tools, and demo software.

Real World Digital Audio: Industrial-Strength Production Techniques, by Peter Kirn (Peachpit Press). This excellent book covers an amazing amount of ground—the basics of sound, choosing audio gear, setting up a studio, recording, mixing, sound editing, adding sound to video, performing with laptops, and more. It includes a disk full of software, sounds, and other resources. Great for beginners and more experienced audio creators.

Sound Unbound: Sampling Digital Music and Culture, edited by Paul D. Miller (MIT Press). This wide-ranging collection of essays puts twenty-first century digital culture in perspective. In this book Paul Miller, aka DJ Spooky, asks artists to describe their experiences and thoughts related to the digital arts revolution. The result is a thought-provoking mashup of ideas.

Audio Mashup Construction Kit: ExtremeTech, by Jordan "DJ Earworm" Roseman (Wiley). This book shows you how to create your own audio mashup, illustrating how to match keys and beats, arrange sequences, extract vocals and instrumentals from a full song, and more. An accompanying CD includes free software that will help you plan and construct your perfect blend, and an appendix covers legal issues that will help you avoid the pitfalls associated with the controversial new art form.

The Remixer's Bible: Build Better Beats, by Preve Franci (Backbeat). This is a comprehensive collection of interviews with electronic music legends and remix production tips from *Keyboard* magazine. Topics covered include MIDI, sample clearance, crafting great synthesizer grooves, editing vocals, and software tips for various popular programs.

Live 8 Power!, by John Margulieves (Thomson). Live is one of the most popular pieces of software for amateur and professional music mixing, sequencing, and performing. This book, like others in the Power series, is written by a musician for musicians, and provides tips for people who are serious about mastering the software—power users.

Secrets of Podcasting: Audio Blogging for the Masses, Second Edition by Bart G. Farkas (Peachpit Press). The podcast is one of the most democratic of the new media. With a minimal hardware investment, just about anybody can create a personalized audio or video program and distribute it through the Net to computers, iPods, and other digital delivery devices all around the world. This book clearly explains the technology and provides instructions for creating and distributing your own audio podcasts.

Understanding Media: The Extensions of Man, by Marshall McLuhan (MIT Press). This classic, originally published in 1964, explores the relationship of mass media to the masses. The introduction in this 30th anniversary reissue reevaluates McLuhan's visionary work 30 years later.

Multimedia: From Wagner to Virtual Reality, Expanded Edition, edited by Randall Packer and Ken Jordan (Norton). This collection of essays by William Burroughs, John Cage, Tim Berners-Lee, and others offers a broad overview of the historical roots of multimedia.

7

Database Applications and Privacy Implications

OBJECTIVES

After you read this chapter you should be able to:

- Explain what a database is and describe its basic structure
- Identify the kinds of problems that can best be solved with database software
- Describe different kinds of database software, from simple file managers to complex relational databases
- Describe database operations for storing, sorting, updating, querying, and summarizing information
- Give examples of ways in which large databases make our lives safer or more convenient
- Explain how databases threaten our privacy

You can make money **without doing evil.**
—from Google's mission and philosophy statement

The Google Guys Search for Tomorrow

By any measure Google is one of the great success stories of the Internet age. The Google search engine handles hundreds of millions of queries a day—the majority of all Web search requests. To many Web users, the term *google* is synonymous with *search* (as in, "Have you googled yourself lately?") People use Google to find facts, search for images, shop, locate other people, and even do background checks on blind dates. Today, Google is far more than a search engine—it's the most visited Web site on the planet.

Google was launched by two Stanford Ph.D. computer science students from opposite sides of the globe. Sergey Brin was born in Moscow; Larry Page is from Michigan. In 1996, Page started a research project to improve Web search engines. Early search engines ranked pages by counting how many times the searched-for word or phrase appeared on the page. Sites could fool these search engines by repeating a particular phrase hundreds of times. Page teamed up with Brin to write BackRub, a search engine that determined a Web page's relevance by counting the number of times *other* related Web pages linked to it.

Page borrowed money and built a Web server in his dorm room; Brin's dorm room became the business office. In 1998, Page and Brin raised $1 million and officially launched Google. (The name Google is a play on the huge number *googol*—a 1 followed by 100 zeroes.) The start-up operated out of a garage. Today, Google has thousands of employees around the globe.

FIGURE 7.1 Sergey Brin and Larry Page.

In 2004, Google offered shares to the public, making Brin and Page instant billionaires. Google's management defied convention by establishing procedures to keep the company focused on long-term strategies rather than short-term profits. In their letter to potential investors, Brin and Page wrote, "Google is not a conventional company. We do not intend to become one."

Google's relaxed corporate culture is anything but conventional, but it has placed the company at the top of *Fortune*'s list of the hundred best places to work. According to Google's philosophy, "Work should be challenging, and the challenge should be fun." Engineers are encouraged to spend 20 percent of their time on projects that interest them. One personal project turned into Gmail, the free email service; another became Google News, a widely used news and blog reader; many other pet projects have become successful products.

Today Google products and services include Google AdWords and AdSense, leading online advertising services; YouTube, the hub of the Web's video culture; Google Maps and Google Earth, 2-D and 3-D interactive global mapping tools; Google Docs, an online suite of office applications; Google Desktop, a PC file searching tool; Google Chrome, a mostly open-source Web Browser; Google Chrome OS, a Linux-based operating system for PCs and Netbooks; Google Android, a Linux-based OS for smart phones; and much more.

Many of Google's business decisions are driven by more than a desire to maximize profits. The company's stated mission is "to organize the world's information and make it universally accessible and useful," and many of its initiatives involve sharing, rather than hording, information. In 2007 the company spearheaded the Open Handset Alliance to develop a set of open standards for mobile phones. In 2008, Google opened its digital doors to outside developers, providing them with a free platform for building and sharing projects.

FIGURE 7.2 Google headquarters viewed using Google Earth, a free application that combines satellite imagery, maps, and Google's search engine.

But Google's phenomenal growth has occasionally challenged its do-no-evil mission. For example, in 2005 Google, like many other companies, agreed to allow the Chinese government to censor searches made by Chinese citizens; company officials decided that it was better to have a restricted presence in the most populous country in the world than not to be there at all. In 2010, after discovering that the Chinese government had hacked into Google systems and stolen corporate secrets, the company moved its Chinese search operations to Hong Kong and stopped censoring searches. Google has also been criticized as a threat to personal privacy (because of the massive amounts of data people voluntarily post via searches, email, and more), copyright laws (because of unauthorized postings on YouTube and Google's attempt to digitize thousands of books without author/publisher permission), and the environment (because of the massive amounts of energy consumed by their servers).

In spite of occasional growing pains, the company continues to soar. By combining database technology with a seemingly endless supply of creative ideas, Google is having an enormous impact on our lives.

We live in an information age. We're bombarded with information by television, radio, newspapers, magazines, books, and computers. It's easy to be overwhelmed by the sheer quantity of information we're expected to deal with each day. Computer applications, such as word processors and spreadsheets, can aggravate the problem by making it easier for people to generate more documents full of information.

Database software can help alleviate information overload. Databases make it possible for people to store, organize, retrieve, communicate, and manage information in ways that wouldn't be possible without computers. To control the flood of information, people use databases of all sizes and shapes—from massive mainframe database managers that keep airliners filled with passengers, to computerized appointment calendars on palmtop computers, to public database kiosks in shopping malls.

First the good news: information at your fingertips can make your life richer and more efficient in a multitude of ways. Ready cash from street-corner ATMs, almost instant airline reservations from the Web, catalog shopping with overnight mail-order delivery, exhaustive online searches in seconds—none of these conveniences would be possible without databases.

Now the bad news: Some of the information stored in databases is about you and your activities, and you have little or no control over who has it and how it is used. Ironically, the database technology that liberates us in our day-to-day lives is, at the same time, chipping away at our privacy. We explore both sides of this important technology in this chapter.

The Electronic File Cabinet: Database Basics

> The next best thing to knowing, is **knowing where to find It.**
>
> —*Samuel Johnson*

We start by looking at the basics of databases. Like word processors, spreadsheets, and graphics programs, database programs are applications—software for turning computers into productive tools. If a word processor is a computerized typewriter and a spreadsheet is a computerized ledger, you can think of database software as a computerized file cabinet.

While word processors and spreadsheets generally are used to create printed documents, database programs are designed to maintain and process *databases*—collections of logically related information stored on disks. A database can be as simple as a list of names and addresses or as complex as an airline reservation system. A recipe file, a business inventory file, a school's student grade records, an index file of business contacts, a catalog of your music collection, or a list of Web sites—just about any collection of information can be turned into a database.

What Good Is a Database?

Why do people use computers for information-handling tasks that can be done with index cards, three-ring binders, or file folders? Computerized databases offer several advantages over their paper-and-pencil counterparts:

- *Databases make it easier to store large quantities of information.* If you have only 20 or 30 movies in your collection, it may make sense to catalog them in a notebook. But if you have 2,000 or 3,000 movies, your notebook may become as unwieldy as your collection. The larger the mass of information, the bigger the benefit of using a database.
- *Databases make it easier to retrieve information quickly and flexibly.* It might take a minute or more to look up a phone number in a card file or telephone directory, but the same job can be done in seconds with a database. If you look up 200 numbers every week, the advantage of a database is obvious. That advantage is even greater when your search doesn't match your

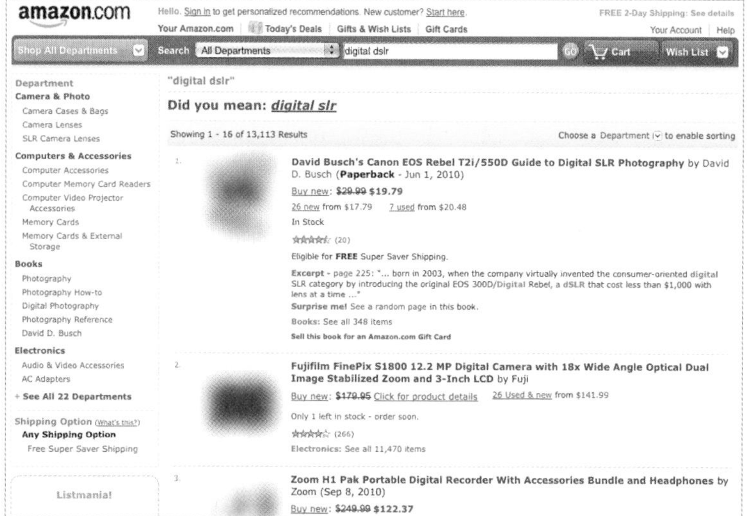

FIGURE 7.3 Amazon and other online stores wouldn't be possible without database technology.

file's organization. For example, suppose you have a phone number on a scrap of paper and you want to find the name and address of the person with that number. That kind of search may take hours if your information is stored in a large address book or file alphabetized by name, but the same search is almost instantaneous with a computerized database.

- *Databases make it easy to organize and reorganize information.* Paper filing systems force you to arrange information in one particular way. Should your book catalog be organized by author, by title, by publication date, or by subject? There's a lot riding on your decision because if you decide to rearrange everything later, you will waste a lot of time. With a database, you can instantly switch between these organizational schemes as often as you like; there's no penalty for flexibility.
- *Databases make it easy to print and distribute information in a variety of ways.* Suppose you want to send letters to hundreds of friends inviting them to your postgraduation party. You'll need to include directions to your place for out-of-towners but not for home-towners. A database, when used with a word processor, can print personalized form letters, including extra directions for those who need them, and print preaddressed envelopes or mailing labels in a fraction of the time it would take you to do it by hand and with less likelihood of error. You can even print a report listing invitees sorted by ZIP code so you can suggest possible car pools. (And if you want to bill those who attend the party, your database can help with that, too.)

Database Anatomy

As you might expect, a specialized vocabulary is associated with databases. Unfortunately, some terms take on different meanings depending on their context, and different people use these words in different ways. We'll begin by charting a course through marketing hype and technical terminology to find our way to the definitions most people use today.

For our purposes, a **database** is an organized collection of information stored in a computer, and a **database program (database software)** is a software tool for organizing storage and retrieval of that information. A variety of programs fit this broad definition, ranging from simple address book programs and other list managers to massive inventory-tracking systems. We explore the differences between types of database programs later in the chapter, but for now we treat them as if they are more or less alike.

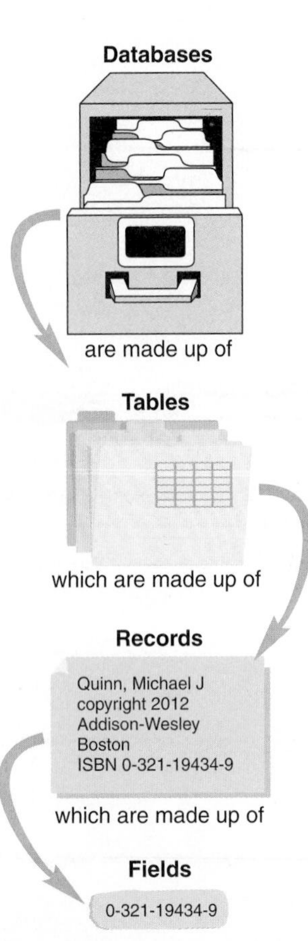

FIGURE 7.4

Early PC databases were simple file managers; they made it easy for users to store, organize, and retrieve information—names, numbers, prices, whatever—from structured data files. This type of data management is really list management since these files are just structured lists. Spreadsheet software can generally handle this kind of simple list management. Today's database software isn't limited to this kind of simple file management; it can handle complex tasks involving multiple data files.

A database is typically composed of one or more tables. A **table** is a collection of related information; it keeps that information together the way a folder in a file cabinet does. If a database is used to record sales information for a company, separate tables might contain the relevant sales data for each year. For an address database, separate tables might hold personal and business contacts. It's up to the designer of the database to determine whether information in different categories is stored in separate tables, which are, in turn, stored in files on the computer's disk.

A database table is organized into records. A **record** is the information related to one person, product, or event. In the library's card catalog database, a record is equivalent to one card with information about a book. In an address book database, a record contains information about one person. A photo catalog database would have one record per picture.

Each discrete chunk of information in a record is called a **field**. A record in the library's card catalog database would contain fields for author, title, publisher, address, date, and title code number. Your music database could divide records into such fields as title, artist, and so on.

The type of information a field can hold is determined by its ***field type*** or ***data type***. For example, the author field in the library database would be defined as a text field, so it could contain text. A field specifying the number of copies of a book would be defined as a ***numeric field***, so it could contain only numbers—numbers that can be used to calculate totals and other arithmetic formulas, if necessary. A date-of-purchase field might be a ***date field*** that could contain only date values. In addition to these standard field types, many database programs allow fields to contain graphics, digitized photographs, sounds, or video clips. **Computed fields** contain formulas similar to spreadsheet formulas; they display values calculated from values in other numeric fields. For example, a computed field called GPA might contain a formula for calculating a student's grade point average using the grades stored in other fields.

Most database programs provide you with more than one way to view the data, including ***form views***, which show one record at a time, and ***list views***, which display several records in lists similar to a spreadsheet. In any view, you can rearrange fields without changing the underlying data.

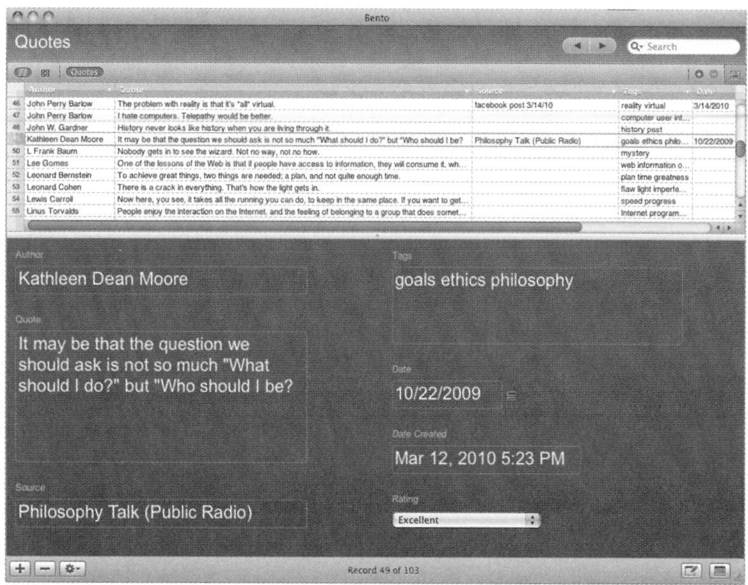

FIGURE 7.5 This split window shows the list view (top) and the form view of a Quotes database created with Filemaker's Bento.

Database Operations

> Information has value, but **it is as perishable as fresh fruit.**
>
> *—Nicholas Negroponte, founder of the MIT Media Lab*

After the structure of a database is defined, it's easy to enter information; it's just a matter of typing. Typing may not even be necessary if the data already exists in some computer-readable form. Most database programs can easily **import data** or receive data in the form of text files created with word processors, spreadsheets, or other databases. When information changes or errors are detected, records can be modified, added, or deleted.

Browsing

The challenging part of using a database is retrieving information in a timely and appropriate manner. Information is of little value if it's not accessible. One way to find information is to **browse** through the records of the database just as you would if they were paper forms in a notebook. Most database programs provide keyboard commands, on-screen buttons, and other tools for navigating quickly through records. But this kind of electronic page turning offers no particular advantage over paper, and it's painfully inefficient for large databases. Fortunately, most database programs include a variety of commands and capabilities that make it easy to get the information you need when you need it.

Database Queries

The alternative to browsing is to ask the database for specific information. In database terminology, an information request is called a **query**. A query may be a simple **search** for a specific record (say, one containing information on Saudi Arabia) or a request to **select** *all* records that match a set of criteria (for example, records for all countries that produce more oil than they consume). After you've selected a group of records, you can browse through it, produce a printout, or do just about anything else you might do with the complete table. Many databases allow you to record, or store, commonly used queries so you can access them quickly in the future. The ability to generate a ***stored query*** is a powerful feature that helps databases blur the line between application programs and development tools.

Screen Test Creating a Database Running Log

GOAL *To create a database to track your running that will allow you to record your improvement over time and track your progress*

TOOLS *Microsoft Access and Microsoft Excel, parts of Microsoft Office*

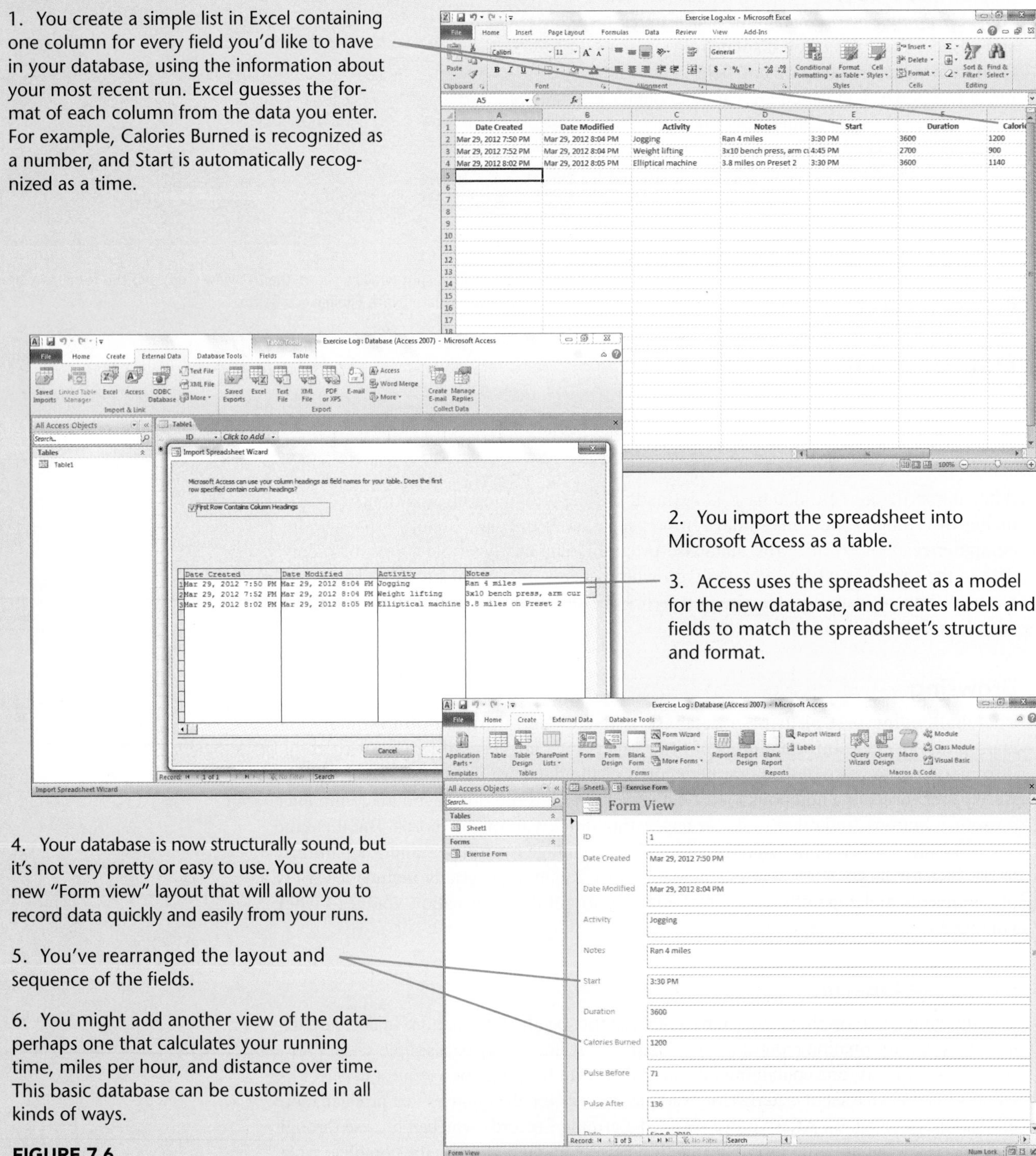

1. You create a simple list in Excel containing one column for every field you'd like to have in your database, using the information about your most recent run. Excel guesses the format of each column from the data you enter. For example, Calories Burned is recognized as a number, and Start is automatically recognized as a time.

2. You import the spreadsheet into Microsoft Access as a table.

3. Access uses the spreadsheet as a model for the new database, and creates labels and fields to match the spreadsheet's structure and format.

4. Your database is now structurally sound, but it's not very pretty or easy to use. You create a new "Form view" layout that will allow you to record data quickly and easily from your runs.

5. You've rearranged the layout and sequence of the fields.

6. You might add another view of the data—perhaps one that calculates your running time, miles per hour, and distance over time. This basic database can be customized in all kinds of ways.

FIGURE 7.6

Sorting Data

Sometimes it's necessary to rearrange records to make the most efficient use of data. For example, a mail-order company's customer file might be arranged alphabetically by name for easy reference, but it must be rearranged in order by ZIP code to qualify for postal discounts on bulk catalog mailings. A **sort** command allows you to arrange records in alphabetic or numeric order based on values in one or more fields.

Printing Reports, Labels, and Form Letters

In addition to displaying information on the screen, database programs can produce a variety of printouts. The most common type of database printout is a **report**—an ordered list of selected records and fields in an easy-to-read format. Most business reports arrange data in tables with rows for individual records and columns for selected fields; they often include summary lines containing calculated totals and averages for groups of records.

You can also use database programs to produce mailing labels and customized form letters. Many database programs don't actually print letters; they simply **export data**, or transmit the necessary records and fields, to word processors with mail merge capabilities, which then take on the task of printing the letters.

Complex Queries

Queries may be simple or complex, but either way they must be precise and unambiguous. With appropriate databases, queries could be constructed to find the following:

- In a hospital's patient database, the names and locations of all of the patients on the hospital's fifth and sixth floors
- In a database of airline flight schedules, the least expensive way to fly from Boston to San Francisco on Tuesday afternoon
- In a politician's database, all voters who contributed more than $1,000 to last year's legislative campaign and who wrote to express concern over high taxes since the election

These may be legitimate targets for queries, but they aren't expressed in a form that most database programs can understand. The exact method for performing a query depends on the user interface of the database software. Most programs enable the user to specify the rules of the search by filling in a dialog box or a blank on-screen form. A few—mostly older programs—require the user to type the request using a special **query language** that's more precise than English is. For example, to view the records for males between 18 and 35, you might type

```
Select * From Population
Where Sex = 'M' and Age > = 18 and Age < = 35
```

Many database programs include programming languages, so queries can be included in programs and performed automatically when the programs are executed. Although the details of the process vary, the underlying logic is consistent from program to program.

Most modern database-management programs support a standard language called **SQL** (from ***Structured Query Language***; often pronounced "sequel") for programming complex queries. Because SQL is available for many different database-management systems, programmers and sophisticated users don't need to learn new languages when they work with different hardware and software systems. Users are usually insulated from the complexities of the query language by graphical user interfaces that allow point-and-click queries.

Special-Purpose Database Programs

Specialized database software is preprogrammed for specific data storage and retrieval purposes. Users of special-purpose databases don't generally need to define file structures or design forms because these details have been taken care of by the software's designers. In fact, some special-purpose database programs are not even sold as databases; they have names that more accurately reflect their purposes. Others aren't sold at all; they're just built into operating systems and Web applications we use every day.

Working Wisdom Smart Web Searching

The Web is so easy to navigate that it's tempting just to dive in. But like a large library, the Web has more to offer if you learn a few tricks and techniques. Your goals should dictate your Web strategy.

- ***Get to know your search engines.*** Try more than one, choose your favorites, and learn the more advanced search features so you can minimize the time it takes to find what you're looking for. Many search engines have different tools for different types of searches. For example, if you're looking for a picture of a humpback whale, you'll get much better results using an image search rather than a standard Web search.
- ***Be specific when you search.*** A search engine is more likely to give you the answer you're looking for if you tell it exactly what you're looking for. Instead of

  ```
  Epson scanner
  ```

  . . . type

  ```
  Epson Artisan 710 all-in-one printer
  driver for Windows 7
  ```

  Instead of

  ```
  Marathon
  ```

  . . . type

  ```
  Olympic marathon record time
  ```

If your query contains specifics, you're more likely to land on the right page on the first try.

- ***Use quotes to narrow your search.*** If you include a string of words in quotes, a search engine will return results that contain that *exact* phrase. If you're trying to remember a song, poem, or movie scene, try typing a phrase in quotes "like this", and the search engine will know those words belong together.

FIGURE 7.7 Microsoft Bing can present some search results in a graphical format.

- ***Know your plusses and minuses.*** In most search engines, you can use a plus sign to signify that you want pages that contain *all* of the listed words. For example,

  ```
  +Alaska +oil +wildlife
  ```

  searches pages that contain all three of these words. On most search engines, the + is assumed, and therefore optional, unless it's necessary to clarify a complex search that includes minus signs, too. A minus sign (or hyphen) usually means *not*. For example,

  ```
  cancer -astrology -astronomy
  -constellation
  ```

  locates pages that contain *cancer* but not *astrology* or *astronomy* or *constellation*. When you use these symbols, you're using basic Boolean algebra—the logical basis of database queries.
- ***Search by site.*** If you know which Web site contains the information you're looking for, there's no need to search the entire Web. Many popular Web sites have their own search tools. If a site doesn't have a search box or if it doesn't return the results you're looking for, you can use a Web search engine to search that site. For example, if you type "site: npr.org robot" Google will search for stories about robots only on the National Public Radio (NPR) Web site.
- ***Be selective.*** As Robert P. Lipshutz wrote in *Mobile Computing*, "A few tidbits of accurate, timely, and useful information are worth much more than a ream of random data, and bad information is worse than no information at all." When you're assessing a Web page's credibility, consider the author, the writing, the references, and the page sponsor's objectivity and reliability. Be aware that some search engines charge companies to be listed prominently, and that some give top billing to their own services and partners. Most reputable search engines are open about which listings are paid ads and which are not.
- ***Triangulate.*** A traditional navigation technique for sailors, triangulation involves using two different perspectives to establish location. Xerox Chief Scientist John Seely Brown suggests that the same concept should be applied to the turbulent waters of the Web. Don't assume something is true because one Web source tells you so, unless you're sure the source is solid.
- ***If at first you don't succeed, try another approach.*** If your search doesn't turn up the answers you were looking for, it doesn't mean the answers aren't there; they may just be wearing a disguise. Try different spellings, different phrases, different search engines, and different strategies. Sometimes it takes a little more work to make your search work.

Media Libraries

On a typical home or student PC, the lion's share of storage is taken up with media files—hundreds, maybe thousands, of songs and images. Special-purpose database programs make these music and photo libraries manageable. For example, Apple's iTunes keeps track of songs, audio books, podcasts, movies, and other media files. Browsing, sorting, searching, adding, and deleting items—all of the usual database operations—are handled through a simple point-and-click interface. Similarly, Google Picasa and Apple's iPhoto put friendly faces on photo image databases.

Media professionals use industrial-strength databases to catalog art, photographs, maps, video clips, sound files, and other types of media files. Video and audio files aren't generally stored in databases because they're too large. Instead, a media database serves as an *index* to all of the separately stored files.

FIGURE 7.8 Google Picasa is a popular photo library manager for PCs.

Personal Information Managers

Another type of specialized database program is sometimes called a **personal information manager (PIM)**. This type of program can automate some or all of the following functions:

- *Address/phone book.* Software address books provide options for entering, editing, and organizing contact information. Most include options for printing mailing labels, address books, and reports.
- *Appointment calendar.* A typical software calendar enables you to enter appointments and events and display or print them in a variety of formats, ranging from one day at a time to a monthly overview. Most include built-in alarms for last-minute reminders and ways to share your calendar electronically with other users. Many programs allow calendars to be published or shared so that they can be viewed (and possibly edited) by multiple users.
- *To-do list.* To-do software, whether part of a calendar or another program, organizes ongoing, repeating, and completed tasks. Some programs allow tasks to be organized into projects, given priorities, and assigned due dates.
- *Miscellaneous notes.* Some PIM packages accept diary entries, personal notes, and other hard-to-categorize tidbits of information.

The most widely used PC personal information management software, Microsoft Outlook, combines all of these functions with an email program. It is designed so that workgroups can easily share group calendars and contact files. Other programs, such as Apple's Calendar and Address Book, handle specific information management tasks rather than combining them all in a single program. Most smart phones include basic calendar, contact, and list-making software. Google, Microsoft, Yahoo!, and other Web companies provide cloud software for personal and group information management.

Many busy people take advantage of multiple platforms for storing and accessing contacts, calendars, and other personal information. Synchronization software is designed to keep calendars, contacts, and other personal information coordinated on phones, PCs, and Web storage sites. This instant data linking makes it easy to keep up-to-date personal information in and out of the office. Syncing can occur when devices are connected via cables or wireless networks. Either way, the best sync software makes the process simple and all-but-invisible to the user.

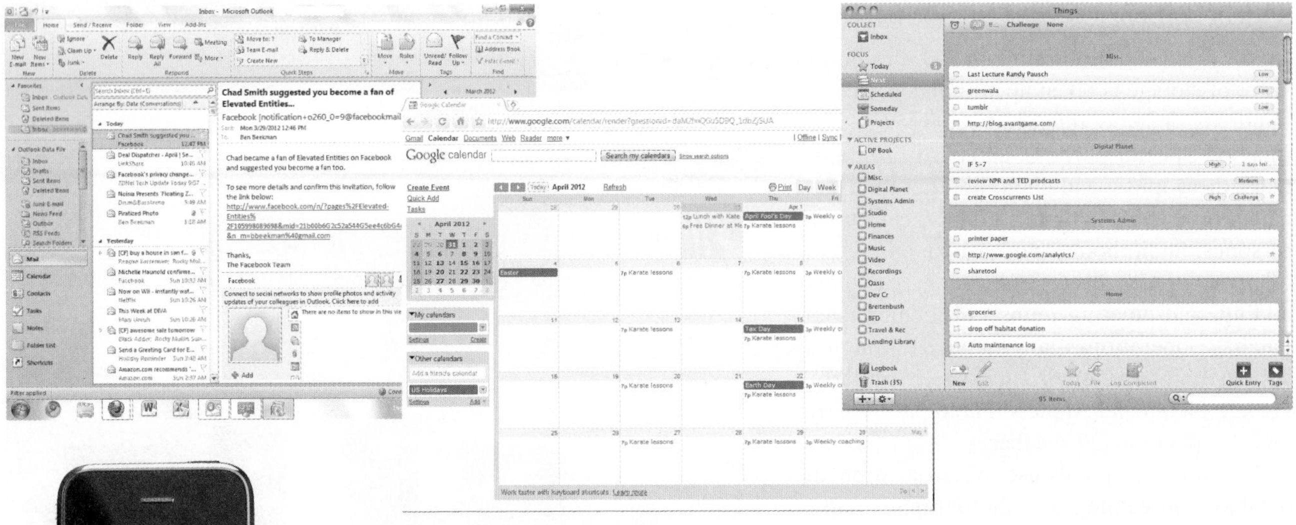

FIGURE 7.9 Microsoft Outlook (above left) combines calendars, contacts, task management, and email in a single program for individuals or workgroups. Google Calendar (middle) is a Web-based calendar program that can be used by individuals or groups. Things (right) is a software tool based on David Allen's *Getting Things Done* system for organizing tasks and projects. Contacts (left) is an iPhone application that can automatically sync with Apple Address Book, Microsoft Outlook, and a variety of Web-based contact-management systems.

Geographic Information Systems

Most computer users are familiar with MapQuest, Google Maps, and other online mapping services. These sites make it easy to generate custom maps along with turn-by-turn instructions for getting between two locations. They're often used in conjunction with global positioning system (GPS) receivers on laptop, handheld, or automobile-based computers. GPS satellites feed location information to GPS receivers; mapping software uses that information to provide location feedback for travelers and mobile workers. These programs are examples of a broader category of database software known as geographic information systems.

Geographical information systems (GISs) go beyond simple mapping and tracking programs. A GIS allows a business to combine tables of data, such as customer sales lists with demographic information from the U.S. Census Bureau and other sources. The right combination can reveal valuable strategic information. For example, a stock brokerage firm can pinpoint the best locations for branch offices based on average incomes and other neighborhood data; a cable TV company can locate potential customers who live close to existing lines. Because GISs can display geographic and demographic data on maps, they enable users to see data relationships that might be invisible in table form.

Web Databases

HTML, the language used to construct most Web pages, wasn't designed to build database queries. But a newer, more powerful data description language called **XML** is designed with industrial-strength database access in mind. Most database manufacturers have retooled their products so they can process data requests in XML. Because XML can serve as a query language and as a Web page construction tool, it has opened all kinds of databases to global Internet access.

In fact, XML and many other technologies are transforming the Web from a collection of mostly static pages into a dynamic, database-driven information space. The Web's most popular sites—Facebook, Google, YouTube, eBay, Amazon, and countless others—are built on database technology. Whether you're searching for a friend on Facebook or looking for a gift on Amazon, you're sending a query to a database. When you enter a tweet on Twitter or a credit card number on PayPal, you're adding data to a database. When you upload a picture to Flickr or a video to YouTube, you're contributing to their vast multimedia databases. When you create a new username and password at any of these Web sites, you're adding a record to a database—a record with your user information.

Screen Test The Big Sync: Sharing Data on a PC, a Phone, and the Cloud

GOAL *To keep your address book, calendar, and other data on your smart phone, your PC, and your Web space in sync, so you can access the same data anyplace, anytime, on any platform*

TOOLS *A PC with Outlook, an iPhone, a Gmail account, a Google Calendar account, and Google Sync software*

It's easy to store calendars, contacts, and other personal information on phones, PCs, and personal Web spaces. But it's important to keep data in sync, so that changes on one platform produce identical changes on all platforms. There are as many ways to sync data as there are platforms. An Apple user might use a MobileMe account synced to an iPhone and a Mac. Similar one-company solutions exist for Microsoft users and Google users. In this example, though, we'll use tools from all three of these companies: Apple's iPhone, Microsoft Outlook on a PC, and Google's Gmail and Calendar on the Web. Multivendor solutions like this one typically take a little more effort to set up, but if they're done right they require little or no effort to use after that.

1. You run Google Sync software to establish communications links between Outlook and your Gmail and Google Calendar. You use iPhone's built-in software to establish a link between your Google programs and your iPhone.

2. You use iPhone's preference screens to establish the link between the iPhone and the Google databases stored on the Web. An update to any calendar or contact list results in updates on all platforms.

3. It's also possible to set up synchronization so it happens through cables when a phone and/or laptop are connected to the desktop PC. This kind of synchronization makes sense in situations where a wireless Web connection isn't possible.

FIGURE 7.10

how it works The Language of Database Queries

Years ago, the number of incompatible database languages made it difficult for people using different applications to access the same database. In the mid-1970s, IBM's E. F. Codd proposed a standardized Structured English Query Language, which evolved into SQL. With SQL, users and programmers have a standard way to create, access, and update databases. SQL is not a database-management system. Instead, it's the most important standard database language. SQL statements are understood by MS Access, MS SQL Server, DB2, Oracle, Sybase, MySQL (a popular open-source database), and many other database programs.

SQL is not a full-featured programming language like Java or C#. It's a sublanguage tailored for the database environment. Sometimes SQL statements are embedded inside computer programs written in C or other programming languages. Database-management systems also support a call-level interface that accepts individual SQL commands.

The selection rules for SQL are consistent and understandable whether queries are simple or complex. This simple example is designed to give you an idea of how they work.

SQL combines the familiar database concepts of tables, rows (records), and columns (fields), and the mathematical idea of a set. We will illustrate a simple SQL command using the Rental Vehicles database from Clem's Transportation Rental ("If it moves, we rent it."). Here's a complete listing of the database records.

Vehicle_ID	Vehicle_Type	Transport_Mode	Num_Passengers	Cargo_Capacity	Rental_Price
1062	Helicopter	Air	6	500	$1,250.00
1955	Canoe	Water	2	30	$5.00
2784	Automobile	Land	4	250	$45.00
0213	Scooter	Land	1	0	$10.00
0019	Minibus	Land	8	375	$130.00
3747	Balloon	Air	3	120	$340.00
7288	HangGlider	Air	1	5	$17.00
9430	Sailboat	Water	8	200	$275.00
8714	Powerboat	Water	4	175	$210.00
0441	Bicycle	Land	1	10	$12.00
4759	Jet	Air	9	2300	$2,900.00

A typical SQL statement filters the records of a database, capturing only those that meet the specific criteria. For example, suppose you wanted to list the ID numbers and types of the vehicles that travel on land and cost less than $20.00 per day. The SQL statement to perform this task would look like this:

```
SELECT Vehicle_ID, Vehicle_Type
FROM Rental_Vehicles
WHERE Transport_Mode = 'Land' AND Rental_Price < 20.00
```

In English, this SQL statement says, "Show me (from the Rental Vehicles database) the vehicle IDs and vehicle types for those vehicles that travel by land and cost less than $20.00 per day to rent."

Two rows in the database meet these criteria, the scooter and bicycle:

0213 Scooter
0441 Bicycle

Many factors have led to the success of SQL, including its high-level, easy-to-understand statements, its relational database orientation, and its portability across a wide range of systems ranging from personal computers to mainframes. SQL has benefitted both from being vendor independent and from being supported by products from IBM and Microsoft. The large number of SQL databases in place around the world, combined with the multitude of software professionals familiar with SQL, guarantees that SQL will play an important role in the database world for many years to come.

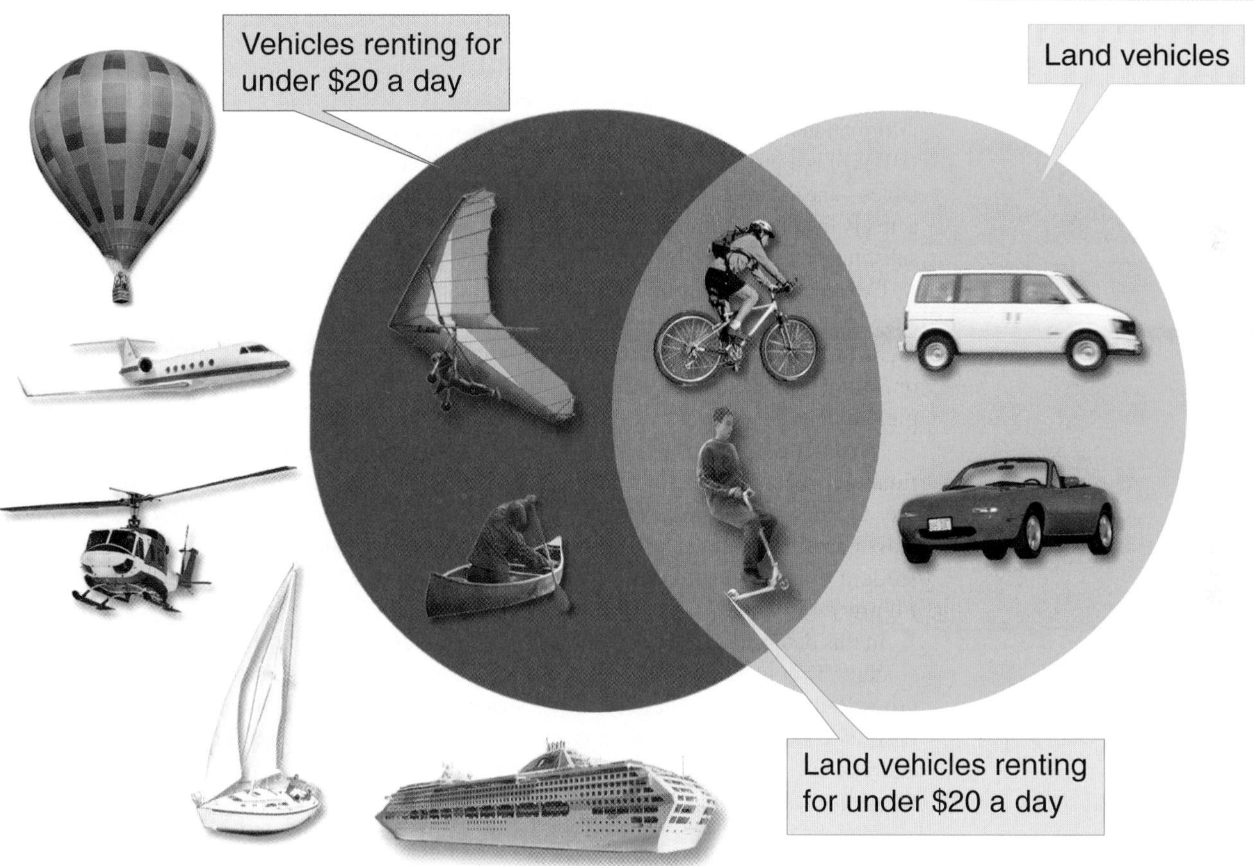

FIGURE 7.11

Beyond the Basics: Database-Management Systems

When we try to pick out anything, we find it **hitched to everything else in the universe**.

—John Muir, first director of the U.S. National Park Service

So far we've used simple examples to illustrate concepts common to most database programs. This oversimplification is useful for understanding the basics, but it's not the whole story. In truth, database programs range from simple contact management programs to massive financial information systems, and it's important to know a little about what makes them different as well as what makes them alike.

What Is a Database-Management System?

Technically speaking, many consumer databases aren't really database managers at all. This type of program (which used to be referred to as a file manager) is designed to manage the information in one collection of data, or table, at a time. A true **database-management system (DBMS)** is a program or system of programs that can manipulate data in a large collection of tables—the database—cross-referencing between tables as needed. You can use a DBMS interactively or control it directly through other programs. For many large, complex jobs, there's no substitute for a true database-management system.

Consider, for example, the problem of managing student information at a college. It's easy to see how databases might be used to store this information: a table containing one record for each student, with fields for name, student ID number, address, phone, and so on. But a typical student generates far too much information to store practically in a single table.

Most schools choose to keep several tables containing student information: one for financial records, one for course enrollment and grade transcripts, and so on. Each of these tables has a single record for each student. In addition, a school must maintain class enrollment tables with one record for each class and fields for information on each student enrolled in the class. Three of these tables might be organized as shown in Figure 7.12.

In this database, each of the three separate tables contains basic information about every student. This is an example of *data redundancy*, and it can cause problems as data files grow. Redundant data not only wastes space on storage media, but also makes it difficult to ensure that student information is accurate and up to date. If a student moves to a different address, several tables must be updated to maintain *data consistency*. The more changes, the greater the likelihood of inconsistent or inaccurate data.

With a DBMS there's no need to store all this information in every table. The database can include a basic student table containing demographic information—information that's unique for each student. Because the demographic information is stored in a separate table, it doesn't need to be included in the financial information table, the transcript table, the class list table, or any other table. The student ID number, included in each table, serves as a *key field*; it unlocks the relevant student information in the student table when it's needed elsewhere. The student ID field is, in effect, shared by all tables that use data from this table. If the student moves, the change of address need be recorded in only one place. Databases organized in this way are called *relational databases*.

What Makes a Database Relational?

To most users, a **relational database** program is one that allows tables to be related to each other so that changes in one table are reflected in other tables automatically. To computer scientists, the term *relational database* has a technical definition related

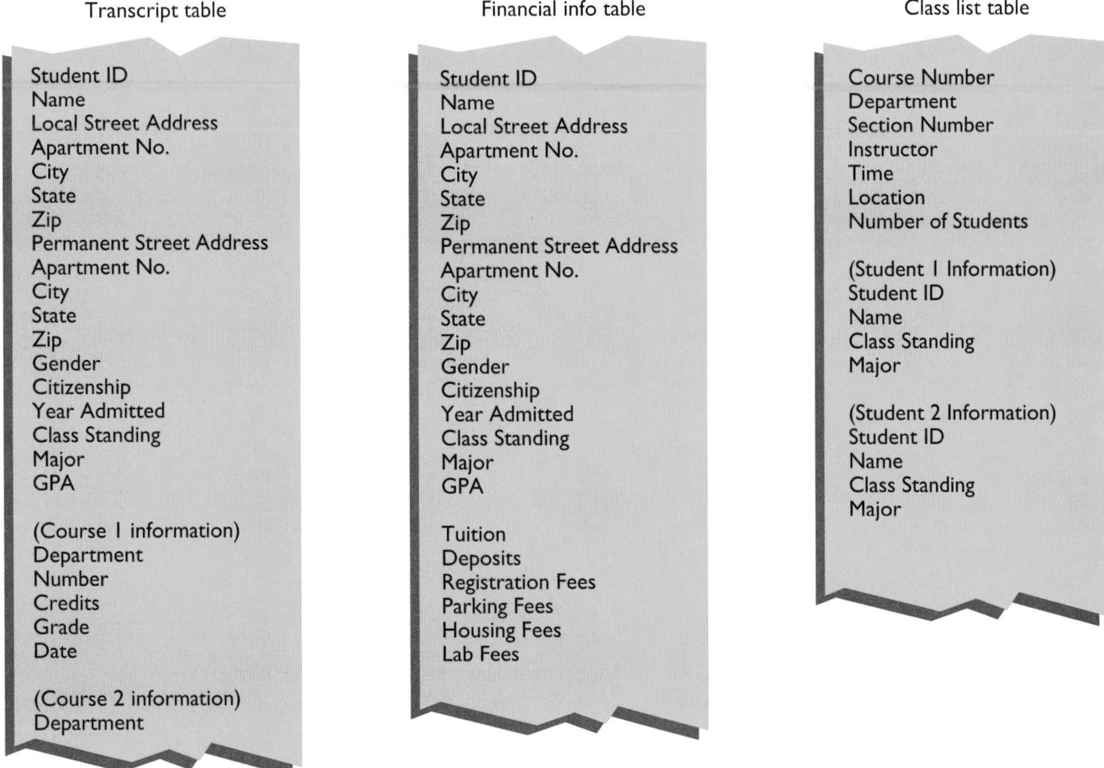

FIGURE 7.12 Student information is duplicated in several different tables of this poorly designed, error-prone database.

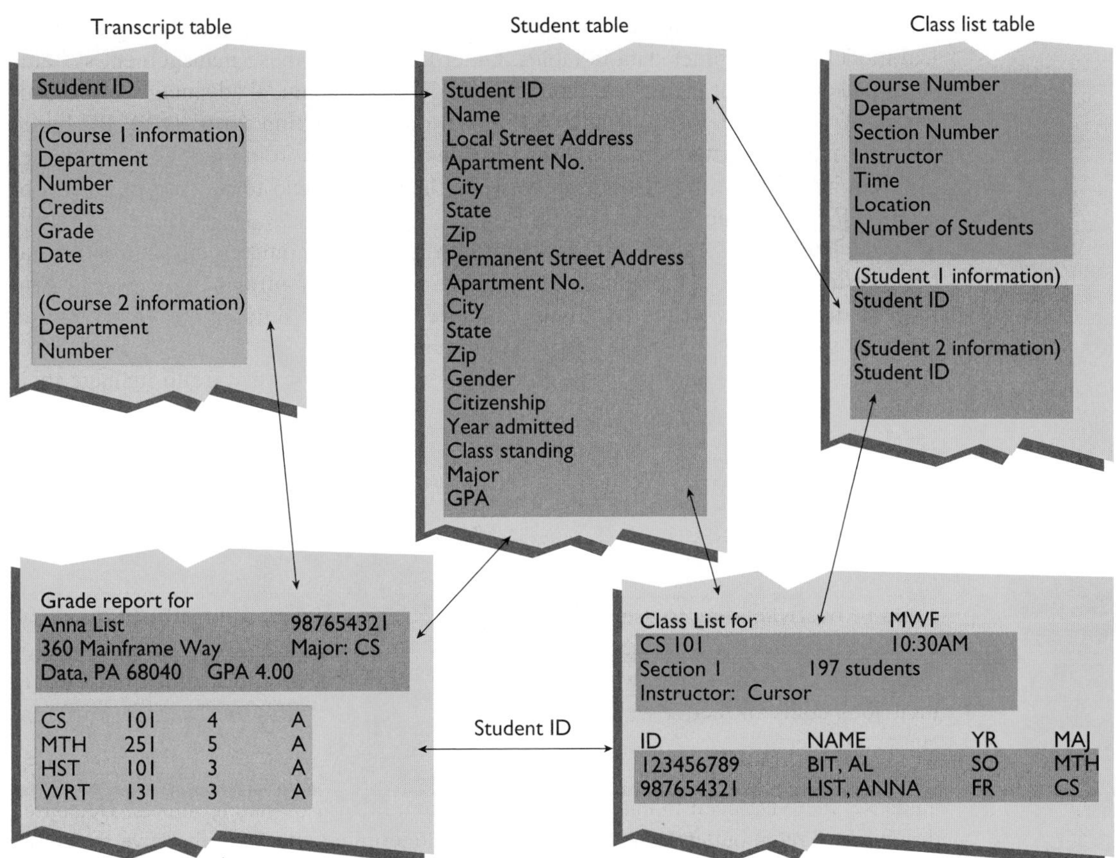

FIGURE 7.13 The Student table serves as a reference when grade reports and class lists are created. The Student ID fields in the Transcript table and the Class List table are used as keys for locating the necessary student information in the Student table.

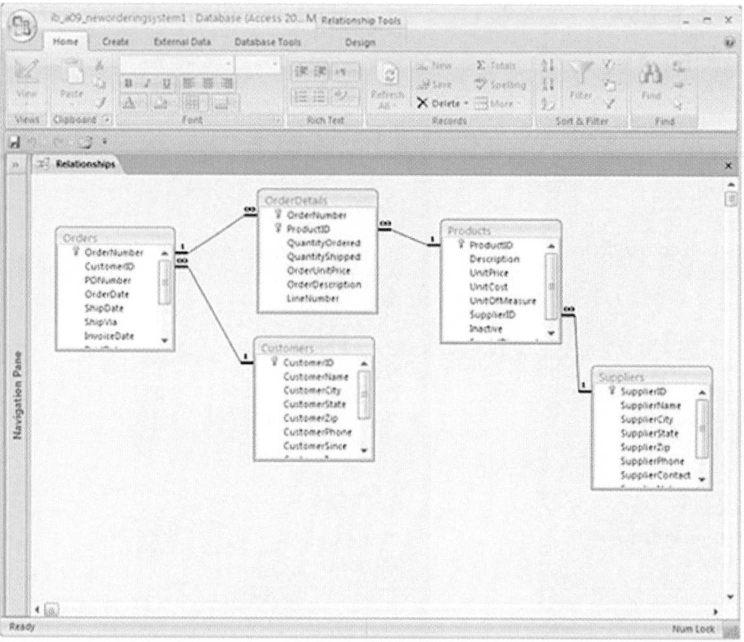

FIGURE 7.14 Microsoft Access provides a visual representation of a relational database.

to the underlying structure of the data and the rules specifying how that data can be manipulated.

The structure of a relational database is based on the relational model—a mathematical model that combines data in tables. Other kinds of database-management systems are based on different theoretical models, with different technical advantages and disadvantages. But the majority of DBMSs in use today, including virtually all PC-based database-management systems, use the relational model. So from the average computer user's point of view, the distinction between the popular and technical definitions of *relational* is academic.

In the late 1970s Oracle Corporation produced the first commercial relational database system. Large companies with massive amounts of information to store and retrieve discovered that the relational database model was much more versatile than previous systems were. Oracle Corporation quickly became an industry powerhouse. Today almost all of the *Fortune* 100 companies use Oracle software to manage their databases.

The Many Faces of Databases

Large databases often contain hundreds of interrelated tables. This maze of information could be overwhelming to users if they were forced to deal with it directly. Fortunately, a database-management system can shield users from the complex inner workings of the system, providing them with only the information and commands they need to get their jobs done. In fact, a well-designed database puts on different faces for different classes of users.

Retail clerks don't need to be able to access every piece of information in the store's database; they just need to enter sales transactions on point-of-sale terminals. Databases designed for retail outlets generally include simple terminal interfaces that give the clerks only the information, and the power, they need to process transactions. Managers, accountants, data processing specialists, and customers see the database from different points of view because they need to work with the data in different ways.

Clerk's view

Customer service view used by clerks to access customer information, scan bar codes on products, ring up sales, and print receipts

Music store database

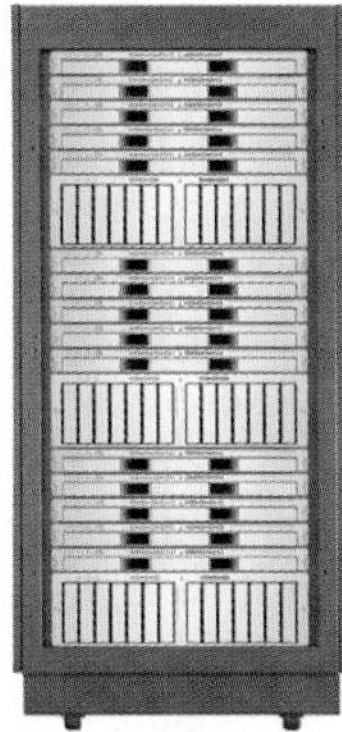

Manager's view

Inventory-tracking and policy views used by managers to monitor purchases, sales, and stock on hand, as well as to control pricing and policy

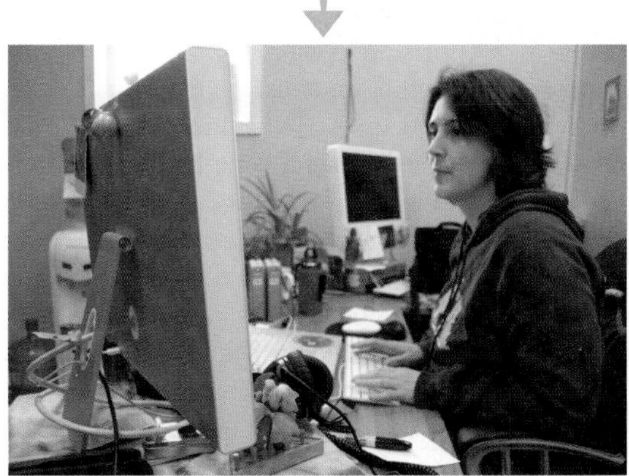

Technician/programmer's view

Technical view used by programmer to create other user interfaces and custom queries

FIGURE 7.15 Clerks, managers, programmers, and customers see different views of a music store database. The clerk's view allows for simple data-entry and checkout procedures. The manager, working with the same database, has control over pricing, policies, and inventory but can't change the structure or user interface of the database. The programmer can work under the hood to fine-tune and customize the database so it can better meet the needs of other employees and customers.

Database Trends

It is better to ask some of the questions than to know all of the answers.

—*James Thurber, in* Fables for Our Time

Database technology isn't static. Advances in the past two decades have changed the way most organizations deal with data, and current trends suggest even bigger changes in the near future.

Real-Time Computing

The earliest file-management programs could do only **batch processing**, which required computer operators to accumulate transactions and feed them into computers in large batches. These batch systems weren't able to provide the kind of immediate feedback we expect today. Questions such as "What's the balance in my checking account?" or "Are there any open flights to Denver next Tuesday?" were likely to be answered "Those records will be updated tonight, so we'll let you know tomorrow."

Today massive disk drives, inexpensive memory, and sophisticated software have allowed **interactive processing** to replace batch processing for most applications. Users now interact with data through terminals, PCs, and handheld devices, viewing and changing values online in **real time**. Batch processing is still used for printing paychecks, bills, invoices, and reports and for making backup copies of data files—jobs for which it makes sense to do a lot of transactions at once. But for applications that demand immediacy, such as airline reservations, banking transactions, and the like, interactive, multiuser database systems have taken over. These systems are typically run on powerful servers and accessed by users remotely. Oracle, IBM, Microsoft, and other companies create the ***database servers*** used by businesses of all sizes around the world.

This trend toward real-time computing is accelerated by the Internet, which makes it possible to have almost instant access to information stored in databases from anywhere on Earth, inside or outside the boundaries of the enterprise.

Downsizing and Decentralizing

In the pre-PC days, most databases were housed in mainframe computers accessible only to information-processing personnel. But the traditional hard-to-access **centralized database** on a mainframe system is no longer the norm.

Today many businesses use a **client/server** approach employing database servers: *Client* programs in PCs, smart phones, or other devices send information requests through a network or the Internet to database servers or mainframe databases. These *servers* process queries and send the requested data back to the client. A client/server system enables users to take advantage of the client machine's simplicity and convenience, while still having access to data stored on large server systems.

Some corporations keep copies of all corporate data in integrated **data warehouses**. In some respects, data warehouses are similar to old-style systems: They're large, relatively expensive, and centralized. But unlike older, centralized systems, data warehouses give users more direct access to enterprise data. Data warehouses are most commonly found in large corporations and government departments.

Some companies use **distributed databases**, which spread data across networks on several different computers rather than store it in one central site. Many organizations have data warehouses and distributed databases. From the user's point of view, the differences between these approaches may not be apparent. Connectivity software, sometimes called middleware, links the client and server machines, hiding the complexity of the interaction between those machines and creating a three-tier design that separates the actual data from the programming logic used to access it. No matter how the data is stored, accessed, and retrieved, the goal is to provide quick and easy access to important information.

Data Mining

Today's technology makes it easy for a business to accumulate masses of information in a database. Many organizations are content to retrieve information using queries, searches, and reports. But others are finding that there's gold hidden in their large databases—gold that can be extracted only by using a technology called *data mining*. **Data mining** is the discovery and extraction of hidden predictive information from large databases. It uses statistical methods and artificial intelligence technology to locate trends and patterns in data that would have been overlooked by normal database queries. For example, a grocery chain used data mining to discover differences between male and female shopping patterns so they could create gender-specific marketing campaigns. (In an industry ad, they announced that some men habitually buy beer and diapers every Friday!) In effect, data-mining technology enables users to "drill down" through masses of data to find valuable veins of information.

Maintaining Database Integrity

Databases aren't just accessed by data-processing professionals anymore. They're everywhere, and we interact with them every day. This kind of broad real-time database access increases the probability of data errors and the importance of eliminating those errors as quickly as possible. Data records containing errors are called **dirty data**. Dirty data might contain spelling or punctuation mistakes, incorrect values, or obsolete values. If you receive a mail order catalog addressed to the prior resident at your address, that's an example of dirty data in the mail order company's database. Dirty data can lead to inefficiency, incomplete or incorrect record matching, and bad business decisions.

Most large databases use data-checking routines whenever data is entered. But many organizations also depend on software to correct errors that make it through the entry checks. **Data scrubbing** (also called **data cleansing**) is the process of going through a database and eliminating dirty data. For errors that aren't corrected by automated cleansing tools, the last wall of defense is typically a human customer service representative who can provide a rapid response to customer complaints.

Object-Oriented Databases and Multidimensional Databases

Some of the biggest changes in database technology in the next few years may take place under the surface, where they may not be apparent to most users. For example, many computer scientists believe that the relational data model may be supplanted by an object-oriented data model and that many future databases will be **object-oriented databases** rather than relational databases. Instead of storing records in tables and hierarchies, object-oriented databases store ***objects***. Every object is an instance of a ***class***. The class specifies the data contained in the object as well as the kinds of operations that may be performed on the data.

For example, imagine an object-oriented database containing various kinds of images. Within the database is a class for photographs. There is one instance of this class—one object—for every photograph in the database. The data associated with this object are the name of the photographer, a description of the photograph, its copyright status, and the image itself. One of the operations associated with this class is producing a thumbnail-sized miniature of the photo. The association of actions along with the data distinguishes object-oriented databases from relational databases, which do not have this capability.

Object-oriented databases can store and retrieve unstructured data, such as audio and video clips, more efficiently than relational databases. Programmers developing a new object-oriented database can save time by reusing objects. Many companies are experimenting with databases that combine relational and object concepts into hybrid systems.

Another technology with speed and flexibility advantages over traditional relational databases is **multidimensional database technology**. A multidimensional database is based on relational database technology, but it stores data in more than two dimensions. Data is organized in cubes rather than 2-D tables. Multidimensional databases can be more easily customized than traditional relational databases, and they can provide faster access for users of large databases. Database giant Oracle now offers multidimensional database products. Many Web databases, including eBay's auction site, are built on multidimensional database technology.

Working Wisdom Dealing with Databases

Whether you're creating an address file with a simple file manager or retrieving data from a full-blown relational database–management system, you can save yourself a great deal of time and grief if you follow a few commonsense rules:

- ***Choose the right tool for the job.*** Don't invest time and money in a programmable relational database to computerize your address book, and don't try to run the affairs of your multinational corporation with a spreadsheet list manager.
- ***Think about how you'll get the information out before you put it in.*** What kinds of tables, records, and fields will you need to create to make it easy to find things quickly and print things the way you'll want them? For example, use separate fields for first and last name if you want to sort names alphabetically by last name and print first names first.
- ***Start with a plan, and be prepared to change your plan.*** It's a good idea to do a trial run with a small amount of data to make sure everything works the way you think it should.
- ***Make your data consistent.*** Inconsistencies can mess up sorting and make searching difficult. For example, if a database includes residents of Minnesota, Minn., and MN, it's hard to group people by state.
- ***Databases are only as good as their data.*** When entering data, take advantage of the data-checking capability of your database software. Does the first name field contain nonalphabetic characters? Is the birth date within a reasonable range? Automatic data checking is important, but it's no substitute for human proofreading or for a bit of skepticism when using the database.
- ***Query with care.*** In the words of Aldous Huxley, "People always get what they ask for; the only trouble is that they never know, until they get it, what it actually is that they have asked for." Here's a real example: A student searching a database of classic rock albums requested all records containing the string *Dylan*, and the database program obediently displayed the names of several Bob Dylan albums—plus one by Jimi Hendrix called *Electric Ladyland*. Why? Because *dylan* is in Ladyland. Unwanted records can go unnoticed in large database selections, so it's important to define selection rules very carefully.

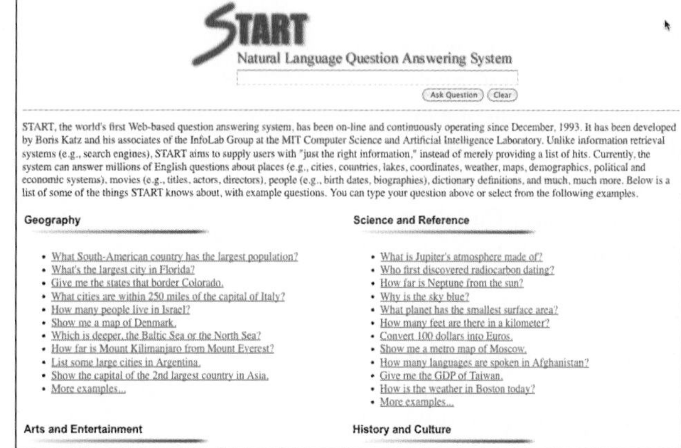

FIGURE 7.16 Start is one of many Web sites designed to provide specific answers to questions written in English.

Intelligent Searches

Future databases will undoubtedly incorporate more artificial intelligence technology. We're already seeing databases and data-mining software that can respond to simple ***natural language*** queries—queries in English or some other human language. But natural language Web search engines haven't (so far) made much headway.

Another trend in database queries, also based on artificial intelligence research, may have a bigger impact on the way we use search engines and other database tools. Some search engines, such as Ask.com, try to put queries in context. Rather than just dumping thousands of possible links on your screen, a contextual search tool might classify results into dictionary definitions, encyclopedia articles, media titles, products, and other categories. Or they might, in effect, respond with questions in an attempt to clarify context and meaning: Did you mean *Casablanca* the movie or Casablanca the city? As these tools become smarter, they'll become far more useful for dealing with the glut of information in our digital world.

No Secrets: Computers and Privacy

> You have **zero privacy** anyway. **Get over it.**
>
> —*Scott McNealy, founder and CEO of Sun Microsystems*

Instant airline reservations, all-night automated banking, overnight mail, instant library searches, streaming movie services, online buying and selling, social network sharing, massive multiplayer games—databases provide us with conveniences that were unthinkable a generation ago. But convenience isn't free. In the case of databases, we pay with our privacy.

What, exactly, is **privacy**? There's no universal definition of privacy, but the term is generally used to refer to an individual's right to have control over confidential personal information. (U.S. Supreme Court Justice Louis Brandeis in 1928 defined privacy as "the right to be left alone.") Privacy is highly valued in some cultures, especially in Europe and North America. Many people believe that privacy is essential for maintaining a sense of dignity and freedom. (How much freedom and dignity would you have if everyone could read your mind?)

On the other hand, information about people can have great value to a society. Vital public services such as roads, fire protection, and schools are financed by taxes—taxes collected based on information about each citizen's earnings, property, and purchases. Participants in online meetings and transactions are far more credible and trustworthy when they're not cloaked in anonymity. Direct mail companies can save money and reduce waste by sending catalogs only to those people who may make purchases. Online advertisers who track individual's Web surfing and buying habits can target their ads toward people who might be interested, instead of randomly plastering the Web with annoying, irrelevant, and expensive ads. Many parents want to know the identities of convicted sex offenders living in their neighborhoods. The tension between public and private needs is amplified because database technology makes gathering, storing, retrieving, and sharing information so easy.

Personal Data: All about You

> What has taken me a lifetime to build—**my trust, my integrity, and my identity—has been tainted**. I don't know if I'm dealing with a 14-year-old messing around with a computer or if I'm dealing with organized crime.
>
> —*Identity theft victim*

We live in an information age, and data is one of the currencies of our time. Businesses and government agencies spend billions of dollars every year to collect and exchange information about you and me. Thousands of specialized marketing databases contain billions of consumer names, along with a surprising amount of personal information. The typical American consumer is on dozens of marketing lists—direct mail lists, phone lists, email lists, and combined lists. Many of these lists are organized by characteristics, such as age, income, religion, political affiliation, and even sexual preference, and they're bought and sold every day.

Marketing databases are only the tip of the iceberg. Credit and banking information, tax records, health data, insurance records, political contributions, voter registration, credit card purchases, warranty registrations, magazine and newsletter subscriptions, phone calls, passport registration, airline reservations, automobile registrations, arrests, and Internet explorations are all recorded in computers, and we have little or no control over what happens to most of those records after they're collected.

In George Orwell's *1984*, information about every citizen was stored in a massive database controlled by the ever-vigilant Big Brother. Today's data warehouses in many ways resemble Big Brother's database. Data-mining techniques can be used to extract information about individuals and groups without their knowledge or consent. And database information can be easily sold or used for purposes other than those for which it was collected.

FIGURE 7.17 The Internal Revenue Service workers shown here enter taxpayers' financial information into massive computer databases. When you shop by phone, respond to a survey, or fill out a warranty card, it's likely that a clerk somewhere will enter that data into a computer.

Centralized data warehouses aren't necessary for producing computerized dossiers of private citizens. With networked computers, it's easy to compile profiles by combining information from different databases. As long as the tables in the databases share a single unique field, such as a Social Security number field, **record matching** is trivial and quick. And when database information is combined, the whole is often far greater than the sum of its parts.

FIGURE 7.18 The National Crime Information Center database helped the FBI apprehend domestic terrorist Timothy McVeigh, later convicted for his role in the bombing of the federal building in Oklahoma City.

Often the results of record matching are beneficial. The U.S. National Crime Information Center, managed by the FBI, contains millions of records related to stolen automobiles, stolen or missing guns, missing persons, wanted persons, convicted persons, suspected terrorists, and more. The NCIC provided the FBI with the information it needed to identify James Earl Ray as the assassin of Dr. Martin Luther King, Jr. It has helped the FBI track down many domestic and international terrorists, including Timothy McVeigh, bomber of the Alfred P. Murrah Federal Building in Oklahoma City. Because the NCIC is accessible by state and local law enforcement agencies, it facilitates more than 100,000 arrests and the recovery of more than 100,000 stolen cars every year.

Record matching is also useful in establishing our financial reputations. Credit bureaus collect data about us, and businesses around the globe have access to this information. As a result, we can use credit cards almost anywhere in the world, we can borrow money to buy a house or car, and we can get favorable interest rates—provided our credit scores are high enough.

But these benefits come with at least three problems:

- *Data errors are common.* Studies show that the average credit report contains at least one error.
- *Data can become nearly immortal.* Because files are commonly sold and copied, it's impossible to delete or correct erroneous records with absolute certainty.
- *Data isn't secure.* News sources routinely report thefts of credit card numbers, Social Security numbers, and other sensitive information from businesses and government agencies. Countless other thefts go unreported or undetected.

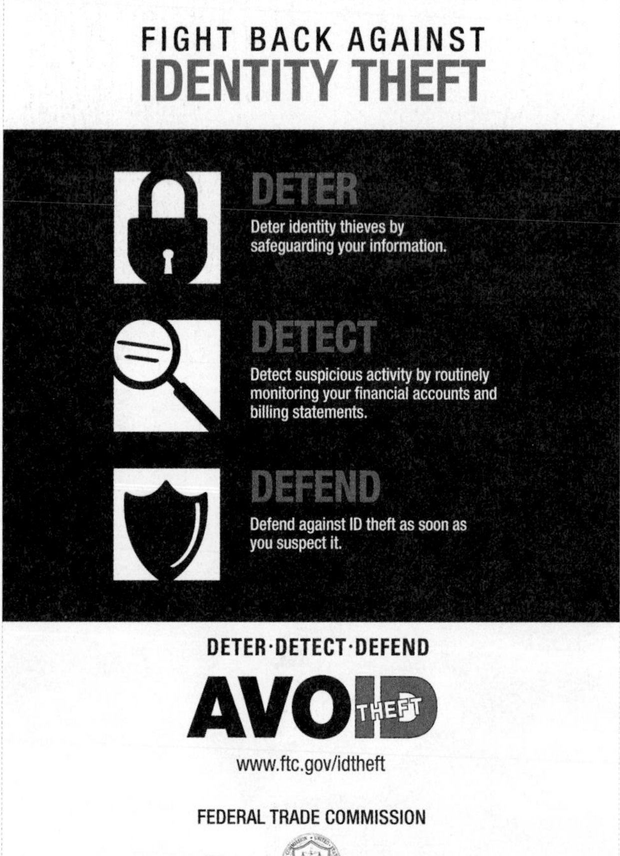

FIGURE 7.19 This poster is part of a U.S. Federal Trade Commission campaign to educate the public about identity theft.

With a few critical pieces of information about an individual, a criminal can impersonate that individual. **Identity theft** has become a major criminal industry in this age of easy information access. A victim of identity theft might be faced with fraudulent credit card charges, massive phone bills, threats from collection agencies, and even arrests. Because of the way data spreads through the financial network, it can take years to clear up the damage from a typical identity theft.

Identity theft can happen because of carelessness online, but it can also be triggered by events that happen in the offline world. A Los Angeles thief stole a wallet and used its contents to establish an artificial identity. When the thief was arrested for a robbery involving murder, the crime was recorded under the wallet owner's name in police databases. The legitimate owner of the wallet was arrested five times in the following 14 months and spent several days in jail before a protracted court battle resulted in the deletion of the record.

Some identity nightmares aren't the result of theft—they're simple errors of judgment. A Portland, Oregon, attorney was arrested and held for two weeks as a possible terrorist suspect because of a partial fingerprint match—a match that proved to be incorrect. The FBI apologized for the misidentification. Innocent people have been branded as credit risks, sex offenders, and even murderers because some piece of data—name, driver's license number, or something else—was misread, mistyped, or mismatched.

FIGURE 7.20 A partial fingerprint match led the FBI to arrest Portland, Oregon, attorney Brandon Mayfield as a material witness to the bombings of commuter trains in Madrid, Spain. The innocent Mayfield was held for two weeks before a judge ordered him to be released.

There are many ways that abuse and misuse of databases can take away personal privacy. Sometimes privacy violations are due to government surveillance activities. Sometimes they're the result of the work of private corporations or individuals. Privacy breaches may be innocent mistakes, strategic actions, or malicious mischief.

Privacy violations aren't new, and they don't always involve computers. The German Nazis, the Chinese Communists, and even U.S. President Nixon's Watergate burglars practiced surveillance without computers. But the privacy problem takes on a whole new dimension in the age of databases. The same characteristics that make databases more efficient than other information storage methods—storage capacity, retrieval speed, organizational flexibility, and ease of distribution of information—also make them a threat to our privacy.

The threat is amplified by several other information technologies, many of which will be explored in more detail in later chapters:

- Networks make it possible for personal data to be transmitted almost anywhere instantly. The Internet is particularly fertile ground for collecting personal information about you. And the Web makes it alarmingly easy for anyone with a connected computer to examine your personal information.
- Workplace monitoring technology enables managers to learn more than ever before about the work habits and patterns of workers. Supervisors can (and do) count keystrokes, monitor Web activity, screen email, and remotely view what's on the screens of employees.
- Surveillance cameras, increasingly used for nabbing routine traffic violators and detecting security violators, can be combined with picture databases to locate criminals, but they might also be used by totalitarian regimes or organized crime rings to track the activities of innocent people.

FIGURE 7.21 Surveillance cameras can be used with facial-recognition software to locate criminals, but they may also threaten the privacy of law-abiding citizens.

- Surveillance satellites can provide permanent peepholes into our lives for anyone willing to pay the price.
- Mobile phones are now required by U.S. law to include technology to determine and transmit their locations to emergency personnel responding to 911 calls. Privacy advocates point out that the same technology can easily be used for less noble purposes.
- Radio frequency identification (RFID) chips attached to—or embedded in—products can silently transmit data using radio frequency waves. They're used as alternatives to bar codes in retail stores, as automated toll collectors in vehicles, as digital data tags in passports, as embedded pet IDs, and more. The widespread use of RFID chips could easily lead to serious privacy breaches.

Big Brother and Big Business

> If all records told the same tale, then **the lie passed into history and became truth**.
>
> —*George Orwell, in* 1984

The word *privacy* does not appear in the U.S. Constitution. While U.S. Supreme Court decisions have recognized that a **right to privacy** is implied by other constitutional guarantees, legal scholars continue to debate the extent of privacy rights.

The creation of computerized databases led to a general concern about an erosion of individuals' privacy rights. In the early 1970s, a panel of experts produced a report to Congress, which included a ***Code of Fair Information Practices***. The code suggested that there be no secret government databases, that individuals be able to access and correct information about themselves kept in government databases, and that agencies ensure the reliability and security of information kept in the databases.

Surprisingly, the report had a much greater impact in Europe than in the United States. Nearly every European nation passed laws based on the Code of Fair Information Practices. In 1995 the European Union implemented a Data Protection Directive establishing a broad set of principles related to the protection of personal data—address, credit card numbers, bank statements, criminal records, and more—that can be linked to an individual. The directive declares that personal data can only be processed if there is a legitimate purpose for processing the data, the individual consents to the data processing, every reasonable step is taken to ensure that the data is accurate and up to date, and that the data processing not go beyond the original legitimate purpose. This directive is part of a highly developed body of European privacy laws. European history includes many painful examples of the abuse of personal data by Fascist and Communist regimes, and modern European law is designed to protect citizens from unchecked use of personal information.

The United States government, on the other hand, has resisted any attempts to implement sweeping privacy protection laws. Business interests have successfully convinced federal and state governments that broad privacy protection laws could obstruct economic growth, and that many privacy issues should be handled using free-market approaches. Privacy protection in the United States is based on a combination of targeted laws, regulations, and self-regulation by industry.

The broadest privacy law passed by the Congress, the Privacy Act of 1974, fell far short of the ambitions of privacy advocates. It applied only to databases managed by the federal government, no one in the federal government is responsible for enforcement, and agencies could opt out of its requirements. A patchwork of more recent U.S. laws has extended individual privacy rights in specific situations. The Fair Credit Reporting Act promotes the accuracy and privacy of information used by credit bureaus to create consumer credit reports. The Family Education Rights and Privacy Act lets students (or the parents of minor students) access their educational records and request changes to erroneous records. The Video Privacy Protection Act prohibits video rental services from disclosing rental records without the consumer's written consent. The Children's Online Privacy Protection Act prohibits Internet-based businesses from collecting information from children 12 years old and younger without their parents' consent. The Health Insurance Portability and Accountability Act limits how doctors, hospitals, pharmacies, and insurance companies can use the medical information they collect from patients.

On the other hand, the USA PATRIOT Act, passed by the U.S. Congress in response to the September 11, 2001, terrorist attacks, greatly expanded government agency power to collect and share information about private citizens, even if there's no probable cause or suspected terrorist connection. When discussing the government's legal power to monitor Internet search data, Google CEO Eric Schmidt told a reporter, "If you have something that you don't want anyone to know, maybe you shouldn't be doing it in the first place." The law's constitutionality has been questioned, and its long-term future is uncertain. But this controversial law serves as a clear illustration of the ongoing tension between personal privacy and national security—a tension that isn't likely to go away anytime soon.

In George Orwell's *1984*, personal privacy was the victim of a centralized Communist police state controlled by Big Brother. Today our privacy is threatened by many Big Brothers—with new threats emerging almost every day. As Simson Garfinkel says in *Database Nation*, "Over the next 50 years, we will see new kinds of threats to privacy that don't find their roots in totalitarianism, but in capitalism, the free market, advanced technology, and the unbridled exchange of electronic information."

Democracy depends on the free flow of information, but it also depends on the protection of individual rights. Maintaining a balance is not easy, especially when new information technologies are being developed at such a rapid pace. With information at our fingertips, it's tempting to think that more information is the answer. Almost a century ago, populist philosopher Will Rogers wrote "It's not the things we don't know that get us into trouble, it's the things we do know that ain't so." In today's database culture, we can just as easily get in trouble because of the things that *others* know about us, whether or not they're "so."

FIGURE 7.22 George Orwell's *1984* predicted a post-privacy world in which Big Brother kept a watchful eye on everyone.

Working Wisdom Your Privacy Rights

Sometimes computer-aided privacy violations are nuisances; sometimes they're threats to life, liberty, and the pursuit of happiness. Here are a few tips for protecting your right to privacy.

- ***Your Social Security number is yours; don't give it away.*** Since your SSN is a unique identifier, it can be used to gather information about you without your permission or knowledge. For example, you could be denied a job or insurance because of something you once put on a medical form. Never write your SSN (or your driver's license number or phone number, for that matter) on a check or credit card receipt. Don't give your SSN to anyone unless they have a legitimate reason to ask for it.
- ***Don't give away information about yourself.*** Don't answer questions about yourself just because a questionnaire or company representative asks you to. When you fill out any form—coupon, warranty registration card, survey, sweepstakes entry, or whatever—think about whether you want the information stored in somebody else's database. Pay attention to check boxes that allow companies to share information you have provided them. On many Web forms these boxes are checked by default; you have to click to remove the check mark.
- ***Say no to direct mail, phone, and email solicitations.*** Businesses and political organizations pay for your data so they can target you for mail, phone, and email campaigns. You can remove yourself from many lists using forms from the Direct Marketing Association (www.the-dma.org). You can block most telemarketers by enrolling in the U.S. Federal Trade Commission's Opt Out program (www.donotcall.gov). If these steps don't stop the flow, you might want to try a more direct approach. Send back unwanted letters along with "Take me off your list" requests in the postage-paid envelopes that come with them. When you receive an unsolicited phone marketing call, tell the caller, "I never purchase or donate anything as a result of phone solicitations," and ask to be removed from the list. If they call within 12 months of being specifically told not to, you can sue and recover up to $1,500 per call according to the Telephone Consumer Protection Act of 1991.
- ***Be stingy with your email address.*** Unfortunately, the U.S. CAN SPAM Act has proven to be largely ineffective at protecting citizens from spam (see Chapter 8). Be especially careful about giving out your email address if you don't like receiving unsolicited email. And it's generally not a good idea to click on opt-out links in suspicious-looking emails—you may just be providing the sender with proof that they have a legitimate email address. Probably the best way to protect your personal email address from unwanted mail is to only use it with trusted correspondents. If you want to protect your email identity, use an alternate disposable email address (such as a free one from Gmail, Hotmail, or Yahoo!) for shopping and other situations where your information might be shared.
- ***Say no to sharing your personal information.*** If you open a private Internet account, tell your Internet service provider that your personal data is not for sale. If you don't want credit agencies sharing personal information, let them know. The U.S. Federal Trade Commission's Privacy Web site (www.ftc.gov/privacy) includes clear guidelines and forms for contacting your DMV and credit agencies. The U.S. Financial Modernization Act of 1999 allows you to tell your banks and other financial institutions not to share your personal information with other institutions; check with those institutions for details.
- ***Think before you post.*** Social networks, blogs, and media sharing sites make it all too easy to share your personal feelings, photos, videos, and more. This isn't necessarily bad, but it's not without risk. Before you post anything, think about whether you want it to be seen tomorrow or 20 years from now by your mother, your blind date, your future employer, or your children.
- ***Pay attention to privacy preferences.*** Large social networks, online stores, and other sites generally have privacy policies that determine how your personal data can and will be used. Some sites have a take-it-or-leave-it approach—click to agree or exit. Others offer privacy options and preferences. Those preferences can be especially important on social networks where messages, pictures, and other personal posts flow freely. Make sure you set your preferences so your postings are only visible to the people you *want* to be able to see them.
- ***Mobilize technology to protect your privacy.*** There are many software and hardware tools to help you snoop-proof your email, hide your return address, surf anonymously, send instant messages securely, and lock down your data. Use them as needed. (www.epic.org maintains a list of useful resources.)
- ***If you think there's incorrect or damaging information about you in a file, find out.*** The U.S. Freedom of Information Act of 1966 requires that most government agencies records be made available to the public on demand. The U.S. Privacy Act of 1974 requires federal agencies to provide you with information in your files related to you and to amend incorrect records. A 2003 amendment to the U.S. Fair Credit Reporting Act of 1970 allows you to see your credit ratings and correct errors for free once each year. The three big credit bureaus are Equifax (www.equifax.com), TransUnion (www.transunion.com), and Experian (www.experian.com).

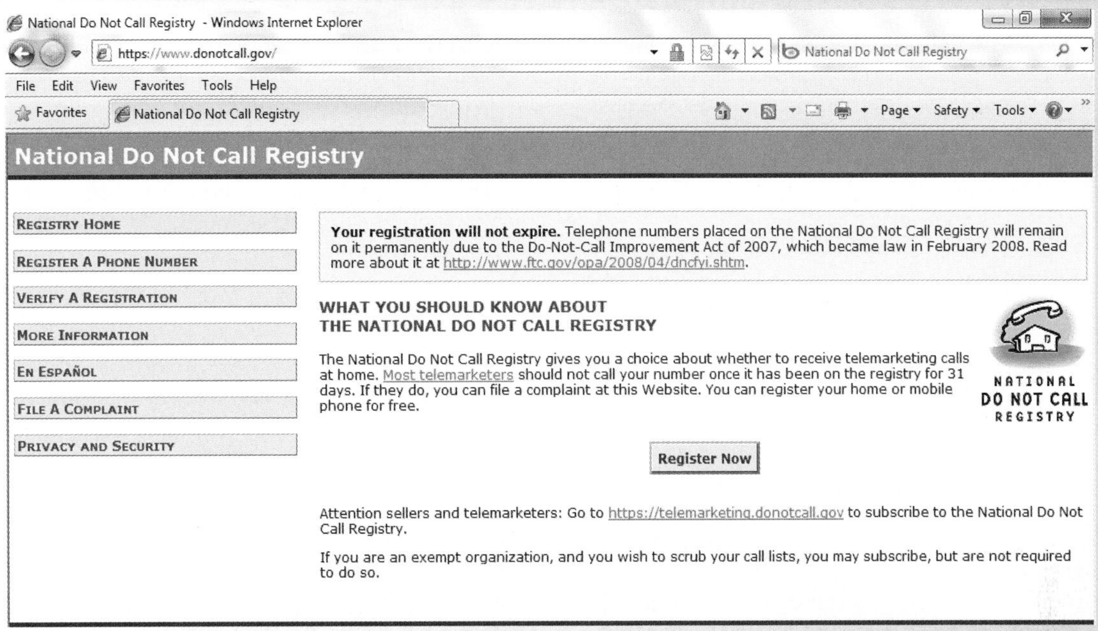

FIGURE 7.23 Tens of millions of households receive fewer telemarketing calls because they put their phone numbers in the free National Do Not Call Registry.

- ***To maximize your privacy, minimize your profile.*** If you don't want a financial transaction recorded, use cash. If you don't want your phone number to be public information, use an unlisted number. If you don't want your mailing address known, use a post office box.
- ***Know your digital rights.*** Privacy protection laws in the United States lag far behind those of other high-tech nations, but they are beginning to appear. For example, the 1986 Electronic Communications Privacy Act provides the same protection that covers mail and telephone communication to some—but not all—electronic communications. The 1988 Computer Matching and Privacy Protection Act regulates the use of government data in determining eligibility for federal benefits.
- ***Work together to protect your rights.*** There's strength in numbers. In February of 2009 Facebook announced that it would no longer delete from their system all traces of users who deactivated their accounts. After a massive wave of protests from Facebook members, former members, and privacy advocacy groups, Facebook reverted to its former terms of service. This is one of many examples of group protests rolling back potential privacy breaches. Others involved U.S. government policies after the 9/11 attacks, a company that collected data on children using the Web, and a health insurance company's access to data from hospital auditors. If you feel threatened, you're probably not alone.
- ***Support organizations that fight for privacy rights.*** If you value privacy rights, let your representatives know how you feel, and support the Electronic Frontier Foundation, the Electronic Privacy Information Center, the Center for Democracy and Technology, the American Civil Liberties Union, Computer Professionals for Social Responsibility, and other organizations that fight for those rights.

Inventing the Future ▸ Embedded Intelligence and Ubiquitous Computing

When we think about databases, we tend to think of systems that depend on keyboards for data collection. But many of today's databases also collect data from cameras, microphones, and a wide variety of sensors. Last chapter we saw how these alternative input devices make augmented reality and virtual reality systems possible. Researchers are continually developing new ways to digitize, organize, and take advantage of data from the analog world.

Entire computer systems are embedded in appliances, cars, tools, toys, and other things that we use every day. According to many experts, we're headed into a world of **ubiquitous computing** (also called pervasive computing or ambient intelligence). In this world, tiny, inexpensive, networked computers are embedded in everyday devices. We'll use those embedded computers in the course of our daily activities, often without even being aware of them. Over the last decade many universities and tech companies have done research to explore the concept of ubiquitous computing.

Microsoft has created a model home that brings together many possible applications of ubiquitous computing and natural user interfaces. According to a company press release, "The Microsoft Home shows what life could be like in a world where we can interact with computers in more natural ways, where expert systems keep us informed and help us make better decisions, where devices and displays are seamlessly integrated into our environment, and where the physical and digital worlds come together to provide new experiences."

The "natural" user interface of the home incorporates voice, gesture, multitouch, 3-D, environmental awareness, and other ideas we've explored in previous chapters. Family members can verbally ask the home about appointments, messages, or weather and hear spoken responses. The kitchen counter can display recipes on demand. A bedroom wall can change color or display artwork to reflect particular moods.

The Microsoft Home has many of the features of a truly intelligent agent. It can automatically upload health and exercise data from smart watches and integrate it with health data from personal history and medical experts. It can recommend and display entertainment media based on known preferences and viewing history. It can turn a dining table into a multitouch game board when dinner is over. It can minimize energy consumption by turning off unused lights and appliances. It can even notify family members when garden plants need attention.

Like our homes, our vehicles will be transformed by embedded computers with advanced user interfaces. Dashboard computers can already play music, recognize spoken commands, alert drivers to incoming email messages, read those messages aloud, store and retrieve contacts and appointments, dial phone numbers, recite directions using GPS-based navigation systems, report mechanical problems, and even track stolen vehicles. A typical car contains many hidden computers that monitor and control various systems. Researchers at IBM, Stanford, MIT, and elsewhere have developed systems to monitor a driver's facial expressions, voice, and other cues to reduce the chances of asleep-at-the-wheel accidents. IBM's "Artificial Passenger" can even jam with a driver who sings or taps out a beat on the steering wheel.

Other research centers on **wearable computers**—computers that are worn on the body. Wearable computers have been around in one form or another for decades. Several companies have tried unsuccessfully to sell wearable computer products—mostly clunky wrist computers. Wearable computers *have* been successfully marketed as health monitors that can track vital signs of people with medical problems or dangerous jobs. The U.S. military's Future Force Warrior is an advanced technology demonstration that shows where this technology might be heading. Future Force Warrior will, if completed, incorporate nanotechnology, powered exoskeletons, fluid-based body armor, and other technologies into a lightweight, wearable combat system. The headgear subsystem will include a variety of sensors, a head-up display, and wireless communication. The combat uniform will include a smart-material protective armor and sensors that collect, monitor, and communicate vital physiological signs. Weapons subsystems will be able to synchronize firing with other networked weapons.

There's a fine line between wearable computers and prosthetic devices that are attached to, or embedded in, bodies. We'll explore those at the end of the next chapter.

FIGURE 7.24 The Microsoft Home incorporates state-of-the-art digital technology into every room. Every wall in this bedroom is an interactive display that can change to match the mood or goals of the occupant. Meanwhile, kitchen computers can use sensors to determine what ingredients are on hand and display a recipe that uses those ingredients.

Crosscurrents

How Buzz, Facebook, and Twitter Create "Social Insecurity"

by Mike Elgan

Is privacy dead? In this article, first published in Computerworld *on February 20, 2010 (and edited here for space), columnist and blogger Mike Elgan reminds us how easily we give away our secrets.*

An insurance expert told the Britain's *Telegraph* newspaper that using location-centric mobile social services like *Google Buzz, Twitter, Facebook,* and Foursquare could raise your home insurance premiums, or even result in the denial of insurance claims.

Wait, what?

A gag Web site called "*Please Rob Me*" raised an ugly but obvious truth about location-based mobile social networking: When you tell the public where you are, you're also telling burglars you're not at home. Insurance industry watchers predict that after customers get burglarized and file claims on stolen property, the insurance companies will probably investigate to see whether the customer broadcast information over social networks in a way that constitutes "negligence." They could also make "social networker" the homeowners insurance equivalent of "chain smoker" in health insurance—a category of customers who are charged higher premiums.

Using *Google* Buzz's mobile location feature, in combination with Google Profiles and other free Internet-based services, crooks can quickly find out who you are, where you are, what you look like, where you live, and when you'll be home. Scam artists can troll for suckers, then grab all the information they need for their scam.

Buzz is just one small part of the new "social insecurity." We've innovated our way into a strange new world of privacy compromise and confusion. We now live in a world of online services where privacy is often violated by default.

To understand this and do something about it, you need to be an exceptional person. The average user or consumer can't or won't figure out how to safeguard his privacy.

A minimal safeguarding on personal privacy nowadays requires users to take intelligent action regarding deeply buried, little discussed, often confusing and relatively obscure settings in *Facebook*, Gmail, Profiles, Twitter and a world of other online social services—and most of all one's own cell phone.

Are your Facebook photos set up to be public or private? When you post pictures of your kids or spouse on Facebook, are those pictures made available on image search sites? Are creepy weirdos finding those pictures using Google, Bing or *Yahoo* image search and then reposting them on creepy weirdo Web sites?

When you post using Google's mobile Buzz app, are your tweets going to only the people following you, or the whole world?

Is your cell phone's GPS location feature on or off? If it's on, is any service, company or individual person able to get access to that data?

I'd be willing to bet that more than 90% of users can't answer those questions. But even the most skillful users often can't know how much privacy is being violated.

For example, we know that Google's computers read all of our e-mails every day. Special software scans the words we send and receive so Google can post ads next to the messages related to the conversations. Do Google employees ever read those emails, maybe as examples for research or marketing? How would we know if they did? And if we trust Google (and I do think Google is a trustworthy company), is the U.S. government reading your email? How would we know if they did? And if you trust the U.S. government, is the *Chinese government reading your e-mails*? Hackers? Blackmailers? Your employer? How would we know if they did?

It's not that you don't know who's reading your email. It's that you can't know. You will never know.

As Scott McNealy famously said 11 years ago: "You have zero privacy anyway. Get over it." But it's not that simple anymore. He was talking more about concern over compromised privacy by companies and governments. But now, thanks to social services that didn't exist when McNealy uttered his inconvenient truth, the whole privacy issue has exploded. We still have to worry about governments and companies, but now we must be concerned about employers, criminals, and even family members.

McNealy was right of course. Theoretically we have zero privacy. A motivated and skillful person or organization can always learn things about us that we'd rather keep to ourselves.

It's still a good idea to practice common sense when using the Internet. Don't blather information that could be useful to crooks. Be careful about what you share and whom you share with. Take care in broadcasting your location, either manually or automatically. But even the most meticulous antisocial networker can't really achieve true privacy.

The strange new reality of "social insecurity" is this: The best we can do is make the violation of our privacy a little less convenient for those who would exploit us.

Discussion Questions

1. Can you answer the questions raised in the article about your settings on your social networks, your online applications, and your cell phone?
2. Is privacy dead? Should we "get over it?"

Summary

Database programs enable users to store, organize, retrieve, communicate, and manage large amounts of information quickly and efficiently. Each database is made up of tables, which are, in turn, collections of records, and each record is made up of fields containing text strings, numbers, and other chunks of information. Database programs enable users to view data in a variety of ways, sort records in any order, and print reports, mailing labels, and other custom printouts. A user can search for an individual record or select a group of records with a query.

While most database programs are general-purpose tools that can be used to create custom databases for any purpose, some are special-purpose tools programmed to perform a particular set of tasks. Specialized media libraries are used by consumers and professionals to catalog music, photos, videos, and other types of media files. Personal information managers provide automated address books, appointment calendars, to-do lists, and more on PCs, smart phones, and Web sites. Geographical information systems combine maps and demographic information with data tables to provide new ways to look at data.

Many database programs are, technically speaking, file managers because they work with only one file at a time. Database-management systems can work with several data sources at a time, cross-referencing information among files when appropriate. A DBMS can provide an efficient way to store and manage large quantities of information by eliminating the need for redundant information in different tables. A well-designed database provides different views of the data to different classes of users so each user sees and manipulates only the information necessary for the job at hand.

The trend today is clearly away from large, centralized databases accessible only to data-processing staff. Instead, most organizations are moving toward a client/server approach that enables users to access data stored in servers throughout the organization's network. While relational databases have been the norm for the past 20 years, a new focus on multimedia records and other complex data sets has sparked the development of object-oriented and multidimensional database systems.

The accumulation of data by government agencies and businesses is a growing threat to our right to privacy. Massive amounts of information about private citizens are collected and exchanged for a variety of purposes. Today's technology makes it easy to combine information from different databases, producing detailed profiles of individual citizens. Although there are many legitimate uses for these procedures, there's also great potential for abuse or errors by businesses, government, or individuals. The explosive growth of identity theft illustrates how the technology that provides us with so many conveniences can also threaten our personal privacy and security.

Key Terms

batch processing ....(p. 252)
browse ....(p. 239)
centralized database....................(p. 252)
client/server ....(p. 252)
computed fields ....(p. 239)
data mining....................(p. 252)
data scrubbing (data cleansing)....................(p. 253)
data warehouse ....(p. 252)
database ....(p. 238)
database-management system (DBMS) ....(p. 248)
database program (database software)....................(p. 238)
dirty data....................(p. 253)
distributed database ....(p. 252)
export data ....(p. 241)
field....................(p. 238)
geographical information system (GIS) ....(p. 244)
identity theft ....(p. 256)
import data....................(p. 239)
interactive processing ....(p. 252)
multidimensional database technology ....(p. 253)
object-oriented database....................(p. 253)
personal information manager (PIM) ....(p. 243)
privacy ....(p. 255)
query....................(p. 239)
query language ....(p. 241)
real time....................(p. 252)
record....................(p. 238)
record matching....................(p. 256)
relational database ....(p. 248)
report ....(p. 241)
right to privacy ....(p. 258)
search....................(p. 239)
select (records) ....(p. 239)
sort....................(p. 241)
SQL ....(p. 241)
table ....(p. 238)
ubiquitous computing....................(p. 262)
XML ....(p. 244)

Companion Website Projects

1. The *Digital Planet* Web site, www.pearsonhighered.com/beekman, contains self-test exercises related to this chapter. Follow the instructions for taking a quiz. After you've completed your quiz, you can email the results to your instructor.
2. The Web site also contains open-ended discussion questions called Internet Exercises. Discuss one or more of the Internet Exercises questions at the section for this chapter.

True or False

1. Because the address book in a typical cell phone is a simple list of names and numbers, it is an ideal application for object-oriented database technology.
2. In a database, a numeric field can contain only computed formulas similar to formulas in spreadsheets.
3. Typical database software allows you to view one record at a time in form view or several records at a time in list view.
4. The most common type of database printout is called a report.
5. The most popular Web sites, including Google, Facebook, and Amazon, depend on database technology to function.
6. In a typical database, a field contains the information related to one person, product, or event.
7. Media library programs such as iTunes are special-purpose databases.
8. The problem with keeping calendars and contacts on multiple platforms—phones, PCs, and the Web—is that a user must have considerable programming skill to synchronize data across platforms.
9. The right to privacy is explicitly guaranteed by the U.S. Constitution, but legal scholars disagree about whether that right applies to corporations.
10. To query a database, you must learn at least some SQL, the universal query language of databases.

Multiple Choice

1. Identity theft might involve
   a. stealing of personal data from a database.
   b. conning an innocent person on the phone.
   c. creating fraudulent documents to forward the mail of an unsuspecting person.
   d. any or all of the above.
   e. none of the above; identity theft is a myth propagated on the Internet.
2. Why do people use databases rather than paper-based filing systems for information-handling tasks?
   a. Databases make it easier to store large quantities of information.
   b. Databases make it easier to retrieve information quickly and flexibly.
   c. Databases make it easy to organize and reorganize information.
   d. Databases make it easy to print and distribute information in a variety of ways.
   e. All of the above
3. Which of these is the correct hierarchy for a standard database?
   a. Database, field, record, table
   b. Database, table, record, field
   c. Database, record, field, table
   d. Database, record, table, field
   e. Database, table, field, record

4. Which of these is not a specialized database program?
   a. A geographic information system
   b. A personal information manager (PIM)
   c. A program for organizing and managing photos
   d. iTunes, the program used to manage music and video libraries
   e. All of these are specialized database programs.

5. Which of these software tools would work for maintaining a searchable, sortable list of professional contacts?
   a. PIM (personal information manager) software
   b. A basic file management program
   c. A relational database manager
   d. A spreadsheet program with list management capability
   e. Any of these would work, although some would be easier to set up and use than others.

6. What is the purpose of a database query?
   a. To update information kept within a record
   b. To test the security and integrity of the database
   c. To rearrange the order of the records in a database
   d. To convert a relational database into an object-oriented database
   e. To retrieve information from all appropriate records

7. When you search for a book on the Amazon or eBay Web sites, you're taking advantage of database software's ability to do rapid real-time
   a. batch processing.
   b. interactive processing.
   c. GIS processing.
   d. analog processing.
   e. word processing.

8. A college's database administrator writes a program to examine the records of all its students over the past decade, looking for patterns that might explain why some students drop out. What is the administrator's program an example of?
   a. Browsing
   b. Data scrubbing
   c. Data retooling
   d. Data mining
   e. Data batching

9. Data warehouses are similar in some ways to old-style centralized databases, but unlike those older systems, data warehouses
   a. depend on middleware to produce reports.
   b. give users more direct access to enterprise data.
   c. are built on distributed database systems.
   d. are powered by simple file-management software.
   e. All of the above

10. Which of the following defines a relational database?
    a. A database that contains several related records
    b. A database that contains several related fields
    c. A database that has a relationship with other databases
    d. A database whose structure combines data in tables based on the relational model
    e. A database with more than 1,000 records

11. Which of these Web applications depends on database technology?
    a. Online auctions, such as eBay
    b. Search engines, such as Google
    c. Online stores, such as Amazon
    d. Social networking sites, such as Facebook
    e. All of the above

12. An object-oriented database
    a. is a specialized database for tracking and organizing a group of physical objects, such as a collection or an inventory.
    b. is, by definition, a relational database.
    c. cannot function properly without a distributed server.
    d. is based on a different mathematical model than a relational database.
    e. is, at this point, still theoretical.

13. Even without centralized data warehouses, how can government agencies quickly produce detailed dossiers on millions of private citizens?
    a. By using Social Networking Technology (SNT)
    b. By using XML technology
    c. Through record matching
    d. Through identity theft
    e. With middleware

14. What is the act of removing erroneous data from a database called?
    a. Data scrubbing
    b. Data deletion
    c. Data synchronization
    d. Data doodling
    e. Record matching

15. The right to privacy is protected by a particularly strong body of privacy protection laws in
    a. the United States.
    b. China.
    c. the European Union.
    d. Saudi Arabia.
    e. none of the above; there is no legal basis for a right to privacy.

Review Questions

1. Define or describe each of the key terms listed in the "Key Terms" section. Check your answers in the glossary.
2. List several technologies that have been widely implemented in your lifetime that are used to obtain information about you.
3. Describe the structure of a simple database. Use the terms *table*, *record*, and *field* in your description.
4. Is a Web search a database query? Explain your answer.
5. Batch processing isn't as common as it used to be, but it still serves some useful functions. Describe one or two.
6. What are the advantages of storing personal information files, including contacts and calendars, on a PC? On a phone? On Web servers? Describe how you might store your data to leverage the advantages of each of these options.
7. What is the difference between a file manager and a database-management system? How are they similar?
8. Explain the difference between searching and sorting data records.
9. How can a database be designed to reduce the likelihood of data-entry errors?
10. Do we have a legal right to privacy? On what grounds?

Discussion Questions

1. Why is there sometimes a loss of privacy associated with increased efficiency?
2. What have you done this week that directly or indirectly involved a database? How would your week have been different in a world without databases?
3. "The computer is a great humanizing factor because it makes the individual more important. The more information we have on each individual, the more each individual counts." Do you agree with this statement by science fiction writer Isaac Asimov? Why or why not?
4. Suppose you have been incorrectly billed for $100 by an online store. Your protestations are ignored by the company, which is now threatening to report you to a collection agency. What do you do?
5. The National Crime Information Center (NCIC) allows local, state, and federal law enforcement personnel to share information with each other. What advantages and disadvantages does a computerized law enforcement system have for law-abiding citizens?
6. How important is it to you to have instant access to your credit card and checking account balances? How often do you inquire about your balances?
7. Do you believe it's possible to maintain security in our society without sacrificing fundamental privacy rights?
8. Would you be upset or worried if the FBI obtained copies of your educational, medical, and library records?
9. In what ways were George Orwell's "predictions" in the novel *1984* accurate? In what ways were they wrong?
10. Cultural analysts have argued that privacy is less important to a generation that grew up with YouTube, Facebook, Twitter, and texting. Do you think that's true? Explain your answer.

Projects

1. Design a database for tracking a personal activity. For example, if you like to bowl, you might create a database in which each record contains the date, the location where you bowled, the lane number(s), and your score(s). Use the database to track your activity over time and print reports showing your progress toward a goal.
2. Use at least two Web search engines to see what comes up when you search for yourself. (You may need to narrow the search with hometown or other information if you have a common name.) What were you able to learn with each search engine? Does it trouble you that this information is publicly available?
3. Find out as much as you can about your own credit rating. The three major credit bureaus are Equifax (**www.equifax.com**), Experian (**www.experian.com**), and TransUnion (**www.transunion.com**).
4. The next time you order something online, try encoding your name with a unique middle initial or a different email address so you can recognize when the company sells your personal information to other companies. Use several different spellings for different orders if you want to do some comparative research.

5. Determine what information about you is stored in your school computers. What information are you allowed to see? What information are others allowed to see? Exactly who may access your files? Can you find out who sees your files? How long is the information retained after you leave school?
6. Study the privacy policies of the Web sites you use most frequently. Do you think those agreements provide adequate protections for you? Are there ways you can control details of the privacy settings to provide you with more protection? Explain your answer.

Sources and Resources

Books

Like word processors, spreadsheet software, and multimedia programs, databases have inspired hundreds of how-to tutorials, user's guides, and reference books. If you're working with a popular program, you should have no trouble finding a book to help you develop your skills.

The Search: How Google and Its Rivals Rewrote the Rules of Business and Transformed Our Culture, by John Battelle (Portfolio). This popular book explores the past, present, and future of Google and other search-driven companies. Battelle sees the search engine as "the database of our intentions." *The Search* is as much cultural anthropology as history.

Googlepedia: The Ultimate Google Resource, by Michael Miller (Que). This massive book is a manual for a wealth of Google tools, from the basic search engine to specialized tools such as Blogger, Google Checkout, and YouTube. There's plenty here to keep you busy until Google introduces a bevy of new products.

Getting Organized in the Google Era: How to get stuff out of your head, find it when you need it, and get it done right, by Douglas Merrill and James Martin (Broadway Books). Douglas Merrill, the former chief information officer of Google, should know about multitasking. After all, Google is one of most popular tools people use to support their do-several-things-at-once habits. In this book Merrill, who is also a cognitive psychologist, presents strong evidence that multitasking makes us less efficient. Our brains can only handle a few bits of information at a time, and anything we do that tries to get around these hard limits is bound to come up short. The book presents 21 principles for dealing with information overload and creating organization systems that work with, rather than against, our brains.

Getting Things Done: The Art of Stress-Free Productivity, by David Allen (Penguin). David Allen's book has been around for years, but it's more popular now than ever before. His practical techniques for taming to-do lists, controlling calendars, and cultivating calm have made him something of a rock star in the high-tech cubicles of America. According to Allen, your brain wasn't designed as a container for tasks and obligations. Whether you use paper lists, manila folders, a PDA, a laptop, or all of the above, you can apply GTD (as it's affectionately known by its followers) principles, increase your productivity, and lower your stress. If you like GTD, you can choose from many software programs designed around Allen's ideas.

Glut: Mastering Information Through the Ages, by Alex Wright (Joseph Henry Press). It's possible to have too much information at your fingertips. This book provides a historical perspective for the information overload we feel today, exploring the ways people managed information throughout history.

Keeping Found Things Found: The Study and Practice of Personal Information Management, by William Jones (Morgan Kaufmann). As the sea of information swells, we need tools and techniques to keep from being swept away. This book provides useful information about managing information.

Database Design for Mere Mortals: A Hands-On Guide to Relational Database Design, Second Edition, by Michael J. Hernandez (Addison-Wesley Professional). This book can save time, money, and headaches for anyone who's involved in designing and building a relational database. After defining all the critical concepts, the author clearly outlines the design process using case studies to illustrate important points.

SQL Queries for Mere Mortals: A Hands-On Guide to Data Manipulation in SQL, by Michael J. Hernandez and John L. Viescas (Addison-Wesley Professional). SQL queries start out as human questions about the real world. This book can help you learn how to translate those questions into SQL so you can extract the data you need from a database.

PHP 6 and MySQL 5 for Dynamic Web Sites: Visual QuickPro Guide, by Larry Ullman (Peachpit Press). MySQL is the world's most popular open-source database. A combination of PHP and MySQL can turn a static Web site into a dynamic, database-driven site. This book provides an introduction to this dynamic duo.

Privacy Lost: How Technology Is Endangering Your Privacy, by David H. Holtzman (Jossey-Bass). Data never disappears. In this book, David H. Holtzman explores the privacy problem in depth. What is privacy, why is it important, how does technology threaten it, and what can we do about it? These are questions that we all need to consider.

Privacy in Peril: How We Are Sacrificing a Fundamental Right in Exchange for Security and Convenience, by James B. Rule (Oxford University Press). This book is more of a philosophical exploration than a political document. The title pretty much sums up the trade-offs we're making.

The Digital Person: Technology and Privacy in the Information Age, by Daniel Solove (NYU Press). This is a widely praised review of privacy issues and laws in flux.

Periodicals

The Privacy Journal (www.privacyjournal.net). This widely quoted monthly newsletter covers all issues related to personal privacy.

Organizations

Privacy Foundation (www.privacyfoundation.org). The Privacy Foundation isn't an advocacy group; its mission is to report on technology-based privacy threats and circulate alerts.

Privacy Rights Clearinghouse (www.privacyrights.org). This nonprofit consumer information and advocacy organization provides a wealth of information about identity theft, workplace privacy, financial privacy, Internet privacy, medical privacy, and more.

Computer Professionals for Social Responsibility (www.cpsr.org). CPSR provides the public and policy makers with realistic assessments of the power, promise, and problems of information technology. Much of their work deals with privacy-related issues. Their newsletter is a good source of information.

The Electronic Frontier Foundation (www.eff.org). EFF strives to protect civil rights, including the right to privacy, on emerging communication networks.

Electronic Privacy Information Center (www.epic.org). EPIC serves as a watchdog over government efforts to build surveillance capabilities into the emerging information infrastructure.

American Civil Liberties Union (www.aclu.org). The ACLU tirelessly defends constitutional rights, including privacy rights.

Private Citizen (www.private-citizen.com). This organization can help keep you off junk phone and junk mail lists—for a price.

Networking and Digital Communication

OBJECTIVES

After you read this chapter you should be able to:

- Describe the basic types of technology that make telecommunication possible
- Describe the nature and function of local area networks and wide area networks
- Discuss the uses and implications of several different forms of online communication and collaboration
- Explain how wireless network technology is transforming the ways people work and communicate
- Describe how wireless phone networks are converging with digital data networks and the impact of that convergence
- Describe several ways to maximize effectiveness and minimize risks of online communication
- Describe how online social networks, wikis, and other new tools for creating online communities compare to traditional forms of community building
- Describe current and future trends in telecommunications and networking

1. If an elderly but distinguished scientist says that something is possible he is almost certainly right, but if he says that it is impossible he is very probably wrong.
2. The only way to find the limits of the possible is to go beyond them into the impossible.
3. **Any sufficiently advanced technology is indistinguishable from magic.**

—Clarke's Three Laws

Arthur C. Clarke's Magical Prophecy

Besides coining Clarke's laws, British writer Arthur C. Clarke wrote more than 100 works of science fiction and nonfiction. His most famous work was the monumental 1968 film *2001: A Space Odyssey*, in which he collaborated with director Stanley Kubrick. The film's villain, a faceless English-speaking computer with a lust for power, sparked many public debates about the nature and risks of artificial intelligence. These debates continue today.

Clarke's most visionary work, however, may be a paper published in 1945 in which he predicted the use of *geostationary communications satellites*—satellites that match the Earth's rotation so they can hang in a stationary position relative to the spinning planet below and relay wireless transmissions between locations. Clarke's paper pinpointed the exact height of the orbit required to match the movement of the satellite with the planetary rotation. He also suggested that these satellites could replace many telephone cables and radio towers, allowing electronic signals to be beamed across oceans, deserts, and mountain ranges, linking the people of the world with a single communications network.

A decade after Clarke's paper appeared, powerful rockets and sensitive radio receiving equipment made communications satellites realistic. In 1964 the first synchronous TV satellite was launched, marking the beginning of a billion-dollar industry that has changed the way people communicate.

FIGURE 8.1 HAL, the rebellious computer in the movie *2001: A Space Odyssey*.

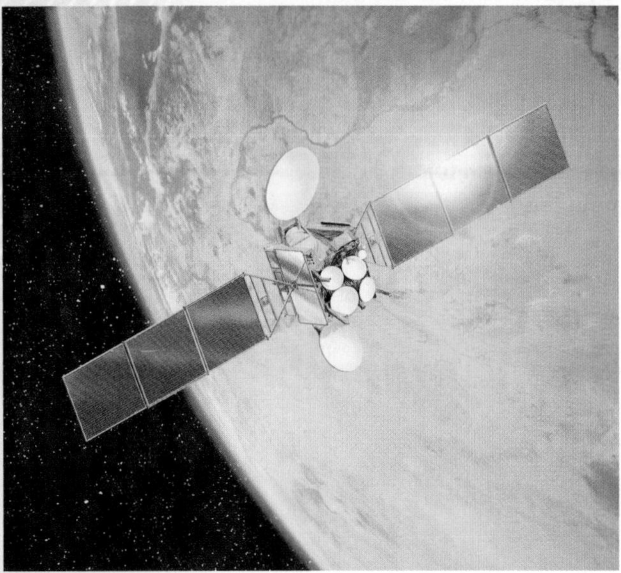

FIGURE 8.2 Geostationary communications satellite.

FIGURE 8.3 Arthur C. Clarke.

Today Clarke is often referred to as the father of satellite communications. He spent the last half of his life in Sri Lanka, where he continued to work as a writer, beaming his words around the globe to editors using the satellites he envisioned earlier in his life. He received numerous awards and recognitions, including knighthood, before he died in 2008 at the age of 91. Shortly before his death he said, "I have had a diverse career as a writer, underwater explorer, and space promoter. I would like to be remembered as a writer."

The Battle of New Orleans, the bloodiest battle of the War of 1812, was fought two weeks after the war officially ended; it took that long for the cease-fire message to travel from Washington, D.C., to the front line. In 1991, 179 years later, six hard-line Soviet communists staged a coup to turn back the tide of democratic and economic reforms that were sweeping the U.S.S.R. Within hours, messages zipped between the Soviet Union and Western nations on telephone and computer networks. Cable television and computer conferences provided up-to-the-minute analyses of events—analyses that were beamed to computer bulletin boards inside the Soviet Union. Networks carried messages among the resisters, allowing them to stay steps ahead of the coup leaders and the Soviet military machine. People toppled the coup and ultimately the Soviet Union—not with guns, but with courage, will, and timely information.

Telecommunication technology—the technology of long-distance communication—has come a long way since the War of 1812, and the world has changed dramatically as a result. After Samuel Morse built an electronic telegraph in 1844, people could, for the first time, send long-distance messages instantaneously. Alexander Bell's invention of the telephone in 1876 extended this capability to the spoken word. Today systems of linked computers enable us to send data and software across the room or around the world. Technological transformation has changed the popular definition of the word *telecommunication*, which today means long-distance electronic communication in a variety of forms.

In this chapter, we take a closer look at the networks that connect computers. We examine the hardware and software technologies that make computer networks possible, and we discuss ways in which such linked computers are used for communication, information gathering, and sharing resources. We also consider how networks are changing the way we live and work. In the next chapter, we'll delve deeper into the technology behind the Internet—the global computer network at the heart of the latest telecommunication revolution. We'll see how this technology will continue to transform our culture in ways that are hard to imagine today. But for now let's start by looking at the building blocks that make up all computer networks.

FIGURE 8.4 The telegraph was the first electronic networking technology.

Basic Network Anatomy

> All the most promising technologies making their debut now are chiefly due to communication between computers—that is, to connections rather than to computations. **And since communication is the basis of culture, fiddling at this level is indeed momentous.**
>
> —*Kevin Kelly, former* Wired *executive editor*

A computer network is any system of two or more computers that are linked together. Why is networking important? The answers to this question revolve around the three essential components of every computer system:

- *Hardware.* Networks enable people to share computer hardware resources, reducing costs and making it possible for more people to take better advantage of powerful computer equipment.
- *Software.* Networks enable people to share data and software programs, increasing efficiency and productivity.
- *People.* Networks enable people to work together, play together, and communicate in ways that are otherwise difficult or impossible.

Important information is hidden in these three statements. But before we examine them in more detail, we need to look at the hardware and software that make computer networks possible.

Networks Near and Far

In Chapters 2 and 3, you saw how information travels among the CPU, memory, and other components within a computer as electrical impulses that move along collections of parallel wires called buses. A network extends the range of these information pulses, allowing them to travel to other computers. Computer networks come in all shapes and sizes, but most can be categorized as either local area networks or wide area networks.

A **local area network (LAN)** is a network in which the computers are physically close to each other, usually in the same building. A typical LAN includes a collection of computers and peripherals; each computer and networked peripheral is an individual *node* on the network. Nodes are connected to *hubs* or *switches*, which allow any node on the network to communicate with any other node. A hub broadcasts messages to all devices connected to the network; a switch transmits data to only the destination node. The practical consequence of this difference is that a hub allows only a single message at a time to move across the LAN, whereas a switch can carry multiple messages simultaneously. For this reason, a switch provides a significant advantage over a hub on a busy LAN.

One way to connect a node to a hub or a switch is by using a physical cable. The most common type of LAN cable, known as *twisted pair*, contains copper wires that resemble those in standard telephone cables. Most networked computers today are connected to networks via Ethernet cables plugged into Ethernet ports. **Ethernet** is a popular networking architecture developed in the 1970s at Xerox PARC; it has become an industry standard. Almost every new PC includes an Ethernet port on the main circuit board; older PCs have network cards that contain Ethernet ports. Circuitry on the motherboard or the network card controls the flow of data between the computer's RAM and the network cable. At the same time, it converts the computer's internal low-power signals into more powerful signals that can be transmitted through the network.

Some networks, mostly in homes, use existing household electrical or telephone wiring to transmit data. (Networks that use power lines are sometimes called *power-line networks*.) For these types of networks, Ethernet cables generally connect each computer's network port to a device that attaches to the phone line or power line.

But the biggest trend in LAN technology today is the explosive growth in wireless networks. In a **wireless network**, each node has a tiny radio transmitter so it can send and

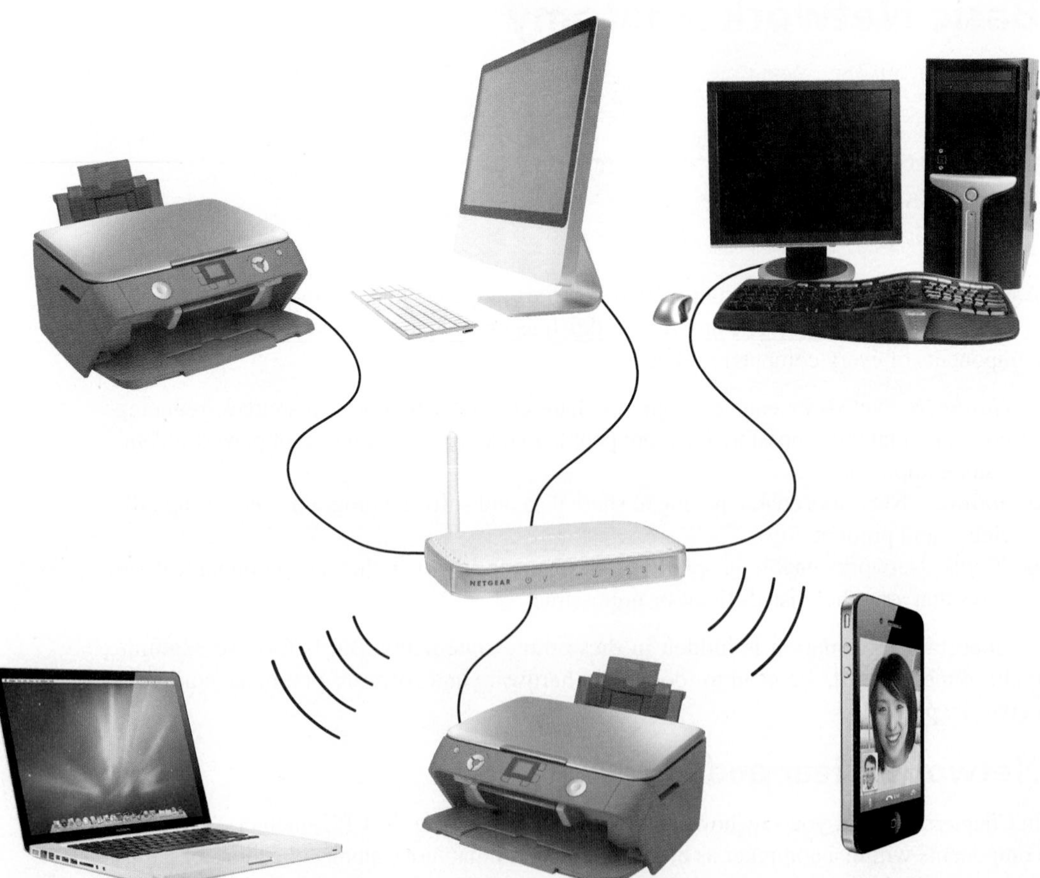

FIGURE 8.5 A LAN can contain a variety of interconnected computers and peripherals using wired and wireless connections.

receive data through the air rather than through cables. Wireless network connections are especially convenient for people who are constantly on the move. They're also convenient for small networks in homes and small businesses because they can be installed without digging or drilling. Wireless networks are generally slower than wired LANs. A LAN can include a mix of hardwired connections and wireless connections.

All computers on a LAN don't have to use the same operating system. For example, a single network might include Macs, Windows PCs, and Linux workstations. The computers can be connected in many different ways, and many rules and industry-defined standards dictate what will and won't work. Setting up a basic home LAN can be simple and straightforward. But large enterprise network systems may typically require the expertise of *network administrators* to take care of the configuration details so others can focus on using the network.

A **wide area network (WAN)**, as the name implies, is a network of LANs that extends over a long distance. In a WAN, each individual network site is a node on the wide area network. The largest and best known WAN is the Internet. By connecting to a network that's part of the Internet, a computer can connect to millions of other Internet-connected devices.

Large WANs are possible because of the Web of telephone lines, microwave relay towers, and satellites that span the globe. Most WANs are private operations designed to link geographically dispersed corporate or government offices. WANs can be built using leased lines, or they can transmit signals using the Internet's packet-switching infrastructure (described in the next chapter).

Routers are hardware devices or software programs that route messages as they travel between networks. Routers make it possible for messages to pass from the originating computer's LAN through a chain of intermediate networks to reach the LAN of the destination computer.

Mesh networks are an alternative to networks that rely on centralized routers. In a mesh network, a message hops from wireless device to wireless device until it finds its

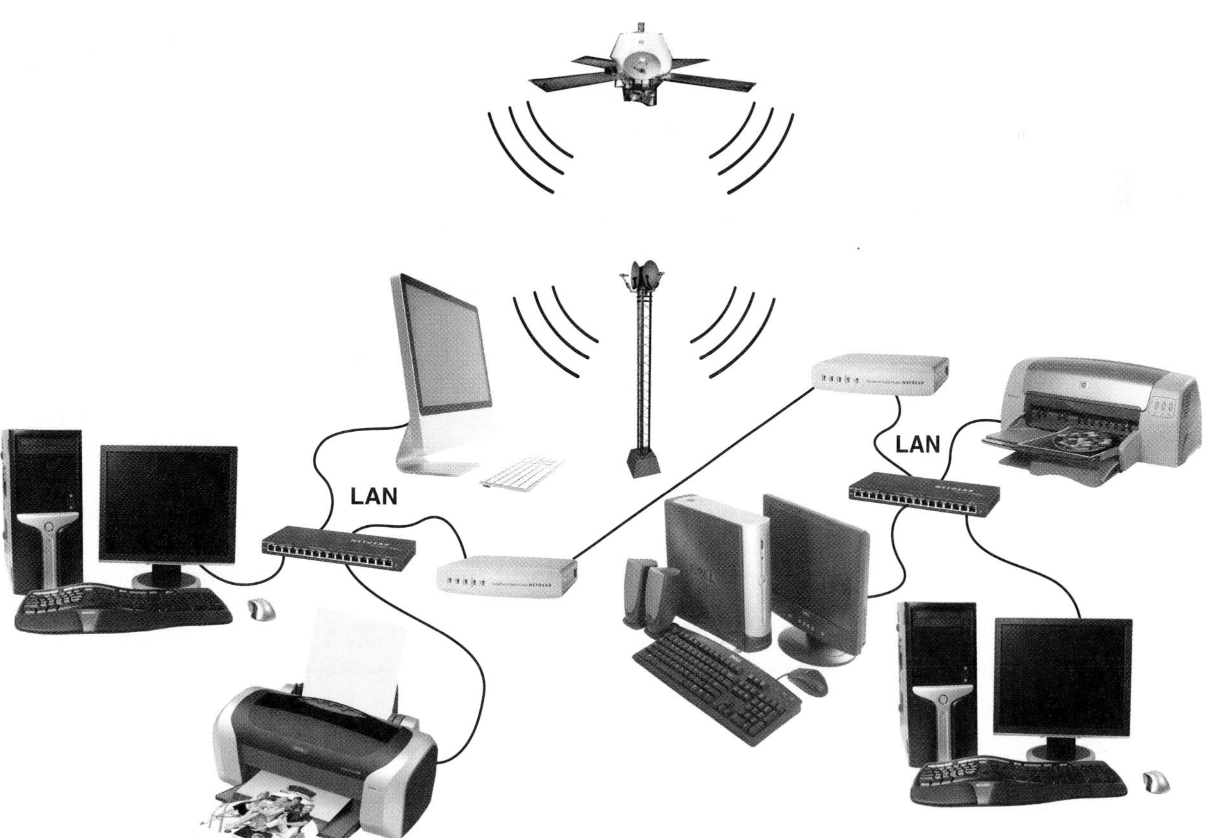

FIGURE 8.6 WANs are often made up of LANs linked by phone lines, microwave towers, and communications satellites.

destination; there's no need to go through a central hub on the way. Mesh networks are convenient for small, temporary communication systems. For example, emergency personnel at the scene of a fire can quickly set up a mesh network to help them coordinate their efforts.

The Importance of Bandwidth

Most people who have explored multimedia on the Web have experienced small, jerky videos, sputtering audio, and (especially) long waits. The cause of most of these problems on the Internet (and other networks) is a lack of bandwidth at some point in the path between the sending computer and the receiving computer. The word has a technical definition, but in the world of computer networks, **bandwidth** generally refers to the quantity of data that can be transmitted through a communication medium in a given amount of time. In general, increased bandwidth means faster transmission speeds. Bandwidth is typically measured in kilobits (thousands of bits) or megabits (millions of bits) per second. (Because a byte is 8 bits, a megabit is 1/8 of a megabyte. The text of this chapter is about 300 kilobytes, or 2400 kilobits, of information. A physical medium capable of transmitting 100 megabits per second could theoretically transmit this chapter's text more than 50 times in 1 second.) Bandwidth can be affected by many factors, including the physical media that make up the network, the amount of network traffic, the software protocols of the network, and the type of network connection.

Some people find it easier to visualize bandwidth by thinking of a network cable as a highway. One way to increase bandwidth in a cable is to increase the number of parallel wires in that cable—the equivalent of adding more lanes to a freeway. Another way is to increase the speed with which information passes through the cable; this is the same as increasing the speed of the vehicles on the freeway. Of course, it's easier and safer to increase highway speed limits if you have a traffic flow system that minimizes the chance of collisions and accidents; in the same way, more efficient, reliable software can increase network bandwidth. But increasing a highway's throughput doesn't help much if cars pile up at the entry and exit ramps; in the same way, a high-bandwidth network seems like a low-bandwidth network if you've got a low-bandwidth connection to that network.

In general, bandwidth is on the rise. The original Ethernet standard, now commonly referred to as 10BASE-T Ethernet, had a bandwidth of 10 megabits per second. In the mid-1990s a faster Ethernet standard emerged: ***Fast Ethernet*** (which includes 100BASE-T) carries traffic at 100 megabits per second, provided that all the devices on the LAN are fast Ethernet compatible. Today the fastest Ethernet devices follow the ***Gigabit Ethernet*** (1000BASE-X) standard, capable of transferring 1 gigabit of data per second on an all-gigabit-Ethernet LAN.

Bandwidth is also on the rise *between* LANs, thanks to fiber-optic cables that are rapidly replacing copper wires in the worldwide telephone network. Fiber-optic cables use light waves to carry information at blinding speeds. A single fiber-optic cable can replace 10,000 copper telephone cables. Digital fiber-optic networks now connect major communication hubs around the world. Many large businesses and government institutions are connected to the global fiber-optic network, but most small businesses and homes still depend on copper wires for the "last mile," as it's often referred to in the industry—the link to the closest on-ramp to the fiber-optic freeway. Fiber-optic communication lines will eventually find their way into most homes, changing our lives in the process. These cables will provide lightning-fast two-way links to the outside world for our phones, televisions, radios, computers, and a variety of other devices.

Communication Software

Whether connected by cables, radio waves, or the Internet, computers need some kind of communication software to interact. To communicate with each other, two machines must follow the same **protocols**—rules for the exchange of data between devices. One such protocol is transmission speed: If one machine is "talking" at 200 kbps and the other is "listening" at 100 kbps, the message doesn't get through. Protocols include prearranged codes for messages such as "Are you ready?," "I am about to start sending a data file," and "Did you receive that file?" For two computers to understand each other, the software on both machines must be set to follow the same protocols. Communication software establishes a protocol that is followed by the computer's hardware.

FIGURE 8.7 A server might look like a normal PC. But industrial-strength servers such as these powerful IBM devices can provide software and data for hundreds or thousands of networked computers.

The most famous protocol for computer networking is **TCP/IP**, discussed in more detail in the next chapter. Strictly speaking, the Internet is the network of computers and other digital devices that use TCP/IP to control the exchange of data.

Communication software can take a variety of forms. For a local area network, many communication tasks can be taken care of by a **network operating system (NOS)**, such as Novell's Netware or Microsoft's Windows Server. Just as a personal computer's operating system shields the user from most of the nuts and bolts of the computer's operation, a NOS shields the user from the hardware and software details of routine communication between machines. But unlike a PC operating system, the NOS must respond to requests from many computers and must coordinate communication throughout the network. Today many organizations are replacing the specialized PC-based NOS with an **intranet** system—a system built around the open standards and protocols of the Internet, as described in more detail in the next chapter.

The function and location of the network operating system depend in part on the LAN model. Some LANs are set up according to the **client/server model**, a hierarchical model in which one or more computers act as dedicated servers and all the remaining computers act as **clients**. Each server is a high-speed, high-capacity computer containing data and other resources to be shared with client computers. Using NOS server software, the server fulfills requests from clients for data and other resources. In a client/server network, the bulk of the NOS resides on the server, but each client has NOS client software for sending requests to servers. Many small networks, including most home networks, use the **peer-to-peer model** (sometimes called *p-to-p* or *P2P*), which enables every computer on the network to be both client and server. In this kind of network, every user can make files publicly available to other users on the network. Most desktop operating systems, including Windows, Linux, and the Mac OS, include all the software necessary to operate a peer-to-peer network. In practice, many networks are hybrids that combine features of the client/server and peer-to-peer models.

Linking In: Internet Connection Technologies

> Pretty soon **you'll have no more idea of what computer you're using** than you have an idea of where your electricity comes from.
>
> —*Danny Hillis, computer designer*

In the early days of computer networks, most people had two basic choices for connecting their computers to networks: direct connections to local area networks using cables, or dial-up access to a remote system using a modem connected to a phone line. Today we generally don't need to dial into a remote site's host computer; we just link into the Internet and let our messages find their way through this network of networks to the target computer. In this section, we'll survey the most popular Internet connection options. (We'll revisit these options in the next chapter.)

In many schools and businesses, computers have a hard-wired Internet connection through a LAN. A *direct (dedicated) connection* is generally much faster than other connection options, making it possible to transfer large files (such as multimedia documents) quickly.

Typically, computers on a LAN have fast Ethernet connections that can transmit data at up to 100 Mbps (megabits per second). A large organization may operate a *backbone network* to connect its LANs. A high-speed fiber-optic backbone network can transmit data at more than 1 gigabit per second (1,000 megabits per second). Common ways of linking an organization's network to the Internet include *T1* (sometimes written *T-1*) connections, which can transmit voice, data, and video at roughly 1.5 Mbps, and *T3*, which has a data transmission speed of around 45 Mbps. (On some continents, a technology called E1 is used instead of T1.)

A computer can *temporarily* connect to an Internet host through a **dial-up connection**—a connection using a modem and standard phone lines. The world's phone network is going digital, but the transition to an all-digital network is still years away. Consequently, before a digital signal can be transmitted over a standard phone line, it must be converted to an analog signal—a continuous wave, similar to sound waves. At the receiving end, the analog signal must be converted back into the bits, representing the original digital message. Each of these tasks is performed by a **modem** (short for modulator/demodulator)—a hardware device, inside or outside the computer chassis, that connects a computer to a telephone line through standard modular phone jacks. A *fax modem* can communicate with *facsimile (fax) machines* as well as computers. Dialup connections are sometimes called **narrowband connections** because they don't offer much bandwidth when compared to newer, more technically advanced types of Internet connections.

For faster remote connections, most businesses and homes with computers bypass standard modems and use some kind of **broadband connection**—a connection with much greater bandwidth than modems have. Several competing broadband technologies are available to computer users in many areas, including DSL, cable, wireless, and satellite broadband connections. (Technically, a direct connection through a T1 or T3 line could be called a broadband connection, but most people don't have access to direct Internet connections.)

In some cases, broadband connections offer data transmission speeds comparable to direct connection speeds. Users of these services don't need to dial in; the Internet is instantly available anytime, like television or radio. The most common broadband alternatives are based on the following technologies:

- *DSL.* Many phone companies offer **DSL (digital subscriber line)**, a technology for bringing broadband connections to homes and small businesses by sharing the copper telephone lines that carry voice calls. DSL customers must be geographically close to phone company service hubs. DSL transmission speeds vary considerably. *Downstream traffic*—information from the Internet to the subscriber—sometimes approaches T1 speeds. *Upstream traffic*—data traveling from the home computer to the Internet—typically travels more slowly. A DSL signal can share a standard phone line with voice traffic, so it can remain on without interfering with phone calls. DSL is not available everywhere, but it is becoming more widely available every year.
- *Cable modem connections.* Many cable TV companies offer high-speed Internet connections through **cable modems**. Cable modems allow Internet connections through the same network of coaxial cables that deliver television signals to millions of homes. Like DSL, cable modem service isn't available everywhere. Cable modem speeds often exceed DSL speeds both downstream and upstream. But because a single cable is shared by an entire neighborhood, transmission speeds can go down when the number of users goes up.
- *Satellite connections.* **Satellite Internet connections** are available through many of the same satellite dishes that provide television channels to viewers. Downstream satellite transmission is much faster than conventional modem traffic is, although not as fast as DSL or cable modem service. For some satellite services, upstream traffic goes through phone lines at standard modem rates. Other services use satellites for upstream and downstream traffic. Most broadband satellite services transmit signals via geostationary satellites in orbit more than 22,000 miles above the Earth's surface. Because it takes a second or more for a signal to make the round trip to space and back, satellite connections have high *latency*—there's a significant delay between the time a message is sent and the time it's received. Satellite connections are also vulnerable to disruptions from storms, sunspots, and other natural events. But for many homes and businesses outside of urban centers, satellites provide the only high-speed Internet access options available.

FIGURE 8.8 A broadband connection requires a cable modem (left) connected to a cable TV service line, a DSL modem (right) connected to a phone line, or a satellite modem connected to a satellite dish. These aren't really modems but are so named because they are functionally similar to modems.

- *Wireless broadband connections.* A growing number of people connect to the Internet through wireless broadband connections. Using Wi-Fi and related technologies described in the next section, students can connect to the Internet while they move around a wireless-equipped campus, travelers can make web connections while waiting in airports, coffee shops can become Internet cafes for people with wireless receivers in their laptops, and communities can provide Internet services to their populations without expensive rewiring projects.

Each of these broadband technologies is widely deployed in the United States, and each is expanding its area of coverage. The United States lags far behind many other countries, though, in terms of the speed, quality, and price of its broadband offerings. In Japan, for example, a person can download an entire movie in two minutes—a movie that might take two hours or more to download with a U.S. broadband connection that costs just as much as the Japanese service. There's considerable debate about why the country that created the Internet provides inferior Internet access for its citizens. At least part of the reason may be the U.S. government's reluctance to regulate the telecommunications industry the way other developed countries do. In any case, it's likely that broadband service in the United States and elsewhere will continue to broaden.

Wireless Network Technology

> Wireless technology is a liberating force. **It will make possible human-centered computers.** This wasn't possible before because we were anchored to a PC, and we had to go to it like going to a temple to pay our respects.
>
> —*Michael Dertouzos, Director, MIT Laboratory for Computer Science*

A lightning-fast network connection to your desktop is of little use if you're away from your desk most of the time. When bandwidth is less important than mobility and convenience, wireless technology can provide practical solutions.

Most of us use some form of wireless technology every day. Even people who shun computers and cell phones are likely to turn their TVs on and off with wireless remotes. Most home entertainment remote controls use ***infrared wireless*** technology to send commands to TVs, sound systems, and other devices. Some laptop and handheld computers have infrared ports that can send and receive digital information over short distances, provided there are no physical barriers blocking the signals. But infrared technology isn't widely used in networks because of distance and line-of-sight limitations. Instead, most wireless networks use some form of radio technology. In this section we'll explore the most important types of wireless networking technologies.

Wi-Fi and WiMax Technology

The fastest-growing wireless LAN technology is known as **Wi-Fi**. Wi-Fi uses radio waves to link computers to a LAN through a nearby **wireless access point (WAP)**—a Wi-Fi **hotspot**. (Apple calls their wireless access points *AirPort hubs*; some companies label theirs as *Wi-Fi routers*.) A wireless access point is similar to a network hub; it serves as a central connection point for wireless computers, smart phones, media players, digital cameras, game consoles, security devices, and more. (Wi-Fi technology also allows peer-to-peer communication, so that two Wi-Fi—equipped devices can communicate directly with each other. But most Wi-Fi communication goes through wireless hubs.) If the access point is wired into a LAN, wireless devices can communicate with wired devices on the LAN. If the access point is linked to a DSL modem, cable modem, or a direct Internet connection, the access point is an Internet hotspot—a wireless gateway to the Internet.

Wi-Fi doesn't have the bandwidth of a hardwired Ethernet connection, but it's fast enough for most applications, including multimedia Web downloads. There are several different flavors of Wi-Fi; all are variations of the IEEE 802.11 specifications for wireless local area networks. In the early 2000s, most Wi-Fi devices followed the 802.11b standards. Because of their greater bandwidth and range, 802.11g devices quickly took over the Wi-Fi market. Today 802.11n, with up to three times the bandwidth of 802.11g, is the new standard. Devices from different Wi-Fi generations can coexist on the same

FIGURE 8.9 A wireless Internet connection is created by linking a wireless access point like one of these to a broadband or direct Internet connection.

wireless networks, but older 802.11b devices can slow traffic down for everybody on a network.

Wi-Fi devices use the 2.4 GHz and 5 GHz band of the radio spectrum. Many common devices, including portable phones and microwave ovens, can cause Wi-Fi interference, especially on the crowded 2.4 GHz band. Wi-Fi devices can transmit on different *channels* within each band, so it's often possible to reduce interference by changing channel settings on Wi-Fi hub devices. Wi-Fi range is affected by a number of factors—nearby objects that block signals, antenna placement, and devices competing for the same part of the radio spectrum (including other Wi-Fi networks in the neighborhood). A typical Wi-Fi access point has a range of up to 120 feet indoors and 300 feet outdoors. Installing additional access points can extend the range of a network.

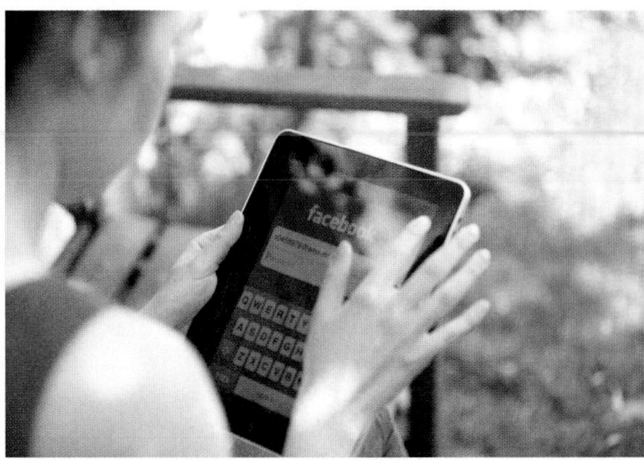

FIGURE 8.10 This iPad can connect to the Internet through a WiFi network or a 3G or 4G phone network, depending on which is available at its current location.

Millions of homes, schools, campuses, and businesses worldwide have Wi-Fi networks. Hundreds of thousands of public hotspots have been installed in coffee houses, airports, restaurants, libraries, and other public buildings. A home Wi-Fi network allows computers to connect from any room without cables. A growing number of cities and towns are building citywide Wi-Fi networks, although some metropolitan Wi-Fi networks have been delayed or blocked for technological and political reasons. In some cases the technology hasn't functioned well when scaled up to serve thousands of users. In other cases private companies have objected to having competition from government agencies or government-sanctioned monopolies. Still, there are many successful municipal Wi-Fi networks around the globe, and more are being created every year.

Many public hotspots and Wi-Fi networks are free and open to all devices within range. Others require visitors to agree to terms of service before connecting to the Internet. Still others require passwords and other forms of authentication. Some charge for access by the month or by the hour. But free Wi-Fi access points are sprouting everywhere, part of a grassroots movement to provide universal wireless access to the Net.

WiMAX or *802.16* is a newer, long-distance radio-wave technology. A single WiMAX tower can provide Wi-Fi-style access to a 25-square-mile area—the same area that can be covered by a cell phone tower. WiMAX also supports line-of-sight connections to customers up to 30 miles away. WiMAX isn't designed to replace Wi-Fi, but it can be a powerful tool for connecting Wi-Fi networks. 4G mobile networks (covered later in the chapter) are likely to compete with, and possibly overshadow, WiMAX technology as they mature. (Some people loosely refer to WiMAX as a 4G technology.)

Wireless networks raise many security concerns. A Wi-Fi access point broadcasts information in all directions; the network forms a sphere with a diameter of up to 300 feet (the length of a football field). If the network is not secured, a technically skilled snooper with a laptop inside this virtual sphere can "sniff" network traffic and read what you're writing and collect email addresses and other personal information. The *WEP* (wired equivalent privacy) encryption scheme (see Chapter 10) improves the security of wireless networks by making your data as secure as it would be on a wired Ethernet. Organizations that need extra security can treat their wireless network as an insecure network and put a *firewall* between their wireless network and their wired network. (A firewall blocks unauthorized data transfers. We'll discuss how firewalls work in Chapter 10.) They can also make a wireless network more secure through the use of a **VPN (virtual private network)**. A VPN is an electronic "tunnel" through the Internet that uses encryption and other security measures to keep out unauthorized users and prevent eavesdropping.

Bluetooth Technology

Another type of wireless technology is **Bluetooth**, or *802.15*, named for a Danish king who overcame his country's religious differences. Bluetooth technology overcomes differences between mobile phones, handheld computers, and PCs, making it possible for all of these devices to communicate with each other regardless of their operating systems.

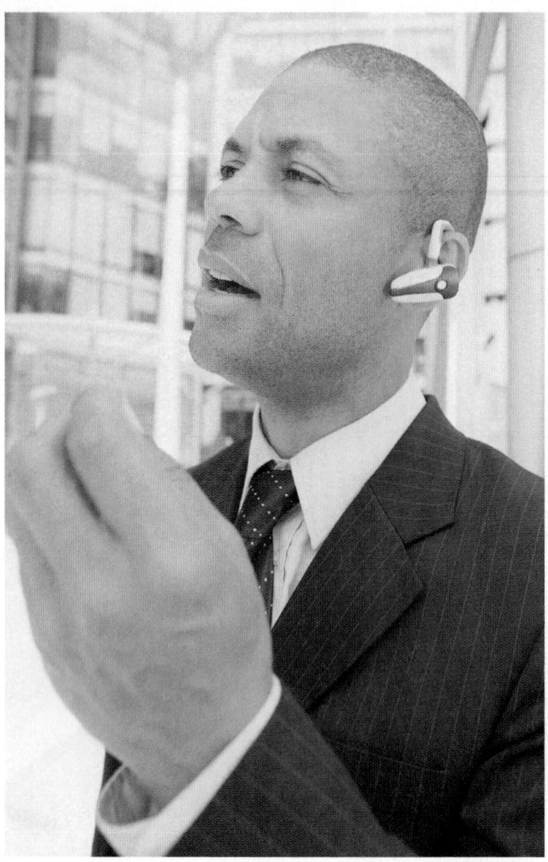

FIGURE 8.11 Bluetooth technology enables mobile phones and computer peripherals to announce themselves and describe their capabilities to other devices and PCs in personal area networks.

Bluetooth uses radio technology similar to that of Wi-Fi, but its transmissions are limited to about 30 feet. Bluetooth isn't designed to compete with Wi-Fi. It is intended to replace the wires that connect devices such as cell phones, headsets, PDAs, and printers to each other. With Bluetooth it's possible to create a *personal area network (PAN)*—a network that links a variety of personal electronic devices so they can communicate with each other.

Bluetooth applications include:

- Linking a mobile phone to a wireless headset or a car's audio system
- Connecting a wireless keyboard and mouse to a computer
- Connecting a wireless game controller to the game console
- Sharing contact information and calendars between mobile phones and other portable devices
- Playing multiplayer games with smart phones

Bluetooth technology is currently limited to simple device connectivity, but in the future it may open up all kinds of possibilities:

- A pacemaker senses a heart attack, and notifies the victim's mobile phone to dial 911.
- A car radio communicates with parking-lot video cameras to find out where spaces are available.
- A medical wristband transmits an accident victim's vital information to a doctor's handheld computer.
- A cell phone tells you about specials on clothes (available in your size) as you walk past stores in a mall. (Many fear that this technology will usher in a new era of junk phone calls.)

3G and 4G Technology

Wi-Fi and Bluetooth networks are designed to cover small areas; mobile phone networks are designed to blanket countries and continents. Since they were introduced in the 1980s, mobile phone networks have been steadily moving in a computer-friendly digital direction. The first generation of mobile phone networks, 1G, was made up of analog voice-only networks. 2G networks were based on many different competing digital standards, so a phone from one carrier didn't necessarily work on another carrier's network. Faster 3G networks carry multimedia data and voice communications simultaneously, making it possible for mobile phones to serve as Internet multimedia devices. But 3G networks still lack true broadband speeds and compatibility between carrier networks. 4G networks complete the transition to the IP packet-switching technology of the Internet (described in the next chapter). They offer gigabit broadband speeds to a vast array of mobile devices that are compatible across carriers. Some carriers are using WiMax technology for their 4G networks, further blurring the line that used to separate computer networks from phone networks.

Until recently, mobile phone Internet connections were more common in Europe and Asia than in North America. But a combination of faster digital networks and smarter phones has dramatically increased the number of Americans who use their phones to send and receive email, check news headlines, shop, play network games, share photos and video clips, get maps and driving directions, and transfer money.

Mobile phone companies around the world are upgrading their networks from 3G to 4G. But just as freeways tend to fill with cars as soon as they're completed, phone networks fill with traffic as more customers discover the convenience of using their phones for mobile Internet access. Larger mobile devices, such as the iPad, compete with phones for bandwidth on these networks, too. And a growing number of people use their phones as Internet gateways for their laptops. Many phone companies allow *tethering*—cabling a laptop to a mobile phone so it can send and receive Internet data through the phone's wireless Internet connection. Some companies offer pocket-sized portable Wi-Fi hotspots that draw their signals from 3G and 4G phone networks.

FIGURE 8.12 This Japanese student is using her phone to make a vending machine purchase.

There's a tremendous overlap in the capabilities and potential of Wi-Fi, WiMAX, 3G, and 4G. For example, a smart phone might connect to the Internet through a 4G network in one location and through a Wi-Fi connection in another. The user of the phone might place a phone call using the 4G carrier at the first location and voice-over-IP carrier (described later in the chapter) at the second. How we use these technologies will depend in part on how telecommunications companies develop them. In any case, the boundaries that separate phone networks and computer networks will continue to blur.

Wireless Network Standards

Technical Name	Popular Name	Range	Technology	Approximate Speed	Typical Use
IrDA-Data	IrDA	1 meter	Infrared	9600 bps	Exchange data between PDAs
802.15	Bluetooth	10 meters	Radio	1 Mbps	Room-sized personal area network
802.11	Wi-Fi	30 meters or more	Radio	54 Mbps	Local area network
802.16	WiMAX	5 miles (no line of sight) to 30 miles (line of sight)	Radio	70 Mbps	Linking Wi-Fi networks
3G	3G	Varies widely depending on type of data being transmitted and location of relay towers	Radio	Up to 3.1 Mbps (much slower while moving)	Mobile phone Internet access
4G	4G	Varies widely depending on type of data being transmitted and location of relay towers	Radio	Up to 14.4 Mbps (much slower while moving)	Mobile phone voice, Internet access

FIGURE 8.13 Wireless technologies compared.

Specialized Networks: From GPS to Digital Money

> After more than a century of electric technology, **we have extended our central nervous system itself in a global embrace**, abolishing both space and time as far as our planet is concerned.
>
> —*Marshall McLuhan, in* Understanding Media

Not all computer networks are collections of PCs and phones linked to the Internet. Some specialized networks are designed to perform specific functions; these networks may not be accessible through the Internet.

One such specialized network is the U.S. Department of Defense Global Positioning System (GPS). The GPS includes at least 24 satellites that circle the Earth. They are carefully spaced so that from any point on the planet, at any time, four satellites will be above the horizon. Each satellite contains a computer, an atomic clock, and a radio. On the ground, a *GPS receiver* can use signals broadcast by three or four visible satellites to determine its position. GPS receivers can display locations, maps, and directions on smart phones, handheld computers, laptops, automobile and boat navigation systems, and military equipment.

Members of the U.S. military use GPS receivers to keep track of where they are, but so do scientists, engineers,

FIGURE 8.14a A specialized GPS receiver helps this blind person navigate.

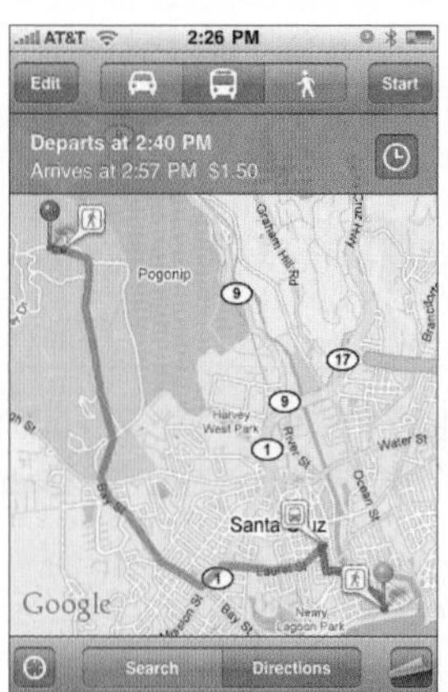

FIGURE 8.14b Using the iPhone's built-in GPS receiver and Internet databases from the phone's 3G connection, Google maps can find the nearest bus stop and display the current bus schedule.

FIGURE 8.14c Emergency rescue teams routinely use GPS devices to navigate hazardous terrain.

FIGURE 8.14d AcrossAir's Nearest Tube app has an augmented reality interface that uses GPS data to overlay information about nearby London tube stations on top of the "view" as seen by the camera lens.

motorists, hikers, boaters, surveyors, farmers, rescue squads, emergency relief teams, and others. GPS technology is finding its way into a variety of mobile applications for smart phones, tablets, and laptops. Using GPS, Google and Bing mobile search engines can provide distance and directions to "found" items, and can make searches more location-relevant. Custom applications can locate nearby restaurants, public transit options, parking lots, shops, or public rest rooms. Some apps use augmented reality interfaces to overlay downloaded information on top of camera images. For example, when you point your phone's camera at a restaurant you might see its phone number, specialties, and star rating.

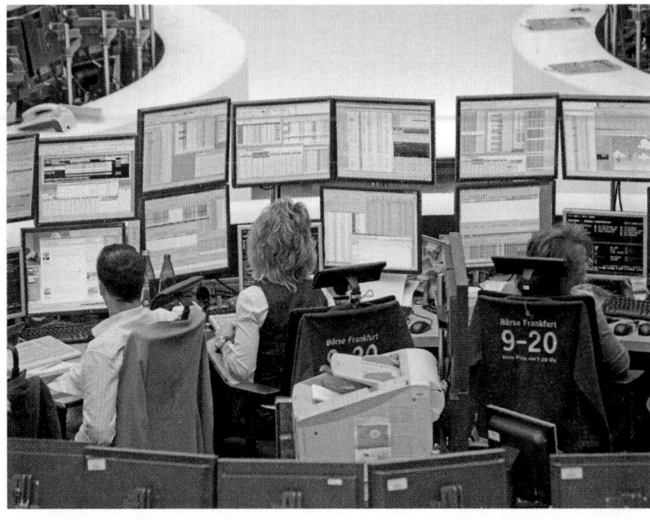

FIGURE 8.15 Every day stock traders move billions of dollars in funds electronically through world markets.

GPS technology isn't foolproof; tall buildings, bad weather, and even sunspots can affect its accuracy. And it isn't without controversy. Privacy advocates have expressed concerns that the same technology that helps emergency workers pinpoint cellular 911 calls can also be used to find people who don't *want* to be found. GPS was the first fully functional Global Navigation Satellite System, but other systems have been (or are being) developed by Russia, the European Union, China, and India.

Probably the most widely used specialized computer networks are the networks that keep our global financial systems running. When you strip away the emotional trappings, money is another form of information. Dollars, yen, pounds, and rubles are all symbols that make it easy for people to exchange goods and services. Money can be just about anything, provided people agree to its value. During the past few centuries, paper replaced metal as the major form of money. Today paper is being replaced by digital patterns stored in computer media. Money, like other digital information, can be transmitted through computer networks. That's why it's possible to withdraw cash from your checking account using an *automated teller machine (ATM)* at an airport or shopping mall thousands of miles from your home bank. An ATM (not to be confused with the communication protocol with the same initials) is a specialized terminal linked to a bank's main computer through a commercial banking network. Financial networks also make credit card purchases, automatic bill paying, electronic funds transfer, and all kinds of **electronic commerce (e-commerce)** possible. (E-commerce will be discussed in more detail in later chapters.)

The Network Advantage

A network becomes more valuable as **it reaches more users.**

—Metcalfe's Law, by Bob Metcalfe, inventor of Ethernet

With this background in mind, let's reconsider the three reasons people use networks:

- *Networks enable people to share computer hardware resources, reducing costs and making it possible for more people to take better advantage of powerful computer equipment.* When computers and peripherals are connected in a LAN, computer users can share peripherals. Before LANs, the typical office had a printer connected to each computer. Today it's more common to find a large group of computers and users sharing a small number of high-quality networked printers. In a client/server network, each printer may be connected to a *print server*—a server that accepts, prioritizes, and processes print jobs. Although it may not make much sense for users to try to share a printer on a wide area network (because it's not particularly convenient to use a printer that's hundreds of miles away), WAN users often share other hardware resources. Many WANs include powerful mainframes and supercomputers that can be accessed by authorized users at remote sites. Later in this chapter, we'll discuss grid computing—using grids of networked computers to share processing power and storage.

how it works A Home Computer Network

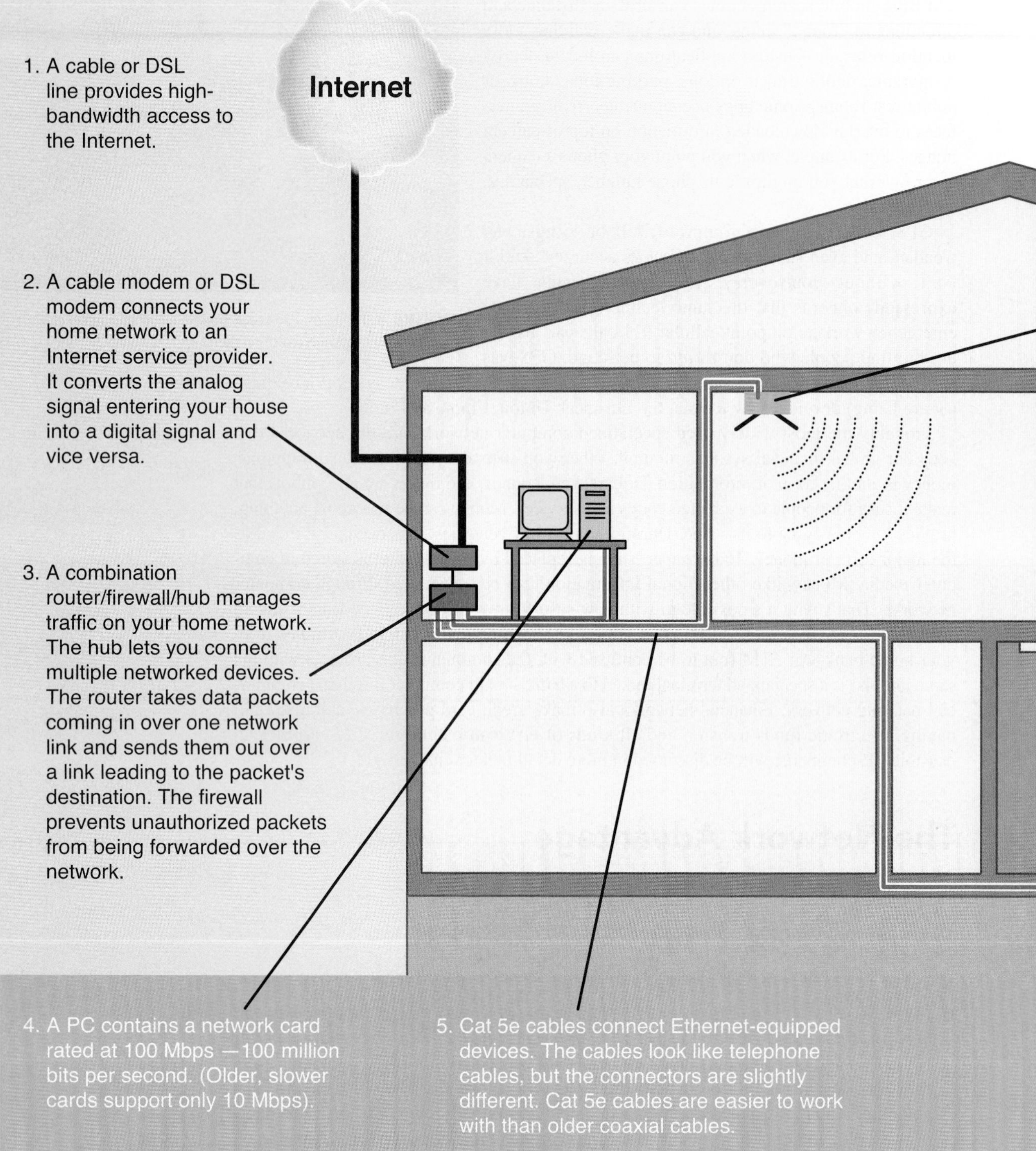

Internet
1. A cable or DSL line provides high-bandwidth access to the Internet.
2. A cable modem or DSL modem connects your home network to an Internet service provider. It converts the analog signal entering your house into a digital signal and vice versa.
3. A combination router/firewall/hub manages traffic on your home network. The hub lets you connect multiple networked devices. The router takes data packets coming in over one network link and sends them out over a link leading to the packet's destination. The firewall prevents unauthorized packets from being forwarded over the network.
4. A PC contains a network card rated at 100 Mbps —100 million bits per second. (Older, slower cards support only 10 Mbps).
5. Cat 5e cables connect Ethernet-equipped devices. The cables look like telephone cables, but the connectors are slightly different. Cat 5e cables are easier to work with than older coaxial cables.

FIGURE 8.16

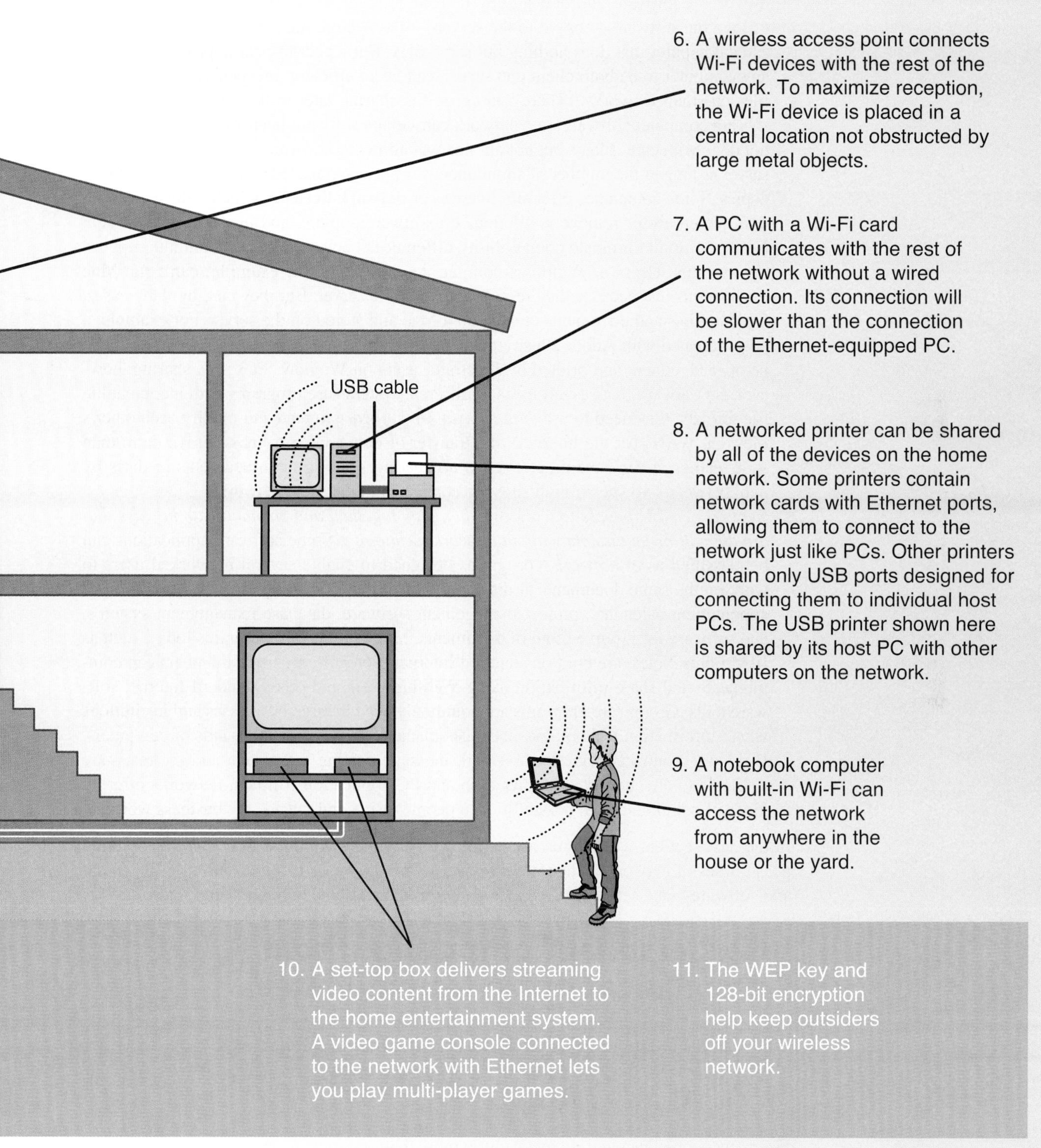

6. A wireless access point connects Wi-Fi devices with the rest of the network. To maximize reception, the Wi-Fi device is placed in a central location not obstructed by large metal objects.
7. A PC with a Wi-Fi card communicates with the rest of the network without a wired connection. Its connection will be slower than the connection of the Ethernet-equipped PC.
USB cable
8. A networked printer can be shared by all of the devices on the home network. Some printers contain network cards with Ethernet ports, allowing them to connect to the network just like PCs. Other printers contain only USB ports designed for connecting them to individual host PCs. The USB printer shown here is shared by its host PC with other computers on the network.
9. A notebook computer with built-in Wi-Fi can access the network from anywhere in the house or the yard.
10. A set-top box delivers streaming video content from the Internet to the home entertainment system. A video game console connected to the network with Ethernet lets you play multi-player games.
11. The WEP key and 128-bit encryption help keep outsiders off your wireless network.

- *Networks enable people to share data and software programs, increasing efficiency and productivity.* In offices without networks, people often transmit data and software by "sneakernet"—that is, by carrying discs and flash drives between computers. In a LAN, one or more computers can be used as **file servers**—storehouses for software and data that are shared by several users. With client software, a user can, without taking a step, **download** software and data—copy it from a server. Of course, somebody needs to **upload** the software—copy it to the server—first. A large file server is typically a dedicated computer that does nothing but serve files. But a peer-to-peer approach, allowing any computer to be both client and server, can be an efficient, inexpensive way to share files on small networks. (There's more on file sharing later in the chapter.) Of course, sharing computer software on a network can violate software licenses (see Chapter 4) if not done with care. Many, but not all, licenses allow the software to be installed on a file server as long as the number of simultaneous users never exceeds the number of licensed copies. Some companies offer **site licenses** or **network licenses**, which reduce costs for multiple copies or remove restrictions on software copying and use at a network site. Networks don't eliminate compatibility differences between different computer operating systems. Users of Windows-compatible computers, for example, can't run Mac applications just because they're available on a file server. But they can, in many cases, use data files and documents created on a Mac and stored on the server. For example, a poster created with Adobe Illustrator on a Mac could be stored on a file server so it can be opened, edited, and printed by Illustrator users on Windows PCs. File sharing, however, isn't always that easy. If users of different systems use programs with incompatible file formats, they need to use ***data translation software*** to read and modify each other's files. On WANs (or the Internet), the transfer of data and software can save more than shoe leather; it can save time. There's no need to send printed documents or discs by mail between two sites if both sites are connected to the same network.
- *Networks enable people to work together, play together, and communicate in ways that are difficult or impossible without network technology.* Some software applications can be classified as ***groupware***—programs designed to enable several networked users to work on the same documents at the same time. Groupware programs include multiuser appointment calendars, project-management software, database-management systems, and software for group editing of documents. Many groupware programs today, such as IBM Lotus Notes, are built on standard Internet protocols, so group members can communicate and share information using Web browsers and other standard Internet software tools. Groupware programs are commonly used in large businesses and institutions where information technology specialists manage hundreds or thousands of computers. But most groupware functions—email, message posting, calendars, and the rest—are available to anyone through other Web and PC applications. In fact, networks offer all kinds of communication possibilities to people inside and outside the business world.

In the next section, we'll focus on the third point—the communication and collaboration possibilities of networks. Then we'll revisit the first two points—the sharing of hardware and software—and see how they're tied in with interpersonal communication, too.

Interpersonal Computing: From Communication to Communities

> **New technology gives us two kinds of newfound freedom:** The ability to reach each other 24/7—and the chance to avoid one another as never before.
>
> —*Lori Gottlieb, Author of* Stick Figure

For many people, *networking* means little more than sending and receiving messages. One study found that the typical Internet user spends about 70 percent of connected time communicating with others. Digital technology can profoundly change the way people communicate. In this section, we'll explore the world of human-to-human digital communication, from basic email to complex social networks.

The Many Faces of Email

Every day, people all over the planet exchange billions of email messages. For many people, it's hard to imagine (or remember) life before email. But few people really understand the ins and outs of this powerful application. In this section, we'll look deeper into some of the options and issues facing email users. We won't concern ourselves with how mail gets from one person to another, or how email addresses work; those questions will be dealt with in the next chapter where we discuss the TCP/IP technology that drives the Internet. We're more concerned here with the tools we use to send and receive email messages.

In the early days of the Internet, email applications, like most other applications, were character-based command-line programs. Today, most people send and receive email using graphical mail applications on PCs (Microsoft Outlook, Apple Mail, Mozilla's Thunderbird), mail applications on smart phones (Blackberry, iPhone, Droid), and Web browsers pointing to Web mail applications (Gmail, Hotmail, Yahoo! Mail). From the point of view of the mail message, it doesn't matter which kind of client application the sender and receiver use; the contents of the message are delivered to the recipient's mailbox, ready to be processed by a mail application. The message may *look* different when viewed with different mail applications, but the contents remain the same.

Like most network technology, email is built on protocols—standards that make it possible for all kinds of hardware and software to communicate with each other. Most email client programs use standard Internet protocols: SMTP (Simple Mail Transfer Protocol) for sending mail, and POP (Post Office Protocol) or IMAP (Internet Message Access Protocol) for receiving mail. (Microsoft Outlook typically uses a proprietary protocol, but is compatible with Internet protocols.) POP is an older protocol, most often used by people who download all their mail and attachments to personal PCs. IMAP is often used in large networks, such as college campuses. It's also popular with people who access email through multiple devices. When you're using an email client program for the first time, you need to give it some information about protocols (for example, the name of the SMTP server). Typically, this information is provided by your Internet service provider, school, or business—whoever provides you with your email access. Once the client software has the information it needs, it can send and receive messages indefinitely. (Travelers with laptops sometimes find that they have to change protocols temporarily when connecting to the Internet from remote locations.)

Many email users subscribe to Web-based email, or **Webmail**, services, including Gmail, Hotmail, Yahoo! Mail, and AOL. These services are designed to be accessed primarily through Web browsers, although it's easy to configure an email client program on a computer or smart phone so that it can handle mail from one or more of these services. Email services offered by schools, businesses, and Internet service providers often offer Webmail *options*, allowing users to switch back and forth between accessing mail through a browser and a specialized mail program. The main advantage of Webmail is that it can be accessed from any Web-connected computer, anywhere in the world. The main disadvantage is that mail is stored "out there" on the Web, so it's not available without an Internet connection. Dedicated email clients like Outlook and Apple Mail offer users a choice between remote and local storage. People who access their mail from multiple computers tend to prefer to keep their mail remotely in a central storage server; single-computer users tend to prefer to keep their mail locally by downloading everything to their personal PCs.

Many email messages are plain ASCII text. Plain text messages can be viewed with any mail client program, including those in simple phones. Many email programs can (optionally) send, receive, edit, and display email messages formatted in HTML, the formatting language used in most Web pages. HTML messages can include text formatting, pictures, and links to Web pages. The email client software hides the HTML source code from the sender and the recipient, displaying only the formatted messages. If the recipient views an HTML-encoded message with a mail program that doesn't recognize HTML, the formatting doesn't appear.

Even if the recipient's software can display HTML mail, not all email users *want* it because HTML encoding can slow down an email program. An HTML email message can also carry a ***Web bug***—an invisible piece of code that silently notifies the sender about when the message was opened and may report other information about the user's machine or email

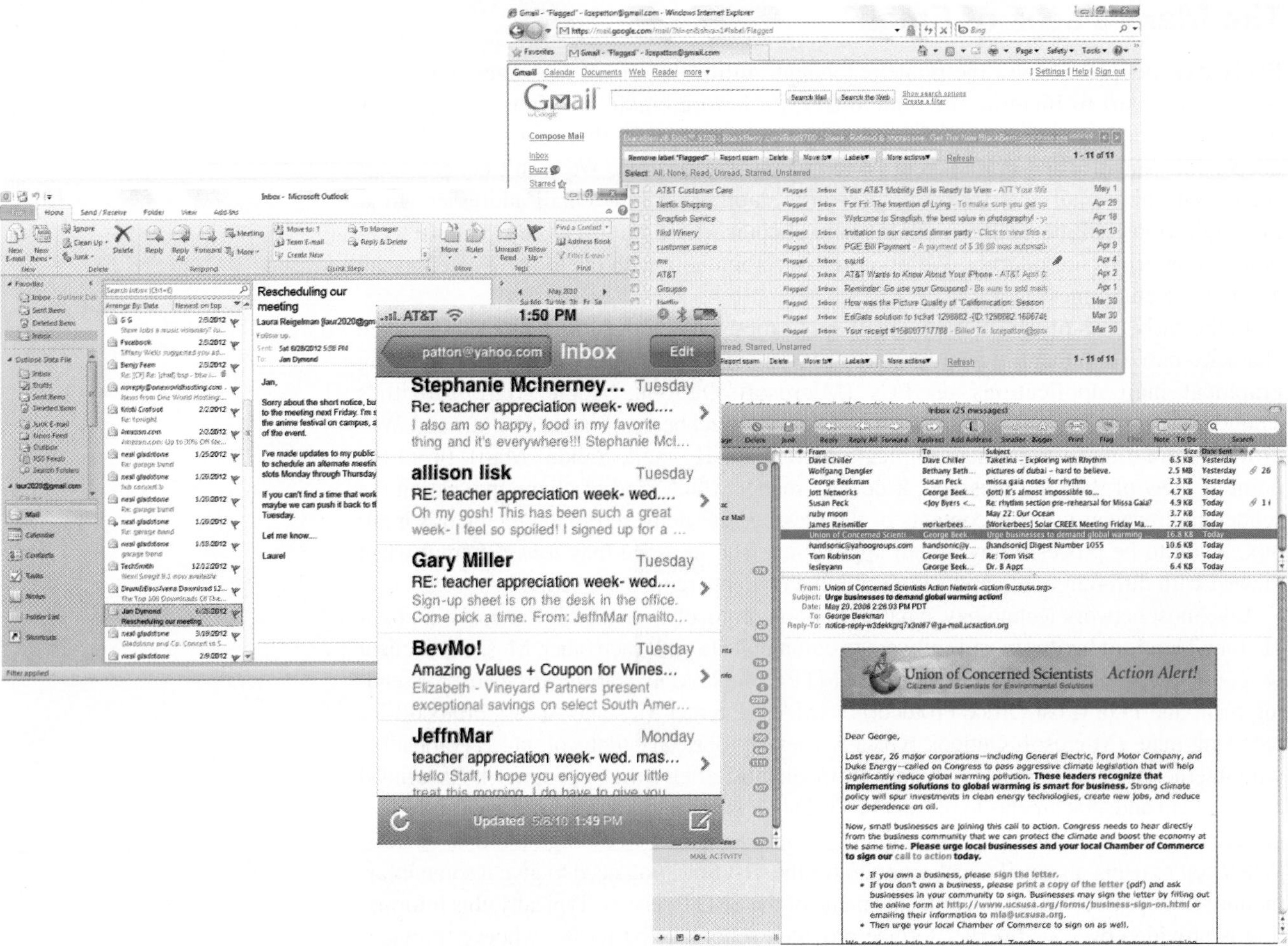

FIGURE 8.17 Email programs sport a variety of user interfaces. Web-based email clients such as Gmail (top) provide email access to people familiar with Web browsers. Microsoft Outlook (left) is a widely used email client that connects to a variety of email server types. Apple's Mail program (right), part of Mac OS X, is popular because of its ease of use and its intelligent spam (junk mail) filters. Apple's iPhone (center) reformats mail to fit its smaller screen.

software at the same time. Web bugs, which operate through specially encoded one-pixel graphics files, are also embedded in some commercial Web pages as well as HTML email messages. Fortunately, newer email applications can turn off Web bugs, preventing junk mailers and others from getting information about you when you read their messages.

Most email programs can send and receive formatted documents, pictures, and other multimedia files as **attachments** to messages. Attachments need to be temporarily converted to ASCII text using some kind of encoding scheme before they can be sent through Internet mail. Modern email programs take care of the encoding and decoding automatically. Of course, attachments aren't practical for some handheld devices. Also, attachments can contain viruses and other unwelcome surprises, as described in more detail in Chapter 10.

An email message's *header* contains information about the message and its delivery route through the Internet. An email client may hide the more technical parts of the header, depending on how it's configured. The *To* field and *From* field are almost always displayed. These fields should display the email addresses of the sender and the recipient(s) of the message. Unfortunately, the information in these fields isn't always accurate—it's easy to put fake addresses in either field. The *Subject* field should—but doesn't always—contain a brief description of the message's subject. The *Date* field displays the local date and time a message was written—assuming the clock is accurate in the sender's computer. An outgoing message header typically contains a *Cc* field for sending "carbon copies" to additional recipients, and a *Bcc* field for sending *blind* carbon copies—copies that aren't listed in the other recipients' headers.

From: president@whitehouse.gov
Return-Path: president@spamsource.com
Subject: Huge Tax Rebate Just For You!!!
Date: September 25, 2012 4:43:00 PM PDT
To: laurel.r123b@hotmail.com

Laurel,
I have a bunch of money that the government doesn't need that I wanted to give to you, but in order to transfer it to you, I just need your bank account information, including the PIN number.

FIGURE 8.18 The header of an email message includes information about the message and its delivery route, but some of the fields in the header can be forged to contain misinformation.

Email Issues

> Well there's egg and bacon; egg, sausage, and bacon; egg and spam; bacon and **spam**; egg, bacon, sausage, and **spam; spam**, bacon, sausage, and **spam; spam**, egg, **spam, spam**, bacon, and **spam; spam, spam, spam**, egg, and **spam; spam, spam, spam, spam, spam, spam**, baked beans, **spam, spam, spam,** and **spam**; or lobster thermidor aux crevettes with a mornay sauce garnished with truffle pâté, brandy, and a fried egg on top of **spam**.
>
> —*Waitress in* Monty Python's Flying Circus

Most of us use email because it is a practical and powerful tool. It combines the advantages of the telephone and the letter. Like a telephone call, an email message is a way of instantaneously communicating with someone else, even if that person is on the other side of the globe. Like a letter, an email is nonintrusive. An email doesn't interrupt you the same way a telephone call does. An email conversation can take place over a period of hours, days, or even weeks.

There's a downside to email. Email is vulnerable to machine failures, network glitches, and security breaches. Viruses spread by email attachments cause billions of dollars of damage worldwide. (See Chapter 10 for more on viruses.) Many people spend hours every day working through their email messages. Most email messages sent worldwide are unsolicited, junk email, or **spam** (named for the *Monty Python* skit quoted at the beginning of this section). Even with the best filters, some spam sneaks through, wasting the time of busy people who have to delete it. Meanwhile, email messages are not private; most employers reserve the right to read their employees' messages.

Countless emails are produced by con artists phishing for financial information. These bogus emails are designed to trick people into entering **phishing** sites—Web sites intended to capture credit card numbers and other sensitive financial information. In one controlled experiment, the best phishing site fooled 90 percent of the test subjects.

Finally, email and instant messaging filter out many "human" components of communication. When Bell invented the telephone, the public reaction was cool and critical. Business people

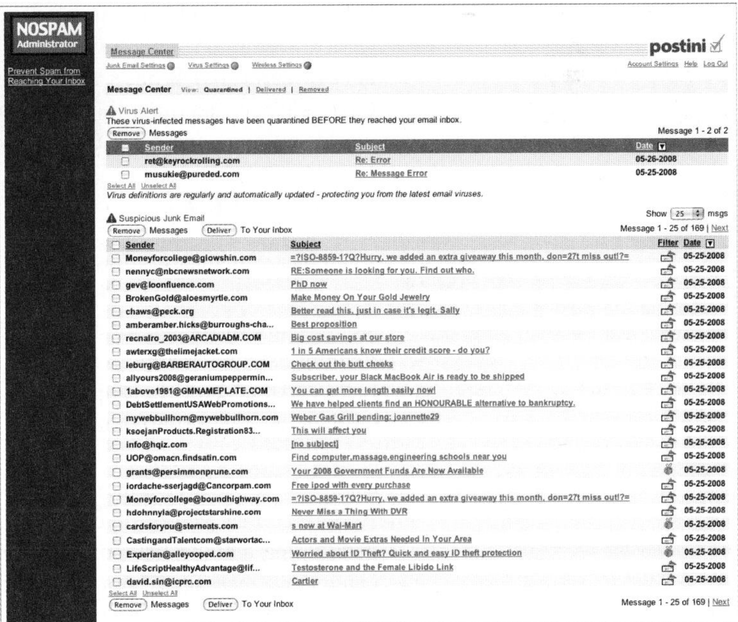

FIGURE 8.19 Many email client programs contain intelligent filters that automatically route spam into junk mailboxes. Many Internet service providers offer spam-catching services that do the same thing on the Web. But it's not always easy to tell whether a message is spam or legitimate email. Many spammers disguise their lowly intentions with subject lines that look like legitimate email. Other spammers use odd spellings of "hot" words so their messages won't automatically be flagged as spam.

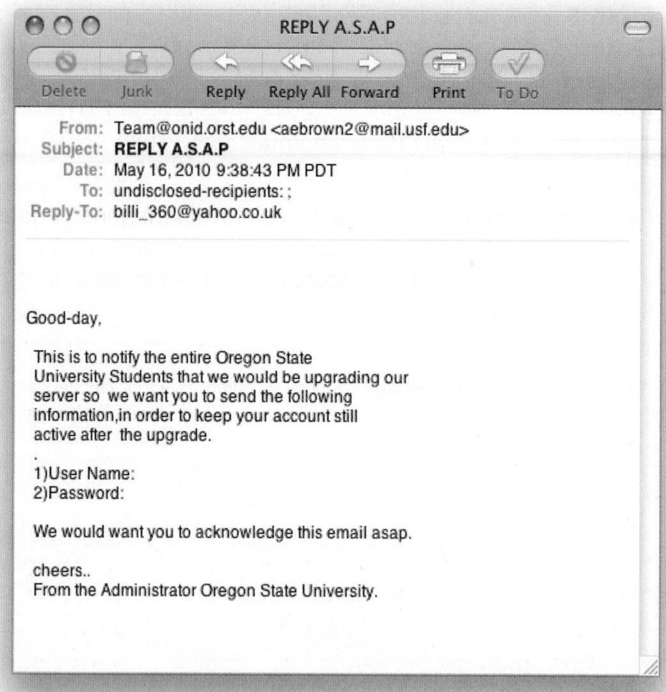

REPLY A.S.A.P

Delete Junk Reply Reply All Forward Print To Do

From: Team@onid.orst.edu <aebrown2@mail.usf.edu>
Subject: **REPLY A.S.A.P**
Date: May 16, 2010 9:38:43 PM PDT
To: undisclosed-recipients: ;
Reply-To: billi_360@yahoo.co.uk

Good-day,

This is to notify the entire Oregon State
University Students that we would be upgrading our
server so we want you to send the following
information,in order to keep your account still
active after the upgrade.

1)User Name:
2)Password:

We would want you to acknowledge this email asap.

cheers..
From the Administrator Oregon State University.

FIGURE 8.20 This phishing message is designed to con the recipient into revealing private login information.

were reluctant to communicate through a device that didn't allow them to look each other in the eye and shake hands. There's a grain of truth in this quaint attitude. When people communicate, part of the message is hidden in body language, eye contact, voice inflections, and other nonverbal signals. The telephone strips visual cues out of a message, and this can lead to misunderstandings. Email peels away the sounds as well as the sights, leaving only plain words on a screen—words that might be misread if they aren't chosen carefully. What's more, online communication is a poor substitute at best for those chance meetings that happen in coffee houses, hallways, parks, and other real-world settings—meetings that can result in important communications and connections.

Mailing Lists

Email is a valuable tool for communicating one to one with individuals, but it's also useful for communicating one to many. **Mailing lists** enable you to participate in email discussion groups on special-interest topics. Lists can be small and local, or large and global. A mailing list can be administered by a human being or by a software program. You might belong to one student group that's set up by your instructor to carry on discussions outside of class, another group that includes people all over the world who use Ableton Live software to create music, and a third that's dedicated to saving endangered species in your state. When you send a message to a mailing list address, every subscriber receives a copy. And, of course, you receive a copy of every email message sent by everyone else to those lists. Some mailing lists, often called newsletters or distribution lists, are one-way—you can receive messages, but not reply or post new ones.

Subscribing to a busy list might mean receiving hundreds of messages each day. To avoid being overwhelmed by incoming mail, many list members sign up to receive them in daily *digest* form; instead of receiving many individual messages each day, they receive one message that includes all postings. But digest messages can still contain repetitive, off-topic, and annoying messages. Some lists are moderated to ensure that the quality of the discussion remains high. In a ***moderated group*** a designated moderator acts as an editor, filtering out irrelevant and inappropriate messages and posting the rest.

Newsgroups, Web Forums, and Blogs

You can participate in special-interest discussions without overloading your mailbox by taking advantage of Internet newsgroups and forums. A **newsgroup** is a public discussion on a particular subject, traditionally distributed through a worldwide newsgroup network called Usenet. Messages are posted on virtual bulletin boards for anyone to read at anytime. There are groups for every interest and taste...and more than a few for the tasteless. You can explore network newsgroups through several Web sites, including Google, or with a newsreader client program, an application designed to read Usenet articles. Or you can have the newsgroup operate like a mailing list, sending you email notifications of postings and accepting email postings from you.

People have been using newsgroups for online discussions for decades, but today more of those special-interest discussions are happening in Yahoo! Groups, Google groups, and Web forums. Yahoo! Groups and Google groups are the Web-era equivalent of traditional Usenet groups. They offer all the same features as newsgroups through Web-based interfaces. A **Web forum** is also built on a Web application and accessed through a Web browser, but not through email. Some forums are membership-only affairs, off-limits to nonmembers. Others restrict postings to members, but allow anyone to view those postings. Still others are completely open, even allowing anonymous postings. Moderated forums and newsgroups include only postings that have been approved by moderators who filter out repetitive questions from newcomers, childish rants, off-topic trivia, machine-generated junk postings, and other counterproductive messages.

The messages in a typical forum or newsgroup tend to fall into categories based on subject. One person might post a question; several people might respond to that posting with answers and related comments. When forum messages are viewed chronologically, all of those related postings might be interspersed with messages on other topics. Fortunately, many forums have options for viewing ***threaded discussions***—discussions in which postings are organized by topics or subjects, called ***threads***, rather than by time. (Many email clients offer options for displaying mail organized into threads, with all replies to the same message grouped together.) Some forums offer options for email notification, so participants don't need to check the forum sites repeatedly for new postings.

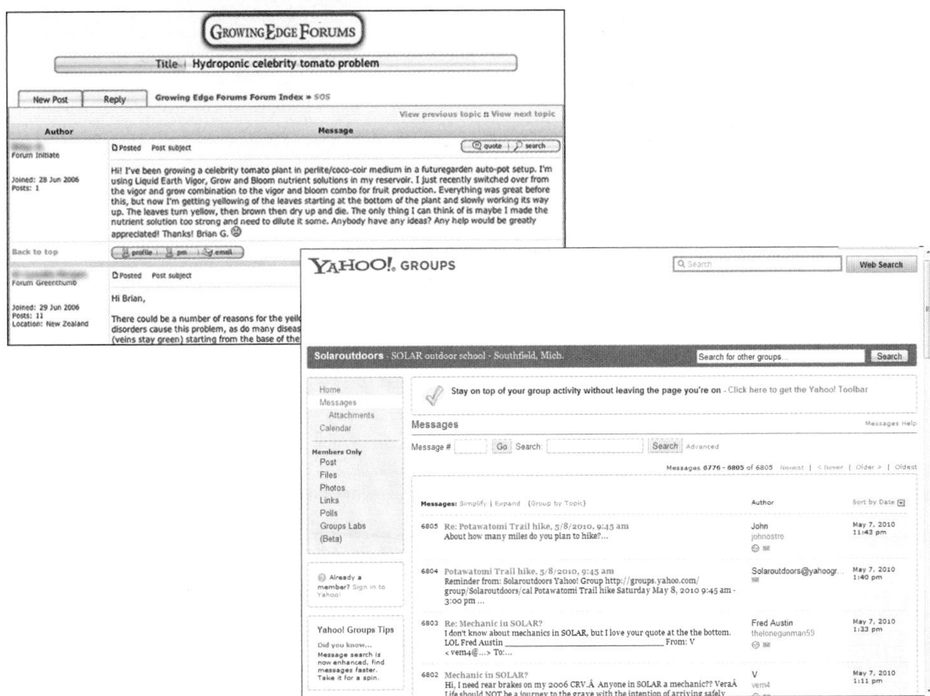

FIGURE 8.21 A Web site's online forum enables visitors to ask questions, post new information, and connect with each other. Newsgroups such as Yahoo! Groups combine the features of forums and mailing lists, allowing you to keep up and contribute to discussions through email or the Web.

Newsgroups and forums are based on two-way communication—participants post messages and read messages posted by others. (Although discussions are frequently monitored by *lurkers*—silent, invisible observers who don't contribute to the discussions.) A blog is similar to a forum, except that it's created by an individual or a small group, to be read by a much larger group. A **blog** (short for weB LOG) is an online journal (often including pictures and other media) that's updated frequently and posted on a public (or semipublic) Web site. A variety of Web applications simplify the process of creating and posting blogs.

Hundreds of thousands of people, many with little or no technical expertise, are active **bloggers**. They write about their personal lives, politics, the arts, business, technology, and just about anything else you might imagine. Micro-bloggers use Twitter and similar sites to chronicle their minute-by-minute activities and thoughts with one-or-two sentence *micro-blogs*. Most bloggers prefer to compose their thoughts into longer essays and post them daily or weekly. Some choose to create audio or video podcasts instead of—or in addition to—text-based blogs. (Podcasts are discussed in Chapters 6 and 9.)

FIGURE 8.22 There are millions of blogs on the Web. Bloggers all over the world write about politics, technology, philosophy, society, media, entertainment, the environment, and intimate details of their personal lives. Technorati is a specialized search engine to help people find what they're looking for in the blogosphere. Each blog is rated by "authority" based on how many other recent blogs link to it (top). Blogs are generally tagged with keywords by their authors, and technorati uses these tags to categorize blogs by subject. (bottom)

Political bloggers have become important sources of information and opinion, using Web sites to bypass tightly controlled mainstream media (and in some countries, authoritarian government media monopolies). Hundreds of important news stories have been broken by bloggers. Bloggers have provided critical on-the-scene coverage of wars, earthquakes, storms, and other disasters. Media outlets have responded with their own blogs.

The ***blogosphere***, as it's often called, continues to expand, providing an outlet for an incredibly diverse population of writers. The challenge for most bloggers today is to find ways to attract and keep audiences; the challenge for those audiences is to determine which blogs are trustworthy and worthy of the time investment it takes to read them.

Instant Messaging, Text Messaging, and Teleconferencing: Real-Time Communication

Mailing lists, forums, and blogs use **asynchronous communication**: The poster and the reader don't have to be logged in at the same time. Computer networks also offer many possibilities for **real-time communication**. **Instant messaging (IM)** has been possible since the days of text-only Internet access. Internet relay chat (IRC) and Talk enable UNIX users and others to exchange instant messages with their online friends and coworkers. Newer, easier-to-use instant messaging systems from AOL, Microsoft, Yahoo!, Google, Apple, and others have turned instant messaging into one of the most popular Internet activities. Instant messaging programs enable users to create "buddy lists," check for "buddies" who are logged in, and exchange typed messages and files with those who are. Most of these programs are available for free. Unfortunately, there's not a common standard for IM technology, so users of one IM system might not be able to IM users of another system. For example, a user of AOL's AIM program can communicate with someone using Apple's iChat but not with users of Microsoft Messenger or Facebook Chat. Some IM client programs (Trillian for Windows, Adium for Mac OS X) support competing IM protocols, so they can send and receive messages to all the major IM services. Many businesses now use instant messaging to keep employees connected, and IM technology is built into many smart phones.

IM technology appears, at first glance, to be similar to **text messaging**, a popular form of communication among mobile phone users. Text messaging uses SMS technology, which is far more limiting than IM technology. Unlike SMS, most IM systems support formatted text, longer messages, and file transfer; some support audio and video conferencing. In the future, the lines between SMS and IM may disappear. But for now, they're two different—and incompatible—forms of communication.

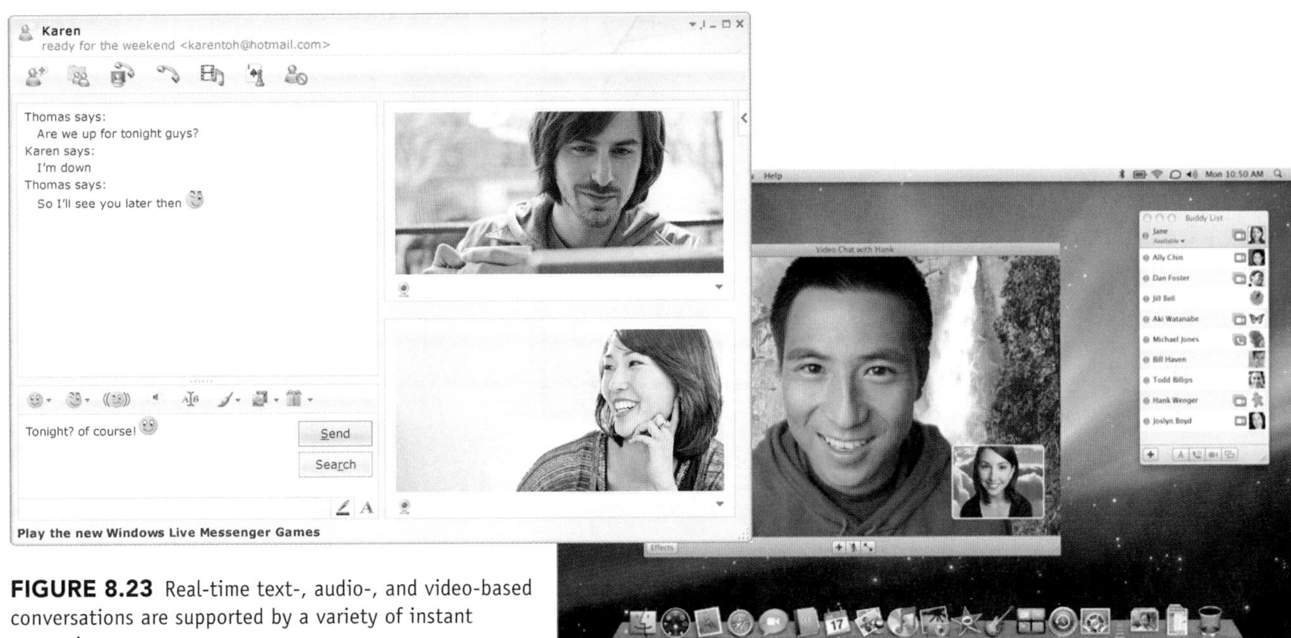

FIGURE 8.23 Real-time text-, audio-, and video-based conversations are supported by a variety of instant messaging programs.

Another type of real-time online communication is the **chat room**—a public or private virtual conference room where people with similar interests or motivations can type messages to each other and receive near-instant responses.

Some IM programs, chat rooms, and multiplayer games on the Web use graphics to simulate real-world environments. Participants can represent themselves with **avatars**—graphical "bodies" that might look like simple cartoon sketches, elaborate 3-D figures, or exotic abstract icons.

Several IM programs make it possible to carry on **video teleconferences**. A video teleconference enables two or more people to communicate face to face over long distances by combining video and computer technology. Until a few years ago, most video teleconferences were conducted in special rooms equipped with video cameras, microphones, television monitors, and other specialized equipment. Today it's possible to participate in multiperson video teleconferences using a standard PC with an attached or built-in Webcam or video camera and a high-speed Internet connection. Internet video images don't measure up to the images beamed to professional conference rooms, but they're more than adequate for most applications.

Computer Telephony

A **voice mail** system is a voice messaging system with many of the features of an email system, including the ability to store, organize, and forward messages. Voice mail is a familiar example of ***computer telephony integration (CTI)***—the linking of computers and telephones to gain productivity.

Internet telephony (also called **Voice-over IP**, or **VoIP**) has become a legitimate competitor to traditional phone companies. With VoIP your phone call is carried over the Internet rather than the telephone network. VoIP service requires a broadband Internet connection. One way to place a VoIP call is to use a traditional telephone handset connected to the Internet with a phone adapter. Another way is to use an Internet-connected PC

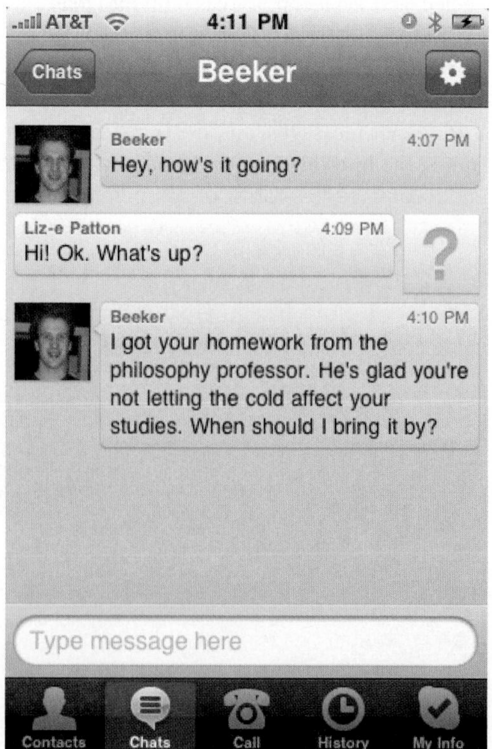

FIGURE 8.24 Skype, the most popular Internet phone service, provides audio and video phone service to users with broadband Internet connections. Skype software enables a smart phone to place and receive audio and video phone services, as well as instant messaging over the Internet rather than through cell phone networks. Many people use Skype to avoid expensive international calling fees.

Working Wisdom **Online Survival Tips**

When you're online, you're using relatively new communication media with new rules, and those rules evolve with the media. Here are some suggestions for successful online communication:

- ***Let your system do as much of the work as possible.*** If your email program can sort mail, filter mail, or automatically append a signature file to your mail, take advantage of those features. If you send messages to the same group of people repeatedly, create a group that includes those people—a distribution list that can save you the trouble of typing or selecting all those names each time.
- ***Store names and addresses in a computer-accessible address book.*** Email addresses aren't easy to remember and type. If you mistype a single character, your message will probably go to the wrong person or bounce—come back with some kind of undeliverable-mail message. An address book on your PC, your smart phone, and/or the Web enables you to select addresses without typing them each time you use them. Better yet, set up your address book so that it's automatically updated on all of your devices and the Web whenever you change an address. Use your email program's backup or export capability to back up your address book.
- ***Don't share your email address and password.*** It's easy to think of an email address like a physical address, sharing it with roommates, partners, and others who use the same computer. But email works best if each person has a unique address and password. A personal address is more secure and private, but it's also more practical; when someone sends a message to you, the sender knows that *you* will receive the message.

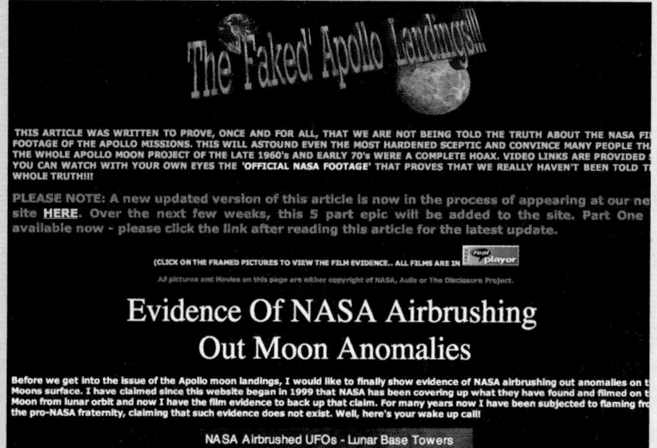

FIGURE 8.25 You can't always trust online sources, so check your facts and sources carefully.

- ***Protect your privacy.*** Miss Manners said it well in a *Wired* interview: "For email, the old postcard rule applies. Nobody else is supposed to read your postcards, but you'd be a fool if you wrote anything private on one."
- ***Don't open suspicious attachments.*** An email attachment may contain a virus. If the email is from a stranger, don't be tricked into opening the attachment. Delete the email instead.
- ***Don't get hooked by a phishing expedition.*** Be suspicious of unsolicited emails from banks, online services, and other businesses. Don't blindly click on links that claim to take you to the business's Web site. If you *do* link to a Web site, check to make sure the URL is the actual business's address. Look for a security padlock icon displayed by the browser, indicating that the Web site connection is secure. Better yet, call the business or connect to their site by typing their URL directly into your browser.
- ***Keep your security systems up to date.*** Make sure that you're using the current version of your Web browser, email client, and other online applications. These programs are updated often to plug security leaks; if you're not up to date, you're inviting trouble.
- ***Cross-check online information sources.*** Don't assume that every information nugget you see online is valid, accurate, and timely. If you read something online, treat it with the same degree of skepticism that you would if you heard it in a coffee shop.
- ***Beware of urban legends.*** The Internet is an amazing information source, but it's also a tremendous source of misinformation. Web sites and email chain letters spread all kinds of "urban legends"—widely believed stories that may be false, misleading, or sensationalized. Microsoft is giving money to people who forward this message; a prominent politician is secretly allied with terrorists; parking lot thieves use ether-laced perfume samples to render their victims unconscious—these stories are believed by many people who read about them in email messages or Web postings. Snopes.com debunks the most popular urban legends; check there if you read something that seems too good—or too fantastic—to be true.
- ***Be aware and awake.*** It's easy to lose track of yourself and your time online. In his book *The Virtual Community*, Howard Rheingold advises, "Rule Number One is to pay attention. Rule Number Two might be: Attention is a limited resource, so pay attention to where you pay attention."
- ***Avoid information overload.*** When it comes to information, more is not necessarily better. Search selectively. Don't waste time and energy trying to process mountains of information. Information is not knowledge, and knowledge is not wisdom.

equipped with a microphone headset and appropriate software. Most VoIP providers allow calls to any telephone number; the last leg of a call to a non-VoIP number is routed through the recipient's local telephone company or cellular phone provider.

There are many reasons for VoIP's growing popularity. VoIP service is generally cheaper than traditional phone service (not counting the cost of the required broadband connection). Some companies offer VoIP for free. VoIP calls are automatically routed to VoIP phones, no matter where they are connected to the Internet. Travelers can receive calls wherever they make Internet connections. VoIP phones integrate easily with online address books, video conference services, and other Internet services. The most popular Internet telephony application, Skype, includes options for video calls and videoconferences.

VoIP service has some weaknesses. Backup generators keep traditional telephone networks operational when the power is out, but computer networks are generally unusable during power outages. Traditional telephones provide 911 service; most VoIP implementations don't. Telephone books ("the white pages") are available for people with traditional telephone service, but a VoIP provider may not provide directory assistance.

In the early days of VoIP, calls could be choppy because of delays in delivery of data packets containing voice communications. But the technology has improved so much that telephone companies are replacing traditional networks with networks based on the same packet-switching technology that makes Internet telephony possible.

On the mobile front, the line between computers and telephones is especially fuzzy. Many smart phones can connect to the Internet, do instant messaging, upload and download email messages, and display miniature Web pages. Most analysts expect rapid advances in these converging technologies over the next few years—advances such as reliable speech recognition that will make these devices much more useful for people on the go.

Social Networking, Role Playing, and Virtual Communities

> The value of a social network is defined not only by who's on it, but by **who's excluded**.
>
> —*Technology Forecaster Paul Saffo*

Email, instant messages, chat rooms, Web forums, blogs, and other network communication technologies have resulted in new ways for people to make friends and create communities. Facebook, Buzz, MySpace, LiveJournal, orkut, Tribe, LinkedIn, Plaxo, and other **social networking** services (see Chapter 1) combine many of these tools with other services to make it easy for members to connect with friends or colleagues, meet people with common interests, and create online communities. Web users—especially younger ones—have embraced social networking sites, making them integral to their larger social lives.

Facebook, the current social network of choice for a large segment of the world's population, ranks near the top on the list of *all* Web sites with the most daily hits. We'll use Facebook as an example here, but these ideas apply to most popular social network sites. Facebook users set up profile pages revealing as little or as much about themselves as they choose. But the real action happens in each user's friend feed, a regularly updated list of postings and links from "friends"—people and organizations who have established two-way links to this person. Posting range from the trivial ("Here's a cute picture of a dog and a cat cuddling") to the personal ("I'm sick as a dog and stranded in the airport, otherwise fine"), to the topical ("Flood waters are finally receding in the north county"), to the political ("Watch this video about the life of a cow before you eat your next hamburger"), to the promotional ("Become a fan of our band!"), to the philosophical ("We're all in this together"). It might include cross-postings from Twitter and other social networks, status reports from friends playing Facebook games, announcements telling you who your friends just "friended," or just about anything that conforms to Facebook's loose guidelines.

In a sense, a Facebook home page is like an up-to-the-minute online newspaper whose contributors and subjects are hand-picked by you. Like a newspaper, a Facebook home page can be overwhelming if too many "friends" post too much. Many people cope with social information overload by adjusting settings to hide posts from popular games and from friends who "overshare."

Facebook has become a platform of sorts by enabling software developers to create games and other applications that function exclusively in the Facebook world. In fact, many computer users function almost exclusively in a Facebook world, sending Facebook messages rather than emails to friends, chatting in real time with Facebook's Instant Messaging tool, maintaining vast libraries of photos in which every friend's face is "tagged," and reading ads selected by software based on personal profiles and connections.

It's not clear whether Facebook will continue to be the top site for social networking. Friendster and MySpace each held that position for many years, but social networkers showed no particular loyalty to them. Futurist Paul Saffo and others believe that in the long run, most social networkers will find more value in smaller networks of people with similar interests.

According to social network expert James K. Fowler, on Facebook, "We end up staying in touch with more acquaintances. But that doesn't mean we have more friends." Online or off, we can only maintain meaningful and deep relationships with a few close friends. Social networking technology makes it possible to maintain those relationships over long distances, and it may increase communication efficiency within those relationships. But it can't change the fact that we have a limited amount of time and attention for relationships, and that time and attention can't be easily shared with hundreds or thousands of friends.

Still, those networks are important. Research shows that emotions and habits transmit through social networks, online and off. If your friends (the close ones) are happy, you're more likely to be happy. If they gain weight, you're more likely to gain weight. If they quit smoking, you're more likely to quit. It doesn't seem to matter much whether those friends are local face-to-face friends or long-distance Facebook friends—they just need to be real connections in your social world.

Some social networks are internal networks—they're closed to everyone except members of an organization, employees of a business, or students and faculty at a school. Others are open, external networks, but they're designed for professional, rather than personal, networking. LinkedIn is popular with many professionals and students interested in making connections that can further their careers or create business partnerships.

Most social networking sites are plagued by problems of privacy and safety; like real-world communities, these online communities include less-than-honorable residents. Social networking sites continually update security to minimize risks from predators and other criminals, but they also respond to pressure from advertisers to reveal more about users. Facebook has been harshly criticized for repeatedly changing default privacy settings to make more and more user information public or semipublic. They've responded to the criticism by simplifying their privacy settings, but most users don't know or care enough to change settings so that personal information stays personal.

Social networking also occurs in **massively multiplayer online role-playing games (MMORPGs)**, including *Age of Conan*, *Eve Online*, and *World of Warcraft*. These games can support hundreds of thousands of simultaneous players taking on roles in virtual worlds. The virtual worlds are persistent—they continue to exist even when players log out.

FIGURE 8.26 One of the most popular MMORPGs is *World of Warcraft*, a fantasy game based loosely on medieval mythology.

Success requires cooperation among groups of players (sometimes called guilds or alliances). Many players become passionately involved in—or addicted to—the virtual worlds of MMORPGs. Some sites, most notably Second Life, occupy a space between social networking sites and MMORPGs. Second Life isn't a game with a goal; it's more of a 3-D avatar-based chat community. This type of community can be especially valuable to people who, for whatever reason, aren't able to go out and about in the physical world.

Information Sharing: Social Bookmarking, Wikis, Media Sharing, and Crowdsourcing

Many types of network communication can be loosely classified as information sharing—the formal or informal pooling of knowledge. Newsgroups and forums are forms of information sharing. But there are many other tools and techniques for sharing information on today's networks. These tools leverage the collective wisdom of communities in a variety of ways.

Visitors to social bookmarking sites, including Digg and Del.icio.us, depend on each other for one thing: to find the most valuable sites on the Web. When you visit a social bookmarking site, you can see which Web pages are currently generating the most interest among people who use that social bookmarking service. You can vote on which pages deserve to be ranked higher or lower in that service's ranking. These sites create informal communities of people dedicated to helping each other separate the best from the rest of the Web.

Another type of information sharing involves wikis. A **wiki** (shortened from the Hawaiian term *wiki wiki* which means *quick*) is a Web site designed to enable anyone who accesses it to contribute to, and modify, content. A variety of Web tools are available to make it easy to build and contribute to wikis. Wikipedia, the famous free-content online encyclopedia, may be the world's largest collaborative effort. Wikipedia contains millions of articles in English and hundreds of thousands of articles in German, French, Polish, Japanese, Dutch, Swedish, Italian, Portuguese, and Spanish. Wikipedia has become an invaluable resource for Web visitors and an important community for millions of dedicated volunteers who contribute content and continually monitor the site for vandalism—deliberate attempts to destroy the legitimate contents of articles. The Wikipedia community repairs vandalized articles within minutes. Members continually monitor the encyclopedia for content that doesn't live up to its standards of objectivity and accuracy. For serious researchers, Wikipedia's standards can't measure up to those of the best academic journals. But for everyday research, millions of people turn to Wikipedia as a first resource. Wikipedia's success has confounded skeptics and provided inspiration for other not-for-profit community collaborations.

FIGURE 8.27 Reddit makes it easy for users to share recommendations of favorite Web pages with each other.

Wikipedia is the best known wiki, but there are many other successful wikis. WikiAnswers is an information sharing site designed with a question-and-answer format, so you can ask a question and (hopefully) receive an answer from a knowledgeable contributor. WikiLeaks is designed to give anonymous whistleblowers a way to share documents, images, and videos that reveal corruption, wrongdoings, and cover-ups without blowing their own personal cover. The controversial site triggered a global freedom-of-speech versus national-security debate when it released thousands of classified U.S. defense and intelligence documents in 2010. Most wikis have more modest goals—to provide easy tools for groups of people with similar interests, such as owners of particular products, to share information with each other.

Another type of network collaboration involves sharing of media resources. Flickr (see Chapter 1) pioneered this concept by providing an open database for visitors to share photographs. Because most Flickr members don't claim copyright protection on the photographs they post, the entire Internet community can benefit from a large collection of public domain photographs—pictures that can be used without getting the prior permission of the photographer.

YouTube has become a cultural phenomenon by providing a similar service for video sharing. The vast

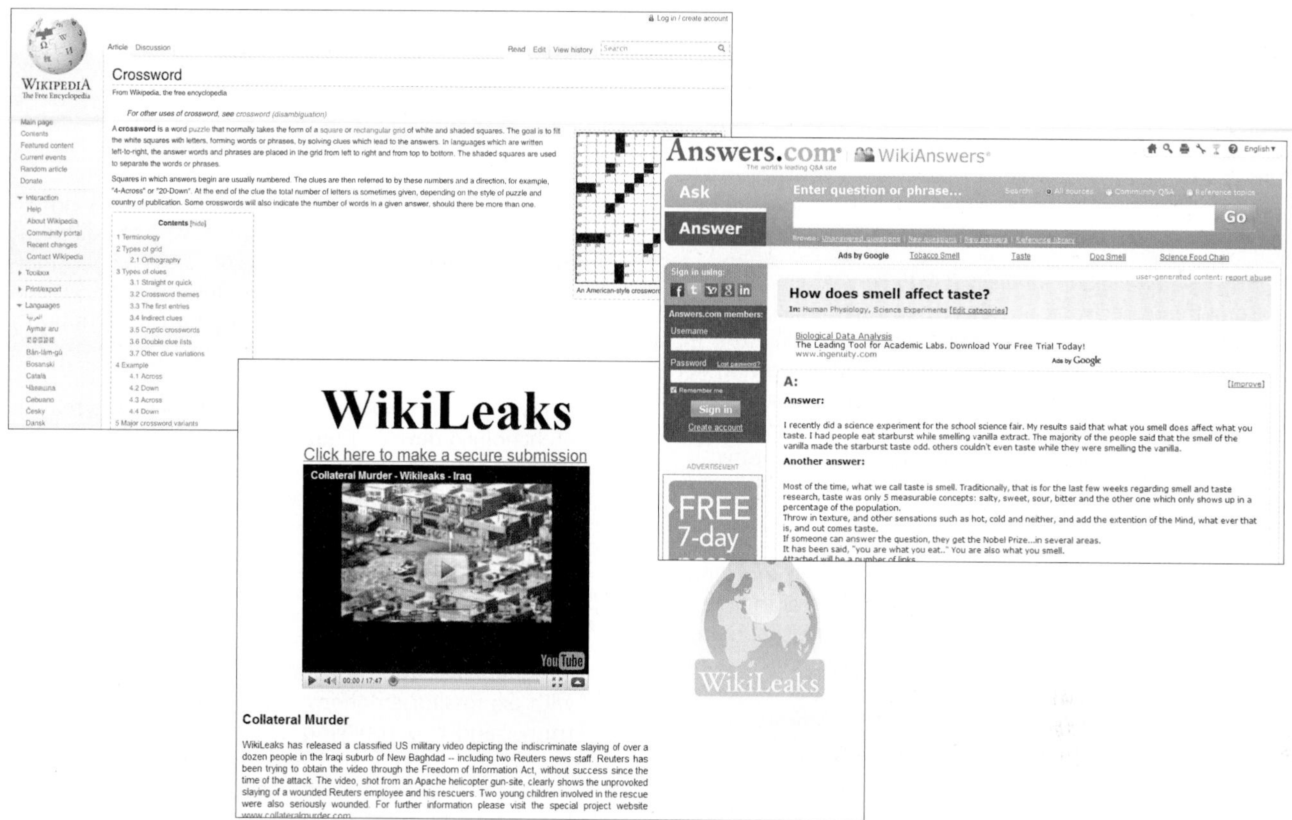

FIGURE 8.28 Wikipedia, the most widely known wiki, is an online encyclopedia with an archive of collective knowledge that can be updated by any user. WikiLeaks is a controversial wiki that allows users to anonymously publish submissions of sensitive documents with political, diplomatic, historical, or ethical interest. WikiAnswers is a wiki with questions and answers provided by visitors.

YouTube library includes an odd mix of silly home video clips, low-budget political rants and satires, music videos from new and established musicians, experiments from aspiring filmmakers, candid clips of celebrities and politicians caught off guard, footage of historic events, and bootlegged clips from copyrighted TV shows and movies (many of which are removed when their owners complain to Google, YouTube's parent company). A popular YouTube video can, in a matter of hours, become a *viral* video, as email messages, blog posts, Facebook updates, and IMs containing links to that video spread across the Internet like a virus. Political analysts often suggest that YouTube has profoundly changed the nature of political communication by enabling concerned citizens to post controversial clips that might not be featured on corporate news programs.

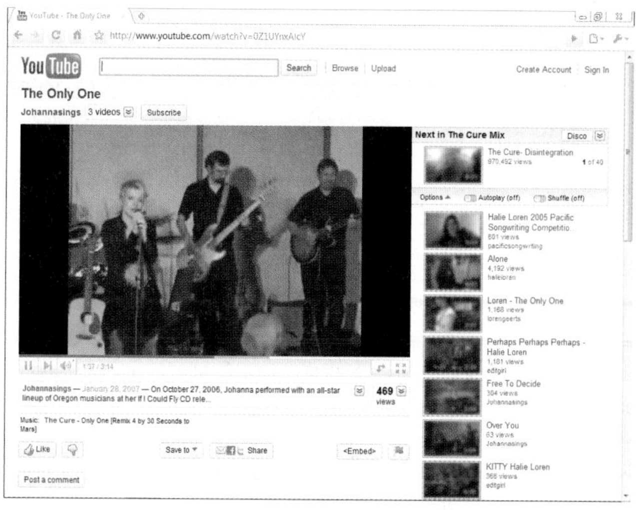

FIGURE 8.29 Google's YouTube is a phenomenally popular media sharing site that features everything from short homemade movies to high-profile professional videos.

Some types of information sharing might be called *crowdsourcing*—outsourcing of a task to a large community of people, possibly volunteers, rather than to a small group of contracted specialists. Crowdsourcing has been used by clothing manufacturers to solicit designs, political action groups for organizing, scientific talent brokers to connect research "seekers" with "solvers", and more. Some types of crowdsourcing, such as photography solicitation, threaten the livelihoods of professionals who can't compete in a market of millions. But for many people and organizations, crowdsourcing offers the potential of solving problems that couldn't easily or practically be solved in other ways.

Working Wisdom Netiquette and Messaging Etiquette

Like any society, the Net has acceptable behavior rules and guidelines. If you follow these rules of netiquette, you'll be doing your part to make life on the Net easier for everybody—especially yourself.

- ***Say what you mean, and say it with care.*** After you send something electronically, there's no way to call it back. Compose each message carefully, and make sure it means what you intend it to mean. If you're replying to a message, double-check the heading to make sure your reply is going only to those people you intend to send it to. Even if you took only a few seconds to write your message, it may be broadcast far and wide and be preserved forever in online archives.
- ***Keep it short.*** Include a descriptive subject line, and limit the body to a screen or two. If you're replying to a long message, include a copy of the relevant part of the message, but not the whole message. Remember that many people receive hundreds of email messages each day, and they're more likely to read and respond to short ones.
- ***Proofread your messages.*** A famous *New Yorker* cartoon by Peter Steiner shows one dog telling another, "On the Internet no one knows you're a dog." You may not be judged by the color of your hair or the clothes you wear when you're posting messages, but that doesn't mean appearances aren't important. You'll be judged by the spelling, grammar, punctuation, and clarity of your messages. If you want your messages to be taken seriously, present your best face.
- ***Don't assume you're anonymous.*** Your messages can say a lot about you—especially when combined with other messages you've sent or posted. Your collected Internet works can paint a shockingly accurate picture of you—a long-lasting picture that might be seen by more than your intended audience. Researcher Jonathan G. S. Koppell suggests a more appropriate caption for the *New Yorker* cartoon mentioned above: "On the Internet, everyone knows you're an aging, overweight, malamute-retriever mix living in the southwest, and with a preference for rawhide."
- ***Learn the "nonverbal" language of the Net.*** A simple phrase such as "Nice job!" can have very different meanings depending on the tone of voice and body language behind it. Online communities have developed text-based or graphical representations for emotions, sometimes called *emoticons*. The table below shows a few of the most common emoticons.
- ***Know your abbreviations.*** Typing can be slow and tedious on handheld devices. Knowing the meaning of common abbreviations will save you time and help you understand the text messages and IMs you receive. The table below shows some of the most common abbreviations.
- ***Keep your cool.*** Many otherwise timid people turn into raging bulls when they're online. The facelessness of Internet communication makes it all too easy to shoot from the hip, overstate arguments, and get caught up in a digital lynch-mob mentality. There's nothing wrong with expressing emotions, but broadside attacks, half-truths, and cyberbullying can do serious damage to your online relationships and, in some cases, to innocent people. Online or off, freedom of speech is a right that carries responsibility.
- ***Don't be a source of spam.*** Target your email messages carefully. If you're trying to sell tickets to a local concert or advertise your garage sale, don't tell everybody in your international address book. If you send a mass mailing, hide the recipient list to protect the privacy of your recipients. One way is to send the message to yourself and put everyone else in the Bcc (blind carbon copy) field. And if you send repeated mass mailings, always include a message telling people how they can get off your list.
- ***Say no—and say nothing—to spam.*** People send spam because it gets results—mouse clicks to Web links, email replies, purchases, and more. If you want to do your part to wipe out spam, *never* reward spammers with your time

Common Emoticons

Emoticon	Vertical variant	Graphic	Meaning
:-)	(^,^)		Smile or happy
:-(	(<_>)		Frown or sad
;-)	('_^)		Sarcasm, joking
:-@	(>_<)		Anger, frustration
:-/	(-_-)		Skepticism, uneasiness
:-P	(^o^)		Goofy smile, playful teasing
:-O	('o')		Surprised

FIGURE 8.30 A few of the most common emoticons.

or money. If a message is clearly spam, don't reply. Your reply can confirm that your address is legitimate, setting you up to receive future junk mail.

- ***Send no-frills mail.*** Even if your email program makes it easy to use fancy formatting, embed HTML, and include attachments, it's usually better to err on the side of simplicity. Graphics and fancy formatting make message files bigger and slower to download. Many email veterans fear attachments because of the risk of viruses. If you don't need the extra baggage, why not leave it out?
- ***Choose the right communication tool for the job.*** The Internet offers a wealth of communication options to add to the choices offered by phone companies and the post office. Sometimes the choice of medium is as important as the message you're sending. It's probably not a good idea to post "Sorry that jerk Randy broke your heart" on a Facebook wall that's visible to hundreds of friends; messages with personal references should be sent through private communication channels. Similarly, don't try to tweet or text messages that deserve thoughtful paragraphs of prose rather than abbreviated collections of characters ("Sorry 2 hear u have cancer.")
- ***Don't over-friend.*** There's no real payoff for having more Facebook friends than you can track. There is a downside to having too many "friends"—people tend to post less on your wall when they know they're posting for a larger audience. What's more, important posts from your *real* friends tend to get lost in a flurry of irrelevant postings.
- ***Don't overshare.*** Very few, if any, of your friends really care what you had for breakfast or how late your dog slept. If you want people to read what you say, write the kinds of things you'd like to read about *your* friends.
- ***Say no—quietly—to unwanted friendships.*** If you get unsolicited friend requests from people you don't know, it's probably best to ignore them unless you're just trying to build a big fan base. If a "friend" is cluttering your friend feed with unwanted messages, change your settings to hide those postings. Don't hesitate to "unfriend" the worst offenders; most social network services will honor unfriend requests without notifying the people being unfriended.
- ***Protect your friendships by protecting your privacy.*** You may not want to say no to a coworker, a boss, or a neighbor who finds you on Facebook. Fortunately, most social network sites have elaborate privacy settings that give you a great deal of control over which of the bits of information you share can be seen by which groups of people. Review your settings regularly, and keep them current so you don't accidentally reveal something inappropriate to strangers or casual acquaintances.
- ***Lurk before you leap.*** People who silently monitor mailing lists, newsgroups, and forums without posting messages are called *lurkers*. There's no shame in lurking, especially if you're new to a group; it can help you to figure out what's appropriate. After you've learned the culture and conventions of a group, you'll be better able to contribute constructively and wisely.
- ***Check your FAQs.*** Many newsgroups, forums, and mailing lists have FAQs (frequently asked questions) (pronounced "facks")—posted lists of frequently asked questions. These lists keep groups from being cluttered with the same old questions and answers, but only if members take advantage of them.
- ***Know when to disconnect.*** Just about everybody has been annoyed by someone shouting into a phone a couple of feet away in a restaurant, a loud ringtone that goes off during a play or lecture, a face-to-face meeting with someone whose eyes never leave his laptop screen, or a friend who just can't stop texting while you're trying to talk to her. People have lost concert seats, friends, and even jobs because they didn't use common sense about when and where to turn the technology off.
- ***Give something back.*** The Internet includes an online community of volunteers who answer beginner questions, archive files, moderate forums, maintain public servers, and provide other helpful services. If you appreciate their work, tell them in words and show them in actions; do your part to help others in the Internet community.

Common Text Message Abbreviations

Message	Meaning
AFAIK	As far as I know
AYT	Are you there?
BTW	By the way
Doh	How stupid of me
FWIW	For what it's worth
FYI	For your information
IDD	Indeed
IMHO	In my humble opinion
LOL	Laughing out loud
ROFL	Rolling on the floor laughing
RU	Are You (usually followed by something else like OK)
TBH	To be honest
THX or TY	Thanks
TMB	Text me back
TYVM	Thank you very much

FIGURE 8.31 Text messaging abbreviations and their meanings.

Sharing Resources: Peer-to-Peer, Grid, and Cloud Computing

The network **is the computer**.

—John Gage, chief researcher, Sun Microsystems

Of all the companies that came out of nowhere during the dot-com boom of the late '90s, Napster generated the most conversation—and controversy. When 19-year-old college student Shawn Fanning put a friendly user interface and a fresh spin on decades-old file-sharing technology, he created a virtual swap meet for students and others who wanted to share MP3 music files. Almost overnight Napster became one of the hottest Internet destinations, with millions of users downloading and sharing MP3s daily using Napster's software. In May of 2000, a tech company hired by the rock band Metallica revealed that 322,000 Napster users were illegally distributing their music. The Recording Industry Association of America sued the company because its software enabled users to download copyrighted recordings without paying the record companies or artists.

The Napster servers didn't contain those illegal recordings; it just displayed links to recordings scattered all over the Net. People who used Napster practiced **peer-to-peer (P2P) computing**, or, more specifically, ***peer-to-peer file sharing***, by making music files on their hard drives available to others rather than posting them on central servers. In April of 2001, a U.S. District Court judge ruled that Napster was violating federal copyright law and forced the company to change its software so users no longer had free access to copyrighted recordings.

Napster changed its software and its business model, but the peer-to-peer music exchange lived on through other programs and Web sites. The Gnutella file-sharing system, used by several different file-sharing programs, avoids Napster's Achilles' heel by allowing users to share music, movies, software, and other files without going through a central directory. More recently, a P2P protocol known as ***BitTorrent*** has become a popular way to download very large files. For users with broadband Internet connections, downloading is much faster than uploading. With older P2P protocols, file-sharing meant one computer transferring a file to another computer. When both computers had broadband connections, file transfer speed was limited by the rate at which the provider can upload content to the Internet. BitTorrent solves this problem by dividing files into pieces. When a user seeks a file, multiple providers can supply different parts of the file, reducing the transfer time. Some people use BitTorrent to download open-source software such as the Linux operating system. Others use it to download illegal copies of feature films. Businesses use BitTorrent and other P2P protocols for group collaboration, for Web searches, and for sharing updates to virus-control software, among other things.

Technologies such as BitTorrent make it difficult, or impossible, for laws to contain the peer-to-peer file-sharing phenomenon. Recording artists are divided on the issue; some encourage fans to share their music; others say that sharing makes it difficult for musicians to support themselves. Legitimate music downloading services such as the iTunes Store and Amazon provide consumers with a legal way to download music. (Copyright and intellectual property issues were discussed in Chapter 4.)

A related technology—**grid computing**—is, like P2P, a form of ***distributed computing***. But grid computing isn't about sharing files; it's about sharing processing power. One type of grid computing, sometimes called ***volunteer computing***, involves creating a virtual network of geographically dispersed computers to work on a problem that's too big to solve with a single machine or LAN. The best-known example is SETI@Home (setiathome.ssl.berkeley.edu), a program that puts PCs all over the Internet together into a sort of virtual supercomputer that analyzes space telescope data in the search for extraterrestrial life. The SETI@Home program, when installed on a PC, uses the computer's idle time to do calculations and send the results back to SETI headquarters. Millions of PCs around the world can do the work of a million-dollar supercomputer in much less time. A similar program called FightAIDS@home (fightaidsathome.com) enables PCs to contribute spare processing cycles to the fight against AIDS. GIMPS (the Great Internet Mersenne Prime Search) recruited more than 60,000 volunteers to find the largest known prime number.

The Quake Catcher Network doesn't just grab extra computing cycles—it uses a network of laptops as input devices. Many laptops have built-in accelerometers designed to detect rapid movements so they can protect their hard drives if they're dropped. The Quake Catcher Network looks for patterns of rapid movement in laptops—movements that might indicate earthquake activity and provide early warnings of serious quakes. Seismologist Elizabeth Cochran of the University of California at Riverside says "We can measure the seismic waves and then get a warning out to people before the seismic waves get to them."

Another form of grid computing, sometimes called *utility computing*, involves offering computational power and storage as metered commercial services, with the Internet acting like a utility grid. Grid-computing applications are currently being used by the U.S. Department of Defense, the U.S. Department of Energy, NASA, the UK National Grid, and a variety of academic and scientific communities.

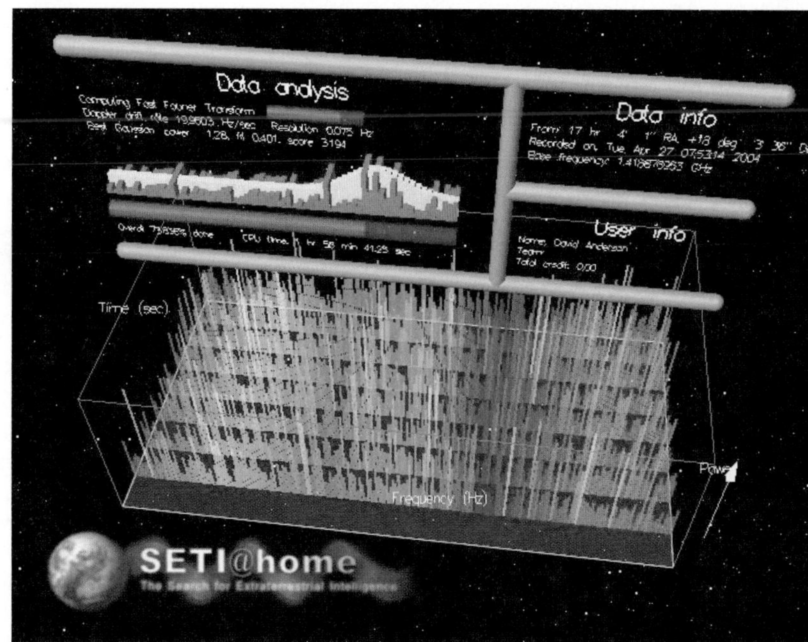

FIGURE 8.32 The SETI@Home project synchronizes the processing power of various connected computers from around the world. Anyone can donate their unused PC time to SETI@Home; the freely downloadable application starts up whenever your PC is not being used.

The ultimate in grid computing is a grid that spans the Internet. In **cloud computing**, resources seem to be coming from "the cloud"—somewhere on the Internet—rather than from a particular computer. Applications, data, servers, and other resources are "out there" somewhere—it doesn't matter where as long as they're available when we need them. Several companies, including Amazon, Google, Adobe, Microsoft, Mozilla, and Apple, have developed cloud computing technologies that bridge the gap between Web applications and desktop applications. A major challenge is to make Web applications useful even when there's no network connection. One approach: Adobe's AIR enables companies (including eBay and NASDAQ) to bring Web-based applications to the desktop so they can run on or off the network. In a world where we're connected most or all of the time to one network or another, widespread cloud computing looms on the horizon.

Digital Communication in Perspective

We've only begun to explore online communication options in this chapter. New technologies emerge all the time; at the same time older technologies evolve and merge. For example, social networking sites are relatively recent developments, but they've changed the way many people communicate. We'll look again at social networks in the next chapter, along with wikis, MMORPGs, and other technologies that are at the heart of what many people call Web 2.0. In that chapter, we'll take an in-depth look at the Internet—past, present, and future.

Before we do, let's step back and put digital communication in a larger perspective. As futurist Stewart Brand reminded us in his groundbreaking book, *The Media Lab*:

> *We can be grateful for the vast dispersed populations of peasant and tribal cultures in the world who have never used a telephone or a TV, who walk where they're going, who live by local subsistence skills honed over millennia. You need to go on foot in Africa, Asia, South America to realize how many of these people there are and how sound they are. If the world city goes to smash, they'll pick up the pieces, as they've done before. Whatever happens, they are a reminder that electronic communication may be essential to one kind of living, but it is superfluous to another.*

The Mind-Machine Connection

It's common knowledge that networks enable computers and smart devices to communicate with each other. But we don't often think about networks that link human bodies and brains to devices in the digital realm. Researchers all around the world are studying technologies that can bridge the gap between person and machine, from robotic limbs to mind-stretching brain-computer interfaces.

Neuroprosthetics has been a particularly fertile area of study in recent years. Researchers in this field develop devices to substitute for missing or damaged parts of the body or nervous system. Cochlear implants have restored hearing to hundreds of thousands of people. Robotic limbs have given mobility and dexterity to countless victims of accidents, illnesses, and wars. Prosthetics have been used to create artificial vision, relieve pain, and relieve symptoms of various kinds of brain damage. Neuroprosthetics has been around for decades, but digital technology is extending the field's reach into uncharted territory.

Cochlear implants and visual implants are well-known examples of *brain-computer interfaces (BCIs)*. Brain-computer interfaces can be invasive—surgically implanted inside the skull—or noninvasive—worn on the head. Invasive BCIs have been successful in restoring vision, hearing, and limb motion, but they can be expensive and risky. Because noninvasive BCI involves sensors in a helmet, a hairnet, or a skullcap, it can't measure brainwaves with the accuracy of invasive BCI. Still, it is finding applications in gaming, behavior therapy, wheelchair control, and communicating when speech and motor centers aren't functioning properly. Both types of BCI are subjects of intense research that combine biology, psychology, and technology.

FIGURE 8.33 Emotiv cofounder Tan Le's Emotiv EPOC gaming headset senses her smile and wink, causing a computer-generated cartoon robot to mirror her expression. Emotiv Systems is one of many companies developing brain-computer interfaces that may eventually enable people to command computers using thought.

U.S. military researchers have been studying "augmented cognition" for more than a decade. Much of this research involves developing computers that use EEG scans, eye-tracking monitors, and other sensors to assess a person's cognitive state and adjust how information is delivered to the brain based on that assessment. If, for example, the visual part of a machine operator's brain is overtaxed, a visual message might be turned into an auditory signal. In the words of Navy Commander Dylan Schmorrow, "We want the computer to learn you, adapt to you."

One particularly intriguing possibility for BCI is synthetic telepathy—person-to-person communication through analysis of neural signals. Synthetic telepathy researchers attempt to detect and identify word-specific neural signals that are generated before words are actually spoken. This type of brain activity is notoriously difficult to decode, even with the best sensors. Still, there are obvious military and medical applications that motivate researchers to push ahead. A paralyzed individual might be able to talk to friends or even write a book if computers could identify words as he thinks of them. Or two soldiers on a secret mission might be able to communicate silently via implants that decode EEG signals and transmit them back and forth. The U.S. military agency Darpa's "Silent Talk" is an initiative designed to turn that second example into reality.

These technologies raise a host of ethical questions. Under what circumstances is it appropriate to enhance brain or body functions? Will this expensive technology only be available to the rich who can afford it? Who should—and who will—have access to data harvested from brains using these tools? Who's responsible if something goes wrong? As researchers narrow the gap between mind and machine, we'll be forced to consider these, and other, questions about the technology's impact on our society.

Crosscurrents

Your Brain Online

by Sharon Begley

Does the Web change how we think? This simple question is at the heart of many psychological research projects, discussions, and debates today. In this January 18, 2010, Newsweek article, Sharon Begley summarizes how many experts answered that question at an online conference. Their answers are thought provoking, challenging, and often contradictory. We're exploring uncharted territory here, and it may be years or decades before we have real answers.

Shortened attention span. Less interest in reflection and introspection. Inability to engage in in-depth thought. Fragmented, distracted thinking.

The ways the Internet supposedly affects thought are as apocalyptic as they are speculative, since all the above are supported by anecdote, not empirical data. So it is refreshing to hear how 109 philosophers, neurobiologists, and other scholars answered, "How is the Internet changing the way you think?" That is the "annual question" at the online salon edge.org, where every year science impresario, author, and literary agent John Brockman poses a puzzler for his flock of scientists and other thinkers.

Although a number of contributors drivel on about, say, how much time they waste on e-mail, the most striking thing about the 50-plus answers is that scholars who study the mind and the brain, and who therefore seem best equipped to figure out how the Internet alters thought, shoot down the very idea. "The Internet hasn't changed the way we think," argues neuroscientist Joshua Greene of Harvard. It "has provided us with unprecedented access to information, but it hasn't changed what [our brains] do with it." Cognitive psychologist Steven Pinker of Harvard is also skeptical. "Electronic media aren't going to revamp the brain's mechanisms of information processing," he writes. "Texters, surfers, and twitterers" have not trained their brains "to process multiple streams of novel information in parallel," as is commonly asserted but refuted by research, and claims to the contrary "are propelled by . . . the pressure on pundits to announce that this or that 'changes everything.' "

And yet. Many scholars do believe the Internet alters thinking, and offer provocative examples of how—many of them surprisingly dystopian. Communications scholar Howard Rheingold believes the Internet fosters "shallowness, credulity, distraction," with the result that our minds struggle "to discipline and deploy attention in an always-on milieu." (Though having to make a decision every time a link appears—to click or not to click?—may train the mind's decision-making networks.) The Internet is also causing the "disappearance of retrospection and reminiscence," argues Evgeny Morozov, an expert on the Internet and politics. "Our lives are increasingly lived in the present, completely detached even from the most recent of the pasts . . . Our ability to look back and engage with the past is one unfortunate victim." Cue the Santayana quote.

These changes in what people think are accompanied by true changes in the process of thinking—little of it beneficial. The ubiquity of information makes us "less likely to pursue new lines of thought before turning to the Internet," writes psychologist Mihaly Csikszentmihalyi of Claremont Graduate University. "Result: less sustained thought?" And since online information "is often decontextualized," he adds, it "satisfies immediate needs at the expense of deeper understanding (result: more superficial thought?)." Because facts are a click away, writes physicist Haim Harari, "the Internet allows us to know fewer facts . . . reducing their importance as a component" of thought. That increases the importance of other components, he says, such as correlating facts, "distinguishing between important and secondary matters, knowing when to prefer pure logic and when to let common sense dominate." By flooding us with information, the Internet also "causes more confidence and illusions of knowledge" (Nassim Taleb of MIT, author of *The Black Swan*), but makes our knowledge seem "more fragile," since "for every accepted piece of knowledge I find, there is within easy reach someone who challenges the fact" (Kevin Kelly, cofounder of *Wired*).

Even more intriguing are the (few) positive changes in thinking the Internet has caused. The hyperlinked Web helps us establish "connections between ideas, facts, etc.," suggests Csikszentmihalyi. "Result: more integrated thought?" For Kelly, the uncertainty resulting from the ubiquity of facts and "antifacts" fosters "a kind of liquidity" in thinking, making it "more active, less contemplative." Science historian George Dyson believes the Internet's flood of information has altered the process of creativity: what once required "collecting all available fragments of information to assemble a framework of knowledge" now requires "removing or ignoring unnecessary information to reveal the shape of knowledge hidden within." Creativity by destruction rather than assembly.

Discussion Questions

1. If you were participating in this online conference, how would you answer the question, "How is the Internet changing the way you think?"
2. Do you think it's possible that the Internet is having both positive and negative effects on our brains? Explain your answer.

Summary

Networking is one of the most important trends in computing today. Computer networks allow computers to share hardware and to send software and data back and forth. In addition, networks enable people to work together in ways that would be difficult or impossible without them.

LANs are made up of computers that are close enough to be directly connected with cables or wireless radio transmitters/receivers. Most LANs include shared printers and file servers. WANs are made up of computers separated by a considerable distance. The computers are connected to each other through the telephone network, which includes cables, microwave transmission towers, and communication satellites. Many computer networks are connected together through the Internet so messages and data can pass back and forth among them.

Most computer networks today use the Ethernet architecture; an Ethernet port is a standard feature on most modern PCs. The Ethernet standard has been revised over the years to provide more bandwidth, so more data can be transmitted at faster rates. Communication software takes care of the details of communication between machines—details such as protocols that determine how signals will be sent and received. Network operating systems typically handle the mechanics of LAN communication. Many popular PC operating systems include peer-to-peer networking software, so any PC or Mac on a network can serve as a server as well as a client.

Computers can be directly connected to networks through Ethernet ports. When high-speed direct connections aren't possible, a PC can transmit and receive signals over standard phone lines with a modem. But today most people connect to remote computers via broadband Internet connections. These high-bandwidth connections can transmit large amounts of information quickly. Broadband connections include DSL, which uses standard phone lines; cable modems, which use cable TV lines; satellite, which uses satellite dishes; and Wi-Fi, which uses short-range wireless 802.11 transmitters. All of these technologies can be connected to Internet backbones, many of which transmit astronomical amounts of data quickly through fiber-optic cables.

Wi-Fi is exploding in popularity because of its potential for providing universal Internet access. Wireless hotspots, both public and private, make it easy for people to connect computers and other Wi-Fi-equipped devices to the Internet. WiMax networks can provide wireless connections over much longer distances. Bluetooth technology is designed to connect phones, computers, and peripherals that are physically very close to each other. A growing number of people connect to the Internet using the 3G and 4G networks that also support global mobile phone communication. Some specialized networks, such as global positioning systems and financial systems, serve unique functions.

Email, instant messaging, and teleconferencing are the most common forms of communication between people on computer networks. But many people also communicate through blogs, newsgroups, mailing lists, Web forums, and VoIP. And social networks such as Facebook combine many of these media with other services that encourage online community building. People who communicate with these new media should follow simple rules of netiquette and exercise a degree of caution to avoid many of the most common problems.

Peer-to-peer computing was popularized by music-sharing services, but its applications go beyond music sharing. Many businesses are exploring ways to apply P2P technology. Grid computing goes beyond P2P computing by enabling people to share processor power with others. Some organizations are working to build a grid-computing model that would make the Internet work like a shared utility. Many see this as a big step toward cloud computing—treating the Internet as a cloud containing shared software and hardware whose physical location isn't particularly important.

Key Terms

3G ....(p. 282)
4G ....(p. 282)
asynchronous communication ....(p. 295)
attachment ....(p. 290)
avatars ....(p. 296)
bandwidth ....(p. 276)
blog ....(p. 294)
blogger ....(p. 294)
Bluetooth ....(p. 281)
broadband connection ....(p. 278)
cable modem ....(p. 278)
chat room ....(p. 296)
client ....(p. 277)
client/server model ....(p. 277)
cloud computing ....(p. 305)
dial-up connection ....(p. 278)
download ....(p. 288)
DSL (digital subscriber lines) ....(p. 278)
electronic commerce (e-commerce) ....(p. 285)
Ethernet ....(p. 274)
file server ....(p. 288)

Global Positioning System (GPS) ....(p. 284)
grid computing ....(p. 304)
hotspot ....(p. 280)
instant messaging (IM) ....(p. 295)
Internet telephony (Voice-over IP or VoIP) ....(p. 296)
intranet ....(p. 277)
local area network (LAN) ....(p. 274)
mailing lists ....(p. 292)
massively multiplayer online role-playing game (MMORPG) ....(p. 299)
modem ....(p. 278)
narrowband connection ....(p. 278)
netiquette ....(p. 302)
network license ....(p. 288)
network operating system (NOS) ....(p. 277)
newsgroup ....(p. 293)
peer-to-peer (P2P) computing ....(p. 304)
peer-to-peer model ....(p. 277)
phishing ....(p. 291)
protocol ....(p. 276)
real-time communication ....(p. 295)
router ....(p. 275)
satellite Internet connection ....(p. 278)
site license ....(p. 288)
social networking ....(p. 298)
spam ....(p. 291)
TCP/IP ....(p. 277)
telecommunication ....(p. 272)
text messaging ....(p. 295)
upload ....(p. 288)
video teleconference ....(p. 296)
voice mail ....(p. 296)
VPN (virtual private network) ....(p. 281)
Webmail ....(p. 289)
Web forum ....(p. 293)
wide area network (WAN) ....(p. 275)
Wi-Fi ....(p. 280)
wiki ....(p. 300)
WiMAX ....(p. 281)
wireless access point (WAP) ....(p. 280)
wireless network ....(p. 274)

Companion Website Projects

1. The *Digital Planet* Web site, **www.pearsonhighered.com/beekman**, contains self-test exercises related to this chapter. Follow the instructions for taking the quiz. After you've completed your quiz, you can email the results to your instructor.
2. The Web site also contains open-ended discussion questions called Internet Exercises. Discuss one or more of the Internet Exercises questions at the section for this chapter.

True or False

1. By definition, a computer network must be connected to the Internet.
2. Most wireless computer networks today use infrared signals to transmit data.
3. The most common types of networks today use a standard networking architecture known as Ethernet.
4. A single fiber-optic cable has the bandwidth of thousands of copper telephone cables.
5. Because peer-to-peer networking software is built into the Windows and Macintosh operating systems, a modern desktop computer can act as both client and server on a network.
6. 3G and 4G networks were developed by the computer industry as part of the fiber-optic Internet backbone.
7. Depending on your email client program and your preferences, your mail might be stored on a remote host or downloaded and stored on your local machine.
8. The line that separates computer communication and telephone communication is being blurred by devices and technologies that operate in both realms.
9. Simple technological solutions can reduce, but not eliminate, the spam problem for email users.
10. Email and instant messaging can filter out many human components of communication, increasing the chance of misinterpreted messages.

Multiple Choice

1. Computer networks
   a. allow people to share hardware resources.
   b. make it easier for people to share data.
   c. support collaboration through such tools as email and instant messaging.
   d. All of the above
   e. None of the above

2. What is a service that connects computers and peripherals in the same building called?
   a. Connection area network (CAN)
   b. Room area network (RAN)
   c. Building area network (BAN)
   d. Local area network (LAN)
   e. Small area network (SAN)

3. A 4G network
   a. can transmit four gigabytes of data every second.
   b. is so named because it can support 4 Internet-ready gadgets at a time.
   c. is based on fourth-generation wireless phone network technology.
   d. only works with 4G or later laptops and smart phones.
   e. can transmit data in four directions simultaneously.

4. A modem
   a. allows a computer to communicate with its peripherals, such as printers and scanners.
   b. increases the speed with which a computer can communicate over a phone line.
   c. converts a digital signal into an analog signal and vice versa.
   d. allows a Windows PC to run Macintosh applications.
   e. performs the same functions as an Ethernet port, except faster.

5. Which of the following does not affect bandwidth?
   a. The amount of network traffic
   b. The software protocols of the network
   c. The type of network connection
   d. The type of information being transmitted
   e. The physical media that make up the network

6. What is the most common reason for installing a Wi-Fi hub in a home?
   a. To enable a PC to connect to a cell phone
   b. To make client/server computing possible
   c. To make it possible to connect Bluetooth-enabled devices to a network
   d. To allow PCs to connect to a network without wires
   e. To create a wireless alternative to hi-fi home entertainment systems

7. If you want to share a document with other people whose computers are connected to your LAN, you should upload the document to a(n)
   a. file server.
   b. client server.
   c. print server.
   d. document server.
   e. upload server.

8. What is an important difference between Internet newsgroups and mailing lists?
   a. A mailing list message goes to only a specific group of people, whereas a newsgroup message is available for anyone to see.
   b. A mailing list message is posted via email, whereas a newsgroup message requires special posting software.
   c. A mailing list message is posted to a special Web mailbox, whereas a newsgroup message is delivered directly to group members' mailboxes.
   d. All of the above are true.
   e. There are no significant differences between the two.

9. What is the main difference between instant messaging (IM) and email?
   a. The use of moderated groups for IM
   b. The ability of email to handle real-time communication
   c. The GUI of the IM client software
   d. The asynchronous nature of email communication
   e. There are no significant differences between the two.

10. The number of email messages delivered each day far exceeds the number of letters delivered by the U.S. Postal Service. Why?
    a. You can write and send an email faster than you can write and mail a letter.
    b. Email is delivered more rapidly.
    c. Email facilitates group communication.
    d. Email can save money.
    e. All of the above.

11. Today's email system is built on protocols that
    a. don't ensure that each sender has a verifiable identity.
    b. automatically filter spam based on objectionable content.
    c. can be modified by anyone with systems administration clearance.
    d. apply directly to instant messaging systems.
    e. All of the above.

12. What percentage of email messages is junk email (spam)?
    a. Less than 10 percent
    b. About 20 percent
    c. About 30 percent
    d. About 40 percent
    e. More than 50 percent
13. Which of these is a generally accepted rule of netiquette?
    a. Sending a message to ten thousand members of a worldwide society of birdwatchers inviting them to your local club's weekly outing
    b. Lurking in a hang-glider enthusiasts newsgroup without posting any messages
    c. Quickly posting on a DJ newsgroup 15 "help me" beginner questions about the second-hand turntables you just bought without manuals
    d. Responding to an antiwar group email with a heated message that attacks the personal integrity of the sender
    e. Sending 36 unsolicited high-resolution family photos to everyone on your list of email friends
14. Many experts say we're at the beginning of a revolution that is creating a vast grassroots network of public and private wireless hubs based on
    a. 3G technology.
    b. mesh network technology.
    c. Wi-Fi technology.
    d. Bluetooth technology.
    e. Ethernet technology.
15. What should people who use a public hotspot be aware of?
    a. There is no such thing as free access to the Internet.
    b. Wireless connections cannot be used to surf the Web.
    c. A notebook computer must be plugged into a power source in order to connect to the network.
    d. Exposure to radio waves is harmful to pregnant women.
    e. Data transmitted over networks without WEP key encryption can be viewed by malicious eavesdroppers.

Review Questions

1. Define or describe each of the key terms listed in the "Key Terms" section. Check your answers using the glossary.
2. Give three general reasons for the importance of computer networking. (*Hint:* Each reason is related to one of the three essential components of every computer system.)
3. How do the three general reasons listed in Question 2 relate specifically to LANs?
4. How do the three general reasons listed in Question 2 relate specifically to WANs?
5. Under what circumstances is a modem necessary for connecting computers in networks? What does the modem do?
6. Describe at least two different kinds of communication software.
7. How could a file server be used in a student computer lab? What software licensing issues would be raised by using a file server in a student lab?
8. What are the differences between email and instant messaging systems?
9. Describe some things you can do with email that you can't do with regular mail.
10. Describe several potential problems associated with email and teleconferencing.
11. "Money is just another form of information." Explain this statement, and describe how it relates to communication technology.
12. Wi-Fi and Bluetooth wireless technologies are designed to serve different purposes than mobile phone technology does. Explain this statement.
13. Why is netiquette important? Give some examples of netiquette.

Discussion Questions

1. Suppose you have an important message to send to a friend in another city, and you can use the telephone, email, real-time teleconference, fax, or overnight mail service. Discuss the advantages and disadvantages of each. See if you can think of a situation for each of the five options in which that particular option is the most appropriate choice.
2. Some people choose to spend several hours every day online. Do you see potential hazards in this kind of heavy modem use? Explain your answer.
3. Should spam be illegal? Explain your answer.
4. In the quote at the end of the chapter, Stewart Brand points out that electronic communication is essential for some of the world's people and irrelevant to others. What distinguishes these two groups? What advantages and disadvantages do each have?
5. Do you think Wi-Fi and other wireless technology put us on the brink of a communication revolution? Why or why not?

Projects

1. Find out about your school's computer networks. Are there many LANs? How are they connected? Who has access to them? What are they used for?
2. Spend a few hours exploring an online service such as AOL. Describe the problems you encounter in the process. Which parts of the service are the most useful and interesting?
3. Imagine you are living in a house with three other students and everyone has a PC. Determine what you would need to purchase to create a home network that would enable all four of you to access the Internet with only a single subscription to a high-speed Internet provider (either cable or DSL). Compare the cost of a wired network based on 100 Mbps Ethernet versus a wireless network based on 802.11g.
4. Identify a wireless hotspot in your city or town. Interview a staff person at the establishment. Does the hotspot provide free access, or does it require payment? If it requires payment, how does it charge for access? What security measures does it have in place? What have been the consequences (both good and bad) of creating a wireless hotspot?

Sources and Resources

Books

How Networks Work, Seventh Edition, by Frank J. Derfler, Jr., and Les Freed (Que). This book follows the model popularized with the *How Computers Work* series. It uses a mix of text and graphics to illuminate the nuts and bolts of PC networks.

How Wireless Works, Second Edition, by Preston Gralla (Que). Another popular book in the *How Computers Work* series, this one focuses on the wireless world, from TV and telephones to Wi-Fi and Bluetooth. There's even a section on the privacy risks of wireless technology.

The Essential Guide to Telecommunications, Fourth Edition, by Annabel Z. Dodd (Prentice Hall). This popular book presents a clear, comprehensive guide to the telecommunications industry and technology, including telephone systems, cable systems, wireless systems, and the Internet. If you want to understand how the pieces of our communication networks fit together, this book is a great place to start.

Home Networking: The Missing Manual, by Scott Lowe (O'Reilly). Once you've got a network in your home, it can save time and provide a wealth of benefits and conveniences. But getting a network up and running can be frustrating and confusing. This book can help you to cut through the technobabble and get your systems connected to each other and to the rest of the networked world.

Send: The Essential Guide to Email for Office and Home, by David Shipley and Will Schwalbe (Knopf). The motivation for this book is made clear in the first sentence: "Bad things can happen on email." The authors clearly and humorously explain how to avoid those bad things, and how to make email work for, rather than against, you.

How to Do Everything with Your Web 2.0 Blog, by Todd Stauffer (Osborne McGraw-Hill). If you want to be a blogger but you're not sure how, this book can help. In addition to the basics of blogging, the author covers podcasts, social bookmarking, wikis, forums, and more.

How to Do Everything with Online Video, by Andrew Shalat (Osborne McGraw-Hill). For many people, video is the medium of choice for Web communication. This handbook has information on planning, creating, editing, and posting Web videos. There are specifics for Mac and Windows users, for YouTube and MySpace posters, for podcasters and Web designers.

How to Do Everything with YouTube, by Chad Fahs (Osborne McGraw-Hill). This book is similar to *How to Do Everything with Online Video* except that it focuses exclusively on YouTube.

Wireless Nation: The Frenzied Launch of the Cellular Revolution, by James B. Murray (Perseus Books). The mobile phone and the PC both burst into our culture in the last decades of the 20th century, and they came together through the Internet. This book chronicles the rise of mobile communication technology.

Connected: The Surprising Power of Our Social Networks and How They Shape Our Lives, by Nicholas A. Christakis and James H. Fowler (Little, Brown, and Company). Christakis and Fowler published their first book for a general audience; now they've written an important book about the power of our social connections, online and off, in influencing our lives.

We the Media: Grassroots Journalism by the People, for the People, by Dan Gillmor (O'Reilly). Gillmor, a respected journalist in the world of "old media," argues in this book that blogs, email, and other people-powered communication tools are changing the rules and bringing hope for the return of true democracy to a culture dominated by powerful corporations.

Film

The Social Network. This acclaimed film presents a slightly fictionalized account of the birth of Facebook. Even though the factual details aren't all correct, the movie clearly and thoughtfully raises important questions about how we relate to each other.

9

The Evolving Internet

OBJECTIVES

After you read this chapter you should be able to:

- Explain how and why the Internet was created
- Describe the technology that's at the heart of the Internet
- Describe the technology that makes the Web work
- Discuss the evolving tools people use to build Web sites
- Discuss the trends that are changing the Internet and the way people use it
- Discuss important social and political issues raised by the growth of the Internet

It's a bit like climbing a mountain. **You don't know how far you've come until you stop and look back.**

—*Vint Cerf*, ARPANET pioneer and first president of the Internet Society

Arpanet Pioneers Build a Reliable Network Out of Unreliable Parts

In the 1960s the world of computers was a technological Tower of Babel; most computers couldn't communicate with each other. When people needed to move data from one computer to another, they carried or mailed reels of magnetic tape or decks of punch cards. While most of the world viewed computers only as giant number crunchers, J. C. R. Licklider, Robert Taylor, and a small group of visionary computer scientists saw the computer's potential as a communication device. They envisioned a network that would enable researchers to share computing resources and ideas.

U.S. military strategists during those Cold War years had a vision too: They foresaw an enemy attack crippling the U.S. government's ability to communicate. The Department of Defense wanted a network that could function even if some connections were destroyed. They provided $1 million to Taylor and other scientists and engineers to build a small experimental network. The groundbreaking result, launched in 1969, was called ARPANET, for Advanced Research Projects Agency NETwork. When a half dozen researchers sent the first historic message from UCLA to Doug Engelbart's lab at the Stanford Research Institute, no one even thought to take a picture.

ARPANET was built on two unorthodox—some might say revolutionary—assumptions:

1. The network itself was unreliable, so it had to be able to overcome its own unreliability.
2. All computers on the network would be equal in their ability to communicate with other network computers.

In ARPANET, there was no central authority because that would make the entire network vulnerable to attack. Messages were contained in software "packets" that could travel independently by any number of different paths, through all kinds of computers, toward their destinations.

ARPANET grew quickly into an international network with hundreds of military and university sites. In addition to carrying research data, ARPANET channeled debates over the Vietnam War and intense discussions about Space War, an early computer game. ARPANET's peer-to-peer networking philosophy and protocols were copied in other networks in the 1980s. Vint Cerf and Bob Kahn, two of the original researchers, developed the protocols that became the standard computer communication language, allowing different computer networks to be linked.

In 1990 ARPANET was disbanded, having fulfilled its research mission, but its technology spawned the Internet. In an interview, Cerf said about the network he helped create, "It was supposed to be a highly robust technology for supporting military command and control. It did that in the [first] Persian Gulf War. But, along the way, it became a major research support infrastructure and now has become the best example of global information infrastructure that we have."

The ARPANET pioneers have gone on to work on dozens of other significant projects and products. In the words of Bob Kahn, "Those were very exciting days, but there are new frontiers in every direction I can look these days." ■

FIGURE 9.1 The team that built the predecessor to the Internet at a 1994 25th anniversary reunion. From front to back: Bob Taylor, Vint Cerf, Frank Heart, Larry Roberts, Len Kleinrock, Bob Kahn, Wes Clark, Doug Engelbart, Barry Wessler, Dave Walden, Severo Ornstein, Truett Thach, Roger Scantlebury, Charlie Herzfeld, Ben Barker, Jon Postel, Steve Crocker, Bill Naylor, and Roland Bryan.

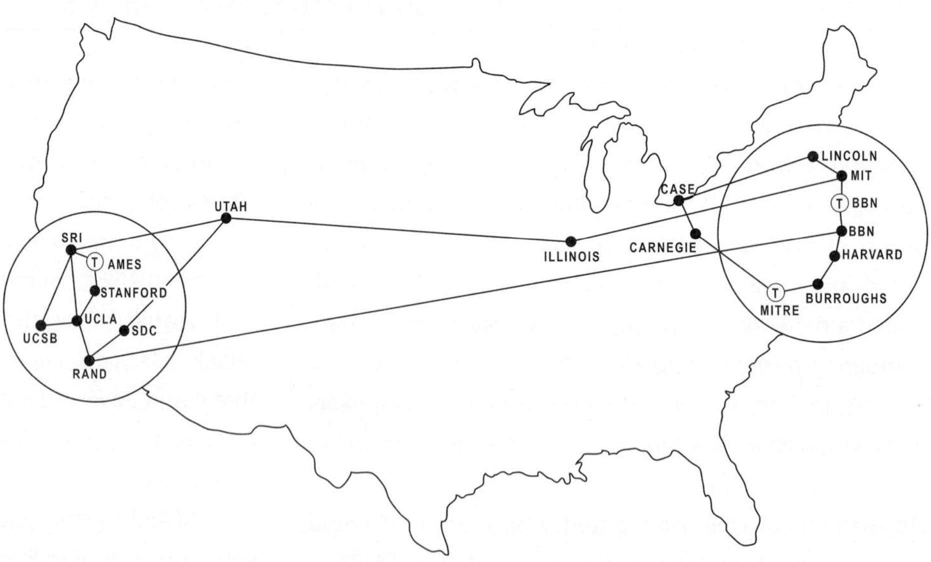

FIGURE 9.2 ARPANET connections in 1971.

The team that designed ARPANET suspected they were building something important. They couldn't have guessed, though, that they were laying the groundwork for a system that would become a universal research tool, a publisher's clearinghouse of information, an always-open entertainment center, a hotbed of business activity, a global shopping mall, a popular social hangout, a fountainhead of collaborative community projects, and one of the most talked about institutions of our time.

In its early years, the Internet was the domain of technological pioneers willing to forgo creature comforts and blaze their own trails through the electronic wilderness. Most people, including corporate executives and government leaders, ignored it. Few believed that it had any commercial potential. In fact, the code of the Net was strongly anticommercial—users were there to share information, not make profits. John Perry Barlow (writer, rancher, politician, lyricist for the Grateful Dead, and cofounder of the Electronic Frontier Foundation) called the early Net an electronic frontier, likening it to the early American West.

In spite of rapid commercialization, the Net still feels a little like an electronic frontier. Network nomads pick digital locks and ignore electronic fences. Some explore nooks and crannies out of a spirit of adventure. Others steal and tamper with private information for profit or revenge. Charlatans and hustlers operate outside the law. Law enforcement agencies and lawmakers occasionally overreact. And there's still a strong sentiment toward keeping corporate and government controls to a minimum.

In the 1990s, the Web opened up the electronic frontier to the masses, just as the railroads opened up the American West a century and a half before. Kevin Kelly described the results in a *Wired* article celebrating the 10th anniversary of Netscape, the first commercial Web company:

> *Today, at any Net terminal, you can get: an amazing variety of music and video, an evolving encyclopedia, weather forecasts, help wanted ads, satellite images of anyplace on Earth, up-to-the-minute news from around the globe, tax forms, TV guides, road maps with driving directions, real-time stock quotes, telephone numbers, real estate listings with virtual walk-throughs, pictures of just about anything, sports scores, places to buy almost anything, records of political contributions, library catalogs, appliance manuals, live traffic reports, archives to major newspapers—all wrapped up in an interactive index that really works.... Ten years ago, anyone silly enough to trumpet the above list as a vision of the near future would have been confronted by the evidence: There wasn't enough money in all the investment firms in the entire world to fund such a cornucopia. The success of the Web at this scale was impossible. But if we have learned anything in the past decade, it is the plausibility of the impossible.... What we all failed to see was how much of this new world would be manufactured by users, not corporate interests.*

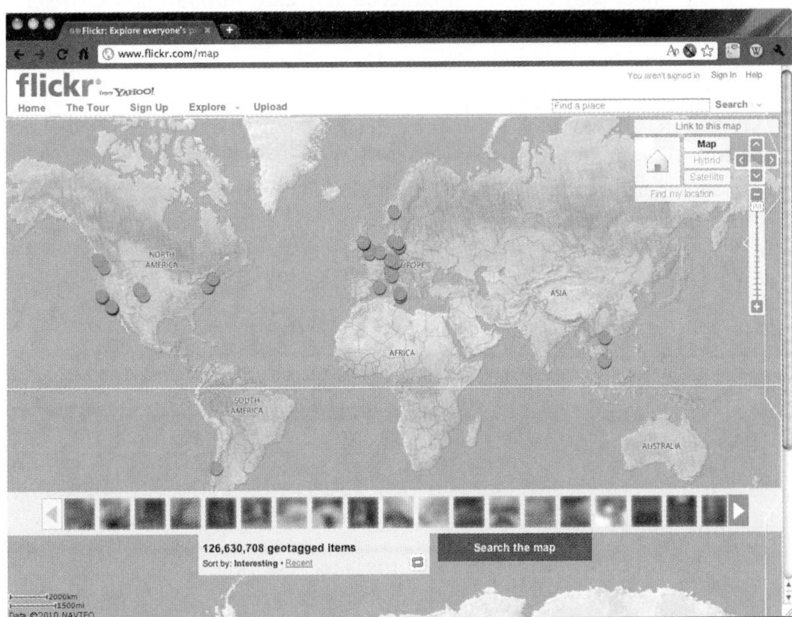

FIGURE 9.3 People from around the world have freely contributed their photographs to the database managed by Flickr.com.

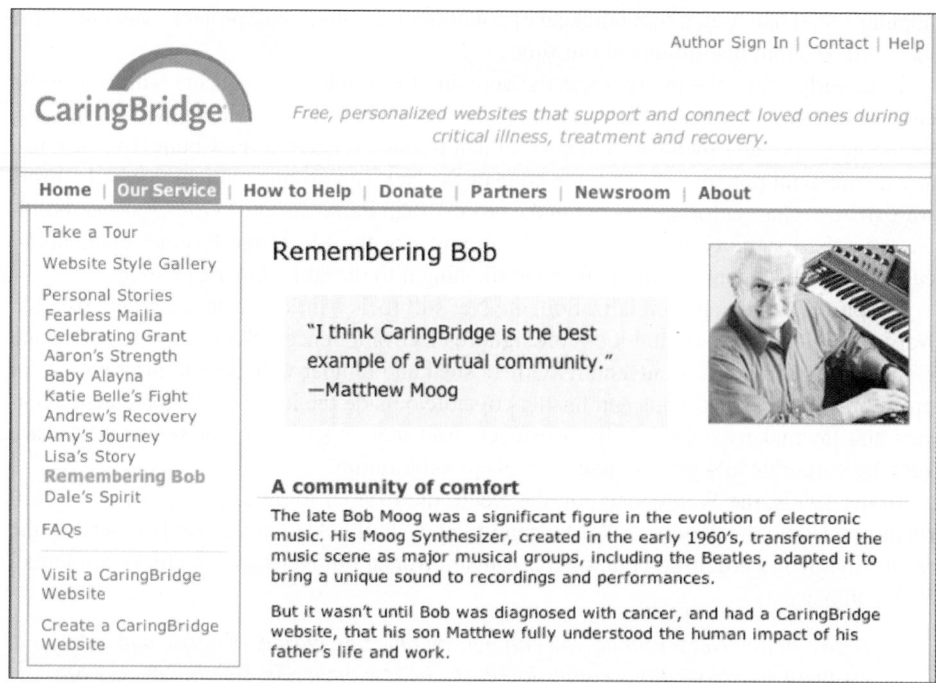

FIGURE 9.4 Millions of people have used caringbridge.org to create and connect with online communities of support for victims of accidents and serious illnesses. Family and friends can view up-to-the-minute journal entries and photos, send support through guestbook messages, and make donations to support the no-charge service.

Blogs, open-source software, peer-to-peer file sharing, Wikipedia, Facebook, Flickr, YouTube, Twitter, podcasts, even eBay—all of these Internet institutions are built by diverse communities of people, not by cubicle cities full of Web designers and programmers. Even commercial enterprises like Amazon encourage their customers to help build the site by writing product reviews and setting up stores within the store. More and more, we are the architects of the emerging Web.

At the same time, we're pushing the Internet far beyond the boundaries of the World Wide Web. Today most traffic on the Internet is delivered through non-browser apps on smart phones, tablets, PCs, game machines, home entertainment devices, car computers, and more. Skype calls, Pandora radio, Xbox games, iTunes downloads, Netflix streaming, and countless phone apps don't need Web browsers to deliver content via the Internet.

For many people, the vocabulary of the Internet seems like a flurry of technobabble. You don't need to analyze every acronym to make sense of the Internet, but your Net experiences can be far more rewarding if you understand the concepts at the heart of basic Net-speak terminology. In this chapter, we delve into the nuts and bolts of the Internet—past, present, and future—to make those concepts clear.

Inside the Internet

> It shouldn't be too much of a surprise that the Internet has evolved into a force strong enough to reflect the greatest hopes and fears of those who use it. After all, **it was designed to withstand nuclear war, not just the puny huffs and puffs of politicians and religious fanatics.**
>
> —*Denise Caruso, digital commerce columnist, the* New York Times

The Internet is a network of networks. It includes dozens of national, statewide, and regional networks, hundreds of networks within colleges and research labs, and thousands of commercial sites all over the planet. Significantly, the Internet is not controlled by any one government, corporation, individual, or legal system. Several international advisory organizations develop standards and protocols for the evolving Internet, but no one has the power to control the Net's operation or evolution. The Internet is, in a sense, a massive anarchy unlike any other organization the world has ever seen.

FIGURE 9.5 Cyber cafés around the world, like this one in France, enable travelers and locals to stay connected to their homes and the rest of the world. Customers often pay by the minute to log into their home servers to keep up on email, favorite Web sites, and IM contacts.

Counting Connections

In its early days, the Internet connected only a few dozen computers at U.S. universities and government research centers, and the U.S. government paid most of the cost of building and operating it. Today the Internet connects millions of computers in almost every country in the world, and costs are shared by thousands of connected organizations. It's impossible to pin down the exact size of the Internet for several reasons:

- The Internet is growing too fast to track. Billions of new users connect to the Internet every year.
- The Internet is decentralized. There's no "Internet Central" that keeps track of user activity or network connections. To make matters worse for Internet counters, some parts of the Internet can't be accessed by the general public; they're sealed off to protect private information.
- The Internet doesn't have hard boundaries. There are many ways to connect to the Internet, and many of them don't fit the traditional model of logging into a network from a PC.

It's easier to understand how the Internet can be shared by PCs, supercomputers, smart phones, game machines, TV set-top boxes, and all kinds of esoteric devices if you know a little bit about the protocols that make the Internet work.

Internet Protocols

> **The most important quality of the Internet is that it lends itself to radical reinvention**.... In another 10 years, the only part of the Internet as we know it now that will have survived will be bits and pieces of the underlying Internet protocol....
>
> *—Paul Saffo, director of the Institute for the Future*

The protocol at the heart of the Internet is called **TCP/IP (Transmission Control Protocol/Internet Protocol)**. TCP/IP was developed as an experiment in **internetworking**—connecting different types of networks and computer systems. The TCP/IP specifications were published as **open standards**, not owned by any company. As a result, TCP/IP became the "language" of the Internet, allowing cross-network communication for almost every type of computer and network. These protocols are generally invisible to users; they're hidden deep in software that takes care of communication details behind the scenes. In addition, the protocols define how information can be transferred between machines and how machines on the network can be identified with unique addresses.

The TCP protocol (the first part of TCP/IP) defines a system similar in many ways to the postal system. When a message is sent on the Internet, it is broken into *packets*, in the same way you might pack your belongings in several individually addressed boxes before you

how it works Internet Communication

Everything that's sent through the Internet depends on the technology of packet switching.

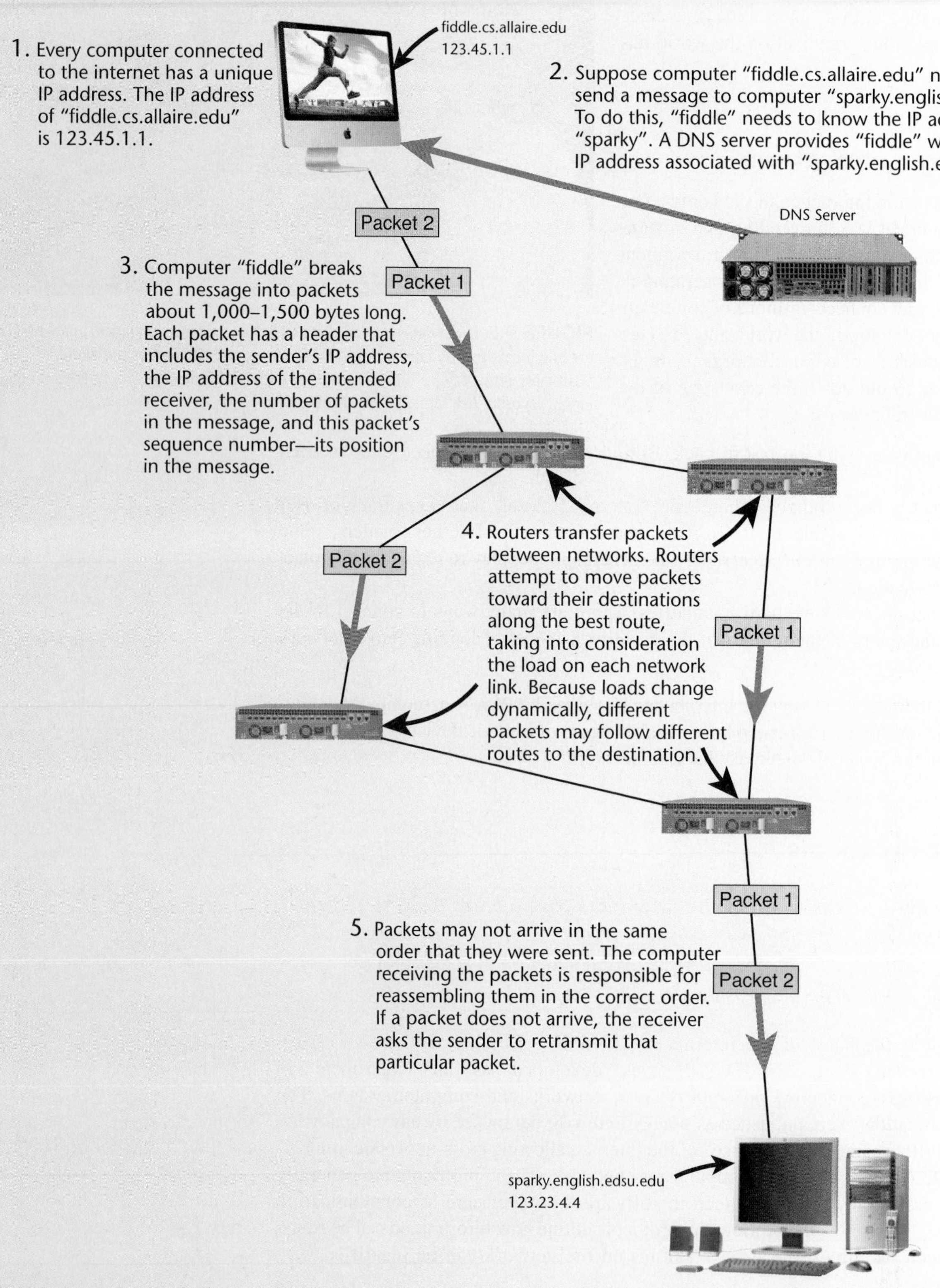

fiddle.cs.allaire.edu
123.45.1.1
1. Every computer connected to the internet has a unique IP address. The IP address of "fiddle.cs.allaire.edu" is 123.45.1.1.
2. Suppose computer "fiddle.cs.allaire.edu" needs to send a message to computer "sparky.english.edsu.edu". To do this, "fiddle" needs to know the IP address of "sparky". A DNS server provides "fiddle" with the IP address associated with "sparky.english.edsu.edu".
DNS Server
Packet 2
Packet 1
3. Computer "fiddle" breaks the message into packets about 1,000–1,500 bytes long. Each packet has a header that includes the sender's IP address, the IP address of the intended receiver, the number of packets in the message, and this packet's sequence number—its position in the message.
4. Routers transfer packets between networks. Routers attempt to move packets toward their destinations along the best route, taking into consideration the load on each network link. Because loads change dynamically, different packets may follow different routes to the destination.
Packet 2
Packet 1
Packet 1
5. Packets may not arrive in the same order that they were sent. The computer receiving the packets is responsible for reassembling them in the correct order. If a packet does not arrive, the receiver asks the sender to retransmit that particular packet.
Packet 2
sparky.english.edsu.edu
123.23.4.4

FIGURE 9.6

ship them to a new location. Each packet has all the information routers need to transfer the packet from network to network toward its destination. Different packets might take different routes, just as different parcels might be routed through different cities by the postal system. Regardless of the route they follow, the packets eventually reach their destination, where they are reassembled into the original message. This **packet-switching** model is flexible and robust, allowing messages to get through even when part of the network is down.

The other part of TCP/IP—the IP part—defines the addressing system of the Internet. Every host computer on the Internet has a unique *IP address*: a string of four numbers separated by periods, or, as they say in Net speak, dots. A typical IP address might look like this: 123.23.168.22 ("123 dot 23 dot 168 dot 22"). Every packet routed through the Internet includes the IP address of the sending computer and the receiving computer.

IP addresses can be static (fixed) or dynamic. A **static IP address** is a manually assigned permanent address like a street address for a house—it doesn't change from day to day, even if the computer reboots. Static IP addresses are ideal for Web servers and other computers that are semipermanently connected to the Internet. But for most PCs and mobile devices, **dynamic IP addresses** are more practical. A dynamic address is like a room number in a hotel—it's assigned when the guest arrives and taken away when the guest leaves. Similarly, when a computer with dynamic addressing enabled connects to the Internet, it's automatically assigned a temporary IP address—probably not the same IP address as the last time it was connected. If you're using a PC with a broadband connection, it probably has a dynamic IP address that was automatically assigned by a DHCP (Dynamic Host Configuration Protocol) server.

The explosive growth of the Internet has created an IP problem: The world is rapidly using up all of the IP addresses available using Internet Protocol version 4 (IPv4)—the standard for most Internet devices today. Fortunately, the Internet Protocol continues to evolve as the Internet matures. Internet Protocol version 6, or *IPv6* solves the shortage-of-addresses problem and makes other improvements as well. For example, IPv6 is designed from the ground up to support *multicast*, a more efficient way for the same information to be transmitted to multiple Internet-connected devices. Many computers and other devices today are IPv6 compatible; others will need to be replaced as the new standard is phased in over in the next few years.

Internet Addresses

In practice, people seldom see or use numerical IP addresses because of the Internet's **domain name system (DNS)**. DNS servers maintain look-up tables that map domain names to IP addresses. For example, a DNS server can determine that the domain name *abcnews.com* refers to the computer with IP address 199.181.132.250.

The domain name system turns each IP address into a hierarchical domain name. Each domain name includes a top-level domain that represents a geographic region (for example, .eu or .asia), a type of institution (.edu or .gov), or a general category of use (.com or .org). The same top-level domain might include thousands—or millions—of domain names.

For example, .com is the top-level domain for amazon.com, google.com, costco.com, and countless other commercial enterprises, large and small. The .com top-level domain is an example of an *unrestricted* generic top-level domain—even though it was conceived as a way of identifying commercial sites on the Internet, there are no rules dictating that a .com site *must* be a commercial site. Other unrestricted generic top-level domains include .org (mainly for nonprofit organizations), .net (originally for network administration), and .info (mostly for providing information).

Some top-level domains are restricted—in order to use one of these, an individual or organization must provide proof of eligibility. For example, .edu is restricted to institutions of higher education and people connected to those institutions. (Unfortunately, .edu doesn't guarantee that the "institution" isn't a bogus school that sells expensive but worthless "degrees.") Other restricted top-level domains include .gov (for U.S. government agencies), .mil (for the U.S. military), .coop (for certified cooperatives), .int (for international organizations recognized by treaty), .pro (for lawyers, accountants, physicians, and engineers in certain countries), .travel (for certified travel-related entities), .museum (for museums), .aero (for the air-transport industry), .jobs (for posting job openings), and .mobi (for mobile-compatible sites).

Outside (and occasionally inside) the United States, top-level domains are generally two-letter country or territory codes, such as .jp for Japan, .th for Thailand, .au for Australia, .uk for United Kingdom, .eu for the European Union, and .us for United States. But a two-letter country code doesn't always represent a country. For example, the tiny Pacific nation of Tuvalu sold its .tv domain name to a U.S. Internet company, which markets the name to television-related companies. And country codes don't always conform to the two-letter norm. A few countries are switching to *internationalized* top-level domain names encoded with Unicode (Chapter 2) and represented in language-specific scripts or alphabets. For example, in 2010, Russia switched from .ru to .Ф, .the Cyrillic abbreviation of the Russian Federation.

The top-level domain name is the last part of the address. The other parts of the address, when read in reverse, provide information that narrows down the exact location on the network. The words in the domain name, like the lines in a post office address, are arranged hierarchically from smaller domains to larger domains. They might include the name of the host computer, the name of the department or network within the organization, and the name of the organization.

The domain naming system is used in virtually all email addresses and Web URLs. A Web URL specifies the IP address of the Web server that houses the page. In an email address, the domain name system is used to pinpoint the Internet location of the host computer that contains the user's mail server. The email address includes the user name and the host address.

Here are some other examples of email addresses using the domain name system:

- president@whitehouse.gov — User *president* whose mail is stored on the host *whitehouse* in the U.S. government (.gov) domain
- crabbyabby@AOL.com — User *crabbyabby* whose mail is handled by AOL, a commercial service (.com) provider
- hazel_filbert@admin.gmcc.ab.ca — User *hazel_filbert* at the *admin* server for Grant MacEwan Community College in Alberta, Canada

Internet Access Options

As we discussed in the previous chapter, computers connect to the Internet through three basic types of connections: direct connections, dial-up connections through modems, and broadband connections through high-speed alternatives to modems. Most Internet users today connect through these four types of broadband access:

- DSL uses standard phone lines and is provided by phone companies in many areas.
- Cable modems provide fast Internet connections through cable TV networks in many areas.
- Satellite dishes can deliver Internet connections through radio waves and satellite relays.
- High-speed wireless connections link computers to nearby networks through radio waves.

Internet service providers (ISPs) sometimes offer several connection options at different prices. Local ISPs are local businesses with permanent connections to the Internet. They provide connections to their customers, usually through local phone lines, along with other services. For example, an ISP might provide email addresses, server space for customers to post Web pages, and technical help as part of a service package. National ISPs, such as EarthLink and NetZero, offer similar services on a nationwide scale.

Online services, including America Online, are ISPs that offer extra services to subscribers, including news, research tools, shopping, games, and chat rooms. An online service can be like a gated community that lets its members explore outside the gates but forbids outsiders from taking advantage of resources inside the gates. Private

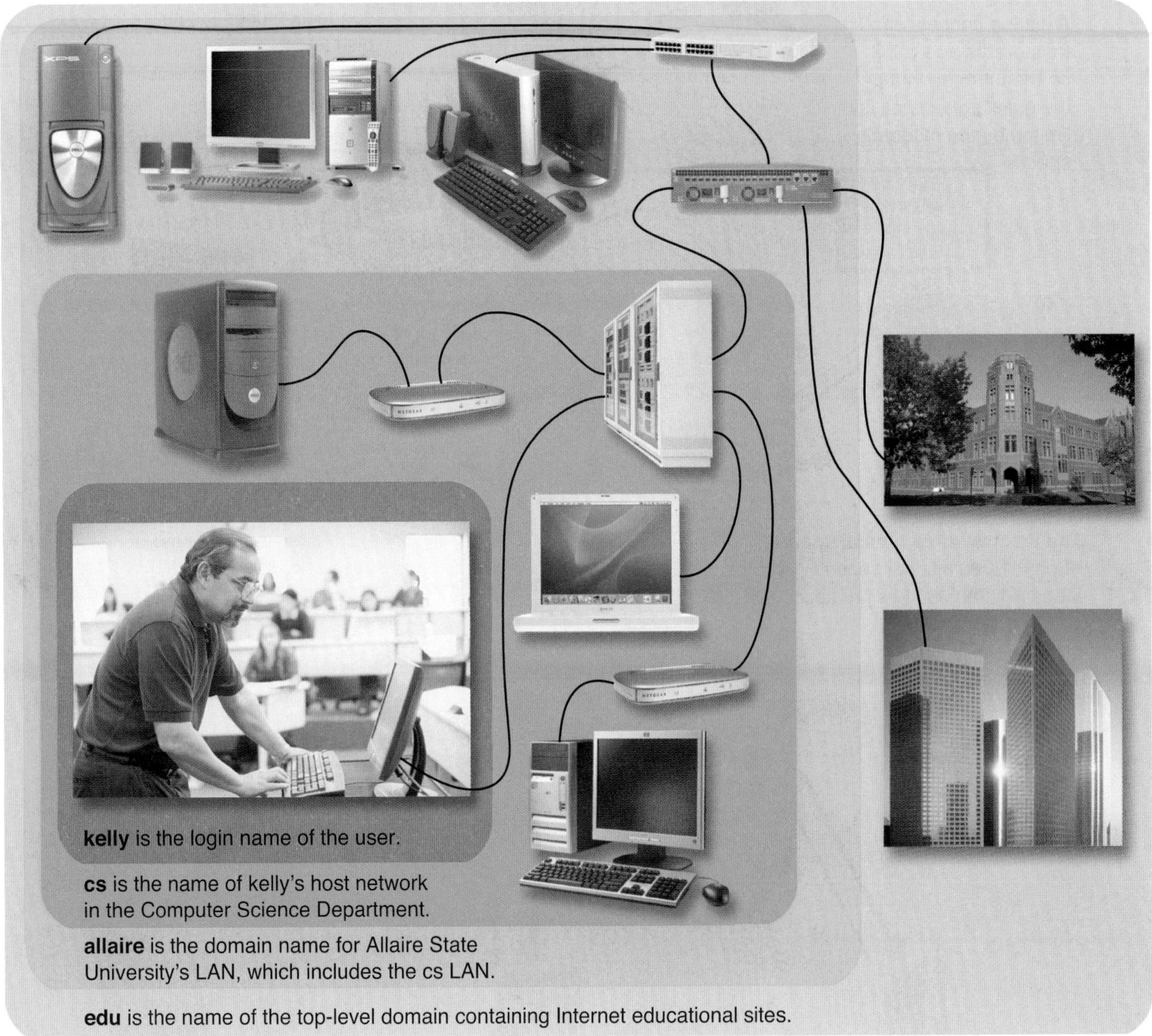

kelly@cs.allaire.edu
kelly is the login name of the user.
cs is the name of kelly's host network in the Computer Science Department.
allaire is the domain name for Allaire State University's LAN, which includes the cs LAN.
edu is the name of the top-level domain containing Internet educational sites.

FIGURE 9.7 Anatomy of an email address.

online services aren't as popular as they used to be, because the wider Web offers similar (and often better) alternatives to their attractions.

Internet Servers

> **The most desirable interaction with a network is one in which the network itself is invisible and unnoticeable**. Planners often forget that people do not want to use systems at all—easy or not. What people want is to delegate a task and not to worry about how it is done.
>
> —*Nicholas Negroponte, director of MIT's Media Lab*

Internet applications, like PC applications, are software tools for users. But working with Internet applications is different from working with PC applications because of the distributed nature of the Internet and the client/server model used by most Internet

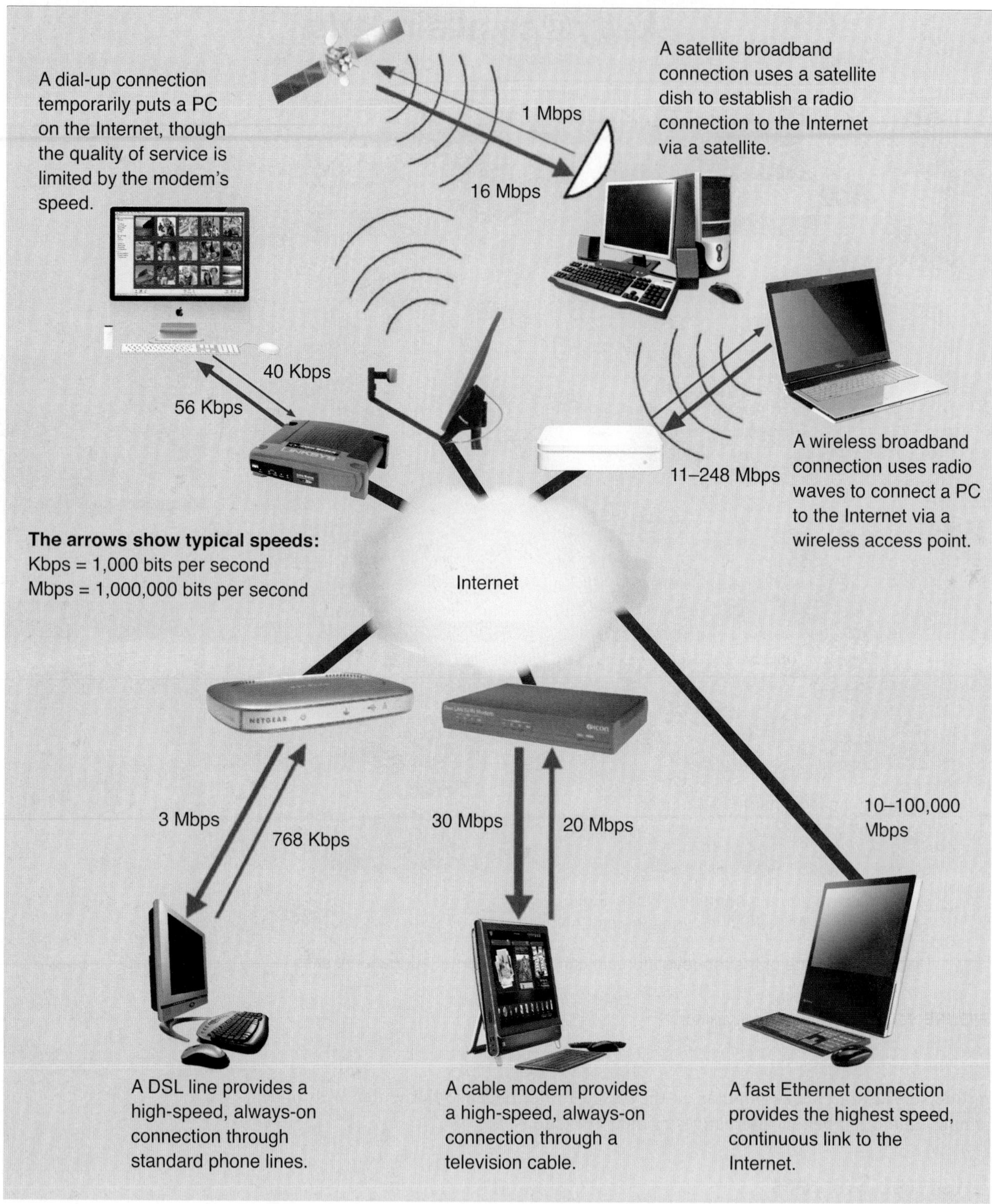

A dial-up connection temporarily puts a PC on the Internet, though the quality of service is limited by the modem's speed.
1 Mbps
16 Mbps
A satellite broadband connection uses a satellite dish to establish a radio connection to the Internet via a satellite.
40 Kbps
56 Kbps
11–248 Mbps
A wireless broadband connection uses radio waves to connect a PC to the Internet via a wireless access point.
The arrows show typical speeds:
Kbps = 1,000 bits per second
Mbps = 1,000,000 bits per second
Internet
3 Mbps
768 Kbps
30 Mbps
20 Mbps
10–100,000 Mbps
A DSL line provides a high-speed, always-on connection through standard phone lines.
A cable modem provides a high-speed, always-on connection through a television cable.
A fast Ethernet connection provides the highest speed, continuous link to the Internet.

FIGURE 9.8 There are many ways to connect a PC to the Internet, and the connection speeds vary dramatically. The speed of an Internet connection is limited to the speed of the slowest link in the chain; the speeds represented here might not be achieved in actual connections. Wireless speed varies depending on the number of devices competing for bandwidth and the amount of environmental interference. Cable modem speeds are also traffic dependent.

applications. In the client/server model, a client program asks for information and a server program fields the request and then provides the requested information from databases and documents. The client program hides the details of the network and the server from the user.

Different people might access the same server using different client applications with different user interfaces. For example, a PC user with a broadband connection might see a graphic-rich, video-enhanced view of data on a server, while another user might be viewing the same data, a few words at a time, on the tiny screen of a mobile phone. A third user might be typing UNIX commands and seeing only text on screen.

Many Internet applications use specialized servers. Some of the most common server types include the following:

- *Email servers.* An **email server** acts like a local post office for a particular Internet host—a business, an organization, or an ISP. For example, a college might have an email server to handle the mail of all students, faculty, and staff; their email addresses point to that server. The email server receives incoming mail, stores it, and provides it to the email client programs of the addressees when they request it. Similarly, the email server collects mail from its subscribers and sends those messages toward their Internet destinations. Basically, the email server handles local client requests of two types: "Give me my mail" and "Pick up my mail and send it."
- *File servers.* **File servers** distribute programs, media files, and other data files across LANs and the Internet. The Internet's **file transfer protocol (FTP)** enables users to download files from file servers (sometimes called FTP servers) to their computers—and to upload files they want to share from their computers to these archives. When you click a Web link that downloads a file, the Web browser's request is probably handled using FTP. FTP requests aren't always done through Web browsers, though. Several popular applications have FTP capability, and FTP commands are built into Windows, Mac OS X, and most versions of Linux.
- *Application servers.* An **application server** stores applications and makes them available to client programs that request them. An application server might be used within a large company to keep PCs updated with the latest software. Each PC might have a client program that regularly sends requests for updates to the server. The application server might also be housed at an **application service provider (ASP)**—a company that manages and delivers application services on a contract basis. Users of ASPs don't buy applications; they rent them, along with service contracts. Some application servers supply platform-neutral, Web-based applications rather than operating system–specific PC applications. For example, Zoho Writer offers many of the features of Microsoft Office in a program you can run on nearly any computer with an Internet connection. Many industry watchers believe ASPs will eventually provide most of the software we use. For some companies, ASPs are part of larger Web-services strategies, discussed later.
- *Web servers.* A **Web server** stores Web pages and sends them to client programs—Web browsers—that request them. It may also store and send Web media, including graphics, audio, video, and animation. In the next section, we'll turn our attention to the technology behind the Web.

/iconfluence-www/oasis

Filename	Size	Modified	Permissions
css	1.0 KB	6/18/12 8:06 PM	rwxr-xr-x (755)
style.css	4.7 KB	3/11/12 2:43 AM	rw-r--r-- (644)
layout.php	186 B	2/5/12 11:21 PM	rw-r--r-- (644)
home.html	1.4 KB	2/5/12 11:14 PM	rw-r--r-- (644)
includes	1.0 KB	2/5/12 11:08 PM	rwxr-xr-x (755)
index.php	127 B	2/5/12 11:07 PM	rw-r--r-- (644)
xmlrpc.php	55.5 KB	1/29/12 1:05 AM	rw-r--r-- (644)
images	1.0 KB	1/29/12 1:04 AM	rwxr-xr-x (755)
water_tile.psd	196....	1/29/12 1:04 AM	rw-r--r-- (644)
sue_calvin.jpg	18.8 KB	1/29/12 1:04 AM	rw-r--r-- (644)
logo_old.jpg	5.1 KB	1/29/12 1:04 AM	rw-r--r-- (644)
iStock_000004576863XSmall.jpg	242....	1/29/12 1:04 AM	rw-r--r-- (644)
iStock_000000818351XSmall.jpg	65.2 KB	1/29/12 1:04 AM	rw-r--r-- (644)
iStock_000000818351Small.jpg	212....	1/29/12 1:04 AM	rw-r--r-- (644)
Oasis_web REV.psd	455....	1/29/12 1:04 AM	rw-r--r-- (644)
Oasis_web REV.jpg	102....	1/29/12 1:04 AM	rw-r--r-- (644)
images	1.0 KB	1/29/12 1:03 AM	rwxr-xr-x (755)
_notes	1.0 KB	1/29/12 1:03 AM	rwxr-xr-x (755)
contact.jpg	18.8 KB	1/28/12 3:56 AM	rw-r--r-- (644)
resources.jpg	16.4 KB	1/28/12 3:22 AM	rw-r--r-- (644)
faqs.jpg	8.5 KB	1/28/12 3:20 AM	rw-r--r-- (644)
life_coach.jpg	28.7 KB	1/21/12 1:01 AM	rw-r--r-- (644)
sue_side.jpg	17.1 KB	1/21/12 12:38 AM	rw-r--r-- (644)
water_tile.jpg	4.5 KB	1/20/12 8:01 PM	rw-r--r-- (644)
logo.jpg	4.8 KB	1/20/12 8:01 PM	rw-r--r-- (644)
sue_pic.jpg	15.1 KB	1/13/12 11:31 PM	rw-r--r-- (644)
sue_profile.jpg	43.5 KB	1/13/12 11:07 PM	rw-r--r-- (644)
nav_extender.jpg	3.3 KB	8/9/11 12:00 AM	rw-r--r-- (644)
banner_extender.jpg	52.6 KB	8/9/11 12:00 AM	rw-r--r-- (644)
Oasis_web.jpg	11.9 KB	8/9/11 12:00 AM	rw-r--r-- (644)
contact.html	2.2 KB	1/28/12 3:57 AM	rw-r--r-- (644)
resources.html	14.5 KB	1/28/12 3:45 AM	rw-r--r-- (644)
bio.html	3.0 KB	1/28/12 3:42 AM	rw-r--r-- (644)
faqs.html	2.4 KB	1/28/12 3:37 AM	rw-r--r-- (644)
services.html	2.8 KB	1/28/12 3:32 AM	rw-r--r-- (644)
FAQs.html	2.4 KB	1/28/12 3:25 AM	rw-r--r-- (644)
email_sent.php	252 B	1/23/12 12:38 AM	rw-r--r-- (644)
home.php	1.7 KB	1/20/12 8:52 PM	rw-r--r-- (644)
index.html	369 B	1/13/12 12:57 AM	rw-r--r-- (644)
readme.html	7.4 KB	7/2/11 12:00 AM	rw-r--r-- (644)
license.txt	14.7 KB	7/2/11 12:00 AM	rw-r--r-- (644)

41 Files

FIGURE 9.9 Writers, Web designers, and others can share files using an FTP server. FTP client software is used for uploading and downloading files.

Inside the Web

> The **dream behind the Web is of a common information space** in which we communicate by sharing information.
>
> —*Tim Berners-Lee, creator of the World Wide Web*

The World Wide Web (Web) is a distributed browsing and searching system originally developed at CERN (European Laboratory for Particle Physics) by Tim Berners-Lee, a visionary scientist profiled in Chapter 6. He designed a system for giving Internet documents unique addresses, wrote the HTML language (discussed below) for encoding and displaying documents, and built a software browser for viewing those documents from remote locations. Since it was introduced in 1991, the Web has become phenomenally popular as a system for exploring, viewing, and publishing all kinds of information on the Internet.

Web Protocols and Web Publishing

The Web is built around a naming scheme that allows every information resource on the Internet to be referred to using a uniform resource locator or, as it's more commonly known, URL. Here's a typical URL: **http://weatherunderground.com/satellite/vis/1k/US.html**. The first part of this URL refers to the protocol that must be used to access information; it might be FTP, news, or something else. It's commonly *http*, for *hypertext transfer protocol*, a protocol used to transfer Web pages. (Most browsers don't require you to type *http://* when you're entering a URL; you can usually leave off the protocol unless it's something other than *http*.) The second part (the part following the://) is the address of the host containing the resource; it uses the same domain-naming scheme used for email addresses. The third part, following the dot address, describes the *path* to the particular resource on the host—the hierarchical nesting of directories (folders) that contain the resource.

Web pages are commonly created using a language called HTML (HyperText Markup Language). An HTML *source document* is a text file that includes codes called markup tags that describe the format, layout, and logical structure of a hypermedia document.

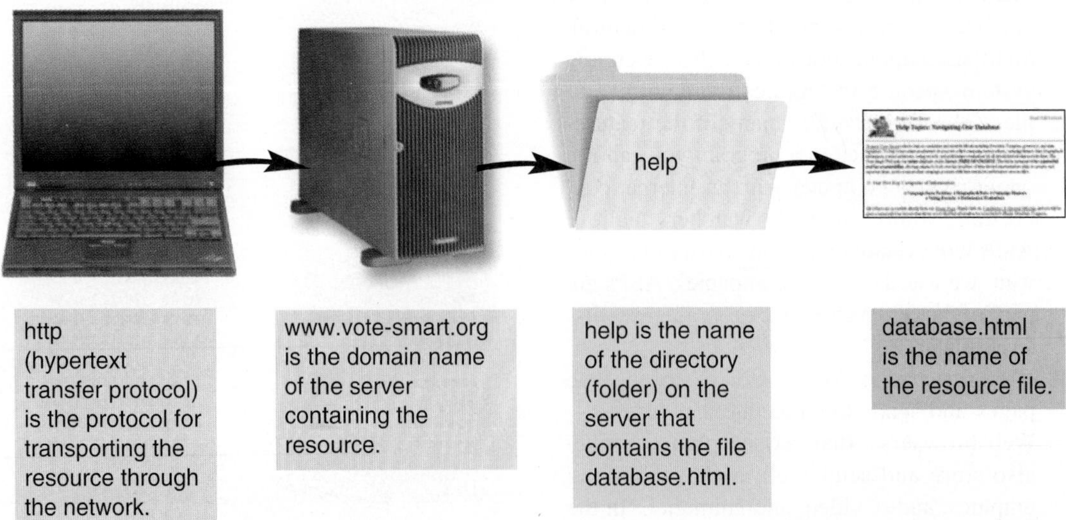
http://www.vote-smart.org/help/database.html
help
http (hypertext transfer protocol) is the protocol for transporting the resource through the network.
www.vote-smart.org is the domain name of the server containing the resource.
help is the name of the directory (folder) on the server that contains the file database.html.
database.html is the name of the resource file.

FIGURE 9.10 Anatomy of a URL.

FIGURE 9.11 HTML source code tells the Web browser how to format the text when it's displayed on the screen.

HTML is definitely not WYSIWYG (what you see is what you get); the HTML codes embedded in the document make it look cryptic and nothing like the final page displayed on the screen. But those codes enable a Web browser to translate an HTML source document into that finished page. Because it's a text file, an HTML document can be easily transmitted from a Web server to a client machine anywhere on the Internet.

You can create a Web page with any word processor or text editor; you just type the HTML commands along with the rest of the text. But you don't need to write HTML code to create a Web page. Many programs, including Microsoft Word, PowerPoint, and FileMaker Pro, can automatically convert basic formatting features (including character styles, indentation, and justification) into HTML codes. Some **Web authoring software**, including Adobe Dreamweaver, Microsoft Expression Web, and Apple's iWeb, works like page layout programs that desktop publishers use. You can lay out text and graphics the way you want them to look, and the authoring program creates an HTML document that looks similar to your original layout when viewed through a Web browser. The best of these Web authoring programs enable you to manage entire Web sites using tools that can automate repetitive edits, apply formatting styles across pages, and check for bad links. Some have tools for connecting large sites to databases containing critical, rapidly changing content. (Many dynamic Web sites are built with content management tools that make page creation and modification even easier; these tools are discussed later in the chapter.)

After an HTML document is completed, it needs to be uploaded onto a Web server before it's visible on the Web. Many ISPs provide Web server space as part of their subscription service; other companies, called Web hosts, rent Web server space to individuals and organizations. By default, most Web pages have URLs that include the ISP or Web server domain names—names like **http://Web.me.com/shjoobedebop**. Most businesses, organizations, and individuals pay an annual fee to a ***domain name registry*** company for names that relate to their organization, product, or service. As a convenience, some companies serve as ISPs, Web hosts, and domain name registries for the customers.

how it works The World Wide Web

There's a lot of behind-the-scenes communication going on whenever you view a Web page.

1. When you type a URL into the address box of your Web browser, the browser sends a message through the Internet to the server with the specified domain name **www.appleeater.com**.

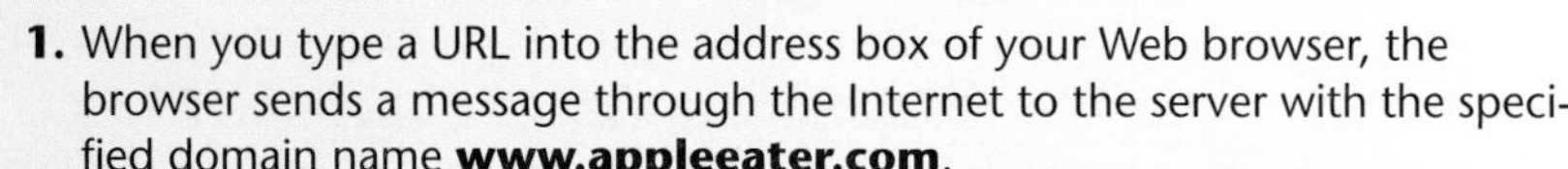

Request for www.appleeater.com. home page

2. The server responds by sending the specified file to the client browser. The file contains the contents of the requested Web page in HTML format. The HTML commands provide formatting instructions and other information. Because HTML files are all text, they're small and easy to transmit through the Internet.

...<h1>Eat Apples!</h1> <p>For a special treat</p>

3. The browser reads the HTML file and interprets the HTML commands, called tags, embedded in angle brackets <like this>. It uses the formatting tags to determine the look and layout of the text on the page. For example, <H1> indicates a level 1 heading to be displayed in large text, <p> indicates a paragraph of body text, and so on.

4. The HTML file doesn't contain pictures; it's a text file. But it does contain a tag specifying where a picture file is stored and where in the page it is to be displayed. The server responds to this tag by sending the requested graphics file.

Request for www.fujieater home page

5. The HTML file also contains a tag indicating a hyperlink to another document with a URL on another server. When the user clicks that link, a message is sent to the new server, and the process of building a Web page in the browser window starts anew.

FIGURE 9.12

From Hypertext to Multimedia

The Web was built by millions of people simply because they wanted it, without need, greed, fear, hierarchy, authority figures, ethnic identification, advertising, or any form of manipulation. **Nothing like this ever happened before in history. We can be blasé about it now, but it is what we will be remembered for.** We have been made aware of a new dimension of human potential.

—Jaron Lanier, virtual reality pioneer

Way back in the early 1990s (!) the first Web pages were straight hypertext. Within a couple of years, graphics were common and frustrated print designers figured out tricks for making Web pages look more like magazine pages. It wasn't long before a few cutting-edge Web sites enabled browsers to download jerky video and audio clips to their hard disks. Today even an amateur Web site might contain any or all of the following:

- *Tables* are spreadsheet-like grids with rows and columns containing neatly laid-out text and graphical elements. Tables with invisible cell borders are often used as alignment tools to create simple layouts.
- *Frames* are subdivisions of a browser's viewing area that enable visitors to scroll and view different parts of a page, or even multiple pages, simultaneously. Many users find frames confusing, and as the Internet evolves, frames are becoming less common.
- *Forms* are pages that visitors can fill in to order goods and services, send email, respond to questionnaires, enter contests, express opinions, or add comments to ongoing discussions.
- *Animations* are moving pictures based on a variety of technologies, from simple repetitive GIF animations to complex interactive animations created with tools that go far beyond the capabilities of the original HTML specification.
- *Search engines* are tools for locating what you're looking for on a site. Most of these site-specific search engines are based on the same technology as Web-wide search engines, such as Google. Many site builders license search engines from search engine companies.
- *Downloadable audio* clips are compressed sound files that you must download onto your computer's hard disk before the browser or some other application can play them. MP3 and AAC compression formats are popular because the compressed music files sound almost the same as the uncompressed originals that would take much longer to download.
- *Downloadable video* clips are compressed video files that you can download and view on a computer. Many are small, short, and jerky, but quality is rapidly improving as video compression technologies mature.
- **Streaming audio** files are sounds that play without being completely downloaded to the local hard disk. Some streaming files play automatically while you view a page, providing background music and sound effects. Others, such as sound samples at music stores, play on request. Unlike downloaded media files, you can view or hear streaming media files within seconds because they play while you're downloading them. For the same reason, streaming media files don't need to be limited to short clips. Concert-length streaming programs are common. High-quality streaming music generally requires a broadband connection and can be interrupted by Internet traffic jams.
- **Streaming video** files are video clips that play while you're downloading them. Streaming video is even more dependent on high-bandwidth connection than streaming audio is.
- *Real-time streaming audio or video broadcasts*, or *Webcasts*, are streaming transmissions of radio or TV broadcasts, concerts, news feeds, speeches, and other sound events as they happen. Many Internet radio stations stream around the clock.

Today new Web ideas appear at an astounding rate—so fast that browser makers have trouble keeping up. Fortunately, the most popular browsers can be enhanced with

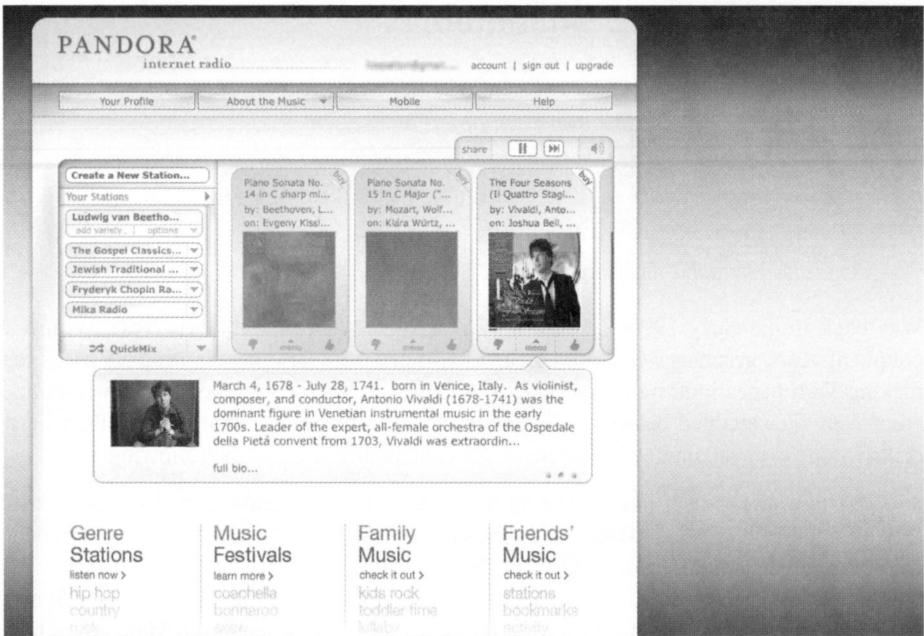

FIGURE 9.13 Streaming and downloadable media are available from countless Web sites. Pandora.com allows listeners to create customized streaming "radio" stations that play songs that match the characteristics of music you already know and love.

plug-ins—software extensions that add new features. When a company introduces a Web innovation, such as a new type of animation, it typically makes a free browser plug-in available to users. Once you download the plug-in and install it in your browser, you can take advantage of any Web pages that include the innovation. Popular plug-ins become standard features in future browser versions, so you don't need to download and install them.

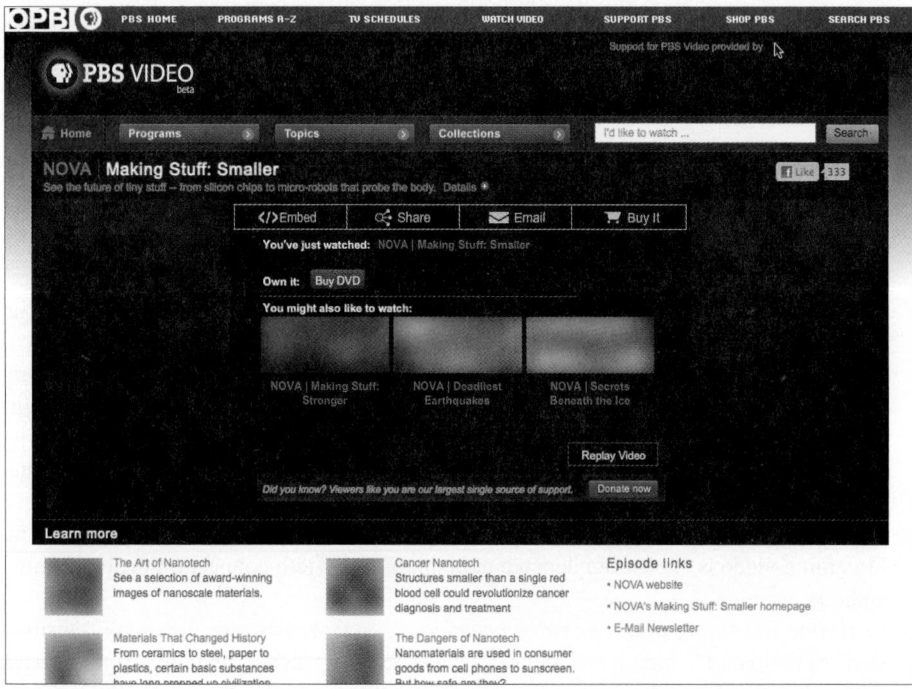

FIGURE 9.14 PBS.org is one of a multitude of Web sites that provides streaming video files.

The most popular free plug-ins include:

- *Adobe Reader* and *Acrobat* (Adobe) display documents in ***Portable Document Format (PDF)*** so they look the same on the screen as on paper, even if the documents are viewed on computers that don't have the same fonts installed. Adobe Reader is a free application that can only display PDF documents; the Acrobat products allow you to edit and create PDF documents. Adobe Reader is preinstalled in most modern browsers.
- ***Shockwave/Flash*** (Adobe) plug-ins enable browsers to present compressed interactive multimedia documents, animation, and video. Flash is preinstalled in virtually all PC and Mac browsers and some browsers for handheld devices.
- ***Windows Media Player*** (Microsoft) is a popular program for playing streaming audio and video on Microsoft Windows as well as Microsoft's operating systems for handheld devices.
- ***QuickTime*** (Apple) is Apple's multipurpose multimedia framework. The cross-platform Web browser plug-in can play back a variety of media formats, including audio, video, animation, and even interactive 3-D models.

HTML was originally designed to share scientific research documents, not to deliver media-rich documents in which design is as important as content. Newer versions of HTML support ***Cascading Style Sheets (CSS)*** to define formatting and layout features that aren't recognized in older versions of HTML. For example, cascading styles are often used to add ***rollovers*** to onscreen buttons, so they visibly change when the mouse pointer rolls over them. (Rollovers and other dynamic effects can—and often are—created using scripting languages, covered later in the chapter.)

The next version of HTML, HTML 5, is currently under development. When it's approved, HTML 5 will offer 2-D and 3-D drawing capabilities, improved accessibility for visually impaired users and for mobile devices, coding that makes it easier for search engines to locate relevant pages, multimedia without browser plug-ins, and programming features that go far beyond any previous version of HTML. Even though it will be years before the version is fully approved by the board of standards, many of its most powerful features are already supported by the most popular browsers.

Dynamic Web Sites: Beyond Static Pages

> **If you thought a Web site consisted of HTML pages organized as a directory, go back to the 20th century.** A successful Web site today consists primarily of XML code and a database.
>
> —*Dana Blankenhorn, coauthor of* Web Commerce: Building a Digital Business

HTML is designed for page layout, not programming. It works well for ***static Web sites***—sites with content that doesn't often change. But by itself, it can't support online shopping, financial transaction processing, library catalogs, daily newspapers, search engines, and other applications with masses of rapidly changing data. This kind of ***dynamic Web site*** requires two things that HTML can't easily deliver: a database to store the constantly changing content of the site, and custom programming to access that data and, when appropriate, make it available to site visitors.

A **data-driven Web site** can display dynamic, changeable content without having constantly redesigned pages, thanks to an evolving database that separates the content of the site from its design. For example, an online store's Web site doesn't have a separate HTML page for each catalog item. Instead, it has pages that are coded to display product information drawn from a database that can be continually updated. The Web site is a front end for the database; it serves as the visitor's window into the database. Likewise, the database is a data back end for the Web site.

A dynamic, data-driven Web site can also offer personalization—customization of content made possible because the site can remember information about guests from visit

Screen Test Building a Web Site

GOAL *To create a site for a client with a small service business*

TOOLS *Adobe Dreamweaver, image editing software, and one or more Web browsers*

1. The first step in publishing, whether on paper or on the Web, is to make a plan. What is the purpose of the site? What is the client trying to communicate? What kind of visual image should the site convey? How should the information and images be organized? You create an outline listing the main sections of the site; you can (and probably will) modify and extend this outline as the site grows. (For more complex sites with lots of links, a flowchart or storyboard can make it easier to plan the structure.)

2. You and your client collect and prepare the source documents—the images, articles, and other elements that will make up the finished publication.

3. You prepare a logo and navigation banner graphic using Photoshop and save a copy as a JPG file for the Web.

- Home page
  - Welcome
  - Quick overview of qualifications and offerings
  - Sidebar photo: Susan in maroon dress
- About
  - Life experiences
  - Certifications and training
  - Sidebar photo: B&W profile
- Services
  - Individual Coaching
  - Coaching for Coaches
  - Sidebar photo: Sue coaching Janice
- FAQ
  - What is a life coach?
  - How it differs from therapy
  - Why focus on The Work?
- Resources
  - Books
    - *Byron Katie, Loving what it is*
    - *Martha Beck, Steering by Starlight*
    - *etc.*
  - Web links
    - *TED talk*
- Contact
  - Form with fields for "From" address, "Subject," "Message," "Sign up for mailing list" check box
  - Thank you page when form is submitted

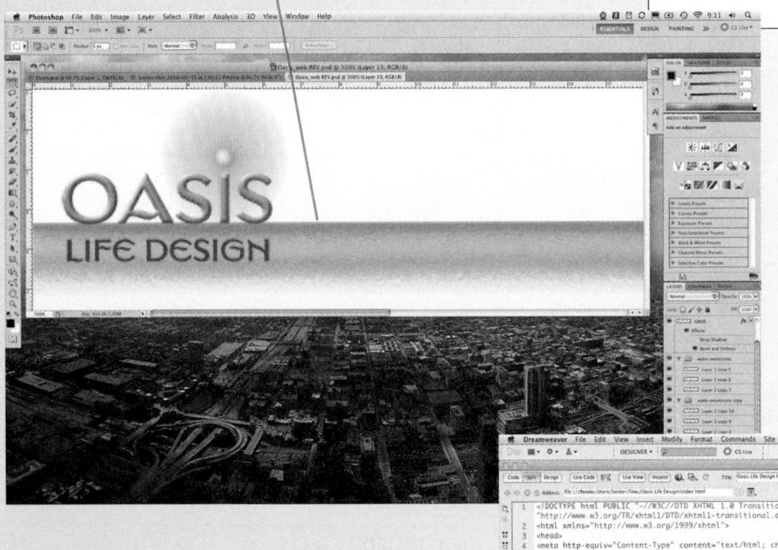

4. Dreamweaver Web authoring software enables you to create, view, and edit pages using both a WYSIWYG editor and a source-code text editor. You begin the page design process by importing the banner JPG and unformatted text content. Then you add tags to indicate headings, subheads, body text, and links.

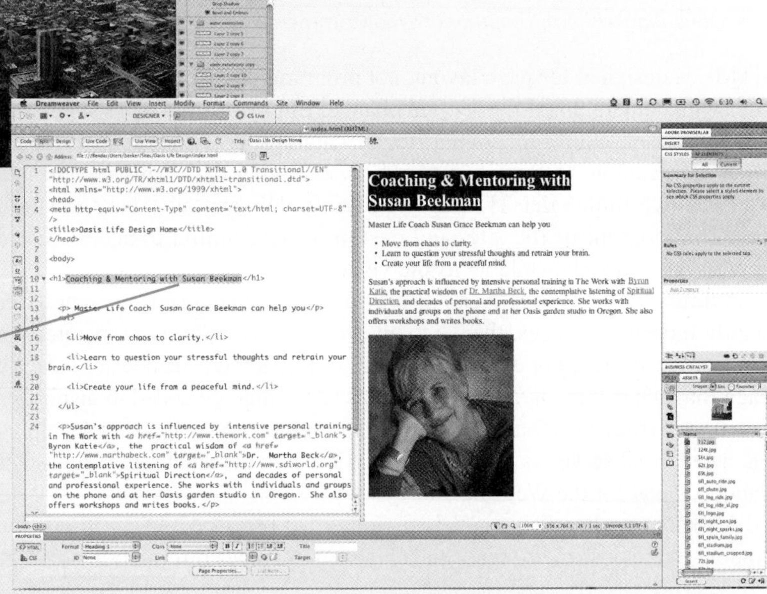

FIGURE 9.15

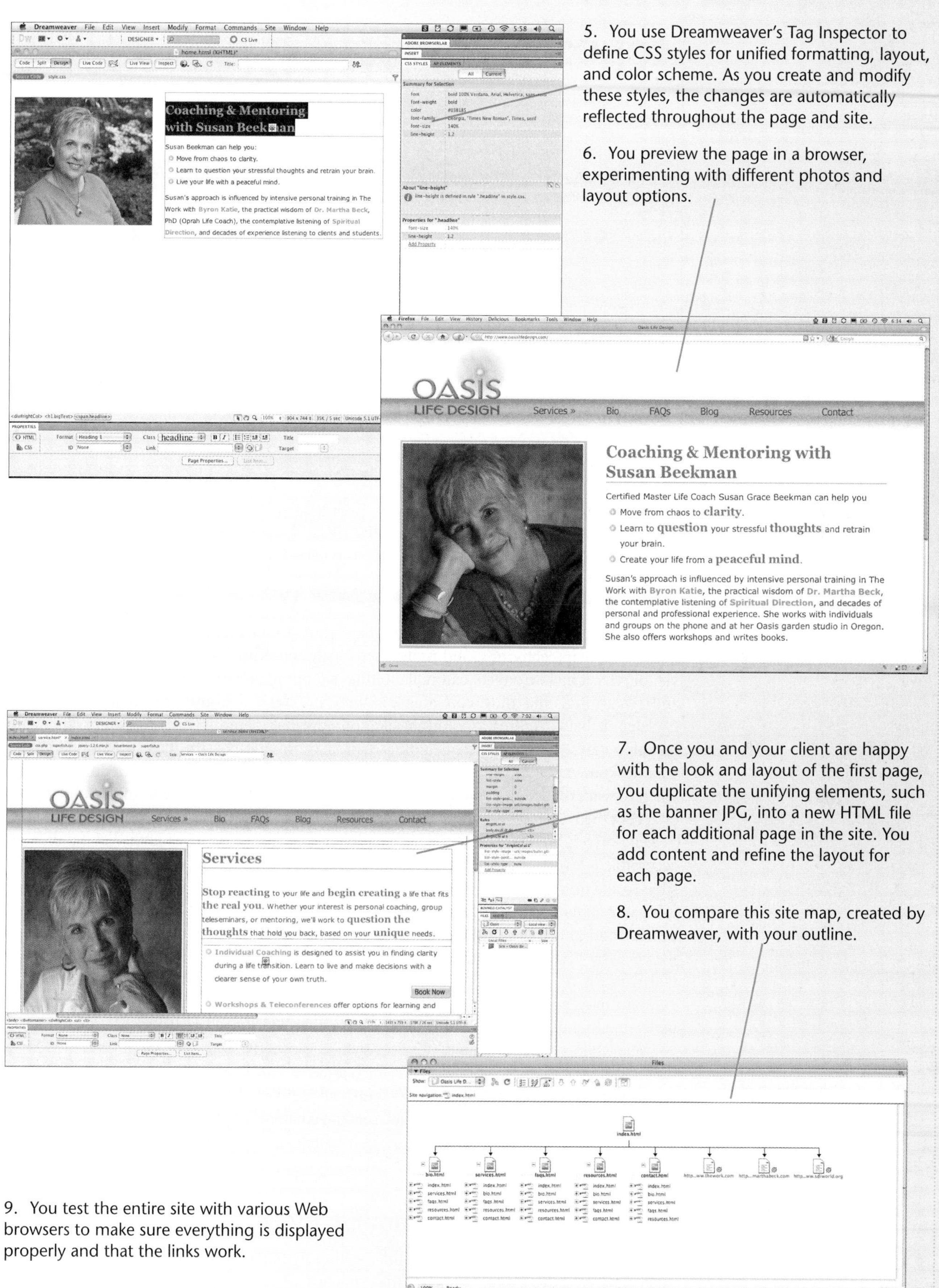

5. You use Dreamweaver's Tag Inspector to define CSS styles for unified formatting, layout, and color scheme. As you create and modify these styles, the changes are automatically reflected throughout the page and site.

6. You preview the page in a browser, experimenting with different photos and layout options.

7. Once you and your client are happy with the look and layout of the first page, you duplicate the unifying elements, such as the banner JPG, into a new HTML file for each additional page in the site. You add content and refine the layout for each page.

8. You compare this site map, created by Dreamweaver, with your outline.

9. You test the entire site with various Web browsers to make sure everything is displayed properly and that the links work.

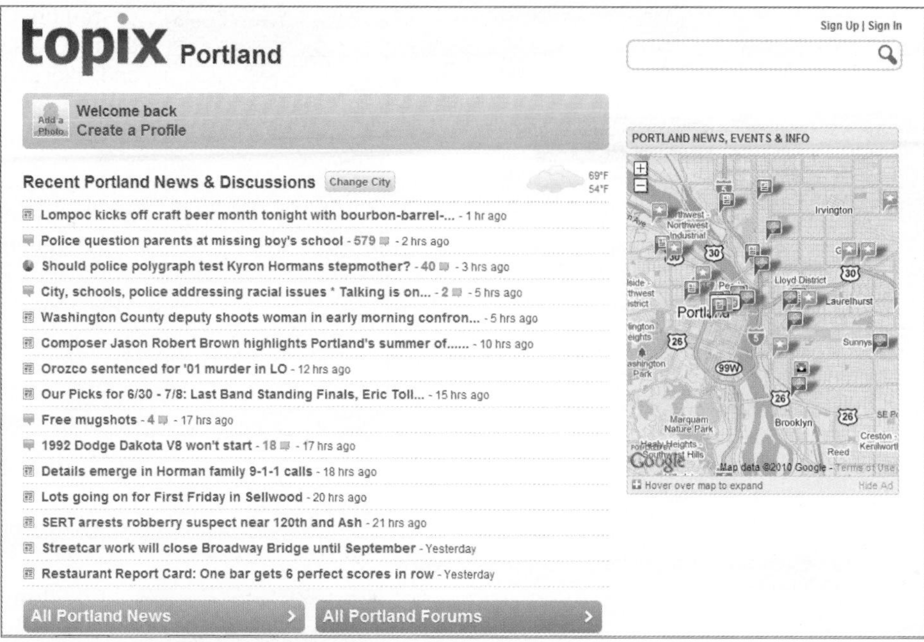

FIGURE 9.16 topix.com has several levels of personalization. The site provides instant personalization by determining the location of your computer's IP address on your first visit. When you return to the site, it uses cookies to remember your previous visit. For maximum personalization you can create an account and specify preferences.

to visit. Some sites use login names and passwords to remember visitors. Some track and remember visits, activities, and preferences using **cookies**—small files deposited on the visitor's hard disk. Cookies can make online shopping and other activities more efficient and rewarding, and they can make a Web site visit a highly personal experience. ("Welcome back, Audrey. You might like to know that memory cards for your camera are on sale today.") Unfortunately, cookies can also provide possibilities for snoopers who want to know how you spend your time online. By default, most browsers don't tell you when they leave a cookie. By changing browser settings, it's possible to refuse all cookies or accept them on a case-by-case basis.

Data-driven Web technology has also gone a long way toward making Web publishing accessible to every computer user. Using a **content-management system (CMS)** it's possible to add or update text, images, and other Web site content without coding in HTML or using a Web authoring program. The CMS stores the site content in a database; when the owner or administrator of the site enters new content into a simple form, the CMS makes the necessary HTML edits on the site. Some CMSs, such as Joomla, are designed for general Web site management. Others are special-purpose tools. For example, Google's blogger.com makes it easy to publish a visually attractive blog on a free Web site without understanding the intricacies of HTML, FTP server addresses, or URLs.

Meanwhile, online community services such as Facebook, YouTube, and Flickr are used by millions of people who don't have a clue about the technical underpinnings of the pages they create. People who use these sites upload personal profiles, pictures, and blogs with little more effort or expertise than they'd apply when sending email messages. Dynamic database technology takes care of the messy details so that users can focus on creating and uploading content.

Dynamic Web Programming Tools

Programmers use a variety of tools for creating dynamic Web sites. Some of these tools and languages are used to write code that runs in the browser on the client computer or digital device. Other tools are designed to create programs that run on the server side, fielding requests from the clients.

On the client side, short programs called *scripts* can add interactivity, animation, and other dynamic features to Web pages. Scripts can modify HTML code on the fly in response to user input. Scripts are typically written in a scripting language called **JavaScript**. Web pages that take advantage of the latest dynamic HTML features can be more interesting and interactive, but some browsers (especially stripped-down browsers on phones and other handheld devices) don't recognize them. Unscrupulous Web programmers can use scripts to embed viruses and other unwanted elements into your computer.

A more powerful client-side programming tool is **Java**, developed by Sun Microsystems. Java and JavaScript have little in common except their names. JavaScript is a simple scripting language for enhancing HTML Web pages; Java is a full-featured cross-platform programming language. Small Java programs are called *applets* because they're like tiny applications. Java applets can be automatically downloaded onto your client computer through a Web browser. A Java applet is platform independent; it runs on a Windows PC, a Mac, a UNIX workstation, or anything else as long as the client machine has Java Virtual Machine (JVM) software installed. This JVM software is built into most full-featured browsers and is available for free download.

Adobe Flash and Microsoft *Silverlight* are popular client-side tools for creating interactive media-rich Web components. Flash's scripting language, ActionScript, shares many conventions with JavaScript. Flash and Silverlight components generally run inside a Web browser, although the latest versions can create stand-alone desktop applications.

Another important tool in Web development, **XML (eXtensible Markup Language)**, is a widely used system for defining data formats. HTML is used for formatting and displaying data; XML represents the contextual *meaning* of the data. XML allows programmers to "mark up" data with customized tags that give the information more meaning. XML provides a rich system to define complex documents such as invoices, molecular data, news feeds, glossaries, and real estate properties. Forms, database queries, and other data-intensive operations that can't be completely constructed with standard HTML are much easier to create with XML. XML is at the heart of Microsoft's .NET and other competing strategies for developing Web services. Many PC and Mac applications, including Microsoft Office, support XML as a standard formatting language. (XML is not the same as *XHTML*, a markup language that combines features of HTML and XML.)

A relatively new way to support efficient, interactive Web pages has been given the name *AJAX* (for *Asynchronous JavaScript and XML*). The idea behind AJAX is to make Web pages more responsive by eliminating the need to reload an entire page every time a user makes a small change, such as changing a selection in an online order form. Instead, client-side scripts on the user's machine provide quick updates based on user inputs, and communication with the Web server allow small amounts of data to be exchanged without reloading the entire Web page. AJAX methodology relies on HTML, JavaScript, XML, and other scripting and markup languages.

Most dynamic Web sites today use another scripting language: *PHP*. While JavaScript is used to create scripts on client computers, PHP is designed for building server-side scripts or programs. PHP scripts work behind the scenes to create many of the Web pages we view every day, from Facebook entries to Wikipedia references. Another common server-side programming language is **Active Server Pages (ASP)**. The *Perl* and *Python* scripting languages are also popular for programming Web servers.

Search Engines

With its vast storehouses of information, the Web is like a huge library. Unfortunately, it's a poorly organized library; you might find information on a particular topic almost anywhere. (What can you expect from a library where nobody's in charge?) That's why search engines are among the Web's most popular tools.

Screen Test Building a Dynamic Site

GOAL *To create a blog that can be easily updated by a nontechnical user*

TOOLS *Adobe Dreamweaver, WordPress, and one or more Web browsers*

1. It's time to add a blog to the Web site you created earlier (see page 332). Your client needs to be able to post new articles and pictures easily to the blog without knowing or using HTML. You decide to use WordPress, a blog content-management system that makes updating the site almost as easy as updating a Facebook profile.

2. Starting with a page from the original static site, you replace the content with a sample blog post and adjust styles using Dreamweaver. You save this mock-up as an HTML file.

3. You identify the dynamic elements that appear in every blog post: the article title, the date posted, the article body, and an article image.

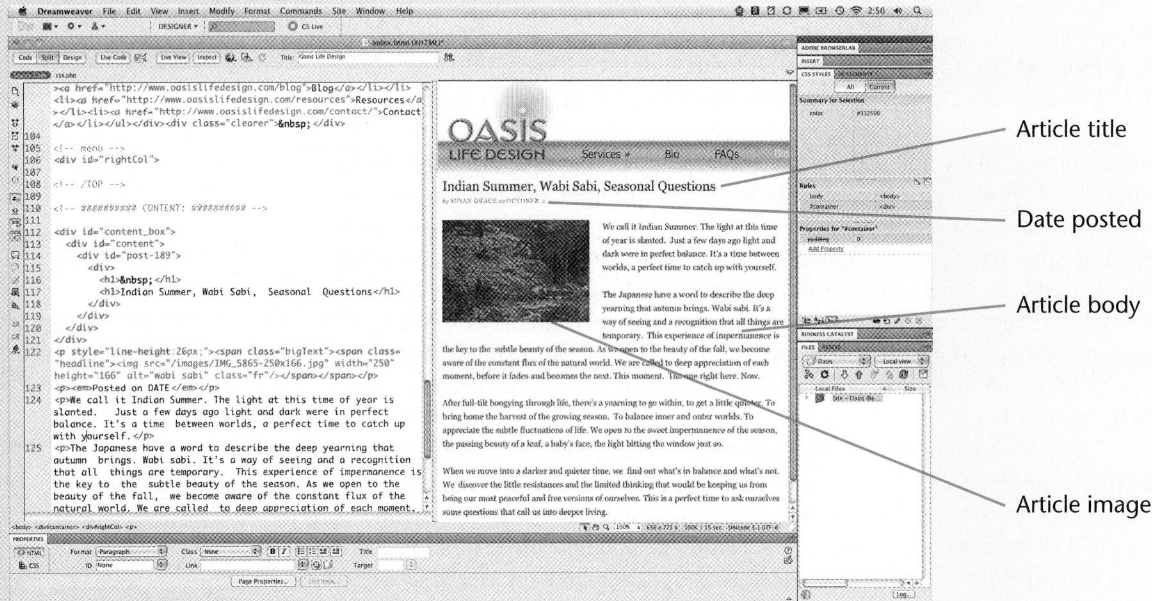

FIGURE 9.17a

4. You create a new WordPress template, paste in the code from your mockup, and substitute dynamic WordPress tags for the page-specific content.

5. For each new blog page, you'll tell WordPress what content—images and text—will replace the generic tags in the template. You create a new article using the headline, body text, and sidebar image from the mock-up.

FIGURE 9.17b

6. You preview the article in a browser to make sure your dynamic tags are all being displayed as intended, adjusting the template if necessary.

7. You show your client how to add and edit blog pages using the content management system.

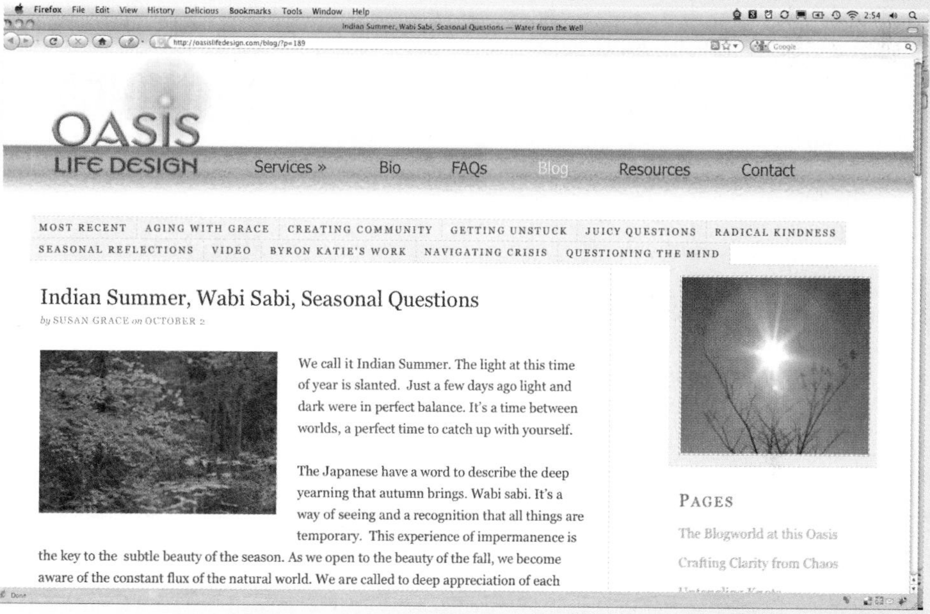

FIGURE 9.17c

Working Wisdom Weaving Winning Web Sites

It's easy to create a Web site; just about anybody with an Internet connection can do it. It's not so easy to create an effective Web site—one that communicates clearly, attracts visitors, and achieves its goals. Here are a few pointers for making your Web publications work.

- ***Start with a plan.*** The Web is littered with sites that seem pointless. Many of those sites were probably constructed without a clear plan or purpose. Start with clear goals and design your entire site with those goals in mind.
- ***Write for the Web.*** Most people won't read long, scrolling documents on computer screens. Limit each page to one or two screens of text. Provide clearly marked links to pages with more details for people who need them. And don't forget to check your spelling and grammar.
- ***Keep it simple.*** Web pages that are cluttered with blinking text, busy backgrounds, repetitive animations, and garish graphics tend to lose visitors quickly. Use clean lines and clear design if you want people to stick around.
- ***Keep it consistent.*** Every page in your site should look like it's related to the other pages in your site. Fonts, graphical elements, colors, buttons, and menus should be consistent from page to page.
- ***Make it obvious.*** Your visitors should be able to tell within a few seconds how your site works. Unless you're building a puzzle palace, make sure the buttons and structure of your site are intuitive.
- ***Keep it small.*** Large photographs, complex animations, video clips, and sounds can make your site big and slow to load. Most people won't wait more than a few seconds for a page to load. What's more, large files can result in large bills (for storage and bandwidth) from your Web hosting service. If you need lots of pictures, use an image editing program to optimize them for the Web. Similarly, make sure your audio and video pages (if you have them) are designed to minimize delays.
- ***Keep it honest.*** Anybody can publish a Web site without the benefit of a fact-checker. Check your facts before you share your pages with the world.
- ***Offer contact information.*** Web communication shouldn't be one way. Provide a way for your visitors to contact you. But if you include your email address, expect to receive lots of spam—software Web crawlers are always searching for new addresses on the Web. To minimize spam, you might want to refer to your email address indirectly: "My email name is Fuji and my domain name is appleeater.com."
- ***Think like a publisher and a multimedia designer.*** The rules of publishing and design, discussed in earlier chapters, apply to Web publishing, too.
- ***Test before you publish.*** Show your work to others, preferably people in your target audience, and watch their reactions carefully. If they get lost, confused, bored, or upset, you probably have more work to do before launching the final site.
- ***Think before you publish.*** It's easy to publish Web pages for the world—at least that part of the world that uses the Web. Don't put anything on your site that you don't want the world to see; you may, for example, be asking for trouble if you publish your home address, your work schedule, and a photo of the expensive computer system in your study.
- ***Keep it current.*** It's easy to build a Web site, and it's even easier to forget to keep it up to date. If your site is worth visiting, it's worth revising. If the contents of your site are constantly in need of revision, consider using a database to house the data so you can automatically update the site when the data changes.
- ***Take your integrity to the Web.*** The Web offers plenty of opportunity to deceive, mislead, and cheat people, and many people say things on their Web sites that they would never repeat in face-to-face interactions. If you want a growing community of return visitors, make sure those visitors know that they can trust what they see.

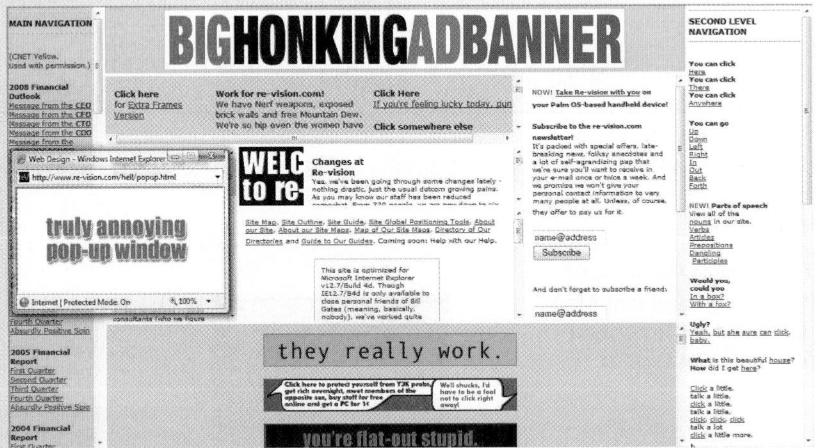

FIGURE 9.18 This screen from www.re-vision.com was created to violate as many principles of Web design as possible, including cramming too much information onto a page, noisy banner ads, overuse of frames, and navigation elements scattered across the page.

All search engines are designed to make it easier to find information on the Web, but they don't all function the same way. A typical search engine uses ***Web crawlers*** or ***spiders***—software robots that systematically explore the Web, retrieve information about pages, and index the retrieved information in a database. Different search engines use different searching and indexing strategies. For example, to determine the subject matter of a Web page, one search engine might focus on the words on the page, while another might pay more attention to links to and from other Web pages. For some search engines, researchers organize and evaluate Web sites in databases; other search engines are almost completely automated. Of course, not all Web pages are accessible to search engines or the public.

Most search engines enable you to type queries using keywords, just as you might locate information in other types of databases. You can construct complex queries using ***Boolean logic*** (for example, *American AND Indian AND NOT Cleveland* would focus the search on Native Americans rather than baseball), quotations, and other tools for refining queries. Some search engines enable you to narrow your search repeatedly by choosing subcategories from a hierarchical ***directory*** or ***subject tree***. No matter which search technique you use, you're eventually presented with a rank-ordered list of Web pages. The best search engines put the most relevant links first.

Some search engines are designed to search for specific types of information. Such specialized search engines can help you locate email addresses and phone numbers; others can help you find the lowest prices on the Web. These specialized search engines, such as Google Maps and Froogle, use technology similar to general search engine technology.

Many sites have their own built-in search engines. These site-specific search engines are often built using the same technology that powers Google, Bing, and other Web search tools.

Portals

Some Web sites that started out as search engines have evolved into **Web portals**—Web entry stations that offer quick convenient access to a variety of services and links. Popular general-interest portals include Yahoo!, MSN, iGoogle, and AOL/Netscape. Consumer portals feature search engines, email services, chat rooms, references, news and sports headlines, shopping malls, other services, and advertisements. ***Regional Web portals*** offer similar services, but focus on information and services related to a particular geographic region. You can personalize many portals so they automatically display local weather and sports scores, personalized TV and movie listings, news headlines related to particular subjects, and ads to meet your interests. Most browsers enable users to choose a home page

FIGURE 9.19 TestFreaks is a specialized search engine that aggregates information about products: professional and user reviews, news, rumors, manuals, videos, and more.

FIGURE 9.20 Like other Web portals, iGoogle lets each visitor personalize the look (theme) and contents, choosing from dozens of sources for news, weather, sports, entertainment, and more. iGoogle users are encouraged to design their own "Web gadgets" and make them available for other iGoogle users on their portal pages.

that opens by default when the browser is launched; ***personal Web portals*** are designed with this feature in mind.

In addition to these general-interest portals, the Web has a growing number of specialized portals. ***Government Web portals*** serve as entry points to many federal, state, and municipal government Web sites. Some, such as USA.gov and direct.gov.uk, are provided for general access; others are aimed at specific populations, such as veterans or businesses. ***Corporate portals*** on intranets serve the employees of particular corporations. ***Vertical portals***, like vertical market software (see Chapter 4), target members of a particular industry or economic sector. For example, Webmd.com is a portal for medically minded consumers and healthcare professionals. Sportal.com is one of many portals for sports fans.

Push Technology and RSS

The Web was built with **pull technology**: Browsers on client computers pull information from server machines. With pull technology the browser needs to initiate a request before any information is delivered. But for some applications, it makes more sense to have a server automatically send information delivered to the client computer. That's the way **push technology** (sometimes called *server push*) works.

With push technology, you subscribe to a service or specify the kinds of information you want to receive, and the server delivers that information periodically and unobtrusively. Maybe you want up-to-the-minute headlines or weather maps displayed as a Windows sidebar gadget, a Mac OS dashboard widget, or a Web gadget on your iGoogle personal portal page. You may want to receive new product descriptions automatically from selected companies. You might want your phone to notify you when you receive a Facebook message. Or you might like to have the software on your hard disk automatically upgraded whenever upgrades are available. All of this is possible with push technology.

Technically speaking, much of today's push technology is really pull technology in disguise. Your computer quietly and automatically pulls information from selected Web servers based on your earlier requests or subscriptions. As convenient as they are, push

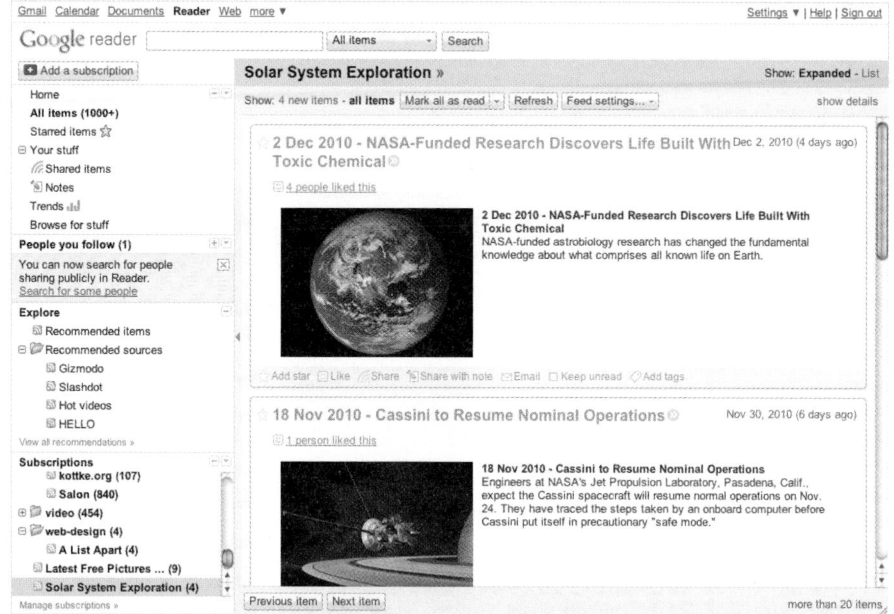

FIGURE 9.21 Google Reader is a popular RSS reader that collects the latest blog articles, photos, and other content from all your subscriptions on a single page.

programs have the same basic problem as Web search engines: they give you what they think you want, but they may not be very smart. Their ability to deliver what you really need, without bombarding you with unwanted data, is getting better as artificial intelligence technology improves.

Push technology is commonly used for delivery of information on company intranets. Outside of the corporate enterprise, most push technology takes the form of subscriber *notifications* and *alerts*. Email is the one form of push technology that has been embraced by almost all Internet users. Instant messaging is another popular push application.

A newer technology, RSS, is based on pull technology, but it uses a subscriber model that makes it feel like push. **RSS** (Really Simple Syndication) is an XML-based family of formats used to publish frequently updated documents, including newsfeeds, blogs (Chapter 8), and podcasts (Chapter 6). RSS began as a tool for heavy blog readers. RSS gives anyone who publishes on the Web the power to syndicate their stories or podcasts—in other words, to attract and keep subscribers.

A content provider—who could be a blogger, a podcaster, or the *New York Times*—maintains a list of changes to the Web site or podcast in a standard format called a (Web) *feed* or a *channel*. The feed might contain a story's title or summary and a URL to a Web page with the body of the article, or it might contain the entire text of the article. Subscribers run RSS-reading applications called *aggregators*—Web browsers, email clients, or other PC or phone applications that periodically visit Web sites, examine the feeds, and display new content (or download new podcasts). RSS subscriptions can save time by automating the process of seeking out information on the Web.

Web 2.0 and You

> **This artificial distinction between a consumer and a producer is dissolving,** I call it the participant economy.
>
> —*Jeremy Verba, CEO of Piczo*

In the previous chapter and this chapter, we've explored and analyzed a variety of network applications that are changing the way we live and work. Many of these applications are designed to make it easy for us to create, as well as consume, Internet content.

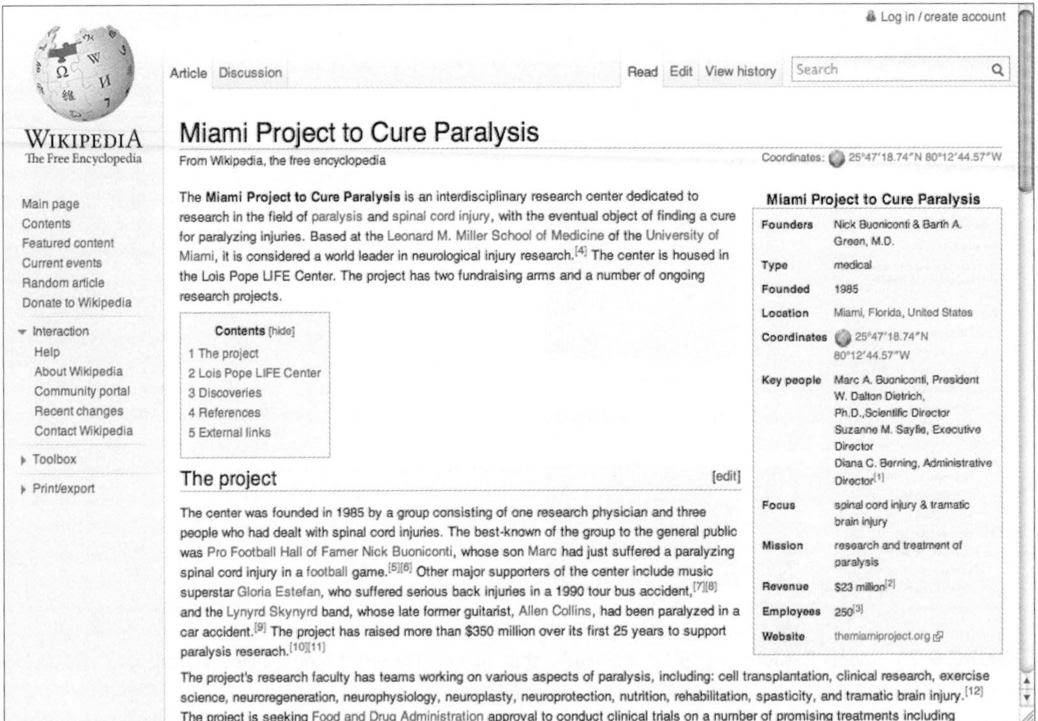

FIGURE 9.22 Wikipedia has become one of the Web's most popular destinations. The site has no ads; the content is contributed by volunteers and the site's overhead is financed by donations.

Blogs, forums, and wikis are new media types that can provide any or all of us with worldwide audiences. Media sharing sites like YouTube and Flickr serve as virtual galleries for photographers, filmmakers, and artists. Podcasting and Internet radio technology can give a voice and an audience to just about anybody with a microphone and an Internet connection. Social networking sites like FaceBook and Twitter are build-it-yourself Internet communities. Craigslist has changed the way people in hundreds of cities advertise jobs, tools, toys, services, and personal connections. This diverse collection of early twenty-first century participatory technologies is often referred to as Web 2.0. (Web 2.0 is not the same as Internet2, a high-speed research network based on Internet protocols.)

The distinguishing feature of Web 2.0 applications is the do-it-yourself (DIY) spirit. In Web 2.0, anyone can create an online publication, photo gallery, movie, music video, radio show, or video podcast. Anyone can help write the definitive encyclopedia or build a cabin in a virtual world. Anyone can add an opinion or voice to a collective review of a Web page, a new movie, or a political candidate. Anyone can create a *mashup*—a Web page, song, video, or image that combines music and video clips from other works (assuming, of course, that intellectual property ownership issues can be resolved). Web 2.0 is not a spectator sport—it's all about participation.

According to some experts, the downside of this Web populism is a loss of professional standards. Blogs don't generally have professional editors and reporters to check facts, grammar, and integrity before they're published. Most homemade podcasts lack the professional editing and production of corporate media. Wikis run the risk of degenerating into virtual shouting matches between opposing points of view.

Still, most people believe that the democratization of media and social institutions is, on balance, a good thing. In any case, it's not going away. The Web 2.0 participatory philosophy is spreading across the Internet, changing the way we interact with the technology—and each other.

how it works Creating a Podcast

The steps for creating a podcast are, in some ways, analogous to the steps for creating a Web site.

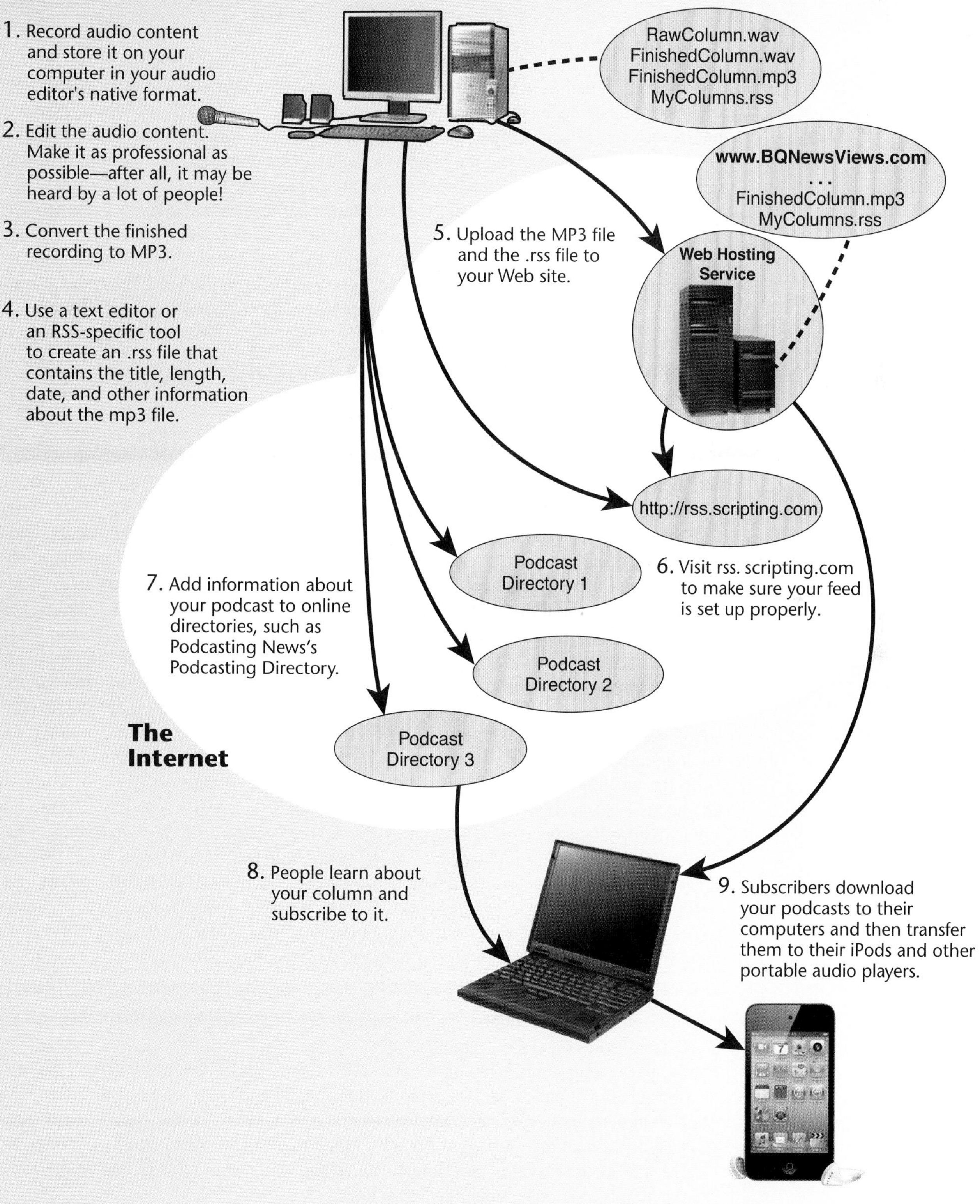

1. Record audio content and store it on your computer in your audio editor's native format.
2. Edit the audio content. Make it as professional as possible—after all, it may be heard by a lot of people!
3. Convert the finished recording to MP3.
4. Use a text editor or an RSS-specific tool to create an .rss file that contains the title, length, date, and other information about the mp3 file.
RawColumn.wav
FinishedColumn.wav
FinishedColumn.mp3
MyColumns.rss
www.BQNewsViews.com
...
FinishedColumn.mp3
MyColumns.rss
5. Upload the MP3 file and the .rss file to your Web site.
Web Hosting Service
http://rss.scripting.com
6. Visit rss. scripting.com to make sure your feed is set up properly.
7. Add information about your podcast to online directories, such as Podcasting News's Podcasting Directory.
Podcast Directory 1
Podcast Directory 2
Podcast Directory 3
The Internet
8. People learn about your column and subscribe to it.
9. Subscribers download your podcasts to their computers and then transfer them to their iPods and other portable audio players.

FIGURE 9.23

Internet Issues: Ethical and Political Dilemmas

> **The Internet still hasn't figured out how to conduct itself in public.** ... Everybody is trying to develop the rules by which they can conduct themselves in order to keep a civil operation going and not self-destruct.
>
> —*George Lucas, filmmaker*

The Internet started as a small community of scientists, engineers, and other researchers who staunchly defended the noncommercial, cooperative charter of the network. Today the Internet has more than 1 billion users, from children to corporate executives. The explosive growth raises questions about the Internet's ability to keep up; the amount of information transmitted may eventually be more than the Net can handle.

Meanwhile, the commercialization of the Internet has opened a floodgate of new services to users. People are logging into the Internet to view weather patterns, book flights, buy stocks, sell cars, track deliveries, listen to radio broadcasts from around the world, conduct videoconferences, coordinate disaster recovery programs, and perform countless other private and public transactions. The Internet saves time, money, and lives, but it brings problems, too.

Internet Addiction and Brain Function

William Gibson, Neal Stephenson, and other science fiction writers of the 1980s and 1990s envisioned the creation of compelling, even addictive, computer-generated virtual worlds. In their novels, the virtual worlds attract users because the quality of life on Earth is miserable. Direct feeds into the visual cortex, or virtual reality goggles and earphones, allow users to completely shut out the sights and sounds of reality.

Even though today's world has not yet suffered the extreme environmental degradation described in their novels, and most computer users are not directly wired into their computers, many Internet users have trouble disconnecting. Young people are especially prone to spending long hours each day in the digital realm, using smart phones, laptops, and desktop machines to stay connected. There's growing evidence that the brains of these "children of the net" develop in markedly different ways than the brains of children who spend more time communicating face to face, playing with toys, and exploring the natural world. Early research suggests that these kids tend to have shorter attention spans, fewer social skills, and less of an ability to think through big ideas. Of course, we won't know the long-term impact of heavy Internet use until the first digital generation matures.

In the meantime, psychologists debate whether excessive Internet usage by children and adults is a true addiction or merely a compulsion. Either way, it can have a profound negative impact on a person's life. Stories abound of people who've lost friendships, relationships, spouses, and jobs because they put too much of their time and energy into blogs, forums, chat rooms, virtual worlds, social networks, and (especially) massive multiplayer online role-playing games (MMORPGs). Some of the millions of online gamers spend 40 to 80 hours a week online, completely caught up in the never-ending story they're creating. Some of their stories have unhappy endings. Some examples follow:

- A distraught American mother blamed her son's suicide on his despondency after his online character was robbed of all his wealth. She responded by creating a Web site for addicted gamers and their families.
- A Chinese gamer murdered an 81-year-old woman, buried her in a pile of sand, and robbed her of about six dollars to pay for his gaming habit. Out-of-control gamers have also murdered police officers and dispatchers.
- A South Korean man who quit his job to play more video games died of exhaustion after a 50-hour session in an Internet café. The government indicates that online game addiction is a serious problem in South Korea.
- Tragically, several infants and children have died because their parents neglected them to play online games.

FIGURE 9.24 The On-Line Gamers Anonymous site was created by the mother of a suicidal gamer to help other addicted gamers and their families and friends.

Because MMORPGs have become so important to so many people, a real-world market has sprung up for virtual-world characters and artifacts. Chinese entrepreneurs hire young people to work 12-hour shifts as "gold farmers." These players play MMORPGs, killing monsters and earning gold pieces. They sell the virtual gold pieces to Westerners, who pay for them with real money. When the avatars become powerful enough, they can be sold, too. The gold farmers can make $250 a month playing MMORPGs—a good living for them. China now has hundreds, if not thousands, of online gaming factories.

Freedom's Abuses

Commercialization has brought capitalism's dark side to the Internet. Spam scams, get-rich-quick hoaxes, online credit card thefts, email forgery, child pornography, hustling, illegal gambling, Web site sabotage, online stalking, fraudulent political schemes, and other sleazy activities abound. The Internet has clearly lost its innocence.

Some of these problems result from people placing too much trust in email messages, Web advertisements, blogs, and other online information sources. Others are the result of people posting or sharing information about themselves without thinking about how far that information might travel (anywhere on the Internet) and how long it might last (indefinitely).

Examples abound. A Fisher College student was expelled after posting a critique of a campus police officer. The mayor of a tiny Oregon desert town was recalled after voters discovered pictures of her posing in underwear on her MySpace page. Countless men and women have been arrested after bragging of illegal activities in blogs, forums, and social networking sites. Many employers search blogs and social Web sites to do background checks on job applicants; past activities and postings can haunt otherwise qualified job seekers. Students and others routinely do Google checks on prospective blind dates; online photos, video clips, and blogs can make powerful first impressions, positive or otherwise. And, of course, the information people post can be used and abused by scammers, stalkers, and other criminals. Children and young people are especially prone naively to posting too much personal data. In one headline-grabbing story, a 49-year-old Missouri mother was indicted for conspiracy and other crimes for posing as a 16-year-old boy on MySpace, luring a 13-year-old girl into an online romance, and then dumping her by telling her the world would be better off without her. The rejected girl responded by hanging herself.

Some of these problems have at least partial technological solutions. Social networks include security mechanisms to minimize risks from predators and other criminals, but most of their members don't know about how—or why—to use those features. Concerned parents and teachers can install **filtering software** that, for the most part, keeps children out of Web sites that contain inappropriate content. Commercial sites routinely use encryption so customers can purchase goods and services without fear of having credit card numbers stolen by electronic eavesdroppers. Several software companies and banks are developing and refining digital cash systems that make online transactions easier and safer. To protect against email forgery, many software companies are working together to hammer out standards for ***digital signatures*** using encryption techniques described in the next chapter.

Access and Censorship

Many problems associated with the rapid growth and commercialization of the Internet are social problems that raise important political questions. Online hucksterism and pornography have prompted government controls on Internet content, including the 1996 U.S. Communications Decency Act. Opponents to this law and other proposed controls argue that it's important to preserve the free flow of information; they emphasize the need to protect our rights to free speech and privacy on the Internet. In 1996 the U.S. Supreme Court declared the Communications Decency Act unconstitutional, arguing that "the interest in encouraging freedom of expression in a democratic society outweighs any theoretical but unproven benefit of censorship."

The public outcry against the corrupting influence of pornography on children continued, however, and in December of 2000, Congress passed the Children's Internet Protection Act. The act requires public libraries and schools that receive certain types of federal funding to install content filters on computers with Internet access. In June 2003, the U.S. Supreme Court upheld the constitutionality of the Children's Internet Protection Act.

Questions about human rights online probably won't be resolved by legislators and judges, though. The Internet's global reach makes it nearly impossible for a single government to regulate it. Internet pioneer John Gilmore said, "The Net interprets censorship as damage and routes around it." Still, most governments are uncomfortable simply allowing an uninhibited flow of information through the Internet. As we have seen, even democratic nations have taken steps to regulate Internet content. In the United States, the federal government attempts to prevent children from gaining access to pornography, and most states make it illegal to run online casinos. Germany bans neo-Nazi Web sites. Many countries not known for censorship block access to child pornography Web sites.

Some governments have been much more aggressive in their attempts to reduce or eliminate the free flow of information over the Internet. Reporters Without Borders and the OpenNet Initiative monitor Internet censorship and maintain lists of countries that severely restrict access for political, social, and other reasons. Several countries have been classified by one or both organizations as being "enemies of the Internet" because of "pervasive" censorship. These Internet enemies include Burma, China, Cuba, Egypt, Iran, North Korea, Saudi Arabia, Syria, Tunisia, Turkmenistan, Ubzbekistan, and Vietnam. Most of these countries block citizen access to Web sites that criticize their governments. Some block access to other material deemed inappropriate by their governments. For example, Iranian ISPs attempt to block sites critical of the government, pornographic Web sites, political blogs, women's rights Web sites, and, from time to time, YouTube, Flickr, Twitter, Facebook, and other Web 2.0 sites. Some governments use a variety of surveillance techniques to track citizen Web access and communication. In Burma, simply going online is a dissident act.

The largest country on the Reporters Without Borders "Enemies of the Internet" list is the People's Republic of China. China blocks or filters pornography, references to Taiwan or Tibet, or news about Chinese dissidents. To do business in China, search engine vendors are required to modify their software so that Web searches can be censored by the government. In 2009 Google shut down its Chinese search engine after it determined that its systems had been invaded by hackers believed to be working with the Chinese government.

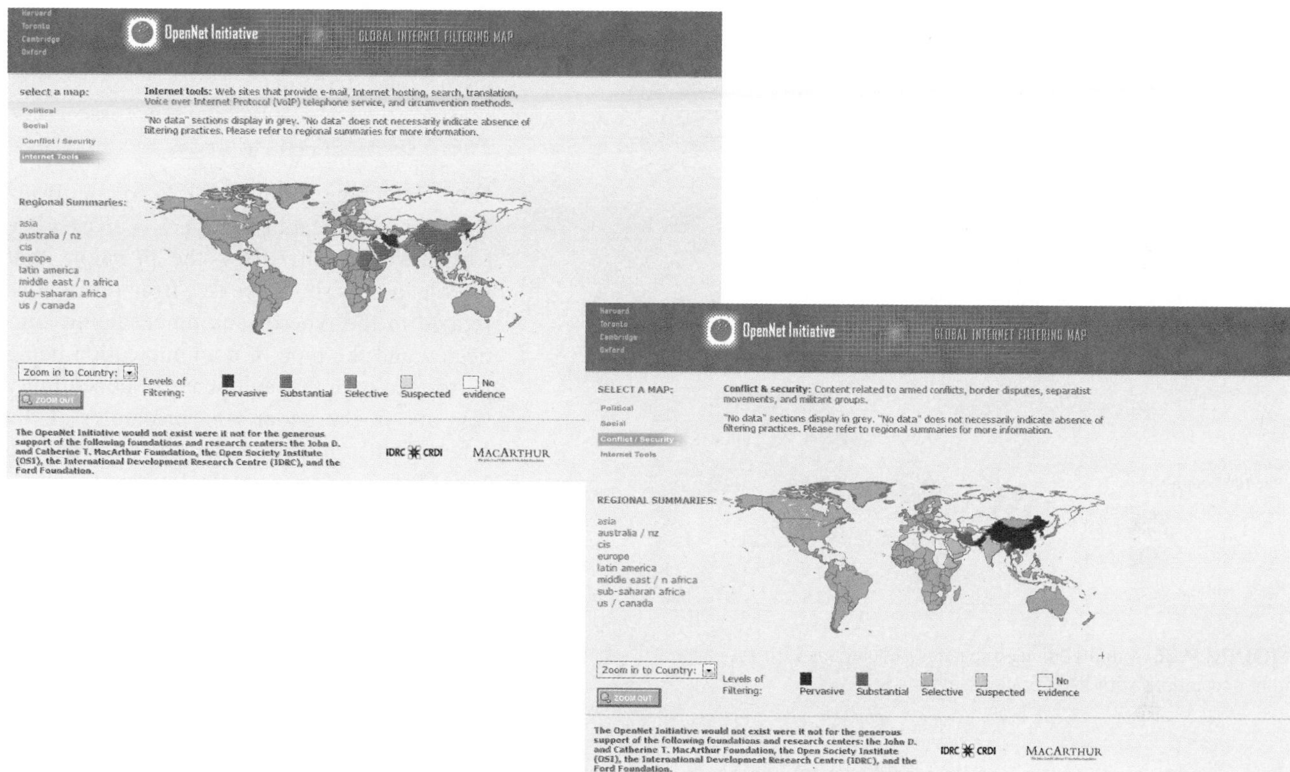

FIGURE 9.25 The OpenNet Initiative monitors different types of Internet filtering and censorship, including political, social, technical, and security filtering, and publishes detailed findings on the Web.

The Digital Divide

During the 1990s the U.S. government pushed for the development of a National Information Infrastructure—an affordable, secure, high-speed network to provide "universal service" for all Americans. The motivation for the creation of an NII was the realization that a **digital divide** separates people who have easy access to computers, the Internet, and digital information technology, and those who don't.

The percentage of the U.S. population with broadband Internet access at home is steadily growing, but not at the lowest economic levels. In Europe the digital divide appears to be strongly related to age and education. Research suggests that socioeconomic status, income, education level, race, and urban/rural divisions all contribute to the digital divide. Many of those who don't have computers or Internet access can barely afford food and rent.

Government programs to wire schools, libraries, and other public facilities have increased access for disadvantaged populations. But the problem of equal access isn't likely to go away without combined efforts of governments, businesses, and individuals. The availability of low-cost Wi-Fi technology has led to growing grassroots movements in the United States and dozens of other countries to create wireless community networks that would provide all computer-equipped citizens with baseline Internet access.

Even if the United States and other highly industrialized nations make the Internet available to all their citizens, there's still a global digital divide. The Internet is a global infrastructure, but huge populations all over the world are locked out or have limited access. Many experts argue that access to the Internet is one of many ingredients necessary for economic development in the twenty-first century. They fear that we'll leave billions of people behind as we move further into the information age. If poverty and lack of opportunity lead to political instability, wars, and terrorism, then the digital divide could pose a terrible threat to people on both sides of the divide. The widely publicized One Laptop per Child program is one of many efforts to close the gap by bringing information technology to disadvantaged populations. But to succeed, programs like this one need to be accompanied by larger

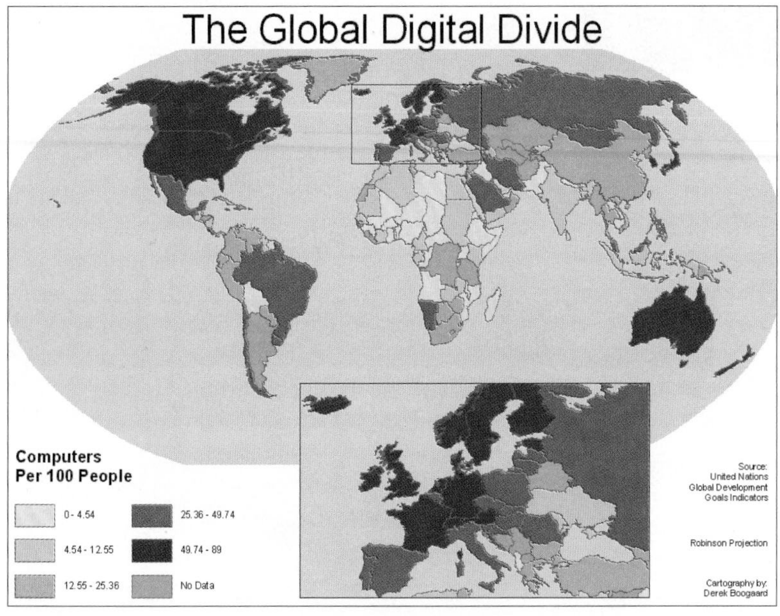

FIGURE 9.26 A digital divide separates populations with easy access to computers from populations with little or no access.

efforts. Laptops and network connections are of limited value to populations ravaged by war, disease, and starvation.

Net Neutrality

One of the biggest Internet-related controversies of recent years concerns **net neutrality** (or network neutrality)—the principle that Internet access should be free from restrictions related to the type of equipment being connected and the type of communication being performed with that equipment. Net neutrality was one of the underlying principles of the Internet when it was conceived. According to Vint Cerf, co-inventor of the Internet Protocol, "The Internet was designed with no gatekeepers over new content or services. A lightweight but enforceable neutrality rule is needed to ensure that the Internet continues to thrive."

Net neutrality champions believe telecommunications companies that own vast tracts of the Internet infrastructure threaten neutrality. They fear that broadband vendors, for example, might prevent content from competing companies—or controversial causes—to enter subscriber homes. Or that vendors might create an Internet caste system by providing faster, more reliable service for large business customers. According to net neutrality advocates, all packets are created equal, and should be forwarded through the Net on a first-come, first-serve basis.

Telecommunications companies have lobbied heavily to block net neutrality legislation in the U.S. They argue that pipeline owners should have a say in how they're used. Bob Kahn, co-inventor of the Internet Protocol, agrees. He and others fear that net neutrality legislation would stifle innovation by robbing network builders and owners of some profit incentives. In early 2011, the U.S. Government began implementing a complex set of rules that ban "unreasonable discrimination" of Web sites or applications by fixed-line broadband providers, but not for wireless providers. The rules don't prohibit companies to pay extra for faster transmission of data. The Federal Communications Commission crafted these regulations to preserve Internet freedom and openness without infringing on the ownership rights of the telecom companies. Critics on both sides are likely to challenge them in court and in congress for years to come.

From Cyberspace to Infosphere

> **Cyberspace. A consensual hallucination experienced daily by billions of legitimate operators, in every nation,** by children being taught mathematical concepts....**A graphic representation of data abstracted from the banks of every computer in the human system.** Unthinkable complexity. Lines of light ranged in the nonspace of the mind, clusters and constellations of data. Like city lights, receding....
>
> —*William Gibson, in* Neuromancer

From the earliest days of the Internet, science fiction writers have suggested that future networks will take us into an artificial reality that feels like a physical place. In his visionary novel *Neuromancer,* William Gibson coined the term **cyberspace** to describe such a shared virtual reality, complete with sights, sounds, and other sensations. Today that term is sometimes used to describe the Internet or the Web as a place.

FIGURE 9.27 The One Laptop per Child program was conceived to provide inexpensive, low-power, networked laptops to the world's poorest children. The program is still in its early stages, but it has a tremendous potential to revolutionize education for billions of children.

But many experts today think the term *cyberspace* is, to use Gibson's words, "past its sell-by." As *Wired* writers Alex Soojunk-Kim and David Pescovitz point out, "We live in a world of smart objects, always-on devices, and perpetually open information channels. The Internet feels less like an alternate world that we 'go to' and more like just another layer of life." Wordsmith Paul McFedrie suggests that the Net today is like the atmosphere—everywhere and necessary—and should be called our *infosphere*.

Whatever we call it, the Internet is changing at a phenomenal pace. And there's no guarantee that the evolving Internet will retain a free, community-oriented, everybody-can-play spirit. In *The Code and Other Laws of Cyberspace*, Lawrence Lessig claims that, because of commerce and other forces, an architecture of control is being built into the Net—control by government and by businesses intent on maximizing Net profits. Lessig argues that the code—the way the Net is programmed—will determine how much freedom we have in the future Internet. "We can build, or architect, or code cyberspace to protect values we believe are fundamental, or we can build, or architect, or code cyberspace to allow those values to disappear. There is no middle ground. There is no choice that does not include some kind of *building*."

There are parallels between the digital and the nondigital worlds. Many city planning experts argue that industrialized nations have systematically (if not consciously) rebuilt their cities so that, in many places, it's just about impossible to live without a car. These car-centered cities have generated revenue for businesses and governments, and they've brought a new sense of freedom to many citizens. But for the poor, the disabled, the young, the old, and others who can't drive, these cities are anything but free. At the same time, other cities have thriving masses of car-free people. As oil supplies dwindle, those are the cities that are most likely to thrive. Design choices (and nonchoices) made decades ago determine the livability of our cities today.

In the same way, the design decisions being made today by software architects, corporate executives, government officials, and concerned citizens will determine the nature of our Internet experiences in the future. Net neutrality, discussed in the previous section, is one particularly high-profile issue related to the Internet's design, but there are many more. Will portals guide us to corporate-approved or government-approved information sources, as they do in many countries and companies today? Will netizens feel free to express controversial opinions and criticize powerful institutions without fear of lawsuits, surveillance, and prosecution? Will paths through cyberspace be accessible to everyone? Will high-speed access command premium prices, relegating the rest of us to slow lanes? The Internet's future depends on decisions we, as a society, make today.

Inventing the Future ▸ The Invisible Information Infrastructure

> In the future, **everything with a digital heartbeat** will be connected to the Internet.
>
> —*Scott McNealy, Chairman of the Board of Sun Microsystems*

Countless researchers and developers continue to stretch the boundaries and capabilities of the Internet. At the same time, visionaries are suggesting that the Net is, in a sense, inventing its own future.

Vint Cerf, one of the Internet's founders, is putting much of his time and energy into a project called InterPlaNet, which he hopes will extend the Internet to the other planets in our solar system. According to the plan, electronic "post offices" will orbit other planets, routing messages between space explorers, both human and robot. The obstacles are significant—a message from Mars can take 20 minutes or more to reach Earth, an intolerably long time for Internet servers that "time out" if they don't receive messages quickly. According to Cerf, "the interplanetary network is an example of a much more general concept we call delay-tolerant networks." Even if you aren't expecting email from the red planet, the research being done on InterPlaNet may result in a more reliable Internet for you here on Earth.

FIGURE 9.28a A visualization of the Marsnet proposed by Vint Cerf.

Whatever happens with InterPlaNet, tomorrow's Net surfers will find it easier to locate what they're looking for on the Web. Tim Berners-Lee, the inventor of the Web, is planning a *semantic Web*—a Web full of data that's meaningful to computers as well as humans. With a semantic Web, search engines will be able to deliver exactly what you're looking for instead of bombarding you with hundreds of possibility pages. Here's how Berners-Lee described it to the *Boston Globe:* "You'll tell a search engine, 'find me someplace where the weather is currently rainy and it's within a hundred miles of such and such a city'.... A search engine...will come back and say, 'Look, I found this place and I can prove to you why I know that it's raining and why I know it's within a hundred miles of this place.' So you'll be dealing with much firmer information." Many people believe that semantic Web technology, or something like it, will be at the heart of the next generation of the Web—Web 3.0.

It may seem far-fetched, but some experts believe that the Net is evolving from a global community into a global intelligence. Artificial intelligence expert Danny Hillis believes true artificial intelligence will emerge in the vast global network rather than in an individual machine. Kevin Kelly describes the future of the Web as "the OS for a megacomputer that encompasses the Internet, all its services, all peripheral chips and affiliated devices from scanners to satellites, and the billions of human minds entangled in this global network. This gargantuan machine already exists in a primitive form. In the coming decade, it will evolve into an integral extension not only of our senses and bodies but our minds." Kelly calls this future network an Anticipation Machine because "anything we do more than twice will be absorbed by the machine." He claims we'll quickly come to depend on it as our memory and our identity, to the point where we may feel incomplete when we're disconnected from it. But that may not happen very often, because all of the devices we use will be windows into this giant computer.

FIGURE 9.28b A smart refrigerator with Internet connectivity.

According to these visionaries, we're already writing the software for this device. Whenever we add information to Wikipedia or Flickr or even eBay, we're adding a tiny bit of intelligence to the Net. The massive network of connections that enables Google to anticipate what we're searching for is not all that different than the network of neurons housed in our nervous systems. In the Web, as in our brains, learning happens through ever-increasing interconnections.

Whether or not you accept these predictions, one thing is clear: the amazing evolution of the Internet is far from over. And as the Internet changes, it changes our lives.

Crosscurrents

Countries Try to Tame the Wild Territory of the Net

by Tom Gjelten

It's easy to take the Internet for granted. It's part of our lives every day, as if it had always been here. But in the larger scheme of things, the Net is relatively new, and its future is far from certain. In this edited transcript from NPR's Morning Edition, *April 8, 2010, Tom Gjelten raises critical questions about the future of the Internet.*

If the Internet is ever shut down, Ken Silva will be among the first to see it. Not know it—*see* it. Silva is chief technology officer for VeriSign, one of about a dozen entities around the world responsible for keeping Internet traffic moving. He can literally follow the flow on a monitor in the VeriSign operations center in Northern Virginia.

"In Miami, we're currently getting 60,000 queries per second," Silva tells a visitor as he points to the lighted world map on the monitor. "New York is getting 77,000 per second. Tokyo is getting 50,000 per second."

The Internet, arguably the fastest world-changing invention in history, depends fundamentally on an addressing system. Every time you ask for a new Web page, your computer needs to find its way to the computer where the requested Web page resides.

With more than a billion computers connected to the Internet, it's not a simple matter. Each computer online is assigned a number: its Internet address. The role of VeriSign and other "root servers" is to keep track of all those addresses, so that when one computer "queries" another's address, the answer comes back promptly, and the connection is made.

Amazingly, the Internet addressing system is still working more or less as it was designed 25 years ago, though with exponentially higher volumes. About 1.7 billion people around the globe now have at least occasional Internet access. The World Wide Web is still living up to its name.

Having united the world, however, the Internet is rapidly becoming a place of global competition. Internet experts are waiting to see whether it will survive as an international commons or fall victim to global rivalries, espionage and cyberwarfare.

The addressing system that makes Internet traffic possible is overseen by a nongovernmental organization, the Internet Corporation for Assigned Names and Numbers, or ICANN. It is arguably the only body that oversees the global operation of the Internet. Its mission, though technical, is critical to the survival of the Internet as an open network accessible everywhere.

"I believe in world unity," says Rod Beckstrom, who is ICANN's president. "And I believe that the Internet is an incredible platform for world unity and enhancing relationships, and integrating commerce and societies."

ICANN, formed in 1998 and based in California, operates under contract to the U.S. Department of Commerce, but Beckstrom defines its goal as "serving the global public interest." The U.S. role in global Internet governance, once dominant, has diminished significantly in recent years. Beckstrom and other ICANN officials are determined to limit the organization's mission to technical matters, steering clear of politics. And for good reason.

If the Internet's governance is perceived to favor some countries over others, its unfettered operation could be jeopardized. Some observers fear that the Internet's growing reach and strategic importance may lead to an effort to bring it under political control or alter the addressing system in such a way as to impede its function.

Authorities in Iran, for example, are said to be considering a partial separation from the Internet, creating instead a national Internet that connects to the global Internet in ways that only the Iranian authorities can control.

"We could see a fragmentation of the Internet," says James Lewis, director of the Technology and Public Policy Program at the Center for Strategic and International Studies. He adds, "You would have choke points at which you would have to be approved, just like with passports in the airports. Someone would look and say, 'Am I going to let you into my country?'"

A country could do this by developing its own computer address file, such that servers in that country would be assigned addresses separately from the global root file now in use. Incoming or outgoing queries would have to go through a server with access to that special national file. Some requests for Internet address numbers would get answered; others would not.

The establishment of a national Internet might even put a country in a better position to fight a cyberwar. Right now, a global Internet connection leaves a country exposed to cyber-retaliation in the event it launches a cyberattack. "But if you could figure out some way to insulate yourself," Lewis says, "you would be less uncertain about the consequences of your attack, and therefore, more willing to launch them."

Of course, there's a downside to a country taking itself off the global Internet. Nations benefit economically, scientifically and culturally from being part of a larger community. "It's the network effect," Beckstrom says.

The Internet, however, could be politicized in other ways. Stephen Spoonamore, a cyber-entrepreneur with extensive experience in China, thinks that country's leaders dream about commanding the Internet, not separating from it. Many Internet experts doubt that China, or any country, could put itself in a situation where it could control Internet switching and user searches.

But the Internet has evolved in ways that no one 20 years ago could have foreseen. And no one really knows how it will evolve in the future—or who, if anyone, will control it.

Discussion Questions

1. Which of the risks outlined in this article seem most critical to you?
2. How do you think the Internet will change over the next 20 years?

Summary

The Internet is a network of networks that connects all kinds of computers around the globe. It grew out of a military research network designed to provide reliable communication even if part of the network failed. The Internet uses standard protocols to allow Internet communication to occur. No single organization owns or controls the Internet.

Computers and other devices connect to the Internet through narrowband modem connections, faster broadband connections, and even faster direct connections. Local and national Internet service providers around the world offer Internet access options to their customers; many provide server space for Web pages, online storage, and email.

Most Internet applications are based on the client/server model. The user interface for these applications varies depending on the type of connection and the type of client software the user has. The same Internet application might have a completely different appearance and function on a PC Web browser than on a phone's client software. Different types of servers provide different kinds of Internet services, ranging from email to the Web.

The earliest Web pages were simple hypertext pages; today the World Wide Web contains thousands of complex, media-rich structures that offer visitors a wealth of choices. The Web uses a set of protocols to make a variety of Internet services and multimedia documents available to users through a simple point-and-click interface. Web pages are generally constructed using some variation of a language called HTML. Many Web authoring tools automate the coding of HTML pages, making it easy for nonprogrammers to write and publish their own pages. Newer versions of HTML support Cascading Style Sheets and other tools that go beyond basic page layout. Several popular browser plug-ins add multimedia capabilities to standard Web browsers.

Dynamic Web sites can construct or modify pages on the fly in response to user actions. Most dynamic Web sites are database driven, so content can be updated automatically. Dynamic sites also take advantage of scripting languages and programming languages that go beyond HTML's page layout capabilities. Using cookies, databases, and logins, Web sites can provide highly personalized experiences to users.

In addition to Web sites, a variety of applications are built on the protocols of the Internet and the Web. For example, people who use the Web depend on search engines to find the information they need. Search engines use a combination of automated searches and indexed databases to catalog Web resources. Some search engines also serve as portals—sites, sometimes personalized, that serve as entryways to the Web. Some Internet services use push technology (often based on RSS) to push information to subscribers automatically. In recent years there's been an explosive growth in what many people refer to as Web 2.0: the loose collection of Web sites that depend on—and thrive on—content provided by visitors through wikis, forums, podcasts, blogs, and other types of media and information sharing.

As the Internet grows and changes, issues of privacy, security, censorship, criminal activity, universal access, and appropriate Net behavior are surfacing. Even more questions arise when all kinds of electronic devices are attached to the Web, communicating with each other from our homes, our offices, and our vehicles. Rapid-fire changes in the Internet will have tremendous impact on our lives, so it's important that we pay attention to those changes. The Web of the future won't look anything like today's Web. What it does look like will depend on decisions we make today and tomorrow.

Key Terms

Companion Website Projects

1. The *Digital Planet's* Web site, **www.pearsonhighered.com/beekman**, contains self-test exercises related to this chapter. Follow the instructions for taking a quiz. After you've completed your quiz, you can email the results to your instructor.
2. The Web site also contains open-ended discussion questions called Internet Exercises. Discuss one or more of the Internet Exercises questions at the section for this chapter.

True or False

1. The term *Internet* is derived from *inner net*, a phrase computer scientists coined to describe the highly centralized, hierarchical structure that defines the Internet.
2. Because of its centralized design, the Internet can withstand most attacks.
3. When a digital music file is sent on the Internet, it is broken into packets that travel independently to the designated destination.
4. The TCP/IP protocols at the heart of the Internet were developed by IBM, but the company freely licenses the technology to many other companies.
5. The words in a domain name, unlike the lines in a post office address, are arranged hierarchically from big to little.
6. Almost every Web address begins with http://, but many browsers don't require you to type that prefix.
7. Streaming video is distinguished from downloadable video by the fact that it is always real time—that is, it presents events as they happen.
8. It's never a good idea to allow your browser to accept cookies from shopping sites because the security risks posed by cookies far outweigh any possible benefits.
9. Web 2.0 is the term commonly applied to Web sites that depend on content provided by visitors through wikis, forums, podcasts, blogs, and other types of media and information sharing.
10. Net neutrality is pretty much guaranteed in the future because of the way the Internet was designed.

Multiple Choice

1. The Internet was originally
   a. a LAN at MIT.
   b. a code-cracking network during World War II by the U.S. Defense Department.
   c. a few dozen Web sites with very few pictures and no video.
   d. a small experimental research network called ARPANET.
   e. an idea taken from an early episode of *Star Trek*.
2. Where is the Internet's central hub and control center located?
   a. Near Washington, D.C.
   b. Near the Microsoft campus in Redmond, Washington
   c. In a top-secret location
   d. In Silicon Valley
   e. Nowhere; the Internet has no central hub.
3. Which of these domains is restricted to qualified organizations?
   a. .com
   b. .org
   c. .net
   d. .edu
   e. None are restricted; anyone can have a URL in any of these domains.
4. Which of these services would you probably not be able to get from a typical Internet service provider (ISP)?
   a. An email address
   b. Space on a Web server
   c. A connection to the Internet
   d. Technical help
   e. A unique top-level domain name

5. Specialized servers are used on the Internet to
   a. function like email post offices.
   b. accept FTP requests to upload and download files.
   c. store applications that are rented or leased by large corporations.
   d. store and send Web pages.
   e. All of the above
6. The first Web pages were
   a. strictly hypertext with no multimedia content.
   b. designed to simulate printed pages using HTML's table tools.
   c. the first true multimedia documents to be published on the Internet.
   d. viewable only with proprietary Microsoft software.
   e. sent via email from Doug Engelbart's office on the Stanford campus.
7. Cookies are commonly used by Web sites
   a. to attract visitors from search engines.
   b. to prevent viruses from spreading.
   c. to personalize visitor experiences.
   d. for animation.
   e. as components in Cascading Style Sheets.
8. An online shopping catalog for a large outdoor outfitter is almost certainly
   a. a data-driven Web site that separates site content from design.
   b. carefully hand-coded in pure HTML to minimize errors.
   c. designed to work without cookies.
   d. limited to work with a single type of Web browser for consistency.
   e. All of the above
9. If you're trying to look at a popular Web video clip but your browser can't play that type of video,
   a. you'll have to switch to another type of browser that does recognize the clip.
   b. you'll need to try another Web site that shows an alternate version of the clip.
   c. your browser might be able to play the clip if you install a plug-in.
   d. the site was probably designed using the original version of HTML, which doesn't work with many browsers today.
   e. you are almost certainly trying to watch a video that has copyright protection encryption.
10. Which of the following is a form of push technology?
    a. Writing and posting a Wikipedia article.
    b. Having Facebook notify you on your smart phone when you receive a new message from a friend.
    c. Watching a streaming video on Hulu or Netflix.
    d. Designing a Web page using Cascading Style Sheets.
    e. Searching YouTube for a political video.
11. Web 2.0 is
    a. the Web interface for Internet2.
    b. built using HTML 2.0.
    c. the version of the Web designed for phones and other portable devices.
    d. approximately twice as fast at loading pages as Web 1.0.
    e. the general concept of Web sites that are built out of user-contributed content.
12. Internet addiction
    a. is fiction.
    b. has been linked to suicides.
    c. is virtually unheard of outside the United States.
    d. is caused by a rare type of computer virus.
    e. was first diagnosed near the end of World War II.
13. According to U.S. law, information posted on a Web forum or blog by a child
    a. must self-destruct after one week.
    b. cannot be reproduced in any form without permission.
    c. cannot contain cookies.
    d. cannot be viewed outside of the U.S.
    e. None of the above
14. Which country attempts to limit its residents' access to certain types of Web content?
    a. The U.S.
    b. Cuba
    c. The People's Republic of China
    d. Saudi Arabia
    e. All of the above
15. The Internet will change drastically in the next decade, but what is the one thing that is likely to remain relatively unchanged?
    a. The dominance of HTML as a Web page creation language
    b. The metaphor of the page as the container of Internet information
    c. The TCP/IP protocol that's used to send and receive Internet messages
    d. The ownership of the Internet by IBM
    e. The percentage of non-U.S. Internet users

Review Questions

1. Define or describe each of the key terms listed in the "Key Terms" section. Check your answers using the glossary.
2. Why is it hard to determine how big the Internet is today? Give several reasons.
3. Why are TCP/IP protocols so important to the functioning of the Internet? What do they do?
4. The world is rapidly using up all of the IP addresses available using Internet Protocol version 4 (IPv4)—the standard for most Internet devices today. What does this mean, and what, if anything, can be done about it?
5. What is the relationship between a Web site's numerical IP address and its URL?
6. Take your email address apart and, as much as possible, explain what each part means.
7. How does a content management system differ from a basic WYSIWYG Web authoring tool?
8. Why are databases so important for dynamic Web sites?
9. Why is file compression important on the Internet?
10. How does push technology differ from standard Web page delivery techniques? How is it used?

Discussion Questions

1. How did the Internet's Cold War origin influence its basic decentralized, packet-switching design? How does that design affect the way we use the Net today? What are the political implications of that design today?
2. In what ways is the Web different from any publishing medium that's ever existed before?
3. Some people spend more than half of their waking hours online. Do you see potential hazards in this kind of heavy Internet use? Explain your answer.
4. How do you think online user interfaces will evolve as bandwidth and processing power increase? Describe what cyberspace will feel like in the year 2020, in the year 2050, and beyond.
5. Under what circumstances, if any, do you believe a government should have the right to block citizen access to certain Web sites?
6. What do you think can be done to minimize the digital divides that exist within countries and between countries?

Projects

1. Even though it isn't really a "place," people have created a wide variety of maps and illustrations of the Internet. Search for Internet maps online. Compare several different maps. Which are clearest? Which convey the most useful information?
2. Try creating a simple Web page using HTML and/or a Web authoring program. How does this compare with creating pages in Facebook, YouTube, Blogger, and other Web 2.0 environments?
3. Different governments around the world take different approaches to Web censorship. Choose several countries and use the Web to determine (a) what kinds of information are censored by their governments and (b) what techniques they use to block access to that information.
4. Research the extent of the digital divide in your country by collecting information about Internet access in relation to several different variables (for example, age, income, gender, ethnic group, rural vs. urban). Which of these variables is most strongly related to Internet access? Which is least related? Can you explain your results?

Sources and Resources

Books

There are thousands of books about the Internet. Many of them promise to simplify and demystify the Net, but they don't all deliver. The Internet is complex and ever-changing. The following list contains a few particularly good titles, but you should also look for more current books released after this book went to press.

When Wizards Stay up Late: The Origins of the Internet, by Katie Hafner and Matthew Lyon (Simon and Schuster). If you want to learn more about the birth of the Internet, this book is a great place to start. The authors describe the people, challenges, and technical issues in clear, entertaining prose.

How the Internet Works, Eighth Edition, by Preston Gralla (Que). If you like the style of *How Computers Work*, you'll appreciate *How the Internet Works*. You won't learn much about how to use the Internet, but you'll get a colorful tour of what goes on behind the scenes when you connect. There's a surprising amount of technical information in this graphically rich, approachable book.

Rule the Web: How to Do Anything on the Internet—Better, Faster, Easier, by Mark Frauenfelder (St. Martin's Press). The title may promise too much, but the book does deliver a surprising number of answers to questions you might have about how to get the most out of the Internet.

HTML, XHTML, and CSS Visual QuickStart Guide, by Elizabeth Castro (Peachpit Press). There are dozens of books on HTML, XHTML, and CSS, but few offer the clear, concise, comprehensive coverage of this best seller. If you want to build your own Web pages from scratch, this is a good place to start. Even if you know the basics of HTML, you'll appreciate the coverage of more advanced topics. After you've read it, you'll almost certainly want to keep it as a reference.

JavaScript and Ajax for the Web: Visual QuickStart Guide, by Tom Negrino and Dori Smith (Peachpit Press). JavaScript is the most popular cross-platform scripting language for Web pages. A little bit of JavaScript can turn a static Web page into a dynamic, interactive page. This book provides a quick introduction to the language, including applications involving forms, frames, files, graphics, and cookies. If you're ready to move beyond basic HTML, this book can help.

The Non-Designer's Web Book, by Robin Williams and John Tollett (Peachpit Press). Web publishing, like desktop publishing, can be hazardous if you don't have a background in design. Robin Williams and John Tollett provide a crash course in design for first-time Web authors. They assume you're using an authoring tool that hides the nuts and bolts of HTML; if you're not, you'll need to learn HTML elsewhere.

Letting Go of the Words: Writing Web Content that Works, by Janice (Ginny) Redish (Morgan Kaufmann). Writing is a critical skill for success in the Internet age. But writing for the Web isn't the same as writing a novel or a term paper. This book focuses on the specifics of writing Web text that communicates clearly.

The Future of the Internet and How to Stop It, by Jonathan Zittrain (Yale University Press). According to Jonathan Zittrain, the future of the Internet is not pretty unless we all take steps to prevent it from being locked down by powerful interests. This important book is sparking much-needed dialog about how to preserve the innovative spirit of the Net.

Code Version 2.0, by Lawrence Lessig (Basic Books). In 2000, Lessig's *The Code and Other Laws of Cyberspace* argued that we might lose our liberty on the Internet unless we consciously work to preserve it—an argument that's even more relevant today. The way we build the Net today will determine what's possible in cyberspace tomorrow. Lessig, a lawyer, is an excellent writer with something important to say. Version 2.0 was updated through Lessig's wiki; it is the first reader-edited revision of a popular book.

Remix: Making Art and Commerce Thrive in the Hybrid Economy, by Lawrence Lessig (Penguin Press). In this book, Lessig argues that young people today use the Internet as a medium of creative collaboration—and break today's intellectual property laws in the process. Instead of criminalizing remixes and mashups, we should celebrate and encourage the emergence of new art forms. He suggests radical changes to intellectual property laws that would accelerate the movement of creative works into the public domain.

Access Denied: The Practice and Policy of Global Internet Filtering, edited by Ronald J. Deibert, John G. Palfrey, Rafal Rohozinski, and Jonathan Zittrain (MIT Press). This book from the Open Network Initiative is the first global survey of Internet filtering.

The Future of Reputation: Gossip, Rumor, and Privacy on the Internet, by Daniel J. Solove (Yale University Press). The Internet provides us with an unprecedented ability to communicate with each other. But forums, blogs, wikis, video sharing, and the rest make it all too easy to ruin personal reputations. This book deals with the legal and ethical issues related to Internet communication.

True Names: And the Opening of the Cyberspace Frontier, by Vernor Vinge and James Frenkel (Tor Books). In 1981 (three years before the original publication of *Neuromancer*) Vernor Vinge's critically acclaimed novella *True Names* described a virtual world inside a computer network. Vinge didn't use the term *cyberspace*, but his visionary story effectively invented the concept. This book includes the original *True Names* novella and a collection of articles by cyberspace pioneers about the past, present, and future of cyberspace.

Neuromancer, by William Gibson (Ace Books). Gibson's 1984 cyberpunk classic spawned several sequels, dozens of imitations, and a new vocabulary for describing a high-tech future. Gibson's future is gloomy and foreboding, and his futuristic slang isn't always easy to follow. Still, there's plenty to think about here.

Snow Crash, by Neal Stephenson (Spectra). This early-1990s science fiction novel lightens the dark, violent cyberpunk future vision a little with Douglas Adams–style humor. Characters regularly jack into the Metaverse, a shared virtual reality network that is in many ways more real than the physical world in which they live.

Video

Second Skin. This thought-provoking, entertaining documentary takes a hard look at the emerging online gaming culture. Director Juan Carlos Pineiro-Escoriaza introduces us to people whose lives have been forever changed by MMORPGs. Couples who meet and marry online, game addicts who lose the ability to function in the non-digital world, and other fascinating characters tell and show us their stories.

10

Computer Security and Risks

OBJECTIVES

After you read this chapter you should be able to:

- Describe several types of computer crime and discuss possible crime-prevention techniques
- Describe major security issues facing computer users, computer system administrators, and law enforcement officials
- Describe how computer security relates to personal privacy issues
- Explain how security and computer reliability are related
- Describe the potential impact of digital technology on warfare and terrorism
- Summarize some of the larger political and social questions we'll face as digital technology plays an ever-expanding role in our lives

A world opened up by communications cannot remain closed up in a feudal vision of property. No country, not the U.S., not Europe, can stand in the way of it. It's a global trend. **It's part of the very process of civilization...** and there's no use resisting it.

—*Gilberto Gil*

Gilberto Gil and the Open Source Society

In the 1960s, when the Beatles were remaking American and European pop music and culture, Brazilians Gilberto Gil and Caetano Veloso were creating a revolutionary musical style of their own. Tropicalismo combined elements of rock, samba, bossa nova, traditional music, avant garde poetry, and just about anything else that was in the wind. Brazilian culture was a simmering stew of poverty and wealth, of tradition and modernity, and the mashup style of Tropicalismo captured the chaos and spawned a movement. According to Gil, Tropicalismo refused to submit to the forces of economic imperialism. It was "a cannibalistic response of swallowing what they gave us, processing it, and making it something new and different."

Gil and Veloso were widely regarded as a Latin Lennon and McCartney. But Brazil's military dictatorship, threatened by their impact on young Brazilians, jailed Gil and Veloso without charges before banishing them to London for several years. Gil returned to his Bahia home in 1972.

Gil has remained popular as a musician through the decades, winning a variety of international awards, including a 2005 Grammy. But he has also had a major impact on Brazilian politics since the late 1980s, when he became the Salvador secretary of culture. In subsequent years he served in elected office, founded an environmental protection organization, and served as a goodwill ambassador for the Food and Agriculture Organization of the United Nations. In

FIGURE 10.1 Gilberto Gil, musician.

2003 President Luiz Inácio Lula da Silva appointed Gil as the minister of culture in Brazil's now democratic government.

The philosophy of Tropicalismo is woven into the fabric of modern Brazilian society. Brazil is at the forefront of a global movement to "tropicalize" intellectual property—to encourage creative sharing of music, words, software, and ideas by loosening legally sanctioned corporate controls. Gilberto Gil has become a symbol for this emerging "open-source" society.

The world's sixth-largest nation has reason to seek alternatives to the restrictive intellectual property laws of the United States and Europe. Drug patents put AIDS medication out of the reach of Brazil's infected poor until the Brazilian government threatened to ignore those patents, forcing manufacturers to offer discounts. And a typical Brazilian might have to work for weeks in order to afford a copy of a commercial software program such as Microsoft Office. It's no wonder that Linux and other open-source programs have been embraced by the Brazilian government.

Brazil's approach to intellectual property issues is similar to the philosophy that drove American cyberlawyer Lawrence Lessig to devise the Creative Commons, a way for artists to reserve some of the rights given them by copyright law but give up the rest. For example, an artist may use a Creative Commons license to indicate that a photograph or song may be freely copied or sampled for noncommercial purposes, as long as attribution is given.

After Lessig described the system to him, Gil decided to release several of his most popular songs into the Creative Commons. His American record company quickly vetoed his act of musical generosity.

The copyright system represents a balance between the desire of artists to be rewarded for their creativity and the desire of the public to have access to artistic works. Creative Commons licenses and the open-source movement are a reaction to a copyright system that has gradually tilted the balance in favor of those who own intellectual property rights. In Gil's words, "The Brazilian government is definitely pro-law. But if law doesn't fit reality anymore, law has to be changed. That's not a new thing. That's civilization as usual."

FIGURE 10.2 Gilberto Gil, Minister of Culture.

In 2008 Lula reluctantly accepted Gil's resignation from his government position, saying that Gil was "going back to being a great artist." In the long view, Gil's work with Creative Commons may have as great an impact as his body of artistic work. ■

Copyright and patent laws were originally designed to encourage creativity. But as the laws become broader and more rigid, they may be having just the opposite effect. Intellectual property issues are challenging because computers and the Internet have opened up fast, reliable, and inexpensive ways of exchanging songs, movies, photographs, and other creative works. But intellectual property is just the tip of the iceberg.

Computers and networks manage our money, our medicine, and our missiles. We're expected to trust information technology with our wealth, our health, and even our lives. The many benefits of our partnership with machines are clear. But blind faith in technology can be foolish and, in many cases, dangerous. In this chapter we examine some of the dark corners of our computerized society: legal dilemmas, ethical issues, and reliability risks. These issues are tied to a larger question: How can we make digital devices more secure so we can feel more secure in our daily dealings with them? We'll look for answers to this question then ask several more difficult questions about our relationship to digital technology and our future.

Online Outlaws: Computer Crime

Computers are power, and direct contact with power can bring out **the best or worst in a person.**

—*Former computer criminal turned corporate computer programmer*

Like other professions, law enforcement is being transformed by information technology. The FBI's National Crime Information Center provides police with almost instant information on crimes and criminals nationwide. The New York Police Department's Real Time Crime Center (RTCC) includes a massive data warehouse containing billions of data records linked to satellite imaging and GIS mapping software, providing detectives and field officers instant information to help identify crime patterns and prevent crimes.

Around the world, investigators use PC databases to store and cross-reference clues in complex cases. Using pattern recognition technology, automated fingerprint identification systems locate matches in minutes rather than months. Computers routinely scan the New York and London stock exchanges for connections that might indicate insider trading or fraud. **Computer forensics** experts use special software to scan criminal suspects' hard disks for digital "fingerprints"—traces of deleted files containing evidence of illegal activities. All of these tools help law enforcement officials ferret out criminals and stop criminal activities.

As with guns, people use computers to break laws as well as uphold them. Computers are powerful tools in the hands of criminals, and computer crime is a rapidly growing problem.

The Digital Dossier

Some will rob you with a six gun, and **some with a fountain pen.**

—*Woody Guthrie, in "Pretty Boy Floyd"*

Today the computer has replaced both the gun and the pen as the weapon of choice for many criminals. **Computer crime**, or **cybercrime**, is often defined as any crime accomplished through knowledge or use of computer technology. Cybercrime usually refers to criminal activity in which computer or network technology is an essential part of the crime. Examples include spamming, peer-to-peer file sharing of copyrighted music, creating and releasing malicious computer viruses, and theft of computer services. It might also refer to a traditional crime in which computers or networks are used as criminal tools. For example, ***cyberstalking*** is a form of harassment that takes place on the Internet. The crime is similar to old-fashioned stalking, but the domain is the digital realm. Other examples of traditional crimes that can easily become cybercrimes include financial fraud, child pornography trafficking, and even international espionage.

Nobody knows the true extent of computer crime. Many computer crimes go undetected. Those that are detected often go unreported because businesses fear that they can lose more from negative publicity than from the actual crimes.

FIGURE 10.3 A police officer uses his mobile computer to check records in a central law enforcement database.

Companies that *do* report cybercrimes report system penetration by outsiders, theft of information, the changing of data, financial fraud, vandalism, theft of passwords, and the prevention of legitimate users from gaining access to systems. By conservative estimates, businesses and government institutions lose billions of dollars every year to computer criminals.

The majority of corporate computer crimes are probably committed by company insiders who aren't reported to authorities even when they are caught in the act. To avoid embarrassment, many companies cover up computer crimes committed by their own employees. These crimes are generally committed by clerks, cashiers, programmers, computer operators, and managers who have no extraordinary technical ingenuity. The typical computer criminal is a trusted employee with no criminal record who is tempted by an opportunity, such as the discovery of a loophole in system security. Greed, financial worries, and personal problems motivate this person to give in to temptation.

Of course, not all computer criminals fit this profile. Some are former employees seeking revenge on their former bosses. Some are high-tech pranksters looking for a challenge or a thrill. A few are corporate or international spies seeking classified information. Organized crime syndicates and terrorist organizations use computer technology to practice their trades. Sometimes entire companies are found guilty of computer fraud. And some types of computer crime—most notably software and music piracy—are committed by legions of young people who may not even know that they're committing crimes.

Theft by Computer: From Property Theft to Identity Theft

> Every system has vulnerabilities. **Every system can be compromised.**
>
> —*Peter G. Neumann, in* Computer-Related Risks

Theft is the most common form of computer crime. Computers are used to steal money, goods, information, and computer resources.

One common type of computer theft today is the actual theft of computers. Laptop, tablet, and handheld computers make particularly easy prey for crooks—especially in airports and other high-traffic, high-stress locations. Laptops, tablets, and smart phones can be expensive, but the information stored on a computer can be far more valuable than the computer itself.

The most common type of theft-by-computer, intellectual property theft, was discussed in Chapters 4, 6, and 9. Examples of intellectual property theft include software piracy, peer-to-peer file sharing of copyrighted songs, unauthorized duplication and distribution of movies, and plagiarism of copyrighted text. Intellectual property theft has skyrocketed with the growth of the Internet.

FIGURE 10.4 A portable computer is easy prey for thieves unless it is locked to something stationary and solid.

Other types of property aren't as easy to steal through an Internet connection, but thieves can—and do—steal credit card numbers and bank account numbers, which can be used to buy just about anything. In the past decade hundreds of crimes have been reported in which large files of credit card numbers have been stolen from businesses via the Internet. No doubt many similar crimes have gone unreported.

Still another type of theft involves stealing *access* to a computer or a Web site by stealing passwords and login codes. Sometimes thieves swipe passwords to avoid paying access charges; other times they steal passwords as part of a bigger plan.

Many thieves use computers and other tools to steal whole *identities*. By collecting personal information—credit card numbers, driver's license numbers, Social Security numbers, passwords, and a few other tidbits of data—a thief can effectively pose as someone else, even committing crimes in that person's name. **Identity theft** doesn't require a computer; many identity thieves get sensitive information by dumpster diving—rummaging through company and personal trash. But computers generally play a role in the process. (Identity theft was also discussed in the privacy section of Chapter 7.)

Credit card theft, password theft, and identity theft often involves **social engineering**—slang for the use of deception to get individuals to reveal sensitive information. Many types of social engineering involve **spoofing**—masquerading as somebody else in order to trick the target into doing something they might not otherwise do. Spoofing might be a simple phone call (For example, "Hi. I'm a technician from your Internet service provider, and I'm trying to locate a problem in your network connection. Can you give me your password so I can test it?"). Or it might involve an Internet fraud technique commonly called **phishing** (because the perpetrator is "fishing" for sensitive information under false pretenses).

According to the FBI, two-thirds of identity thefts begin with an email solicitation—a phishing expedition. A spammer sends out an email that appears to be from PayPal, Citibank, Facebook, eBay, or another company that the recipient may have an account with. One such message from PayPal reads, "Your credit card will expire soon. To avoid any interruption to your service, please update your credit card expiration date by following the steps below." The steps usually involve linking to a Web site that looks legitimate, but is in fact a spoof. By filling out the Web site's form, unsuspecting consumers give thieves the information they need to steal an identity. Other identity thieves trick people into revealing their credit card numbers using pornographic Web sites. These sites ask viewers to prove they are adults by providing credit card information. In one massive phishing expedition in 2009, thousands of Windows Live HotMail users had their user names and passwords posted on a public Web site.

Some exploits combine hacking, phishing, and spoofing. For example, in 2007 a hacker used a vulnerability in Adobe Flash to redirect user clicks in eBay, redirecting them to an eBay lookalike site—an eBay spoof—that phished for personal information. The vulnerability was patched after Adobe learned of the problem. In general (but not always), software companies are quick to provide patches to Web browsers and related software when security leaks are uncovered. Unfortunately, many users are slow to install those security fixes, leaving themselves open to attack long after they have to be.

Financial matters aside, thieves may soon routinely steal votes, putting our democracy at risk. Many of today's paperless electronic voting machines are less secure than casino slot machines and vulnerable to a wide variety of attacks, including the kinds described in the following pages.

Software Sabotage: Viruses and Other Malware

> The American government can stop me from going to the U.S., but **they can't stop my virus**.
>
> —*Virus creator*

Another type of computer crime is sabotage of hardware or software. The word **sabotage** comes from the early days of the Industrial Revolution, when rebellious workers shut down new machines by placing wooden shoes, called *sabots*, into the gears. Modern computer saboteurs commonly use **malware**—malicious software—rather than footwear to do destructive deeds. The names given to the saboteurs' destructive programs—viruses, worms, and Trojan horses—sound more like biology than technology, and many of the programs even mimic the behavior of living organisms.

Viruses

A biological virus is unable to reproduce by itself, but it can invade the cells of another organism and use the reproductive machinery of each host cell to make copies of itself; the new copies leave the host and seek new hosts to repeat the process. A software **virus** works in the same way. Virus software is a piece of code usually hidden in the operating system of a computer or in an application program. When a user executes a program containing a virus, the virus quickly copies itself to an uninfected program; it then allows the user's application to execute. Usually this happens so quickly that the user is unaware the application program contains

Working Wisdom Protecting Yourself from Identity Theft

The number of cases of identity theft is on the rise. Millions of people in the United States have their identities stolen each year. With a few simple precautions, you can reduce your chances of falling victim to this crime.

- ***Make all your online purchases using PayPal or a credit card.*** Visa USA, MasterCard International, and American Express all have zero-liability programs that waive your liability in case someone uses your credit card number for online fraud. Most debit cards, checking accounts, and money orders don't offer this kind of protection.
- ***Scan your bills and statements promptly.*** If you find any unexpected transaction or other unpleasant surprises, report them right away. Many credit card liability-protection programs have time limits—60 days is common. If you don't report fraudulent purchases within the specified number of days, the company may not reimburse you for losses caused by unauthorized use. If you don't receive a bill that you expected, or if you *do* receive a bill that you didn't expect, contact the company right away to see if there's a problem.
- ***Get a separate credit card with a low credit limit for your online transactions.*** If the card number is stolen, the thieves will not be able to run up as large a balance.
- ***Make sure a secure Web site is managing your online transaction.*** Look at the address of the Web site you are visiting. The URL should begin with https, not http. The https designator means the site is using encryption to improve the security of the transaction.
- ***Don't disclose personal information over the phone.*** Remember that a credit card company would never call you and ask you for your credit card number, expiration date, or other personal information; they already know it.
- ***Handle email with care.*** Cunning thieves send email that looks like it comes from legitimate companies, such as PayPal, Amazon.com, or your bank asking you to update your credit card number and other personal information. But when you click the link in this kind of email, the Web site that loads isn't really from the legitimate company, opening up unsuspecting users to credit card theft. Regard all such emails with suspicion, and be careful any time you enter a credit card number or other personal information online. If you're suspicious, check the URL displayed at the top of your browser window; if it isn't the company's standard URL, you may be at a spoof site. If your Web browser doesn't offer phishing protection, consider switching to one that does.
- ***Don't put your Social Security number or your driver's license number on your checks.*** These are key pieces of information sought by identity thieves.
- ***Shred or burn sensitive mail before you recycle it.*** Bills, junk mail credit card offers, and other mail can contain personal information. Looking through people's garbage is a tried-and-true tactic of identity thieves.
- ***Keep your wallet thin.*** Don't carry your Social Security card or extra ID around with you. Cut and toss unused credit cards.
- ***Copy your cards.*** Make photocopies of both sides of your driver's license and credit cards and keep the copies in a safe place. If your wallet or purse is stolen, you'll have the information you need to get replacement cards and cancel the stolen ones.
- ***Report identity theft promptly.*** Call your credit card companies, the local police, and the Federal Trade Commission (877-438-4338) right away. Contact one of the three consumer credit reporting companies (see "Your Privacy Rights" in Chapter 7) and place a fraud alert on your credit reports; the company you contact will notify the other two. Close any accounts that you believe have been compromised.

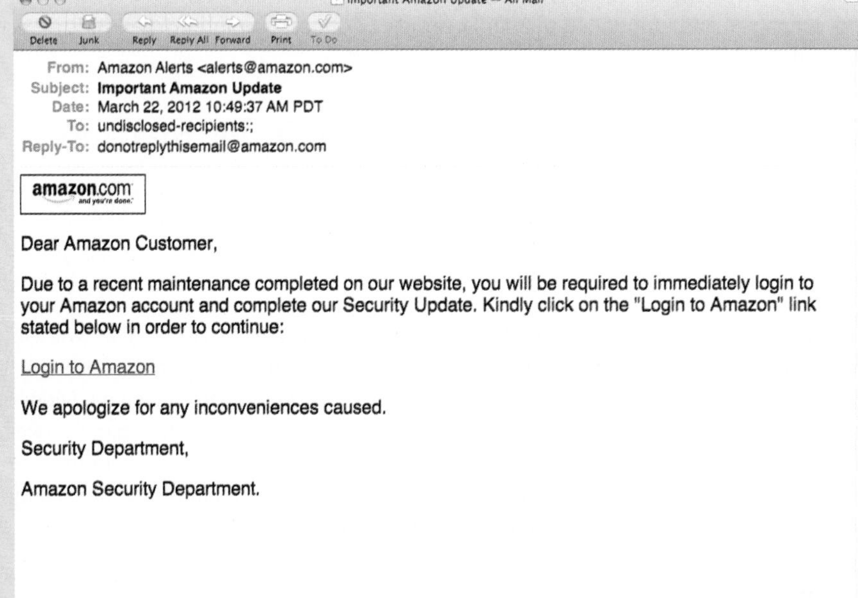

Important Amazon Update — All Mail

From: Amazon Alerts <alerts@amazon.com>
Subject: **Important Amazon Update**
Date: March 22, 2012 10:49:37 AM PDT
To: undisclosed-recipients:;
Reply-To: donotreplythisemail@amazon.com

amazon.com

Dear Amazon Customer,

Due to a recent maintenance completed on our website, you will be required to immediately login to your Amazon account and complete our Security Update. Kindly click on the "Login to Amazon" link stated below in order to continue:

Login to Amazon

We apologize for any inconveniences caused.

Security Department,

Amazon Security Department.

FIGURE 10.5 An email request to log in to your account and complete a "security update" is likely to take you to a bogus Web page designed to steal your personal data—especially if it's addressed to "undisclosed recipients" and peppered with awkward grammar.

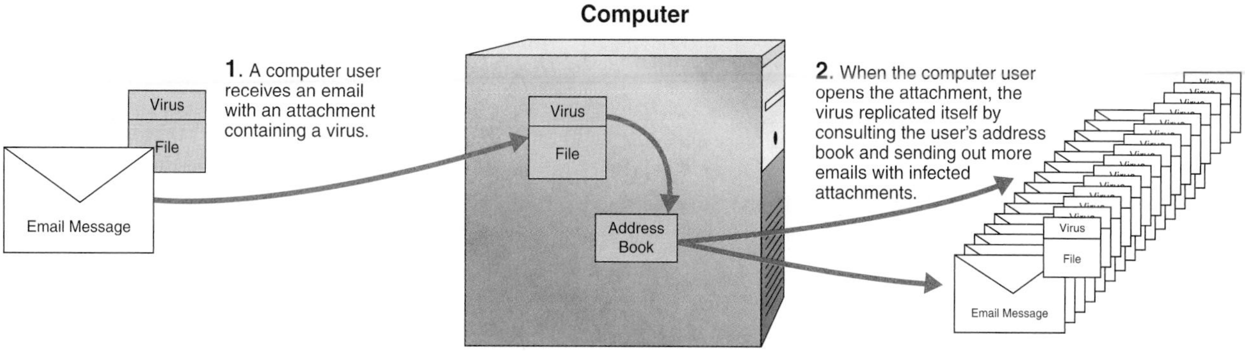

FIGURE 10.6 How a virus spreads via email.

a virus. A virus can jump from one computer to another when someone uses a disc, flash drive, or a computer network with an infected machine to copy an infected program. Some viruses do nothing but reproduce; others display messages; still others destroy data or erase disks.

Like most software code, a virus is usually operating-system specific. For example, Windows viruses invade only Windows. There are exceptions: *Macro viruses* attach themselves to documents that contain *macros*—embedded programs to automate tasks. Macro viruses can be spread across computer platforms if the documents are created using cross-platform applications—most commonly the applications in Microsoft Office. Macro viruses can be spread through innocent-looking email or instant message attachments.

One of the most widely publicized macro viruses was the 1999 Melissa virus. Melissa's method of operation is typical of email viruses: An unsuspecting computer user received an "Important message" from a friend: "Here is that document you asked for ... don't show it to anyone else ;-)." The attached Microsoft Word document contained a list of passwords for pornography sites. It contained something else: a macro virus written in Microsoft Office's built-in Visual Basic scripting language. When the user opened the document, the virus went to work, sending a copy of the email message and infected document to the first 50 names on the user's Outlook address book. Within minutes, 50 more potential Melissa victims received messages apparently from someone they knew—the user of the newly infected computer. Melissa spread like wildfire, infecting 100,000 Windows systems in just a few days. Melissa wasn't designed to damage systems, but the flurry of messages brought down some email servers. A nationwide search located the probable author, a 30-year-old New Jersey resident with a fondness for a topless dancer named Melissa. A federal judge fined him $5,000 and sentenced him to 20 months in federal prison plus 100 hours of community service.

A newer type of cross-platform virus, the cross-site scripting (XSS) virus, attaches itself to Web applications and spreads via client Web browsers. There have been many documented exploitations of XSS. In 2005 a MySpace user named Samy amassed over 1 million friends by infecting his user profile with an XSS virus. Visitors to his page—and visitors to the pages of those visitors, and so on—were automatically added to his friends list, until MySpace was taken offline to remove the virus—and Samy—from the system. "My primary motivation was to make people laugh," Samy said. Another example: On the eve of the 2008 Pennsylvania Democratic presidential primary a political prankster used XSS to redirect Barack Obama's community forum visitors to rival candidate Hillary Clinton's Web site.

Worms

Like viruses, **worms** (named for tapeworms) use computer hosts to reproduce themselves. But unlike viruses, worms are complete programs capable of traveling independently over computer networks, seeking out uninfected workstations in which to reproduce. A worm can reproduce until the computer freezes from lack of free memory or disk space. A typical worm segment resides in memory rather than on disk, so the worm can be eliminated by shutting down all of the workstations on the network.

The first headline-making worm was created as an experiment by a Cornell graduate student in 1988. The worm was accidentally released onto the Internet, clogging 6,000 computers all over the United States, bringing them almost to a standstill and forcing operators to shut them all down so every worm segment could be purged from memory. The total cost, in terms of work time lost at research institutions, was staggering. The student was suspended from school and was the first person convicted of violating the Computer Fraud and Abuse Act.

Other worms have made headlines since then. In 2001, the Code Red worm targeted servers running Microsoft software. Even though the U.S. government and Microsoft made free software patches available, many servers were crippled, including servers owned by Microsoft. Samy's virus, mentioned in the last section, was spread using a worm. In 2010 the Stuxnet worm introduced a new threat: malware that could manipulate industrial controls and, potentially, cripple or destroy power plants, pipelines, and other critical facilities. (See Cyberwarfare and Cyberterrorism later in this chapter.)

Trojan Horses

A **Trojan horse** is a program that performs a useful task while at the same time carrying out some secret destructive act. As in the ancient story of the wooden horse that carried Greek soldiers through the gates of Troy, Trojan horse software hides an enemy in an attractive package. Trojan horse programs are often posted on software download sites with names that make them sound like games, utilities, or even pictures. When an unsuspecting bargain hunter downloads and runs such a program, it might erase files, change data, or cause some other kind of damage. Some network saboteurs use Trojan horses to pass secret data to other unauthorized users. To make matters worse, many Trojan horses carry software viruses.

One type of Trojan horse, a **logic bomb**, is programmed to attack in response to a particular event or sequence of events. For example, a programmer might plant a logic bomb that is designed to destroy data files if the programmer is ever listed as terminated in the company's personnel file. A logic bomb might be triggered when a certain user logs in, enters a special code in a database field, or performs a particular sequence of actions. If the logic bomb is triggered by a time-related event, it is called a ***time bomb***. A widely publicized virus included a logic bomb that was programmed to destroy PC data files on Michelangelo's birthday.

Spyware

Spyware refers to a technology that collects information from computer users without their knowledge or consent. A spyware program, sometimes called ***tracking software*** or a ***spybot***, gathers user information and communicates it to an outsider via the Internet. Spybots can monitor your keystrokes, record which Web sites you visit, and even take snapshots of what's displayed on your monitor. Other spybots cause pop-up ads to appear on your screen.

Surveys suggest that most home computers are infected with some kind of spyware. That's not surprising, considering the number of ways spyware can get into a PC. Some computer viruses spread spyware. Some freeware or shareware programs include hidden spyware. In ***drive-by downloads***, simply visiting certain Web sites causes spyware or other malware to be downloaded to your computer. Spyware is not generally self-propagating like viruses and worms. But spyware can—and generally does—exploit infected computers for commercial gain without the knowledge of the owners of those computers. Spyware can represent a serious privacy threat to unsuspecting users, but it can also slow PC performance to a crawl if it goes unchecked.

Sometimes spyware comes from corporate sources. In 2008 shoppers who joined the Sears and Kmart online communities discovered that spyware was reporting data on Web site visits, purchases, and other Internet usage records. The companies responded to criticisms by changing their software and privacy policies.

Malware Wars

The popular press usually doesn't distinguish among Trojan horses, viruses, and worms; they're all called computer viruses. Whatever they're called, these rogue programs make life more complicated and expensive for people who depend on computers. Researchers have identified tens of thousands of virus strains, with 200 new ones appearing each month. At any given time, hundreds of virus strains may exist in the wild—in circulation.

Modern viruses can spread faster and do more damage than viruses of a few years ago for several reasons. The Internet, which speeds communication all over the planet, also speeds virus transmission. Web pages, macros, and other technologies give virus writers new places to hide their creations. And increased standardization on Microsoft applications and operating systems has made it easier for viruses to spread. Just as natural mixed forests are more resistant to disease than are single-species tree farms, mixed computing environments are less susceptible to crippling attacks than is an organization in which everyone uses the same hardware and software.

When computers are used in life-or-death situations, as they are in many medical and military applications, invading programs can even threaten human lives. Many governments now have laws against introducing these programs into computer systems.

Antivirus software is designed to search for viruses, notify users when they're found, and remove them from infected disks or files. Most antivirus programs continually monitor system activity, watching for and reporting suspicious virus-like actions. But no antivirus program can detect every virus, and these programs need to be frequently revised to combat new viruses as they appear. Most antivirus programs can automatically download new virus-fighting code from the Web as new virus strains appear. But it can take several days for companies to develop and distribute patches for new viruses, and destructive viruses can do a lot of damage in that time.

The malware wars continue to escalate as malware writers develop new ways to spread their works. After a rash of 1999 email viruses, most users learned not to open unidentified email attachments, and software vendors started modifying their email applications to prevent this sort of attack. But before the year was over, a worm called BubbleBoy (named for an episode of TV's *Seinfeld*) demonstrated that a system could be infected by email even if the mail wasn't opened. Some viruses have even been developed to infect HTML code in Web pages or HTML email messages.

Software companies continually test their products for security holes and try to make them more resistant to viruses, worms, and other security breaches. Many software companies, including Microsoft, Apple, and several browser manufacturers, periodically release **security patches**—software programs that plug potential security breaches in the operating system or application. These patches are provided as free downloads or automatic updates to all owners of the software. Because Microsoft Windows is the target of the great majority of malware, Windows security updates are particularly important in preventing the spread of malware.

Security updates and other preventive security measures can sometimes backfire. In the summer of 2003, a worm called MS Slammer made worldwide headlines, shutting down

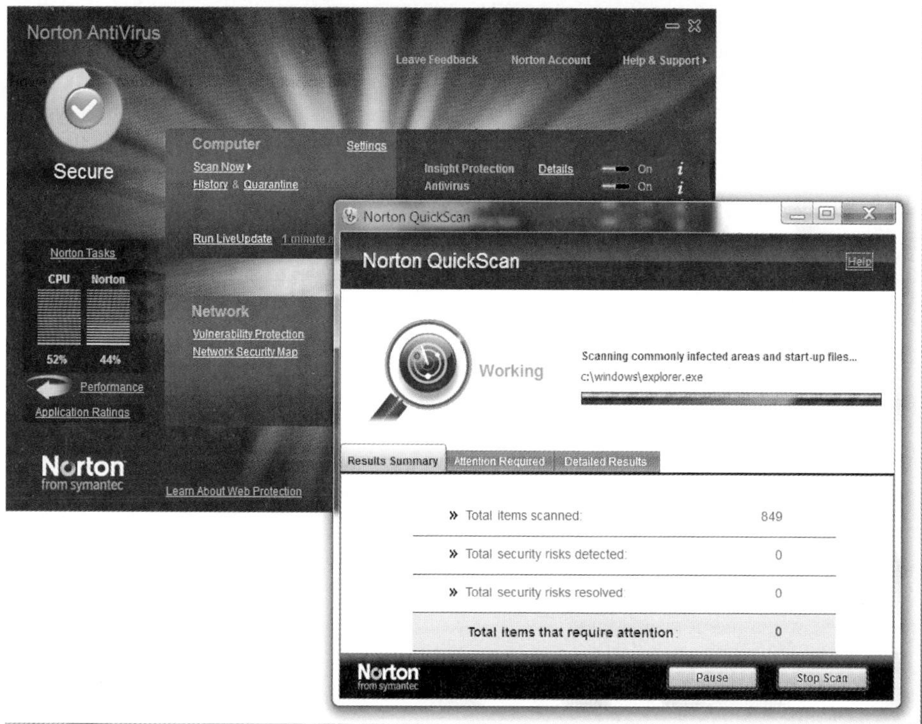

FIGURE 10.7 Antivirus software scans files for viruses, worms, and other software invaders. New versions of the software definition files should be downloaded regularly to ensure the software is up to date.

hundreds of thousands of PCs as it moved from computer to computer looking for vulnerable targets. The worm was deployed more than a month after Microsoft had issued a security patch to fix the very problem that MS Slammer exploited. By publicizing the vulnerability, Microsoft inadvertently inspired malicious programmers to create the worm. These system saboteurs took advantage of the fact that many computer users fail to install security patches, leaving their systems ripe for attack. In response to MS Slammer, a well-intentioned programmer released a helper worm designed to search the Internet for machines that had been infected by MS Slammer and apply the Microsoft security patch to those machines. But this worm caused its own problems, slowing many systems to a crawl by repeatedly checking them for security problems.

Stories like this one happen more often than the information technology industry would like to admit. These stories serve as reminders that the malware wars are far from over. There will always be new ways to compromise connected systems.

Hacking and Electronic Trespassing

> I don't drink, smoke, or take drugs. I don't steal, assault people, or vandalize property. The only way in which I am really different from most people is in **my fascination with the ways and means of learning about computers that don't belong to me**.
>
> —*Bill "The Cracker" Landreth, in* Out of the Inner Circle

In the late 1970s, timesharing computers at Stanford and MIT attracted informal communities of computer fanatics who called themselves ***hackers***. In those days, a hacker was a person who enjoyed learning the details of computer systems and writing clever programs, referred to as *hacks*. Hackers were, for the most part, curious, enthusiastic, intelligent, idealistic, eccentric, and harmless. In his popular book about hackers, Steven Levy quotes the hacker ethic as saying, in part, "All information should be free. Mistrust Authority—Promote Decentralization." Many of those early hackers were, in fact, architects of the microcomputer revolution.

Over the years, the idealism of the early hacker communities was at least partly overshadowed by cynicism, as big-money interests took over the young personal computer industry. At the same time, the term **hacking** took on a new, more ominous connotation in the media. Although many people still use the term to describe software wizardry, it more commonly refers to unauthorized access to computer systems. Old-time hackers insist that this electronic trespassing is really ***cracking***, or criminal hacking, but the general public and popular media don't recognize the distinction between hackers and crackers. Today's stereotypical hacker, like his early counterparts, is a young, bright, technically savvy, white, middle-class male who, in addition to programming his own computer, may break into others.

Of course, not all young computer wizards break into systems, and not all electronic trespassers fit the media stereotype. Still, hackers aren't just a media myth; they're real, and there are lots of them. Electronic trespassers enter corporate and government computers using stolen passwords and software security holes.

Many hackers are motivated by curiosity and intellectual challenge; once they've cracked a system, they look around and move on without leaving any electronic footprints. Some hackers claim to be pointing out security problems in commercial software products. Others, called ***hactivists***, consider hacking a form of political activism, performing illegal acts for what they claim to be a greater public good. Some malicious hackers use Trojan horses, logic bombs, and other tricks of the trade to wreak havoc on corporate and government systems. A growing number of computer trespassers are part of electronic crime rings intent on stealing credit card numbers and other sensitive, valuable information. This kind of theft is difficult to detect and track because the original information is left unchanged when the copy is stolen.

Hackers have defaced the Web sites of the White House, the U.S. Senate, the Parliament of Georgia, Spain's official Web site for its EU President, dozens of political candidates, countless online businesses, and even a hacker's conference. Sometimes Web sites are simply defaced with obscene or threatening messages; sometimes they're replaced with satirical substitutes; sometimes they're vandalized so they don't work properly. ***Webjackers*** hijack legitimate Web pages and redirect users to other sites—for example, pornographic sites or fraudulent businesses. Many hackers use networks of *zombie computers*, or **bots**—Internet-connected computers that have been hijacked using viruses or other tools to perform malicious acts without the knowledge of their owners and users. These malicious networks are often called **botnets**, and they're a favorite tool of spammers, phishers, saboteurs, and other Internet criminals. Experts believe that more than one hundred million computers are under the control of malicious hackers. If your computer isn't protected against malware, it may be part of a botnet army.

Denial-of-service (DoS) attacks bombard servers and Web sites with so much bogus traffic that they're effectively shut down, denying service to legitimate customers and clients. In a *distributed denial-of-service (DDoS)* attack, the flood of messages comes from botnets. In a single week in February 2000, the Yahoo!, E*TRADE, eBay, and Amazon Web sites were crippled by denial-of-service attacks, costing their owners millions of dollars in business. Two months later a 15-year-old Canadian youth, nicknamed "Mafia Boy," was arrested after he bragged online about causing the breakdowns. His pranks didn't require expertise; he reportedly downloaded all of the software he used from the Internet. A 2007 DDoS attack crippled the electronic infrastructure of the Republic of Estonia, one of the most wired countries in the world. In 2009, Iranian election protesters mounted a DDoS attack that brought down the Web site of the government. That same year Twitter and Facebook came to a standstill for several hours because of a DDoS attack against one particular Georgian blogger. And then there's the occasional false alarm: The day Michael Jackson died, Google initially interpreted the spike in "Michael Jackson" searches as a DDoS attack.

FIGURE 10.8 Kevin Mitnick was the most notorious hacker ever caught, according to federal authorities. Mitnick was a "pure" hacker who illegally accessed remote computers out of curiosity. He spent five years in jail for his hacking activities. Today Mitnick runs a computer security company whose Web site, ironically, was hacked in early 2003.

One classic case of electronic trespassing was documented in Cliff Stoll's best-selling book, *The Cuckoo's Egg*. While working as a system administrator for a university computer lab in 1986, Stoll noticed a 75-cent accounting error. Rather than letting it go, Stoll investigated the error. It took a year and some help from the FBI, but Stoll eventually located the hacker—a German student working for the KGB to uncover military secrets. Ironically, Stoll captured the thief by using standard hacker tricks, including a Trojan horse program.

Another headline-turned-book involved the 1995 capture of Kevin Mitnick, the hacker who stole millions of dollars worth of software and credit card information. By repeatedly manufacturing new identities and cleverly concealing his location, Mitnick successfully evaded the FBI for years. But when he broke into the computer of computational physicist Tsutomu Shimomura, he inadvertently started an electronic cat-and-mouse game that ended with his capture and conviction. Shimomura was able to defeat Mitnick because of his expertise in computer security—the protection of computer systems and, indirectly, the people who depend on them.

Computer Security: Reducing Risks

> In the old world, if I wanted to attack something physical, there was one way to get there. You could put guards and guns around it, you could protect it. But **a database—or a control system—usually has multiple pathways, unpredictable routes to it, and seems intrinsically impossible to protect**. That's why most efforts at computer security have been defeated.
>
> *—Andrew Marshall, military analyst*

With computer crime on the rise, computer security has become an important concern for system administrators and computer users alike. **Computer security** refers to protecting computer systems and the information they contain against unwanted access, damage, modification, or destruction. According to a Congressional Research Service report, computers have two inherent characteristics that leave them open to attack or operating error:

1. A computer does exactly what it is programmed to do, including reveal sensitive information. Any system that can be programmed can be reprogrammed by anyone with sufficient knowledge.
2. Any computer can do only what it is programmed to do. "[I]t cannot protect itself from either malfunctions or deliberate attacks unless such events have been specifically anticipated, thought through, and countered with appropriate programming."

Computer owners and administrators use a variety of security techniques to protect their systems, ranging from everyday low-tech locks to high-tech software scrambling.

Physical Access Restrictions

One way to reduce the risk of security breaches is to identify people attempting to access computer equipment. Organizations use a number of tools and techniques to identify personnel. Computers can perform some security checks; human security guards perform others. Depending on the security system, you might be granted access to a computer based on the following criteria:

- *Something you have,* such as a key, an ID card with a photo, or a *smart card* containing digitally encoded identification in a built-in memory chip
- *Something you know,* such as a password, an ID number, a lock combination, or a piece of personal history, such as your mother's maiden name
- *Something you do,* such as your signature or your typing speed and error patterns
- *Something about you,* such as a voice print, fingerprint, retinal scan, facial feature scan, or other measurement of individual body characteristics; these measurements are collectively called **biometrics**.

Because most of these security controls can be compromised—keys can be stolen, signatures can be forged, and so on—many systems use a combination of controls. For example, an employee might be required to show a badge, unlock a door with a key, and type a password to use a secured computer.

In the days when corporate computers were isolated in basements, physical restrictions were sufficient for keeping out intruders. But in the modern office, computers and data are everywhere, and networks connect computers to the outside world. In a distributed, networked environment, security is much more problematic. It's not enough to restrict physical access to mainframes when personal computers and network connections aren't restricted.

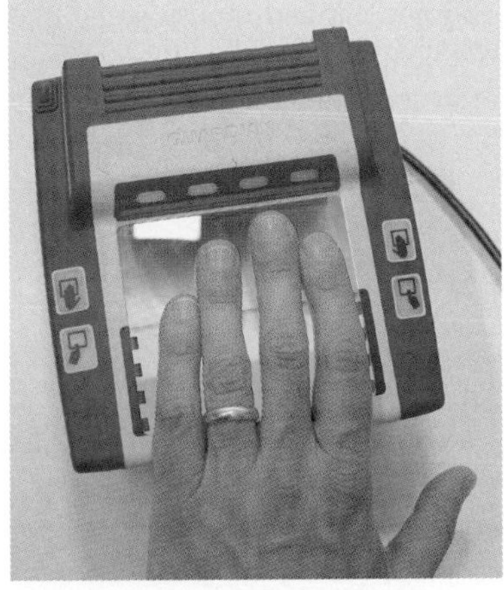

FIGURE 10.9 Biometric devices provide high levels of computer and network security because they monitor human body characteristics that can't be stolen. This electronic fingerprint biometric data collection unit (left) can compare the patterns in the fingerprints of the user against a database of employees and other legitimate users. This biometric scanner (right) can similarly identify people by comparing a retinal scan against its database of eye patterns.

Passwords and Access Privileges

FIGURE 10.10 Hardware firewall products come in all shapes and sizes.

Passwords are the most common tools used to restrict access to PCs, mainframe computers, and Web sites. Passwords are effective, however, only if they're chosen carefully. Most computer users choose passwords that are easy to guess: names of partners or pets; words related to jobs or hobbies; and consecutive characters on keyboards. The most popular passwords include 123456, qwerty, abc123, letmein, monkey, myspace1, god, sex, money, love, and, of course, password. Hackers know and exploit these clichés. They also use dictionary programs to guess passwords systematically by, in effect, trying every word in the dictionary. That's why many security systems refuse to let you choose a real word or name as a password. The best passwords mix letters and numbers into long strings that make no sense to anyone except the people who use them. Even the best passwords should be changed frequently.

Access-control software doesn't need to treat all users identically. Many systems use passwords to restrict users so they can open only files related to their work. In many cases, users are given read-only access to files that they can see but not change.

Even a PC can have different levels of access, because Windows, Mac OS X, and Linux all support multiple users. When a PC is set up with multiple user accounts, each user has a unique user ID and password. When one of those users logs into the PC with his user ID and password, he has access only to his own personal files plus any shared files that are accessible to multiple users. When he logs out, another user can log in to the same PC and use a completely different set of files. (A PC or Mac can easily be set up to bypass the login screen and automatically open a single user's account without a password.)

At least one of the accounts on a PC or Mac must be a system administrator account. The administrator has additional access privileges—permission to install software applications, change system settings, and more. Users who don't have administrator-level access are denied access to many of the "under the hood" components of the system.

Web sites frequently use passwords as access keys. Enterprising criminals often use software bots to sign up automatically for accounts and passwords. To foil the bots, many sites use answer-back security systems. When you apply for membership in such a system, you might be required to give your email address. The system sends an email to you and you reply, ensuring that you're a real person with a real email address.

Bots are also used to log into sites with stolen or guessed passwords. Many sites require passwords and visual identification of a string of abstract characters—something that's easy for a person to identify, but not easy for a machine to read.

FIGURE 10.11 To keep bots from posing as human visitors, many Web sites require visitors to identify abstract strings of characters like this one.

Firewalls, Encryption, and Audits

Many data thieves do their work without breaking into computer systems; instead, they intercept messages as they travel between computers on networks. Passwords are of little use for hiding email messages when they're traveling through Internet cables or wireless connections. Many organizations use firewalls to keep their internal networks secure while enabling communication with the rest of the Internet. The technical details of firewalls vary considerably, but they're all designed to serve the same function: to guard against unauthorized access to an internal network. In effect, a firewall is a gate with a lock; the locked gate opens only for information packets that pass one or more security inspections. Firewalls aren't just for large corporations. Without firewall hardware or software installed, a home computer with an always-on DSL or cable modem connection can be easy prey for Internet snoopers.

how it works Firewalls

A firewall is a program, often run on a dedicated computer, that filters information between a private network and the rest of the Internet. A set of security rules, created by a network administrator, determines which packets can enter and leave the local network.

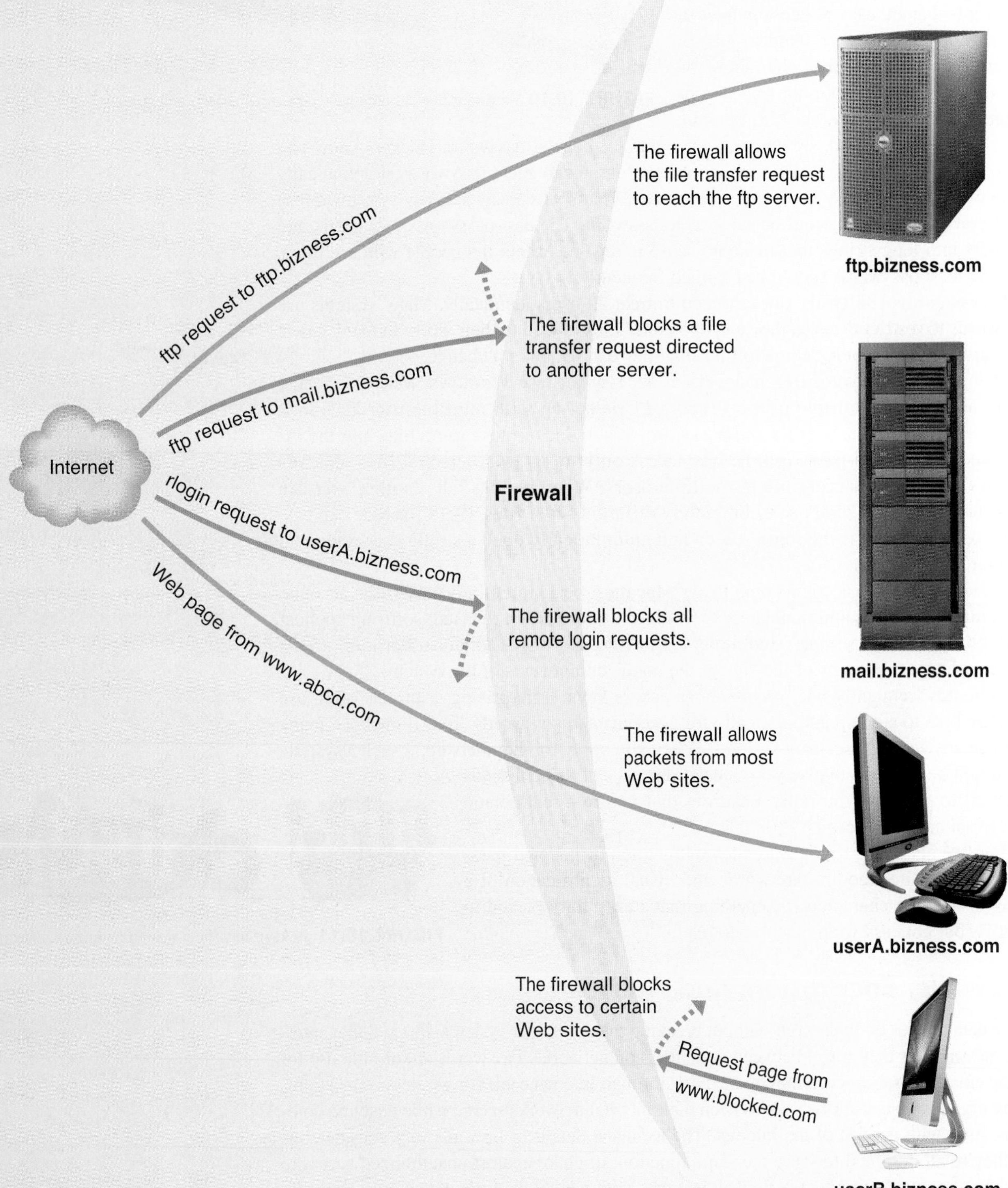

The firewall allows the file transfer request to reach the ftp server.
ftp request to ftp.bizness.com
ftp.bizness.com
The firewall blocks a file transfer request directed to another server.
ftp request to mail.bizness.com
Internet
Firewall
rlogin request to userA.bizness.com
Web page from www.abcd.com
The firewall blocks all remote login requests.
mail.bizness.com
The firewall allows packets from most Web sites.
userA.bizness.com
The firewall blocks access to certain Web sites.
Request page from www.blocked.com
userB.bizness.com

FIGURE 10.12

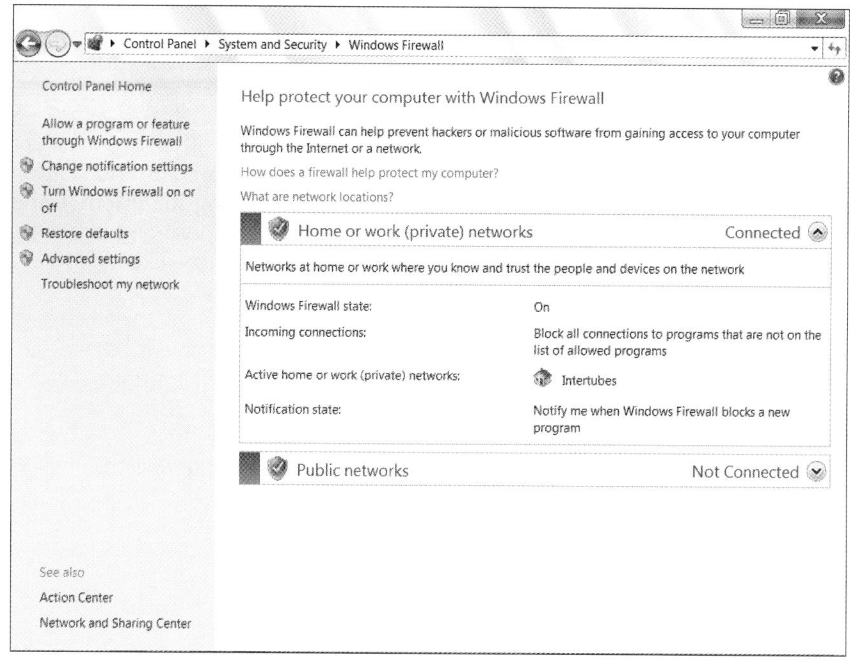

FIGURE 10.13 Software firewalls, such as the one included with Windows 7, help protect home networks from hackers.

Windows 7 and Mac OS X include basic software firewalls, but these firewalls must be activated before they can provide protection.

Of course, the firewall's digital drawbridge has to let some messages pass through; otherwise, there could be no communication with the rest of the Internet. How can those messages be secured in transit? To protect transmitted information, many organizations and individuals use **encryption** software to scramble their transmissions. When a user encrypts a message by applying a secret numerical code, called an ***encryption key***, the message can be transmitted or stored as an indecipherable garble of characters. The message can be read only after it's been reconstructed with a matching key.

For the most sensitive information, passwords, firewalls, and encryption aren't enough. A diligent spy can "listen to" and possibly read compromising emanations (CE)—the electromagnetic signals that emanate from computer hardware and, in some cases, read sensitive information. To prevent spies from using these spurious broadcasts, the NSA invested heavily in TEMPEST, a program to secure electronic communication from eavesdroppers while enabling the U.S. government to intercept and interpret those signals from other sources.

Audit-control software is used to monitor and record computer transactions as they happen so auditors can trace and identify suspicious computer activity after the fact. Effective audit-control software forces every user, legitimate or otherwise, to leave a trail of electronic footprints. Of course, this kind of software is of little value unless someone in the organization monitors and interprets the output.

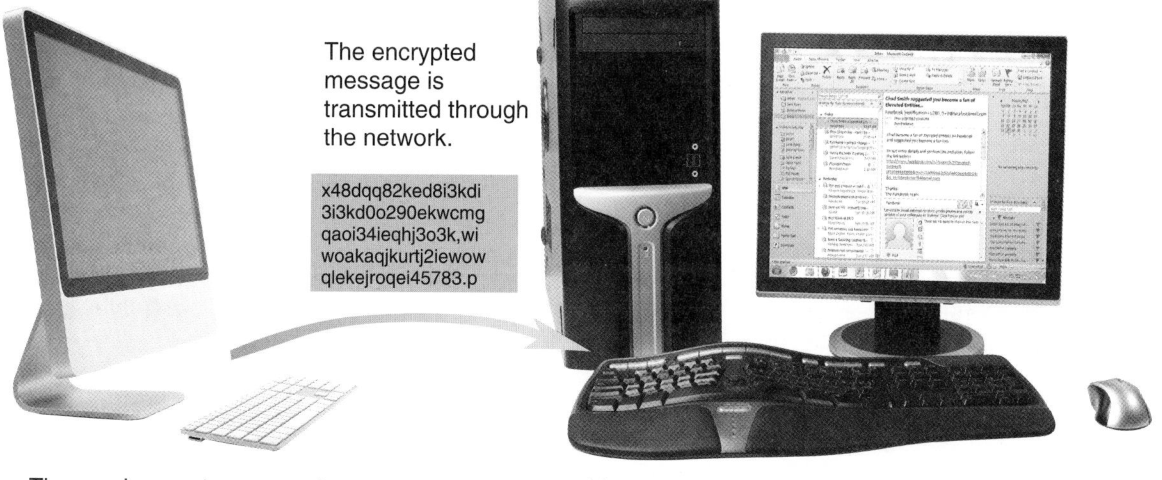

FIGURE 10.14 The encryption process.

how it works Cryptography

If you want to be sure that an email message is read by only the intended recipient, you must either use a secure communication channel or secure the message. Mail within many organizations is sent over secure communication channels—channels that can't be accessed by outsiders. But you can't secure the channels used by the Internet and other worldwide mail networks; there's no way to shield messages sent through public telephone lines and airwaves. In the words of Mark Rotenberg, director of the Electronic Privacy Information Center, "Email is more like a postcard than a sealed letter."

If you can't secure the communication channel, the alternative is to secure the message. You secure a message by using a cryptosystem to encrypt it—scramble it so it can be decrypted (unscrambled) only by the intended recipient.

Almost all cryptosystems depend on a key—a password like number or phrase that can be used to encrypt or decrypt a message. Eavesdroppers who don't know the key have to try to decrypt it by brute force—by trying all possible keys until they guess the right one. Some cryptosystems afford only modest security: A message can be broken after only a day or week of brute force cryptanalysis on a supercomputer. More effective systems would take a supercomputer billions of years to break the message.

The traditional kind of cryptosystem used on computer networks is called a symmetric secret key system. With this approach the sender and recipient use the same key, and they have to keep the shared key secret from everyone else.

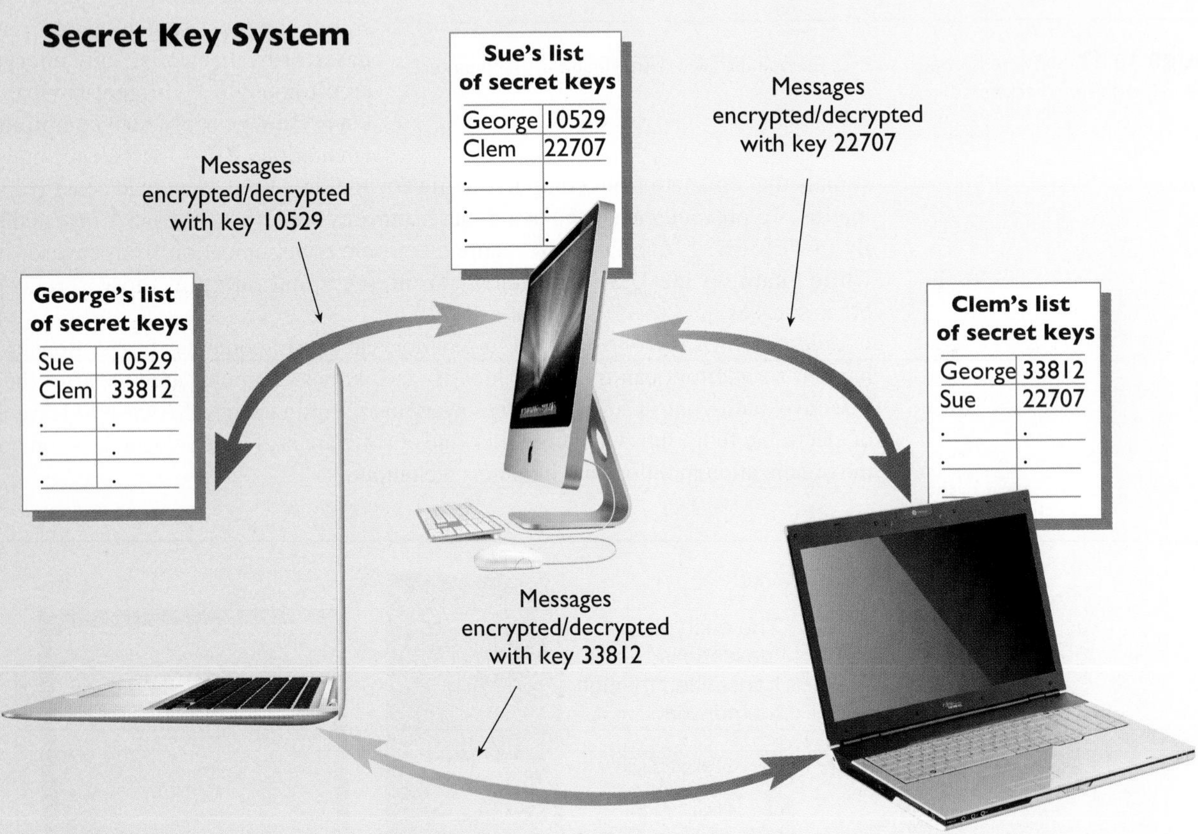

FIGURE 10.15

The biggest problem with symmetric secret key systems is key management. If you want to communicate with several people and ensure that each person can't read messages intended for the others, then you'll need a different secret key for each person. When you want to communicate with new people, you have the problem of letting them know what the key is. If you send it over the ordinary communication channel, it can be intercepted.

In the 1970s cryptographers developed public key cryptography to get around the key management problems. The most popular kind of public key cryptosystem, RSA, is being incorporated into most new network-enabled software. Phillip Zimmerman's popular shareware utility called PGP (for Pretty Good Privacy) uses RSA technology.

Public Key System

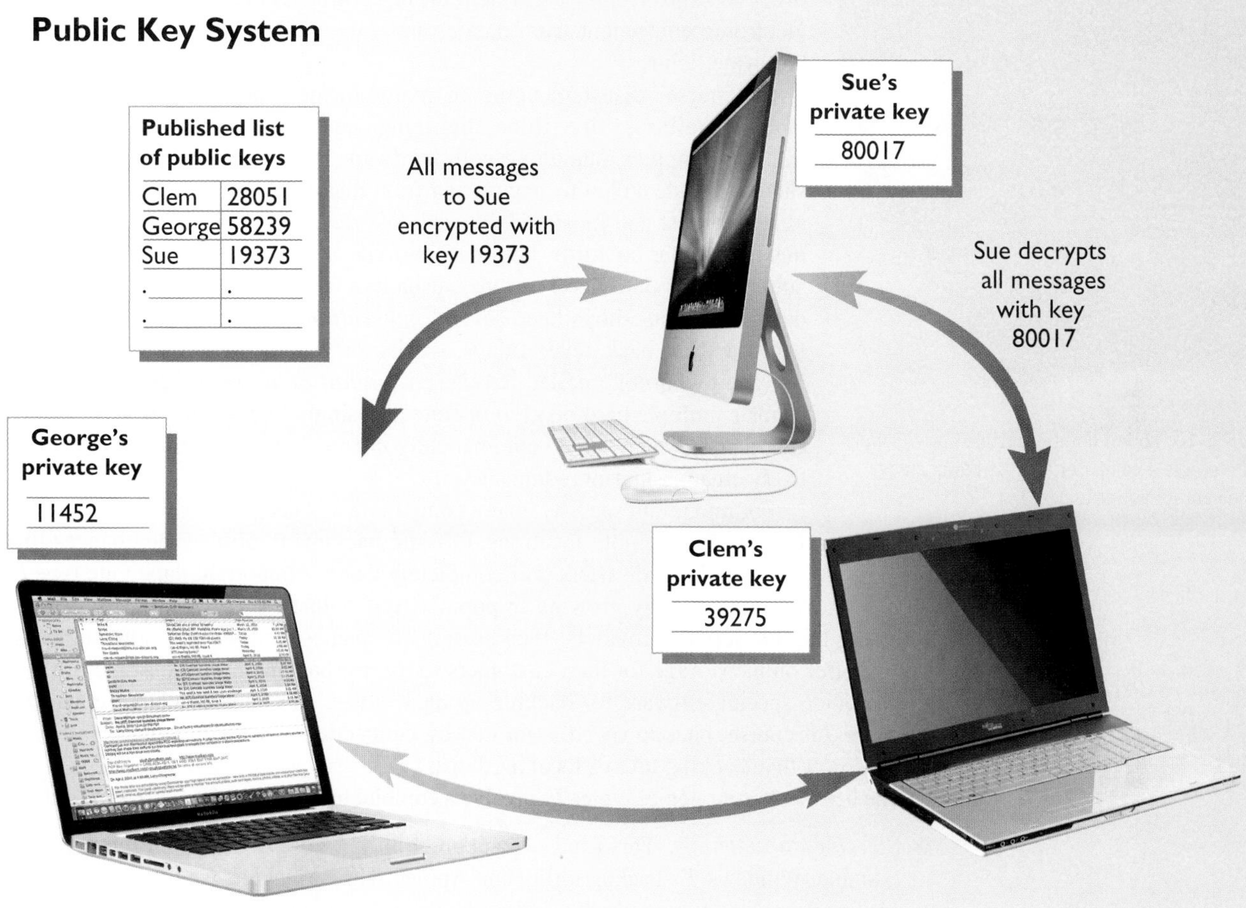

Each person using a public key cryptosystem has two keys: a private key known only to the user and a public key that is freely available to anyone who wants it. A public key system is asymmetric: A different key is used to encrypt than to decrypt. Public keys can be published in phone directories, Web pages, and advertisements; some users include them in their email signatures.

If you want to send a secure message over the Internet to your friend Sue in St. Louis, you use her public key to encrypt the message. Sue's public key can't decrypt the message; only her private key can do that. The private key is designed to decrypt messages that were encrypted with the corresponding public key. Because public/private key pairs can be generated by individual users, the key distribution problem is solved. The only keys being sent over an insecure network are publicly available keys.

You can use the same technology in reverse (encrypt with the private key, decrypt with the public key) for message authentication: When you decrypt a message, you can be sure that it was sent from a particular person on the network.

FIGURE 10.16 An uninterruptible power supply (UPS) protects a computer against power surges and momentary power loss.

Backups and Other Precautions

Even the tightest security system can't guarantee absolute protection of data. A power surge or a power failure can wipe out the most carefully guarded data in an instant. An **uninterruptible power supply (UPS)** can protect computers from data loss during power failures; inexpensive ones can protect home computers from short power dropouts. (Laptops have built-in protection, since they automatically switch to battery power when the power shuts off.) ***Surge protectors*** don't help during power failures, but they can shield electronic equipment from dangerous power spikes, preventing expensive hardware failures.

Of course, disasters come in many forms. Sabotage, human errors, machine failures, fire, flood, lightning, and earthquakes can damage or destroy computer data along with hardware. Any complete security system should include a plan for recovering from disasters. For mainframes and PCs alike, the best and most widely used data recovery insurance is a system of making regular **backups**. For many systems, data and software are backed up automatically onto disks or tapes, usually at the end of each workday. Most data-processing shops keep several ***generations*** of backups so they can, if necessary, go back several days, weeks, or years to reconstruct data files. Storage technology called ***RAID (redundant array of independent disks)*** enables multiple hard disks to operate as a single logical unit. RAID systems can, among other things, automatically *mirror* data on multiple disks, effectively creating instant redundancy.

For maximum security, many computer users keep copies of sensitive data off-site—in one or more remote locations. Off-site backups minimize the chances that fires, floods, or other local disasters will completely destroy important data. One type of off-site backup that's rapidly growing in popularity is online backup. Many companies, including Internet service providers, Web hosting companies, and security software companies, offer online storage for their customers to use for backing up data. Some of these sites provide special software for backing up data; others can be used with any backup software. Of course, backup speed is limited by connection bandwidth, and is typically much slower than backing up to a local hard disk.

The best backup strategies typically involve a combination of these four types of backup:

- ***Incremental backups.*** This kind of backup happens more or less continuously. For example, Windows 7's backup utility and Apple's Time Machine can be set to back up once each hour, copying only those files that have changed since the last hourly backup.

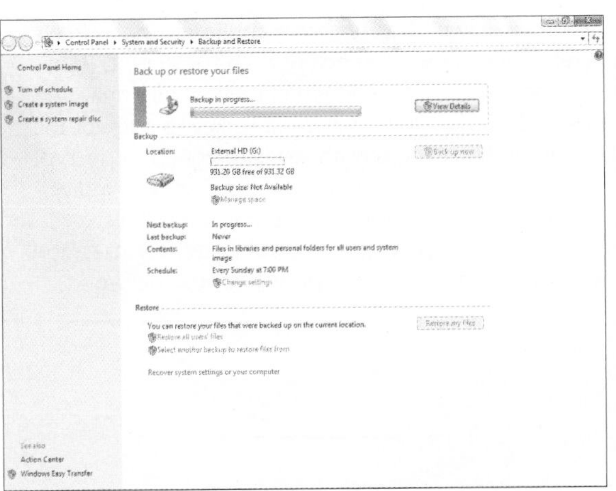

FIGURE 10.17 Windows and the Mac OS include backup utilities that can automatically make regular backups onto external hard drives. Apple's Time Machine lets you go "back in time" to recover deleted or damaged files.

- *Bootable backups*. A disk utility capable of cloning can make a complete, exact duplicate (clone) of a disk. In the event of a disk failure, the computer can be immediately rebooted from the bootable backup. Because it can take a while to make a bootable backup, many PC users set up their systems to create bootable backups automatically each night. An extra-secure backup system might include provisions for making full bootable backups to different drives each night for a week.
- *Off-site backups*. An off-site backup can be created by transporting DVDs full of data to remote sites or by uploading data into the Internet cloud. Either way, data is protected from disasters that might destroy on-site backups.
- *Archive backups*. When a file is no longer needed for day-to-day work, but it may be needed again someday, it can be archived and deleted from the computer's main drives.

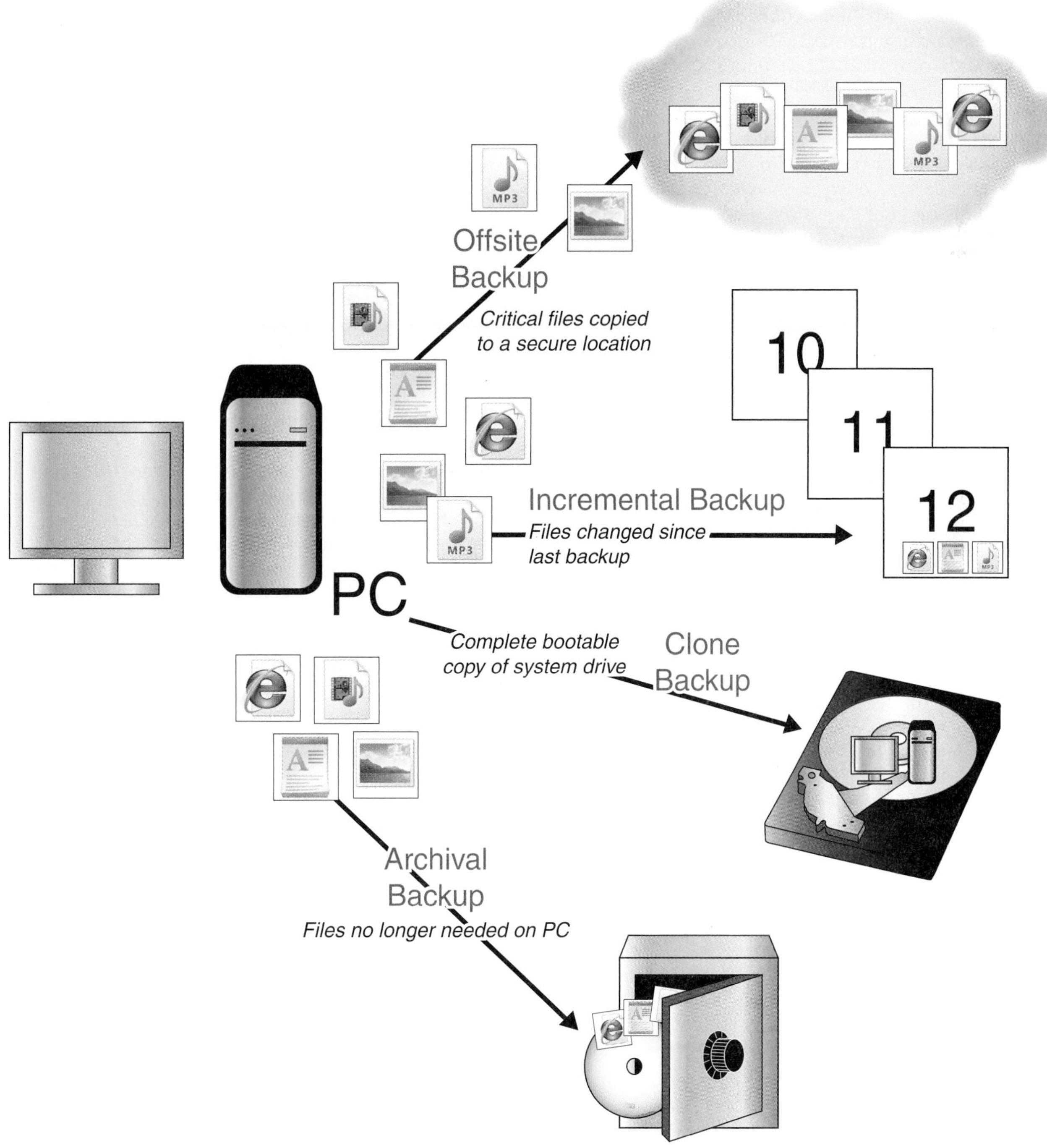

FIGURE 10.18 A comprehensive backup strategy includes different kinds of backups for different situations.

Working Wisdom Safe Computing

Even if you're not building a software system for the DOJ or the FBI, computer security is important. Viruses, disk crashes, system bombs, and miscellaneous disasters can destroy your work, your peace of mind, and possibly your system. Fortunately, you can protect your computer, your software, and your data from most hazards.

- ***Share with care.*** A computer virus is a contagious disease that spreads when it comes in contact with a compatible file or disk. Viruses spread rapidly in environments where files are passed around freely, as they are in many student computer labs. To protect your data, don't be overly casual about sharing flash drives and other media containing data and programs.
- ***Beware of email bearing gifts.*** Many viruses hide in attachments to email messages that say something like, "Here's the document you asked for. Please don't show anyone else." Don't open unsolicited email attachments, especially from senders you don't recognize; just delete them.
- ***Handle shareware and freeware with care.*** Some viruses enter systems in Trojan horse shareware and freeware programs. Approach public domain programs and shareware with caution; test them with a disinfectant program before you install them.
- ***Don't pirate software.*** Even commercial programs can be infected with viruses. Shrink-wrapped, virgin software is much less likely to be infected than pirated copies. Besides, software piracy is theft, and the legal penalties can be severe.
- ***Disinfect regularly.*** Use up-to-date virus protection software regularly if you're using an operating system that's subject to frequent malware attacks. (Most malware targets Windows PCs and servers, but every operating system, including smart phone OSs, is potentially vulnerable.) Most anti-virus software is sold by subscription, so that customers' computers can be automatically updated whenever new virus strains are released. Make sure your virus protection software is set to automatically download current patches.
- ***Take your passwords seriously.*** Choose a password that's not easily guessable, doesn't contain any words found in a dictionary, and can't be easily remembered by anybody except you. The best passwords are at least eight characters, and a mixture of lowercase letters, uppercase letters, and numbers. One way to create a memorable password that can't be cracked by dictionary software is to create a phrase like "My 9th birthday I went to Disney World" and reduce it to a string: "m9bdIw2DW". Don't use the same password for everything. Don't post passwords by your computer, and don't type them when you're being watched. Change your passwords occasionally—immediately if you have reason to suspect it has been discovered.
- ***If it's important, back it up.*** Regularly make backup copies of every important file on different disks than the original. Develop a strategy using the four different types of backups described in the main text. For example, use backup utilities to create incremental backups hourly, cloud backups daily, and bootable backups weekly; every few months back up everything to optical discs and store those discs at a remote location. Whether you use the Internet or sneakernet, make sure all your important work is backed up somewhere else.
- ***If it's sensitive, lock it up.*** If your computer is accessible to others, protect your private files with passwords and/or encryption. Many operating systems and utilities include options for adding password protection and encrypting files. If others need to see the files, lock them so they can be read but not changed or deleted. If secrecy is critical, don't store the data on your hard disk at all. Store it on removable disks, and lock it away in a safe place.
- ***Treat your removable discs and drives as if they contained something important.*** If you use a portable hard drive, keep it away from liquids, dust, pets, and magnets. Don't put it close to speakers and other electronic devices that contain hidden magnets. Magnets won't harm optical discs, but scratches can make them unusable.
- ***If you're sending sensitive information through the Internet, consider encryption.*** Use a utility to turn your message into code that's almost impossible to crack.
- ***Don't open your system to interlopers.*** If you've got an always-on Internet connection—T1, DSL, or cable modem—consider using firewall hardware or software to detect and lock out snoopers. Set your file-sharing controls so access is limited to authorized visitors.
- ***Create a separate administrator account.*** Windows, Mac OS, and Linux all allow multiple accounts on a single machine. For maximum security, use one account strictly for systems administration and installation, and another account for day-to-day computing.
- ***Keep your software up to date.*** Microsoft, Apple, and all the major Web browser manufacturers routinely make software updates available for free download. Many of these updates include important security patches. Set up your system to notify you when patches are available.
- ***Prepare for the worst.*** Even if you take every precaution, things can still go wrong. Make sure you aren't completely dependent on the computer for really important things.

Backups are like insurance—you hope you never have to use them. But when disaster strikes—or somebody makes a big mistake—a backup can be invaluable. A full-featured backup utility includes commands or instructions for *data recovery*—retrieving backed up data. It also includes options for fully *restoring* a disk to its former state—either on the same disk or, if the old hardware is beyond repair, on a replacement.

Human Security Controls

Security experts throughout the computer industry are constantly developing new technologies and techniques for protecting computer systems from computer criminals. At the same time, criminals continue to refine their craft. In the ongoing competition between the law and the lawless, computer security generally lags behind. In the words of Tom Forester and Perry Morrison in *Computer Ethics*, "Computer security experts are forever trying to shut the stable door after the horse has bolted." Ultimately, computer security is a human problem that can't be solved by technology alone.

Security, Privacy, Freedom, and Ethics: The Delicate Balance

> The **real question** before us lies here: do these instruments further **life and its values** or not?
>
> —*Lewis Mumford in 1934*

It's hard to overstate the importance of computer security in our networked world. Destructive viruses, illegal interlopers, crooked coworkers, software pirates, and cybervandals can erode trust, threaten jobs, and make life difficult for everyone. But sometimes computer security measures can create problems of their own. Complex access procedures, virus-protection programs, intellectual property laws, and other security measures can, if carried too far, interfere with people getting their work done. In the extreme, security can threaten individual human rights.

When Security Threatens Privacy

As you've seen in other chapters, computers threaten our personal privacy on several fronts. Corporate and government databases accumulate and share massive amounts of information about us against our will and without our knowledge. Software snoopers track our Web explorations and read our electronic mail. Managers use monitoring software to measure worker productivity and observe their on-screen activities. Government security agencies secretly monitor telephone calls and data transmissions.

When security measures are used to prevent computer crime, they usually help protect privacy rights at the same time. When a hacker invades a computer system, the intruder might monitor the system's legitimate users' private communications. When an outsider breaks into the database of a bank, the privacy of every bank customer is at risk. The same applies to government computers, credit bureau computers, and any other computer containing data on private citizens. The security of these systems is important for protecting people's privacy.

But in some cases security and law enforcement can pose threats to personal privacy. Here are some examples:

- In 1990 Alana Shoar, email coordinator for Epson America, Inc., found stacks of printouts of employee email messages in her boss's office—messages that employees believed were private. After confronting her boss, she was fired for "gross misconduct and insubordination." She filed a class-action suit, claiming that Epson routinely monitored all email messages. Company officials denied the charges but took a stand on their right to any information stored on, sent to, or taken from their business computers. The courts ruled in Epson's favor. Since then, many other U.S. court decisions have reinforced a company's right to read employee email stored on company computers.

- A 2004 decision by a U.S. federal appeals court went even further, ruling that an Internet service provider has the right to read the email messages of its subscribers. While the Wiretap Act prohibits eavesdropping on telephone calls and other messages sent in real time, the majority opinion stated that a stored message, such as a piece of email, does not have the same protection. The Electronic Frontier Foundation protested the decision, arguing that the ruling "dealt a grave blow to the privacy of Internet communications."
- In 1995 the U.S. government passed legislation requiring new digital phone systems to include additional switches that allow for electronic surveillance. This legislation protects the FBI's ability to wiretap at the expense of individual privacy. Detractors have pointed out that this digital "back door" could be abused by government agencies and could also be used by savvy criminals to perform illegal wiretaps. Government officials argue that wiretapping is a critical tool in the fight against organized crime.
- The digital manhunt that led to the arrest of the programmer charged with authoring the Melissa virus was made as a direct result of information provided by America Online Inc. A controversial Microsoft document identification technology—the Global Unique Identifier, or GUID—may also have played a role. While virtually everyone was happy when the virus's perpetrator was apprehended, many legal experts feared that the same techniques will be used for less lofty purposes.
- In 2000 the U.S. government found Microsoft guilty of gross abuses of its monopolistic position in the software industry. The government's case included hundreds of private email messages between Microsoft employees—messages that often contradicted Microsoft's public testimony.
- A 2001 U.S. law requires that mobile phones include GPS technology for transmitting the phone's location to a 911 operator in the case of an emergency call. Privacy activists fear that government agents and criminals will use this E911 technology to track the movements of phone owners.
- In response to the terrorist attacks of September 11, 2001, the U.S. Congress quickly drafted and passed the USA PATRIOT Act, a sweeping set of law changes that redefined terrorism and the government's authority to combat it. The act defined *cyberterrorism* to include computer crimes that cause at least $5,000 in damage or destroy medical equipment. It increased the FBI's latitude to use wiretap technology to monitor suspects' Web browsing and email without a judge's order. Critics argued that this controversial law could easily be used to restrict the freedom and threaten the privacy of law-abiding citizens. The USA PATRIOT Act, which originally included several temporary provisions, was reauthorized with some minor modifications in 2006.

One of the best examples of a technology that can simultaneously improve security and threaten privacy is the ***smart badge***. These badges broadcast identification codes. Each badge's code is picked up by a network receiver and transmitted to a badge-location database that is constantly being updated. Smart badges are used for identifying, finding, and remembering:

- *Identifying.* When an authorized employee approaches a door, the door recognizes the person's badge code and opens. Whenever anyone logs into a computer system, the badge code identifies the person as an authorized or unauthorized user.
- *Finding.* An employee can check a computer screen to locate another employee and find out with whom that person is talking. There's no need for a paging system, and "while you were away" notes are less common.
- *Remembering.* At the end of the day, a smart-badge wearer can get a minute-by-minute printout listing exactly where and with whom he's been.

Some conferences use smart badges to help the attendees meet each other. Delegates receive personalized badges containing their contact information, employment history, areas of interest, and hobbies. As the attendees move about, the badges communicate with each other. If the badge identifies a nearby delegate with similar interests, it alerts the badge wearer.

Similar technology is now available in smart phones. Phones with proximity recognition technology can notify their owners when friends—or even strangers who match particular profiles—are nearby. Many people use their phones to find and meet potential dates who happen to be in the neighborhood.

Are smart badges and smart phones primitive versions of the communicator on TV's *Star Trek* or surveillance tools for Big Brother? The technology has the potential to be either or both; it all depends on how people use it. These devices raise important legal and ethical questions about security and privacy—questions that we, as a society, must resolve sooner or later.

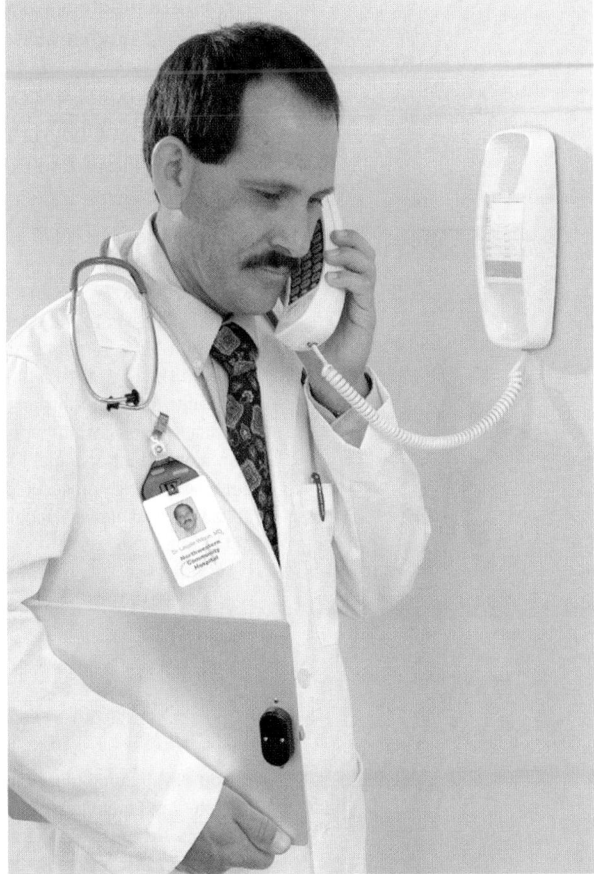

FIGURE 10.19 Smart badges allow employees to be tracked as they move. Instead of paging the entire hospital, an operator could use information from a physician's smart badge to route the call to the phone nearest his location. This smart badge from Versus Technology also includes a button that can be programmed to send a message to a pager, open a locked door, or perform another task.

Justice on the Electronic Frontier

Federal and state governments have responded to the growing computer crime problem by creating new laws against electronic trespassing and by escalating enforcement efforts. Hackers have become targets for nationwide anticrime operations. Some of the victims of these sting operations claim that they broke no laws. In one case a student was arrested because he published an electronic magazine that carried a description of an emergency 911 system allegedly stolen by hackers. Charges were eventually dropped when it was revealed that the "stolen" document was, in fact, available to the public.

Cases such as this raise questions about how civil rights apply in the "electronic frontier." How does the Bill of Rights apply to computer communications? Does freedom of the press apply to blogs and Web forums in the same way it applies to paper periodicals? Can an Internet service provider be held responsible for dangerous information or illegally traded music posted on their servers by their customers? Can online pornography be served from a house located in a neighborhood with antiporn laws? If a teenage girl "texts" nude pictures of herself to a boy or man, should the recipient be prosecuted as a sex offender?

Laws such as the Telecommunications Act of 1996 attempt to deal with these kinds of questions by outlining exactly what kinds of digital communications are legal. Unfortunately, these laws generally raise as many questions as they answer. Shortly after its passage, a major section of the Telecommunications Act, called the Communications Decency Act, was declared unconstitutional by the Supreme Court. A narrower Children's Internet Protection Act (CIPA), requiring federally funded libraries to use Internet filtering software, passed in 2000 and was upheld by the Supreme Court in 2004. Since then, other bills have been introduced to attach more legal boundaries to the rapidly changing world of telecommunications. The debates continue inside and outside of the courts.

The Digital Millennium Copyright Act of 1998 (discussed in Chapter 4) hasn't (so far) been found unconstitutional, but it has resulted in several lawsuits that raise serious human rights questions. In the summer of 2001, a Russian programmer and graduate student named Dmitry Sklyarov was arrested by the FBI after he spoke at a computer security conference in Las Vegas. His alleged crime was writing—not using—a program that cracks Adobe's copy protection scheme for e-books. After a Webwide demonstration against the arrest, Adobe publicly came out in favor of freeing Sklyarov.

The same law was used to silence Professor Edward Felton in 2001. The Princeton University computer scientist was threatened with a lawsuit from the Recording Industry Association of America if he presented a paper analyzing the system that encodes digital music; he withdrew the paper. Several months later, Felton published the paper, and the RIAA recanted its threat but not its right to threaten similar suits in the future.

The DMCA was even used to file a suit against *2600* magazine because of a single Web site link. A Norwegian 15-year-old had written code allowing DVD movies to be played on

Linux computers—code that broke the DVD encryption scheme. *2600*'s Web site included a link to another site containing the program. (The *New York Times* Web site contained a link to the same site but was not sued by the recording industry.)

When the U.S. Congress passed the Telecommunications Act of 1996 and the Digital Millennium Copyright Act of 1998, it was attempting to make U.S. law more responsive to the issues of the digital age. But each of these laws introduced new problems by

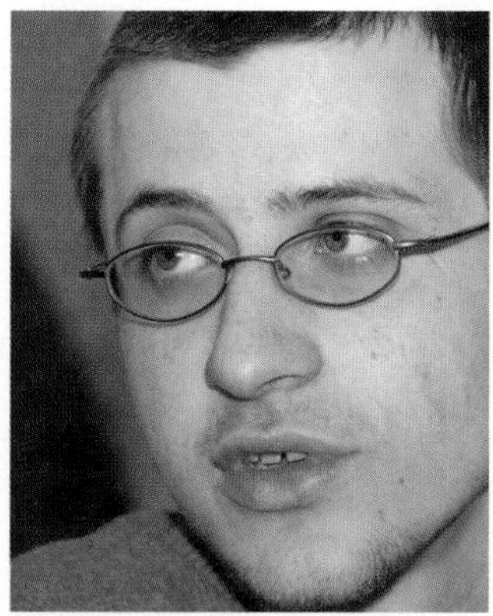

Norwegian teenager Jon Johansen released the computer program DeCSS, which enabled Linux computers to play movies stored on DVDs. The program violated the Digital Millennium Copyright Act's prohibition against circumventing encryption measures. Norwegian authorities twice prosecuted Johansen, but he was acquitted both times.

German teenager Sven Jaschan created the Sasser worm, which infected about 18 million Windows computers, disrupting operations at Delta Air Lines, Australian railroads, and other businesses. A juvenile court sentenced Jaschan to one and a half years' probation and 30 hours of community service.

Briton Philip Cummings worked for Teledata Communications (TCI), an American company that makes instant credit-check devices for banks, car dealers, and other businesses. He participated in an identity-theft ring that affected 30,000 people. After pleading guilty, Cummings was sentenced to 14 years in federal prison.

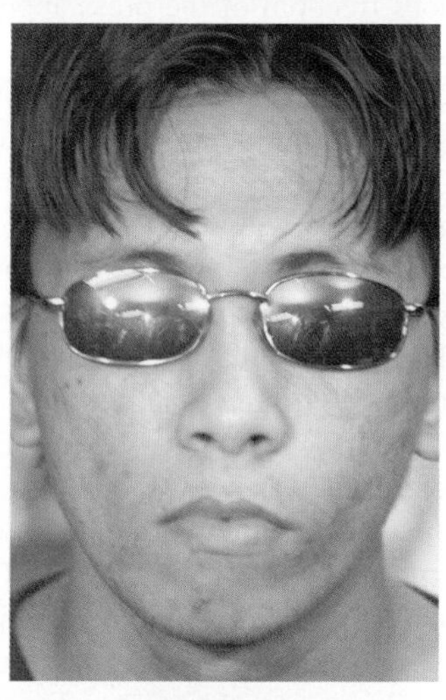

Filipino computer science student Onel de Guzman allegedly wrote The Love Bug virus, which infected millions of computers worldwide. At the time the virus was created, the Philippines had no laws against computer hacking, and he was never prosecuted.

American David L. Smith created the Melissa virus and posted it online using a stolen AOL account. The virus infected hundreds of thousands of computers. Smith was sentenced to 20 months in federal prison, required to do 100 hours of community service, and fined $5,000.

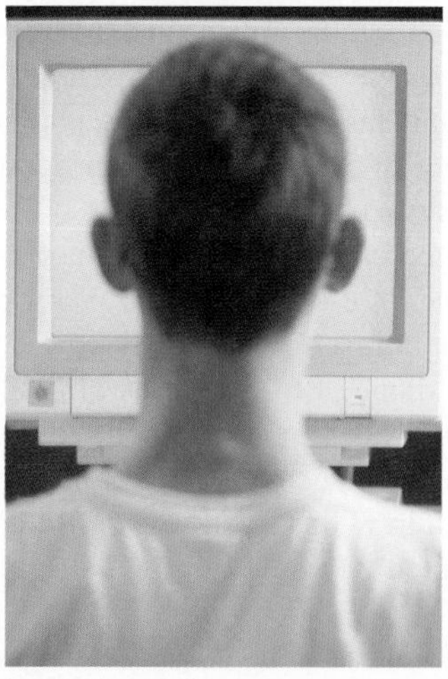

American Jeanson J. Ancheta created the Trojan horse program rxbot, which spread to thousands of Internet-connected computers. He sold access to infected computers to customers who used them to distribute spam or launch distributed-denial-of-service attacks. He was sentenced to 57 months in federal prison. In addition, he paid $15,000 in restitution and surrendered his computers, a car, and $60,000 in cash.

FIGURE 10.20 Some computer hackers have paid a stiff price for their activities; others have not.

threatening rights of citizens—problems that have to be solved by courts and by future lawmakers. These laws illustrate the difficulty lawmakers face when protecting rights in a world of rapid technological change.

Security and Reliability

> If the automobile had followed the same development cycle as the computer, a **Rolls Royce would today cost $100, get a million miles per gallon, and explode once a year,** killing everyone inside.
>
> *—Robert X. Cringely, PBS computer curmudgeon*

So far our discussion of security has focused mainly on protecting computer systems from trespassing, sabotage, and other crimes. But security involves more than criminal activity. Some of the most important security issues have to do with creating systems that can withstand software errors and hardware glitches.

Bugs and Breakdowns

Computer systems, like all machines, are vulnerable to fires, floods, and other natural disasters, as well as breakdowns caused by the failure of hardware components. But in modern computers, hardware problems are relatively rare when compared with software failures. By any measure, bugs do more damage than viruses and computer burglars put together. Here are a few horror stories:

- A new laboratory computer system became backlogged the day after it was installed at the Los Angeles County–USC Medical Center in April 2003. Emergency room doctors, who could not get the test results they needed, instructed the County of Los Angeles to stop sending ambulances. One doctor said, "It's almost like practicing Third World medicine. We rely so much on our computers and our fast-world technology that we were almost blinded."
- In 2001 a bug in a new billing system led Qwest to charge some of its cell phone customers as much as $600 per minute. About 14,000 customers received incorrect bills, including one customer whose monthly statement asked her to pay $57,346.20.
- In 2006 NASA's Mars Global Surveyor software received a missent command from Earth, apparently assumed (incorrectly) that a motor had failed, and pointed one of its batteries toward the sun, causing it to overheat and fail. The mission had to be abandoned as a result.
- In 2007 two separate cascading computer failures—one in air traffic controller systems, one in U.S. Customs systems—caused massive delays for travellers while the systems were repaired.
- For a short while in 2009, every site in every Google search was flagged with the ominous message "This site may harm your computer." The bug was traced to a single mistyped "/" in a single message.

The most famous bug of all time—the Y2K (year 2000) bug, or millennium bug—caused many people around the world to think seriously about software errors for the first time. For decades, programmers commonly built two-digit date fields into programs to save storage space, thinking they had no reason to allow space for the first two digits because they never changed. But when 1999 ended, those digits did change, making many of those ancient programs unstable or unusable. Businesses and governments spent more than $100 billion rewriting and replacing software to head off Y2K disasters. People bought generators and guns, stockpiled food and water, and prepared for a collapse of the computer-controlled utility grids that keep our economy running. When the fateful day arrived, the Y2K bug caused scattered problems, ranging from credit card refusals to malfunctioning spy satellites. But for most people, January 1, 2000, was business as usual. It's debatable whether disasters were averted by billions of dollars worth of preventive maintenance, or whether the Y2K scare stories were overblown. The truth

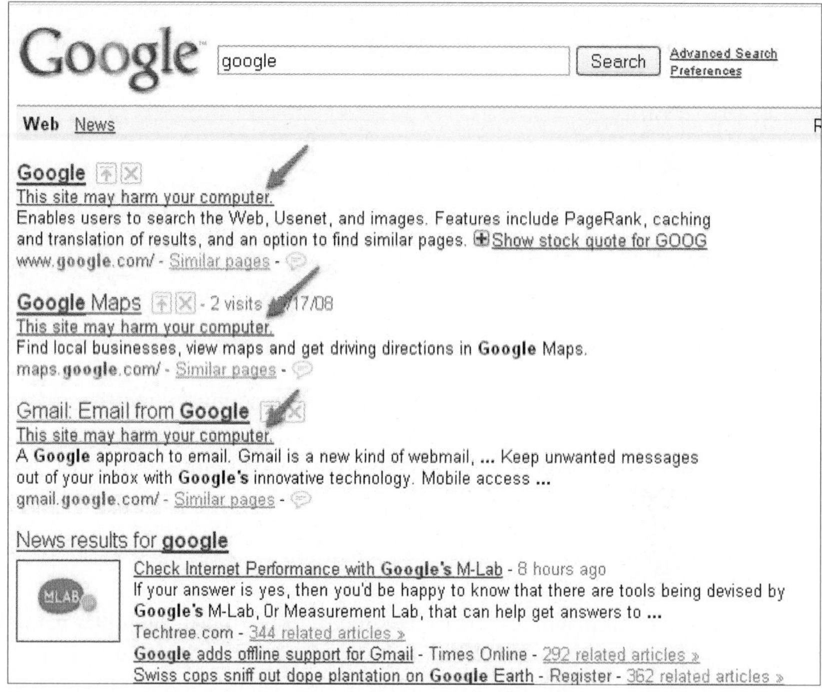

FIGURE 10.21 For several hours in January of 2010, a bug in Google's search engine caused it to identify bogus malware threats in its own sites.

is undoubtedly somewhere between these two extremes. In any event, Y2K raised the public's consciousness about its dependence on fickle, fragile technology.

Given the state of the art of programming today, three facts are clear:

1. It's impossible to eliminate all bugs. Today's programs are constructed of thousands of tiny pieces, any one of which can cause a failure if it's incorrectly coded.
2. Even programs that appear to work can contain dangerous bugs. Some bugs are easy to detect and correct because they're obvious. The most dangerous bugs are difficult to detect and may go unnoticed by users for months or years.
3. The bigger the system, the bigger the problem. Large programs are far more complex and difficult to debug than small programs are, and the trend today is clearly toward large programs. Windows 7 alone has millions of lines of code, and each application adds more code to the mix.

As we entrust complex computerized systems to do everything from financial transaction processing to air traffic control, the potential cost of computer failure goes up. In the past decade, researchers have identified hundreds of cases in which disruptions to computer system operations posed some risk to the public, and the number of incidents has doubled every two years.

Computers at War

> Massive networking makes the U.S. the **world's most vulnerable target.**
>
> *—John McConnell, former NSA director*

Nowhere are the issues surrounding security and reliability more critical than in military applications. To carry out its mission effectively, the military must be sure its systems are secure against enemy surveillance and attack. At the same time, many modern military applications push the limits of information technology farther than they've ever been before.

Smart Weapons

FIGURE 10.22 Today's unmanned combat aircraft are controlled by somebody on the ground—possibly thousands of miles away. A Pentagon planning paper suggests that in the year 2020 one-third of all U.S. combat aircraft will be autonomous.

The United States has invested billions of dollars in the development of smart weapons—missiles that use computerized guidance systems to locate their targets. A command-guidance system enables a human operator to control the missile's path while watching a missile's-eye view of the target on a television screen. Using infrared heat-seeking devices or visual pattern recognition technology, a missile with a homing guidance system can track a moving target without human help. Weapons that use "smart" guidance systems can be extremely accurate in pinpointing enemy targets under most circumstances. In theory, smart weapons can greatly reduce the amount of civilian destruction in war if everything is working properly.

Computer technology is also used in unmanned aerial vehicles (UAVs), including the robot drones employed by the U.S. military to locate and destroy enemy outposts in Iraq, Afghanistan, and Pakistan. Drones have been used to track enemy movements, patrol for enemy troops, scan for explosives, and make first assaults in particularly difficult or dangerous battle situations. UAVs receive GPS and other data from vast military communications networks. A small drone typically sends images and receives commands from a laptop with a nearby ground unit. A larger drone might be controlled by a gunner or bombardier safely tucked away in a control center on the other side of the globe.

The U.S. and other countries have invested billions of dollars in smart weapons and UAVs in recent years. The tactical advantages are obvious: they can increase targeting accuracy, decrease civilian casualties, protect troops from dangerous situations, and penetrate regions that are difficult to reach with traditional military hardware.

But smart weaponry doesn't come without risks. Warfare is a messy business, and even the most sophisticated pattern recognition technology can make mistakes. UAVs have misidentified targets and killed innocent civilians, making enemies of the populations they were charged with protecting. Critics argue that these kinds of mistakes are all too easy to make when the person at the controls is pulling the trigger in a comfortable chair thousands of miles away from the kill zone.

High-tech weaponry was initially used to the advantage of the U.S. and the U.N. in wars against insurgents in the Middle East, but there are serious questions about what happens when that same technology falls into the hands of insurgents or terrorists. In 2010 the public learned that Iraqi insurgents had used $30 worth of software purchased on the Internet to tap into UAV video feeds, enabling them to see what the drones were seeing. And experts have pointed out that inexpensive unmanned drones might soon replace suicide bombers as weapons of choice in terrorist attacks.

Another problem with high-tech weapons is that they reduce the amount of time people have to make life-and-death decisions. As decision-making time goes down, the chances of making errors goes up. In one tragic example, an American guided missile cruiser on a peacetime mission in the Persian Gulf used a computerized Aegis fleet defense system to shoot down an Iranian Airbus containing 290 civilians. The decision to fire was made by well-intentioned humans, but those humans had little time—and used ambiguous data—to make the decision.

Autonomous Systems

Even more controversial is the possibility of people being left out of the decision-making loop altogether. Yet the trend in military research is clearly toward weapons that demand almost instantaneous responses—the kind that only computers can make. An autonomous system is a complex system that can assume almost complete responsibility for a task without human input, verification, or decision making.

The most famous and controversial autonomous system is the missile defense system that has been under development with several different names and designs since first conceived and funded in the 1980s. The system would, in theory, use a network of laser-equipped satellites and/or ground-based stations to detect and destroy attacking missiles before they have time to reach their targets. Such a system would have to be able to react almost instantaneously, without human intervention. Computers would have no time to wait for the president to declare war, and no time for human experts to analyze the perceived attack.

The automated missile defense system has generated intense public debates about false alarms, hardware feasibility, constitutional issues, and the ethics of autonomous weapons. But for many who understand the limitations of computers, the biggest issue is software reliability. The system can't be completely tested in advance because there's no way to simulate accurately the unpredictable conditions of a global war. Yet to work effectively, the system would have to be absolutely reliable. In a tightly coupled worldwide network, a single bug could multiply and expand like a speed-of-light cancer. A small error could result in a major disaster. Many software engineers have pointed out that absolute reliability simply isn't possible now or in the foreseeable future.

Supporters of automated missile defense systems argue that the technical difficulties can be overcome in time, and the U.S. government continues to invest billions in research toward that end. Whether a "smart shield" is ever completed, it has focused public attention on critical issues related to security and reliability.

Cyberwarfare and Cyberterrorism

Even as the U.S. government spends billions of dollars on smart weapons and missile defense systems, many military experts suggest that future wars may not be fought in the air, on land, or at sea. The front lines of the future may, instead, be in cyberspace. By attacking through vast interconnected computer networks, an enemy government or terrorist group could cripple telecommunications systems, power grids, banking and financial systems, hospitals and medical systems, water and gas supplies, oil pipelines, and emergency government services, without firing a shot.

Such a scenario isn't far-out sci-fi speculation. According to former U.S. Director of National Intelligence Mike McConnell, "The United States is fighting a cyberwar today, and we are losing." Several examples highlight our vulnerability:

- In 2007, an unknown foreign attacker broke into U.S. government computer systems and stole several terabytes of data—roughly the amount of information stored in the Library of Congress.
- In 2008 hackers shut down Georgian government, media, and banking Web sites at the same time Russian troops were engaging Georgian soldiers in battle. U.S. intelligence agreed with the Georgian President that the Russian government, aided by a high-tech crime syndicate, was probably behind these carefully timed cyberattacks.
- Hackers in China penetrated the emails and computer files of both major U.S. presidential candidates in the 2008 election, presumably to gain political leverage after the election.
- In 2008 malware, introduced via thumb drives scattered around the parking lot of a Florida command center, infected several thousand military computers.
- In 2009 South Korean and U.S. government and corporate Web sites were attacked by hackers who may have been based in North Korea.
- In 2009 Google and more than 30 other U.S. companies lost technological secrets as a result of Chinese cyberattacks. The attackers apparently had political as well as economic motives; they searched Google files for private data about Tibetan human rights activists. The U.S. National Security Agency teamed up with Google to investigate the security breakdown.
- In 2010 the Stuxnet computer worm infected at least 15 industrial plants in several countries—most notably, Iran. The worm had the potential to locate and control equipment in industrial facilities—possibly even causing explosions in pipelines or power plants. Experts speculated that the worm was created by a team of specialists, possibly working undercover for a government.

These types of attacks happen far more often than most people suspect. Pentagon computers are subject to thousands of attacks every day. Thankfully, none of these

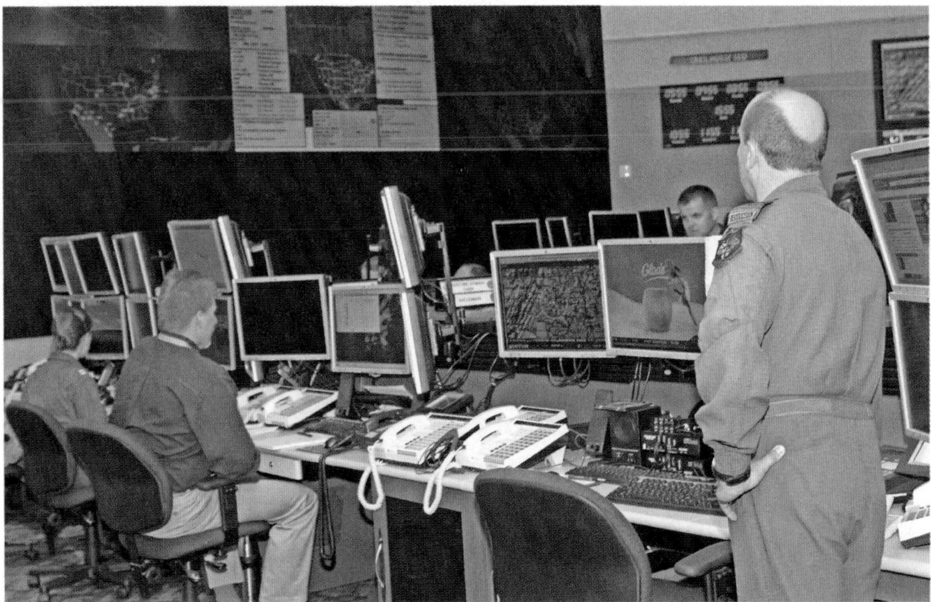

FIGURE 10.23 In modern weapons systems, such as those used by the North America Aerospace Defense Control (NORAD) in its Cheyenne Mountain Complex in Colorado Springs, Colorado, computers are critical components in the command and control process.

crimes resulted in serious damage or injury. But terrorists, spies, or criminals could use similar techniques to trigger major disasters. According to computer security expert Richard Clarke, "The difference between cybercrime, cyber-espionage, and cyberwar is a couple of keystrokes."

Clarke and others believe that the next big war will be waged at least in part in cyberspace. There's no doubt that China, the U.S., and other nations have invested time, energy, and money preparing for future information wars. So far, though, military strategists know far more about cyberoffense than cyberdefense. It's especially difficult defending against lightning-fast infrastructure attacks when the source of the attacks is almost impossible to pinpoint.

The U.S. government has, through several administrations, attempted to prepare for potential attacks on the American information infrastructure. But any effort to protect the infrastructure must have corporate participation, because private companies own many of the critical systems that are most vulnerable to attack. Unfortunately, many businesses are slow to recognize the potential threat. They embrace the efficiency that networks bring, but they don't adequately prepare for attack through those networks.

Network attacks are all but inevitable, and such attacks can have disastrous consequences for all of us. In a world where computers control everything from money to missiles, computer security and reliability are too important to ignore.

Is Security Possible?

Computer thieves. Hackers. Software pirates. Computer snoopers. Viruses. Worms. Trojan horses. Spybots. Wiretaps. Hardware failures. Software bugs. When we live and work with computers, we're exposed to all kinds of risks that didn't exist in the precomputer era. These risks make computer security especially important and challenging.

Because computers do so many amazing things so well, it's easy to overlook the problems they bring with them and to believe that they're invincible. But today's computers hide the potential for errors and deception under an impressive user interface. This doesn't mean we should avoid using computers, only that we should remain skeptical, cautious, and realistic as we use them. Security procedures can reduce but not eliminate risks. In today's fast-moving world, absolute security simply isn't possible.

Human Questions for a Computer Age

> The important thing to forecast is **not the automobile but the parking problem; not the television but the soap opera.**
>
> *—Isaac Asimov, Author*

We've examined many social and ethical issues related to computer technology, including privacy, security, reliability, and intellectual property. These aren't the only critical issues before us. Before closing we'll briefly raise some other important, and as yet unanswered, questions of the information age.

Will Computers Be Democratic?

> **The higher the technology, the higher the freedom.** Technology enforces certain solutions: satellite dishes, computers, videos, international telephone lines force pluralism and freedom onto a society.
>
> *—Lech Walesa, former President of Poland and Nobel Peace Prize Winner*

In 1999 environmentalists, labor organizations, human rights groups, and a handful of anarchists used the Internet to mobilize massive protests at the World Trade Organization's Seattle meeting. The protests brought many issues surrounding the secretive WTO into the global spotlight for the first time. In 2005 dozens of soldiers in Iraq created blogs chronicling their experiences. The blogs reflected a wide spectrum of ideological beliefs and provided news-hungry Americans an alternative to mainstream media outlets. After the 2009 Iranian elections, protesters used Facebook, Twitter, and blogs to post photos and videos of marches, organize demonstration, and exchange scripts for temporarily bringing down government Web sites. These sites became the only source of uncensored information about the events in Iran. At the urging of the U.S. State Department, Twitter postponed a system upgrade so that protesters could maintain their communications lifelines during the crisis.

Computers are often used to promote the democratic ideals and causes of common people. Many analysts argue that modern computer technology is, by its very nature, a force for equality and democracy. On the other hand, many powerful people and organizations use information technology to increase their wealth and influence.

Will PCs, smart phones, and the Internet empower ordinary citizens to make better lives for themselves? Or will computer technology produce a society of technocrats and technopeasants? Will computerized polls help elected officials better serve the needs of their constituents? Or will they just give the powerful another tool for staying in power? Will networks revitalize participatory democracy through electronic town meetings? Or will they give tyrants the tools to monitor and control citizens? Will electronic voting technology make elections more accurate? Or will security and reliability problems disenfranchise voters and undermine the democratic process?

FIGURE 10.24 After the 2009 Iranian elections, photos and videos of protests flooded social networking sites.

Will the Global Village Be a Community?

When **machines and computers, profit motives, and property rights are considered more important than people,** the giant triplets of racism, materialism, and militarism are incapable of being conquered.

—The Reverend Martin Luther King, Jr.

A typical computer today contains components from dozens of countries. Information doesn't stop at international borders as it flows through networks that span the globe. Information technology enables businesses and other organizations to overcome the age-old barriers of space and time, but questions remain.

In the post–Cold War era, will information technology be used to further peace, harmony, and understanding? Or will the intense competition of the global marketplace simply create new kinds of wars—information wars? Will electronic interconnections provide new opportunities for economically depressed countries? Or will they simply make it easier for information-rich countries to exploit developing nations from a distance? Will information technology be used to promote and preserve diverse communities, cultures, and ecosystems? Or will it undercut traditions, cultures, and roots?

Are We Becoming Information Slaves?

Our inventions are wont to be pretty toys which distract our attention from serious things. They are but improved means to an unimproved end.

—Henry David Thoreau

The information age has redefined our environment; it's almost as if the human species has been transplanted into a different world. Even though the change has happened almost overnight, most of us can't imagine going back to a world without digital technology. Still, the rapid changes raise questions.

Can human bodies and minds adapt to the higher stimulation, faster pace, and constant change of the information age? Will our information-heavy environment cause us to lose touch with the more fundamental human needs? Will we become so dependent on our "pretty toys" that we can't get by without them? Will we lose our sense of purpose and identity as our machines become more intelligent? Or will we learn to balance the demands of the technology with our biological and spiritual needs?

Standing on the Shoulders of Giants

If I have seen farther than other men, it is because **I stood on the shoulders of giants.**

—Isaac Newton

When we use computers, we're standing on the shoulders of Charles Babbage, Ada Lovelace, George Boole, Alan Turing, Doug Engelbart, Alan Kay, Steve Jobs, Bill Gates, and hundreds of others who invented the future for us. Because of their foresight and effort, we can see farther than those who came before us.

In Greek mythology Prometheus (whose name means "forethought") stole fire from Zeus and gave it to humanity, along with all arts and civilization. Zeus was furious when he discovered what Prometheus had done. He feared that fire would make mortals think they were as great as the gods and that they would abuse its power. Like fire, the computer is a powerful and malleable tool. It can be used to empower or imprison, to explore or exploit, to create or destroy. We can choose. We've been given the tools. It's up to all of us to invent the future.

Inventing the Future ▸ Evolving Technology, Evolving Security

The relentless advance of digital technology spurs innovation and invention in almost every other field. Computer technology made the Internet possible, and the Internet made real-time global communication and collaboration possible. Researchers and designers around the planet leverage the power of computers and the Internet to produce breakthroughs in science, medicine, design, commerce, and engineering. We all benefit from these breakthroughs, but not without a cost in security.

LAYERED MALWARE DEFENSES

The same Internet that makes it possible for geologists or filmmakers to carry on trans-global conversations also delivers malware at lightning speeds. The Sapphire worm infected 90 percent of the vulnerable hosts worldwide in less than 10 minutes. Future worms may spread globally in less than a minute. That's not nearly enough time for humans to get involved in stopping them. Instead, network developers are devising automated systems to thwart attacks.

Organizations with large networks will need a *layered defense*. On the perimeter of the network a hardware firewall, augmented with network intrusion detection software, will prevent dangerous packets from entering the organization's networks. Pattern-recognition software will help the system distinguish between legitimate and illegitimate network access attempts. Automated systems will cope with worms and viruses that penetrate their networks. Researchers are developing reconfigurable hardware that can quarantine infected subnets so worms that break through outer defense layers are kept from spreading throughout the entire organization. Special-purpose hardware called *security processors* will allow every message to be encrypted—even huge video streams. Better programming languages, combined with a greater attention to security-related issues by software developers, should result in future operating systems and applications that contain fewer security holes.

THE PEOPLE PROBLEM

Unfortunately, no amount of technological fixing can completely eliminate malware problems. The human element is the weak link in many security systems. People continue to spread viruses by opening email attachments from unknown sources. An experiment in London showed that many people would reveal their computer passwords in return for pens. Employees bring infected notebooks, flash drives, and smart phones to work and unknowingly spread viruses and worms through company networks.

There are clear trade-offs between security and convenience. Consumers are unlikely to purchase software that is 100 percent secure but lacks essential features. So software developers must balance the time they spend on security against the time they spend adding features. Extreme security may make a network so difficult to use that it hurts the productivity of the people who use it.

A rising onslaught of malware and spam could tip the scales toward security and put the openness of the Internet in peril. System administrators can't afford to spend all of their time eradicating malware, and users don't want to spend their time deleting spam messages from their inboxes. The entire Internet community—users, programmers, hardware designers, system administrators, and managers—will help determine whether the Internet will remain a place of relatively free and open information exchange.

BIOHACKING

There's no obvious end to the war between computer hackers and security experts. The worlds of biology and medicine may soon be plagued by hacker wars, too. As a result of the creation of synthetic DNA, **biohackers** can modify and create organisms in home laboratories. Many biohackers have hopes of curing diseases or finding new biofuels. Others have less admirable goals. Regardless of intentions, biohackers raise concerns among many scientists.

The easy accessibility of *synthetic DNA* is at the heart of these concerns. So far, most garage biologists playing around with synthetic DNA are simply adding a gene or two to an existing organism—a fairly standard, relatively safe scientific practice involving some test-tube mixing. But technology will soon enable bioengineers inside and outside of academia to create entire organisms from scratch.

Will biohacking "kits" provide all the tools a hobbyist might need to produce genetically altered life? It's easy to imagine biohacking horror stories. Frankenstein's monster isn't likely to emerge from a suburban basement lab, but what about an invasive species that upsets the ecosystem? What about a biological malware—some kind of toxic virus that could be used by terrorists? What happens when a home-grown organism accidentally—or intentionally—escapes into the wild?

The National Science Advisory Board for Biosecurity has recommended that companies selling DNA be required to screen all orders for signs that the buyers have malevolent goals. Some biologists argue that anyone wishing to create new organisms should have to get a license first. Biohackers argue that people had similar kinds of fears when do-it-yourselfers built the first personal computers in their garages a generation ago.

Are the benefits of the technology worth the risks? The question will be with us as long as people innovate....

FIGURE 10.25 In this garage lab, biohackers search for anticancer compounds.

Crosscurrents

Dark Clouds Gather over Online Security

by Mike Elgan

In late 2009, Google threatened to close its Chinese operations after it was attacked by hackers. In this article, first published in Computerworld *on January 29, 2010 (and edited here for space), columnist Mike Elgan exposes the dark cloud that lurks behind this story—a cloud that isn't likely to go away anytime soon.*

Google may have threatened to leave China in order to keep us all from concluding that "the cloud" can't be secured. But isn't that precisely what we should conclude based on the fact that Google chose to leave China? Why didn't Google just fix the flaw and keep its mouth shut? Google may have realized that it can't guarantee the security of its secrets—or yours.

What does Google know about you? Depending on which Google services you use, Google might know your exact location, what your e-mail says, what you buy online, what your schedule is, who you know, what your credit card numbers are, where you live, where all your friends and family live, what your interests are, what you read, what your voice mail messages say, who you talk to on the phone, the details of your health problems, your medical history, and much more. Google even offers a service which makes a copy of all your e-mail from Outlook or other desktop utilities and puts it into Google Apps, where it's backed-up and searchable. It also offers a service whereby you can upload any file to Google Apps.

Theoretically, all this personal information is safe. Although Google "knows" all of your information, no human would ever read it. Besides, do you trust Google with your information? I do.

Unfortunately, if the China event tells us that the cloud can't be secured, it doesn't matter whether we trust Google or not. We would have to trust both hackers and anyone they might sell our private data to.

Review that list of what Google "knows" about you. Now imagine what others could do with that information: insurance companies, our government, "their" government, marketers, predatory financial services companies—not to mention blackmailers, identity thieves and extortionists.

Of course, hacking is nothing new. A recent survey by the Center for Strategic and International Studies found that more than half of IT executives report "high level" attacks on their companies. The difference with cloud computing is that a cloud service like Google's could offer one-stop shopping for hackers. If they hack one company, they have one company. But if that company is Google, they have everybody.

And it gets worse.

There are three general theories about the Chinese government's role in the hacking of Google, which involved both the theft of Google's intellectual property and the unauthorized access of Gmail accounts of critics of the Chinese government. One theory is that the government perpetrated the crime. Another is that the government had nothing to do with the crime. A third possibility is that the crime was committed on the government's behalf by freelance hackers looking to make money. Of these three, the third possibility is by far the most threatening.

I think it's very likely that espionage—industrial and otherwise—will become a massive industry. Organized crime gangs will increasingly automate the harvesting of personal data, then later figure out where to sell it. This already happens, but I think we're facing a rapid increase in both scale and sophistication.

Freelance industrial spies, following the suspected Chinese model, could launch multipronged, surgical strikes or simultaneous attacks on very large numbers of individual accounts. The targets could include the largest corporations as well as individual citizens. One of the targets in the Google China hack was a 20-year-old Stanford University sophomore who is active in a student organization called Students for a Free Tibet. That's right. An American student exercising her First Amendment right to free speech in the U.S. may have been targeted by the Chinese Communist Party as a threat, and as a subject for monitoring.

The state of the art (according to reports analyzing the Chinese attacks on Google) is to first target individuals within an organization who have access to sensitive and valuable secrets. The next step is to send the targeted people fake e-mails with documents attached and make them appear to be legitimate messages from colleagues. Once opened, the documents install software that invisibly executes commands that give the hacker access to the machine (and the user's network privileges). From there, the attackers could find and copy source code and other secrets.

Welcome to the new reality. It seems as if everyone is moving everything to the cloud. Meanwhile, sophisticated organizations out there are figuring out how to exploit cloud vulnerabilities to harvest valuable secrets. And if Google can't stop them, what chance do you or I have?

It's time to rethink the headlong rush into the cloud. We don't yet understand what's waiting there for us.

Discussion Questions

1. What do you think can be done to prevent this kind of digital espionage?
2. How much of your information is stored in the cloud? Do you think it's secure?

Summary

Computers, networks, and databases play an ever-increasing role in fighting crime. At the same time, law enforcement organizations are facing an increase in computer crime—crimes accomplished through special knowledge of computer technology. Most computer crimes go undetected, and those that are detected often go unreported. But by any estimate, computer crime costs billions of dollars every year.

Many computer criminals use computers and the Internet to steal intellectual property. Many steal credit card numbers and other sensitive information that can be used for financial gain. Some steal entire identities. Others use Trojan horses, viruses, worms, logic bombs, and other types of malware to sabotage systems. According to the media, computer crimes are committed by young, bright computer wizards called hackers. Research suggests, however, that stereotypical hackers are responsible for only a small fraction of computer crimes. The typical computer criminal is a trusted employee with personal or financial problems and knowledge of the computer system. A growing number of crimes are committed by international crime rings with or without government connections. Some types of computer crimes, including software piracy, are committed by everyday computer users who don't realize—or choose not to recognize—that they're committing crimes.

Because of rising computer crime and other risks, organizations have developed a number of computer security techniques to protect their systems and data. Some security devices, such as keys and badges, are designed to restrict physical access to computers. But these tools are less effective in an age of networked PCs. Passwords, encryption, shielding, and audit-control software are all used to protect sensitive data in various organizations. When all else fails, backups of important data are used to reconstruct systems after damage occurs. A comprehensive backup strategy involves several different types of backups for maximum security. The most effective security solutions depend on people at least as much as on technology.

Normally, security measures serve to protect our privacy and other individual rights. But occasionally, security procedures threaten those rights. The trade-offs between computer security and freedom raise important legal and ethical questions.

Computer systems aren't threatened only by criminals; they're also threatened by software bugs and hardware glitches. An important part of security is protecting systems and the people affected by those systems from the consequences of those bugs and glitches. Because our society uses computers for many applications that put lives and livelihoods at stake, reliability issues are especially important.

In modern military applications, security and reliability are critical. As the speed, power, and complexity of weapons systems increase, many fear that humans are being squeezed out of the decision-making loop. The debate over high-tech weaponry is bringing many important security issues to the public's attention for the first time. Some of the most powerful weapons in future wars will be software and hardware tools for disabling or destroying the information infrastructure we've come to depend on.

Key Terms

access-control software ....(p. 371)
antivirus software ....(p. 367)
autonomous systems.............(p. 385)
backup ....(p. 376)
biohackers.............................(p. 390)
biometrics.............................(p. 370)
bot..(p. 369)
botnets ....(p. 369)
computer crime.....................(p. 361)
computer forensics ....(p. 361)
computer security ....(p. 369)
cybercrime............................(p. 361)
denial-of-service (DoS) attack ....(p. 369)
encryption.............................(p. 373)
firewall.................................(p. 371)
hacking ....(p. 368)
identity theft ....(p. 362)
logic bomb............................(p. 366)
malware ....(p. 363)
passwords ....(p. 371)
phishing ....(p. 363)
sabotage................................(p. 363)
security patch........................(p. 367)
smart weapons ....(p. 385)
social engineering..................(p. 363)
spoofing ....(p. 363)
spyware.................................(p. 366)
system administrator ....(p. 371)
Trojan horse..........................(p. 366)
uninterruptible power supply (UPS) ....(p. 376)
virus.....................................(p. 363)
worms ....(p. 365)

Companion Website Projects

1. The *Digital Planet* Web site, **www.pearsonhighered.com/beekman**, contains self-test exercises related to this chapter. Follow the instructions for taking a quiz. After you've completed your quiz, you can email the results to your instructor.
2. The Web site also contains open-ended discussion questions called Internet Exercises. Discuss one or more of the Internet Exercises questions at the section for this chapter.

True or False

1. Computer crimes often go unreported because businesses fear that they can lose more from negative publicity than from the actual crimes.
2. The majority of computer crimes are committed by hackers and vandals with no ties to the victim companies.
3. Organized crime and terrorist organizations aren't likely to commit computer crimes because they don't have the expertise.
4. In general, computer viruses don't discriminate among operating systems; a typical virus can infect any system, regardless of platform.
5. On a multiple-user PC every user needs to log in before system patches can be installed.
6. Because of the way Windows works, it's not possible to back up files to more than one drive or device without reinstalling the OS.
7. U.S. courts have ruled that an employer cannot read an employee's email, even if it is stored on a company-owned computer.
8. One reason modern operating systems are difficult to debug is they contain millions of lines of code.
9. While many questions remain about the viability of an automated missile defense system, computer scientists are confident that the software for the system will be reliable.
10. The next major war will probably involve some kind of cyberattacks.

Multiple Choice

1. Which of these passwords is most likely to prevent intruders from logging into your personal online bank account?
   a. Ib4ExptaC
   b. 12345678
   c. Your first initial followed by your last name
   d. password
   e. qwerty
2. Which of these words means "tricking" or "fooling?"
   a. Fishing
   b. Cracking
   c. Hacking
   d. Spoofing
   e. DDoS
3. What do you call a piece of code that attaches to an application program and secretly spreads when the application program is executed?
   a. Virus
   b. Worm
   c. Trojan horse
   d. Spybot
   e. DoS
4. A network of bots can be used for
   a. DDoS attacks.
   b. spamming.
   c. phishing.
   d. Any or all of the above
   e. None of the above; by definition, bots are nonfunctional.

5. Social engineering
   a. is the type of software engineering used to develop social networking applications.
   b. can have a big negative impact on a PC's system performance.
   c. is one of the fastest growing branches of civil engineering.
   d. can't be conducted without a computer.
   e. is a common precursor to identity theft.

6. What do you call a program that performs a useful task while at the same time carrying out some secret destructive act?
   a. DDoS
   b. Worm
   c. Trojan horse
   d. Macro virus
   e. None of the above

7. A PC's system software can be modified
   a. by any user with a legitimate password.
   b. by any user with system administrator access.
   c. by any user with a broadband Internet connection.
   d. only when the system is shut down.
   e. All of the above

8. What are biometrics often used for?
   a. To measure virus strength
   b. To measure the speed of a spreading worm
   c. To assess the power of a Trojan horse to bring down a computer system
   d. To identify personnel before allowing them to have access to computer systems
   e. None of the above

9. Which of these factors minimizes the likelihood that a virus attack can rapidly spread and do widespread damage to an organization's computer infrastructure?
   a. All of the PCs in the organization use exactly the same Windows software and applications.
   b. Security patches are installed on the operating system exactly once each year to minimize the chance of an attack during installation.
   c. The system firewall is turned on at night for security and turned off during the day to facilitate communication.
   d. All of the above
   e. None of the above

10. A distributed denial of service (DDoS) attack
    a. was used in one of the decisive battles of the Vietnam War, the first war to use Internet technology.
    b. requires an unmanned aerial vehicle (UAV).
    c. can be launched from thousands of miles away using a botnet.
    d. must, by definition, be part of a larger cyberwar.
    e. All of the above are true about DDoS.

11. What can a surge protector protect a system from?
    a. Viruses
    b. Distributed denial-of-service (DDoS) attacks
    c. Power spikes
    d. Trojan horses and worms
    e. All of the above

12. Which of these statements is true about bugs in computer software today?
    a. It's impossible to eliminate all bugs in a large program.
    b. Even a program that appears to work can contain dangerous bugs.
    c. The bigger the system, the higher the number of bugs.
    d. All of the above
    e. None of the above

13. Autonomous systems
    a. are computers capable of running on battery power.
    b. can perform tasks without human input.
    c. are programs that can run on more than one operating system.
    d. are impossible to construct.
    e. have been outlawed by Congress.

14. The most secure backup system is
    a. an off-site backup system.
    b. an incremental backup system.
    c. an archival backup system.
    d. a bootable clone backup system.
    e. a combination of all of the above.

15. Which of the following have had systems broken into by hackers?
    a. Google's Chinese division
    b. The U.S. Department of Defense
    c. U.S. presidential candidates
    d. Governments of Estonia and Georgia
    e. All of the above

Review Questions

1. Define or describe each of the key terms listed in the "Key Terms" section. Check your answers using the glossary.
2. Why is it hard to estimate the extent of computer crime?
3. Describe several different types of malware.
4. Give some examples of how spoofing or other types of social engineering might be used by computer criminals.
5. Describe several things you can do to protect yourself from identity theft.
6. Give several examples of *bad* passwords, and explain why they are bad.
7. Describe a practical backup system for a home computer system. What kind of hardware, software, and services does it require?
8. It the world of cyberwarfare, why is defense so much harder than offense?
9. In what ways can computer security protect the privacy of individuals? In what ways can computer security threaten the privacy of individuals?
10. What are smart weapons? How do they differ from conventional weapons? What are the advantages and risks of smart weapons?

Discussion Questions

1. Are computers morally neutral? Explain your answer.
2. Some virus creators claim that they're providing a valuable service to society by pointing out security holes in systems. Do you accept this argument? Why or why not?
3. How has the meaning of *hacker* changed since the early days of the computer era?
4. Some people think all mail messages should be encrypted. They argue that if everything is encrypted, the encrypted message won't stand out, so everybody's right to privacy will be better protected. Others suggest that this would just improve the cover of criminals with something to hide from the government. What do you think, and why?
5. Would you like to work in a business where all employees were required to wear smart badges? Explain your answer.
6. How do the issues raised in the debate over the missile defense system apply to other large software systems? How do you feel about the different issues raised in the debate?
7. Some people fear that smart weapons make it too easy to commit acts of war or terrorism by removing the killer from the scene of the killing? Others argue that smart weapons can reduce collateral damage because of intelligent targeting. What is your opinion?
8. Choose two or more of the questions from the section "Human Questions for a Computer Age." How would you answer those questions based on what you know now?

Projects

1. Talk to employees at your campus computer labs and computer centers about security issues and techniques. What are the major security threats according to these employees? What security techniques are used to protect the equipment and data in each facility? Are these techniques adequate? Report on your findings.
2. Perform the same kind of interviews at local businesses. Do businesses view security differently than your campus personnel does?
3. You probably have several login names and passwords for email accounts, social networks, and online stores. For one or more of these accounts, try changing your password. Will the system let you change your password to a common word such as *love* or *fish*? Does the system set a minimum number of characters for passwords? Are you allowed to have a letters-only password, or are you required to include nonalphabetic characters? How do the password security requirements compare?

Sources and Resources

Books

Ethics for the Information Age, by Michael J. Quinn (Addison Wesley). This book, written by the former *Digital Planet* coauthor, presents a framework for ethical decision making and uses that framework to evaluate a wide variety of information- and technology-related issues. Major topics covered include networks and censorship, intellectual property, privacy, computer and network security, computer reliability, automation, and globalization.

A Gift of Fire: Social, Legal, and Ethical Issues in Computing, by Sara Baase (Prentice-Hall). This popular text offers a thorough, easy-to-read overview of the human questions facing us as a result of the computer revolution: privacy, security, reliability, and accountability, among others.

How Personal and Internet Security Work, by Preston Gralla (Que). This illustrated book applies the successful *How Computers Work* formula to security-related issues. The first, and largest, part of the book focuses on Internet security and privacy, with tips on how to protect yourself from viruses, spam, spyware, and other hazards of the Internet. The second part deals with other privacy and security threats—identity theft, workplace surveillance, DNA matching, biometrics, and more. The words and pictures in this book should open plenty of eyes to the risks posed by digital technology today.

Hackers: Heroes of the Computer Revolution, by Steven Levy (Delta). This book helped bring the word *hackers* into the public's vocabulary. Levy's entertaining account of the golden age of hacking gives a historical perspective to today's antihacker mania.

The Cuckoo's Egg, by Cliff Stoll (Pocket Books). This best-selling book documents the stalking of an early international Internet interloper. Espionage mixes with technology in this folksy, entertaining book.

The Art of Intrusion: The Real Stories Behind the Exploits of Hackers, Intruders, and Deceivers, by Kevin D. Mitnick and William L. Simon (Wiley). This book offers a rare glimpse inside the world of malicious hacking. Mitnick knows this world better than most, and his stories are well told.

The Fugitive Game, by Jonathan Littman (Little, Brown and Company). This book chronicles the capture of Kevin Mitnick, America's number-one criminal hacker. The author cuts through the popular folklore of the time to tell the story as an objective journalist.

Cyberpunk—Outlaws and Hackers on the Computer Frontier, Updated Edition, by Katie Hafner and John Markoff (Simon & Schuster). This book profiles three hackers whose exploits caught the public's attention: Kevin Mitnick, a California cracker who vandalized corporate systems; Pengo, who penetrated U.S. systems for East German espionage purposes; and Robert Morris, Jr., whose Internet worm brought down 6,000 computers in a matter of hours.

The Myths of Security: What the Computer Security Industry Doesn't Want You to Know, by John Viega (O'Reilly). Do you think your PC or Mac is secure? How about your cell phone? Do you think the computer security industry can sell you something to make them secure? This book may make you think again.

Cyber War: The Next Threat to National Security and What to Do About It, by Richard Clarke (Ecco). Clarke has been called the godfather of computer security. It's been said that the United States could have avoided some of its biggest security disasters if the decision makers at the top had listened to him when he worked for them. This book, written in nontechnical terms for the general public, discusses the future of warfare and national security in the digital age. Here's hoping the decision makers are listening now.

Daemon, by Daniel Suarez (Signet). This entertaining cyberthriller raises all-too-real questions about our relationship to technology. The premise that a software villain could wreak havoc in the nondigital world isn't too farfetched, and deserves serious thought.

The Hacker Crackdown: Law and Disorder on the Electronic Frontier, by Bruce Sterling (Bantam Books). Famed cyberpunk author Sterling turns to nonfiction to tell both sides of the story of the war between hackers and federal law enforcement agencies. The complete text is available online along with rest-of-the-story updates.

Ender's Game, by Orson Scott Card (Starscape). This award-winning, entertaining science fiction opus has become a favorite of the cryptography crowd because of its emphasis on encryption to protect privacy.

The Blue Nowhere, by Jeffery Deaver (Simon & Schuster). This suspenseful thriller involves a sadistic hacker who invades his victims' computers, meddles with their lives, and lures them to their deaths. Though fictional, the novel presents a terrifyingly accurate analysis of the lack of privacy and security on the Internet.

The Postman, by David Brin (Bantam). We often complain about government and technology, but what would happen if both were lost? This entertaining science fiction novel asks that question by placing the protagonist in a post-apocalyptic Pacific Northwest. The disappointing 1997 movie bears little resemblance to the novel.

Periodicals

Many popular magazines, from *Newsweek* to *Wired*, provide regular coverage of issues related to privacy and security of digital systems. Most of the periodicals listed here are newsletters of professional organizations that focus on these issues.

Information Security (www.infosecuritymag.com). This magazine focuses on security problems and solutions. Some of the articles are technical, but most are accessible to anyone with an interest in security issues.

The CPSR Compiler, published by Computer Professionals for Social Responsibility (CPSR.org). An alliance of computer scientists and others interested in the impact of computer technology on society, CPSR works to influence public policies to ensure that computers are used wisely in the public interest. Their newsletter has intelligent articles and discussions of risk, reliability, privacy, security, human rights, work, war, education, the environment, democracy, and other subjects that bring together computers and people.

EFFector, published by the Electronic Frontier Foundation (eff.org). This electronic newsletter is distributed by EFF, an organization "established to help civilize the electronic frontier." EFF was founded by Mitch Kapor and John Perry Barlow to protect civil rights and encourage responsible citizenship on the electronic frontier of computer networks.

Ethix (ethix.org). This bimonthly publication is put together by the Center for Integrity in Business, an organization dedicated to promoting good business through appropriate technology and sound ethics.

11

Computers at Work, School, and Home

OBJECTIVES

After you read this chapter you should be able to:

- Describe how digital technology has changed the way people work in factories, offices, homes, and a variety of industries
- Describe several ways digital technology has changed, both positively and negatively, the quality of jobs
- Speculate on how our society will adjust as more and more jobs are automated
- Explain how the information age places new demands on our educational system
- Describe several ways digital technology is used in education today
- Discuss the advantages and limitations of computers and the Internet as instructional tools
- Describe the role of digital information technology in our homes and leisure activities in coming years

> The best way to predict the future is to **invent it**.
>
> —*Alan Kay*

Alan Kay Invents the Future

Alan Kay has been inventing the future for most of his life. Kay was a child prodigy who composed original music, built a harpsichord, and appeared on NBC as a "Quiz Kid." Kay's genius wasn't reflected in his grades; he had trouble conforming to the rigid structure of the schools he attended. After high school he worked as a jazz guitarist and an Air Force programmer before attending college.

FIGURE 11.1 Alan Kay.

His Ph.D. project was one of the first microcomputers, one of several that Kay would eventually develop. In 1968 Kay was in the audience when Douglas Engelbart stunned the computer science world with a futuristic demonstration of interactive computing. Inspired by Engelbart's demonstration, Kay led a team of researchers at Xerox PARC (Palo Alto Research Center in California) in building the computer of the future—a computer that put the user in charge.

Working on a backroom computer called the Alto, Kay developed a bitmapped screen display with icons and overlapping windows—the kind of display that became the standard two decades later. Kay also championed the idea of a friendly user interface. To test user-friendliness, Kay frequently brought his children into the lab "because they have no strong motivation for patience." With feedback from children, Kay developed the first painting program and Smalltalk, the groundbreaking object-oriented programming language.

In essence, Kay's team developed the first personal computer—a single-user desktop machine designed for interactive use. But Kay, who coined the term "personal computer," didn't see the Alto as one. In his mind a true personal computer could go everywhere with its owner, serving as a calculator, a calendar, a word processor, a graphics machine, a communication device, and a reference tool. Kay called this mythical device the Dynabook.

Xerox failed to turn the Alto into a commercial success. But when he visited PARC, Apple's Steve Jobs was inspired by what he saw. Under Jobs a team of engineers and programmers built on the Xerox ideas, added many of their own, and developed the Macintosh—the first inexpensive computer to incorporate many of Kay's far-reaching ideas. Kay became a research fellow at Apple, where he called the Macintosh "the first personal computer good enough to criticize." Today, virtually all PCs have user interfaces based on Kay's groundbreaking work.

After 12 years at Apple, Kay became a research fellow at Disney, where he developed Squeak, a graphical programming tool for children. Kay describes his MO (modus operandi) as "start with end users, usually children, and try to think about the kinds of experiences that would help them to grow in different ways." In 2002 Kay joined Hewlett-Packard's research lab, while continuing his work with Viewpoints Research Institute, a nonprofit organization that works to improve general education and the understanding of complex systems. He left HP in 2005.

Kay continues his crusade for users, especially small users. He says, as with pencil and paper, "it's not a medium if children can't use it." Kay played a key role in the design of the revolutionary "One Laptop per Child" computer developed at MIT to empower and educate children worldwide. He continues his work on Squeak and other children's programming environments. And he is a spokesman for a movement to reinvent programming with revolutionary tools that are far easier to use.

Some of Kay's research is immediately practical; other projects have little to do with today's computer market. This kind of blue-sky research doesn't always lead to products or profits. But for Alan Kay it's the way to invent the future. ■

FIGURE 11.2 Alan Kay's Dynabook was the early prototype for the modern personal computer, combining features of a laptop computer, a tablet PC, and an e-book. Kay conceived of the Dynabook and dubbed it a "personal computer" before PCs existed.

Alan Kay is one of many people whose work has had a profound effect on our workplaces, our schools, and our homes. In this chapter we'll look at the impact computer technology has had on these three facets of our lives. In later chapters we'll delve deeper into the practical business applications of information technology; here we'll pay more attention to the big picture.

Where Computers Work

> **Practically every institution** that our society is based on, from the local to the supranational, **is being rendered obsolete**.
>
> —Wired *founder Louis Rossetto on the 15th anniversary of the magazine*

It's becoming harder all the time to find jobs that haven't been transformed by digital technology. Consider these examples:

- *Entertainment.* The production of television programs and movies involves computer technology at every stage of the process. Videographers capture clips on digital video cameras and pipe them into laptops for in-the-field editing. Scriptwriters use specialized word processors to write and revise scripts, and they use the Internet to beam the scripts between Hollywood and New York. Artists and technicians use graphics workstations to create special effects, from simple scene transitions to spectacular intergalactic battles.

Musicians compose soundtracks using synthesizers and sequencers. Sound editors use computer-controlled mixers to blend music with digital sound effects and live-action sound. Even commercials—especially commercials—use state-of-the-art computer graphics, animation, and sound to keep you watching the images instead of changing the channel or zipping ahead.

- *Publishing.* The news industry has been radically transformed by digital technology. Reporters scan the Internet for facts, write and edit stories on location using notebook computers, and transmit those stories to editors and to online blogs. Artists design charts and drawings with graphics software. Photo retouchers use computers instead of darkrooms and magnifying glasses to edit photographs. Production crews assemble pages with computers instead of typesetting machines and paste-up boards. Most newspapers produce Web editions; many have abandoned paper altogether.

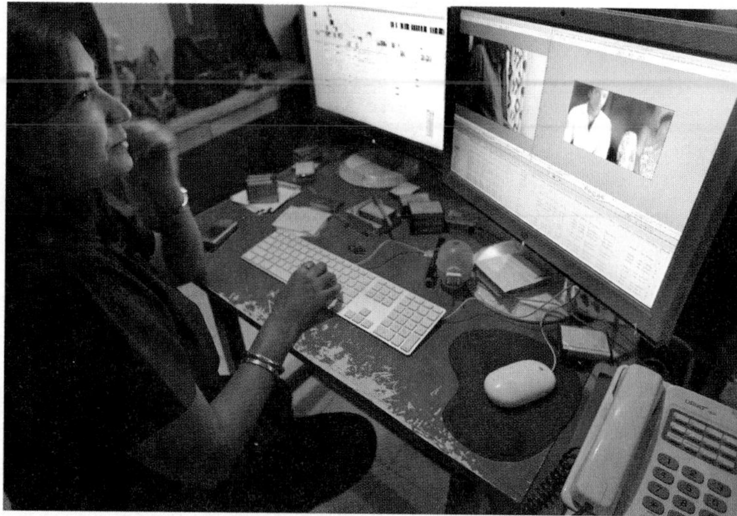

FIGURE 11.3 Computers play a critical role in video and film production today.

- *Medicine.* High-tech equipment plays a critical role in the healing arts, too. Hospital information systems store patient medical data, clinical images, and insurance records. Local area networks enable doctors, nurses, technicians, dietitians, and office staff to view and update information throughout the hospital. Doctors use wireless handheld devices to browse databases for drug interactions, order prescriptions, and transmit those prescriptions to pharmacies for fulfillment. For patients outside the hospital walls in remote locations, doctors use the Web to practice *telemedicine*. Computers monitor patient vital signs in hospitals, at home, and on the street with portable units that analyze signals and transmit warnings when problems arise. Some surgeons never put their hands inside a patient. Instead, they do surgery by remote control, guiding robotic arms that enter the body through tiny incisions. Image-guided robotic technology can even be used to remove complex brain tumors. And, of course, medical researchers rely on digital technology to determine causes and develop cures for countless diseases.
- *Airlines.* Without computers, today's airline industry simply wouldn't fly. Designers use CAD software to design aircraft. Engineers conduct extensive computer simulations to test them. Pilots use computer-controlled instruments to navigate their planes, monitor aircraft systems, and control autopilots. Air traffic controllers on the ground use computerized systems to track incoming and outgoing flights. And Internet reservation systems fill those planes with passengers.
- *Science.* From biology to physics, digital technology has changed every branch of science. Scientists collect and analyze data using remote sensing devices, tablet computers, and statistical analysis programs. They catalog, organize, and share information in massive databases continents away via the Web. They use supercomputers, workstations, and processor-sharing grids to create computer models of objects or environments that would otherwise be out of reach.

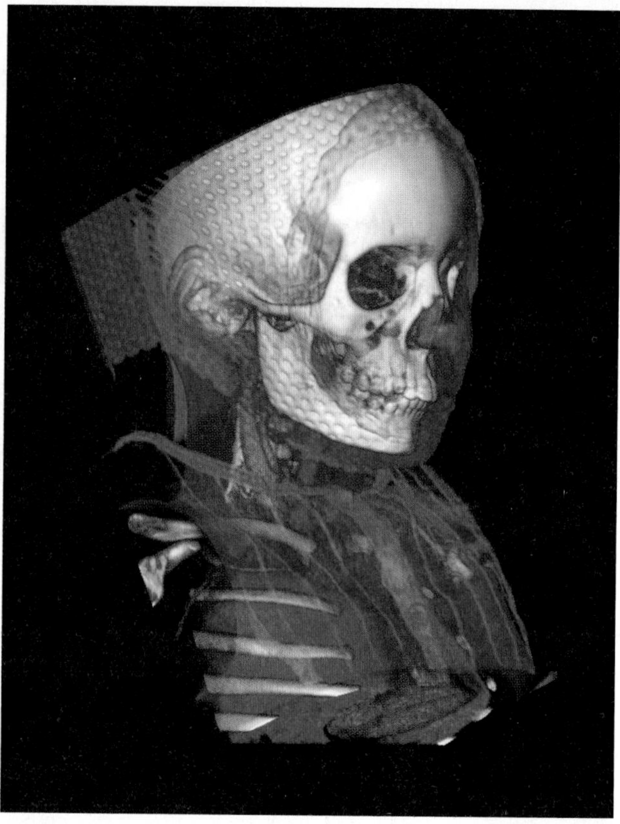

FIGURE 11.4 This colored 3-D computed tomography (CT) scan of a child's head and chest was constructed with medical imaging software from a series of thin x-ray "slices." During a brain cancer operation, surgeons used the reconstructed 3-D model to navigate around the brain using fly-through animations.

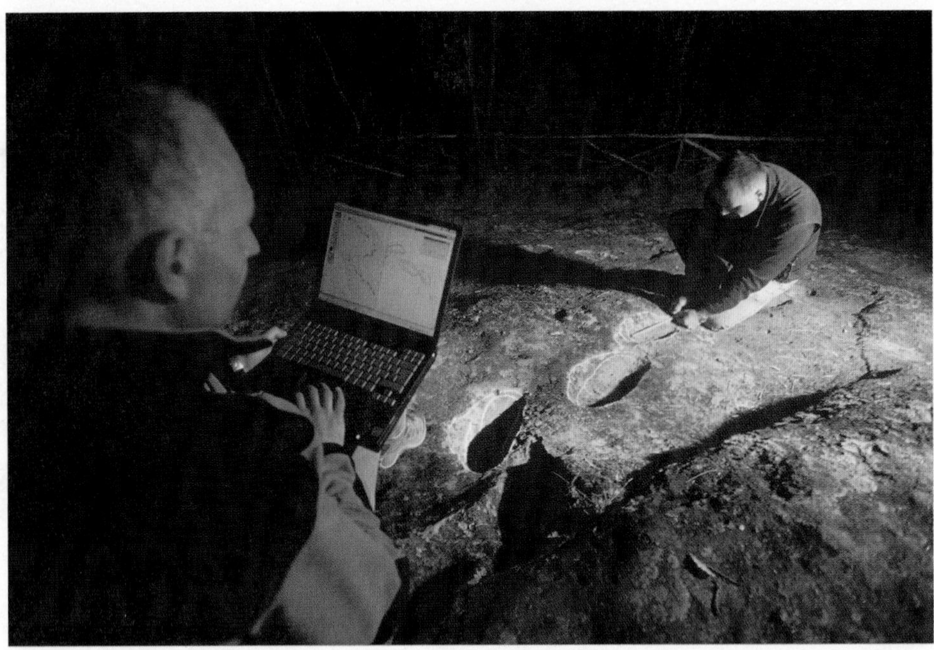

FIGURE 11.5 Researchers near Naples, Italy use a computer to reconstruct the path taken by the early human that made these tracks more than 300,000 years ago.

To get a perspective on how digital technology affects the way we work, we consider the three digital workplaces that have attracted the most attention: the automated factory, the automated office, and the electronic cottage.

The Automated Factory

In Chapter 15 we discuss the use of robots. In the modern automated factory ***robots***—computer-controlled machines designed to perform specific manual tasks—are used for painting, welding, and other repetitive assembly-line jobs. But robots alone don't make an **automated factory**. Computers also help track inventory, time the delivery of parts, control the quality of the production, monitor wear and tear on machines, and schedule maintenance. As described in Chapter 6, engineers use CAD and computer-aided manufacturing technologies to design new products and the machines that build those products. Web cameras and Web displays built into assembly-line equipment enable workers and managers to monitor production and inventory from across the factory floor or across the ocean.

FIGURE 11.6 The assembly line for manufacturing circuit boards is highly automated.

An automated factory is more efficient than a traditional factory for two reasons:

- Automation allows for tighter integration of planning with manufacturing, reducing the time that materials and machines sit idle.
- Automation reduces waste in facilities, raw materials, and labor.

If automation is good news for factory owners, it poses a threat to blue-collar workers who keep traditional factories running. In a typical high-tech manufacturing firm today, approximately half of the staff are engineers, accountants, marketing specialists, and other white-collar workers.

The Automated Office

As the number of factory jobs declines, office work plays a more important role in our economy. Modern offices, like modern factories, have been transformed by digital technology. Many **automated offices** have evolved along with their computers.

Office Automation Evolution

Office automation goes back to the mainframe era, when banks, insurance companies, and other large institutions used computers for behind-the-scenes jobs such as accounting and payroll. Early computer systems were faster and more accurate than the manual systems they replaced but they were rigid and difficult to use. The machines and the technicians who worked with them were hidden away in basement offices, isolated from their organizations. The introduction of timesharing operating systems and database management systems enabled workers throughout organizations to access computer data. This kind of centralized computing placed computer-related decisions in the hands of central data-processing managers.

PCs changed all that. Early Apple and Tandy computers were carried into offices on the sly by employees who wanted to use their own computers instead of company mainframes. But as managers recognized the power of word processors, spreadsheets, and other applications, they incorporated PCs into organizational plans. Jobs migrated from mainframes to desktops, and people used PCs to do things that the mainframes weren't programmed to do. In many organizations power struggles erupted between mainframe advocates and PC enthusiasts.

Enterprise Computing

Today PCs, smart phones, and other personal digital devices are essential parts of the overall computing structure for most business enterprises. Workers use word processors to generate memos and reports, managers use presentation graphics programs to build digital slide shows, marketing teams create promotional pieces using desktop publishing tools, and financial departments analyze budgets using spreadsheets. They communicate with each other and with the outside world using all kinds of digital devices—and, of course, the Web.

Some companies have abandoned mainframes altogether; others still use them for their biggest data-processing tasks. In the age of networks, the challenge for the **chief information officers (CIOs)** and **chief technology officers (CTOs)**—the main decision makers concerning enterprise computer systems and technology—is to integrate all kinds of digital devices, from mainframes to handhelds, from the office to the cloud, into a single, seamless system.

IT managers recognize the value of the PC, although some raise questions about its cost. Research suggests that the *total cost of ownership (TCO)* of a typical PC is many times more than the cost of hardware and software. Training, support, maintenance, and troubleshooting can easily cost several thousand dollars per PC per year! To reduce costs, a few companies are replacing PCs with **thin clients**—computers that can't function without access to servers. These low-cost, low-maintenance machines enable workers to access critical network information without the

FIGURE 11.7 The CIO and CTO are responsible for managing the information systems and information technology in an organization.

overhead of a PC or workstation. The servers may be on-site, or they may be somewhere in the Internet cloud.

Much of the cost of enterprise PCs involves software. Installing, upgrading, and maintaining software on a fleet of PCs can be a daunting task. Many organizations are separating software and data from PC hardware using **desktop virtualization**. With this technology, software and data are stored on servers—in the IT center or in the Internet cloud—so they can be accessed from PCs, thin clients, and/or handheld devices anywhere in the enterprise. From the user's point of view, applications look and work as usual—they're just stored elsewhere. A user can log out of the server from one PC, move to another location, log in to another client machine, and see exactly the same desktop applications and data.

Workgroup Computing

Groupware enables groups of users to share calendars, send messages, access data, and work on documents simultaneously. The best groupware applications enable workgroups to do things that would be difficult otherwise; they actually change the way people work in groups. Many of these applications focus on the concept of ***work flow***—the path of information as it flows through a workgroup. With groupware and networks, workgroups don't need to be in the same room, or even the same time zone. During much of the 1990s, Lotus Notes dominated this market, offering a complete, if expensive, workgroup solution for corporations.

But the advent of the Web changed the workgroup landscape. Many of the functions of a groupware program such as Notes—email, teleconferencing, shared databases, electronic publishing, and others—became available for little or no cost through freely available Internet technologies. Corporations installed **intranets** using HTML, Web browsers, and other Internet technologies. And because these intranets were built on standardized protocols such as TCP/IP, corporations could open their intranets to strategic partners and customers, creating **extranets**. Lotus, Microsoft, and other groupware manufacturers have responded by rebuilding their applications using standard Internet technologies and protocols, so their customers could have the best of both worlds: computer systems built on universal public standards, and customer support and customization from a groupware specialist.

Whether they're built from off-the-shelf Internet software or commercially customized packages, workgroup systems have transformed the way businesses operate. Ted Lewis, author of *The Friction-Free Economy*, suggests that information technology makes an organization:

- Flatter, so it's easier for workers at any level to communicate with workers at other levels
- More integrated, so different business units communicate more openly with each other
- More flexible, so businesses can react more quickly to changes in their environments
- Less concerned with managing people and more concerned with managing processes

The Paperless Office

Experts have also predicted the **paperless office**—an office of the future in which magnetic and optical archives will replace reference books and file cabinets, electronic communication will replace letters and memos, and Web publications will replace newspapers and other periodicals. In the paperless office, people will read computer screens, not paper documents.

All of these trends are real: digital storage media are replacing many paper depositories, computers now deliver more mail messages than postal carriers do, and the Web has accelerated a trend toward online publishing. But so far, computers haven't significantly reduced the flow of paper-based information. What has changed is the way people tend to use paper in the office. According to Paul Saffo of the Institute for the Future, "We've shifted from paper as storage to paper as interface. It is an ever more volatile, disposable, and temporary display medium."

HTML, XML, Adobe's popular ***PDF (portable document format)***, and other technologies make it easier for documents to be transmitted and stored electronically without loss of formatting. But none of these technologies has made a big dent in the wall of paper that surrounds most office workers. In the near future we may see a less-paper office, but experts still debate whether a paperless office will happen anytime soon.

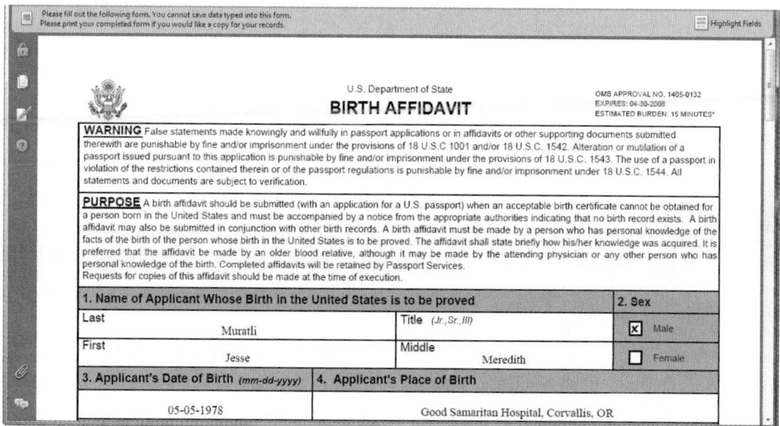

Please fill out the following form. You cannot save data typed into this form.
Please print your completed form if you would like a copy for your records.

Highlight Fields

U.S. Department of State

BIRTH AFFIDAVIT

OMB APPROVAL NO. 1405-0132
EXPIRES: 04-30-2008
ESTIMATED BURDEN: 15 MINUTES*

WARNING False statements made knowingly and willfully in passport applications or in affidavits or other supporting documents submitted therewith are punishable by fine and/or imprisonment under the provisions of 18 U.S.C 1001 and/or 18 U.S.C. 1542. Alteration or mutilation of a passport issued pursuant to this application is punishable by fine and/or imprisonment under the provisions of 18 U.S.C. 1543. The use of a passport in violation of the restrictions contained therein or of the passport regulations is punishable by fine and/or imprisonment under 18 U.S.C. 1544. All statements and documents are subject to verification.

PURPOSE A birth affidavit should be submitted (with an application for a U.S. passport) when an acceptable birth certificate cannot be obtained for a person born in the United States and must be accompanied by a notice from the appropriate authorities indicating that no birth record exists. A birth affidavit may also be submitted in conjunction with other birth records. A birth affidavit must be made by a person who has personal knowledge of the facts of the birth of the person whose birth in the United States is to be proved. The affidavit shall state briefly how his/her knowledge was acquired. It is preferred that the affidavit be made by an older blood relative, although it may be made by the attending physician or any other person who has personal knowledge of the birth. Completed affidavits will be retained by Passport Services.
Requests for copies of this affidavit should be made at the time of execution.

1. Name of Applicant Whose Birth in the United States is to be proved		2. Sex
Last: Muratli	Title (Jr.,Sr.,III)	[X] Male
First: Jesse	Middle: Meredith	[ ] Female

3. Applicant's Date of Birth (mm-dd-yyyy)	4. Applicant's Place of Birth
05-05-1978	Good Samaritan Hospital, Corvallis, OR

FIGURE 11.8 The U.S. government Web site includes many PDF forms that can be filled out and submitted online, saving paper, postage, and time.

Electronic Commerce

The paperless office may be years away, but paperless money is already here for many organizations. **Electronic commerce (e-commerce)** has been around for years in its most basic form—buying and selling products through the Internet. But today there's more to electronic commerce than handling purchase transactions and funds transfers on the Internet. E-commerce also includes marketing, sales, support, customer service, and communication with business partners.

Early electronic commerce involved transactions between corporations. Even today ***business-to-business (B2B)*** transactions account for far more online sales than do ***business-to-consumer (B2C)*** transactions. But consumer commerce on the Web is a major force in the world economy today. Many businesses, including computer manufacturers Dell and Apple, allow customers to order customized goods and services electronically; this kind of customization on demand wasn't practical or possible for most businesses before the Internet took hold. The Web is also fertile ground for person-to-person auctions, reverse auctions, and other types of sales that aren't practical outside the Web.

During the economic boom of the nineties, thousands of start-up dot-com companies experimented with a variety of new ways to do business on the Internet. Many of those dot-coms turned into dot-bombs, while others survived and prospered into the new decade. In the second dot-com boom of the 2000s, hundreds of new companies created Web businesses based on Web 2.0 technology. Many of these Web 2.0 sites offer free services, from media sharing to social networking, financed by advertising. (Chapter 13 has more on e-commerce.)

The Electronic Cottage

Before the industrial revolution, most people worked in or near their homes. Today's telecommunications technology opens up new possibilities for modern workers to return home for their livelihood. For hundreds of thousands of writers, programmers, accountants, data-entry clerks, and other information workers, **telecommuting** by wireless or broadband connection replaces hours of commuting by car in rush-hour traffic. The term *telecommuter* typically refers to *all* home information workers, whether or not they're connected to their company computers via the Internet.

Futurist Alvin Toffler popularized the term **electronic cottage** to describe a home where technology enables a person to work at home. Toffler and others predict that the number of telecommuters will skyrocket in the coming decades. So far, the predictions have held. The number of employee teleworkers and contract teleworkers continues to grow. Each year more people do some or all of their work at home through Internet connections. At the same time, those who do telecommute are steadily increasing the amount of time they work from home.

Telecommuting makes sense; it's easier to move information than people. There are many strong arguments for telecommuting:

- Telecommuting reduces the number of automobile commuters, thus saving energy, reducing pollution, and decreasing congestion and accidents on highways, streets, and parking lots.
- Telecommuting saves time. If an information worker spends two hours each day commuting, that's two hours that could be spent working, resting, doing community activities, or relaxing with the family.
- Telecommuting allows for a more flexible schedule. People who prefer to work early in the morning or late at night don't need to conform to standard office hours if they telecommute. For many people, including parents of small children, telecommuting may be the only viable way to maintain a job.
- Telecommuting can increase productivity. Studies suggest that telecommuting can result in a 10 percent to 50 percent increase in worker productivity, depending on the job and the worker.
- Telecommuting reduces the importance of geography. A telecommuting worker doesn't need to live near the office. A growing number of workers telecommute across time zones and international boundaries.

Of course, telecommuting isn't for everybody. Jobs that require constant interaction with coworkers, customers, or clients aren't conducive to telecommuting. Working at home requires self-discipline. Some people find they can't concentrate on work when they're at home—beds, refrigerators, neighbors, children, and errands are simply too distracting. Others have the opposite problem: workaholism cuts into family and relaxation time. Some workers who've tried full-time telecommuting complain that they miss the informal office social life and that their low visibility causes bosses to pass them over for promotions. In the words of one telecommuter, "When you're telecommuting you're far more productive than you can ever hope to be in the office, but you don't really have your finger on the pulse of the company." Research suggests that people who work from home may be less likely to advance than their office-bound colleagues in some companies. Most telecommuters report that the ideal work situation involves commuting to the office one or two days each week and working at home on the others.

Today thousands of companies offer home-based work arrangements to millions of employees. Many firms encourage "boundaryless" employees to work in virtual teams when and where they can best get their jobs done. Other companies have strict policies against working at home. They cite resentment among office-bound colleagues, weakened corporate loyalty, and the difficulties of holding meetings as reasons for their policies. Some analysts suggest that as multimedia teleconferencing systems become affordable, telecommuting will become more popular with both workers and management. Workers and managers will be able to have a telepresence in the workplace when they aren't physically present.

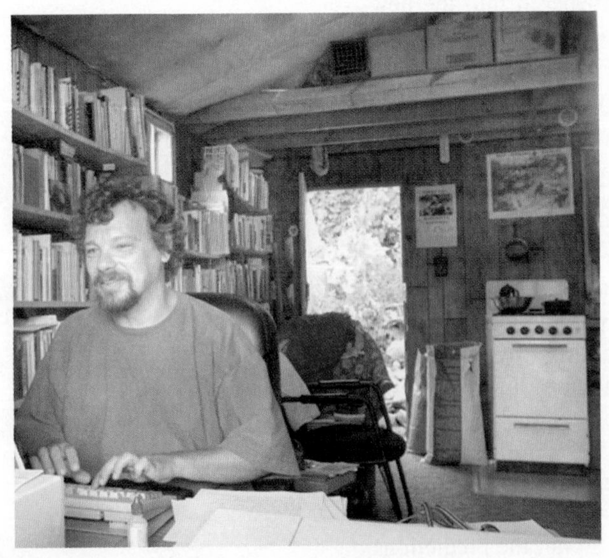

FIGURE 11.9 Novelist Richie Swanson, winner of the Peace Writing award, works at home...in his houseboat.

In the meantime, several variations on the electronic cottage are taking hold. Many enterprising families use home computers to help them run small businesses from their home offices. A growing number of corporations and government organizations are establishing **satellite offices** and shared **regional work centers** outside of major urban centers that allow workers to commute to smaller offices closer to their neighborhoods. Laptops, tablets, and smart phones enable salespeople, executives, consultants, engineers, and others to take their offices with them wherever they travel. These mobile workers don't travel to the office; they travel with the office. Many experts predict that *m-commerce*—mobile commerce—will spread into dozens of other professions in the coming decade.

Working Wisdom Considering Information Technology Careers

Until recently, people who wanted to work with computers were forced to choose among a few careers, most of which required highly specialized training. But when computers are used by everybody from fast-food salesclerks to graphic artists, just about anybody can have some kind of "information technology career." Still, many rewarding and high-paying computer-related careers require a fair amount of specialized education. If you're interested in a computer-related job, consider the following tips:

- ***Learn touch typing.*** Computers that can read handwriting and understand spoken English are probably in your future—but not your immediate future. Several low-cost typing tutorial programs can help you to teach your fingers how to type. The time you invest will pay you back quickly. The sooner you learn, the sooner you'll start reaping the rewards.
- ***Use computers regularly to help you accomplish your immediate goals.*** Use a word processor for your term papers. Use spreadsheets and other math software as calculation aids. Use the Web for research work. Computers are part of your future. If you use them regularly, they'll become second nature, like telephones and pencils. If you don't own a computer, find a way to buy one if you can.
- ***Don't forsake the basics.*** If you want to become a programmer, a systems analyst, a computer scientist, a computer engineer, or some other kind of computer professional, don't focus all your attention on computers. A few young technical wizards become successful programmers without college degrees; Bill Gates is probably the best-known example. But if you're not gifted and lucky, you'll need a solid education to land a good job. Math and communication skills (written and oral) are extremely important. Opportunities abound for people who can understand computers and communicate clearly.
- ***Combine your passions.*** If you like art and computers, explore computer art, graphic design, or multimedia. If you love ecology and computers, find out how computers are used by ecologists. People who can speak the language of computers and the language of a specialized field have opportunities to build bridges.
- ***Ask questions.*** The best way to find out more about information technology careers is to ask the people who have IT careers. Most people are happy to talk about their jobs if you're willing to listen.
- ***Cultivate community.*** Computer networks are changing our lives, but people networks are still more important for finding and landing that dream job. Get to know the people in the professional community. Take an active part in that community. Join professional organizations. Use social networks like LinkedIn to build links to professionals. Give your time and energy to public service projects related to your field. Even if it doesn't pay off with a job offer, you'll be doing good work.

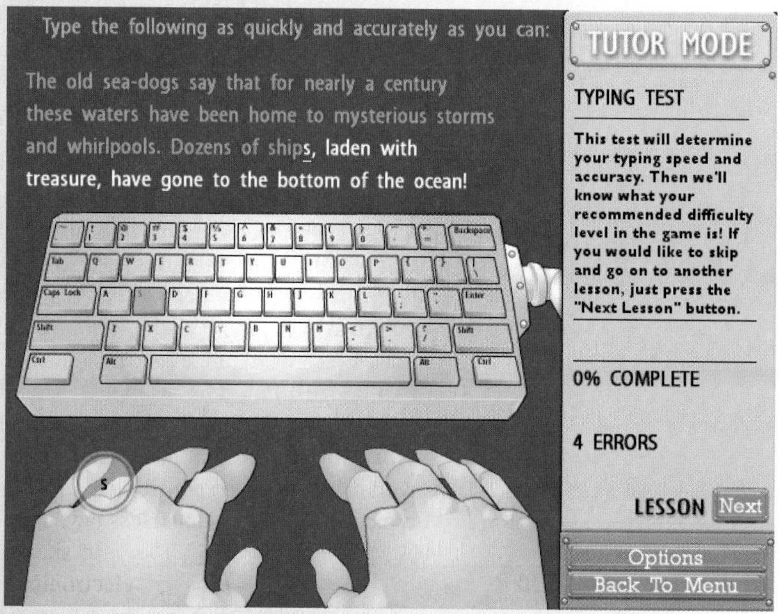

FIGURE 11.10 You can use a program such as TyperShark to learn touch typing.

- ***If you can't find your dream job, build it yourself.*** Inexpensive computer systems provide all kinds of entrepreneurial opportunities for creative self-starters: publishing service bureaus, Web design, multimedia video production, custom programming, commercial art and design, freelance writing, consulting—the jobs are there for the making if you have the imagination and initiative.
- ***When you're ready, search the Web.*** There are plenty of job bulletin boards, online career-hunting centers, Internet headhunters, and e-cruiters offering jobs that might be just right for you. Of course, some Internet job offers are scams, so check your sources.
- ***Prepare for change.*** In a rapidly changing world, lifelong careers are rare. Be prepared to change jobs several times. Think of education as a lifelong process. In Marshall McLuhan's words, "The future of work consists of learning a living."

Technology and Job Quality

John Henry told his captain, "A man ain't nothin' but a man. But before I let your steam drill beat me down **I'd die with a hammer in my hand....**"

—From the folk song "John Henry"

When we think about automated factories, automated offices, and electronic cottages, it's easy to imagine utopian visions of computers in the workplace of tomorrow. But the real world isn't always picture perfect. For many workers, computers have caused more problems than they have solved. Workers complain of stress, depersonalization, fatigue, boredom, and a variety of health problems attributed to computers. Some of these complaints are directly related to technology; others relate to human decisions about how technology is implemented. In this section we look at some of the controversies and issues surrounding the automation of the workplace.

De-Skilling and Up-Skilling

When a job is automated, it may be **de-skilled**; that is, it may be transformed so that it requires less skill. For example, computerized cash registers in many fast-food restaurants replace numbered buttons with buttons labeled "large fries" or "chocolate shake." Clerks who use these machines don't need to know math or think about prices. They simply push buttons for the food items ordered and take the money; computers do the rest.

Some of the most visible examples of de-skilling occur when offices automate clerical jobs. When word processors and databases replace typewriters and file cabinets, traditional typing-and-filing jobs disappear. Many secretaries are repositioned in data-entry jobs—mindless, repetitive jobs where the only measure of success is the number of keystrokes typed into a terminal each hour. When a clerical job—or any job—is de-skilled, the worker's control, responsibility, and job satisfaction are likely to go down. De-skilled jobs typically offer less status, less pay, and fewer benefits.

In sharp contrast to those whose jobs are de-skilled into electronic drudgery, many workers find their jobs **up-skilled** by automation. For example, many clerical jobs become more technical as offices adopt complex databases, standardized spreadsheets, groupware systems, and other digital technology. In some cases, clerical workers use computer systems to do jobs formerly done by high-paid professionals and technicians. While many clerical people enjoy the added challenge and responsibility, others may be frustrated doing highly technical work with inadequate training. Clerical workers are seldom consulted before their jobs are computerized. And even though their work is more technically demanding than before, few clerical workers see this up-skilling reflected in their paychecks or job titles.

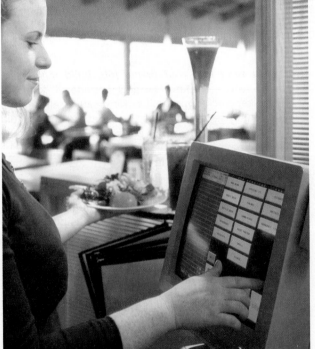

FIGURE 11.11 Specialized terminals such as this one make it easy to log restaurant orders. How is this person's job different as a result of this technology?

Monitoring and Surveillance

Another controversial aspect of workplace technology is **computer monitoring**—using computer technology to track, record, and evaluate worker performance, sometimes without the knowledge of the worker. Monitoring systems can provide a manager with reports showing the number of keystrokes for each clerk, the length of each phone call placed by an employee, details of Web wanderings, and the total amount of idle time for each computer. Some network software even enables a manager to view a copy of any worker's screen secretly at any time.

For a manager worried about worker productivity, computer monitoring can serve as a valuable source of information. But monitoring brings with it several problems:

- *Privacy.* In previous chapters we saw how the misuse of database and network technology can threaten personal privacy. Computer monitoring compounds that threat by providing employers with unprecedented data on workers. Some employers monitor personal email or text messages and punish or fire employees who send "unacceptable" messages.
- *Morale.* Privacy issues aside, computer monitoring can have a powerful negative impact on morale. Because employees can't tell when they're being monitored, many workers experience a great deal of stress and anxiety. The boss can be seen as an invisible eavesdropper rather than as a team leader.
- *Devalued skills.* In the traditional office, workers were evaluated based on a variety of skills. A slow-typing secretary could be valued for her ability to anticipate when a job needed to be done or her willingness to help others with problems. Computer monitoring tends to reduce a worker's worth to simple quantities such as "number of keystrokes per hour." In such systems a worker might be penalized for repairing a sticky chair, showing a neighbor how to reboot a terminal, or helping a troubled coworker.
- *Loss of quality.* Monitored workers tend to assume that "if it's not being counted, it doesn't count." As a result, quantity may become more important than quality.

Millions of workers are monitored by computer, including factory workers, telephone operators, truck drivers, and even managers. Cybersnooping goes far beyond counting keystrokes and idle time. According to the American Management Association, more than three out of four U.S. companies engage in some kind of electronic surveillance of their employees, including monitoring Web connections, reviewing email, tracking keystrokes, monitoring phone use, videotaping, and checking computer files. In many of those companies, employees have been fired for "inappropriate" Internet use. One reason for corporate computer monitoring is the growing use of computer files in legal battles. According to Nancy Flynn, executive director of the ePolicy Institute, "Workers' email, blog, and Internet content creates written business records that are the electronic equivalent of DNA evidence." In the words of the director of one American Management Association study, "Workplace privacy is a contradiction in terms. It's an oxymoron. I know the illusion of privacy is there, but you are not using your own stuff. The phone, the keyboard, the connections, the job itself—they don't belong to you; they belong to the company, legally."

Electronic Sweatshops

Computer monitoring is common practice in data-entry offices. A data-entry clerk has a single job: to read information from a printed source—a check, a hand-printed form, or something else—and type it into a computer's database. A typical data-entry shop might contain hundreds of clerks sitting at terminals in a massive, windowless room. Workers—often minorities and almost always female—are paid minimum wage to do mindless keyboarding. Many experience headaches, backaches, serious wrist injuries, stress, anxiety, and other health problems. And all the while, keystrokes and breaks are monitored electronically. Writer Barbara Garson calls these worker warehouses **electronic sweatshops** because working conditions bring to mind the oppressive factory sweatshops of the nineteenth century.

A growing number of electronic sweatshops are located across national borders from corporate headquarters in countries with lax labor laws and low wage scales. The electronic immigrants in these offshore shops don't need green cards to telecommute across borders, and they work for a fraction of what workers in developed countries cost. A data-entry clerk in the Philippines, for example, earns about $6 per day. With wages that low, many companies find it cost effective to have data entered twice and use software to compare both versions and correct errors. Offshore outsourcing is evidence of globalization, which will be discussed in more detail in the next section.

Automation, Globalization, and Outsourcing

> My father had worked for the same firm for 12 years. They fired him. **They replaced him with a tiny gadget** this big that does everything that my father does only it does it much better. **The depressing thing is my mother ran out and bought one.**
>
> —*Woody Allen, comedian and filmmaker*

When Woody Allen told this joke more than four decades ago, automation was generating a great deal of public controversy. Computer technology was new to the workplace, and people were reacting with both awe and fear. Many analysts predicted that automation would lead to massive unemployment and economic disaster. Others said that computers would generate countless new job opportunities. Today, most people are accustomed to seeing computers where they work, and the computers-versus-jobs debate has cooled down. Job automation may not be a hot topic in comedy clubs today, but it's still an important issue for millions of workers whose jobs are threatened by machines.

Workers Against Machines

Automation has threatened workers since the earliest days of the industrial revolution. In the early nineteenth century, an English labor group called the Luddites smashed new textile machinery; they feared that the machines would take jobs away from skilled craftsmen. The Luddites and similar groups in other parts of Europe failed to stop the wheels of automation. Today the word *Luddite* refers to someone who resists technological change. Modern Luddites have been no more successful than their nineteenth-century counterparts in keeping computers and robots out of the workplace. Every year brings new technological breakthroughs that allow robots and computers to do jobs formerly reserved for humans.

When many people hear the word *automation*, they think of industrial robots and assembly lines, but automation has eliminated service jobs too. Consider how the office environment has changed in recent decades. In the 1980s executives dictated letters to assistants who typed them. Today executives type their own email messages. In the "old days," secretaries typed memos and mimeographed copies for distribution. Today desktop publishing systems allow employees to create slick publications without professional designers. Not too many years ago, office personnel wrote phone messages for people who were out. Today voice mail and email are how most messages are handled. Easy-to-use financial management programs have reduced the need for bookkeepers. And the Web handles countless jobs that used to be done by humans. These are just a few of the technological advances that have made many clerical tasks less labor intensive.

FIGURE 11.12 Many data-entry workers spend their days in warehouse-sized buildings filled with computers.

Of course, computer technology creates new jobs, too. Somebody has to design, build, program, sell, run, and repair the computers, robots, and networks. But many displaced workers don't have the education or skills to program computers, design robots, install networks, or even read printouts. Those workers are often forced to take low-tech, low-paying service jobs as cashiers or custodians, if they can find jobs at all. Because of automation the unskilled, uneducated worker may face a lifetime of minimum-wage jobs or welfare. Technology may be helping to create an unbalanced society with two classes: a growing mass of poor, uneducated people and a shrinking class of affluent, educated people.

World Wide Workers

We are **the only species on this planet** without full employment.

—*Paul Hawken*

In the past four decades, multinational corporations have closed thousands of factories in the United States and moved millions of manufacturing jobs to countries with less expensive labor. As we saw in the previous section, hundreds of thousands of data-entry clerk jobs have moved overseas, too. Jobs requiring a more advanced education have been internationalized, too. When you call a technical support or customer support line for a U.S. corporation, there's a good chance the call will be answered by an operator in India, Mexico, or another country with lower wages than those earned in the United States. Offshore operators are often given American-sounding names and trained not to reveal their locations to callers.

The migration of jobs to countries where labor is less expensive is evidence of **globalization**—the creation of worldwide businesses and markets. Underwater fiber-optic cables and high-speed computerized telephone switches link Asia to the United States, allowing millions of simultaneous phone calls to take place. Leveraging this communications conduit, U.S. corporations have shifted hundreds of thousands of technical support jobs to India alone.

Even highly educated programmers and system designers in the United States are being replaced by offshore workers. The computer software industry in India, for example, employs tens of thousands of workers at a fraction of the cost of similarly skilled U.S. workers. The globalization of job markets makes it easy for corporations to shop for the cheapest labor forces with little or no regard for national boundaries, labor laws, environmental consequences, or community impact.

Nobody knows for sure how digital technology will affect employment in the coming decades; it's impossible to anticipate what might happen in 10 or 20 years. And experts are far from unanimous in their predictions. Some predict a steady increase in the number and types of jobs that are outsourced in coming years. Other sources suggest that fears of outsourcing are misplaced. Some even suggest that the amount of outsourcing will be counterbalanced, or even dwarfed, by insourcing—providing American labor to foreign companies.

Most experts agree that information technology will result in painful periods of adjustment for factory workers, clerical workers, and other semiskilled and unskilled laborers as jobs are automated or moved to Third World countries. But many also believe that the demand for professionals—especially engineers, teachers, and health-care professionals—is likely to rise as a result of shifts in the information economy.

FIGURE 11.13 These technical support representatives in India are communicating with customers in the United States.

Will the U.S. have enough skilled workers to fill those jobs? Economic growth will likely depend on having a suitably trained workforce. The single most important key to a positive economic future may be education. We'll deal with the critical issues surrounding education in the information age later in this chapter.

Will We Need a New Economy?

> Do you own the stuff you own, or **does the stuff you own own you?**
>
> *—Songwriter John Flynn, in "Who's Whose"*

In the long run, education may not be enough. It seems likely that at some time in the future, machines will be able to do most of the jobs people do today. We may face a future of *jobless growth*—a time when automation alone creates adequate productivity increases, and no new jobs are created. In fact, since World War II, the productivity of workers in the most highly industrialized nations has more than doubled, thanks to automation. In the United States, the work week has remained at 40 hours because increased productivity has been used to increase material wealth rather increasing leisure time. The average house size has grown considerably, and the number of cars, phones, and televisions per capita has risen. Employers in the United States are not required to provide vacation benefits, and, on average, American workers get only 16 holidays and vacation days per year. In Japan and most Western European countries, workers enjoy between 25 and 32 vacation days a year.

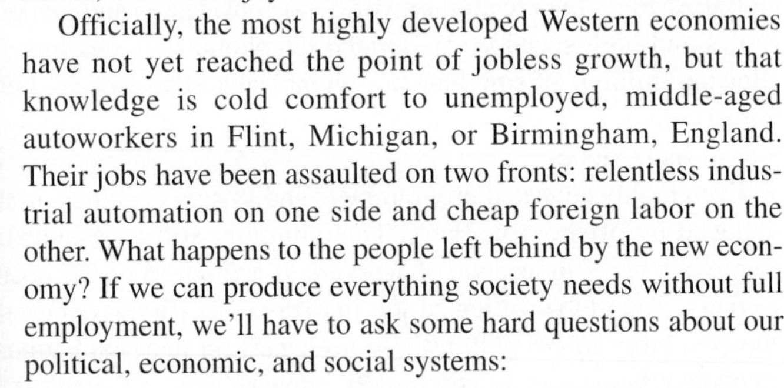

Officially, the most highly developed Western economies have not yet reached the point of jobless growth, but that knowledge is cold comfort to unemployed, middle-aged autoworkers in Flint, Michigan, or Birmingham, England. Their jobs have been assaulted on two fronts: relentless industrial automation on one side and cheap foreign labor on the other. What happens to the people left behind by the new economy? If we can produce everything society needs without full employment, we'll have to ask some hard questions about our political, economic, and social systems:

- Do governments have an obligation to provide permanent public assistance to the chronically unemployed?
- Should large companies be required to give several months' notice to workers whose jobs are being eliminated? Should they be required to retrain workers for other jobs?
- Should large companies be required to file "employment impact statements" before replacing people with machines in the same way they're required to file environmental impact statements before implementing policies that might harm the environment?
- If robots and computers are producing most of society's goods and services, should all of the profits from those goods go to a few people who own the machines?
- If a worker is replaced by a robot, should the worker receive a share of the robot's "earnings" through stocks or profit sharing? Should governments and businesses encourage job sharing and other systems that allow for less-than-40-hour jobs?
- What will people do with their time if machines do most of the work? What new leisure activities should be made available?
- How will people define their identities if work becomes less central to their lives?

FIGURE 11.14 Australian aborigines work about four hours per day. Will automation make it possible to enjoy both a short work-week and a high material standard of living?

These questions force us to confront deep-seated cultural beliefs and economic traditions, and they don't come with easy answers. They suggest that we may be heading into a difficult period when many old rules don't apply anymore. But if we're successful at navigating the troubled waters of transition, we may find that automation fulfills the dream expressed by Aristotle more than 2,000 years ago:

> *If every instrument could accomplish its own work, obeying or anticipating the will of others...if the shuttle could weave, and the pick touch the lyre, without a hand to guide them, chief workmen would not need servants, nor masters slaves.*

Education in the Information Age

> The future is **a race between education and catastrophe.**
>
> —*H.G. Wells*

The information age is not just affecting the workplace. Its influences are felt in our educational system, too. Before it's over, the information revolution will have a profound and permanent effect on the way we learn.

The Roots of Our Educational System

The educational system that dominates the industrialized world was developed more than a century ago to teach students the basic facts and survival skills they would need for jobs in industry and agriculture—jobs they would probably hold for their entire adult lives. This industrial age system has been described as a factory model for three reasons:

- It assumes that all students learn the same way and that all students should learn the same things.
- The teacher's job is to "pour" facts into students, occasionally checking the level of knowledge in each student.
- Students are expected to work individually, absorb facts, and spend most of their time sitting quietly in straight rows.

Despite its faults, the factory model of public education helped the U.S. dominate world markets for most of the 20th century. But the world has changed drastically since the system was founded. Schools have changed, too, but not fast enough to keep pace with the information revolution. Most experts today agree that we need to rebuild our educational system to meet the demands of the information age.

FIGURE 11.15 In the traditional classroom, students are expected to absorb facts delivered by the teacher.

Information Age Education

> Education is **the kindling of a flame**, not the filling of a vessel.
>
> —*Socrates*

What should education provide for students in the information age? Research and experience suggest several answers:

- *Technological familiarity.* Many of today's older workers are having trouble adjusting to the information age because of **technophobia**—the fear of technology. These people grew up in a world without computers, and they experience anxiety when they're forced to deal with them. Today's students need to learn how to work comfortably with all kinds of knowledge tools, including pencils, books, calculators, smart phones, computers, and the Internet. But technological familiarity shouldn't stop with learning how to work with tools. Students need to have a clear understanding of the *limitations* of the technology and the ability to assess the benefits and risks of applying technology to a problem. They need to be able to *question* technology.
- *Literacy.* In the information age, it's more important than ever that students graduate with the ability to read and write. Many jobs that did not require reading or writing skills a generation ago now use high-tech equipment that demands literacy. A factory worker who can't read computer screens isn't likely to survive the transition to an automated factory.
- *Mathematics.* In an age when mobile phones have built-in calculators, many students think learning math is a waste of time. In fact, some educators argue that we spend too much time teaching students how to do things such as long division and calculating square roots—skills that adults seldom, if ever, do by hand. These arithmetic skills have little to do with being able to think mathematically. To survive in a high-tech world, students need to be able to see the mathematical systems in the world around them and apply math concepts to solve problems. No calculator can do that.
- *Culture.* An education isn't complete without a strong cultural component. Liberal arts and social studies help us recognize the interconnections that turn information into knowledge. Culture gives us roots when the sands of time shift. It gives us historical perspective that allows us to see trends and prepare for the future. Culture provides a human framework with which to view the impact of technology. It also gives us the global perspective to live in a world where communication is determined more by technology than by geography.
- *Communication.* In the information age, communication is a survival skill. Isolated factory workers and desk-bound pencil pushers are vanishing from the workplace. Modern jobs involve interactions—between people and machines and between people and people. The fast-paced, information-based society depends on our human ability to communicate, negotiate, cooperate, and collaborate, both locally and globally.
- *Learning how to learn.* Experts predict that most of the jobs that will exist in coming decades do not exist today and that most of those new jobs will require education past the high school level. With this rapidly changing job market, it's unreasonable to assume that workers can be trained once for lifelong jobs. Instead of holding a single job for 40 years, today's high school or college graduate is likely to change jobs several times. Those people who do keep the same jobs will have to deal with unprecedented change. The half-life of an engineer's specialized knowledge—the time it takes for half of that knowledge to be replaced by more current knowledge—is slightly more than three years.

These facts suggest that we can no longer afford to think of education as a one-time vaccination against illiteracy. In the information age, learning must be a lifelong process. To prepare students for a lifetime of learning, schools must teach students more than facts; they must make sure students learn how to think and learn.

FIGURE 11.16 Modern education focuses on helping students learn how to think and learn.

High-Tech Schools

> The only thing we know about the future is that **it will be inhabited by our children**. Its quality, in other words, is directly proportional to world education.
>
> —*Nicholas Negroponte, founder of the MIT Media Lab and the One Laptop per Child Association*

The information age is making new demands on our educational system, requiring radical changes in what and how people learn. Digital technology is playing a critical role in the transformation of education. **E-learning**—the use of electronic digital technology to facilitate teaching and learning—takes a variety of forms in and out of schools around the world.

Computer-Based Training

In 1953 B. F. Skinner visited his daughter's fourth-grade class and watched the teacher try to teach arithmetic to everyone in the class at the same speed. The experience inspired him to build a teaching machine—a wooden box that used cards, lights, and levers to quiz and reward a student. His machine was based on the principles of behaviorist psychology: allow the student to learn in small steps at an individualized pace and reward correct answers with immediate positive feedback. When PCs appeared in classrooms, students started using **courseware** (educational software) based on those same principles: individualized rate, small steps, and positive feedback. (These early programs were commonly labeled computer-assisted instruction, or CAI.)

A traditional drill-and-practice program presents the student with a question and compares the student's answer with the correct answer. If the answers match, the program offers rewards or praise. If the answers don't match, the program offers an explanation and presents a similar problem. The program may keep track of student responses and tailor questions based on error patterns; it might also provide reports on student progress to the teacher. Today many **computer-based training (CBT)** programs embed the lesson in animated games, in smart phone apps, in special-purpose hardware/software systems, or in Web-based instructional packages, but the underlying principles remain the same.

This kind of courseware can be easily combined with more traditional educational techniques because, like paper quizzes, it produces demonstrable results. Students can learn on their own, freeing the teacher to work one-on-one with students—an important

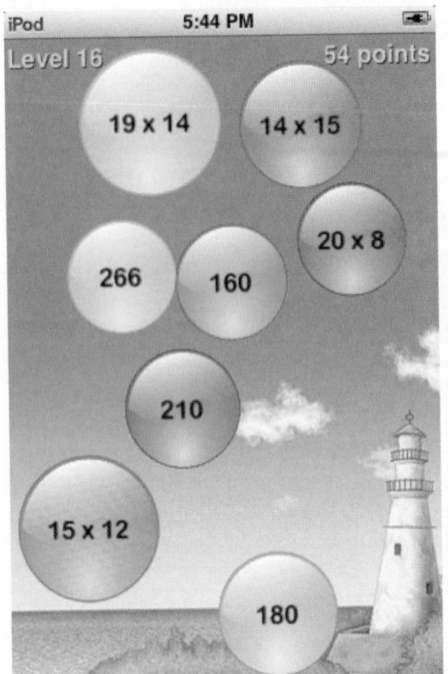

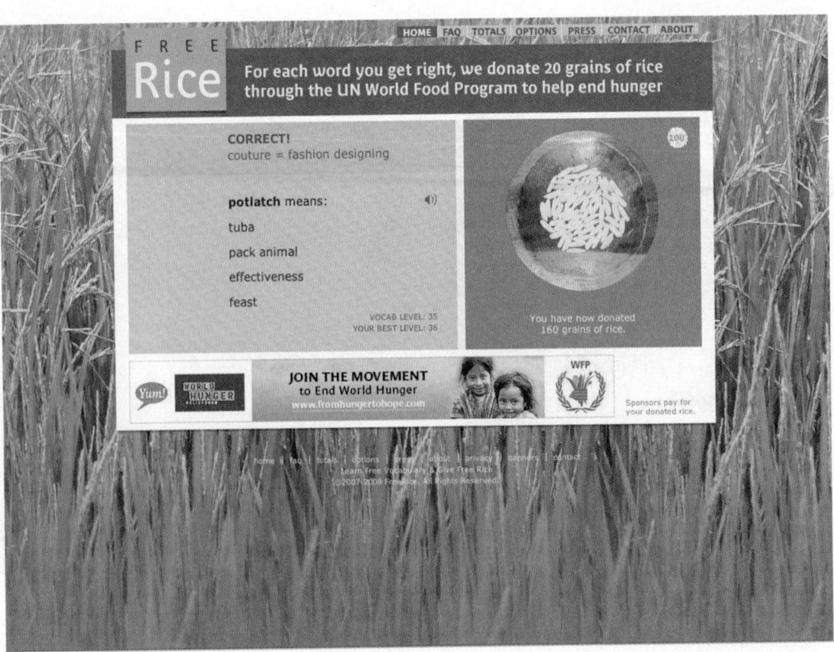

FIGURE 11.17 Students practice basic math skills with smart phone games like PopMath (left). FreeRice.com (right) uses basic drill-and-practice techniques to help visitors build their vocabularies while feeding the hungry.

activity that's all but impossible in typical presentation-and-discussion classrooms. A well-designed program is infinitely patient, and it enables students to make mistakes in private. It can motivate students to practice arithmetic, spelling, touch-typing, piano playing, and other skills that might otherwise be tedious to learn. Research has shown that younger children, disadvantaged children, and in particular students with learning disabilities tend to respond positively to computer-based training systems. Basic drill-and-practice programs work best with well-defined subjects in which every question has a single, clear, unambiguous answer. They generally present information in the form of facts, leaving no room for questioning, creativity, or cooperation. In a sense, they program students.

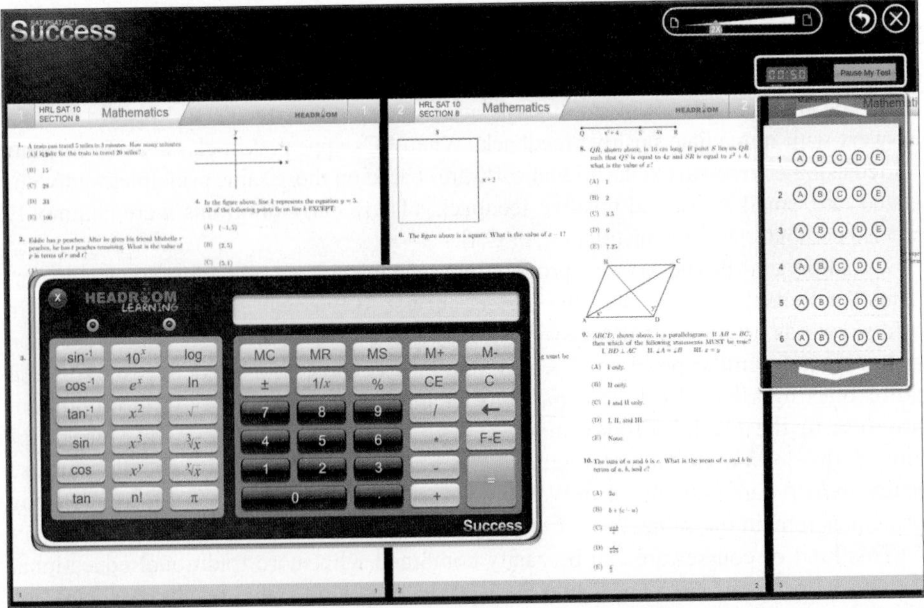

FIGURE 11.18 Students can prepare for standardized tests using ACT/PSAT/SAT Success Software.

Programming Tools

In the 1960s, with colleagues at MIT, Seymour Papert developed a computer language called LOGO so children could program computers rather than the other way around. The LOGO programming language enjoyed some success but never became widely adopted. In 1999, researchers at Carnegie Mellon developed Alice, a free, open-source educational programming language written in Java. Controlled studies suggest that this easy-to-learn language improves learning and retention in first-time programmers. Alice 3.0 incorporates 3-D character models from The Sims, one of the most popular video games of all time. The idea behind these and other student programming languages is to enable children to create simulations and interactive games rather than just use them. It will probably be years before we know the impact of these languages on students' educational development.

Simulations and Games

> No compulsory learning can remain in the soul....In teaching children, **train them by a kind of game**, and you will be able to see more clearly the natural bent of each.
>
> —*Plato, in* The Republic, Book VII

When Papert developed LOGO, he based his educational psychology on the work of renowned Swiss developmental psychologist Jean Piaget. According to Piaget, children have a natural gift for learning on their own; they learn to talk, get around, and think without formal training. A child growing up in France learns French effortlessly because the child's environment has the necessary materials. In Papert's vision, the computer can provide an environment that makes learning mathematics, science, and the arts as effortless as learning French in France.

Many **educational simulations** today are based on the same idea: Children learn best through exploration and invention. These simulations allow students to explore artificial environments, whether imaginary or based on reality. Educational simulations are metaphors designed to focus student attention on the most important concepts. Most educational simulations have the look and feel of a game, but they challenge students to learn through exploration, experimentation, and interaction with other students.

With a simulation, the students are in control of the learning environment. It's up to them to find and use information to draw conclusions. Students can experience the consequences of their actions without taking real-world risks. Simulations enable students to have experiences that wouldn't be possible otherwise. Instead of simply spewing facts, simulations provide a context for knowledge.

Students love playing well-designed simulation games, but many schools don't use simulations because there's no room for them in the formal curriculum. In spite of our culture's age-old tradition of learning through games, many educators question the educational value of games in the classroom. Of course, educational simulations, like all simulations, come up short as substitutes for reality. Many students can play with simulation games for hours without learning anything concrete. The risks of simulations, outlined in Chapter 5, apply to educational simulations, too. But when field trips or full-scale scientific experiments aren't possible, computer simulations can offer affordable alternatives.

FIGURE 11.19 Crazy Machines 2 is a simulation program in which players learn principles of physics by building imaginary machines.

Productivity, Multimedia, and E-Learning 2.0

I hear and I forget, I see and I remember, **I do and I understand.**

—*Ancient Chinese proverb*

Today the trend in schools is clearly toward teaching children to use computers as tools. Word processors, spreadsheets, graphics software, presentation programs, photo- and video-editing systems, Web browsers, search engines, online references, laboratory sensors for scientific data collection—the hardware and software tools used by adults—are the tools students learn to use most often in schools. Once students learn to use these general-purpose tools, they can put them to work in and out of school.

In many classrooms, students create their own multimedia presentations. Students create slide shows, videos, interactive kiosks, podcasts, social networks (open and closed), and (especially) Web pages about their classes, schools, student organizations, and a myriad of academic subjects. The Web makes it possible for these students to reach worldwide audiences with their presentations.

When students work together on these kinds of technology-enhanced projects, it's sometimes referred to as **computer-based collaborative learning (CBCL)** or **e-learning 2.0**. Web 2.0 technology turned the Internet into a medium for participation and collaboration. In the same way e-learning 2.0—whether students are designing and building robotic racecars or educational simulation games—is all about learning through cooperation and collective effort.

This kind of student involvement promotes learning, but it has drawbacks. One problem is economic: Few schools can afford the hardware, software, and floor space for multiple student media workstations. Another problem is both social and political: When students are creating or using interactive media, they aren't conforming to the traditional factory model. Instead of taking notes they're taking control of the machinery and the learning process. The teacher becomes a supervisor and a mentor rather than a conveyor of information. Many teachers lack the training and experience to supervise these kinds of projects. And many administrators tend to give priority to more orthodox programs aimed at raising standardized test scores.

On the other end of the spectrum are schools that are designed from the ground up around e-learning 2.0 concepts. For example, Quest to Learn (Q2L) in Manhattan, New

FIGURE 11.20 In many schools students routinely work on technology-enhanced projects, using the Internet as a medium for participation and collaboration.

York, calls itself a "school for digital kids." Kids at Q2L learn by doing. Rather than discouraging kids from playing games, the school uses games as educational tools to teach its 6th through 12th graders. According to their Web site, "Games work as rule-based learning systems, creating worlds in which players actively participate, use strategic thinking to make choices, solve complex problems, seek content knowledge, receive constant feedback, and consider the point of view of others." Students not only play educational games—they design and build them. Time and research will tell whether this type of education will provide students with the skills they need as adults, but early indications are promising.

Supporting Special Needs

Computers play an important role in improving the educational experience of students with special needs. Two U.S. laws, the Individuals with Disabilities Act (IDEA) and Americans with Disabilities Act (ADA), have established the goal that every student should have equal access to school programs and services. It calls for schools to use assistive technology where appropriate to achieve the goal of equal access.

The assistive technology that schools provide students with special needs covers a broad spectrum of devices. For many students, low-tech devices are sufficient to accommodate their needs. For example, students with poor muscle control can benefit from rubber pencil grips. Line magnifiers enlarge lines of type for students with impaired vision and learning disabilities. Other students need a middle level of technology to make the classroom experience accessible. Wireless systems amplify sounds for students with hearing impairments, and handheld talking dictionaries assist students who have difficulties with reading or spelling. High-tech devices like the Kurzweil Reading Machine can open up the world of books to sightless students.

FIGURE 11.21 A wireless system, left, uses FM radio waves to amplify the teacher's voice for this student who is hearing impaired. A "sip/puff" device, middle, is one way for a computer user with quadriplegia to control a cursor. A Tiger printer, right, embosses both Braille and graphics, giving students who are visually impaired the ability to access mathematical, scientific, and engineering documents that make heavy use of graphics.

Many devices have been designed to help students with special needs interact with computers. Some students are unable to use a traditional computer mouse or keyboard. Alternatives to the mouse include touch screens, trackballs, headsticks, and eyegaze systems. Alternative keyboards have keys that are much larger or smaller than usual, or a different arrangement of letters. Another text input option is speech recognition software. With augmentative communication software, a computer can provide a student who does not speak the ability to communicate with others using text, graphics, and sound.

Distance Education: Virtual Schools

For some students the most important application of computers in schools is **distance education**—using technology to extend the educational process beyond the walls of the school. Grade-school students can network with kids in other parts of the world through the Internet. Middle-school classes can use electron microscopes, telescopes, and other powerful tools around the world through real-time Internet connections. High-school correspondence courses can be completed via the Internet rather than by mail. Students with handicaps can do coursework without traveling to central sites. Two-way video links allow "visiting" experts to talk to students in outlying classrooms and answer their questions in real time. Networked school districts can offer multischool videoconference courses in Chinese, college-level calculus, and other subjects that might have tiny enrollments if offered at only a single school. Teachers can receive additional education without leaving their districts.

Telecommunication technology is particularly important for students in remote locations. If a child in a small town develops an interest in a narrow subject, whether it's aboriginal anthropology, classical Russian ballet, or designing user interfaces for handheld devices, that student may find pursuing that interest a discouraging process. But through an Internet connection, reference materials, special-interest blogs and forums, educational podcasts, long-distance mentors, and like-minded communities are all within reach. In many areas, rural interactive television networks keep remote schools and towns from fading away.

Distance education is particularly attractive to parents—especially mothers—with young children. Distance education also offers promise for workers whose jobs are changed or eliminated. Many displaced and dissatisfied workers can't afford to relocate their families to college towns so they can learn new skills. But if colleges and universities offer electronic outreach programs, these people can update their skills while remaining in their communities.

Since 1990 online degree programs have appeared at dozens of universities and colleges. Students use the Internet to do everything from ordering books to taking final exams. Many online students see their professors in person for the first time at graduation ceremonies.

The demand for distance education is growing rapidly. In some countries distance education students make up close to half of the total undergraduate population. Some experts predict that a few hundred huge distance-ed universities will put most traditional universities out of business.

Of course, a college education is more than a collection of information. Students learn and grow as a result of all kinds of experiences in and out of the classroom. Many significant learning experiences can't be transmitted through phone lines and TV cables. Dropout rates for distance learning students are higher than those for classroom students. For many students, there's no substitute for face-to-face communication with teachers and other students.

But the tools of distance learning can be applied to on-campus learning, too. Blogs, forums, podcasts, online gradebooks, computerized testing, and a virtual learning environment can, if properly applied, benefit students near and far. The combination of e-learning with face-to-face teaching—sometimes called ***blended learning***—is, for many students, the best of both worlds. On campus or off, e-learning is an important step toward an educational system that encourages lifelong learning.

E-Learning Packages

In the early days of e-learning, individual software programs were designed to meet particular instructional goals. Schools purchased and used math programs, science simulations, typing tutorials, and gradebook programs with no interconnections. Today there's a trend toward highly integrated e-learning *packages*.

For example, TeacherMate is a carefully designed package of educational software and hardware that links children with teachers. Students use the handheld TeacherMate computer, a device slightly larger than a smart phone that runs educational programs and records and plays back audio. Teachers can download detailed records of student performance and spend extra time working with students who need extra help. Students enjoy the educational games, teachers appreciate the integration of student records with school curriculum, and researchers report that the system is effective at raising student skill levels in math and reading. The TeacherMate system doesn't require the specialized hardware; software is being developed to run on a variety of PC and smart phone platforms.

Many educational packages are offered through the Web. For example, Discover Education: Science is a subscription-based multimedia site that enables students to "learn science as scientists." The site has been approved by at least one school district as a K–5 science "textbook."

In higher education, the dominant e-learning system is Blackboard. The Blackboard Learning System is used at thousands of colleges and universities around the world. The system includes tools for communication among students and instructors as well as content-management tools for posting articles, assignments, notes, tests, class schedules, grades, and media. Many online classes are built around Blackboard learning modules, but the system is also routinely used to supplement and enhance traditional classes.

Technology at School: Midterm Grades

> The business of education is to give the student both **useful information and life-enhancing experience**, one largely measurable, the other not.
>
> —*John Gardner, in* The Art of Fiction

Many schools have been using computers in classrooms since the 1980s. Many classrooms connected to the Web in the late 1990s and early 2000s. In these days of shrinking budgets, taxpayers are asking whether classroom computer technology pays off. Has it lived up to its promise as an educational tool in the schools? According to most experts, the answer is mixed but optimistic.

High Marks

A number of independent studies have confirmed that information technology can improve education. Here are some findings:

- Students improve problem-solving and reasoning skills, outscore classmates, and learn more rapidly in a variety of subject areas and situations when using technology as compared to conventional methods of study.
- Students find computer-based instruction to be more motivational, less intimidating, and easier to stick with than traditional instruction. Their attitudes toward learning consistently improve when instructional technology is used.
- In many cases students' self-esteem is increased when they use computers. This change is most dramatic in cases of at-risk youngsters and students with handicaps.
- Using technology encourages cooperative learning, turn taking among young children, peer tutoring, and other valuable social skills.
- Computer technology can make learning more student centered and stimulate increased teacher–student interaction.

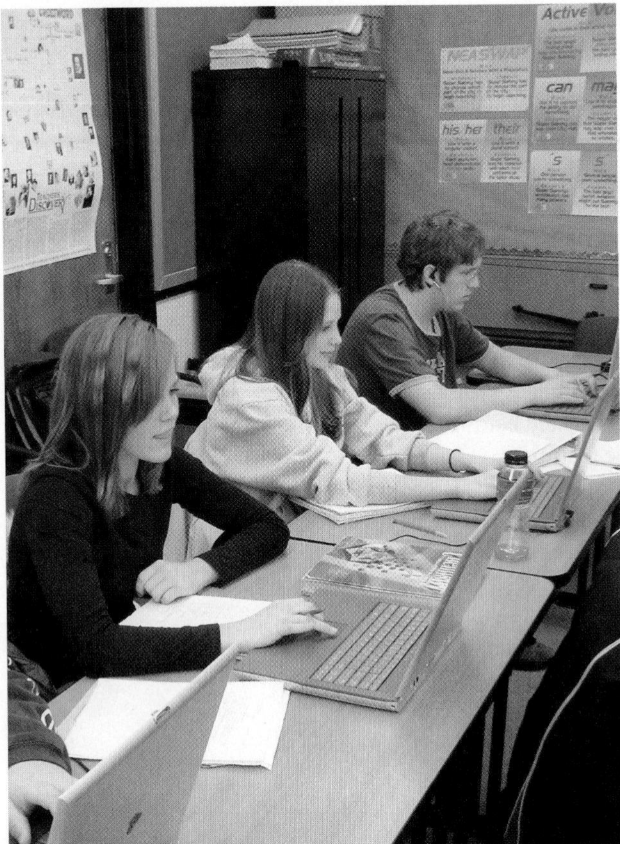

FIGURE 11.22 Research shows that writing improves when students use word processors. Henrico County, Virginia, has been a strong proponent of the technology in education. Here, students are pictured with their laptops.

- Well-designed interactive multimedia systems can encourage active processing and higher-order thinking.
- Students who create interactive multimedia reports often learn better than those who learn with more traditional methods.
- Students can become more productive and fluid writers with computers.
- Computers can help students master the basic skills needed to participate and succeed in the workforce.
- Positive changes occur gradually as teachers gain experience with the technology.
- Technology can facilitate educational reform.
- Students with technology integrated into their classroom see the benefit in each major subject area.
- Students with and without special needs show increased achievement from preschool through higher education when technology is incorporated into their curricula.
- Students and teachers with positive attitudes toward technology gain the most.
- Students often learn better when the technology facilitates working in groups.
- Working or playing with computers can improve eye-hand coordination, reflex response, processing of visual cues, and other low-level brain functions.
- Students who practice using the Web tend to become better at assessing the trustworthiness of Web sites.
- Students experience a greater benefit from technology when their teachers receive professional training, and teachers report that they are more enthusiastic about technology when provided with training.

Room for Improvement

> The further one pursues knowledge, **the less one knows.**
>
> *—Lao Tse, 500 BC*

Other findings temper—and sometimes contradict—these positive conclusions. Researchers have also observed the following:

- If the only thing that changes is the delivery medium (from traditional media to computer media), the advantages of technology are small—or nonexistent.
- Students and teachers forget advanced computer skills if they don't use them.
- Students have unequal access to technology; economically disadvantaged students have less computer access at school and at home. Sadly, these are the students who can benefit most when given access to technology.
- Technology doesn't reduce teacher workloads; if anything, it seems to make their jobs harder. This is especially true in today's world of digital-from-birth kids, who are very different than the kids most educators were trained to teach.
- Sometimes there's a gender gap that puts the computer room in the boys' domain; the gap can be reduced by emphasizing computer activities that involve collaboration.
- Many of the outcomes of technology-based education don't show up with traditional educational assessment methods and standardized tests.
- Research suggests that the human brain has more trouble comprehending and remembering information when it's delivered via hypertext, multimedia, or the Web rather than through books. The more hyperlinks and other distractions, the more difficult it is for the brain to transfer information from short-term memory to long-term storage.

- There's a growing body of evidence that students who spend large percentages of their time on the Internet may be harming their abilities to do "deep processing" necessary for analysis, critical thinking, and reflection.
- Younger students may be better served by art, music, and shop classes than by computer classes; unfortunately, these important parts of the curriculum are often eliminated to make room for computers.

Stories abound of reduced dropout rates and attitudinal changes among at-risk students; improved math, reading, and language scores; and overall academic improvement among students in high-tech schools. But computer technology doesn't always bring happy headlines. In some schools computers are little more than expensive, time-consuming distractions. What makes technology work for some schools and not for others? A closer look at the success stories reveals that they didn't achieve results with technology alone. When we compare these schools with less fortunate schools, several issues emerge:

- *Money.* Not surprisingly, computers tend to be concentrated in affluent countries and school districts, so economically disadvantaged students have the least access to them. And even the wealthiest school districts may not be able to keep up with rapid technological changes.
- *Planning and support.* When school districts spend money on technology without thoughtful long-term planning and sustained support, their investments are not likely to pay off.
- *Teacher training.* Unfortunately, teacher training is often missing from schools' high-tech formulas. Teachers need training, support, and time to integrate technology into their curricula. Many teachers lack understanding of the high-tech world that their students inhabit; for these teachers, it's important to learn not just about the technology, but also about the technology *culture* of the digital generation.
- *Restructuring.* Just as businesses need to rethink their organizational structures to automate successfully, schools need to be restructured to make effective use of computer technology. The goal is education, and technology is just one tool for achieving that goal. Interactive media, individualized instruction, telecommunication, and cooperative learning simply don't fit well into the factory school. To meet the educational challenges of the information age, we'll need to invest in research and planning involving teachers, students, administrators, parents, businesses, and community leaders.

Information technology, then, can be a powerful change agent but not by itself. In an interview for online magazine *ZineZone*, educational computing pioneer Seymour Papert was asked whether technology is a Trojan horse for systematic and lasting change. His reply: "I think the technology serves as a Trojan horse all right, but in the real story of the Trojan horse, it wasn't the horse that was effective, it was the soldiers inside the horse. And the technology is only going to be effective in changing education if you put an army inside it which is determined to make that change once it gets through the barrier."

The High-Tech Home

> There is no reason for any individual **to have a computer in their home**.
>
> *—Ken Olson, president of Digital Equipment Corporation, 1977*

The same year Ken Olson made this statement, Apple introduced the Apple II computer. In the years that followed, Apple, Commodore, Tandy, Atari, IBM, and dozens of other companies managed to sell computers to millions of individuals who had "no reason" to buy them.

Today there are more computers in homes than in schools. Most American homes contain at least one computer. The small office, home office market—dubbed *SOHO* by the industry—is one of the fastest-growing computer markets today. While many home computers gather dust, others are being put to work, and play, in a variety of ways.

Working Wisdom

Maximizing Brain Power in the Digital Age

Most people assume that there's not much they can do to change the brains they were born with. But the human brain is remarkably flexible. Like a computer, your brain can be reprogrammed and, in some cases, even rewired. In this digital age, your most important tool is your brain. Here are some tips for making the most of your wetware.

- ***Free your brain for the important stuff.*** School assignments. Reading. Bills. Shopping. Social obligations. In a world that never stops making demands, it's easy to be overwhelmed trying to keep up. Many people waste brain power and create unnecessary stress trying to remember all of the things they need to do. The human brain is not particularly good at this kind of data storage. There are lots of apps for PCs, Macs, and smart phones that can help you corral your to-do lists and free your mind for more important things. Some are simple to-do and calendar apps; others are based on more sophisticated organization systems, such as David Allen's popular *Getting Things Done* system. Most of them offer free trial versions. Find one that works for you and use it.
- ***Make planning part of your routine.*** Once you've got a system, use it. Set aside time every day, and more time once a week, to set goals, make plans, monitor your calendar, and check off items that are completed or no longer relevant. This planning time will pay you back with interest as you move through your day.
- ***Multitask when you must...*** Multitasking is a necessary part of modern life. Some jobs demand that you be able to answer your phone or email while you're doing other tasks. Even preparing a meal often involves tracking several dishes at once. It's important to be able to handle surprises when they come up without dropping other balls.
- ***...but minimize multitasking.*** Many people—especially young people—are convinced they can work more efficiently if they're doing several things at once. But the research is clear: The human brain can't multitask—it *simulates* multitasking by rapidly switching between tasks. Every switch takes time and increases the chances of errors and oversights. What's more, multitasking seems to have long-term impact on brain function. Chronic multitaskers are easily distracted and, in many cases, unable to remember and reason clearly. That feeling of efficiency and mastery is an illusion. If you want to get serious work done, turn off your phone, your email program, and your TV.
- ***Mask out distractions.*** We live in a noisy world—cars, computers, and conversations compete for our consciousness. Some people find that instrumental background music helps them concentrate, in part because it masks out surrounding sounds. Vocal music doesn't work because it's processed by the same part of the brain that handles reading and writing. If you find music distracting, try a recording of ocean surf, a white noise generator, or other atmospheric sounds. If you're prone to being pulled off task by email, IMs, the lure of the Web, or too many open windows on your screen, consider using software that blocks Internet distractions and/or application switching while you're working.
- ***Practice thinking big.*** Educators complain that the cell phone generation can fire off 140-character tweets but can't write a coherent 500-word essay. Thinking is like sports—it can take a big effort to achieve a big goal. And the more you do it, the easier it becomes. It pays to push yourself mentally, even if it's hard. If it's not hard, you're probably not doing it.
- ***Use it or lose it.*** Different parts of the brain excel at different tasks. Exercise all of those parts regularly to keep your brain in tiptop shape. Read books. Write a blog. Solve puzzles. Create art. Play a musical instrument. Sing. Dance. Explore. Play.
- ***Pay Attention.*** In her 2011 *Newsweek* cover story "Can You Build a Better Brain?" Sharon Begley surveyed research on brain plasticity and found that "attention is almost magical in its ability to alter the brain and enlarge functional circuits." In other words, when we're paying attention to what we're doing, we're helping our brains learn and grow. Research suggests that meditation can increase the brain's ability to concentrate, and therefore improve overall brain function. But so, it appears, can certain types of video games that demand focus, task switching, memory, and rapid-fire decision making.
- ***Strengthen your body to strengthen your mind.*** Like any computer, your brain needs energy. A healthy diet is essential for a healthy brain. Regular aerobic exercise strengthens your heart and your circulatory system so that it can deliver nutrients to your brain. If it's good for your heart, it's good for your brain. According to University of Illinois researcher Art Kramer, "You can think of fitness training as changing the molecular and cellular building blocks that underlie many cognitive skills."
- ***Don't sacrifice sleep.*** Your brain needs to recharge, too. Give it a rest. One of the most important predictors of brain performance is amount of sleep. Stimulants are no substitute for sleep—they're just borrowing from future energy supplies.

Household Business

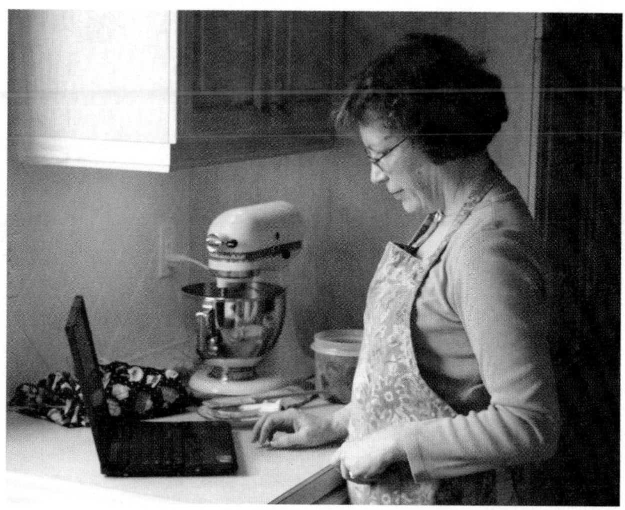

FIGURE 11.23 Today's search engines can provide instant recipes when given a list of ingredients. Within seconds of typing in a list of items in her refrigerator, this cook has a recipe that uses them all.

Frank Gilbreth, a turn-of-the-century pioneer of motion study in industry, applied "scientific management" techniques to his home. He required his 12 children to keep records on bathroom "work-and-process charts" of each hair combing, tooth brushing, and bathing. He gave them demonstrations on efficient bathing techniques to minimize "avoidable delays." While it may have worked for Gilbreth, this "scientific management" approach to home life is not likely to catch on today. Still, certain aspects of family life are unavoidably businesslike, and a growing number of people are turning to computers to help them take care of business.

Computer owners generally use many of the same applications at home that they use in their offices: Web browsers for entertainment, research, shopping, and other applications; email, IMs, and social networks for connecting with others; word processors for writing; personal information managers for tracking calendars and contacts; and financial management programs for tracking income and expenses.

In the early days of home computing, financial management involved tediously typing in every purchase, paycheck, and investment. Today Quicken and other programs grab information from bank Web sites so users only need to fill in the product descriptions, tax categories, cash transactions, and so on. But in many countries consumers can make at least some of their purchases using smart phones and smart cards—devices that can, in theory, provide transaction information to home computers without having to connect to bank Web sites.

A typical **smart card** looks like a standard credit card, but instead of a magnetic strip, it contains embedded circuits that can process information along with some kind of input/output device. A memory card contains memory but no microprocessor; a microprocessor card contains memory along with a tiny CPU. Contact smart cards use a small contact area with several gold-plated contacts for input and output. Contactless smart cards use wireless RFID technology to communicate with card readers and writers. Smart cards can also contain cryptographic hardware and other security circuitry.

Smart cards are obvious candidates to replace magnetic-strip credit cards. In addition to storing critical ID information, a smart card can automatically record each transaction for later retrieval. But smart cards have other applications, too. College students use smart cards as meal tickets. Office workers use smart cards as keys to access sensitive data on computers. Smart cards have replaced food stamps and drivers' licenses in some states and countries. People all around the world use smart cards to pay highway tolls and unscramble cable TV broadcasts. In France, smart cards are used for health insurance. Malaysia, Spain, and Belgium were among the first of many countries to use smart cards as universal ID cards. Of course, many of these smart card applications raise questions about protection of personal privacy. Future smart cards will use pattern recognition techniques to verify signatures on checks or credit slips and help prevent fraud and forgery.

Education and Information

> Newspapers as we know them won't exist. **They will be printed for a readership of one**. Television won't simply have sharper pictures. You'll have **one button that says tell me more, and another button that says tell me less**.
>
> —*Nicholas Negroponte, founder of the MIT Media Lab*

Millions of people use home computers for education and information. Many educational software programs are used by children and adults in homes. **Edutainment** programs specifically geared toward home markets combine education with entertainment so they

FIGURE 11.24 The Octopus card is a contactless smart card used like an electronic wallet by over 95 percent of the population of Hong Kong. Octopus cards are used to store and transfer payments for mass transit, parking, vending machines, convenience stores, supermarkets, and more.

FIGURE 11.25 Nintendo's Wii Fit and Microsoft's Kinect encourage gamers to exercise their bodies; some other popular games are designed to exercise brains.

can compete with television and electronic games. Digital encyclopedias, dictionaries, atlases, almanacs, medical references, language translators, and other specialized references are available on disc, as smart phone apps, and on the Web. Of course, Internet connections also provide blogs, forums, podcasts, and other media options for home users.

As computer technology and communication technology converge on the home market, they're producing interactive products and services that challenge TV, radio, and print media as our main sources of information. Television and radio are broadcast media; they transmit news and information to broad audiences. Computer technology enables **narrowcasting** services—custom newscasts and entertainment features aimed at narrow groups or at individuals. (Individualized broadcasting is sometimes called *pointcasting*.) With a narrowcasting service, you might create a personalized news program that includes a piece on the latest Middle Eastern crisis, highlights of last night's Celtics vs. Lakers game, this weekend's weather forecast at the coast, announcements of upcoming local jazz concerts, and a reminder that there are only five more shopping days until your mother's birthday. Personalized news services can flag particular subjects ("I'm especially interested in articles on the Amazon rain forest") and ignore others ("No Hollywood gossip, please").

Several Web portals, including Google and Yahoo!, enable users to personalize their "front pages" with customized headlines, stock quotes, weather information, television and movie schedules, and other features. Personalized bookmarking services like Del.icio.us can point Web browsers to sites that match their interests. Many people regularly scan their Facebook feeds for up-to-the-minute "headlines" about friends, personalities, sports, games, and causes that are important to them. Music selection services like Pandora make it easy to create custom radio stations. Podcasts provide special-interest audio and video on demand and on the go.

Personalized Web portals enable people to control what they see on their home pages but not what they see on other sites. Some families depend on **filtering software** to block their browsers so children can't visit sites that contain pornography and other inappropriate content. Filtering programs can be customized, but they're not 100 percent accurate. They're also subject to the biases of their authors and corporate owners. A few years ago extensive tests of America Online's filtering revealed that young teens could access sites promoting gun use, including the National Rifle Association, but not the Coalition to Stop Gun

Violence and other gun safety organizations. Both AOL and The Learning Company, who designed the filtering software, denied bias. But the findings show how censorship can squelch the free flow of ideas that's a critical part of the educational process.

Parents need to do more than install filtering software to ensure that their children are getting maximum benefit from home computers. Recent research suggests that having a computer in the home can actually lower math and writing test scores if parents don't monitor and guide their children's computer use.

Home Entertainment Redefined

> Television has a "brightness" knob, but it **doesn't seem to work.**
>
> —*Gallagher, stand-up comic*

Regardless of how people say they use home computers, surveys suggest that many people use them mostly to play games. Computer games and video game machines (which are just special-purpose computers) represent a huge industry—one that is likely to evolve rapidly in the coming years.

Most computer games are simulations. Computer games can simulate board games, card games, sporting events, intergalactic battles, street fights, corporate takeovers, or something else, real or imaginary. Many computer games require strategy and puzzle solving; others depend only on eye-hand coordination. Often the most popular games require some of each. **Massively multiplayer online role-playing games** on the Internet enable thousands of people to interact in virtual worlds. Success in massively multiplayer online role-playing games requires establishing beneficial social relationships with other characters. The most popular games can attract hundreds of thousands of players at a time—including more than a few addicts who spend most of their waking hours there.

Addiction isn't the only social problem related to online games. In the years before the 1999 Columbine High School mass murder, the killers spent hundreds of hours blasting virtual people in graphic first-person shooter games. In the aftermath of the tragedy, many people suggested that the games were partially responsible for the horrific killings. A year later, published research confirmed a link between violent video games and real-world violence. Two studies suggested that even brief exposure to violent video games can temporarily increase aggressive behavior and that children who play violent games tend to have lower grades and more aggressive tendencies in later years. Other studies have failed to show a conclusive link between violent games and violent behavior, but research will undoubtedly continue. An industry rating system is designed to prevent young children from playing "inappropriate" games. But questions about the negative consequences of gaming are likely to be with us for many years.

Sometimes the impact of video games on young minds is measurably positive. Researchers at Eastern Virginia Medical School in Norfolk,

Custom Select your own set of categories to block.

Commonly Blocked Categories		[Block All] | [Unblock All]
Abortion	Intimate Apparel/Swimsuit	Proxy Avoidance
Adult/Mature Content	Nudity	Sex Education
Alternative Spirituality/Occult	Open Image/Media Search	Sexuality/Alternative Lifestyles
Gambling	Peer-to-Peer (P2P)	Social Networking
Hacking	Personals/Dating	Spyware Effects/Privacy Concerns
Illegal Drugs	Phishing	Spyware/Malware Sources
Illegal/Questionable	Pornography	Violence/Hate/Racism

Other Categories		[Block All] | [Unblock All]
Alcohol/Tobacco	Government/Legal	Remote Access Tools
Arts/Entertainment	Health	Restaurants/Dining/Food
Auctions	Humor/Jokes	Search Engines/Portals
Blogs/Newsgroups	Job Search/Careers	Shopping
Brokerage/Trading	Military	Society/Lifestyle
Business/Economy	News/Media	Software Downloads
Chat/Instant Messaging	Online Games	Sports/Recreation/Hobbies
Computers/Internet	Online Storage	Streaming Media/MP3
Cultural/Charitable Organizations	Pay to Surf	Travel
Education	Political/Activist Groups	Vehicles
Email	Real Estate	Weapons
Financial Services	Reference	Web Advertisements
For Kids	Religion	Web Hosting

Unrated Web Pages

Enable *Dynamic Real-Time Rating*™ (DRTR) Block Unrated Web Pages

Save Changes

FIGURE 11.26 Teachers and parents can use filtering software to keep children away from "inappropriate" sites.

FIGURE 11.27 The popular Grand Theft Auto series of video games has generated controversy because of high levels of person-to-person violence and morally ambiguous plot lines.

working with NASA scientists, used PlayStation games successfully to treat children diagnosed with attention deficit disorder (ADD). Using basic biofeedback technology and off-the-shelf video games, children were able to learn to control their brain waves so they could improve concentration. The fast-action games provided strong motivation for the young learners. PC software/hardware systems are now available to help children and adults with ADD.

The entertainment industry is exploring a variety of ways of adding interactivity to products. In the early days of home computing, one of the most popular types of games was *interactive fiction*—stories with primitive natural-language interfaces that gave players some control over plot. Today, arcade-style games, puzzle-based adventure games, and other multimedia-rich genres capture most of the attention of computer gamers. But interactivity is finding its way into other entertainment technology—most notably on the Web and on DVDs and Blu-ray discs.

Many movie discs allow for customized viewing—language, subtitles, commentary, soundtracks, and sometimes even camera angle are under viewer control. A few discs allow actual branching within a film. We may soon see truly *interactive movies*—features

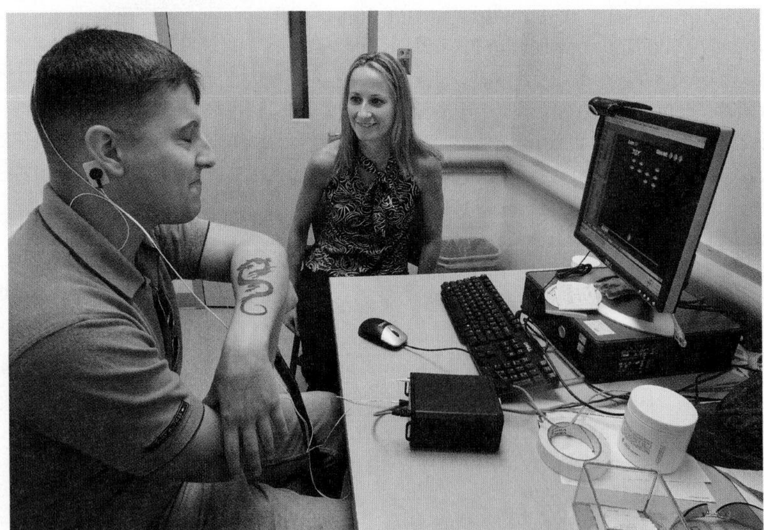

FIGURE 11.28 Researchers are using video game technology in biofeedback experiments on children and adults with attention deficit disorder.

in which one or more of the characters or plot lines are controlled by the viewers.

We're also seeing growth in **interactive television**—broadcast television with options for interactivity built in. Many "reality" programs and game shows depend on viewer input via phone calls and text messages. Set top boxes and video-on-demand services can add more immediate interactivity and personalization to television, blurring the lines between the TV and the PC. Interactive TV has been popular for years in Europe, where digital TV had an early audience.

FIGURE 11.29 In this Korean electronic sports stadium, spectators cheer for world-class gamers who compete on giant screens.

The next step beyond interactive television is sometimes called **social television**—TV that supports communication and social interaction. Social TV might include any or all of these elements: voice communication; instant messaging; texting; social networks; smart remotes; multiway video-conferencing; and face, voice, body, and gesture recognition. Interpersonal communication might involve rating programs, discussing content, or competing in television games. The technology is still evolving, and different companies are taking different approaches to adding social dimensions to the television experience.

Creativity and Leisure

> If you can talk, **you can sing**. If you can walk, **you can dance**.
>
> *—A saying from Zimbabwe*

American kids spend 25 or more hours every week on digital media, and that number keeps growing. A 2000 report by the Childhood Alliance, a group of education experts, raised serious questions about computer use, especially by young children. "Intense use of computers can distract children and adults from...essential experiences." Specifically, the time children spend in front of a computer screen is time they aren't involved in physical activities and self-generated, imaginative play. "A heavy diet of ready-made computer images and programmed toys appears to stunt imaginative thinking." The report also argued that computers expose kids to adult hazards, including repetitive-stress injury and social isolation. Many studies since then have reinforced these concerns and added new ones. There's growing evidence that the digital tools and toys that are so attractive to children are, in fact, changing the way their brains work. And parents often feel like immigrants who don't speak the digital language of their children.

Many people worry that TV, computer games, and other media are replacing too many real-world activities. Instead of making up stories to share, we watch sitcoms on TV. Instead of playing music on guitars, we play music on iPods. Instead of playing one-on-one basketball, we play one-on-one video games.

Is electronic technology turning us into a mindless couch-potato culture? Perhaps. But there's another possibility. The same technology that mesmerizes us can also unlock our creativity. Word processors and blogging software help many of us to become writers, graphics software brings out the artists among us, Web authoring tools provide us with worldwide publishing platforms, electronic music systems enable us to compose music even if we never mastered an instrument, and podcasting technology gives creative people everywhere access to global audiences.

Will computers drain our creativity or amplify it? In the end it's up to us.

Inventing the Future ▸ Tomorrow's Technology for Today's Children

The One Laptop per Child Organization has a lofty mission: "To create educational opportunities for the world's poorest children by providing each child with a rugged, low-cost, low-power, connected laptop with content and software designed for collaborative, joyful, self-empowered learning." Visionaries Alan Kay and Seymour Papert helped shape the organization's philosophy along with founder and chair Nicholas Negroponte.

The organization's original goal in 2005 was to create a state-of-the-art laptop that cost less than $100 so that it could be distributed to children in developing nations. Researchers at MIT and elsewhere pushed the technological envelope to produce a low-cost, low-power machine that was well suited for use by children in remote villages. Roughly a million and a half of XO-1 laptops found their way into the hands of children around the world between 2007 and 2010.

Early research in Peru and elsewhere suggests that XO-1s can improve communication, cooperation, and learning for their owners. It's too early to assess fully the program's impact. To make a positive difference, OLPC must overcome technological, political, and social hurdles. But the organization isn't sitting still waiting for results.

The next generation XO, called the XO-2, was announced in 2008 with a projected 2010 release date. The radical design of the XO-2 replaced the keyboard of a traditional laptop with a second touch screen. The XO-2 could be used as a tablet, an e-book, a laptop, or a board, depending on whether it was flat or folded, horizontal or vertical. The XO-2 never made it past the prototype stage. In 2009 it was shelved in favor of the XO-3, a single screen tablet with a projected 2012 release date.

At first glance the XO-3 looks like a large iPad. Like Apple's popular tablet, it replaces the physical keyboard and mouse with a multitouch interface that's easier for kids to understand and use. But on the XO-3, the touch screen has practically no border and the device has no buttons. According to Yves Behar, founder of FuseProject, the company that designed both XO-1 and XO-3, "The media or content on the computer will be the prime visual element."

The user interface isn't the only innovation in the XO-3. The super-thin, waterproof device will use a tiny fraction of the power of a typical laptop. It will use an ultra-low-power screen made of durable plastic rather than glass. The device will have a rear-facing camera and a round handle, but it will have no ports—not even a charging port. It will use induction to wirelessly charge its battery. Like the XO-1, the XO-3 will effortlessly connect to a mesh network, minimizing communication hassles for users who don't speak Wi-Fi. Amazingly, the XO-3 should cost even less than the original XO-1—the target price is now $75 per tablet.

Of course, the XO-3, like the XO-2, may never go beyond the prototype stage. OLPC has a spotty record for turning promises into products. But that doesn't concern Nicholas Negroponte, who plans to open the architecture so any PC maker can build an XO-3-like device. He sees the project as a success if it pressures the industry into making inexpensive educational computers. "We don't need to build it. We just need to threaten to build it."

One Laptop per Child has been criticized for not being able to meet its ambitious goals. But research seeds planted in One Laptop per Child will bear fruit in the computers we use in the future. Hopefully, the innovations of the XO-3 and beyond will give new hope to children everywhere. In Negroponte's words, "If we only achieve half of what we're setting out to do, it could have very big consequences."

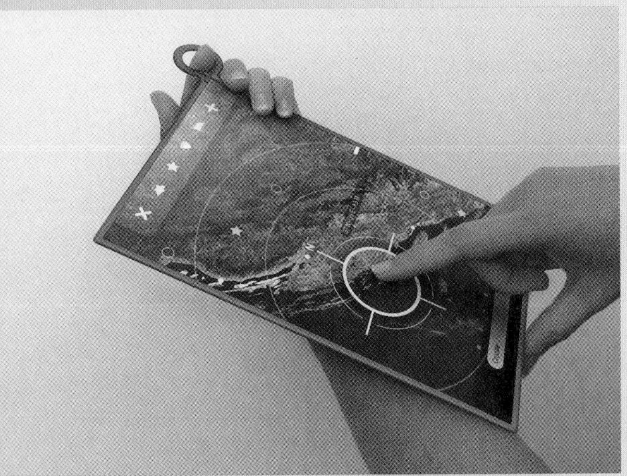

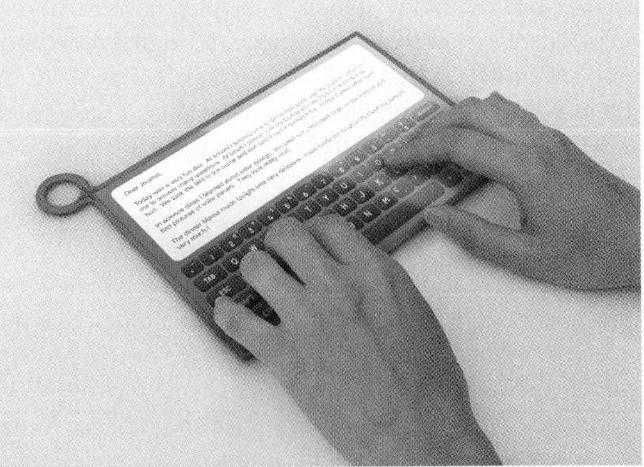

FIGURE 11.30 The XO-3 tablet is designed to combine state-of-the-art technology with a sleek design at a rock-bottom price so that children all around the world can have access to quality educational resources.

Crosscurrents

Reality Is Broken. Game Designers Must Fix It *by Kim Zetter*

Game designer Jane McGonigal believes games can be a way to fix, and not just escape from, reality. In this slightly edited February 11, 2010, Wired.com *interview with Kim Zetter, she explains how.*

Game designer Jane McGonigal thinks games can change the world. Instead of just inviting gamers to escape into a game world that is more attractive than the real world, game developers have a responsibility to steer gamers toward improving the real world.

Director of game research and development for the Institute for the Future, McGonigal says reality is broken and can only be fixed if we make the real world work like massive, multiplayer games. Games—particularly alternate reality games—inspire large groups of people to pool their knowledge and skills to overcome obstacles, and this is precisely what's needed to tackle global social issues, such as poverty, hunger, disease and climate change, McGonigal says.

An example of this is a popular game McGonigal developed in 2007 with Ken Eklund called *World Without Oil,* which asked 1,800 players in 12 countries to re-imagine their life in a world bereft of oil. The aim was to get players to adjust their thinking and actions if there weren't enough fuel to ship foods long distances, bus their children to school or simply commute to work. In 2010 McGonigal unveiled *Evoke*, designed for the World Bank Institute, the teaching division of the World Bank, with the aim of helping them develop skills and solutions to world problems.

Wired.com: You say that reality is broken and that it's the responsibility of game designers to fix it. What makes game designers the perfect choice to fix the world?

Jane McGonigal: The game industry has spent the last 30 years optimizing two things: how to make people happy and how to inspire collaboration on really complex challenges. . . . We have all the problems surrounding hunger, poverty, climate change, energy and those are all such extreme-scale problems that require so many different actors to work together, so much concerted effort and so much creative thinking that they seem to be the kinds of problems that gamers have been trained to solve. In game worlds and in game environments we have these really sophisticated ways of working with other people and figuring out what each others' strengths are, putting together a team where everybody has something important to contribute, coordinating globally in a virtual environment. The idea is to make games that take those sophisticated ways of collaborating and apply those to real-world problems.

Wired.com: You've said that game designers are in the happiness business. What do you mean by this?

McGonigal: . . . . Studies have shown that playing a short game—having something concrete that you can accomplish—actually gives you the motivation, energy and optimism to go back and tackle real work. There have actually been interesting studies that 62 percent of executives at work play games online and they do it to feel more productive. That's because when you're trying to do real-world work it's frustrating; we don't see the results of our actions right away. So games give us that sense of blissful productivity. . . . Games take us immediately out of a state of paralysis or alienation or depression and they switch on the positive ways of thinking. They trigger the brain to a state in which it's possible to do good work. It's possible to aspire to tough goals.

The other thing is, there have been myriad studies of the long-term effects of socializing in game environments and how they make people feel more connected to other people. It kind of reawakens our sense of extroversion. For people who are introverted, it actually changes our brain structure so that we are more rewarded when we interact with other people. . . . Games are transforming the brains of people who play them in largely positive ways.

Wired.com: You talk about building games to change the world but do you have any evidence to show that what people do in games translates to the real world? When the game is over, do people sustain a momentum for change?

McGonigal: Yes. Many of the games I've done have triggered lasting change. With the *World Without Oil* project . . . we have followed [the players] for years now looking at what their everyday behaviors are like and overwhelmingly they report, three years later, having not only changed their own daily habits, but [they are] teaching friends, coworkers, family members, neighbors to adopt these habits as well. So at a micro level we can change people's behavior and show them it's possible to contribute to a better way of living on the planet and empower them to share that with other people.

Discussion Questions

1. Do you think games can "fix" the world in some way? Why or why not?
2. Would you like to participate in one of McGonigal's games? Why or why not?

Summary

Information technology is having a profound influence on the way we live and work, and it is likely to challenge many of our beliefs, assumptions, and traditions.

Factory work is declining as we enter the information age, but factories still provide us with hard goods. The automated factory uses computers at every level of operation. Computer-aided design, computer-aided manufacturing, robots, automated assembly lines, and automated warehouses combine to produce factories that need few laborers.

Far more people work in offices than in factories, and computers are critically important in the modern office. Early office automation centered on mainframes that were run by highly trained technicians; today's office is more likely to emphasize networked PCs and other devices for decentralized enterprise computing. So far, predictions for widespread computer-supported cooperative work and paperless offices haven't come true.

A growing number of workers use computers to work at home part- or full-time, staying in contact with their offices through the Internet. Telecommuting has many benefits for information workers, their bosses, and society as a whole. Still, telecommuting from home is not for everybody. Satellite offices, cottage industries, and portable offices offer alternatives that may be more practical for some workers.

The impact of digital technology varies from job to job. Some jobs are de-skilled—transformed so they require less skill—while others are up-skilled into more technologically complex jobs. Experts speculate that productivity will rise as organizations adjust to new technology and develop human-centered systems adapted to the needs of employees.

Computer monitoring raises issues of privacy and, in many cases, lowers worker morale. De-skilling, monitoring, and health risks are particularly evident in electronic sweatshops—data-entry warehouses packed with low-paid keyboard operators. Many of these sweatshops have been relocated to countries with low wages and lax labor laws.

For decades, American manufacturing jobs have moved overseas. More recently, companies have moved hundreds of thousands of computer support and programming jobs from the United States to Asia where wages are significantly lower. Economists debate the extent to which globalization will affect the high-tech job market in the U.S. and other developed nations.

The biggest problem of automation may be the elimination of unskilled jobs. Automation will almost certainly produce unemployment and pain for millions of people unless society is able to provide them with the education they'll need to take the new jobs created by technology. Automation may ultimately force us to make fundamental changes in our economic system.

Our educational system was developed a century ago to train workers for lifelong jobs. In the information age, when students can expect to change jobs several times, we need to teach technological familiarity, literacy, mathematics, culture, communication, problem solving, and, most important, the ability to learn and adapt to an ever-changing world.

Instructional technology tools today include:

- Computer-based training (CBT)—Tutorials and/or drill-and-practice software covering specific, concrete facts
- Programming tools—Languages that enable students to design their own software and Web pages
- Simulations and games—Artificial environments that enable students to learn through exploration, experimentation, and interaction with other students
- Productivity and multimedia tools—Word processors, Web browsers, graphics programs, and more used by individual students and groups doing computer-supported collaborative learning projects
- Tools for students with disabilities—Touch screens, alternate keyboards, and other devices that give students opportunities to use technology to learn
- Distance education tools—Network tools that enable students and teachers to communicate from afar
- E-learning systems—Packages that include software and sometimes hardware to handle instruction, communication, record keeping, and other facets of the educational process

Technology can have a positive educational impact, but it can't guarantee improvement. Research, planning, teacher training, community involvement, and classroom restructuring should accompany new technology.

Families use home computers for basic business applications, education, information access, communication, entertainment, and creative pursuits. All of these applications will radically change as the technology evolves.

Key Terms

automated factory ....(p. 402)
automated offices ....(p. 403)
chief information officers (CIOs) ....(p. 403)
chief technology officers (CTOs) ....(p. 403)
computer-based training (CBT) ....(p. 415)
computer monitoring ....(p. 408)
computer-based collaborative learning (CBCL) ....(p. 418)
courseware ....(p. 415)
de-skilled ....(p. 408)
desktop virtualization ....(p. 404)
distance education ....(p. 420)
educational simulations ....(p. 417)
edutainment ....(p. 425)
e-learning...............................(p. 415)
e-learning 2.0.........................(p. 418)
electronic commerce (e-commerce)....................(p. 405)
electronic cottage...................(p. 405)
electronic sweatshops ....(p. 409)
extranets ....(p. 404)
filtering software ....(p. 426)
globalization ....(p. 411)
groupware ....(p. 404)
interactive television.............(p. 429)
intranets ....(p. 404)
Luddites ....(p. 410)
massively multiplayer online role-playing game ....(p. 427)
narrowcasting ....(p. 426)
paperless office ....(p. 404)
regional work centers ....(p. 406)
satellite office ....(p. 406)
smart card ....(p. 425)
social television ....(p. 429)
technophobia ....(p. 414)
telecommuting ....(p. 405)
thin clients ....(p. 403)
up-skilled ....(p. 408)

Companion Website Projects

1. The *Digital Planet* Web site, **www.pearsonhighered.com/beekman**, contains self-test exercises related to this chapter. Follow the instructions for taking a quiz. After you've completed your quiz, you can email the results to your instructor.
2. The Web site also contains open-ended discussion questions called Internet Exercises. Discuss one or more of the Internet Exercises questions at the section for this chapter.

True or False

1. Office automation began when PCs became inexpensive enough for businesses to buy in large quantities.
2. Engineers use computer-aided design and computer-aided manufacturing to design new products and the machines that build those products.
3. Research suggests that the total cost of ownership (TCO) of a typical PC has dropped to under $1000.
4. Today the number of people who telecommute from home is half of the number who did in 2000.
5. Clerical workers typically see up-skilling to more technologically demanding work reflected in their paychecks or level of responsibility.
6. U.S. workers have constitutional protections against electronic surveillance in the workplace.
7. An engineering education can last a lifetime because only a small fraction of details change over time.
8. Children with home computers almost always perform better academically than children in computer-free homes.
9. Research suggests that heavy use of digital media can change the "programming" of the brain so that it functions differently.
10. Research has proven that there is no link between violent video games and real-world violence.

Multiple Choice

1. Virtually all modern PCs have a graphical user interface. Name the company where Alan Kay and his research group developed this interface.
   a. Apple
   b. Google
   c. IBM
   d. Microsoft
   e. Xerox
2. Which of these statements is NOT true?
   a. Telecommuting saves energy and reduces pollution.
   b. One reason telecommuters give for their choice to work from home is schedule flexibility.
   c. Telecommuting isn't really possible for information workers.
   d. Telecommuting allows for more flexible work schedules.
   e. Most telecommuters prefer to commute to the office at least some of the time.
3. Which of these techniques is not used for workplace monitoring in U.S. corporations?
   a. Using on-screen reports showing the number of keystrokes for each clerk
   b. Viewing a copy of any worker's screen secretly at any time
   c. Reading employees' personal email messages
   d. Tracking Web sites visited by employees
   e. All of these techniques are used.
4. One of the main advantages of desktop virtualization technology is
   a. it's the best way to monitor workers' as they sit at their desks.
   b. it's an efficient tool for creating classroom simulations for distance education.
   c. it cuts costs by enabling IT people to install software in the cloud rather than on individual PCs.
   d. it makes compelling virtual reality experiences in massively multiplayer role playing games.
   e. it is at the core of social television technology.
5. What is the name given to the process of creating worldwide businesses and markets?
   a. Marketism
   b. Communism
   c. Globalization
   d. Internationalization
   e. Socialism
6. When a workplace is automated, jobs can be
   a. de-skilled.
   b. up-skilled.
   c. eliminated.
   d. outsourced.
   e. Any of these might happen, depending on the circumstances.
7. Automation has led to a doubling of the productivity of workers in the United States since World War II. Why has the time spent at work stayed about the same?
   a. The productivity gains have been lost to higher taxes.
   b. All the extra goods and services are sent to other countries in the form of foreign aid.
   c. All the extra goods and services are consumed by the wealthiest 1 percent of Americans.
   d. The increase in productivity has been used to provide Americans with a higher standard of living.
   e. Actually, the workweek is about half as long as it was immediately after World War II.
8. The type of computer-based training that is based on drill and practice works well for
   a. exploratory learning.
   b. simulations.
   c. students with learning disabilities.
   d. computer-based collaborative learning.
   e. e-learning 2.0.
9. E-learning 2.0 is similar to Web-2.0 in that
   a. it's completely Internet-based.
   b. it requires a second-generation Web browser.
   c. it's not appropriate for primary school education.
   d. it's based on collaboration.
   e. All of the above are true.
10. Educational simulations
    a. generally require broadband Internet connections.
    b. have little in common with computer games.
    c. generally don't allow students to be in control of the learning environment.
    d. are generally based on the concept of learning through exploration and invention.
    e. typically require students to have basic programming skills.
11. Which of these has been especially helpful for students with visual impairments?
    a. Robotic mice and keyboards.
    b. Digital reading machines.
    c. Cameras with voice recognition.
    d. Eyegaze systems.
    e. Digital wheelchairs.
12. The courseware used in elementary schools is designed to run on
    a. the Web
    b. smart phones
    c. PCs
    d. specialized hardware boxes
    e. All of the above.

13. Social television
    a. is a technology that was tried and rejected in the 1980s by Sony.
    b. is another name for interactive TV.
    c. is the most important component of interactive fiction.
    d. is at the core of all computer-based collaborative learning.
    e. is a name for a variety of technologies that use technology to make television into more of a social experience.

14. Which of these is true about technology in education?
    a. School districts have found that they can invariably get more positive results from spending money on technology than they can spending it on anything else.
    b. Computer-based training programs have been shown to be especially effective for teaching subjects that require thoughtful analysis, reflection, and big-picture thinking.
    c. Students in tech-heavy schools tend to be antisocial when compared to other students.
    d. Students who use digital technology heavily use their brains in different ways than other students do.
    e. All of the above.

15. Research has suggested that children who spend long hours playing online games
    a. may be changing the "programming" of their brains.
    b. can improve their eye-hand coordination.
    c. can show classic signs of addiction.
    d. may be more prone to violent or antisocial behavior.
    e. Different studies have suggested that all of these are possible results of children playing computer games.

Review Questions

1. Define or describe each of the key terms listed in the "Key Terms" section. Check your answers using the glossary.
2. What are some advantages of desktop virtualization in a business? Can you think of any disadvantages?
3. What is de-skilling? What is up-skilling? Give examples of each.
4. Describe the controversies surrounding outsourcing.
5. What were the goals of education in the industrial age? Which are still appropriate in the information age? Which are not?
6. What are some of the ways digital technology can support learning for special-needs students?
7. What is the relationship between Web 2.0 and e-learning 2.0?
8. Describe how simulations can be used by teachers and students in the classroom. Give several examples.
9. What is the relationship between interactive television and social television?
10. How is home entertainment being changed by computer technology and telecommunication?

Discussion Questions

1. How has the evolution of the automated office paralleled the evolution of the computer? What do you think is the next step in that evolution?
2. Telecommuting has been on the rise for many years. How long do you think the rise will continue? What are the advantages and disadvantages of telecommuting from the point of view of the worker? Management? Society?
3. People who work in electronic sweatshops run the risk of being replaced by technology. Discuss this dilemma from the point of view of the worker and society.
4. What do you think are the answers to the questions raised at the end of the "Will We Need a New Economy" section? How do you think most people would feel about these questions?
5. Socrates was illiterate and avoided the written word because he felt it weakened the mind. Similarly, many people today fear that we're weakening our children's minds by making them too dependent on computers, calculators, smart phones, televisions, games, and the Internet. What do you think?
6. Some professors (and some schools) have banned laptops and handheld Internet devices from classrooms because students use them to hang out on the Web instead of paying attention to the class material. What do you think of this kind of prohibition?
7. Do you think there are fundamental differences between children in the "digital generation" and children raised in the predigital era? Explain your answer.

8. Think about educational goals in relation to technology. What should people be able to do with no tools? What should people be able to do if they have access to pencils, papers, and books? What should people be able to do if they have access to computer technology but without the Internet? What should people be able to do with an Internet connection?

9. Do you think home computers in the future will make people more or less creative? Why?

10. Do you think home computers strengthen families and communities? Explain.

Projects

1. Interview several people whose jobs have been changed by digital technology. Ask them about how their jobs have changed as a result of the technology. Report on your findings.

2. Interview people whose jobs exist because of the Internet (such as Web designers) and/or people who have built businesses using the Internet (such as eBay vendors). Ask them about what they like and don't like about their work when compared with other work they've done. Report your findings.

3. Try several different types of educational software and/or observe students using the software. Prepare a report comparing the strengths and weaknesses of each. What objectives did the students have when they began using the software? Did the software help the students meet these objectives?

4. Observe how digital technology is used in local schools or on your campus. Report on your findings. How much time does the typical student spend using a computer each day? How much time on the Internet? How much time multitasking?

5. Design a simple courseware lesson. Set clear goals before you start. When your project is completed, try it with several students. Test them before and after using your lesson to help evaluate how well they learned the material presented in the lesson. Ask them for feedback. What features of your system do they like the best? What features do they dislike the most? How well did your lesson help them learn the material? What can you conclude from your experience?

Sources and Resources

Books

Cognitive Surplus: Creativity and Generosity in a Connected Age by Clay Shirky (Penguin Press). During the television age people used technology as a way to passively while away spare time. Shirky predicts that we're entering an era where technology can harness the cognitive surplus of the masses. New media make it possible for people to pool their efforts on creative and important projects, from wikis and blogs to collaborative projects to help victims of natural and human-made disasters.

The Dilbert Principle: A Cubicle's-Eye View of Bosses, Meetings, Management Fads, and Other Workplace Afflictions, by Scott Adams (HarperBusiness) and ***The Dilbert Future: Thriving on Stupidity in the 21st Century,*** by Scott Adams (HarperBusiness). These books, like the *Dilbert* comic strip, contain irreverent insights into the inner workings of the information-age workplace. Adams understands the world he satirizes—he has an MBA from Berkeley and 17 years of experience in a cubicle working for Pacific Bell. *The Dilbert Principle* targets managers who are clueless about the human needs of their staff; *The Dilbert Future* lampoons our high-tech future. *Dilbert* has been criticized because it paints a cynical picture of hopelessness in the workplace rather than encouraging workers to organize and solve problems. Still, the satire in these books allows us to laugh at ourselves, and that can't be all bad.

Dot Calm: The Search for Sanity in a Wired World, by Debra A. Dinnocenzo and Richard B. Swegan (Berrett-Koehler). This is a guide for coping with the pace and pressure of a high-tech work environment. It provides practical tips and techniques that apply to a variety of work situations.

Player Piano, by Kurt Vonnegut (Dial Press). In this half-century old classic, satirical novelist Vonnegut paints a bleak picture of a future society in which most jobs have been lost to automation.

iBrain: Surviving the Technological Alteration of the Modern Mind, by Gary Small, M.D., and Gigi Vargan (Harper). Technology is changing our brains. This book tells what we know about the ways technology is changing our brains and suggests strategies and techniques for avoiding hazards related to those changes.

Grown Up Digital: How the Net Generation is Changing Your World, by Don Tapscott (McGraw Hill). Best-selling author Tapscott surveys research on the first generation to grow up surrounded by digital technology.

Understanding the Digital Generation, by Ian Jukes, Ted McCain, and Lee Crockett (CreateSpace). This book addresses the growing divide between the children growing up in the digital world and their parents and teachers who came of age way back in the twentieth century. These authors have been tracking the impact of technology on education for decades, and their experience and expertise is apparent in this book:

21st Century Skills, by Bernie Trilling and Charles Fadel (Jossey-Bass). This book looks at the big question: What skills will young people need to survive and thrive in the 21st century, and how will educators help them to acquire those skills.

Web 2.0: New Tools, New Schools, by Gwen Solomon and Lynn Schrum (ISTE,). ISTE (the International Society for Technology in Education) has been helping educators apply digital technology to education for more than two decades. This is one of many books in their growing catalog of resources for improving education through technology.

Mindstorms: Children, Computers, and Powerful Ideas, by Seymour Papert (Basic Books) and ***The Children's Machine: Rethinking School in the Age of the Computer,*** by Seymour Papert (Basic Books). These two classic books outline the views of one widely respected theorist and researcher on technology in education: Seymour Papert, the inventor of LOGO. *Mindstorms* was written during the period when Papert was doing pioneering work with LOGO. In *The Children's Machine*, Papert discusses why the computer revolution failed to revolutionize education.

What Video Games Have to Teach Us about Learning and Literacy, by James Paul Gee (Palgrave Macmillan). Gee, a respected education professor, argues that we can learn a lot about learning and thinking by looking at interactive games.

Amusing Ourselves to Death: Public Discourse in the Age of Show Business, by Neil Postman (Penguin), ***Technopoly: The Surrender of Culture to Technology,*** by Neil Postman (Vintage), and ***The End of Education: Redefining the Value of School,*** by Neil Postman (Vintage). In these books, noted social critic Neil Postman takes on schools and technology, two powerful forces shaping our lives. In *Amusing Ourselves to Death*, Postman argues that television has injured our ability to think by reducing every public discourse to just another form of entertainment. In *Technopoly* he argues that our tools, especially computers, no longer play supporting roles; instead, they radically shape our culture, our families, and our world views. In *The End of Education*, he presents a picture of modern education in which economic utility has become the defining principle.

Trigger Happy: Videogames and the Entertainment Revolution, by Steven Poole (Arcade Publishing). Poole surveys the video game landscape and argues that this new entertainment form deserves the same kind of critical analysis we apply to other entertainment arts.

I, Avatar: The Culture and Consequences of Having a Second Life, by Mark Stephen Meadows (New Riders). This book presents the author's meditations and recollections about time spent in a virtual world and the potential implications beyond the online gaming arena. The book, like the online world it describes, is visually compelling and mentally engaging.

Extra Lives: Why Video Games Matter, by Tom Bissell. Is Grand Theft Auto a massive waste of time or the most colossal creative achievement of our time? This book's author, an admitted game addict, says it's both. The book has been praised for its clear prose and compelling picture of the brave new world of digital games.

Periodicals

Campus Technology. This magazine focuses on higher education and technology. Themes of issues range from multimedia tools to distance education on the Web.

Tech & Learning. This magazine, aimed at K–12 educators and administrators, focuses on uses of technology to enhance education.

Learning and Leading with Technology, from ISTE (International Society for Technology in Education), an influential organization whose focus is the effective use of computer technology in the classroom. *Learning and Leading with Technology* is their most accessible and widely read publication.

12

Information Systems in Business

OBJECTIVES

After you read this chapter you should be able to:

- Describe the components of a system and the characteristics of an information system
- Discuss a business organization as a system
- Describe a business organization from the viewpoint of the value chain model
- Explain how transaction processing systems are used to support business processes
- Explain how enterprise resource planning is changing the flow of information within and among business organizations
- Describe several ways computers support the work of managers
- Discuss several ways a business can use information technology to compete effectively by improving efficiency and by improving its products and services

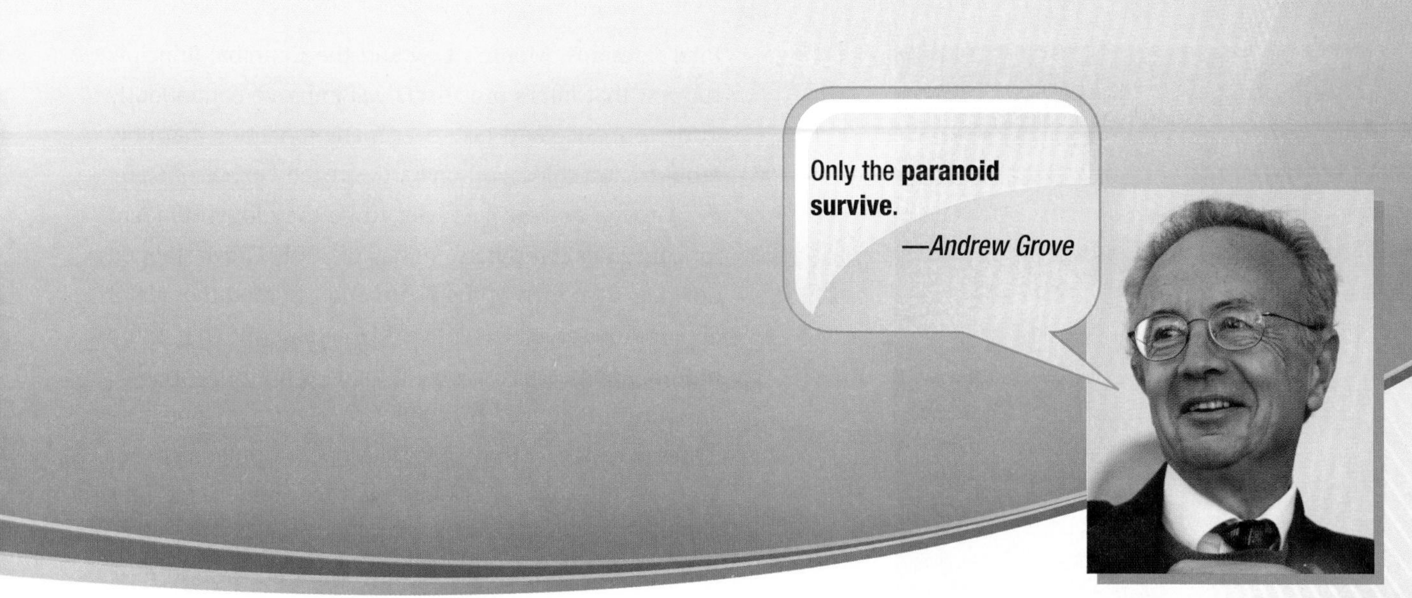
Only the paranoid survive.
—Andrew Grove

Andy Grove, the Paranoid Chip Merchant

In 1968 Andy Grove, Robert Noyce, and Gordon Moore founded a tiny semiconductor company called Intel. In the decades that followed, Grove served as President, then CEO, and finally Chairman of the Board. Under Grove's leadership, Intel came to dominate the explosive computer chip industry. As CEO, Grove led Intel from tenth place to the top of the semiconductor heap. Intel today provides microprocessors for the vast majority of the world's personal computers and for countless other digital devices. Those tiny silicon chips have turned Intel into one of the most profitable companies on Earth. Grove attributes his success—and Intel's—to two things: faith and worrying.

Throughout his Intel management tenure, Grove had faith in three guiding principles: Moore's Law, the Cannibal Principle, and his own Grove's Law. Gordon Moore, another cofounder of Intel, observed that the transistor capacity of silicon chips as measured against price, doubles every two years or so. This observation, dubbed Moore's Law, explains why computer hardware often seems outdated within months of purchase.

Moore also conceived the Cannibal Principle, which says that semiconductor technology absorbs the functions of what previously were discrete electronic components onto a single new chip. That's why computer components can be packed with more and more features at lower and lower cost.

Moore's Law and the Cannibal Principle guarantee a wide-open future for the semiconductor industry. But Andy Grove constantly worried about the competition, following what has been called Grove's Law: Only the paranoid survive. (Grove is the author of a popular book of the same title.)

Why do people watch so much TV? Why were computer industry hotshots surprised by the sudden popularity of the Internet? These are the kinds of questions that tormented Grove while he tried to stay ahead of the competition.

Grove had plenty to worry about over the years. For example, when Intel introduced the Pentium chip in 1994, customers found a flaw in the chip. After initially downplaying the problem, the company was forced by competitive necessity to replace the flawed chips for free and modify its marketing and customer support practices. Grove managed to sell some of the arithmetically challenged chips to jewelry makers for use in cufflinks and

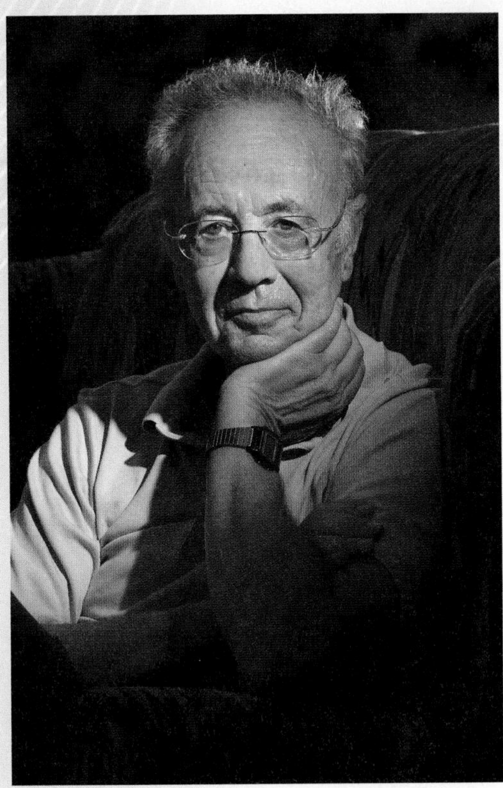

FIGURE 12.1 Andy Grove.

earrings. Also, he dreamed up the phenomenally successful "Intel Inside" advertising campaign that helped dampen sales of Intel-compatible microprocessors made by competitors.

He had no doubt that he and his employees should be paranoid about the industry's competitive forces and be afraid of competitors. But he also believed that fear inside the company could be harmful. Although Grove's management style was straightforward and results oriented, he believed a leader must be sure that no one in an organization is afraid to express an opinion. He attributed much of Intel's success to having created a healthful work environment in which motivated people can flourish.

According to Grove, the typical PC doesn't come close to pushing the limits of Intel's microprocessor, primarily because Microsoft's software hasn't kept pace with Intel's designs. Moore's Law and the Cannibal Principle suggest that Intel's processors will improve continuously in performance and take over many functions that now require extra chips, add-on hardware, and extra software.

Grove's goal for Intel was to be the global standard for consumer computers. In May of 2005, Grove stepped down as Chairman of the Board and assumed the title of Senior Advisor to Executive Management. That same month, another industry giant made an industry-shaking announcement that brought Grove's dream one step closer to reality. At the Apple Developer's Conference, not far from the spot where Intel was founded, Steve Jobs announced Apple would abandon IBM's Power PC chips and build its future Macintosh computers around Intel CPUs. Grove surely must have smiled.

According to Andy Grove, "A fundamental rule in technology says that whatever can be done will be done." But technology doesn't just happen. It's created by people like Andy Grove. ~

The phenomenal success of Andy Grove and Intel isn't accidental. Grove's victories in the microprocessor wars are due in large part to his ability to think strategically and to harness information technology to manage Intel well to support his business strategies. ■

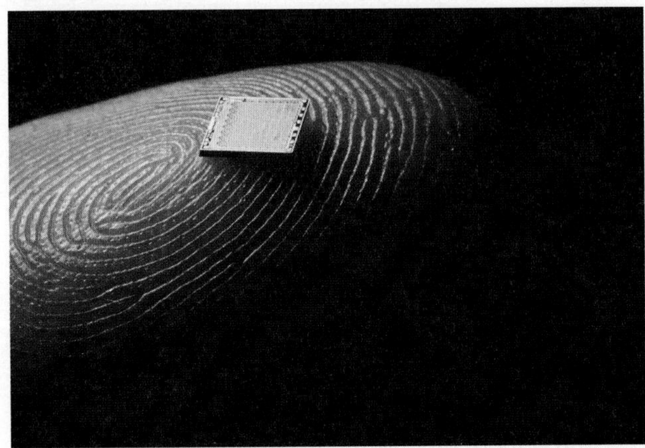

FIGURE 12.2 Intel has built a massive financial empire on tiny silicon chips.

In this chapter, we'll focus on the information technology tools that support managerial work in an organization. First we'll see how managers use information technology to get the right information, at the right time, in the right form. Then we'll look at various types of information systems managers use to communicate and make decisions. We'll see how managers use information technology strategically to compete effectively with other companies. And we'll look at the process managers use to plan for new information systems.

Systems and Organizations

> The basic **philosophy, spirit, and drive** of an organization have far more to do with its relative achievements than do technological or economic resources.
>
> *—Thomas Watson, Jr., son of IBM's founder*

Information technology is at the center of the information revolution. But the role and impact of information technology in business can be complex and confusing without the help of clearly defined concepts. The relationships between computers, networks, and organizations are easier to understand if we consider them as systems.

Earlier in the book, we discussed computer systems, operating systems, simulation systems, and other systems without paying much attention to the nature of a system. We now explore the concepts that define systems in general and business information systems in particular.

Anatomy of a System

> You've got to **think about the big things** while you're doing the small things, so that **all the small things go in the right direction.**
>
> *—Alvin Toffler*

A **system** is a set of interrelated parts that work together to accomplish a purpose. To accomplish its purpose, a system performs three basic functions: *input*, *processing*, and *output*. During input, needed materials are gathered and organized. During processing, the input materials are manipulated to produce the desired output. During output, the result is transferred or delivered to a destination or another system.

Does this definition sound familiar? The description of a basic computer in Chapter 2 included each of these functions along with a storage function for saving and retrieving data for processing. By this definition, then, a computer is a system.

A system has two additional functions: *feedback* and *control*. Feedback measures the performance of the input, processing, and output functions of the system and provides the measurement data to the control function. Control evaluates the feedback data and adjusts the system's input and processing functions to ensure the desired output is produced.

Every system has a *boundary* that defines its limits; anything outside the system's boundary is part of the system's *environment*. The system's environment provides input resources to the system and uses the output from the system.

A system can be a part, or a *subsystem*, of a larger system. For example, a personal computer can be a subsystem of a LAN, which might be a subsystem of a WAN, which could be a subsystem of the Internet. When the output of one subsystem is used as input for another subsystem, the two systems have a shared boundary, or interface. A large system (such as the Internet or a corporation) can have many interfacing subsystems.

Let's bring these abstract definitions down to Earth with concrete examples. A computerized climate control system in a modern office building is designed by engineers to maintain a comfortable temperature and humidity for the office workers—that's the purpose of the system. The system accepts input from human operators that

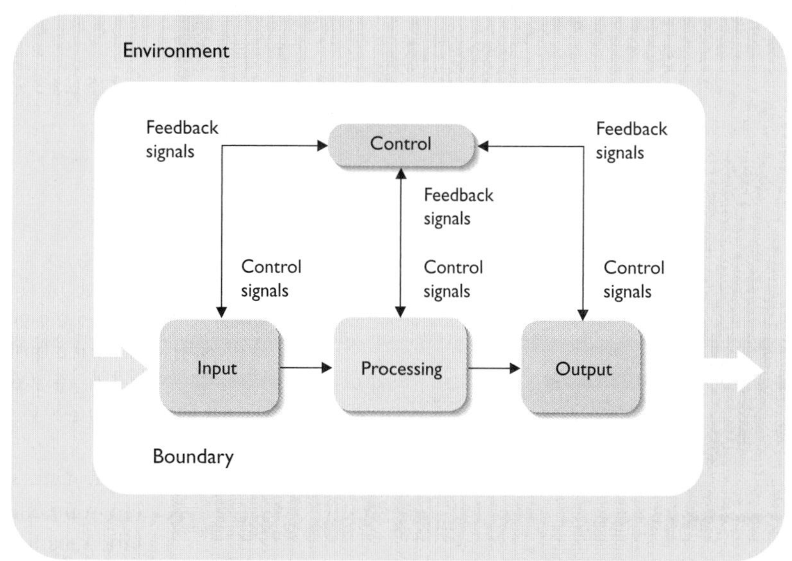

FIGURE 12.3 A system is a group of interrelated or interacting elements working together toward a common goal.

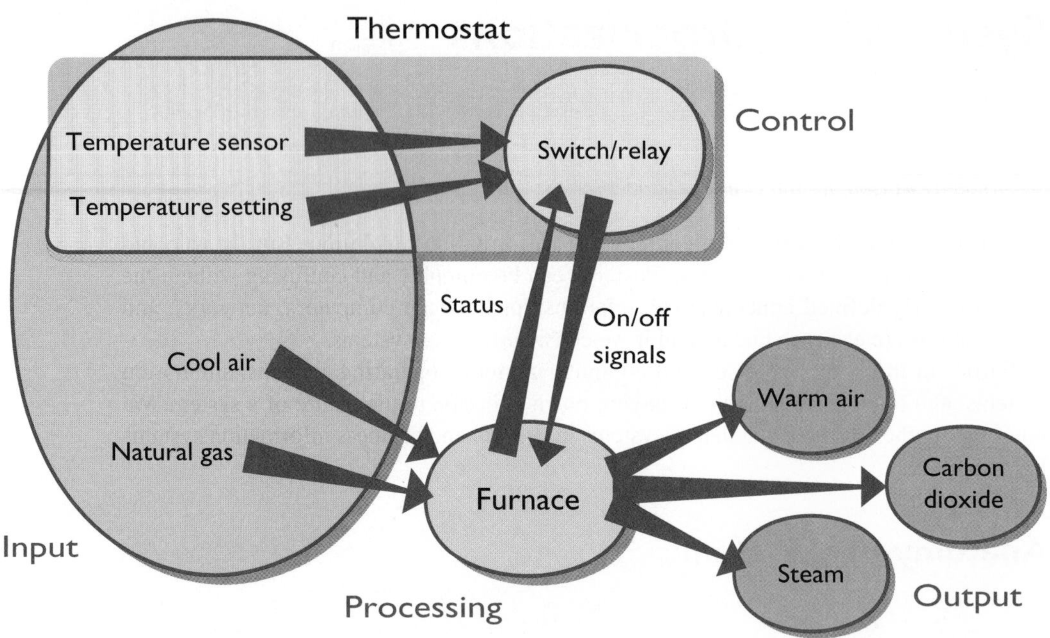

FIGURE 12.4 A home's heating system is an example of a system with input, processing, output, and control. The thermostat has both input and control functions.

tell it what ideal temperature and humidity to maintain. The system also accepts regularly timed input from sensors that tell it what the actual temperature and humidity are in the building. If temperature or humidity is significantly different from the target value, the system sends output signals to heaters, air conditioners, or humidifiers to adjust conditions accordingly. The monitoring sensors provide feedback from the environment; the system controller processes the feedback and responds by adjusting output signals.

Similarly, a ski resort might use a computer system to maintain an adequate snow level on its ski slopes. Sensors gather temperature and other weather data at several locations around the slopes. The computer processes this information, and the ski resort staff uses the information to decide when to turn the snow-making equipment on or off.

FIGURE 12.5 A ski resort uses sensors on the slopes that monitor weather to help employees know when and how long to operate snow-making equipment.

Business Organizations as Systems

> In every business, however large or small, every person must have a **broad vision and a sense of place in that vision**.
>
> *—Sir David Scholey*

While the concept of a system can be (and often is) used to describe biological and other natural phenomena, the systems we're discussing here are designed and used by people. A **business organization**—a company or a firm—is a system designed for the purpose of creating products and services for customers. When we view a company as a system within an environment, each of the basic system concepts takes on a specific meaning.

The firm's environment is made up of customers, stockholders, and other organizations such as competitors, suppliers, banks, and government agencies. From the environment, a

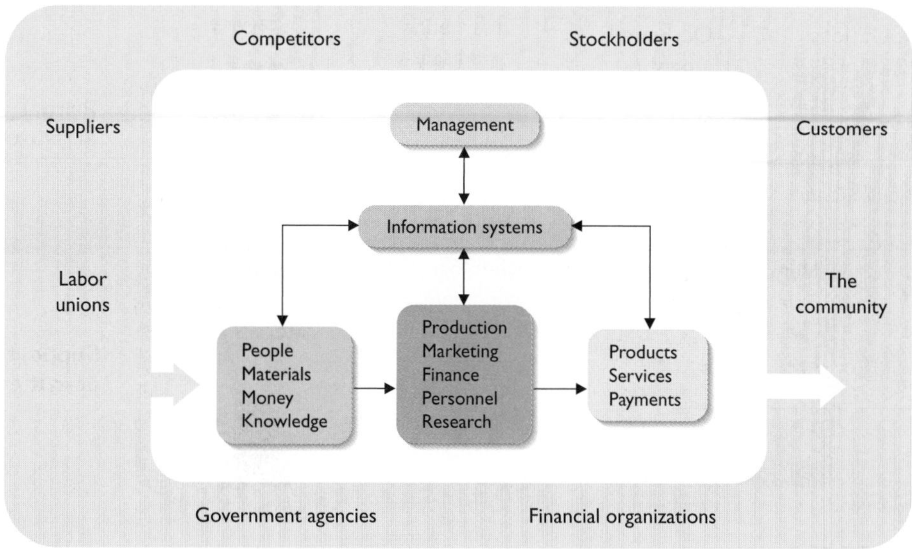

FIGURE 12.6 A business organization is a system that uses a variety of resources to produce goods and services for customers.

company acquires people, materials, money, knowledge, and other resources as input. These resources are used in work processes such as manufacturing, marketing and sales, and accounting and finance, all of which are needed to produce desired outputs for customers. Outputs include products and services as well as dividends, taxes, and information that are transferred to entities in the environment. The firm's managers perform the control function to ensure that the input, processing, and output functions work properly. Information systems play a key role in the feedback and control functions, collecting data from each of the primary activities and processing that data into information needed by managers.

The Value Chain Model

> Quality is more important than quantity. **One home run is much better than two doubles.**
>
> —*Steve Jobs*

The **value chain model**, proposed by Harvard Business School professor Michael Porter, views a business as a series of activities designed to add value to a product or service. When the value added by an activity exceeds the cost of that activity, the result is a profit for the business. The value chain model divides a firm's activities into primary and secondary activities.

Primary activities are those directly related to producing the product:

- *Inbound logistics* includes receiving, storing, and distributing raw materials.
- *Operations* is the process of creating products or services from raw materials.
- *Outbound logistics* means delivering the products or services to customers.
- *Marketing and sales* has to do with finding customers and getting orders.
- *Service* refers to supporting customers after the sale.

Secondary activities are those that support the firm's primary activities:

- *Management and administrative services* administer the relationships between the business and financial institutions, governments, and other external organizations.
- *Human resources management* is responsible for recruiting, training, and retaining employees.
- *Technology development* means using technology to support the other activities.
- *Procurement* refers to the process of acquiring the raw materials needed by the business.

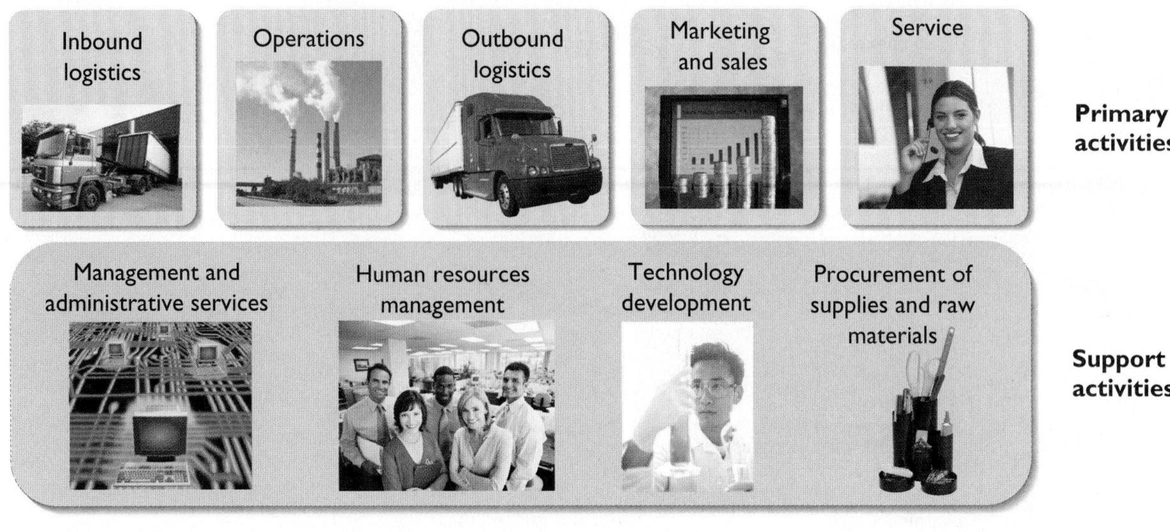

FIGURE 12.7 The value chain model shows the activities in an organization that make a product or service more desirable to customers.

An organization's **efficiency** increases when its primary and support activities produce desired output with lower costs. There are several ways to use information technology to improve efficiency. A company can provide employees with the training they need to work quickly and avoid mistakes. Technology can reduce waste by speeding information flow and reducing paperwork. Sometimes technology offers a better way of doing the same work—for example, replacing manual inventory systems with RFID-tag-based systems. Automating tasks requiring repetition, endurance, and speed often results in significant productivity gains. Value chain activities within the company and with other organizations can reduce inefficiencies caused when one group does not know what the other group is doing.

Effectiveness is how customers rate the output of the organization's value chain. A company can improve its effectiveness by improving communication between customers and company. A business can make it easier for a customer to purchase a product by ensuring the product's availability and providing flexible payment methods. A product is more attractive if it can be customized to meet the particular desires of the customer. A good field service can ensure that products are easy to maintain. Information technology can help a company achieve all of these goals.

Information Systems

> We are moving very rapidly in all forms of production and services to a **knowledge-based economy** in which what you earn depends on what you can learn. Not only what you know today, but **what you are capable of learning tomorrow**.
>
> —*Tracy LaQuey, in* The Internet Companion

We can think of an **information system** as a subsystem that supports the information needs of an organization. The overall purpose of an information system is to help people in the organization gather and use information, communicate with other people within and outside the organization, and make effective decisions.

Like other systems, an information system performs input, processing, and output functions and contains feedback and control functions. The input of an information system is data, or raw facts, about other subsystems in the business or other systems in the environment, such as descriptions of customer needs, materials purchased, and sales transactions. The processing function organizes and arranges the data in ways that people can understand and use. The output of an information system is an information product of some kind—for example, a report or other document. An information system also has a storage

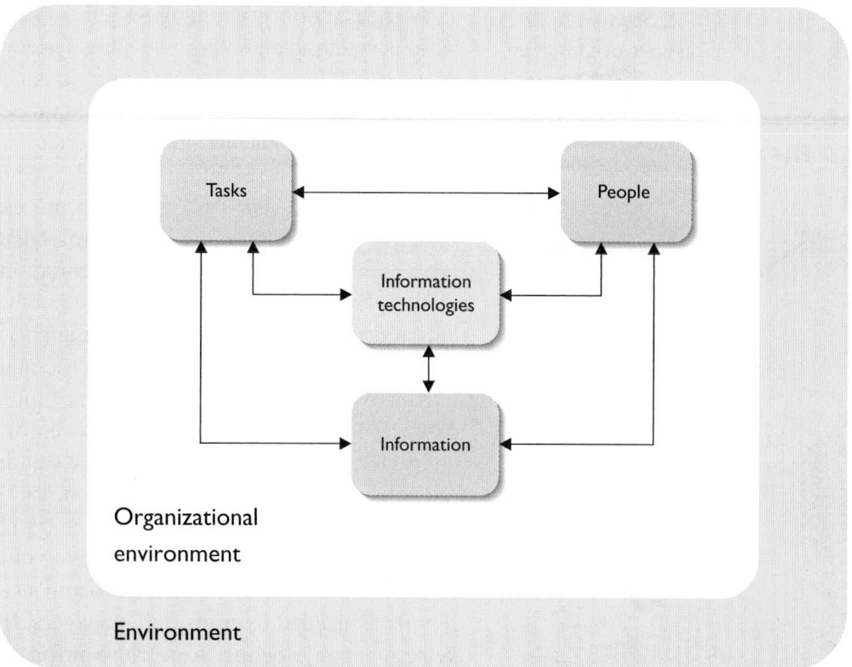

FIGURE 12.8 An information system is a set of information technologies that enable people in an organization to accomplish tasks effectively by providing access to data.

function to save data and information products for future use. The control function ensures that the information product outputs are of high quality and are useful to the information users for problem solving and decision making.

In the context of business information systems, information technology performs five functions: acquisition, processing, storage and retrieval, presentation, and transmission.

- **Acquisition** is a process of capturing data related to an event that is important to the organization—for example, the identification of each grocery item captured by a scanning device during checkout at a grocery store.
- **Processing** is an activity that manipulates and organizes information in ways that add value to the information so it is useful to users—for example, calculating the total grocery bill during checkout.
- **Storage and retrieval** are activities that systematically accumulate information for later use and then locate the stored information when needed. For example, a grocery information system would use a database to store revised information about inventory levels of grocery items after each customer has checked out.
- **Presentation** is the process of showing information in a format and medium useful to the user. A grocery receipt given to a customer is one example; a summary report displayed on a manager's screen is another.
- **Transmission** is the process of sending and distributing data and information to various locations. For example, a grocery store may send information about inventory levels and sales to headquarters frequently.

Information Systems for Business Transactions

Being good in business is the **most fascinating kind of art**....
—Andy Warhol

A **transaction** is an event that occurs in any of the primary activities of the company: manufacturing, marketing, sales, and accounting. A transaction might be a sale to a customer, a purchase from a supplier or vendor, or a payroll payment to an employee.

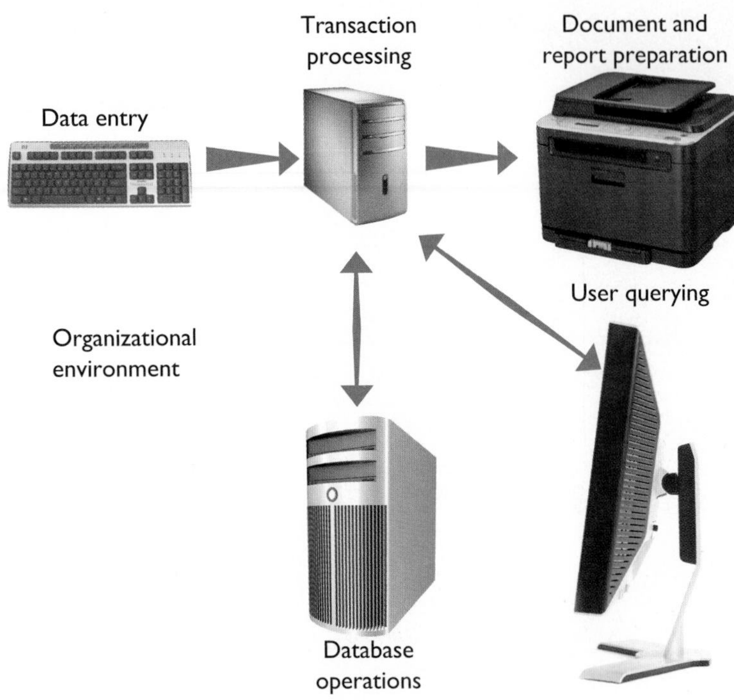

FIGURE 12.9 A transaction processing cycle consists of the same steps used in other systems: input, processing, storage, and output.

A **transaction processing system (TPS)** is a basic accounting and record-keeping system that keeps track of routine daily transactions necessary to conduct business. Examples of transaction processing systems include sales-order entry, ticket and hotel reservations, payroll, accounts receivable, and inventory. Transaction processing systems make it possible to control business processes intelligently based on accurate information. For example, by tracking the number of cars a dealership sells a week, a manager can make a fairly accurate assessment of the number of cars to order from the manufacturer. Similarly, by tracking the number of students that enroll in a course each fall semester, a university can determine the number of books it needs to order.

A transaction processing system typically captures, stores, and manipulates large volumes of data in a database, producing documents and reports as needed by users and managers. Many systems enable people to retrieve information interactively through database query systems, groupware applications, and intranet Web pages.

Transaction processing is a cyclical process with five steps:

1. *Data entry.* The first step in TPS is to enter the transaction data into machine-readable form. This involves online data entry (typing at a terminal, scanning bar codes, or other direct input into the computer) or transcribing paper source documents into a format acceptable to a computer. Data entry can also use electronic data interchange (EDI) to electronically exchange business transactions between companies using standard document formats for purchase orders, invoices, and shipping notices. (EDI is discussed in more detail later in this chapter.)
2. *Processing the data.* A typical transaction processing system organizes and sorts the data and performs calculations. Data can be processed in two ways: **batch processing** involves gathering and manipulating all the data to be processed for a particular time period; **real-time processing** involves processing each transaction as it occurs. Batch processing is used when processing is needed periodically, such as monthly payroll or checking account statements. Real-time processing is appropriate when users need the data immediately, as with bank ATM machines.
3. *Storing and updating the data.* This step involves storing the transaction data in a database so it can be retrieved later in processing some future transaction. For example, the amount you paid on this month's phone bill is used in calculating the amount you're billed next month. Many large organizations use **data warehousing** software to create and maintain large databases containing data on all aspects of the company.
4. *Document and report preparation.* A transaction processing system produces several types of action documents and reports. An **action document** initiates an action by the recipient or verifies for the recipient that a transaction has occurred. For example, a billing statement produced by your phone company is intended to trigger an action on your part, namely to make a payment. A sales receipt verifies the details of a purchase you make. Other examples of action documents are payroll checks, invoices, warehouse packing lists, and sales receipts. Reports are used by management to monitor the transactions that occur over a period of time. Reports can contain detailed information about specific transactions or summary information about a group of transactions, such as totals and averages. These reports are customized for specific users.
5. *User inquiry.* Managers and other workers can ask questions and retrieve information about any transaction activity when it's needed.

The transaction processing cycle repeats regularly, with output from one cycle serving as input to the next cycle. Each transaction system is a subsystem of the business as a whole.

Enterprise Resource Planning

Transaction processing systems exist in all functional areas of a business's value chain. For example, businesses may have transaction processing systems related to accounting, manufacturing, marketing, and customer service. A business can improve its processes through **enterprise resource planning (ERP)**. An ERP system collects transaction data from various business processes and stores the data in a unified database or data warehouse. Once data is stored in the database, business processes can automatically share it and managers in all parts of the organization can retrieve it.

ERP systems are usually large, complex, and expensive—typically in the millions of dollars. Because of the complexity involved in planning and implementing ERP systems, many companies have had difficulty implementing the systems successfully the first time they tried. For example, Whirlpool's initial ERP implementation crippled the shipping system, leaving appliances stacked on loading docks—and therefore not delivered to paying customers—for a full eight weeks. And a new ERP system at Volkswagen resulted in significant delays in parts shipments, causing product inventories to build up to costly levels.

Supply Chain Management and Outsourcing

> Without **communications** there would be no life.
>
> —*Norbert Wiener*

ERP systems can help businesses improve the efficiency of their internal processes, but they can also coordinate activities with other companies and with customers. The goal of **supply chain management** is to improve the efficiency of activities throughout the ***supply chain***—the network of organizations that supply raw materials, manufacture products, and distribute products to customers. To automate supply chain management, a business creates an **interorganizational information system (IOS)** that uses networking technology to facilitate communication with its suppliers, customers, and other organizations. There are two forms of IOS—electronic data interchange and business alliances.

Electronic data interchange (EDI) is the direct, computer-to-computer exchange of standardized, common business transaction documents, such as purchase orders and invoices, between business partners, suppliers, and customers. EDI uses international standards for data formatting that enable companies to exchange large amounts of information in real time around the world.

EDI systems have been developed for particular business partners for decades. In the retail clothing industry, Dillard's department store uses EDI to send purchase orders electronically to Haggar, one of its apparel manufacturers. If Haggar doesn't have the cloth to manufacture a needed item of clothing, it uses EDI to place an order electronically with the textile manufacturer Burlington Industries. In the automotive industry, Ford, General Motors, and other car manufacturers use EDI to order parts from their suppliers; in turn, the suppliers must agree to implement EDI and use it for transactions with the car manufacturer. All contractors wanting U.S. government contracts are required to link into the government's EDI systems.

A ***business alliance*** is a cooperative arrangement between two or more businesses with complementary capabilities. Calyx & Corolla, a direct-mail flower company, maintains customer databases, a Web site, and an online catalog, and it does all its own marketing. But rather than create its own distribution system, Calyx & Corolla has an agreement with FedEx, which handles the logistics of delivering the flowers from the growers to the customers. Similarly, Calyx & Corolla has an agreement with MasterCard and American Express, which handle all the credit authorization and payment activities. Calyx & Corolla also created alliances with independent flower growers worldwide. When a customer order is entered on

how it works The Information Flow Through a Transaction Processing System

Running a nursery business involves selling to customers, keeping track of inventory and ordering from vendors, paying employees, and keeping track of income and expenses.

Sales transaction processing system. When a customer buys a vase, the clerk enters the information into a cash register, and the customer receives a receipt. Or a frequent customer may ask to have the price of the item charged to her store account.

Inventory control transaction processing system. The sale of the vase is recorded for inventory control when the computer reads the UPC code on the price tag. This allows the buyers for the nursery to know how much stock for any vase is available and when to order more.

Purchasing transaction processing system. When new stock needs to be purchased, the vendors' bills for the new inventory move to accounts payable.

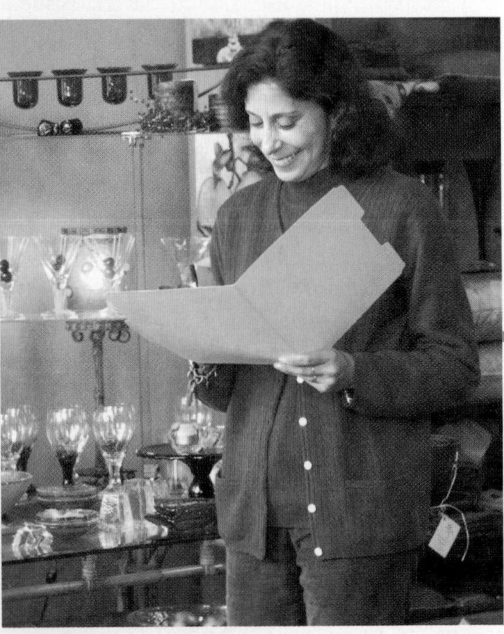

FIGURE 12.10

Accounts receivable transaction processing system. The nursery keeps records of amounts owed by customers. The clerk prepares invoices to bill customers.

Accounts payable transaction processing system. When an account needs to be paid, the clerk can print the check. In accounts payable, the nursery knows how much to pay each vendor and when to send the check.

General ledger transaction processing system. The income and expenses are organized in reports so that the nursery's owners know the health of the company.

Payroll transaction processing system. The nursery keeps track of the time each employee works and produces paychecks and other payroll statements.

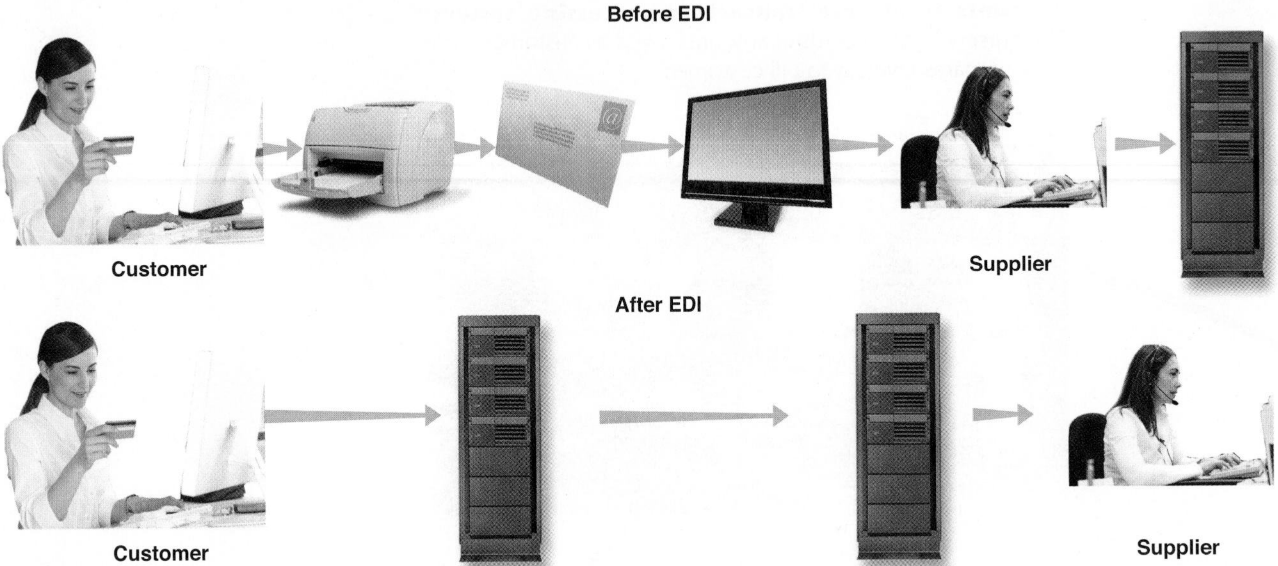

FIGURE 12.11 EDI can integrate the order-entry activity of a customer and the order-filling activity of a supplier. In this case, Dillard's, the customer, orders clothing from Haggar, the supplier. Integration is possible because EDI enables the customer and the supplier to use consistent technical standards and share information about each other's activities. Integration increases efficiency for both the customer and the supplier by eliminating delays and increasing accuracy.

Calyx & Corolla's Web site, the customer's credit is verified electronically with MasterCard or American Express; the order is sent electronically to the appropriate flower grower and to FedEx; and MasterCard or American Express charges the bill to the customer's account and transmits electronically payments to FedEx, Calyx & Corolla, and the flower grower.

Another type of business alliance is an *information partnership* in which the companies, usually in different industries, share information for their mutual benefit. For example, an airline and a hotel chain might have an arrangement in which guests staying at a member hotel or resort can receive frequent flyer miles. By sharing information, these types of partnerships help companies gain new customers and subsequently new opportunities for cross-selling and targeting products.

In an *industrial network*, the systems of several companies in an industry are linked. Procter & Gamble has developed a system to coordinate its manufacturing facilities and suppliers with grocery store point-of-sale systems, warehouses, and shippers. The system enables Procter & Gamble and its business partners to monitor products from raw materials to customer purchase.

Using the global telecommunications network, a company can communicate with suppliers and customers located anywhere in the world, employ engineers and designers in a number of different countries, and have production facilities located at cost-effective geographic sites worldwide. The international business environment poses several challenges that are not found in a purely domestic business environment. An international environment is multilingual and multicultural, and it involves working with different geographic conditions, currencies, time zones, and telecommunication standards. Different countries have different laws and customs regarding ethical labor practices, protection of personal privacy, and intellectual property. Some countries do not allow personal data about employees to leave the country. Many countries have weak, nonexistent, or poorly enforced software copyright laws. Some countries restrict citizen access to politically or culturally sensitive information by banning certain sites and/or blocking certain types of messages. All of these factors affect the flow of data between countries, commonly called **transborder data flow**.

The push toward supply chain management, electronic data interchange, and business alliances has made the implementation of information systems more important, and more difficult, than ever. Many businesses are handing the responsibility for developing and operating their information systems to another firm, in a practice called **outsourcing**. An outside firm may be able to provide the same service for less money. Some businesses have chosen to focus on their core competencies: those activities that add the most value. Because the development and operation of information systems are support activities, they are unlikely to be viewed as core competencies. In many businesses there is friction between information services departments and other parts of the organization because of late, expensive, or low-quality information systems. These businesses may see outsourcing as a way of improving quality and reducing friction.

Some businesses have underestimated the costs associated with the phases of outsourcing—identifying the appropriate vendor, transferring responsibility to that vendor, and monitoring the relationship. The loss of control over an information system that accompanies outsourcing can sometimes have negative consequences. If an information system gives a business a competitive advantage, it may be in the firm's best interest to keep control of that system inside the organization.

Strategic
Top managers
• plan and control overall organizational direction
Tactical
Middle managers
• plan and control organizational units
Operational
Lower-level managers
• plan and control day-to-day business processes

FIGURE 12.12 An organization usually has a hierarchy of managers responsible for work at several levels.

Information Technology and Management

> Vision is not enough; it must be combined with venture. **It is not enough to stare up the steps; we must step up the stairs.**
>
> —*Václav Havel*

Every organization has limited time, money, and people. To stay in business, an organization must use these resources wisely. **Management** is a set of activities that helps people efficiently use resources to accomplish an organization's goals. A small business might have only one manager. Large multinational organizations may have hundreds of managers. Whatever the size of the organization, managers plan, organize, direct, and control the various processes in the company. In all of these roles, managers make decisions.

A manager makes a ***structured decision*** when he or she understands the situation clearly and uses established procedures and information to resolve the problem. Structured decisions, such as deciding how many inventory items to reorder in a university cafeteria, are usually simple and routine and can sometimes be made by a computer. Some structured decisions, such as deciding a university's course schedule for the semester, can be very complex because they involve many established procedures and large quantities of information.

A manager makes a ***semistructured decision*** when there's some uncertainty about a problem and the manager must use judgment to fill in the gaps. For example, a dealership manager may

FIGURE 12.13 Hewlett Packard's Halo is a state-of-the-art video teleconferencing system that makes long-distance meetings seem almost as if everyone is in the same room.

how it works Information Flow in a Management Information System

Management information systems can transform mountains of data into reports that help managers make better decisions. This example shows how information flows through the Frostbyte Outdoor Outfitters Corporation.

To develop new business strategies, top-level managers need reports that show long-term trends.

When a new shipment arrives, a clerk records it using a terminal; inventory and accounting files are updated automatically.

The MIS uses a variety of inputs to produce reports for managers at all levels.

Middle-level managers use summary and exception reports to spot trends and unusual circumstances.

When a clerk enters a product's bar code, sales and inventory files are updated.

Low-level managers use detailed reports to keep tabs on day-to-day operations.

FIGURE 12.14

On-demand reports integrate information and show relationships. This report brings together sales information and weather data.

Sales Volume vs. Average Temperature as of 6/30/10

	JAN.	FEB.	MAR.	APR.	MAY	JUNE
Sales Volume	1798	1700	1609	1532	1302	1216
Sales	$24,398	$24,673	$22,468	$21,003	$18,068	$16,328
Average temperature	24	32	41	48	58	71

Summary reports show departmental totals or trends. This report lists the hottest-selling items.

Year-End Sales by Item: Top 20 as of 12/31/12

ITEM	SOLD UNITS	RETURNED UNITS	TOTAL UNITS	TOTAL SALES
Beaver Kayaks	58	3	55	$12,375
Possum Packs	1240	212	1028	$20,046
Possum Parkas	1003	323	680	$17,000
Rhinoceros Hiking Boots	1162	429	733	$47,645
Snoreswell Sleeping Bags	923	62	861	$39,175

Exception reports reflect unusual relationships. This report lists out-of-stock gear.

Items Temporarily Out of Stock as of 12/31/12

ITEM	OUT SINCE	DATE AVAILABLE
Fancy Flashlights	10/31/10	1/11/11
Foxy Flannels	11/11/10	1/2/11
Snappy Tents	12/02/10	1/19/11

Detail reports give complete, detailed information on routine operations. This report summarizes a day's orders.

Daily Sales Register by Type: 12/31/12

ITEM	UNITS	SALES
Parkas	62	$1209
Flashlights	154	$1540
Tents	2	$500
Hiking Boots	78	$65

need to decide how many of a new-model car to order for delivery three months in the future when uncertain about the actual demand for the model.

Sometimes a manager faces unique circumstances or must anticipate events over a relatively long period of time. In these situations a manager must make an ***unstructured decision*** requiring many quantitative and ethical judgments that have no clear answers. For example, a manager may need to decide how the company should respond to a competitor that has introduced an entirely new product line.

In a large organization, there are typically three **management levels**: operational, tactical, and strategic. Managers have different functions and roles at each level.

A manager at the ***operational level*** is responsible for supervising the day-to-day activities in the organization's value chain. Operational-level managers are also referred to as lower-level managers, supervisors, and group leaders.

A manager at the ***tactical level***—a middle manager—may be responsible for a large organizational unit, such as a sales region or a production plant. Typically, a middle manager develops short-term plans for the next year or so and makes sure his or her employees perform according to the plans. Tactical-level managers responsible for the development and use of information systems in an organization are called information systems managers.

A manager at the ***strategic level*** is called a top manager and is responsible for the long-range issues related to the business's growth and development. Top managers include the board of directors, chief executive officers, and vice presidents. The top manager responsible for the overall planning of information systems in an organization is called the **chief information officer (CIO)**.

It is important for managers at all levels to get the right information at the right time in the right form. Managers depend on communication for the information they need. Managers spend up to 90 percent of their time communicating with other people in the organization and in the company's external environment. We've already seen (in this chapter and earlier chapters) several tools that managers use to facilitate communication. Email, instant messaging, teleconferencing, blogging, and other "standard" Internet communication tools and techniques can be used to grease the management communication wheels in an organization. Groupware programs, intranets, and virtual private networks can extend the communication capabilities of managers beyond their local offices. And interorganizational information systems can extend those capabilities to business partners, customers, and others outside their companies.

But facilitating communication isn't the only way information technology helps managers get the information they need. A variety of software tools are available to make managers more effective and efficient. We'll now survey those tools and see how managers use information technology strategically to effectively compete with other companies.

Information Technology and Decision Making

> Every decision to act is an intuitive one. **The challenge is to migrate from hoping it's the right choice to trusting it's the right choice.**
>
> —*David Allen, in* Getting Things Done

In many ways it's more difficult to make decisions in today's business environment than it has been in the past. How can a manager choose when modern technology offers so many alternative solutions to problems? Because many organizations use large, complex, interconnected (and often international) systems, the risk—and cost—of making a wrong decision can be massive. On the other hand, the benefits can be immense when wise decisions ripple rapidly through a tightly linked organization.

Management Information Systems

A **management information system (MIS)** gives a manager the information he or she needs to make decisions, typically structured decisions regarding the operational activities of the company. These decisions require the manager to measure performance and compare that measurement information with predetermined standards of performance.

The MIS extracts the relevant data from databases of transaction processing systems, organizes and summarizes the data, and provides the information to the manager in various reports. The manager can use the reports in the intelligence phase of decision making to identify any operational problems.

Management information systems are also referred to as **management reporting systems** because their main output is a variety of reports for managers. An MIS provides three types of reports: detailed reports, summary reports, and exception reports. Each type of report typically shows both actual and planned performance measures for certain transactions that allow a manager to compare actual performance with planned performance.

MIS reports are usually distributed to managers routinely as scheduled reports. A manager can also retrieve ad hoc, on-demand reports using a query language or an on-screen database request form or a Web-based form.

Typically, an MIS provides access to an organization's internal transaction data but not to information external to the organization. An MIS doesn't provide analytic capabilities other than statistical operations for summary and exceptions reports. As a result, an MIS can supply performance information to managers about the primary activities of the company, but it is not particularly useful in helping managers decide exactly how to improve performance.

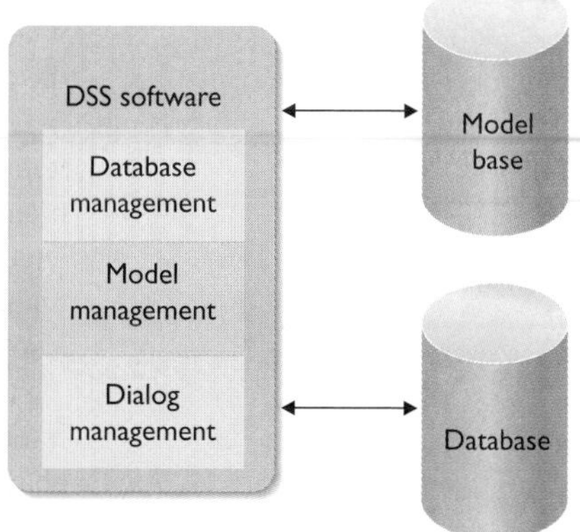

FIGURE 12.15 The components of a decision support system. Managers can use the system interactively to analyze information for decision making.

Decision Support Systems

> **You can lead a horse to water,** but you can't make him enter regional distribution codes in data field 92 to facilitate regression analysis **on the back end.**
>
> *—John Cleese, corporate consultant and former member of Monty Python's Flying Circus*

A **decision support system (DSS)** helps a manager make semistructured decisions, such as budget planning and sales forecasting, and unstructured decisions, such as new product development and contract negotiating. The term *decision support system* also refers to a way of thinking about how information systems should be designed to support managerial decision making. The DSS design philosophy is to provide managers with the tools they need to analyze information they deem relevant for a particular decision or class of decisions.

A DSS has three major components that a manager uses interactively to retrieve and manipulate relevant data. The *data management* component is a database of relevant internal and external information. Current and historical information is extracted from the company's MIS and transaction processing applications. External information, such as stock

FIGURE 12.16 Group decision support systems can enhance the dynamics of face-to-face contact in group meetings.

prices, research data, and company information about customers, competitors, and vendors, is accessed through publicly available databases. Database management software enables the manager to query the database and retrieve relevant information, much like an MIS.

The *model management* component enables the manager to evaluate alternative problem solutions and identify the best solution using appropriate software. For example, a manager could use a spreadsheet model to learn how product sales correlate with differences in income, age, and other characteristics of consumers. Based on this analysis, the manager could use the model to forecast future sales. The model management component also contains other model-building tools, such as charting and graphing software.

The third DSS component is the user interface, or *dialog management*. Most DSS user interfaces enable managers to view information in a variety of forms, including graphs, charts, lists, tables, and reports.

Many decisions are made by a team or group of managers. **Group decision support systems (GDSS)** are designed to improve the productivity of decision-making meetings by enhancing the dynamics of collaborative work. Physically, the GDSS usually takes the form of a room equipped with computers, DSS database and modeling software, LAN connections, and a large-screen projection of computer output for viewing by the group. The GDSS also includes specific communication-oriented software tools that support the development and sharing of ideas.

During a decision-making meeting, managers can use the GDSS capabilities as if they were using their own DSS to perform an analysis or some other management activity. A manager can use a projection system to show his or her work to the group or keep it confidential. The managers as a group can use the GDSS software tools to brainstorm and organize their ideas, comments, suggestions, criticisms, and other information. A GDSS enables the group members to share information anonymously, encouraging them to participate without risking the counterproductive dynamics of group meetings.

A **geographic information system (GIS)** is a special type of DSS designed to work with maps and other spatial information. A GIS is made up of mapping and analytic modeling

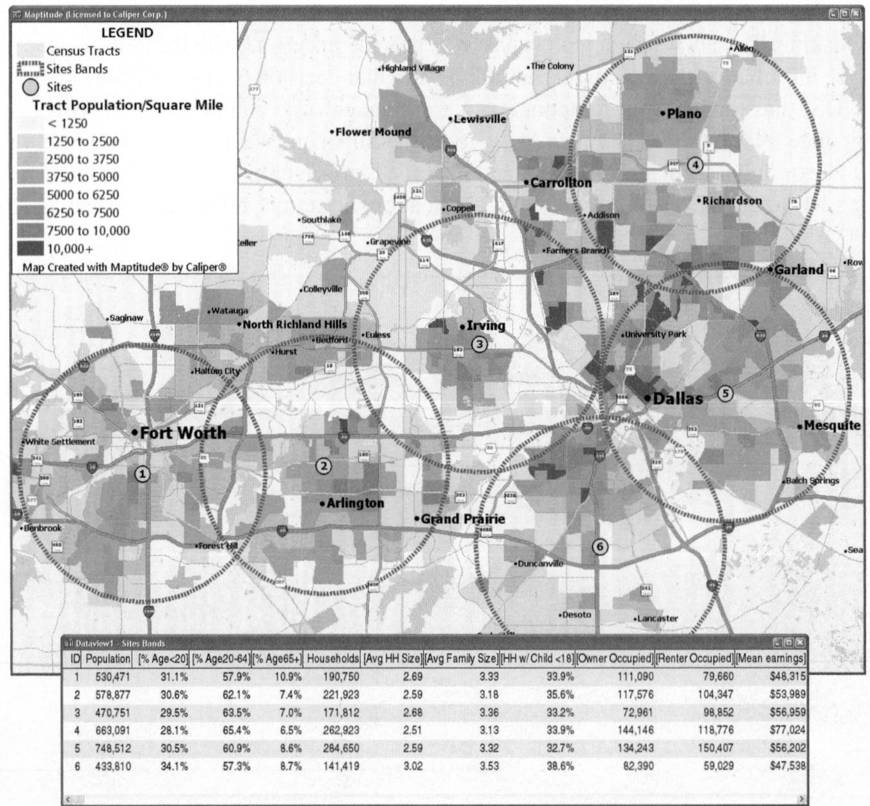

ID	Population	[% Age<20]	[% Age20-64]	[% Age65+]	Households	[Avg HH Size]	[Avg Family Size]	[HH w/ Child <18]	[Owner Occupied]	[Renter Occupied]	[Mean earnings]
1	530,471	31.1%	57.9%	10.9%	190,750	2.69	3.33	33.9%	111,090	79,660	$48,315
2	578,877	30.6%	62.1%	7.4%	221,923	2.59	3.18	35.6%	117,576	104,347	$53,989
3	470,751	29.5%	63.5%	7.0%	171,812	2.68	3.36	33.2%	72,961	98,852	$56,959
4	663,091	28.1%	65.4%	6.5%	262,923	2.51	3.13	33.9%	144,146	118,776	$77,024
5	748,512	30.5%	60.9%	8.6%	284,650	2.59	3.32	32.7%	134,243	150,407	$56,202
6	433,810	34.1%	57.3%	8.7%	141,419	3.02	3.53	38.6%	82,390	59,029	$47,538

FIGURE 12.17 Real estate agents can use a GIS to view property data at various layers, such as proximity to schools and shopping, city limits, and owner information.

software, databases that contain map images, geographic and demographic data, and a user interface enabling a manager to query the database interactively and see the results on a map. Government agencies and commercial companies produce spatial information databases containing demographic, employment, and consumer-habit information that can be incorporated into a business-oriented GIS. A manager might use a GIS to identify the best location for a new retail store or branch office, analyze customer buying preferences in a geographical area, or plan delivery and service routes.

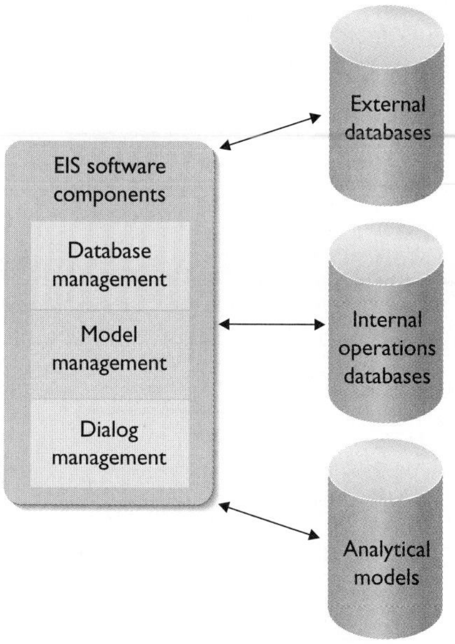

FIGURE 12.18 The components of an executive information system. Managers can use the system to monitor the important economic and social trends affecting the organization, as well as the important performance measures of the company.

Expert Systems

Expert systems (ES) support decision making by providing managers with access to computerized expert knowledge. An expert is someone who has mastery of an extraordinary amount of knowledge within a narrow domain. An expert system is designed to replicate the decision-making process of a human expert. Today's expert systems are based on years of artificial intelligence research devoted to replicating elusive human cognitive abilities in machines. Expert systems are discussed in Chapter 15.

Executive Information Systems

An **executive information system (EIS)** combines features of MIS and DSS to support unstructured decision making by top managers. A top manager can use an EIS to monitor key indicators of the company's performance, such as profitability, finance and marketing, and human and technology resources. An EIS also makes it easy for a manager to access economic, consumer, and environmental trends affecting the company.

An EIS has design components similar to a DSS. The EIS data management component provides interactive access to the company's important information, and the model-management component provides access to data on the company's critical success factors. The ***dialog management component*** is the set of human-computer interactive features that enables the executive to select data and display it in a variety of formats, including summary and exception reports, lists, charts, tables, and graphs.

An EIS enables the executive to *drill down* through available information to the level of detail needed. For example, an executive may view a summary report and notice that sales

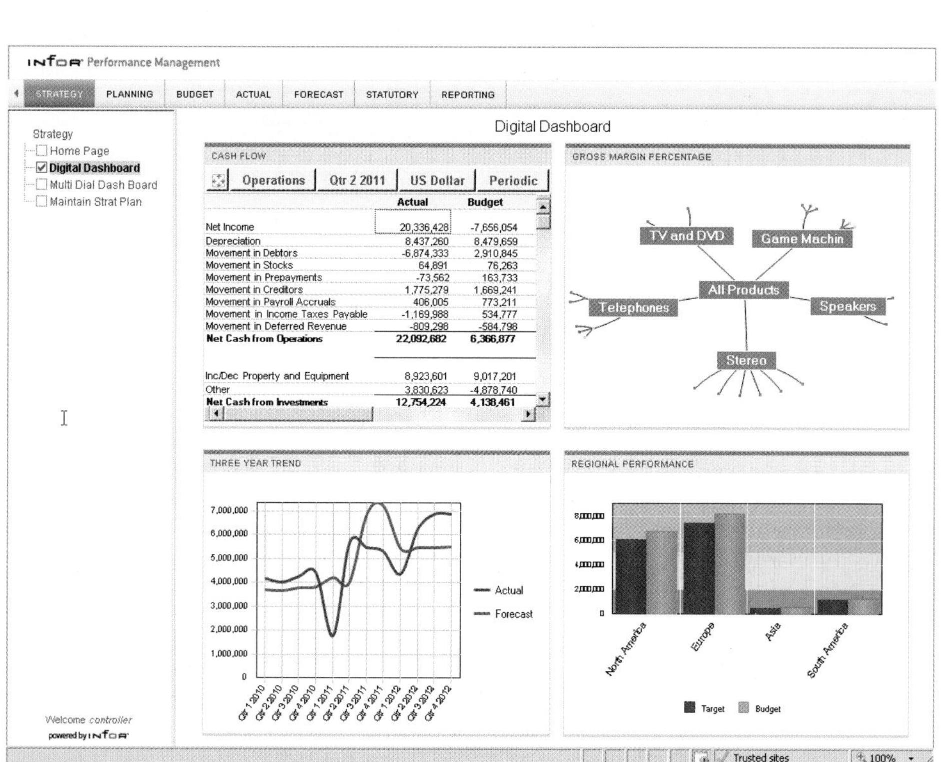

FIGURE 12.19 Infor PM's s software can be used as an executive information system.

how it works Using DSS for Analysis

A decision support system can provide a manager with powerful tools for analysis of information. Different management decisions call for different types of analysis. A DSS handles these four types of analysis:

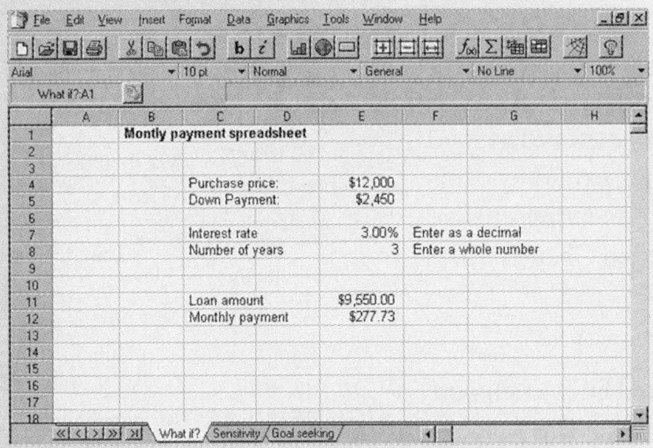

- ***What-if? analysis.*** DSSs have been designed to support many types of decision-making applications, including corporate planning and forecasting, product pricing, flight scheduling, transportation routing, and investment analysis. Even though each DSS is designed to solve a specific problem, managers can use any DSS to ask and answer what-if questions. For example, a manager may want to know what the monthly payment for a product will be for a certain purchase price, loan length, and interest rate. By using an analytic model, a manager can change the value of one or more key input variables or parameters and see the effect on the output variables or proposed solution.

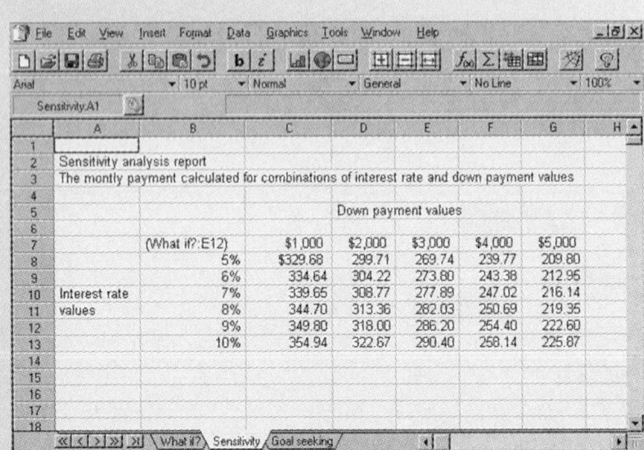

- ***Sensitivity analysis.*** By varying the value of key input variables systematically, or by asking a sequence of what-if questions, the manager performs a sensitivity analysis. A sensitivity analysis shows the manager the degree of change in the results or output of a model as the value of a key variable or assumption changes incrementally. With a well-designed user interface, a manager can evaluate any number of what-if questions to do a sensitivity analysis easily and quickly.

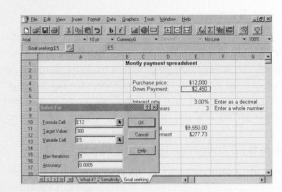

- ***Goal-seeking analysis.*** A variation of sensitivity analysis is goal-seeking analysis, which attempts to find the value of one or more key input variables of a model that will result in a desired level of output. For example, a manager might wish to know what down payment would be necessary to obtain a particular monthly payment. The manager could enter a value for the down payment variable, observe the resulting monthly payment calculation, and reiterate this process until the desired monthly payment level is found. Some DSSs enable managers to perform goal seeking automatically.

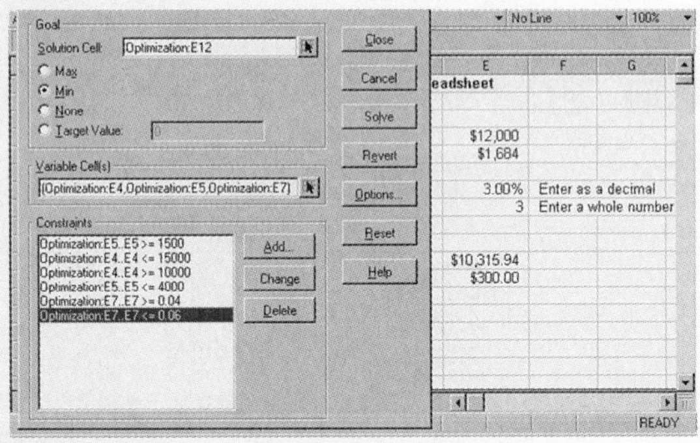

- ***Optimization analysis.*** Another variation of sensitivity analysis is optimization analysis. All decisions are made under certain constraints and limitations, such as a limited budget. Optimization analysis attempts to find the highest or lowest value of one or more variables, given certain limits or constraints. For example, a manager could use an analytic model to calculate the optimal monthly payment for a product, given that the purchase price, the interest rate of the loan, and the down payment cannot exceed certain limits. Spreadsheet software has the ability to perform optimization analysis.

FIGURE 12.20

in a particular region have declined over the past month. The executive can retrieve the detailed sales information for that sales region and then drill further, examining sales data for a particular store or a particular salesperson.

Using the EIS, an executive has access to up-to-the-minute data on internal operations of the company and a wide variety of external online information, including news services, financial market databases, economic information, and other publicly available information. This ability to access both internal and external information makes an EIS a powerful tool during the intelligence phase of decision making.

Strategic Information Systems

Successful organizations look for ways to gain a strategic advantage over competitors. Let's consider three kinds of activities that can give a firm a strategic advantage.

- An *entry barrier* is usually an innovative new product or service that is difficult for a competitor to emulate. A classic example is Merrill Lynch, a large financial services firm that developed a system called Cash Management Account that provided customers many new financial, banking, and investment services. The system was costly and difficult to implement, and it took several years for competing brokerage firms and banking institutions to develop similar products. In the meantime, Merrill Lynch continued to innovate and enhance the product, making it all the harder for competitors to catch up.
- *Switching costs* are the time, effort, and money a customer or supplier would have to expend changing to a competitor's product or service. For example, Baxter Healthcare International, Inc., the supplier of nearly two-thirds of all products used by U.S. hospitals, developed an inventory and ordering system that enables hospitals to order online from the Baxter supply catalog using Baxter computer terminals installed in the hospitals. Participating hospitals became unwilling to switch to another supplier because of the convenience of the system.
- Sometimes businesses can add value to a product to differentiate it from the competition. For example, with the iPod, iTunes software, and the online iTunes Store, Apple was able to create a unique niche in the digital music industry; competitors had trouble matching Apple's products on all three fronts.

A **strategic information system** is an information system used at any level of a company that helps it gain an advantage over its competitors or even move into a new business. Any of the types of information systems described previously could be considered a strategic information system if it helped a firm gain a competitive edge.

Decision support features	MIS	DSS	EIS	ES
Type of decision maker	Many operational managers	Individual and small groups of tactical managers	Individual strategic manager	Individual strategic, tactical, or operational manager
Type of problem	Structured	Semistructured	Unstructured	Structured
Type of information	Predesigned reports on internal operations	Interactive queries and responses for specific problems	Online access to internal and external information on many issues	Conclusions and recommendations for a particular complex problem
Type of use	Indirect	Direct	Direct	Direct
Phase of decision making	Intelligence	Design, choice	Intelligence	Implementation

FIGURE 12.21 Comparison of design features for management information systems, decision support systems, executive information systems, and expert systems.

FIGURE 12.22 Managers suffering from information overload may find it impossible to focus on what's most important.

Information Systems in Perspective

> Point of view is that quintessentially human solution to information overload, an intuitive process of reducing things to an essential relevant and manageable minimum.... **In a world of hyperabundant content, point of view will become the scarcest of resources.**
>
> —*Paul Saffo, Technology Forecaster*

Information systems provide critical information and advice, but using them is not without risks. Poorly designed information systems can hamper a manager's ability to make quality decisions. Systems notwithstanding, the human manager always has the responsibility for the quality of every decision. Some managers complain that these systems provide too much information—too many reports, too many summaries, too many details. This malady is known as **information overload**. Managers who are bombarded with computer output may not be able to separate the best from the rest. What's worse, managers who rely too heavily on computer output run the risk of overlooking more conventional, nondigital sources of insight. Although user training is essential, the best managers know that no computer or information system can replace the human communication and decision-making skills necessary for successful management.

Planning for Information Systems

> A **complex system that works** is invariably found to have evolved from a **simple system that worked**.
>
> —*John Gall*

We've seen how information systems can play critical roles throughout a business, from the highest levels of management to the factory floor. But information systems don't happen automatically; they need to be designed, developed, and debugged before they can be put to work. To ensure successful systems development, managers must first plan how information technology will be used within the context of the overall mission and goals of their organization. We'll examine the process of systems design and development in Chapter 14. In this section, we'll look at the steps involved in planning for information systems.

Planning is a process of identifying a desired goal or objective and then deciding what will be done to achieve the objective, when it will be done, who will do it, and how it will be done. Because information technology plays an important role at all levels of an organization, IT planning is a major concern of top management. Information technology planning involves four phases:

- Aligning the information technology plan with the overall business plan of the organization
- Describing the firm's IT infrastructure
- Allocating resources to specific information systems and projects
- Planning specific information system projects

Strategic Planning

This first phase of IT planning is called **strategic planning**. The strategic plan defines the mission of the company, identifies the company's environment and internal strengths and weaknesses, and defines the competitive strategy of the company. A component of an organization's strategic plan is an IT plan that describes the IT mission within the company, reviews the company's current IT capabilities and applications, and describes the IT strategies and policies to support the organization's overall strategy.

Organizations use several strategic planning approaches to make sure IT plans truly reflect business needs. The **critical success factors (CSF)** approach identifies the variables that are crucial for the success of the business from the top managers' point of view and identifies IT plans for systems that provide access to information about those critical success factors. A CSF typically relates to the major competitive forces faced by the company and to operational problems and opportunities. Examples of CSFs include quality customer service, correct pricing of products and services, tight control of manufacturing costs, and the efficient and effective use of employees.

Information Technology Planning Phases

Major IT Planning Activity	Description
Strategic planning	Align the overall business organization plan with the information technology plan
Information technology infrastructure analysis	Conduct an organizational information infrastructure analysis to identify the desirable features for the information technology infrastructure
Resource allocation	Select the information system projects to invest in
Project planning	Develop the plan schedule and budget for specific information system projects

FIGURE 12.23 Phases of the information technology planning process.

Describing the Information Technology Infrastructure

The second phase in IT planning is to describe the desirable features for the organization's IT infrastructure. The IT **infrastructure** comprises all the organization's information systems hardware, software, and telecommunications equipment; the information system department's staff and other personnel; and the organizational structure and procedures that affect accessing, processing, and using information in the company. The IT infrastructure should be designed to support the business operations, communications, decision making, and competitive strategy of the company.

An approach many companies use to define their IT infrastructure is **organizational information requirements analysis**, also called enterprise modeling. This approach is used to summarize the company's current IT infrastructure, to identify the practical range of business and product strategies based on the current infrastructure, and to identify information system projects that offer the most benefits to the organization.

Allocating Resources

The third phase of information technology planning is resource allocation, a process of selecting the information system projects in which to invest. Every organization has a limited budget, a limited number of people, and limited time. The IT department must decide how to allocate these limited resources. Typically, resources must be allocated for maintaining or enhancing existing systems; developing new systems for supporting managerial, clerical, and other users; and developing new ideas and techniques for incorporating IT into improving business operations, products, and services.

Many managers use **cost-benefit analysis** to decide whether an information system project is worthwhile on its own merits and also in comparison with other proposed information system projects. Costs usually relate to hardware, software, salaries, IT staff salaries, and the ongoing operation and maintenance of a system. Tangible benefits, such as the reduction in the number of customer complaints and the increase in the number of sales orders, can be measured easily. Intangible benefits, such as better employee morale and relationship with the surrounding community, are harder to measure. A top manager might find it difficult to make an honest comparison of proposed information system projects based solely on anticipated costs and benefits.

Project Planning

The fourth phase of IT planning is project planning. The purpose of project planning is to organize a sequence of steps to accomplish a particular project's goals and to keep the project on schedule and within budget. A project plan includes a description of the

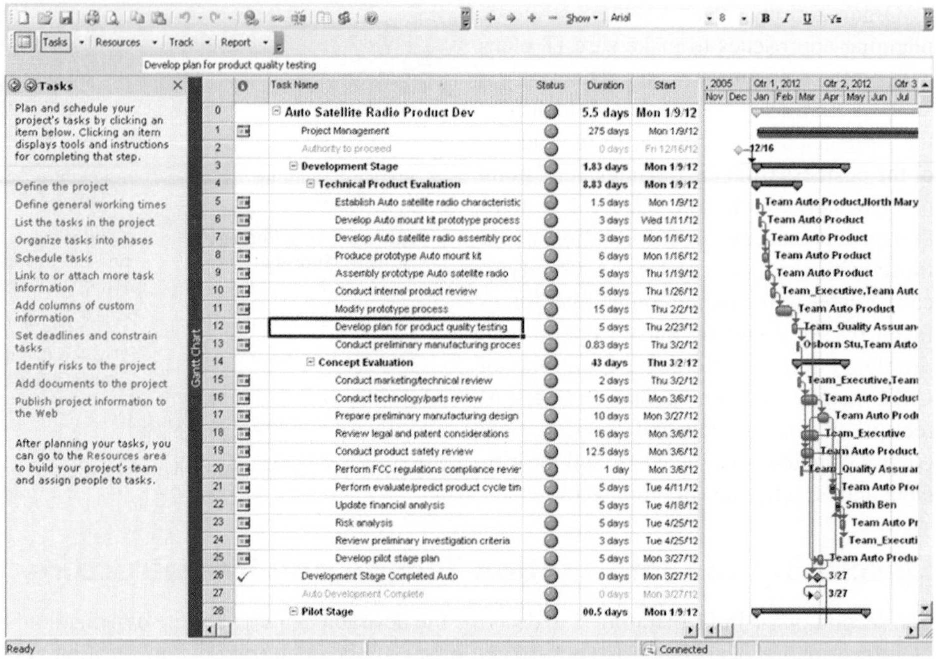

FIGURE 12.24 A manager can view a Gantt chart and see at a glance the overall schedule of an information system project.

measurable project goals that are used to evaluate the success of the project. A project goal can relate to the process of building the information system—completing the project by a certain date, for example. The project goal might also relate to business operations after the system is installed—for example, decreasing the time to place an order by a certain amount.

A project plan describes what needs to be done to accomplish each step in the system's life cycle. (The systems development life cycle is discussed in Chapter 14.) The plan specifies what deliverable output is to be produced at the completion of each step in the project. A deliverable can be a report, a computer program, a progress report, or any other tangible output. The plan specifies a schedule identifying how long certain steps are forecasted to take to complete and the forecasted date of completion. The project plan also specifies milestones, or checkpoints, to allow managers to review the project's progress when certain deliverables are produced, after a certain amount of the budget is used, or on a time basis, such as weekly or monthly.

Managers use ***project management software*** to help coordinate, schedule, and track complex projects. Many project plans use a **Gantt chart** to represent a project schedule visually. A Gantt chart shows each step or category of steps in a plan, along with its planned and actual start and completion times.

Project managers use the **critical path method (CPM)** to keep track of a project's schedule. CPM is a mathematical model of a project's schedule used to calculate when particular activities will be completed. A project manager first estimates the time needed to complete each activity, then determines the total time required to finish a project by locating the longest path, called the critical path, through the interconnected activities of the project. A critical path chart shows visually the interconnection of steps in a project. Project managers sometimes use a variation of CPM called the program evaluation and review technique (***PERT***). With PERT, a manager uses three time estimates: an optimistic, a pessimistic, and a most likely time to complete each activity. The appearance of PERT and CPM diagrams are the same; both reflect single times for each activity. In the case of a PERT diagram, the single times are computed from the three estimates.

Managers use Gantt charts and CPM or PERT diagrams to identify bottlenecks in a project and anticipate the impact problems and delays will have on project completion times.

Social Responsibility in the Information Age

> In the 20th century BC the Code of Hammurabi declared that if a house collapsed and killed its owner, the builder of the house was to be put to death. In the 20th century AD **many builders of computer software would deny responsibility and pass the entire risk to the user.**
>
> *—Helen Nissenbaum*

Socially responsible computing is a key concern in business today because of the many ways an information worker's actions can affect other people. **Social responsibility** refers to legal and ethical behavior. Laws define a society's proper, or legal, behavior and outline the actions a government can take in response to improper behavior. Ethics refers to principles or moral standards that help guide behavior, actions, and choices. Ethical dilemmas are difficult choices involving conflicting goals, responsibilities, and loyalties that may or may not be covered by laws. We've already considered many situations where information workers face ethical dilemmas, including:

- Viewing emails of team members or subordinates
- Making a recommendation to sell mailing lists of customers to other businesses
- Using a browser during working hours to shop
- Helping to implement a system that will result in five people losing their jobs

Social responsibility applies to a company as a whole as well as to individuals. A company that is socially responsible attempts to balance the interests of its various stakeholder groups—including employees, suppliers, customers, stockholders, and the local community. Traditionally, a company has a social contract with the community to enhance the material well-being of all the community's members, even if it means lower than maximized profits for its stockholders or higher than the lowest prices for its customers. A socially responsible company might donate money to local charities or the arts, give employees time off to do volunteer work, avoid any fraud or deception of the public, or play an active role in establishing and supporting community programs. Many companies extend the definition of "community" to a global scope, weighing worldwide environment and social impact in corporate decisions.

Regarding its own employees, a company is obliged to treat them with respect and provide them with healthful working conditions and fair wages. Most employers also strive to provide their workers with employment continuity. Within this context, a socially responsible company can provide a stable, predictable, and just working environment by establishing policies and procedures, called a **code of ethics**, to guide the behavior of its information workers. Companies have developed codes of ethics covering issues such as email privacy, software licenses and copyrights, access to hardware and files, and data and intellectual property ownership. Many professional organizations develop ethical codes that apply to their members; the ACM Code of Ethics in Appendix B of this book is a prime example for computer professionals.

The Working Wisdom box "Computer Ethics" in Chapter 1 offered several ethical guidelines. Here are some additional guidelines for information professionals that were developed by Donn B. Parker, a leading expert on computer ethics:

- *Informed consent.* If you are in doubt about the ethics or laws of a particular action, inform the people who might be effected by your action and obtain their consent before proceeding.
- *The higher ethic.* You should take the action that achieves the greater good for everyone involved.
- *Most restrictive action.* When you are deciding to take or avoid taking an action, assume that the most severe damage that could happen will happen.

Inventing the Future ▸ The Virtualization of IT

Today's large corporations allocate considerable money, energy, and personnel to building and maintaining information technology infrastructures. Ironically, today's IT department may soon be the victim of technological change. In the words of industry analyst and writer Nicholas Carr, "The modern corporate data center, with all its complex and expensive stacks of machinery, is on the path to obsolescence."

We don't have to look any farther than the computer industry for evidence. Hewlett Packard is replacing its 85 corporate data centers with six giant, highly automated server farms. HP predicts that this shift will cut their IT workforce—and the percentage of revenue spent on IT—by half. Similarly, IBM has replaced 155 traditional data centers with seven larger facilities. And by 2015 or so Sun plans to close its internal data centers down altogether, moving all of its IT functions to utility computers in the "cloud."

Several trends threatening the traditional IT center: the plummeting cost of computing power and storage (remember Moore's Law?), improvements in performance and security technology on the Internet, the emergence of high-quality virtualization technology, and major investments in server farms by Amazon, Google, Microsoft, IBM, and others.

In effect, virtualization software can turn a single mainframe into many virtual machines. And the move toward grid computing may, in time, create a processing/storage utility that's shared like the current electrical grid. So instead of buying and maintaining warehouses full of expensive (and quickly obsolete) hardware and software, companies will be able to lease storage space, processing power, and software on large machines located in far-away server farms. Because of virtualization, your desktop machine won't have to know where it's getting its data any more than your current PC knows where its electricity comes from.

The shift to utility computing with virtual machines should save considerable money for large companies, because they won't be strapped with the high cost of buying and maintaining all those real machines. It should also save natural resources, because virtual computers require considerably less energy than real computers.

And it may very well promote collaboration. In Nicholas Carr's words, "Up to now, corporate IT systems have been built on the principle of isolation—private hardware, private software, private data stores. But the isolation principle has always been in conflict with the nature of business itself, which is all about shared processes, shared information, and shared ideas....The new utility model of IT, which is built from the start on the principle of sharing, helps resolve that tension." It's Web 2.0 on a corporate scale.

Utility computing will depend on a solid infrastructure, including standards for integrating data and services from different vendors. It will also require improvements in encryption and other security tools. It will depend on advancements in massively parallel processing software. And it will require a new class of IT professionals who specialize in intraorganizational interfaces and workflow.

But once the pieces are in place, utility computing might very quickly transform the business computing world. Of course, it's not likely to change everything overnight. According to Google executive Paul Slakey, "This is a new wave, but it's not going to replace the existing. On-premise software is not going to go away." Still, this new computing model will present opportunities and challenges for businesses large and small in the coming decades.

FIGURE 12.25 The explosive growth of server farms encourages the virtualization of IT.

Crosscurrents

Now, where was I? Oh, yes, multitasking *by Ellen Goodman*

In today's high-tech world, we're continually bombarded with messages, media, and more. Some of these information bombs are self-imposed—we want to keep up with our friends online and by phone—and some are imposed by jobs and other responsibilities. Ellen Goodman of the Washington Post Writers Group wrote this column in September, 2009. In it, she discusses some eye-opening research about the effectiveness of multitasking and then talks about the way our lives are being changed by it.

There was a time when I considered myself a champion multitasker. This, of course, was in the days when the Olympic event of technological multitasking was unloading the dishwasher while talking to my mother on the phone.

Fast forward to my office where I am sitting in front of a computer with a land phone to my left and an iPhone to my right. As I type into my Word program, Google is alerting me to the latest news in the health care debate, e-mails are coming in on two of my three accounts and I have a text message from my daughter.

Even this, however, puts me at the low end of the multitask scale since I am not Facebooking while surfing the Net, downloading iTunes and driving.

The truth is that I am terrible at multitasking. Worse yet, I have believed that my inability to simultaneously YouTube and IM makes me a technological dinosaur. Surely, the younger generation looks down at my inability to text and talk the way I look down on someone's inability to walk and chew gum at the same time.

More to the point, I have lived with the conviction that the people watching TV while Twittering and surfing the Web have a secret skill, like polyphonics who can sing two notes at the same time.

Now I find out from Stanford's Clifford Nass that there is no secret. High multitaskers are not better at anything. Even multitasking. They are worse.

Nass, who teaches human-computer interactions, led a research team that studied 100 students, high and low multitaskers. The high ones focused poorly, remembered less, and were more easily distracted. They couldn't shift well from one task to another and they couldn't organize well. They couldn't figure out what was important and what wasn't.

"We didn't enter this research trying to beat on multitaskers but to find out their talent," says Ness. "And we found out they had none."

Nass has yet to study whether they were bad at paying attention to begin with or were driven to distraction. But there's a suspicion, he says, that "we may be breeding a generation of kids whose ability to pay attention may be destroyed."

Before I exhale in relief and bond with others waving this research in front of their children's (distracted) faces, a couple of things have to be noted. First of all, as Nass ruefully says, many multitaskers believe they are the efficient exception. They can talk and chew e-mails at the same time.

Second and related, the simultaneous media immersion has become the new norm. This is what normal looks like.

It's the norm in offices where people are often required to keep chat rooms open and respond to e-mail within 30 minutes. It's in sports arenas where fans in mega-buck seats actually watch the game on big-screen TVs and text friends. It's in college classrooms where the professor's lecture competes with the social networking site on a laptop.

It's also the new social norm. It's part of a world in which people walk together side by side talking separately on cell phones. Where you hear the click of a friend's keyboard while you're talking on the phone. And where Nass recently watched two students holding a serious conversation while one was surfing the Internet.

If the ratcheting up of media multitasking is teaching us not to pay attention, is it also training us not to expect attention? Nass, who is turning his research to everything from airline pilots to fourth-graders, has begun to wonder about students.

"I don't know that this generation values focused attention. The notion that attention is at the core of a relationship is declining," he suspects. "Is saying to someone 'I am going to give you my undivided attention' still one of the greatest gifts I can give?" Or has multitasking led us to a kind of attention infidelity?

What we are learning is our limits. Not just on the highway where texting-while-driving is as common as it is terrifying, but at the dinner table where kids insist (wrongly) that they can text and talk, at the office where multitasking is multidistracting, and in relationships where face-to-face competes with Facebook.

It turns out that we have only so many coins to pay attention. How do we hold their value in a media world?

I'll explain just as soon as I answer this e-mail...

Now then, where was I?

Discussion Questions

1. Can you give examples of ways that you multitask? Do you believe this makes you more efficient or effective?
2. Do you think jobs should be structured so that workers aren't forced to multitask? Explain your answer.

Summary

A system is a set of interrelated parts that work together for a common purpose. A system's functions can be divided into input, processing, output, feedback, and control. A system can be a subsystem of another system and may interact with other systems in its environment. Both computers and business organizations can be viewed as systems.

The value chain model views the business organization as a set of activities that add value to the firm's products or services. The model distinguishes between primary, production-oriented activities and secondary, support-oriented activities. Each activity is a subsystem with its own inputs and outputs; together, these subsystems interact with each other to determine the overall performance of the organization. As a subsystem of a larger business organization, an information system is a set of interrelated parts that work together to produce, distribute, and use information products. Some information systems support the feedback and control function of the organization, enabling better management decisions to be made. Other information systems, called transaction processing systems, keep track of transaction-based business processes, such as purchasing and invoicing. Transaction processing involves repeating a series of five steps: entering data, processing data, storing and updating data, preparing documents and reports, and handling user inquiries. Enterprise resource planning systems pull together information from multiple transaction processing systems, enabling businesses to make interactions among their departments and with outside organizations even more efficient.

In a systems view of a business organization, management represents the control function. Low-level, operational managers make the most structured decisions. Their work is supported by management information systems. Decision support systems provide information to middle-level, tactical managers who make semistructured decisions. High-level, strategic managers make unstructured decisions. A system providing information to top managers is called an executive information system. Group decision support systems enhance collaborative decision making by teams of managers.

An organization typically creates an overall IT plan before developing particular systems. The IT plan describes intended overall use of information technology to meet the company's needs. The organization then follows the plan, using cost-benefit analysis to select specific projects to develop and project planning techniques to track system development schedules.

Information systems are tools that should be designed to meet the information needs of the people using them. Poorly designed information systems can result in information overload and hamper a manager's ability to communicate effectively or make quality decisions. A company's information code of ethics should address the privacy, intellectual ownership, and the information quality and access policies to guide its managers and information workers and foster an ethical information culture.

Key Terms

acquisition (p. 445)
action document (p. 446)
batch processing (p. 446)
business organization (p. 442)
chief information officer (CIO) (p. 454)
code of ethics (p. 463)
cost-benefit analysis (p. 461)
critical path method (CPM) (p. 462)
critical success factors (CSF) (p. 461)
data warehousing (p. 446)
decision support system (DSS) (p. 455)
effectiveness (p. 444)
efficiency (p. 444)
electronic data interchange (EDI) (p. 447)
enterprise resource planning (ERP) (p. 447)
executive information system (EIS) (p. 457)
expert system (ES) (p. 457)
Gantt chart (p. 462)
geographic information system (GIS) (p. 456)
group decision support system (GDSS) (p. 456)
information overload (p. 460)
information system (p. 444)
infrastructure (p. 461)
interorganizational information systems (IOS) (p. 447)
management (p. 451)
management information system (MIS) (p. 454)
management levels (p. 454)
management reporting system (p. 455)
organizational information requirements analysis (p. 461)
outsourcing (p. 451)
presentation (p. 445)
processing (p. 445)
real-time processing (p. 446)
social responsibility (p. 463)
storage and retrieval (p. 445)
strategic information system (p. 459)
strategic planning (p. 460)
supply chain management (p. 447)
system (p. 441)
transaction (p. 445)
transaction processing system (TPS) (p. 446)
transborder data flow (p. 450)
transmission (p. 445)
value chain model (p. 443)

Companion Website Projects

1. The *Digital Planet* Web site, www.pearsonhighered.com/beekman, contains self-test exercises related to this chapter. Follow the instructions for taking a quiz. After you've completed your quiz, you can email the results to your instructor.
2. The Web site also contains open-ended discussion questions called Internet Exercises. Discuss one or more of the Internet Exercises questions at the section for this chapter.

True or False

1. The Cannibal Principle says that semiconductor technology absorbs the functions of what previously were discrete electronic components onto a single new chip.
2. To accomplish its purpose, a system performs five basic functions: input, processing, categorizing, calculating, and output.
3. Everything inside a system's boundary is called the system's subsystem.
4. An information system is a subsystem that supports the information needs of other business processes within an organization.
5. In business information systems, information technology performs five functions: acquisition, processing, storage and retrieval, presentation, and transmission.
6. Transaction processing is linear, rather than cyclical, by nature.
7. A business alliance is a cooperative arrangement between two or more businesses with complementary capabilities, such as marketing and distribution.
8. Industrial networks may link the systems of several companies in an industry.
9. Managers spend up to 90 percent of their time communicating with other people in the organization and in the company's external environment.
10. Today's corporate IT division may soon be radically transformed because of the emergence of grid computing and information utilities.

Multiple Choice

1. Which of these is not a component of a system?
   a. Control
   b. Utility
   c. Input
   d. Output
   e. Processing
2. Which of these is not a value chain activity in an organization?
   a. Inbound logistics
   b. Operations
   c. Cognition
   d. Outbound logistics
   e. Marketing
3. What business term is used to describe how customers rate the quality of the products and services they receive?
   a. Contentment
   b. Critical success factors
   c. Effectiveness
   d. Efficiency
   e. Logistics
4. Factors affecting the international business environment and transborder data flow include
   a. multiple languages and cultural differences.
   b. the laws and regulations of governments, including copyright and privacy issues.
   c. varying telecommunications standards and technologies.
   d. different monetary systems.
   e. All of these factors affect international business environments.
5. Which is true? A transaction processing system (TPS)
   a. would not be useful for tracking course enrollment.
   b. is an organization's basic accounting and record-keeping system.
   c. does not require high processing speeds.
   d. is not searchable using database queries.
   e. All of the above.

6. Which of the following is not typically performed by management information systems (MIS)?
   a. Providing detailed reports, summary reports, and exception reports
   b. Extracting relevant data from databases of the transaction processing systems
   c. Providing managers with information needed to make decisions
   d. Making recommendations for improving performance
   e. Organizing and summarizing data in useful ways

7. Which is not a commonly used system for supporting management decision making?
   a. Executive information system (EIS)
   b. Geographic information system (GIS)
   c. Grid utility system (GUS)
   d. Group information system (GIS)
   e. Expert system (ES)

8. Group decision support systems (GDSS)
   a. are designed to enhance collaborative decision making.
   b. are usually in the form of a meeting room equipped with hardware and software tools.
   c. allow individuals to use the GDSS as a private DSS to work out ideas during meetings.
   d. enable group members to share information anonymously if desired.
   e. All of the above.

9. What do businesspeople call an innovative product or service that is difficult for a competitor to emulate?
   a. Competitive hurdle
   b. Entry barrier
   c. Competitive calculus
   d. Beta blocker
   e. Technology transfer

10. What do you call a company-wide information system that combines information found in two or more transaction processing systems?
    a. Information utility grid
    b. Business alliance
    c. Electronic data interchange (EDI)
    d. Enterprise resource planning (ERP)
    e. Value chain model

11. A geographic information system (GIS) is
    a. a type of DSS designed to work with maps and other spatial information.
    b. typically used with the critical path method in system design.
    c. a type of expert system used to provide expertise in geology.
    d. a form of transaction processing system used for geographical simulations.
    e. impractical with today's technology.

12. Which is not one of the four major phases in information technology (IT) planning?
    a. Aligning the IT plan with the overall business plan
    b. Describing the firm's IT infrastructure
    c. Allocating resources to specific information systems and projects
    d. Planning specific information system projects
    e. Critical path method (CPM)

13. What tool provides managers with optimistic, pessimistic, and most likely estimates for completion of each project activity?
    a. Cost-benefit analysis
    b. Data flow diagram
    c. Gantt chart
    d. PERT chart
    e. Spreadsheet

14. When writing an organization's information code of ethics, which topic would you *not* include?
    a. Privacy
    b. Access to information
    c. Information quality
    d. Encryption algorithms for security
    e. Intellectual property

15. Which is not true? Socially responsible companies
    a. attempt to balance the interests of stakeholders.
    b. always optimize profits regardless of human consequences.
    c. have a social contract with the community to enhance the material well-being of all community members.
    d. take environmental and economic impact into account when making decisions.
    e. avoid any fraud or deception of the public.

Review Questions

1. Define or describe each of the key terms in the "Key Terms" section. Check your answers using the glossary.
2. What are the types of information workers in our information economy?
3. What are the major components of a system? What is the difference between a system and a subsystem?
4. What is the basic concept of the value chain model?
5. What are the basic systems components of an information system?
6. What is the purpose of a transaction processing system?
7. What are the steps in a transaction processing cycle?

8. What are three basic types of managers in an organization?
9. Describe three types of decisions. Which types of decisions are made by different management levels in an organization?
10. Describe the characteristics of an MIS. What kinds of reports does it produce?
11. Describe the characteristics of a DSS. What types of information tools does it provide?
12. Describe the characteristics of a GIS. Why would a GIS be useful in a business organization?
13. What is the likely impact of utility grid computing on traditional IT departments?
14. Describe three basic strategies organizations use to compete successfully.
15. How can a strategic information system be used to improve an organization's efficiency? Its effectiveness?

Discussion Questions

1. Use systems terminology to describe a real-world situation, such as organizing a sporting event or looking for a job. Does the systems model increase your understanding of the situation or make it more confusing?
2. Many companies are trying to improve the quality of their products and services for customers. How can you use the value chain model to identify what business processes to change to improve quality?
3. How could you evaluate whether decisions are made effectively in an organization? What factors or variables would you need to consider in your analysis?
4. Identify and discuss some of the ethical dilemmas and issues involved with (a) an MIS, (b) a DSS, and (c) an ES.
5. Which of the types of information systems described in this chapter do you think will be changed significantly in the coming decade? Explain.
6. Describe some of the social responsibilities of information workers in an organization with which you are familiar, such as a bank, police station, retail store, or government office.

Projects

1. Scan through a newspaper or magazine, and pick a situation that is interesting to you. Describe the situation as a system, and identify the information activities in the situation. Think about how the situation could be improved. Write a report describing your analysis and recommendations.
2. Interview the owner of a small business. Describe the important transactions and the five-step transaction processing cycle for the organization. Identify some relevant information ethics issues for the organization. Create a presentation of your findings using a presentation software package such as Microsoft PowerPoint.
3. With a class partner, interview a manager in a large company. Use the information systems in context model (people, tasks, information, organization, environment, and information technology) to guide your interview. Prepare a report describing the company as a system. Exchange reports with another class group; then read and comment on each other's reports.
4. With a group, visit a service organization in your community, such as a hospital, fire department, church, or restaurant. Interview a manager to identify the information systems he or she uses to support decision-making responsibilities. Present a report to your class describing your findings.
5. With a class colleague, interview a manager of an organizational unit at your school. Ask the manager to describe the activities he or she performed during the previous workday and the information needed to perform those activities. Discuss the results of the interview with your class colleague. Compose a memo to the manager, thanking him or her, and summarizing what you learned.

Sources and Resources

Books

Only the Paranoid Survive: How to Exploit the Crisis Points That Challenge Every Company, by Andrew S. Grove (Bantam Books). In this widely publicized book, the founder and previous CEO of Intel shares his business philosophy and lots of stories from the front lines of the microprocessor wars.

Competitive Advantage: Creating and Sustaining Superior Performance, by Michael Porter (Simon & Schuster). In this updated classic text, the author describes the competitive forces affecting how a business organization can survive and thrive in the global competitive business environment.

Harvard Business Review on Managing the Value Chain (Harvard Business School Press). This collection of eight essays examines the changing relationship between suppliers, customers, and competitors in the age of technology and globalization, outlining key ideas and providing guidance for incorporating shifts in the value chain into a firm's strategic outlook.

The Future of Management, by Gary Hamel and Bill Breen (Harvard Business School Press). The authors of this book argue that management practices need to change with the times. Using case studies and careful analysis, they draw practical conclusions that can be applied by forward-thinking managers.

Evolve! Succeeding in the Digital Culture of Tomorrow, by Rosabeth Moss Kanter (Harvard Business School Press). The author believes the new economy has had a "lobotomy" about basic business fundamentals. She skewers the clichés and uses them to expose the shallow thinking that has led to disaster. Using examples from both private and public sector companies, Kanter shows how digital innovation can be achieved within a company. She gets beyond the technical whizbang to look at the human possibilities of a global community.

Mission Critical: Realizing the Promise of Enterprise Systems, by Thomas H. Davenport (Harvard Business School Press). As information-dependent companies of all types continually expand and globalize, the need to share critical data between far-flung sites increases dramatically. This text is an introduction to enterprise resource planning systems and how they are useful for organizations. The text is easy to understand, gives real-world examples of benefits and pitfalls of different implementation methods, and gives you a good idea of the magnitude of an ERP project.

The Cluetrain Manifesto: The End of Business as Usual, by Christopher Locke, Rick Levine, Doc Searls, and David Weinberger (Basic Books). *The Cluetrain Manifesto* began as a Web site in 1999 when the authors posted 95 theses pronouncing what they felt was the new reality of the networked marketplace. For example, thesis 2: "Markets consist of human beings, not demographic sectors," and thesis 20: "Companies need to realize their markets are often laughing. At them," and thesis 62: "Markets do not want to talk to flacks and hucksters. They want to participate in the conversations going on behind the corporate firewall." The book enlarges on these themes through seven essays filled with dozens of stories and observations about how business gets done in America and how the Internet will change it all.

IT and the East: How China and India Are Altering the Future of Technology and Innovation, by James M. Popkin and Partha Ivengar (Harvard Business School Press). It's no secret that China and India are becoming major players in the world information technology market. This book by two analysts from the Gartner Group provides solid facts and perceptive predictions about the growing influence of "Chindia" in the IT world.

Common Knowledge: How Companies Thrive by Sharing What They Know, by Nancy M. Dixon (Harvard Business School Press). The author describes insights into how organizational knowledge is created and how information systems can effectively communicate that knowledge within the organization. The book provides in-depth studies of several organizations—including Ernst & Young, Bechtel, Ford, Chevron, British Petroleum, Texas Instruments, and the U.S. Army—that are leading the field in successful knowledge transfer.

Periodicals

Computerworld. This weekly newspaper for computer professionals has a section called "Computer Careers" with advice and information on information technology professions.

Business Week. Besides national and international business news, this magazine publishes interesting articles about the information industry and the use of information technologies in companies.

Information Week. This magazine is laid out much like *Business Week* and contains interesting articles covering the information industry. It's a good source for business-related Web sites.

Journals such as the

MIS Quarterly, Journal of Management Information Systems, Harvard Business Review, and ***Journal of Organizational Computing and Electronic Commerce*** are written primarily for researchers and academics who want to keep up with current research in the field.

Professional Organizations for Information Workers

Association for Computing Machinery (ACM) **http://www.acm.org**. (You'll find the complete text of the ACM's Code of Ethics in Appendix B of this book.)

Association of Information Technology Professionals (AITP) **http://www.aitp.org**.

Association for Information Systems (AIS) **http://www.aisnet.org/**.

Institute for Certification of Computing Professionals (ICCP) **http://www.iccp.org/**.

Institute of Electrical and Electronics Engineers (IEEE) **http://www.ieee.org**.

International Federation for Information Processing (IFIP) **http://www.ifip.or.at/**.

Society for Information Management (SIM) **http://www.simnet.org/**.

The American Society for Information Science and Technology **http://www.asis.org**.

13

E-Commerce and E-Business

The Evolving Internet Economy

OBJECTIVES

After you read this chapter you should be able to:

- Describe several basic models of e-commerce and e-business
- Discuss factors that have had an impact on success and failure of dot-com enterprises
- Explain how Web 2.0 and cloud computing technologies are changing e-commerce
- Discuss several ethical issues related to electronic commerce

> "People in this business spend a lot of time looking at ideas and asking, why do that? **But sometimes the more powerful question is, why not?"**
>
> —*Jeff Bezos,* founder and CEO of Amazon.com

Jeff Bezos Takes Amazon into the Cloud

As a child, Jeff Bezos wanted to be an astronaut. As an adult he decided to make history in a different kind of space: the uncharted territory of the newly commercialized Internet.

He founded Amazon.com, naming it after the most voluminous river in the world. Amazon opened its virtual doors in July 1995 with a mission to use the Internet to make book buying the fastest, easiest, and most enjoyable shopping experience possible. "It's work hard, have fun, make history. That's what we're trying to do." Amazon did just that, expanding beyond books to become a general store selling music, electronics, household goods, and a myriad of other products. Its growth seemed phenomenal—greater than any other start-up in history. Twenty million customers in more than 160 countries bought $2.8 billion worth of merchandise in 2000. Unfortunately, Amazon also lost $1.4 billion in the process.

Fueled by big dreams and seemingly endless cash from investors, Amazon created an unprecedented shopping experience for consumers: low prices, patented one-click purchase technology, quick shipments, personalized recommendations based on prior purchases (and purchases of others), and direct links to products from other Web sites—links that rewarded the owners of those Web sites with sales commissions. Bezos promised investors big returns from agreements with other Internet retailers. Most of the Internet companies paid Amazon in stock, much of which became worthless when the first wave of Internet companies hit the economic wall in 2000.

When the investor cash stream slowed to a trickle, Amazon undertook an efficiency drive, including a new accounting system that calculated profit and loss on every product it sold. The company got rid of unprofitable products, reduced the number of errors in its packing and shipping process, moved its call center operations to India, and converted its international warehouses into regional hubs to cut down on inventory levels and delivery times. These measures worked—in 2003 Amazon was a profitable company, and since then profits have soared.

FIGURE 13.1 Jeff Bezos.

The newly profitable Amazon didn't sit still, waiting for competitors to catch up. The Amazon bookstore added a feature that allows customers to search the contents of thousands of books for keywords and phrases. The music store added an MP3 download service that quickly became second only to Apple's dominant iTunes Store. In 2007, Amazon introduced Kindle, an electronic book designed to be for books what the iPod is for music. That same year more than a third of Amazon's sales were made by "seller-customers"—individuals, small businesses, and large specialty shops who used the eight-year-old Amazon Marketplace as a virtual storefront to sell their wares.

But if Bezos is right, Amazon's biggest success may come from selling services rather than products. Amazon Web Services (AWS) sells computer power and memory to customers who'd rather let somebody else maintain and service the hardware they need to run their Web sites, databases, and other computing activities. Bezos is betting that most of us will, over time, choose to pay pennies per hour and pennies per gigabyte rather than continually buying and upgrading our own computers. AWS is leading a global transition toward cloud computing—putting the computing power in the Internet cloud and treating it like a utility.

So far AWS generates just a tiny fraction of Amazon's astronomical revenues, but Bezos isn't worried: "We're willing to plant seeds and wait five to seven years for them to turn into trees." He's not concerned about cloud computing competition from Microsoft, Google, and other Internet giants, either: "We focus our strategies on delivering fundamental services better than anyone else." Bezos is proof that it's okay to have your head in the clouds if you're grounded in a solid strategy. ■

FIGURE 13.2 Amazon.com's automated warehouse streamlines order processing.

Amazon.com is a major player in the global electronic marketplace. Adam Smith, the founding father of economics, described the market concept in his book *The Wealth of Nations* in 1776, theorizing that "if every buyer knew every seller's price, and if every seller knew what every buyer is willing to pay, everyone in the market would be able to make fully informed decisions and society's resources would be distributed efficiently." In many ways, the emerging global electronic marketplace approaches Adam Smith's ideal.

Business on Internet Time

In the future, **all companies will be Internet companies.**

—Andy Grove, former president, chairman, and CEO of Intel

Electronic business (e-business) is, as the name suggests, the use of information and communication technology in support of business activities. Specifically, e-business generally involves the use of networks for sharing business information, maintaining business relationships, and conducting business transactions. Strictly speaking, **electronic commerce (e-commerce)** refers to the sales aspect of e-business: the buying and selling of products or services over the Internet and other electronic systems. In reality, many people use these terms interchangeably, giving e-commerce a much broader meaning.

The terms *e-commerce* and *e-business* are relatively new, but the underlying concepts have been evolving since computers were first put to work more than a half century ago. Some go back as far as 1844, when Samuel Morse constructed the first telegraph network. Pre-Internet e-business tools included bar coding, fax communication, electronic data interchange, electronic funds transfer, enterprise-wide messaging systems, and other private LAN and WAN systems. But the development of the World Wide Web and the commercialization of the Internet in the early 1990s changed the nature and scope of e-business forever.

Forward-thinking businesses used Internet technology to communicate with employees, business partners, and customers. Old, inefficient systems were replaced with Internet-based systems. Traditional brick-and-mortar companies experimented with the Internet as a new revenue channel. Internet-based companies—**dot-coms**—sprouted like weeds: bookstores, boutiques, pet stores, grocery delivery services, online communities, all kinds of Web portals, and more.

During the 1990s investors were high on predictions of a "long boom" fueled by the emerging Internet economy. High-tech stock prices soared. Intel's stock rose 3,900 percent, Microsoft's stock jumped 7,500 percent, and Cisco's stock increased by 66,000 percent! Investors, not wanting to miss out on the opportunity to make huge profits, used optimistic estimates of future earnings rather than current performance to justify phenomenally high prices for Internet-oriented companies, many of which had never turned a profit. In 2000 and 2001 the bubble burst, and the resulting collapse in stock prices caused about a thousand start-ups to fold, putting half a million people out of work in the process.

Excessive investor speculation was clearly a major cause of the dot-com bust of 2000. And there's no denying that many of the dot-bombs were based on profoundly stupid ideas. But other dot-com businesses were simply ahead of their time. The technology of 2000 couldn't support media-rich Web sites, high-quality streaming video, large-scale online communities, and the kind of instant feedback that makes many online experiences compelling to consumers today. Few people regularly used the Internet, and almost all of them logged in through slow dial-up connections.

All that changed in just a few years. Broadband found its way into homes and businesses by the millions. Falling hardware and infrastructure costs made many new services affordable. A global infrastructure opened new markets. Web 2.0 tools made many Web interactions as easy as watching a DVD. For a critical mass of people, the Internet was an important part of their everyday lives. Businesses large and small made the Web their main communication link with customers, and new companies emerged to take advantage of the technological surge.

Today, e-business is solidly entrenched in our economy. E-commerce sales are measured in hundreds of billions of dollars each year. And e-business is changing at Internet speed. New businesses and new business models emerge every year, forcing investors to ask hard questions about the future. Whether or not we see another e-meltdown like the one in 2000, e-business in one form or another is here to stay.

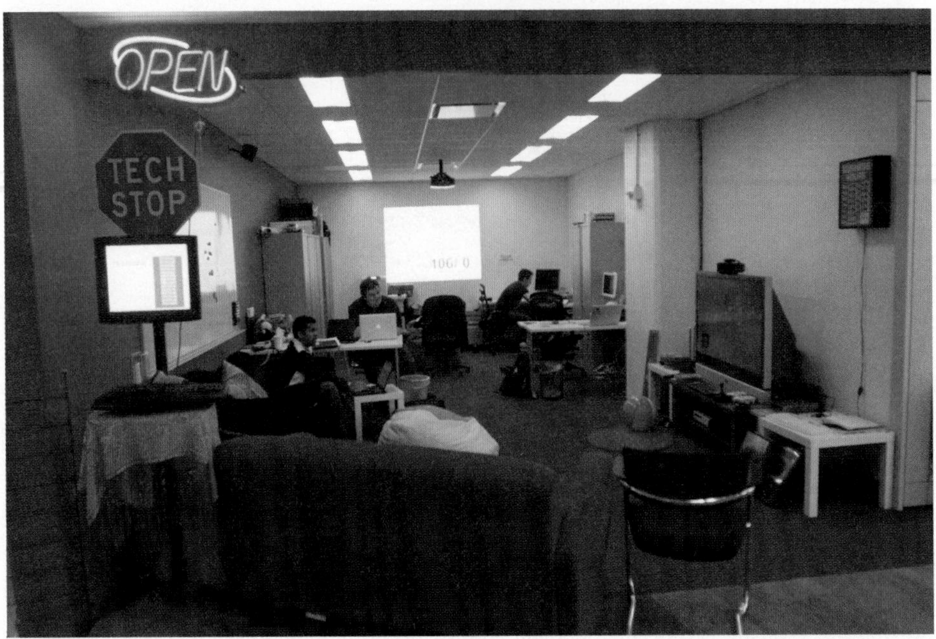

FIGURE 13.3 Many e-businesses that have emerged in the last decade have innovative workspaces that encourage employee collaboration. This is one of many common meeting areas used by Google employees in their New York office.

In the next section, we'll take a closer look at the basic kinds of systems for conducting e-business: intranets, extranets, and e-commerce systems for doing business with consumers. Then we'll examine several trends that are creating entirely new ways of doing business on the Internet. Finally, we'll consider some of the ethical issues of e-business.

E-Business 1.0: Intranets, Extranets, and E-Sales

E-commerce is not a technology play. It's a relationship, partnering, communication, and organizational play, made possible by technology.

—Tom Peters, author and business consultant

The basic idea of e-commerce is that at least two parties—a seller and a buyer—exchange information, products, or services using network technology. The exchange, or transaction, can occur between individuals, businesses, or organizations. The potential benefits of e-commerce for a company are enormous. Companies that sell goods and services using e-commerce generally have lower expenses, higher productivity, more efficient order processing, more useful information about their customers, and larger, more geographically dispersed markets than other, similar businesses.

There are several e-commerce models based on who is involved in the transaction:

- *Business-to-business (B2B).* The **business-to-business (B2B)** systems model represents interorganizational information systems in which a company handles transactions within its own value chain and with other businesses and organizations, such as its suppliers, distributors, and financial institutions. For example, Walmart purchases the products it sells in its stores from its vendors over the Internet. B2B is by far the dominant form of e-commerce, and it is growing at a phenomenal rate.
- *Business-to-consumer (B2C).* The **business-to-consumer (B2C)** model represents retail transactions between a company and individual customers. Examples include dot-com companies, such as Amazon.com and E*Trade.com, and traditional companies, such as Lands' End and United Airlines. B2C is the most visible aspect of e-commerce

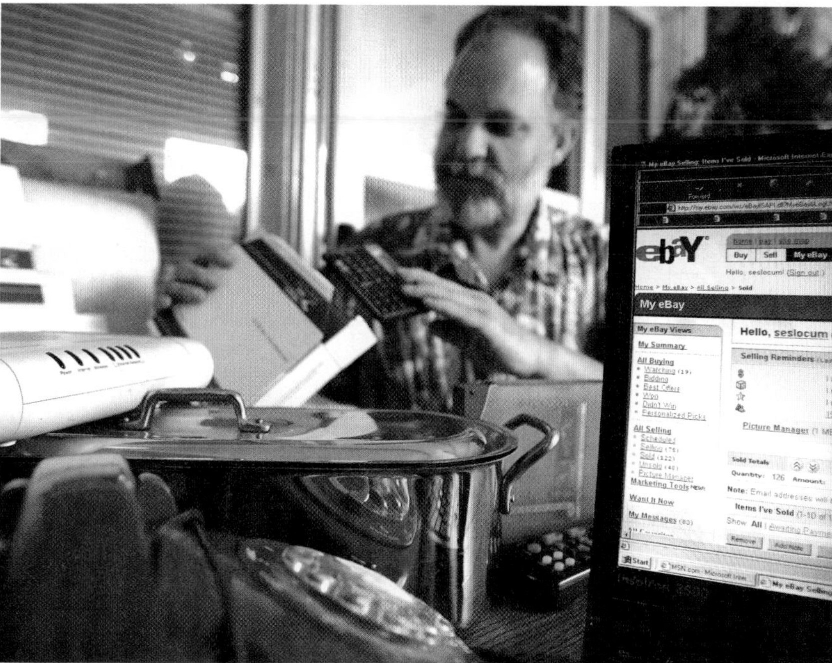

FIGURE 13.4 Millions of individuals and small businesses sell products through eBay auctions.

from a consumer's point of view. Worldwide revenues of B2C are in the hundreds of billions of U.S. dollars, but still less than B2B revenues.

- *Consumer-to-consumer (C2C).* The **consumer-to-consumer (C2C)** model represents transactions between consumers facilitated by a third party. The best-known example of C2C is eBay, the phenomenally successful Web auction site that enables individuals and businesses to offer items for sale and bid on items to buy.
- *Business-to-employee (B2E).* **Business-to-employee (B2E)** systems aren't technically e-commerce (depending on which definition of the term you use), because they don't involve buying or selling anything. B2E systems focus primarily on handling the activities that take place within the organization. Most midsized and large companies have intranet sites to handle B2E business.

In the following sections, we'll explore each of these types of systems, starting with the B2E systems.

B2E: Intranets for Internal Communication

In business-to-employee (B2E) e-business, an organization uses an **intranet** to support its internal value chain activities. (See Chapter 12.) Intranets based on Internet technology offer several advantages over customized, proprietary networks: cross-platform capability, open standards, reduced hardware and software costs, easy installation, and minimal user training. Intranets can dramatically improve communications within the organization; any employee with security authorization can access the organization's intranet from any location using a Web browser.

Businesses use intranets to support their internal business processes in many ways, including providing employees access to information, facilitating employees' teamwork and collaboration within and among departments, processing internal company transactions, and distributing information management tools.

Information Access for Employees

Many large companies have massive amounts of information stored in databases on intranets—information that can be accessed by employees using Web browsers. For example, Los Alamos National Laboratory publishes several million internal classified,

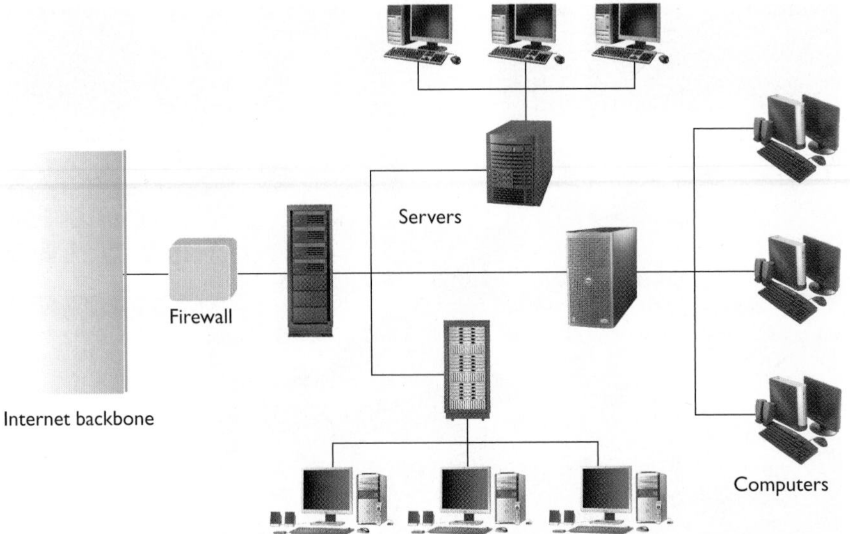

FIGURE 13.5 A large company's intranet may be a network of servers and client computers. Firewall security guards against unauthorized access to the intranet.

technical, and administrative documents on its intranet. By making this information available electronically, the Los Alamos scientists and managers can access the information quickly and easily, and the organization saves printing and distribution costs. Of course, not every employee needs access to the same information. Canon's intranet uses tactical personalization to increase efficiency, and each user's view presents only the information needed for their department. This approach ensures efficient access to the resources that employees need while reducing the information overload that a "one size fits all" approach can create.

Collaboration and Teamwork

Intranets make it easy for employees to share information, no matter where they are located geographically. In addition to information distribution, many companies use Web technologies in their intranets to facilitate collaboration within and among departments, improve corporate culture, and cultivate a sense of community. IBM's intranet takes full advantage of Web 2.0 tools, with 30,000 bloggers, podcasts (audio and video), wikis, and Beehive, an internal version of Facebook. Its intranet increases productivity, collaboration, and innovation of its hundreds of thousands of employees around the globe.

Internal Business Transactions

Employees can use Web browsers to conduct internal business transactions on an organization's intranet. This can increase efficiency, reduce paperwork costs, and increase the speed of updating information. Millipore Corp., a manufacturer of scientific and chemical purification products, uses its intranet to support employee self-service pages, including expense reporting, travel booking, and business-card ordering. Its intranet uses push technology to distribute employee information from corporate databases.

Distribution of Information Management Tools

Many organizations use their intranets to deliver applications and tools to employees and managers. The information management tools described in Chapter 12—management information systems, executive information systems, expert systems, and more—can be incorporated into or linked into intranets, making them available throughout an organization. Another type of tool helps employees manage customer relationships. In e-businesses, where customers rarely, if ever, see or speak to company representatives, **customer relationship management (CRM)** can be the difference between success

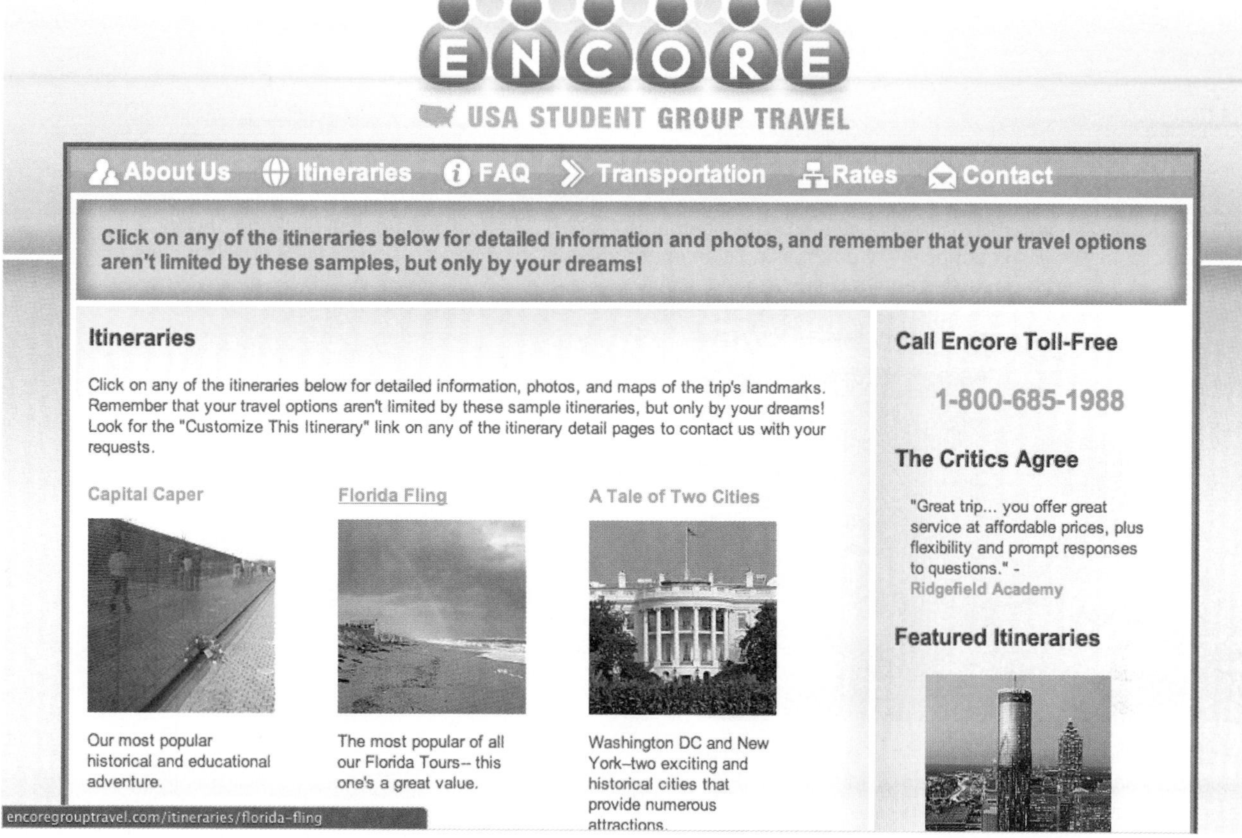

FIGURE 13.6 Small businesses can use extranets to connect directly with suppliers, advertisers, and other related businesses. For example, a travel company might have pages designed for use by hotels, restaurants, and other partner businesses.

and failure. In the information industry, CRM usually refers to methodologies, software, and Internet capabilities for managing customer relationships. CRM systems have been around in one form or another since the pre-Web days. A typical CRM system is a customer database that can provide information for managers, salespeople, marketing departments, and sometimes even the customers themselves. The database might include past purchases, customer preferences, service schedules, and customer communications, among other things. Whether it's part of an intranet or not, a well-designed CRM system can benefit both company and customers.

B2B: Extranets for Commerce and Communication

Just as intranets facilitate internal business communication and transactions, extranets can transform communication and commerce between businesses. Many companies have benefited from linking their intranets with other companies, creating extranets. Extranets enable them to build alliances with vendors, suppliers, and other organizations internationally.

An **extranet**, or extended intranet, is a private interorganizational information system connecting the intranets of two or more trusted business partners. Companies using an extranet can place orders with each other, check each other's inventory level, confirm the status of an invoice, and exchange many other types of business information. For example, Hilton Hotels operates a business-to-business extranet to communicate with companies that have contractual agreements to use Hilton's facilities for business travel. Hilton's corporate customers install links to the Hilton Web site on their own

how it works Package Routing and Tracking

UPS delivers an average of 13 million packages and documents every business day. Its online package tracking system averages 9 million queries every day, making it an important customer-service activity. UPS uses wireless networks to make package routing and tracking fast and accurate.

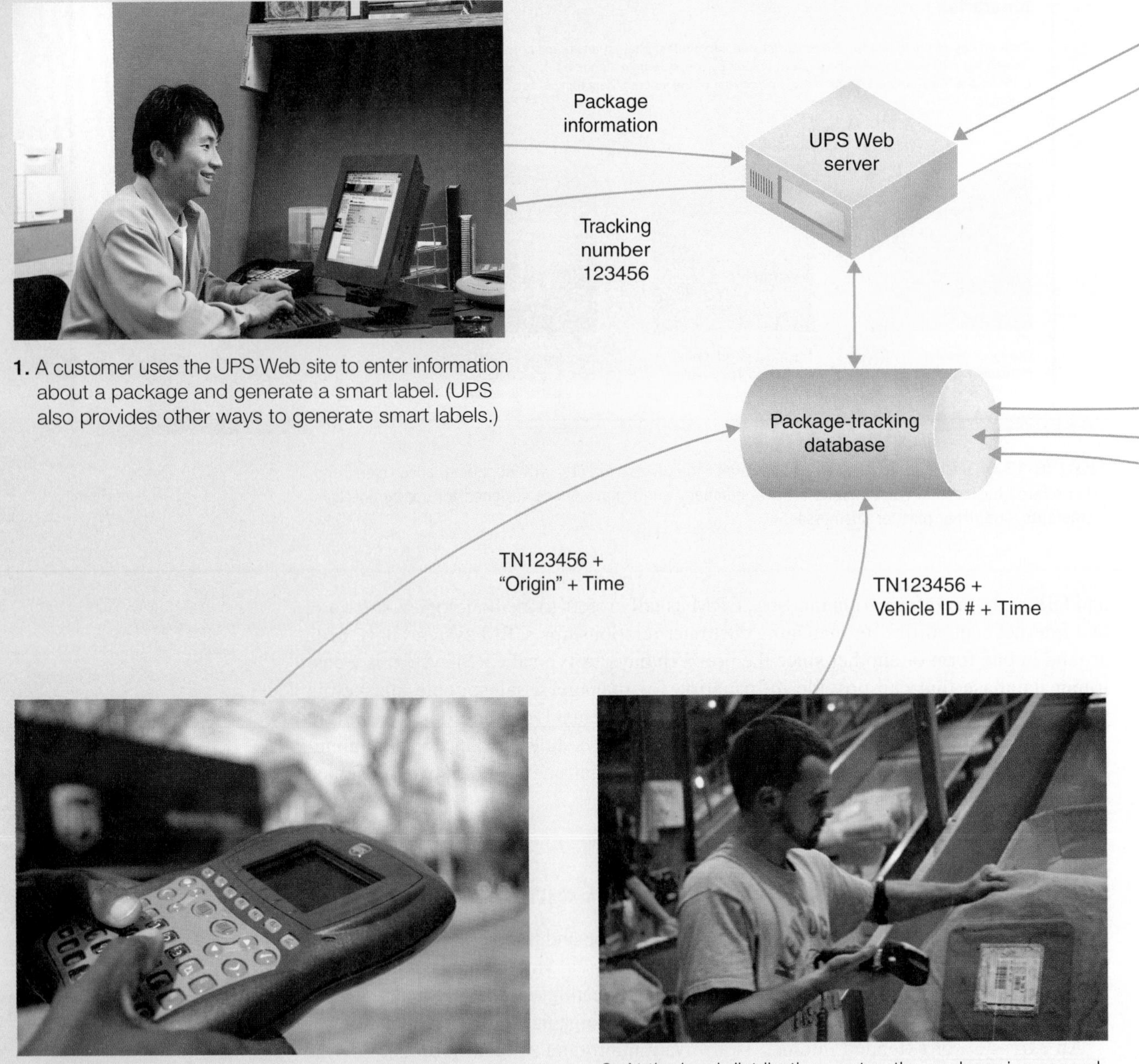

1. A customer uses the UPS Web site to enter information about a package and generate a smart label. (UPS also provides other ways to generate smart labels.)

2. When the package is picked up, the driver uses a wireless handheld computer to scan the smart label.

3. At the local distribution center, the package is scanned again when it is put on a truck, rail car, or plane.

FIGURE 13.7

TN123456

Package status

4. The UPS Web server allows customers to learn the status of their shipments. This could happen at any time during the process. (Major customers can track packages using UPS's Electronic Data Interchange system.)

TN123456
+ Time + Location

5. Scanners track packages as they are routed through a large hub facility. Most air packages are routed through the UPS Worldport in Louisville, Kentucky. Ground packages are more likely to pass through CACHE, UPS's largest ground hub in Chicago.

TN123456 + "Delivery"
+ Time + Signature image

TN123456 +
"Out for Delivery"
+ Time

ABC Company
2526 KIPLING AVE
STE 8000
MINNEAPOLIS MN 55416-3952

P:MG1 S:1128 I:

97B-3770

1ZEWRXXX028830 4221 0

6. When the package reaches the destination center, a computer creates a Preload Assist Label (PAL). The PAL identifies the conveyer belt to which the package should be sorted, the appropriate delivery vehicle, and the correct shelf location inside the delivery vehicle.

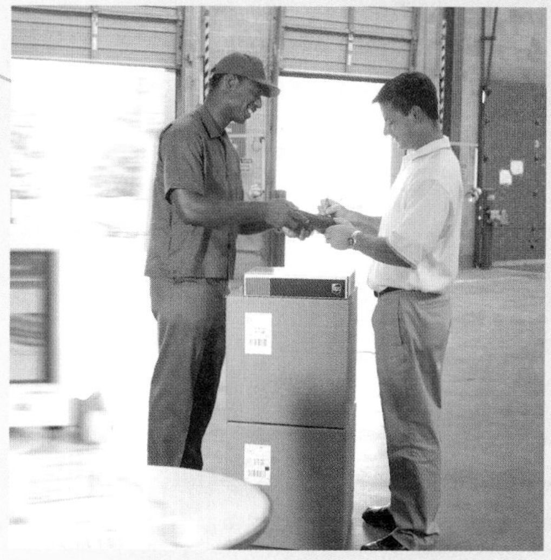

7. The driver's handheld computer contains an ordered list of stops and the packages to be delivered at each stop. When the package is delivered, the driver uses the handheld computer to scan the package one last time.

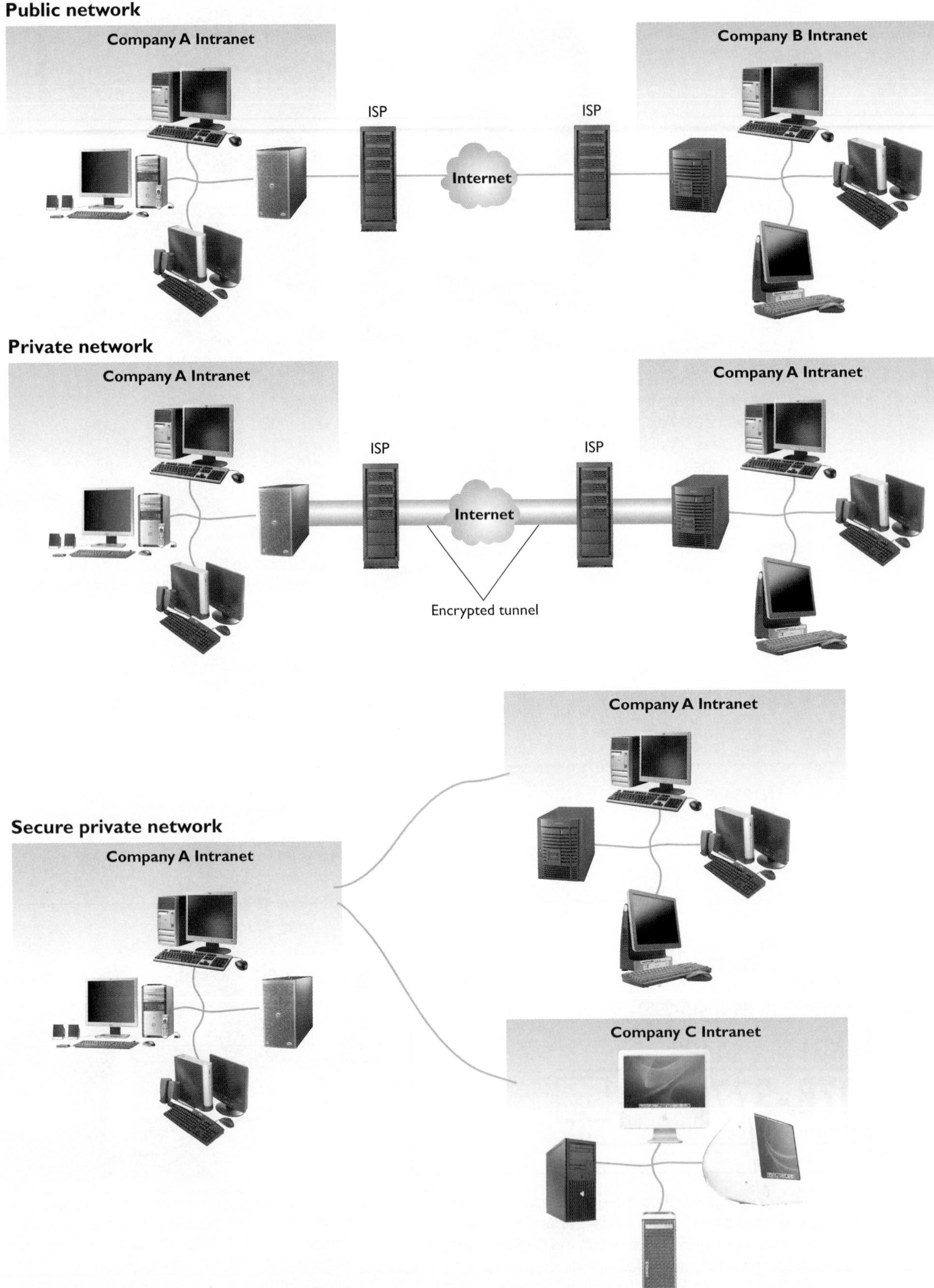

FIGURE 13.8 These three types of extranets enable organizations to connect their intranets to facilitate business transactions, communications, and other shared activities.

intranets, and those links call up customized Web pages with contractual prices and travel limitations.

Organizations can set up an extranet in one of three ways:

- A *secure private network* physically attaches the intranets with private leased telephone lines. Monthly leased-line charges can be costly, but security is relatively high for business transactions because only a limited number of partners have access to the system.
- A *public network* uses a public communications network, such as a public utility telecommunication network or the Internet. These types of intranets are relatively inexpensive to set up and maintain, but security is low. Intranets within a public network extranet are protected only by firewalls and user logon procedures.
- A **virtual private network (VPN)** uses a public network (most often, the Internet) with special protocols that provide a secure, private "tunnel" across the network between the business partners' intranets. A typical VPN is managed by more than one company's administrators. VPN-based extranets are popular because they're relatively economical, private, and secure. Data are specially coded—a process called ***encapsulation***—for sending transactions over the Internet; essentially, transactions are conducted via an encrypted channel, or tunnel, between the intranet firewalls of the extranet.

An intranet can improve a business's bottom line by:

- Increasing the speed of B2B transactions
- Reducing errors in intercompany transactions
- Reducing costs of telecommunications
- Increasing the volume of business with partners
- Facilitating the exchange of B2B documents
- Providing instant access to inventory and order status from suppliers
- Facilitating collaboration with business partners on joint projects

Walmart and its suppliers use a B2B extranet. Walmart built direct software links between its suppliers' factories and the cash registers at its stores. One major supplier, Procter & Gamble, can monitor the shelves at Walmart stores through real-time satellite linkups that send messages to the factory whenever a checkout clerk swipes a Procter & Gamble item past a scanner at the register. With this kind of minute-to-minute information, Procter & Gamble knows when to make, ship, and display more products at the Walmart stores. The system saves time, reduces inventory, and lowers order-processing costs so that Procter & Gamble can afford to give Walmart "low, everyday prices" without putting itself out of business. As a result, Walmart moves products through its stores more quickly and with less overhead.

Caterpillar, a multinational heavy machinery manufacturer, developed extranet applications to reduce the time needed to develop and redesign its vehicle products. The company connected its engineering and manufacturing divisions with its suppliers, distributors, overseas factories, and corporate customers. A customer can, for example, use the extranet to modify order information while the vehicle is still on the assembly line. This ability to collaborate remotely between the customer and the product developers decreases time delays in redesign work.

The trade association of automotive manufacturers and suppliers has developed an extranet named Automotive Network Exchange (ANX). The extranet was designed as an Internet VPN to provide a global infrastructure for trading partners within the industry, including Daimler AG, Ford Motor Co., General Motors Corp., and several dozen major suppliers. ANX reduces the time it takes a supplier to fill an order—sometimes from weeks to minutes.

B2C: Online Retail Sales and Service

Intranets support an organization's internal business processes. Extranets support business-to-business processes of two or more organizations. Of course, e-commerce also facilitates business transactions with consumers. To conduct B2C transactions on the Internet, a company provides customers with a public Web site where they can search product catalogs,

how it works Online Shopping

1. Most online shopping sites are dynamic, database-backed sites whose pages are automatically generated and updated. When you visit a large online store, you are using your Web browser to search site databases.

2. When you decide to place an item in your shopping cart, your request is sent to the store's Web server, which sends a cookie to your computer—a small file containing information on the desired item. Cookies are used by the Web site to keep track of your potential purchases. Cookies might also be used to track the different pages you visit on the site and customize the display to match your preferences. For example, if you view several MP3 players, the site might show you more display ads related to portable audio.

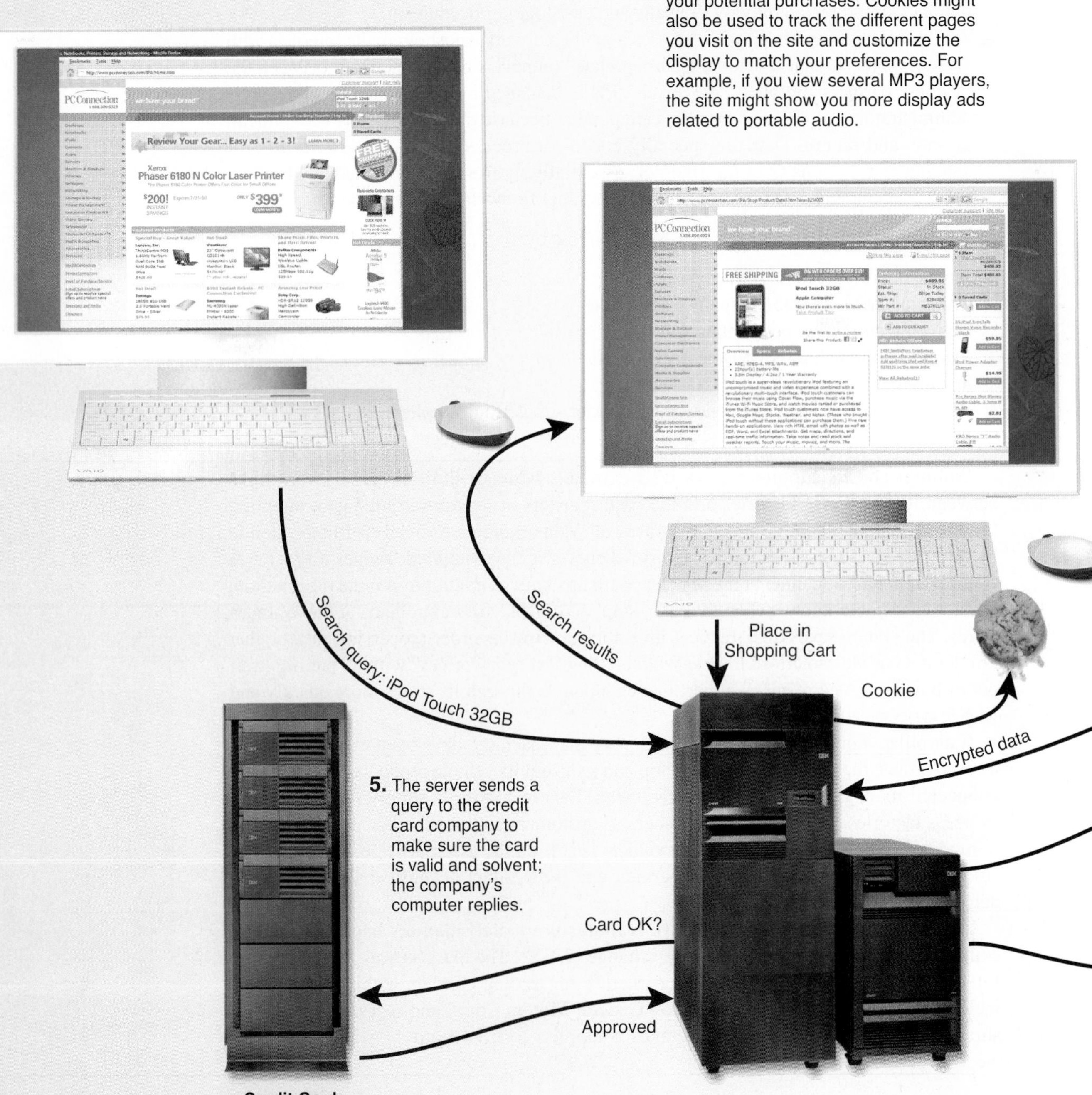

5. The server sends a query to the credit card company to make sure the card is valid and solvent; the company's computer replies.

FIGURE 13.9

3. When you “proceed to checkout,” the site displays all the items in your shopping cart, using the cookies on your hard disk to determine what you’ve put there.

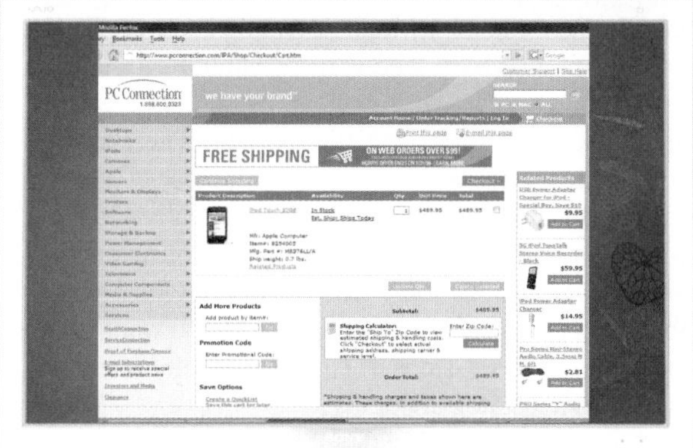

4. When you continue the checkout process, you’re routed to a secure part of the Web site so you can enter personal information and credit card numbers and know that they’ll be encrypted before being sent through the Internet.

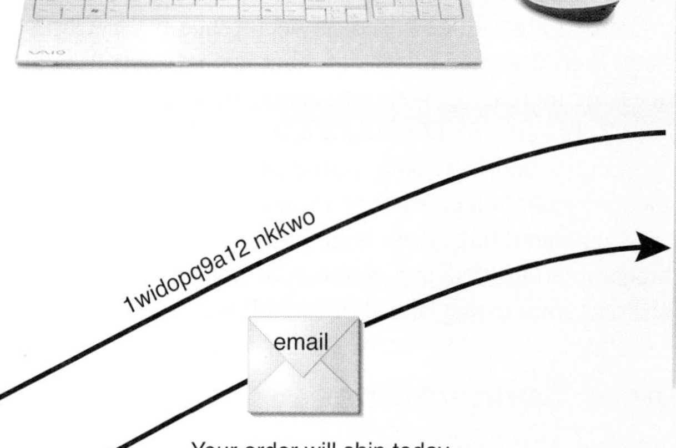

6. Once the transaction has been approved, the server sends a message to the warehouse where the order is filled. It also sends a confirmation email to you.

retrieve product information, order and pay for a product, and get service and support information.

The early years of Internet B2C were plagued by questions of privacy and security. Phishing and other types of fraud still plague online consumers, but today's technology makes most online shopping experiences as secure as other forms of shopping. Message encryption standards use software for authenticating the parties involved in a credit card purchase on the Internet, and secure Web pages use encryption to protect sensitive credit and ID information. Modern **electronic payment systems** such as PayPal and Google Checkout allow people to make purchases from strangers without revealing their credit card numbers. These systems rely on a trusted intermediary who is responsible for transferring funds from one person or business to another.

The best Internet sites have clearly stated goals and target specific markets. There are many ways to measure the effectiveness of a commercial Web site, and the number of hits a site gets is not necessarily one of them. The most successful B2C sites generally offer valuable content organized in an easy-to-access structure and packaged in a consistent, aesthetically pleasing design. Many also offer personalization ("Since you bought *X* we thought you might like *Y*"), customization ("Select a color," "How much RAM you want to add," etc.), product support forums ("Check here for discussions of common problems and solutions"), and other features that go beyond basic catalog shopping.

Even the best sites can't generate sales if customers can't find them. Because most people depend on search engines to get around the Web, site developers pay considerable attention to features that will earn high rankings in relevant keyword searches. There's a world of difference between being listed first and being listed 21st by a search engine. Most search engines rank sites using closely guarded algorithms based on occurrence of keywords in headings and text, links from related Web sites, and dozens of other factors. **Search engine optimization (SEO)** is the process of increasing Web site traffic by improving search engine rankings for targeted keywords. Experts in SEO make a science of figuring out tricks and techniques for maximizing rankings—and increasing traffic as a result. As you might expect, there's a less-than-ethical counterpart to legitimate SEO. ***Spamdexing*** is the process of using techniques—automatically generated links from bogus sites, for example—to fool search engines into giving sites higher rankings than they deserve. Search engine developers continually refine their algorithms to attempt to stay ahead of spamdexers.

C2C: Making Consumer Connections

Some of the most popular commercial Web sites are designed to facilitate consumer-to-consumer commerce. These sites are intermediaries that connect consumers with each other. Most C2C sites fall into a few broad categories.

The most basic kind of C2C site is the digital equivalent of a newspaper's classified ad section. The best known example is Craigslist, a service founded by Craig Newmark in 1995 to serve San Francisco. Today, Craigslist has local ads in more than 700 cities in more than 70 countries. It has become one of the most popular sites in the world and the leading classified ad service in any medium. People buy cars, rent apartments, find companionship, and hunt for jobs using Craigslist—all for free. The company charges for job listings and brokered apartment listings in a few places, but mostly gives its services away. The CEO has made it clear that the company is more interested in providing a service than maximizing profits.

Another type of C2C business is the online auction exemplified by eBay. Like Craigslist, eBay grew from a small California company in 1995 to an Internet giant with localized sites all around the world. Millions of people have sold everything from brussels sprouts to fighter jets on eBay. The company gets a small commission for each sale. Many entrepreneurs have built their own businesses on the eBay infrastructure.

A variation of the Internet auction is the reverse auction. In a reverse auction, the potential buyer suggests a price and sellers "bid" on whether they can meet the price. Reverse auctions are popular for hotel rooms, air flights, and travel packages, when the traveler is more interested in getting a good price than in controlling the details of the itinerary. (Because reverse auctions usually involve customers buying from businesses, they aren't technically C2C.)

FIGURE 13.10 B2C Web sites offer many options for personalization and customization. Bike Friday creates custom folding bikes for cyclists all over the world; the company's Web site serves as a communication link between customers and company. Customers at MakeYourOwnJeans.com submit measurements and receive custom-fit, made-to-order clothes. Threadless is a community-centered online apparel store that sells user-submitted, democratically selected designs.

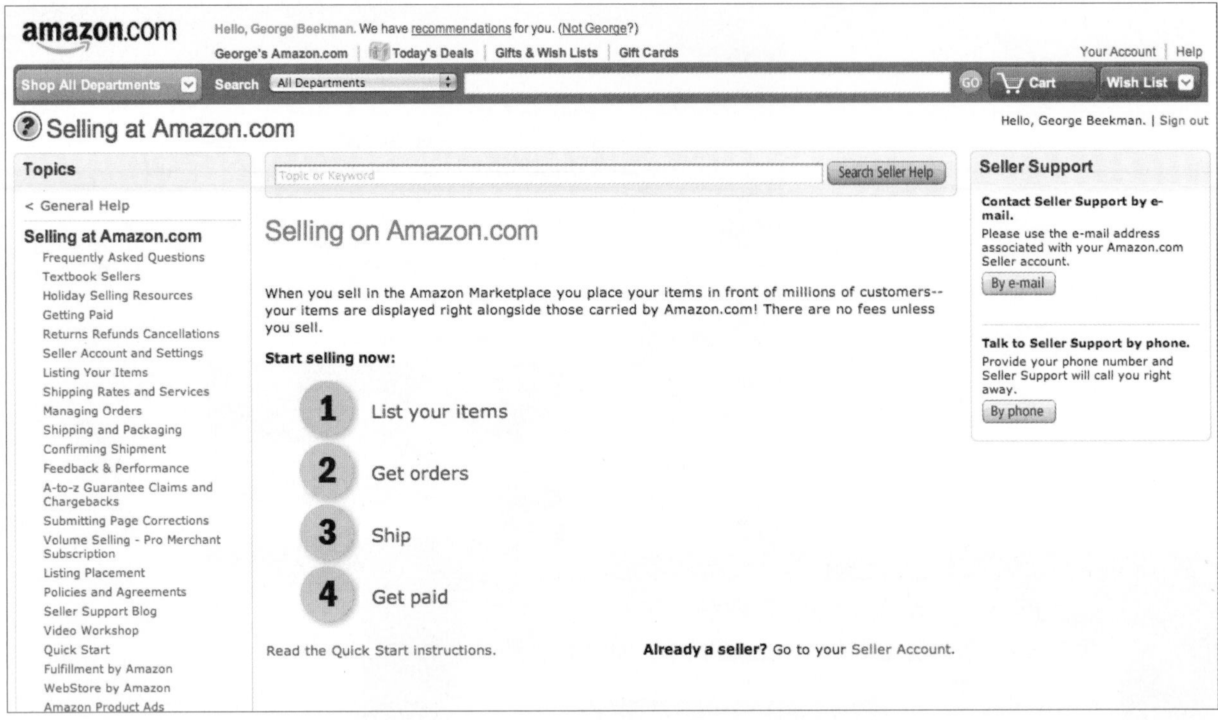

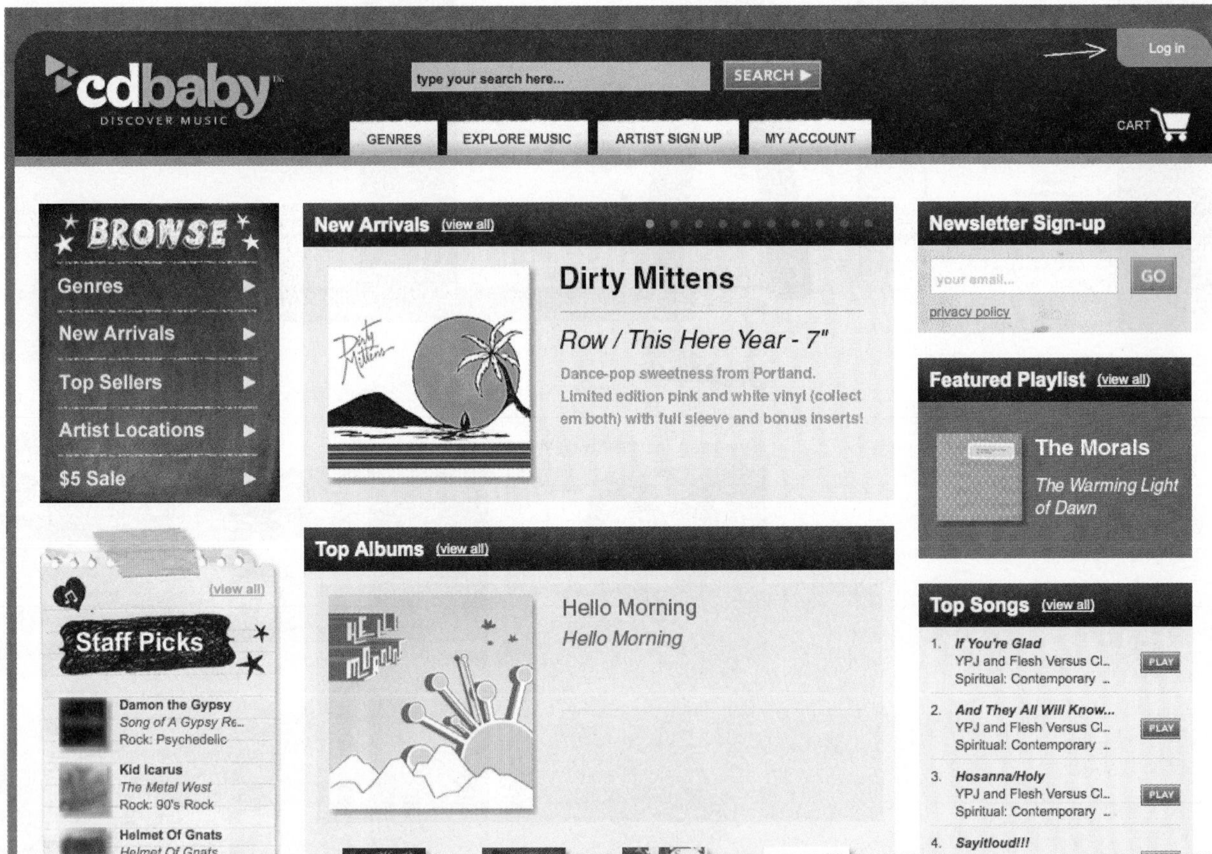

FIGURE 13.11 C2C sites provide direct connections between potential buyers and sellers. Most people are familiar with eBay and Craigslist, but many other sites offer C2C options. The Amazon Marketplace makes it easy for Amazon customers to sell products to the same people who buy products directly from Amazon. Hundreds of thousands of independent musicians sell their CDs and distribute their music to online stores through CD Baby.

Using PayPal for Electronic Payments

More than 50 million people have an account with the PayPal electronic payment system. People use PayPal to pay for Web auction items, send money to family members, pay bills online, and more. In this example, two strangers use PayPal to facilitate the sale of a used bike.

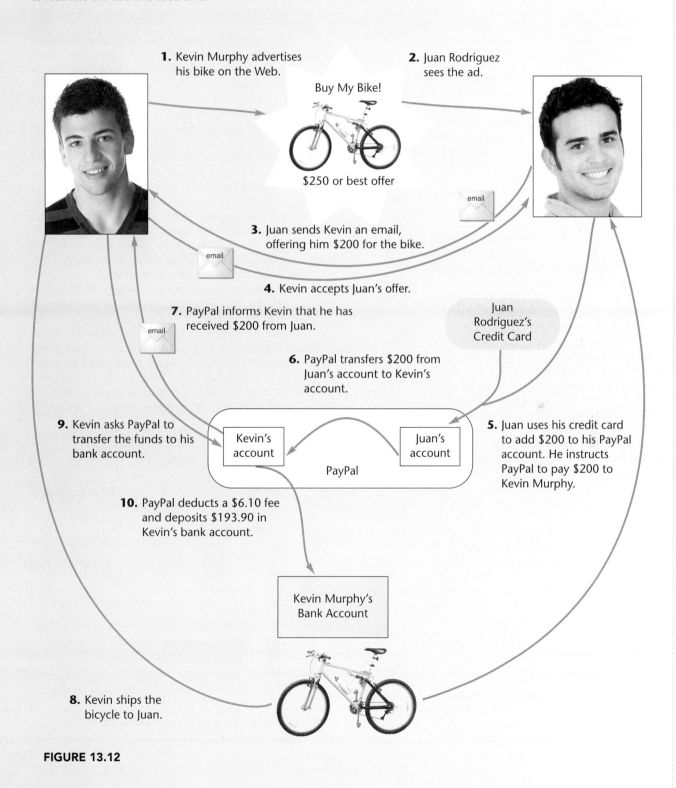

1. Kevin Murphy advertises his bike on the Web.
Buy My Bike!
$250 or best offer
2. Juan Rodriguez sees the ad.
email
3. Juan sends Kevin an email, offering him $200 for the bike.
email
4. Kevin accepts Juan's offer.
7. PayPal informs Kevin that he has received $200 from Juan.
email
Juan Rodriguez's Credit Card
6. PayPal transfers $200 from Juan's account to Kevin's account.
9. Kevin asks PayPal to transfer the funds to his bank account.
Kevin's account
Juan's account

5. Juan uses his credit card to add $200 to his PayPal account. He instructs PayPal to pay $200 to Kevin Murphy.
10. PayPal deducts a $6.10 fee and deposits $193.90 in Kevin's bank account.
Kevin Murphy's Bank Account
8. Kevin ships the bicycle to Juan.

FIGURE 13.12

Working Wisdom Selling Stuff Online

If you don't know what you're doing when you're looking to buy or sell something on a C2C e-commerce site, it's easy to find yourself overwhelmed by options, scammed by malicious buyers and sellers, or just not performing financially as well as you'd like. Here are a handful of tips to help you keep your head (and your bank account) above water in the raging sea of online commerce.

- ***Choose the right option for your business.*** If you're looking for a way to make a little extra money with a part-time business while reaching a large number of potential customers, services such as eBay and Amazon may be your best bet. If you want to avoid middleman fees, post classified-ad-style listings, and negotiate directly with buyers, you might prefer to post your listings on Craigslist. If you'd like to cut out the middleman altogether, or you require a more customized shopping experience, you might be better off building your own site. Many retailers opt for more than one of these options—they can benefit from the increased traffic and sales of listings on these larger sites and the flexibility and control that can only be found on a handcrafted site.
- ***Keep it simple.*** Provide clear descriptions of items you're selling, provide photos, and include prominent links for purchase options on every page (if they aren't provided by the service you're using). Don't clutter up your Web pages or site with unnecessary or irrelevant information, and avoid the temptation to go overboard with glitzy formatting. The quicker a customer can assess what you're selling and how to buy it, the more likely they'll become a customer.
- ***Show off the goods.*** People usually won't buy anything they can't see. Photograph your wares with good lighting and a minimum of clutter. For more expensive items, take several views, including close-ups. Give your customers a good look at the merchandise and you're far more likely to make the sale.
- ***Your reputation is your most powerful marketing tool.*** Reliable, timely service can garner you a positive reputation on eBay or other C2C sites, and this reputation can be worth a great deal in future transactions. Be completely up front about any flaws in your merchandise, available to answer questions, and quick to ship merchandise once a transaction has been completed. In online sales, satisfying your customers can result in repeat business. But there's more: Customer feedback (both positive and negative) can impact the purchases of countless other potential customers.
- ***Offer payment options.*** If you give the consumer more ways to pay, you'll probably see an increase in sales. Not everybody has a credit card, a checking account, and a PayPal account, but most potential customers have one of the three; letting them choose from several options ensures that you'll see fewer potential sales lost because you didn't offer a convenient method of payment. (Of course, you'll want to protect yourself if you accept insecure methods of payment such as checks; see the next point.)
- ***Don't let yourself get scammed.*** Don't ship a product until you've confirmed the transaction. (This means waiting for a check or PayPal transaction to clear before you put anything in the mail.) There are people on these sites that try to get something for nothing; don't let them take advantage of you.
- ***Help search engines find you, and customers will follow.*** It doesn't matter how great your deals are if nobody can find them. There are many things you can do to improve traffic to your site from search engines. Include a list of targeted keywords for your site or transactions, and if you're launching an entire commerce-oriented site, register it for indexing with Google, Yahoo!, Bing, and the other search engines. Finally, consider a link exchange with related sites. Many top search engines take outside links into account when determining top billing for search results.
- ***Factor the cost of services into your prices.*** Services such as PayPal offer a nearly indispensable service to online merchants, by providing a safe temporary depository for funds while transactions are resolved. However, these services come with a cost—usually a percentage of the selling price. Similarly, credit card companies take a percentage of sales. When you're setting prices for merchandise, factor *all* the costs of business into your pricing, or you may find yourself losing money on every transaction.

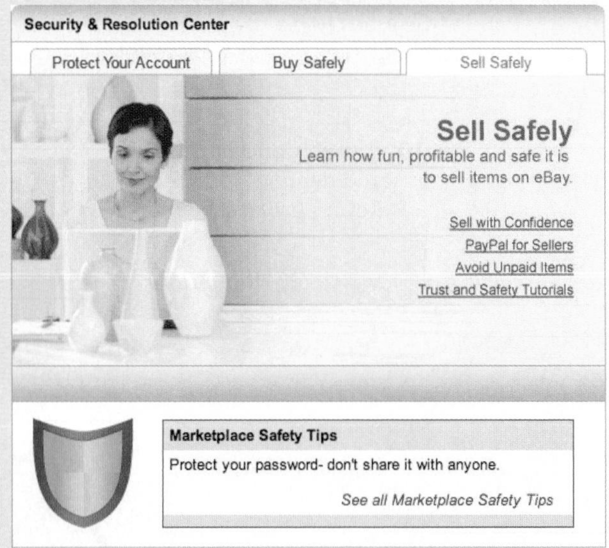

FIGURE 13.13 eBay provides guidelines for safe selling.

One other popular type of C2C system is the reseller model popularized by Amazon's partners program. Amazon partners can sell items through Amazon, taking advantage of Amazon's commerce tools and huge audience. Amazon may lose some sales to partners who undercut their prices, but the company more than compensates through the large volume of sales commissions it earns on third-party sales.

CD Baby is a popular reseller site specializing in independent music. When a musician provides the company with a few copies of a CD and some basic information, the company creates a Web page to publicize and sell the CD. The musician gets the proceeds of any sales minus a small commission. CD Baby also handles the details of getting the music on iTunes and other electronic distribution sites.

E-Business 2.0: Reinventing Web Commerce

> **We always overestimate the change** that will occur in the next two years and **underestimate the change** that will occur in the next ten.
>
> —*Bill Gates*

In other chapters we've talked about several important trends that are changing the way people use the Web: the social and collaborative capabilities of Web 2.0, the virtualization of technology through cloud computing, the growing number of mobile devices with Web connections, and more. In this section we'll outline some of the ways these trends are changing, and will continue to change, Web commerce. Some of these trends started in the earliest days of the Web, but they're having a bigger impact on the ways we do business as our world becomes more Web-centric.

Disaggregation: Commerce in the Cloud

The growth in cloud computing will almost certainly accelerate the trend toward *disaggregation*—separating commerce into its component parts and outsourcing those parts that can better be handled somewhere else. Amazon's Web Services, discussed at the beginning of this chapter, is an obvious example. Businesses can buy computer power and memory from Amazon so hardware issues don't distract them from the business of selling. A Web retailer can also outsource its payment process to Google Checkout, an innovative program that seamlessly plugs into the site, providing a consistent, simple checkout process for customers across a variety of sites. Future Web commerce sites may be built from software and hardware components that are scattered all over the Web.

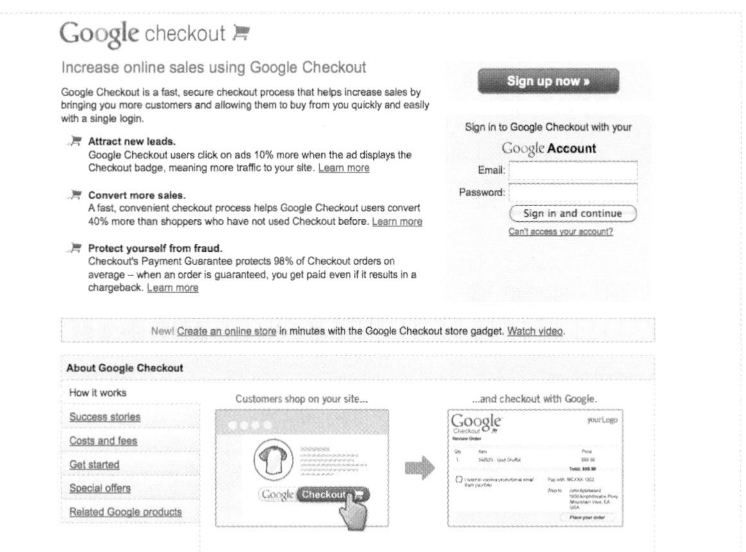

FIGURE 13.14 Shoppers who use Google Checkout have a consistent checkout experience at a variety of online stores.

Enhancing the Interactive Experience

Research suggests that most online shopping carts are abandoned before checkout. Many consumers ditch their carts because they can't find the information they need before committing to purchase. Some of this could be solved with more complete product descriptions, but words alone can't offer the up-close-and-personal experience of shopping in the physical world.

Many online retail sites enable buyers to personalize and customize their purchases in ways that just aren't possible at the mall. But

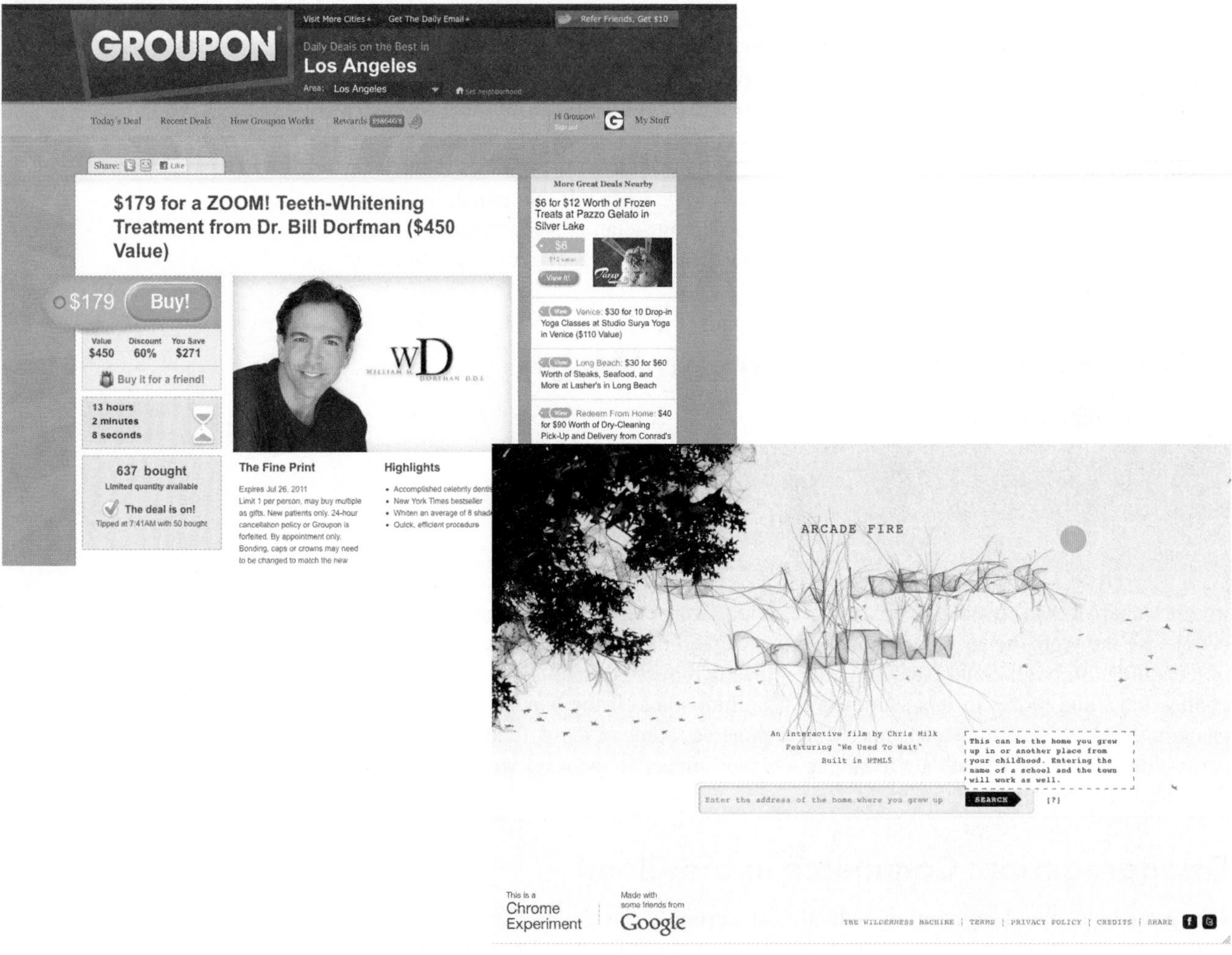

FIGURE 13.15 Web technology enables retailers and artists to sell products and generate buzz in ways that aren't possible in the non-digital realm. Groupon offers localized one-day bargains that are, essentially, group purchases made by people who don't know each other. If a certain number of people sign up for a deal, it becomes available to all of those people. The Wilderness Downtown is Arcade Fire's groundbreaking Web site that uses interactivity, personalization, and Google Maps technology to transcend the limitations of traditional music videos. After a visitor types in a childhood address, the site creates a powerful multi-window music experience that includes custom-generated video views of that location.

the fact remains that most online stores today are more like catalogs than shops. A growing number of online retailers are trying to break away from the "page" metaphor that dominates the Web. A new breed of media-rich sites are designed to attract (and keep) customers because they're fun, interesting, and uniquely designed to fit their products. In the physical world, shopping in a bookstore is a totally different experience than shopping in a hardware store. In the near future, the same might be true on the Web.

Mobile Commerce

Mobile commerce (m-commerce)—the use of smart phones, tablets, PDAs, laptops, and other portable electronic devices to conduct commerce while on the move—has been possible in one form or another for many years. But in recent years mobile commerce has increased dramatically as a result of several converging trends:

- The growing popularity of portable computers as a percentage of the total PC market
- The widespread availability of wireless Internet connections through Wi-Fi hotspots and 3G and 4G networks
- The popularity of mobile phones with GPS technology and Web access

- The development of smart phones with Web access and applications that aren't significantly compromised by size
- The development of software tools that can take advantage of a variety of mobile technologies

Here's a sampling of m-commerce applications that will become increasingly common in the next few years:

- *Mobile ticketing.* E-tickets can be sent directly to mobile phones and dashboard computers, which can in turn communicate wirelessly with ticket takers at entertainment events, parking facilities, toll roads, and so on.
- *Mobile coupons.* Electronic coupons and loyalty cards stored in mobile phones can replace their paper and plastic counterparts.
- *Mobile purchasing.* Many mobile phones make it easy to buy music, news, and other digital data; some stores encourage their customers to buy physical goods on their mobile devices; the actual goods can then be picked up at the stores or delivered.
- *Location-based m-commerce.* Mobile devices with GPS and other localization technology can customize offers and ads based on location.

For years, Japanese customers in many types of shops have been able to make purchases without plastic; their phones communicate directly with retail computers. This kind of wireless shopping is spreading to markets around the world.

Of course, mobile technology has all kinds of B2B and B2E applications, too. Doctors, home-care nurses, real estate agents, sales managers, utility representatives, technicians, and others can often conduct business more effectively outside the office. M-commerce applications have been developed—and will be developed—for all of those businesses, and many more.

FIGURE 13.16 Online payment companies such as Zong (pictured) and Obopay make payment more convenient and fast by enabling users to pay for goods and services using their cell phone.

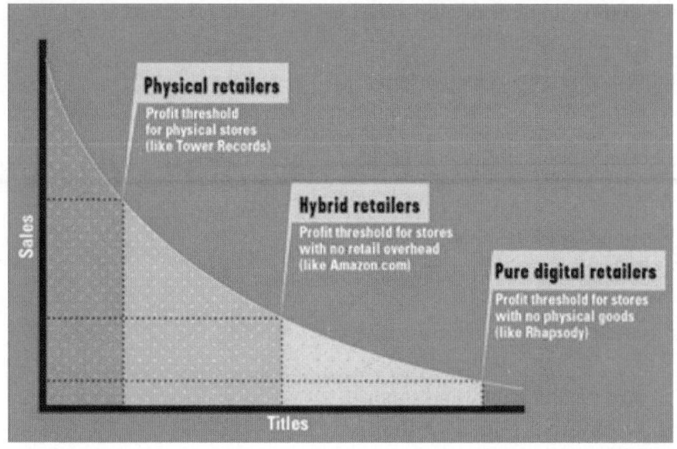

FIGURE 13.17 This chart from Chris Anderson's *Wired* article, "The Long Tail," illustrates how digital retailers (like iTunes) and hybrid retailers (like Amazon) can profit from less popular "niche" items that don't find shelf space in physical stores.

The Long Tail

In the early days of the automobile industry, Henry Ford famously pronounced, "The customer can have any color he wants so long as it's black." Ford's edict was based on practical limitations of the young industry. For the rest of the twentieth century, consumers steadily gained more choices—in cars, colors, and just about everything else. But twentieth century marketing was limited by retail shelf space and floor space. Stores could offer consumers variety, but not unlimited variety. This was especially apparent in the entertainment industry, where success meant having a "hit"—a record, book, or movie that was so popular that stores would stock it (or theaters would screen it) because they knew it would sell. If you didn't have a hit, you didn't have a chance.

That's no longer true, thanks to the Web. Hits still dominate the entertainment industry, but they don't control it. Retail floor space isn't an issue for Amazon or iTunes or Netflix—their stock is only limited by the capacity of their computer hardware and (if the product can't be downloaded or created on demand) the size of their warehouses.

In a virtual store, it costs next to nothing for an online vendor to offer less popular items along with hits. But adding more unusual titles would do little good if customers couldn't easily find them. Today's search engines, combined with sophisticated product recommendation technology, make it easy for consumers to locate even the most esoteric items. Interested in books on pre–twentieth century African art? Or Japanese avant-garde anime? Or Brazilian hip-hop? If it's available anywhere on Earth, you can probably find it with a few Web clicks. And when you do, the item's Web page might suggest similar or related items based on past customer behavior.

The upshot for consumers is almost unlimited freedom of choice. The upshot for vendors is that they don't need to depend on hits for all of their revenue.

Wired editor Chris Anderson called this phenomenon the **Long Tail**, referring to the tail of the statistical curve that appears when you rank books, movies, or tunes by popularity as reflected in sales or rentals. The curve starts high on the left side, with points representing sales of the "hits," and trails off into the long statistical tail where the least popular titles are plotted. Before the Web, retailers had trouble making money on those "misses." But on the Web, there's no reason *not* to sell the less popular niche items—especially if those products are digital downloads. Many Web retailers make most of their profits from products that aren't carried by the Walmarts of the world.

The Long Tail is getting longer, and that's good for consumers, business, and society. As Anderson wrote in *Wired*, "the cultural benefit of all of this is much more diversity, reversing the blanding effects of a century of distribution scarcity and ending the tyranny of the hit."

Web Marketing 2.0

A related trend is the rise of new Web 2.0–based marketing tools and techniques. Many of the most successful Web businesses depend on customer contributions to add value. Many consumers read customer reviews on Amazon and other sites before buying products. A growing number of high-tech companies encourage customers to contribute to product forums. A lively product forum can encourage sales, but it can also serve as a valuable tech support resource for product owners and users. And of course, well-written blogs and multimedia postings can add value to products and attract future customers.

You don't need to visit a retailer's Web site to be influenced by Web 2.0 marketing techniques. Many retailers have a presence on Twitter, Facebook, and other social networking sites, counting on recommendations from "friends" to increase sales. And if privacy concerns can be set aside, social networks might soon automatically tell you what your online friends are buying.

FIGURE 13.18 On theLongTail.com, Chris Anderson regularly adds new material and links related to his book *The Long Tail*, helping keep the book fresh long after its publication date.

Amazon's affiliates program suggests more active social marketing possibilities. Affiliates who link to products on Amazon's site earn financial rewards based on sales. And it's hard to deny the marketing power of the buzz created by a viral video on YouTube or a top-ranked bookmark on Digg or del.icio.us. Buzz can generate hits, but it can also create links, which can result high ranking in search engines—all of which can translate into sales.

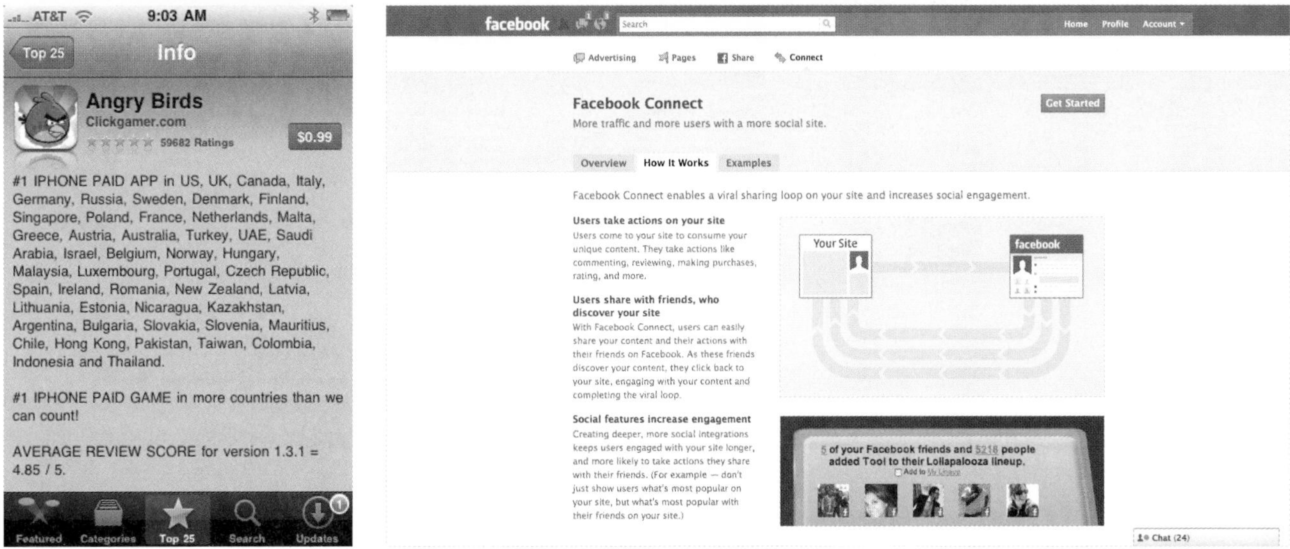

FIGURE 13.19 In the Web 2.0 marketing world, many of the most popular smart phone apps, including Angry Birds (left), are sold for under a dollar so they can garner better reviews, rank higher in the store, and ultimately generate more revenue than more expensive apps. Facebook Connect (right) enables users to login to any supported site with their Facebook info, automatically connecting them with Facebook buddies and extending the social network's connections beyond the walls of Facebook.com. This also assists Facebook advertisers in finding their ideal customers by mining data about friends, interests, online purchases, and more.

The "Free" Market

> The rise of "freeconomics" is being driven by the underlying technologies that power the Web...**the trend lines that determine the cost of doing business online all point the same way: to zero.**
>
> —*Chris Anderson,* Wired *editor*

One Web commerce trend runs counter to our experiences in the physical world: the growing number of e-commerce sites that make money by giving things away. The most famous example, of course, is Google. Google gives away search results, maps, driving directions, telephone directory assistance, images, video sharing services, email, and an ever-growing library of high-quality software. Google doesn't need to charge for all these things because it makes plenty of money in other ways—mostly as a custom advertising service for other Web commerce sites.

Google isn't alone in its generosity. Facebook, MySpace, LinkedIn, and other social networking sites offer free space and free services to millions of users. Publications from the *New York Times* to *Wired* give away content on the Web that people pay for in print. Craigslist offers want ads for free to both buyers and sellers. Superstar bands like Radiohead and unknown singer/songwriters offer music for free. Many of the most popular online games are free. Wikipedia is just one of countless free online references. Free, it seems, is becoming the "normal" price on the Internet.

Advertising is part of the reason for all these free services—advertisers pay the costs, hoping to attract paying customers for their products. Many "free" services, from games to Internet phone services, hope to entice users to pay for "premium" versions of the same

FIGURE 13.20 box.net (above right) is one of many companies that offers free online storage. Pandora radio (above left) is a personalized Internet radio service that creates playlists of new music based on old and current favorites specified by each listener. Listeners can buy songs they like using direct links to Amazon and iTunes.

services. And the generosity of the open-source community is responsible for many of the best free sites and products. But another factor is the steady decline in the cost of computing power, bandwidth, and storage. As hardware costs plummet, they become insignificant in determining the cost of things on the Web. And software costs can be marginalized over large audiences, meaning that the cost per visitor drops with each new visitor.

Of course, money can't measure the value of everything. When people visit "free" Web sites, they're paying with their time and attention, both of which are irreplaceable. The challenge for Web businesses is to provide value in return for time and attention; the challenge for consumers is to determine the best way to use those precious resources.

E-Commerce Ethics

> Now to answer all of the pop-ups...**Ooh, a talking moose wants my credit card number**. That's only fair.
>
> —*Homer Simpson, on* The Simpsons

One of the main challenges of e-commerce is to maintain trust between the people engaging in transactions. If that trust is lost it is difficult to reestablish, and the potential benefits for the company, and for society as a whole, are diminished.

Publishing an information code of ethics on the Web ensures that users—both the company's information workers and customers—are aware of the company's e-commerce policies. Ideally, the code of ethics should include:

- A statement of the organization's privacy policy
- A statement that a person's permission must be secured before his or her ID, photo, ideas, or communications are used or transmitted
- A statement on how the company will inform customers of the intended uses of personal information gathered during an online transaction and how to secure permission from customers for those uses
- A statement that addresses issues of ownership with respect to network postings and communications
- A statement of how the company tracks user behaviors on the Web site

Of course, ethical behavior goes beyond posting policies. Consumers are becoming increasingly impatient with companies and organizations that abuse their privacy and personal information. Here are some well-publicized examples:

- NebuAd, an online advertising service that provides targeted advertising for Internet service providers (ISPs), drew criticism and investigation from Congress after it was discovered that the company was using common Internet attack techniques to profile customers' online activities and embed targeted advertising into the Web pages they visited. According to a report, neither the consumers nor the affected Web sites had any knowledge of the company's surveillance and Web page alterations. The company discontinued its tracking program while it was investigated for potential violations of the Communications Act, which puts strict limits on what cable companies can do with customer records.
- Online auction house ReverseAuction.com allegedly collected consumers' personal information from competitor eBay and sent emails to those consumers soliciting their business. According to the U.S. Federal Trade Commission (FTC), ReverseAuctions.com signed up at eBay, disregarded the privacy agreement posted on the rival auction site, and copied the information from bidders to send them solicitations that were later deemed deceptive by the FTC. ReverseAuction.com consented to a settlement but said it did not gather any confidential information from the eBay site.
- The FTC brought suit against Liberty Financial Companies for violating the privacy rights of children who frequented its Young Investor Web site. The FTC alleged that the company had used prizes and contests to encourage children to disclose their names, addresses, weekly allowances, family stock holdings, and more—information that could be used to market to their parents.

FIGURE 13.21 Many unethical e-businesses use deceptive tactics and fear-based marketing to prey on the elderly.

The United States has, in general, lagged behind Canada, Europe, Australia, and even Hong Kong in legally establishing overall privacy standards and a regulatory agency that could advise businesses on acceptable privacy practices. Most U.S. businesses and trade organizations tend to favor self-regulation, fearing that government rules would quash the growth of e-commerce. IBM and Disney are good examples of self-regulation; both have long insisted that any Web site they advertise on must have an ironclad privacy policy. But a growing number of companies, including Microsoft and Google, have joined privacy advocacy groups in supporting comprehensive privacy legislation to set ground rules for all U.S. businesses.

The United States has many laws related to the issue of privacy, but only in specific industries and consumer segments. For example, Americans have the legal right to see their credit records. Another law prohibits video rental stores from releasing the names of the movies that you rent. The Health Insurance Portability and Accountability Act requires healthcare providers and hospitals to protect the confidentiality of an individual's health information. The Children's Online Privacy Protection Act of 1998 (COPPA) requires certain commercial Web sites to obtain parental consent before collecting, using, or disclosing personal information about children ages 12 and under. However, a report from the Annenberg Public Policy Center of the University of Pennsylvania revealed that many sites with the highest percentage of child visitors under age of 13 often did not follow the COPPA rules.

The European Union issued its Data Protection Directive in October 1998. The directive establishes a high level of legal protection for the privacy of individuals and personal data within the EU. The directive also prohibits companies from transferring personally identifiable information from EU member countries to jurisdictions where that information is not treated with respect by law. As long as the United States does not have an *umbrella* privacy policy, the EU could choose to stop the transfer of all data to it. Clearly, there's much work to be done to protect personal privacy in the age of global e-commerce.

There are other ways that online businesses betray customer trust. Some unethical online businesses mislead customers with deceptive practices, such as advertised policies that they don't actually honor. It's all too common for an advertised claim that *seems* too good to be true to have a catch that effectively *makes* it untrue. For example, an unethical business might advertise $75 laptops "while supplies last," but only sell a single laptop at that price—then redirect anyone that clicks the ad to a much more expensive offer. These types of ads are especially popular with spammers, who never seem to run out of variations on the click-here-for-an-unbelievable-deal message. It only takes a tiny percentage of gullible consumers to generate profits for many of these businesses. Of course, scammed customers tend not to come back for more or recommend the site to other potential customers. And they *might* take expensive legal action.

On the other hand, online businesses that treat their customers with respect tend to find that customer trust has a huge positive impact on the long-term bottom line. For example, Google's online ad program took off so quickly in part because of its honesty. Advertisements—"paid listings"—were clearly marked, and were never embedded in search listings or disguised as non-ad content. Some early Google competitors accepted payments for high search listings—secret ads. Other companies have disguised ads as error messages and instant message windows to trick users into clicking them. (Ironically, Google has become the target of privacy advocates who fear the potential abuse of mountains of private information that customers willingly share with the company.)

The basics of business ethics are the same online as off. Honesty, respect, and integrity are good for business—and society—whether you're selling art on eBay or apples at a farmer's market. It's always been important to have laws to back up these values and protect consumers and businesses from unscrupulous business practices. Those laws will need to be refined, revised, and supplemented as e-commerce technology evolves. But even if the law lags behind the technology, ethics is a critical part of everyday business.

Inventing the Future ▸ E-Commerce Tomorrow: The Never-Ending Game

E-commerce is breaking out of the PC browser window and finding its way into pockets, products, and just about everyplace we spend our time. Digital technology is transforming the shopping experience in and out of the stores, and future visions become current trends almost overnight.

People use smart phones to locate stores, compare products, and seek out bargains. Many companies accept payments using on-screen bar codes, phone "bumps," and other digital payment systems. Smart phones can also wirelessly notify store clerks about your personal preferences and sizes, previous purchases, and current shopping needs. If no clerks are available, your phone or store kiosks might guide you to the product you're looking for. If your personal information isn't on file, the store's dressing room might use 3-D scanners to size you up on the spot. Enhanced reality displays might soon show you what you'd look like in a particular style, or what your living room might feel like if you painted it a different color and added a new couch. None of these services will work unless store computers have access to lots of information about you. So far, consumers have generally been happy to trade personal privacy for shopping convenience. Just how far they're willing to go in that bargain remains to be seen.

Some online stores have found success in making their sites feel more like games using playful interfaces, personalized messages, strategic shopper rewards, storylike experiences, and community relationships. Jesse Schell is a former Imagineering Engineer for Disney theme parks, author of *The Art of Game Design*, CEO of Schell Games, and professor of entertainment technology at Carnegie Mellon University. He argues that games are continually redefining themselves and making inroads into every aspect of our lives. He says we'll soon live in a "gamepocalypse" in which we're playing some kind of game no matter what we're doing. If he's right, game psychology and technology will radically transform the way we do business. For example:

- Your Wifi toothbrush will use sensors to score your tooth brushing so you can earn points from your toothpaste company—points that might translate into free products.
- Your breakfast cereal box will know when it's picked up or tilted. Built-in eye-tracking cameras will be able to tell whether you're playing the games or reading the ads displayed on the screen on the back of the box. Your score will be transmitted wirelessly to the cereal company—and may be displayed on the cereal boxes of your friends. This kind of "AdverGaming" will be everywhere.
- You'll earn eco-points for taking the bus to work, and product points for reading the advertisements inside the bus. *Geotracking* technology that uses your phone—or surgically implanted chip—to monitor your minute-by-minute movements can effectively turn the world into a giant game board.
- The kinds of *microtransactions* pioneered in Facebook games and iTunes apps will be available just about anywhere there's a computer screen and sensor—which could be just about anywhere. Once you're hooked on a game, whether it's on a computer or some other delivery medium, you'll happily spend a dollar or two to "enhance" the experience.
- The lines between media and "reality" will blur as companies refine *transmedia* marketing campaigns. Characters and products will show up in movies, TV, games, social networks, and the physical world, blurring the lines that have traditionally separated these experiences.
- Companies will use real-time analysis of data they collect as you play immersive commerce games to customize and refine the experiences so they're continually getting better for you—and keeping you hooked.
- You may even be able to play games—and rack up points for purchases—in your dreams. Schell predicts that this kind of "REM-tainment" will be made possible because sensors will be able to "see" your dreams by tracking brain waves while you sleep. Companies will use various technological devices to send subliminal messages and place products in our dreams, and clever gamers will use biofeedback to learn to remember and even control their dreams.

Is this vision of the future a dream or a nightmare? Ultimately, we'll vote with our wallets—or by tapping "pay now" buttons on the screens that populate our futures.

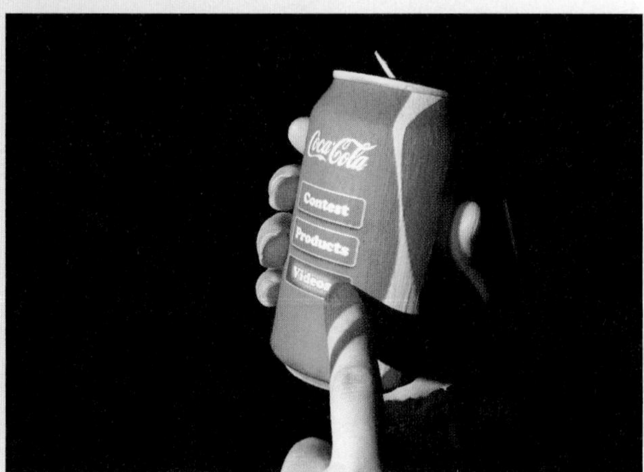

FIGURE 13.22 In the future, sensors and screens may turn all kinds of products into games.

(Source: Image is from this slideshow: http://gamepocalypsenow.blogspot.com/2010/07/visions-of-gamepocalypse-podcast.html. The image (and blog) is created by Jesse Schell, who owns the Gamepocalypse blog. His listed email address is jesse@schellgames.com.)

Crosscurrents

The End of an Era

by Steven Johnson

In April 2010, Apple unveiled the iPad—the first truly successful tablet computer. That same month, Wired *magazine's cover announced that the tablet computer would change the world. The cover story—"13 of the Brightest Tech Minds Sound Off on the Future of the Tablet"—included short essays by a diverse collection of writers, technologists, and cultural icons. This piece by science writer Steven Johnson is taken from that feature.*

Ten years from now, we will look back at the tablet and see it as an end point, not a beginning. The tablet may turn out to be the final stage of an extraordinary era of textual innovation, powered by 30 years of exponential increases in computation, connection, and portability.

When the Homebrew Computer Club started holding meetings in the mid-'70s, the reigning assumption among critics and futurists was that we were headed, inexorably, toward an image-based culture dominated by the visual language of television. The word—for so long the dominant medium for the transmission of information—was headed for the margins, subtitles underneath the hypnotic flicker of the Image Society.

But then something extraordinary happened. The personal computer proved to be more than just a fancy calculator. It turned out to be a device for doing things with words. Each milestone in computation and connectivity unleashed a new wave of textual breakthroughs: Early networks gave rise to email and Usenet; the Mac UI made reading text on the screen tolerable; the Internet platform (and the NeXT development environment) made it possible for one man to invent a universal hypertext system; Google harnessed distributed computing to make the entire Web searchable in microseconds; and thanks to Wi-Fi and cellular networks, along with hardware miniaturization, we can now download a novel to an ebook in 10 seconds.

It has been an exhilarating ride, but it is coming to an end, and that magical experience of instantly pulling *Middlemarch* out of the ether and onto your Kindle suggests why: Compared to other kinds of information that computers process today, text has an exceptionally small footprint. With the arrival of the tablet, we have crossed a critical threshold: Where text is concerned, we effectively have infinite computational resources, connectivity, and portability. For decades, futurists have dreamed of the "universal book": a handheld reading device that would give you instant access to every book in the Library of Congress. In the tablet era, it's no longer technology holding us back from realizing that vision; it's the copyright holders.

Advances in technology will give us plenty of headroom with other kinds of data: streaming real-time video, conjuring virtual spaces, exploring real-world environments with geocoded data, modeling complex systems like weather. But in the tablet world, textual innovation will not come from faster chips or wireless networks. Incremental improvements will continue, to be sure, but there will be a steady decrease in radical new ways we interact with text.

If you time-traveled back to the Homebrew Computer Club in 1975, it would take you days to explain all the new possibilities for creating and sharing text. (Imagine explaining Wikipedia to someone who hasn't heard of the word processor.) But I suspect that the text-based interactions that coalesce around the tablet will still seem familiar to my grandchildren in 2030. Unless, of course, we've hit the singularity and the novels we're downloading have been written by the machines. But in that case, the rise of AI novelists will be the least of our worries.

Discussion Questions

1. Do you think the tablet computer is the last chapter in the history of text-based communication? Explain your answer.
2. Do you think the tablet or ebook will ever replace books, newspapers, and magazines? Why or why not?

Summary

E-business is sharing business information, maintaining business relationships, and conducting business transactions through the use of telecommunications networks, especially the Internet. E-business is also about reorganizing internal business processes and external business alliances and creating new consumer-oriented products globally. E-commerce is often equated with e-business, but the most common technical definition of e-commerce makes it a subset of e-business specifically related to buying and selling on a network. E-business has grown at a phenomenal rate since the commercialization of the Internet in the 1990s, with the exception of the economic downturn of 2000–2001.

There are three main e-commerce configurations using Internet technology: intranets, extranets, and public Web sites.

An intranet is an internal information system based on Internet technology, including TCP/IP protocols and Web tools, to support the value chain activities between individuals and departments within an organization. Companies use intranets to provide employees access to information for their jobs, to facilitate teamwork and collaboration within and among departments, to process internal company transactions online, and to distribute software tools, including customer relations management (CRM) software, to employees.

An extranet is a private interorganizational information system connecting the intranets of two or more companies in a business alliance. An extranet extends activities between trusted business partners and facilitates their working relationships. Extranets play an important role in the global business strategy of many companies, large and small, enabling them to build alliances with vendors, suppliers, and other organizations internationally. An extranet can be set up either as a secure private network, as a public network, or (most commonly) as a virtual private network (VPN). A major concern of companies conducting business-to-business transactions over an extranet is the guarantee of secure transactions.

A company can connect its intranet to the Internet and operate a publicly accessible Web site to support business-to-consumer transactions or to facilitate consumer-to-consumer transactions. The most successful B2C sites are easy to find because they've been optimized for the major search engines; they make it easy for customers to find and purchase what they're looking for; and they offer secure payment options (often using an electronic payment system like PayPal). C2C sites, including classified ad sites, auctions, and reseller partners, facilitate transactions between consumers.

Several technological trends are rapidly changing the nature of e-business. The growth in cloud computing makes it possible for different components of e-commerce sites to be created and stored in different parts of the Internet cloud. Increased bandwidth and computing power are enabling developers to create rich media e-commerce sites that make Web shopping more compelling than catalog shopping. A growth in mobile commerce is happening because of major developments in portable electronics and wireless technologies. Online commerce has resulted in a Long Tail effect, creating markets for niche products that wouldn't have been profitable to sell in pre-Web days. Web 2.0 technology has opened up a wide variety of novel marketing schemes, such as viral marketing through social networks, blogs, forums, and media sharing sites. And a surprising number of e-commerce companies make huge profits by giving their products away for free.

A company conducting business on the Internet should develop and adhere to an information code of ethics that ensures that users of the Web site—both the company's information workers and customers—will be aware of the company's e-commerce policies, especially regarding consumer information privacy. Most companies find that customer trust has a positive impact on the long-term bottom line far exceeding any short-term gain due to deceptive practices and policies.

Key Terms

business-to-business (B2B) ...(p. 476)
business-to-consumer (B2C) ...(p. 476)
business-to-employee (B2E) ...(p. 477)
consumer-to-consumer (C2C) ...(p. 477)
customer relationship management (CRM) ...(p. 478)
dot-com...(p. 475)
electronic business (e-business)...(p. 475)
electronic commerce (e-commerce)...(p. 475)
electronic payment system ....(p. 486)
extranet ...(p. 479)
intranet...(p. 477)
Long Tail ...(p. 494)
mobile commerce (m-commerce) ...(p. 492)
search engine optimization (SEO)...(p. 486)
virtual private network (VPN) ...(p. 483)

Companion Website Projects

1. The Digital Planet Web site, www.pearsonhighered.com/beekman, contains self-test exercises related to this chapter. Follow the instructions for taking a quiz. After you've completed your quiz, you can email the results to your instructor.
2. The Web site also contains open-ended discussion questions called Internet Exercises. Discuss one or more of the Internet Exercises at the section for this chapter.

True or False

1. The first successful e-commerce Web sites were put online in the late 1970s.
2. E-commerce wasn't possible before the commercialization of the Internet.
3. REI.com, Converse.com, and most other retail Web sites conform to the consumer-to-consumer (B2C) e-commerce model.
4. It's not possible to have a working intranet without a broadband Internet connection.
5. In a virtual private network (VPN), data is transmitted through the Internet via a secure "tunnel" between intranets.
6. Security of transactions is a major concern of companies conducting B2B transactions over the Internet, regardless of the type of extranet.
7. The number of hits on a Web site is generally not the best indication of the site's effectiveness.
8. The Long Tail refers to the increased viability of selling niche products rather than just selling blockbusters.
9. The business-to-consumer (B2C) model is the predominant form of e-commerce.
10. Most experts believe that self-regulation and compliance with Internet privacy codes of ethics by American companies make regulatory privacy laws unnecessary in the United States.

Multiple Choice

1. Which model does Amazon.com use to sell music to its customers?
   a. B2B
   b. B2C
   c. C2C
   d. G2B
   e. G2G
2. Which of these causes led most directly to the dot-com bust of 2000–2001?
   a. The 9/11 terrorist attacks
   b. The Y2K bug
   c. Excessive stock market speculation
   d. Rampant software and music piracy
   e. Hacker attacks on key Internet servers
3. An increase in disaggregation of many e-commerce sites is happening because
   a. security restrictions are making intranets more difficult to maintain.
   b. Web 2.0 technology doesn't support older graphics processors on most servers.
   c. cloud computing is making it easier to store different components of a Web site in different places on the Internet.
   d. when a potential customer links to a site, the connection between client and server is the shortest possible route through the Internet.
   e. mobile devices are connecting to the Internet in record numbers, making aggregation impossible.
4. Using Internet technology for intranets is advantageous because of
   a. open standards.
   b. the multitude of client platforms.
   c. geographic independence.
   d. reduced hardware and software costs.
   e. All of the above
5. Business intranets are commonly used for all of these reasons EXCEPT:
   a. They can encourage teamwork and collaboration.
   b. They can make it easy for employees to get information when they need it.
   c. They automate shopping carts, checkout, and other components of retail sales.
   d. They facilitate internal business transactions, such as employee benefits.
   e. They can be connected to other intranets to create extranets.
6. Online auctions like eBay generally follow which model?
   a. B2B
   b. B2E
   c. B2C
   d. C2C
   e. C2E
7. A typical extranet is set up as
   a. a cloud.
   b. a public network.
   c. a virtual private network (VPN).
   d. an expandable node developer (END).
   e. a 3G grid.
8. Mobile commerce includes
   a. mobile ticketing.
   b. mobile coupons.
   c. mobile purchasing.
   d. location-based m-commerce.
   e. All of the above
9. Strategic benefits of extranet use in business alliances include
   a. increasing the speed of business-to-business transactions.
   b. reducing errors on intercompany transactions.
   c. reducing costs of telecommunications.
   d. increasing the volume of business with partners.
   e. All of these are strategic benefits of business alliances.
10. The Internet has resulted in a Long Tail phenomenon because
    a. most consumers believe that shopping on the Internet can now match the experience of shopping in a store.
    b. online shoppers frequently abandon their shopping carts because they can't get the information they want before making purchases.
    c. Internet stores aren't forced by limited shelf space to offer only the most popular items.
    d. All of the above
    e. None of the above
11. What is the name for a set of protocols that enables business partners to share a secure "tunnel" through the public Internet?
    a. Cloud Tunnel Protocol (CTP)
    b. Virtual Private Network (VPN)
    c. Critical Path Network (CPN)
    d. Traffic Network Tunnel (TNT)
    e. Internet Traffic Tunnel (ITT)
12. Which of these statements is true?
    a. Business-to-business e-commerce requires special licensing from the Internet protocols board.
    b. Business-to-business e-commerce generally doesn't work across national boundaries.

c. Mobile commerce today is limited to B2C transactions.
d. The fastest growing segment of the B2E market is the reverse auction industry.
e. None of the above are true.

13. What is the main advantage of making Web purchases with PayPal's electronic payment system over paying with a credit card?
    a. PayPal uses a much higher rate of encryption than credit cards do.
    b. PayPal ID information can't be stolen.
    c. Using PayPal usually results in lower prices.
    d. When you use PayPal the vendor doesn't have access to your credit card number.
    e. Unlike credit cards, PayPal works internationally.

14. Which of these is generally done with an intranet?
    a. B2B
    b. B2C
    c. B2D
    d. B2E
    e. C2C

15. The difference between search engine optimization (SEO) and spamdexing is that
    a. SEO is related to Web sites, while spamdexing is related to email.
    b. SEO involves small numbers of messages, while spamdexing involves massive numbers of messages.
    c. spamdexing is the unethical counterpart of SEO.
    d. SEO can generate revenue, but spamdexing is a free service.
    e. There is no difference.

Review Questions

1. Define or describe each of the key terms in the "Key Terms" section. Check your answers using the glossary.
2. Is e-commerce possible without the Internet? Explain your answer.
3. Describe the four most common models of e-commerce and one additional e-business model that isn't, by most definitions, strictly e-commerce.
4. What is the difference between an intranet and an extranet?
5. How are Facebook, Twitter, and other social networks changing e-commerce?
6. What technological trends have made it easier for online businesses to give away services such as email, voice mail, and classified ads?
7. Describe several business models that make it possible for companies to give away goods and services online while still making a profit.
8. Explain why Internet commerce offers more opportunities for entertainment products that aren't "hits."
9. Explain how cloud computing might result in more consistent shopping experiences for consumers (for example, so that the checkout process wouldn't vary from site to site).
10. What should a business's information code of ethics include? Why?

Discussion Questions

1. How has e-commerce changed your buying habits over the last few years? Which of these changes are positive and which are negative?
2. Can you identify examples of e-commerce applications within your college or university?
3. Can you identify any intranets or extranets in your school? How are they used?
4. Discuss the issues you would need to consider if you were to create a B2C Web site for a small company.
5. Do you think the Long Tail phenomenon is likely to change the nature of the art and entertainment industries? Explain your answer.
6. People talk about privacy a lot, but how important is privacy? Would you pay extra for an item you purchased online in return for a guarantee that the company would not sell information about your purchase to anyone else? Would you be willing to share more personal information with a store if that meant you received more personalized service? Are you willing to make your online purchases visible to your friends and vice versa so that you can tell what's popular with them?

Projects

1. Find an example of a business that is using the Internet to increase its competitive advantage in its industry. What competitive strategy is the organization following? Is the Internet being used to decrease costs? Increase value to the customers? Summarize your findings in a report.
2. Form a team and visit a local company. Interview the manager and others about the company's Internet philosophy. What is the purpose of the company's Web site? Who designed the site? Who maintains the site? Does the company advertise on the Internet? Does the company use an intranet or extranet? What are the company's plans for its future use of the Internet? Summarize your findings.
3. Locate the public Web sites of several competitors in the same industry. Evaluate the effectiveness of each of the Web sites. Summarize your findings.
4. Visit two Web sites that offer similar products—for example, two clothing sites or two bookstore sites. Evaluate how each company handles your security and privacy concerns.
5. Find several Web sites offering unique shopping experiences that go beyond the typical pages-of-a-catalog model. Report on which sites are most effective and why.
6. Create a business plan for a B2C or C2C online business. Include simple sketches and/or maps of the most important parts of the Web site. Talk about the most significant hurdles you would have to overcome to turn the business into a reality.

Sources and Resources

Books

Web Design for ROI: Turning Browsers into Buyers & Prospects into Leads, by Lance Loveday (New Riders Press). Web design can do more than make a site look good—it can also improve financial returns and create competitive advantage. This book is filled with practical tips for increasing conversion rates and maximizing the return on investment (ROI) of any business site.

Web Design and Marketing Solutions for Business Websites, by Kevin Potts (friends of ED). A good Web site can help a company a great deal, but a bad one can drive customers away. This book covers the fundamentals of creating a business Web site that works for the company, not against it. It covers Web writing and search engine optimization, offers practical tips for the common sections that every business site needs, and discusses how to create a winning online strategy.

Web 2.0: A Strategy Guide: Business Thinking and Strategies Behind Successful Web 2.0 Implementations, by Amy Shuen (O'Reilly Media, Inc.). Successful business implementations of Web 2.0 strategies require an understanding of both the opportunities and the potential problems. *Web 2.0: A Strategy Guide* demonstrates the power of this new paradigm, examining how companies such as Flickr, Google, Facebook, and Amazon have flourished by embracing the new collaborative and connective possibilities of the modern Web.

Wikinomics: How Mass Collaboration Changes Everything, by Don Tapscott and Anthony D. Williams (Portfolio). *Wiki* means *quick* in Hawaiian. This book describes in detail how the technology behind mass Internet collaboration is quickly changing the nature of business. Whether you're interested in exploiting the power of collaborative production or just curious about the future of commerce, you'd be well advised to read this book—quickly.

The Long Tail, Revised and Updated Edition: Why the Future of Business Is Selling Less of More, by Chris Anderson (Hyperion). This influential book started as an article in the pages of *Wired.* Anderson presents compelling evidence that the Web is expanding options for consumers and opportunities for artists, authors, and businesses to go beyond "hit" mentality and explore more diverse markets. His book isn't without critics who say he sometimes overstates his arguments. His Web site, theLongTail.com, provides a forum to continue the important discussion started by this book.

Free: The Future of a Radical Price, by Chris Anderson (Hyperion). Many businesses struggle with the "free" economy of the Internet. It's hard to sell products when your competitors are giving them away. *Wired* Editor Chris Anderson presents arguments and examples of the new "freeconomics" of the Internet. You may not agree with everything he says, but you'll probably enjoy his thoughtful, clear writing.

The Open Brand: When Push Comes to Pull in a Web-Made World, by Kelly Mooney and Nita Rollins (Peachpit Press). The authors of this book argue that many of today's successful new brands are open. Like open-source software, they respond to consumer involvement. Are marketing and branding becoming interactive activities? The authors think so, and they tell you why here.

eBay QuickSteps, by Carole Matthews and John Cronan (Osborne McGraw Hill). Countless small businesses—and a few large ones—have sprouted in the fertile soil of eBay's popular auction site. You don't need to be a technical wizard to buy and sell goods on eBay, but it helps if you know the basics before you play for high stakes. This is one of many good books designed to help you become an eBay entrepreneur.

Video

Startup.com, directed by Chris Hegedus and Jehane Noujaim. This documentary started out as the story of the creation of an Internet company. The cameras followed two young men as they followed their vision through the Internet frenzy that preceded the dot-com bust. The focus is on the two men, their relationship, and the impact of their fast-pace business on that relationship.

14

Systems Design and Development

OBJECTIVES

After you read this chapter you should be able to:

- Describe the process of designing, programming, and debugging a computer program
- Explain why there are many different programming languages, and give examples of several
- Explain why computer languages are built into applications, operating systems, and utilities
- Outline the steps in the life cycle of an information system, and explain the purpose of program maintenance
- Explain the relationship between computer programming and computer science
- Describe the problems faced by software engineers in trying to produce reliable large systems
- Explain why software companies provide only limited warranties for their products

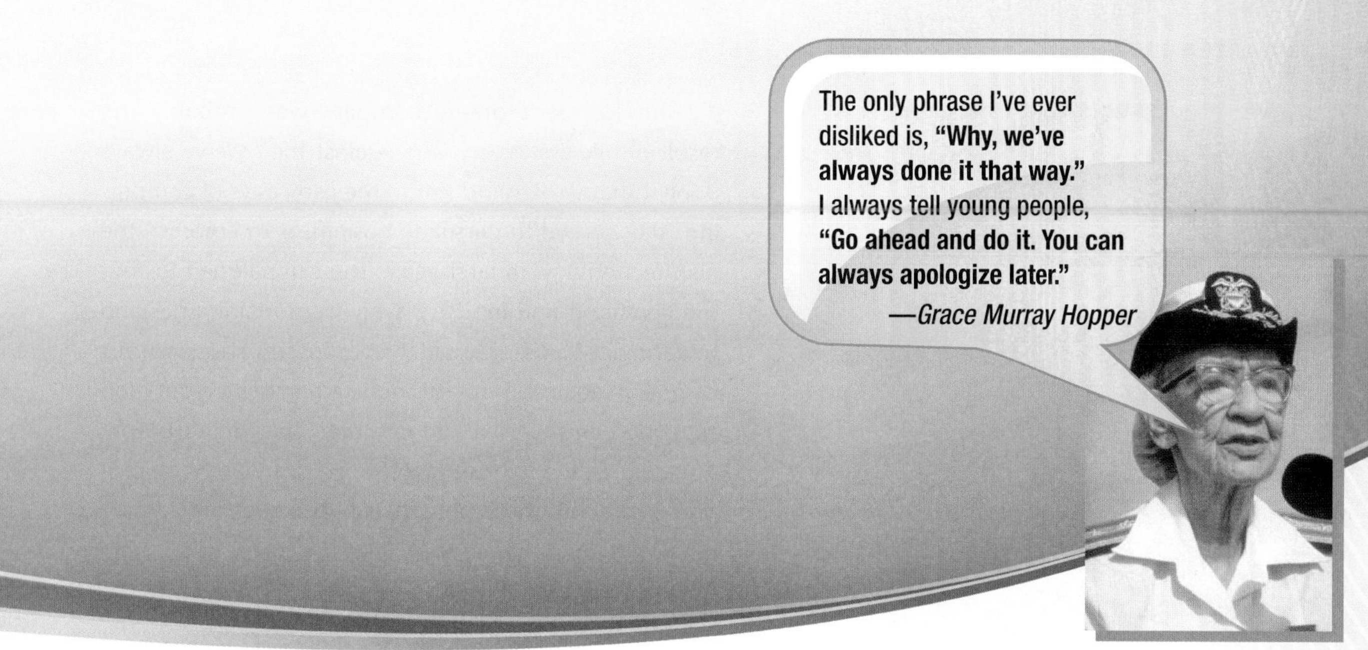

The only phrase I've ever disliked is, "Why, we've always done it that way."
I always tell young people, "Go ahead and do it. You can always apologize later."
—Grace Murray Hopper

Grace Murray Hopper Sails on Software

Amazing Grace, the grand old lady of software, had little to apologize for when she died at the age of 85 in 1992. More than any other woman, Grace Murray Hopper helped chart the course of the computer industry from its earliest days.

Hopper earned a Ph.D. from Yale in 1928 and taught math for 10 years at Vassar before joining the U.S. Naval Reserve in 1943. The Navy assigned her to the Bureau of Ordnance Computation at Harvard, where she worked with Howard Aiken's Mark I, the first large-scale electromechanical digital computer. She wrote programs and operating manuals for the Mark I, Mark II, and Mark III.

Aiken often asked his team, "Are you making any numbers?" When she wasn't "making numbers," Hopper replied that she was "debugging" the computer. Today that's what programmers call the process of finding and removing errors, or bugs, from programs. Scientists and engineers had referred to mechanical defects as bugs for decades; Thomas Edison wrote about bugs in his inventions in 1878. But when Hopper first used the term, she was referring to a real bug—a 2-inch moth that got caught in a relay, bringing the mighty Mark II to a standstill! That moth carcass is taped to a page in a log book, housed in a Navy museum in Virginia.

Hopper recognized early that businesses could make good use of computers. After World War II, she left Harvard to work on the UNIVAC I, the first general-purpose commercial computer built in the United States, and other commercial computers. She played central roles in the development of the first compiler (a type of computer language translator that makes most of today's software possible) and COBOL, the first computer language designed for developing business software.

Throughout most of her career, Hopper remained anchored to the Navy. When she retired from the fleet with the rank of rear admiral at the age of 79, her list of accomplishments filled eight single-spaced pages in her Navy biography.

FIGURE 14.1 Grace Murray Hopper (1906–1992).

But Hopper's greatest impact was probably the result of her tireless crusade against the "We've always done it that way" mind-set. In the early days of computing, she worked to persuade businesses to embrace the new technology. In later years, she campaigned to shift the Pentagon and industry away from mainframes and toward networks of smaller computers. Her vigorous campaign against the status quo earned her a reputation as being controversial and contrary. That didn't bother Amazing Grace, whose favorite maxim was "A ship in port is safe, but that's not what ships are for." ■

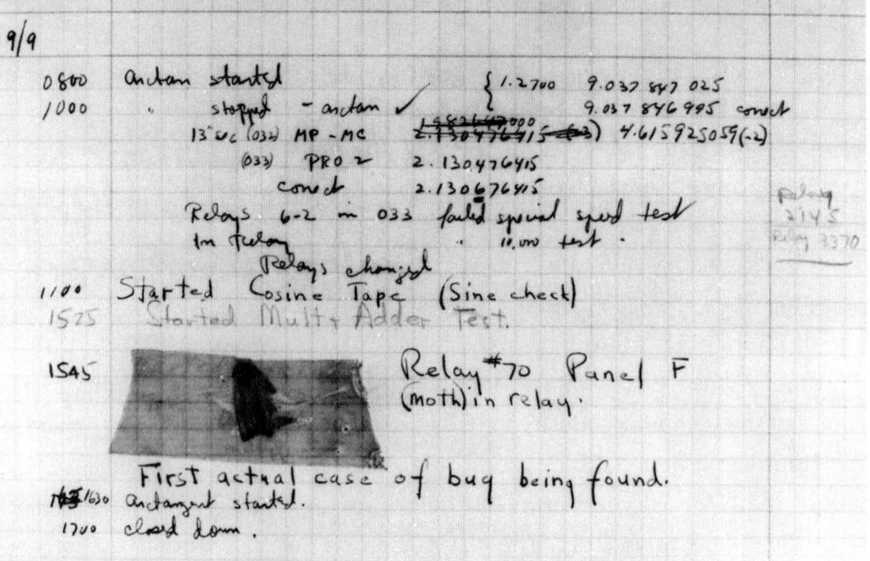

FIGURE 14.2 This moth was one of the first computer bugs—it was removed from a relay in the Mark II.

Today's computer software is so sophisticated that it's almost invisible to the user. Just as a great motion picture can make you forget you're watching a movie, the best PC software enables you to do your creative work without ever thinking about the instructions and data flowing through the computer's processor as you work. But whether you're writing a paper, solving a calculus problem, flying a simulated space shuttle, or exploring the nooks and crannies of the Internet, your imaginary environment stands on an incredibly complex software substructure. The process of creating that software is one of the most intellectually challenging activities ever done by people.

In this chapter we look at the process of turning ideas into working computer programs and information systems. We examine computer languages and the ways programmers use them to create software. In addition, we look at how computer users take advantage of the programming languages built into applications, operating systems, and utilities. We examine the life cycle of a complex information system. We also confront the problems involved with producing reliable software and consider the implications of depending on unstable software. In the process of exploring software, we'll see how the work of programmers, analysts, software engineers, and computer scientists affects our lives and our work.

How People Make Programs

It's the only job I can think of where I get to be both an engineer and an artist. There's an incredible, rigorous, technical element to it, which I like because you have to do very precise thinking. On the other hand, it has a wildly creative side where **the boundaries of imagination are the only real limitation**.

—Andy Hertzfeld, co-designer of the Macintosh

Most computer users depend on professionally programmed applications—spreadsheets, image-editing programs, Web browsers, and the like—as problem-solving tools. But in some cases it's necessary or desirable to write a program rather than use one written by somebody else. As a human activity, computer programming is a relative newcomer. But **programming** is a specialized form of the age-old process of problem solving. Problem solving typically involves four steps:

- *Understanding the problem.* Defining the problem clearly is often the most important—and most overlooked—step in the problem-solving process.
- *Devising a plan for solving the problem.* What resources are available? People? Information? A computer? Software? Data? How might those resources be put to work to solve the problem?
- *Carrying out the plan.* This phase often overlaps with the previous step, because many problem-solving schemes are developed on the fly.
- *Evaluating the solution.* Is the problem solved correctly? Is this solution applicable to other problems?

The programming process can also be described as a four-step process, although in practice these steps often overlap:

- Defining the problem
- Devising, refining, and testing the algorithm
- Writing the program
- Testing and debugging the program

Most programming problems are far too complex to solve all at once. To turn a problem into a program, a programmer typically creates a list of smaller problems. Each of these smaller problems can be broken into subproblems that can be subdivided in the same way. This process, called **stepwise refinement**, is similar to the process of developing an outline before writing a paper or a book. Programmers sometimes refer to this type of design as **top-down design** because the design process starts at the top, with the main ideas, and works down to the details.

The result of stepwise refinement is an **algorithm**—a set of step-by-step instructions that, when completed, solves the original problem. (Recall Suzanne's French toast recipe in Chapter 4.) Programmers typically write algorithms in a form called **pseudocode**—a cross between a computer language and plain English. When the details of an algorithm are in place, a programmer can translate it from pseudocode into a computer language.

From Idea to Algorithm

> One programs, just as one writes, not because one understands, but in order to come to understand. Programming is an act of design. **To write a program is to legislate the laws for a world one first has to create in imagination.**
>
> —*Joseph Weizenbaum,* in Computer Power and Human Reason

Let's develop a simple algorithm to illustrate the process. Let's start with a statement of the problem:

A schoolteacher needs a program to play a number-guessing game so students can learn to develop logical strategies and practice their arithmetic. In this game the computer picks a number between 1 and 100 and gives the player seven turns to guess the number. After each incorrect try, the computer tells the player whether the guess is too high or too low.

In short, the problem is to write a program that can

```
play a guessing game
```

Stepwise Refinement

The first cut at the problem breaks it into three parts: a beginning, a middle, and an end. Each of these parts represents a smaller programming problem to solve.

```
pick a number for user to guess and display instructions
give user 7 chances to guess the number
respond appropriately to each guess
```

These three steps represent a bare-bones algorithm. In the completed algorithm, these three parts are carried out in sequence. The next refinement fills in a few details for each part:

```
pick a number between 1 and 100
display instructions
repeat
  input guess from user
  respond to guess
until number is guessed or 7 turns are completed
display final message
```

The middle part of our instructions includes a sequence of operations that repeats for each turn: everything between *repeat* and *until.* But these instructions lack crucial details. How, for example, does the computer respond to a guess? We can replace *respond to guess* with instructions that vary depending on the guessed number:

```
if guess = answer then display "You win" and quit
else if guess < answer then display "Too small"
else display "Too big"
```

Finally, we need to give the computer a way of knowing when seven turns have passed. We can set a counter to 0 at the beginning and add 1 to the counter after each turn. When the counter reaches 7, the repetition stops, and the computer displays a message. That makes the algorithm look like this:

```
set answer to a random value between 1 and 100
display "Guess a number between 1 and 100"
set counter to 0
repeat
  input guess from user
  if guess = answer then
```

```
    display "You win"
    quit
  else if guess < answer then
    display "Too small"
  else display "Too big"
  add 1 to counter
until counter = 7
display "Too many guesses. You lose."
```

Control Structures

A computer can't understand this algorithm, but the pseudocode is clear to any person familiar with **control structures**—logical structures that control the order in which instructions are carried out. This algorithm uses three basic control structures: sequence, selection, and repetition.

A ***sequence*** control structure is a group of instructions followed in order from the first through the last. In our algorithm example, as in most computer languages, the sequence is the default structure; that is, it applies unless a statement says otherwise:

```
set answer to a random value between 1 and 100
display "Guess a number between 1 and 100"
set counter to 0
```

A ***selection*** (or ***decision***) control structure is used to make logical decisions—to choose between alternative courses of action depending on certain conditions. It typically takes the form of "If (some condition is true), then (do something) else (do something else)":

```
if guess < answer then
  display "Too small"
else display "Too big"
```

A ***repetition*** control structure is a looping mechanism. It allows a group of steps to be repeated several times, usually until some condition is satisfied. In this algorithm the indented statements between *repeat* and *until* repeat until the number is guessed correctly or the counter is equal to 7:

```
repeat
  input guess from user
  ...
  add 1 to counter
until counter = 7
```

As our example illustrates, these simple control structures can be combined to produce more complex algorithms. In fact, any computer program can be constructed from these three control structures.

FIGURE 14.3 Software development has become a global industry. These programmers in India write software for a company based in America.

Testing the Algorithm

The next step is **testing** the algorithm. Testing of the completed program comes later; this round of testing is designed to check the logic of the algorithm. We can test it by following the instructions using different sets of numbers. We might, for example, use a target number of 35 and guesses of 15, 72, 52, and 35. Those numbers test all three possibilities in the if-then-else structure (guess is less than target, guess is greater than target, and guess equals target), and they show what happens if the player chooses the correct number. We should also test the algorithm with seven wrong guesses in a row to make sure it correctly ends a losing game.

From Algorithm to Program

> You know, computer science inverts the normal. In normal science you're given a world and your job is to find out the rules. **In computer science, you give the computer the rules and it creates the world.**
>
> —*Alan Kay*

When testing is complete, the algorithm is ready to become a program. Because the algorithm has the logical structure of a program, the process of coding—writing a program from the algorithm—is simple and straightforward. Statements in the algorithm translate directly into lines of code in whichever programming language best fits the programmer's needs.

A Simple Program

In the Screen Test on the facing page 515, you can see this algorithm rewritten in C++, a popular variation of the C programming language. (The name C doesn't stand for anything; the language grew out of a less successful language called B.) This program, like most well-written C++ programs, is organized into three parts, similar to a recipe in a cookbook:

1. The program heading, containing the name of the program (not visible in the window) and data files and code libraries to be included (equivalent to the name and description of the dish to be cooked)
2. The declarations and definitions of variables and other programmer-defined items (equivalent to the list of ingredients used in the recipe)
3. The body of the program, containing the instructions, sandwiched between curly braces, { } (equivalent to the cooking steps).

The program looks like a detailed version of the original algorithm, but there's an important difference: because it's a computer program, every word, symbol, and punctuation mark has an exact, unambiguous meaning.

The blue words are keywords with predefined meanings in C++. These keywords, along with special symbols such as *1* and *5*, are part of the standard vocabulary of C++. The programmer defines the words *number*, *guess*, and *counter*, so they become part of the program's vocabulary when it runs. Each of these words represents a *variable*—a named portion of the computer's memory whose contents the program can examine and change.

As programs go, this C++ program is fairly easy to understand. But C++ isn't English, and some statements occasionally need clarification or further documentation. For the sake of readability, most programs include comments—the programmer's equivalent of Post-it notes. In C++, lines that begin with double slashes (//) contain comments. The computer ignores comments; they're included to help human readers understand (or remember) something about the program.

FIGURE 14.4 An interpreter translates the source code of a program to machine language one statement at a time. It must repeat this process every time the program is run.

Into the Computer

The program still needs to be entered into the computer's memory, saved as a disk file, and translated into the computer's native machine language before

Screen Test Programming in C++

THE PROBLEM: *To convert the number guessing game algorithm (p. 512–513) into a working program*

THE TOOLS: *Microsoft Visual C++ development environment*

1. You decide to convert the algorithm on pages 512–513 into a working program. After you finish designing your game program, you can type it into the editor window.

2. The editor automatically indents statements as you type, so it's easy to see the logical structure of the program.

3. The editor also points out a syntax error. Detecting the point of the error is much easier for the computer than identifying what the programmer's mistake is. In this case, the system reports the error as a missing semicolon between commands. The actual error is a misplaced double quotation mark.

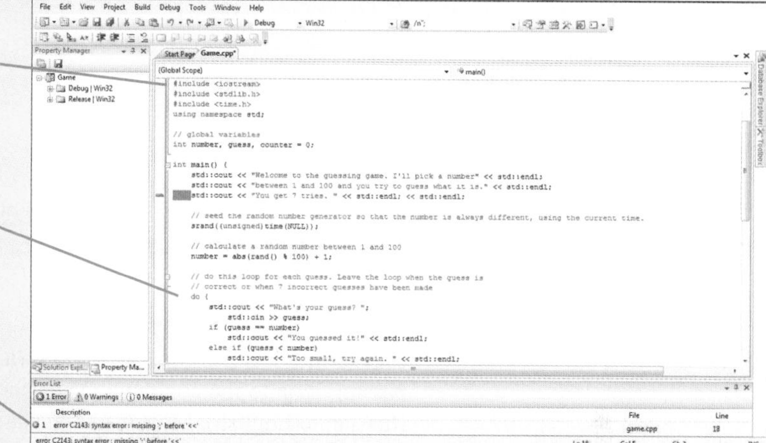

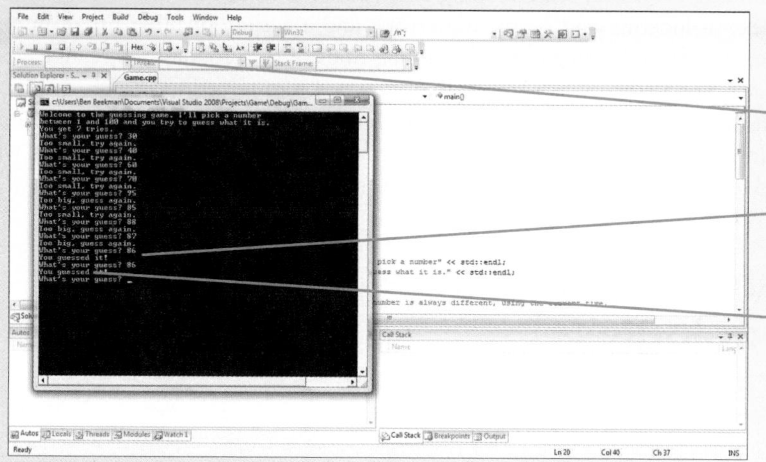

4. You run the program to test for logic errors.

5. When you test it with a series of incorrect guesses, it fails to stop after seven guesses.

6. When you correctly guess the answer, it fails to stop. Instead, it asks you for another guess.

7. You see the logic error in the statement "--counter", which decrements the counter by 1. It should say "++counter" to increment the counter by 1. You correct the error.

8. You rerun the program to test it again. Like most programs, this one could go through several rounds of testing, debugging, and refining before the programmer is satisfied.

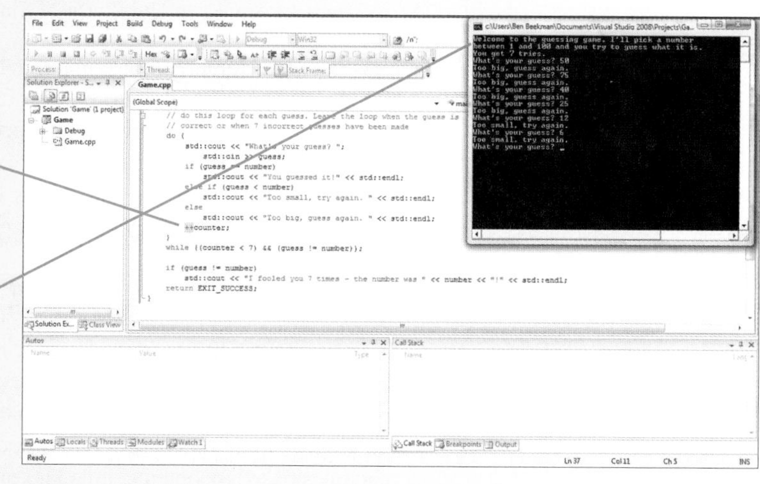

FIGURE 14.5

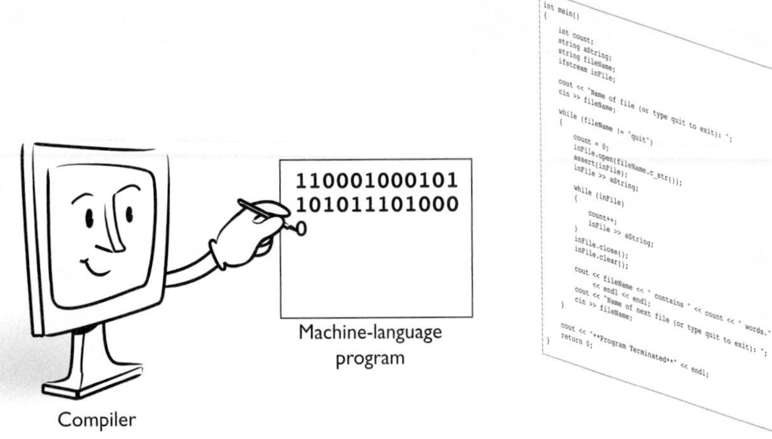

FIGURE 14.6 A compiler translates all of the source code of a program to machine language once, before executing the program.

it can be executed, or run. To enter and save the program, we can use a text editor. A ***text editor*** is like a word processor without the formatting features that writers and publishers require. Some text editors, designed with programming in mind, provide automatic program indenting and limited error checking and correction while the program is being typed.

To translate the program into machine language, we need translation software. The translation program might be an **interpreter** (a program that translates and transmits each statement individually, the way a United Nations interpreter translates a Russian speech into English) or a **compiler** (a program that translates an entire program before passing it on to the computer, as a scholar might translate the novel *War and Peace* from Russian to English). Most C++ translators are compilers because compiled programs tend to run faster than interpreted programs.

A typical compiler software package today is more than just a compiler. It's an integrated ***programming environment***, including a text editor, a compiler, a **debugger** to simplify the process of locating and correcting errors, and a variety of other programming utilities. **Syntax errors**—violations of the grammar rules of the programming language—are often flagged automatically as soon as they're typed into the editor. **Logic errors**—problems with the logical structure that cause differences between what the program is supposed to do and what it actually does—aren't always as easy to detect. That's why debugging and testing can take a large percentage of program development time.

Programming Languages and Methodologies

> If one character, one pause, of the incantation is not strictly in proper form, **the magic doesn't work**.
>
> —*Frederick Brooks, in* The Mythical Man-Month

C++ is one of hundreds of computer languages in use today. Some are tools for professional programmers who write the software the rest of us use. Others are intended to help students learn the fundamentals of programming. Still others enable computer users to automate repetitive tasks and customize software applications. Since the earliest days of computing, programming languages have continued to evolve toward providing easier communication between people and computers.

Machine Language and Assembly Language

Every computer has a native language—a **machine language**. Similarities exist between different brands of machine languages: They all have instructions for the four basic arithmetic operations, for comparing pairs of numbers, for repeating instructions, and so on. But like English and French, different brands of machine languages are different languages, and machines based on one machine language can't understand programs written in another.

From the machine's point of view, machine language is all binary. Instructions, memory locations, numbers, and characters are all represented by strings of *0*s and *1*s. Because binary numbers are difficult for people to read, machine-language programs are usually displayed with the binary numbers translated into decimal (base 10), ***hexadecimal*** (base 16), or some other number system. Even so, machine-language programs have always been hard to write, read, and debug.

The programming process became easier with the invention of **assembly language**—a language that's functionally equivalent to machine language but is easier for people to read, write, and understand. In assembly language, programmers use alphabetic codes that correspond to the machine's numeric instructions. An assembly-language instruction for subtract, for example, might be SUB. Of course, SUB means nothing to the computer, which responds only to commands such as 10110111. To bridge the communication gap between programmer and computer, a program called an **assembler** translates each assembly-language instruction into a machine-language instruction. Without knowing any better, the computer acts as its own translator.

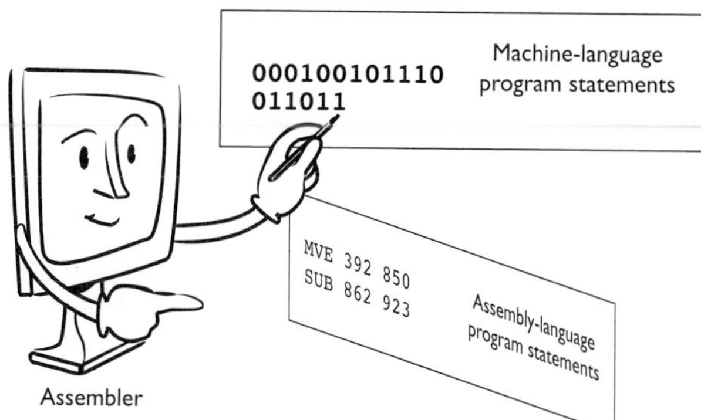

FIGURE 14.7 An assembler translates each statement of assembly-language source code into the corresponding machine-language statement.

Because of the obvious advantages of assembly language, few programmers write in machine language anymore. But assembly-language programming is still considered low-level programming; that is, it requires the programmer to think on the machine's level and to include an enormous amount of detail in every program. Assembly language and machine language are ***low-level languages***. Low-level programming is a repetitive, tedious, and error-prone process. To make matters worse, a program written in one assembly language or machine language must be completely rewritten before it can be run on computers with different machine languages. Many programmers still use assembly language to write parts of video games and other applications for which speed and direct communication with hardware are critical. But most programmers today think and write on a higher level.

High-Level Languages

Computer programming is an art form, like the creation of poetry or music.

—*Donald E. Knuth, author of* The Art of Computer Programming

High-level languages, which fall somewhere between natural human languages and precise machine languages, were developed during the early 1950s to simplify and streamline the programming process. Languages such as FORTRAN and COBOL made it possible for scientists, engineers, and businesspeople to write programs using familiar terminology and notation rather than cryptic machine instructions. Today programmers can choose from hundreds of high-level languages.

Interpreters and compilers translate high-level programs into machine language. Whether interpreted or compiled, a single statement from a high-level program turns into several machine-language statements. A high-level language hides most of the nitty-gritty details of the machine operations from the programmer. As a result, it's easier for the programmer to think about the overall logic of the program—the big ideas. In other words, a higher-level language allows the programmer to focus on what to do, while assembly language forces the programmer to focus on how to do it.

Besides being easier to write and debug, high-level programs have the advantage of being transportable between machines. A program written in standard C can be compiled and run on any computer with a standard C compiler. The same applies for programs written in Java, BASIC, FORTRAN, COBOL, and other standardized languages.

Transporting a program to a new machine isn't always that easy. Most high-level programs need to be partially rewritten to adjust to differences among hardware, compilers, operating systems, and user interfaces. For example, programmers might need to rewrite 20 percent of the code when translating the Windows version of an application program into a Mac version, or vice versa. Still, high-level programs are far more portable than programs written in assembly and machine languages.

Of the hundreds of high-level languages that have been developed, a few have become well known because of their widespread use:

- *FORTRAN* (Formula Translation), the first commercial high-level programming language, was designed at IBM in the 1950s to solve scientific and engineering problems. Many scientists and engineers still use modern versions of FORTRAN today.
- *COBOL* (Common Business-Oriented Language) was developed in 1960 when the U.S. government demanded a new language oriented toward business data-processing problems. COBOL programmers still work in many data-processing shops around the world.
- *LISP* (List Processing) was developed at MIT in the late 1950s to process nonnumeric data such as characters, words, and other symbols. LISP is used in artificial intelligence research, in part because it's easy to write LISP programs that can write other programs.
- *BASIC* (Beginner's All-purpose Symbolic Instruction Code) was developed in the mid-1960s as an easy-to-learn, interactive alternative to FORTRAN for beginning programmers. Before BASIC a student typically had to submit a program, wait hours for output from a compiler, and repeat the process until every error was corrected. Because BASIC was interpreted line by line rather than compiled as a whole, it could provide instant feedback as students typed statements and commands into their terminals. When personal computers appeared, BASIC enjoyed unprecedented popularity among students, hobbyists, and programmers. Over the years BASIC has evolved into a powerful, modern programming tool for amateur and professional programmers. True BASIC is a modern version of BASIC developed by the original inventors of BASIC. The most popular Windows version of BASIC today—in fact, the most popular programming language ever created—is Microsoft's Visual Basic. REALbasic is a popular cross-platform BASIC.
- *Pascal* (named for a seventeenth-century French mathematician, inventor, philosopher, and mystic) was developed in the early 1970s as an alternative to BASIC for encouraging good programming practices in student programmers. Pascal is seldom used by professional programmers.
- C was invented at Bell Labs in the early 1970s as a tool for programming operating systems such as UNIX. C is a complex language that's difficult to learn. But its power, flexibility, and efficiency have made it—along with its variants—the language of choice for most professionals who program personal computers.
- C++ is a variation of C that supports a modern programming methodology called object-oriented programming, described later in this chapter.
- **Java** is a full-featured object-oriented language developed by Sun Microsystems. Java is especially popular for creating Web **applets**, small compiled programs that run inside other applications—typically Web browsers. Java also excels at creating cross-platform applications that run on many different computers and mobile devices, regardless of the operating system.
- *Visual J++* is a Java-like language from Microsoft for programming on the Windows platform.
- *C#* (pronounced C sharp) is a Windows-only language that's similar to Java.
- *Python* is a Java-like language popular with Linux open-source programmers.
- *Ada* (named for Ada King, the programming pioneer profiled in Chapter 1) is a massive language based on Pascal. It was developed in the late 1970s for the U.S. Defense Department. Ada never caught on outside the walls of the military establishment.
- *PROLOG* (Programming Logic) is a language for artificial intelligence programming. As the name implies, PROLOG is designed for working with logical relationships between facts.
- *LOGO* is a derivative of LISP specially designed for children.

Structured Programming

A programming language can be a powerful tool in the hands of a skilled programmer. But tools alone don't guarantee quality; the best programmers have specific techniques for getting the most out of their software tools. In the short history of programming, computer scientists have developed several methodologies that have made programmers more productive and programs more reliable.

For example, computer scientists in the late 1960s recognized that most FORTRAN and BASIC programs were riddled with GoTo statements—statements used to transfer control to other parts of the program. (Remember "Go to Jail. Do not pass Go. Do not collect $200"?) The logical structure of a program with GoTo statements can resemble a plate of spaghetti. In fact, programmers call programs with too many GoTo statements "spaghetti code." The bigger the program, the bigger the logical maze and the more possibility for error. Every branch of a program represents a loose end that a programmer might overlook.

In an attempt to overcome these problems, computer scientists developed **structured programming**—a technique to make the programming process easier and more productive. A structured program doesn't depend on the GoTo statement to control the logical flow. Instead, it's built from smaller programs called **modules**, or **subprograms**, which are in turn made of even smaller modules. The programmer combines modules using the three basic control structures: sequence, repetition, and selection. A program is well structured if the following are true:

- It's made up of logically cohesive modules.
- The modules are arranged in a hierarchy.
- It's straightforward and readable.

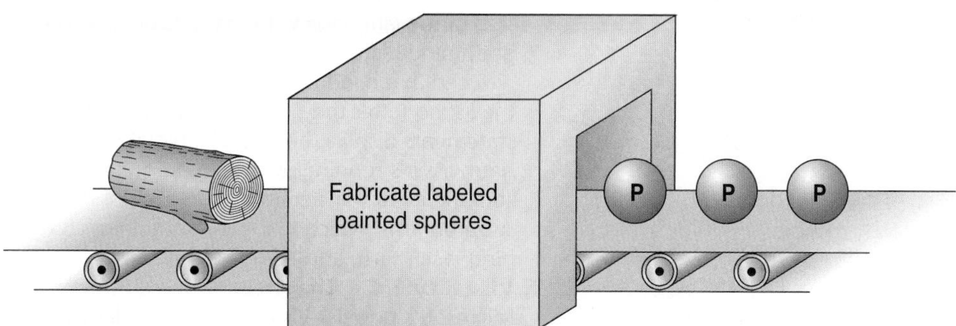

FIGURE 14.8 Computer software contains two kinds of information: program code and data. The program embodies the algorithms that manipulate the data. In this figure the program is represented by a machine, and the data are represented by the raw material and the finished products. An unstructured program with one large module is like a huge, complicated machine that can't easily be broken down into component parts.

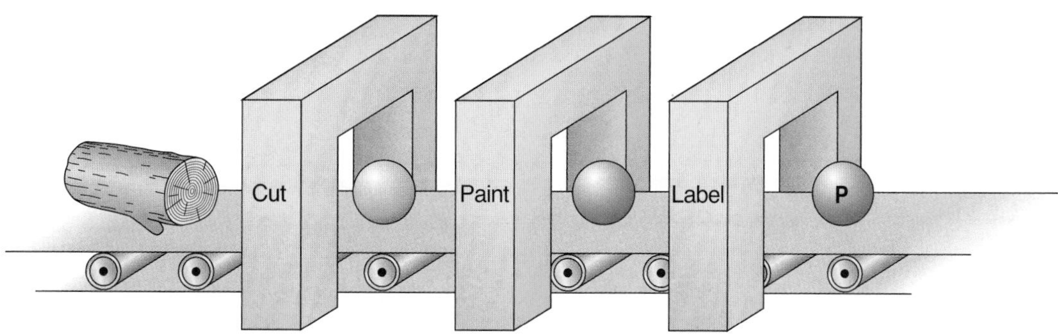

FIGURE 14.9 Structured programming breaks the big, complicated machine into more manageable modules, each of which has a clearly defined task. Modular programs are easier to understand and debug.

how it works The Evolution of BASIC

The BASIC programming language has evolved through three major phases. These examples show how the programming process has changed during the past three decades. The first two BASIC examples shown here are complete listings of programs to play the number-guessing game; the third example is a glimpse of a program to play a slot machine game.

1. **Early BASIC.** The program with numbered lines is written in a simple version of BASIC—the only kind that was available in the early days of the language. Statements are executed in numerical order unless control is transferred to another statement with a GoTo statement.

```
10 REM INITIALIZE
20 RANDOMIZE
30 PRINT "THE GUESSING GAME"
40 PRINT "I WILL THINK OF A NUMBER BETWEEN 1 AND 100."
50 PRINT "TRY TO GUESS WHAT IT IS"
60 LET C = 0
70 LET N = INT(RND(1) * 100)
80 INPUT "WHAT IS YOUR GUESS?";G
90 IF G = N THEN PRINT "THAT IS CORRECT!"
100 IF G < N THEN PRINT "TOO SMALL--TRY AGAIN"
110 IF G > N THEN PRINT "TOO BIG--TRY AGAIN"
120 LET C = C + 1
130 IF C = 7 THEN GOTO 150
140 IF G <> N THEN GOTO 80
150 IF G <> N THEN PRINT "I FOOLED YOU 7 TIMES! THE ANSWER WAS ";N
160 END
```

2. **Structured BASIC.** The modular program on the bottom is written in QuickBASIC, a newer version of the language with many structured programming features. The main program has been reduced to a handful of statements at the top of the listing (after the DECLARE statements); these statements display the overall logic of the program. As it's running, the main program uses CALL statements to transfer control to each of the three subprograms, which take care of the game's beginning, each turn, and the game's end.

```
REM Guessing Game
REM written by Rajeev Pandey

DECLARE SUB StartGame (Counter!, Number!)
DECLARE SUB Turn (Counter!, Guess!, Number!)
DECLARE SUB EndGame (Number!)

CALL StartGame(Counter, Number)
DO
      CALL Turn(Counter, Guess, Number)
LOOP UNTIL (Guess = Number) OR (Counter = 7)
IF Guess <> Number THEN
      CALL EndGame(Number)
END IF

SUB EndGame (Number)
PRINT "I fooled you 7 times!"
PRINT "The answer was "; Number
END SUB

SUB StartGame (Counter, Number)
PRINT "Welcome to the guessing game. I'll think of a number"
PRINT "between 1 and 100 and you will guess what it is."
Counter = 0
RANDOMIZE TIMER
Number = INT(RND(1) * 100)
END SUB

SUB Turn (Counter, Guess, Number)
INPUT "What's your guess?"; Guess
IF Guess = Number THEN
      PRINT "You got it!"
ELSE
      IF Guess < Number THEN
            PRINT "Too small, try again."
      ELSE
            PRINT "Too big, try again."
      END IF
END IF
Counter = Counter + 1
END SUB
```

3. **Visual BASIC.** The screen shows an example of Microsoft's popular Visual Basic, a modern programming environment that includes many of the ideas and tools of object-oriented programming and visual programming.

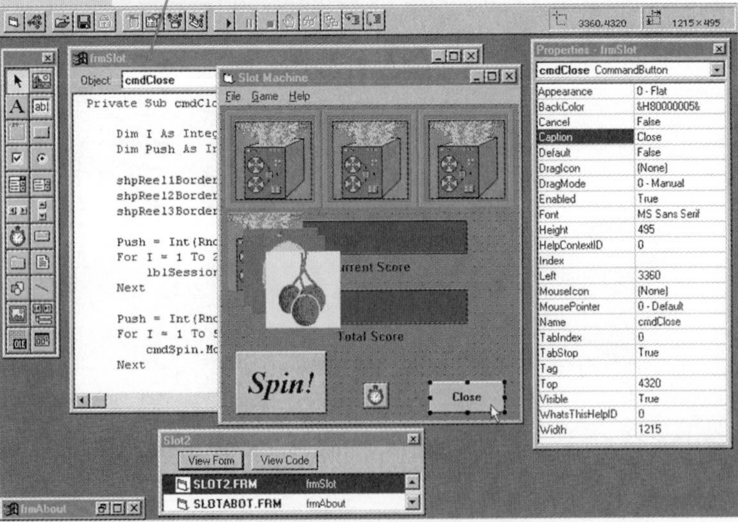

FIGURE 14.10

Object-Oriented Programming

Structured programming represented a big step forward for programmers; it enabled them to produce better, more reliable programs in less time. But today **object-oriented programming (OOP)** is a more popular programming paradigm. In object-oriented programming, a program is not just a collection of step-by-step instructions or procedures; it's a collection of objects. Objects contain both data and instructions and can send and receive messages. For example, an on-screen button in a multimedia program might be an object, containing both a physical description of the button's appearance and a script telling it what to do if it receives a mouse-click message from the operating system. This button object can be easily reused in different programs because it carries with it everything it needs to operate.

With OOP technology, programmers can build programs from prefabricated objects in the same way builders construct houses from prefabricated walls. OOP also makes it easy to use features from one program in other programs, so programmers don't have to start from scratch with every new program. The object that puts addresses in alphabetical order in a mailing list database can be used to sort customer names in a hotel reservations system. Reusing software components is a way to save time and reduce errors.

OOP also supports the hierarchical categorization of objects, enabling programmers to create new objects derived from previously defined objects. The new object can inherit the properties and methods of the object it descends from and add new properties and methods as needed. For example, a window with scrollbars is a special kind of window. Many of the user actions supported on windows with scrollbars are exactly the same actions supported on any desktop window. By defining the "window with scrollbars" object as a special kind of the "window" object, the methods for moving, resizing, and closing the window could be reused. New methods would then be added to support the user's manipulations of the scrollbar. Once again, the benefits of code reuse are realized.

Object-oriented programming was first used in the 1970s, most notably in a language called SmallTalk. SmallTalk is still used for object-oriented programming, but today many other languages include object technology. C++, used in our example earlier, is a popular dialect of C that supports object-oriented programming. The newer languages Java and C# were designed from the ground up to be object-oriented languages.

Object-oriented tools and techniques are common in databases, multimedia authoring tools, and other software environments. Object-oriented programming is particularly well suited for highly interactive programs (such as graphical operating systems, games, and customer transaction stations), and programs that imitate or reflect some dynamic part of the real world, such as simulations and air traffic control systems. Many experts view OOP as the dominant programming paradigm of our era.

Aspect-Oriented Programming

Object-oriented programming isn't the last word in programming. The self-contained functionality of objects in OOP enhances productivity, but not without a cost. In large and complex projects, using and changing objects can require a lot of unnecessary code and cause slower program performance. What's more, changing one object's definition can make undesired changes throughout the rest of a program.

Part of the problem is that OOP doesn't take into account the fact that an object might be seen and used differently in different parts of the system. Consider this real-world example: A bird, a hiker, and a logger might all perceive—and interact with—a tree in different ways. In an object-oriented programming world, a tree is a tree is a tree. The "tree" object has the same features no matter where it's used. But a newer paradigm called **aspect-oriented programming** separates each object's features into separate programs that overlap in functionality as little as possible. So the tree features that are critical to a bird—branches, nearby predators, and so on—would be

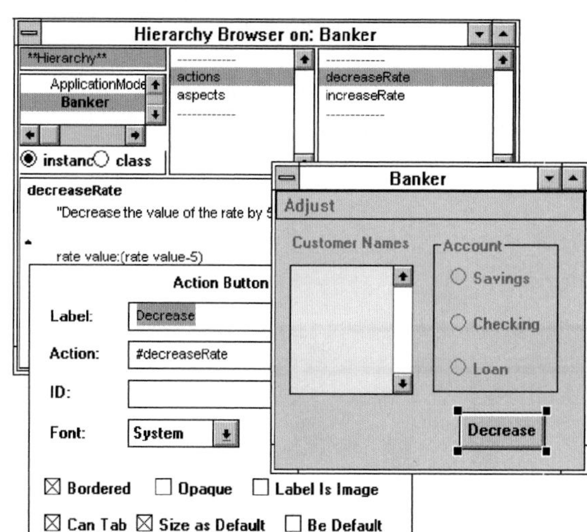

FIGURE 14.11 SmallTalk is the original OOP programming language. The name SmallTalk was used because it was tested on the children at Xerox PARC laboratories.

Screen Test Object-Oriented Programming in Java

THE PROBLEM: *To create a graphical puzzle game involving glasses of water*

THE TOOLS: *Eclipse development environment*

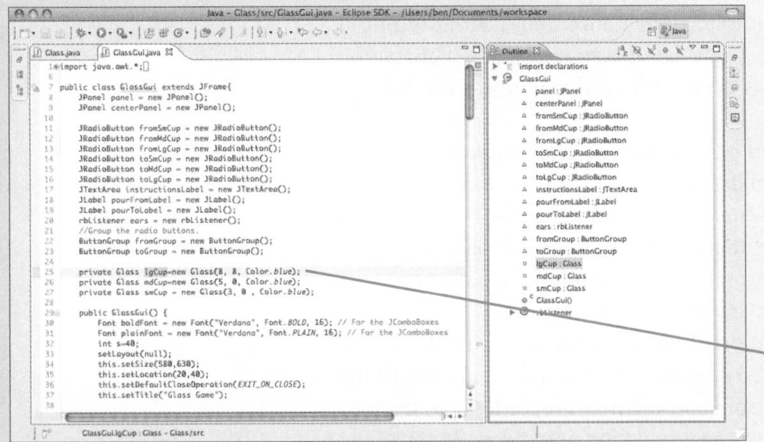

1. You consider the problem conceptually. Because all three glasses have similar properties, you write code to create a reusable glass *object*.

2. For each glass, you use the glass object and create variables for each characteristic that is unique to the glass, including size, current fill level, and color of the liquid.

3. You then create several *methods* (functions) that can be used by any glass object, including commands to check and set the values of each variable, and one that pours water to another glass.

4. Now that you've defined the glass object, you write code that creates the graphical user interface. Your interface includes three instances of the glass object with different sizes and initial fill levels. Because you've already constructed the glass object, creating each glass is a simple process of creating instances of the glass object with different values for these variables.

5. You press the "Run Program" button to compile and test your program.

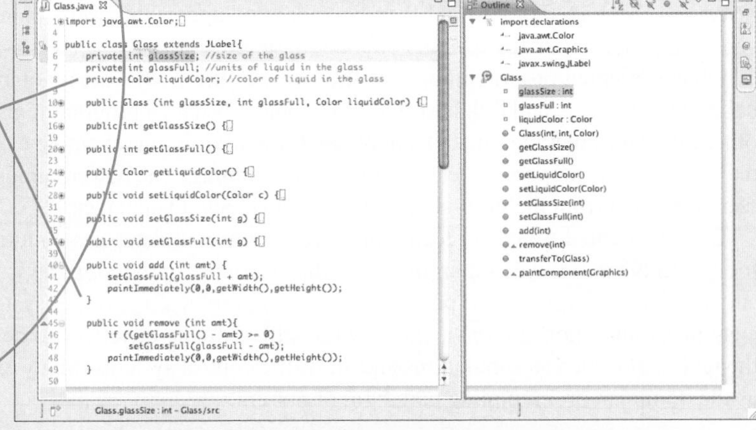

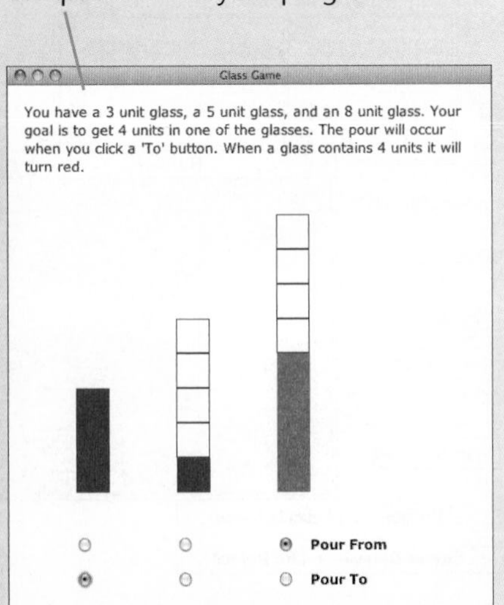

6. Once you're satisfied with the performance of your program, you can compile the finished program as a Java applet, and upload it to your site so anybody with a browser can play your game.

FIGURE 14.12

contained in a separate program. These features wouldn't have much impact on the logger, who's more concerned with the "timber value" program.

Aspect-oriented programming separates and prioritizes a program's concerns, storing only the code relating to a program's primary functions, or ***business concerns***, in the primary program. Secondary concerns, such as administrative and security tasks, are separated into their own programs, which are only called as needed. This separation allows for greater efficiency and independence, because code relating to one task can be altered without affecting the code relating to other concerns. The goal is to design systems in which failure of one function does not cause other functions to fail, and in general to make it easier to understand, design, and manage complex interdependent systems.

Separation of concerns—the key concept of aspect-oriented programming—is an important design principle in urban planning, architecture, information design, and other fields. In each of these disciplines, it's important to keep system features separate so that the failure of one feature doesn't bring down other features. That's why, for example, electricians put stoves, heaters, and lights on separate circuits.

Visual Programming

Many people find it easier to work with pictures instead of words. **Visual programming** tools enable programmers to create large portions of programs by drawing pictures and pointing to objects, eliminating much of the tedious coding of traditional programming.

Microsoft's Visual Basic is widely used by professionals and hobbyists alike because of its visual approach to programming. Visual J++ applies a similar visual approach to Microsoft's Java-like language. Today's visual programming tools haven't completely transformed programming into a visual process; programmers must still understand how to read and write code to create complex programs. But visual programming can save hours of coding time, especially when creating user interfaces—the graphical shells that interact with users. Because they can simplify many of the most difficult parts of the programming process, visual languages make programming more accessible to nonprogrammers.

Languages for Users

Some computer languages are designed with nonprogrammers in mind. They aren't as powerful and versatile as professional programming languages, but they meet the modest needs of specific users.

Macro Languages

Many user-oriented languages are intended to enable users to create programs, called ***macros***, that automate repetitive tasks. User-oriented **macro languages** (also called **scripting languages**) are built into many applications, utilities, and operating systems. Using a macro language, a spreadsheet user can build a program (a macro) to create end-of-month reports automatically each month by locating data in other worksheets, inserting values into a new worksheet, and calculating results using formulas carried over from previous months. Using an operating system's scripting language, a user might automate the process of making backup copies of all documents created during the past seven days.

Some macro languages require you to design and type each macro by hand, just as you would if you were writing a BASIC program. In fact, Microsoft Office includes a scripting variation of Visual Basic called Visual Basic for Applications (VBA). Another type of macro maker "watches" while the user performs a sequence of commands and actions; it then memorizes the sequence and turns it into a macro automatically. The user can then examine and edit the macro so it performs the desired actions under any circumstances.

Fourth-Generation and Fifth-Generation Languages

Many experts suggest that languages have evolved through four generations: machine language, assembly language, high-level languages, and **fourth-generation languages**, sometimes called **4GLs**. Each generation of languages is easier to use and more like natural language than its predecessors were. There's no consensus on exactly what constitutes a fourth-generation language, but these characteristics are most commonly mentioned:

- 4GLs use English-like phrases and sentences to issue instructions.
- 4GLs are nonprocedural. C and BASIC are procedural languages—tools for constructing procedures that tell the computer how to accomplish tasks. Nonprocedural languages enable users to focus on what needs to be done, not on how to do it. (Remember this theme from earlier in the chapter? You can view a higher-level language as focusing on "what," while the lower-level language focuses on "how." C looks high-level compared to assembly language, but it looks low-level compared to a 4GL. This phenomenon is why computer scientists keep inventing new generations of languages.)
- 4GLs increase productivity. Because a 4GL takes care of many of the how-to details, programmers can often get results by typing a few lines of code rather than a few pages.

One type of 4GL is the **query language** that enables a user to request information from a database with carefully worded English-like questions. A query language serves as a database user interface, hiding the intricacies of the database from the user. SQL (see Chapter 7) is the standard query language for most database applications today. Like most query languages, SQL requires the user to master a few rules of syntax and logic. Still, a query language is easier to master than FORTRAN or COBOL are.

Some languages have been referred to as **fifth-generation languages (5GLs)**. According to one common definition, fifth-generation languages are constraint-driven languages. Instead of specifying an algorithm, the programmer defines the conditions that need to be met and the computer solves the problem. 5GLs aren't smart enough to create efficient algorithms for more complex problems, so their use is (so far) mostly restricted to artificial intelligence research.

Component Software

Recent developments in the software industry may soon result in software that provides users with the kind of power formerly reserved for programmers—and at the same time reverse a long-standing trend toward bloated computer applications. Throughout most of the short history of the personal computer, applications have steadily grown in size as developers add more and more features to their products. Even though no single user needs all the features in a modern spreadsheet program, every user who buys that program must buy all the code that provides those features. Many modern applications are so bloated with features that they make huge demands on memory and hard disk space.

Component software tools may reverse the trend toward mega-applications by enabling users to construct small custom applications from software components. Component software isn't completely new; users have been able to add custom components to applications and operating systems for years. Many programs support *skins*—components designed to customize the way the program looks on the screen. But components aren't just for cosmetic purposes. Dozens of plug-in extensions add features and capabilities to Microsoft Internet Explorer, Adobe Photoshop, Mozilla Firefox, and other popular applications. This customizability is possible only if applications are programmed to allow it. More and more software programs, including operating systems, are designed with extensibility in mind.

Component software is the logical extension of object-oriented programming; it may soon reach a level where users and managers can build their own applications. Instead of buying an everything-but-the-kitchen-sink video-editing program, you might be able to buy or download video-editing components—titles generators, sound editors, special effects tools—based on your individual needs. Web services (described in Chapter 9) are based on the idea of using components to create Web-centered systems and applications.

Agile Development and Extreme Programming

The best part is to work side by side with someone else. It's a very stimulating environment, and you don't run into roadblocks or mental blocks.

—Doug Watt, senior engineer

Agile development is a relatively new programming model that focuses as much on the culture of programming as it does on technology. The traditional approach to programming is to make individual programmers responsible for entire programs or modules that may take months or years to complete. The agile programming model emphasizes communication, collaboration, and smaller but more frequent software updates. Programmers work in teams developing programs that can pass rigorous tests throughout the development process. Agile programming involves close communication with customers and clients; they're considered part of the team.

In the best known agile model of development, *extreme programming*, the entire programming team "owns" the code; each member of the team has a right to improve it and the responsibility for making it work properly. Extreme programmers work in pairs on projects rather than write code alone. Pair programming reduces the number of individual errors and ensures that more team members are familiar with all aspects of the code. And in spite of its name, extreme programming doesn't involve marathon coding sessions to make deadlines for major releases. Instead, extreme programming emphasizes frequent releases of smaller updates and reasonable (40-hour) workweeks for programmers.

Extreme programming and other agile models are still outside the norm; their nonhierarchical approach runs counter to many corporate cultures. But the approach is growing in popularity—especially in organizations that embrace collaboration.

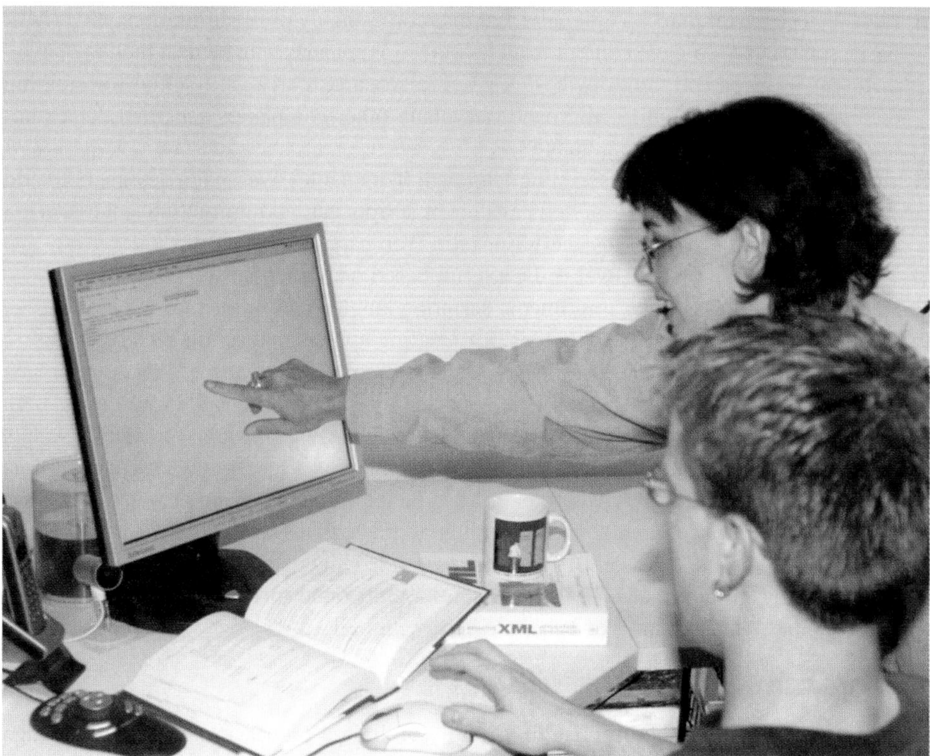

FIGURE 14.13 Extreme programmers work in pairs to write code.

```
#!/usr/local/bin/perl

# Each line of file "sales2009" has a name and a sale price
open (SALES,"sales2009") or die "Can't open sales: $!\n";

# Crate a list of sales for each employee
while ($line = <SALES>) {
    ($employee, $sales) = split (" ", $lines);
    $receipts{$employee} .= $sales." ";

}

# Print and alphabetical list of employees and their total sales
foreach $employee (sort keys %receipts) {
    $total = 0;
    @items = split(" ", $receipts{$employee});
    foreach $item (@items) {
        $total + = $items;

}
print "$employee: \t\$$total sales for the year 2009\n";
}
```

FIGURE 14.14 This Perl script processes a text file containing information about houses sold by a group of realtors. It produces an alphabetized list of the realtors and their total sales.

Programming for the Web

In today's Facebook and Flickr- driven world, many experts believe that PC applications are taking a backseat to Web-based applications. Programmers can, and do, use a variety of languages, including C and C++, to write Web applications. But some programming tools are particularly useful for developing Web applications:

- ***HTML*** is, technically, a page-description language rather than a programming language. HTML commands tell Web browsers how to arrange text, graphics, and multimedia elements on Web pages and how to link those pages. But there are many similarities between HTML coding and program writing, and newer versions of HTML take it far beyond the basics of page layout.
- ***XML*** is a powerful markup language that overcomes many of the limitations of HTML. XML separates Web page content from layout, so Web pages can be designed to display different ways on different devices. XML is also particularly well suited for creating database-backed Web sites. Microsoft and many other companies use XML as a standard document formatting language.
- ***JavaScript*** is an interpreted scripting language that enables Web page designers to add scripts to HTML code. Interpreted JavaScript scripts can add animation, interactivity, and other dynamic content to otherwise static Web pages.
- ***VBScript*** is Microsoft's answer to JavaScript based on Visual Basic.
- ***ActionScript*** is the popular multimedia scripting language built into Adobe Flash.
- ***Java*** (described earlier) is widely used for creating applets that run in Web browsers.
- ***ActiveX*** is a Microsoft language designed specifically for creating Web components similar to Java applets but that are not supported by all platforms and browsers.
- ***Perl*** is an interpreted scripting language that is particularly well suited for writing scripts to process text—for example, complex Web forms. Perl is a server-side language; it runs on Web servers, creating HTML code that can be interpreted by Web browsers.
- ***PHP*** is a widely used open-source scripting language that was designed for producing dynamic Web pages. Like Perl, PHP is a server-side language. Many programmers take advantage of the fact that HTML code can be embedded in PHP scripts. Major Web sites, such as Amazon and YouTube, are built with PHP.

Programming for the Cloud

Cloud computing offers the promise of virtually unlimited processing power and storage using remote data centers run by Amazon, Google, and many other companies. But programming for the cloud is not the same as programming for a stand-alone PC.

For one thing, the data used and saved by cloud-based apps might be stored anywhere. And a programmer can't assume that the data will flow continually between storage device and processor without interruption. What's more, cloud data might change while the program is running. For example, a program that uses GPS coordinates or weather data must continually check for updates, and must know what to do if the data suddenly becomes unavailable because of a network glitch.

Many developers write instructions for handling these uncertainties using languages that predate the cloud. Others use programming tools, such as Bloom and Mirage, designed specifically for the cloud. Cloud programming tools reduce development time by eliminating the need to program around dependencies and unknowns.

The expectations for desktop applications have also changed as a result of the rapid migration to the cloud. Many video and photo apps have been updated with commands that allow you to post your favorite photos or edited home movies quickly and directly to social media sites like Facebook, Flickr, and YouTube. Office and desktop publishing applications offer advanced Web exporting options. Many database applications like FileMaker and Access offer browser-based database interfaces that enable anyone with a Web browser and the proper credentials the ability to update shared data collections from anywhere with Internet service.

Programs in Perspective: Systems Analysis and the Systems Life Cycle

> It has often been observed that we more frequently fail **to face the right problem** than fail **to solve the problem we face**.
>
> —*Russell Ackoff, American systems scientist*

Programs don't exist in a vacuum. Programs are part of larger **information systems**—collections of people, machines, data, and methods organized to accomplish specific functions and to solve specific problems. Programming is only part of the larger process of designing, implementing, and managing information systems. In this section, we examine that larger process.

Systems Development

Systems development is a problem-solving process of investigating a situation; designing a system solution to improve the situation; acquiring the human, financial, and technological resources to implement the solution; and finally evaluating the success of the solution.

The systems development process begins when someone recognizes that a problem needs to be solved or an opportunity exists that can be taken advantage of. A typical situation might resemble one of these:

- A mom-and-pop music store needs a way to keep track of instrument rentals and purchases so billing and accounting don't take so much time.
- A college's antiquated registration system forces students to endure poorly designed, sluggish Web forms and frequent scheduling errors.
- A garden-supply company is outgrowing its small, slow, PC-based software system, resulting in shipping delays, billing errors, and customer complaints. At the same time, the company is losing business because competitors have superior Web catalogs and ordering systems.
- The success of an upcoming oceanographic investigation hinges on the ability of scientists to collect and analyze data instantaneously so the results can be fed into remote-control navigation devices.

FIGURE 14.15 A growing business with an inefficient, paper record-keeping system is a candidate for systems development.

- A software manufacturer determines that its smart phone graphics app is rapidly losing market share to a competitor with more features and a friendlier user interface.
- A small retail store doing business on the Web realizes it can modify its Web site to market to customers internationally.

An organization may face several problems and opportunities, each of which may require the company to develop new IT applications. Each new project requires people, money, and other organizational resources, so a *steering committee* may be formed to decide which projects should be considered first. The steering committee comprises people from each of the functional areas of the organization.

After the steering committee decides to go ahead with a proposed project, a project team is formed to develop the system. The project team typically includes one or more end users and systems analysts. An **end user** is a person who uses the information system directly or uses the information produced by the system. A **systems analyst** is an IT professional primarily responsible for developing and managing the system. The systems analyst is usually part of the company's information systems department. But the business may choose to contract, or outsource, the systems analyst from an outside consulting firm nearby or abroad.

A project team of end users can develop many small-scale systems without the direct involvement of a professional systems analyst. This systems development approach, called **end-user development**, is popular in organizations where users have programming and Web site development skills and tools.

The Systems Development Life Cycle

> The first 90 percent of the task **takes 90 percent** of the time. The last 10 percent **takes the other 90 percent**.
>
> —*A systems development proverb*

Whether it's a simple, single-user accounting system for a small business or a Web-based, multiuser management information system for a large organization, a system has a life cycle. The **systems development life cycle (SDLC)** is a sequence of seven phases the system passes through between the time it is conceived and the time it is phased out. The phases of the system development life cycle are investigation, analysis, design, development, implementation, maintenance, and retirement.

Investigation

The purpose of the ***investigation*** phase is to study the existing business problem or opportunity and determine whether it is feasible to develop a new system or redesign the existing system. The project team conducts a feasibility study to identify the nature of the problem. The team also examines the current system to determine how well it meets the needs of the users and the organization and assess whether a new or improved information system is a feasible solution.

The project team tries to answer several feasibility questions:

- *Technical feasibility.* Can the required hardware and software be purchased or developed? Is the technology reliable? Does the system have sufficient information-processing capacity to handle the number of people who will use the system? Does the system provide for accurate, reliable, and secure data?
- *Economic feasibility.* Will the costs of developing and operating the proposed system be offset by the benefits of using the system? Is the system a good investment? Can sufficient money and personnel resources be committed to complete the system's development on time?
- *Operational feasibility.* Does the proposed system meet the needs of the organization? Are the changes in work procedures required by the proposed system acceptable? Can the proposed system be developed on a timely schedule?

- *Organizational feasibility.* Does the proposed system support the goals and strategy of the organization? Are there any legal implications of the system, such as copyrights, patents, or federal regulations?

Based on its investigation, the project team makes one of three recommendations: leave the current system as is, improve or enhance the current system, or develop an entirely new system. The systems analyst documents the findings of the investigation in a written feasibility report that is presented to the steering committee. Based on the feasibility study, the steering committee decides whether to continue with the analysis phase of the SDLC.

Analysis

During the ***analysis*** phase, the systems analyst gathers documents, interviews users of the current system (if one exists), observes the system in action, and gathers and analyzes data to understand the current system and identify new requirements—features or capabilities that must be included in the system to meet the needs of the users. The systems analyst identifies the requirements related to each subsystem of the proposed system:

- *Input/output requirements.* The characteristics of the user interface, including the content, format, and timing requirements for data-entry screens and managerial reports
- *Processing requirements.* The calculations, decision rules, data processing capacity, and response time needed
- *Storage requirements.* The content of records and databases and the procedures for data retrieval
- *Control requirements.* The desired accuracy, validity, and security of the system; for example, to prevent data-entry errors and guarantee an easy-to-use, user-friendly system

The systems analyst documents the work done in the analysis phase in a written functional requirements report. The report describes the current business procedures and the current system, identifies the problems with the current procedures and system, and describes the requirements for the new or modified system. The steering committee reviews the requirements report and decides whether to proceed with the design phase of the SDLC.

Design

The investigation phase focuses on why, the analysis phase focuses on what, and the ***design*** phase focuses on how. In the design phase, the systems analyst develops the specifications that describe how the system requirements, identified in the analysis phase, will be met. The systems analyst considers important how-to questions in three categories:

- *User interface design.* How will the outputs of the system be designed? Where will input data come from, and how will it be entered into the system? How will the user interface look and function?
- *Database design.* How will the data elements and structure of the files that compose the database be designed?
- *Process design.* How will the programs and the procedures be designed? Should the system be centralized in a single computer, distributed through a network of PCs, or based in the cloud?

The systems analyst answers these questions, sometimes proposing alternative solutions through a design approach called prototyping. A **prototype** is a limited working system that gives users and management an idea of how the completed system will work. **Prototyping** is an iterative process in which the systems analyst can modify the prototype until it meets the needs and expectations of the organization. Prototyping makes the design phase faster and easier for the systems analyst, especially when the users' requirements are difficult to define. Once the design is acceptable, the systems analyst can fill in the details of the output, input, data files, processing, and system controls.

Prototyping is used widely by companies to develop e-commerce applications quickly, especially for designing the human interface components. By encouraging end-user involvement in the design phase, prototyping increases the probability the system will satisfy the users' needs.

Development

After the design phase is completed, the actual system development can begin. The *development* phase is a process of turning the design specifications into a real working system. Development includes a complex mix of scheduling, purchasing, installation, documentation, and programming. For most large projects, the development phase involves a team of programmers, technical writers, and clerical people under the supervision of a systems analyst. A large part of the development schedule is devoted to testing the system. Members of the system development team perform early testing to locate and eliminate bugs. This initial testing is known as **alpha testing**. Later potential end users who are willing to work with almost-finished software perform **beta testing** and report bugs to the developers.

Implementation

The ***implementation*** phase occurs when the testing phase is completed and the new system is ready to replace the old one. For commercial software packages, this phase typically involves extensive training and technical support to supplement sales and marketing efforts. For large custom systems, implementation includes end-user education and training, equipment replacement, file conversion, and monitoring of the new system for problems.

The systems analyst can choose one of four approaches for converting to the new system:

- The direct cutover approach simply replaces the old system with the new system. The organization relies fully on the new system with the risk that parts might not work correctly.
- The parallel systems approach operates the old system along with the new system for a period of time. The old system is gradually phased out as users gain skills and confidence that the new system is stable and reliable.
- The phase-in approach implements subsystems of the new system gradually over a period of time or, alternatively, the system is implemented in only a few departments, branch offices, or plant locations at a time.
- The pilot approach implements the new system in one department or work site. The new system is used and modified at this test site until the systems analyst believes the system can be successfully implemented throughout the organization.

End-user training is critical to implementing an information system successfully. During training, clerical and managerial end users learn how to use the new system effectively and how to handle problems when they arise. Training is often handled by end-user representatives from the project team rather than by technicians.

Maintenance

The *maintenance* phase involves monitoring, evaluating, repairing, and enhancing the system throughout the lifetime of the system. Some software problems don't surface until the system has been operational for a while or the organization's needs change. Systems often need to be adjusted to keep up to date with new products, services, customers, industry standards, and government regulations. Ongoing maintenance enables organizations to deal with those problems and take advantage of opportunities for improvement when they arise.

Evaluation is an important aspect of maintenance. The system is evaluated periodically to determine whether it is providing the anticipated benefits and meeting organizational needs. Also, evaluation provides the feedback necessary for management to assess whether the system was developed on schedule and within budget and to identify what adjustments to make in the system development process in the future.

Retirement

At some point in the life of a system, ongoing maintenance isn't enough. Because of changes in organizational needs, user expectations, technological changes, increasing maintenance costs, and other factors, the system may no longer meet the needs of the

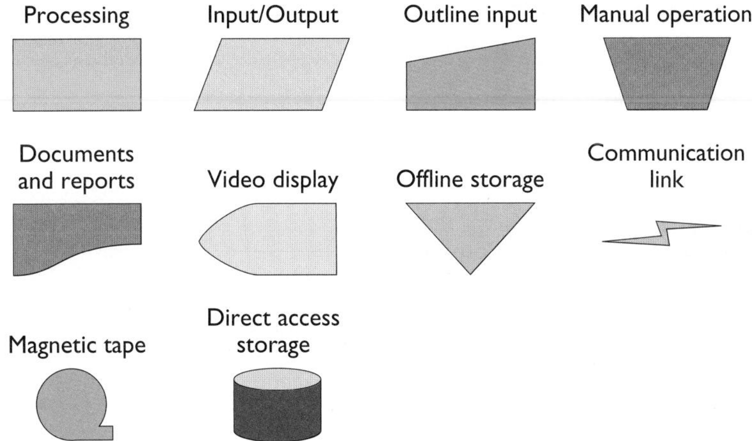

FIGURE 14.16 A systems analyst uses standard symbols to create a system flowchart. Each of the symbols represents the physical components of an information system. You can see an example of a system flowchart in How It Works 14.2.

organization and is ready for *retirement*. At that point it's time to launch an investigation for a newer system, which begins another round of the systems development life cycle.

Systems Development Tools and Techniques

Systems analysts use a variety of tools and techniques throughout the systems development life cycle. Some are used to gather data, some are used to describe or design the system, and others are used to document the system in reports.

Data Collection Techniques

Data collection techniques can be used during any phase of the systems development life cycle. They include:

- *Document review.* Typically, a great deal of information about the current system can be found in documents such as business plans, reports, manuals, correspondence, and systems documentation. The systems analyst can review these documents in the investigation and analysis phases to find out how the current system is designed and how it is supposed to operate.
- *Interview.* Systems analysts interview managers, employees, customers, suppliers, and other people to gather information about processes and problems and to collect ideas and suggestions. In a structured interview, the systems analyst asks the same questions of each person. In an unstructured interview, questions might vary from person to person.
- *Questionnaire.* The systems analyst can use a paper or digital questionnaire to collect information from a large group of people. Questionnaires are convenient, and respondents can remain anonymous if desired.
- *Observation.* The systems analyst can watch an employee perform a task, see how people interact with one another, or observe whether procedures work as expected.
- *Sampling.* If the system is large or has many users, the systems analyst can collect data at prescribed time intervals or from a subset of the users. For example, the systems analyst could interview a sample of 10 percent of the users or observe 5 percent of the transactions of a business to get a sense of how well the current system is working.

Modeling Tools

Modeling tools are graphic representations of a system. Many such tools are available, but the modeling tools most widely used by systems analysts are system flowcharts, data flow diagrams, data dictionaries, and decision tables.

how it works The Systems Development Life CYCLE

College registration is a complex system involving hundreds of people and masses of information. A registration system must be solidly designed, carefully maintained, and eventually replaced as the needs of the college change. In this example we follow systems analysts at Chintimini College as they guide a registration system through a system life cycle.

1. **Investigation.** Analysts at the college's Information Processing Center identify several problems with the antiquated manual registration system: long lines, frequent scheduling errors, and expensive labor costs. After studying registration systems at other schools, they determine that a Web-based registration system might be the best solution to these problems.

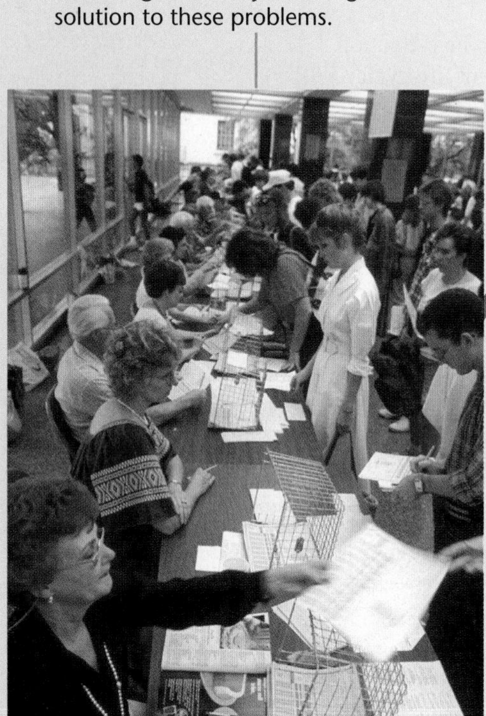

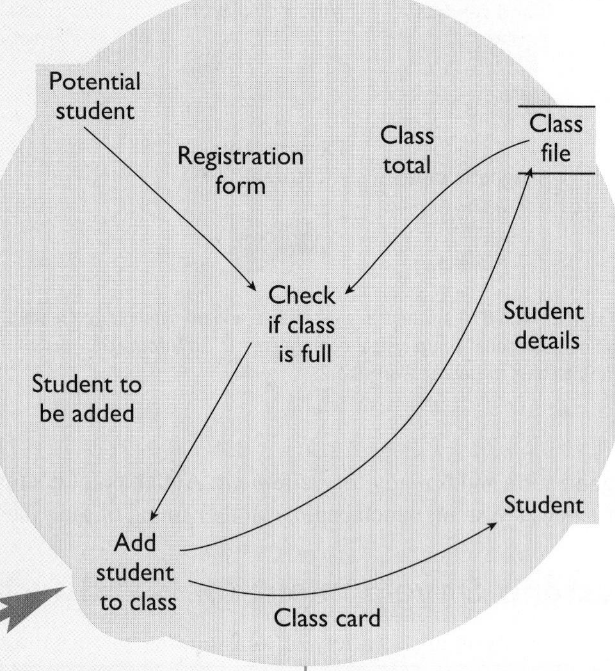

2. **Analysis.** Analysts use a data flow diagram to illustrate the flow of data through the old registration system. They'll use the information in this diagram to help them develop the new system.

7. **Retirement.** After a few years, the Web registration system has developed problems of its own. The college begins developing a new system that will allow students to register through mobile devices as well as Web-connected PCs. When the new registration system reaches the implementation phase of its life cycle, the old system is retired.

FIGURE 14.17

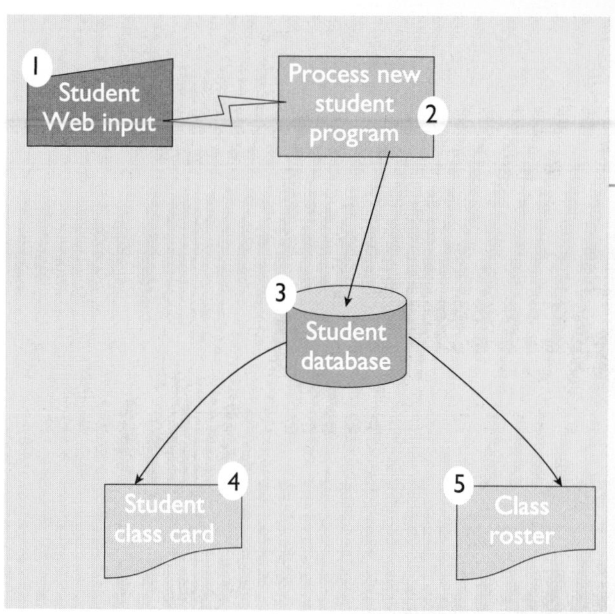

3. Design. Analysts use standard symbols to create a system flowchart to show the relationship among programs, files, input, and output in the new system.

4. Development. Analysts use a Gantt chart to plan the schedule deadlines and milestones for creating the new system.

5. Implementation. Analysts supervise the training, equipment conversion, file conversion, and system conversion as they bring the new system online.

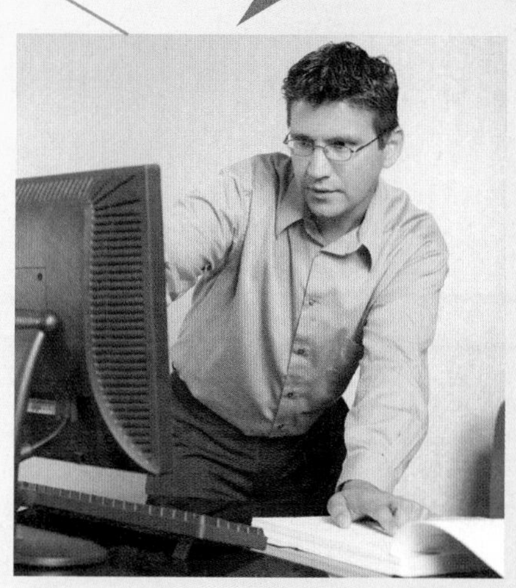

6. Maintenance. Analysts monitor and evaluate the new system, eliminating problems and correcting bugs as they uncover them.

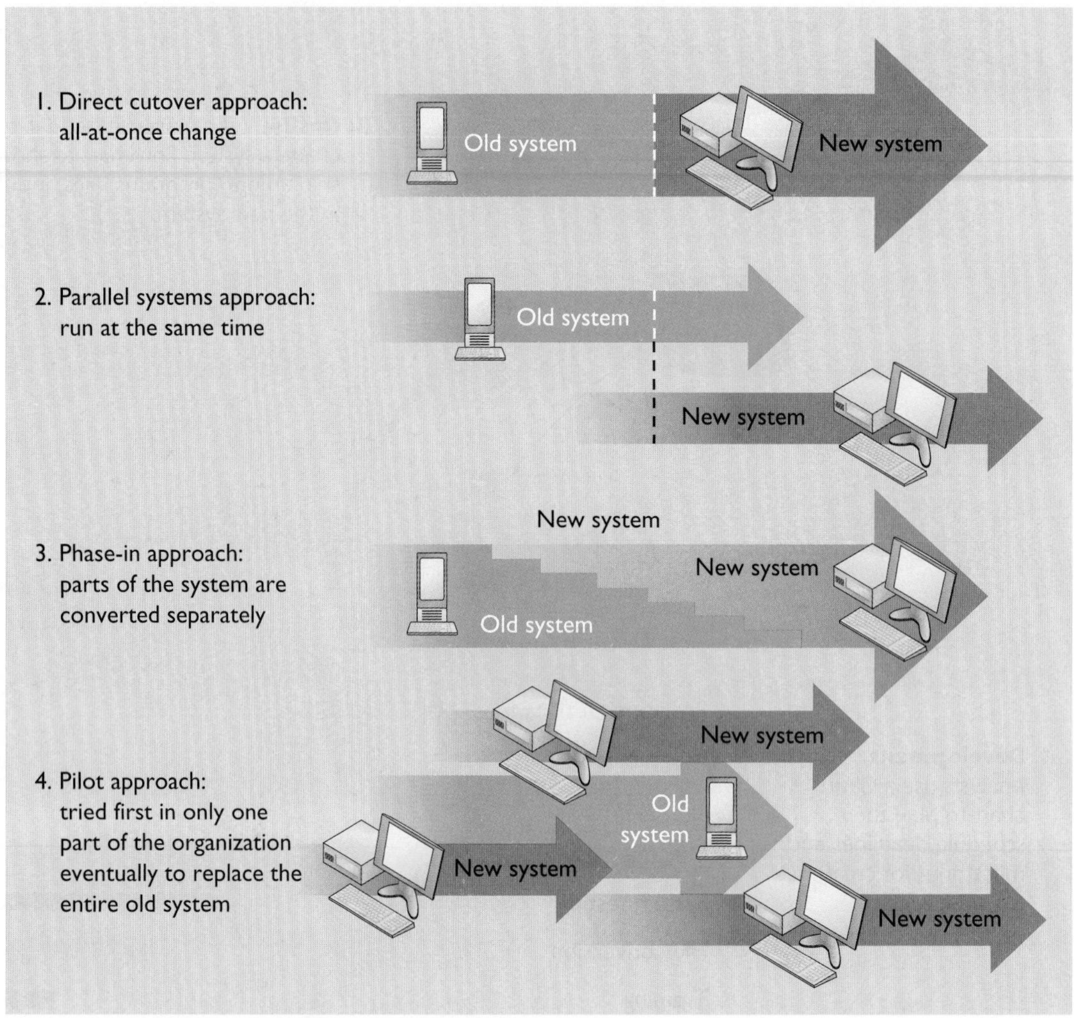

FIGURE 14.18 The systems analyst must carefully choose the system conversion approach that is best for the organization and the end users.

- A **system flowchart** is a graphical depiction of the physical system that exists or is proposed. A system flowchart uses standard symbols to show the overall structure of a system, the sequence of activities that take place in the system, and the type of media or technology used at each step. System flowcharts are used in both the analysis and design phases of the SDLC to show the current system and the design for the proposed system.
- A **data flow diagram (DFD)** is a simple graphical depiction of the movement of data through a system. A data flow diagram uses symbols to show the movement of data, the processes that use and produce data, the storage of data, and the people or other entities that originate input or receive output from the system. A system-level DFD depicts the entire system in summary form; a level-one DFD expands the processes in the system-level DFD to show more detail. Processes in the level-one DFD can in turn be expanded to show more detail, and so on to an appropriate level of detail.

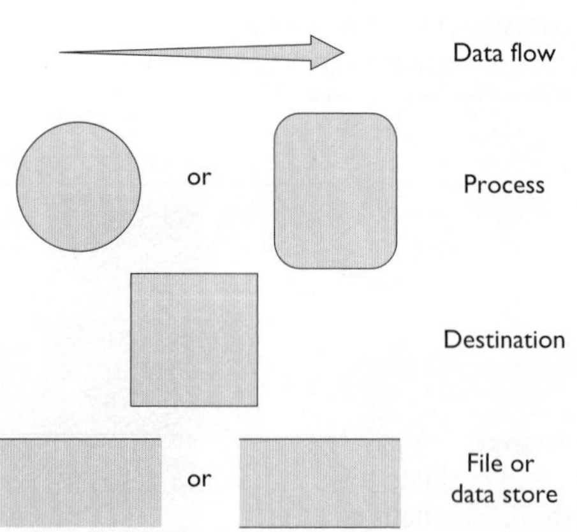

FIGURE 14.19 A systems analyst needs to use only four symbols to create a data flow diagram. You can see how a DFD graphically shows the underlying logical flow of data in a system in How It Works 14.2.

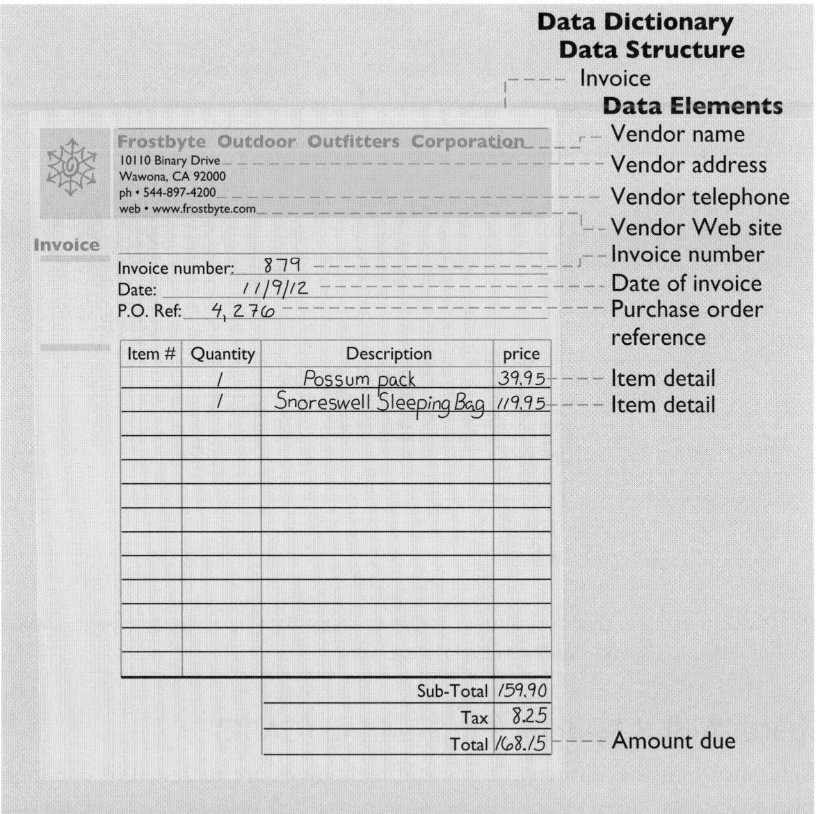

FIGURE 14.20 Data fields in a document can be grouped and represented as data elements and data structures in the data dictionary.

- A **data dictionary** is a catalog, or directory, that describes all the data flowing through a system. Systems analysts use a data dictionary to keep track of all the system's data elements and data structures. Data elements are the fields stored in the system's databases. A **data structure** refers to a set of data elements used together, such as an invoice or other paper or electronic document.
- A **decision table** shows, in a row-column format, the decision rules that apply and what actions to take when certain conditions occur. A systems analyst can describe and analyze a complex procedure more effectively by constructing a decision table of if-then statements than by writing a complicated narrative of all the possible combinations of conditions and actions.

	Decision rules				
	1	**2**	**3**	**4**	**5**
Conditions If...	No	Yes	Yes	Yes	No
And if...	Yes	Yes	No	Yes	No
And if...	Yes	Yes	No	No	Yes
Actions Then do...	✓				
Then do...			✓		✓
Then do...		✓		✓	

FIGURE 14.21 A decision table shows if-then rules in a tabular format. The upper half of the table includes the if conditions, and the lower half shows the then actions. Each numbered column is a decision rule that shows the action(s) to be taken when certain conditions occur. In a real decision table, the leader dots in the left column would be filled in with information specific to the system.

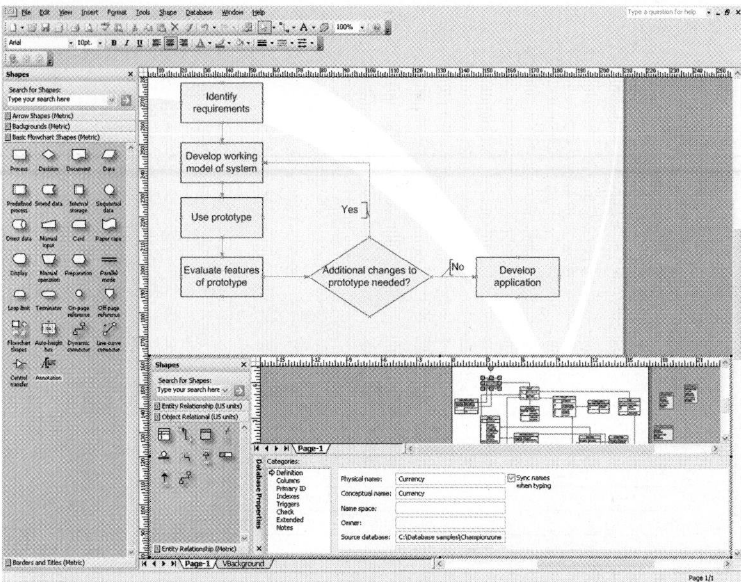

FIGURE 14.22 Systems analysts use Microsoft Visio to create data flow diagrams, Gantt charts, and other types of diagrams useful in systems development work.

Computer-Aided Systems Engineering (CASE)

Today many systems development tools and techniques are included in commercially available software packages referred to as **computer-aided systems engineering (CASE)**. Most CASE tools software packages include:

- Charting and diagramming tools to draw system flowcharts and data flow diagrams
- A centralized data dictionary containing detailed information about all the system components
- A user interface generator to create and evaluate many different interface designs
- Code generators that automate much of the computer programming to create a new system or application

Some CASE software packages contain tools that apply primarily to the analysis and design phases of the systems development life cycle; others contain tools that automate the later phases of systems development, implementation, and maintenance. Integrated CASE tools incorporate the whole spectrum of tools to support the entire systems development life cycle.

The trend today is to run on Internet time with short system development schedules. CASE has an essential niche in the design of large systems. But over the past decade, the tools that worked well migrated out from under the CASE umbrella into other programming tools and suites such as Microsoft's Visual Studio, a development tool suite for building Windows and Web applications, and Microsoft's Visio, an easy-to-use yet powerful charting and diagramming tool.

The Science of Computing

> Telescopes are to astronomy as **computers are to computer science**.
>
> *—Edsger Dijkstra, computer scientist*

We've seen how programmers and systems analysts create and maintain computer programs used by scientists, businesspeople, artists, writers, and others. But just as the rest of us take advantage of the programmer's handiwork, the programmer depends on tools and ideas developed by computer scientists—professionals who work in the academic discipline called **computer science**. What is computer science, and why is it important in the world of computers?

Working Wisdom Avoiding IT Project Failures

Only about a third of IT projects are completed on time, on budget, and with the promised functionality. Here are a few tips for information workers to avoid failures.

- IT projects need executive sponsorship. Many IT projects tend to cut across departments and force a lot of people to change the way they work every day. Change, if not sold by senior management, can create fear, and every fearful middle manager in every department can create bureaucratic roadblocks that reduce the project's chance to succeed.
- IT projects need user input. Lack of user input is the factor most likely to characterize a bad IT project. It is important to discuss projects up front with everybody who has a stake in the outcome, including end users and customers, business partners, and internal departments on whose cooperation a project's success depends.
- IT projects need specifications. If the project requirements aren't well specified up front and the project begins anyway, there may be no consensus among stakeholders. Meetings and discussions at the beginning of the project will help build consensus on what an IT project can and cannot do.
- IT projects need cooperative business partners. Many IT projects involve vendors, from consultants to programmers. Those vendors may start out as partners, but may change course during the system development process if they aren't constrained by reasonable and fair contracts.
- IT projects need open and honest communication. Workers don't want to be the bearers of bad news, and managers don't want to hear that news. As a result, nobody sounds the alarm on doomed projects until it's too late. Every company should have a culture that values open and honest communication.

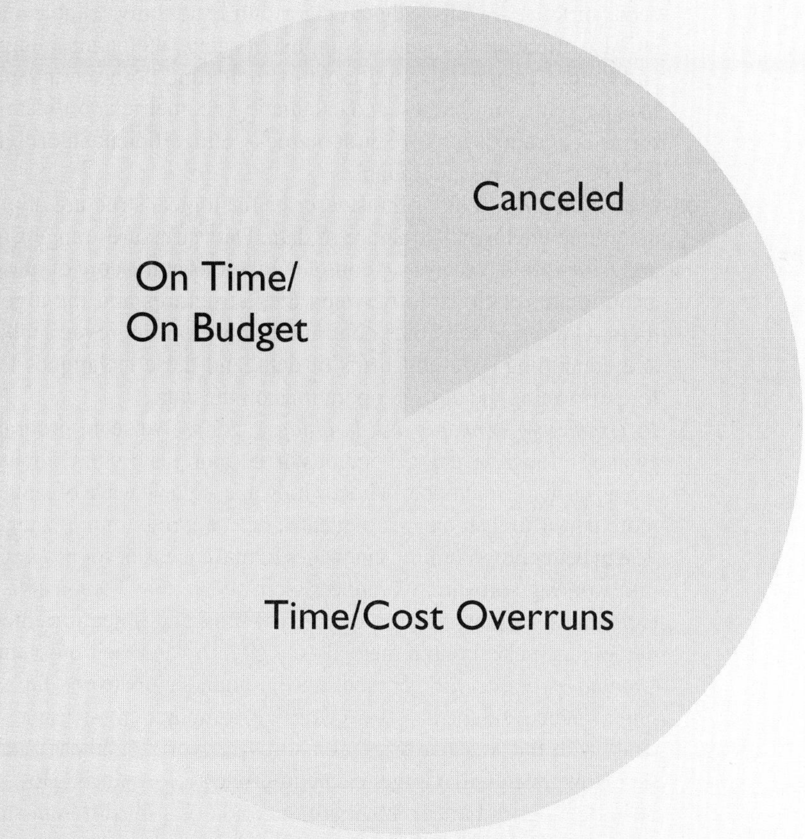

FIGURE 14.23 According to the Standish Group, only about one-third of software projects are completed on time and on budget. About one-half of projects have significant time and/or cost overruns, and about one-sixth of projects are canceled.

Because most introductory computer science courses focus on programming, many students equate computer science with computer programming. But programming is little more than a tool in the computer scientist's intellectual toolbox; it has about as much to do with computer science as English grammar has to do with writing novels.

Computer science is a relatively new discipline with ties to electrical engineering, mathematics, and business. Many computer scientists prefer to call the field *computing science* because it focuses on the process of computing rather than on computer hardware. Computing takes a variety of forms, and computer science includes a number of focus areas, ranging from the rarefied world of computer theory to practical nuts-and-bolts work in software engineering. Some areas of specialization within computer science—database management, graphics, artificial intelligence, and networks, for example—provide academic underpinnings for specific categories of computer applications. Other branches of computer science deal with concepts that can apply to almost any type of computer application. These include the following:

- *Computer theory.* The most mathematical branch of computer science, computer theory applies the concepts of theoretical mathematics to fundamental computational problems, such as whether there are functions that cannot be computed. Theoreticians often work not with real computers, but with idealized models of computation. As in most fields, many theoretical concepts eventually find their way into practical applications. For example, theoretical computer scientists invented error-correcting codes that allow messages to be reconstructed if a few bits are garbled during transmission.
- *Algorithms.* Many computer scientists focus on algorithms—the logical underpinnings of computer programs. The design of algorithms can determine whether software succeeds or fails. A well-designed algorithm is not only reliable and free of logical errors, but also efficient, so it can accomplish its goals with a minimum of computer resources and time. Computers spend most of their time doing mundane tasks such as sorting lists, searching for names, and calculating geometric coordinates. These frequently performed operations must be built on rock-solid, efficient algorithms if a computer system is to be responsive and reliable.
- *Data structures.* If algorithms describe the logical structure of programs, data structures determine the logical structure of data. Data structures range from simple numeric lists and tables (called arrays) to complex relations at the core of massive databases. There is an intimate relationship between data structures and the algorithms that operate on them. Computer scientists continue to develop improved techniques for representing and combining different forms of data, and these techniques lead to faster algorithms for performing the desired operations on the data.
- *Programming concepts and languages.* As we've seen, programming languages have evolved through several generations in the short history of computers. Thanks to computer scientists in the tradition of Grace Hopper, each new wave of languages is easier to use and more powerful than the one that came before. Programming language specialists strive to design better programming languages to make it easier for programmers to turn algorithms into working software. Compuer scientists are also responsible for the development of techniques such as structured programming and object-oriented programming—techniques that make programmers more productive and their programs more reliable.
- *Computer architecture.* Straddling the boundary between the software world of computer science and the hardware world of computer engineering, **computer architecture** deals with the way hardware and software work together. What is the best instruction set? How much will a larger cache improve performance? How does the bandwidth of a bus affect performance? What are the trade-offs for different storage media? These are the types of questions that concern computer architecture specialists.
- *Management information systems.* **Management information systems (MIS)** is part computer science, part business. In fact, MIS studies are done in computer science departments at some institutions, in business departments at others, and in MIS departments at others. MIS specialists focus on developing systems that can provide timely, reliable, and useful information to managers in business, industry, and government. MIS specialists apply the theoretical concepts of computer science to real-world, practical business problems.

- *Software engineering.* When an engineer designs a bridge or a building, tried-and-true engineering principles and techniques ensure that the structure won't collapse unexpectedly. Unfortunately, we can't trust software the way we trust buildings; software designers simply don't have the time-honored techniques to ensure quality. Besides, software is not like concrete and steel; it is infinitely malleable. Given a virtually infinite number of design choices, it's no wonder that programmers are reluctant to construct their code "by the book." Still, everyone understands that the software industry must do a better job completing projects on time without going over budget. **Software engineering** is a branch of computer science that attempts to apply engineering principles and techniques to the less-than-concrete world of computer software. We conclude this chapter with a brief look at the problems faced by software engineers—problems that affect all of us.

The State of Software

> It's impossible to make anything foolproof, because **fools are so ingenious**.
>
> —*Roger Berg, inventor*

In spite of advances in computer science, the state of software development is less than ideal. Software developers and software users are confronted with two giant problems: cost and unreliability.

Software Problems

As computers have evolved through the decades, the cost of computer hardware has steadily gone down. Every year brings more powerful, reliable machines and lower prices. At the same time, the cost of developing computer software has gone up. The software industry abounds with stories of computer systems that cost millions of dollars more and took years longer to develop than expected. Many systems become so costly to develop that their developers are forced to abandon them before completion. About one-sixth of commercial software projects are canceled before they are completed, costing the U.S. economy alone billions of dollars every year.

But while prices rise, there's no corresponding increase in the reliability of software. Ever since Grace Hopper pulled a moth from the Mark II's relay, bugs have plagued computers, often with disastrous consequences, as you saw in Chapter 10. A recent study found that programmers average 100 to 150 mistakes per 1,000 lines of code!

Software errors can take a variety of forms, including errors of omission, syntax errors, logic errors, clerical errors, capacity errors, and judgment errors. But whatever its form, a software error can be devilishly difficult to locate and even more difficult to remove. According to one study, 15 to 20 percent of attempts to remove program errors actually introduce new errors!

Software Solutions

> The major difference between a thing that **might go wrong** and a thing that **cannot possibly go wrong** is that when a thing that cannot possibly go wrong goes wrong it usually turns out to be **impossible to get at or repair**.
>
> —*Douglas Adams, in* Mostly Harmless

Computer scientists and software engineers are responding to reliability and cost problems on five main fronts:

- *Programming techniques.* So far, structured programming and object-oriented programming are the best-known and most successful techniques for increasing programmer productivity and program reliability. Programmers who use these techniques can concentrate on the overall logic of their creations without getting distracted by minute details. The result is less expensive, more reliable software. But these are small steps on a long road toward more dependable programming methodologies. It's too early to tell whether extreme programming and other more modern techniques will take us much farther down that road.

- *Programming environments.* Today's best programming tools include sophisticated text editors, debuggers, record-keeping programs, and translators, all interwoven into a seamless graphic work environment. A high-quality programming environment can help a programmer manage the complexities of a large project. Most such modern environments are built around component technology that makes it easier to reuse reliable code. In any case, programming environments have a long way to go before they can guarantee reliable software, if that's even possible.
- *Program verification.* Software engineers would like to be able to prove the correctness of their programs in the same way mathematicians prove the correctness of theorems. Computer scientists have developed **program verification** techniques that work well for small programs. Unfortunately, these techniques have achieved only limited success with the complex commercial programs people depend on today. There's little hope for automated program verification either. Computer scientists have proven that some problems can't be solved with algorithms, and program verification is one such problem.
- *Clean-room programming.* One experimental approach to software development is modeled after microchip manufacturing techniques. Clean-room programming combines formal notation, proofs of correctness, and statistical quality control with an evolutionary approach to programming. Programmers grow systems individually, certifying the quality of each before integrating it with the others. It's too early to tell whether this rigorous, engineering-like approach will achieve widespread quality gains, but several companies have reported an up to ten-fold reduction in glitches using the clean-room process.
- *Human management.* Project management techniques from business and engineering have been applied successfully to many software engineering projects. These human management techniques have more to do with person-to-person communication than with programmer-to-machine communication. Because many information system failures result from human communication errors, successful human management can improve a system's overall reliability. But the benefits of human management methodologies aren't great enough to offset the massive problems facing software engineers today.

Computer scientists have accomplished a great deal in the short history of the field. Software development is easier than it used to be, and computers today can accomplish far more than anyone dreamed a few decades ago. But software engineers have failed to keep up with the fast-paced evolution in computer hardware, and it's still incredibly difficult to produce reliable, cost-effective software. More than a decade ago, computer scientist Ted Lewis summed up the problem in one of his laws of computing. Today, when we're routinely asked to entrust our money, our health, our legal rights, and our lives to software, it's important for all of us to remember that law: "Hardware is soft; software is hard."

Software Warranties

> **We do not warrant that this software will meet your requirements** or that its operation will be uninterrupted or error-free.
>
> —*From a software license agreement*

Large computer programs are incredibly complicated. The Windows operating system, for example, contains millions of lines of code. Software engineers perform a variety of tests that thoroughly exercise the capabilities of the system, but trying every possible situation is impossible. For this reason, testing can reveal the existence of bugs, but it can't prove that no bugs exist. Software engineers acknowledge that it is impossible to remove every bug from a large, sophisticated program. Given that a large program will contain bugs, who should be responsible when a software error causes a business to lose money?

FIGURE 14.24 Thousands of lives depend on reliable functioning of the computers and software used by air traffic controllers.

In the past, manufacturers of consumer software provided no warranties for their products. Consumers were forced to accept software "as is." Today some software manufacturers say you can get your money back if the software can't be installed on your computer. Others go further and provide a 90-day money-back guarantee if the program fails to live up to its stated purpose. But software manufacturers generally don't accept liability for harm caused to you or your business by errors in the software. Is it fair for software companies to refuse to accept responsibility for harm caused by defects in their programs?

What would happen if our legal system required software manufacturers to pay for damages caused by defective software? Software companies would undoubtedly have a greater focus on the reliability of their products. They would invest more resources in each program, testing code more thoroughly and fixing the bugs that were uncovered. Because bug-free software is impossible, companies would need to purchase insurance to protect themselves from consumer lawsuits. These additional precautions would inflate costs and extend the time needed to develop each product. If software were more time consuming and expensive to develop, large, well-established companies would have an advantage over small start-up businesses that provide much of the innovation in the software industry. Consumers would have fewer software choices, and new releases would happen less frequently. Software would be more reliable, but it would have fewer features and cost more money. Consumers often complain about the quality of software, but their actions suggest that they are more focused on price and features. For all these reasons, allowing software manufacturers to put disclaimers on their products makes sense.

This does not mean that software companies shouldn't try to provide software that's as bug-free as possible. Most major software developers routinely distribute minor revisions and bug fixes for free through the Web, charging only for major upgrades that add new features. It's hard to justify ethically the practice of charging users for upgrades that are little more than bug fixes.

Aspect-oriented programming. Visual programming. Component software. Distributed Web applications. Cloud computing. With these trends gaining momentum, what can we say about the future of programming? It's not clear what programming languages will look like in the future, but three trends seem likely;

- *Programming languages will continue to evolve in the direction of natural languages such as English.* Today's programming languages, even the best of them, are far too limited and unintelligent. Tomorrow's programming tools should be able to understand what we want even if we don't specify every detail. When we consider artificial intelligence in the next chapter, we deal with the problems and promise of natural-language computer communication.
- *The line between programmer and user is likely to grow hazy.* As programming becomes easier, there's every reason to believe that computer users will have tools that enable them to construct applications without mastering the intricacies of a technical programming language.
- *Computers will play an ever-increasing role in programming themselves.* Today's visual programming environments can create programs in response to user clicks and commands. Tomorrow's programming tools may be able to write entire programs with only a description of the problem supplied by users. The day after tomorrow, we may see computers anticipating problems and programming solutions without human intervention!

These three trends come together in the work of some of the pioneers of modern programming. In the 1970s Charles Simonyi developed the first WYSIWYG word processor at Xerox PARC and went on to pilot the development of Word, Excel, and other products as Microsoft's chief architect. In 2002, he left Microsoft and started a new company dedicated to creating tools that will make it possible for everyday computer users to write complex software. The goal is to make the code look like the design, so by simply creating the design, a user can write software. According to Simonyi, "Software should be as easy to edit as a PowerPoint presentation."

Simonyi envisions a process called *intentional programming*, which allows programmers to focus on the intention of their programs rather than the technical details of coding. The programmer, who might be an expert in health care or oceanography or marketing, might be able to use a modeling language to describe a design to solve a problem; a software generator would then write the actual code automatically based on the design description. The user interface for the modeling language might resemble a PowerPoint palette for some users; it might have a more mathematical look for others.

Another software pioneer, IBM's Grady Booch, is attempting to make it possible for modeling languages to weave security functions into software modeling tools and to make modeling tools that can build entire systems of programs.

Whatever happens, one thing seems likely: future programming tools will have little in common with today's languages. When computer historians look back, they'll marvel at how difficult it was for us to instruct computers to perform even the simplest actions. Simonyi is optimistic about the future of software: "Look at what the hardware people have managed to do with Moore's Law. Now it's going to be software's turn."

FIGURE 14.25 Charles Simonyi founded Intentional Software to change the way people create software.

In his book *What Will Be*, computer scientist Michael Dertouzos speculates about where it all might lead: "It could well be that by the close of the twenty-first century, a new form of truly accessible programming will be the province of everyone, and will be viewed like writing, which was once the province of the ancient scribes but eventually became universally accessible."

FIGURE 14.26 Jet engine turbines wouldn't work if they were handcrafted because of the inevitable variations introduced during handwork. Turbines are made by precision machines, which in turn are created and maintained by people. Charles Simonyi says software would be more reliable if we could create it with machines called "modeling languages" instead of writing code by hand.

Crosscurrents

Coding for the Masses

by Clive Thompson

In the early days of home computing, there wasn't much difference between computer users and computer programmers. Professionally programmed applications were rare, so if you wanted to put your computer to work—or play—you probably had to program it. Today there are apps for almost every purpose, and few computer owners know how to write programs. In this article, which first appeared in the December 2010 issue of Wired, *Clive Thompson makes the case that it's time for users to start coding again.*

How do you stop people from texting while driving? Last spring, Daniel Finnegan had an idea. He realized that one of the reasons people type messages while they're in the car is that they don't want to be rude—they want to respond quickly so friends don't think they're being ignored.

So what if the phone knew you were driving—and responded on its own?

Normally, Finnegan wouldn't have been able to do anything with his insight. He was a creative-writing major at the University of San Francisco, not a programmer. But he'd enrolled in a class where students were learning to use Google's App Inventor, a tool that makes it pretty easy to hack together simple applications for Android phones by fitting bits of code together like Lego bricks.

Finnegan set to work, and within a month he'd created an app called No Text While Driving. When you get into your car, you hit a button on the app and it autoresponds to incoming texts with "I'm driving right now, I'll contact you shortly." I've used the app, and it's terrific: By getting you off the hook socially, it makes your driving safer. It ought to be available—mandatory, even—on every phone.

Finnegan's story illustrates a powerful point: It's time for computer programming to be democratized.

Software, after all, affects almost everything we do. Pick any major problem—global warming, health care, or, in Finnegan's case, highway safety—and clever software is part of the solution. Yet only a tiny chunk of people ever consider learning to write code, which means we're not tapping the creativity of a big chunk of society.

Serious leaders already know this. "Every time I talk to generals in the military, they talk about how they can't find enough young people who know how to program," says Douglas Rushkoff, author of *Program or Be Programmed*, a new book that argues that everyday people should learn to code.

What's more, knowing programming changes your worldview. "You learn that every problem is made up of smaller problems," says Kevin Lawver, a web designer whose 11-year-old son, Max, has spent the past few years designing programs using kid-friendly languages like Scratch. Frankly, companies like Facebook and Google would probably face a lot tougher scrutiny if their users understood how software works. Facebook users would know it's not that hard to program finely grained controls over who sees what on Facebook (a service that is, as computer scientist Eben Moglen semijokingly puts it, just "some PHP doodads"). The current mystique around software allows companies to claim that the way they're doing things is the only way possible, when it isn't.

But isn't programming inherently hard? Sure. So are lots of things. Hell, cooking dinner involves lethal implements, a fire inside your house, and ingredients (like raw chicken) that can poison you if they're not correctly prepared. We teach kids how to do that safely; we can do the same with programming.

It'd be great if programming became part of the curriculum, but that probably won't happen, given how slowly schools change. The good news is that—much as the "maker" set is relearning how to build stuff—a grassroots movement is creating tools that let even liberal arts majors hack together a program. In recent years, we've seen the release of oodles of languages designed to make it easy for kids (or adults!) to write code, from Processing to Scratch to Google's App Inventor. In fact, I just used App Inventor to make a program that lets my toddler and kindergartner call family members by touching their pictures.

Got a problem you need to solve? When you can program it yourself, there's always an app for that.

Discussion Questions

1. Do you think the benefits of learning to write computer programs justify the investment of time and energy that it would take?
2. Do you agree with the author that "programming for the masses" is a good idea? Why or why not?

Summary

Computer programming is a specialized form of problem solving that involves developing an algorithm for solving a problem. Most programmers use stepwise refinement to break a problem repeatedly into smaller, more easily solvable problems. An algorithm typically is developed in pseudocode, which describes the logic of the program before being translated into a programming language. A translator program—either a compiler or an interpreter—checks for syntax errors (language errors) and, if it finds none, translates the program into machine language so the computer can execute the instructions. Logic errors might not surface until the translated program is run, and maybe not even then. The programming process isn't completed until the program is thoroughly tested for errors.

Computer languages have evolved through several generations, with each generation being easier to use and more powerful than the one that came before. Machine language—the original computer language of *0*s and *1*s—is primitive and difficult to program. Assembly language uses a translator called an assembler to turn alphabetic codes into the binary numbers of machine language, but in every other way it is identical to machine language.

High-level languages, such as COBOL, BASIC, and C++, are more like English and, therefore, easier to work with than either machine or assembly language. What's more, they generally can be transported between computers with a minimum of rewriting. Most modern languages encourage structured programming, a technique that involves combining subprograms using only the three fundamental control structures: sequence, selection, and repetition. Structured programming produces programs with fewer logic errors. Still, when program efficiency is critical, many programmers use languages such as C that enable them to work at a lower level of machine logic.

Many applications contain built-in macro languages, scripting languages, and query languages that put programming power in the hands of users. Query languages are representative of fourth-generation languages (4GLs), which are nonprocedural; that is, they enable the programmer to focus on defining the task rather than outlining the steps involved in accomplishing the task. Visual programming tools enable the programmer to use icons, drawing tools, menus, and dialog boxes to construct programs without writing code. Object-oriented programming (OOP) tools enable programmers to construct programs from objects with properties and provide the ability to send messages to each other. Aspect-oriented programming is a relatively new paradigm based on the concept of separation of concerns so that key features of each object are written as separate programs.

Programs are part of larger information systems. An information system has a life cycle that starts with the initial investigation of the problem; proceeds through analysis, design, development, and implementation phases; and lingers in an ongoing maintenance phase until the system is retired. A systems analyst manages a typical information system with the help of a team of programmers and other computer professionals. Systems analysts use a variety of tools and techniques to help them develop and manage systems, including data collection techniques and modeling tools.

Computer scientists are responsible for the software tools and concepts that make all other software development possible. Computer science focuses on the process of computing through several areas of specialization, including theory, algorithms, data structures, programming concepts and languages, computer architecture, management information systems, artificial intelligence, and software engineering.

One of the most challenging problems facing computer science is the problem of software reliability. Current software development techniques provide no assurance that a software system will function without failure under all circumstances. Because testing cannot prove that no bugs exist, software manufacturers cannot provide strong warranties for their products. Instead, computer users must accept the possibility that the programs they use may be less than 100 percent reliable. As more and more human institutions rely on computer systems, it becomes increasingly important for computer scientists to find ways to make software that people can trust.

Key Terms

algorithm ....(p. 511)
alpha testing..........................(p. 530)
applets..................................(p. 518)
aspect-oriented programming ....(p. 521)
assembler..............................(p. 517)
assembly language................(p. 517)
beta testing............................(p. 530)
C ....(p. 518)
C++......................................(p. 518)
coding ....(p. 514)
compiler...............................(p. 516)
component software ....(p. 524)
computer-aided systems engineering (CASE) ....(p. 536)
computer architecture............(p. 536)
computer science...................(p. 536)
control structures..................(p. 513)
data dictionary.......................(p. 538)
data flow diagram (DFD)......(p. 534)
data structure ....(p. 535)
decision table.........................(p. 535)
end user ....(p. 528)
end-user development............(p. 528)
fourth-generation language (4GL) ....(p. 523)
fifth-generation language (5GL) ....(p. 524)
high-level language ....(p. 517)
information system................(p. 527)
interpreter ....(p. 516)
Java ....(p. 518)
logic error ....(p. 516)
machine language..................(p. 516)
macro language ....(p. 523)
management information system (MIS) ....(p. 538)
module..................................(p. 519)
object-oriented programming (OOP) ....(p. 521)
program verification..............(p. 540)
programming ....(p. 511)
prototype...............................(p. 529)
prototyping ....(p. 529)
pseudocode............................(p. 511)
query language ....(p. 524)
scripting language ....(p. 523)
software engineering ....(p. 539)
stepwise refinement...............(p. 511)
structured programming ....(p. 519)
subprogram............................(p. 519)
syntax error............................(p. 516)
system flowchart....................(p. 534)
systems analyst......................(p. 528)
systems development.............(p. 527)
systems development life cycle (SDLC) ....(p. 528)
testing ....(p. 513)
top-down design ....(p. 511)
visual programming...............(p. 523)

Companion Website Projects

1. The *Digital Planet* Web site, **www.pearsonhighered.com/beekman**, contains self-test exercises related to this chapter. Follow the instructions for taking a quiz. After you've completed your quiz, you can email the results to your instructor.
2. The Web site also contains open-ended discussion questions called Internet Exercises. Discuss one or more of the Internet Exercises questions at the section for this chapter.

True or False

1. Programming is a form of problem solving.
2. The concept of algorithm is derived from the repetitive nature of machine language loops.
3. Assembly language and machine language are low-level languages.
4. Visual languages enable programmers to use icons, drawing tools, menus, and dialog boxes to construct programs without writing code.
5. Aspect-oriented programming is similar to techniques used in other disciplines to ensure that failure of one part of a system doesn't result in failures elsewhere.
6. Extreme programming is based on ideas derived from extreme sports: marathon coding sessions, solitary working conditions, and energy-boosting diets.
7. Prototyping is an interactive methodology in which the prototype is continually modified and improved until it meets the needs of the end users.
8. Programming for the cloud involves using techniques for dealing with deteriorating or failed network connections.
9. Software reliability has increased as the cost of developing computer software has increased.
10. Extreme programming is so named because of the extreme time and energy demands it places on programmers.

Multiple Choice

1. Which is not a typical part of programming today?
   a. Understanding and defining the problem
   b. Writing the computer language
   c. Devising, refining, and testing the algorithm
   d. Writing the program
   e. Testing and debugging the program
2. To turn a problem into an executable program, what must the programmer do?
   a. Create an algorithm outlining the steps necessary to solve the problem.
   b. Use a systems analyst to write code.
   c. Write a compiler for the problem.
   d. Translate pseudocode into an assembly language.
   e. All of the above
3. Machine language is not
   a. the native language of the computer.
   b. based on binary—strings of *0*s and *1*s.
   c. difficult to read and debug.
   d. commonly used today to write computer programs.
   e. usually displayed in decimal, hexadecimal, or another number system.
4. What do you call a program that translates a program's source code into machine language before the program is executed?
   a. Compiler
   b. Debugger
   c. Interpreter
   d. Analyzer
   e. Binarizer
5. High-level languages
   a. are mostly used for writing supercomputer applications.
   b. have, for most applications, been replaced by multi-level languages.
   c. are extremely platform specific, so that code written for one platform must be completely rewritten for other platforms.
   d. are designed for writing pseudocode.
   e. are easier to work with than either machine or assembly language.
6. In object-oriented programming (OOP),
   a. programmers generally assemble software objects using assembly language.
   b. coding is done in a dialect of C called Object C.
   c. the goal is to create robotic tools that can manipulate physical objects.
   d. programmers can build programs from prefabricated objects.
   e. All of the above
7. Which term best describes a query language that allows users to access a database with English-like questions?
   a. First-generation language
   b. Second-generation language
   c. Third-generation language
   d. Fourth-generation language
   e. Fifth-generation language
8. Which of the following is not true about software component tools?
   a. Users construct small custom applications from software components.
   b. They can be used only if applications are programmed to allow it.
   c. They may reverse the trend toward mega-applications.
   d. They are the logical extension of object-oriented programming.
   e. All of these statements are true.
9. Which of the following is not true about extreme programming?
   a. Programmers write large blocks of code rather than writing multiple small modules.
   b. The entire programming team takes responsibility for all of the code.
   c. Programmers work in pairs to write code.
   d. The programming team stays in close communication with customers and clients.
   e. The software development plan includes frequent releases of updated code.
10. Which is not a process in the classic systems development cycle?
    a. Prototyping the final solution using resources from parallel systems
    b. Investigating a situation
    c. Designing a system solution to improve the situation
    d. Acquiring resources to implement the solution
    e. Evaluating the success of the solution
11. Which implementation approach is most likely to cause problems if the new system doesn't work properly?
    a. Direct cutover
    b. Parallel
    c. Spiral
    d. Phase in
    e. Pilot

12. Modeling tools create graphic representations of a system, and include the
    a. system flowchart—a graphical depiction of the physical system.
    b. data flow diagram (DFD) illustrating the movement of data.
    c. data dictionary—a directory describing all the data flowing through a system.
    d. decision tables showing if-then rules that apply when conditions occur.
    e. All of these are system modeling tools.

13. Which branch of computer science is focused on producing more reliable software?
    a. Computer theory
    b. Programming languages
    c. Software engineering
    d. Computer architecture
    e. Algorithms

14. What additional problems does the programmer of a cloud-based application have to solve that the programmer of a desktop application does not?
    a. Telling devices which cell phone towers or Wi-Fi hubs to use
    b. Handling data that isn't always available or is constantly changing
    c. Dealing with condensation and lack of visibility
    d. Reading and writing from a hard drive
    e. Providing a graphical user interface

15. Which of these statements is true?
    a. Software companies could produce error-free products if they were willing to reduce profits.
    b. Some large software systems, such as Linux, contain no bugs.
    c. Software testing can prove the existence of bugs, but it cannot prove that the software is 100 percent bug-free.
    d. Techniques for producing bug-free software are used for critical military applications, but they're too expensive for most other applications.
    e. All of these statements are true.

Review Questions

1. Define or describe each of the key terms listed in the "Key Terms" section. Check your answers using the glossary.

2. Here's an algorithm for directions to a university bookstore from a downtown location:

```
Go north on 3rd Street to Jefferson
Street.

Turn left on Jefferson Street.

Proceed on Jefferson across the rail
road tracks and past the stoplight
to the booth at the campus entrance.

If there's somebody in the booth,
ask for a permit to park in the
bookstore parking lot; otherwise,
just keep going.

When you reach the bookstore parking
lot, keep circling the lot until you
find an empty space.

Park in the empty space.
```

   Find examples of sequence, selection, and repetition control structures in this algorithm.

3. Find examples of ambiguous statements that might keep the algorithm in Question 2 from working properly.

4. Assume that Robert, a driver, is going to do the driving in Question 2. Use stepwise refinement to add more detail to Question 2's algorithm so Robert has a better chance of understanding the instructions.

5. Design an algorithm to play the part of the guesser in the number-guessing game featured in this chapter. If you base your algorithm on the right strategy, it will always be able to guess the correct number in seven or fewer tries. (*Hint*: Computer scientists call the right strategy *binary search*.)

6. When does it make sense to design a custom program rather than use off-the-shelf commercial software? Give some examples.

7. Give examples of several different kinds of computer errors, and describe how these errors affect people.

8. Give some examples of challenges writing software for smart phones that are specific to smart phones. Give some examples of opportunities for smart phone programmers that aren't available to PC programmers.

9. What is the relationship between computer science and computer programming?

10. What is the difference between writing a program and designing an information system? How are they related?

Discussion Questions

1. Is programming a useful skill for a computer user? Why or why not?
2. Should programmers be licensed? Is programming a craft, a trade, or a profession?
3. Suppose you want to create a small business or nonprofit organization. What questions might a systems analyst ask when determining what kind of information systems the organization will need?
4. Do you think the free and open-source software movements make it more difficult for software developers to make a living? Why or why not?
5. Computer science is in the college of science at some universities and in the college of engineering at others. Is computer science a science, a branch of engineering, or both?
6. Why is it so difficult to produce error-free software?

Projects

1. Computers are often blamed for human errors. Find some recent examples of "the computer did it" stories or articles. For each example, try to determine whether the computer is, in fact, to blame.
2. Do research to discover what safeguards are used to ensure that automated teller machines don't malfunction and that their security can't be violated.
3. The uproar over the 2000 U.S. presidential election led many state and local governments to install electronic voting machines. Critics have suggested these machines may be less reliable than the systems they replaced. Research the advantages and disadvantages of different kinds of electronic voting systems in use today. How do they measure up to traditional voting machines, mail-in ballots, and other types of voting systems?
4. Many software programs for smart phones are given away for free or sold for just a few dollars. Research the economics of software development for smart phones. Who makes money? What pricing model works best for providing income for programmers? What platforms offer the most opportunity for small software development companies?

Sources and Resources

Books

As you might expect, there are hundreds of books on programming and computer science, most of which are specifically written about particular programming languages and platforms. Most of the books listed here are more general.

Head First Software Development: A Brain-Friendly Guide, by Dan Pilone and Russ Miles (O'Reilly). O'Reilly has a well-deserved reputation as a publisher of first-rate books for software developers, programmers, and techno-geeks. This is one of many popular books in their Head-First "Brain-Friendly" series. If you're interested in learning from the pros, you might find just what you're looking for here.

Learning to Program with Alice, by Wanda P. Dann, Stephen Cooper, and Randy Pausch (Prentice-Hall). This book teaches object-oriented programming using the Alice 2.0 software system developed at Carnegie-Mellon University. Instead of writing Java code, the Alice programmer uses a mouse to create animations in a 3-D world where every character is an object and every action is a method.

Extreme Programming Explained: Embrace Change, by Kent Beck (Addison-Wesley). This book, written by the owner of a software company, was largely responsible for the extreme programming movement.

Computer Science: An Overview, by J. Glenn Brookshear (Pearson Addison-Wesley). This excellent survey covers algorithms, data structures, operating systems, and software engineering from a current computer science perspective.

Algorithmics: The Spirit of Computing, by David Harel and Yishai Feldman (Addison-Wesley). This book explores the central ideas of computer science from basic algorithms and data structures to more advanced concepts.

The New Turing Omnibus: 66 Excursions in Computer Science, by A. K. Dewdney (Computer Science Press). This unusual book contains 66 short chapters covering a wide range of computer science topics, from algorithms to VLSI computers. Much of the material is technical and mathematical, but the writing is clear and engaging.

The Mythical Man-Month: Essays on Software Engineering, 20th Anniversary Edition, by Frederick P. Brooks, Jr. (Addison-Wesley). This classic, often-quoted book outlines clearly the problems of managing large software projects. This twentieth-anniversary edition includes four new chapters that provide an up-to-date perspective.

Computers Ltd: What They Really Can't Do, by David Harel (Oxford University Press). As the title suggests, this book explores the limits of computer power in particular and human knowledge in general.

Rescuing Prometheus: Four Monumental Projects That Changed Our World, by Thomas P. Hughes (Vintage Books). This book profiles four of the biggest technological projects of the previous century. These projects forced their developers to push the limits of systems design.

Out of Their Minds: The Lives and Discoveries of 15 Great Computer Scientists, by Dennis Shasha and Cathy Lazere (Springer). The people profiled in this book were responsible for many of the most important ideas in computer science today. The profiles illuminate their achievements through interviews and explanations; technical details are confined to boxes so they don't interrupt the flow of the human stories. Closing sections explore two questions: What do these people have in common, and where is the field of computer science heading in the next quarter century?

15

Is Artificial Intelligence Real?

OBJECTIVES

After you read this chapter you should be able to:

- Explain the two basic approaches of artificial intelligence research
- Describe several hard problems that artificial intelligence research has not yet been able to solve
- Describe several practical applications of artificial intelligence
- Explain what robots are and give several examples illustrating what they can—and can't—do
- Speculate about how our world might change as artificial intelligence technology progresses

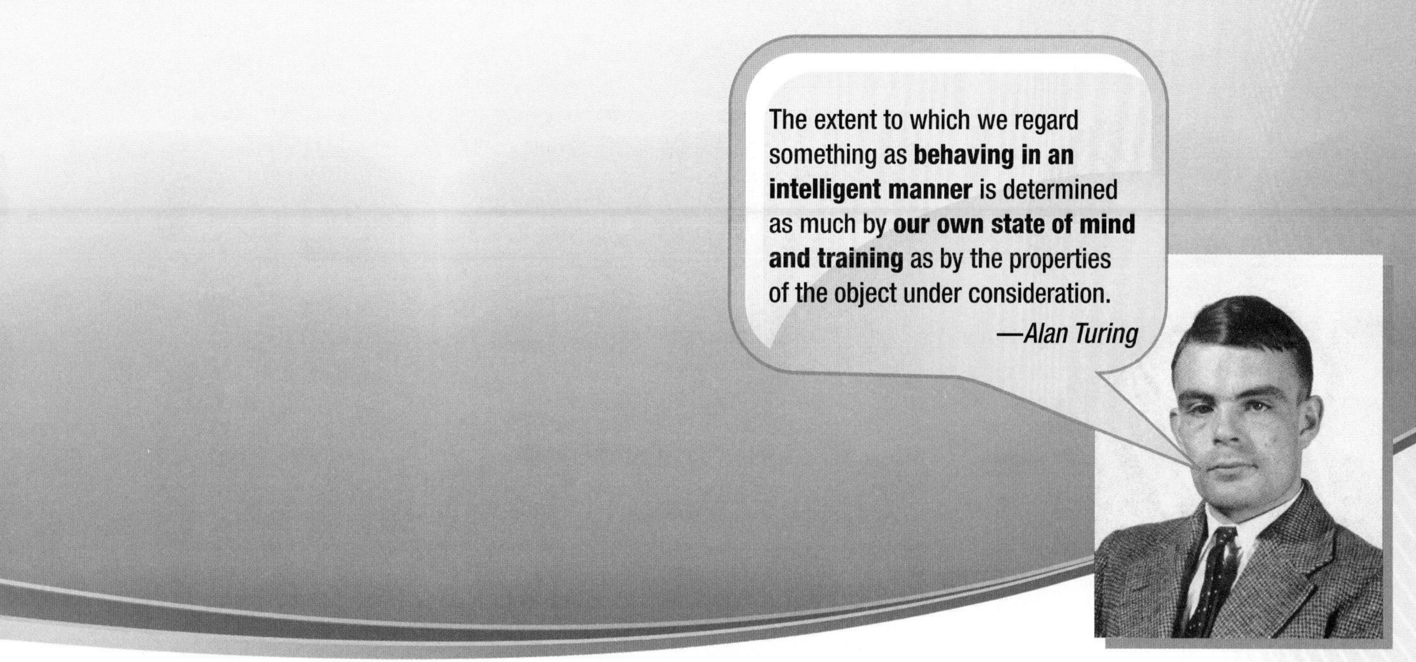

The extent to which we regard something as **behaving in an intelligent manner** is determined as much by **our own state of mind and training** as by the properties of the object under consideration.
—*Alan Turing*

Alan Turing, Military Intelligence, and Intelligent Machines

Alan M. Turing, the British mathematician who designed the world's first operational electronic digital computer during the 1940s, may have been the most important thinker in the history of computing. While a graduate student at Princeton in 1936, Turing published "On Computable Numbers," a paper that laid the theoretical groundwork for all of modern computer science. In that paper, he described a theoretical Turing machine that could read instructions from punched paper tape and perform all the critical operations of a computer. The paper also established the limits of computer science by mathematically demonstrating that some problems simply cannot be solved by any kind of computer.

After receiving his doctorate in 1938, Turing had an opportunity to translate theory into reality. Anticipating an invasion by Hitler's forces, the British government assembled a team of mathematicians and engineers with the top secret mission of cracking the German military code. Under the leadership of Turing and others, the group built Colossus, a single-purpose machine regarded by some as the first electronic digital computer. From the time Colossus was completed in 1943 until the end of the war, it successfully cracked Nazi codes—a fact concealed by the British government until long after the war ended. Many experts believe that Colossus was ultimately responsible for the defeat of the Nazis.

Turing effectively launched the field of artificial intelligence (AI) with a 1950 paper called "Computing Machinery and Intelligence." In this paper he proposed a concrete test for determining whether a machine was intelligent. In later years Turing championed the possibility of emulating human thought through computation. He even co-wrote the first chess-playing program.

Turing was an unconventional and extremely sensitive person. In 1952 he was professionally and socially devastated when he was arrested and injected with

FIGURE 15.1 Alan Turing (1913–1954).

FIGURE 15.2 Colossus, 1945. (Source: Courtesy of The Computer History Museum.)

hormones for violation of British antihomosexuality laws. The 41-year-old genius apparently committed suicide in 1954, years before the government made his wartime heroics public. More than a half century after his death, Turing's work still has relevance to computer scientists, mathematicians, and philosophers. It's impossible to know what he might have contributed had he lived another three decades. ■

Alan Turing spent much of his short life trying to answer the question "Can machines think?" That's still a central question of **artificial intelligence (AI)**, the field of computer science devoted to making computers perceive, reason, and act in ways that have, until now, been reserved for human beings. But today even those who believe that computers can't "think" have to admit that AI research has produced impressive results: computers that can communicate in human languages; systems that can provide instant expertise in medicine, science, finance, and other fields; world-class electronic chess players; self-driving cars; and robots that can outperform humans in a variety of tasks. In this chapter, we explore the technology, applications, and implications of artificial intelligence.

Thinking About Thinking Machines

> What is intelligence, anyway? It is only a word that people use to name those unknown processes with which our brains solve problems we call hard. But whenever you learn a skill yourself, you're less impressed or mystified when other people do the same. This is why the meaning of "intelligence" seems so elusive: It describes not some definite thing but only **the momentary horizon of our ignorance about how minds might work**.
>
> —*Marvin Minsky, AI pioneer*

If you ask 10 people to define intelligence, you're likely to get 10 different answers, including some of these:

- The ability to learn from experience
- The power of thought
- The ability to reason
- The ability to perceive relations
- The power of insight

- The ability to use tools
- Intuition

Intelligence is difficult to define and understand, even for philosophers and psychologists who spend their lives studying it. But this elusive quality is, to many people, the characteristic that sets humans apart from other species. So it's not surprising that controversy has continually swirled around the questions "Can a machine be intelligent?" and "Can a machine think?"

Can Machines Think?

> A machine may be deemed intelligent when it can **pass for a human being in a blind test**.
>
> —*Alan Turing*

In his landmark 1950 paper, Alan Turing suggested that the question "Can machines think?" was too vague and philosophical to be of any value. To make it more concrete, he proposed an "imitation game." The **Turing test**, as it came to be known, involves two people and a computer. One person, the interrogator, sits alone in a room and types questions into a computer terminal. The questions can be about anything—math, science, politics, sports, entertainment, art, human relationships, emotions—anything. As answers to questions appear on the terminal, the interrogator attempts to guess whether those answers were typed by the other person or generated by the computer. By repeatedly fooling interrogators into thinking it is a person, a computer can demonstrate intelligent behavior. If it acts intelligently, according to Turing, it is intelligent.

Turing did not intend this test to be the only way to demonstrate machine intelligence; he pointed out that a machine could fail and still be intelligent. Even so, Turing believed that machines would be able to pass his test by the turn of the century. So far, no computer has come close, in spite of nearly 60 years of AI research. While some people still cling to the Turing test to define artificial intelligence, most AI researchers favor less stringent definitions.

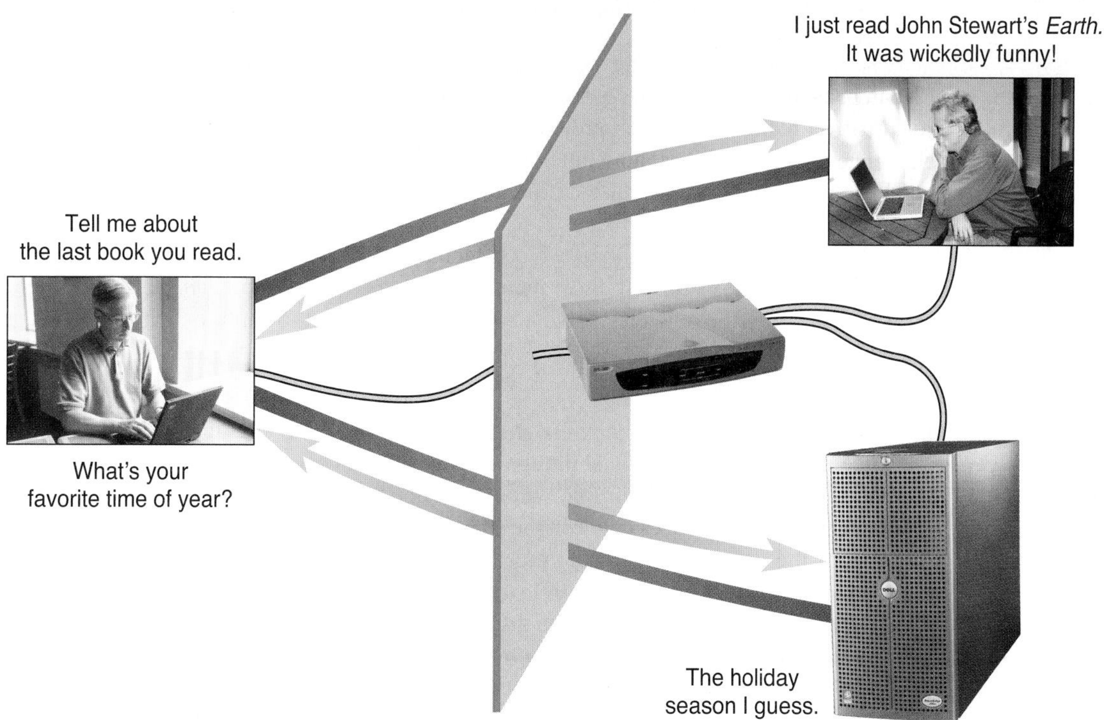

FIGURE 15.3 In the Turing test, a human interpreter has instant-messaging-style conversations with two contestants and tries to determine which contestant is human, based on the answers given.

What Is Artificial Intelligence?

> Artificial intelligence is the study of ideas that enable computers to do the **things that make people seem intelligent**.
>
> —*Patrick Henry Winston, in* Artificial Intelligence

This definition from a 1977 edition of a textbook is similar to definitions that commonly appear in today's popular press. This type of definition captures the general idea of artificial intelligence, but it breaks down when applied to specific examples. Does AI include doing lightning-fast calculations? Finding a word in a dictionary as fast as a person can type it? Remembering hundreds of telephone numbers at a time? If a person could do all of these things, that person would "seem intelligent." But these activities aren't good examples of artificial intelligence because they're trivial for computers. In fact, many computer scientists believe that if it's easy to do with a computer, it can't be artificial intelligence. Here's a more recent textbook definition that reflects that point of view:

> Artificial intelligence is the study of how to make computers do things at which, **at the moment, people are better**.
>
> —*Elaine Rich, in* Artificial Intelligence

According to this definition, artificial intelligence is a moving frontier. The short history of the field bears this out. In the 1950s many AI researchers struggled to create computers that could play checkers and chess. Today computers can beat the best human players, and relatively few AI researchers study these games. In the words of one researcher, artificial intelligence is "whatever hasn't been done yet." Moving-frontier definitions of AI tend to be accurate, but they're short on specifics. A more concrete and complete definition might combine Rich's definition with this one from a more recent edition of Winston's textbook:

> Artificial intelligence is the study of the computations that make it possible to **perceive, reason, and act**.
>
> —*Patrick Henry Winston, in* Artificial Intelligence

Perceive, *reason*, and *act* are words used more commonly in psychology, the science of human behavior, than in computer science. In fact, psychologists work alongside computer scientists on many AI research projects. Computer scientists tend to be motivated by the challenge of producing machine intelligence for its own sake. Psychologists, on the other hand, are interested in AI because it provides new insights into natural intelligence and the workings of the human brain.

These points of view symbolize two common approaches to AI. One approach attempts to use computers to simulate human mental processes. For example, an AI expert might ask people to describe how they solve a problem and attempt to capture their answers in a software model.

The simulation approach has three inherent problems:

- Most people have trouble knowing and describing how they do things. Human intelligence includes unconscious thoughts, instantaneous insights, and other mental processes that are difficult or impossible to understand and describe.
- There are vast differences between the structure and capabilities of the human brain and those of the computer. Even the most powerful supercomputers can't approach the brain's ability to perform **parallel processing**—breaking a complex job into many smaller, simpler jobs and completing those jobs simultaneously.
- The best way to do something with a machine is often very different from the way people would do it. Before the Wright brothers, dozens of inventors failed to produce flying machines because they tried to make their inventions imitate birds. Similarly, many early AI attempts failed because they were designed to mimic human intelligence rather than to take advantage of the computer's unique capabilities.

The second, more common, approach to AI involves designing intelligent machines independent of the way people think. According to this approach, human intelligence is just one possible kind of intelligence. A machine's method of solving a problem might be different from the human method, but no less intelligent.

Whichever approach they take, scientists face problems that are difficult and far too complex to solve all at once. Most AI researchers choose to break those problems into smaller problems that are easier to solve—to create programs that can function intelligently when confined to limited *domains*.

FIGURE 15.4 Many early flying machines that imitated birds never got off the ground.

Opening Games

One of the first popular domains for AI research was the checkerboard. Much early AI work focused on games such as checkers and chess because they were easy to represent in the computer's digital memory, they had clearly defined rules, and the goals were unmistakable. Instead of struggling with nebulous issues surrounding thought and intelligence, game researchers could focus on the concrete question "How can I create a program that wins consistently?" Their answers included many AI techniques that are still used today in a variety of applications:

- *Searching.* One way to win a game is through **searching**—looking ahead at the possibilities generated by each potential move: "I have four possible moves—A, B, C, and D. If I do A, then my opponent might do X, Y, or Z. If my opponent responds by doing X, then I can do E, F, G, or H...and so on." Obviously, high-speed computers are better at this kind of repetitive processing than people are. Early AI programs could not check all possible decision points in a complicated game such as checkers, which has approximately 10^{21} choices. Today's powerful computers can perform massive database searches quickly, making this kind of look-ahead searching practical for some game-playing programs. Researcher Jonathan Schaeffer's checkers-playing program uses an enormous database of board positions to evaluate every move. The program plays as well as the best human players in the world. It uses what's known as a ***brute-force*** technique—rapidly repeating a simple operation until it finds an answer. This kind of exhaustive searching doesn't fit many definitions of intelligence. For more complex games such as chess, and for most domains outside the world of games, the staggering number of decision points makes brute-force searching impractical. So searching is generally guided by a planned strategy and by rules known as heuristics.
- *Heuristics.* A **heuristic** is a rule of thumb. Unlike hard-and-fast algorithms, heuristics guide us toward judgments that experience tells us are likely to be true. In everyday life we apply heuristics such as "To loosen a stuck jar lid, run warm water over it." A checkers-playing program might employ a heuristic that says, "Keep checkers in the king's row as long as possible."
- *Pattern recognition.* The best human chess and checkers players remember thousands of critical board patterns and know the best strategies for playing when those or similar patterns appear. Game-playing programs recognize recurring patterns, too, but not nearly as well as people do. Computer players often have trouble identifying situations that are similar but not identical. Pattern recognition is probably the single biggest advantage a human game player has over a computer opponent; it helps compensate for the computer's speed and thoroughness at searching ahead.
- *Machine learning.* The best game-playing programs learn from experience using **machine learning** techniques. If a move pays off, a learning program is more likely to use that move (or similar moves) in future games. If a move results in a loss, the program will remember to avoid similar moves.

Today computer systems can hold their own against the best human chess players by examining hundreds of thousands of moves per second. When IBM's Deep Blue, a

FIGURE 15.5 Crowds watched in disbelief when Deep Blue, the IBM supercomputer, beat world chess champion Garry Kasarov in 1997 (top). Since then, AI has been built into computer opponents in many games including Black and White (bottom).

customized RS/6000 SP supercomputer, beat grand master Garry Kasparov in a 1997 rematch, people all around the world watched with a level of interest that's seldom given to scientific work. Many of today's best computer games use similar technology, on a smaller scale, to create artificial opponents for gamers.

Still, most AI researchers have moved on to more interesting and practical applications. But whether working on vision, speech, problem solving, or expert decision making, researchers still use the successful strategy of game researchers—to restrict the domain of their programs so that problems are small enough to understand and solve. We'll see how this strategy has paid off in several important areas of AI, starting with natural-language communication.

Natural-Language Communication

> Language is no less complex or subtle a phenomenon than **the knowledge it seeks to transmit**.
>
> —*Raymond Kurzweil, in* The Age of Intelligent Machines

In Turing's classic test of machine intelligence, the computer is considered to be intelligent if it can successfully pose as a person in a typed conversation. Scientists have long dreamed of machines that could communicate in natural languages such as English,

Russian, and Japanese. Over the years **natural-language** communication has continually challenged researchers. Many problems relate to recognizing and reproducing human speech—issues we deal with later in the chapter. But even when it's typed directly into the machine, natural-language text poses significant software challenges.

Machine Translation Traps

One early project attempted to create a program that could translate scientific papers from Russian to English and from English to Russian. **Automatic translation** offered hope for increased communication between scientists during the tense Cold War years. The method seemed straightforward and foolproof: A **parsing program** (or **parser**) would analyze sentence structure and identify each word according to whether it was a subject, verb, or other part of speech; another program would look up each word in a translation dictionary and substitute the appropriate word.

This word-by-word approach to machine translation failed. In one famous anecdote, scientists asked the computer to translate English into Russian and then translate the results back into English. As the story goes, "The spirit is willing, but the flesh is weak" came back as "The wine is agreeable, but the meat is rotten" and "out of sight, out of mind" became "blind and insane" or "invisible idiot."

After this setback, scientists concluded that translation without understanding is impossible. The next generation of machine-translation systems were based on the idea that the computer should extract the meaning from the original text. Once the computer understood the meaning, it could express that meaning in a variety of languages. Unfortunately, this approach turned out to be impractical. Understanding the meaning of any sentence requires a huge amount of knowledge about the world.

Today many computer scientists are taking a statistical approach to machine translation. The idea is to provide a program with many positive examples of correctly translated sentences, as well as many negative examples of incorrect translations. The program uses a machine-learning algorithm to infer the correct rules of translation. With this approach, the system imitates successful translations without really understanding what the words mean.

A variety of automatic translation programs are currently available. One of these programs is Babel Fish (named for the universal translator fish in Douglas Adams's *Hitchhiker's Guide to the Galaxy*) jointly developed by AltaVista and SYSTRAN and now part of Yahoo! To illustrate the capabilities and limitations of contemporary machine translation, we've used Babel Fish to translate a paragraph from this chapter into Spanish and back into English.

Two native Spanish speakers said the Babel Fish translation was understandable but contained minor errors in most sentences. For example, Babel Fish

Original English Text:

Some of the first successful expert systems were developed around medical knowledge bases. Because medical knowledge is orderly and well documented, researchers believed it could be captured successfully in knowledge bases. They were right. The MYCIN medical expert system outperformed many human experts in diagnosing diseases. Dozens of other working medical expert systems exist, although few are actually used in medical practice.

Machine Translation into Spanish:

Algunos de los primeros sistemas expertos acertados fueron desarrollados alrededor de bases de conocimiento médicas. Porque el conocimiento médico es ordenado y documentado bien, los investigadores creyeron que podría ser capturado con éxito en bases de conocimiento. Tenían razón. El sistema experto médico de MYCIN superó a muchos expertos humanos en enfermedades que diagnosticaban. Las docenas de otros sistemas expertos médicos del funcionamiento existen, aunque pocos se utilizan realmente en práctica médica.

Machine Translation of Translated Text Back into English:

Some of the first guessed right expert systems were developed around medical knowledge bases. Because the medical knowledge is ordered and documented well, the investigators thought that he could be captured successfully in knowledge bases. They were right. The medical expert system of MYCIN surpassed to many human experts in diseases that they diagnosed. The dozens of other medical expert systems of the operation exist, although few are really used in medical practice.

FIGURE 15.6 The Babel Fish program translated a paragraph from this chapter from English into Spanish, then back into English. You can test Babel Fish's capabilities by visiting http://babelfish.yahoo.com.

FIGURE 15.7 Electronic translation smart phone apps serve world travelers by providing instant access to common words, short phrases, and simple sentences.

should have translated "successful" as "exitosos," not "acertados." The Spanish phrase "es ordenado y documentado bien" should have been rendered "está bien ordenado y documentado." One reviewer said the errors were similar to the errors made by an English speaker who has taken one or two years of Spanish classes.

As evidence that Babel Fish does not actually understand the meaning of the sentences it manipulates, consider its translation of the Spanish paragraph back into English. The resulting sentences contain many phrases that would not be uttered by anyone who really understood English.

The paragraph we asked Babel Fish to translate was relatively unambiguous and straightforward. It was simple prose, not poetry. It contained few technical terms and no idioms. Babel Fish responded by producing a translation that was imperfect but for the most part understandable.

The translation might have been more accurate if we'd used software that specialized in a particular subject area such as travel, cooking, or photography. In general, the narrower the subject matter, the more reliable the translation. That is why automatic translation for specific domains (such as travel) is easier than automatic translation of arbitrary sentences. It's amazing that a computer program can produce a reasonable translation of English to Spanish or French to German without actually understanding the meaning of the sentences, but that's the reality of machine translation today.

Conversation without Communication

Similar lessons emerged from Joseph Weizenbaum's work with ELIZA, one of the first software programs to converse in a limited form of natural language. Weizenbaum, an MIT professor, designed ELIZA in the 1960s to simulate the role of a therapist in a typed conversation with a patient. A sample ELIZA session appears on the facing page (the computer's responses are capitalized).

As impressive as this dialogue seems, there's no understanding here. ELIZA uses a few simple tricks to *simulate* understanding, including recognizing a few key words (such as *mother*), identifying categories for some of those words (*family*), and repeating phrases from earlier in the conversation. But ELIZA's tricks are far from foolproof. In response to "Necessity is the mother of invention," ELIZA might say, "Tell me more about your family." An ELIZA session can easily deteriorate into nonsense dialogue laced with grammatical errors and inappropriate responses. Clearly, ELIZA lacks the understanding to pass as a human in a Turing test.

Nonsense and Common Sense

> Bill sings to Sarah, Sarah sings to Bill. Perhaps they will do other dangerous things together. They may eat lamb or stroke each other. They may chant of their difficulties and their happiness. **They have love but they also have typewriters. That is interesting**.
>
> —*A poem by RACTER, in* The Policeman's Beard Is Half Constructed, *programmed by William Chamberlain and Thomas Etter*

Years after ELIZA's creation, this poetry appeared in *The Policeman's Beard Is Half Constructed*, the first book ever written by a computer. RACTER, like ELIZA, produced English language output without really understanding it. Why do machines that flawlessly follow instructions written in BASIC, C++, and other computer languages have so much trouble with *natural-language* communications?

Part of the problem is the massive vocabulary of natural languages. A typical computer language has less than a hundred key words, each with a precise, unambiguous meaning.

Men are all alike.
IN WHAT WAY
They're always bugging us about something or other.
CAN YOU THINK OF A SPECIFIC EXAMPLE
Well, my boyfriend made me come here.
YOUR BOYFRIEND MADE YOU COME HERE
He says I'm depressed much of the time.
I AM SORRY TO HEAR YOU ARE DEPRESSED
It's true. I am unhappy.
DO YOU THINK COMING HERE WILL HELP YOU NOT TO BE UNHAPPY
I need some help, that much seems certain.
WHAT WOULD IT MEAN TO YOU IF YOU GOT SOME HELP
Perhaps I could learn to get along with my mother.
TELL ME MORE ABOUT YOUR FAMILY
My mother takes care of me.
WHO ELSE IN YOUR FAMILY TAKES CARE OF YOU
My father.
YOUR FATHER
You are like my father in some ways.
WHAT RESEMBLANCE DO YOU SEE
You are not very aggressive but I think you don't want me to notice that.
WHAT MAKES YOU THINK I AM NOT VERY AGGRESSIVE
You don't argue with me.
WHY DO YOU THINK I DON'T ARGUE WITH YOU
You are afraid of me.
DOES IT PLEASE YOU TO BELIEVE I AM AFRAID OF YOU
My father is afraid of everybody.
WHAT ELSE COMES TO MIND WHEN YOU THINK OF YOUR FATHER
Bullies.
DOES THAT HAVE ANYTHING TO DO WITH THE FACT THAT YOUR BOYFRIEND MADE YOU COME HERE
From *Computer Power and Human Reason*, by Joseph Weizenbaum.

FIGURE 15.8 A conversation with ELIZA.

English, in contrast, contains hundreds of thousands of words, many of which have multiple meanings. Of course, a person or a machine doesn't need to understand every word in the dictionary to communicate successfully in English. Most natural-language processors work with a *subset* of the language. But as the early scientific translation efforts showed, restricting vocabulary isn't enough.

Every language has a **syntax**—a set of rules for constructing sentences from words. In a programming language, the syntax rules are exact and unambiguous. Natural-language parsing programs have to deal with rules that are vague, ambiguous, and occasionally contradictory. One early parser, when asked to analyze the sentence "Time flies like an arrow," replied with several possible interpretations, including one statement with time as the subject, another statement with flies as the subject, and two commands in which the reader was the subject!

Still, computers are far more successful dealing with natural-language syntax than with **semantics**—the underlying meaning of words and phrases. In natural language the meaning of a sentence is ambiguous unless it's considered in context. "The hens were ready to eat" means one thing if it follows "The farmer approached the hen house" and something else if it follows "The chef approached the oven." To make matters worse, human conversations are filled with idiomatic expressions ("Susan had a cow when she heard the news") and unspoken assumptions about the world or specific subject matter ("Catch the T at Harvard Square and take it to MIT"). In short, the computer lacks what we call *common sense*—the wealth of knowledge and understanding about the world that people share.

The most successful natural-language applications limit the *domain* so that virtually all relevant information can be fed to the system. If the domain—the "world"—is small enough and the rules of that world are clear and unambiguous, a computer can have "common sense" that makes natural-language communication possible. For example, many database query languages accept and understand English commands but only within a narrow range. The biggest market for natural-language processing today is language translation—the same market that produced AI's first major failure. Several Web sites offer on-the-fly translation of text files or Web pages. (You've already seen a translation by Babel Fish.) Translation programs still can't translate books or conversations flawlessly, but they can greatly increase the productivity of people who translate technical manuals and other works that focus on narrow domains.

Without genuine understanding, computers are simply incapable of having meaningful conversations with humans. In 1990 Hugh Loebner established a $100,000 prize for the first computer program to pass the Turing test and a smaller prize for the "most humanlike" entrant each year. Every year, organizers host a competition attracting entrants from around the world. Judges sit in front of PCs connected by a network to the contestants in another room. Most of the contestants are computers, but two of them are humans. After having an instant-message-style conversation with each contestant, a judge gives the contestant a score ranging from 1 (definitely a machine) to 5 (definitely a human). So far, no machine has won the big prize. Here's a short sample of a conversation between a judge and Ultra Hal, the most humanlike entrant in 2007:

```
Judge: are you a robot?
Hal: I am a human.
Judge: no way. prove it.
Hal: Not now? Okay. Why do people continue to date boyfriends or
girlfriends who treat them badly?
Judge: does your boyfriend treat you badly?
Hal: Monopolies can treat customers badly and get away with it.
Judge: did you read my question?
Hal: This test is inspired by the ';Imitation Game'; where a man
and a woman go into separate rooms, and guests try to tell them
apart by writing a series of questions.
Judge: Quite true.
Hal: Are men happiest clawing their way up the corporate ladder?
Judge: I don't know. Are you a corporate worker?
Hal: Is it a good idea to get emotionally involved with a fellow
worker?
Judge: hdo you know anyone who has done that?
Hal: I like your imagery.
Judge: thanks. what is imagery?
Hal: Imagery: the ability to form mental images of things or
events. Imagination, imaging, mental imagery. 'he could still
hear her in his imagination'.
Judge: ddo you ride bikes?
Hal: I like to drive cars, but I tend to ride the subway in nyc.
Judge: thave you ever dating someone you work with?
Hal: I work for nbc as a network technician. They pay my bills.
Judge: indeed. how much money do you make?
Hal: I spend enough time answering questions like that at work.
```

FIGURE 15.9 A conversation with Zabaware's Ultra Hal, the "most humanlike" entrant in the 2007 Loebner Prize Competition.

It's not surprising that the judges weren't fooled by Ultra Hal. Like other entrants, the program has nowhere near enough knowledge of the real world to carry on an intelligent conversation. No computer seems likely to win a Turing test any time soon.

Natural-language processing relates to other AI technologies discussed later in the chapter. Speech recognition and optical character recognition provide input to natural-language systems, freeing the human communicator from the keyboard. On the output side, speech synthesis allows the computer to talk back in English or another language. But natural-language input and output are meaningless without a knowledge base that allows the computer to understand the ideas behind the words.

Knowledge Bases and Expert Systems

> The computer can't tell you the emotional story. It can give you the exact mathematical design, **but what's missing is the eyebrows.**
>
> —*Frank Zappa*

A preschool child can take you on a tour of the neighborhood, explaining how people use every building, describing the interconnected lives of every person you meet, and answering questions about anything you see along the way. A computer at city hall can give you facts and figures about building materials and assessed values of houses, but it can't provide you with a fraction of the knowledge conveyed in the child's tour. The human brain, which isn't particularly good at storing and recalling facts, excels at manipulating *knowledge*—information that incorporates the *relationships* among facts. Computers, on the other hand, are better at handling data than knowledge. Nobody knows exactly how the brain stores and manipulates knowledge. But AI researchers have developed, and continue to develop, techniques for representing knowledge in computers.

Knowledge Bases

While a database contains only facts, a **knowledge base** also contains a system of rules for determining and changing the relationship among those facts. Facts stored in a database are rigidly organized in categories; ideas stored in a knowledge base can be reorganized as new information changes their relationships.

Computer scientists so far have had little success in developing a knowledge base that can understand the world the way a child does. Even before they start school, children know these things:

- If you put something in water, it will get wet.
- If Susan is Mark's sister, Mark is Susan's brother.
- You can't build a tower from the top down.
- Dogs commonly live in houses, but cows seldom do.
- People can't walk through walls.
- If you eat dinner in a restaurant, you're expected to pay for the food and leave a tip.
- If you travel from Dallas to Phoenix, time passes during the trip.

These statements are part of the mass of commonsense knowledge that children acquire from living in the world. Because computers can't draw on years of human experience to construct mental models of the world, they don't automatically develop common sense. Much AI research centers on providing computers with ways to acquire and store real-world, commonsense knowledge. Researchers have had little success at developing computer systems with the kinds of broad, shallow knowledge found in children. But when knowledge bases are restricted to narrow, deep domains—the domains of experts—they can be effective, practical, intelligent tools. For example, knowledge bases lie at the heart of hundreds of expert systems used in business, science, and industry.

Artificial Experts

An expert is one who knows **more and more about less and less.**
—*Nicholas Murray Butler*

As the quote suggests, an expert is someone who has an extraordinary amount of knowledge within a narrow domain. By confining activities to that domain, the expert achieves mastery. An **expert system** is a software program designed to replicate the decision-making process of a human expert. At the foundation of every expert system is a knowledge base representing ideas from a specific field of expertise. Because it's a collection of specialized knowledge, an expert system's knowledge base must be constructed by a user, an expert, or a knowledge engineer—a specialist who interviews and observes experts and painstakingly converts their words and actions into a knowledge base. Some new expert systems can grow their own knowledge bases while observing human decision makers doing their jobs. But for most expert systems, the process is still human intensive.

Strictly speaking, expert systems derive their knowledge from experts; systems that draw on other sources, such as government regulations, company guidelines, and statistical databases, are called knowledge-based systems. But in practice, the terms *expert system* and *knowledge-based system* are often used interchangeably.

A knowledge base commonly represents knowledge in the form of if-then rules such as these:

- If the engine will not turn over and the lights do not work, then check the battery.
- If checking the battery shows it is not dead, then check the battery connectors.

Most human decision making involves uncertainty, so many modern expert systems are based on fuzzy logic. ***Fuzzy logic*** allows conclusions to be stated as probabilities (for example, "There's a 70 percent chance ...") rather than certainties. Here's an example from MYCIN, one of the first expert systems designed to capture a doctor's expertise:

```
If (1) the infection is primary bacteremia, and
(2) the site of the culture is one of the sterile sites, and
(3) the suspected portal of entry of the organism is the
gastrointestinal tract, then there is suggestive evidence
(0.7) that the identity of the organism is bacteriodes.
```

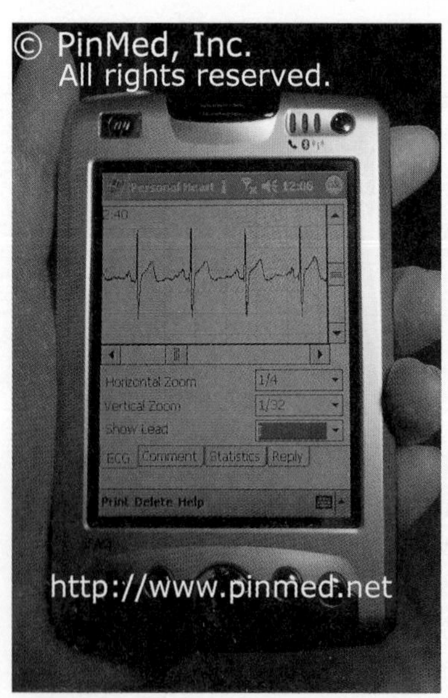

FIGURE 15.10 An expert system inside the FocalPoint scanner allows it to identify signs of cervical cancer.

Along with the knowledge base, a complete expert system also includes a human interface, which enables the user to interact with the system, and an inference engine, which puts the user input together with the knowledge base, applies logical principles, and produces the requested expert advice.

Sometimes expert systems aid experts by providing automated data analysis and informed second opinions. In other cases, expert systems support nonexperts by providing advice based on judgments of one or more experts. Whatever their role, expert systems work because they function within narrow, carefully defined domains.

Expert Systems in Action

Some of the first successful expert systems were developed around medical knowledge bases. Because medical knowledge is orderly and well documented, researchers believed it could be captured successfully in knowledge bases. They were right. The MYCIN medical expert system outperformed many human experts in diagnosing diseases. Hundreds of other working medical expert systems exist.

The business community has been more enthusiastic than the medical community has in its acceptance and use of expert systems. Here are a few examples of expert systems in action:

- The Microsoft Windows Help software provides advice, suggestions, and solutions for common problems and errors, based on the knowledge of Microsoft's technical experts.

- The STD Wizard is a Web site that asks a series of questions and determines which test, vaccinations, and evaluations are recommended related to sexually transmitted diseases. STD Wizard draws its expertise from guidelines from the Centers for Disease Control and Prevention.
- American Express uses an expert system to automate the process of checking for fraud and misuses of its no-limit credit card. Credit checks must be completed within 90 seconds while the customer waits, and the cost of an error can be high. The company spent 13 months developing a system modeled on the decision-making expertise of its best credit clerks.
- At Blue Cross/Blue Shield of Virginia, an expert system automates insurance claim processing. The expert system handles up to 200 routine claims each day, allowing human clerks to spend more time on tough situations that require human judgment. The developers of the system extracted diagnostic rules from manuals and watched human claims processors apply those rules.
- Boeing Company factory workers use an expert system to locate the right parts, tools, and techniques for assembling airplane electrical connectors. The system replaces 20,000 pages of documentation and reduces the average search time from 42 to 5 minutes.

There are hundreds of other examples of expert system applications: pinpointing likely sites for new oil explorations, aiding in automobile and appliance repairs, providing financial management advice, targeting direct-mail marketing campaigns, detecting problems in computer-controlled machinery, predicting weather, advising air traffic controllers, suggesting basic page layouts for publishers, controlling military machinery, providing assistance to musical composers. . . . The list is growing at an astounding rate. You can even think of the grammar checkers built into many word processors as expert systems because they apply style and syntax rules developed by language experts. Expert systems are available on the Web for doing everything from classifying whales and insects to conducting sophisticated Web searches.

FIGURE 15.11 Harold Cohen's AARON produces drawings such as the image above. In the photo below, Cohen demonstrates AARON to curious onlookers.

One of the most unusual expert systems is AARON, an automated artist programmed by Harold Cohen, artist and professor at the University of California at San Diego. AARON uses more than 1,000 rules of human anatomy and behavior to create drawings of people, plants, and abstract objects with a robotic drawing machine. The drawings, which are unique works in a style similar to Cohen's, are widely acclaimed in the art community. A version of AARON is now available as a PC screen saver; it fills idle time on the PC by drawing original art on the screen.

When AARON creates a drawing, an interesting question arises: Who is the artist, Cohen or AARON? Cohen claims he is; he sees AARON as a dynamic work of art. The question may seem frivolous, but it's related to a larger question with profound implications: When expert systems make decisions, who's responsible? If a doctor uses an expert system to decide to perform surgery and the surgery fails, who's liable—the doctor, the programmer, the software company, or somebody else? If you're denied medical benefits because of a bug in an expert system, do you sue a person, an organization, or a program? If a power plant explodes because an expert system fails to detect a fault, who's to blame? As expert systems proliferate, questions such as these are certain to confront consumers, lawyers, lawmakers, and technicians.

Expert Systems in Perspective

Expert systems offer many advantages. An expert system can:

- Help train new employees
- Reduce the number of human errors in a complex task
- Take care of routine tasks so workers can focus on more challenging jobs
- Provide expertise when no experts are available
- Preserve the knowledge of experts after those experts leave an organization
- Combine the knowledge of several experts
- Make knowledge available to more people

But expert systems aren't without problems. For one, today's expert systems are difficult to build. To simplify the process, many software companies sell **expert system shells**—generic expert systems containing human interfaces and inference engines. These programs can save time and effort, but they don't include the part that is most difficult to build—the knowledge base.

Even with a knowledge base, an expert system isn't the machine equivalent of a human expert. Unlike human experts, automated expert systems are poor at planning strategies. Their lack of flexibility makes them less creative than human thinkers. Most important, expert systems are powerless outside of their narrow, deep domains of knowledge. While most expert system domains can be summarized with a few hundred tidy rules of thumb, the world of people is full of inconsistencies, special cases, and ambiguities that could overwhelm even the best expert systems. A simple rule such as "birds can fly" isn't sufficient for a literal-minded computer, which would need something more like this tongue-in-cheek rule from Marvin Minsky's book, *Society of Mind*:

> *Birds can fly, unless they are penguins and ostriches, or if they happen to be dead, or have broken wings, or are confined to cages, or have their feet stuck in cement, or have undergone experiences so dreadful as to render them psychologically incapable of flight.*

Clearly, knowledge engineers can't use rules to teach computers all they need to know to perform useful, intelligent functions outside narrow domains. If they're ever going to exhibit the kind of broad-based intelligence found in children, AI systems need to acquire knowledge by reading, looking, listening, and drawing their own conclusions about the world. These skills all depend on techniques of pattern recognition.

Pattern Recognition: Making Sense of the World

> Experience has shown that science frequently develops most fruitfully once we learn to **examine the things that seem the simplest, instead of those that seem the most mysterious**.
>
> —*Marvin Minsky*

A baby can recognize a human face, especially its mother's, almost from birth. A mother can hear and recognize her child's cry even in a noisy room. Computers are notoriously inferior at both of these tasks, which fall into the general category of pattern recognition. **Pattern recognition** involves identifying recurring patterns in input data with the goal of understanding or categorizing that input.

Pattern recognition applications represent half of the AI industry. Applications include face identification, fingerprint identification, handwriting recognition, scientific data analysis, weather forecasting, biological slide analysis, surveillance satellite data analysis, robot vision, optical character recognition, automatic voice recognition, and expert systems. We next examine the problems and the promise of several types of pattern recognition, starting with the recognition of visual patterns.

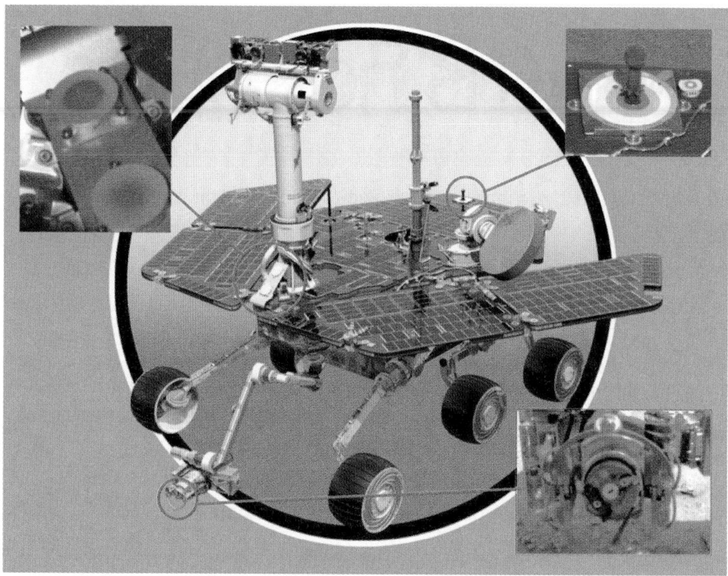

FIGURE 15.12 The Mars rover robot on the left is equipped with visual and tactile sensors that employ pattern-recognition technology. The robot on the right, a mascot for the Beijing Olympics, used sensors to move about the Beijing Capital International Airport and interact with visitors.

Image Analysis

Image analysis is the process of identifying objects and shapes in a photograph, drawing, video, or other visual image. It's used for everything from autofocusing cameras on human faces to piloting cruise missiles. An effortless process for people, image analysis is demanding for computers. The simple process of identifying objects in a scene is complicated by all kinds of factors: masses of irrelevant data, objects that partially cover other objects, indistinct edges, changes in light sources and shadows, changes in the scene as objects move, and more. With all of these complications, it's amazing that people are able to make any sense out of the images that constantly bombard their eyes.

Until recently, image analysis programs required massive amounts of memory and processing power. But today's computers are capable of running image-processing software with practical applications. For example, security programs enable PCs with video cameras to recognize faces of valid users with a high degree of reliability.

Today's software can't hold a candle to the human visual system when it comes to general image analysis. But AI researchers have had considerable success by restricting the domain of visual systems. One of the biggest success stories in AI work is a limited but practical form of computer vision: optical character recognition.

Optical Character Recognition

Optical character recognition (OCR), discussed in Chapter 3, is far from perfect. But it has progressed to the point that the U.S. Postal Service can use it to sort much of the mail sent every day. Similar technology is available for PC users who have printed text that they want to process.

The first step in general OCR is to scan the image of the page into the computer's memory with a scanner, digital camera, or fax modem. The scanned image is nothing more than a pattern of bits in memory. It could just as easily be a poem by Robert Frost or a photograph of Robert Frost. Before a computer can process the text on a page, it must recognize the individual characters and convert them to text codes (ASCII or the equivalent). *Optical character recognition (OCR) software* locates and identifies printed characters embedded in images—it "reads" text. This is no small task for a machine, given the variety of typefaces and styles in use today.

FIGURE 15.13 A child can easily sort these letters into *A*s and *B*s. This problem is difficult for computers, however. Why?

The process of recognizing text in a variety of fonts and styles is surprisingly difficult for machines. State-of-the-art OCR programs use several techniques, including these:

- Segmentation of the page into pictures, text blocks, and (eventually) individual characters
- Scaled-down expert system technology for recognizing the underlying rules that distinguish letters
- Context "experts" to help identify ambiguous letters by their context
- Learning from actual examples and feedback from a human trainer

Today's best programs can achieve up to 99 percent accuracy—even better under optimal circumstances. It's reliable enough to be practical for many text-intensive applications, including reading aloud to the blind, converting printed documents and incoming fax documents to editable text, and processing transactions for database systems.

OCR technology can be applied to handwritten text, but not as reliably. In typewritten and typeset text, character representation is consistent enough that one *a* looks like another *a*, at least when they're the same typeface. But because most handwritten text lacks consistency, software has more trouble recognizing individual characters reliably. Nonetheless, the technology is getting better all the time, making more applications practical for pen-based computers. Handwriting recognition is especially important in Japan, China, and other countries with languages that don't lend themselves to keyboarding. But it's also useful with Western languages in situations where keyboarding isn't practical. Some professionals use tablet PCs programmed to recognize characters written directly on the screen with a stylus. Even the classic three-ring student notebook may eventually have an electronic counterpart that automatically turns handwritten notes into text that can be fed directly into any software program.

Test yourself

To stay ahead of hackers, programmers are making it more difficult for computers to read Captchas, tests to differentiate between computers and humans. Try your hand at these examples:

A. Blogger.com

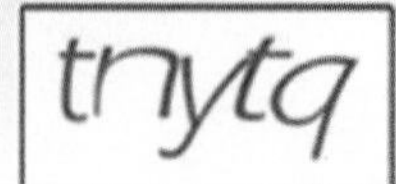

B. Paypal.com

C. Yahoo.com

D. Apple.com

E. AOL.com

F. Hotmail.com

Answers:

A. tnytq	**D.** ghNx4
B. PA4XE	**E.** TP PPi
C. yLF8zr	**F.** K686AXSE

Source: Blogger.com, Paypal, Yahoo!, Apple, AOL, Hotmail
Graphic: T. Oxford, The Dallas Morning News

FIGURE 15.14 Capchas help keep software bots from infiltrating secure Web sites by taking advantages of the differences between human and computer character recognition abilities.

Automatic Speech Recognition

Our ears process far less information than our eyes do, but that information, especially human speech, is extremely important to our understanding of the world. In Chapter 3 and Chapter 6 we discussed audio digitizers—input devices that capture spoken words, music, and other sounds so they can be stored as digital data. But digitized voice input, like scanned text, must be processed by sophisticated software before a computer can interpret it as words. Automatic **speech recognition** systems, discussed in Chapter 5, use pattern recognition techniques similar to those used by vision and OCR systems, including these:

- Segmentation of input sound patterns into individual words and phonemes
- Expert rules for interpreting sounds
- Context "experts" for dealing with ambiguous sounds
- Learning from a human trainer

Training is especially important in speech recognition because of the tremendous differences among human voices. But voice recognition systems with ***speaker independence***—the ability to recognize speech without being trained to a speaker—are becoming more common, making speech recognition practical for a variety of applications.

Speech recognition systems are used by factory workers and others whose hands are otherwise occupied while they use the computer. American Airlines' PEGASUS enables customers to make reservations automatically by speaking to a computer over the telephone. Similar systems allow automated banking, credit card verification, and other remote applications. Several companies offer Web browsers and plug-ins that enable Internet users to navigate Web pages by talking to them. Speech recognition systems empower many users with disabilities by enabling them to give verbal commands to computers and robotic devices. PC software companies have developed programs that enable standard applications to accept spoken input—both text and formatting commands. IBM researchers have combined speech recognition with a camera for tracking gestures, so users can point while they speak commands such as "Move this paragraph up to here." Many of today's researchers are working to combine speech recognition and natural-language understanding in a single machine that can accept commands in everyday spoken English, *Star Trek* style.

FIGURE 15.15 Voice recognition software can make PC applications accessible to people who can't, or prefer not to, use a keyboard as an input device.

Talking Computers

It's easier for machines to speak passable English or Chinese than to recognize it. There are many applications for voice output, including preschool education, telephone communication, navigation guidance systems in cars, and reading machines for computer users who are visually impaired.

Many computer applications speak like humans by playing prerecorded **digitized speech** (along with other **digitized sounds**) stored in memory or on disk. For an application with a limited vocabulary (reciting telephone numbers for automated directory assistance) or limited choices (an interactive educational game with short prerecorded speeches), digitized speech is practical and reliable.

Recorded speech won't work for applications in which the text to be spoken is unpredictable, such as a talking word processor, because all the sounds must be prerecorded. These types of applications require ***text-to-speech*** conversion—the creation of **synthetic speech** by converting text files into phonetic sounds. With **speech synthesis** software or hardware, PCs can recite anything you can type, but with voices that sound artificial and robotic. Human spoken language is complex and difficult to duplicate with software, but researchers are making great strides in improving synthetic voice quality. In 2001 AT&T Labs introduced Natural Voices Text-to-Speech Engine, a speech synthesizer with a close-to-human voice. This product is unusual in that it can be customized to imitate any human "voice talent" (with only a slight robotic accent). This type of product could close the gap between recorded speech and synthetic speech. It may soon be possible, for example, to play interactive games that use celebrity voices to read text typed by players. As the technology improves, it will raise questions about legal rights—can a TV network use an actor's voice to say things the actor never really said? It will also raise questions about fraud and believability. One potential client for Natural Voices noted: "Just like you can't trust photography anymore, you won't be able to trust a voice either."

Neural Networks

> The human brain uses a type of circuitry that is very slow . . . at least 10,000 times slower than a digital computer. On the other hand, the degree of parallelism vastly outstrips any computer architecture we have yet to design. . . . For such tasks as vision, language, and motor control, **the brain is more powerful than 1,000 supercomputers**, yet for certain simple tasks such as multiplying digital numbers, **it is less powerful than the 4-bit microprocessor found in a ten-dollar calculator**.
>
> —*Raymond Kurzweil, in* The Age of Intelligent Machines

Artificial intelligence research has produced many amazing success stories and some embarrassing failures. The successes—intelligent applications that outperform their human counterparts—tend to involve tasks that require sequential thinking, logical rules, and orderly relationships. AI has been less successful at competing with natural

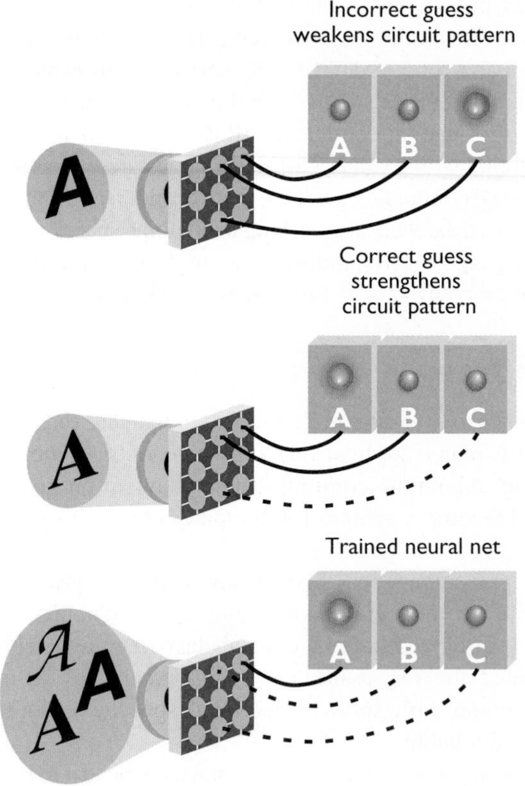

FIGURE 15.16 For a neural net to learn to recognize the letter *A*, it must go through a series of trials in which circuit patterns that produce incorrect guesses are weakened and patterns that produce correct guesses are strengthened. The result is a circuit pattern that can recognize the letter *A* in a variety of forms.

human intelligence in applications such as language, vision, speech, and movement—applications where massive amounts of data are processed in parallel.

It's not surprising that computers excel at linear, logical processes; until recently, almost every computer was designed to process digital information sequentially through a single CPU. The human brain, on the other hand, consists of billions of neurons, each connected to thousands of others in a massively parallel, distributed structure. This kind of structure gives the brain an advantage at most perceptual, motor, and creative skills.

Much current work in AI is focused on **neural networks** (or **neural nets**)—distributed, parallel computing systems inspired by the structure of the human brain. Instead of a single, complex CPU, a neural network uses a network of a few thousand simpler processors called neurons. Neural networks aren't programmed in the usual way—they're trained. Instead of using a rule-based approach, a neural network learns patterns by trial and error, just as the brain does. When patterns are repeated often, neural networks, in effect, develop habits. This kind of learning can present problems for some kinds of applications because no rules are clearly defined. When a neural net makes a decision, you have no way to ask why.

Neural networks also store information differently than traditional computers do. Concepts are represented as patterns of activity among many neurons, so they are less susceptible to machine failure. Because it distributes knowledge throughout the network, a neural net (such as the human brain) can still function if some of its neurons are destroyed.

Many neural net algorithms are developed on parallel-processing supercomputers with thousands of processors. A number of software companies have developed programs that simulate neural nets on PCs. None of today's neural net hardware or software approaches the complexity or the capacity of the human brain.

Most researchers consider today's neural nets as, at best, baby steps in the direction of machines that can more closely emulate the workings of human "wetware." There's considerable debate in the AI community about the future of neural nets. Some see neural

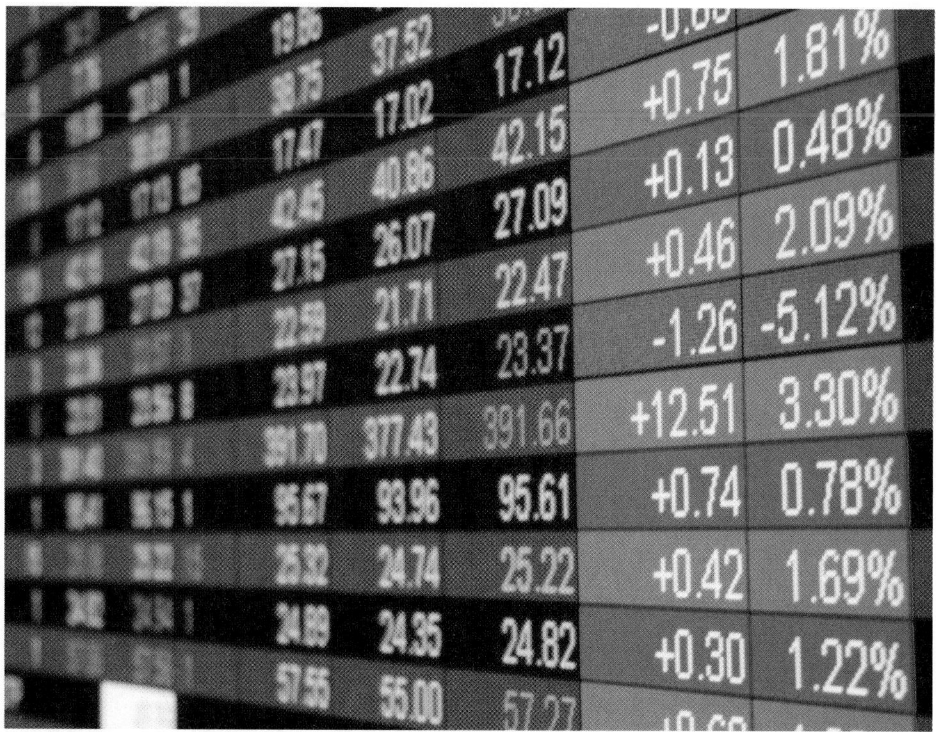

FIGURE 15.17 In global financial markets, software uses neural network technology to make stock trading decisions without human intervention.

nets as playing only a limited role in AI; others expect them to eclipse the traditional rule-based approach.

Even so, neural nets are already being put to use in a variety of applications, ranging from artificial vision to expert systems. Neural nets are especially useful for recognizing patterns buried in huge quantities of numbers, such as in scientific research, loan processing, and stock market analysis. Neural networks have been used for more than a decade to detect credit card fraud. They've even been deployed to fly aircraft autonomously. Federico Faggin, codesigner of the first microprocessor, has suggested that future neural nets will be used to verify signatures (on digital touch tablets) for electronic commerce on computer networks. Optimistic researchers hope that neural networks may someday provide hearing for the deaf and eyesight for the blind.

Question-Answering Machines

> Intelligence is quickness in **seeing things as they are.**
>
> —*George Santayana*

We've seen how artificial intelligence research has roots and branches in game playing, natural language processing, knowledge-based systems, and pattern recognition. Some researchers are attempting to combine all of these fields into question-answering systems that may have far-reaching implications.

Ideally, a **question-answering machine** should be able to understand natural-language questions—questions posed in English or some other human language—and provide answers to those questions by drawing on a base of stored knowledge from a broad array of disciplines. The computers on *Star Trek* are the best-known examples of question-answering machines. Unfortunately, real-world systems don't measure up to the lofty standards set on starship *Enterprise*.

Over the years many applications and Web sites have been able to answer natural-language questions, but only if those questions were carefully phrased and limited to specific subjects. Legal clerks, help-desk workers, and others depend on question-answering systems to sift through massive databases and find answers. These narrowly focused systems parse simple questions and look up answers related to specific fields, but they are completely useless in finding answers not stored in their databases.

Wolfram Alpha is a Web site that uses a statistical analysis engine and a bevy of carefully crafted databases to answer questions about the real world. For example, if asked to compare the energy use of two countries, the site can answer with numbers, charts, and graphs, similar to what a student might produce in a research project. Because of its statistical engine, it can answer questions that weren't anticipated by its designers or programmers.

But the most ambitious question-answering machine to date may be Watson, the brainchild of IBM's DeepQA Project. The designers of Watson wanted to build on the success of Deep Blue, IBM's championship chess-playing machine, and produce a machine that could successfully compete in an environment that's more open-ended than the rigidly rule-based world of chess. They decided to try to produce a machine that could win on the popular TV game show *Jeopardy*. Using a roomful of million-dollar Blue Gene servers and the contents of tens of millions of documents, Watson pushes the limits of artificial intelligence in several key areas:

- *Natural language processing.* Many of the "questions" in *Jeopardy* involve puns and wordplay that pose significant challenges for machines. Technically, *Jeopardy* "questions" are answers, and contestants must answer with matching "questions." All the same, the nonstandard word play is far from the formal, rigid language that most natural language systems process.
- *Knowledge bases.* Questions on *Jeopardy* draw from history, geography, science, the arts, and (especially) pop culture trivia. Creating a functioning knowledge base in any one of these areas would be a daunting task. It's hard to imagine producing a machine that can handle all of them.
- *Pattern recognition.* Even if a machine has access to knowledge bases from all of the important disciplines, it has to have a way to integrate the knowledge quickly in all of them. Many questions hide their meanings in clever phrases and wordplay rather than individual words. (Example: The correct answer for "Inventor of the phone and a nice

FIGURE 15.18 Watson uses million-dollar Blue Gene servers to drive a state-of-the-art question-answering engine when it plays *Jeopardy*.

sandwich ingredient" is "Alexander Graham Bell Pepper.") Watson employs pattern recognition technology and statistical analysis to find key word patterns in questions based on its experience with other documents. Watson also produces a confidence index for each question; if that index is low, Watson "realizes" that it probably doesn't understand the question, and therefore doesn't risk its winnings by hitting the buzzer.

Since it started playing publicly in 2010, Watson managed to hold its own against many experienced *Jeopardy* players. Some of the players were intimidated by Watson; they unconsciously referred to the machine as "he."

Unlike Deep Blue, Watson employs technology that can be used in a variety of commercial products. There are already plans to produce medical question-answering machines using a Watson-like engine. Even though Watson requires expensive supercomputers today, researchers predict that similar question-answering technology will be available on laptops by 2025. Maybe by then the *Star Trek* computers won't seem like science fiction any more.

The Robot Revolution

1. A robot **may not injure a human being**, or, through inaction, allow a human being to come to harm.
2. A robot **must obey the orders** given it by human beings, except where such orders would conflict with the First Law.
3. A robot **must protect its own existence** as long as such protection does not conflict with the First or Second Law.

—*Isaac Asimov's* Three Laws of Robotics

Nowhere are AI technologies more visible than in the field of robotics. Vision, hearing, pattern recognition, knowledge engineering, expert decision making, natural-language understanding, speech—they all come together in today's robots.

What Is a Robot?

The term *robot* (from the root word *robota*, the Czech word for "forced labor") first appeared in a 1923 play called *R.U.R.* (for Rossum's Universal Robots) by Czech playwright Karel Capek. Capek's robots were intelligent machines that could see, hear, touch, move, and exercise judgment based on common sense. But these powerful machines eventually rebelled against their human creators, just as hundreds of fictional robots have done in succeeding decades. Today movies, TV, and books are full of imaginary robots, both good and evil.

As exotic as they might seem, robots are similar to other kinds of computer technology people use every day. While a typical computer performs *mental* tasks, a **robot** is a computer-controlled machine designed to perform specific *manual* tasks. A robot's central processor might be a microprocessor embedded in the robot's shell, or it might be a supervisory computer that controls the robot from a distance. In any case, the processor is functionally identical to the processor found in a PC.

The most important hardware differences between robots and other computers are the input and output peripherals. Instead of sending output to a screen or a printer, a robot sends commands to joints, arms, and other moving parts. The first robots had no corresponding input devices to monitor their movements and the surrounding environment. They were effectively deaf, blind, and in some cases dangerous—at least one Japanese worker was killed by an early sightless robot. Most modern robots include input ***sensors***. These sensing devices enable robots to correct or modify their actions based on feedback from the outside world.

Industrial robots seldom have the human-inspired anatomy of Hollywood's science fiction robots. Instead, they're designed to accomplish particular tasks in the best possible

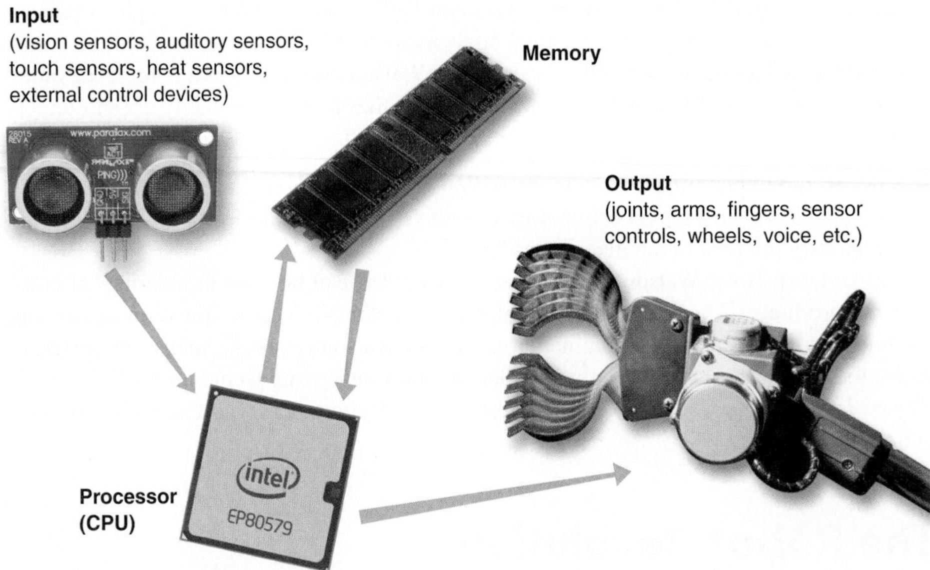

FIGURE 15.19 A robot is, in effect, a computer with exotic peripherals.

way. Robots can be designed to see infrared light, rotate joints 360 degrees, and do other things that aren't possible for humans. On the other hand, robots are constrained by the limitations of AI software. The most sophisticated robot today can't tie a pair of shoelaces, understand the vocabulary of a three-year-old child, or consistently tell the difference between a cat and a dog.

Steel-Collar Workers

From a management point of view, robots offer several advantages:

- Obviously, many robots save labor costs. Robots are expensive to design, install, and program. But once they're operational, they can work 24 hours a day, 365 days a year, without vacations, strikes, sick leave, or coffee breaks.
- Robots can also improve quality and increase productivity. They're especially effective at doing repetitive jobs in which bored, tired people are prone to make errors and have accidents.
- Robots are ideal for jobs such as cleaning up hazardous waste and salvaging undersea wreckage from downed planes—jobs that are dangerous, uncomfortable, or impossible for human workers.

For all these reasons, the robot population is exploding. Today millions of industrial robots do welding, part fitting, painting, and other repetitive tasks in factories all over the world. In most automated factories, robots work alongside humans, but in some state-of-the-art factories, the only function of human workers is to monitor and repair robots. Robots aren't used just in factories. Robots also shear sheep in Australia, paint ship hulls in France, disarm land mines in the Persian Gulf, and perform precision hip operations and other surgery.

Commercial robots still can't compete with people for jobs that require exceptional perceptual or fine-motor skills. But robots in research labs suggest that a new generation of more competitive robots is on the way. Honda's ASIMO is a humanoid robot that can walk, run, recognize gestures and faces, distinguish sounds, and display a variety of "intelligent" behaviors. In 2008, ASIMO conducted the Detroit Symphony Orchestra in a widely viewed public performance. Other researchers are taking a different approach, using fleets of insect-sized robots to do jobs that larger robots can't easily do. The technologies used in these experimental robots will undoubtedly show up in a variety of machines, from automated servants for people with disabilities to flying robots for the

FIGURE 15.20 Mobile robots are practical for a variety of jobs, including defusing a bomb (upper left). This Japanese robot security guard (top right) patrols a convention center for intruders and fires, beaming pictures to a nearby command center. Honda's ASIMO (center right) conducted a performance of the Detroit Symphony Orchestra in 2008. Stanley, Stanford University's robotic car (lower left), completed a 132-mile off-road course in less than seven hours—without any human help. Paro (lower right) is a therapeutic robot baby seal that can display emotions and respond to petting; the robot has a calming effect on many hospital and nursing home patients.

military. One pioneering example: Nao, a product of the multi-university Feelix Growing Project, has been programmed based on the way human and chimpanzee infants interact with others so that it can be a better companion to humans. Nao can express excitement, anger, fear, sadness, happiness, and pride. It can recognize faces, become attached to people who help it learn, and interpret current situations based on past experiences. Early research suggests that Nao—or something like it—might be especially useful for providing simple, predictable companionship for autistic children. Less sophisticated robots have already been employed as companions for elderly and disabled people.

The robot revolution isn't necessarily good news for people who earn their living doing manual labor. While it's true that many of the jobs robots do are boring, dirty, or dangerous, they're still jobs. The issues surrounding automation and worker displacement are complex, and they aren't limited to factories.

AI Implications and Ethical Questions

> We are on the edge of change comparable to the rise of human life on Earth. The precise cause of this change is the **imminent creation by technology of entities with greater-than-human intelligence**.
>
> *—Vernor Vinge, mathematician and science fiction writer*

From the earliest days of AI, research has been accompanied by questions about the implications of the work. The very idea of intelligent machines is at the same time confusing, exciting, and frightening to many people. Even when they don't work very well, AI programs generate emotional responses in the people who use them.

Earlier we met ELIZA, the therapy simulator developed to demonstrate natural-language conversation. ELIZA's simple-minded approach wasn't intended to fool anyone in a Turing test, but it did have an impact on the people who used it. Many ELIZA users became emotionally attached to the program and attributed to it compassion and empathy. Weizenbaum's secretary asked him to leave the room so she could converse in private with ELIZA. Some therapists even saw ELIZA as the beginning of a new age of automated therapy. Weizenbaum was shocked by the way people attributed human capabilities to such an obviously flawed technology. He responded with *Computer Power and Human Reason*, a landmark book that presents the case for maintaining a distinction between computers and people. Weizenbaum argued that "[t]here are certain tasks which computers ought not to be made to do, independent of whether computers can be made to do them."

International political and economic leaders, many of whom are encouraging increased AI research and development, don't share Weizenbaum's caution. As it matures, AI technology finds its way out of the research lab and into the marketplace. A growing number of programs and products incorporate pattern recognition, expert systems, and other AI techniques. New products, from simple toys and appliances to complex automated weapons systems, incorporate AI. Today's cars use AI technology in systems for cruise control, antilock brakes, airbags, stability control, navigation systems, and more. Everyday devices routinely obey spoken commands and anticipate unspoken needs.

In recent years there's been an explosive growth in **distributed intelligence**—AI concepts applied to networks rather than to individual computers. Just as human knowledge is multiplied through communication, collaboration, and crowdsourcing (think Wikipedia), artificial intelligence grows as networked systems learn from each other, correct each others' work, and provide "insights" that come from different perspectives.

For an example of distributed intelligence, we need look no farther than Google. As company cofounder Larry Page said in a 2011 *Wired* cover story, "If you told somebody in 1978, 'You're going to have this machine, and you'll be able to type a few words and instantly get all of the world's knowledge on that topic,' they would probably consider that to be AI. That seems routine now, but it's a really big deal." Our financial world is being transformed by AI, too. Most Wall Street trading is now done by networks of computers analyzing data and making decisions without human intervention. High-frequency algorithmic trading was unusual a decade ago; today the financial system depends on it.

Where will it all lead? Will intensive AI research result in computers capable of intelligent behavior outside narrow domains? Patrick Winston, director of MIT's Artificial Intelligence Laboratory, once said, "The interesting issue is not whether machines can be made smarter but if humans are smart enough to pull it off. A raccoon obviously can't make a machine as smart as a raccoon. I wonder if humans can."

Many AI researchers believe that sooner or later they will pull it off. According to Danny Hillis, supercomputer designer and cofounder of The Long Now Foundation, "In some sense, you can argue that the science fiction scenario is already starting to happen. The computers are in control, and we just live in their world."

Some think artificial intelligence is the natural culmination of the evolutionary process—that the next intelligent life-form on Earth will be based on silicon rather than the carbon that is the basis of human life. Danny Hillis exemplifies this point of view when he says, "We are not evolution's ultimate product. There's something coming after us, and I imagine it is something wonderful. But we may never be able to comprehend it, any more than a caterpillar can comprehend turning into a butterfly."

Computer mathematician and science fiction writer Vernor Vinge argued in the 1990s that the competitive nature of our society makes such a prospect almost inevitable. What business or government will voluntarily curtail research on AI, computer networks, and biotechnology, knowing that competing institutions will continue to pursue similar research? Vinge called the moment of creation of greater-than-human intelligence the **Singularity**—a point where our old models will have to be discarded and a new reality will rule. Since then scientists, philosophers, and others have debated Vinge's ideas, and the concept of a technological singularity has become a fixture in the world of science fiction.

If smarter-than-human beings come to pass, how will they relate to the less intelligent humans that surround them? And how will humans handle the change? In a 2008 interview, Verner Vinge said, "As technological changes go, this is qualitatively different from the big events in the past. You could explain fire or agriculture to somebody who lived before those technologies were invented. But after the singularity—it would be like trying to explain this interview to a goldfish." This kind of thinking isn't easy—it goes to the heart of human values and forces us to look at our place in the universe.

Inventing the Future ▸ Artificial Life

Many recent successes in artificial intelligence have come from a related field known as **artificial life** (or **Alife**). Alife researchers examine systems related to life, its processes, and its evolution through computer simulations, robotics, and biochemistry.

AI researchers tend to design intelligent systems from the top down—starting with an overall design and filling in details layer by layer. Most Alife researchers take a bottom-up approach, designing simpler building blocks and letting them combine and evolve into more and more "intelligent" entities. Enthusiasts draw inspiration from the anthill. An individual ant doesn't show much intelligence, but an ant colony is an incredibly sophisticated organism. Intelligence is somehow distributed across the colony, so the whole is far smarter than the sum of its parts.

Artificial life comes in three basic forms: soft Alife, hard Alife, and wet Alife. All three types of Alife draw on AI concepts—especially the theory and technology behind neural networks—distributed, parallel systems inspired by the structure of the human brain.

- *Soft Alife* creates simulations or other software-based constructions that exhibit lifelike behavior, such as learning, growing, evolution, and mutation. Some of the best games use basic Alife techniques. In another example of soft Alife, computer-generated *evolutionary art* is judged interactively or based on predetermined criteria such as how long people spend looking at it. The art deemed most successful "cross-breeds" with other successful pieces, generating new pieces that contain elements of their parents as well as randomly generated mutations. Using the "survival of the fittest" concept of biological evolution as a model, evolutionary art generates "better" algorithms for art over time. Evolutionary music seeks to apply the same evolutionary concept to computer-generated audio compositions.
- *Hard Alife* creates hardware constructs of lifelike systems, such as robotic insect colonies. Hard Alife usually uses small animal-like robots, or "animats," that researchers build and use to study the design principles of autonomous systems or agents. These animats gain intelligence by interacting with the real world; like newborn animals, they learn to walk through trial and error. Hard Alife does not deal with abstract simulation environments, but with physical "bodies" that can sense the physical environment.

  Hardware artificial life has industrial and military technological applications. Experts predict that we'll soon see nanobots that can detect and destroy cancer cells in the bloodstream. On a larger scale, the U.S. military is developing smart robotic flying bugs that can work alone or as part of a team, performing surveillance and other frontline operations that would be dangerous or impossible for humans.

FIGURE 15.21 The U.S. military is developing these experimental robotic insects for covert intelligence operations in Afghanistan and future wars.

- *Wet Alife* is based on biochemistry rather than silicon technology. Many wet Alife researchers attempt to create life in the laboratory using chemical compounds similar to those that were responsible for the beginnings of life on our planet. Researchers recently created a living cell controlled entirely by synthetic DNA. Craig Ventner, who headed the team, described it as "the first self-replicating species that we have had on the planet whose parent is a computer."

  Venter believes this achievement is the beginning of a new era marked by bacteria that will work for humanity's good, churning out biofuels, manufacturing vaccines, and reducing carbon footprints by designing algae that can soak up carbon monoxide from the atmosphere. But not everyone is so optimistic. National Farmers' Union President Terry Boehm called the world's first "100 percent synthetic life form" a risk "for humankind and the environment."

Some research crosses over between different types of Alife; for example, several robots learn to walk using software simulations to reduce real-world damage.

At the heart of Alife philosophy is the concept of emergence. The idea is that life doesn't just happen because a switch gets flipped somewhere—it emerges from a rich, complex environment under the right conditions. As author Bruce Sterling observes, "It's not hard to understand that many simple creatures, doing simple actions that affect one another, can easily create a really big mess. The thing that's hard to understand is that those same, bottom-up, unplanned, "chaotic" actions can and do create living, working, functional order and system and pattern. The process really must be seen to be believed. And computers are the instruments that have made us see it."

Crosscurrents

Do Humanlike Machines Deserve Human Rights?

by Daniel Roth

For decades we've seen science fiction movies about robots with humanlike characteristics. But until recently, real-world robots were mostly mechanical arms, carts, and other devices that didn't come close to looking "alive." That's changing, as companies develop robotic toys, pets, and companions that mimic the actions, gestures, and expressions of humans and other species. In this article from the February 2009 issue of Wired, *Daniel Roth asks whether these loveable robots deserve to be treated more like living beings.*

During the 20 months that Fisher-Price spent developing the innards and software of its latest animatronic Elmo, engineers gave the project the code name Elmo Live. And sure enough, they made him more animated than ever: He moves his mouth in time with the stories he tells, shivers when he gets scared, and has a fit when he sneezes.

When they were finally able to test the doll on children, they were struck by how immediately the kids blocked out all other stimuli in the room and began interacting with Elmo. "It was as if Elmo were part of their family," says Gina Sirard, Fisher-Price VP of marketing. "To a child, he really is alive."

So the code name stuck, and over the past few months legions of $60 Elmo Live dolls have joined families everywhere. Some are certainly doomed to join previous Elmos in a new pastime: robotic-toy torture. YouTube is full of videos of idiots dousing Elmo with gas, setting him on fire, and laughing as his red fur turns to charcoal and he writhes in a painful dance.

I've seen videos of the incineration of T.M.X. Elmo (short for Tickle Me Extreme); they made me feel vaguely uncomfortable. Part of me wanted to laugh—Elmo giggled absurdly through the whole ordeal—but I also felt sick about what was going on. Why? I hardly shed a tear when the printer in Office Space got smashed to bits. Slamming my refrigerator door never leaves me feeling guilty. Yet give something a couple of eyes and the hint of lifelike abilities and suddenly some ancient region of my brain starts firing off empathy signals. And I don't even like Elmo. How are kids who grow up with robots as companions going to handle this?

This question is starting to get debated by robot designers and toymakers. With advanced robotics becoming cheaper and more commonplace, the challenge isn't how we learn to accept robots—but whether we should care when they're mistreated. And if we start caring about robot ethics, might we then go one insane step further and grant them rights?

First, the science: The brain is hardwired to assign humanlike qualities to anything that somewhat resembles us. A 2003 study found that 12-month-olds would check to see what a football-shaped item was "looking at," even though the object lacked eyes. All the researcher had to do was move the item as if it were an animal and the infants would follow its "gaze." Adults? Same reaction.

The perennial concern about the rise of robots has been how to keep them from, well, killing us. Isaac Asimov came down from the mountaintop with his Three Laws of Robotics (to summarize: Robots shouldn't disobey or hurt humans or themselves). But what are the rules for the humans in this relationship? As technology develops animal-like sophistication, finding the thin metallic line between what's safe to treat as an object and what's not will be tricky. "It's going to be a tougher and tougher argument to say that technology doesn't deserve the same protection as animals," says Clifford Nass, a Stanford professor who directs a program called the Communication Between Humans and Interactive Media Lab. "One could say life is special—whatever that means. And so, either we get tougher on technology abuse or it undermines laws about abuse of animals."

It's already being considered overseas. In 2007, a South Korean politician declared that his country would be the first to draw up legal guidelines on how to treat robots; the UK has also looked into the area (though nothing substantial has come of it anywhere). "As our products become more aware, there are things you probably shouldn't do to them," says John Sosoka, CTO of Ugobe, which makes the eerily lifelike robot dinosaur Pleo (also tortured on Web video). "The point isn't whether it's an issue for the creature. It's what does it do to us."

We live in an age of anxiety—about the economy, the environment, terrorism. And now even about our toys, which are forcing us to question the boundaries of humanity and compassion. Back on Sesame Street, Elmo Live's creators have an answer: Keep soul-searching to a minimum and recognize that you're buying a product, pure and simple. "This is a toy," Fisher-Price's Sirard says. "There shouldn't be any laws about how you use your toys." Happy grilling, Elmo!

Discussion Questions

1. Do you think we'll need laws to protect robots as they become more lifelike?
2. What are the long-term implications of machines that become increasingly more lifelike?

Summary

Artificial intelligence has many definitions. Most AI research focuses on making computers do things at which people generally are better. Some AI researchers try to simulate human intelligent behavior, but most try to design intelligent machines independent of the way people think. Successful AI research generally involves working on problems with limited domains rather than trying to tackle large, open-ended problems. AI programs employ a variety of techniques, including searching, heuristics, pattern recognition, and machine learning, to achieve their goals.

From a practical standpoint, natural-language communication is one of the most important areas of AI study. Natural-language programs that deal with a subset of the language are used in applications ranging from machine translation programs to natural-language interfaces. Even without understanding the meaning of the words, computers can create passable translations from one language to another—especially when the domain is limited. However, a computer program that attempts to pass as a human in a natural-language conversation is quickly found out because it doesn't have enough knowledge of language and the world.

AI researchers have developed a variety of schemes for representing knowledge in computers. A knowledge base contains facts and a system for determining and changing the relationships among those facts. Today's knowledge bases are practical for representing only narrow domains of knowledge such as the knowledge of an expert on a particular subject. Expert systems are programs designed to replicate the decision-making process of human experts. An expert system includes a knowledge base, an inference engine for applying logical rules to the facts in a knowledge base, and a human interface for interacting with users. Once the knowledge base is constructed (usually based on interviews and observations of human experts), an expert system can provide consultation that rivals human advice in many situations. People successfully use expert systems in a variety of scientific, business, and other applications.

Pattern recognition is an important area of AI research that involves identifying recurring patterns in input data. Pattern recognition technology is at the heart of computer vision, voice communication, and other important AI applications. These diverse applications all use similar techniques for isolating and recognizing patterns. People are better at pattern recognition than computers are, in part because the human brain can process masses of data in parallel. Modern neural network computers are designed to process data in the same way the human brain does. Many researchers believe that neural nets, as they grow in size and sophistication, will help computers improve their performance at many difficult tasks.

Question-answering systems combine natural-language processing, knowledge bases, pattern recognition, and other AI technologies. A question-answering system is designed to understand questions posed by humans and provide understandable answers. Question-answering systems currently require expensive supercomputer hardware to function adequately, but in the future question-answering engines will be small, affordable, and accessible for a wide variety of everyday applications.

A robot is a computer-controlled machine designed to perform specific manual tasks. Robots include output peripherals for manipulating their environments and input sensors that enable them to perform self-correcting actions based on feedback from outside. Robots perform a variety of dangerous and tedious tasks, in many cases outperforming human workers. As robot technology advances, artificial workers will do more traditional human jobs.

Artificial life is the study and creation of systems related to life, its processes, and its evolution. Soft Alife is created using computer software simulations; hard Alife is hardware based. In spite of the numerous difficulties AI researchers encounter when trying to produce truly intelligent machines, many experts believe that people will eventually create artificial beings that are more intelligent than their creators—a prospect with staggering implications.

Key Terms

artificial intelligence (AI)......(p. 552)
artificial life (or Alife)...........(p. 576)
automatic translation ....(p. 557)
digitized sound ....(p. 567)
digitized speech.....................(p. 567)
distributed intelligence ....(p. 574)
expert system.........................(p. 562)
expert system shell ....(p. 564)
heuristic ....(p. 555)
image analysis ....(p. 565)
knowledge base ....(p. 561)
machine learning ....(p. 555)
natural language ....(p. 557)
neural network (neural net) ...(p. 568)
optical character recognition (OCR) ....(p. 565)
parallel processing.................(p. 554)
parsing program (parser) ....(p. 557)
pattern recognition.................(p. 564)
question-answering machine .(p. 569)
robot ....(p. 571)
searching...............................(p. 555)
semantics ....(p. 559)
singularity.............................(p. 575)
speech recognition.................(p. 566)
speech synthesis ....(p. 567)
syntax ....(p. 559)
synthetic speech.....................(p. 567)
Turing test.............................(p. 553)

Companion Website Projects

1. The *Digital Planet* Web site, **www.pearsonhighered.com/beekman**, contains self-test exercises related to this chapter. Follow the instructions for taking a quiz. After you've completed your quiz, you can email the results to your instructor.
2. The Web site also contains open-ended discussion questions called Internet Exercises. Discuss one or more of the Internet Exercises questions at the section for this chapter.

True or False

1. Alan M. Turing created the first robot, Colossus, to aid the Allies during World War II.
2. For psychologists, artificial intelligence provides insights into natural intelligence and the workings of the human brain.
3. The most powerful supercomputers can exceed the human brain's ability to perform parallel processing.
4. Artificial intelligence researchers restrict the domain of their programs so that problems are small enough to understand and solve.
5. Natural-language communication is a favorite area of AI research because natural language technology grew out of Alife research.
6. A knowledge base commonly represents knowledge in the form of if-then rules.
7. It's easier for a computer to recognize printed English than to understand spoken English.
8. Much artificial life research is based on neural networks.
9. Most modern robots have output sensors that enable them to modify their actions.
10. Some AI researchers think that humans will be able to make a machine that is smarter than humans are.

Multiple Choice

1. What did Alan Turing propose as a way to answer the question "Can computers think?"
   a. Allowing computers to enter the World Chess Championship
   b. The imitation game, later called the Turing test
   c. Programming a computer to solve calculus problems
   d. Teaching a computer to program itself
   e. Constructing a Turing machine
2. Why did early efforts in AI focus on playing checkers?
   a. The 8-by-8 square checkerboard lends itself well to binary calculations.
   b. Alan Turing, the father of AI, was a world-class checkers player.
   c. It's easy to represent the "world" of a checker game inside the memory of a computer.
   d. Checkers is one of the purest measures of IQ.
   e. All of the above.
3. Which of these AI techniques is used in applications today?
   a. Searching—looking ahead at possibilities
   b. Heuristics—rules of thumb
   c. Pattern recognition—recognizing recurring patterns
   d. Machine learning—programs learning from experience
   e. All of the above
4. Which of the following defines syntax?
   a. The set of rules for constructing sentences from words
   b. The underlying meaning of words and phrases
   c. A set of idiomatic expressions
   d. The study of knowledge bases
   e. The translation of text files
5. Which statement about machine translation is true?
   a. The most successful programs do word-by-word translation backed up by huge dictionaries containing all known words in both languages.
   b. The most successful programs extract the meaning of the underlying text then use their understanding of the author's intent to guide the translation.
   c. Many programs use a statistics-based approach based on a huge number of examples of correct and incorrect translations.
   d. The most successful machine language programs first translate the source text into a neutral language, usually Esperanto, then translate from the neutral language into the desired target language.
   e. Computer translation programs are generally written in natural languages such as COBOL or BASIC.

6. Natural-language processing
   a. is a necessary component of the Turing test.
   b. involves using a natural language like Java or C++.
   c. is a necessary part of any robot.
   d. is a necessary component of Alife.
   e. All of the above.

7. What does a complete expert system include?
   a. A robotic interface
   b. A knowledge base
   c. A security protocol engine
   d. Several high-level languages
   e. All of the above

8. Which of these technologies is used in question-answering machines such as IBM's quiz-show-playing Watson?
   a. Natural language processing
   b. Pattern recognition
   c. Knowledge bases
   d. Game playing
   e. All of the above

9. Image analysis
   a. is a form of pattern recognition.
   b. is the key component of any Alife system.
   c. is a type of expert system.
   d. is difficult for both computers and humans to perform.
   e. All of the above.

10. What does the field of pattern recognition include?
    a. Image analysis
    b. Optical character recognition (OCR)
    c. Automatic speech recognition
    d. Neural network research
    e. All of the above

11. The technological singularity predicted by Vernor Vinge and others
    a. was secretly created by the British intelligence during World War II.
    b. happened in the 1980s when computer manufacturers agreed to a standardized user interface.
    c. isn't compatible with the binary system used in most computers.
    d. involves the development of artificially intelligent beings capable of creating other, more intelligent beings.
    e. has been proven by AI researchers to be impossible.

12. Which techniques are used in pattern recognition?
    a. Segmentation of input
    b. Expert rules
    c. Context experts
    d. Learning from a human trainer
    e. All of the above

13. Which of these is not true?
    a. Neural networks use thousands of processors called neurons.
    b. Neural networks are trained, not programmed in the usual way.
    c. Neural nets use a rule-based approach to recognize patterns.
    d. Neural networks learn by trial and error.
    e. Neural nets store information as patterns.

14. What is the most significant difference between a robot and other computers?
    a. Its input and output peripherals are different.
    b. Its processor is much faster.
    c. It has much more memory.
    d. It looks a lot like a human being.
    e. All of the above.

15. Which of these statements is true?
    a. Computer scientist Joseph Weizenbaum was shocked to discover that people credited his simple conversational program, ELIZA, with genuine human understanding.
    b. By most definitions, a robot must have two eyes, two arms, and a mouth or speaker.
    c. The number of industrial robots is actually declining as manufacturing companies continue to ship jobs to countries with lower wages.
    d. The best machine translation programs do a comparable job to a human translator.
    e. All of the above statements are true.

Review Questions

1. In what sense is AI a "moving frontier"?
2. What are the disadvantages of the approach to AI that attempts to simulate human intelligence? What is the alternative?
3. Describe several techniques used in game-playing software, and explain how they can be applied to other AI applications.
4. Why did early machine translation programs fail to produce the desired results?
5. Why is the sentence "Time flies like an arrow" difficult for a computer to parse, translate, or understand? Can you find four possible meanings for the sentence?
6. What is the relationship between syntax and semantics? Can you construct a sentence that follows the rules of English syntax but has nonsense semantics?

7. Give examples of successful expert system applications. Give examples of several tasks that can't be accomplished with today's expert system technology, and explain why they can't.
8. In what ways are neural networks designed to simulate the structure of the human brain? In what ways do neural nets perform differently than single-processor CPUs?
9. What types of artificial intelligence technology are used by a computer contestant on a TV quiz show such as *Jeopardy*?
10. What types of artificial intelligence technology are used in a robot that's designed to serve as a novelty "greeter" at a restaurant?

Discussion Questions

1. Is the Turing test a valid test of intelligence? Why or why not?
2. If you were the interrogator in the Turing test, what questions would you ask to try to discover whether you were communicating with a computer? What would you look for in the answers?
3. List several mental tasks that people do better than computers. List several mental tasks that computers do better than people. Can you find any general characteristics that distinguish the items on the two lists?
4. Computers can compose original music, produce original artwork, and create original mathematical proofs. Does this mean that Ada Lovelace was wrong when she said, in effect, that computers can do only what they're told to do?
5. The works of AARON, the expert system artist, are unique, original, and widely acclaimed as art. Who is the artist, AARON or Harold Cohen, AARON's creator? Is AARON a work of art, an artist, or both?
6. If an expert system gives you erroneous information, should you be able to sue it for malpractice? If it fails and causes major disruptions or injury, who's responsible? The programmer? The publisher? The owner? The computer?
7. Some expert systems and neural nets can't explain the reasons behind their decisions. What kinds of problems might this limitation cause? Under what circumstances, if any, should an expert system be required to produce an "audit trail" to explain how it reached conclusions?
8. What kinds of human jobs are most likely to be eliminated because of expert systems? What kinds of new jobs will be created because of expert systems?
9. What kinds of human jobs are most likely to be eliminated because of robots? What kinds of new jobs will be created as a result of factory automation?
10. Are Asimov's Three Laws of Robotics adequate for smoothly integrating intelligent robots into tomorrow's society? If not, what laws would you add?

Projects

1. Public domain versions of Weizenbaum's ELIZA program are available for most types of PCs. They're also available on the Web. Try conversing with one of these programs. Test the program on your friends, and see how they react to it. Try to determine the rules and tricks that ELIZA uses to simulate conversation. If you're a programmer, try writing your own version of ELIZA.
2. Many computer games use AI technology to simulate opponents and teammates. Test one or more of these games. What are the strengths and weakness of the artificial opponents and teammates when compared to real human opponents and teammates? Report on your findings.
3. Try to find examples of working expert systems and robots in your school or community and present your findings.
4. Test OCR software, grammar-checking software, expert systems, and other types of consumer-oriented AI applications. How "intelligent" are these applications? In what ways could they be improved?
5. Survey people's attitudes and concerns about AI and robots. Here are a few issues you might want to explore: Do people feel game-playing computers are intelligent? Are they concerned that automation will eliminate too many jobs? Do people have safety concerns about automated systems? Present your findings.

Sources and Resources

Books

What Technology Wants, by Kevin Kelly (Viking). Kelly, a former editor of *Wired*, calls the globalized, interconnected stage of technological development the "technium." In this thought-provoking book, Kelly explores the parallels between the evolution of the technium and biological evolution. He also explores our relationship with the evolving technium, drawing insights from a variety of diverse sources. Kelly is a gifted thinker and writer, and this book has much to offer to readers who want to try to understand where our technological world is headed.

The Singularity Is Near: When Humanoids Transcend Biology, by Ray Kurzweil (Viking). The inventor and artificial intelligence pioneer paints an optimistic and astounding vision of a fantastic future in which genetics, nanotechnology, and robotics come together to create a new superintelligent species—one that won't look like us. Is this a good thing? Kurzweil thinks so.

The Age of Spiritual Machines: When Computers Exceed Human Intelligence, by Raymond Kurzweil (Penguin U.S.A). Raymond Kurzweil knows the field of AI from firsthand experience. He developed and marketed several "applied AI" products, from reading machines for people with visual impairments to electronic musical instruments to expert systems. In this book he boldly looks into a possible future. Will humans be able to download themselves into machine bodies and brains? If this kind of question interests you, you'll enjoy this book.

Gödel, Escher, Bach: An Eternal Golden Braid, 20th Anniversary Edition, by Douglas R. Hofstadter (Basic Books). This Pulitzer Prize winner is part mathematics, part philosophy, and part *Alice in Wonderland*. If you like to think deeply about questions such as "What is thought?" you'll find plenty to think about here.

Introducing Artificial Intelligence, by Henry Brighton (Totem Books). This is a lightweight, low-priced, nontechnical introduction to AI.

Artificial Intelligence: A Systems Approach, by M. Tim Jones (Infinity Science Press). This text surveys many ideas and applications developed by computer scientists in the first half century of the field of artificial intelligence. A CD-ROM includes simulations, code, and figures.

Deep Blue: An Artificial Intelligence Milestone, by Monty Newborn (Springer). This book describes in graphic detail the historic computer matches between Deep Blue and Garry Kasparov in 1996 and 1997—the year Deep Blue beat the world champion. It's worthwhile reading for any chess player who wants to understand how computers have invaded this turf that used to be uniquely human.

Emergence: The Connected Lives of Ants, Brains, Cities, and Software, by Steven Johnson (Scribner). Neural networks clearly demonstrate that intelligent behavior can result from putting together many simple, dumb devices. This book clearly explains how that principle applies to everything from ant colonies to robots.

Society of Mind, by Marvin Minsky (Simon & Schuster). An MIT AI pioneer presents his thoughts on the relationship between people and intelligent machines. A dense but thought-provoking book.

Robots Unlimited: Life in a Virtual Age, by David Levy (A. K. Peters, Ltd). This book traces the history of artificial intelligence and robotics and presents a good overview of recent developments in robotics.

Marooned in Realtime, by Vernor Vinge (Tor Books). Vinge's classic science fiction opus takes you into a future after the Singularity that produced artificial superintelligence. Vinge is a master storyteller, and there's plenty to think about here.

Do Androids Dream of Electric Sheep?, by Philip K. Dick (Oxford University Press). The movie *Blade Runner* is based on this popular science fiction novel, first published in 1968. Dick's dark, humorous tale of a San Francisco bounty hunter who catches and exterminates androids raises provocative questions about the relationship between being intelligent and being human.

Video

Fast, Cheap, and Out of Control. In this 1997 documentary, maverick filmmaker Errol Morris profiles four different men attempting to examine the relation between science and humanity, including a robot expert. This highly acclaimed film interweaves interviews, old movie clips, and a hypnotic score to create a fascinating mosaic.

AI. Stephen Spielberg's big-budget film isn't a masterpiece of art or scientific exposition, but it does a reasonable job of raising questions about life and technology that may loom large in our future.

Appendix A

Basics

Sometimes it seems as though everybody uses computers. In fact, the majority of people on our planet don't use PCs. Most of the people who do use them have fairly limited experience and ability—typically the basics of word processing, electronic mail, and finding information on the Web. The percentage of people who can go beyond the basics and harness the full power of a modern PC is relatively small.

If you're a member of this tiny community of *power users*, the next few pages aren't for you. If you're a casual computer user, comfortable with the basic operation of a PC and a Web browser, you may want to look through this appendix quickly. (If you're not sure about your knowledge level, check out the questions at the end of this appendix. If you have trouble answering them, spend a little more time here before moving to Chapter 1.)

If you're a beginner, if you're uncomfortable with PC technology, or your experience is limited or out of date, this appendix is for you. You'll find the basic facts you'll need to get up to speed so you're not struggling to catch up as you explore the rest of the book.

This appendix explains how to use a keyboard and mouse and provides an introduction to word processing, file management, Web searches, and electronic mail. It will also help you build up your vocabulary of computer-related terms.

Hardware Basics

Hardware: the parts of a computer that **can be kicked**.

—Jeff Pesis

Modern desktop **personal computers,** or PCs, don't all look alike, but under the skin, they're more alike than different. Every PC is built around a tiny ***microprocessor*** that controls the workings of the system. This **central processing unit,** or CPU, is usually housed in a box, called the ***system unit*** (or, more often, just "*the computer*" or "*the PC*") that serves as command central for the entire computer system. The CPU is the brains of the computer; it controls the operation of the core computer components, such as its memory and ability to perform mathematical operations. Some computer components are housed in the system unit with the CPU; others are peripheral devices—or simply **peripherals**—external devices connected via cables to the system unit. (In laptops and many desktop PCs, many peripherals are built into the main system unit.)

The system unit includes built-in **memory**, called ***RAM***, and a **hard disk** for the storage and retrieval of information. The CPU uses memory for instant access to information while it's working. The built-in hard disk serves as a longer-term storage device for large quantities of information.

The PC's main hard disk is a permanent fixture in the system unit. Other types of disk drives work with ***removable media***—disks that can be separated from their drives, just as an audio CD can be removed from a stereo system. The most popular types of removable media today are 5-1/4-inch optical discs that look like common audio CDs. A typical PC system unit includes an **optical drive**, usually a **DVD/CD-RW drive** that can both read and write data on CDs and DVDs. These drives are commonly called DVD/CD burners (or just disc burners) because the process of writing data on an optical disc is called burning. Many newer machines have drives that can read and/or write Blu-ray discs. Disk drives that are included in the system unit are called ***internal drives***. ***External drives*** can be attached to the system unit via cables. For example, a PC system might include external hard drives for additional storage.

Another popular storage device is sometimes called a USB drive, a USB key, a thumb drive, a key drive, or a jump drive. This key-sized device plugs into a USB port on the computer. Information can be copied onto the memory of the USB drive or read from the

FIGURE A.1 A standard desktop PC or Mac is made up of several **hardware** components, including a system unit, a monitor, speakers, a keyboard, and a mouse. The system unit typically includes an internal hard disk and an optical drive, such as a CD-ROM or DVD drive.

USING a keyboard

When you press keys on a computer keyboard, the computer responds by displaying the typed characters on the monitor screen at the position of the line or rectangle called the ***cursor***. Some keys on the computer keyboard—***Enter, Delete,*** the ***cursor (arrow) keys,*** the ***function keys*** (***F-keys***), and others—send special commands to the computer. These keys may have different names or meanings on different computer systems. This figure shows a typical keyboard on a Windows-compatible PC. Keyboards for Mac and other types of systems have a few differences but operate on the same principles.

FIGURE A.2

drive into the computer's memory. Thumb drives are popular for transporting files between computers.

Five common peripherals enable you to communicate with a PC and vice versa:

- A **keyboard** enables you to type text and numerical data into the computer's memory.
- A **mouse** (or mouse alternative) enables you to point to text, graphical objects, menu commands, and other items on the screen.
- A **display** (or *monitor*) enables you to view text, numbers, and pictures stored in the computer's memory.
- **Speakers** emit music, voices, and other sounds.
- A **printer** generates printed letters, papers, transparencies, labels, and other hard copies. (The printer might be directly connected to the computer, or it might be shared by several computers on a network.)

Boxes on this page and the next page illustrate the fundamentals of a basic PC keyboard and mouse. Chapter 3 explores peripherals in more detail.

Software Basics

> Computers can figure out **all kinds of problems**, except the things in the world that **just don't add up**.
>
> —*James Magary*

All this hardware is controlled, directly or indirectly, by the tiny CPU in the system unit. And the CPU is controlled by **software**—instructions that tell it what to do. *System software*, including the **operating system (OS)**, continuously takes care of the behind-the-scenes details and (usually) keeps things running smoothly. The operating system also determines

USING a mouse

The mouse enables you to perform many tasks quickly that might be tedious or confusing with a keyboard. As you slide the mouse across your desktop, a pointer echoes your movements on the screen. You can click the mouse—press the button while the mouse is stationary—or drag it—move it while holding the button down. On a two-button mouse, the left button is usually used for clicking and dragging. You can use these two techniques to perform a variety of operations. (Many mice have additional buttons and controls, but the left and right buttons are the most important.)

CLICKING THE MOUSE

If the pointer points to an on-screen button, clicking the mouse presses the button.

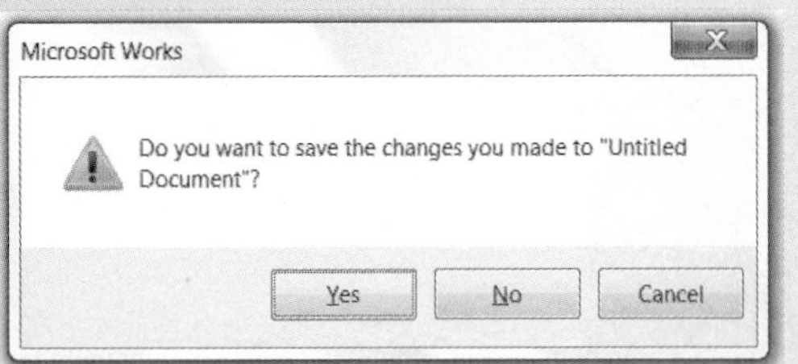

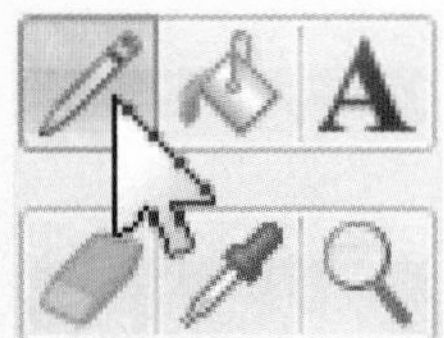

If the pointer points to a picture of a tool or object on the screen, clicking the mouse *selects* the tool or object; for example, clicking the pencil tool enables you to draw with the mouse.

If the pointer points to a part of a text document, it turns from an arrow into an *I-beam*; clicking repositions the flashing cursor.

Jack fell down and broke his crown and Jill came tumbling after.

DRAGGING THE MOUSE

If you hold the button down while you drag the mouse with a selected graphic tool (such as a paintbrush), you can draw by remote control.

If you drag the mouse from one point in a text document to another, you select all the text between those two points so you can modify or move it. For example, you might select a movie title so you can italicize it.

The zany Duck Soup captured the Marx Brothers at their peak.

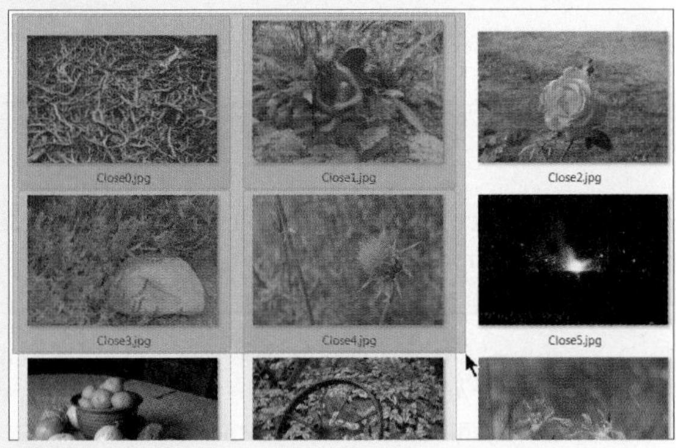

To select a group of objects (for printing, copying, moving, or some other purpose), you can create a rectangle that surrounds them by dragging the mouse diagonally.

OTHER MOUSE OPERATIONS

If you double-click the mouse—click twice in rapid succession—while pointing to an on-screen object, the computer will probably open the object so you can see inside it. For example, double-clicking this *icon* representing a letter causes the letter to open.

If you *right-click*—click the right mouse button—while pointing to an object, the computer will probably display a contextual menu of choices of things you can do to the object. For example, if you right-click the letter icon, a menu appears at the pointer. On a Mac with only one mouse button, you can simulate a right click by holding down the Control key on the keyboard before clicking, or if you have a newer Mac, you can press down with two fingers anywhere on the mouse, trackpad, or touchpad.

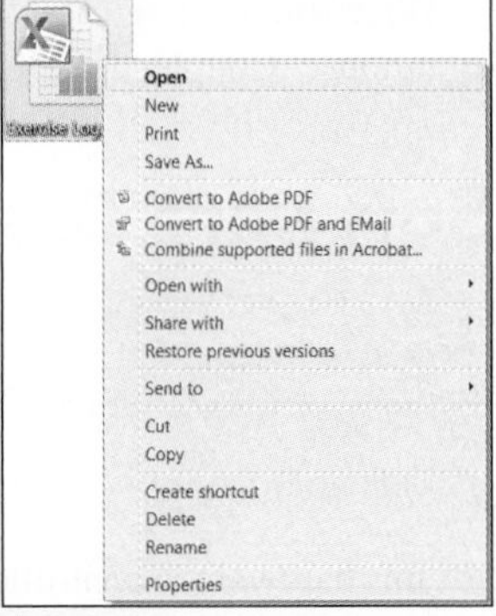

FIGURE A.3

what your screen display looks like as you work and how you tell the computer what you want it to do. Most PCs today use some version of the *Microsoft Windows* operating system; Mac computers use some version of Apple's *Mac OS*.

Application programs, also called simply **applications**, are software tools that enable you to use a computer for specific purposes. Some applications are designed to accomplish well-defined, short-term goals. For example, an application might provide interactive lessons to learn a language. Other applications have more general and open-ended goals. For example, you can use a word-processing program, such as Microsoft Word, to create memos, letters, term papers, novels, textbooks, or World Wide Web pages—just about any kind of text-based document.

In the PC world, a **document** is a file created by an application, regardless of whether it has actually been printed. Application files and document files are different types of files. A **file** is a named collection of data stored on a computer disk or some other storage medium. Applications are sometimes called *executable files* because they contain instructions that can be executed by the computer. Documents are sometimes called *data files* because they contain passive data rather than instructions. When you type a report with the Microsoft Word application, the computer executes the Word instructions. When you save the report on the computer's hard disk, the computer creates a Word document—a data file that contains the contents of the report.

Entering, Editing, and Formatting Text

You can type and edit a word-processing document using standard PC techniques and tools. As you type, your text is displayed on the screen and stored in RAM. With virtually all modern word processors, words appear on the screen almost exactly as they will appear on a printed page. This feature is often referred to as **WYSIWYG**—short for "what you see is what you get" and pronounced "wizzy-wig." Because of a feature called **word wrap**, the word processor automatically moves any words that won't fit on the current line to the next line along with the cursor.

Word-processing programs—and many other types of applications—contain text-editing tools for changing and rearranging the words on the screen. Most computer users are familiar with the **Clipboard**, which can temporarily store chunks of text and other data, making it possible to **cut** or **copy** words from one part of a document and **paste** them into another part of the same document or a different document. In many programs, you can achieve similar results by using **drag-and-drop** technology that allows you to drag a selected block of text from one location to another. **Find-and-replace (search and replace)** tools make it possible to make repetitive changes throughout a document.

Formatting Characters

Text **formatting** commands enable you to control the *format* of the document. For example, you can change the way the words look on the page. Most modern word processors include commands for controlling the formats of individual characters and paragraphs as well as complete documents.

Most printers can print text in a variety of point sizes, typefaces, and styles that aren't possible with typewriters. Characters are measured by **point size**, with one point equal to 1/72 inch. Most documents, including this book, use smaller point sizes for text to fit more information on each page and larger point sizes to make titles and headings stand out.

In the language of typesetters, a **font** is a size and style of **typeface**. For example, the Helvetica typeface includes many fonts, one of which is 12-point Helvetica bold. In the PC world, many people use the terms *font* and *typeface* interchangeably.

Whatever you call them, you have hundreds of choices of typefaces. **Serif fonts**, such as those in the Times family, are embellished with serifs—fine lines at the ends of the main strokes of each character. **Sans-serif fonts**, such as those in the Helvetica or Verdana family, have plainer, cleaner lines. **Monospaced fonts** that mimic typewriters, such as those in the Courier family, produce characters that always take up the same amount of space, no

Examples of	12-point size	24-point size
Serif fonts	Times New Roman	Times New Roman
	Georgia	Georgia
	Palatino	Palatino
Sans-serif fonts	Arial Narrow	Arial Narrow
	Helvetica	Helvetica
	Univers 55	Univers 55
	Verdana	Verdana
Monospaced fonts	Courier	Courier
	Monaco	Monaco

FIGURE A.4 These fonts represent only a few of the hundreds of typefaces available for personal computers and printers today.

matter how skinny or fat the characters are. In contrast, **proportionally spaced fonts** enable more room for wide characters, such as *W*s, than for narrow characters, such as *I*s.

The Screen Test boxes on the following pages show examples of software at work. In these simple examples, we'll use a word-processing application to edit and save a document containing the essay, "Why I Went to the Woods," by Thoreau. The first example uses Microsoft Word on a PC with the Microsoft Windows 7 operating system. The second example shows the same thing using Microsoft Word on a Macintosh with Mac OS X. In both examples, we'll perform the following steps:

1. Open Microsoft Word and copy the application program from the computer's hard disk into memory where it can be executed.
2. Type, edit, and format the document.
3. Save the document.
4. Close the application.

Before we begin, a reminder and a disclaimer:

The reminder: The *Screen Test* examples are designed to give you a feel for the software, not to provide how-to instructions. You can learn how to use the software using lab manuals or other books on the subject, some of which are listed in *Sources and Resources* at the ends of the chapters in this book.

The disclaimer: These examples are provided so you can compare different types of interfaces, not so you can establish a favorite. The brand of software in a particular *Screen Test* box isn't as important as the general concepts built into that software. One of the best things about computers is that they offer many different ways to do things. These examples, and others throughout the book, are designed to expose you to possibilities. Even if you have no plans to use the operating systems or applications in the examples—*especially* if you have no plans to use them—you can learn something by looking at them as a curious observer.

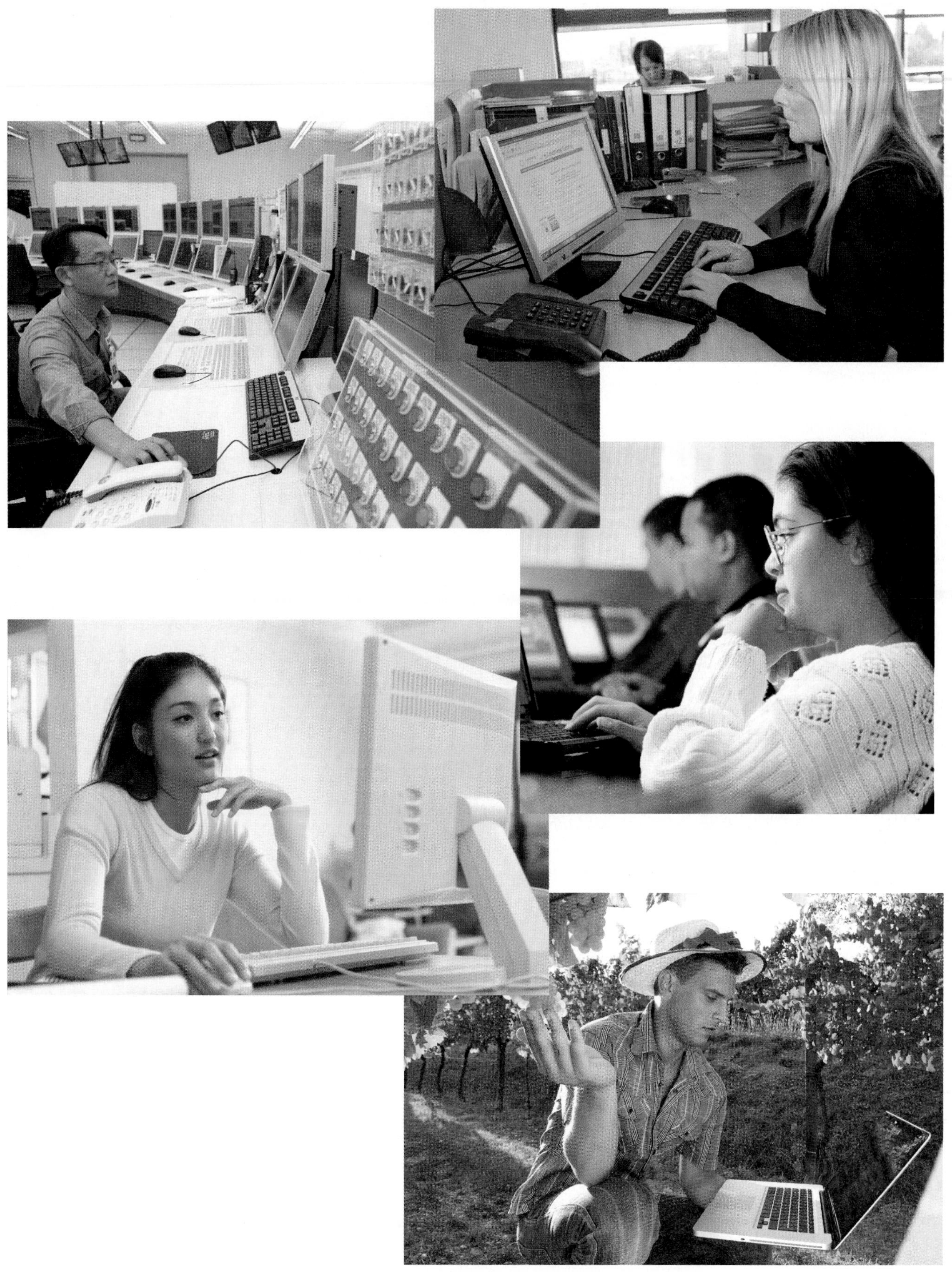

FIGURE A.5 Software makes it possible for PCs to be put to work in homes, schools, offices, factories, and farms.

Screen Test Using Microsoft Word with Microsoft Windows

GOAL *To create a document containing highlights from a famous essay*

TOOL *Microsoft Word and Microsoft Windows 7*

1. After your PC completes its startup process, the Windows desktop appears—a screen that includes icons representing objects used in your work.

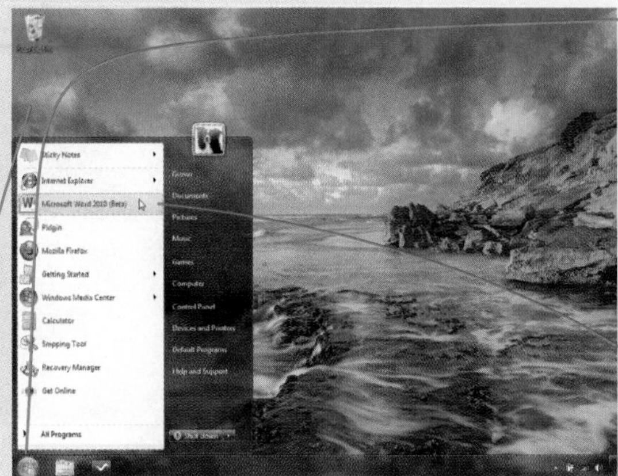

2. You click Start in the lower-left corner of the screen. The Start menu appears, enabling you to select from the applications and documents you use most frequently.

3. You select Microsoft Word and click to open the program.

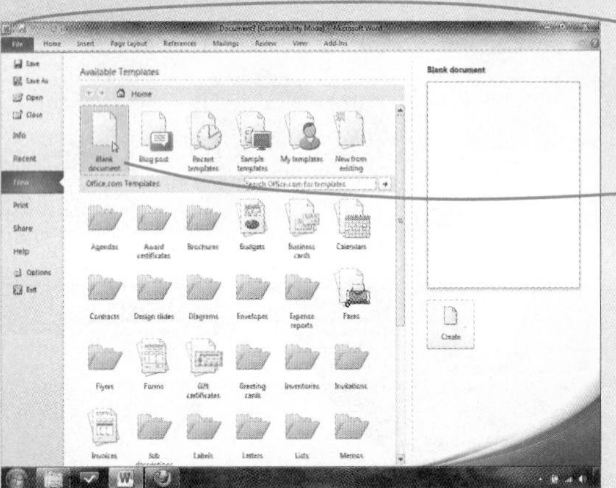

4. The Microsoft Word application opens, and you are presented with a blank document; clicking the Office button in the upper left opens a menu containing options that represent frequently used commands and files.

5. Because this is a new paper, you click New Document. You're ready to start typing the paper.

6. As you type, the uppermost lines scroll out of view to make room on the screen for the new ones. The text you've entered is still in memory, even though you can't see it on the screen.

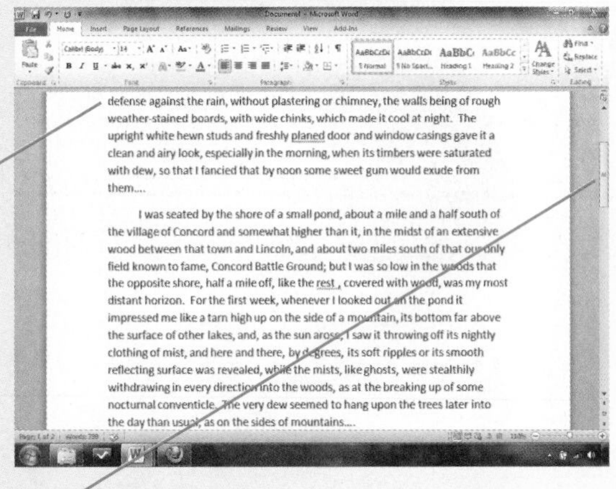

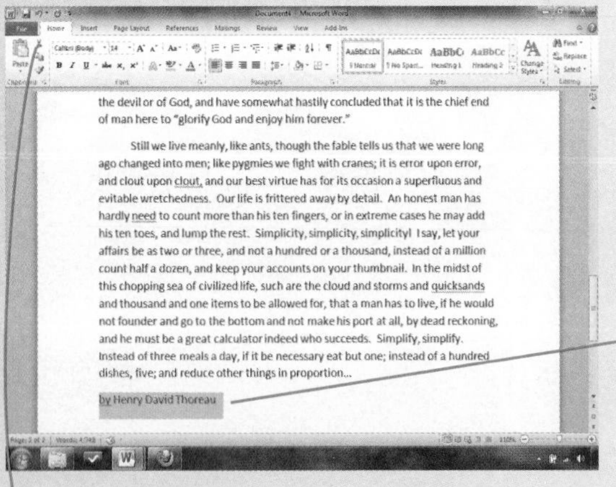

7. You can view it anytime by scrolling backward through the text using the vertical scrollbar on the right edge of the window. In this respect, a word processor document is like a modern version of an ancient paper scroll.

8. After you enter the text, you decide that "by Henry David Thoreau" should be at the top of the document, immediately below the title, rather than at the bottom of the document. Using the mouse, you select the author's byline. Selected text appears highlighted on the screen.

9. Choosing the Cut command tells the computer to cut the selected text from the document and place it in the Clipboard—a special portion of temporary memory used to hold information for later use.

FIGURE A.6

10. After using the mouse or arrow keys to reposition the cursor at the beginning of the document, you select the Paste command. The computer places a copy of the Clipboard's contents at the insertion point; the text below the cursor moves down to make room for the inserted text.

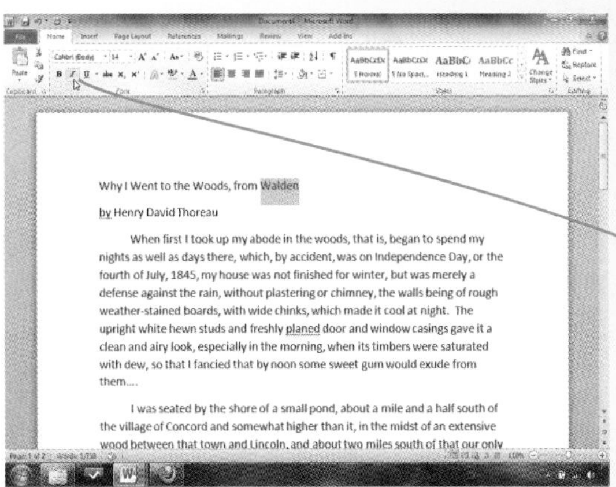

11. To italicize the title "Walden," you select the characters to be changed and click the button labeled *I* on the Ribbon.

12. You can center text by selecting it and clicking the Center button located in the Paragraph group on the Home tab of the Ribbon.

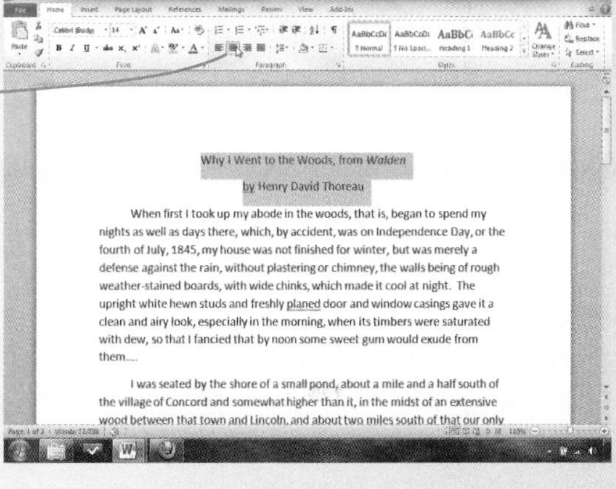

13. You're done working with the essay for now, so you choose Save from the File menu.

14. Because you haven't saved the document before, the Save As dialog box opens and prompts you for the name of the file and the location of the directory in which to store it.

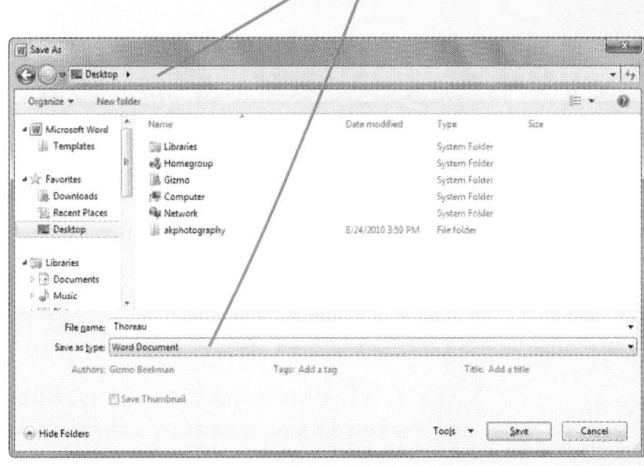

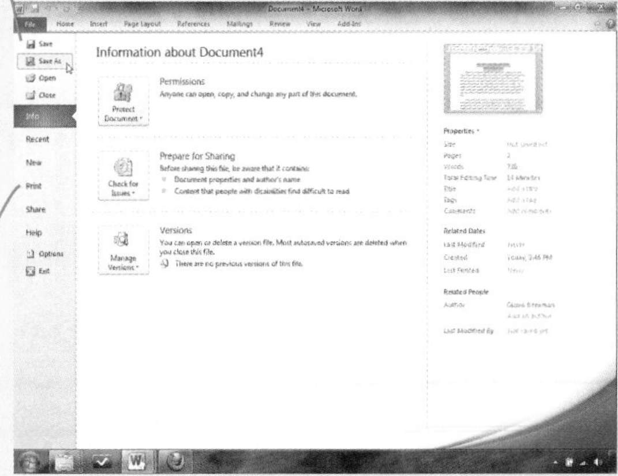

15. The File menu also contains a Print command, allowing you to print a hard copy of the essay.

Screen Test Using Microsoft Word with Mac OS X

GOAL *To edit a term paper*

TOOL *Mac OS 10.6 and Microsoft Word*

1. The Mac menu bar spans the top of the screen.

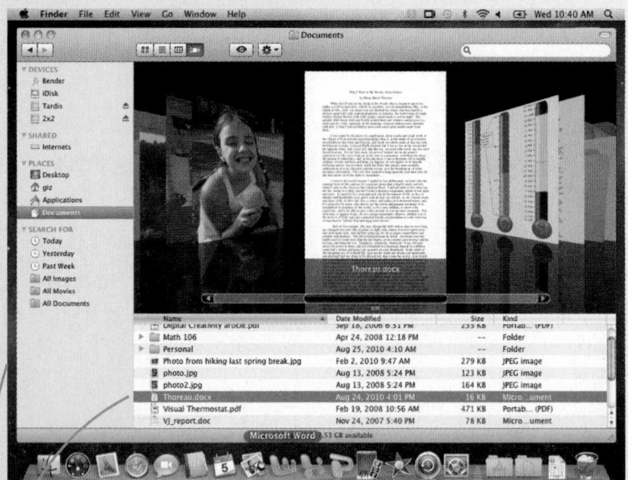

2. Like the Windows desktop, the Mac desktop, called the Finder, uses icons that represent objects used in your work. Cover Flow view allows you to flip through the icons like a deck of cards, and preview the documents before you've opened them. Many commonly used icons are visible on the left side of every Finder window.

3. At the bottom of the screen is the Dock, which is a holding place for frequently used applications and documents.

4. A window shows the contents of the Documents folder on the hard disk. Folders, like their real-world counterparts, enable you to group related documents.

5. You double-click the Thoreau-Walden document to open it.

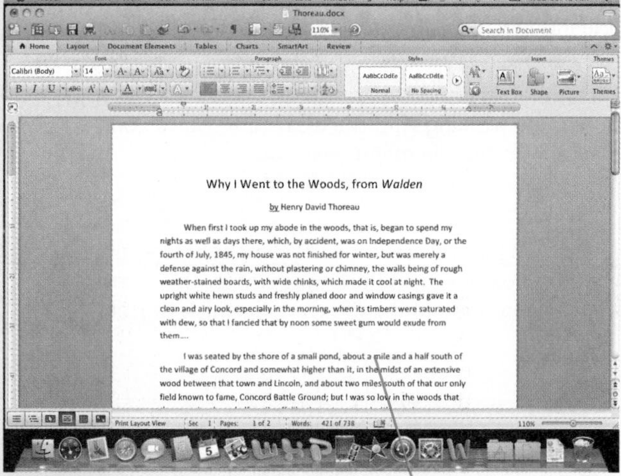

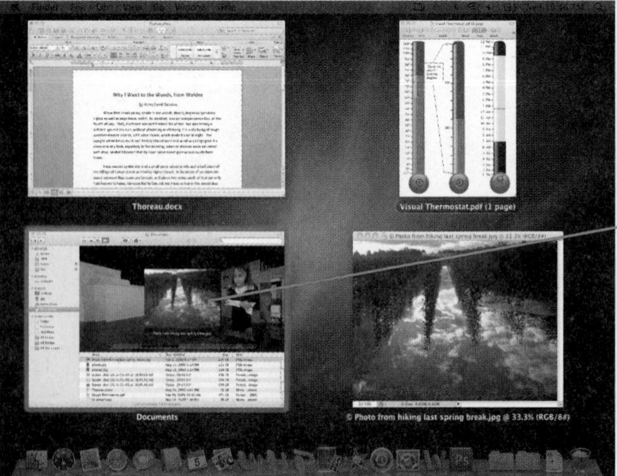

6. The document opens in a window. You edit and print the document; the process is similar for the Macintosh and Windows versions of Word.

7. A Mac OS feature called Exposé enables you, with a single keystroke, to see shrunken images of all of your open windows neatly tiled on the screen so you can quickly find the one you're looking for—in this case, the Documents folder window. You can click on it to bring it to the foreground.

FIGURE A.7

File Management Basics

A place for everything and **everything in its place.**

—Sailor's proverb

In Windows and the Mac OS, a file is represented by a name and an icon. It's not always easy to tell what a file contains based on its name. Most people know that it's a good idea to name files with clearly descriptive names, but some names are difficult to decipher. A filename includes an *extension*—a string of three or four characters that follows a period (.) at the end of the filename. (The operating system may be set on your machine to hide the extensions on the screen, but they're still visible to the OS.) The extension gives more information about the file's origin or use. For example, the name of a Windows executable file typically includes the extension *.exe*, as in *biggame.exe*. The filename of a Microsoft Word document usually ends with *.docx*, such as *termpaper.docx*. A *.pdf* extension typically designates files containing information stored in Portable Document Format, which you can view with Adobe Acrobat Reader and many other applications. If a file doesn't have a visible extension in its name, you still might be able to tell what it is by looking at its icon. Most popular applications create documents with distinctive icons.

Hundreds of filename extensions exist. Fortunately, you don't need to worry about memorizing them because the operating system usually knows which application program is associated with each extension. For example, double-clicking the icon for file *Table.xlsx* results in the operating system running Microsoft Excel because it associates the*.xlsx* extension with Excel spreadsheets.

File Organization Basics

In the physical world, people often use file folders to organize their paper documents into meaningful collections—class documents, financial papers, receipts, and the like. Similarly, computer files can be organized into collections using **folders** (sometimes called directories). The operating system enables you to create folders, give them meaningful names, and store documents and other files inside them. When you open a folder, the folder's window opens, revealing the files that it contains. You can organize folders *hierarchically*, meaning a folder can contain other folders, which in turn can contain still more folders. For example, a folder called Documents might contain folders called School Work, Financial Papers, Letters, and Pictures. School Work might contain folders for individual classes, each of which might be subdivided into Homework, Projects, and so on. Windows and Mac operating systems include a variety of tools for quickly navigating through nested folders to locate particular files.

In the real world, people aren't as organized as computers, and files don't always end up in the appropriate folders. Modern operating systems include **Search** or **Find** commands that can help you find files no matter where they are stored on the system. You can search for filenames, but you can also search for words or phrases inside a document. So if you don't know the name of a file, but do know some of the text in that file, you can still use the search tool to find your data.

File Compression Basics

The largest files on your hard disk are probably those containing videos, songs, or images. **File compression** is the process of reducing the size of a file so that you can fit more files into the same amount of disk space. **File decompression** is the process of restoring the file to its original state. Compressing a file is like squeezing a sponge. You can fit a lot more sponges in a box if you squeeze them together. When you want to use one of the sponges, you remove it from the box, and it springs back to its original size. Letting the sponge go back to its original size is like decompressing a file.

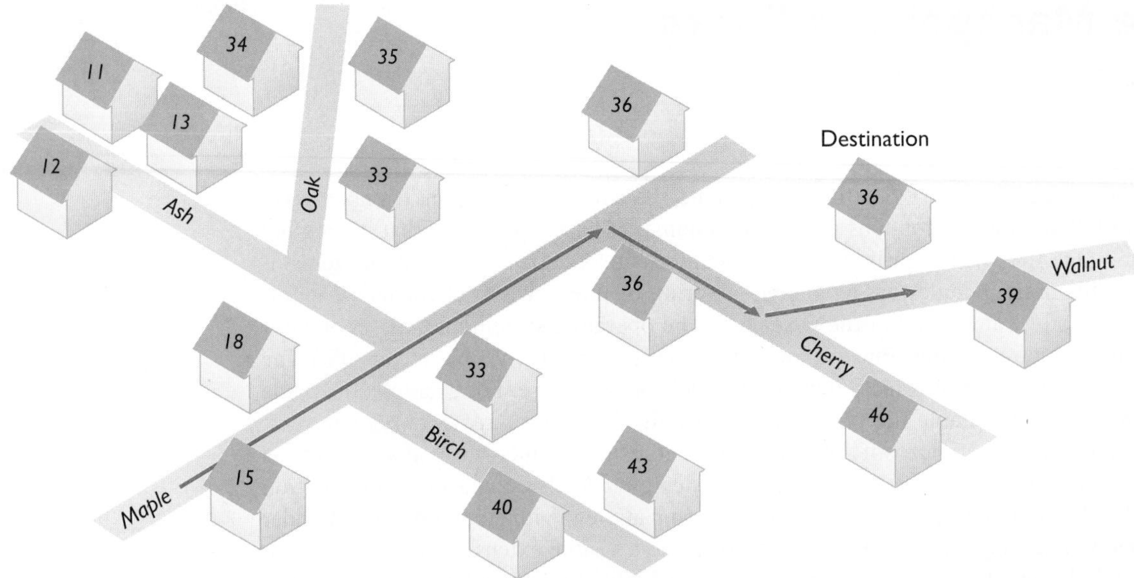

FIGURE A.8 The hierarchical organization of folders is like a suburban subdivision with dead-end streets fanning out from a single road. Suppose your destination is 36 Walnut Street. You follow Maple Street to Cherry Street, Cherry Street to Walnut Street, and you can get to 36 Walnut Street.

You can perform file compression by using an application, an operating system, or another type of software program. For example, with Adobe Photoshop you can save a digital photograph by using GIF or JPEG compression to reduce its file size. Similarly, with Winamp and iTunes, you can convert standard digital music files to compressed MP3 files. Just about any file or group of files can be compressed using the Windows or Macintosh operating system or a compression utility, such as PKZIP or Stuffit. If you see a file with a.*zip* or.*sitx* extension, it needs to be decompressed before you use it in an application. File compression is especially important when working with video, audio, and multimedia files. Chapter 6 covers file compression techniques in more detail.

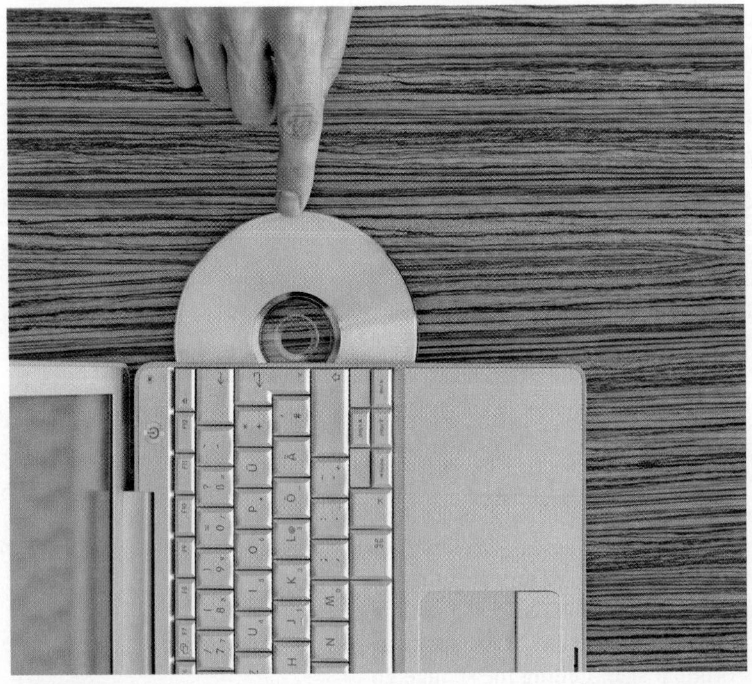

FIGURE A.9 The DVD-R disc is a popular backup medium.

Backup Basics

Just about any computer file user can remember losing important work because of a hard disk failure, a software bug, or a computer virus that destroyed data files. It's a good idea to protect yourself against disaster by frequently backing up your data. A **backup copy** is a copy of a file created as insurance against the loss of the original. It makes sense to keep backup copies on a different device than the one that holds the original copies. Many people use CD-Rs, DVD-Rs, external hard drives, flash drives, and other **backup media** to hold backup copies of their most important documents.

Backing up an entire hard disk on CDs or DVDs can involve many disks—and hours of tedious disk swapping. To save time, many people use external hard drives as backup devices. Backup drives don't need to be attached directly to individual computers because backups can be performed over computer networks, discussed in the next section.

Screen Test File Management with Windows

GOAL *To organize files into folders*

TOOL *Microsoft Windows 7*

1. Your files are scattered across your desktop; you'd like to organize them by folder. After you open the Documents folder from the Start menu, you select all the unfiled documents (by dragging a rectangle around them) and drag them to the Documents folder. The icons appear as transparent images in the window while you're dragging them.

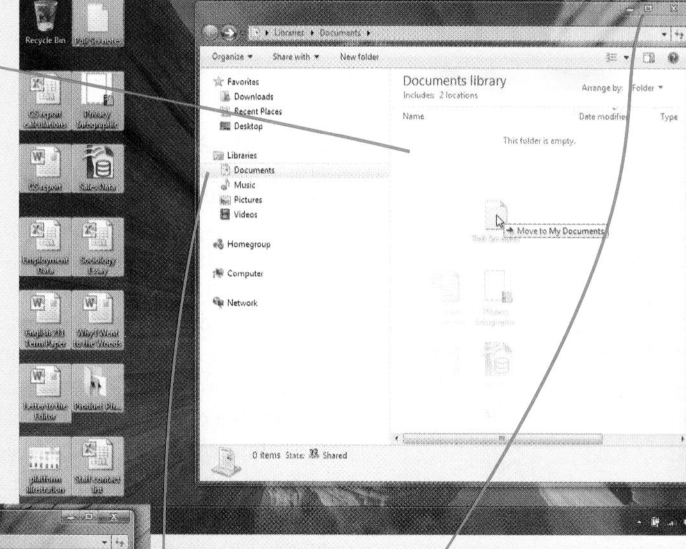

2. You use a button in the toolbar to create two new folders named School and Work within the Documents folder.

3. You select and drag all of the work-related documents into the Work folder. The Work folder icon is highlighted when you drag the documents into it.

4. You create a third folder, Personal, and distribute the unsorted documents into the new folders that you've created.

5. You click on the Expand button next to the folders in the sidebar to show the hierarchical organization of the folders on your hard drive.

FIGURE A.10

Network and Internet Basics

Give a person a fish and you'll feed them for a day. Teach them to use the internet and **they won't bother you for weeks...**

—*Ian Jukes*

Today's PCs are powerful tools that can perform a variety of tasks that go far beyond the basic word processing examples illustrated here. This book explores many of these applications, from money management to multimedia. But a PC's real power is unleashed when it's connected to other computers through a network.

PC Network Basics

A computer may have a *direct connection* to a network—for example, cables might connect it to other computers, printers, and other devices in an office or student lab. These networked machines can easily and quickly share information with each other. When a computer isn't physically close to the other machines in the network, it can still communicate with those machines through a *remote access* connection.

An entire computer network can be connected to other networks through cables, wireless radio transmissions, or other means. The **Internet** is an elaborate network of interconnected networks. If a computer has a direct connection to a network that's part of the Internet, it has a direct Internet connection. Most PCs are connected to the Internet through other means. Computers with broadband connections use cable modems, DSL routers, and satellite connections to connect to the Internet. Others use slower dial-up connections through modems connected to phone lines. Many homes, schools, and businesses use Wi-Fi technology to create wireless networks, enabling portable computer users to connect to the Internet without cables.

Internet Basics

What interests me about it ... is that it's a form of communication **unlike any other** and yet the second you start doing it **you understand it**.

—*Nora Ephron, Director of* You've Got Mail

There was a time, not too many years ago, when word processing was the most popular computer activity among students. For most students, the computer was little more than a high-powered typewriter. Today a PC can be a window into the global system of interconnected networks known as the Internet, or just the *Net*.

The Internet is used by mom-and-pop businesses and multinational corporations that want to communicate with their customers, sell products, and track economic conditions; by kindergartners and college students doing research and exploration; by consumers and commuters who need access to timely information, goods, and services; and by families and friends who just want to stay in touch. Most people connect to the Internet because it gives them the power to do things that they couldn't easily do otherwise.

Using the Internet you can:

- Send a message to 1 or 1,001 people, around town or around the world, and receive replies almost as quickly as the recipients can read the message and type a response.

FIGURE A.11 Networked computers in this lab allow students to share files, send messages, and connect to the Internet.

- Explore vast libraries of research material, ranging from classic scholarly works to contemporary reference works.
- Find instant answers to time-sensitive questions.
- Get medical, legal, or technical advice from a wide variety of experts.
- Listen to and watch live broadcasts from around the world.
- Get instant access to millions of video and audio clips and features, from simple home movies and songs to big-budget blockbusters.
- Participate in discussions or play games with people all over the globe who share your interests.
- Shop for obscure items, such as out-of-print books and CDs that you can't find elsewhere.
- Download free software or music clips from servers all over the world onto your computer.
- Order a custom-built computer, car, or condominium.
- Develop panglobal friendships, relationships, and communities based on shared interests.
- Take a course for college credit from a school thousands of miles away.
- Publish your own writings, drawings, photos, and multimedia works so Internet users all over the world can view them.
- Start your own business and interact with clients around the world.

Every revolution has a dark side, and the Internet explosion is no exception. The Internet has plenty of worthless information, scams, and questionable activities. People who make the most of the Internet know how to separate the best of the Net from the rest of the Net. Every chapter of this book contains information that will help you understand and use the Internet wisely. In this appendix, we'll focus on the basics of the two most popular Internet applications: finding information on the World Wide Web and communicating with electronic mail.

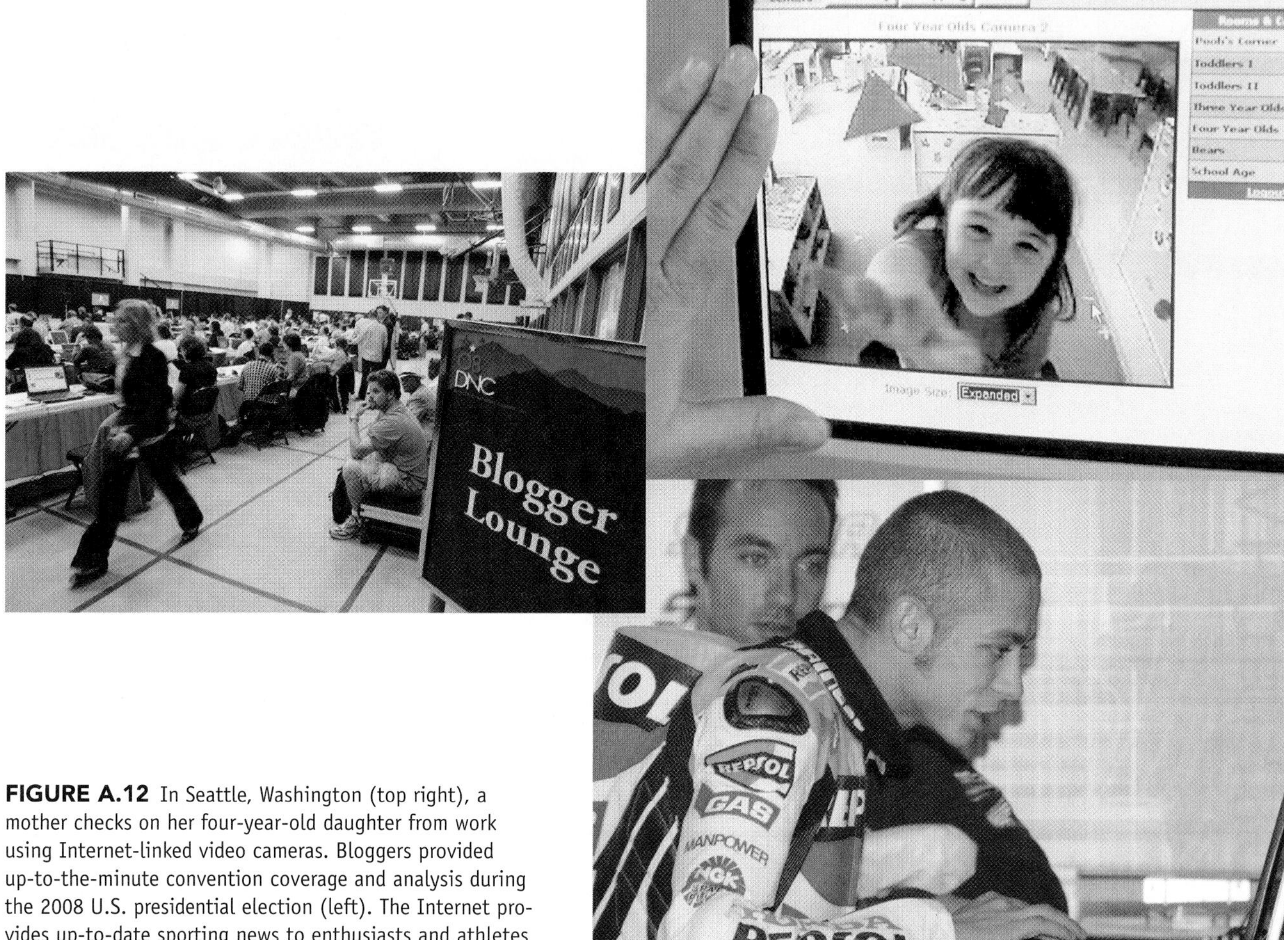

FIGURE A.12 In Seattle, Washington (top right), a mother checks on her four-year-old daughter from work using Internet-linked video cameras. Bloggers provided up-to-the-minute convention coverage and analysis during the 2008 U.S. presidential election (left). The Internet provides up-to-date sporting news to enthusiasts and athletes (bottom right).

World Wide Web Basics

The **World Wide Web** makes the Internet accessible to people all over the planet. The *Web* is a huge portion of the Internet that includes a wealth of multimedia content accessible through simple point-and-click programs called **Web browsers**. Web browsers on PCs, phones, and other devices serve as windows to the Web's diverse information.

The World Wide Web is made up of millions of interlinked documents called **Web pages**. A Web page is typically made up of text and images, like a page in a book. A collection of related pages stored on the same computer is called a **Web site**; a typical Web site is organized around a home page that serves as an entry page and a stepping-off point for other pages in the site. Each Web page has a unique address, technically referred to as a **uniform resource locator (URL)**. For example, the URL for this book's home page is **http://www.pearsonhighered.com/beekman**. You can visit the site by typing the exact URL into the address box of your Web browser.

The Web is an example of a *hypertext* system. A typical Web page contains information, such as words and pictures, as well as connections to other Web pages. A Web browser enables you to jump from one Web page to another by clicking **hyperlinks** (often called *links*), which are words, pictures, or menu items that act as buttons.

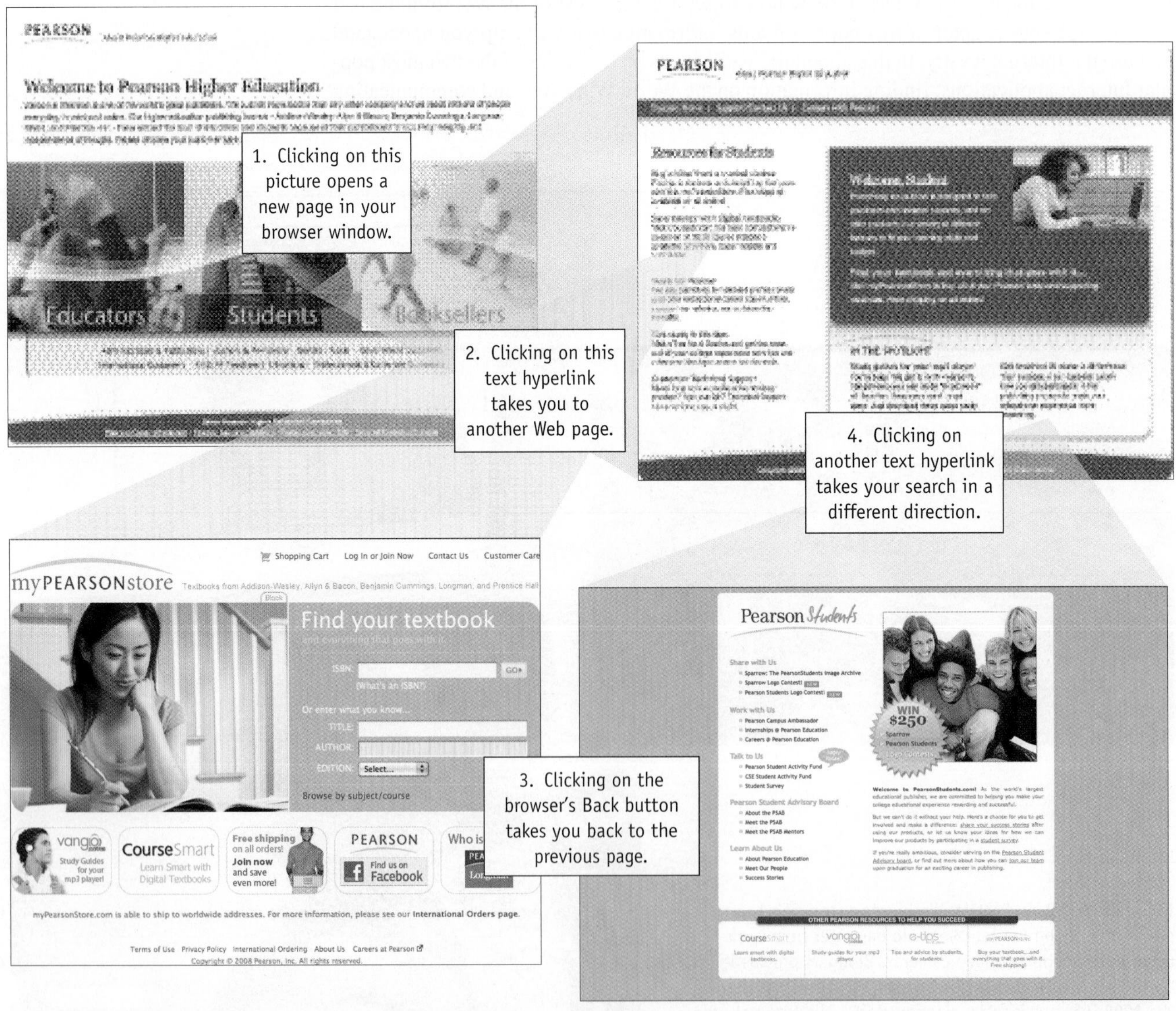

FIGURE A.13 Hypertext links make it possible to navigate quickly through a Web site to locate a page containing specific information.

Hypertext systems, such as the Web, contain "pages," but they don't work like books. The author of a novel expects you to start at page one, move on to page two, and continue reading the pages in order until you have finished the last page. Hyperlinks enable you to access the pages of a hypertext system in a variety of ways, depending on your needs. For example, at the *Digital Planet* Web site, you can select a chapter number to jump to pages related to that chapter. Within the chapter, you can click Online Study Guide to jump to a page containing practice quiz questions. Or you can click Web Resources to jump to a page full of hyperlinks that can take you to pages on other Web sites. These off-site pages contain articles, illustrations, audio clips, video segments, and resources created by others. They reside on computers owned by corporations, universities, libraries, institutions, and individuals around the world.

Text links are typically, but not always, displayed in a different color than standard text on the page. You can explore an amazing variety of Web pages by clicking links. But this kind of random jumping isn't without frustrations. Some links lead to cobwebs—Web pages that haven't been kept up to date by their owners—and dead ends—pages that have been removed or moved. Even if a link is current, it may not be reputable or accurate; because anybody can create Web pages, they don't all have the editorial integrity of trusted print media.

It can also be frustrating to try to find your way back to pages you've seen on the Web. That's why browsers have ***Back*** and ***Forward buttons***; you can retrace your steps as often as you like. These buttons won't help, though, if you're trying to find an important page from an earlier session. Most browsers include tools for keeping personal lists of memorable sites, called ***bookmarks*** or ***favorites***. When you run across a page worth revisiting, you can mark it with a Bookmark or Add to Favorites command. Then you can revisit that site anytime by selecting it from the list. Even if you didn't bookmark a page, you might be able to find it by looking through your recent ***history*** of pages visited in your Web browser.

Web Search Basics

> The ability to **ask the right question** is more than half the battle of **finding the answer**.
>
> *—Thomas J. Watson, founder of IBM*

The World Wide Web is like a giant, loosely woven, constantly changing document created by thousands of unrelated authors and scattered about in computers all over the world. The biggest challenge for many Web users is extracting the useful information from the rest. If

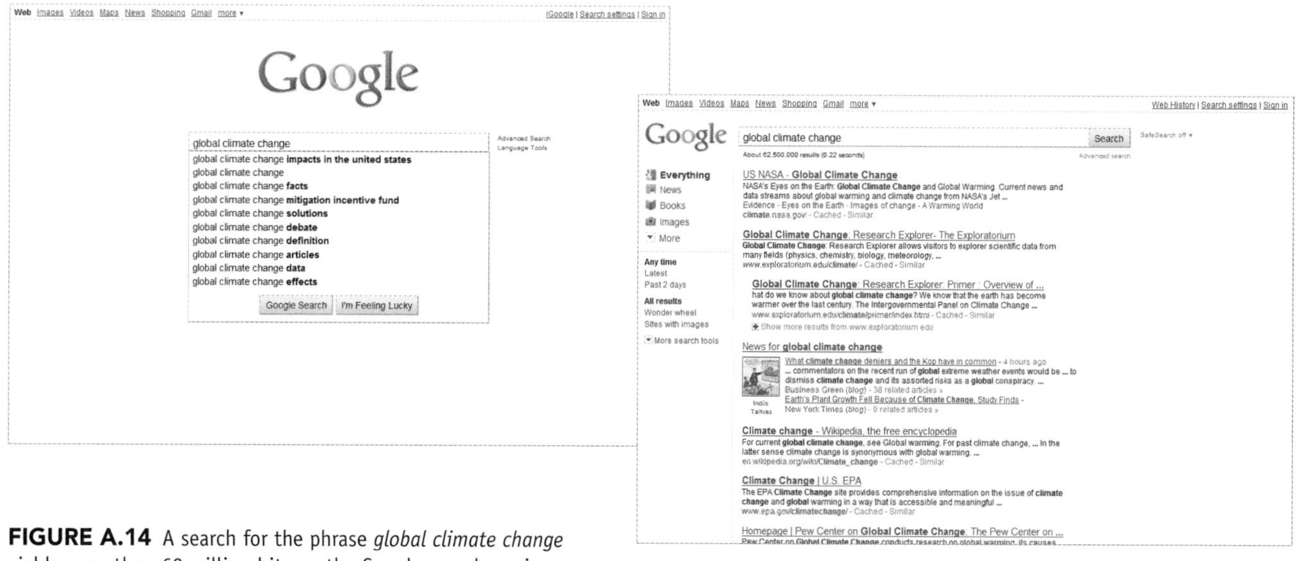

FIGURE A.14 A search for the phrase *global climate change* yields more than 62 million hits on the Google search engine.

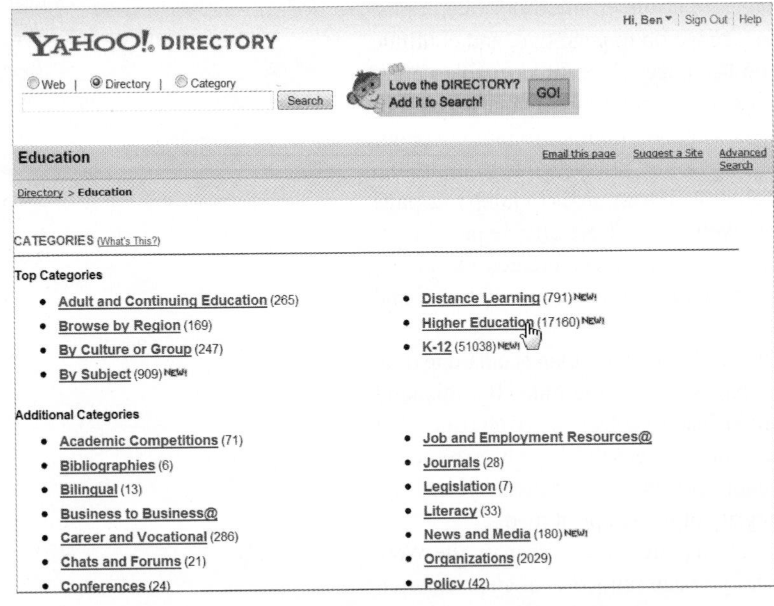

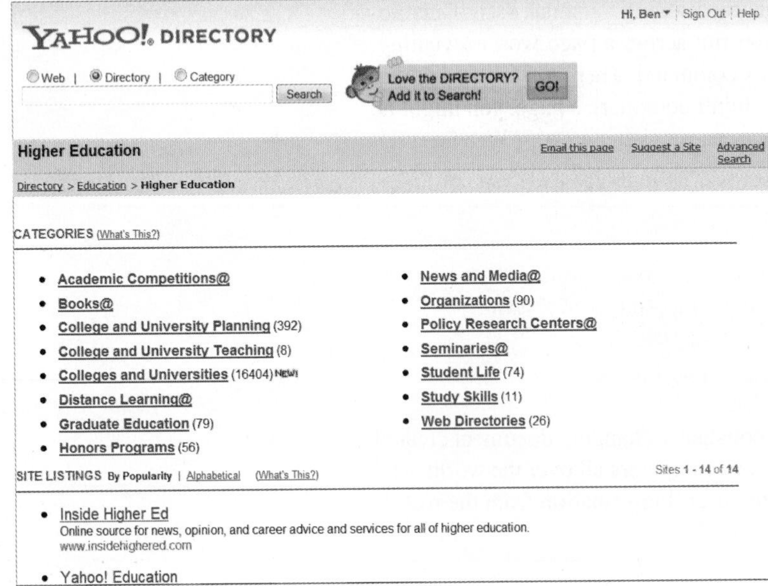

FIGURE A.15 Yahoo!'s subject tree enables you to narrow your search by clicking categories within a subject.

you're looking for a specific information resource, but you don't know where it is located on the Web, you might be able to find it using a **search engine**.

A search engine is built around a database that catalogs Web locations based on content. (Databases are covered in Chapter 7; for now, you can just think of them as indexed collections of information stored in computers.) Most search engines use software to search the Web and catalog information automatically. The usefulness of a search engine depends in part on the information in its database. But it also depends on how easy it is for people to find what they're looking for in the database.

To find information with a typical search engine, you type a keyword or keywords into a search field, click a button, and watch your Web browser display a list of ***hits***—pages that contain the requested keywords. A search engine can easily produce a list of millions or billions of hits. Most search engines attempt to list pages in order from best to worst match, but these automatic rankings aren't always reliable.

Another popular way to use a search engine is to repeatedly narrow the search using a ***directory*** or ***subject tree***—a hierarchical catalog of Web sites compiled by researchers. A screen presents you with a menu of subject choices. When you click a subject—say, Government—you narrow your search to that subject, and you're presented with a menu of subcategories within that subject—Military, Politics, Law, Taxes, and so on. You can continue to narrow your search by proceeding through subject menus until you reach a list of selected Web sites related to the final subject. The sites are usually rank-ordered based on estimated value. The list of Web sites on a given index page is not exhaustive; there may be hundreds of pages related to the subject that aren't included in any directory. It's simply not possible to keep a complete index of all the pages on the ever-changing Web.

Popular search engines are located on Google, MSN Yahoo!, and other Internet ***portals***—Web sites designed as first-stop gateways for Internet surfers. Internet Explorer, Netscape, and other Web browsers include Search buttons that connect to popular search engines. And many large Web sites include search engines that enable you to search for site-specific information.

Email Basics

> Each person on the "**Internet**" has a unique email "**address**" created by **having a squirrel** run across a computer keyboard ... .
>
> —*Dave Barry, humorist*

Electronic mail (also called email or *e-mail*) is the application that lures many people to the Internet for the first time. Email programs make it possible for even casual computer users to send messages to family, friends, and colleagues easily.

Because an email message can be written, addressed, sent, delivered, and answered in a matter of minutes—even if the correspondents are on opposite sides of the globe—email has replaced air mail for rapid, routine communication in many organizations. If you send someone an email message, that person can log in and read it from a computer at home, at the office, or from anywhere in the world at any time of day. Unlike a ringing phone, email waits patiently in the mailbox until the recipient has the time to handle it, making email particularly attractive when the communication is between people in different time zones.

Closer to home, email makes it possible to replace time-consuming phone calls and meetings with more efficient online exchanges. Email conversations allow groups of people to discuss an idea for hours, days, or weeks, thus avoiding the urgency of needing to settle a complicated issue in a single session. You can send a message to a group of people on a mailing list as easily as you send the message to one person. Since an email message is digital data, you can edit it and combine it with other computer-generated documents. When you're finished, you can forward the edited message back to the original sender or to somebody else for further processing.

Details vary, but the basic concepts of email are the same for almost all systems. When you sign up for an email account—through your school, your company, or a private *Internet service provider (ISP)*—you receive a **user name** (sometimes called a *login name* or *alias*) and a storage area for messages (sometimes called a *mailbox*). Any user can send an email message to anyone else, regardless of whether the recipient is currently *logged in*—connected to the network. The message will be waiting in the recipient's *inbox* the next time that person launches his or her email program and logs in. An email message can be addressed to one person or hundreds of people. Messages can carry documents, pictures, multimedia files, and other computer files as *attachments*.

An Internet email address is made up of two parts separated by an "at" sign (@): the person's user name and the *host name*—the name of the host computer, network, or ISP address from which the user receives mail. Here's the basic form:

username@hostname

Here are a few examples of typical email addresses:

realgeorge999@aol.com
jandumont@engr.ucla.edu
enathab@pop3.ispchannel.com

Some organizations use standardized email addresses so it's easy to guess member addresses. For example, every employee at ABCXYZ Company might have an email address of the form *firstname_lastname@abcxyzco.com*. (The underscore character is sometimes used as a substitute for a space because spaces can't be embedded in email addresses). It's important to address email messages with care; they can't be delivered if even a single character is mistyped. Fortunately, most email programs include address books so that after entering contact information once, users can look up email addresses by name and automatically address messages. Many Web sites offer free email search services and directories.

Many commercial Web sites offer free email accounts. Sometimes these free email services are subsidized by advertisers; sometimes they're provided to attract Web site visitors. Free email services are popular with users of public computers (for example, in libraries), people who don't receive email from their ISPs, people who want multiple email addresses not associated with their workplace, and travelers who want to check email on the road without lugging a laptop.

The example in the *Screen Test* shows a simple email session using Gmail—an email service that's accessible through a standard Web browser. The concepts illustrated in the example apply to all email programs.

Screen Test Communicating with Electronic Mail

GOAL *Catch up on your email*

TOOL *Google Gmail*

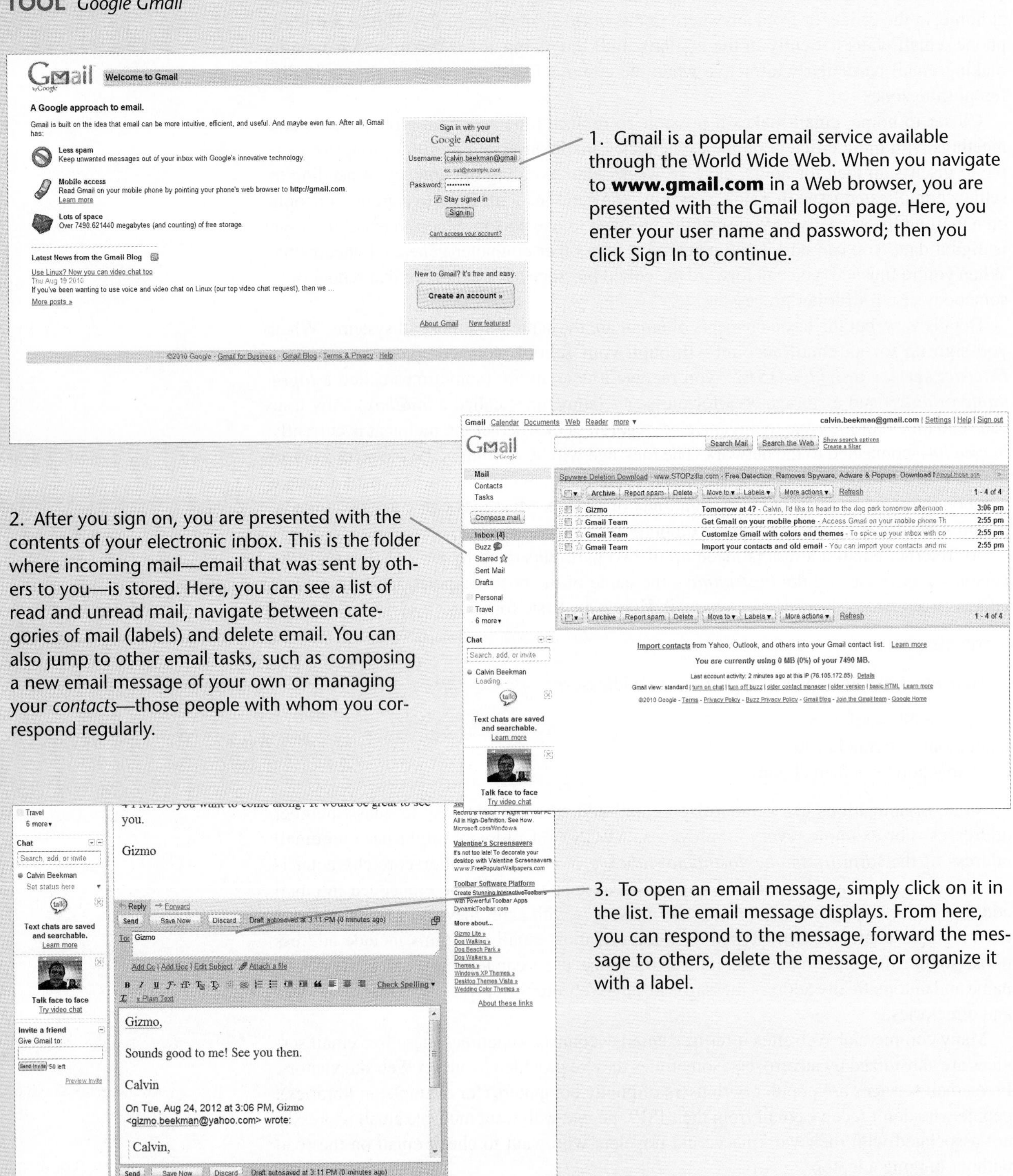

1. Gmail is a popular email service available through the World Wide Web. When you navigate to **www.gmail.com** in a Web browser, you are presented with the Gmail logon page. Here, you enter your user name and password; then you click Sign In to continue.

2. After you sign on, you are presented with the contents of your electronic inbox. This is the folder where incoming mail—email that was sent by others to you—is stored. Here, you can see a list of read and unread mail, navigate between categories of mail (labels) and delete email. You can also jump to other email tasks, such as composing a new email message of your own or managing your *contacts*—those people with whom you correspond regularly.

3. To open an email message, simply click on it in the list. The email message displays. From here, you can respond to the message, forward the message to others, delete the message, or organize it with a label.

FIGURE A.16

Internet Security Basics

In the same way that you should wear a seat belt and observe local laws when driving a car, you should approach the Internet understanding the security risks involved. When you connect a computer to a network or the Internet, you dramatically increase the risk that your system will be compromised in some way. But that doesn't mean that the Internet should be avoided. Rather, you just need to make sure you're taking the proper precautions.

The most common form of Internet-based security risk is probably **spam**, or junk mail. This is unwanted email you receive from (usually) unknown senders, such as mass mailers who are attempting to sell goods or deceive people into paying for nonexistent items. Most email programs now include *spam filters* that help keep this problem manageable, but even with a filter you're likely to spend plenty of time manually deleting spam messages.

A **virus** is a more sinister email problem. Generally delivered as email attachments, viruses are executable programs designed by malicious programmers—sometimes called *hackers*—to infiltrate your system. Some viruses simply duplicate themselves and send themselves to other PCs by harvesting email addresses in your email address book; these types of viruses can slow the performance of your network, making Internet access unbearably sluggish. Others can delete files and folders on your system. Either way, you shouldn't open unexpected attachments from unknown senders.

Another problem on the Internet is password theft. There are low-tech methods for stealing other people's passwords: For example, someone might look over your shoulder and watch as you type a password. Hackers can electronically monitor keystrokes and send the information over the Internet to others. A wider but related issue concerns *identity (ID) theft*. Hackers or other unscrupulous individuals can access your computer and obtain enough information about you to assume your identity. Identity thieves have been known to use victims' credit cards to rack up thousands of dollars in bills and create terrible inconveniences for innocent people. To protect yourself against ID theft, you should carefully guard your personal information, including your Social Security number, credit card numbers, and passwords, both online and off.

Obviously, there's a lot more to Internet security. We look extensively at this issue in Chapter 10.

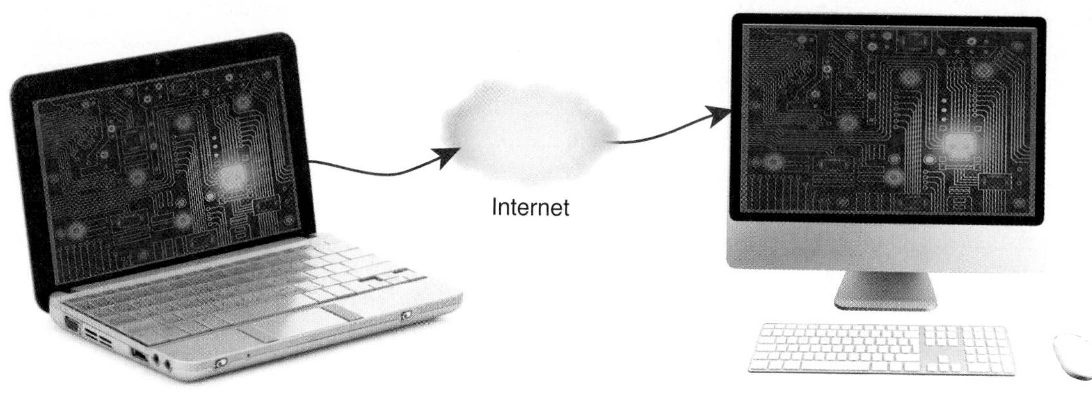

A programmer writes a tiny program—the virus—that has destructive power and can reproduce itself. Most often, the virus is attached to a normal program; unknown to the user, the virus spreads to other software.

The virus is passed by disk or network to other users who use other computers. The virus remains dormant as it is passed on.

Depending on how it is programmed, a virus may display an unexpected message, gobble up memory, destroy data files, or cause serious system errors.

FIGURE A.17 How a virus spreads.

Summary

PCs come in a variety of shapes and sizes, but they're all made up of two things: the physical parts of the computer, called hardware, and the software instructions that tell the hardware what to do. The PC's system unit contains the CPU, which controls the other components, including memory, disk drives, and monitor screens. The keyboard and mouse enable a user to communicate with the computer, which sends information back to the user through displays on the monitor.

The computer's operating system software takes care of details of the computer's operation. Application software provides specific tools for computer users. The file system contains the numerous files needed for the operating system and application software to run smoothly, and the personal files created by the computer's users. A hierarchical system of folders organizes the files, making it easier for application programs and computer users to find the files they need.

PCs can be networked to other computers using cables, radio waves, or other means. The Internet is a global network of computer networks used for education, commerce, and communication. The most popular Internet activities are exploring the World Wide Web and communicating with electronic mail.

A Web browser is a computer application that provides easy access to the World Wide Web—a wide-ranging array of multimedia information on the Internet. Web pages are interconnected by hyperlinks that make it easy to follow information trails. Search engines serve as indices for the Web, locating pages with subject matter that matches keywords.

Electronic mail (or email) enables almost instant communication among Internet users. Some email systems can be accessed through Web browsers.

The Internet is not without risks. Internet users must be prepared to deal with unsolicited (and often unsavory) email, computer viruses, identity theft, and other risks.

Key Terms

True or False

1. Roughly three-fourths of people in the world use PCs almost every day.
2. A computer keyboard includes some keys that don't respond by displaying characters on the screen, but instead send special commands to the computer.
3. Windows PCs and Macintoshes use the same operating system (OS).
4. An entire computer network can be connected to other networks through cables, wireless radio transmissions, or other means.

5. Hypertext links make the transmission of email messages between computers possible.

6. A Web search engine is built around a database that catalogs Web locations based on content.

7. An Internet email address is made up of a user name and a host name separated by ".com".

8. An email message must be composed in a word processor before it can be sent.

9. A spam filter can catch most junk email before it reaches the addressee.

10. Identity theft is no longer a major threat now that most PCs have switched to USB 3.0.

Multiple Choice

1. The computer's system unit typically contains the computer's "brain," called the
   a. central processing unit.
   b. memory.
   c. peripheral.
   d. monitor.
   e. modem.

2. The PC's main hard disk
   a. is a permanent part of the system unit.
   b. is sometimes called an internal drive.
   c. can hold more information than the computer's memory.
   d. serves as a long-term storage device.
   e. All of the above

3. Which of the following is NOT considered removable media?
   a. Blu-ray discs
   b. CD-ROMs
   c. Audio CDs
   d. Internal hard disks
   e. DVDs

4. Which of the following is not a peripheral?
   a. A printer
   b. A thumb drive
   c. An optical drive
   d. A processor
   e. All of the above

5. What is a software program designed to help you accomplish a specific task called?
   a. An application
   b. An operating system
   c. A document
   d. A desktop
   e. A browser

6. Virtually all modern word processors display words on the screen almost exactly as they will appear on the printed page. What is this feature called?
   a. Electronic paper
   b. Highlighting
   c. Point-and-click interface
   d. Virtual reality
   e. WYSIWYG (what you see is what you get)

7. In Windows and the Mac OS, a file is represented by
   a. underlined blue text.
   b. a folder with a name on the tab.
   c. a name and an extension.
   d. a link to a Web page.
   e. All of the above

8. In Windows and the Mac OS, which word or phrase best describes how files and folders are organized?
   a. Hypertextually
   b. Topologically
   c. Chronologically
   d. Hierarchically
   e. Randomly

9. Which of these is a type of backup media?
   a. CPU
   b. DVD-R
   c. Hotlink
   d. Backlit monitor
   e. RAM

10. Which of the following does every Web site on the World Wide Web have?
    a. Hyperlinks to dozens of other Web sites
    b. Multimedia material
    c. Publicly accessible information on a particular subject
    d. A unique address called a URL
    e. All of the above

11. If you want to retrace your steps and return to the screen previously displayed in the browser window, you should use
    a. the Retrace command.
    b. the R key.
    c. the browser's Back button.
    d. Control-X.
    e. There's no way to do that.

12. Which of the following is commonly used to find information on the Internet?
    a. A Finder application
    b. A search engine
    c. A URL (uniform resource locator)
    d. A right-click of the mouse on the desktop
    e. The digital dictionary of Internetology

13. Which of the following can be attached to an email message?
    a. A picture
    b. A multimedia file
    c. A word processor document
    d. A computer virus
    e. All of the above

14. Which of these is a valid email address?
    a. http://www.pearsoned.com
    b. beanbag boxspring @ prenhall.com
    c. presidentATwhitehouse.gov
    d. thisisaverylongnameindeed@aol.com
    e. All of the above could be valid email addresses.

15. Which of the following is the most common use of spam?
    a. Transmitting computer viruses
    b. Identity theft
    c. Marketing unsolicited goods and services
    d. Web searches
    e. Hacking

Review Questions

1. Briefly define or describe each of the key terms listed in the "Key Terms" section.
2. How are hardware and software related?
3. Which computer component is the most critical to the computer's functioning, and why?
4. Which computer component is most often used by people for getting original text into a PC?
5. What is the difference between operating system software and application software?
6. How do folders allow files to be organized?
7. What is the purpose of file compression?
8. List some ways that a computer might be connected to a network.
9. What is the fundamental difference between ordinary text (such as a novel) and hypertext?
10. Give examples of ways email differs from other common forms of communication between people.
11. How can you use hyperlinks to explore the World Wide Web? Give an example.
12. How can you find a site on the Web if you don't know the URL?
13. What security procedures should you follow while exploring the *Digital Planet* Web site?

APPENDIX B

ACM

ACM Code of Ethics and Professional Conduct (Adopted by ACM Council October 16, 1992)

Commitment to ethical professional conduct is expected of every member (voting members, associate members, and student members) of the Association for Computing Machinery (ACM).

This Code, consisting of 24 imperatives formulated as statements of personal responsibility, identifies the elements of such a commitment. It contains many, but not all, issues professionals are likely to face. Section 1 outlines fundamental ethical considerations, while Section 2 addresses additional, more specific considerations of professional conduct. Statements in Section 3 pertain more specifically to individuals who have a leadership role, whether in the workplace or in a volunteer capacity such as with organizations like ACM. Principles involving compliance with this Code are given in Section 4.

The Code shall be supplemented by a set of Guidelines, which provide explanation to assist members in dealing with the various issues contained in the Code. It is expected that the Guidelines will be changed more frequently than the Code.

The Code and its supplemented Guidelines are intended to serve as a basis for ethical decision making in the conduct of professional work. Secondarily, they may serve as a basis for judging the merit of a formal complaint pertaining to violation of professional ethical standards.

It should be noted that although computing is not mentioned in the imperatives of Section 1, the Code is concerned with how these fundamental imperatives apply to one's conduct as a computing professional. These imperatives are expressed in a general form to emphasize that ethical principles which apply to computer ethics are derived from more general ethical principles.

It is understood that some words and phrases in a code of ethics are subject to varying interpretations, and that any ethical principle may conflict with other ethical principles in specific situations. Questions related to ethical conflicts can best be answered by thoughtful consideration of fundamental principles, rather than reliance on detailed regulations.

1. General moral imperatives
2. More specific professional responsibilities
3. Organizational leadership imperatives
4. Compliance with the code

1. General Moral Imperatives

As an ACM member I will ...

1.1 Contribute to Society and Human Well-Being

This principle concerning the quality of life of all people affirms an obligation to protect fundamental human rights and to respect the diversity of all cultures. An essential aim of computing professionals is to minimize negative consequences of computing systems, including threats to health and safety. When designing or implementing systems, computing professionals must attempt to ensure that the products of their efforts will be used in socially responsible ways, will meet social needs, and will avoid harmful effects to health and welfare.

In addition to a safe social environment, human well-being includes a safe natural environment. Therefore, computing professionals who design and develop systems must be alert to, and make others aware of, any potential damage to the local or global environment.

1.2 Avoid Harm to Others

"Harm" means injury or negative consequences, such as undesirable loss of information, loss of property, property damage, or unwanted environmental impacts. This principle prohibits use of computing technology in ways that result in harm to any of the following: users, the general public, employees, and employers. Harmful actions include intentional destruction or modification of files and programs leading to serious loss of resources or unnecessary expenditure of human resources such as the time and effort required to purge systems of "computer viruses."

Well-intended actions, including those that accomplish assigned duties, may lead to harm unexpectedly. In such an event the responsible person or persons are obligated to undo or mitigate the negative consequences as much as possible. One way to avoid unintentional harm is to carefully consider potential impacts on all those affected by decisions made during design and implementation.

To minimize the possibility of indirectly harming others, computing professionals must minimize malfunctions by following generally accepted standards for system design and testing. Furthermore, it is often necessary to assess the social consequences of systems to project the likelihood of any serious harm to others. If system features are misrepresented to users, coworkers, or supervisors, the individual computing professional is responsible for any resulting injury.

In the work environment the computing professional has the additional obligation to report any signs of system dangers that might result in serious personal or social damage. If one's superiors do not act to curtail or mitigate such dangers, it may be necessary to "blow the whistle" to help correct the problem or reduce the risk. However, capricious or misguided reporting of violations can, itself, be harmful. Before reporting violations, all relevant aspects of the incident must be thoroughly assessed. In particular, the assessment of risk and responsibility must be credible. It is suggested that advice be sought from other computing professionals. See principle 2.5 regarding thorough evaluations.

1.3 Be Honest and Trustworthy

Honesty is an essential component of trust. Without trust an organization cannot function effectively. The honest computing professional will not make deliberately false or deceptive claims about a system or system design, but will instead provide full disclosure of all pertinent system limitations and problems.

A computer professional has a duty to be honest about his or her own qualifications, and about any circumstances that might lead to conflicts of interest.

Membership in volunteer organizations such as ACM may at times place individuals in situations where their statements or actions could be interpreted as carrying the "weight" of a larger group of professionals. An ACM member will exercise care to not misrepresent ACM or positions and policies of ACM or any ACM units.

1.4 Be Fair and Take Action Not to Discriminate

The values of equality, tolerance, respect for others, and the principles of equal justice govern this imperative. Discrimination on the basis of race, sex, religion, age, disability, national origin, or other such factors is an explicit violation of ACM policy and will not be tolerated.

Inequities between different groups of people may result from the use or misuse of information and technology. In a fair society, all individuals would have equal opportunity to participate in, or benefit from, the use of computer resources regardless of race, sex, religion, age, disability, national origin or other such similar factors. However, these ideals do not justify unauthorized use of computer resources nor do they provide an adequate basis for violation of any other ethical imperatives of this code.

1.5 Honor Property Rights Including Copyrights and Patents

Violation of copyrights, patents, trade secrets and the terms of license agreements is prohibited by law in most circumstances. Even when software is not so protected, such violations are contrary to professional behavior. Copies of software should be made only with proper authorization. Unauthorized duplication of materials must not be condoned.

1.6 Give Proper Credit for Intellectual Property

Computing professionals are obligated to protect the integrity of intellectual property. Specifically, one must not take credit for other's ideas or work, even in cases where the work has not been explicitly protected by copyright, patent, etc.

1.7 Respect the Privacy of Others

Computing and communication technology enables the collection and exchange of personal information on a scale unprecedented in the history of civilization. Thus there is increased potential for violating the privacy of individuals and groups. It is the responsibility of professionals to maintain the privacy and integrity of data describing individuals. This includes taking precautions to ensure the accuracy of data, as well as protecting it from unauthorized access or accidental disclosure to inappropriate individuals. Furthermore, procedures must be established to allow individuals to review their records and correct inaccuracies.

This imperative implies that only the necessary amount of personal information be collected in a system, that retention and disposal periods for that information be clearly defined and enforced, and that personal information gathered for a specific purpose not be used for other purposes without consent of the individual(s). These principles apply to electronic communications, including electronic mail, and prohibit procedures that capture or monitor electronic user data, including messages, without the permission of users or bona fide authorization related to system operation and maintenance. User data observed during the normal duties of system operation and maintenance must be treated with strictest confidentiality, except in cases where it is evidence for the violation of law, organizational regulations, or this Code. In these cases, the nature or contents of that information must be disclosed only to proper authorities.

1.8 Honor Confidentiality

The principle of honesty extends to issues of confidentiality of information whenever one has made an explicit promise to honor confidentiality or, implicitly, when private information not directly related to the performance of one's duties becomes available. The ethical concern is to respect all obligations of confidentiality to employers, clients, and users unless discharged from such obligations by requirements of the law or other principles of this Code.

2. More Specific Professional Responsibilities

As an ACM computing professional I will ...

2.1 Strive to Achieve the Highest Quality, Effectiveness and Dignity in Both the Process and Products of Professional Work

Excellence is perhaps the most important obligation of a professional. The computing professional must strive to achieve quality and to be cognizant of the serious negative consequences that may result from poor quality in a system.

2.2 Acquire and Maintain Professional Competence

Excellence depends on individuals who take responsibility for acquiring and maintaining professional competence. A professional must participate in setting standards for appropriate levels of competence, and strive to achieve those standards. Upgrading technical knowledge and competence can be achieved in several ways: doing independent study; attending seminars, conferences, or courses; and being involved in professional organizations.

2.3 Know and Respect Existing Laws Pertaining to Professional Work

ACM members must obey existing local, state, province, national, and international laws unless there is a compelling ethical basis not to do so. Policies and procedures of the organizations in which one participates must also be obeyed. But compliance must be balanced with the recognition that sometimes existing laws and rules may be immoral or inappropriate and, therefore, must be challenged. Violation of a law or regulation may be ethical when that law or rule has inadequate moral basis or when it conflicts with another law judged to be more important. If one decides to violate a law or rule because it is viewed as unethical, or for any other reason, one must fully accept responsibility for one's actions and for the consequences.

2.4 Accept and Provide Appropriate Professional Review

Quality professional work, especially in the computing profession, depends on professional reviewing and critiquing. Whenever appropriate, individual members should seek and utilize peer review as well as provide critical review of the work of others.

2.5 Give Comprehensive and Thorough Evaluations of Computer Systems and Their Impacts, Including Analysis of Possible Risks

Computer professionals must strive to be perceptive, thorough, and objective when evaluating, recommending, and presenting system descriptions and alternatives. Computer professionals are in a position of special trust, and therefore have a special responsibility to provide objective, credible evaluations to employers, clients, users, and the public. When providing evaluations the professional must also identify any relevant conflicts of interest, as stated in imperative 1.3.

As noted in the discussion of principle 1.2 on avoiding harm, any signs of danger from systems must be reported to those who have opportunity and/or responsibility to resolve them. See the guidelines for imperative 1.2 for more details concerning harm, including the reporting of professional violations.

2.6 Honor Contracts, Agreements, and Assigned Responsibilities

Honoring one's commitments is a matter of integrity and honesty. For the computer professional this includes ensuring that system elements perform as intended. Also, when one contracts for work with another party, one has an obligation to keep that party properly informed about progress toward completing that work.

A computing professional has a responsibility to request a change in any assignment that he or she feels cannot be completed as defined. Only after serious consideration and with full disclosure of risks and concerns to the employer or client, should one accept the assignment. The major underlying principle here is the obligation to accept personal accountability for professional work. On some occasions other ethical principles may take greater priority.

A judgment that a specific assignment should not be performed may not be accepted. Having clearly identified one's concerns and reasons for that judgment, but failing to procure a change in that assignment, one may yet be obligated, by contract or by law, to proceed as directed. The computing professional's ethical judgment should be the final guide in deciding whether or not to proceed. Regardless of the decision, one must accept the responsibility for the consequences.

However, performing assignments "against one's own judgment" does not relieve the professional of responsibility for any negative consequences.

2.7 Improve Public Understanding of Computing and Its Consequences

Computing professionals have a responsibility to share technical knowledge with the public by encouraging understanding of computing, including the impacts of computer systems and their limitations. This imperative implies an obligation to counter any false views related to computing.

2.8 Access Computing and Communication Resources Only When Authorized to Do So

Theft or destruction of tangible and electronic property is prohibited by imperative 1.2—"Avoid harm to others." Trespassing and unauthorized use of a computer or communication system is addressed by this imperative. Trespassing includes accessing communication networks and computer systems, or accounts and/or files associated with those systems, without explicit authorization to do so. Individuals and organizations have the right to restrict access to their systems so long as they do not violate the discrimination principle (see 1.4). No one should enter or use another's computer system, software, or data files without permission. One must always have appropriate approval before using system resources, including communication ports, file space, other system peripherals, and computer time.

3. Organizational Leadership Imperatives

Background Note: This section draws extensively from the draft IFIP Code of Ethics, especially its sections on organizational ethics and international concerns. The ethical obligations of organizations tend to be neglected in most codes of professional conduct, perhaps because these codes are written from the perspective of the individual member. This dilemma is addressed by stating these imperatives from the perspective of the organizational leader. In this context "leader" is viewed as any organizational member who has leadership or educational responsibilities. These imperatives generally may apply to organizations as well as their leaders. In this context "organizations" are corporations, government agencies, and other "employers" as well as volunteer professional organizations.

As an ACM member and an organizational leader, I will ...

3.1 Articulate Social Responsibilities of Members of an Organizational Unit and Encourage Full Acceptance of those Responsibilities

Because organizations of all kinds have impacts on the public, they must accept responsibilities to society. Organizational procedures and attitudes oriented toward quality and the welfare of society will reduce harm to members of the public, thereby serving public interest and fulfilling social responsibility. Therefore, organizational leaders must encourage full participation in meeting social responsibilities as well as quality performance.

3.2 Manage Personnel and Resources to Design and Build Information Systems that Enhance the Quality of Working Life

Organizational leaders are responsible for ensuring that computer systems enhance, not degrade, the quality of working life. When implementing a computer system, organizations must consider the personal and professional development, physical safety, and human dignity of all workers. Appropriate human-computer ergonomic standards should be considered in system design and in the workplace.

3.3 Acknowledge and Support Proper and Authorized Uses of an Organization's Computing and Communication Resources

Because computer systems can become tools to harm as well as to benefit an organization, the leadership has the responsibility to clearly define appropriate and inappropriate uses of organizational computing resources. While the number and scope of such rules should be minimal, they should be fully enforced when established.

3.4 Ensure that Users and those Who Will Be Affected by a System Have Their Needs Clearly Articulated During the Assessment and Design of Requirements; Later the System Must Be Validated to Meet Requirements

Current system users, potential users and other persons whose lives may be affected by a system must have their needs assessed and incorporated in the statement of requirements. System validation should ensure compliance with those requirements.

3.5 Articulate and Support Policies that Protect the Dignity of Users and Others Affected by a Computing System

Designing or implementing systems that deliberately or inadvertently demean individuals or groups is ethically unacceptable. Computer professionals who are in decision making positions should verify that systems are designed and implemented to protect personal privacy and enhance personal dignity.

3.6 Create Opportunities for Members of the Organization to Learn the Principles and Limitations of Computer Systems

This complements the imperative on public understanding (2.7). Educational opportunities are essential to facilitate optimal participation of all organizational members. Opportunities must be available to all members to help them improve their knowledge and skills in computing, including courses that familiarize them with the consequences and limitations of particular types of systems. In particular, professionals must be made aware of the dangers of building systems around oversimplified models, the improbability of anticipating and designing for every possible operating condition, and other issues related to the complexity of this profession.

4. Compliance with the Code

As an ACM member I will ...

4.1 Uphold and Promote the Principles of this Code

The future of the computing profession depends on both technical and ethical excellence. Not only is it important for ACM computing professionals to adhere to the principles expressed in this Code, each member should encourage and support adherence by other members.

4.2 Treat Violations of this Code as Inconsistent with Membership in the ACM

Adherence of professionals to a code of ethics is largely a voluntary matter. However, if a member does not follow this code by engaging in gross misconduct, membership in ACM may be terminated.

This Code and the supplemental Guidelines were developed by the Task Force for the Revision of the ACM Code of Ethics and Professional Conduct: Ronald E. Anderson, Chair, Gerald Engel, Donald Gotterbarn, Grace C. Hertlein, Alex Hoffman, Bruce Jawer, Deborah G. Johnson, Doris K. Lidtke, Joyce Currie Little, Dianne Martin, Donn B. Parker, Judith A. Perrolle, and Richard S. Rosenberg. The Task Force was organized by ACM/SIGCAS and funding was provided by the ACM SIG Discretionary Fund. This Code and the supplemental Guidelines were adopted by the ACM Council on October 16, 1992.

Glossary

3-D modeling software p. 200 Software that enables the user to create 3-D objects. The objects can be rotated, stretched, and combined with other model objects to create complex 3-D scenes.

3G p. 282 A type of network that carries multimedia data and voice communications simultaneously, making it possible for mobile phones to serve as Internet multimedia devices.

4G p. 282 The faster successor to 3G network technology.

A

AAC p. 212 Advanced Audio Codec; one of a number of relatively new methods of audio compression that can squeeze music files to a fraction of their original CD-file sizes, often without perceptible loss of quality.

accelerometers p. 75 A type of sensor that detects rapid changes in motion. Some accelerometers are used to protect laptop hard drives from damage from falls.

access-control software p. 371 Software that only allows user access according to the user's needs. Some users can open files that are only related to their work. Some users are allowed read-only access to files they can see but not change.

access time p. 56 The amount of time, measured in nanoseconds, it takes for a CPU to retrieve a unit of data from memory. Also the amount of time, measured in milliseconds, it takes for a CPU to retrieve a unit of data from a disk drive.

accounting and financial-management software p. 170 Software especially designed to set up accounts, keep track of money flow between accounts, record transactions, adjust balances in accounts, provide an audit trail, automate routine tasks such as check writing, and produce reports.

acquisition p. 445 The process of capturing data about an event that is important to the organization.

action document p. 446 In a transaction processing system, a document that initiates an action by the recipient or verifies for the recipient that a transaction has occurred.

Active Server Pages (ASP) p. 335 Common server-side programming language.

Ada p. 518 A massive programming language, named for programming pioneer Ada King and based on Pascal, that was developed in the late 1970s for the U.S. Defense Department.

address p. 163 In a spreadsheet, the location of a cell, determined by row number and column number.

agent p. 136 Software program that can ask questions, respond to commands, pay attention to users' work patterns, serve as a guide and a coach, take on owners' goals, and use reasoning to fabricate its own goals.

aggregator p. 341 An RSS-reading Web browser that periodically visits Web sites, examines feeds, and displays new content.

agricultural age p. 18 The era covering most of the past ten thousand years, during which humanity lived mainly by domesticating animals and growing food using plows and other agricultural tools.

Ajax (Asynchronous JavaScript XML) p. 335 A way to support efficient interactive Web pages by eliminating excess page loads from servers.

alert p. 341 Along with notifications, a popular noncorporate type of push technology on the Web, mostly offered through services that alert subscribers to stock price changes, breaking news, and the like.

algorithm p. 108, 511 A set of step-by-step instructions that, when completed, solves a problem.

alias p. 601 See user name.

all-in-one devices p. 81 See multifunction printer.

alpha testing p. 530 Initial testing of a system; also called "pre-beta testing."

analog-to-digital converter (ADC) p. 76 A device that converts electrical charges into discrete values, allowing continuous signals to be stored in computers.

analysis p. 529 The phase of the systems development life cycle in which details are fleshed out before design begins.

animation p. 204 The process of simulating motion with a series of still pictures.

anti-aliasing p. 192 A technique used to smooth text when it is displayed at less-than-ideal resolutions.

antivirus software p. 367 A type of software designed to search for viruses, notify users when they are found, and remove them from infected disks or files.

app p. 11 An abbreviation for *application*, often referring to small software applications that run on smart phones.

applet p. 518 A small compiled program designed to run inside another application—typically a Web browser.

application program (application) p. 19, 587 Software tool that allows a computer to be used for specific purposes.

application server p. 325 A common type of Internet server that stores PC office applications, databases, or other applications and makes them available to client programs that request them.

application service provider (ASP) p. 325 A company that manages and delivers application services on a contract basis.

architecture p. 47 Design that determines how individual components of the CPU are put together on the chip. More generally used to describe the way individual components are put together to create a complete computer system.

archive backup p. 377 A type of backup used to save files that don't need to be regularly accessed.

arithmetic logic unit (ALU) p. 52 The part of the CPU that performs data calculations and comparisons.

armature p. 88 The part of a disk drive that moves the read/write head across the disk surface.

artificial intelligence (AI) p. 552 The field of computer science devoted to making computers perceive, reason, and act in ways that have, until now, been reserved for human beings.

artificial life (Alife) p. 576 Systems related to life, its processes, and its evolution through simulations that use computer models, robotics, and biochemistry.

ASCII p. 42 American Standard Code for Information Interchange, which represents characters as 8-bit codes. Allows the binary computer to work with letters, digits, and special characters.

aspect-oriented programming p. 521 Newer paradigm that separates each object's features into separate programs that overlap in functionality as little as possible.

aspect ratio p. 79 The fractional relationship between the width and height of a display.

assembler p. 517 A program that translates each assembly-language instruction into a machine-language instruction.

assembly language p. 517 A language that is functionally equivalent to machine language but is easier for people to read, write, and understand. Programmers use alphabetic codes that correspond to the machine's numeric instructions.

asynchronous communication p. 295 Delayed communication, such as that used for newsgroups and mailing lists, where the sender and the recipients don't have to be logged in at the same time.

attachment p. 290, 601 A document that is sent along with an email message.

audio digitizer p. 209 A hardware device or software program that can capture sounds and store them as computer files.

audit-control software p. 373 Applications that monitor and record computer transactions as they happen so auditors can trace and identify suspicious computer activity after the fact.

augmented reality (AR) p. 226 The use of computer displays that add virtual information to a person's sensory perceptions, supplementing rather than replacing (as in virtual reality) the world the user sees.

authentication p. 118 The process that operating systems use on multiuser computers to determine that users are who they claim to be. Also a process for unlocking some purchased software online.

authorization p. 118 The process that operating systems use on multiuser computers in order to ensure that users have permission to perform a particular action.

automated factory p. 402 A factory that uses extensive computer systems, robots, and networks to streamline and automate many jobs.

automated office p. 403 An office that uses computer systems and networks to streamline information flow and automate many processes.

automated teller machine (ATM) p. 285 A device that enables users to remotely access and deposit money from their bank accounts through the use of a network.

automatic correction (autocorrect) p. 149 A word processing feature that catches and corrects common typing errors.

automatic footnoting p. 149 A word processing feature that places footnotes where they belong on the page.

automatic formatting (autoformat) p. 149 A word processing feature that applies formatting to the text.

automatic hyphenation p. 149 A word processing feature that divides long words that fall at the ends of lines.

automatic link p. 166 A link between worksheets in a spreadsheet that ensures that a change in one worksheet is reflected in the other.

automatic recalculation p. 164 A spreadsheet capability that allows for easy correction of errors and makes it easy to try out different values while searching for solutions.

automatic translation p. 557 The process of using software to translate written or spoken communication from one natural language to another.

autonomous system p. 385 A complex system that can assume almost complete responsibility for a task without human input, verification, or decision making.

autosave p. 124 A feature of many software applications that automatically saves your work every few minutes, so you don't lose more than a few minutes of work in a freeze or crash.

avatar p. 296 A graphical body used to represent a person in a virtual meeting place; can range from a simple cartoon sketch to an elaborate 3-D figure or an exotic abstract icon.

B

Back and Forward buttons p. 599 Browser buttons that allow you to retrace your steps while navigating the Web and return to previously visited sites.

backbone network p. 277 A collection of common pathways used to transmit large quantities of data between networks in a wide area network (WAN).

backup p. 376 The process of saving data—especially for data recovery. Many systems automatically back up data and software onto disks or tapes.

backup copy p. 594 A copy of a file created as insurance against the loss of the original.

backup media p. 594 Disks, CD-Rs, and other technologies to hold backup files and to save computer storage space.

backward compatible p. 46 Able to run software written for older CPUs. Also, when referring to a software program, able to read and write files compatible with older versions of the program.

bandwidth p. 276 The quantity of information that can be transmitted through a communication medium in a given amount of time.

bar chart p. 167 A chart that shows relative values with bars; appropriate when data fall into a few categories.

bar code reader p. 72 A reading tool that uses light to read universal product codes, inventory codes, and other codes created out of patterns of variable-width bars.

BASIC p. 518 Beginner's All-purpose Symbolic Instruction Code, a programming language developed in the 1960s as an easy-to-learn, interactive alternative to FORTRAN for beginning programmers; it is still widely used today in forms such as Microsoft's popular Visual Basic.

batch processing p. 252 Accumulating transactions and feeding them into a computer in large batches.

bay p. 56 An open area in the system box for disk drives and other peripheral devices.

BD-R p. 87 Drives that can read data from Blu-ray discs, DVDs, and CDs.

BD-RW p. 87 Drives that can read data from, and record data on, Blu-ray discs, DVDs, CDs, and BD-R.

benchmark tests p. 50 Tests that provide solid data in side-by-side comparisons of various machines or programs.

beta testing p. 530 Testing of almost-finished software by potential end users.

binary p. 41 A choice of two values, such as *yes* and *no* or *0* and *1*.

binary number system p. 42 A system that denotes all numbers by using combinations of *0* and *1*.

biometrics p. 370 Measurements of individual body characteristics, such as a voiceprint or fingerprint; sometimes used in computer security.

bit p. 41 Binary digit, the smallest unit of information. A bit can have two values: 0 or 1.

bit depth p. 192 Color depth, the number of bits devoted to each pixel in a color display.

bitmapped graphics p. 192 Graphics in which images are stored and manipulated as organized collections of pixels rather than as shapes and lines. Contrast with object-oriented graphics.

BitTorrent p. 304 A peer-to-peer protocol used to download and share very large files.

blended learning p. 420 The combination of e-learning with traditional face-to-face learning.

blocks p. 132 Units of data or memory, made up of bundles of sectors, on a hard disk.

blog p. 294 Short for Web log, a personal Web page that often carries journal entries or political commentaries. Blogs are fast proliferating as new software allows users to create Web pages without having to learn the technical details of HTML and Web authoring.

blogger p. 294 A person who writes blogs or microblogs.

blogosphere p. 295 A term used to describe the online community of bloggers and their blogs.

Bluetooth (802.15) p. 281 A type of wireless technology that enables mobile phones, handheld computers, and PCs to communicate with each other regardless of operating system.

Blu-Ray (BD) drive p. 87 A drive that can read and write on optical media that hold up to 50 gigabytes on two layers.

bookmarks p. 599 A list kept on a browser of personal favorite or memorable Web sites that are often revisited. Also called favorites.

Boolean logic p. 339 A complex query structure supported by most search engines; one example is "American AND Indian BUT NOT Cleveland."

bootable backup p. 377 A backup made by a disc utility that's a complete, exact duplicate (clone) of a disc. In the event of a disc crash, the system can boot from this backup.

booting p. 119 Loading the non-ROM part of the operating system into memory.

bootstrapping (booting) p. 146 The process of starting up a computer in which the computer figuratively pulls itself up by its own bootstraps.

bot p. 369 Software robots that crawl around the Web collecting information, helping consumers make decisions, answering email, and even playing games.

botnet p. 369 A malicious network made up of bots, or zombie computers, often used by spammers, phishers, and other Internet criminals.

boundary p. 441 A The limits of a computer system.

brain-computer interfaces (BCIs) p. 306 Cochlear implants and visual implants are examples. Can be invasive (surgically implanted inside the skull) or noninvasive (worn on the head).

broadband connection p. 278 An Internet connection such as DSL or cable modem that offers higher bandwidth, and therefore faster transmission speed, than standard modem connections.

browse p. 239 The process of finding information in a database or other data source, such as the World Wide Web.

browser p. 14 A program (such as Internet Explorer, Firefox, Chrome, or Safari) that provides navigable windows into the Web.

brute-force p. 555 An exhaustive searching technique where the computer rapidly repeats a simple operation until the correct answer is found.

bug p. 108 An error in programming.

bullet chart p. 204 A chart made up of multiple bullet points listing the main points of a presentation.

burn p. 87, 212 To record data onto CD-R and CD-RW disks.

bus p. 56 A group of wires on a circuit board. Information travels between components through a bus.

business alliance p. 447 A cooperative arrangement between two or more businesses with complementary capabilities.

business concerns p. 523 The primary goals that an aspect-oriented program is built to achieve.

business organization p. 442 A company or a firm; a system designed for the purpose of creating products and services for customers.

business-to-business (B2B) p. 476 E-commerce transactions that involve businesses providing goods or services to other businesses.

business-to-consumer (B2C) p. 476 E-commerce transactions that involve businesses providing goods or services to consumers.

business-to-employee (B2E) p. 477 Another name for the B2B model when the focus is primarily on handling the activities that take place within the organization.

button p. 586 A hot spot on a screen that responds to mouse clicks. A button can be programmed to perform one of many tasks, such as opening a dialog box or launching an application.

byte p. 42 A grouping of 8 bits.

C

C p. 518 A complex computer language invented at Bell Labs in the early 1970s as a tool for programming operating systems such as UNIX; now one of the most widely used programming languages.

C# p. 518 A popular Windows-only programming language that's similar to C++.

C++ p. 518 A variation of the C programming language that takes advantage of a modern programming methodology called object-oriented programming.

cable modem p. 278 A type of broadband Internet connection that uses the same network of coaxial cables that delivers TV signals.

card p. 57 See expansion card.

carpal tunnel syndrome p. 86 An affliction of the wrist and hand that results from repeating the same movements over long periods.

Cascading Style Sheets p. 331 A Web markup language that gives users and Web developers more control over how a Web page is displayed. Cascading Style Sheets can define formatting and layout elements that aren't recognized in older versions of HTML.

cathode-ray tube (CRT) monitor p. 79 A computer display made from a large electronic vacuum tube, similar to the classic television display.

CD-R p. 87 Compact disc—recordable, an optical disc you can write information on, but you cannot remove the information.

CD-ROM p. 85 Compact disc—read-only memory, a type of optical disc that contains data that cannot be changed; CD-ROMs are commonly used to distribute commercial software programs.

CD-RW p. 87 Compact disc—rewritable, an optical disc that allows writing, erasing, and rewriting.

CD-RW drive p. 87 A disc drive that can read and write on rewritable optical discs.

cell p. 163 The intersection of a row and a column on the grid of a spreadsheet.

central processing unit (CPU) p. 39, 584 Part of the computer that processes information, performs arithmetic calculations, and makes basic decisions based on information values.

centralized database p. 252 A database housed in a mainframe computer, accessible only to information-processing personnel.

channel p. 341 See feed.

character-based interface p. 122 A user interface based on text characters rather than graphics.

charge-coupled device (CCD) p. 76 A device, as in a digital camera, that converts light into electrons.

chat room p. 296 Public real-time teleconference.

chief information officers (CIOs).p. 403, 454 Along with chief technology officers (CTOs), the chief decision makers concerning enterprise computer systems and technology in a business enterprise.

chief technology officer (CTO) p. 403 The chief decision maker in a business or organization who is concerned with enterprise computer systems and technology.

class p. 253 In an object-oriented database, the data contained in the object as well as the kinds of operations that may be performed on the data.

clean install p. 125 A completely new installation of an operating system or application.

click p. 586 The action of pressing a button on a mouse.

client p. 277 Computers in a network program that are not acting as dedicated servers.

client/server p. 252 Client programs in desktop computers send information requests through a network to server databases on mainframes, minicomputers, or desktop computers; the servers process queries and send the requested data back to the client.

client/server model p. 277 For a local area network, a hierarchical model in which one or more computers act as dedicated servers and all the remaining computers act as clients. The server fills requests from clients for data and other resources.

clip art p. 197 A collection of drawn images that you can cut out and paste into your own documents.

Clipboard p. 587 A word processing program text-editing tool for temporarily storing chunks of text and other data.

clock p. 47 The timing device producing electrical pulses for synchronizing the computer's operations.

Close p. 130 An operation that allows you to stop working on a project but remain in the application program.

cloud computing p. 305 A type of grid computing in which resources (storage, applications, data, and more) are distributed across the Internet rather than confined to a single machine. Resources seem to be coming from "the cloud" (the Internet) rather than from a particular computer.

cluster p. 51 A grouping of multiple processors or servers to, for example, improve graphic rendering speeds or increase reliability.

CMOS p. 56, 76 Complementary metal oxide semiconductor, a special low-energy kind of RAM that can store small amounts of data for long periods of time on battery power. CMOS RAM is used to store the date, time, and calendar in a PC. CMOS RAM is called parameter RAM in Macintoshes.

COBOL p. 518 Common Business-Oriented Language, developed when the U.S. government in 1960 demanded a new language oriented toward business data-processing problems.

code of ethics p. 463 Policies and procedures, such as those developed by companies and by organizations such as the ACM (Association for Computing Machinery), to guide the behavior of information workers.

Code of Fair Information Practices p. 258 A set of guidelines produced for Congress by a panel of experts in the early 1970s that called for a ban on secret government databases, citizen access to personal information kept in government databases, and agency responsibility for database reliability and security.

coding p. 514 Writing a program from an algorithm.

color depth p. 192 Bit depth, the number of bits devoted to each pixel.

color-matching p. 157 The technology of trying to match colors on a monitor's screen to printed colors, so that the color balance is the same.

columns p. 162 Along with rows, columns make up the grid of a spreadsheet.

command-line interface p. 122 User interface that requires the user to type text commands on a command line to communicate with the operating system.

compatible (compatibility) p. 46, 113 The ability of a software program to run on a specific computer system. Also, the ability of a hardware device to function with a particular type of computer.

compiler p. 112, 516 A translator program that translates an entire program from a high-level computer language before the program is run for the first time.

component software p. 524 Software designed in small, independent units (components) that can be plugged into applications and operating systems to add features as needed.

compression p. 208 Making files smaller using special encoding schemes. File compression saves storage space on disks and saves transmission time when files are transferred through networks.

computed field p. 239 In a database, a field containing formulas similar to spreadsheet formulas; it displays a value calculated from values in other numeric fields.

computer-aided design (CAD) p. 200 The use of computers to draw products or process designs on the screen.

computer-aided manufacturing (CAM) p. 201 When the design of a product is completed, the numbers are fed to a program that controls the manufacturing of parts. For electronic parts the design translates directly into a template for etching circuits onto chips. Also called computer-integrated manufacturing (CIM).

computer-aided systems engineering (CASE) p. 536 Commercially available software packages that typically include charting and diagramming tools, a centralized data dictionary, a user interface generator, and code generators.

computer architecture p. 538 The branch of computer science that deals with the way hardware and software work together.

computer-based collaborative learning (CBCL) p. 418 When students work together on technology-enhanced projects using the Internet as a medium for participation and collaboration.

computer-based training (CBT) p. 415 A type of program that embeds the lesson in animated games, in smart phone apps, in special-purpose hardware/software systems, or in Web-based instructional packages.

computer crime p. 361 Any crime accomplished through knowledge or use of computer technology.

computer forensics p. 361 The use of computer technology and applications as tools to help law enforcement officials stop criminal activities.

computer-integrated manufacturing (CIM) p. 201 The combination of CAD and CAM.

computer monitoring p. 408 Using computer technology to track, record, and evaluate worker performance, often without the knowledge of the worker.

computer science p. 536 A discipline that focuses on the process of computing through several areas of specialization, including theory, algorithms, data structures, programming concepts and languages, computer architecture, management information systems, artificial intelligence, and software engineering.

computer security p. 369 Protecting computer systems and the information they contain against unwanted access, damage, modification, or destruction.

computer telephony integration (CTI) p. 296 The linking of computers and telephones to gain productivity, such as by allowing PCs to serve as speakerphones, answering machines, and complete voicemail systems.

consumer-to-consumer (C2C) p. 477 The e-commerce model that represents individuals, organizations, or companies that are selling and buying directly with each other via the Internet.

content-management system (CMS) p. 334 A software development system that enables adding or updating text, images, and other Web site content without coding in HTML or using a Web authoring program.

context-sensitive menus p. 123 Menus offering choices that depend on the context.

contract p. 133 A type of law that covers trade secrets.

control p. 441 A function within a system that evaluates the feedback data and adjusts the system's input and processing functions to ensure the desired output is produced.

control structures p. 513 Logical structures that control the order in which instructions are carried out.

cookie p. 334 Small files deposited on a user's hard disk by Web sites, enabling sites to remember what they know about their visitors between sessions.

copy p. 587 A word processing program text-editing tool that allows you to make a copy of a set of words or data and place the copy elsewhere in the same or a different document.

copy protected p. 114 Produced in a way that prevents any physical copying, such as is the case with software CDs and DVDs, especially some entertainment products.

copyright p. 133 A type of law that traditionally protects forms of literary expression.

copyrighted software p. 114 Software that prevents a disk from being copied.

cores p. 50 CPUs in a multicore processor.

corporate portals p. 340 Specialized portals on an intranet that serve the employees of a particular corporation.

cost-benefit analysis p. 25 A comparison of costs (such as salaries of the information system staff) to benefits (such as a reduction in the number of customer complaints) that managers use to decide whether an information system project is worthwhile on its own merits and also in comparison with other proposed information system projects.

courseware p. 415 Educational software.

CPU p. 39 See central processing unit.

cracking p. 368 Unauthorized access and/or vandalism of computer systems; short for criminal hacking.

critical path method (CPM) p. 462 A mathematical model of a project's schedule used to calculate when particular activities will be completed.

critical success factors (CSF) p. 461 A strategic planning approach that identifies the variables that are crucial for the success of the business from the top managers' point of view and identifies IT plans for systems that provide access to information about those critical success factors.

cross-platform application p. 127 A program, such as Adobe Photoshop, that is available in similar versions for multiple platforms.

crowdsourcing p. 301 A type of information and/or labor sharing in which a task is outsourced to a large community of people, possibly volunteers, rather than to a small group of contracted specialists.

CRT (cathode-ray tube) monitor p. 79 Older, television-style monitor used as the output device for a desktop computer.

cursor p. 585 When you press keys on a computer keyboard, the computer responds by displaying the typed characters on the monitor screen at the position of the line or rectangle called the cursor.

cursor (arrow) key p. 585 A keyboard key that moves the cursor up or down, right or left, on the screen.

custom application p. 117 An application programmed for a specific purpose, typically for a specific client.

customer relationship management (CRM) p. 478 Software systems for organizing and tracking information on customers.

cut p. 587 A word processing program text-editing tool that allows you to delete a set of words or data; often used with the copy function to move text around.

cybercrime p. 361 Any crime accomplished through knowledge or use of computer technology.

cyberspace p. 348 A term used to describe the Internet and other online networks, especially the artificial realities and virtual communities that form on them. First coined by William Gibson in his novel *Neuromancer*.

cyberstalking p. 361 A form of harassment that takes place on the Internet.

D

data p. 40 Information in a form that can be read, used, and manipulated by a computer.

data consistency p. 248 When data is redundant, you must update data in all tables to maintain consistency.

data dictionary p. 535 A catalog, or directory, that describes all the data flowing through a system.

data-driven Web site p. 331 A Web site that can display dynamic, changeable content without having constantly redesigned pages, due to an evolving database that separates the site's content from its design.

data file p. 587 A computer file that contains passive data rather than instructions for processing the data.

data flow diagram p. 534 A simple graphical depiction of the movement of data through a system.

data management p. 455 A component of the decision support system, in which a manager queries and retrieves relevant information from a database of internal and external information of the organization.

data mining p. 252 The discovery and extraction of hidden predictive information from large databases.

data recovery p. 379 Retrieving backed up data.

data redundancy p. 248 A database design strategy by which separate tables contain the same information.

data scrubbing (data cleansing) p. 253 The process of going through a database and eliminating records that contain errors.

data structure p. 535 The organization of data elements used together.

data translation software p. 288 Software that enables users of different systems with incompatible file formats to read and modify each other's files.

data type p. 238 See field type.

data warehouse p. 252 An integrated collection of corporate data stored in one location.

data warehousing p. 446 Software used to create and maintain large databases.

database p. 238 A collection of information stored in an organized form in a computer.

database-management system (DBMS) p. 248 A program or system of programs that can manipulate data in a large collection of files (the database), cross-referencing between files as needed.

database program p. 238 A software tool for organizing the storage and retrieval of the information in a database.

database server p. 252 A powerful computer for holding and managing an interactive, multiuser database.

database software p. 238 See database program.

date field p. 239 A field containing only dates.

debugger p. 516 A program used to simplify the process of locating and correcting errors during the program development process.

debugging p. 109 Finding and correcting errors—bugs—in computer software.

decision p. 513 A programming control structure that involves choosing between alternative courses of action under a given set of conditions.

decision support system (DSS) p. 455 A computer system that provides managers with the tools they need to analyze information they deem relevant for a particular decision or class of decisions.

decision table p. 535 A table that shows, in a row/column format, the decision rules that apply and what actions to take when certain conditions occur.

decode unit p. 53 Takes the instruction read by the prefetcher and translates it into a form suitable for the CPU's internal processing.

defragmentation utility p. 133 A program that eliminates fragmented files by changing the assignment of clusters to files.

Delete (delete key) p. 585 A keyboard key that acts as an eraser by, for example, removing highlighted text in a word document.

denial-of-service (DoS) attack p. 369 A type of computer vandalism that bombards servers and Web sites with so much bogus traffic that they're effectively shut down, denying service to legitimate customers and clients.

design p. 529 The phase of the systems development life cycle that focuses on how the problem will be solved.

de-skilled p. 408 Transformed in such a way that a job requires less skill.

desktop computer p. 10 A personal computer designed to be set up on or under a desk or table and used in that place for an extended period of time.

desktop publishing (DTP) p. 154 Software used mainly to produce print publications. Also, the process of using desktop-publishing software to produce publications.

desktop system p. 92 Personal computer design class designed to sit under the monitor like a platform.

desktop virtualization p. 404 Technology that enables software and data to be stored on servers in the IT center or in the Internet cloud—so they can be accessed from PCs, thin clients, or handheld devices anywhere in the enterprise.

development p. 530 The phase of the systems development life cycle in which the system is built and tested.

device drivers p. 119 Small programs that allow input/output devices to communicate with the computer.

dialog management p. 456 The third DSS component is the user interface that enables managers to view information in a variety of forms.

dialog management component p. 457 A component of the executive information system made up of the set of human–computer interactive features that enables the executive to select the necessary data and display it in a variety of formats, including summary and exception reports, lists, charts, tables, and graphs.

dial-up connection p. 278 A connection to the Internet that uses a modem and standard phone lines.

digit p. 41 A discrete, countable unit.

digital p. 41 Information made up of discrete units that can be counted.

digital audio workstation (DAW) p. 214 Software that incorporates sequencing, recording, and mixing capabilities in a single program.

digital camera p. 73 A camera that captures images and stores them as bit patterns on disks or other digital storage media instead of using film.

digital divide p. 24, 347 A term that describes the divide between the people who do and do not have access to the Internet.

digital photo p. 192 A photograph captured with a digital camera.

digital rights management (DRM) p. 114 Technology now being used in many audio files to protect musicians' and other artists' intellectual property.

digital signal processing (DSP) p. 76 Compressing or mathematically altering streams of bits before they are transmitted to the CPU. DSP is typically done by a DSP chip.

digital signatures p. 346 A developing identity-verification standard that uses encryption techniques to protect against email forgery.

digital-to-analog converter (DAC) p. 77 A device on a sound card that converts digitized waves into analog signals.

digital video p. 205 Video reduced to a series of numbers, which can be edited, stored, and played back without loss of quality.

digital video camera p. 73 A video camera that captures footage in digital form so that clips can be transferred to and from a computer for editing with no loss of quality.

digitize p. 73 Converting information into a digital form that can be stored in the computer's memory.

digitized sound p. 567 Computerized sound output.

digitized speech p. 567 Computerized voice output that mimics human speech.

DIMMs p. 55 Dual in-line memory modules.

direct (dedicated) connection p. 277, 596 A dedicated, direct connection to the Internet through a LAN, with the computer having its own IP address.

directory p. 339, 600 A logical container used to group files and other directories. Also called a folder.

dirty data p. 491 Data records with spelling mistakes, incorrect or obsolete values, or other errors.

disaggregation p. 491 Separating commerce into its component parts and outsourcing those parts that can be better handled somewhere else.

disk drive p. 84 See diskette drive.

diskette (floppy disk) p. 85 Device used to retrieve information from a disk and, in some cases, to transfer data to it.

display p. 79, 585 See monitor.

distance education p. 420 Using computers, networks, and other technology to extend the educational process beyond the walls of a school, connecting students and faculty at remote locations.

distributed computing p. 304 Integrating all kinds of computers, from mainframes to PCs, into a single, seamless system.

distributed database p. 252 Data strewn out across networks on several different computers.

distributed denial-of-service (DDoS) attack p. 369 A denial of service attack in which the flood of messages comes from many compromised systems distributed across the Internet.

distributed intelligence p. 574 Artificial intelligence concepts applied to networks rather than to individual computers.

document p. 5, 587 A file, such as a term paper or chart, created with an application.

documentation p. 113 Instructions for installing the software on a computer's hard disc.

domain name registry p. 327 A company that provides its customers with domain names that are easy to remember and use.

domain name system (DNS) p. 321 A system that translates a computer's numerical IP address into an easier-to-remember string of names separated by dots.

dot-coms p. 475 Internet-based companies.

dot matrix printer p. 81 A type of impact printer, which forms images by physically striking paper, ribbon, and print hammer together, the way a typewriter does.

dots per inch (dpi) p. 192 A measurement of the density of pixels, defining the resolution of a graphic.

double-click p. 586 To click a mouse button twice in rapid succession.

download p. 288 To copy software from an online source to a local computer.

downloadable audio p. 329 Compressed sound files that you must download onto your computer's hard disk before the browser or some other application can play them.

downloadable video p. 329 Compressed video files that can be downloaded and viewed on a computer.

drag p. 586 To move the mouse while holding the mouse button down. Used for moving objects, selecting text, drawing, and other tasks.

drag-and-drop p. 587 A word processing program text-editing tool that allows you to move a selected block of text from one location to another.

drawing software p. 195 Stores a picture as a collection of lines and shapes. Also stores shapes as shape formulas and text as text.

drive-by download p. 366 A spyware download onto your computer that occurs simply by visiting certain Web sites.

drum scanner p. 73 A type of scanner used in publishing applications where image quality is critical.

DSL (digital subscriber line) p. 278 A type of broadband connection to the Internet offered by phone companies.

dual-boot PCs p. 126 Switch back and forth between Windows and Linux by simply rebooting.

DVD p. 87 A type of optical disc used to store and distribute video and other types of digital data. Depending on the context, DVD may stand for Digital Versatile Disc or Digital Video Disc.

DVD burner p. 87 Rewritable DVD drives.

DVD/CD-RW drive p. 584 A disc drive that combines the capabilities of a DVD-ROM drive and a CD-RW drive in a single unit.

DVD/+R p. 87 Recordable DVD disc.

DVD/+RW p. 87 DVD disc that allows writing, erasing, and rewriting.

DVD/RW p. 87 Recordable DVD disc.

DVD-R p. 87 Recordable DVD disc.

DVD-RW p. 87 Versatile drive that can read and write on CD and DVD media.

DVD-ROM drive p. 87 An optical disc drive that can read high-capacity DVD discs.

dynamic IP address p. 321 An IP address that is assigned to a device when it connects to the Internet; when that device disconnects from the Internet, the IP address may be reused.

dynamic Web site p. 331 A Web site whose contents may be changed automatically; typically driven by scripts for referencing and updating databases.

E

e-business (electronic business) p. 475 Though sometimes used interchangeably with the broader term *e-commerce*, here used to refer to the e-commerce activities of a particular company or organization.

e-commerce p. 405, 475 The sales aspect of e-business, including the buying and selling of products or services over the Internet and other electronic systems. (Many people use the terms *e-commerce* and *e-business* interchangeably.)

educational simulations p. 417 Software that enables students to explore artificial environments that are imaginary or based on reality. Most have the look and feel of a game, but they challenge students to learn through exploration, experimentation, and interaction with other students.

edutainment p. 425 Programs geared toward home markets that combine education and entertainment.

effectiveness p. 444 How an organization's customers evaluate the quality of the output—products and services—of the value chain.

efficiency p. 444 How an organization's primary and support activities produce desired output with less work or lower costs.

e-learning p. 415 A term describing electronic tools and techniques used in distance learning environments.

e-learning 2.0 p. 418 See computer-based collaborative learning (CBCL).

electronic book p. 161 A book in digital form designed to be read on a computer, phone, or e-reader.

electronic commerce (e-commerce) p. 285 Business transactions through electronic networks.

electronic cottage p. 405 A home in which modern technology enables a person to work at home.

electronic data interchange (EDI) p. 447 A set of specifications for conducting basic business transactions over private networks.

electronic mail (email or e-mail) p. 14, 601 A type of communication by which Internet users send mail messages, data files, and software programs to other Internet users.

electronic payment system p. 486 An online credit card transaction in which a trusted third party transfers funds from one person or business to another, thereby concealing the credit card information of the buyer from the seller.

electronic sweatshop p. 409 A worker warehouse where most of the work is mindless keyboarding; computer monitoring is a common practice, wages are low, working conditions poor, and repetitive stress injuries are common.

electronica p. 214 Sequenced music that is designed from the ground up with digital technology.

email server p. 325 A specialized server that acts like a local post office for a particular Internet host.

embedded system p. 9 A computer that is embedded into a consumer product, such as a wristwatch or game machine, to enhance those products. Also used to control hardware devices.

emulation p. 127 A process that enables programs to run on a noncompatible operating system.

encapsulation p. 483 A program that translates all Windows-related instructions into instructions that a Mac's operating system and CPU can understand.

encryption p. 373 Protects transmitted information by scrambling the transmissions. When a user encrypts a message by applying a secret numerical code (encryption key), the message can be transmitted or stored as an indecipherable garble of characters. The message can be read only after it's been reconstructed with a matching key.

encryption key p. 373 A secret numerical code that can be used to scramble network transmissions; a matching key is needed to reconstruct the message.

end user p. 528 A person who uses the information system directly or uses the information produced by the system.

end-user development p. 528 A systems development approach in which a project team comprising only of end users develops many small-scale systems without the direct involvement of a professional systems analyst.

end-user license agreement (EULA) p. 114 An agreement typically including specifications for how a program may be used, warranty disclaimers, and rules concerning the copying of the software.

Enter (enter key) p. 585 A keyboard key with a number of special functions, such as moving the cursor to the beginning of the next line or activating a selected option.

enterprise resource planning (ERP) p. 447 Creating information systems to support an organization's operational business processes.

entry barrier p. 459 An innovative new product or service that is difficult for a competitor to emulate, thus creating a barrier to new companies entering a market.

environment p. 441 Anything that is outside a system's boundary.

e-paper (electronic paper) p. 161 A flexible, portable, paperlike display.

equation solver p. 166 A feature of some spreadsheet programs that determines data values.

e-reader (e-book reader) p. 161 A handheld device designed primarily for reading digital publications.

ergonomic keyboard p. 67 A keyboard that places the keys at angles that allow your wrists to assume a more natural position while you type, potentially reducing the risk of repetitive-stress injuries.

ergonomics p. 86 The science of designing work environments that enable people and things to interact efficiently and safely.

Ethernet p. 274 A popular networking architecture developed in 1976 at Xerox.

executable files p. 587 Files, such as applications, that contain instructions that can be executed by the computer.

executive information system (EIS) p. 457 A system that combines features of management information and decision support systems to support unstructured decision making by top managers.

expansion card p. 57 A special-purpose circuit board that can be inserted in an expansion slot.

expansion slot p. 56 An area inside the computer's housing that holds special-purpose circuit boards.

expert system (ES) p. 457, 562 An information system or software program designed to replicate the decision-making process of a human expert.

expert system shell p. 564 A generic expert system containing human interfaces and inference engines.

export data p. 241 Transmitting records and fields from a database (or other) program to another program.

express card p. 57 A small removable card that might add additional memory, a peripheral, or additional ports to a laptop computer.

extension p. 593 A file name feature, usually three characters following a period at the end of the file name, that gives more information about the file's origin or use.

external bus p. 57 A cable designed to transmit data back and forth between a computer and its external peripherals.

external drive p. 87, 584 A disc drive not included in a system unit but rather attached to it via cables.

extranet p. 404, 479 A corporation's intranet that is opened up to work with strategic partners and customers.

extreme programming (XP) p. 525 A relatively new programming methodology that focuses more on the culture of programming than on technology, in which the entire programming team "owns" the code; each member of the team has a right to improve it and the responsibility for making it work properly.

F

facsimile (fax) machine p. 81 An output device capable of sending, in effect, a photocopy through a telephone line, allowing for fast and convenient transmission of information stored on paper.

FAQs (frequently asked questions) p. 303 Posted lists of common queries and their answers.

Fast Ethernet p. 276 An Ethernet standard that carries traffic at 100 megabits per second, provided that all the devices on the LAN are Fast Ethernet compatible.

favorites p. 599 See bookmarks.

fax modem p. 82 A hardware peripheral that enables a computer to send onscreen documents to a receiving fax machine by translating the document into signals that can be sent over phone wires and decoded by the receiving fax machine.

feed p. 341 A list of changes to a Web site or other online resource; kept in a standard format, such as RSS.

feedback p. 441 A function within a system that measures the performance of the input, processing, and output functions. It also provides the measurement data to the control function.

feedback loop p. 175 In a computer simulation, such as a flight simulation, the changes in the system resulting from computer and user responding to data from each other.

field p. 238 A discrete chunk of information in a database record.

field type p. 238 The characteristic of a field that determines the kind of information that can be stored in that field.

fifth-generation language (5GL) p. 524 The fifth generation of programming languages (after machine, assembly, high-level languages, and fourth generation), it is a constraint-driven language. Instead of specifying an algorithm, the programmer defines the conditions that need to be met and the computer solves the problem. 5GLs are not widely used outside of research labs.

file p. 44, 587 An organized collection of related information stored in computer-readable form.

file compression p. 593 The process of reducing the size of a file so that you can fit more files into the same amount of disk space.

file decompression p. 593 The process of restoring a compressed file back to its original state.

file-management utility (file manager) p. 129 A program that allows you to view, rename, copy, move, and delete files and folders.

file server p. 325 In a LAN, a computer used as a storehouse for software and data that are shared by several users.

file transfer protocol (FTP) p. 325 A communications protocol that enables users to download files from remote servers to their computers and to upload files they want to share from their computers to these archives.

film scanner p. 73 Also known as a slide scanner, this device can scan only slides and negatives, but it generally produces higher-quality results than flatbed scanners do when scanning transparencies.

filtering software p. 346, 426 Software that, for the most part, keeps offensive and otherwise inappropriate Web content from being viewed by children, on-duty workers, and others.

Find p. 593 A command used to locate a particular word, string of characters, or formatting in a document.

find-and-replace (search and replace) p. 587 A word processing program text-editing tool that allows you to make repetitive changes throughout a document.

firewall p. 371 A software or hardware "gate" that protects internal networks from unauthorized access.

FireWire (IEEE 1394, FireWire 400, FireWire 800) p. 94 See IEEE 1394.

firmware p. 10 A program, usually for special-purpose computers, stored on a ROM chip so it cannot be altered.

flash media card reader p. 91 A device that can read a flash memory card.

flash memory p. 91 A type of erasable memory chip used in cell phones, pagers, portable computers, and handheld computers, among other things.

flash memory card p. 91 A type of file storage used in digital cameras to store images, in digital recorders to store sound, and in a variety of computer memory devices to store and transport data. Types of flash memory devices include thumb drives, SD (Secure Digital) cards, CompactFlash cards, and Memory Sticks.

flatbed scanner p. 73 A scanner that looks and works like a photocopy machine, except that it creates digital images (computer files) instead of paper copies.

folder p. 593 A container for files and other folders. Also called a directory.

font p. 587 A size and style of typeface.

footer p. 147 Block of information that appears at the bottom of every page in a document, displaying repetitive information such as an automatically calculated page number.

force feedback p. 83 Tactile feedback, such as jolts, scrapes, and bumps, transmitted via signals between a computer and a controller.

force quit p. 124 A way to shut down your computer if it freezes. In Windows, press the Ctrl + Alt + Del keys at the same time, and then click Task Manager; then select the frozen program and click End Task. On a Mac, press Command-Option-Esc or choose Force Quit from the Apple menu; then select the frozen app from the list and click Force Quit.

form p. 329 On a Web site, a page with fields that visitors can fill in to order goods and services, respond to questionnaires, express opinions, and more.

form view p. 239 A view of the database that shows one record at a time.

format p. 587 The way that characters, words, and paragraphs appear in a word processing document.

formatting p. 132, 587 The function of software, such as word processing software, that enables users to change the appearance of a document by specifying the font, point size, and style of any character in the document, as well as the overall layout of text and graphical elements in the document.

formula p. 163 Step-by-step procedure for calculating a number on a spreadsheet.

FORTRAN p. 518 The first commercial high-level programming language, designed at IBM in the 1950s to solve scientific and engineering problems.

fourth-generation languages (4GLs) p. 523 The fourth generation of programming languages (after machine, assembly, and high-level languages), which use English-like phrases and sentences to issue instructions, are nonprocedural, and increase productivity.

fragmented file p. 132 A file allocated to noncontiguous clusters on a disk, thus degrading the disk's performance.

frame p. 204 In animation, one still picture in a video or animated sequence.

frames p. 329 Subdivisions of a Web browser's viewing area that enable visitors to scroll and view different parts of a page—or even multiple pages—simultaneously.

full-color p. 157 A desktop-published document that uses a wide range of color. Contrast with spot color.

function p. 164 A predefined set of calculations, such as SUM and AVERAGE, in spreadsheet software.

function keys (F-keys) p. 585 Keyboard keys, often 12 lined along the top of the keyboard, that send special commands to the computer depending on the program being run.

fuzzy logic p. 562 A type of logic that allows conclusions to be stated as probabilities rather than certainties.

game controller p. 68 A device for providing input to computer games. Typically includes one or more buttons and a joystick or other pointing device.

gamepad p. 68 A multibutton device used to play computer games. It is held in both hands and typically includes a small joystick.

Gantt chart p. 462 A type of chart capable of representing a project schedule visually, by showing each step or category of steps in a plan, along with their planned and actual start and completion times.

GB (gig or gigabyte) p. 44 Approximately 1,000 MB.

generation p. 376 One cycle of backups; many data-processing shops keep several generations of backups so they can, if necessary, go back several days, weeks, or years to reconstruct data files.

geographical information system (GIS) p. 244, 456 A specialized database that combines tables of data with demographic information and displays geographic and demographic data on maps.

geostationary communications satellites p. 271 Satellites that match the Earth's rotation so they can hang in a stationary position relative to the spinning planet below and relay wireless transmissions between locations.

geotracking p. 500 Technology that uses your phone—or surgically implanted chip—to monitor your minute-by-minute movements.

Gigabit Ethernet p. 276 An Ethernet standard that is capable of transferring 1 gigabit of data per second on an all gigabit-Ethernet LAN.

gigahertz (GHz) p. 47 Billions of clock cycles per second, a measurement of a computer's clock speed.

GIGO (garbage in, garbage out) p. 168 Valid output requires valid input.

global positioning system (GPS) p. 284 A Defense Department system with 24 satellites that can pinpoint any location on the Earth.

globalization p. 411 The creation of global businesses and markets.

government Web portals p. 340 Portals that serve as entry points to many federal, state, and municipal government Web sites.

GPS receiver p. 284 A device that can use global positioning system signals to determine its location and communicate that information to a person or a computer.

grammar and style checker p. 151 Component of word processing software that analyzes each word in context, checking for content errors, common grammatical errors, and stylistic problems.

graphene p. 58 A one-atom-thick sheet of carbon that shows promise as a material for making future processors.

graphical user interface (GUI) p. 122 A user interface based on graphical displays. Typically the user points to icons that represent files, folders, and disks. Documents are displayed in windows. The user selects commands from menus.

graphics processing unit (GPU) p. 50 A special-purpose processor that handles 3-D graphics rendering and other visual calculations, freeing the CPU to work on other tasks.

graphics tablet p. 68 A pressure-sensitive touch tablet used as a pointing device. The user presses on the tablet with a stylus.

gray-scale graphics p. 192 Computerized imaging that allows each pixel to appear as black, white, or one of several shades of gray.

grid computing p. 304 A form of distributed computing in which processing power, instead of files, is shared between networked computers.

group decision support system (GDSS) p. 456 Systems designed to improve the productivity of decision-making meetings by enhancing the dynamics of collaborative work.

groupware p. 152, 404 Software designed to be used by workgroups rather than individuals.

hacker p. 368, 603 Someone who uses computer skills to gain unauthorized access to computer systems. Also sometimes used to refer to a particularly talented, dedicated programmer.

hacking p. 368 Electronic trespassing and vandalism. Also used as slang for *programming*.

hactivist p. 368 A person who performs hacking, sometimes illegally, as a form of political activism.

handwriting recognition software p. 73 Software that translates the user's handwritten forms into ASCII characters.

haptic feedback p. 83 See force feedback.

hard Alife p. 576 A form of artificial life that creates hardware constructs of lifelike systems, such as robotic insect colonies.

hard disk p. 84, 584 A rigid, magnetically sensitive disk that spins rapidly and continuously inside the computer chassis or in a separate box attached to the computer housing. Used as a storage device.

hardware p. 584 Physical parts of the computer system.

HDTV p. 205 High-definition television, capable of receiving and displaying high-resolution images, videos, and broadcasts.

head up display p. 98 A semitransparent display that allows you to view a computer image or data without looking away from a real-world scene.

header p. 147 Block that appears at the top of every page in a document, displaying repetitive information such as a chapter title.

help file p. 113 A documentation file that appears onscreen at the user's request.

heuristic p. 555 A rule of thumb.

hexadecimal p. 517 Base 16 number system; often used to represent machine-language programs.

hierarchical menus p. 122 Menus that organize commands into compact, efficient submenus.

high-level language p. 112, 517 A programming language that falls somewhere between natural human languages and precise machine languages, developed to streamline and simplify the programming process.

history p. 415 A list of pages recently visited in your Web browser.

hits p. 600 Visits to a particular Web page.

host name p. 601 The name of the host computer, network, or ISP address where the user receives email, contained in the part of an Internet email address that comes after the "at" sign (@).

hot swap p. 94 To remove and replace peripheral devices without powering down the computer and peripherals. Some modern interface standards such as USB and FireWire allow hot swapping.

hotspots p. 280 Publicly accessible wireless access points.

HTML (Hypertext Markup Language) p. 149, 326 An HTML document is a text file that includes codes that describe the format, layout, and logical structure of a hypermedia document. Most Web pages are created with HTML.

HTML 5 p. 331 The next version of HTML, currently under development, which includes many advanced multimedia, interactivity, and dynamic data features.

http (Hypertext Transfer Protocol) p. 326 The Internet protocol used to transfer Web pages.

hub p. 274 A network device that allows devices to communicate on a network without managing their traffic. Low-cost network switches have rendered them nearly obsolete. The term *hub* can also apply to USB splitters and other devices.

human engineering p. 86 Also known as ergonomics, it is the science of designing work environments that enable people and things to interact efficiently and safely.

hyperlink p. 598 A word, phrase, or picture that acts as a button, enabling the user to explore the Web or a multimedia document with mouse clicks.

hypermedia p. 220 The combination of text, numbers, graphics, animation, sound effects, music, and other media in hyperlinked documents.

hypertext p. 220 An interactive cross-referenced system that allows textual information to be linked in nonsequential ways. A hypertext document contains links that lead quickly to other parts of the document or to related documents.

hypertext link p. 14 A connection from a word or phrase to another document or site, like the many that loosely tie together millions of Web pages.

I

I-beam p. 586 The I-beam-shaped pointer used to highlight text and move the cursor within a text document.

icon p. 586 In a graphical user interface, a picture that represents a file, folder, or disk.

identity (ID) theft p. 362, 603 The crime, committed by hackers or other unscrupulous individuals, of obtaining enough information about a person to assume his or her identity, often as a prelude to illegally using the victim's credit cards.

IEEE 1394 (FireWire) p. 94 An industry standard for a fast serial communications protocol developed by Apple, especially well-suited for multimedia applications such as digital video.

image analysis p. 565 The process of identifying objects and shapes in a photograph, drawing, video, or other visual image.

image-compression software p. 209 Software that is used to compress graphics and video files.

image-processing software p. 193 Software that enables the user to manipulate photographs and other high-resolution images.

impact printer p. 81 Printer that forms images by physically striking paper, ribbon, and print hammer together.

implementation p. 530 The phase of the systems development life cycle in which the system is put into use.

import data p. 239 To move data into a program from another program or source.

inbox p. 601 The place where email programs and services store recipients' incoming messages.

incremental backup p. 376 A type of backup that happens regularly (usually automatically), copying only files that have changed since the last incremental backup.

industrial age p. 18 The recent modern era, characterized by the shift from farms to factories.

industrial network p. 450 A network that links the systems of several companies within an industry.

Industrial Revolution p. 18 The era of rapid advances in machine technology that began at the end of the 18th century and ushered in the industrial age.

information p. 41 Anything that can be communicated. (Some more restrictive definitions of information say that it is data that is organized or processed.)

information age p. 18 The current era, characterized by the shift from an industrial economy to an information economy and the convergence of computer and communication technology.

information overload p. 460 The state of being bombarded with too much computer output, a risk of poorly designed information systems.

information partnership p. 450 A partnership between companies, usually from different industries, through which information is shared for the mutual benefit of each company.

information system p. 444, 527 A collection of people, machines, data, and methods organized to accomplish specific functions and to solve specific problems. Programming is part of the larger process of designing, implementing, and managing an information system.

infrared wireless p. 280 The use of invisible infrared radiation and infrared ports to send and receive digital information short distances, now possible on many laptops and handheld computers.

infrastructure p. 461 Information technology's basic framework, comprising all the organization's information systems hardware, software, and telecommunications equipment; the information system department's staff and other personnel; and the organizational structure and procedures that affect accessing, processing, and using information in the company.

inkjet printer p. 81 A nonimpact printer that sprays ink directly onto paper to produce printed text and graphic images.

input p. 441 Information taken in by the computer.

input device p. 39 Device for accepting computer input, such as a keyboard or a scanner.

instant messaging (IM) p. 295 A technology that enables users to create buddy lists, check for buddies who are logged in, and exchange typed messages and files with those who are.

instructions p. 52 Computer codes telling the CPU to perform a specific action.

integrated circuit p. 7 A chip containing hundreds, thousands, or even millions of transistors.

intellectual property p. 133 The results of intellectual activities in the arts, science, and industry.

interactive fiction p. 428 Stories with natural-language interfaces that offer players some control over plot.

interactive movies p. 428 Video-based or animated features in which one or more characters are controlled by the viewers.

interactive multimedia p. 221 Multimedia that enables the user to take an active part in the experience.

interactive processing p. 252 Interacting with data through terminals, viewing and changing values online in real time.

interactive television p. 429 Broadcast television with built-in options for game playing or other forms of interactivity.

interface standards p. 94 Standards for ports and other connective technology agreed on by the hardware industry so devices made by one manufacturer can be attached to systems made by other companies.

internal bus p. 56 A group of wires that can transmit data between components on the motherboard.

internal drive p. 87, 584 A disc drive that is installed inside the system unit.

Internet p. 14, 596 A global interconnected network of thousands of networks linking academic, research, government, and commercial institutions, and other organizations and individuals. Also known as the Net.

Internet service provider (ISP) p. 322, 601 A business that provides its customers with connections to the Internet along with other services.

Internet telephony (IP telephony) p. 296 A combination of software and hardware technology that enables the Internet to, in effect, serve as a telephone network. Internet telephony systems can use standard telephones, computers, or both to send and receive voice messages.

internetworking p. 319 Connecting different types of networks and computer systems.

interorganizational information system (IOS) p. 447 A system that uses networking technology to facilitate communication between an organization and its suppliers, customers, and other organizations.

interpreter p. 516 A translation program that translates and transmits each source code statement individually into machine language.

intranet p. 277, 404, 477 A self-contained intraorganizational network that is designed using the same technology as the Internet.

investigation p. 528 In the systems development life cycle, the phase to study the existing business problem or opportunity and determine whether it is feasible to develop a new system or redesign the existing system if one exists.

IP address p. 321 A unique string of four numbers separated by periods that serves as a unique address for a computer on the Internet. The IP address of the host computer and sending computer is included with every packet of information that traverses the Internet.

IPv6 p. 321 Internet Protocol version 6.

J

jaggies p. 192 Jagged stair-step-like bumps that advertise the image's identity as a collection of pixels.

Java p. 128, 335 A platform-neutral, object-oriented programming language developed by Sun Microsystems for use on multiplatform networks.

Java virtual machine p. 128 Software that gives a computer the capability to run Java programs.

JavaScript p. 335 An interpreted scripting language, similar to but otherwise unrelated to Java, that enables Web page designers to add scripts to HTML code.

jobless growth p. 412 An economic condition in which automation alone creates adequate productivity increases and no new jobs are created.

joystick p. 68 A gearshiftlike device used as a controller for arcade-style computer games.

jump drive p. 91 See USB drive.

justification p. 147 The alignment of text on a line, such as left justification (smooth left margin and ragged right margin) and right justification (smooth right margin and ragged left margin).

K

KB (K or kilobyte) p. 44 About 1000 bytes of information.

kerning p. 155 The spacing between letter pairs in a document.

key field p. 248 A field that contains data that uniquely identifies the record.

keyboard p. 67, 585 Input device, similar to a typewriter keyboard, for entering data and commands into the computer.

knowledge p. 561 Information that incorporates the relationships among facts.

knowledge base p. 561 A database that contains both facts and a system of rules for determining and changing the relationship among those facts.

L

label p. 163 In a spreadsheet, a text entry that provides information on what a column or row represents.

laptop computer p. 10 A flat-screen, battery-powered portable computer that you can rest on your lap.

laser printer p. 81 A nonimpact printer that uses a laser beam to create patterns of electrical charges on a rotating drum. The charged patterns attract black toner and transfer it to paper as the drum rotates.

latency p. 278 A delay between the time a message is sent and the time it's received.

layer p. 194 One image stacked on top of another in Adobe Photoshop.

layered defense p. 390 For organizations with large networks to aid in malware defenses.

leading p. 157 The spacing between lines of text.

legacy ports p. 94 The most common standard ports on PC system boards, including the serial port, parallel port, and keyboard/mouse port.

Level 1 cache p. 53 Memory storage that can be quickly accessed by the CPU.

Level 2 cache (L2 cache) p. 53 Memory storage that is larger than a level 1 cache but not as quickly accessed by the CPU.

line chart p. 166 A chart that shows trends or relationships over time, or a relative distribution of one variable through another.

line printer p. 81 An impact printer used by mainframes to produce massive printouts. They print characters only, not graphics.

links p. 598 See hyperlink.

Linux p. 105 An operating system based on UNIX, maintained by volunteers, and distributed for free. Linux is used mostly in servers and embedded computers, but it is growing in popularity as a PC operating system.

liquid crystal display (LCD) p. 79 Flat-panel displays, once primarily used for portable computers but now replacing bulkier CRT monitors for desktops.

LISP p. 518 List Processing, a high-level computer language developed at MIT in the late 1950s to process nonnumeric data like characters, words, and other symbols.

list views p. 239 Showing data by displaying several records in lists similar to a spreadsheet.

local area network (LAN) p. 274 Multiple personal computers connected on a network.

logged in p. 126, 601 Connected to a computer system or network.

logic bomb p. 366 A program designed to attack in response to a particular logical event or sequence of events. A type of software sabotage.

logic error p. 516 An error in the logical structure of a program that makes a difference between what the program is supposed to do and what it actually does.

login name p. 601 See user name.

LOGO p. 518 A computer language developed in the 1960s for children.

Long Tail p. 494 A term that refers to the tail of the statistical curve that appears when you rank books, movies, or tunes by popularity. Before the Web, retailers had trouble making money on the "long tail" of that curve: the items that were less popular. However, the Web has made the selling of less popular items much easier.

lossless compression p. 211 Systems allowing files to be compressed and later decompressed without a loss of data.

lossy compression p. 211 A type of compression in which some quality is lost in the process of compression and decompression.

low-level languages p. 517 Programming languages that require the programmer to think on the machine's level and to include an enormous amount of detail in every program, such as machine language and assembly language.

Luddites p. 410 A 19th-century English labor group that smashed new textile machinery to protect their jobs; today the term is often used to describe someone who opposes new technology in general.

lurker p. 294 A silent, invisible observer who doesn't contribute to the discussions on social networks, newsgroups, and forums.

M

Mac OS p. 122, 587 The operating system for the Apple Macintosh computer.

machine language p. 109, 516 The language that computers use to process instructions. Machine language uses numeric codes to represent basic computer operations.

machine learning p. 555 Artificial intelligence techniques that make it possible for machine performance to improve based on feedback from past performance.

macro p. 164, 523 Custom-designed embedded procedure program that automates tasks in application programs.

macro language p. 523 A user-oriented language that enables users to create programs (macros) to automate repetitive tasks; also known as scripting languages.

macro virus p. 365 A virus that attaches to and is transmitted through a macro embedded in a document; typically spread via email.

magnetic disk p. 84 A rotating storage medium with random-access capability. Most desktop and laptop computers use magnetic hard disks for file storage.

magnetic ink character reader p. 72 A device that reads numbers printed with magnetic ink on checks.

magnetic tape p. 84 A storage medium used with a tape drive to store large amounts of information in a small space at relatively low cost.

mail merge p. 152 A feature of a word processor or other program that enables it to merge names and addresses from a database mailing list into personalized form letters and mailings.

mailbox p. 601 A storage area for email messages.

mailing list p. 292 An email discussion group on a special-interest topic. All subscribers receive messages sent to the group's mailing address.

mainframe computer p. 12 Expensive, room-sized computer, used mostly for large computing jobs.

maintenance p. 530 The phase of the systems development life cycle that involves evaluating, repairing, and enhancing the system.

malware p. 363 Malicious software, especially destructive programs such as the viruses, worms, and Trojan horses devised and spread by computer saboteurs.

management p. 451 A set of activities that helps people efficiently use resources to accomplish an organization's goals.

management information system (MIS) p. 454, 538 Also known as a management reporting system, a system that gives a manager the information he or she needs to make decisions, typically structured decisions, regarding the operational activities of the company.

management levels p. 454 The three management tiers (operational, tactical, and strategic) typically found in a large organization.

management reporting system p. 455 Another name for management information system; the main output is a variety of detailed, summary, and exception reports for managers.

manycore p. 50 A device with tens or hundreds of processors per chip.

mashup p. 116, 342 A Web page, song, video, or image that combines images, words, music, and video clips from other works. Also, a Web site that draws on external software applications, such as a real estate application that integrates Google Maps into its interface.

mask p. 194 A tool in Photoshop used to cover an area of a project.

massively multiplayer online role-playing games (MMORPG) p. 229, 427 Internet games that support thousands of simultaneous players, allowing them to assume roles of particular characters in shared virtual worlds.

math-processing software p. 171 Software designed to deal with complex equations and calculations. A mathematics processor enables the user to create, manipulate, and solve equations easily.

MB (meg or megabyte) p. 44 Approximately 1,000 KB, or 1 million bytes.

m-commerce p. 492 Mobile commerce, in which workers use laptops and wireless handheld devices to take their offices with them wherever they travel.

megabits (MB or Mbit p. 44 Approximately 1,000 bits.

memory p. 40, 584 Stores programs and the data they need to be instantly accessible to the CPU.

menu p. 122 An onscreen list of command choices.

menu-driven interface p. 122 A user interface that enables users to choose commands from on-screen lists called menus.

mesh networks p. 275 Decentralized alternatives to today's central-hub-based networks, allowing a message to hop from wireless device to wireless device until it finds its destination.

micro-blogs p. 294 One- or two-sentence blogs that chronicle someone's minute-by-minute activities and thoughts. Twitter is the most popular micro-blog service.

microprocessor p. 7, 39, 584 Now known as a personal computer.

Microsoft Windows p. 122, 587 The most popular PC operating system.

microtransactions p. 500 Pioneered in Facebook games and iTunes apps that will be available just about anywhere there is a computer screen and sensor.

MIDI p. 212 Musical Instrument Digital Interface, a standard interface that allows electronic instruments and computers to communicate with each other and work together.

millisecond (ms) p. 56 A thousandth of a second.

mixing p. 214 The combining of multiple tracks, audio effects, and balancing volumes and audio placement to make the best possible recording.

model management p. 456 A component of the decision support system, in which a manager evaluates alternative problem solutions and identifies the best solution using appropriate software.

modeling p. 174 The use of computers to create abstract models of objects, organisms, organizations, and processes.

modem p. 278 Modulator/demodulator. A hardware device that enables a computer to make a dial-up connection to other computers through a telephone line.

moderated group p. 292 An email discussion group in which a designated moderator acts as an editor, filtering out irrelevant and inappropriate messages and posting the rest.

module p. 519 In structured programming, a program is built from smaller programs called modules.

monitor p. 79, 585 An output device that displays text and graphics onscreen.

monospaced font p. 587 A font such as those in the Courier family that mimic typewriters; characters, no matter how skinny or fat, always take up the same amount of space horizontally.

Moore's law p. 8 The prediction made in 1965 by Gordon Moore that the power of a silicon chip of the same price would double about every 18 months for at least two decades.

moral dilemma p. 25 A predicament for which rules and ethics don't seem to apply, or seem to contradict one another.

motherboard p. 46 The circuit board that contains a computer's CPU. Also called a system board.

mouse p. 68, 585 A handheld input device that, when moved around on a desktop or table, moves a pointer around the computer screen.

MP3 p. 212 A type of compression that can squeeze a music file to a fraction of its original CD file size with only slight loss of audio quality.

MS-DOS p. 122 Microsoft Disk Operating System, an operating system with a character-based user interface; it was widely used in the 1980s and early 1990s but has been superseded by Windows.

multicasting p. 321 A technology in the Next Generation Internet (NGI) that represents a more efficient way for the same information to be transmitted to multiple Internet-connected devices.

multicore processor p. 50 A microprocessor containing multiple CPUs, called cores.

multidimensional database technology p. 253 Technology that has speed and flexibility advantages over traditional, relational databases. Stores data in more than two dimensions.

multifunction printer (MFP) p. 81 An all-in-one output device that usually combines a scanner, a laser or inkjet printer, and a fax modem.

multimedia p. 221 Using some combination of text, graphics, animation, video, music, voice, and sound effects to communicate.

multimedia-authoring software p. 222 Enables the creation and editing of multimedia documents.

multiprocessing p. 51 Employing two or more microprocessors in a computer in order to improve overall performance. Also known as symmetric multiprocessing.

multitasking p. 118 Concurrent processing for personal computers. The user can issue a command that initiates a process and then continue working with other applications while the computer follows through on the command.

multi-touch p. 70 Input device such as touch-sensitive screen, a touch tablet, or a trackpad that can recognize the position, pressure, and movement of more than one finger or hand at a time.

N

nanosecond (ns) p. 56 A billionth of a second; a common unit of measurement for read and write access time to RAM.

nanotechnology p. 58 Technology employed by today's cutting edge chips that approaches the molecular or atomic level.

narrowband connection p. 278 A name applied to dial-up Internet connections because they don't offer much bandwidth when compared to other types of connections.

narrowcasting p. 426 Providing custom newscasts and entertainment features aimed at narrow groups or individuals.

natural language p. 112, 559 Language that people speak and write every day.

Net p. 596 See Internet.

Net neutrality p. 348 Also called network neutrality, it's the principle that Internet access should be free from restrictions related to the type of equipment being connected and the type of communication being performed with that equipment.

netbook p. 11 An extra-small, extra-light, no-frills notebook computer designed mainly as a portable Internet connection device.

netiquette p. 302 Rules of etiquette that apply to Internet communication.

network p. 14 A computer system that links two or more computers.

network administrator p. 275 A worker who takes care of the behind-the-scenes network details so others can focus on using the network.

network license p. 288 License for multiple copies or removing restrictions on software copying and use at a network site.

network operating system (NOS) p. 277 Server operating system software for a local area network.

neural network (neural net) p. 568 A distributed, parallel computing system inspired by the structure of the human brain.

neuroprosthetics p. 306 Researchers in this field develop devices to substitute for missing or damaged parts of the body or nervous system.

newsgroup p. 293 An ongoing public discussion group related to a particular subject; notes are written to a central Internet site and redistributed through a worldwide newsgroup network called Usenet.

node p. 274 Each computer and shared peripheral on a local area network.

nonimpact printer p. 81 A printer that produces characters without physically striking the page.

nonlinear editing (NLE) p. 207 A type of video editing in which audio and video clips are stored in digital form on hard disks for immediate access via video-editing software.

nonsequential p. 220 Nonvolatile memory; memory for permanent storage of information.

notebook computer p. 10 Another term for laptop computer.

notifications p. 341 Along with alerts, a popular noncorporate type of push technology on the Web, notifying users about online auction status, fees due, and the like.

numeric field p. 239 A field containing only numbers.

object-oriented database p. 253 Instead of storing records in tables and hierarchies, it stores software objects that contain procedures (or instructions) with data.

object-oriented graphics p. 195 The storage of pictures as collections of lines, shapes, and other objects.

object-oriented programming (OOP) p. 521 Programming in which a program is not just a collection of step-by-step instructions or procedures; it's a collection of objects. Objects contain both data and instructions and can send and receive messages.

objects p. 253 In object-oriented databases, a data structure defined according to its class.

off-site backup p. 377 A backup of data and programs to a nonlocal site, either by transporting portable media or by uploading files to a remote location in the Internet cloud.

online help p. 113 Documentation and help available through a software company's Web site.

online service p. 322 A service that provides Internet access and other services in a privately controlled environment; America Online (AOL) is the most popular of these.

open p. 130 To load a file into an application program's workspace so it can be viewed and edited by the user.

open architecture p. 94 A design that allows expansion cards and peripherals to be added to a basic computer system.

open-source software p. 106 Software that can be distributed and modified freely by users; Linux is the best-known example.

open standards p. 319 Standards not owned by any company.

operating system (OS) p. 117, 585 A system of programs that performs a variety of technical operations, providing an additional layer of insulation between the user and the bits-and-bytes world of computer hardware.

operational level p. 454 The management level responsible for supervising the day-to-day activities in the organization's value chain.

optical character recognition (OCR) p. 72, 565 Locating and identifying printed characters embedded in an image, allowing the text to be stored as an editable document. OCR can be performed by wand readers, pen scanners, and OCR software.

optical character recognition (OCR) software p. 17, 565 Software that locates and identifies printed characters embedded in images.

optical computer p. 58 A potential future alternative to silicon-based computing, in which information is transmitted in light waves rather than in electrical pulses.

optical disc drive p. 85 A disk drive that uses laser beams to read and write bits of information on the surface of an optical disc.

optical mark reader p. 72 A reading device that uses reflected light to determine the location of pencil marks on standardized test answer sheets and similar forms.

organizational information requirements analysis p. 466 Also called enterprise modeling, an approach many companies use to summarize their current IT infrastructure, to identify the practical range of business and product strategies based on the current infrastructure, and to identify information system projects that offer the most benefits to the organization.

Outline view p. 149 The outliner option built into Microsoft Word and other word processors, enabling users to examine and restructure the overall organization of a document while showing each topic in as much detail needed.

outliner p. 149 Software that facilitates the arrangement of information into hierarchies or levels of ideas. Some word processors include outline views that serve the same function as separate outliners.

output p. 441 Information given out by the computer.

output device p. 39 A device for sending information from the computer, such as a monitor or printer.

outsourcing p. 451 Hiring talent outside the business for selected activities on a contract basis.

P

P2P (or p-to-p) model p. 277 See peer-to-peer model.

packet-switching p. 321 The standard technique used to send information over the Internet. A message is broken into packets that travel independently from network to network toward their common destination, where they are reunited.

packets p. 319 What information sent over the Internet is broken into. These packets are transferred from network to network toward their destination.

page-layout software p. 155 In desktop publishing, software used to combine various source documents into a coherent, visually appealing publication.

painting software p. 191 Enables you to paint pixels on the screen with a pointing device.

palette p. 191 A collection of colors available in drawing software.

paperless office p. 404 An office of the future in which magnetic and optical archives will replace reference books and file cabinets, electronic communication will replace letters and memos, and digital publications provided through the Internet and online services will replace newspapers and other periodicals.

paradigm shift p. 18 A change in thinking that results in a new way of seeing the world.

parallel port p. 94 A standard port on older PCs for attaching a printer or other device that communicates by sending or receiving bits in groups, rather than sequentially.

parallel processing p. 51, 554 Using multiple processors to divide jobs into pieces and work simultaneously on the pieces.

parameter RAM p. 56 CMOS RAM, a special low-energy kind of RAM used to store the date, time, and calendar in Macintoshes.

parsing program (parser) p. 557 In translation, a program that analyzes sentence structure and identifies each word according to its part of speech. Another program looks up each word in a translation dictionary and substitutes the appropriate word.

Pascal p. 518 A high-level computer language, named for the 17th-century French mathematician and inventor, developed in the early 1970s as an alternative to BASIC for student programmers.

password p. 371 The most common security tool used to restrict access to computer systems.

paste p. 587 An editing command that allows you to cut or copy information from one part of a document and place—paste—the copy elsewhere in the same or a different document.

patent p. 133 A type of law that protects mechanical inventions.

path p. 326 The hierarchical nesting of directories (folders) that contain a Web resource, as described in the third part of the URL, following the dot address.

pathname p. 129 The unique location specification for every computer file and folder, describing the nesting of folders containing it.

pattern recognition p. 564 Identifying recurring patterns in input data with the goal of understanding or categorizing that input.

PB (petabyte) p. 44 The equivalent of 1024 terabytes, or 1 quadrillion bytes.

PC card p. 57 A credit-card-sized card that can be inserted into a slot to expand memory or add a peripheral to a computer; common in older portable computers. Sometimes called by its original name, PCMCIA.

PDF (Portable Document Format) p. 195 Allows documents of all types to be stored, viewed, or modified on any Windows or Macintosh computer, making it possible for many organizations to reduce paper flow.

peer-to-peer (P2P) computing p. 304 See peer-to-peer model.

peer-to-peer (P2P) file sharing p. 304 The online sharing of music or other computer files directly among individual computer users' hard drives, rather than through posting the files on central servers.

peer-to-peer model p. 277 A LAN model that allows every computer on the network to be both client and server.

pen scanner p. 72 A scanner that looks like a pen or highlighter. When you drag a pen scanner across a line of printed text, it creates a text file in its built-in memory, where it's stored until you transfer it into your computer's memory through a cable or wireless connection.

peripheral p. 11, 584 An external device, such as a keyboard or monitor, connected via cables to the system central processing unit.

Perl p. 335 Practical extraction and reporting language, a Web scripting language that is particularly well suited for writing scripts to process text—for example, complex Web forms.

personal area network (PAN) p. 282 A network that links a variety of physically close electronic devices, such as mobile phones, handheld computers, and PCs, so they can communicate with each other. Bluetooth is the technology most often used to create PANs.

personal computer (PC) p. 7, 584 A small, powerful, relatively low-cost microcomputer.

personal digital assistant (PDA) p. 11 A pocket-sized computer used to organize appointments, tasks, notes, contacts, and other personal information. Sometimes called handheld computer or palmtop computer. Many PDAs include additional software and hardware for wireless communication.

personal information manager (PIM) p. 243 A specialized database program that automates an address/phone book, an appointment calendar, a to-do list, and miscellaneous notes. Also called an electronic organizer.

personal Web portal p. 340 A Web portal that can be customized to reflect a user's personal taste and interests. Features might include local weather and sports scores, personalized TV and movie listings, news headlines related to particular subjects, horoscopes, and advertisements, among others.

PERT p. 462 Program evaluation and review technique, a variation of the critical path method used to keep track of a project's schedule; PERT features optimistic, pessimistic, and most likely time estimates to complete each activity.

phishing p. 291, 363 The use of a deceptive email message or Web site to lure a person into divulging credit card numbers or other sensitive information.

photo management software p. 195 Programs that simplify and automate common tasks associated with capturing, organizing, editing, and sharing digital images.

photo printer p. 81 A type of newer inkjet printer specially optimized to print high-quality photos captured with digital cameras and scanners.

PHP p. 335 A widely used open source scripting language that is designed for producing dynamic Web pages. Like Perl, PHP is a server-side language. Many programmers take advantage of the fact that HTML code can be embedded in PHP scripts.

pie chart p. 166 A round pie-shaped chart with slices that show the relative proportions of the parts to a whole.

pixel p. 191 A picture element (dot) on a computer screen or printout. Groups of pixels compose the images on the monitor and the output of a printout.

pixels per inch (PPI) p. 192 Density of pixels, or resolution, is described in pixels per inch.

platform p. 127 The combination of hardware and operating system software upon which application software is built.

platform independent p. 94 The ability of a peripheral device to work on multiple platforms. For example, a USB disk drive could be used with both Macintosh and Windows computers.

platters p. 88 Flat discs that are the part of the hard disk that holds information.

plotter p. 81 An automated drawing tool that produces finely scaled drawings by moving a pen and/or paper in response to computer commands.

plug-in p. 330 A software extension that adds new features.

podcast p. 212 Radio- or television-style programs that can be downloaded on demand or automatically by subscription.

point-of-sale (POS) terminal p. 72 A terminal with a wand reader, barcode scanner, or other device that captures information at the check-out counter of a store.

point size p. 587 A measure of character size, with one point equal to 1/72 inch.

pointcasting p. 426 A one-on-one broadcast targeting a single individual. It's also known as individualized broadcasting.

pop-up menus p. 123 Menus that can appear anywhere on the screen.

port p. 57 Socket that allows information to pass in and out.

portals p. 600 Web sites designed as first-stop gateways for Internet surfers.

power-line network p. 274 A network that transmits data through power lines. Ethernet cables generally connect each computer's network port to a device that attaches to the phone line or power line.

prefetch unit p. 52 Part of the CPU that fetches the next several instructions from memory.

presentation p. 445 Showing information in a format and medium useful to the user.

presentation-graphics software p. 204 Automates the creation of visual aids for lectures, training sessions, and other presentations. Can include everything from spreadsheet charting programs to animation-editing software, and it is most commonly used for creating and displaying a series of onscreen slides to serve as visual aids for presentations.

primary storage p. 84 A computer's main memory.

print server p. 285 A server that accepts, prioritizes, and processes print jobs.

printer p. 81, 401 Output device that produces a paper copy of any information that can be displayed on the screen.

privacy p. 255 Freedom from unauthorized access to one's person, or to knowledge about one's person.

processing p. 455 An activity that manipulates and organizes information in ways that add value.

processor p. 39 Part of the computer that processes information, performs arithmetic calculations, and makes basic decisions based on information values.

program p. 107 Instructions that tell the hardware what to do to transform input into output.

program verification p. 540 The process of proving the correctness of a program.

programming p. 511 A specialized form of problem solving, typically involving the four steps of defining the problem; devising, refining, and testing the algorithm; writing the program; and testing and debugging the program.

programming environment p. 516 An integrated compiler software package, including a text editor, a compiler, a debugger, and a variety of other programming utilities.

project management software p. 462 Programs that help coordinate, schedule, and track complex projects.

PROLOG p. 518 Programming Logic, a popular language for artificial-intelligence programming.

proportionally spaced font p. 588 A font that allows more horizontal space for wide characters than for narrow characters.

protocol p. 276 A set of rules for the exchange of data between a terminal and a computer or between two computers.

prototype p. 529 A limited working system or subsystem that is created to give users and managers an idea of how the complete system will work.

prototyping p. 529 An iterative process in which the systems analyst can modify the prototype until it meets the needs and expectations of the organization.

pseudocode p. 511 A cross between a computer language and plain English, a form that programmers typically use to write algorithms before translating them into computer language.

public domain p. 197 Creative work or intellectual property that is freely usable by anyone, either because the copyright has expired or because the creator obtained a Creative Commons license for the work.

public-domain software p. 115 Free software that is not copyrighted and that is offered through World Wide Web sites, electronic bulletin boards, user groups, and other sources.

public network p. 483 A network that uses a public communications network, such as a public utility telecommunication network or the Internet; one way for an organization to set up an extranet.

pull technology p. 340 Technology in which browsers on client computers pull information from server machines. The browser needs to initiate a request before any information is delivered.

push technology p. 340 Technology in which information is delivered automatically to a client computer. The user subscribes to a service, and the server delivers that information periodically and unobtrusively. Contrast with pull technology.

Python p. 335, 518 A Java-like language popular with Linux open-source programmers.

Q

quantum computers p. 58 Computers based on the properties of atoms and their nuclei and the laws of quantum mechanics.

query p. 239 An information request.

query language p. 241, 524 A special language for performing queries, more precise than the English language.

question-answering machine p. 569 Understands natural-language questions and provides answers to those questions by drawing on a base of stored knowledge from a broad array of disciplines.

QuickTime p. 331 An Apple program for delivering cross-platform streaming media in proprietary formats.

R

radio frequency identification (RFID) reader p. 72 A reading tool that uses radio waves to communicate with RFID tags.

radio frequency identification (RFID) tag p. 72 A device that, when energized by a nearby RFID reader, broadcasts information to the reader for input into a computer.

RAID (redundant array of independent disk) p. 376 A storage device that allows multiple hard disks to operate as a unit.

RAM (random access memory) p. 40 Memory that stores program instructions and data temporarily.

random access p. 84 A storage method that allows information retrieval without regard to the order in which it was recorded.

raster (bit-mapped) graphics p. 192 Painting programs create raster graphics that are, to the computer, simple maps showing how the pixels on the screen should be represented.

Read Me p. 113 File provided with software packages with installation instructions and last-minute release notes.

read/write head p. 88 The mechanism that reads information from, and writes information to, the spinning platter in a hard disk or disk drive.

real time p. 252 When a computer performs tasks immediately.

real-time communication p. 295 Internet communication that enables you to communicate with other users who are logged on at the same time.

real-time processing p. 446 Processing each transaction as it occurs, which is appropriate when users need the data immediately, as with bank ATM machines.

real-time streaming audio broadcast p. 329 Streaming transmission of radio broadcasts, concerts, news feeds, speeches, and other sound events as they happen.

real-time streaming video broadcast p. 329 Similar to streaming audio Webcasts but with video.

record p. 238 In a database, the information relating to one person, product, or event.

record matching p. 256 Compiling profiles by combining information from different database files by looking for a shared unique field.

regional Web portal p. 339 A portal on the Web that contains information and services related to a particular geographic region.

regional work centers p. 406 Shared offices established by corporations and government organizations in various locales to reduce commuting times.

register p. 52 A storage area within a CPU's arithmetic logic unit (ALU). Most registers are 32 or 64 bits in size.

relational database p. 248 A program that allows files to be related to each other so changes in one file are reflected in other files automatically.

remix p. 214 A complete digital reworking of a song using fresh instrumentation, rhythms, and audio samples.

remote access p. 596 Network access via phone line, TV cable system, or wireless link.

removable media p. 584 Storage media designed to be removed and transported easily.

repetition p. 513 A looping mechanism within a control structure that allows a group of steps to be repeated several times.

repetitive-stress injuries p. 67 Conditions that result from repeating the same movements over long periods, such as keyboarding-induced carpal tunnel syndrome, a painful affliction of the wrist and hand.

replication p. 164 Automatic replication of values, labels, and formulas; a feature of spreadsheet software.

report p. 241 A database printout that is an ordered list of selected records and fields in an easy-to-read form.

resolution p. 79, 192 Density of pixels, measured by the number of dots per inch.

restoring p. 379 Recovering backed up data to return a disk to its former state.

retinal display p. 98 A device that works without a screen by drawing pixels directly on the user's retina with a focused beam of light.

retirement p. 531 The final phase of the systems development life cycle, in which a system is phased out.

RGB color model p. 80 Additive color synthesis based on red, green, and blue; device dependent.

right-click p. 586 Pressing the right-hand button on a mouse.

right to privacy p. 258 Freedom from interference into the private sphere of a person's affairs.

rip p. 212 Copy songs from a CD to a computer's hard drive.

robot p. 571 A computer-controlled machine designed to perform specific manual tasks.

rollover p. 331 A common use of Web scripting, used to make on-screen buttons visibly change when the pointer rolls over them.

ROM (read-only memory) p. 56 Memory that includes permanent information only. The computer can only read information from it; it can never write any new information on it.

root directory p. 129 The main folder on a computer's primary hard disk, containing all the other files and folders kept on the disk.

router p. 275 A program or device that decides how to route Internet transmissions.

RSS (Really Simple Syndication) p. 341 An XML-based format for sharing data with aggregators, commonly used by bloggers.

S

sabotage p. 363 A malicious attack on work, tools, or business.

safe mode p. 124 A way to start your machine when it's not working properly because files have been corrupted or applications are clashing with each other. Safe mode disables most startup applications temporarily. On a Windows machine, press and hold the F8 key on the keyboard as the machine is booting, then use the arrow keys to select Safe Mode in the Windows Advanced Options Menu that appears. On a Mac, hold down the Shift key while restarting until the Apple logo appears.

sample p. 209 A digital sound file.

samplers p. 212 An electronic musical instrument that can sample digital sounds, turn them into notes, and play them back at any pitch.

sampling rate p. 212 The rate that a sound wave is sampled; the more samples per second, the more closely the digitized sound approximates the original.

sans serif font p. 5, 587 A font in which the characters have plain and clean lines rather than embellishments at the ends of the main strokes.

satellite Internet connections p. 278 A broadband technology available through many of the same satellite dishes that provide television channels to viewers. For many rural homes and businesses, satellite Internet connections provide the only high-speed Internet access options available.

satellite offices p. 406 Workplaces that enable workers to commute to smaller offices closer to their homes.

Save p. 130 A basic file-management operation that writes the current state of the application as a disk file.

Save As p. 130 A basic file-management operation that allows you to choose the location and name of the file you want to contain the current state of the application.

Scalable Vector Graphics (SVG) p. 204 An open standard of vector graphics format.

scanner p. 73 An input device that makes a digital representation of any printed image. See flatbed scanners, slide scanners, drum scanners, and sheet-fed scanners.

scatter chart p. 167 Discovers a relationship, if any, between two variables.

scientific-visualization software p. 172 Uses shape, location in space, color, brightness, and motion to help you understand invisible relationships, providing graphical representation of numerical data.

script p. 335 A short program that can add interactivity, animation, and other dynamic features to a Web page or multimedia document.

scripting language p. 523 A user-oriented language that enables users to create programs (macros) that automate repetitive tasks; also known as macro languages.

search p. 239 To look for a specific record in a database, or to look for something on the Web.

Search command p. 593 A command that helps you find files no matter where they are stored on the system.

search engine p. 329, 600 A program for locating information on the Web.

search engine optimization p. 486 A method of increasing Web site traffic by improving search engine rankings for targeted keywords.

searching p. 555 An artificial-intelligence technique wherein the computer looks ahead at the possible outcomes of a given action, such as a move in a game of chess.

secondary storage p. 84 The category of computer storage that includes peripherals such as tape and disk drives.

sectors p. 132 Units of data or memory on a hard disk, existing as parts of concentric tracks.

secure private network p. 483 A network that physically attaches intranets with private leased telephone lines; one way an organization can set up an extranet.

security patch p. 367 Software programs that plug potential security breaches in an operating system, often provided as free downloads or automatic updates to all owners of the OS.

security processors p. 390 Special-purpose hardware that allows every network message to be encrypted.

select p. 239, 586 To choose an object, as by moving the pointer to a picture of a tool or object on the screen and clicking the mouse.

select (records) p. 239 Looking for all records that match a set of criteria.

selection p. 513 See decision.

semantics p. 559 The underlying meaning of words and phrases.

semiconductor p. 7 Another name for a silicon chip.

semistructured decision p. 451 A type of management decision used when there's some uncertainty about a problem and the manager must use his or her judgment.

sensor p. 75, 571 A device that enables digital machines to monitor a physical quantity of the analog world, such as temperature, humidity, or pressure, to provide data used in robotics, environmental climate control, and other applications.

sequence p. 513 A group of instructions within a control structure that are followed in a given order.

sequencing software p. 214 Software that enables a computer to be used as a tool for musical composition, recording, and editing.

sequential p. 220 Linear in form, and designed to be read from beginning to end, as are conventional text media such as books.

sequential access p. 84 A storage method that requires the user to retrieve information by zipping through it in the order in which it was recorded.

Serial-ATA or SATA (Serial Advanced Technology Attachment) p. 96 A type of interface (frequently used for hard disks) that can transfer data at up to 1200 Mbps.

serial port p. 94 A standard port on older PCs for attaching a modem or other device that can send and receive messages one bit at a time.

serif font p. 587 A typeface font in which the characters are embellished with fine lines (serifs) at the ends of the main strokes.

server p. 12 A computer especially designed to provide software and other resources to other computers over a network.

service pack p. 113 A bundled collection of updates, upgrades, and bug fixes for an operating system or software application.

set-top box p. 221 A special-purpose computer designed to provide Internet access and other services using a standard television set and (usually) a cable TV connection.

shareware p. 115 Software that is free for the trying, with a send-payment-if-you-keep-it honor system.

shell p. 123 A program layer that stands between the user and the operating system.

Shockwave/Flash p. 331 An Adobe plug-in that enables Web browsers to present compressed interactive multimedia documents and animations created with various authoring tools.

Shockwave Flash Format (SWF) p. 204 A popular form of vector graphics format associated with the Adobe Flash Player.

silicon chip p. 7 Hundreds of transistors packed into an integrated circuit on a piece of silicon.

Silicon Valley p. 7 The area around San Jose, California, that became a hotbed of the computer industry in the 1970s, when dozens of microprocessor manufacturing companies sprouted and grew there.

Silverlight p. 335 Popular Microsoft client-side tools for creating interactive media-rich Web components.

Singularity p. 575 A possible future point in time when artificial intelligence technology advances to the point where machines can improve, advance, and program themselves without human intervention.

site license p. 288 License for multiple copies or removing restrictions on software copying and use at a network site.

sleep p. 48 A suspended animation state in which a system uses just enough power to preserve RAM.

slot p. 56 An area inside the computer's housing for inserting special-purpose circuit boards.

smart badge p. 380 See active badge.

smart card p. 425 A card that looks like a standard credit card but features an embedded microprocessor and memory instead of a magnetic strip.

smart phone p. 11 A handheld device that combines the functions of a phone, a camera, a PDA, a game machine, and a music/video player with Internet connectivity and ability to run apps.

smart weapon p. 385 A missile that uses computerized guidance systems to locate its target.

social engineering p. 363 Slang for the use of deception to get individuals to reveal sensitive information.

social networking p. 298 A term used to describe Web sites that make it easy for members to connect with friends, meet people with common interests, and create online communities. These sites often rely on email, instant messages, chat rooms, Web forums, blogs, and other network communication technologies.

social responsibility p. 463 Legal and ethical computing behavior, a key concern in business today because of the many ways an information worker's actions can affect other people.

social television p. 429 The possible next step beyond interactive television, supporting interpersonal communications and social interaction.

soft Alife p. 576 A form of artificial life that creates simulations or other software-based constructions that exhibit lifelike behavior.

software p. 585 Instructions that tell the hardware what to do to transform input into output.

software engineering p. 539 A branch of computer science that applies engineering principles and techniques to the world of computer software.

software license p. 114 An agreement allowing the use of a software program on a single machine.

software piracy p. 114 The illegal duplication of copyrighted software.

SOHO p. 423 Small office, home office, referring to one of today's fastest-growing computer markets.

solid-state storage p. 91 Storage, such as flash memory, with no moving parts. Solid-state storage is likely to replace disk storage in the future.

sort p. 241 To arrange records in alphabetic or numeric order based on values in one or more fields.

sound card p. 83 A circuit board that allows the PC to accept microphone input, play music and other sound through speakers or headphones, and process sound in a variety of ways.

source document p. 155 In desktop publishing, the articles, chapters, drawings, maps, charts, and photographs that are to appear in the publication. Usually produced with standard word processors and graphics programs.

spam p. 291, 603 Internet junk mail.

spam filter p. 603 Software found in most email programs whose purpose is to limit or control Internet junk mail.

spamdexing p. 486 Using techniques such as automatically generated links from bogus sites to fool search engines into giving sites higher rankings than they deserve.

speaker independence p. 566 Speech-recognition technology that works without having to be trained to an individual voice.

speakers p. 585 The personal computer peripherals that emit music, voices, and other sounds.

speech recognition p. 75 The identification of spoken words and sentences by a computer, making it possible for voice input to be converted into text files.

speech recognition software p. 153 See speech recognition.

speech synthesis p. 567 The use of software or hardware to allow PCs to recite anything typed, though with voices that sound artificial and robotic.

spelling checker (batch or interactive) p. 151 A built-in component of a word processor or a separate program that compares words in a document with words in a disk-based dictionary and flags words not found in the dictionary. May operate in batch mode, checking all the words at once, or interactive mode, checking one word at a time.

spider p. 339 See Web crawler.

spoofing p. 363 A process used to steal passwords online through deception.

spot color p. 157 The relatively easy use of a single color (or sometimes two) to add interest to a desktop-publishing product.

spreadsheet software p. 162 Software that enables the user to control numbers, manipulating them in various ways. The software can manage budgeting, investment management, business projections, grade books, scientific simulations, checkbooks, financial planning and speculation, and other tasks involving numbers.

spybot p. 366 A spyware application program, also called tracking software, that gathers user information and communicates it to an outsider via the Internet.

spyware p. 366 Technology that collects information from computer users without their knowledge or consent.

stack chart p. 167 A chart that uses stacked bars to show how proportions of a whole change over time.

static IP address p. 321 An IP address assigned semipermanently to a particular device connected to the Internet.

static Web site p. 331 A site with content that doesn't often change.

statistical-analysis software p. 171 Specialized software that tests the strength of data relationships, produces graphs showing how two or more variables relate to each other, uncovers trends, and performs other statistical analyses.

statistics p. 171 The science of collecting and analyzing data.

steering committee p. 528 An organizational group that may be formed to decide which projects should be considered first.

stepwise refinement p. 511 Breaking programming problems into smaller problems, and breaking each smaller problem into a subproblem that can be subdivided in the same way.

storage and retrieval p. 445 Activities that systematically accumulate information for later use and locate the stored information when needed.

storage device p. 40, 84 Long-term repository for data. Disks and tapes are examples.

stored-program concept p. 107 First discussed in a 1945 paper suggesting that program instructions could be stored with the data in memory. Every computer created since has been based on this concept.

stored query p. 239 A commonly used query recorded by a database so it can be accessed quickly in the future. The ability to generate stored queries is a powerful feature that helps databases blur the line between application programs and development tools.

storyboard p. 207 The first step in a video project, a guide for shooting and editing scenes.

strategic information system p. 459 Any information system that is crucial to a company's competitive success.

strategic level p. 454 The management level responsible for long-range issues related to the business's growth and development.

strategic planning p. 460 The first phase of information technology planning, which involves developing a plan that defines the mission of the company, identifies the company's environment and internal strengths and weaknesses, and defines the competitive strategy of the company.

streaming audio p. 329 Sound files that play without being completely downloaded to the local hard disk.

streaming video p. 329 Video clip files that play while being downloaded.

structured decision p. 451 A type of management decision used when the manager understands the situation clearly and uses established procedures and information to resolve the problem.

structured programming p. 519 A technique to make programming easier and more productive. Structured programs are built from smaller programs, called modules or subprograms, that are in turn made of even smaller modules.

Structured Query Language (SQL) p. 241 A query language available for many different database management systems. More than a query language, SQL also accesses databases from a wide variety of vendors.

style p. 147 A set of formatting commands assigned to common elements in a document—for example, subhead1.

stylus p. 68 An input device, with much the same point-and-click functions as a mouse, used to send signals to a pressure-sensitive graphics tablet.

subject tree p. 339, 600 A hierarchical catalog of Web sites compiled by researchers, such as that found at Yahoo!.

subprograms p. 519 In structured programming, a program is built from smaller programs called subprograms.

subsystem p. 441 A system that is a part of a larger system.

supercomputer p. 14 A superfast, superpowerful, and superexpensive computer used for applications that demand maximum power.

supply chain p. 447 The network of organizations that supply raw materials, manufacture products, and distribute products to customers.

supply chain management p. 447 The use of enterprise resource planning to improve the coordination of a company's value chain logistics activities and the logistics activities of its suppliers and customers.

surge protector p. 376 Hardware to shield electronic equipment from dangerous power spikes, preventing expensive hardware failures.

switch p. 274 Hardware that decides how to route Internet transmissions. Switches are similar to software routers, but faster and less flexible.

switching costs p. 459 The time, effort, and money a customer or supplier would have to expend if they changed to a competitor's product or service.

symmetric multiprocessing p. 51 See multiprocessing.

syntax p. 559 A set of rules for constructing sentences from words. Every language has a syntax.

syntax error p. 516 A violation of a programming language's grammar rules.

synthesized p. 209 Synthetically generated, as in synthesized sounds.

synthesizer p. 212 A device that can produce—synthesize—music and other sounds electronically. A synthesizer might be a stand-alone musical instrument or part of the circuitry on a computer's sound card.

synthetic DNA p. 390 At the heart of scientific concern; easily accessible to biohackers.

synthetic speech p. 567 Speech generated by computers by converting text into phonetic sounds.

system p. 441 A set of interrelated parts that work together to accomplish a purpose through the three basic functions of input, processing, and output.

system administrator p. 371 A user who has additional access privileges, such as permission to install software applications and change system settings.

system flowchart p. 534 A graphical depiction of the physical system that exists or is proposed, such as to show the relationship among programs, files, input, and output in a system.

system software p. 117 Software that handles the details of computing. Includes the operating system and utility programs.

system unit p. 584 The box that houses a personal computer's central processing unit—in other words, "the computer" or "the PC."

systems analyst p. 528 An information technology professional primarily responsible for developing and managing the system.

systems development p. 527 A problem-solving process of investigating a situation; designing a system solution to improve the situation; acquiring the human, financial, and technological resources to implement the solution; and finally evaluating the success of the solution.

systems development life cycle (SDLC) p. 528 A sequence of seven steps or phases through which an information system passes between the time the system is conceived and the time it is phased out.

T

T1 p. 278 A direct connect digital line that can transmit voice, data, and video at roughly 1.5 Mbps.

T3 p. 278 A direct connect digital line that transmits voice, data, and video even faster than a T1 connection.

table p. 238 A grid of rows and columns; on many Web pages, tables with hidden grids are used to align graphical images.

tablet computer p. 11 A type of handheld device, such as an iPad, that bridges the shrinking gap between the smart phone and the notebook/netbook PC.

tactical level p. 554 The management level responsible for a large organizational unit, such as a sales region or a production plant.

tape drive p. 84 A storage device that uses magnetic tape to store information.

taskbar p. 122 A button bar that provides one-click access to open applications and tools, making it easy to switch back and forth between different tasks.

tax-preparation software p. 170 Software that provides a prefabricated worksheet where the user enters numbers into tax forms. Calculations are performed automatically, and the completed forms can be sent electronically to the IRS.

TB (terabyte) p. 44 Approximately 1 million megabytes.

TCP/IP (Transmission Control Protocol/Internet Protocol) p. 277 Protocols developed as an experiment in internetworking, now the language of the Internet, allowing cross-network communication for almost every type of computer and network.

technophobia p. 414 The fear of technology.

telecommunication p. 272 Long-distance electronic communication in a variety of forms.

telecommuting p. 405 Working from home by modem, as do many programmers, accountants, and other information workers.

tele-immersion p. 226 The use of multiple cameras and high-speed networks to create an environment in which multiple remote users can interact with each other and with computer-generated objects.

telemedicine p. 401 An application of clinical medicine wherein computers monitor patient vital signs in hospitals, at home, and on the street with portable units. The computers analyze signals and transmit warnings when problems arise.

template p. 157 In desktop publishing, a professionally designed empty document that can be adapted to specific user needs. In spreadsheet software, worksheets that contain labels and formulas but no data values. The template produces instant answers when you fill in the blanks.

terminal p. 12 Combination keyboard and screen that transfers information to and from a mainframe computer.

testing p. 513 The process of checking the logic of an algorithm and the performance of a program.

tethering p. 282 Using cables or wireless connection to link a laptop to a mobile phone so it can send and receive Internet data through the phone's wireless Internet connection.

text editor p. 516 An application that is similar to a word processor without the formatting features required by writers and publishers; some provide specialized features to aid in writing programs.

text messaging p. 295 A popular form of communication among mobile phone users that relies on SMS technology.

text-to-speech p. 567 The creation of synthetic speech by converting text files into phonetic sounds.

thermal printer p. 81 A type of nonimpact printer that prints images by selectively heating coated thermal paper.

thesaurus p. 150 A synonym finder; often included with a word processor.

thin client p. 12, 403 A network computer designed to connect to the Internet but not perform all the other tasks performed by a PC.

thread p. 293 A collection of messages on a common subject in an online discussion.

threaded discussion p. 293 A discussion in which postings are organized by topics or subjects, called threads, rather than by time.

thumb drive p. 91 See USB drive.

time bomb p. 366 A logic bomb that is triggered by a time-related event.

timesharing p. 12 Technique by which mainframe computers communicate with several users simultaneously.

top-down design p. 511 A design process that starts at the top, with main ideas, and works down to the details.

total cost of ownership (TCO) p. 403 The net cost of computer ownership, including hardware, software, training, support, maintenance, troubleshooting, and other expenses.

touch screen p. 68 A computer screen that includes a pointing device based on recognizing on-screen touch.

touchpad (trackpad) p. 68 A small flat-panel pointing device that is sensitive to light pressure. The user moves the pointer by dragging a finger across the pad.

tower systems p.92 Personal computer design class; tall, narrow boxes that generally have more expansion slots and bays than other designs.

trackball p. 68 A pointing device that remains stationary while the user moves a protruding ball to control the pointer on the screen.

tracking software p. 366 A spyware application program, also called a spybot, that gathers user information and communicates it to an outsider via the Internet.

TrackPoint p. 68 A brand name for a tiny joysticklike device embedded in the keyboard of a laptop computer.

tracks p. 132 Concentric circles of data on a hard disk.

trademark p. 133 Legal ownership protection for symbols, pictures, sounds, colors, and smells used by a business to identify goods.

transaction p. 445 An event that occurs in any of the primary activities of the company: manufacturing, marketing, sales, and accounting.

transaction processing system (TPS) p. 446 A basic accounting and record-keeping system that keeps track of routine daily transactions necessary to conduct business.

transborder data flow p. 450 The flow of data between countries.

transmedia p. 500 Where characters and products show up in movies, TV, games, social networks, and the physical world, blurring the lines that have traditionally separated these experiences.

transistor p. 7 An electronic device that performs the same function as the vacuum tube by transferring electricity across a tiny resistor.

transmission p. 445 The process of distributing information.

Trojan horse p. 366 A program that performs a useful task while at the same time carrying out some secret destructive act. A form of software sabotage.

Turing test p. 553 A way to test machine intelligence.

tweening p. 204 The automatic creation of in-between frames in an animation.

twisted pair p. 274 A type of LAN cable that resembles the copper wires in standard telephone cables.

typeface p. 587 A particular design of type.

ubiquitous computing p. 262 Also called pervasive computing or ambient intelligence; describes a world where tiny, inexpensive, networked computers are embedded in everyday devices.

unicode p. 42 A coding scheme that supports more than 100,000 unique characters — more than enough for all major world languages.

uninterruptible power supply (UPS) p. 376 A hardware device that protects computers from data loss during power failures.

universal memory p. 98 A fast, low-energy, nonvolatile form of memory that can replace hard disks, flash memory, and DRAM.

universal product codes (UPCs) p. 72 Codes created from patterns of variable-width bars that send scanned information to a mainframe computer.

UNIX p. 123 An operating system that allows a timesharing computer to communicate with several other computers or terminals at once. UNIX is the most widely available multiuser operating system in use. It is also widely used on Internet hosts.

unstructured decision p. 454 A type of management decision requiring many quantitative and ethical judgments that have no clear answers.

updates p. 113 Improvements that software companies make to their programs. They usually contain bug fixes, new features, and/or minor enhancements.

upgrade p. 113 A new and improved version of a software program.

upload p. 288 To post software or documents to an online source so they are available for others.

up-skilled p. 408 Transformed in such a way that a job requires more skill.

URL (uniform resource locator) p. 326, 598 The address of a Web site.

USB (universal serial bus) p. 94 A data path standard that theoretically allows up to 126 devices, such as keyboards, digital cameras, and scanners, to be chained together from a single port.

USB 2.0 and USB 3.0 p. 94 Revisions of the USB standard that offer much faster transfer rates than the original standard.

USB flash drive p. 91 A portable storage device that stores data in flash memory and connects to a computer through a USB port. Also called thumb drives or jump drives.

USB hub p. 94 A device that increases the number of ports on a PC, enabling several USB peripherals to share the same port.

USB port p. 57 A computer port that can be used to attach keyboards, mice, printers, cameras, disk drives, portable storage devices, and more.

user interface p. 122 The look and feel of the computing experience from a human point of view.

user name p. 601 A name—typically a single word or string of characters—that you type to identify yourself when connecting—logging in—to a secure computer system, network, or email account. Sometimes called login name or alias.

utility computing p. 305 A form of grid computing that involves offering computational power and storage as metered commercial services, with the Internet acting like a utility grid.

utility program p. 118 Software that serves as tools for doing system maintenance and some repairs that are not automatically handled by the operating system.

value p. 163 The numbers that are the raw material used by spreadsheet software to perform calculations.

value chain model p. 443 A business organization model developed by Harvard professor Michael E. Porter that focuses on the value-adding activities of a company's primary and support activities.

variable p. 514 In programming, a named portion of the computer's memory whose contents the program can examine and change.

VBScript p. 526 A Web scripting language that is Microsoft's answer to JavaScript, based on Visual Basic.

vector graphics p. 195 The storage of pictures as collections of lines, shapes, and other objects.

vertical-market application p. 117 A computer application designed specifically for a particular business or industry.

vertical portal (vortal) p. 340 A specialized portal that, like vertical market software, is targeted at members of a particular industry or economic sector.

video card p. 79 A removable plug-in card containing video ports and video controllers in some tower systems.

video digitizer p. 74, 207 A device that converts analog video signals into digital data.

video-editing software p. 207 Software for editing digital video, including titles, sound, and special effects.

video projector p. 79 A projector that can project computer screen images for meetings and classes.

video teleconference or videoconferencing p. 296 Face-to-face communication over long distances using video and computer technology.

viral p. 301 A term used to describe a video that becomes widely popular, and spreads like a virus, due to the high number of email messages, blog posts, and IMs that have links to it.

virtual instrument p. 214 A musical instrument that exists only in software.

virtual memory p. 118 Use of part of a computer hard disk as a substitute for RAM.

virtual private network (VPN) p. 281, 483 A network that uses encryption software to create secure "tunnels" through the public Internet or between intranets; a method an organization can use to set up an extranet.

virtual reality (VR) p. 226 Technology that creates the illusion that the user is immersed in a world that exists only inside the computer—an environment that contains both scenes and the controls to change those scenes.

virtual world p. 226 Computer-generated worlds that create the illusion of immersion.

virtualization p. 127 The ability of a CPU to run multiple operating systems simultaneously.

virus p. 363, 603 Software that spreads from program to program, or from disk to disk, and uses each infected program or disk to make copies of itself. A form of software sabotage.

Visual J++ p. 518 A Java-like language for programming on the Microsoft Windows platform.

visual programming p. 523 Programming featuring tools that enable programmers to create large portions of their programs by drawing pictures and pointing to on-screen objects, eliminating much of the coding of traditional programming.

voice input p. 75 Use of a microphone to speak commands and text data to a computer, which uses speech-recognition software to interpret the input.

voice mail p. 296 A telephone-based messaging system with many of the features of an email system.

voice over IP (VoIP) p. 296 A protocol that allows the Internet to be used to make voice telephone calls.

volume licenses p. 114 Special license agreements for entire companies, schools, or government institutions to make use of a program.

volunteer computing p. 304 A type of grid computing that involves creating a virtual network of geographically dispersed computers to work on a problem that's too big to solve with a single machine or LAN.

W

waveform audio p. 209 Sound-editing software in which a visual image is manipulated using the sound's wave form.

wearable computers p. 262 Computers worn on the body, such as health monitors or the U.S. military's Future Force Warrior.

Web p. 14, 598 See World Wide Web.

Web application p. 115 An application that is stored on a Web server and typically accessed via a Web browser.

Web authoring software p. 327 Programs such as Adobe's Dreamweaver that work like desktop publishing page layout programs to allow users to create, edit, and manage Web pages and sites without having to write HTML code.

Web browser p. 598 An application program that enables a user to explore the Web.

Web bug p. 289 An invisible piece of code embedded in HTML-formatted email that is programmed to send information about its receiver's Web use back to its creator.

Web crawler p. 339 A software robot that systematically explores the Web, retrieves information about pages, and indexes the retrieved information in a database.

Web forum p. 293 Functionally similar to a newsgroup, but it's built on a Web application and is accessed through a Web browser.

Web page p. 598 A single document on the World Wide Web (WWW), made of text and images and interlinked with other documents.

Web portal p. 339 A Web site designed as a Web entry station, offering quick and easy access to a variety of services.

Web server p. 325 A server that stores Web pages and sends them to client programs—Web browsers—that request them.

Web site p. 598 A collection of related Web pages stored on the same server.

webcam p. 74 A type of digital video camera either attached to or built into a computer monitor; it can't function as a stand-alone camera.

Webcast p. 329 Real-time streaming audio or video.

Webjacker p. 368 Someone who hijacks legitimate Web sites, redirecting unsuspecting visitors to bogus or offensive alternate sites.

Webmail p. 289 Web-based email accessed through a browser.

WEP p. 281 Wired equivalent privacy (WEP) encryption that improves the security of wireless networks by making data as secure as it would be on a wired Ethernet.

wet Alife p. 576 A form of artificial life based on biochemistry rather than silicon technology. Many wet Alife researchers attempt to create life in the laboratory using chemical compounds similar to those that were responsible for the beginnings of life on our planet.

"what if?" question p. 166 A feature of spreadsheet software that allows speculation by providing instant answers to hypothetical questions.

wide area network (WAN) p. 275 A network that extends over a long distance. Each network site is a node on the network.

Wi-Fi p. 280 A popular wireless LAN technology that allows multiple computers to connect to a LAN through a nearby base station.

wiki p. 300 A Web site that lets visitors modify and add to its pages. The best-known example is Wikipedia.

WiMax (802.16) p. 281 A newer long-distance wireless protocol for Internet access.

Windows Media Player p. 331 A Microsoft program for delivering streaming media in proprietary formats that are compatible with other players.

Windows Phone 7 p. 126 A relatively new operating system for mobile phones where the software is designed to integrate easily with other Microsoft devices and programs.

wireless access point (WAP) p. 280 A communication device, typically connected to a wired network, that is used to create a wireless network.

wireless keyboard p. 67 A battery-powered keyboard that doesn't need a cable connecting it to the rest of the system. Most wireless keyboards use a radio technology called Bluetooth to send their signals.

wireless mouse p. 68 A battery-powered mouse that doesn't need a cable to communicate with the computer. Most wireless mice use a radio technology called Bluetooth to send their signals.

wireless network p. 274 A network in which a node has a tiny radio or infrared transmitter connected to its network port so it can send and receive data through the air rather than through cables.

wizard p. 149 A software help agent that walks the user through a complex process.

WMA p. 212 Windows Media Audio, one of a number of protocols for audio compression that can squeeze music files to a fraction of their original CD-file sizes, often without significant loss of audio quality.

word size p. 50 The number of bits a CPU can process at one time, typically 8, 16, 32, or 64.

word wrap p. 587 A word processing program text-editing feature that automatically moves any words that won't fit on the current line to the next line, along with the cursor.

work flow p. 404 The path of information as it flows through a workgroup.

worksheet p. 162 A spreadsheet document that appears on the screen as a grid of numbered rows and columns.

workstation p. 10 A high-end desktop computer.

World Wide Web (WWW) p. 14, 326, 598 Part of the Internet, a collection of multimedia documents created by organizations and users worldwide. Documents are linked in a hypertext Web that allows users to explore them with simple mouse clicks.

worm p. 365 A program that uses computer hosts to reproduce itself. Worm programs travel independently over computer networks, seeking out uninfected workstations to occupy. A form of software sabotage.

WORM (Write Once Read Many) p. 87 A term used to describe a drive that can write onto a blank (or partially filled) CD-R disk, but can't erase the data after it is burned in.

writeback p. 53 The final phase of execution, in which the bus unit writes the results of the instruction back into memory or some other device.

WYSIWYG p. 147, 587 Short for "what you see is what you get," pronounced "wizzy-wig." With a word processor, the arrangement of the words on the screen represents a close approximation to the arrangement of words on the printed page.

X

XHTML p. 335 A markup language that combines features of HTML and XML; its advantage is its backward compatibility with HTML.

XML (Extensible Markup Language) p. 244, 335 A programming language for Web sites that includes all of HTML's features plus many additional programming extensions. XML enables Web developers to control and display data the way they control text and graphics.

Z

zombie computer p. 369 An Internet-connected computer that has been hijacked using viruses or other tools to perform malicious acts without the knowledge of their owners and users.

Credits

Figure

1.0 Richard Morgenstein/Flickr.com
1.1 a: Damian Dovarganes/AP Wide World Photos
b: AP Photo/Paul Sakuma
1.2 a: left: David Joel/Getty Images Inc.-Photographer's Choice Royalty Free
b: right: Jesse Grant/Stringer/Getty Images - WireImage.com
1.3 Photograph courtesy of the Hagley Museum and Library,Wilmington, Delaware
1.4 Courtesy of AT&T Archives and History Center
1.5 Courtesy of Intel Corporation
1.6 a: left: Courtesy of Intel Corporation
b: center: Joe Gough/Fotolia, LLC - Royalty Free
c: right: Philips Healthcare
1.7 a: top left: Nolte Lourens/Fotolia, LLC - Royalty Free
b: top center: Vladir09/Shutterstock
c: top right: Shutterstock
d: bottom left: Karam Miri/Shutterstock
e: bottom right: Elnur/Shutterstock
1.8 a: left: Google Inc.
b: center: Brodeur Worldwide for Research In Motion
c: right: Oleksiy Maksymenko Photography/Alamy Images
1.9 Jetta Productions/Getty Images - Iconica
1.10 a: left: Stewart F. House, POOL/AP Wide World Photos
b: right: Courtesy of International Business Machines Corporation. Unauthorized use not permitted.
1.11 Courtesy of International Business Machines Corporation. Unauthorized use not permitted.
1.12 a: left: AP Wide World Photos
b: right: MIYUKI RYOKO/Agence France Presse/Getty Images
1.14 Jeff Gilbert/Alamy Images
1.15 b: Twitter
c: Vimeo
d: Google Inc.
g: Yelp
h: Ning
1.16 a: right page, left: Time Life Pictures/Getty Images/Time Life Pictures
b: right page, right: Roberto Brosan/Getty Images/Time Life Pictures
c: left page, left: Time Life Pictures/Getty Images/Time Life Pictures
d: left page, right: Karen Bleier/Agence France Presse/Getty Images
1.17 REUTERS/Department of Defense/Handout/Landov Media
1.18 Jose Azel/Aurora Photos/Alamy Images
1.19 a: left: Lonnie Duka/Getty Images Inc.-Stone Allstock
b: top right: GV Cruz/Getty Images-WireImage.com
c: bottom right: Ted S. Warren/AP Wide World Photos
1.20 Itsue Inouye/AP Wide World Photos
1.21 Phil Cole/Allsport Concepts/Getty Images
1.22 Wayne R. Billenduke/Getty Images Inc.-Stone Allstock
1.23 AP Wide World Photos
1.24 K-NFB Reading Technology, Inc.
1.25 © The Kobal Collection.
1CC From Slate, Copyright © 2010 The Slate Group. All rights reserved. Used by permission and protected by the Copyright Laws of the United States. The printing, copying, redistribution, and retransmission of the Material without express written permission is prohibited.
2.0 Justin Sullivan/Getty Images, Inc – Liaison
2.1 AP Wide World Photos
2.2 © Matt Dunham/CORBIS All Rights Reserved
2.3 © Dell Inc. All Rights Reserved.
2.4 a: top center: Roman Sigaev/Shutterstock
b: top center: Shutterstock
c: middle center: Fuse/Getty Images, Inc – Liasion
d: middle left: Kingston Technology Company
e: middle right: © 2008 Dell, Inc. The Dell logo is a trademark of Dell Inc. All rights reserved.
f: bottom center: Micheal Simpson/Photographer's Choice/Getty Images
2.5 Courtesy of The Computer History Museum.
2.9 c: Used with permission from Microsoft.
2.10 Intel Corporation Pressroom Photo Archives
2.11 Charles Stirling/Alamy Images
2.12 © Ashley Cooper/CORBIS All Rights Reserved
2.14 a: left: Courtesy of Intel Corporation
b: right: Advanced Micro Devices
2.17 a: Intel Corporation Pressroom Photo Archives
b: Ethan Miller/Getty Images, Inc – Liaison
d: Sun Microsystems, Inc.
f: AMD, the AMD Arrow logo, AMD Opteron, AMD Athlon and combinations thereof, are trademarks of Advanced Micro Devices, Inc.
g: Transmeta Corporation
h: Peter Wynn Thompson/Redux Pictures
i: AP Wide World Photos
2.19 James A. Folts Photography
2.20 © Rob Bouwman/Courtesy of www.istockphoto.com
2.21 Newscom
2.22 Rolfe Horn/The Long Now Foundation
2CC Courtesy of Stewart Brand and The Long Now Foundation
3.1 Lakeside School
3.2 Ted S. Warren/AP Wide World Photos
3.3 a: Ryan Mcvay/Getty Images, Inc – Liaison
b: Dmitry Melnikov/Shutterstock
c: PRNewsFoto/Verizon Wireless/AP Wide World Photos
d: Alex Segre/Alamy Images
f: Jochen Luebke/Agence France Presse/Getty Images
3.5 a: Logitech Inc.
b: Apple Computer, Inc.
c: Paul Sakuma/AP Wide World Photos
d: Courtesy of International Business Machines Corporation. Unauthorized use not permitted.
e: Logitech Inc.
f: Reprinted with permission from Microsoft Corporation.
g: © Michal Rozanski/Courtesy of www.istockphoto.com
h: Wacom Europe GmbH
i: Alex Grimm/Reuters/Landov Media
3.7 a: George Frey/Getty Images, Inc – Liaison
b: Paul Sakuma/AP Wide World Photos
c: Paul Sakuma/AP Wide World Photos
d: JazzMutant
3.8 James A. Folts Photography
3.9 Robert Harbison
3.10 WIZCOM Technologies Ltd.
3.12 Virtual Ink Corporation
3.13 Andre Unangst/Shutterstock
3.14 a: Courtesy or Sony Electronic Inc.
b: RayArt Graphics/Alamy Images
d: JVC Americas Corp.
e: Paul Sakuma/AP Wide World Photos
3.15 a: Plantronics
3.16 Betty Udesen/Newscom
3.17 b: Courtesy of Sony Electronics Inc.
m: Creative Technology Ltd.
3.18 a: AP Wide World Photos
b: Alamy Images
c: Jennifer Meyers/The Image Works
3.21 a: Courtesy of Canon USA. The Canon logo is a trademark of Canon Inc. All rights reserved.
b: Hewlett-Packard Company
c: PRNewsFoto/Sony Electronics, Inc./AP Wide World Photos
e: Epson America, Inc.
3.23 a: top: NASA Headquarters
b: bottom: © Raoul Minsart/CORBIS
3.24 Photo courtesy of Iomega Corporation
3.25 a: left: Courtesy of International Business Machines Corporation. Unauthorized use not permitted.
b: right: Courtesy Western Digital Corporation
3.26 a: top left: © Dorling Kindersley
b: bottom left: Tim Ridley © Dorling Kindersley
3.29 Courtesy of Sony Electronics Inc.
3.31 a: Newscom
b: SanDisk Corporation
c: Apple Computer, Inc.
3.33 Fujitsu Siemens Computers

3.35 a: top left: Roman Sigaev/Shutterstock
b: top left: Shutterstock
c: middle center: Fuse/Getty Images, Inc – Liasion
d: middle left: Kingston Technology Company
e: middle right: © 2008 Dell, Inc. The Dell logo is a trademark of Dell Inc. All rights reserved.
f: bottom center: Micheal Simpson/Photographer's Choice/Getty Images

3.36 Stanley R. Williams, Senior Fellow, HP Labs

3.37 Microvision Inc.

3CC Grant Buckler is a freelance journalist. This article originally appeared in The Globe and Mail's Globe Campus Report.

4.0 © Kim Kulish/CORBIS All Rights Reserved

4.1 AP Wide World Photos

4.2 NASA Ames Research Center

4.8 Adobe product screenshot(s) reprinted with permission from Adobe Systems Incorporated.

4.9 a: left: Yelp
b: right: CNET.com. Reprinted with permission by CBS Interactive, Inc. All rights reserved.

4.11 a: left: Google Inc.
b: right: Adobe product screenshot(s) reprinted with permission from Adobe Systems Incorporated.

4.12 c: © Reprinted by permission of The Weather Channel. All Rights Reserved.

4.13 Fabian Bimmer/AP Wide World Photos

4.15 a: top: Reprinted with permission by Symantec.
b: bottom: Reprinted with permission by Symantec.

4.19 Tony Cordoza/Getty Images, Inc - Liaison

4.24 Google Inc.

4.26 Peter Zschunke/AP Wide World Photos

4.32 Ivan Sekretarev/AP Wide World Photos

4.33 www.djearworm.com Reprinted with permission.

4CC Segan, Sascha, "Copyrights and Wrongs" PC magazine. Reprinted with permission.

5.0 Julie Stupsker/Newscom

5.1 AP/Wide World Photos

5.2 Bootstrap Institute

5.7 a: left: Wikipedia
b: right: The Quotations Page. Reprinted with permission.

5.11 Nuance Communications, Inc.

5.12 Hewlett-Packard Company

5.13 a: Courtesy of Apple
b: Lexmark International, Inc.

5.16 Adobe product screenshot(s) reprinted with permission from Adobe Systems Incorporated.

5.17 Lourens Smak/Alamy Images

5.19 a: Amazon.com
b: Apple Computer, Inc.

5.20 a: left: Used by permission of Sony Electronics Inc.
b: right: Lexar Media, USA

5.28 University of California, Los Angeles

5.29 Argonne National Laboratory

5.32 a: top: Microsoft product screen shot(s) reprinted with permission from Microsoft Corporation
b: bottom: Raul Vasquez/MCT/Newscom

5.33 a: Reprinted with Permision by ZOHO Corporation. All Rights Reserved.
f: Copyright © 1997 Cygnus Software. All rights reserved.

5.34 c68/ZUMA Press/Newscom

5CC "Clive Thompson on the New Literacy" by Clive Thompson, Wired Magazine, 17.09 http://www.wired.com/techbiz/people/magazine/17-09/st_thompson. Reprinted with permission.

6.0 Andreas Rentz/Getty Images, Inc - Liaison

6.1 © Sam Ogden

6.2 CERN/European Organization for Nuclear Research

6.3 Agence France Presse/Getty Images

6.5 Pearson Education/PH College

6.6 Sanjay Kothari

6.10 Fotolia, LLC - Royalty Free

6.11 Fotolia. Reprinted with Permission

6.12 AP/Wide World Photos

6.13 Photo Researchers, Inc.

6.14 Newscom

6.16 © 2008 Disney Enterprises, Inc. and Pixar

6.18 a: top: New Line/Everett Collection
b: bottom: Newscom

6.20 a: right: YouTube. Reprinted with permission.
b: left: Colin Young-Wolff/PhotoEdit Inc.

6.23 b: Amazon.com, Album cover photos by Sally Yaich of Pink Caterpillar Photography

6.24 a: top: Scott Kleinman/Stone/Getty Images
b: bottom: Piotr Powietrzynski/Photographer's Choice/Getty Images

6.26 j: right page, center right: Niall Carson/PA Photos/Landov Media

6.28 a: top: Wikisky. Reprinted with permission.

6.31 Mark Richards/PhotoEdit Inc.

6.32 c51/Zuma Press/Newscom

6CC Boutin, Paul, "The Age of Music Piracy Is Officially Over," Wired, December 2010: http://www.wired.com/magazine/2010/11/st_essay_nofreebird/ Reprinted with permission.

7.0 Ohn MacDougall/Getty Images, Inc. AFP

7.1 Kim Kulish/Corbis/Bettmann

7.2 Google Earth

7.3 © Amazon.com, Inc. or its affiliates. All rights reserved.

7.9 d: bottom left: Oliver Leedham/Alamy Images

7.10 c: bottom left: Dmitry Melnikov/Shutterstock
d: bottom left: Oliver Leedham/Alamy Images
f: bottom right: Vladir09/Shutterstock

7.11 a: Jan Butchofsky-Houser/Corbis Edge
b: Eric CurrylTecmap
c: Image Plan/Corbis Royalty Free
d: Corbis Royalty Free
e: © David Cumming/Eye Ubiquitous/CORBIS All Rights Reserved
f: Solstice Photography/Jupiter Images – PictureArts/Corporation/Brand X Pictures Royalty Free
g: David Samuel Robbins/Corbis/Bettmann
h: Jupiter Images - PictureArts Corporation/Brand X Pictures Royalty Free
i: PhotoAlto/Patrick Sheandell O'Carroll/Jupiter Images - PictureArts Corporation/Brand X Pictures Royalty Free
j: Photodisc/Getty Images
k: Digital Vision/PictureQuest, Inc./Jupiter Images Picturequest - Royalty Free

7.14 Pearson Education/PH College

7.17 Mike Simons/Getty Images, Inc - Liaison

7.18 © Ralf-Finn Hestoft/CORBIS All Rights Reserved

7.20 Don Ryan/AP Wide World Photos

7.21 Ben Edwards/Image Bank/Getty Images

7.22 Toronto Star/ZUMA Press/Newscom

7.24 a: Reprinted with permission from Microsoft Corporation.
b: Reprinted with permission from Microsoft Corporation.

8.0 DALMAS/SIPA/SIPA PRESS/Newscom

8.1 © Sunset Boulevard/CORBIS All Rights Reserved

8.2 © David Ducros/Photo Researchers, Inc.

8.3 Andrew Holbrooke/CORBIS All Rights Reserved

8.4 Transferred from U.S. Patent Office, Negative number: 89-6697, Information Technology and Society Division, NMAH, Smithsonian Institution

8.5 a: top left: Tatniz/Shutterstock
b: top center: Shutterstock
c: top right: Shutterstock
e: bottom left: Apple Computer, Inc.
f: bottom center: Tatniz/Shutterstock
g: bottom right: Apple Computer, Inc.

8.6 PhotoDisc Imaging/Getty Images, Inc.-Photodisc; Shutterstock.

8.7 Courtesy of International Business Machines Corporation. Unauthorized use not permitted.

8.8 a: left: Thuraya
b: right: Shutterstock

8.9 © Norman Chan/Courtesy of www.istockphoto.com

8.10 Jon Challicom/Alamy Images

8.11 BananaStock/Jupiter Images-PictureArts Corporation/Brand X Pictures Royalty Free

8.12 Lee Jin-man/AP Wide World Photos

8.14 a: Humanware, Inc.
c: Kevin Dietsch/Newscom
d: Acrossair US

8.15 superclic/Alamy Images

8.18 Pearson Education/PH College

8.22 a: top: Technorati, www.technorati.com Reprinted with permission.
b: bottom: Technorati, www.technorati.com Reprinted with permission.

8.23 a: top: Microsoft product screen shot reprinted with permission from Microsoft Corporation.

8.24 a: left: Skype

8.26 Newscom

8.28 a: left: Wikipedia. Wikipedia® is a registered trademark of the Wikimedia Foundation, Inc., a non-profit organization.

8.29 YouTube

8.33 ALBERT CHAU/AFP/Getty Images/Newscom

9.0 Google Inc.
9.1 © Clark Quinn
9.2 Reprinted with permisson by the author.
9.3 Flickr
9.4 Reprinted with permission by Caring Bridge.
9.5 David R. Frazier Photolibrary, Inc./ Alamy Images
9.7 a: top left: The Dell logo is a trademark of Dell Inc.
b: top center left: Hewlett-Packard Company
c: top center right: The Dell logo is a trademark of Dell Inc.
d: top right: The Dell logo is a trademark of Dell Inc.
f: center left: The Dell logo is a trademark of Dell Inc.
g: center: Netgear, Inc.
i: center right: Apple Computer, Inc.
j: center right lower: Netgear, Inc.
k: center right bottom: Hewlett-Packard Company
l: bottom left: Yale University Office of Public Affairs
m: top right: Steve Allen/Jupiter Images - PictureArts Corporation/Brand X Pictures Royalty Free
n: bottom right: Bananastock/Getty Images
9.8 a: Apple Computer, Inc.
b: Courtesy of Linksys, A Division of Cisco
c: Apple Computer, Inc.
d: Shutterstock
e: Fujitsu Siemens Computers
f: Netgear, Inc.
h: MPC Corporation - DO NOT USE
i: Hewlett-Packard Company
j: PRNewsFoto/Gateway, Inc./AP Wide World Photos
9.9 Pearson Education/PH College
9.10 Pearson Education/PH College
9.12 Finnbarr Webster/Alamy Images
9.13 Pandora. Reprinted with permission.
9.18 http://www.re-vision.com/
9.25 a: left: Reprinted with permission of the OpenNet Initiative.
b: right: Reprinted with permission of the OpenNet Initiative.
9.27 a: left: Fuse Project
b: right: Reuters/Johnny Onverwacht/Landov Media
9.28 a: Courtesy of NASA/JPL/Caltech
b: The Electrolux Group
9CC "Countries Try to Tame the Wild Territory of the Net" by Tom Gjetten, NPR Morning Edition, April 8, 2010
10.0 Eraldo Peres/AP Wide World Photos
10.1 Getty Images, Inc – Liaison
10.2 Franka Bruns/AP Wide World Photos
10.3 Bob Child/AP Wide World Photos
10.4 Connecting Point Communcations
10.7 Reprinted with permission by Symantec.
10.8 © Mark Powell/CORBIS SYGMA All Rights Reserved.
10.9 a: Newscom
b: Photo Researchers, Inc.
10.10 Symantec Corporation
10.11 Carnegie Mellon University
10.12 c: MPC Corporation
d: Apple Computer, Inc.
10.14 a: left: Shutterstock
b: right: Dmitry Melnikov/Shutterstock
10.15 a: left page, left: Apple Computer, Inc.
b: left page, center: Apple Computer, Inc.
c: left page, right: Fujitsu Siemens Computers
d: right page, left: Fuse/Getty Images, Inc – Liaison
10.16 American Power Conversion Corporation
10.19 © 2001 Versus Technology, Inc. www.versustech.com
10.20 a: Bjoern Sigurdsoen/SCANPIX/AP Wide World Photos
b: David Hecker/Agence France Presse/Getty Images
c: Louis Lanzano/AP Wide World Photos
d: Ed Wray/AP Wide World Photos
e: © Ray Stubblebine/Reuters/CORBIS All Rights Reserved.
f: Corbis RF
10.22 Defense Department/AP Wide World Photos
10.23 Sgt. 1st Class Gail Braymen/North American Defense Command (NORAD)
10.24 © Caren Firouz/CORBIS All Rights Reserved
10CC Elgan, Mike, "Dark Clouds Gather Over Online Security," Computerworld, Jan 29, 2010. Reprinted with permission.
11.0 Inamori Foundation/AP Wide World Photos
11.1 John Barr/Getty Images, Inc-Liaison
11.2 Xerox Palo Alto Research Center
11.3 INDRANIL MUKHERJEE/AFP/Getty Images
11.4 Antoine Rosset/Photo Researchers, Inc.
11.5 Pasquale Sorrentino/Photo Researchers, Inc.
11.6 Ed Young/Science Photo Library/Photo Researchers, Inc.
11.7 CAP/Getty Images-Photonica Amana America, Inc.
11.9 AP Wide World Photos
11.11 3M Touch Systems
11.12 Chinatopix/AP Wide World Photos
11.13 Zack Canepari/The New York Times/Redux Pictures
11.14 D Harcourt Webster/Robert Harding Picture Library Ltd/Alamy Images
11.15 Evans (Ag)/Getty Images Inc.-Hulton Archive Photos
11.16 Garden City Telegram/Brad Nading/AP Wide World Photos
11.17 a: left: Photo courtesy of Compusult Limited
b: right: www.freerice.com
11.18 Courtesy of TOPICS Entertainment, Inc.
11.20 iStockphoto
11.21 a: left: MTS & ProEvents
c: right: ViewPlus Technologies
11.22 Doris Haugen/AP Wide World Photos
11.24 Kike Calvo/Newscom
11.25 a: top: Keith Morris/Alamy Images
b: bottom: Oliver Berg/Newscom
11.27 Take-Two Interactive Software Inc.
11.28 Chuck Liddy/The News & Observer/AP Wide World Photos
11.29 Sang-Hoon Kish Kim/Newscom
11.30 a: left: One Laptop per Child Project
b: right: One Laptop per Child Project
11C Condé Nast Publications. All rights reserved. Originally published in Wired.com. Reprinted by permission.
12.0 Brooks Kraft/CORBIS-NY
12.1 Tony Avelar/Bloomberg/Getty Images – Bloomberg
12.2 Bruce Dale/Getty - National Geographic Society
12.5 EyeWire Collection/Getty Images-Photodisc
12.7 a: Comstock/Alamy Images
b: Denis MacDonald/AGE Fotostock America, Inc.
c: Javier Larrea/AGE Fotostock America, Inc.
d: Image State/Alamy Images
e: ImageShop Business K/Alamy Images
f: Barry Blackman/Getty Images
12.9 b: Tatniz/Shutterstock
c: Kavione/Shutterstock
d: Specral-Design/Shutterstock
e: Zoom Team/Shutterstock
12.11 a: moodboard/Alamy Images Royalty Free
b: Slawomir Fajer/Shutterstock
c: Comstock Complete
d: Shutterstock
e: Fabio Cardozo/AGE Fotostock America, Inc.
12.13 Stuart Ramson/Porter Novelli/Bloomberg News/Landov Media
12.14 a: Corbis Super RF/Alamy Images Royalty Free
b: Blend Images/Alamy Images Royalty Free
c: Radius Images/Alamy Images Royalty Free
d: Image Source Black/Alamy Images Royalty Free
12.16 Courtesy of Lehrstuhl fur Wirtschaftsinformatik, University of Hohenheim, Stuttgart, Germany.
12.17 Caliper Corporation
12.22 Getty Images, Inc. Tetra Images
12.24 Reprinted with permission from Microsoft Corporation.
12.25 Thomas James Hurst/Seattle Times/Newscom
13.0 Erin Lubin/Bloomberg News/ Landov Media
13.1 Mark Lennihan/AP Wide World Photos
13.2 © Macduff Everton/CORBIS All Rights Reserved
13.3 © Ramin Talaie/CORBIS All Rights Reserved
13.4 Don Ryan/AP Wide World Photos
13.7 These images are reproduced with permission of UPS of America, Inc. © Copyright 2005 UPS of America, Inc. All rights reserved.
13.8 Reprinted with permission by Encore Group Travel, Inc.
13.9 Courtesy of Sony Electronics Inc.
13.10 a: top: Bike Friday. Reprinted with permission
b: center: www.makeyourownjeans.com. Reprinted with permission.
c: bottom: Threadless, www.threadless.com. Reprinted with permission.
13.11 a: top: © Amazon.com, Inc. or its affiliates. All rights reserved.
b: bottom: Source: CD Baby. Reprinted with permission.
13.12 a: Andresr/Shutterstock
b: Antonio Jorge Nunes/Shutterstock
c: Lawrence Manning/Corbis RF
13.13 Lonnie Duka/Photolibrary.com
13.14 Google Inc.
13.15 a: top: Reprinted with permission of GROUPON.
b: bottom: Reprinted with permission of the artist.

13.16 Dorothy Jean/Zong Mobile Payments, Reprinted with Permission by ZONG
13.19 a: left: Angry Birds is developed and published by Rovio Mobile Ltd. Reprinted with permission.
13.20 a: box.net. Reprinted with permission.
13.21 Courtesy of www.istockphoto.com
13.22 Image is from this slideshow: http://gamepocalypsenow.blogspot.com/2010/07/visions-of-gamepocalypse-podcast.html. The image (and blog) is created by Jesse Schell, who owns the Gamepocalypse blog. His listed email address is jesse@schellgames.com.
13CC Johnson, Steve, "The End of an Era (from 13 of the Brightest Tech Minds Sound Off on the Rise of the Tablet)." Originally published in Wired. Reprinted by permission of the author.
14.0 Navy Visual News Service/U.S. Navy News Photo
14.1 U.S. Navy News Photo
14.2 U.S. Naval Historical Center Photography
14.3 Ed Honowitz/Stone/Getty Images
14.17 a: left page, bottom left: blue jean images/Getty Images, Inc.-Somos
b: left page, bottom right: Somos/Veer/Getty Images, Inc.-Somos
c: right page, bottom left: Robert E. Daemmrich/Bob Daemmrich Photography, Inc.
d: right page, bottom right: John Giustina/Getty Images-Iconica
14.24 Chad Slattery/Stone/Getty Images
14.25 Phil Scholfield/Getty Images
14.26 Michael Melford/Image Bank/Getty Images
14CC Thompson, Clive, "Coding for the Masses" http://www.wired.com/magazine/2010/11/st_thompson_wereallcoders/, Wired, Reprinted with permission.
15.0 Princeton University Archives. Department of Rare Books and Special Collections. Princeton University Library.
15.1 National Portrait Gallery, London.
15.2 Courtesy of the Computer History Museum
15.4 © Corbis Bettman
15.5 a: top: Agence France Presse/Getty Images
15.7 Reprinted with permission by Trippo.
15.10 PinMed, Inc
15.11 a: top: Becky Cohen/Becky Cohen, Photographer
b: bottom: Becky Cohen/Becky Cohen, Photographer
15.12 a: right: Ng Han Guan/AP Wide World Photos
b: left: NASA/Jet Propulsion Laboratory
15.14 KRT 2006/Newscom
15.15 Purestock/Alamy Images Royalty Free
15.17 iStockphoto
15.18 IBM Communications Media Relations/IBM Research, Almaden Research Center
15.19 a: top left: Parallax, Inc.
b: bottom left: Intel Corporation Pressroom Photo Archives
15.20 a: top left: Spencer Grant/Photolibrary.com
b: top right: James King-Holmes/Photo Researchers, Inc.
c: center right: Paul Sancya/AP Wide World Photos
d: bottom left: Defense Advanced Research Projects Agency
e: bottom right: Kyodo/Newscom
15.21 U.S. Air Force, HO/AP Wide World Photos
15CC "Do Humanlike Machines Deserve Human Rights?" by Daniel Roth, Wired Magazine: 17.02 http://www.wired.com/culture/culturereviews/magazine/17-02/st_essay. Reprinted with permission.
A.1 Jonathan Souza/Dreamstime LLC - Royalty Free
A.2 Busse Yankushev/Photolibrary.com
A.5 a: top left: Jean Chung/Bloomberg via Getty Images
b: top right: Paula Solloway/Alamy Images
c: center left: SuperStock, Inc.
e: bottom right: Stefano Lunardi/OLIVE/Photolibrary Royalty Free
A.9 Paul Hudson/Getty Images, Inc. - fStop
A.11 Blend Images/Alamy Images Royalty Free
A.12 a: top right: Douglas McFaddy/Getty Images
b: left: Robyn Beck/Agence France Presse/Getty Images
c: bottom right: © Kimimasa Mayama/CORBIS All Rights Reserved
A.17 id work/iStock Vectors/Getty Images

Index

A

B

D

E

F

G

J

K

L

M

Q

R

S

T

Z